AutoCAD
and Its Applications

BASICS

by

Terence M. Shumaker
Faculty Emeritus
Former Chairperson
Drafting Technology
Autodesk Premier Training Center
Clackamas Community College, Oregon City, Oregon

David A. Madsen
President, Madsen Designs Inc.
Faculty Emeritus, Former Department Chairperson Drafting Technology
Autodesk Premier Training Center
Clackamas Community College, Oregon City, Oregon
Director Emeritus, American Design Drafting Association

David P. Madsen
Vice President, Madsen Designs Inc.
Computer-Aided Design and Drafting Consultant and Educator
Autodesk Developer Network Member
American Design Drafting Association Member

2009

Publisher
The Goodheart-Willcox Company, Inc.
Tinley Park, Illinois
www.g-w.com

The Goodheart-Willcox Company, Inc. Brand Disclaimer: Brand names, company names, and illustrations for products and services included in this text are provided for educational purposes only and do not represent or imply endorsement or recommendation by the author or the publisher.

The Goodheart-Willcox Company, Inc. Safety Notice: The reader is expressly advised to carefully read, understand, and apply all safety precautions and warnings described in this book or that might also be indicated in undertaking the activities and exercises described herein to minimize risk of personal injury or injury to others. Common sense and good judgment should also be exercised and applied to help avoid all potential hazards. The reader should always refer to the appropriate manufacturer's technical information, directions, and recommendations; then proceed with care to follow specific equipment operating instructions. The reader should understand these notices and cautions are not exhaustive.

The publisher makes no warranty or representation whatsoever, either expressed or implied, including but not limited to equipment, procedures, and applications described or referred to herein, their quality, performance, merchantability, or fitness for a particular purpose. The publisher assumes no responsibility for any changes, errors, or omissions in this book. The publisher specifically disclaims any liability whatsoever, including any direct, indirect, incidental, consequential, special, or exemplary damages resulting, in whole or in part, from the reader's use or reliance upon the information, instructions, procedures, warnings, cautions, applications, or other matter contained in this book. The publisher assumes no responsibility for the activities of the reader.

Library of Congress Cataloging-in-Publication Data

Shumaker, Terence M.
    AutoCAD and Its Applications: BASICS 2009 / by Terence M. Shumaker, David A. Madsen, David P. Madsen. – 16th ed.
        p. cm.

    Includes bibliographical references and index.
    ISBN 978-1-59070-988-7
    1. Computer graphics. 2. AutoCAD. I. Madsen, David A. II. Madsen, David P.

T385.S461466 2009
620'.0042028553--dc22   2008014975

Introduction

AutoCAD and Its Applications—Basics is a textbook providing complete instruction in mastering fundamental AutoCAD® 2009 tools and drawing techniques. Typical applications of AutoCAD are presented with basic drafting and design concepts. The topics are covered in an easy-to-understand sequence and progress in a way that allows you to become comfortable with the tools as your knowledge builds from one chapter to the next. In addition, *AutoCAD and Its Applications—Basics* offers the following features:

- Step-by-step use of AutoCAD tools.
- In-depth explanations of how and why tools function as they do.
- Extensive use of font changes to specify certain meanings.
- Examples and descriptions of industry practices and standards.
- Screen captures of AutoCAD and Windows features and functions.
- Professional tips explaining how to use AutoCAD effectively and efficiently.
- More than two hundred exercises to reinforce the chapter topics. These exercises also build on previously learned material.
- Chapter tests for review of tools and key AutoCAD concepts.
- A large selection of drafting problems supplementing each chapter. Problems are presented as industrial drawings, engineering sketches, or architectural, civil, electrical, or other related industry drawings.

With *AutoCAD and Its Applications—Basics*, you learn AutoCAD tools and become acquainted with information in other areas:

- Office practices for firms using AutoCAD systems.
- Preliminary planning and sketches.
- Drawing geometric shapes and constructions.
- Special editing operations that increase productivity.
- Making multiview drawings (orthographic projection).
- Dimensioning techniques and practices, based on accepted standards.
- Drawing section views and designing graphic patterns.
- Creating shapes and symbols for different uses.
- Creating and managing symbol libraries.
- Sketching with AutoCAD.
- Plotting and printing drawings.

Learning Objectives identify key items you will learn in the chapter.

Command Entry Graphics show command prompt, toolbar, and pull-down menu entry options. Command options are also shown where applicable.

Illustrations, including AutoCAD "screen shots" and line art illustrations, make learning easy.

Cautions alert you to potential problems.

Reference Material References direct you to charts, tables, and other useful references available on the Student CD.

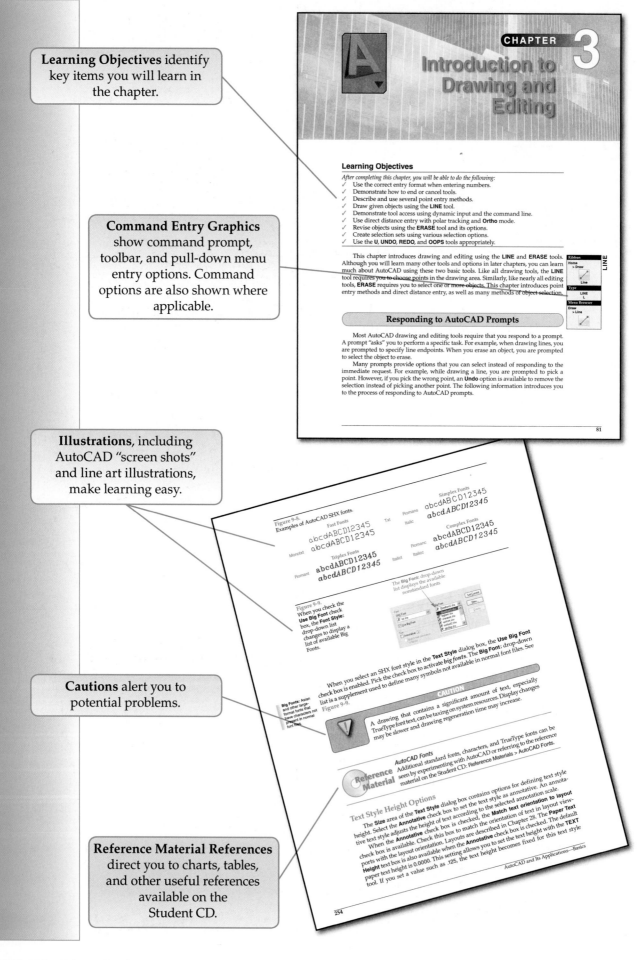

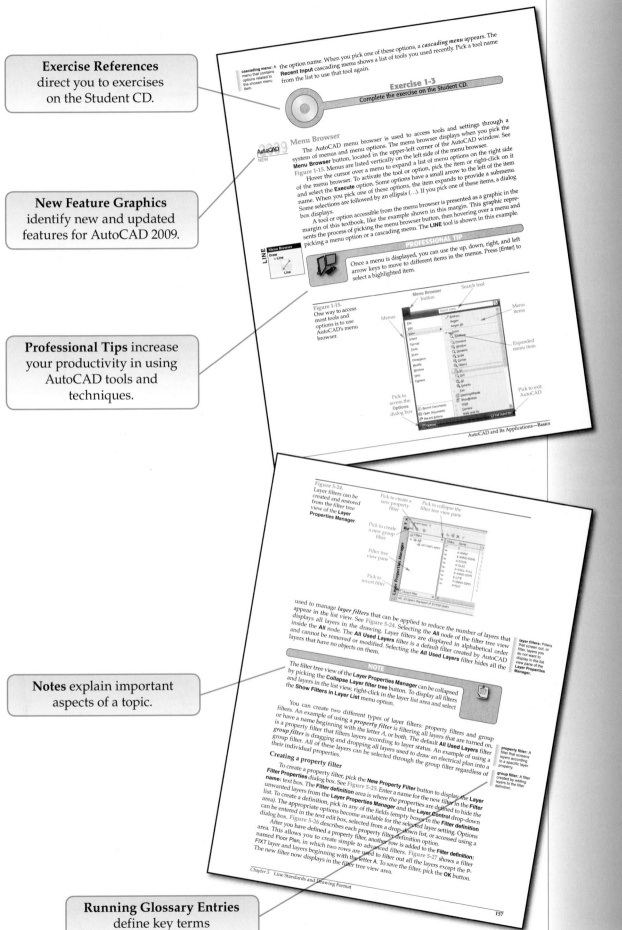

Exercise References
direct you to exercises
on the Student CD.

New Feature Graphics
identify new and updated
features for AutoCAD 2009.

Professional Tips increase
your productivity in using
AutoCAD tools and
techniques.

Notes explain important
aspects of a topic.

Running Glossary Entries
define key terms

Features of the Textbook

Supplemental Material References direct you to additional material on the Student CD that is relevant to the current chapter.

Template Development References direct you to Template Development material on the Student CD.

Express Tool References direct you to Express Tool material on the Student CD.

Chapter Tests reinforce the knowledge gained by reading the chapter and completing the exercises.

Figure 7-26.
Drawing a parallelogram with polar snap.

A   B   C   D

Using polar tracking overrides

It takes some time to set up the polar tracking and the polar snap options, but it is worth the effort if you have several objects to draw that can take advantage of this feature. Use the polar tracking overrides to perform polar tracking when you need to define only one point. Polar tracking overrides work for the specified angle whether polar tracking is on or off. To activate a polar tracking override, type a less than symbol (<) followed by the desired angle when AutoCAD asks you to specify a point. For example, after you access the **LINE** tool and pick a first point, enter <30 to set a 30° override. Then move the crosshairs in the desired 30° direction and enter a distance, such as 1.5 to draw a 1.5-unit line.

Exercise 7-12
Complete the exercise on the Student CD.

Supplemental Material   *AutoSnap and AutoTrack Options*
The **Options** dialog box provides several options for controlling the appearance and function of AutoSnap and AutoTrack. Refer to the Student CD: Supplemental Materials > AutoSnap and AutoTrack Options for more information about options specific to these drawing tools.

Template Development   You will find that you need different object snaps and polar
Chapter 7   tracking settings depending on the type of drawing you are creating. These settings can be specified in your drawing templates to save time and increase efficiency. Refer to the Student CD for detailed instructions to add these settings to your mechanical, architectural, and civil drawing templates.

Express Tools   The **Express** menu on the menu browser includes additional
Chapter 14   tools for improved functionality and productivity during the drawing process. The following Express Tools apply to creating selection sets. Refer to the Student CD: Student Materials > Express Tools > Chapter 14 for information about these tools.

Get Selection Set

Fast Select

Chapter Test

Answer the following questions. Write your answers on a separate sheet of paper or complete the electronic chapter test on the Student CD.

1. Name the editing tools that can be accessed automatically using grips.
2. How can you select a grip tool other than the default **STRETCH**?
3. What is the purpose of the **Base Point** option in the grip tools?
4. Explain the function of the **Undo** option in the grip tools.
5. What happens when you choose the **Exit** option from the grips shortcut menu?
6. Which option of the **ROTATE** grip tool option would you use to rotate an object from an existing 60° angle to a new 25° angle?
7. What scale factor would you use to scale an object to become three-quarters of its original size?
8. Describe the options for editing object properties.
9. Where does the **Quick Properties** panel appear by default when an object is selected?
10. By default, how many properties are shown in the **Quick Properties** panel?
11. Describe three items that might be displayed when you pick a property from a **Quick Properties** panel or **Properties** palette row.
12. Identify at least two ways to access the **Properties** palette.
13. Explain how you would change the radius of a circle from 1.375 to 1.875 using the **Properties** palette.
14. How can you change the linetype of an object using the **Properties** palette?
15. What does it mean when color, linetype, and lineweight are specified as ByLayer?
16. What tool is used to change the properties of objects to match the properties of a different object?
17. Briefly discuss how the Windows copy and paste function works to copy an object from one drawing to another.
18. Name the option that joins a group of objects as a block when they are pasted.
19. When you use the option described in Question 27, how do you separate the objects back into individual objects?
20. Identify four ways to open the **Quick Select** dialog box.

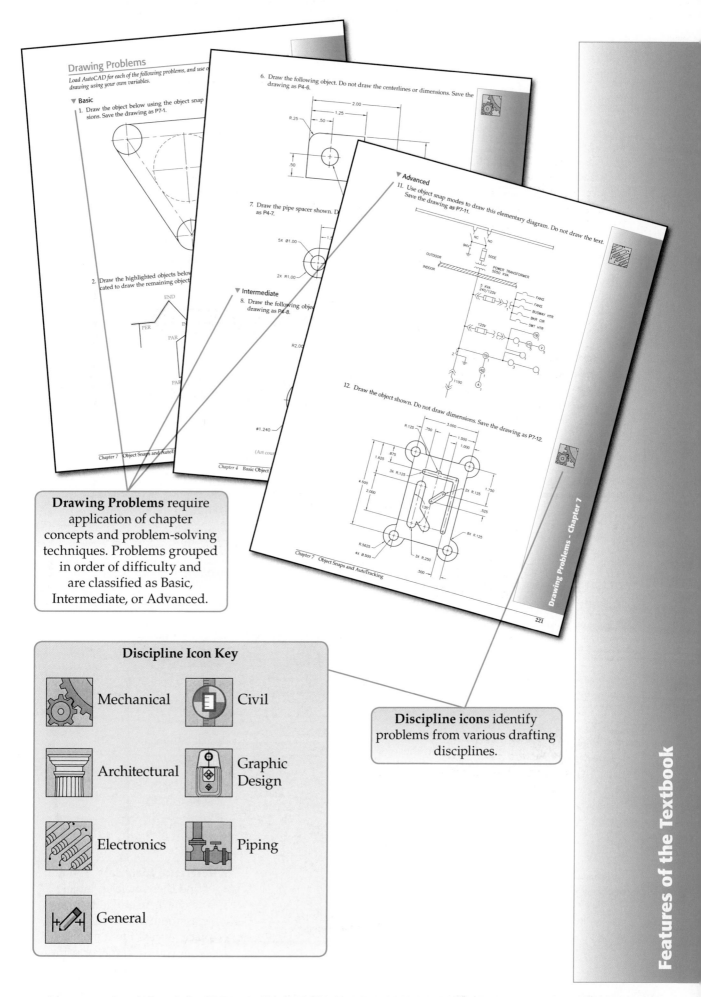

Drawing Problems require application of chapter concepts and problem-solving techniques. Problems grouped in order of difficulty and are classified as Basic, Intermediate, or Advanced.

Discipline icons identify problems from various drafting disciplines.

Discipline Icon Key

Mechanical

Civil

Architectural

Graphic Design

Electronics

Piping

General

Features of the Textbook

Features of the Student CD

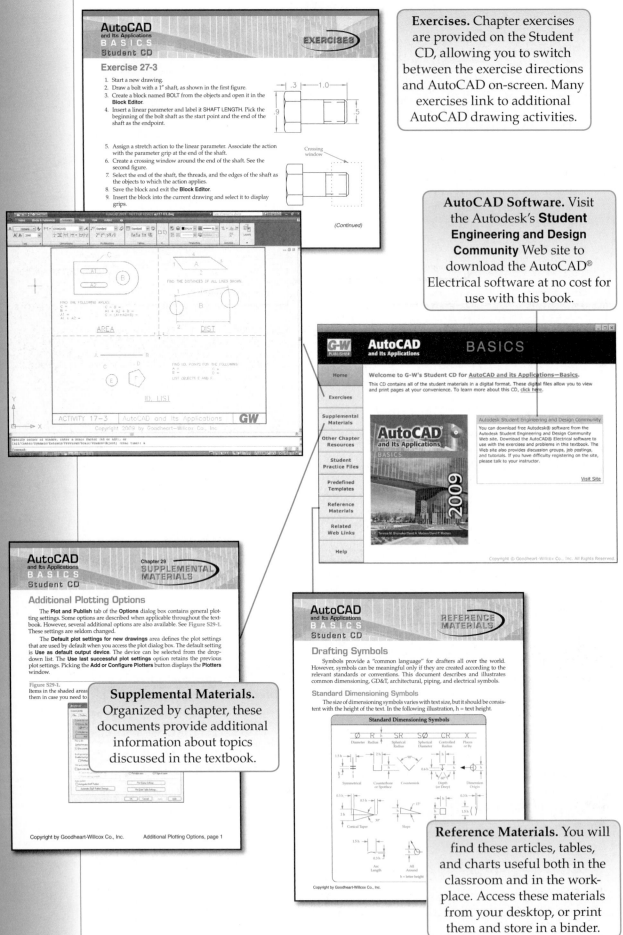

Exercises. Chapter exercises are provided on the Student CD, allowing you to switch between the exercise directions and AutoCAD on-screen. Many exercises link to additional AutoCAD drawing activities.

AutoCAD Software. Visit the Autodesk's **Student Engineering and Design Community** Web site to download the AutoCAD® Electrical software at no cost for use with this book.

Supplemental Materials. Organized by chapter, these documents provide additional information about topics discussed in the textbook.

Reference Materials. You will find these articles, tables, and charts useful both in the classroom and in the workplace. Access these materials from your desktop, or print them and store in a binder.

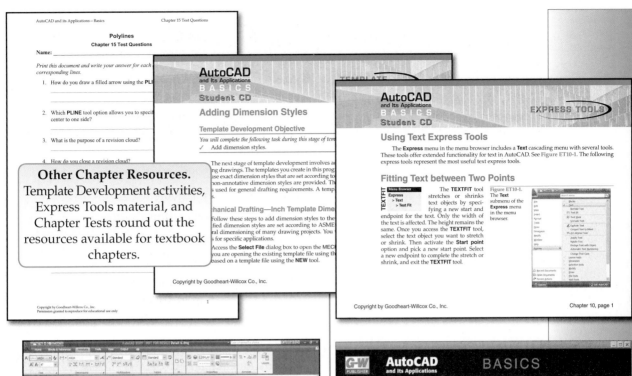

Other Chapter Resources.
Template Development activities, Express Tools material, and Chapter Tests round out the resources available for textbook chapters.

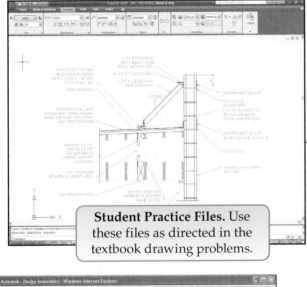

Student Practice Files. Use these files as directed in the textbook drawing problems.

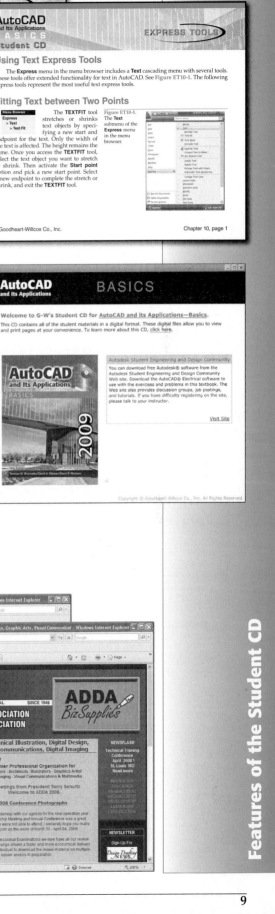

Related Web Sites. Use this to access a wide variety of CAD/Drafting Web sites.

Fonts Used in This Textbook

Different typefaces are used throughout this textbook to define terms and identify AutoCAD commands. The following typeface conventions are used in this textbook:

Text Element	Example
AutoCAD tools	**LINE** tool
AutoCAD menu browser menus	**Draw > Arc > 3 Points**
AutoCAD system variables	**LTSCALE** system variable
AutoCAD toolbars and buttons	**Quick Access** toolbar, **Undo** button
AutoCAD dialog boxes	**Insert Table** dialog box
Keyboard entry (in text)	Type LINE
Keyboard keys	[Ctrl]+1 key combination
File names, folders, and paths	C:\Program Files\AutoCAD 2009\mydrawing.dwg
Microsoft Windows features	Start menu, Programs folder
Prompt sequence	Command:
Keyboard input at prompt sequence	Command: **L** or **LINE**↵
Comment at a prompt sequence	Specify first point: (*pick a point or press* [Enter])

Other Text References

For additional information, standards from organizations such as ANSI (American National Standards Institute) and ASME (American Society of Mechanical Engineers) are referenced throughout the textbook. Use these standards to create drawings that follow industry, national, and international practices.

Also for your convenience, other Goodheart-Willcox textbooks are referenced. Referenced textbooks include *AutoCAD and Its Applications—Advanced* and *Geometric Dimensioning and Tolerancing*. These textbooks can be ordered directly from Goodheart-Willcox.

AutoCAD and Its Applications—Basics covers basic AutoCAD applications. For a textbook covering the advanced AutoCAD applications, please refer to *AutoCAD and Its Applications—Advanced*.

Trademarks

Autodesk, the Autodesk logo, 3ds max, Autodesk VIZ, AutoCAD, DesignCenter, AutoCAD Learning Assistance, AutoSnap, and AutoTrack are either registered trademarks or trademarks of Autodesk, Inc. in the U.S.A. and/or other countries.

Microsoft, Windows, and Windows NT are registered trademarks of Microsoft Corporation in the United States and/or other countries.

Contents in Brief

About the Authors

Terence M. Shumaker is Faculty Emeritus, the former Chairperson of the Drafting Technology Department, and former Director of the Autodesk Premier Training Center at Clackamas Community College. Terence taught at the community college level for over 25 years. He has professional experience in surveying, civil drafting, industrial piping, and technical illustration. He is the author of Goodheart-Willcox's *Process Pipe Drafting* and coauthor of the *AutoCAD and Its Applications* series.

David A. Madsen is president of Madsen Designs Inc (www.madsendesigns.com). David is Faculty Emeritus, the former Chairperson of Drafting Technology and the Autodesk Premier Training Center at Clackamas Community College and former member of the American Design and Drafting Association (ADDA) Board of Directors. David was honored by the ADDA with Director Emeritus status at the annual conference in 2005. David was an instructor and a department chair at Clackamas Community College for nearly 30 years. In addition to community college experience, David was a Drafting Technology instructor at Centennial High School in Gresham, Oregon. David also has extensive experience in mechanical drafting, architectural design and drafting, and construction practices. He is the author of Goodheart-Willcox's *Geometric Dimensioning and Tolerancing* and coauthor of the *AutoCAD and Its Applications* series, *Architectural Drafting Using AutoCAD, AutoCAD Architecture and Its Applications, Architectural Desktop and its Applications, Architectural AutoCAD,* and *AutoCAD Essentials.*

David P. Madsen is the vice president of Madsen Designs Inc. Dave holds a Master of Science degree in Educational Policy, Foundations, and Administrative Studies with a specialization in Postsecondary, Adult, and Continuing Education; a Bachelor of Science degree in Technology Education; and an Associate of Science degree in General Studies and Drafting Technology. Dave has been involved in providing Drafting and Computer-Aided Design and Drafting instruction to adult learners since 1999. Dave also has extensive professional experience in a variety of drafting, design, and engineering disciplines. Dave is the author of Goodheart-Willcox's *Inventor and Its Applications* and coauthor of *AutoCAD and Its Applications, Basics* and *Comprehensive* editions 14 through 16, and *Architectural Drafting Using AutoCAD 2009.*

Acknowledgments

Technical Assistance and Contribution of Materials

Margo Bilson of Willamette Industries, Inc.
Fitzgerald, Hagan, & Hackathorn
Bruce L. Wilcox, Johnson and Wales University School of Technology

Contribution of Photographs or Other Technical Information

Arthur Baker
Autodesk
CADalyst magazine
CADENCE magazine
Chris Lindner
EPCM Services, Ltd.
Harris Group, Inc.

International Source for Ergonomics
Jim Webster
Kunz Associates
Myonetics, Inc.
Norwest Engineering
Schuchart & Associates, Inc.
Willamette Industries, Inc.

Contents

Introduction to AutoCAD

Basic Drawing and Printing

Creating Text and Tables

Editing Drawings

Polylines, Splines, and Multilines

Dimensioning and Tolerancing

Additional AutoCAD Applications

Using Layouts

Student CD Content

Using the Student CD

Express Tools

Exercises

Template Development

Chapter Tests

Reference Materials

Supplemental Materials

Student Practice Files

Predefined Templates

Download Student AutoCAD

Related Web Links

CHAPTER 1

Introduction to AutoCAD

Learning Objectives

After completing this chapter, you will be able to do the following:

✓ Describe the methods and procedures used in computer-aided drafting.
✓ Describe typical applications for AutoCAD.
✓ Explain the value of planning your work and system management.
✓ Load AutoCAD from the Windows desktop.
✓ Demonstrate how to exit AutoCAD.
✓ Describe the AutoCAD interface.
✓ Select AutoCAD tools using a variety of methods.
✓ Use the features found in the **AutoCAD Help** window.

Computer-aided design and drafting (CADD) is the process of using a computer with drafting software to produce drawings according to specific industry and company standards. The terms *computer-aided design (CAD)* and *computer-aided drafting (CAD)* refer to specific aspects of the CADD process. Drafters and designers use CAD to create two-dimensional (2D) drawings, three-dimensional (3D) models, and animations. CAD also offers tools for analyzing and testing designs.

computer-aided design and drafting (CADD): The process of using a computer with drafting software to create and produce drawings.

CAD has surpassed the use of manual, or board, drafting because CAD provides increased speed, power, accuracy, and flexibility. However, designing and drafting effectively with computers requires a skilled CAD operator who is at least as knowledgeable as a manual drafter. Although the uses of CAD designs are limited only by the imagination, you should remember that computer equipment is sensitive, and that the human body reacts to the repetitive motions required when using CAD.

Using AutoCAD

AutoCAD tools are available for drawing objects of any size or shape. Objects can be given colors, patterns, and textures. Drawings can be annotated with text and described using a variety of dimensioning techniques. Careful use of the AutoCAD system is required for the planning and drawing processes. Therefore, it is important to be familiar with AutoCAD tools and to know how they work and when they are best suited for a specific drawing task. There is no substitute for knowing AutoCAD tools.

Learning the Cartesian Coordinate System

Cartesian (rectangular) coordinate system: A system in which point locations in space are defined using three perpendicular axes.

rectangular coordinates: XY or XYZ coordinate values.

origin: The point at which the Cartesian axes intersect.

Drawings and models are constructed in AutoCAD using the *Cartesian (rectangular) coordinate system*. The locations of points are described with XYZ coordinate values. These values, called *rectangular coordinates*, locate any point in three-dimensional (3D) space. XY coordinates locate a point on a flat, two-dimensional (2D) plane, such as a sheet of paper. The *origin* of the coordinate system is where the axes intersect. See **Figure 1-1A.** A distance measured horizontally from the origin is an X value. A distance measured vertically from the origin is a Y value.

3D Coordinates

To locate a point in 3D space, a third axis is needed. The third dimension rises up from the surface of the XY plane and is given a Z value. See **Figure 1-1B.** To describe a coordinate location, the X value is listed first, the Y value is second, and the Z value is third. Each value is separated by a comma. For example, the coordinate location of 3,1,6 represents a point that is three units from the origin in the X direction, one unit from the origin in the Y direction, and six units from the origin in the Z direction.

AutoCAD Applications

Using AutoCAD software and this textbook, you will learn how to construct, lay out, dimension, and annotate 2D drawings. *AutoCAD and Its Applications—Advanced* provides detailed instruction on 3D modeling and 3D rendering. Your studies can help you create a wide variety of drawings, designs, and 3D models in any of the drafting, design, and engineering disciplines.

Objects in AutoCAD drawings can have many properties, such as layers, which contain various object characteristics. Objects can be shown in 2D or 3D, or as 3D exploded assemblies. See **Figure 1-2.** Objects in the drawing can also be given "intelligence" in the form of *attributes*. For example, doors in a drawing can have attributes that define the door material, size, manufacturer, and price. These attributes can be used to automate some parts of the drawing process, such as creating a door schedule.

attributes: Text-based data that is assigned to a specific object. Attributes turn a drawing into a graphical database.

AutoCAD provides you with the ability to construct 3D models that appear as wireframes or have surface colors and textures. You can also create solid models that have physical properties, such as mass and density, that can be used for analysis. 3D models can be colored and shaded to appear in a realistic format. See **Figure 1-3.**

One powerful application of 3D CAD models is animation. The simplest form of animation is to rotate the model dynamically in order to view it from any direction. See **Figure 1-4.** Drawings and models can also be animated so the model appears to move, rotate, and even explode into its individual components. A *walkthrough* is a form of

walkthrough: A computer simulation that follows a path through or around a 3D model.

Figure 1-1.
The Cartesian coordinate system consists of X, Y, and Z axes. The intersection of the X, Y, and Z axes form the origin.

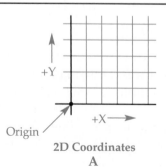

Origin

+X →

+Y

2D Coordinates
A

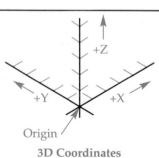

+Z

+Y   +X

Origin

3D Coordinates
B

Figure 1-2.
An example of
an exploded 3D
assembly model.

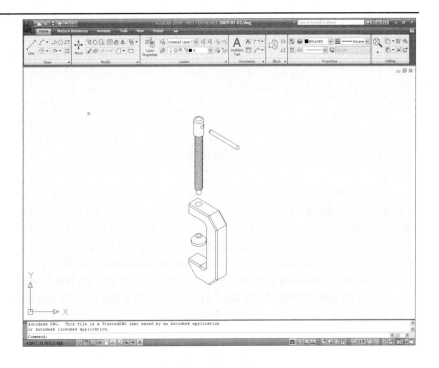

Figure 1-3.
3D models can be created and displayed in many formats, including the wireframe and
realistic formats shown here.

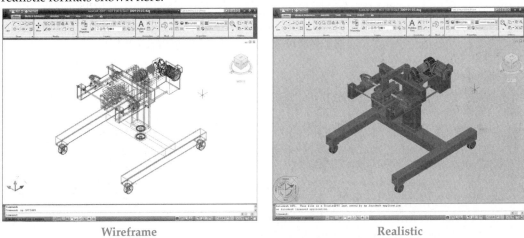

Wireframe   Realistic

Figure 1-4.
A model can be rotated, zoomed in and out, and viewed from any location in 3D space.

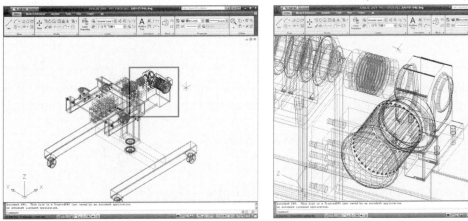

Initial Display   Highlighted Area Rotated and Zoomed In

virtual reality:
A simulation that responds to the viewer's physical movements.

animation in which you use AutoCAD's navigation tools to follow a path through or around a model. These concepts are described in *AutoCAD and Its Applications—Advanced*. The next step in viewing the model is to actually be inside it and have the ability to change objects. This is called *virtual reality*, and it is achieved through the use of 3D models and specialized software and hardware.

Planning Your Work

As you begin your CAD training, plan your drawing sessions thoroughly to organize your thoughts. Developing effective methods for managing your work is critical. Keep the following points in mind as you begin your AutoCAD training:

✓ Plan your work and organize your thoughts.
✓ Learn and use industry, classroom, or office standards.
✓ Save your work often.

If you remember to follow these three points, you will find it easier to use CAD tools and methods, and your experiences with AutoCAD will be more productive and enjoyable.

Planning a Drawing

Drawing planning involves looking at the entire process or project in which you are involved. A plan determines how you approach a project. It includes the drawings to be created, the title and numbering conventions, the information to be presented, and the types of symbols needed to represent information. Take as much time as needed to develop drawing and project goals. Then proceed with the confidence of knowing where you are heading.

Plan your drawing projects carefully. You may want your applications to happen immediately or to be automatic, but if you hurry and do little or no planning, you may become increasingly frustrated. A good drawing plan can save time. During your early stages of AutoCAD training, you should consider creating a planning sheet, especially for your first few assignments. Your planning sheet should document every tool and every coordinate point, or dimension, needed. You may also want to prepare a sketch as part of the planning process. A drawing plan and a sketch can help you:

- Determine the drawing layout.
- Set the overall size of the drawing by laying out views and required free space.
- Confirm the drawing units, based on the dimensions provided.
- Establish drawing settings.
- Preset drawing variables, such as layers, linetypes, and line widths.
- Establish how and when various activities are to be performed.
- Determine the best use of AutoCAD, resulting in an even workload.
- Maximize your use of equipment.

Using Drawing Standards

standards:
Guidelines containing operating procedures, drawing techniques, and record keeping methods.

Most drafting fields, schools, and companies have established *standards*. It is important that standards exist and be used by all CAD personnel. Drawing standards can include the following items:

- Methods of file storage (location and name)
- File naming conventions
- File backup methods and times
- Drawing templates with predefined settings
- Layouts
- Borders and title blocks

- Drawing symbols
- Dimensioning styles and techniques
- Text styles
- Table styles
- Layer settings
- Plot styles

The standards you follow may vary in content. The most important aspect of standards is that people use them. When you follow drawing standards, your drawings are consistent, you become more productive, and the classroom or office functions more efficiently.

The mechanical drafting standards used throughout this textbook are based on the American Society of Mechanical Engineers (ASME) and American National Standards Institute (ANSI) ASME Y series. Other drafting standards used throughout this textbook are based on appropriate discipline-specific standards. For example, architectural, structural, and civil drafting standards are based on standards developed by the American Institute of Architects (AIA), as stated in the United States National CAD Standard.

NOTE

Other drafting standards can be considered when setting up drawing templates. *DIN* refers to the German standard *Deutsches Institut Für Normung,* which was established by the German Institute for Standardization. *Gb* refers to *Guo Biao* (Chinese) standards, *ISO* is the International Organization for Standardization, and *JIS* is the Japanese Industry Standard. DIN, Gb, ISO, and JIS templates are based on metric measurement settings.

DIN: Deutsches Institut Für Normung—a standard established by the German Institute for Standardization.

Gb: Guo Biao (Chinese) standards.

ISO: International Organization for Standardization.

JIS: Japanese Industry Standard.

Saving Your Work

Drawings can be lost due to a software error, hardware malfunction, power failure, or your own mistakes. You should prepare for such an event by saving your work frequently. Develop the habit of saving your work at least every ten to fifteen minutes. The automatic save option, described in Chapter 2, can be set to automatically save your drawings at predetermined intervals. However, even if you use the automatic save function, you should also save your work manually at frequent intervals.

Working Procedures Checklist

As you begin learning AutoCAD, you will realize that several skills are required to become proficient. The following checklist provides you with some hints to help you become comfortable with AutoCAD. These hints also allow you to work quickly and efficiently.

- ✓ Plan all work with pencil and paper before using the computer.
- ✓ Frequently check object and drawing settings, such as layers, styles, and properties, to see which object and drawing aids are in effect.
- ✓ Read the prompts and tooltips displayed by AutoCAD. Consistently check for the correct options, instructions, or keyboard entry of data.
- ✓ Right-click to access shortcut menus; review available options.
- ✓ Think ahead and know your next move.
- ✓ Learn new tools and options. Do not rely on just a few that seem to work. Find tools and options that can increase your speed and efficiency.
- ✓ Save your work every ten to fifteen minutes.
- ✓ Learn to use available resources, such as this textbook, to help solve problems and answer questions. You should also become familiar with the AutoCAD help system.

Exercise 1-1
Complete the exercise on the Student CD.

Starting AutoCAD

AutoCAD 2009 is designed to operate with Windows Vista and Windows XP. If you see illustrations in this textbook that appear slightly different from those on your screen, do not be concerned, because the AutoCAD feature is the same.

When AutoCAD is first installed, Windows creates an AutoCAD 2009 *icon*, which is displayed on the Windows desktop and in the list of programs available from the Start menu. AutoCAD can be started using several different techniques. One of the quickest methods is to double-click on the AutoCAD 2009 desktop icon. A second option is to pick the Start button in the lower-left corner of the Windows desktop, move the cursor to Programs and hold it there or pick, and then select Autodesk, AutoCAD 2009, and finally AutoCAD 2009. See Figure 1-5.

icon: Small graphic representing an application, file, or tool.

Figure 1-5.
Double-click the AutoCAD 2009 icon on the Windows desktop or pick AutoCAD 2009 in the AutoCAD 2009 menu to load the program.

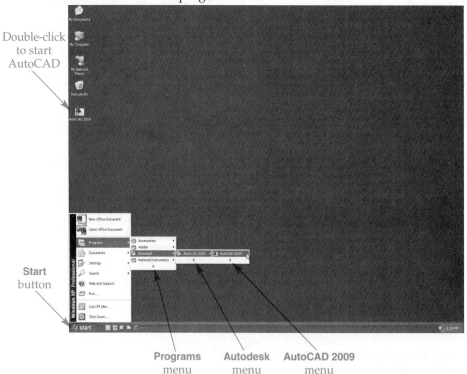

Double-click to start AutoCAD

Start button

Programs menu   Autodesk menu   AutoCAD 2009 menu

Figure 1-6.
You can use any of several techniques to exit AutoCAD when you have finished a drawing session.

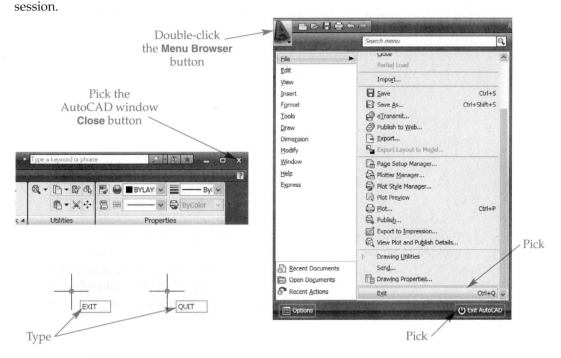

Double-click the **Menu Browser** button

Pick the AutoCAD window **Close** button

Type

Pick

Pick

Exiting AutoCAD

The **EXIT** tool is used to end an AutoCAD session. You can exit AutoCAD by picking the AutoCAD window **Close** button, located in the upper-right corner of the AutoCAD window; double-clicking the **Menu Browser** button, located in the upper-left corner of the AutoCAD window; selecting the **File** menu and then the **Exit** option in the menu browser; selecting the **Exit AutoCAD** button in the menu browser; or typing EXIT or QUIT and pressing the [Enter] key. See **Figure 1-6.**

NOTE

If you attempt to exit before saving your work, AutoCAD gives you a chance to decide what you want to do with unsaved work.

The AutoCAD Interface

Interface items include devices to input data, such as the keyboard and mouse, and devices to display or receive information, such as the monitor. AutoCAD uses a Windows-style *graphical user interface (GUI)* with a menu browser, ribbon, and dialog boxes, along with AutoCAD-specific interface items.

Figure 1-7 shows the appearance of the AutoCAD window when you first launch AutoCAD. AutoCAD's interface items are described in this chapter and throughout this textbook. Become familiar with the unique AutoCAD interface. Learn the format, appearance, and proper use of interface items to help quickly master AutoCAD.

interface: Items that allow users to input data into and receive outputs from a computer system.

graphical user interface (GUI): On-screen features that allow users to interact with a software program.

Figure 1-7.
The default AutoCAD window with the **2D Drafting & Annotation** workspace active.

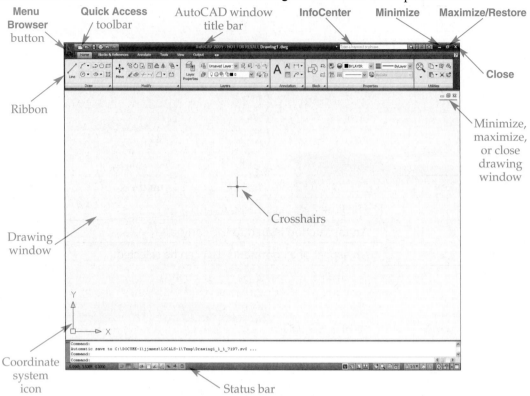

Menu Browser button | Quick Access toolbar | AutoCAD window title bar | InfoCenter | Minimize | Maximize/Restore

Close

Ribbon

Minimize, maximize, or close drawing window

Crosshairs

Drawing window

Coordinate system icon

Status bar

NOTE

As you learn to use AutoCAD, you may want to customize the graphical user interface according to common tasks and specific applications. *AutoCAD and Its Applications—Advanced* provides complete information on customizing the user interface.

Exercise 1-2
Complete the exercise on the Student CD.

Interface Terminology

Figure 1-8 provides a list and description of interface terms used throughout this textbook. Become familiar with these terms and reference Figure 1-8 as you learn AutoCAD.

Workspaces

workspace: Preset work environment containing specific interface items.

Three AutoCAD *workspaces* are available by default: **2D Drafting & Annotation**, **3D Modeling**, and **AutoCAD Classic**. The **2D Drafting & Annotation** workspace is displayed when you first launch AutoCAD. See Figure 1-7. The **2D Drafting & Annotation** workspace displays interface features above and below a large drawing window and contains only those tools and options specific to 2D drawing. The **3D Modeling** workspace contains a large drawing window and the same interface features found in the

Figure 1-8.
Common interface terms and descriptions.

Term	Description
Default	A value maintained by the computer until you change it.
Pick or click	Use the left mouse button to select an item on the screen.
Hover	Use the mouse to move the cursor over an item and hold the cursor at that location to display additional information or options.
Button	One of the ribbon, toolbar, or mouse buttons.
Key	A key on the keyboard.
Function key	One of the keys labeled [F1]–[F12] along the top of the keyboard.
[Enter] (↵)	The [Enter] key on the keyboard.
Command	An instruction issued to the computer.
Option	An aspect of a command that can be selected.
Tool	A command used to perform a specific drawing task. For example, the **LINE** tool is used to draw lines. The terms *command* and *tool* are often used interchangeably.
Drawing window	The largest area in the AutoCAD window, where drawing and modeling occurs. Also known as the *graphics window*.

2D Drafting & Annotation workspace, but it contains tools and options specific to 3D modeling. See Figure 1-9A. The **AutoCAD Classic** workspace, shown in Figure 1-9B, contains the traditional AutoCAD menu bar, toolbars, and the **Tool Palettes** window with tools and options that can be used for both 2D and 3D design applications.

To change workspaces, pick the **Workspace Switching** button on the status bar and select a workspace from the menu. You can also change the workspace by hovering over the **Tools** menu on the menu browser and picking a workspace from the menu or by typing WSCURRENT and the workspace name and pressing the [Enter] key. See Figure 1-10.

NOTE

This textbook focuses on the default **2D Drafting & Annotation** workspace. Only the **2D Drafting & Annotation** workspace interface items are shown throughout this textbook, except in specific situations that require additional items. Interface items and AutoCAD tools and options not shown in a workspace are still available and can be added to the workspace at any time.

Crosshairs

The AutoCAD crosshairs is the primary means of pointing to objects or locations within a drawing. The crosshairs changes to the familiar Windows cursor when you move the crosshairs outside of the drawing area or over an interface item, such as the ribbon.

Figure 1-9.
Each workspace displays different components on the AutoCAD window. A—The **3D Modeling** workspace. B—The **AutoCAD Classic** workspace.

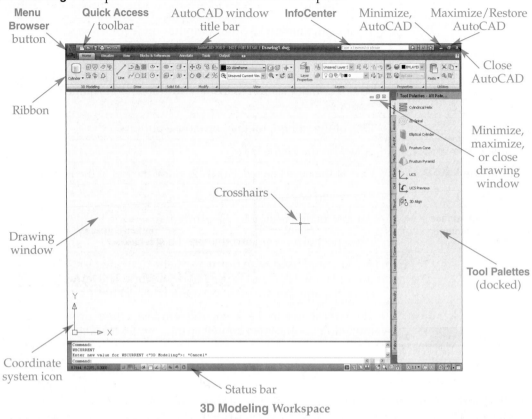

3D Modeling Workspace

A

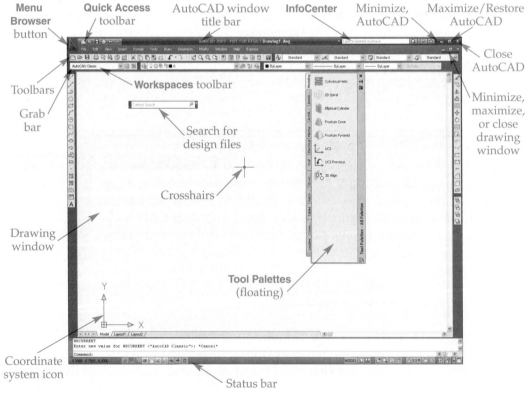

AutoCAD Classic Workspace

B

Figure 1-10.
Options for changing to a different workspace.

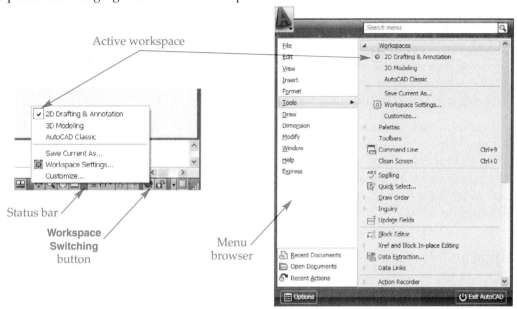

Active workspace

Status bar

**Workspace
Switching**
button

Menu
browser

You can increase or decrease the length of the crosshairs by accessing the **Display** tab of the **Options** dialog box. To display the **Options** dialog box, pick the **Options** button at the bottom of the menu browser. The text box or slider found in the **Crosshair size** area of the **Display** tab controls crosshairs size. The **Options** dialog box is described later in this chapter.

Tooltips

When you hover over an object in the drawing window, and most interface items, a *tooltip* displays. See **Figure 1-11.** The content presented in a tooltip varies depending on

AutoCAD 2009
NEW

tooltip: A pop-up window that provides information about the item over which you are hovering.

Figure 1-11.
Examples of tooltips displayed as you hover the crosshairs or cursor over an item.

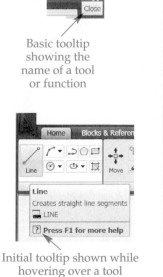

Basic tooltip showing the name of a tool or function

Initial tooltip shown while hovering over a tool

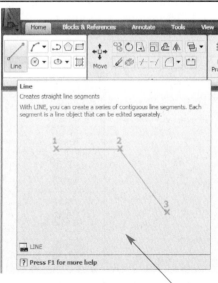

Tooltip expands as you continue to hover

the object or item. Some tooltips show only the item name. Other tooltips list object properties, a description of the tool, the command name, help file reference, and images.

Many tooltips expand as you continue to hover over the tool. The initial tooltip might only display the tool name, a brief description of the tool, and the command name. As you continue to hover, an explanation on how to use the tool and other information may be presented.

Controlling Windows

The AutoCAD program and drawing windows are similar to other windows within the Windows operating system. To minimize, maximize, or close the AutoCAD window or individual drawing windows, pick the small control icon in the upper-left corner, which displays a standard window control menu, or pick the appropriate icon in the upper-right corner. Window sizing operations are the same as those for any other window. Figure 1-12 shows a summary of standard window control functions available for drawing windows.

Floating and docking interface items

float: Describes interface items that can be freely resized or moved about the screen.

Several AutoCAD interface items, including the AutoCAD and drawing windows, can *float* or can be *docked*. Floating features are displayed within a border. Some items, such as the drawing window, have a title bar at the top or side. Floating windows can be moved and adjusted for size in the same manner as any other window. However, the drawing windows can only be adjusted and positioned within the AutoCAD window. Different options and functions are available depending on the particular interface item and whether the item is floating or docked. Typically, the close and minimize or maximize options are available. Some floating items, such as toolbars and panels, include *grab bars*.

docked: Describes interface items that are locked into position on an edge of the AutoCAD window (top, bottom, left, or right).

Locking interface items

grab bars: Two thin bars at the top or left edge of a docked or floating feature; used to move the feature.

AutoCAD interface items can be moved around to suit your work environment. To prevent items from being moved accidentally, some features can be locked in either a floating or docked state. To access locking options, right-click on an item and hover over the **Lock Location** menu option; pick the **Toolbar/Window Positions** button on the status bar; select the **View** tab on the ribbon and then the **Locking** *flyout* from the **Window Elements** panel; or select **Window** and **Lock Location** in the menu browser. The **Lock Location** menu options are displayed in Figure 1-13.

flyout: Set of related buttons that appears when you pick the arrow that appears next to certain tool buttons.

Select an option to lock the interface items that reside in that group as floating or docked. To unlock a group, select the option again. To quickly lock or unlock all of

Figure 1-12.
Drawing window control options.

Window Control Buttons		Resizing Controls	
Button	**Function**	**Cursor**	**Function**
 ▬	Minimize	 ↕	Size window vertically
 ⧉	Restore	↔	Size window horizontally
 ☐	Maximize	 ↘	Size window diagonally
 ✕	Close	 ⬉	Move window
 ⊞	Display window control menu		

Figure 1-13.
Interface items can be locked in position using one of several lock location options.

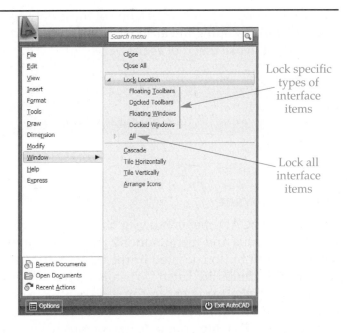

Lock specific types of interface items

Lock all interface items

the interface items, select **Locked** or **Unlocked** from the **All** cascading menu. A locked feature can be moved without unlocking it by holding down the [Ctrl] key while moving the feature.

Shortcut Menus

AutoCAD makes extensive use of *shortcut menus*, also known as *cursor menus, right-click menus,* or *pop-up menus,* to simplify and accelerate tool and option access. When you right-click in the drawing area with no tool active, the first item displayed on the shortcut menu is typically an option to repeat the previously used tool or operation. If you right-click while a tool is active, the shortcut menu contains *context-sensitive menu options.* See **Figure 1-14.** Some menu options have a small arrow to the right of

shortcut menus:
Context-sensitive menus available by right-clicking on interface items or drawing objects. Menu content varies based on the location of the cursor and the current conditions, such as whether a tool is active or whether an object is selected.

context-sensitive menu options:
Options that are specific to the tool that is currently in use.

Figure 1-14.
Shortcut menus provide instant access to tools and options related to the current drawing or editing operation.

Pick to view and select the most recent tools

Cascading menu of recent tools

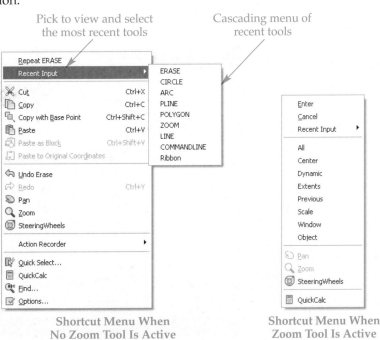

Shortcut Menu When No Zoom Tool Is Active

Shortcut Menu When Zoom Tool Is Active

the option name. When you pick one of these options, a *cascading menu* appears. The **Recent Input** cascading menu shows a list of tools you used recently. Pick a tool name from the list to use that tool again.

Exercise 1-3
Complete the exercise on the Student CD.

Menu Browser

The AutoCAD menu browser is used to access tools and settings through a system of menus and menu options. The menu browser displays when you pick the **Menu Browser** button, located in the upper-left corner of the AutoCAD window. See **Figure 1-15.** Menus are listed vertically on the left side of the menu browser.

Hover the cursor over a menu to expand a list of menu options on the right side of the menu browser. To activate the tool or option, pick the item or right-click on it and select the **Execute** option. Some options have a small arrow to the left of the item name. When you pick one of these options, the item expands to provide a submenu. Some selections are followed by an ellipsis (…). If you pick one of these items, a dialog box displays.

A tool or option accessible from the menu browser is presented as a graphic in the margin of this textbook, like the example shown in this margin. This graphic represents the process of picking the menu browser button, then hovering over a menu and picking a menu option or a cascading menu. The **LINE** tool is shown in this example.

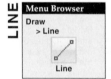

LINE

Menu Browser
Draw
> Line

Line

PROFESSIONAL TIP

Once a menu is displayed, you can use the up, down, right, and left arrow keys to move to different items in the menus. Press [Enter] to select a highlighted item.

Figure 1-15.
One way to access most tools and options is to use AutoCAD's menu browser.

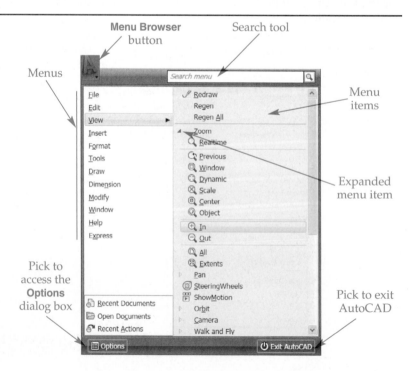

You can also access menus and menu options using menu accelerator keys. One method involves holding down the [Alt] key while pressing the key that corresponds to the underlined character in the menu. Another option involves the use of control keys, which are shown to the right of the option name and allow you to access certain predefined tools by pressing and holding the [Ctrl] key while pressing a second key. Despite the name, using accelerator keys is usually a more difficult means of selecting tools from the menu system.

Shortcut Keys

Many individual character key and key combination shortcuts are available for Windows and Windows-based applications. Refer to the Student CD: Reference Materials > Shortcut Keys for a complete list of keyboard shortcuts.

Searching for commands

The menu browser contains a search tool that can be used to locate and access any AutoCAD command listed in the Customize User Interface (CUI) file. To use the search feature, type the name of the command you want to access in the **Search** text box. As you type, commands that match the letters you enter are displayed. For example, if you type the letter *s*, all commands with an *s* in their name are displayed. Typing additional letters narrows the search, with the most relevant or best-matched command listed first. **Figure 1-16** shows the **Search** text box being used to locate the **SAVE** tool for saving a file. Pick a command from the list of matches to start the command.

Additional menu browser features

The menu browser also includes features for accessing recently opened files, currently opened files, and tools recently accessed from the menu browser. The **Recent Documents** and **Open Documents** menus are described in Chapter 2. Hover the cursor over the **Recent Actions** menu to display and execute tools that have recently been

Figure 1-16.
Use the menu browser to search for a command, and then pick from the list to start the command.

Type the name of a command here

Pick to start the command

Figure 1-17.
Use the **Recent Actions** menu to view and access commands that you have recently selected from the menu browser.

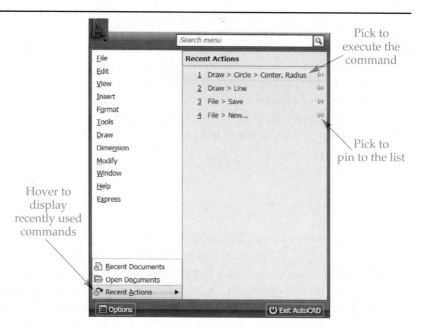

Pick to execute the command

Pick to pin to the list

Hover to display recently used commands

selected using the menu browser. See Figure 1-17. Tools accessed from other interface sources are not displayed.

By default, nine recently accessed tools are displayed, beginning with the most recent tool. Pick an action from the list, or right-click on the action and select **Execute** to start the tool. Other options are also available when you right-click on the action. Pick **Pin** to keep the tool on the recent actions list until the list is cleared. An action that is not pinned is eventually replaced by another tool as you select different tools from the menu browser. You can also pin the action to the list by picking the push pin button to the right of the action. Select the **Clear Recent Actions List** option to remove all tools from the list.

PROFESSIONAL TIP

You can specify the number of previous actions displayed in the menu browser by accessing the **Open and Save** tab of the **Options** dialog box. The setting that controls this function is the **Number of recently-used menu actions** value in the **Menu Browser** area.

Exercise 1-4
Complete the exercise on the Student CD.

Supplemental Material

Menu Bar
The AutoCAD menu bar is the traditional method for accessing the same menus available from the menu browser. Refer to the Student CD: Supplemental Materials > Menu Bar for more information on displaying and using the menu bar.

Figure 1-18.
Use the **Quick Access** toolbar to access commonly used tools quickly and conveniently. Pick a tool button to activate a tool.

Default tools available when a drawing is open

Default tools available when no drawing is open

Quick Access Toolbar

Toolbars are interface items that contain *tool buttons*. Each button on a toolbar displays an image that indicates an AutoCAD tool or tool option. As you move the cursor across a toolbar button, the button may display a border and highlights. Use the tooltip to become familiar with the tool icon. Select a toolbar button to activate the tool.

The **Quick Access** toolbar is displayed by default and is located on the title bar in the upper-left corner of the AutoCAD window to the right of the menu browser button. See Figure 1-18. The **Quick Access** toolbar provides fast, convenient access to some of the most commonly used tools. Activating a tool from the **Quick Access** toolbar is fast because it only requires a single pick. Most other interface items require two or more picks to activate a tool.

When a drawing is open, the default toolbar contains **New**, **Open**, **Save**, **Plot**, **Undo**, and **Redo** buttons. When a drawing is not open, the **New**, **Open**, and **Sheet Set Manager** tool buttons are displayed. The **Quick Access** toolbar can be fully customized by adding, removing, and relocating tool buttons.

toolbars: Interface items that contain tool buttons or drop-down lists.

tool buttons: Interface items used to start tools.

Additional Toolbars
Additional AutoCAD toolbars are available and can be displayed in the AutoCAD window. These toolbars are usually application- or task-specific. Refer to the Student CD: Supplemental Materials > Additional Toolbars for more information on displaying and using toolbars.

palette (modeless dialog box): Special type of window containing tool buttons and other features found in dialog boxes. Palettes can remain open while other tools are in use.

Exercise 1-5
Complete the exercise on the Student CD.

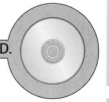

Ribbon

Many AutoCAD features are presented in *palettes*, also known as *modeless dialog boxes*. Palettes can look like extensive toolbars or more like dialog boxes, depending on the function and floating or docked state. They can contain tool buttons, flyouts, and many other features, such as list boxes, *drop-down lists*, and scroll bars. Unlike a dialog box, you do not need to close a palette in order to use other tools and work on the drawing. Some palettes are divided into *control panels*, or *panels*, separated by a line. Large palettes are divided into separate pages or windows, which are commonly accessed using *tabs*.

The ribbon, shown in Figure 1-19, is an example of one of the many AutoCAD palettes. The ribbon is shown by default in the **2D Drafting & Annotation** and **3D Modeling** workspaces. Tabs are displayed along the top of the ribbon. The tabs shown when the

drop-down list: A list of options that appears when you pick a button that contains a down arrow.

control panels (panels): Palette divisions that group tools.

tab: A small stub that sticks out at the top or side of a page or window, allowing you to move quickly to that part of the palette.

Figure 1-19.
The ribbon is an example of a palette that is docked at the top of the drawing window. Palettes are used to access tools, options, properties, and settings.

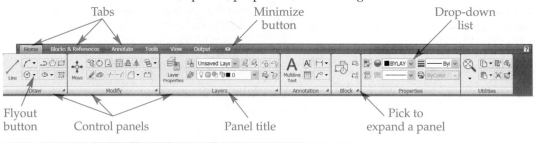

2D Drafting & Annotation workspace is active provide easy access to 2D drawing tools. The tabs shown when the **3D Modeling** workspace is active provide easy access to 3D modeling tools. Each tab is divided into panels that group tools and options for certain drawing or modeling tasks. For example, the **Annotate** tab includes several panels; each panel houses tools for creating, modifying, and formatting annotations, such as text.

The large tool button in a panel signifies the panel tool most often used. In addition to tool buttons, panels can contain flyouts, drop-down lists, and other items. Some panels show a small black arrow in the lower-right corner. If you see this arrow, pick the bottom, or title, of the panel to display a set of additional related buttons. You can show the expanded list on-screen at all times by selecting the push pin button. See **Figure 1-20.**

> **NOTE**
> When you pick an option from a ribbon flyout, the option becomes the new default and appears in the ribbon. This makes it easier to select the same option the next time you use the tool.

The tools provided in the ribbon can also be accessed using the menu browser, menu bar, toolbars, or by typing. The advantage of using the ribbon is that several tools, traditionally accessed by extensive typing, multiple toolbars, or several menus, are brought together in one location in the ribbon. Using the previous example of the **Annotate** tab, you need to type several tools, or access multiple menus or toolbars to find the same annotation tools located in the **Annotate** tab. The ribbon allows you to spend less time looking for tools and options, while reducing clutter in the AutoCAD window and increasing valuable drawing window space.

Basic adjustments to the default ribbon display can be made using shortcut menus. Right-click on a part of the ribbon that is not occupied by a panel to access a shortcut menu with a variety of ribbon display options. Pick **Minimize** and then **Minimize to Tabs** to show only tabs, requiring you to pick a tab to show panels. Pick **Minimize** and then **Minimize to Panel Titles** to show tabs and the titles of each panel. Minimize options can also be activated by pressing the **Minimize** button to the right of the tabs repeatedly.

Figure 1-20.
Some panels can be expanded to provide additional tools and options.

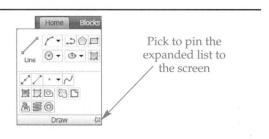
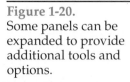

Figure 1-21.
Floating palettes
remain on-screen
as you work in the
drawing area.

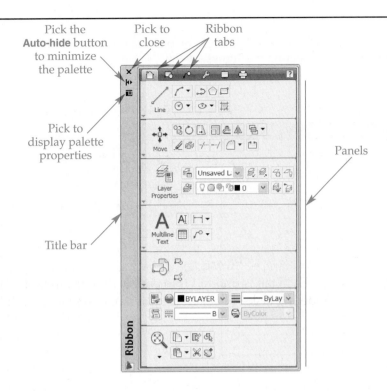

By default, the ribbon is docked horizontally below the AutoCAD window title bar. To change the ribbon to a floating state, as shown in **Figure 1-21**, right-click on the ribbon away from a panel and pick **Undock**. Most undocked palettes, including the ribbon, contain many of the same features. Right-click on the title bar or pick the **Properties** button to select from a list of options that allow you to control how the palette operates and displays within AutoCAD. The **Auto-hide** option allows the palette to minimize out of your way when the cursor is away from the palette.

A tool or option accessible from the ribbon is presented in a graphic located in the margin of this textbook, like the example shown in this margin. The graphic identifies the tab and panel where the tool is located. You may need to expand the panel or pick a flyout to locate the tool. The **LINE** tool is shown in this example.

PROFESSIONAL TIP

Resize a floating ribbon using the resizing arrows that appear when you move the cursor over the ribbon edge. Then pick the **Auto-hide** button to take full advantage of the ribbon while displaying the largest possible drawing area.

NOTE

To return the ribbon and other interface items to their default locations in the **2D Drafting & Annotation** workspace, pick the **Work-space Switching** button on the status bar and reload the **2D Drafting & Annotation** workspace.

Additional Palettes

The ribbon is the only palette displayed in the **2D Drafting & Annotation** workspace. However, many other palettes are used throughout the design and drafting process. All palettes are available by selecting **Tools** and **Palettes** in the menu browser. Most palettes can also be displayed using palette-specific access techniques. For example, to

Figure 1-22.
Tool palettes can be made transparent by picking the **Properties** button or right-clicking in the title bar and selecting the **Transparency...** option.

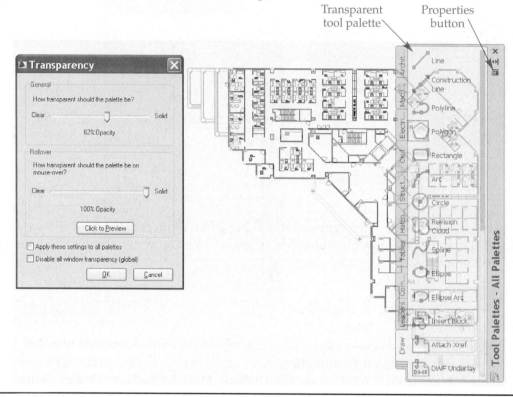

access the **Properties** palette, you can pick **Tools**, **Palettes**, and **Properties** in the menu browser; double-click on most objects in the drawing window; select an object and then select **Properties** from the shortcut menu; or type **PROPERTIES**.

When you display a palette for the first time, it is often in a floating state, though some pallets can be docked. Most of the palette control features available on the ribbon, such as docking and sizing, apply to other palettes. In addition, the **Properties** button or shortcut menu on some palettes include other functions, such as the **Transparency...** option, which makes the palette transparent, allowing drawing geometry behind the palette to be viewed. See **Figure 1-22.**

Additional palettes that you may use include **Properties**, **Layer Properties Manager**, **Tool Palettes**, **QuickCalc**, **External References**, **Sheet Set Manager**, **Markup Set Manager**, **DesignCenter**, **Lights in Model**, **Materials**, **Visual Styles Manager**, and **Advanced Render Settings**. These palettes play a major role in the operation of AutoCAD and are described when applicable throughout this textbook or in *AutoCAD and Its Applications—Advanced*.

NOTE

Deselect the **Allow Docking** palette property or menu option if you do not want to have the ability to dock a palette.

Exercise 1-6
Complete the exercise on the Student CD.

Figure 1-23.
Picking buttons on the application status bar is the quickest and most effective way to manage certain drawing settings.

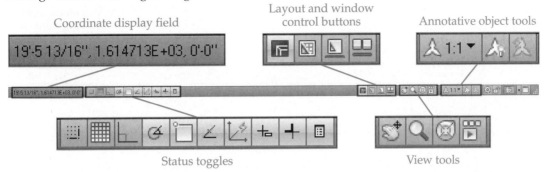

Coordinate display field

Layout and window
control buttons

Annotative object tools

Status toggles

View tools

Status Bars

AutoCAD provides two types of status bars. The application status bar applies to all open drawings. A drawing status bar, when activated, appears above the *command line* and is specific to each drawing.

Application status bar

The application status bar is located along the bottom of the AutoCAD window. See **Figure 1-23.** This status bar is divided into areas that display and control a variety of drawing aids and tools. The application status bar is the quickest and most effective way to manage certain drawing settings.

The coordinate display field, located on the left side of the application status bar, shows the XYZ coordinates of the crosshairs, identifying its location in drawing space. *Status toggle buttons* are located next to the coordinate display field.

> **NOTE**
>
> Status toggle buttons are shown as icons by default. To change the appearance of buttons from icons to names, right-click on any button and deselect the **Use Icons** option. This option only applies to the status toggle buttons.

The buttons on the right side of the application status bar control windows and the drawing environment, activate tools, and adjust annotation scaling. As you may recall, the **Workspace Switching** button is one option for changing and managing workspaces. The **Toolbar/Window Positions** button can be used to lock interface items. The remaining tools and settings available on the application status bar will be described when applicable throughout this textbook.

When you right-click on the application status bar, away from the coordinate display field or a button, a shortcut menu appears that allows you to modify the display of the application status bar. The same options are also available on the **View** tab of the ribbon by selecting the **Window Elements** panel and the **Status Bar** flyout. By default, all application status bar items are displayed. Deselect an option from the menu to hide the coordinate display field or a button.

Drawing status bar

A **Drawing Status Bar** option is available from the shortcut menu and the **Window Elements** panel of the ribbon. When this option is selected, a separate drawing status bar is shown in the drawing window. When the drawing status bar is displayed, the **Annotation Scale**, **Annotation Visibility**, and **AutoScale** tools move from the application status bar to the drawing status bar. See **Figure 1-24.**

command line: Area where commands (tool names) and options may be typed.

status toggle buttons: Buttons that toggle drawing aids and tools on and off.

Figure 1-24.
The drawing status bar, when displayed, is specific to the current drawing. When you have more than one drawing open, each drawing has its own drawing status bar.

Annotative object tools
move to drawing status bar

Drawing
status bar

Application
status bar

```
Command:
Command: STATUSBAR
Enter new value for STATUSBAR <1>: 2
Command:
```

PROFESSIONAL TIP

Right-click on the coordinate display field or a button in the application or drawing status bar to view a shortcut menu specific to the item. Picking options from a status bar shortcut menu is often the most efficient method of controlling drawing settings.

Exercise 1-7
Complete the exercise on the Student CD.

Dialog Boxes

dialog box: A window-like part of the user interface that contains various kinds of information and settings.

Pick any menu selection or button displaying an ellipsis (…) to activate a *dialog box*. An example of a dialog box is shown in **Figure 1-25.** This dialog box is displayed when you pick **Insert** and then **Block…** in the menu browser.

The cursor is used to set variables and select items in a dialog box. In addition, many dialog boxes include images, previews, or other methods to help you to select appropriate options. When you pick a button in a dialog box that is followed by an ellipsis (…), another dialog box appears. You must make a selection from the second dialog box before you can return to the original dialog box. A button with an arrow icon requires you to make a selection in the drawing area.

Dialog boxes contain many of the same features found in other interface items, including icons, text, buttons, and flyouts. See **Figure 1-26.** Become familiar with these features and reference **Figure 1-26** as you learn AutoCAD.

Figure 1-25.
A dialog box is displayed when you pick an item that is followed by an ellipsis. The dialog box shown here appears after you select the **INSERT** tool.

Drop-down
list

Button with ellipsis (…)
displays another dialog box

Check
box

Text
box

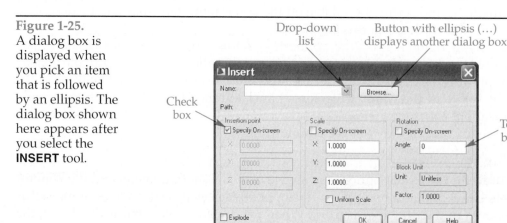

Command buttons

AutoCAD and Its Applications—Basics

Figure 1-26.
Standard dialog box features.

Feature	Example	Function
Command button	 OK Cancel Help	Causes an action to occur immediately. The default button is displayed with a dark border. Pressing the [Enter] key accepts the default. A grayed-out button cannot be selected.
Text box	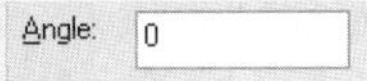 Angle: 0	Allows you to type a name, number, or single line of information.
Check box	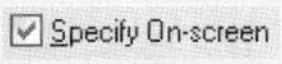 ☑ Specify On-screen	Turns an item on or off. Displays a ✓ when on (active). The option is off when the box is empty. Also known as a *toggle*.
Radio button	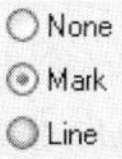 ○ None ◉ Mark ○ Line	Activates a single item in a group of options. Only one item in a group of radio buttons can be active at one time.
Tab	 Hatch | Gradient	Separates dialog box "pages," allowing easy access to each page.
List box	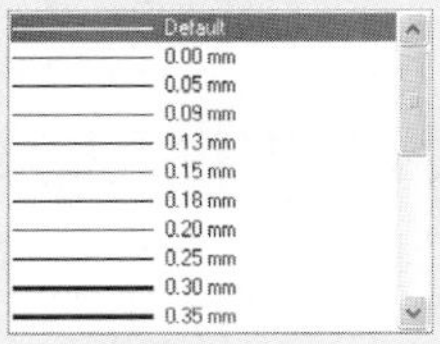 Default / 0.00 mm / 0.05 mm / 0.09 mm / 0.13 mm / 0.15 mm / 0.18 mm / 0.20 mm / 0.25 mm / 0.30 mm / 0.35 mm	Contains a list of items or options from which to select. A long list box displays a scroll bar. Highlight the desired item and press [Enter] or select it with the mouse.
Drop-down list	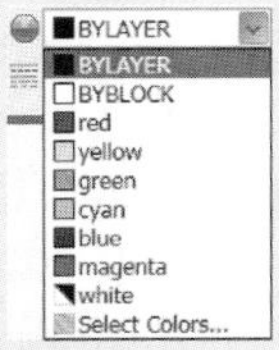 BYLAYER / BYLAYER / BYBLOCK / red / yellow / green / cyan / blue / magenta / white / Select Colors...	Similar to the list box, except only one item is initially shown. Pick the drop-down arrow to display a list below the initial item. Then pick from the expanded list or use the scroll bar (if present) to find an item.
Slider	 Min ─●─── Max	Increases or decreases a value when you slide the bar.
Preview box	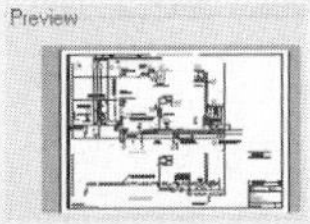 Preview	Displays a "picture," or thumbnail image, of an option or selected item.
Scroll bars and buttons	◁ ▭ ▷	Vertical scroll bars and buttons allow you to scroll up or down a list of items. Horizontal scroll bars and buttons operate in the same manner.
Alert	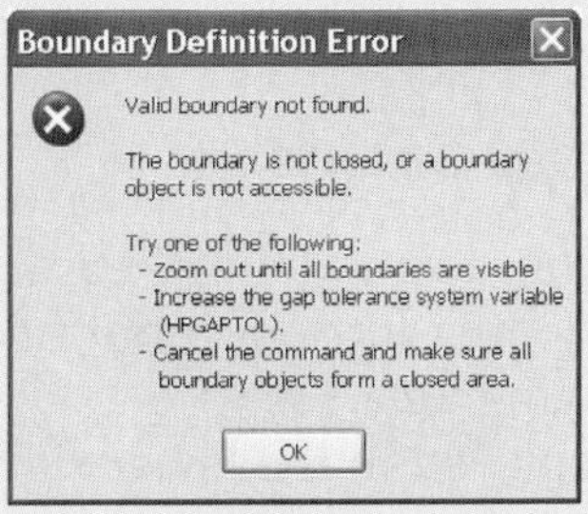 **Boundary Definition Error** ⊗ Valid boundary not found. The boundary is not closed, or a boundary object is not accessible. Try one of the following: - Zoom out until all boundaries are visible - Increase the gap tolerance system variable (HPGAPTOL). - Cancel the command and make sure all boundary objects form a closed area. OK	Indicates a potential problem.
... (Ellipsis button)	 Browse...	Provides access to a related dialog box.

System Options

OPTION

Type

    OPTIONS
    OP

Menu Browser

   Options

Tools
> Options

AutoCAD system options are contained in the **Options** dialog box. System options apply to the entire program and are not specific to any particular file. Many system options help configure your work environment. The **Options** dialog box is referenced throughout this textbook when applicable.

> **NOTE**
>
> The **Options** dialog box is also available by right-clicking when no tool is active and selecting the **Options...** menu option.

Selecting Tools

AutoCAD drawings are created by accessing and using tools. Tools are available by direct selection from interface items such as shortcut menus, the menu browser, the menu bar, toolbars, palettes, or the status bar. An alternative technique is to type the command that activates a tool using dynamic input or the command line.

Accessing tools using the interface items mentioned above can offer advantages over typing commands at the keyboard. One benefit is that you do not need to memorize commands or aliases. Tools and your drawing activities are shown on-screen as you work, using visual icons, tooltips, and prompts. As you work with AutoCAD, you will become familiar with the display and location of tools. As an AutoCAD drafter, you decide which tool selection technique works best for you. A combination of tool selection methods can prove most effective.

> **NOTE**
>
> Even though you may not access tools by typing command names, you must still enter certain values by typing. For example, you may have to enter the diameter of a circle using the keyboard.

Dynamic Input

dynamic input:
Area near the crosshairs where commands may be typed and context-oriented information may be provided.

Dynamic input allows you to keep your focus at the point where you are drawing. When dynamic input is on, a temporary area for tool input and tool information is displayed near the crosshairs in the drawing area.

When you type a command, it is displayed in the lower-right corner of the crosshairs. See **Figure 1-27**. When a tool is in progress, regardless of how the tool is accessed, the next action needed to proceed is displayed, along with additional tool options, an input area, and additional information.

Figure 1-27.
Using dynamic input, tools can be typed in or selected from a temporary input area next to the crosshairs.

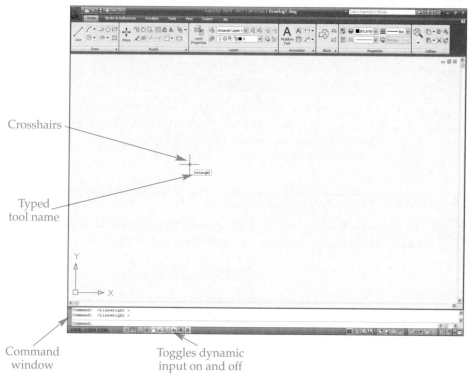

Crosshairs

Typed tool name

Command window

Toggles dynamic input on and off

command aliases (keyboard shortcuts): Abbreviated commands entered at the keyboard.

Depending on the tool that is in progress, different information and options are available in the dynamic input area. In **Figure 1-28,** the **RECTANGLE** tool has been started. The first part of the dynamic input area is the tooltip, which reads Specify first corner point or. In this case, you need to pick in the drawing area, type coordinates to specify the first corner of the rectangle, or use the arrow keys.

Pressing the down arrow key displays the options available for the current tool. See **Figure 1-29.** Options in the list can be selected at any time using the cursor. Pressing the down arrow again cycles through the available options, as indicated by a bullet next to the option. To select an option once it is bulleted, press [Enter]. The next available options and additional information are then displayed in the dynamic input area.

Figure 1-28.
The dynamic input fields after the **RECTANGLE** tool has been started.

Crosshairs   Tooltip   Arrow key   Coordinate

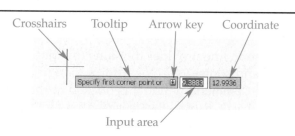

Input area

Figure 1-29.
Pressing the down arrow key exposes additional options for the current tool. Pick an option with the cursor, or use the up and down arrow keys to position the bullet at the desired option and press the [Enter] key to select that option.

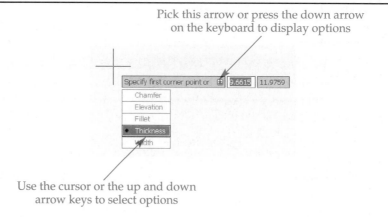

Pick this arrow or press the down arrow on the keyboard to display options

Use the cursor or the up and down arrow keys to select options

Figure 1-30.
The dynamic input fields change while a tool is active. Before you pick the first endpoint of a line, the coordinates of the crosshairs are displayed. After the first endpoint is picked, the distance and angle of the crosshairs relative to the first endpoint are displayed.

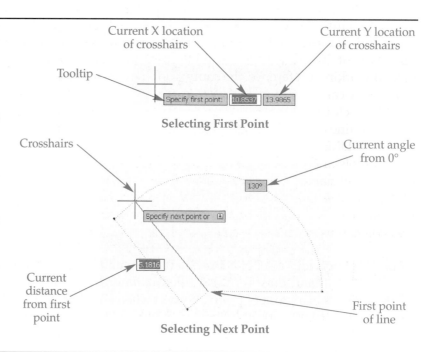

Current X location of crosshairs

Current Y location of crosshairs

Tooltip

Selecting First Point

Crosshairs

Current angle from 0°

Current distance from first point

First point of line

Selecting Next Point

The information displayed in the dynamic input area changes while you are working with the tool, depending on the actions you choose. **Figure 1-30** shows the dynamic input display for the **LINE** tool.

NOTE

Dynamic input can be used instead of the command line, or it can be disabled so that only the command line can be used for tool input and information. Dynamic input can be toggled on and off by picking the **Dynamic Input** button on the status bar or pressing the [F12] key.

Command Line

The command line provides the same function as dynamic input, but it allows you to enter tools and context-specific information in a more traditional window format. By default, the **Command** window is docked at the bottom of the AutoCAD window, above the status bar. It displays the Command: prompt and reflects any command entries you make. It also displays prompts that supply information or that request input.

Commands can be typed and information can be read at the command line when it is turned on. When you start a tool, AutoCAD either performs the specified operation or displays prompts for any additional information needed. The commands that activate AutoCAD tools have a standard format, structured as follows:

Command: **COMMANDNAME**↵
Current settings: Setting1 Setting2 Setting3
Instructional text [Option1/oPtion2/opTion3/...] <default option or value>:

If the command has associated settings or options, these are displayed as shown. The instructional text indicates what you should do at this point, and all available options are shown within the square brackets. Each option has an alias, or unique combination of uppercase characters, that you can enter at the prompt rather than typing the entire option name. If a default option is displayed in the angle brackets (<>), you can press [Enter] to accept it rather than typing the value again.

The command line is displayed in each default AutoCAD workspace, and the **Command** window can float or be docked, resized, and locked. The floating **Command** window contains the **Auto-hide** and **Properties** buttons found on palettes. Depending on your working preference, the command line can be used concurrently with dynamic input, or it can be disabled if you use only dynamic input. To hide the **Command** window, pick the **Close** button on the **Command** window title bar, right-click on the command line and pick **Close**, go to **Tools** > **Command Line** on the menu browser, type COMMANDLINEHIDE, or press [Ctrl]+[9].

All tools and options can be typed using either dynamic input or the command line. All tool names and aliases, along with other access techniques available in the **2D Drafting & Annotation** workspace, are shown in a graphic located in the margin of this textbook. The example displayed in this margin shows the command name and alias you can use to access the **LINE** tool.

PROFESSIONAL TIP

While learning AutoCAD, pay close attention to the prompts displayed at the command line and in the dynamic input area.

Keyboard Keys

Many keys on the keyboard allow you to perform AutoCAD functions quickly. Become familiar with these keys to improve your performance with AutoCAD. Whenever it is necessary to cancel a tool or dialog box, press the *escape key* [Esc] on the keyboard. This key is found on the upper-left corner of most keyboards and is typically labeled Esc. Some tool sequences require that you press the [Esc] key twice to completely cancel the operation.

escape key:
Keyboard key used to cancel a tool or exit a dialog box.

Select previously used tools using the up and down arrow keys. When no tool is active, press the up arrow key to display the previously used tool. If dynamic input is active, previously used tools are displayed near the crosshairs by default. To display previously used tools at the command line, you must pick the command line before pressing the up arrow key, or turn off dynamic input. If you continue to press the up arrow key, AutoCAD continues to backtrack through the tools you have used. Press [Enter] to activate a displayed tool.

Function keys provide instant access to tools. They can also be programmed to perform a series of commands. Function keys are located along the top of the keyboard and are numbered from [F1] to [F12].

Reference Material

Shortcut Keys

Refer to the Student CD: Reference Materials > Shortcut Keys for lists of keyboard entry tools. Keep printouts of these reference sheets handy while you learn AutoCAD.

Exercise 1-9

Complete the exercise on the Student CD.

Getting Help

HELP

Ribbon
?
Type
[F1] KEY
HELP
Menu Browser
Help
?
Help

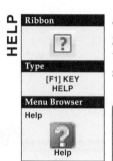

If you need help with a specific tool, option, or AutoCAD feature, use the powerful and convenient help system contained in the **AutoCAD Help** window. The margin graphic shows several ways to access the **AutoCAD Help** window. You can also access the **AutoCAD Help** window from the **InfoCenter**, described later in this chapter, or by selecting **Help** from a shortcut menu.

> **NOTE**
>
> If you are unfamiliar with how to use a Windows help system, spend time now exploring all the topics under **AutoCAD Help** in the **Contents** tab of the **AutoCAD Help** window.

The **AutoCAD Help** window consists of two frames. See Figure 1-31. The left frame, which has three tabs, is used to locate help topics. The right frame displays the selected help topics. The **Contents** tab in the left frame displays a list of book icons and topic names. The book icons represent the organizational structure of books of topics within the AutoCAD documentation. Topics contain the actual help information; the icon used to represent a topic is a sheet of paper with a question mark. To open a book or a help topic, double-click on its name or icon.

Although the **Contents** tab of the **AutoCAD Help** window is useful for displaying all the topics in an expanded table of contents manner, it may not be very useful when you are searching for a specific item. In this case, you should refer to the help file index. This is the function of the **Index** tab. The **Search** tab is used to search the help documents for specific words or phrases.

In addition to the two frames, six buttons reside at the top of the **AutoCAD Help** window. The **Hide/Show** button controls the visibility of the left frame. The **Back** button is used to view the previously displayed help topic. The **Forward** button is used to go forward to help pages you viewed before pressing the **Back** button. The **Home** button takes you to the AutoCAD Help page. The **Print** button prints the currently displayed help topic. The **Options** button presents a menu with a variety of items used to control other aspects of the **AutoCAD Help** window.

Figure 1-31.
The **AutoCAD Help** window.

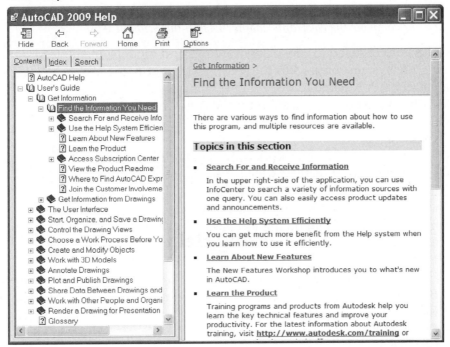

PROFESSIONAL TIP

If you press the [F1] key while you are in the process of using a tool, the help information associated with the active tool is displayed. This *context-oriented help* saves valuable time, since you do not need to scan through the help contents or perform any searches to find the information.

context-oriented help: Help information for the active tool.

Using the InfoCenter

The **InfoCenter**, located on the right side of the title bar, allows you to search for help topics without first displaying the **AutoCAD Help** window. It also provides buttons for access to the **Communication Center** and the **Favorites** list. Type a question in the text box to search for topics. Then select the appropriate topic from the list to display it in the **AutoCAD Help** window. To add a topic to the **Favorites** list, pick the star next to the topic. Pick the **Communication Center** button to access content on a variety of help topics. Pick the **Favorites** button to access any help topics you have stored.

Using the Support Knowledge Base

AutoCAD's product support extends beyond the locally installed help system. The Autodesk Web site provides additional support resources. To access this information, go to **Help** > **Additional Resources** > **Support Knowledge Base** in the menu browser. Your computer must have an Internet connection to access this information. Enter the topic in the text box to search the database.

Exercise 1-10
Complete the exercise on the Student CD.

Chapter Test

Answer the following questions. Write your answers on a separate sheet of paper or complete the electronic chapter test on the Student CD.

1. What system is used to construct drawings and models in AutoCAD?
2. Using the system referred to in Question 1, what is the proper notation for the values $Z = 4$, $X = 2$, and $Y = 5$?
3. Describe at least one application for the AutoCAD software.
4. What is drawing planning?
5. What are standards?
6. Why should you save your work every ten to fifteen minutes?
7. What is the quickest method for starting AutoCAD?
8. Name one method of exiting AutoCAD.
9. What is the name for the interface that includes on-screen features?
10. Define or explain the following terms:
    A. Default
    B. Pick or click
    C. Hover
    D. Button
    E. Key
    F. Function key
    G. [Enter] (↵)
    H. Option
    I. Tool
11. What is a workspace?
12. How do you change from one workspace to another?
13. What is the difference between a docked interface item and a floating interface item?
14. How do you select the locking options to lock the interface items in either their floating and docked state?
15. What is a flyout?
16. How do you access a shortcut menu?
17. What does it mean when a shortcut menu is described as context-sensitive?
18. Explain the basic function of the menu browser.
19. Describe the menu browser's search tool and briefly explain how to use it.
20. What is another name for a palette?
21. What is the function of tabs in the ribbon?
22. Briefly describe an advantage of using the ribbon.
23. Describe the function of the application status bar.
24. What is the meaning of the … (ellipsis) in a menu option or button?
25. What are the two primary methods for accessing AutoCAD tools? List interface items associated with each.
26. Briefly describe the function of dynamic input.
27. How do you hide the **Command** window?
28. Briefly explain the function of the [Esc] key.
29. How do you access previously used tools when dynamic input is on?
30. Name the function keys that execute the following tasks. (Refer to the Shortcut Keys document in the *Reference Materials* section of the Student CD.)
    A. Snap mode (toggle)
    B. Coordinate display (toggle)
    C. Grid mode (toggle)
    D. Ortho mode (toggle)
31. Identify the quickest way to access the **AutoCAD Help** window.

32. Describe the purpose of the book icons in the **Contents** tab of the **AutoCAD Help** window.

33. What is context-oriented help, and how is it accessed?

Problems

▼ Basic

1. Launch AutoCAD and perform the following tasks:
   A. Open the **AutoCAD Help** window.
   B. In the **Contents** tab, expand the **User's Guide** book.
   C. Expand the **Get Information** book.
   D. Expand the **Find the Information You Need** book.
   E. Pick and read each topic in the right pane.
   F. Close the **AutoCAD Help** window, and then close AutoCAD.

2. Launch AutoCAD using the Start button on the Windows task bar.
   A. Move the cursor over the buttons in the status bar and read the tooltip for each.
   B. Slowly move the cursor over each of the ribbon panels and read the tooltips.
   C. Pick the menu browser to display it. Hover over the **File** menu, then use the right arrow key to move to the **File** options. Then use the down arrow key to move through all the menu options.
   D. Press the [Esc] key to dismiss the menu.
   E. Close AutoCAD.

▼ Intermediate

3. Interview your drafting instructor or supervisor and try to determine what type of drawing standards exist at your school or company. Write them down and keep them with you as you learn AutoCAD. Make notes as you progress through this textbook on how you use these standards. Also note how the standards could be changed to better match the capabilities of AutoCAD.

4. Research your drawing department standards. If you do not have a copy of the standards, acquire one. If AutoCAD standards have been created, make notes as to how you can use these in your projects. If no standards exist in your department or company, make notes about how you can help develop standards. Write a report on why your school or company should create CAD standards and how they would be used. Describe who should be responsible for specific tasks. Recommend procedures, techniques, and forms, if necessary. Develop this report as you progress through your AutoCAD instruction and as you read through this textbook.

5. Develop a drawing planning sheet for use in your school or company. List items you think are important for planning a CAD drawing. Make changes to this sheet as you learn more about AutoCAD.

6. Create a freehand sketch of the default AutoCAD window with the **2D Drafting & Annotation** workspace active. Label each of the screen areas. To the side of the sketch, write a short description of each screen area's function.

7. Create a freehand sketch showing three examples of tooltips displayed as you hover the crosshairs or cursor over an item. To the side of the sketch, write a short description of each example's function.

8. Using the search tool on the menu browser, type the letter C and review the information provided in the menu browser. Then add the letter L. How does the information change? Continue typing O, S, and E to complete the **CLOSE** command. Write a short paragraph explaining how you might use this search tool to find a command if you are unsure how the command is spelled or where it is located.

9. Sketch the X and Y axes on a sheet of paper. Label the origin, the positive values for X = 1 through X = 10, and the positive values for Y = 1 through Y = 10. Then sketch the object described by the following coordinate points:
2,2
8,2
8,7
7,7
7,3
6,3
6,6
4,6
4,3
3,3
3,7
2,7
2,2

▼ Advanced

10. Sketch the X and Y axes of the Cartesian coordinate system as you did for the previous problem. Then sketch an object outline of your choice within the axes. List, in order, the rectangular coordinates of the points a drafter would need to specify in AutoCAD to recreate the object in your sketch.

11. Research and write a report of 250 words or less covering the U.S. National CAD Standard.

12. Research and write a report of 250 words or less covering workplace ethics, especially as related to CAD applications and CAD-related software.

13. Research and write a report of 150 words or less covering an ergonomically designed CAD workstation. Include a sketch of what you might consider a high-quality design for a workstation and label its characteristics.

Working with Drawings and Templates

Learning Objectives

After completing this chapter, you will be able to do the following:

✓ Start a new drawing.
✓ Use various save tools and options.
✓ Close a drawing.
✓ Open a saved drawing.
✓ Manage multiple open drawings.
✓ Create a drawing template.
✓ Determine and specify drawing setting, including units, drawing limits, snap, and grid.

In this chapter, you will learn how to start new drawing files, save drawing files, open existing drawing files, and prepare template files. Some of the basic drawing aids used in AutoCAD are also described. You will find the drawing settings explained in this chapter very useful as you begin working with drawing files.

Starting a New Drawing

There are two primary AutoCAD file types: *drawing files*, which have a .dwg extension, and *drawing templates*, which have a .dwt extension. New drawings are typically started from drawing template files, but the actual drawing is created and saved in a drawing file. Drawing templates, often just known as *templates*, store standard drawing settings and objects. All template file settings and contents are included in the new drawing. To help avoid confusion as you learn AutoCAD, remember that a new drawing file references a drawing template file, but the drawing file is where you create drawings.

drawing files: Files in AutoCAD that contain the actual drawing geometry and information.

drawing templates (templates): Files that contain standard drawing settings and objects for use in new drawings.

Figure 2-1.
The **Select template** dialog box allows you to begin a new drawing by selecting a template.

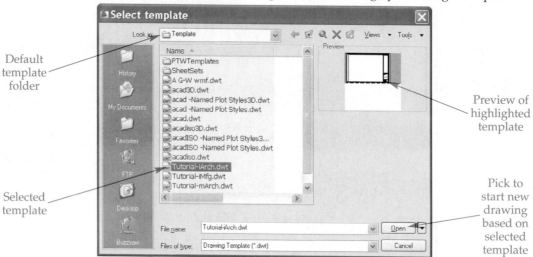

Default template folder

Selected template

Preview of highlighted template

Pick to start new drawing based on selected template

Using the New Tool

| Type |
| NEW |
| [Ctrl]+N |
| Menu Browser |
| File |
| > New... |

The **NEW** tool is the primary tool to start a new drawing that references a template file. The **Select template** dialog box appears when you access the **NEW** tool. See **Figure 2-1**. The **Select template** dialog box lists the templates found in the default template folder. AutoCAD includes a variety of predefined template files. All the files have a .dwt extension. To open a template file, double-click on the file, right-click on the file and pick the **Select** option, or select the file and pick the **Open** button.

The Tutorial drawing templates for architecture and manufacturing are provided with imperial and metric units. These templates include a border and title block. If you want to open a blank file, use the acad.dwt file for English settings or the acadiso.dwt file for metric settings.

> **PROFESSIONAL TIP**
>
> Use the **Options** dialog box to change the default drawing template folder displayed when you access the **NEW** tool. In the **Files** tab of the **Options** dialog box, expand Template Settings, and then expand Drawing Template File Location. Pick the **Browse...** button to select a folder.

Starting a Drawing from Scratch

You can start a drawing "from scratch" without using a template. Starting a drawing from scratch provides a blank drawing without a title block, layouts, or customized drawing settings. Use this option when you plan to make up the drawing session as you go along, such as if you are just sketching or when the start or end of a project is unknown.

To start a drawing from scratch, pick the arrow next to the **Open** button in the **Select template** dialog box. See **Figure 2-2**. Then select **Open with no Template-Imperial** or **Open with no Template-Metric**.

Figure 2-2.
Specifying a template file for the **QNEW** tool.

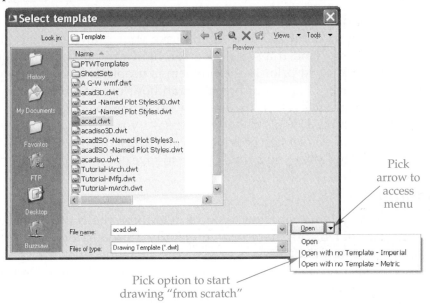

Pick arrow to access menu

Pick option to start
drawing "from scratch"

Starting a Drawing Quickly

AutoCAD provides a "quick start" feature that allows you to begin a drawing using a specific template. Before using quick start, you must specify the template to be used for quick starts. This is done in the **Options** dialog box. In the **Files** tab of the **Options** dialog box, expand Template Settings, and then expand the Default Template File Name for QNEW item. None is displayed by default. See **Figure 2-3.** Pick the **Browse...** button to select a template.

The **QNEW** tool activates the quick start template. If the Default Template File Name for QNEW setting is None, typing **QNEW** opens the **Select template** dialog box. The **QNEW** tool can also be accessed from the **Quick View Drawings** tool described later in this chapter.

Quick Access

QNEW

QNEW

Figure 2-3.
Starting a drawing without a drawing template.

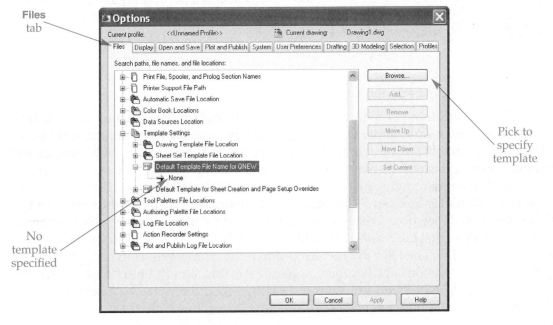

Files tab

Pick to specify template

No template specified

Saving Drawings

You should save your drawing immediately after you start a new drawing. Then, while working in AutoCAD, you should save your drawing every 10 to 15 minutes. This is very important! If a software error, hardware malfunction, or power failure occurs, all work saved prior to the problem is usable. If you save only once an hour, a system or power failure could result in an hour of lost work. Saving your drawing every 10 to 15 minutes results in less lost work if a problem occurs.

Several AutoCAD tools allow you to save your work. Also, any tool or option ending the AutoCAD session provides a warning asking if you want to save changes to the drawing. This gives you a final option to save or not save changes to the drawing.

Naming Drawings

Set up a system that allows you to determine the content of a drawing by the drawing name. Drawing names often identify a product by name and number—for example, VICE-101, FLOORPLAN, or 6DT1009. Drawing titles should be standardized and are most effective when they contain a clear and concise reference to the project, part number, process, sheet number, and revision level.

Although it is possible to give a drawing file an extended name, such as Details for Top Half of Compressor Housing for ACME, Inc., Part Number 4011A, Revision Level C, this is normally not a practical way of sorting drawing information. A standardized naming system that uses a shorter name, such as ACME.4011A.C, provides all the necessary information. If additional information is needed for easier recognition, it can be added to the base name; for example: ACME 4011A.C Compressor Housing.Top.Casting Details.

Remember the following rules and restrictions when naming AutoCAD drawings:
- A maximum of 256 characters can be used.
- Alphabetic and numeric characters and spaces, as well as most punctuation symbols, can be used.
- Characters that cannot be used include: quotation mark ("), asterisk (*), question mark (?), forward slash (/), and backward slash (\).

PROFESSIONAL TIP

Every school or company should have a drawing naming system. Drawing names should be recorded in a part numbering or drawing name log. Such a log serves as a valuable reference long after you forget what the drawings contain.

Using the Qsave Tool

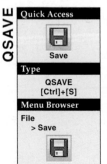

QSAVE

Quick Access

Save

Type

QSAVE
[Ctrl]+[S]

Menu Browser

File
> Save

The **QSAVE** tool is the most frequently used tool for saving your work. **QSAVE** stands for *quick save*. If the current drawing has a name, accessing the **QSAVE** tool updates the file based on the current state of the drawing. In this situation, **QSAVE** issues no prompts and displays no dialog boxes.

If the current drawing has not yet been named, the **QSAVE** tool displays the **Save Drawing As** dialog box. See Figure 2-4. The **Save Drawing As** dialog box is a standard file selection dialog box. To save a file, choose the type of file to save, such as drawing (.dwg) or template (.dwt); select the folder in which the file is to be saved; and type a name for the file. The **Files of type:** drop-down list offers options to save the drawing file in alternative formats. For most applications, this should be set to AutoCAD 2007 Drawing (*.dwg) when you are saving drawings. Use the AutoCAD Drawing Template (*.dwt) when you save a template file.

Figure 2-4.
The **Save Drawing As** dialog box.

Select folder where drawing will be saved

Move up one level from current folder

Create a new folder

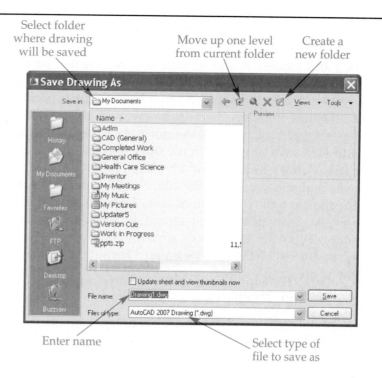

Enter name

Select type of file to save as

When you select the folder in which to store the file, first pick the disk drive from the **Save in:** drop-down list. To move upward from the current folder, pick the **Up one level** button. To create a new folder in the current location, pick the **Create New Folder** button and type the folder name.

> **NOTE**
>
> Drawings created in AutoCAD 2009 are saved as AutoCAD 2007 drawings. You will not see an option for saving a drawing as an AutoCAD 2009 drawing file in the **Files of type:** drop-down list.

If the drawing has not yet been named, the name Drawing1 appears in the **File name:** text box, if the file is the first drawing file started since AutoCAD was launched. Change the name to the desired drawing name. You do not need to include the .dwg extension. Once you specify the correct location and file name, pick the **Save** button to save the drawing file. You can also press the [Enter] key to activate the **Save** button.

Using the Saveas Tool

The **SAVEAS** tool is used when the current drawing already has a name and you need to save it under a different name, or when you need to save the current drawing in an alternative format, such as a previous AutoCAD release format. The **SAVEAS** tool is also used when you *open* a drawing template file to use as a basis for another drawing. This leaves the template unchanged and ready to be used for other drawings.

The **SAVEAS** tool always displays the **Save Drawing As** dialog box. If the current drawing has already been saved, the current name and location are displayed. Confirm that the **Save in:** drop-down list displays the correct drive and folder and that the **Files of type:** drop-down list displays the desired file type. Type the new drawing name in the **File name:** text box and pick the **Save** button.

Type
SAVE
SAVEAS
Menu Browser
File
> Save As...

SAVEAS

Saving Your Work Automatically

AutoCAD can create an automatic backup copy of the active drawing. The backup file has a .bak extension and is automatically created in the same folder where the drawing is located. When you save the drawing, the DWG file is updated, and the BAK file is overwritten by the old DWG file. Therefore, the backup file is always "one save behind" the drawing file.

The backup feature is on by default and can be controlled using the **Create backup copy with each save** check box in the **Open and Save** tab of the **Options** dialog box. See **Figure 2-5.** Before you can open a backup file in AutoCAD, you must rename it. Use Windows Explorer to rename the file, changing the file extension from .bak to .dwg. Once the file has a file extension of .dwg, it can be opened in AutoCAD.

automatic save (autosave): A save procedure that occurs at specified intervals without input from the user.

AutoCAD provides another automatic work-saving tool called *automatic save (autosave)*. Type the amount of time (in minutes) between saves in the **Minutes between saves** text box in the **File Safety Precautions** area of the **Open and Save** tab in the **Options** dialog box, as shown in **Figure 2-5.** The default setting automatically saves every 10 minutes.

The autosave timer starts as soon as a change is made to the drawing. The timer is reset when the drawing is saved. The drawing is automatically saved when you start the first tool after the autosave time has been reached. For example, if you set the timer to 10 minutes, work for 9 minutes, and then let the computer remain idle for 5 minutes, an automatic save is not executed until you return and execute a tool. Therefore, be sure to save your drawing manually if you plan to be away from your computer for an extended period of time.

The autosave feature is intended to be used in case AutoCAD shuts down unexpectedly. Therefore, when you close a drawing file, the autosave file associated with that drawing is automatically deleted. If AutoCAD does shut down unexpectedly, the autosave file remains and can be used. By default, the next time you open AutoCAD after a system failure, the **Drawing Recovery Manager** displays, containing a node for every drawing file to display all of the available versions of the drawing: the original drawing, the recovered drawing saved at the time of the system failure, the autosave file, and the .bak file. Pick each version in the **Drawing Recovery Manager** to view it,

---

Figure 2-5.
Use the **Open and Save** tab in the **Options** dialog box to set up automatic backup files and the autosave feature.

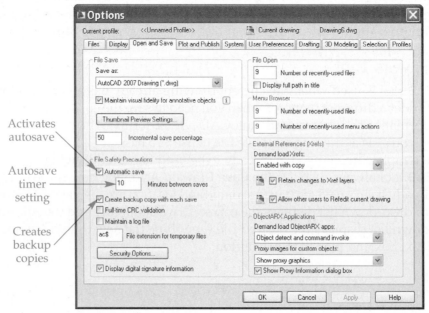

determine which version you want to save, and then save that file. It is possible to save it over the original name of the file.

NOTE

The **Automatic Save File Location** listing in the **Files** tab of the **Options** dialog box determines the folder where the autosave files are stored.

Windows Explorer

Windows Explorer is an effective tool for renaming files, including changing the file extension. Using Windows Explorer to accomplish tasks is mentioned throughout this chapter. Refer to the Student CD: Supplemental Materials > Windows Explorer for more information about using Windows Explorer.

Saving Drawings to Older Release Formats

The drawing file type saved by AutoCAD 2009 is a different file format from the file types saved by some previous releases of AutoCAD. AutoCAD 2009 drawings can be saved in an older file format, such as the AutoCAD 2004 format. This allows you to send AutoCAD 2009 drawings to companies where older releases of AutoCAD are used.

To save a drawing to an older release format, use the **SAVEAS** tool. Using the **Files of type:** drop-down list in the **Save Drawing As** dialog box, select the older release, such as AutoCAD 2004/LT2004 Drawing (*.dwg), to save the drawing in the AutoCAD 2004 format. AutoCAD 2004, 2005, and 2006 all use AutoCAD 2004-format files. When you save a version of a drawing in an earlier format, be sure to give it a name that is different from the AutoCAD 2009 version. This prevents you from accidentally overwriting your working drawing with the older format file.

Closing a Drawing

Use the **CLOSE** tool to exit a drawing file without ending the AutoCAD session. One of the quickest methods of closing a file is to pick the **Close** button from the drawing window title bar. If you close a file before saving your work, an AutoCAD alert box with the message Save Changes to *drawing*.dwg? appears. Pick the **Yes** button to save the drawing. Pick the **No** button to discard any changes made to the drawing since the previous save. Pick the **Cancel** button if you decide not to close the drawing and want to return to the drawing area.

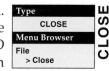

Type	
	CLOSE
Menu Browser	
File	
	> Close

CLOSE

NOTE

You can also close a file by picking the **Close** button available in the **Quick View Drawings** tool, described later in this chapter.

Quick Access

Open...

Type

OPEN
[Ctrl]+[O]

Menu Browser

File
> Open...

Opening Existing Drawings

An existing drawing is one that has been previously saved. Existing drawings that have been closed can be opened in various ways. You can use the **Open** tool, select recently opened files from the menu browser, or open a drawing from Windows Explorer.

Using the Open Tool

You can access any existing drawing using the **OPEN** tool. The **Select File** dialog box, which appears when you access the **OPEN** tool, contains a list of folders and files. See **Figure 2-6.** Double-click on a file folder to open it, and then double-click on the desired file to open it..

When you select an existing drawing, an image of the drawing is displayed in the **Preview** area. This provides an easy way for you to view each drawing without loading it into AutoCAD. After picking a drawing file name to highlight it, you can quickly highlight other files and scan through the drawing previews using the keyboard arrow keys. Use the up and down arrow keys to move vertically between files, and use the left and right arrow keys to move horizontally. The **Select File** dialog box includes a list on left side that provides instant access to certain folders. See **Figure 2-7.**

NOTE

You can also access the **Open** dialog box by picking the open button in the **Quick View Drawings** toolbar, described later in this chapter.

Figure 2-6.
The **Select File** dialog box is used to open a drawing. In this illustration, the AutoCAD 2009\ Sample folder is open. The Architectural – Annotation Scaling and Multileaders drawing has been selected and appears in the File name: text box.

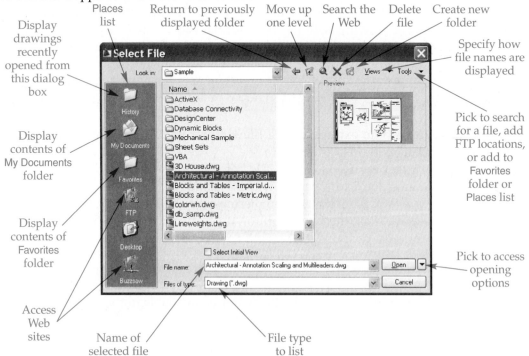

Figure 2-7.
Additional **Select File** dialog box features.

Button	Function	Description
	History	Lists drawing files recently opened from the **Select File** dialog box.
	My Documents	Displays the files and folders contained in the My Documents folder for the current user.
	Favorites	Displays files and folders located in the Favorites folder for the current user.
	FTP	Displays available FTP (file transfer protocol) sites. To add or modify the listed FTP sites, select **Add/Modify FTP Locations** from the **Tools** menu.
	Desktop	Lists the files, folders, and drives located on the computer desktop.
	Buzzsaw	Displays projects on the Buzzsaw Web site. Buzzsaw.com is designed for the building industry. After setting up a project hosting account, users can access drawings from a given construction project on the Web site. This allows the various companies involved in the project to have instant access to the drawing files.

Exercise 2-1

Complete the exercise on the Student CD.

Finding Files

You can search for files by picking **Find...** in the **Tools** drop-down list at the top of the **Select File** dialog box. This accesses the **Find** dialog box, as shown in Figure 2-8. If you know the drawing file name, type it in the **Named:** text box. If you do not know the name, you can use wildcard characters, such as *, to narrow the search.

Figure 2-8.
The **Find** dialog box is used to locate drawing files.

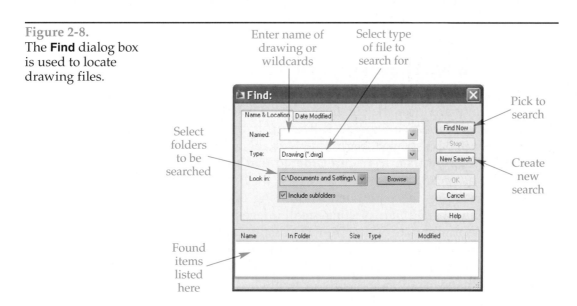

Choose the type of file from the **Type:** drop-down list. You can search for DWG, DWS, DXF, or DWT files from the **Find** dialog box. To search for another type of file, use the Windows Explorer search tool.

To complete a search more quickly, avoid searching the entire hard drive. If you know the folder in which the file is located, specify the folder in the **Look in:** text box. Pick the **Browse** button to select a folder from the **Browse for Folder** dialog box. Check the **Include subfolders** check box if you want the subfolders within the selected folder to be searched.

You can also search for files based on when they were last modified. The **Date Modified** tab provides options to search for files modified within a certain time period. This option is useful if you wish to list all drawings modified within a specific week or month.

PROFESSIONAL TIP

Certain file management capabilities are available in file dialog boxes, similar to those in Windows Explorer. To rename an existing file or folder, pick it once and pause for a moment, then pick the name again. This places the name in a text box for editing. Type the new name and press [Enter].

Right-click on a folder to display a shortcut menu of available options. Use one of the options or pick somewhere off the menu to close it.

CAUTION

Use extreme caution when you are deleting or renaming files and folders. Never delete or rename anything if you are not absolutely certain you should. If you are unsure, ask your instructor or system administrator for assistance.

Exercise 2-2
Complete the exercise on the Student CD.

Opening Recent Drawings from the Menu Browser

Quickly open recently opened documents using the **Recent Documents** menu on the menu browser. Hover the cursor over the **Recent Documents** menu to show the files in the right pane. See **Figure 2-9.** By default, the name and location of 9 recently opened files can be displayed, beginning with the most recent file.

Select **Group by Date** from the **Ordered List** drop-down list to group recently opened files according to the date on which they were last opened, or select **Group by Type** to group by file type, such as drawing or drawing template files. You can display recently opened files as icons, small images, medium images, or large images by picking the appropriate option from the display options flyout.

When you hover the cursor over a file in the list of recent documents, a tooltip with file information and a preview of the file appears to help you select the correct file. Pick a file from the list to open the file, or right-click on the file to list opening options. The **Open Read-Only** and **Partial Open** options are described later in this chapter. Pick

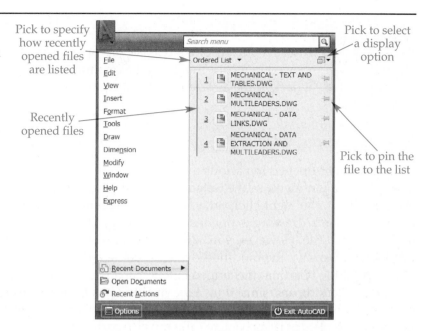

Figure 2-9.
Use the **Recent Documents** menu on the menu browser to quickly locate and open a file that has been opened recently.

Pick to specify how recently opened files are listed

Recently opened files

Pick to select a display option

Pick to pin the file to the list

Pin to keep the file on the recent documents list until the list is cleared. A file that is not pinned is eventually replaced by another file as additional files are opened. You can also pin the file to the list by picking the push pin icon to the right of the file. Select **Clear Recent Documents List** to remove all of the files from the list.

PROFESSIONAL TIP

You can specify the number of previous drawings displayed in the **File** pull-down menu by accessing the **Open and Save** tab of the **Options** dialog box. The setting that controls this function is the **Number of recently-used files** value in the **Menu Browser** area.

NOTE

If you try to open a file after it has been deleted or moved to a different drive or folder, AutoCAD displays the message Cannot find the specified drawing file. Please verify that the file exists. AutoCAD then opens the **Select File** dialog box.

Using Windows Explorer to Open Drawings

You can open drawing files using Windows Explorer in either of two ways. You can double-click on the file, and it opens in AutoCAD. If AutoCAD is not already running, it starts and the file opens. You can also drag-and-drop a file onto the AutoCAD **Command** window. If AutoCAD is not running, you can drag-and-drop the file onto the AutoCAD 2009 icon on your desktop. AutoCAD then starts and opens the drawing file.

Opening Drawings from Previous AutoCAD Releases

In AutoCAD 2009, you can open drawing files created in AutoCAD Release 12 or later. When you open a drawing from a previous release and work on it, AutoCAD automatically updates the drawing to the AutoCAD 2007 file format when you save. After the drawing is saved in AutoCAD 2009, it can be viewed in the **Preview** image tile in the **Select File** dialog box during future applications.

Opening Drawings As Read-Only or Partial Open

Files can be opened in various modes by selecting the appropriate option from the **Open** drop-down menu in the **Select File** dialog box, or from the shortcut menu that appears when you right-click on a file in the **Recent Documents** menu of the menu browser. When a drawing is opened as *read-only*, drawing changes cannot be saved to the original file. However, you can make changes to the drawing and then use the **SAVEAS** tool to save the modified drawing using a different name. This ensures that the original file remains unchanged.

When working with large drawings, you can open only part of a drawing by selecting specific views and layers to be opened. This process is known as a *partial open*. (Views and layers are described in later chapters.) You can also partially open a drawing in the read-only mode.

read-only:
Describes a drawing file that has been opened for viewing only. You can make changes to the drawing, but you cannot save them without using the **SAVEAS** tool.

partial open:
Opening a portion of a file by specifying only the views and layers you need to see.

Working with Multiple Documents

AutoCAD allows you to have multiple drawings and drawing templates open at the same time. Most drafting projects are composed of a number of drawings; each drawing presents different aspects of the project. For example, in an architectural drafting project, required drawings might include a site plan, a floor plan, electrical and plumbing plans, and assorted detail drawings. Another example is a mechanical assembly composed of several unique parts. The required drawings in this example might include an overall assembly drawing, plus individual detail drawings of each component. The drawings in such projects are closely related to one another. By opening two or more of these drawings at the same time, you can easily reference information contained in existing drawings while working in a new drawing. AutoCAD even allows you to copy all or part of the contents from one drawing directly into another using a drag-and-drop operation.

Each drawing you open or start in AutoCAD is placed in its own drawing window. The drawing name is displayed on the drawing window title bar if the drawing window is floating, or on the AutoCAD window title bar if the drawing window is maximized. The drawing windows and the AutoCAD window have the same relationship that program windows have with the Windows desktop. When a drawing window is maximized, it fills the available area in the AutoCAD window. Minimizing a drawing window displays it as a reduced size title bar along the bottom of the drawing area. Pick the title bar of a minimized or floating drawing window to work with, or activate, the drawing. Drawing windows cannot be moved outside the AutoCAD window. Figure 2-10 illustrates drawing windows in a floating state and minimized.

Using the Quick View Drawings Tool

The **Quick View Drawings** tool is one of many AutoCAD tools that can be used to change between open drawings. The visual display of this tool allows you to see and control open drawing files without actually changing drawing windows.

The quickest way to access the **Quick View Drawings** tool is to pick the **Quick View Drawings** button on the status bar. When accessed, the **Quick View Drawings** tool is

Figure 2-10.
Display drawing windows as floating windows when more than one file is open to move quickly from drawing to drawing. Minimized drawing windows are displayed as reduced-size title bars. Pick the title bar to display a window control menu.

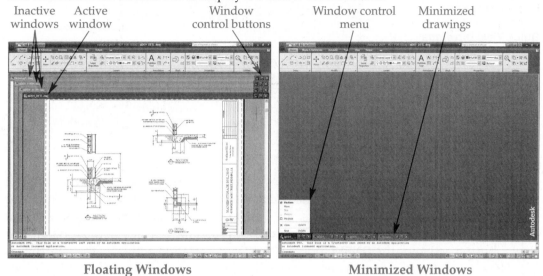

Inactive windows Active window Window control buttons Window control menu Minimized drawings

Floating Windows   Minimized Windows

displayed in the lower center of the AutoCAD window. See **Figure 2-11.** Each open file is represented by a thumbnail image with the file name below. Drawings are arranged in the order in which they were opened, with the file that was opened first on left side of the row. When you initially access the **Quick View Drawings** tool, the current file is highlighted. Pick the thumbnail of a different file to make the selected drawing window current, or move the cursor over a thumbnail to show additional options for controlling the drawing window.

Figure 2-11.
The **Quick View Drawings** tool offers an effective visual method for changing between open drawings.

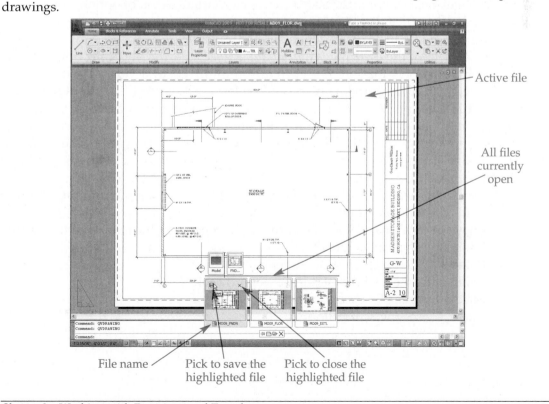

Active file

All files currently open

File name   Pick to save the highlighted file   Pick to close the highlighted file

Figure 2-12.
The **Quick View Drawings** toolbar provides access to basic functions directly from the **Quick View Drawings** feature.

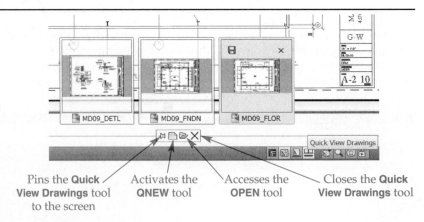

Pins the **Quick View Drawings** tool to the screen | Activates the **QNEW** tool | Accesses the **OPEN** tool | Closes the **Quick View Drawings** tool

The **Quick View Drawings** tool provides a small toolbar below the file thumbnail images. See **Figure 2-12.** By default, the **Quick View Drawings** tool is hidden when you pick a thumbnail to switch drawings. To keep the tool on-screen after you select a thumbnail, pick the **Pin Quick View Drawings** button on the left side of the toolbar. The **New...** button activates the **QNEW** tool and the **Open...** button activates the **OPEN** tool. The **New...** and **Open...** buttons are especially useful for starting a new drawing or opening an existing drawing that relates to the currently opened files. Select the **Close Quick View Drawings** button to close the **Quick View Drawings** tool.

NOTE

If you pin the **Quick View Drawings** tool to the screen, close the tool and then access the tool again, the **Quick View Drawings** tool will still be in the pinned state.

You can also quickly display a specific drawing layout without first activating the drawing window. See **Figure 2-13.** Layouts are used to prepare a drawing for plotting and are fully described in Chapters 28 and 29.

Right-click on a thumbnail image to access a shortcut menu of options for controlling open drawing files. The **Windows** cascading menu provides options for arranging all open files. Choose the **Arrange Icons** option to arrange minimized drawings neatly along the bottom of the drawing window area. Select the **Tile Vertically** option to tile the drawing windows that are not currently minimized in a vertical arrangement, with the active drawing window placed in the left position. Pick the **Tile Horizontally** option to tile the drawing windows that are not currently minimized in a horizontal arrangement, with the active drawing window placed in the top position. Pick the **Cascade** option to arrange the drawing windows in a cascading style. The effects of tiling the drawing windows vary based on the number of windows being tiled and whether they are tiled horizontally or vertically. See **Figure 2-14.**

The shortcut menu that appears when you right-click on a file thumbnail image also contains the following options:

- **Copy File as a Link.** Copies the entire file extension to the clipboard for pasting into a drawing or document.
- **Close All.** Closes all open documents.
- **Close other files.** Closes all files, except the active file.
- **Save All.** Saves all open documents.
- **Close.** Closes the active file.

Figure 2-13.
A—The initial display when you hover over a file thumbnail.
B—The model space and layout thumbnails enlarge when you hover over them.

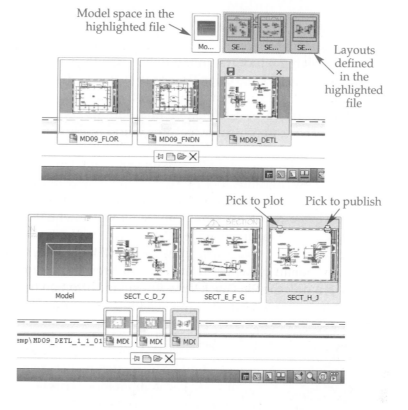

Model space in the highlighted file

Layouts defined in the highlighted file

Pick to plot   Pick to publish

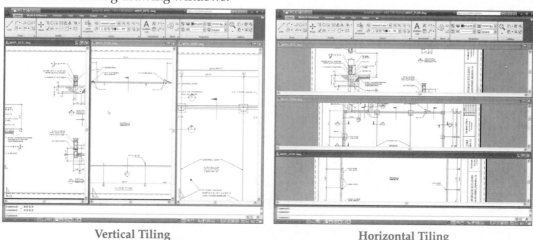

Figure 2-14.
Tiled and cascading drawing windows.

Vertical Tiling

Horizontal Tiling

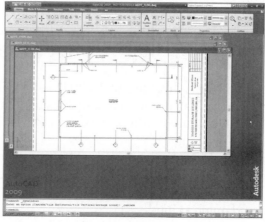

Cascading

Additional Window Control Tools

The **Quick View Drawings** tool provides an excellent method for working with multiple drawings. However, there are other ways to change the active drawing and manage drawing windows. In the ribbon, the **View** tab contains a **Window** panel with several buttons. Pick the **Open Drawings** button to display a menu of all currently open files. Select the file you want to make active from the menu. The **Tile Horizontally**, **Tile Vertically**, **Cascade**, and **Arrange Icons** buttons control the arrangement of all open drawings. These are the same features found in the **Quick View Drawings** tool shortcut menu.

The menu browser includes a **Windows** menu that contains the same items found in the **Quick View Drawings** tool shortcut menu. The **Windows** menu also houses the **Lock Location** cascading menu described in Chapter 1. In addition to the **Windows** menu, the menu browser provides an **Open Documents** menu that displays all currently open AutoCAD files. Documents are listed numerically in the order in which they were opened. You can display open files as icons, small images, medium images, or large images by picking the appropriate option from the display options flyout. The bullet to the left of a file indicates the active document. To activate a different drawing window, pick the file from the list or right-click on the file and select the **Switch** option.

PROFESSIONAL TIP

Another technique for switching between open drawings is to press the [Ctrl] + [F6] key combination. This is a very effective way to cycle quickly through all open drawings.

NOTE

Typically, you can change the active drawing as desired. In some situations, however, you cannot switch between drawings. For example, you cannot activate a different drawing while a dialog box is open. You must either complete the operation or cancel the dialog box before switching is possible.

Exercise 2-3

Complete the exercise on the Student CD.

Creating and Using Drawing Templates

Drawing templates can be incredible productivity boosters. Templates allow you to use an existing drawing as a starting point for a new drawing. This option is extremely valuable for ensuring that everyone in a department, class, school, or company uses the same standards in their drawings.

When you use a well-developed template, values defining the drawing settings are set automatically. Drawing templates usually have the following values and drawing elements:
   ✓ Drawing units and angle values
   ✓ Drawing limits

- ✓ Grid, snap, and other drawing aid settings
- ✓ Standard layouts with a border and title block
- ✓ Text styles
- ✓ Table styles
- ✓ Dimension styles
- ✓ Layer definitions and linetypes
- ✓ Plot styles
- ✓ Commonly used symbols and blocks
- ✓ General notes

Reference Material

Drawing Sheet Sizes

The term *sheet* refers to the paper you use to lay out and plot the final drawing. The *sheet size* is the size of the paper, and is identified by a size designation. Sheet size takes into account the size of the drawing and additional sheet items. In AutoCAD, the sheet size is specified using layouts. The process of using layouts is described in Chapters 28 and 29. Refer to the Student CD: Reference Materials > Drawing Sheet Sizes, Settings, and Scale Parameters for detailed information on this process.

sheet: The paper used to lay out and plot drawings.

sheet size: Size of the paper used to lay out and plot drawings.

Creating Drawing Templates

If none of the predefined AutoCAD drawing templates meet your needs, you can create and save your own custom templates. AutoCAD allows you to save *any* drawing as a template. A drawing template should be developed whenever several drawing applications require the same setup procedure. The template then allows the setup to be applied to any number of future drawings. Creating templates increases drafting productivity by decreasing setup requirements.

You can modify and then save an existing AutoCAD template as a new custom template, or you can construct a template from scratch. As you learn more about working with AutoCAD, you will find many settings that can be included in your drawing templates.

When you have everything needed in the template, the template is ready to save. To save a template, use the **SAVEAS** tool to display the **Save Drawing As** dialog box. To specify that the drawing is to be saved as a drawing template, pick AutoCAD Drawing Template (*.dwt) from the **Files of type:** drop-down list. The file list window then shows all the drawing templates currently found in the Template folder. See Figure 2-15.

You can store custom templates in another location, but it is recommended that they be stored in the Template folder so they automatically appear in the **Select template** dialog box. After specifying the name and location for the new template file, pick the **Save** button in the **Save Drawing As** dialog box. The **Template Options** dialog box is now displayed. See Figure 2-16. Type a description of the template file you are saving in the **Description** area. A brief description usually works best. In the **Measurement** drop-down list, specify whether the units used in the template are English or Metric, and then pick the **OK** button.

The template name should relate to the template, such as Mechanical Template, for mechanical part and assembly drawings. The template might be named for the drawing application, such as Architectural floor plans, or might be as simple as Template 1. The name should be written in a reference manual, along with documentation about what is included in the template. This provides future reference for you and other users.

Figure 2-15.
Saving a template in the AutoCAD Template folder.

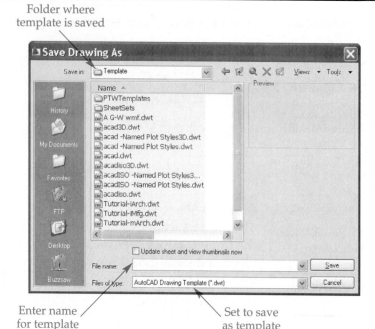

Folder where template is saved

Enter name for template

Set to save as template

Figure 2-16.
Type a description of the new template in the **Template Options** dialog box.

Enter description for template

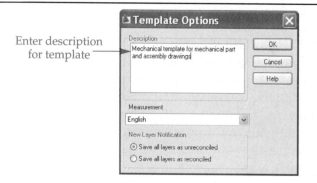

 **PROFESSIONAL TIP**

As you refine your setup procedure, you can open and revise template files. To save a new template over an existing one, use the **SAVE** tool. You can also use the **SAVEAS** tool to save a new template from an existing one.

Template Development Section

Template Development
Chapter 2

The Template Development section of the Student CD contains several predefined templates that you can use to create drawings in accordance with correct mechanical, architectural, and civil drafting standards. **Figure 2-17** describes each of the available templates. The mechanical drafting templates are based on the American Society of Mechanical Engineers (ASME) and American National Standards Institute (ANSI) ASME Y series of drafting standards. The architectural and civil drafting templates are based on appropriate architectural and civil drafting standards, including standards developed by the American Institute of Architects (AIA) and stated in the United States National CAD Standard.

Figure 2-17.
The predefined drawing templates available in the Template Development section of the Student CD.

Template File	Application	Layout Sheet Sizes
MECHANICAL-INCH.dwt	Mechanical drawings dimensioned in decimal inches.	A-size, B-size, C-size, D-size
MECHANICAL-METRIC.dwt	Mechanical drawings dimensioned in metric units.	A4-size, A3-size, A2-size, A1-size
ARCHITECTURAL-US.dwt	Architectural drawings dimensioned in feet and inches.	Architectural C-size, Architectural D-size
ARCHITECTURAL-METRIC.dwt	Architectural drawings dimensioned in metric units.	Architectural A2-size, Architectural A1-size
CIVIL-US.dwt	Civil drawings dimensioned in decimal inches.	C-size, D-size
CIVIL-METRIC.dwt	Civil drawings dimensioned in metric units.	A2-size, A1-size

In addition to the complete, ready-to-use templates in the Template Development section on the Student CD, the Template Development sections at the end of several chapters refer you to the Student CD for important template creation topics and procedures. Use the Template Development feature of this textbook to learn step by step how to prepare templates in accordance with correct mechanical, architectural, and civil drafting standards.

Drawing Settings

Drawing settings determine the general characteristics of a drawing. The most basic drawing settings that can be added to a template include units, limits, grid, and snap. Drawing settings can be changed within a drawing, but it is best to adhere to the settings defined in the template as much as possible.

Setting Drawing Units

Drawing units define the linear and angular measurements used while drawing and the precision to which these measurements are displayed. Drawing units are set in the **Drawing Units** dialog box. See **Figure 2-18.**

> **drawing units:** The standard units for linear and angular measurements and the precision of the measurements.

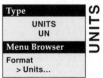

Both linear and angular units are set in the **Drawing Units** dialog box. Linear units are specified in the **Length** area. Select the desired linear units format from the **Type:** drop-down list and use the **Precision:** drop-down list to specify the precision of linear units. Linear unit formats are described in **Figure 2-19.**

The angular unit format and precision is set in the **Type:** and **Precision:** drop-down lists in the **Angle** area of the **Drawing Units** dialog box. Selecting the **Clockwise** check box changes the direction for angular measurements to clockwise from the default setting of counterclockwise.

Pick the **Direction...** button to access the **Direction Control** dialog box. See **Figure 2-20.** The standard **East**, **North**, **West**, and **South** options are offered as radio buttons. Pick one of these buttons to set the compass orientation. The **Other** radio button activates the **Angle:** text box and the **Pick an angle** button. Enter an angle for

Figure 2-18.
Use the **Drawing Units** dialog box to set linear and angular unit values.

Select linear units

Select linear precision

Select angular units

Select angular precision

Pick to change direction of angular measurement

Access the **Direction Control** dialog box

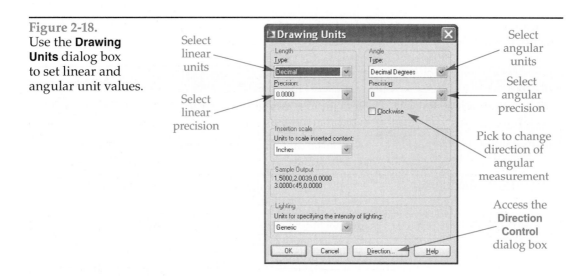

Figure 2-19.
Linear unit formats available in the **Drawing Units** dialog box.

Type	Applications and Features	Example
Decimal	• Decimal inches or millimeters. • Used for mechanical drawings for manufacturing. • Conforms to the ASME Y14.5M dimensioning and tolerancing standard. • Initial default precision: four decimal places.	14.1655
Engineering	• Feet and decimal inches. • Used for civil drafting projects such as maps, plot plans, dam and bridge construction, and topography. • Initial default precision: four decimal places.	1'-2.1655"
Architectural	• Feet, inches, and fractional inches. • Used for architectural and structural drawings. • Initial default precision: 1/16".	$1'\text{-}2\frac{3}{16}''$
Fractional	• Fractional parts of any common unit of measure. • Used for mechanical drawings for manufacturing. • Initial default precision: 1/16".	$14\frac{3}{16}$
Scientific	• Drawings requiring very large or small values. • Used for chemical engineering and astronomy drawings. • E+01 means the base number is multiplied by 10 to the first power. • Initial default precision: four decimal places.	1.4166E+01

Figure 2-20.
The **Direction Control** dialog box.

Set direction of 0°

Specify another angle

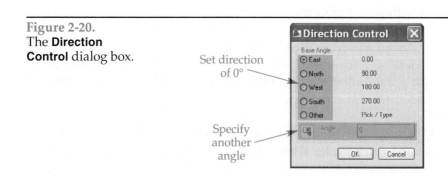

zero direction in the **Angle:** text box. The **Pick an angle** button allows you to pick two points on the screen to establish the angle zero direction.

CAUTION

The default direction of 0° East should be used at all times, unless you have a specific need to change the compass direction angle, such as when direction is measured using azimuths (0° North). The 0° East direction is used throughout this textbook and should be set in order to complete most exercises and problems correctly.

Angular unit formats are described in **Figure 2-21.** After selecting the linear and angular units and precision, pick the **OK** button to exit the **Drawing Units** dialog box.

Exercise 2-4
Complete the exercise on the Student CD.

Figure 2-21.
Angular unit formats available in the **Drawing Units** dialog box.

Type	Applications and Features	Example
Decimal Degrees	• Degrees and decimal parts of a degree. • Used in mechanical drawings for manufacturing. • This is the initial default setting.	45°
Deg/Min/Sec	• Degrees, minutes, and seconds. • Sometimes used in mechanical, architectural, structural, and civil drafting. • 1 degree equals 60 minutes; 1 minute equals 60 seconds.	45°0'0"
Grads	• Grad is the abbreviation for *gradient*. • One-quarter of a circle has 100 grads; a full circle has 400 grads.	50.000g
Radians	• A radian is an angular unit of measurement in which 2π radians = 360° and π radians = 180°. Pi (π) is approximately equal to 3.1416. • A 90° angle has $\pi/2$ radians and an arc length of $\pi/2$. • Changing the precision displays the radian value rounded to the specified decimal place.	0.785r
Surveyor	• Degrees, minutes, and seconds. • Uses bearings. A bearing is the direction of a line with respect to one of the quadrants of a compass. Bearings are measured clockwise or counterclockwise (depending on the quadrant), beginning from either north or south. • An angle measuring 55°45'22" from north toward west is expressed as N55°45'22"W. • Set precision to degrees, degrees/minutes, degrees/minutes/seconds, or decimal display accuracy of the seconds part of the measurement.	N45°E

Adjusting Drawing Limits

An AutoCAD drawing is created at actual size, or full scale, regardless of the type of drawing, the units used, or the size of the final layout on paper. The full-scale drawing is prepared in an environment known as model space. When you finish drawing in model space, you then switch to layout space, where the drawing layout is organized and scaled as necessary to be printed on paper. Model space and layout space are presented in Chapter 28. All material prior to Chapter 28 is presented with the assumption that model space is active.

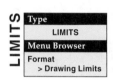

limits: The size of the virtual drawing area in model space.

AutoCAD allows you to specify the size of a virtual drawing area, which is known as the model space drawing limits, or *limits*. Limits are typically set in the template drawing, but they can be changed at any time during the drawing process.

The concept of drawing limits is somewhat misleading, because the AutoCAD drawing area is infinite in size. For example, if you set limits to 17″ × 11″, you can still create objects that extend past the 17″ × 11″ area, such as a line that is 1200′ long. As a result, you can choose not to consider limits while developing a template or creating a drawing. Conversely, as you learn AutoCAD, you may decide that setting appropriate drawing limits is helpful, especially when you are drawing large objects. Regardless of whether you choose to acknowledge limits, you should be familiar with the concept, and recognize that some AutoCAD tools, such as the **ZOOM** and **PLOT** tools, provide options for using limits.

LIMITS
Type
LIMITS
Menu Browser
Format
> Drawing Limits

Model space drawing limits are set using the **LIMITS** tool. Once you access the **LIMITS** tool, you are prompted to specify the coordinates for the lower-left corner of the drawing limits. For now, when setting limits, the lower-left corner is usually 0,0. Press [Enter] to accept the default 0,0 value or enter a new value and press [Enter]. You are now prompted to specify the coordinates for the upper-right corner of the virtual drawing limits. For example, type 17,11 and then press [Enter] to set limits of 17″ x 11″. The first value is the horizontal measurement, and the second value is the vertical measurement of the limits. A comma separates the values.

In general, limits should be set larger than the objects you plan to draw. You can determine limits accurately by identifying the drawing scale, converting the scale to a scale factor, and then multiplying the scale factor by the size of sheet on which you plan to plot the drawing. For now, however, calculate the approximate total widths and lengths of the objects you plan to draw, adding extra space for dimensions and notes. For example, if you are drawing a 48′ × 24′ building floor plan, allow 10′ on each side for dimensions and notes to make a total virtual drawing area of 68′ × 44′.

> **NOTE**
>
> The **LIMITS** tool provides a limits checking feature that, when turned on, restricts your ability to draw outside of the drawing limits. Turn on limits checking by entering or selecting the **ON** option. Turn off limits checking using the **OFF** option.

Setting the Grid

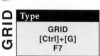

grid: A pattern of dots that appears on-screen to aid in the drawing process.

GRID
Type
GRID
[Ctrl]+[G]
F7

A *grid*, or pattern of dots, can be shown on-screen to help you lay out a drawing. The quickest way to toggle **Grid** mode on and off is to pick the **Grid Display** button on the status bar. When the **Grid** mode is activated, this pattern of dots appears in the drawing area, as shown in **Figure 2-22.** By default, the grid pattern displays only within the drawing limits to help clearly define the working area. The spacing between dots can be adjusted.

Figure 2-22.
Dots represent the grid spacing when **Grid** mode is activated.

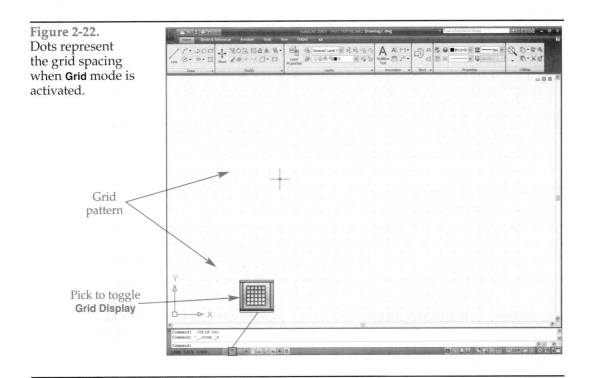

Grid pattern

Pick to toggle **Grid Display**

Figure 2-23 shows the **Snap and Grid** tab of the **Drafting Settings** dialog box. The **Drafting Settings** dialog box can also be displayed by right-clicking on any of the status bar toggle buttons and selecting the **Settings...** option. The right side of this dialog box can be used to set the grid spacing and display. The grid may also be turned on or off by checking the **Grid On** check box. Grid spacing is set in the **Grid spacing** area. Type the appropriate values in the **Grid X spacing:** and **Grid Y spacing:** text boxes.

The options in the **Grid behavior** area of the **Drafting Settings** dialog box allow you to set how the grid appears on screen. When the **Adaptive Grid** check box is selected, and the grid spacing is too dense, AutoCAD adjusts the display automatically so the grid can be shown on-screen. The **Display grid beyond Limits** option determines whether the grid appears only within the set drawing limits. The **Allow subdivision below grid spacing** and **Follow Dynamic UCS** options are used for 3D applications.

Type
DSETTINGS
DS
SE
Menu Browser
Tools
> Drafting
Settings...

DSETTINGS

Figure 2-23.
Grid and snap grid settings can be made in the **Snap and Grid** tab of the **Drafting Settings** dialog box.

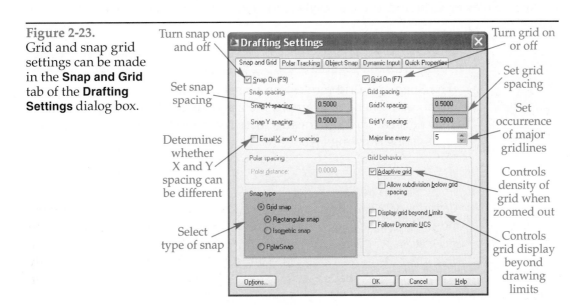

Turn snap on and off

Set snap spacing

Determines whether X and Y spacing can be different

Select type of snap

Turn grid on or off

Set grid spacing

Set occurrence of major gridlines

Controls density of grid when zoomed out

Controls grid display beyond drawing limits

Setting the Snap Grid

SNAP

Type
SNAP
[Ctrl]+[B]
[F9]

snap grid (snap resolution, snap): Invisible grid that allows the crosshairs to move only in exact increments.

Use the **SNAP** tool to the *snap grid*, also known as *snap resolution* or *snap*. The quickest way to toggle snap on and off is to pick the **Snap Mode** button on the status bar. By default, snap is off, and when you move the mouse, the crosshairs moves freely on the screen. Turn snap on to move the crosshairs in specific increments. Using the snap grid is different from using the on-screen grid. Snap controls the movement of the cross-hairs, while the grid is only a visual guide. The grid and snap settings can, however, be used together. The AutoCAD defaults provide the same settings for both.

Snap can also be turned on or off by checking the **Snap On** check box of the **Drafting Settings** dialog box. Refer again to Figure 2-23. The snap increment can be set in the **Snap spacing** area on the left side of the dialog box. Type a value in the **Snap X spacing:** or **Snap Y spacing:** text box to set an equal X and Y increment. To set different values for horizontal and vertical snap increment, deselect the **Equal X and Y spacing** check box. Then type the appropriate values in the **Snap X spacing:** and **Snap Y spacing:** text boxes.

PROFESSIONAL TIP

The most effective use of the **Snap** mode is often to set an equal X and Y spacing to the lowest, or near lowest, increment of the majority of the feature dimensions. For example, this might be .0625 units in a mechanical drawing or 6″ in an architectural application. If many horizontal features conform to one increment and most vertical features correspond to another, then a snap grid can be set up using different X and Y values.

The **Snap type** area of the **Drafting Settings** dialog box allows you to select one of two types of snap grids: **Grid snap** or **PolarSnap**. **PolarSnap** allows you to snap to precise distances along alignment paths when you use polar tracking. Polar tracking is described in Chapter 7. **Grid snap** has two styles: **Rectangular snap** and **Isometric snap**. **Rectangular snap** is the standard style. **Isometric snap** is useful when you are creating isometric drawings as described in Chapter 25. Select the radio button(s) for the appropriate snap type and style and pick the **OK** button. You can also use the **Type** and **Style** options of the **SNAP** tool to change these settings. Use the **Type** option to select **Polar** or **Grid** and use the **Style** option to select **Standard** (rectangular) or **Isometric**.

PROFESSIONAL TIP

The **Snap** and **Grid** modes can be set at different values to comple-ment each other. For example, the grid may be set at .5, and the snap may be set at .25. With these settings, each mode plays a separate role in assisting drawing layout.

Factors to Consider When Setting Drawing Aids

The following factors influence the drawing aid settings you choose to use:

✓ **Drawing units.** If the units are decimal inches, set the grid and snap values to standard decimal increments such as .0625, .125, .25, .5, and 1 or .05, .1, .2, .5, and 1. For architectural units, use standard increments such as 1, 6, and 12 (for inches) or 1, 2, 4, 5, and 10 (for feet).

✓ **Drawing size.** A very large drawing might have a grid spacing of 12 (one foot), or 120 (ten feet), while a small drawing may use a spacing of .125 or less.

✓ **Value of the smallest dimension.** If the smallest dimension is .125, then an appropriate snap value is .125 with a grid spacing of .25.

✓ **Ability to change the settings.** You can change the snap and grid values at any time without changing the location of points or lines already drawn. You should do this when larger or smaller values would assist you with a certain part of the drawing. For example, suppose a few of the dimensions are multiples of .0625, but the rest of the dimensions are multiples of .250. Change the snap spacing from .250 to .0625 when laying out the smaller dimensions.

✓ **Sketches prepared before starting the drawing.** Use the visible grid to help you place views and lay out the entire drawing.

✓ **Efficiency.** Use whatever method works best and quickest for you when setting or changing the drawing aids.

Exercise 2-5
Complete the exercise on the Student CD.

 **Template Development**
Chapter 2

The development of a drawing template requires much thought and consideration. Many factors and settings need to be defined, and appropriate standards should be consulted. Refer to the Student CD for detailed instructions to begin the development of drawing templates for use in mechanical, architectural, and civil drafting.

 ## Chapter Test

Answer the following questions. Write your answers on a separate sheet of paper or complete the electronic chapter test on the Student CD.

1. What is a drawing template?
2. What is the name of the dialog box that opens by default when you access the **NEW** tool?
3. Briefly explain how to start a drawing from scratch.
4. How often should work be saved?
5. Explain the benefits of using a standard system for naming drawing files.
6. Name the tool that allows you to save your work quickly without displaying a dialog box.
7. How do you set AutoCAD to save your work automatically at designated intervals?
8. What tool allows you to save a drawing file in an older AutoCAD format?

9. Identify the tool you would use if you wanted to exit a drawing file, but remain in the AutoCAD session.
10. What is the quickest way to close an AutoCAD drawing file?
11. From which menu browser menu can you select the name of a recently opened drawing file and open it?
12. How can you set the number of recently opened files listed in the menu browser?
13. What does the term *read-only* mean?
14. Describe the advantages of using the **Quick View Drawings** tool to work with multiple open drawings.
15. How do you keep the **Quick View Drawings** tool on-screen after you pick a thumbnail image?
16. How can you close all open drawing windows at the same time?
17. How do you quickly cycle through all the currently open drawings in sequence?
18. What is sheet size?
19. How can you convert a drawing file into a drawing template?
20. How can you access the **Drawing Units** dialog box?
21. Name three settings that can be specified in the **Drawing Units** dialog box.
22. Name the tool used to place a pattern of dots on the screen.
23. How do you set a grid spacing of .25?
24. Name three ways to access the **Drafting Settings** dialog box.
25. How do you activate the **Snap** mode?

Problems

▼ Basic

1. Start a new drawing using the **acad-Named Plot Styles** template supplied by AutoCAD. Save the new drawing as a file named P2-1.dwg.

2. Start a new drawing using the **acadiso** template supplied by AutoCAD. Save the new drawing as a file named P2-2.dwg.

3. Start a new drawing using the **Tutorial-iArch** template supplied by AutoCAD. Save the new drawing as a file named P2-3.dwg.

▼ Intermediate

Problems 4 through 7 can be done if the AutoCAD 2009\Sample file folder is loaded. All drawings listed are found in that folder.

4. Locate and preview the Lineweights drawing. Open the drawing and describe it in your own words.

5. Locate and preview the TrueType drawing. Open the drawing and describe it in your own words.

6. Locate and preview the Tablet drawing. Open the drawing and describe it in your own words.

Drawing Problems – Chapter 2

7. Locate and preview the 3D House drawing. Open the drawing and describe it in your own words.

▼ Advanced

The following problems can be saved as templates for future use.

8. Create a template with decimal units with 0.0 precision, decimal degrees with 0.0 precision, default angle measure and orientation, a snap setting of .1, and a grid setting of .5. Save the template as P2-8.dwt. Enter an appropriate description for the template.

9. Create a template with metric units with 0.0 precision, decimal degrees with 0.0 precision, default angle measure and orientation, a snap setting of 10, and a grid setting of 50. Save the template as P2-9.dwt. Enter an appropriate description for the template.

10. Create a template with architectural units with 0'-0" precision, decimal degrees with 0 precision, a snap setting of 1", and a grid setting of 6". Save the template as P2-10.dwt. Enter an appropriate description for the template.

AutoCAD includes many standard templates. These templates include settings and title blocks for many standard sheet sizes. Three such templates are shown here.

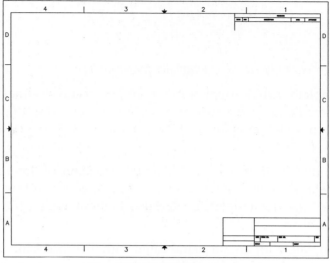

ANSI C Title Block

Architectural Title Block

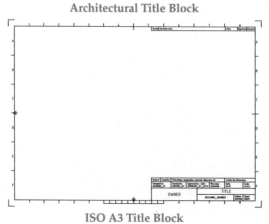

ISO A3 Title Block

CHAPTER 3

Introduction to Drawing and Editing

Learning Objectives

After completing this chapter, you will be able to do the following:
- ✓ Use the correct entry format when entering numbers.
- ✓ Demonstrate how to end or cancel tools.
- ✓ Describe and use several point entry methods.
- ✓ Draw given objects using the **LINE** tool.
- ✓ Demonstrate tool access using dynamic input and the command line.
- ✓ Use direct distance entry with polar tracking and **Ortho** mode.
- ✓ Revise objects using the **ERASE** tool and its options.
- ✓ Create selection sets using various selection options.
- ✓ Use the **U**, **UNDO**, **REDO**, and **OOPS** tools appropriately.

This chapter introduces drawing and editing using the **LINE** and **ERASE** tools. Although you will learn many other tools and options in later chapters, you can learn much about AutoCAD using these two basic tools. Like all drawing tools, the **LINE** tool requires you to choose points in the drawing area. Similarly, like nearly all editing tools, **ERASE** requires you to select one or more objects. This chapter introduces point entry methods and direct distance entry, as well as many methods of object selection.

LINE
Ribbon
Home
> Draw
Line
Type
LINE
L
Menu Browser
Draw
> Line

Responding to AutoCAD Prompts

Most AutoCAD drawing and editing tools require that you respond to a prompt. A prompt "asks" you to perform a specific task. For example, when drawing lines, you are prompted to specify line endpoints. When you erase an object, you are prompted to select the object to erase.

Many prompts provide options that you can select instead of responding to the immediate request. For example, while drawing a line, you are prompted to pick a point. However, if you pick the wrong point, an **Undo** option is available to remove the selection instead of picking another point. The following information introduces you to the process of responding to AutoCAD prompts.

Responding to AutoCAD Prompts with Numbers

Many AutoCAD tools require specific types of numeric data. Some AutoCAD prompts require you to enter a whole number. Other entries require whole numbers that are positive or negative. AutoCAD understands that a number is positive without the plus sign (+) in front of it. However, the minus sign (−) must precede a negative number.

Much of the data you enter may not be whole numbers. In these cases, any real number can be used and expressed as a decimal, as a fraction, or in scientific notation. These numbers can be positive or negative. Examples of acceptable real numbers include:

> 4.250
> −6.375
> 1/2
> 1-3/4
> 2.5E+4 *(25,000)*
> 2.5E-4 *(0.00025)*

For fractions, the numerator and denominator must be whole numbers greater than zero. For example, 1/2, 3/4, and 2/3 are all acceptable fraction entries. Fractional numbers greater than one must have a hyphen between the whole number and the fraction. For example, 2-3/4 is typed for two and three quarters. The hyphen (-) separator is needed because a space acts just like pressing [Enter] and automatically ends the input. The numerator can be larger than the denominator, as in 3/2, *only* if a whole number is not used with the fraction. For example, 1-3/2 is not a valid input for a fraction.

When you enter coordinates or measurements, the values used depend on the units of measurement. AutoCAD understands that values on inch drawings are in inches without placing the inch marks (″) after the numeral. For example, 2.500 is automatically understood to be 2.500″.

When your drawing is set up for metric values, any entry is automatically expressed as millimeters. If you are working in an engineering or architectural environment, any value greater than 1″ is expressed in inches, feet, or feet and inches. The values can be whole numbers, decimals, or fractions. For measurements in feet, the foot symbol (′) must follow the number, as in 24′. If the value is in feet and inches, there is no space between the feet and inch value. For example, 24′6 is the proper input for the value 24′-6″. If the inch part of the value contains a fraction, the inch and fractional part of an inch are separated by a hyphen, such as 24′6-1/2. Never mix feet with inch values greater than one foot. For example, 24′18 is an invalid entry. In this case, you should type 25′6.

NOTE

AutoCAD accepts the inch (″) and foot (′) symbols only when architectural or engineering drawing units have been specified in the drawing.

PROFESSIONAL TIP

Placing the inch mark (″) after an inch value at the prompt line is acceptable, but not necessary. It takes more time and reduces productivity.

Ending and Canceling Tools

Some AutoCAD tools, such as the **LINE** tool, remain active until they are stopped. For example, you can continue to pick points to create new line segments until you end the **LINE** tool. As a result, it is necessary to stop the currently active tool to either reenter it or use another tool. This can occur if you make an incorrect entry and need to restart the tool using the correct method. You can usually end a tool by pressing the [Enter] key or the space bar, or by right-clicking and selecting the **Enter** option.

If you press the wrong key or misspell a word while using a tool or answering a prompt, use the [Backspace] key to correct the error. This works only if you notice your mistake *before* you accept the value. If you do enter an incorrect option or tool, AutoCAD usually responds with an error message. Access the **AutoCAD Text Window** to view lengthy error messages, or review the tools and options you entered. Return to the graphics screen using the same method you used to access the text window, or pick any visible portion of the graphics screen.

You can cancel any active tool or abort any data entry by pressing the [Esc] key. It may be necessary to press the [Esc] key twice to cancel certain tools completely. To simultaneously cancel the active tool and access a new tool, pick a ribbon button or a menu browser option.

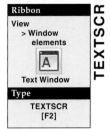

Ribbon
View
> Window
elements

Text Window

Type
TEXTSCR
[F2]

TEXTSCR

Point Entry Methods

Several point entry techniques exist for locating objects, such as the endpoints of lines. Point entry methods use the *Cartesian coordinate system*, which is based on selecting the *location* of the point by specifying its distance from the *origin*. In 2D drafting applications, you draw objects on the XY plane without referencing the Z axis. Using the Z axis is described in *AutoCAD and Its Applications—Advanced*.

In 2D drafting, the origin divides the coordinate system into four quadrants on the XY plane. Points are located in relation to the origin, where X = 0 and Y = 0, or (0,0). See **Figure 3-1**. The origin is usually at the lower-left corner of the drawing. This setup places all points in the upper-right quadrant of the XY plane, where both X and Y coordinate values are positive. See **Figure 3-2**. Methods of establishing points in the Cartesian coordinate system include using absolute coordinates, relative coordinates, and polar coordinates. You must understand the relationship of points in the Cartesian coordinate system, shown in **Figure 3-1**, before using the point entry options, especially relative coordinates.

Cartesian coordinate system: A rectangular system based on selecting distances from three intersecting axes.

location: A point's distance from the origin.

origin: The intersection point of the X, Y, and Z axes.

Figure 3-1.
The Cartesian coordinate system.

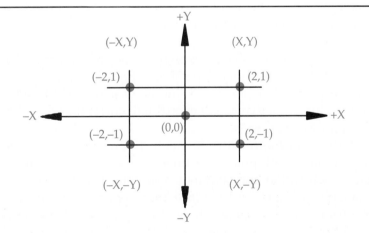

Figure 3-2.
By default, the X and Y coordinate axes are placed so that the upper-right quadrant of the Cartesian coordinate system fills the screen.

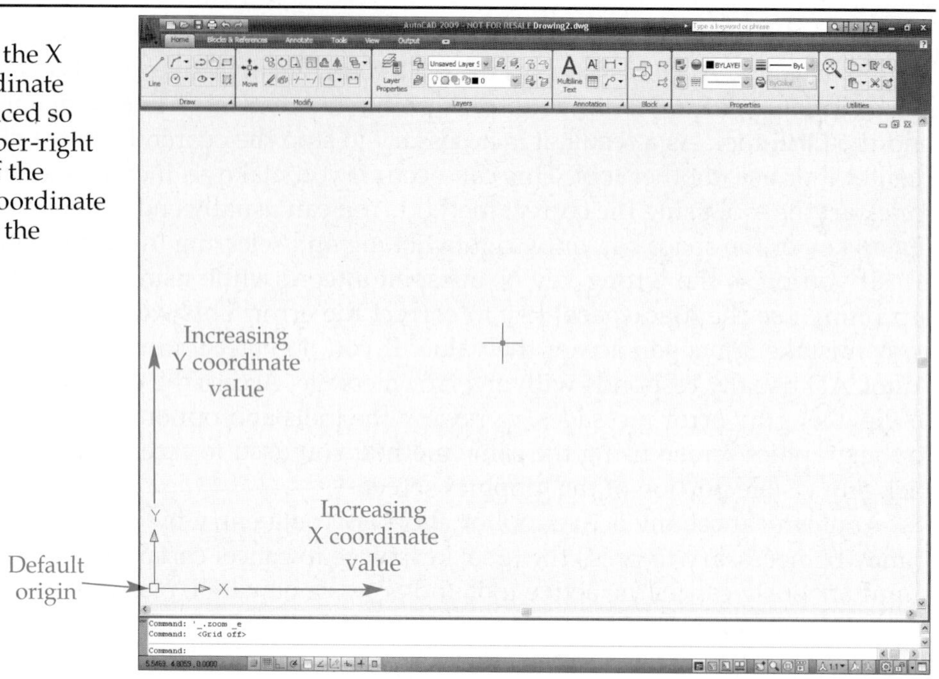

Increasing Y coordinate value

Increasing X coordinate value

Default origin

PROFESSIONAL TIP

The most basic method of point entry is to pick a point using the crosshairs. This is the method introduced early in this chapter. Picking a random point in space is typically not accurate, but you can turn on the **Snap** mode to move the crosshairs in designated increments at specific coordinates. This method can be useful while drawing. The best way to pick points on existing objects using the crosshairs is to use object snaps. Object snaps are described in Chapter 7.

absolute coordinates: Coordinate distances measured from the origin.

Points located using *absolute coordinates* are measured from the origin (0,0). For example, when X = 2 and Y = 2 (2,2), a point is located two units horizontally and two units vertically from the origin. A comma separates the X and Y values. Drawing a line starting at (2,2) and ending the line at (4,4) creates the line shown in Figure 3-3. The first point you pick when drawing a line is often positioned using absolute coordinates. Remember, when the absolute coordinate system is used, each point is located from 0,0. If you enter negative X and Y values, the point is located outside of the upper-right XY plane quadrant.

relative coordinates: Coordinates specified from, or relative to, the previous position, rather than from the origin.

When using *relative coordinates*, you may want to think of the previous point as the "temporary origin." The @ symbol is used to enter relative coordinates. For example, if the first point of a line is located at (2,2) and the second point is positioned using a relative (@2,2) coordinate entry, the second point is located (4,4) from the origin. See Figure 3-3.

polar coordinates: Coordinates based on the distance from a fixed point at a given angle.

Polar coordinate entry is much different than absolute and relative coordinate entry because, with polar coordinate entry, you specify the length of the line and the angle at which the line is drawn. You enter the distance, then the angle. A less than (<) symbol separates the distance and angle values. The angular values used for the polar coordinate format are shown in Figure 3-4. Consistent with standard AutoCAD convention, 0° is to the right, or east. Angles are measured counterclockwise. When preceded by the @ symbol, a polar coordinate point is located relative to the previous point. If the @ symbol is not included, the coordinate is located relative to the origin. For example, to draw a line 2 units long at a 45° angle, starting 2 units from (0,0) at a 45° angle, type 2<45 for the first point, and @2<45 for the second point. See Figure 3-5.

AutoCAD and Its Applications—Basics

Figure 3-3.
Locating points
using absolute and
relative coordinates.

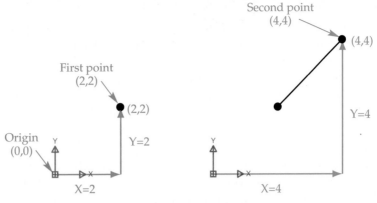

Absolute Coordinate Entry

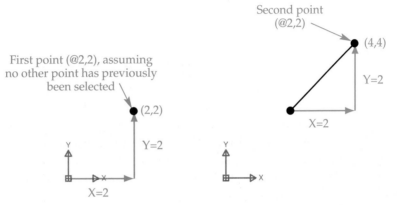

Relative Coordinate Entry

Figure 3-4.
Angles used in
entering polar
coordinates.

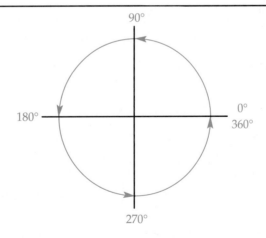

Figure 3-5.
Locating points
using polar
coordinates.

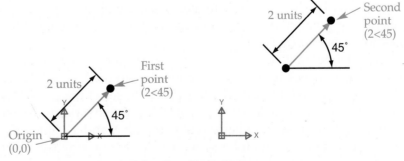

Polar Coordinate Entry

The Coordinate Display

The area on the left side of the status bar shows the coordinate display field. The drawing units setting determines the format and precision of the coordinate display. Picking the coordinate display in the status bar toggles the coordinate display on and off. With coordinates on, the coordinate display constantly changes as the crosshairs moves. With coordinates off, the coordinate display is "grayed out," but still updates to display the coordinates of the last point selected.

You can choose to display relative or absolute coordinates by right-clicking on the coordinate display field and picking the appropriate option. Both modes display the current crosshairs location when a tool is not active. When the **Relative** mode is set and a tool is active, the coordinates display the crosshairs position as polar coordinates relative to the previously picked point. The coordinates update each time you pick a new point. When the **Absolute** mode is selected and a tool is active, the coordinate display changes to represent the location of the crosshairs in relation to the origin.

Drawing Lines

rubberband line: A stretch line that extends from the crosshairs with certain drawing tools to show where an object will be drawn.

point entry: Identifying a point location in AutoCAD's coordinate system.

Individual line segments are drawn between two points using the **LINE** tool. To use the **LINE** tool, first select a start point. As you move the mouse, a *rubberband line* appears connecting the first point and the crosshairs. When the Specify next point or [Undo]: prompt appears, continue selecting additional points if you want to connect a series of lines. Then press the [Enter] key or the space bar, or right-click and select **Enter** to end the **LINE** tool. The process of specifying the endpoints of a line is referred to as *point entry*.

Exercise 3-1

Complete the exercise on the Student CD.

Drawing Using Dynamic Input

Dynamic input is on by default and is one of the most effective tools for entering coordinates. Dynamic input provides the same function as the command line, but it allows you to keep your focus at the point where you are drawing. Point entry methods function a little differently when dynamic input is active, depending on settings. Some additional coordinate entry techniques are also available when dynamic input is active.

When you start the **LINE** tool, dynamic input prompts you to specify the first point. The X coordinate input field is active, and the Y coordinate input field is displayed. See **Figure 3-6.** The X and Y coordinates of the first point can be typed using an absolute, relative, or polar coordinate entry method. Using these methods with dynamic input is known as *pointer input*.

pointer input: The process of entering points using dynamic input.

To define an absolute coordinate entry, type the X value, then press the [Tab] or comma key to lock in the X value and move to the Y coordinate input field. Then type the Y value and right-click or press [Enter] to select the point. The absolute coordinate entry method is the default when you select the first point. To use a relative coordinate entry, type the @ symbol before entering the X and Y values. To apply a polar coordinate entry, type the less than symbol (<) after entering the length of the line in the X coordinate input field. Then enter the angle at which you what to draw the line in the

Figure 3-6.
After you start the **LINE** tool, dynamic input displays these items. When you type the @ symbol to use relative coordinates, the symbol is displayed in the tooltip. When you use polar coordinates, the less than symbol (<) is displayed in the tooltip just before the angle.

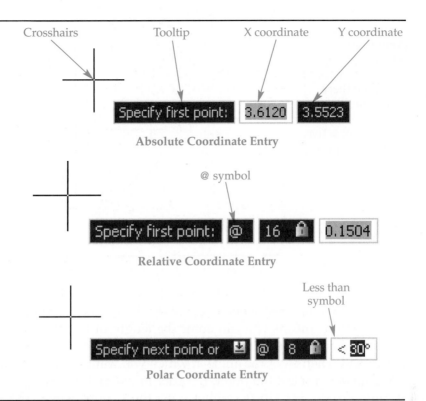

Crosshairs   Tooltip   X coordinate   Y coordinate

Specify first point: 3.6120 3.5523

Absolute Coordinate Entry

@ symbol

Specify first point: @ 16 🔒 0.1504

Relative Coordinate Entry

Less than symbol

Specify next point or @ 8 🔒 < 30°

Polar Coordinate Entry

Y coordinate input field. Dynamic input fields automatically change to anticipate the next entry. Refer again to **Figure 3-6**.

Once you enter the start point of the line, dynamic input provides a feature that allows you to enter the length of a line and the angle at which the line is drawn, similar to polar coordinate entry. This feature is known as *dimensional input*. To use dimensional input, first establish the start point. Now, move the crosshairs away from the start point and, by default, distance and angle input fields appear. See **Figure 3-7**. Enter the length of the line in the active distance input field and press the [Tab] key to lock in the distance and move to the angle input field. Now type the angle at which you want to draw the line and right-click or press [Enter] to select the point. The angular values used for dimensional input are shown in **Figure 3-8**.

Pointer input can also be used to pick additional points once you select the start point of the line. Relative coordinates are used by default, which means you do not need to type the @ symbol before entering the X and Y values. To select the second point using a relative coordinate entry, type the X value, which appears in the distance input field, then type the comma key to lock in the X value and move to the Y coordinate input field that automatically appears. Then type the Y value and right-click or press [Enter] to select the point.

dimensional input: A method of entering points that is similar to polar coordinate entry, but uses dynamic input.

Figure 3-7.
Use the dimensional input feature of dynamic input to define the length and angle of a line.

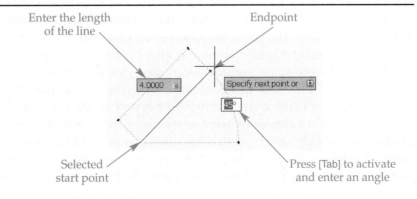

Enter the length of the line   Endpoint

4.0000

Specify next point or

45°

Selected start point   Press [Tab] to activate and enter an angle

Figure 3-8.
Angles used
when applying
dimensional input.
Compare these
angles to the angles
used when dynamic
input is not active,
shown in Figure 3-4.

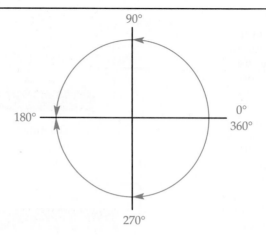

Dimensional input is on by default. To temporarily turn off dimensional input, type the # symbol before entering values. This makes dynamic input default to polar format, which means you can enter the length of the line in the active X coordinate input field and press the [Tab] key to lock in the length and move to the Y coordinate input field. Then enter the angle at which you want to draw the line and right-click or press [Enter] to select the point. In order to use an absolute coordinate entry with the default settings, type the # symbol, enter the X coordinate in the active field, then type the comma key, type the Y value, and press right-click or [Enter] to select the point.

PROFESSIONAL TIP

Use the [Tab] key to cycle through dynamic input fields. You can make changes to values before accepting the coordinates.

Dynamic Input Settings
Options for dynamic input can be found on the **Dynamic Input** tab of the **Drafting Settings** dialog box. Refer to the Student CD: Supplemental Materials > Dynamic Input Settings for more information on adjusting dynamic input options.

Drawing Using the Command Line

Although dynamic input is a very effective tool for locating points because of its on-screen display and ease of use, the command line can also be used. However, you must closely adhere to point entry methods, because neither dimensional input nor quick input settings are available with the command line. Dynamic input can be used at the same time as the command line or can be disabled to use only the command line for tool input and information. Another option is to hide the command line to free additional drawing space and focus on using dynamic input.

Absolute, relative, and polar point entry methods accomplish the same tasks whether they are entered using dynamic input or typed at the command line. The following content provides examples of point entry using the command line. The same examples can be applied to dynamic input. Even if you choose not to use the command line, review these examples to help better understand point entry techniques. You must disable dynamic input in order for these exact command sequences to work appropriately.

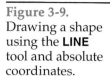

Figure 3-9.
Drawing a shape
using the **LINE**
tool and absolute
coordinates.

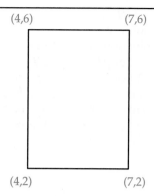

(4,6)   (7,6)

(4,2)   (7,2)

Absolute coordinate entry

Follow these commands and absolute coordinate entries at the command line as you refer to **Figure 3-9**:

```
Command: L or LINE↵
Specify first point: 4,2↵
Specify next point or [Undo]: 7,2↵
Specify next point or [Undo]: 7,6↵
Specify next point or [Close/Undo]: 4,6↵
Specify next point or [Close/Undo]: 4,2↵
Specify next point or [Close/Undo]: ↵
Command:
```

Exercise 3-2
Complete the exercise on the Student CD.

Relative coordinate entry

Follow these commands and relative coordinate entry methods as you refer to **Figure 3-10**:

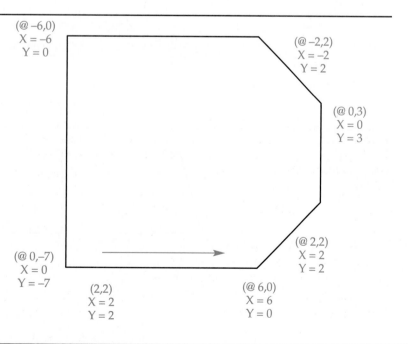

Figure 3-10.
Drawing a shape
using the **LINE**
tool and relative
coordinates. Notice
that negative (–)
values are used and
the coordinates
are entered
counterclockwise
from the first point
(2,2).

(@ –6,0)
X = –6
Y = 0

(@ –2,2)
X = –2
Y = 2

(@ 0,3)
X = 0
Y = 3

(@ 0,–7)
X = 0
Y = –7

(@ 2,2)
X = 2
Y = 2

(2,2)
X = 2
Y = 2

(@ 6,0)
X = 6
Y = 0

```
Command: L or LINE↵
Specify first point: 2,2↵
Specify next point or [Undo]: @6,0↵
Specify next point or [Undo]: @2,2↵
Specify next point or [Close/Undo]: @0,3↵
Specify next point or [Close/Undo]: @-2,2↵
Specify next point or [Close/Undo]: @-6,0↵
Specify next point or [Close/Undo]: @0,-7↵
Specify next point or [Close/Undo]: ↵
Command:
```

Exercise 3-3
Complete the exercise on the Student CD.

Polar coordinate entry

Follow these commands and polar coordinate entry methods as you refer to Figure 3-11:

```
Command: L or LINE↵
Specify first point: 2,6↵
Specify next point or [Undo]: @2.5<0↵
Specify next point or [Undo]: @3<135↵
Specify next point or [Close/Undo]: 2,6↵
Specify next point or [Close/Undo]: ↵
Command: ↵
LINE Specify first point: 6,6↵
Specify next point or [Undo]: @4<0↵
Specify next point or [Undo]: @2<90↵
Specify next point or [Close/Undo]: @4<180↵
Specify next point or [Close/Undo]: @2<270↵
Specify next point or [Close/Undo]: ↵
Command:
```

Exercise 3-4
Complete the exercise on the Student CD.

Figure 3-11.
Using polar
coordinates to draw
a shape.

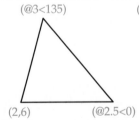
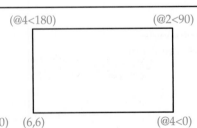

Using Direct Distance Entry

To draw a line using *direct distance entry*, drag the crosshairs in any desired direction from the first point of the line. Then type a numerical value indicating the distance from that point. Direct distance entry is a very quick way to draw lines at a specific length. However, direct distance entry itself is not very useful, because when you move the crosshairs to a location in space, the angle from the first point is inaccurate, unless you incorporate other drawing tools. *Polar tracking* and **Ortho** modes can be used to draw lines at accurate angles using direct distance entry.

Introduction to polar tracking

Polar tracking is on by default and causes the drawing crosshairs to "snap" to predefined angle increments. Pick the **Polar Tracking** button on the status bar or press the [F10] key to toggle polar tracking on and off. Polar tracking provides visual aids. As you move the crosshairs in the desired direction, AutoCAD displays an alignment path and tooltip at the default polar angle increments of 0°, 90°, 180°, or 270°. Polar tracking is an AutoTrack mode. AutoTrack is fully described in Chapter 7.

To use polar tracking in combination with direct distance entry, first access the **Line** tool and specify a start point. Then move the crosshairs in alignment with a polar tracking angle. Type the desired distance value and press [Enter] or right-click and select the **Enter** option to draw the line. See **Figure 3-12.** Polar tracking is described in detail in Chapter 7.

Drawing in ortho mode

Ortho mode constrains points selected while drawing and editing to be only horizontal or vertical. See **Figure 3-13.** Pick the **Ortho Mode** button on the status bar to toggle **Ortho** mode on and off. If **Ortho** mode is turned off, you can temporarily turn it on when drawing an object by holding down the [Shift] key.

To use **Ortho** in combination with direct distance entry, access the **LINE** tool and specify a start point. Move the crosshairs to display a horizontal or vertical rubberband in the direction you want to draw. Then type the desired distance value and press [Enter] or right-click and select the **Enter** option to draw the line. See **Figure 3-14.**

direct distance entry: Entering points by dragging the crosshairs for direction and typing a number for distance.

polar tracking: A drawing aid that causes the drawing crosshairs to "snap" to predefined angle increments.

ortho: From *orthogonal*, which means "at right angles."

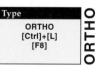

Figure 3-12.
Using polar tracking to draw lines at predefined angle increments.

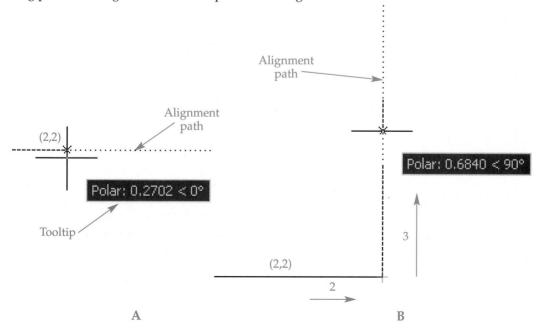

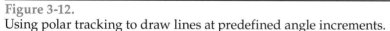

Figure 3-13.
Using **Ortho** mode. Angled lines cannot be drawn with a pointing device while **Ortho** mode is turned on. With **Ortho** mode turned off, angled lines can be drawn.

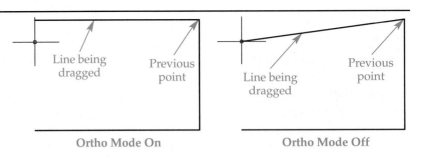

Line being dragged   Previous point   Line being dragged   Previous point

Ortho Mode On   Ortho Mode Off

Figure 3-14.
Using direct distance entry to draw lines a designated distance from a current point. With **Ortho** mode on, move the cursor in the desired direction and type the distance.

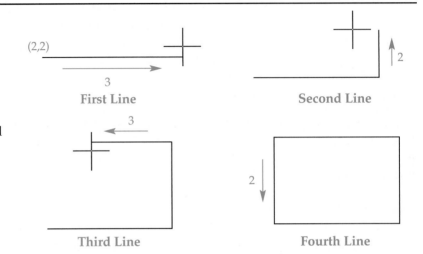

(2,2)

3

First Line   Second Line

3

Third Line   Fourth Line

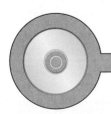

PROFESSIONAL TIP

Practice using the different point entry techniques and decide which method works best for certain situations. Keep in mind that you can mix methods to help enhance your drawing speed. For example, absolute coordinates may work best to locate an initial point. Polar coordinates may work better to locate features in a circular pattern or in an angular relationship. Practice with direct distance entry using polar tracking and **Ortho** mode to see the advantages and disadvantages of each.

Exercise 3-5
Complete the exercise on the Student CD.

Undoing the Previously Drawn Line

When drawing a series of lines, you may find you have made an error. To delete the mistake while still using the **LINE** tool, right-click and select the **Undo** option, pick the **Undo** dynamic input option, or type U and press [Enter]. This removes the previously drawn line and allows you to continue from the previous endpoint. You can use the **Undo** option repeatedly to continue deleting line segments until the entire line is gone. See Figure 3-15.

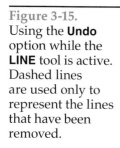
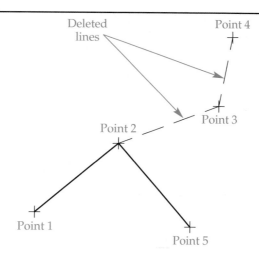

Figure 3-15.
Using the **Undo** option while the **LINE** tool is active. Dashed lines are used only to represent the lines that have been removed.

Deleted lines

Point 4

Point 3

Point 2

Point 1

Point 5

Using the Close Option

To aid in drawing a *polygon* using the **LINE** tool, after you have drawn two or more line segments of a polygon, use the **Close** option to automatically connect the endpoint of the last line segment to the start point of the first line segment. To use this option, right-click and select the **Close** option, pick the **Close** dynamic input option, or type C or CLOSE and press [Enter]. In Figure 3-16, the last line is drawn using the **Close** option.

polygon: Closed plane figure with at least three sides. Triangles and rectangles are examples of polygons.

Using Previously Picked Points

AutoCAD provides several methods for selecting previously picked points. This is a common need while drawing, especially if you draw a line, then exit the **LINE** tool, and decide to go back and connect a new line to the end of a previously selected point. A tool, such as **LINE**, must be active in order to select a previous point.

The quickest way to reselect the last point entered when you see the Specify first point: prompt is to right-click or press the [Enter] key or space bar. This action automatically connects the first endpoint of the new line segment to the endpoint of the previous line. The **Continue** function can also be used for drawing arcs, as described in Chapter 4.

You can access the coordinates of many previously selected points, not just the last selected point. When using dynamic input, press the up arrow key at a point selection prompt to display the coordinates of the last picked point. You can continue to press the up arrow key to cycle through other previously picked points. As you scroll through previous point coordinates, a symbol appears at the location of each point. When the point symbol appears at the coordinates you want to pick, press [Enter] or right-click and choose the **Enter** option. Previous coordinates are also displayed at the command line when a tool is active and you press the up arrow key.

Figure 3-16.
Using the **Close** option to complete a box.

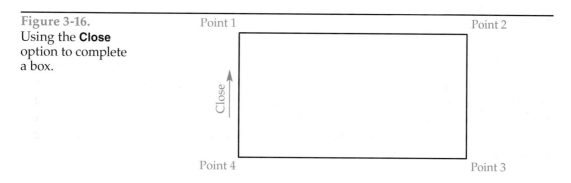

Point 1

Point 2

Close

Point 4

Point 3

Exercise 3-6

Complete the exercise on the Student CD.

Introduction to Editing

editing: Procedure used to modify an existing object.

selection set: A group of one or more drawing objects, typically defined to perform an editing operation.

Many *editing* tools exist to help increase productivity. The basic editing tools **ERASE**, **OOPS**, **UNDO**, **U**, and **REDO** are introduced in the next sections. To edit a drawing, you must select items to modify. A *selection set* is created when you select one or more objects. A selection set can consist of a single object or thousands of objects. You can create a selection set using a variety of selection options, depending on the number and location of objects you want to select. When you become familiar with the selection set options, you will find they increase your flexibility and productivity.

The following information introduces several selection set methods using the **ERASE** tool. Keep in mind, however, that these techniques can be used with most AutoCAD editing tools whenever the Select objects: prompt appears.

Erasing Objects

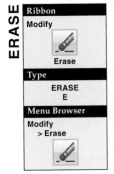

pick box: Small box that replaces the screen crosshairs when objects are to be selected.

The **ERASE** tool is similar to using an eraser in manual drafting to remove unwanted information. With the **ERASE** tool, however, you have a second chance. If you erase the wrong item, you can bring it back with the **OOPS** or **UNDO** tool.

When you access the **ERASE** tool, the Select objects: prompt appears and an object selection target, or *pick box*, replaces the screen crosshairs. Move the pick box over the item to be erased and pick that item. The object is highlighted and the Select objects: prompt is redisplayed. You can then select another object to erase. When you finish selecting objects, erase the selected objects by right-clicking, pressing the [Enter] key, or pressing the space bar. See **Figure 3-17**.

Figure 3-17.
Using the **ERASE** tool to erase a single object.

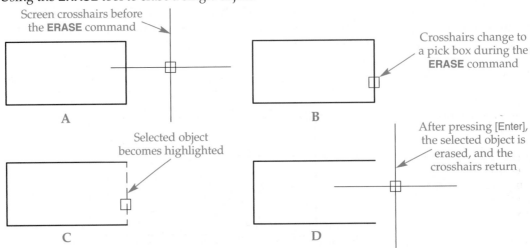

By default, when you move the crosshairs or pick box over an object and pause for a moment, the object changes to a thicker lineweight and becomes dashed. When the crosshairs or pick box is moved off the object, the object display returns to normal. This allows you to preview the object before you select it. When many objects are in a small area, this feature helps you select the correct object the first time and often eliminates the need to cycle through stacked objects.

Exercise 3-7
Complete the exercise on the Student CD.

Window and Crossing Selection

Window and crossing selection can be used to quickly select multiple objects, reducing the need to pick individual objects with the pick box. Window selection allows you to draw a box, or "window," around an object or group of objects to select for editing. Everything entirely within the window is selected at the same time. If portions of objects project outside the window, those objects are not selected.

Crossing selection is similar to window selection, but with crossing selection, objects contained within the box *and objects crossing the box* are selected. The crossing selection box displays a dotted outline with a light green background to distinguish it from the window selection box, which displays a solid outline and light blue background.

The quickest and most effective way to use window or crossing selection is through a feature known as *automatic windowing*, or *implied windowing*, which is on by default. When automatic windowing is on and the Select objects: prompt appears, use the pick box to select a point away from an object. This point establishes the first corner of a window or crossing selection box. The direction in which you move the cursor defines whether the selection is a window or a crossing.

automatic windowing (implied windowing): Selection method that allows you to select multiple objects at one time without entering a selection option.

To apply automatic window selection, use the pick box to select a point clearly above or below and to the left of the object(s) to be erased. The pick box is replaced by a selection box, and the Specify opposite corner: prompt is shown. Move the corner of the selection box to the right and up or down so the box completely covers the object(s) to be erased. Pick to locate the second corner. See **Figure 3-18.** All objects that lie completely within the box become highlighted.

To apply automatic crossing selection, use the pick box to select a point above or below and to the right of the object(s) to be erased. The pick box is replaced by a selection box, and the Specify opposite corner: prompt is shown. Move the corner of the selection box to the left and up or down, across the objects you want to select. Remember, the crossing box does not need to enclose the entire object to erase it, as does the window

Figure 3-18.
Using automatic windowing to select all objects completely inside a window selection box.

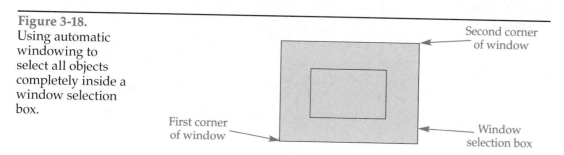

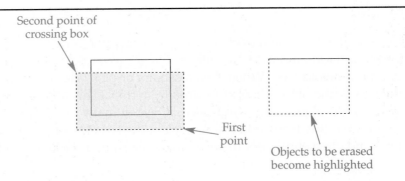

Figure 3-19.
Using crossing selection to select all objects inside and touching the crossing selection box.

Second point of crossing box

First point

Objects to be erased become highlighted

box. The crossing box needs only to cross part of the object. **Figure 3-19** shows how to erase three of the four lines of a rectangle using crossing selection.

Once you select the object(s) you want to erase using automatic window or crossing selection, right-click or press the [Enter] key or space bar to complete the **ERASE** tool. The selected objects are erased and the crosshairs reappears.

NOTE

You can also type W or WINDOW at the Select objects: prompt to use manual window selection, or type C or CROSSING to use manual crossing selection. When you use manual window or crossing selection, the selection box remains in the window or crossing format whether the first pick is left or right of objects and whether you move the cursor to the left or right.

Exercise 3-8
Complete the exercise on the Student CD.

Window Polygon and Crossing Polygon Selection

The window and crossing selection methods use a rectangular selection box, which may not allow you to select needed objects. An alternative is to form a window or crossing selection polygon. To use window polygon selection, type WPOLYGON or WP at the Select objects: prompt. Then pick points to draw a polygon enclosing the objects you want to select. As you pick corners, the polygon drags into place. See **Figure 3-20.**

Figure 3-20.
Using the window polygon selection method to erase objects.

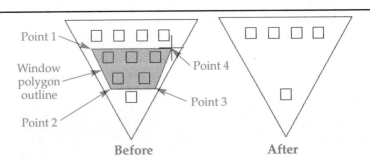

Point 1

Window polygon outline

Point 2

Point 4

Point 3

Before

After

AutoCAD and Its Applications—Basics

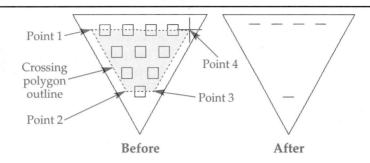

Figure 3-21.
Using crossing polygon selection. Everything enclosed within and crossing the polygon is selected.

Point 1
Crossing polygon outline
Point 2
Point 4
Point 3

Before   **After**

Crossing polygon selection is similar to window polygon selection, but with crossing polygon selection you create a crossing selection. To form a crossing selection polygon, type CPOLYGON or CP at the Select objects: prompt. Then pick points to draw a polygon. See **Figure 3-21.**

Fence Selection

Fence selection is another method used to select several objects at the same time. When using fence selection, you place a fence, or connected lines, through the objects you want to select. Only the objects the fence passes through are included in the selection set. To use fence selection, type FENCE or F at the Select objects: prompt. Then pick points to draw a fence through the objects you want to select. The fence can be straight or staggered, as shown in **Figure 3-22.**

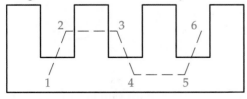

Exercise 3-9
Complete the exercise on the Student CD.

Figure 3-22.
Using fence selection to erase objects. The fence can be either straight or staggered.

2   3   6
1   4   5

Before   **After**

Last Selection

Last selection allows you to select the last object drawn. To use last selection, type LAST or L at the Select objects: prompt. The last selection feature selects only the last item drawn. You must repeatedly access a tool, such as **LINE**, and use last selection every time to select individual items in reverse order. This is extremely slow compared to selecting the objects using other methods.

Selecting All Objects

Sometimes, you want to select every object in the drawing. To do this, type ALL at the Select objects: prompt, or pick the **Select All** button from the **Utilities** panel on the **Home** tab of the ribbon. Everything in the drawing that is not on a frozen layer is selected, even objects that are outside of the current drawing window display. Layers are described in Chapter 5.

Cycling through Stacked Objects

stacked objects:
Objects that overlap in the drawing; when you pick with the mouse, the topmost object is selected by default.

cycle: Repeatedly select a series of stacked objects until the desired object is highlighted.

One way to deal with *stacked objects* is to let AutoCAD *cycle* through the overlapping objects. Cycling works best when several objects cross at the same place or are very close together. To cycle through stacked objects, first access a tool, such as **ERASE**. Next, with the Select objects: prompt shown, move the pick box over the intersection of the stacked objects. Hold down the [Shift] key and repeatedly press the space bar to cycle through the stacked objects. When the desired object is highlighted, pick (left-click) to select the item. See **Figure 3-23**.

Removing from and Adding to the Selection Set

A common mistake while editing a drawing is to accidentally select an object you do not want to select. The quickest way to remove one or more objects from the current selection set is to hold down the [Shift] key and reselect the objects. This is possible only for individual picks and automatic windows. For automatic windowing, the [Shift] key must be held down while picking the first corner and then can be released while picking the second corner. If you accidentally remove the wrong object from the selection set, release the [Shift] key and pick it again.

Another option for removing objects from a selection set is to type REMOVE or R at the Select objects: prompt. This enters the **Remove** option and changes the Select objects: prompt to Remove objects:, allowing you to pick the objects you want to remove from the selection set. To switch back to the selection mode, type ADD or A at the Remove objects: prompt. This enters the **Add** option and restores the Select objects: prompt and allows you to select additional objects.

Figure 3-23.
Cycling through a series of stacked circles until the desired object is highlighted.

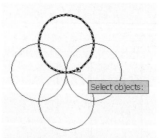

Original group of objects with top item highlighted

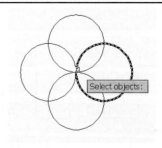

Hold down shift key and press the space bar to cycle through objects

AutoCAD and Its Applications—Basics

Exercise 3-10
Complete the exercise on the Student CD.

Selection Display Options

Options for selection display can be found on the Selection tab of the Options dialog box. Refer to the Student CD: Supplemental Materials > Selection Display Options for detailed information on adjusting selection display options. Note that many of the settings apply to selection options described later in this textbook.

Using the U Tool

The **U** tool undoes the effect of the previously entered tool. The **U** tool is different from the **Undo** option of the **LINE** tool and the **Undo** option of certain other tools. It allows you to undo the action of the previous tool after the tool has been completed. You can reissue the **U** tool to continue undoing tool actions, but you can only undo one tool at a time. The actions must be undone in the order in which they were used.

NOTE

The **U** tool can also be activated by right-clicking in the drawing area and selecting **Undo** *current* from the shortcut menu.

Exercise 3-11
Complete the exercise on the Student CD.

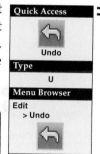

Using the Undo Tool

The **UNDO** tool is different from the **U** tool. The **UNDO** tool offers several options that allow you to undo a single tool or a number of tools at once. When you enter the **UNDO** tool, the prompt reads Enter the number of operations to undo or [Auto/Control/BEgin/End/Mark/Back] <1>:. The default option allows you to designate the number of previous tool sequences to remove. For example, if you enter 1, the previous tool sequence is undone. If you enter 2, the previous two tool sequences are undone. AutoCAD tells you which tools were undone with a message on the command line.

The **UNDO** tool contains several other options. When the **Auto** option is on, any tools that are part of a group and are used to perform a single operation are removed together. For example, when a tool contains other tools, all the tools in that group are removed in a single operation. The **Auto** option is active by default. If it is turned off, each tool in a group of tools is treated individually.

The **Control** option allows you to specify the maximum number of operations the **UNDO** tool can reverse. You can even disable the **UNDO** tool altogether. To use the **Control** option, select the **Control** dynamic input option or type **Control** or **C**. Selecting the **All** suboption keeps the full range of **UNDO** tool options active. This is the default setting. The **None** suboption disables the **U** and **UNDO** tools. The **One** suboption limits **UNDO** to one operation only. If you attempt to enter a number higher than one when this suboption is active, you get an error message.

The **Combine** option determines whether **Pan** and **Zoom** operations are combined and treated as a single operation. The **Layer** option determines whether changes made in the **Layer Properties Manager** are combined into a single operation.

PROFESSIONAL TIP

When you use the **UNDO** tool, AutoCAD maintains an "undo" file. This file saves previously used tools so that they can be undone. All **UNDO** entries saved before disabling **UNDO** with the **None** suboption of the **Control** option are discarded, which frees up some disk space. This may be valuable information to keep in mind if you ever get close to having a full disk. Using the **One** suboption of the **UNDO** tool's **Control** option allows you to keep using the **U** and **UNDO** tools to a limited extent, while freeing up disk space holding current information about **UNDO**.

The **BEgin** and **End** options of the **UNDO** tool are used together to perform several undo operations at once. They allow you to group a series of tool sequences and treat them as a single operation. Once the group is defined, the **U** tool is used to remove the tools that you used after entering the **BEgin** option but before entering the **End** option. These options are useful if you anticipate the possible removal of several tools entered consecutively. For example, if you think you want to undo the actions of the next three tools altogether, start by entering the **BEgin** option of the **UNDO** tool. Execute the three drawing tools. Then enter the **End** option of the **UNDO** tool. Since the three tools were executed between the **BEgin** and **End** options, the **U** tool treats them as one operation and undoes all three. The **BEgin** option must precede the tool sequence and the **End** option must immediately follow the last tool in the group to be undone.

The **Mark** option of the **UNDO** tool allows you to insert a marker in the undo file. The **Back** option of the **UNDO** tool undoes all tools issued after the marker was inserted. For example, if you do not want certain work to be undone by the **Back** option, enter the **Mark** option after completing the work. Then continue working. To undo all work since the marker was inserted, reissue the **UNDO** tool and enter the **Back** option. If no marker has been inserted, everything in the entire drawing is undone. AutoCAD issues the prompt This will undo everything. OK? <Y>. If you want everything you have drawn and edited to be undone, right-click or press [Enter]. If not, type N or NO and press [Enter], or press the [Esc] key.

The **Mark** option of the **UNDO** tool can be used to assist in the design process. For example, if you are working on a project and have completed a portion of the design, you can mark the spot with the **Mark** option and then begin work on the next design phase. If anything goes wrong with this part of the design, you can use the **Back** option to remove everything back to the mark.

Be very careful when using the **Back** option of the **UNDO** tool. Entering this option can undo everything in the entire drawing. You can bring back what you have undone if you use the **Redo** tool immediately after using the **Back** option of the **UNDO** tool. If you use any other tool, even **Redraw**, after using **UNDO Back**, the drawing is lost forever. The **Redo** tool is explained next.

Redoing the Undone

The **REDO** tool is used to reverse the action of the **UNDO** and **U** tools. The **REDO** tool works only *immediately* after undoing something. The **REDO** tool does *not* bring back line segments that were removed using the **Undo** option of the **LINE** tool. If multiple actions were undone, any or all of the tools that were undone can be redone using the **REDO** list.

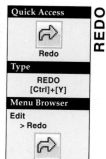

Using the Oops Tool

The **OOPS** tool brings back the last object you *erased*. Unlike the **U** and **UNDO** tools, **OOPS** only returns the objects erased in the most recent procedure. It has no effect on other modifications. It is issued by typing OOPS. If you erased several objects in the same tool sequence, all of the objects are brought back to the screen.

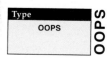

The **OOPS** tool can be used in combination with the previous selection option. This is usually done when more than one sequential editing operation needs to be carried out on a specific group of objects. In this case, the **Previous** selection option can be used to select the same object(s) you just edited. For example, a group of objects is erased, and then the **OOPS** tool is used to recover them. Then type Previous or P at the Select objects: prompt to reselect all the objects selected during the original erase.

Exercise 3-12

Complete the exercise on the Student CD.

Chapter Test

Answer the following questions. Write your answers on a separate sheet of paper or complete the electronic chapter test on the Student CD.

1. When you enter a fractional number in AutoCAD, why is a hyphen required between a whole number and its associated fraction?
2. List two ways to discontinue drawing a line.
3. Name three types of coordinates used for point entry.
4. What does the absolute coordinate display 5.250,7.875 mean?
5. What does the polar coordinate display @2.750<90 mean?
6. How can you turn on the coordinate display field if it is off?
7. Give the tools and entries to draw a line from Point A to Point B to Point C and back to Point A. Return to the Command: prompt:
   A. Command: _____
   B. Specify first point: _____
   C. Specify next point or [Undo]: _____
   D. Specify next point or [Undo]: _____
   E. Specify next point or [Close/Undo]: _____
8. What two general methods of point entry are available when dynamic input is active?
9. Explain, in general terms, how direct distance entry works.
10. What are the default angle increments for polar tracking?
11. How can you turn on the **Ortho** mode?
12. Explain how you can continue drawing another line segment from a previously drawn line.
13. When you access the **ERASE** tool, what replaces the crosshairs?
14. How does the appearance of window and crossing selection boxes differ?
15. List five ways to select an object to erase.
16. Define *stacked objects*.
17. How many tool sequences can you undo at one time with the **U** tool?
18. What is the difference between pressing the **UNDO** button on the **Quick Access** toolbar and entering the **UNDO** tool?
19. Name the tool used to bring back an object that was previously removed using the **UNDO** tool.
20. Name the tool used to bring back the last object(s) erased before starting another tool.

Drawing Problems

▼ Basic

1. Start a new drawing using one of your templates. Use the **LINE** tool and draw the following objects on only the left side of the screen. Accurately draw the specified objects with grid and snap turned off.
   - Right triangle.
   - Isosceles triangle.
   - Rectangle.
   - Square.

   Save the drawing as P3-1.

2. Draw the same objects specified in Problem 1 on the right side of the screen. This time, make sure the snap grid is turned on. Observe the difference between having snap on for this problem and off for the previous problem. Save the drawing as P3-2.

3. Draw an object by connecting the following point coordinates. Use dynamic input to enter the coordinates. Save your drawing as P3-3.

Point	Coordinates	Point	Coordinates
1	2,2	8	@-1.5,0
2	@1.5,0	9	@0,1.25
3	@.75<90	10	@-1.25,1.25
4	@1.5<0	11	@2<180
5	@0,-.75	12	@-1.25,-1.25
6	@3,0	13	@2.25<270
7	@1<90		

4. Use direct distance entry and polar tracking to draw the outline shown. Each grid square is one unit. Do not draw the grid lines. Save the drawing as P3-4.

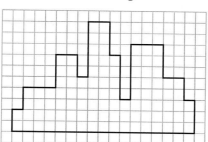

5. Use the dimensional input feature of dynamic input to draw the hexagon shown. Each side of the hexagon is 2 units. Begin at the start point, and draw the lines in the direction indicated by the arrows. Do not draw dimensions. Save the drawing as P3-5.

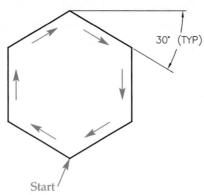

30° (TYP)

Start

▼ Intermediate

6. Draw the following shapes using absolute, relative, and polar coordinate entry methods. Draw Object A three times, using a different point entry system each time. Set the units to decimal and the precision to 0.0 when drawing Object A. Draw Object B once, using at least two methods of coordinate entry. Set the units to fractional and the precision to 1/16 when drawing Object B. Do not draw dimensions. Save the drawing as P3-6.

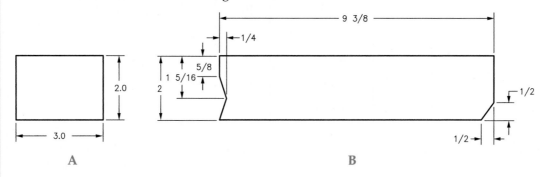

9 3/8

1/4

5/8

1 5/16

2.0

2

3.0

1/2

1/2

A

B

For Problems 7–8, draw the given part. Do not draw dimensions. Save the drawings as P3-7 *and* P3-8.

7.

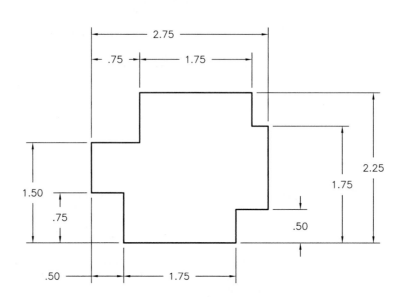

2.75

.75

1.75

1.50

.75

2.25

1.75

.50

.50

1.75

AutoCAD and Its Applications—Basics

8.

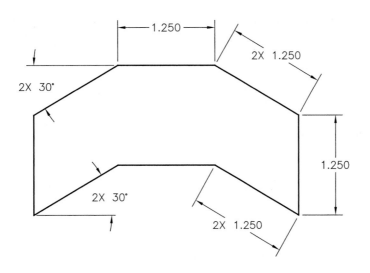

9. Draw the objects shown in A and B. Begin at the start point and then discontinue the **LINE** tool at the point shown. Complete each object using the **Continue** option. Do not draw dimensions. Save the drawing as P3-9.

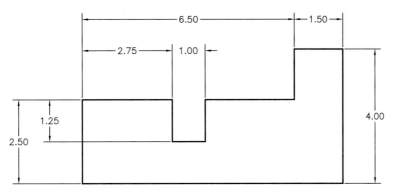

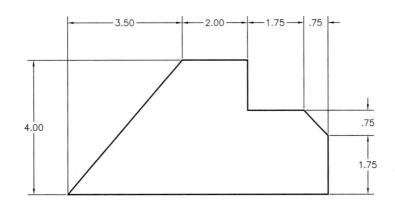

▼ Advanced

For Problems 10–12, draw the given part. Do not draw dimensions. Save the drawings as P3-10, P3-11, *and* P3-12.

10.

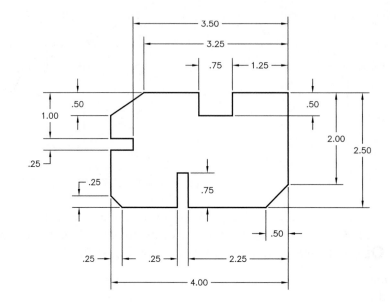

11.

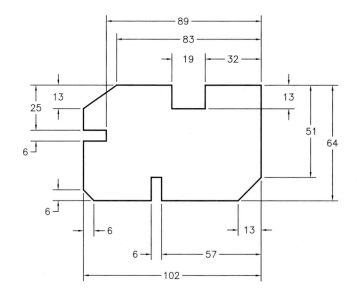

12.

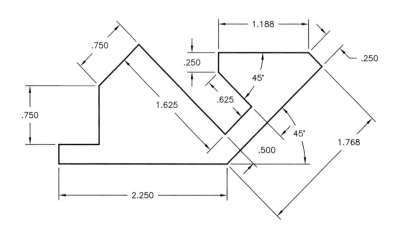

CHAPTER 4

Basic Object Tools

Learning Objectives

After completing this chapter, you will be able to do the following:

✓ Explain the role of the rubberband line in creating basic objects.
✓ Draw circles using the **CIRCLE** tool options.
✓ Draw arcs using the **ARC** tool options.
✓ Use the **ELLIPSE** tool to draw ellipses and elliptical arcs.
✓ Draw polygons using the **POLYGON** tool.
✓ Draw rectangles using the **RECTANGLE** tool options.
✓ Draw donuts using the **DONUT** tool.

AutoCAD provides drawing tools that allow you to create and document any design. You have already learned to use the **LINE** tool to draw objects. This chapter describes additional tools used for drawing basic shapes. These tools include **CIRCLE**, **ARC**, **ELLIPSE**, **POLYGON**, **RECTANGLE**, and **DONUT**. AutoCAD provides many ways to create objects, depending on the shape you want to create and information you already know.

NOTE

This chapter presents the ribbon and menu browser as the primary means of accessing basic object tool options. When you select a specific **CIRCLE**, **ARC**, or **ELLIPSE** tool option from the ribbon or menu browser, all prompts are specific to the selected option. When you access a tool using dynamic input or the command line, you must enter specific options when prompted

---

Using Basic Object Tools

When you draw basic shapes, AutoCAD prompts you to select coordinates, just as when you draw lines. For example, the prompt Specify center point: appears when you are drawing a circle using the **Center, Radius** or **Center, Diameter** methods. Your response to this prompt is similar to your response to the Select first point: prompt that appears when you use the **LINE** tool. You can pick a location in space with the crosshairs or use absolute, relative, or polar coordinate entry.

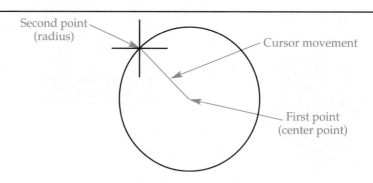

Figure 4-1.
Dragging a circle to its desired size. The circle attached to the crosshairs stretches like a rubberband until you pick a point to define the radius.

Second point (radius)

Cursor movement

First point (center point)

Some basic object tools give you the option of entering specific values to define the size and shape of the object. For example, after locating the center point of a circle when using the **Center, Radius** option of the **CIRCLE** tool, the prompt Specify radius of circle: appears. Usually, the most effective response to this type of prompt is to type a value; in this example, the value would be the radius of the circle. An alternative is to use dimensional input or absolute, relative, or polar coordinate entry. Refer to Chapter 3 to review appropriate numerical responses to AutoCAD tools and point entry methods.

As you may recall, a *rubberband* line connecting the first point and the cross-hairs appears while you are using the **LINE** tool. The rubberband image is "dragged" across the screen before you pick the second endpoint. The **CIRCLE**, **ARC**, **ELLIPSE**, **POLYGON**, and **RECTANGLE** tools also display a rubberband image to help you decide where to place the object. For example, when you draw a circle using the **Center, Radius** option, a circle image appears on the screen after you pick the center point. This image gets larger or smaller as you move the pointer. When you pick the circle size, a circle replaces the rubberband image. See **Figure 4-1.**

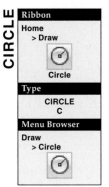

Ribbon
Home > Draw
Circle
Type
CIRCLE C
Menu Browser
Draw > Circle

Drawing Circles

The **CIRCLE** tool provides several methods for drawing circles. The option you choose is based on how you want to locate the circle and the information you already know or want to use to construct the circle. The ribbon and menu browser are presented as the primary locations for accessing circle tool options in this chapter. See **Figure 4-2.**

Drawing a Circle by Radius

Use the **Center, Radius** option of the **CIRCLE** tool to specify the center point and the radius of a circle. After selecting the **Center, Radius** option, define the center point. Then type a value for the radius and press the [Enter] key or space bar, or right-click and pick the **Enter** option. You can also define the radius using point entry. See **Figure 4-3.**

NOTE

The radius value you enter is stored as the new default radius setting, allowing you to quickly draw another circle with the same radius.

AutoCAD and Its Applications—Basics

Figure 4-2.
The **Circle** options can be accessed from the ribbon or the menu browser.

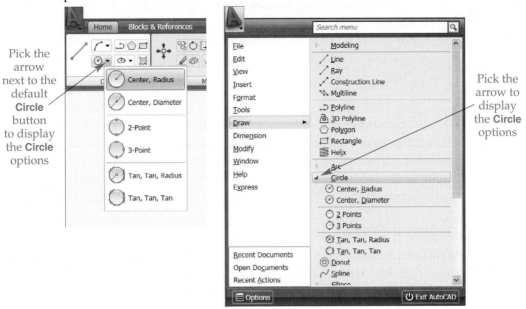

Pick the arrow next to the default **Circle** button to display the **Circle** options

Pick the arrow to display the **Circle** options

Figure 4-3.
Drawing a circle by specifying the center point and radius.

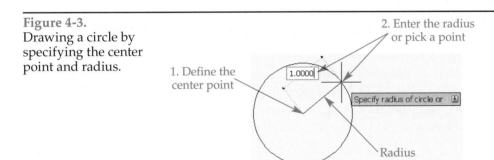

2. Enter the radius or pick a point

1. Define the center point

Radius

Drawing a Circle by Diameter

A circle can also be drawn by specifying the center point and the diameter. The **Center, Diameter** option is convenient because most circular holes, shafts, and features are specified by diameter. After selecting the **Center, Diameter** option, define the center point. Then type a value for the diameter and press the [Enter] key or space bar, or right-click and pick the **Enter** option. You can also define the diameter using point entry. In the **Center, Diameter** option, the crosshairs measures the diameter, but the rubberband circle passes midway between the center and the crosshairs. See **Figure 4-4.**

Figure 4-4.
When you use the **Center, Diameter** option, AutoCAD calculates the circle's position as you move the crosshairs.

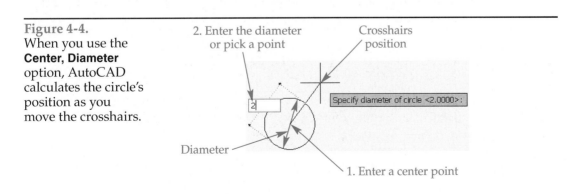

2. Enter the diameter or pick a point

Crosshairs position

Diameter

1. Enter a center point

Drawing a Two-Point Circle

A two-point circle is drawn by picking two points on opposite sides of the circle to define its diameter. The **2-Point** option is useful if the diameter of the circle is known, but the center is difficult to find. One example of this is locating a circle between two lines. The process of drawing a two-point circle is very similar to drawing a line. After selecting the **2 Points** option, enter or select a point for the first endpoint of the circle's diameter. Then enter or select the second endpoint of the circle's diameter. See **Figure 4-5**.

Drawing a Three-Point Circle

The **3-Point** option is the best method to use if you know three points on the circumference of a circle. After selecting the **3-Point** option, enter or select three points in any order to define the circumference of the circle. See **Figure 4-6**.

Drawing a Circle Tangent to Two Objects

tangent: A line, circle, or arc that comes into contact with another circle or arc at only one point.

point of tangency: The point shared by tangent objects.

object snap: A tool that snaps to exact points, such as endpoints or midpoints, when you pick a point near these locations.

The **Tan, Tan, Radius** option creates a circle of a specified radius *tangent* to two objects. You can draw a circle tangent to given lines, circles, or arcs. The circle is automatically positioned at the *point of tangency*. The **Tan, Tan, Radius** option uses an *object snap* known as **Deferred Tangent** to assist you in picking a point exactly on and tangent to other objects. Object snaps are covered in detail in Chapter 7. After accessing the **Tan, Tan, Radius** option, hover the crosshairs over the first line, arc, or circle to which the new circle will be tangent. Pick when the deferred tangent symbol appears. Repeat the process to select the second line, arc, or circle to which the new circle will be tangent. Then, enter or select the radius of the circle. See **Figure 4-7**.

Figure 4-5.
Drawing a circle by selecting two points.

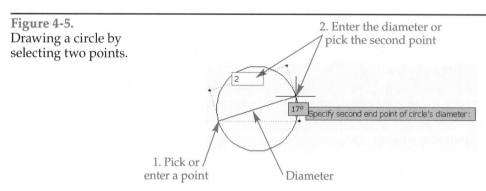

Figure 4-6.
Drawing a circle by picking three points that lie on the circle.

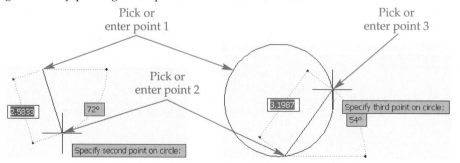

Figure 4-7.
Two examples of
drawing circles
tangent to two given
objects using the
Tan, Tan, Radius
option.

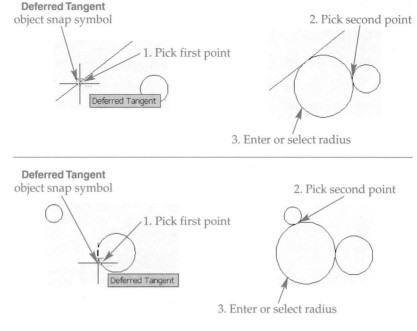

Deferred Tangent
object snap symbol

1. Pick first point

2. Pick second point

Deferred Tangent

3. Enter or select radius

Deferred Tangent
object snap symbol

1. Pick first point

2. Pick second point

Deferred Tangent

3. Enter or select radius

NOTE

If the radius you enter while using the **Tan, Tan, Radius** option is too small, AutoCAD displays the message Circle does not exist.

Drawing a Circle Tangent to Three Objects

The **Tan, Tan, Tan** option allows you to draw a circle tangent to three existing objects. This option creates a three-point circle using the three points of tangency. Like the **Tan, Tan, Radius** option, the **Tan, Tan, Tan** option uses the **Deferred Tangent** object snap to assist you in picking a point exactly on and tangent to other objects. After accessing the **Tan, Tan, Tan** option, pick three lines, arcs, or circles to which the new circle will be tangent. You must pick each item when the deferred tangent symbol appears, but the order in which you pick the items is not critical. See **Figure 4-8.**

NOTE

Unlike the **Tan, Tan, Radius** option, the **Tan, Tan, Tan** option does not automatically recover when a point prompt is answered with a pick where no tangent exists. In such a case, the **Tangent** object snap must be manually reactivated to make additional picks. The **Tangent** object snap is described in Chapter 7. For now, type TAN and press [Enter] at the point selection prompt to return the pick box so you can pick again.

Exercise 4-1

Complete the exercise on the Student CD.

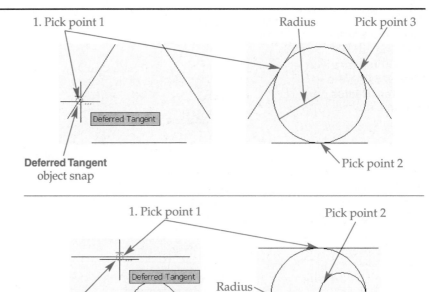

Figure 4-8.
Two examples of drawing circles tangent to three given objects.

1. Pick point 1

Radius   Pick point 3

Deferred Tangent

Deferred Tangent
object snap

Pick point 2

1. Pick point 1

Pick point 2

Deferred Tangent

Radius

Deferred Tangent
object snap

Pick
point 3

Drawing Arcs

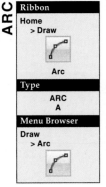

arc: Any portion of a circle.

ARC

Ribbon
Home
> Draw

Arc

Type
ARC
A

Menu Browser
Draw
> Arc

Arcs are commonly dimensioned with a radius, but they can be drawn by a number of different methods using the **ARC** tool. The option you use for drawing an arc is based on how you want to locate the arc and the information you already know or want to use to construct the arc. The ribbon and menu browser are presented as the primary locations for accessing arc tool options in this chapter. See **Figure 4-9.**

Figure 4-9.
Selecting an **Arc** option from the ribbon or menu browser.

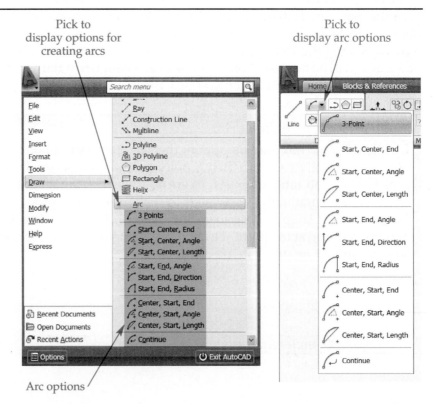

Pick to
display options for
creating arcs

Pick to
display arc options

Arc options

Figure 4-10.
Drawing an arc by picking three points. A three-point arc can be drawn clockwise or counterclockwise.

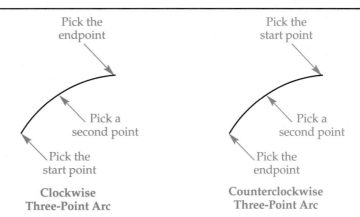

Pick the endpoint

Pick a second point

Pick the start point

Clockwise
Three-Point Arc

Pick the start point

Pick a second point

Pick the endpoint

Counterclockwise
Three-Point Arc

Drawing Three-Point Arcs

Use the **3-Point** option when you know the start point, a second point along the arc, and the endpoint of the arc. The arc can be drawn clockwise or counterclockwise and is dragged into position when you specify the endpoint. After selecting the **3-Point** option, enter or select the start point of the arc. Then enter or select a second point anywhere along the arc. Enter or pick the endpoint to complete the arc. See **Figure 4-10.**

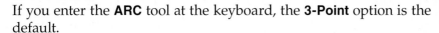

NOTE

If you enter the **ARC** tool at the keyboard, the **3-Point** option is the default.

Using the Start, Center, End Option

Use the **Start, Center, End** option when you know the start point, center point, and endpoint of an arc. In this method, arcs are drawn counterclockwise. After selecting the **Start, Center, End** option, pick the start point of the arc. Then pick the center point of the arc to establish the arc's radius. Pick the endpoint to complete the arc. The endpoint does not have to be on the radius of the arc. See **Figure 4-11.**

Figure 4-11.
Using the **Start, Center, End** option. Notice that the endpoint does not have to be on the arc.

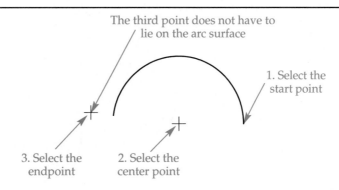

The third point does not have to lie on the arc surface

1. Select the start point

3. Select the endpoint

2. Select the center point

Figure 4-12.
Using the **Start, Center, Angle** option. The positive or negative value of the included angle affects the location of the arc endpoint.

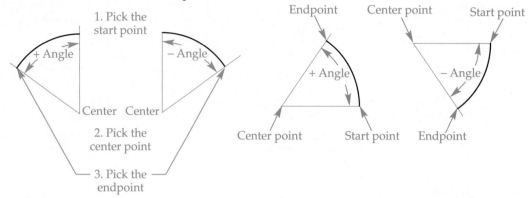

Using the Start, Center, Angle Option

included angle:
The angle formed between the center, start point, and endpoint of an arc.

When you know the arc's *included angle*, the **Start, Center, Angle** option may be the best choice. The arc is drawn counterclockwise, unless a negative angle is specified. After selecting the **Start, Center, Angle** option, pick the start point of the arc. Then pick the center point of the arc to establish the arc's radius. Enter or pick the included angle to complete the arc. An included angle selection does not have to be on the radius of the arc. **Figure 4-12** shows examples of creating **Start, Center, Angle** arcs using a 45° included angle.

Using the Start, Center, Length Option

chord length: The linear distance between two points on a circle or arc.

Use the **Start, Center, Length** option to specify the *chord length* of an arc. In this method, arcs are drawn counterclockwise. A positive chord length gives the smallest possible arc with that length. A negative chord length results in the largest possible arc. After selecting the **Start, Center, Length** option, select the start point of the arc. Then select the center point of the arc to establish the arc's radius. Pick the chord length to complete the arc. **Figure 4-13** shows examples of creating **Start, Center, Length** arcs using a .765 chord length.

Figure 4-13.
Using the **Start, Center, Length** option. The positive or negative value of the chord length determines the overall length of the arc.

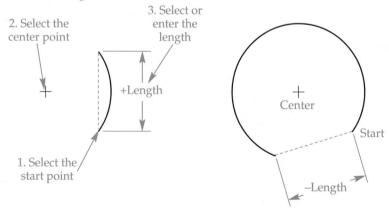

Chord Length Table
A chord length table is provided on the Student CD: Reference Materials > Standard Tables.

Exercise 4-2

Complete the exercise on the Student CD.

Using the Start, End, Angle Option

Use the **Start, End, Angle** option to draw an arc if you know the start point, endpoint, and included angle. After you access the **Start, End, Angle** option, select the start point of the arc and then the endpoint of the arc. Enter or pick the included angle to complete the arc. A positive included angle draws the arc counterclockwise, and a negative draws the arc clockwise. See Figure 4-14.

Using the Start, End, Direction Option

Use the **Start, End, Direction** option to draw an arc if you know the start point, endpoint, and direction tangent to the arc from the start point. After you access the **Start, End, Direction** option, select the start point and endpoint of the arc. Enter the direction to complete the arc. The arc starts tangent to the direction specified. The distance between the points and the tangent direction you select determine the location and size of the arc. See Figure 4-15.

Figure 4-14.
Using the **Start, End, Angle** option. The positive or negative angle value determines the size and location of the arc.

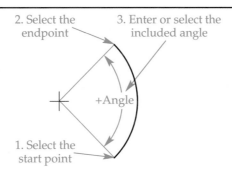

Figure 4-15.
Using the **Start, End, Direction** option.

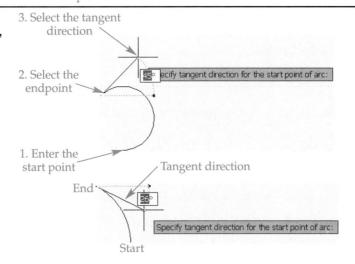
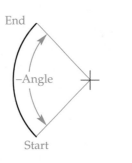

Figure 4-16.
Using the **Start, End, Radius** option with a positive and negative radius.

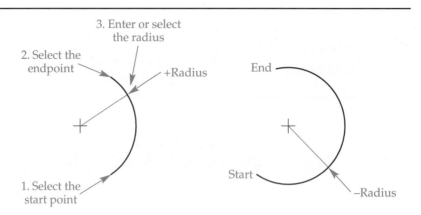

3. Enter or select the radius

2. Select the endpoint

+Radius

1. Select the start point

End

Start

−Radius

Using the Start, End, Radius Option

Use the **Start, End, Radius** option when you know the start point, endpoint, and radius of the arc. Arcs can only be drawn counterclockwise with this option. After you access the **Start, End, Radius** option, select the start point and the endpoint of the arc. Enter the radius to complete the arc. A positive radius value for the **Start, End, Radius** option results in the smallest possible arc between the start point and endpoint. A negative radius creates the largest arc possible. See **Figure 4-16**.

Exercise 4-3
Complete the exercise on the Student CD.

Using the Center, Start, End Option

The **Center, Start, End** option is a variation of the **Start, Center, End** option. Use the **Center, Start, End** option when it is easier to begin by locating the center. After selecting the **Center, Start, End** option, select the center point of the arc. Then enter the start point of the arc to establish the arc's radius. Select the endpoint to complete the arc. See **Figure 4-17**.

Using the Center, Start, Angle Option

Use the **Center, Start, Angle** option when it is easier to begin by locating the center. After you access the **Center, Start, Angle** option, select the center point of the arc. Then select the start point of the arc to establish the arc's radius. Enter the included angle to complete the arc. **Figure 4-18** shows examples of creating **Center, Start, Angle** arcs using a 45° included angle.

Figure 4-17.
Using the **Center, Start, End** option. Like the **Start, Center, End** option, this option does not require the endpoint to be on the arc.

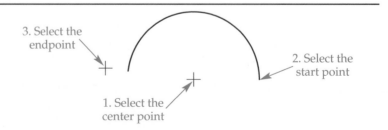

3. Select the endpoint

2. Select the start point

1. Select the center point

Figure 4-18.
Using the **Center, Start, Angle** option. The positive or negative value of the included angle affects the location of the arc endpoint.

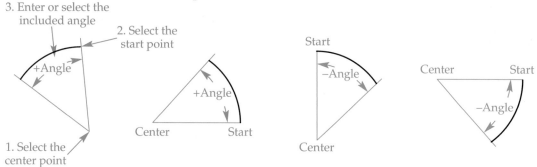

Using the Center, Start, Length Option

The **Center, Start, Length** option provides another way to begin an arc by locating the center. After you access the **Center, Start, Length** option, select the center point of the arc. Then enter or select the start point of the arc to establish the arc's radius. Enter the chord length to complete the arc. Figure 4-19 shows examples of creating **Center, Start, Length** arcs using a .765 chord length.

Continuing Arcs from a Previously Drawn Arc or Line

An arc can be continued from the endpoint of a previously drawn arc or line using the **Continue** option available from the ribbon or menu browser. When you access the **Continue** option, the arc is automatically attached to the endpoint of the previously drawn arc or line, and the: Specify endpoint of arc: prompt appears. Pick the endpoint to create the arc.

When a series of arcs are drawn using the **Continue** option, each arc is tangent to the previous arc. The start point and direction are taken from the endpoint and direction of the previous arc. See Figure 4-20. When you use the **Continue** option to begin an arc at the endpoint of a previously drawn line, the arc is tangent to the line. See Figure 4-21. This is a quick way to draw an arc tangent to a line for a variety of applications, such as slots.

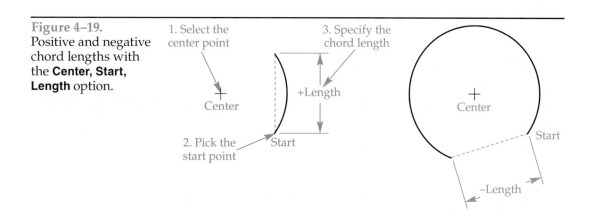

Figure 4–19. Positive and negative chord lengths with the **Center, Start, Length** option.

Figure 4–20.
Using the **Continue**
option to draw three
tangent arcs.

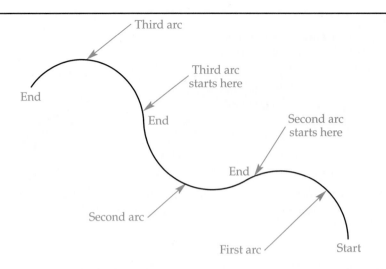

Third arc

Third arc
starts here

End

End

Second arc
starts here

End

Second arc

First arc

Start

Figure 4–21.
An arc continuing
from the previous
line. Point 2 is the
start of the arc, and
Point 3 is the end of
the arc. The arc and
line are tangent at
Point 2.

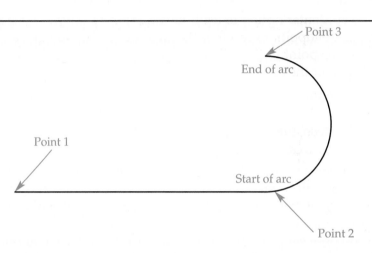

Point 3

End of arc

Point 1

Start of arc

Point 2

NOTE

The **Continue** option can also be accessed by beginning the **ARC**
tool and then pressing the [Enter] key, pressing the space bar, or
selecting **Enter** from the shortcut menu when prompted to specify
the start point of the arc.

Exercise 4-4
Complete the exercise on the Student CD.

Drawing Ellipses

ellipse: An oval
shape that contains
two centers of equal
radius.

major axis: The
longer of the two
axes in an ellipse.

minor axis: The
shorter of the two
axes in an ellipse.

When a circle is viewed at an angle, it appears as an *ellipse* and contains both a
major axis and a *minor axis*. For example, a 30° ellipse is created if a circle is rotated
30° from the line of sight. The parts of an ellipse are shown in Figure 4-22.

Figure 4–22.
The parts of an
ellipse.

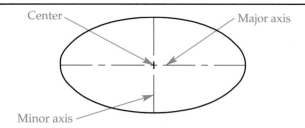

The **ELLIPSE** tool provides several methods for drawing elliptical shapes. The option you choose is based on how you want to locate the ellipse, the information you already know or want to use to construct the ellipse, and whether the ellipse is whole or partial.

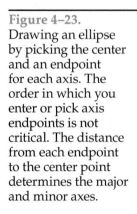

Ribbon
Home
> Draw
Ellipse

Type
ELLIPSE
EL

Menu Browser
Draw
> Ellipse

Using the Center Option

The **Center** option is used to construct an ellipse by specifying the center point and one endpoint for each of the two axes. After you access the **Center** option, select the center point of the ellipse. Then select the endpoint of one of the axes. Enter the endpoint of the other axis to complete the ellipse. See **Figure 4-23.**

Using the Axis, End Option

The **Axis, End** option establishes the first axis and one endpoint of the second axis. The first axis can be either the major or minor axis, depending on what you enter for the second axis. After selecting the **Axis, End** option, select the endpoint of one of the axes. Then select the other endpoint of the same axis. Enter a distance from the midpoint of the first axis to the end of the second axis to complete the ellipse. See **Figure 4-24.**

Figure 4–23.
Drawing an ellipse by picking the center and an endpoint for each axis. The order in which you enter or pick axis endpoints is not critical. The distance from each endpoint to the center point determines the major and minor axes.

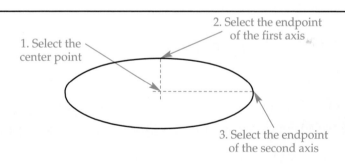

Figure 4–24.
Constructing the same ellipse by choosing different axis endpoints.

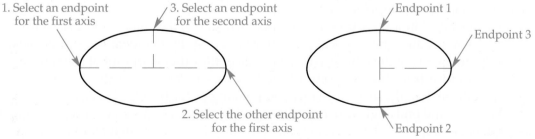

Figure 4–25.
Ellipse rotation angles.

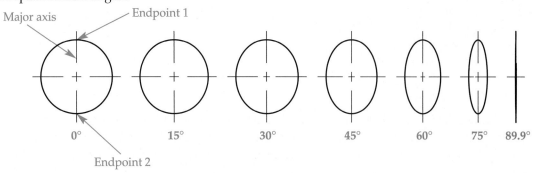

Major axis

Endpoint 1

0° 15° 30° 45° 60° 75° 89.9°

Endpoint 2

Using the Rotation option

When the Specify distance to other axis or: prompt appears, you can select the **Rotation** option instead of picking the second axis endpoint. When you use the **Rotation** option, AutoCAD assumes you have selected the major axis with the first axis endpoint. The next prompt requests the angle at which the corresponding circle is rotated from the line of sight to produce the ellipse. Enter an angle to complete the ellipse.

For example, if you respond by entering 30 for a 30° rotation, an ellipse is created based on a circle that is rotated 30° from the line of sight. A 0 response draws an ellipse with the minor axis equal to the major axis, which is a circle. AutoCAD rejects any rotation angle between 89.99994° and 90.00006° or between 269.99994° and 270.00006°. **Figure 4-25** shows the relationship among several ellipses having the same major axis length, but different rotation angles.

NOTE

The **Rotation** option works with both the **Center** option and the **Axis, End** option.

Exercise 4-5
Complete the exercise on the Student CD.

Drawing Elliptical Arcs

Ribbon
Home
> Draw

Elliptical Arc

Menu Browser
Draw
> Ellipse
> Arc

The **Arc** option of the **ELLIPSE** tool is used to draw elliptical arcs. Creating an elliptical arc is just like drawing an ellipse, but with two steps that define the start point and endpoint of the elliptical arc. Several options are available for defining the size and shape of an elliptical arc.

The default elliptical arc uses axis endpoints to define the ellipse, and then start and end angles to produce the elliptical arc. After selecting the **Elliptical Arc** option, select the endpoint of one of the ellipse axes. Then select the other endpoint of the same axis. Enter a distance from the midpoint of the first axis to the end of the second axis to form an ellipse. Finally, select the start and end angles for the elliptical arc.

The start and end angles are the angular relationships between the ellipse's center and the arc's endpoints. The angle of the elliptical arc is established from the angle of the first axis. For example, a 0° start angle begins the arc at the first endpoint of the first axis. A 45° start angle begins the arc 45° counterclockwise from the first endpoint

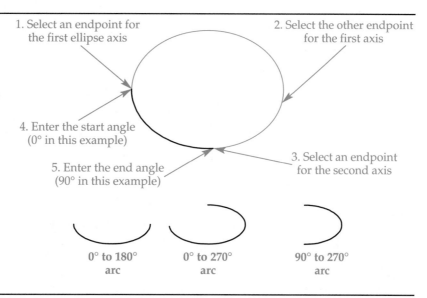

Figure 4–26. Drawing elliptical arcs. Note the three examples at the bottom created by three different angle settings.

1. Select an endpoint for the first ellipse axis

2. Select the other endpoint for the first axis

4. Enter the start angle (0° in this example)

5. Enter the end angle (90° in this example)

3. Select an endpoint for the second axis

0° to 180° arc

0° to 270° arc

90° to 270° arc

of the first axis. End angles are also established counterclockwise from the start point. Figure 4-26 shows an elliptical arc drawn using a 0° start angle and a 90° end angle and displays sample arcs with different start and end angles.

Using the Parameter option

When the Specify start angle or [Parameter]: prompt appears, you can enter the **Parameter** option instead of picking the start angle of the elliptical arc. When you use the **Parameter** option, AutoCAD uses a different means of vector calculation to create the elliptical arc, but the results are similar to other elliptical arcs. The **Parameter** option requires the same input used for drawing other elliptical arcs until the Specify start angle or [Parameter]: prompt. Enter the **Parameter** option, and then select the start parameter point. Enter or select the end parameter point to complete the elliptical arc.

Using the Included angle option

The **Included angle** option establishes an included angle beginning at the start angle. This option requires the same input used for drawing other elliptical arcs until the Specify end angle or [Parameter/Included angle]: prompt appears. Enter the **Included angle** option, and then enter the included angle to complete the elliptical arc.

Rotating an elliptical arc around its axis

The **Rotation** option for drawing an elliptical arc is similar to the **Rotation** option for drawing a full ellipse. This option allows you to rotate the elliptical arc about the first axis by specifying a rotation angle. Refer to **Figure 4-25** for examples of various rotation angles. This option requires the same input used for drawing other elliptical arcs until the Specify distance to other axis or [Rotation]: prompt appears. Enter the **Rotation** option, and then enter the rotation around the major axis. Enter the start angle for the elliptical arc, and then enter the end angle to complete the elliptical arc. The **Parameter** and **Included angle** options can also be applied.

Using the Center option

The **Center** option for drawing an elliptical arc lets you establish the center of the ellipse. After you access the **Center** option, select the center point of the ellipse. Then select the endpoint of one of the ellipse axes. Pick the endpoint of the other axis to form the ellipse. Enter the start angle for the elliptical arc, and then select the end angle to complete the elliptical arc. See **Figure 4-27**. The **Rotation, Parameter,** and **Included angle** options can also be applied.

Figure 4-27.
Drawing elliptical arcs with the **Center** option.

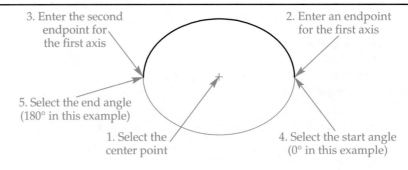

3. Enter the second endpoint for the first axis

2. Enter an endpoint for the first axis

5. Select the end angle (180° in this example)

1. Select the center point

4. Select the start angle (0° in this example)

Exercise 4-6
Complete the exercise on the Student CD.

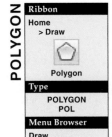

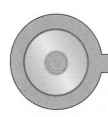

POLYGON

Ribbon
Home
> Draw

Polygon

Type
POLYGON
POL

Menu Browser
Draw
> Polygon

Drawing Regular Polygons

The **POLYGON** tool is used to draw any *regular polygon* with up to 1024 sides. When you access the **POLYGON** tool you are first prompted for the number of sides. For example, if you wanted to draw an octagon, which is a regular polygon with eight sides, you would enter 8.

Next, you must decide how you want to describe the size and location of the polygon. The default setting involves choosing the center and radius of an imaginary circle. To use this method, after entering the number of polygon sides, enter or pick a location for the polygon center point. You are then asked if you want to form an *inscribed polygon* or a *circumscribed polygon*. After selecting the appropriate option, enter the radius to create the polygon. See **Figure 4-28.**

regular polygon:
A closed geometric figure with three or more equal sides and equal angles.

inscribed polygon:
A polygon that is drawn inside an imaginary circle so that its corners touch the circle.

circumscribed polygon: A polygon that is drawn outside of an imaginary circle so that the sides of the polygon are tangent to the circle.

NOTE

The number of polygon sides you enter, the **Inscribed in circle** or **Circumscribed about circle** option you select, and the radius you enter are stored as the new default settings, allowing you to quickly draw another polygon with the same characteristics.

Figure 4-28.
Polygons can be inscribed in a circle (left) or circumscribed around a circle (right).

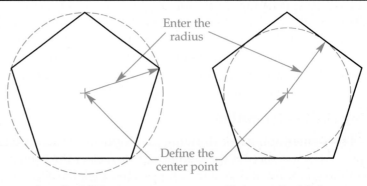

Enter the radius

Define the center point

Inscribed Polygon

Circumscribed Polygon

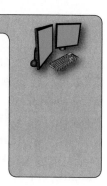

Regular hexagons are six-sided polygons commonly drawn to represent bolt heads and nuts on mechanical drawings. Keep in mind that these features are normally dimensioned across the flats. Use the **Circumscribed about circle** option to draw a polygon to be dimensioned across the flats. The radius you enter is equal to one-half the distance across the flats. Use the **Inscribed in circle** option when the distance across the corners is specified for a polygon confined within a circular area.

Using the Edge Option

Use the **Edge** option to construct a polygon if you do not know the center point location or the radius of the imaginary circle, but you do know the size and location of a polygon edge. After you access the **POLYGON** tool and enter the number of sides, choose the **Edge** option at the Specify center of polygon or [Edge]: prompt. The process of drawing an **Edge** polygon is similar to drawing a line. Select a point for the first endpoint of one of the polygon's sides. Then select the second endpoint of the polygon side. See Figure 4-29.

Polygons are *polylines* and can be edited using the **PEDIT** (polyline edit) tool. The **PEDIT** tool is described in Chapter 15 of this textbook.

polyline: A series of lines and arcs that constitute a single object.

Exercise 4-7
Complete the exercise on the Student CD.

Figure 4–29.
Use the **Edge** option of the **POLYGON** tool to construct a polygon according the location and size of an edge.

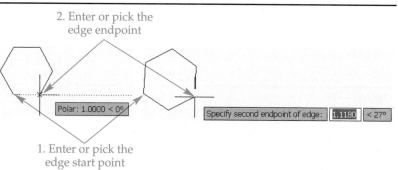

2. Enter or pick the edge endpoint

Polar: 1.0000 < 0°

Specify second endpoint of edge: 1.1180 < 27°

1. Enter or pick the edge start point

Drawing Rectangles

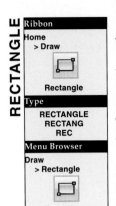

RECTANGLE

Ribbon
Home
> Draw

Rectangle

Type
RECTANGLE
RECTANG
REC

Menu Browser
Draw
> Rectangle

The **RECTANGLE** tool allows you to draw rectangles easily. To use the **RECTANGLE** tool, enter or pick one corner and then the opposite diagonal corner. See Figure 4-30.

Drawing Chamfered Rectangles

Use the **Chamfer** option to include *chamfered* corners in the initial rectangle construction. This is a brief introduction to adding chamfers while creating rectangles. Adding chamfers is covered in detail in Chapter 12.

chamfer: In mechanical drafting, a small angled surface used to relieve a sharp corner.

The **Chamfer** option requires you to specify chamfer distances, or distances from the corner. See Figure 4-31A. When prompted, enter the first chamfer distance, followed by the second chamfer distance. After setting the chamfer distances, you can either draw the rectangle or select another option. However, using the **Fillet** option overrides the **Chamfer** option.

The default chamfer distances are the chamfer distances that were used to draw the previous rectangle. If the default for the first chamfer distance is zero, and you enter a different value, the new distance becomes the default for the second chamfer distance. If the default chamfer distances are nonzero values, however, a new value entered for the first distance does *not* become the default for the second distance. If you set chamfer distances to a value greater than 0, any new rectangles created are automatically chamfered. New rectangles continue to be created with chamfers until you reset the chamfer distances to 0 or use the **Fillet** option to create rounded corners.

Drawing Rounded Rectangles

fillet: A rounded interior corner.

round: A rounded exterior corner.

Use the **Fillet** option to include rounded corners in the initial rectangle construction. AutoCAD uses the term *fillet* to describe both *fillets* and *rounds*. This is a brief introduction to adding rounds while creating rectangles. Adding fillets is covered in detail in Chapter 12.

Figure 4–30.
Using the
RECTANGLE tool.

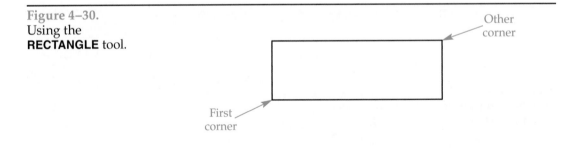

Other corner

First corner

Figure 4–31.
Rectangles can be chamfered or rounded when they are created.

Chamfer distance

Radius

Chamfered Rectangle
A

Rounded Rectangle
B

The **Fillet** option requires you to specify the round radius. See **Figure 4-31B**. When prompted, enter the round radius. After setting the round radius, you can either draw the rectangle or select another option. However, using the **Chamfer** option overrides the **Fillet** option.

If you set the round radius to a value greater than 0, any new rectangles created receive rounded corners. New rectangles continue to be created with rounds until you reset the round radius to 0 or use the **Chamfer** option to create chamfered corners.

Drawing Rectangles with Line Width

The **Width** option of the **RECTANGLE** tool is used to adjust the rectangle's line width, or "boldness." This should not to be confused with lineweight, which is described in Chapter 5. When you choose the **Width** option, you are prompted to enter the line width. For example, to create a rectangle with lines that are .5 wide, enter .5.

After setting the rectangle width, you can either draw the rectangle or select additional options to use those options in combination with the **Width** option. If a width is set, any new rectangles drawn use the width you entered. Reset the **Width** option to create new rectangles using a standard "0 width" line.

Specifying Rectangle Areas

When you know the area of a rectangle and the length of one of its sides, you can draw the rectangle using the **Area** option. This option is available after the first corner point of the rectangle is picked, when the Specify other corner point or [Area/ Dimensions/Rotation]: appears. Enter the **Area** option, and then specify the total area for the rectangle. Enter a value that corresponds to the current units. For example, enter 45 to draw a rectangle with an area of 45 in^2. Next, choose the **Length** option if you know the length of a side, or the X value, or choose the **Width** option if you know the width of a side, or Y value. When prompted, enter the length or width to complete the rectangle. AutoCAD calculates the unspecified dimension automatically and draws the rectangle.

Specifying Rectangle Dimensions

An alternative to using point entry to specify the opposite corner of a rectangle is to enter the length and width of a rectangle using the **Dimensions** option. The option is available after the first corner of the rectangle has been picked. Enter the **Dimensions** option, and then specify the length of a side, which is the X value. Next, enter the width of a side, which is the Y value. After you specify the length and width, AutoCAD asks for the other corner point. If you want to change the dimensions, select the **Dimensions** option again. If the dimensions are correct, specify the other corner point to complete the rectangle. The second corner point determines which of four possible rectangles is drawn. See **Figure 4-32**.

Drawing a Rotated Rectangle

A rectangle can be drawn at any angle by specifying a rotation angle after selecting the first point. Use the **Rotation** option available after the first corner of the rectangle has been picked. By default, you are prompted to specify the rotation angle. Enter or select an angle to rotate the rectangle. Then pick the opposite corner of the rectangle. An alternative is to choose the **Pick points** option when the Specify rotation angle or [Pick points] appears. If you select the **Pick points** option, you are prompted to select two points to define the angle. When a new value is specified for the **Rotation** option, it becomes the default angle.

Figure 4–32.
The orientation of the rectangle relative to the first corner point is determined by the second corner point.

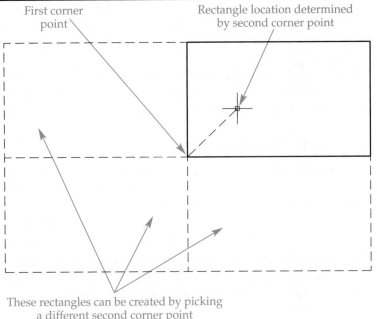

First corner point

Rectangle location determined by second corner point

These rectangles can be created by picking a different second corner point

Additional Rectangle Options

Two other options are available for the **RECTANGLE** tool. The **Elevation** option sets the elevation of the rectangle along the Z axis. The default value is 0. The **Thickness** option gives the rectangle depth along the Z axis. The default value is 0. Like other rectangle options the **Elevation** and **Thickness** options remain effective for multiple uses of the **RECTANGLE** tool.

NOTE

Rectangles are polylines and can be edited using the **PEDIT** tool. Since a rectangle is a polyline, it is treated as one object until it is exploded. After it is exploded, the individual sides can be edited separately. The **PEDIT** and **EXPLODE** tools are described in Chapter 15 of this textbook.

PROFESSIONAL TIP

A combination of rectangle settings can be used to draw a single rectangle. For example, you can enter a width value, chamfer distances, and length and width dimensions, all to create a single rectangle.

Exercise 4-8
Complete the exercise on the Student CD.

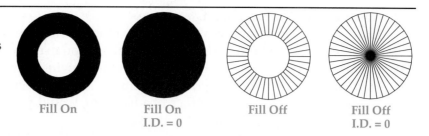

Figure 4–33.
The appearance of a donut depends on its inside and outside diameters and the current **FILL** mode.

Fill On Fill On I.D. = 0 Fill Off Fill Off I.D. = 0

Drawing Donuts and Filled Circles

The **DONUT** tool allows you to draw a thick or filled circle. See **Figure 4-33**. Donuts drawn in AutoCAD are actually polyline arcs with width. Polylines are covered in detail in Chapter 15.

After selecting the **DONUT** tool, enter the inside diameter and then the outside diameter of the donut. Enter a value of 0 for the inside diameter to create a completely filled donut, or solid circle. After you define the inside and outside donut diameters, the donut attaches to the crosshairs, and the Specify center of donut or <exit>: prompt appears. Pick a location to place the donut. The donut is located using its center point. You can then pick another center point to draw the same size donut in a new location. The **DONUT** tool remains active until you right-click, press the [Enter] key or the space bar, or cancel.

When **FILL** mode is turned off, donuts appear as segmented circles or concentric circles. The **FILL** tool can be used *transparently* by entering 'FILL while the **DONUT** tool is active. Enter **ON** or **OFF** as needed. The fill display for previously drawn donuts is updated when the drawing is regenerated.

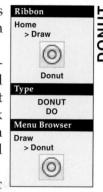

Ribbon
Home > Draw
⊚
Donut

Type
DONUT DO

Menu Browser
Draw > Donut
⊚

transparently:
While another tool is already in progress.

DONUT

Exercise 4-9
Complete the exercise on the Student CD.

Chapter Test

Answer the following questions. Write your answers on a separate sheet of paper or complete the electronic chapter test on the Student CD.

1. Describe the rubberband display shown when you draw a **Center, Radius** circle. What is the purpose of the rubberband?
2. When you use the **CIRCLE** tool, what are the options for responding to the prompt Specify radius of circle?
3. Explain how to create a circle with a diameter of 2.5 units.
4. What option of the **CIRCLE** tool creates a circle of a specific radius that is tangent to two existing objects?
5. Define the term *point of tangency*.
6. Explain how to draw a circle tangent to three objects.
7. Briefly explain how to create a three-point arc.
8. What is the default option if the **ARC** tool is entered at the keyboard?
9. Define the term *included angle* as it applies to an arc.
10. Explain the procedure to draw an arc beginning with the center point and having a 60° included angle.
11. List the three input options that can be used to draw an arc tangent to the endpoint of a previously drawn arc.

12. Name the two axes found on an ellipse.
13. Briefly describe the procedure to draw an ellipse using the **Axis, End** option
14. What is the **ELLIPSE** rotation angle that causes you to draw a circle?
15. Identify two ways to access the **Arc** option for drawing elliptical arcs.
16. Explain how to draw a hexagon measuring 4″ (102 mm) across the flats.
17. Given the distance across the flats of a hexagon, would you use the **Inscribed** or **Circumscribed** option to draw the hexagon?
18. Name the tab and panel on the ribbon where the **RECTANGLE** tool is found.
19. Name at least three tools you could use to create a rectangle.
20. Name the tool option used to draw rectangles with rounded corners.
21. Name the tool option designed for drawing rectangles with a specific line thickness.
22. Describe a method for drawing a solid circle.
23. Explain how to draw two donuts with an inside diameter of 6.25 and an outside diameter of 9.50.
24. Explain how to turn the **FILL** mode off.
25. Give the easiest keyboard shortcut for the following tools:
    A. **CIRCLE**
    B. **ARC**
    C. **ELLIPSE**
    D. **POLYGON**
    E. **RECTANGLE**
    F. **DONUT**

Drawing Problems

Start AutoCAD and use a template or a setup option of your choice. Do not draw dimensions or text. Use your own judgment and approximate dimensions if needed.

▼ Basic

1. Use the **LINE** tool and the **CIRCLE** tool options to draw the objects below. Do not include dimensions. Save the drawing as P4-1.

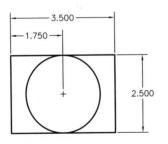

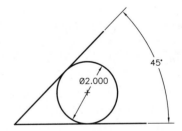

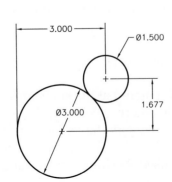

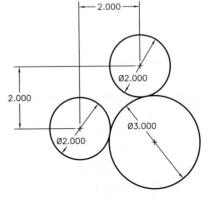

2. Use the **CIRCLE** and **ARC** tool options to draw the object below. Do not include dimensions. Save the drawing as P4-2.

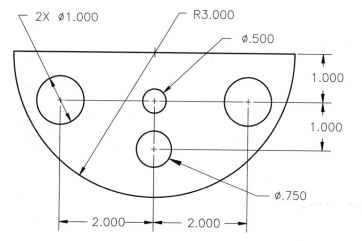

3. Draw the spacer below. Do not draw the centerlines or dimensions. Save the drawing as P4-3.

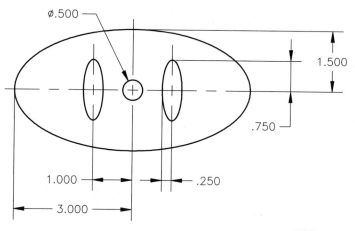

4. Draw the following object. Do not draw the dimensions. Save the drawing as P4-4.

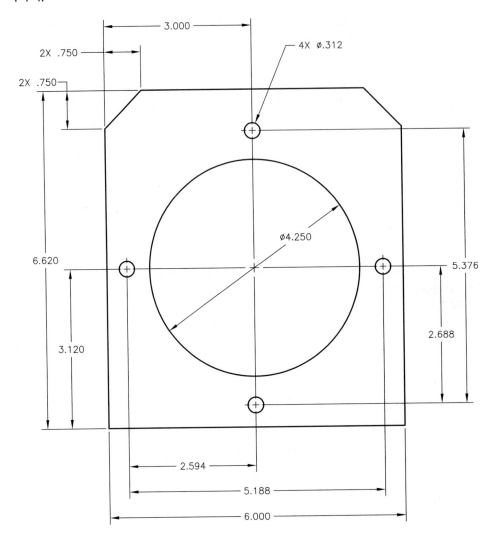

5. Draw the following object. Do not draw the centerlines or dimensions. Save the drawing as P4-5.

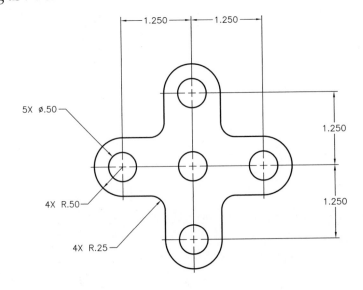

Drawing Problems – Chapter 4

6. Draw the following object. Do not draw the centerlines or dimensions. Save the drawing as P4-6.

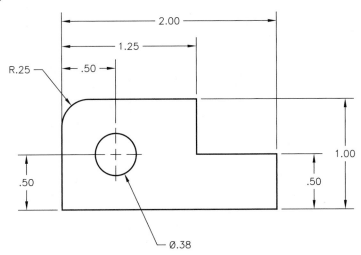

7. Draw the pipe spacer shown. Do not include the dimensions. Save the drawing as P4-7.

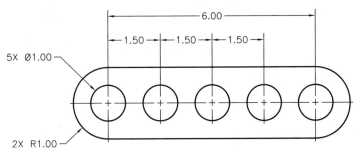

▼ Intermediate

8. Draw the following object. Do not include centerlines or dimensions. Save the drawing as P4-8.

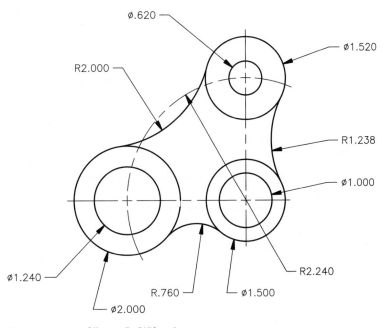

(Art courtesy of Bruce L. Wilcox)

9. Draw the pressure cylinder shown below. Use the **Arc** option of the **ELLIPSE** tool to draw the cylinder ends. Do not include the dimensions. Save the drawing as P4-9.

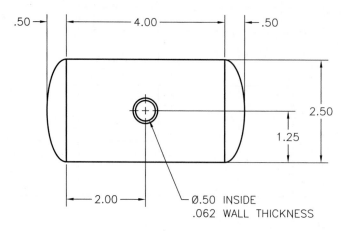

10. Draw the gasket shown below. Do not draw the dimensions. Save the drawing as P4-10.

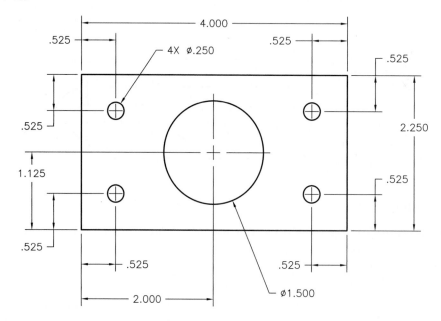

11. Draw the following object. Do not draw the centerlines or dimensions. Save the drawing as P4-11.

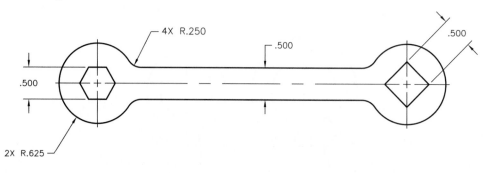

AutoCAD and Its Applications—Basics

12. Draw the following object. Do not draw the centerlines or dimensions. Save the drawing as P4-12.

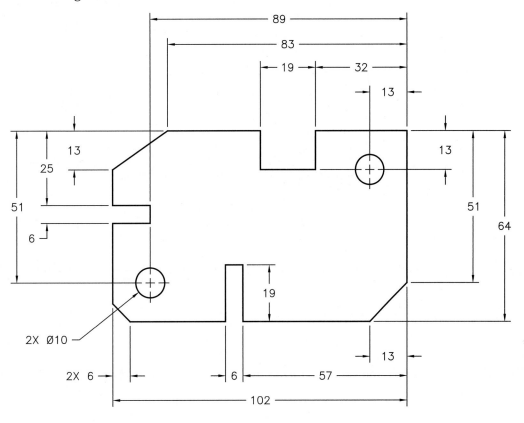

13. Draw the pipe fitting shown. Save the drawing as P4-13.

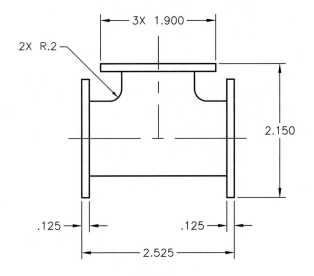

14. Draw the ellipse template shown. Save the drawing as P4-14.

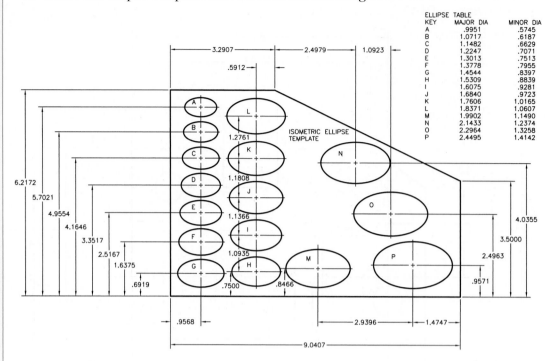

ELLIPSE TABLE

KEY	MAJOR DIA	MINOR DIA
A	.9951	.5745
B	1.0717	.6187
C	1.1482	.6629
D	1.2247	.7071
E	1.3013	.7513
F	1.3778	.7955
G	1.4544	.8397
H	1.5309	.8839
I	1.6075	.9281
J	1.6840	.9723
K	1.7606	1.0165
L	1.8371	1.0607
M	1.9902	1.1490
N	2.1433	1.2374
O	2.2964	1.3258
P	2.4495	1.4142

15. Draw the gasket shown. Do not include the dimensions. Save the drawing as P4-15.

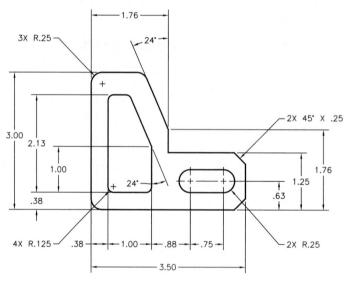

Drawing Problems - Chapter 4

▼ Advanced

16. Draw the object shown below. Do not draw the centerlines or dimensions. Save the drawing as P4-16.

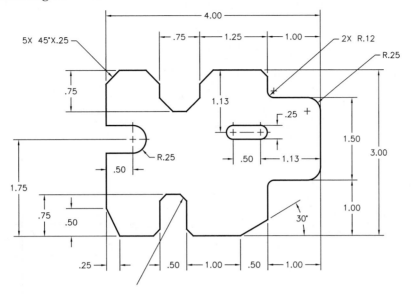

17. You have just been given the sketch of a new sports car design (shown below). You are asked to create a drawing from the sketch. Use the **LINE** tool and selected shape tools to draw the car. Do not be concerned with size and scale. Consider the tools and techniques used to draw the car, and try to minimize the number of objects. Save your drawing as P4-17.

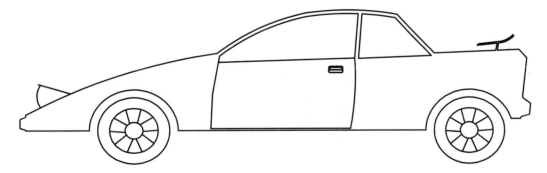

18. You have just been given the sketch of an innovative new truck design (shown below). You are asked to create a drawing from the sketch. Use the **LINE** tool and selected shape tools to draw a truck resembling the sketch. Do not be concerned with size and scale. Save your drawing as P4-18.

19. Draw the following object. Do not draw the centerlines or dimensions. Save the drawing as P4-19.

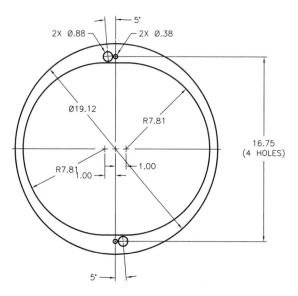

20. Draw this elevation using the **Arc**, **Circle**, and **Rectangle** tools. Do not be concerned with size and scale. Save the drawing as P4-20.

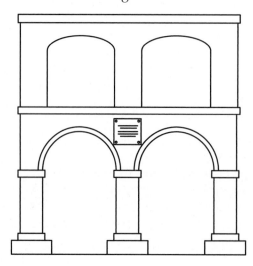

CHAPTER 5

Line Standards and Drawing Format

Learning Objectives

After completing this chapter, you will be able to do the following:
- ✓ Describe basic line conventions for drafting.
- ✓ Create and manage drawing layers.
- ✓ Set up and use a variety of linetypes.
- ✓ Draw objects on separate layers.
- ✓ Filter a list of layers.
- ✓ Use **DesignCenter** to copy layers and linetypes between drawings.
- ✓ Make prints of your drawings.

An important part of basic drawing setup involves assigning and organizing line-types and other object characteristics to conform to accepted standards and conventions. AutoCAD uses a layer system to simplify the process of assigning and modifying object elements. In addition, you can use layer display options to help create several different drawing sheets, views, and displays from a single drawing.

This chapter introduces line conventions and the AutoCAD layer system. It also provides a brief introduction to printing and plotting so that you can begin printing and plotting your drawings. Printing and plotting is covered in detail in Chapter 29.

Line Standards

Drafting is a graphic language that uses lines, symbols, and words to describe products to be manufactured. *Line conventions* are standards based on line thickness and type. These standards are designed to enhance the readability of drawings. This section introduces the line standards that you will apply later in this chapter when you begin loading linetypes and defining layers, as well as throughout your drafting career.

line conventions:
Standards related to line thickness and type.

The American Society of Mechanical Engineers (ASME) is responsible for the drafting standards approved by the American National Standards Institute (ANSI). These standards recommend two line widths to establish contrasting lines in a drawing. Lines are described as thick or thin. Thick lines are twice as thick as thin lines, with recommended widths of 0.6 mm and 0.3 mm, respectively. **Figure 5-1** shows recommended line width and type as defined in ASME Y14.2M, *Line Conventions and Lettering.*

Figure 5-1.
Line conventions. (Adapted from ASME Y14.2M)

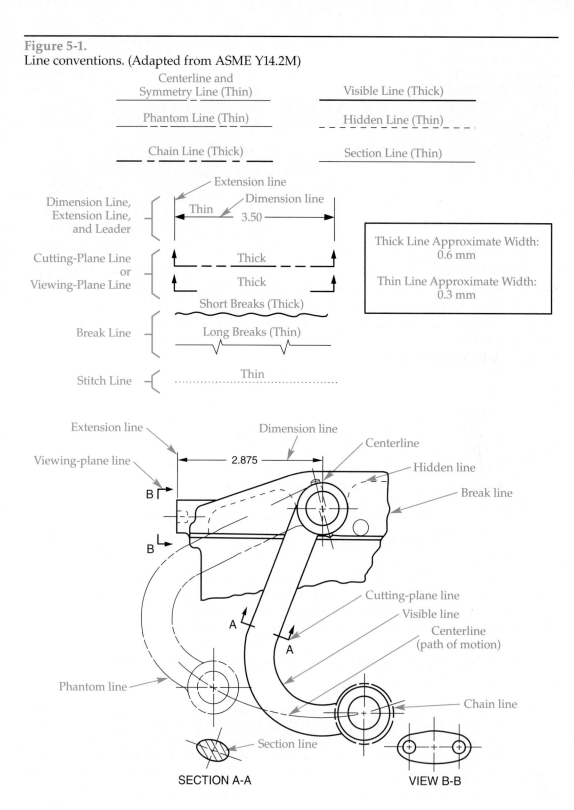

Object and Hidden Lines

Object lines, also called *visible lines*, are the most commonly used lines in drawings. These lines should be twice as thick as thin lines. See **Figure 5-2.**

Hidden lines, sometimes called *dashed lines*, are drawn thin to contrast clearly with thick object lines. See **Figure 5-2.** When properly drawn at full size, the dashes are .125″ (3 mm) long and spaced .06″ (1.5 mm) apart. Be aware that if the drawing is to be greatly reduced or scaled down during the plotting process, the dashes may appear too small.

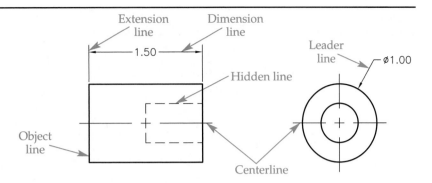

Figure 5-2.
This drawing shows
standard line styles
and line thicknesses
used in drafting.

Centerlines

Centerlines are thin, as shown in **Figure 5-2**. The recommended dash lengths are .125″ (3 mm) for the short dashes and .75″ to 1.5″ (19 mm to 38 mm) for the long dashes. These lengths can be altered, depending on the size of the drawing. Spaces approximately .06″ (1.5 mm) long should separate the dashes. The small centerline dashes should cross only at the center of a circle. Centerlines should extend .125″ to .25″ (3 mm to 6 mm) past objects.

Extension Lines

Extension lines are thin and begin a short distance from an object. They should extend .125″ (3 mm) beyond the last dimension line. See **Figure 5-2**. Extension lines can cross object lines, hidden lines, and centerlines, but they should not cross dimension lines. Centerlines become extension lines when they are used to show the extent of a dimension. When this is done, there is no space where the centerline joins the extension line.

Dimension Lines and Leader Lines

Dimension lines are thin and, in mechanical drafting, are normally broken near the center for placement of the dimension numeral. See **Figure 5-2**. The dimension line normally remains unbroken in architectural and structural drawings. The dimension numeral is placed on top of an unbroken dimension line. Arrows terminate the ends of dimension lines, except in architectural drafting, where slashes (ticks) or dots are often used.

Leader lines are thin and often terminate with an arrowhead at the feature. They have a small shoulder at the note, as shown in **Figure 5-2**.

Cutting-Plane, Viewing-Plane, and Section Lines

Cutting-plane lines and *viewing-plane lines* are thick and identify the location of a section or view. See **Figure 5-3**. Cutting-plane and viewing-plane lines can be drawn in one of two ways, as shown in **Figure 5-1**. *Section lines* are thin and are usually drawn in a pattern as shown in **Figure 5-3**.

Break, Phantom, and Chain Lines

A portion of a very long part can be broken out using *break lines*. Several types of break lines are shown in **Figure 5-4**. *Phantom lines* are thin lines with two short dashes alternating with long dashes. The short dashes are .125″ (3 mm) long, and the long dashes range from .75″ to 1.5″ (19 mm to 38 mm) in length, depending on the size of the drawing. Spaces between dashes are .06″ (1.5 mm). See **Figure 5-5**. *Chain lines* are thick lines of alternating long and short dashes. See **Figure 5-6**.

centerlines: Thin lines made up of alternating long and short dashes that locate the centers of circles and arcs and show the axis of cylindrical or symmetrical shapes.

extension lines: Lines that extend from the object being measured to the dimension line to show the extent of the dimension.

dimension lines: Thin lines placed between extension lines to show the distance being measured.

leader lines: Thin lines used to connect a specific note to a feature on a drawing.

cutting-plane lines: Thick lines that identify the location and viewing direction of a section view.

viewing-plane lines: Thick lines that identify the location of a view.

section lines: Thin lines, usually drawn in a pattern, that are used in a section view to show where material has been cut away.

break lines: Lines that show where a portion of an object has been removed for clarity or convenience.

phantom lines: Thin lines that identify repetitive details, show alternate positions of moving parts, and locate adjacent positions of related parts.

chain lines: Thick lines that indicate special features or unique treatment for a surface.

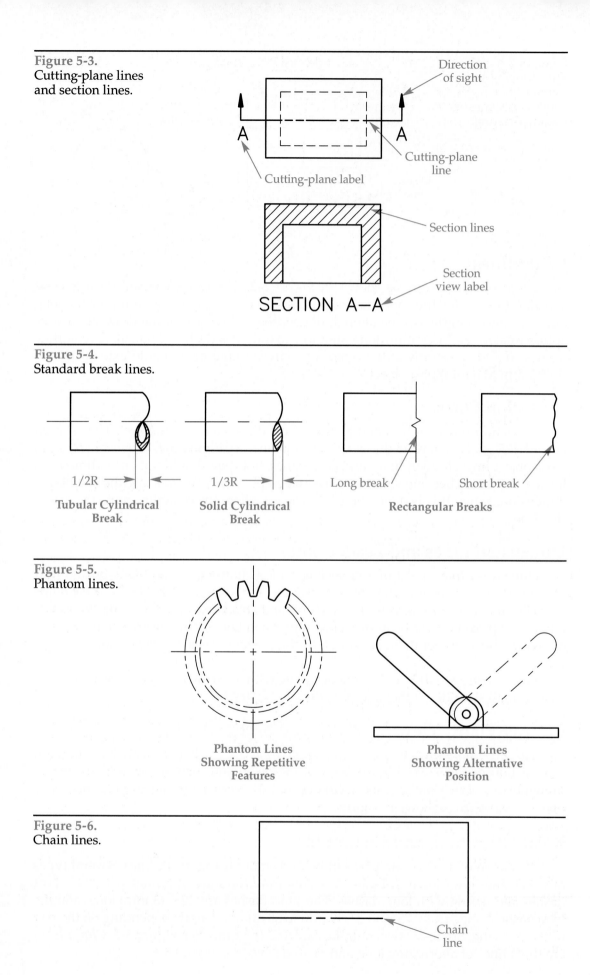

Figure 5-3.
Cutting-plane lines and section lines.

Direction of sight

A A

Cutting-plane label

Cutting-plane line

Section lines

Section view label

SECTION A–A

Figure 5-4.
Standard break lines.

1/2R

1/3R

Long break

Short break

Tubular Cylindrical Break

Solid Cylindrical Break

Rectangular Breaks

Figure 5-5.
Phantom lines.

Phantom Lines Showing Repetitive Features

Phantom Lines Showing Alternative Position

Figure 5-6.
Chain lines.

Chain line

Introduction to Layers

In AutoCAD, different elements or components of a drawing are separated using an *overlay system*. The overlay system components are referred to as *layers*. All the layers can be displayed together, or "overlaid," to reflect the entire design drawing. Individual layers can be displayed or hidden to show specific details or components of the design.

overlay system:
A system of separating drawing components by layer.

layers:
Components of AutoCAD's overlay system that allow users to separate objects into logical groups for formatting and display purposes.

Increasing Productivity with Layers

Using layers increases productivity in several ways:
- ✓ Each layer can be assigned a different color, linetype, and lineweight to correspond to line conventions and to help improve clarity.
- ✓ Changes can be made to a layer promptly, affecting all objects drawn on the layer.
- ✓ Selected layers can be turned off or frozen to decrease the amount of information displayed on the screen or to speed screen regeneration.
- ✓ Each layer can be plotted in a different color, linetype, or lineweight, or it can be set not to plot at all.
- ✓ Specific information can be grouped on separate layers. For example, a floor plan can be drawn on specific floor plan layers, the electrical plan on electrical layers, and the plumbing plan on plumbing layers.
- ✓ Several plot sheets can be created from the same drawing file by controlling layer visibility to separate or combine drawing information. For example, a floor plan and electrical plan can be reproduced together and sent to an electrical contractor for a bid. The floor plan and plumbing plan can be reproduced together and sent to a plumbing contractor.

Layers Used in Different Drafting Fields

Typically, the type of drawing you create determines the function of each layer. In mechanical drafting, each different type of line or object is usually assigned to a specific layer. For example, visible object lines might be drawn on an Object layer that is black in color and uses a solid (continuous) linetype that is 0.6 mm wide. Hidden lines might be drawn on a green Hidden layer that uses a 0.3 mm hidden linetype. Architectural and civil drawings may have hundreds of layers, each used to produce a specific item. For example, full-height walls on a floor plan might be drawn on a black A-WALL-FULL layer that uses a 0.6 mm solid linetype. Plumbing fixtures added to a floor plan might be drawn on a blue P-FIXT layer that uses a 0.3 mm solid linetype.

Layers can be created for any type of drawing, including detail parts, assemblies, floor plans, foundation plans, partition layouts, plumbing systems, electrical systems, structural systems, roof drainage systems, reflected ceiling systems, HVAC systems, site plans, profiles, topographic maps, and details. Interior designers may use floor plan, interior partition, and furniture layers. In electronics drafting, each level of a multilevel circuit board can be drawn on its own layer.

Creating and Using Layers

Ribbon

Home
> Layers

Layer Properties

View
> Palettes
> Layer
   Properties

Type

LAYER
LA

Menu Browser

Format
> Layer

The **LAYER** tool opens the **Layer Properties Manager** palette, which is used to create and delete layers and control layer properties. See **Figure 5-7**. The **Layer Properties Manager** is divided into two panes. The list view pane on the right side of the palette lists layers and provides layer property controls. Layer properties are displayed in a column format in the list view. Properties in each column are shown either as an icon or as an icon and a name. See **Figure 5-8**. Pick a property to change layer settings. The tree view pane on the left side of the palette displays filters that can be used to limit the number of layers displayed in the list view pane.

Figure 5-7.
The **Layer Properties Manager**. Layer 0 is AutoCAD's default layer.

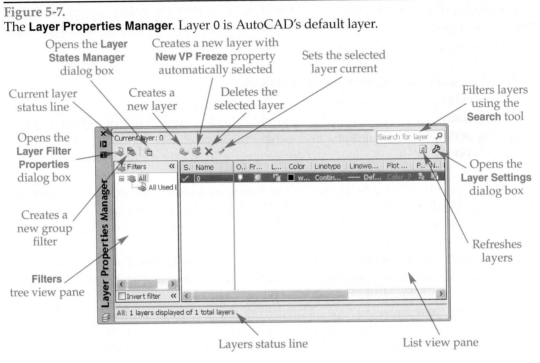

Figure 5-8.
Layer settings can be changed by picking the icons in the **Layer Properties Manager**.

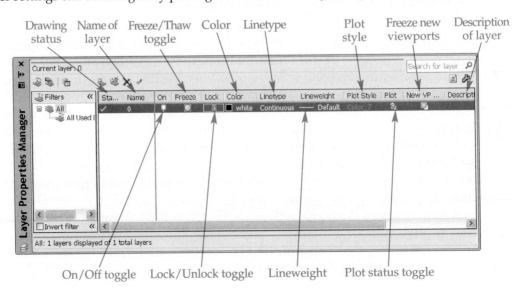

Only one layer is required in an AutoCAD drawing. This default layer is named 0 and cannot be deleted, renamed, or purged from the drawing. The 0 layer is primarily reserved for drawing blocks, as described later in this textbook. Each object should be drawn on a layer specific to the object. For example, draw visible object lines on an Object layer, draw floor plan walls on an A-WALL layer, and draw construction lines on a Construction layer.

Defining New Layers

The **Name** column in the list view shows the name of all the layers in the drawing. Layers should be added to a drawing to meet the needs of the current drawing project. To add a new layer, select an existing layer from the list that contains properties similar to those you want to assign to the new layer. (If this is the first new layer in a default template, only the 0 layer is available to reference.) Then pick the **New Layer** button, right-click in the list view and select the **New Layer** option, or press [Alt] + [N]. A new layer appears, using a default name of Layer1. See **Figure 5-9.** The layer name is highlighted when the listing appears, allowing you to type a new name. Pick away from the layer in the list or press the [Enter] key to accept the layer.

Layers should be given names to reflect drawing content. Layer names can have up to 255 characters and can include letters, numbers, and certain other characters, including spaces. Some examples of typical mechanical, architectural, and civil drafting layer names include:

Mechanical	Architectural	Civil
Object	A-WALL-FULL	C-BLDG
Hidden	A-GLAZ	C-WATR
Center	A-DOOR	C-TOPO
Dimension	E-LITE	C-PROP
Construction	P-FIXT	C-NGAS
Section	S-FNDN	C-SSWR
Border	M-FURN	C-ELEV

Layers are usually named according to specific industry or company standards. However, for very simple drawings, layers might be named by linetype and color. For example, the layer name Continuous-White can have a continuous linetype drawn in white. The layer usage and color number, such as Object-7, may be used to indicate an object line with color 7. Another option is to assign the linetype a numerical value. For example, object lines can be 1, hidden lines can be 2, and centerlines can be 3. If you use this method, keep a written record of your numbering system for reference.

Figure 5-9.
A new layer is named Layer1 by default.

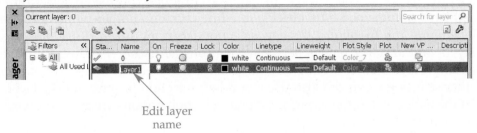

Edit layer
name

Figure 5-10.
Layer names are automatically placed in alphanumeric order when you create new layers or change layer names.

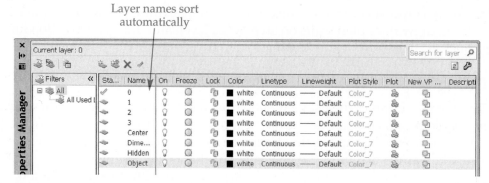

Layers can also be given more complex names. The name might include the drawing number, color code, and layer content. The layer name Dwg100-2-Dimen, for example, could refer to drawing DWG100, color 2, and the fact that this layer is used for dimensions. The American Institute of Architects (AIA) has established a layer naming system for architectural and related drawings. This standard is found in the document *CAD Layer Guidelines*, published by AIA.

Layer names are automatically arranged alphanumerically as new layers are created. See **Figure 5-10.** Pick any column heading in the list view sort layer names in ascending or descending order.

The **Layer Properties Manager** is a palette, so new layers and changes made to existing layers are automatically saved and applied to the drawing. There is no need to "apply" changes or close the palette to see the effects of the changes in the drawing.

PROFESSIONAL TIP

If you need to create multiple layers, accelerate the process by pressing the comma key after typing each layer name to create another new layer.

Exercise 5-1
Complete the exercise on the Student CD.

Selecting Multiple Layers

Using the **Layer Properties Manager**, you can select multiple layers to speed the process of deleting or applying the same properties to several layers. To select multiple layers in the list view, you can use the same techniques you use to select files. You can highlight a single name by picking it, while picking another name deselects the previous name and highlights the new selection. You can use the [Shift] key to select two layers and all layer names between them on the listing. Holding the [Ctrl] key while picking layer names highlights or deselects each selected name without affecting any other selections. You can also use a window selection to select all the layers that contact the window. The following additional selection options are available when you right-click in the list view:

- **Select All.** Selects all layers.
- **Clear All.** Deselects all layers.

- **Select All but Current.** Selects all layers except the current layer.
- **Invert Selection.** Deselects all selected layers and selects all deselected layers.

Exercise 5-2
Complete the exercise on the Student CD.

Layer Status

The icon in the **Status** column describes the status, or existing use of a layer. A green check mark indicates that this is the *current layer*. The current layer is also identified in the current layer status line at the top of the **Layer Properties Manager**.

In a drawing that has many layers, you may need to see at a glance which layers contain objects. The **Layer Settings** dialog box provides an option to display different icons depending on whether a layer contains objects. When this option is turned on, a blue sheet of paper, or **In Use** icon, in the **Status** column means that objects have been drawn with the layer, and the layer is not current. The **In Use** icon can also mean that the layer cannot be deleted or purged from the drawing, even if no objects are drawn with the layer. A white sheet of paper, or **Not In Use** icon, in the **Status** column indicates that the layer is not being used in any way by the drawing, the layer is not current, and no objects have been drawn with the layer.

Setting a layer current

To set a different layer current using the **Layer Properties Manager**, double-click the layer name, pick the layer name in the layer list and select the **Set Current** button, or right-click on the layer and choose the **Set Current** menu option.

You can also make a different layer current without using the **Layer Properties Manager** by selecting it in the **Layer Control** drop-down list located on the **Home** tab of the ribbon. The name of the current layer is displayed in the box. Pick the drop-down arrow to display a layer list, and select a layer name from the list to set that layer current. See **Figure 5-11.** When many layers are defined in the drawing, the vertical scroll bar can be used to move up and down through the list. Selecting a layer name to set as current automatically closes the list and returns you to the drawing. When a tool is active, the drop-down button is grayed out and the list is not available.

Current

current layer:
The active layer. Whatever you draw is placed on the current layer.

Figure 5-11.
The **Layer Control** drop-down list allows you to change the current layer and change the properties of layers.

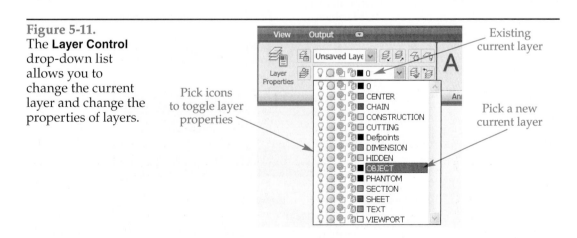

Changing an object's layer

Occasionally, you may accidentally create an object on the wrong layer. You can use the **Layer Control** drop-down list to move an object from one layer to another. Select the object, then pick the drop-down arrow to display the list of layers, and select a new layer. The object moves to the layer you specified.

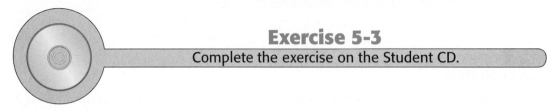

Exercise 5-3
Complete the exercise on the Student CD.

Setting Layer Color

Each layer can be assigned a unique color to help distinguish the objects drawn on those layers. Layer colors are commonly used to differentiate drawing items on-screen. Colors are often not used when plotting a drawing, as is the case when drawings are plotted using black ink only. Even if the drawing is not plotted in color, however, adding color to layers is still very important for drawing clarity, organization, workability, and format. Alternatively, layer colors can affect the appearance of drawings plotted in color and can control object properties such as lineweight.

The number of layer colors available depends on your graphics card and monitor. Color systems usually support at least 256 colors, while many graphics cards support up to 16.7 million colors. Layer colors should highlight the important features on the drawing and not cause eyestrain.

The **Color** column of the list view indicates the color applied to each layer. To change the color of an existing layer, pick the color swatch. This displays the **Select Color** dialog box, shown in **Figure 5-12.** This dialog box includes an **Index Color** tab, a **True Color** tab, and a **Color Books** tab from which a color can be selected. Each tab uses a different method of obtaining colors for assignment to a layer.

The default tab is the **Index Color** tab, which includes 255 color swatches from which you can choose. This tab is commonly referred to as the AutoCAD Color Index (ACI) because layer colors are coded by name and number. The first seven colors in the ACI include both a numerical index number and a name:

Figure 5-12.
The **Select Color** dialog box is used to choose a layer color.

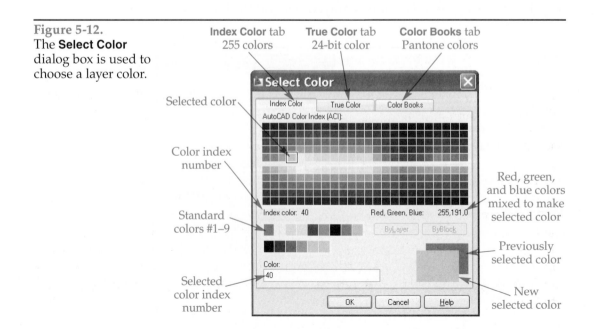

AutoCAD and Its Applications—Basics

Number	Color
1	red
2	yellow
3	green
4	cyan
5	blue
6	magenta
7	white

To select a color, you can either pick the color swatch displaying the desired color or type the color name or ACI number in the **Color:** text box. The color white (number 7) shows up black with the default white drawing window background. The "white" name comes from the concept of using a black drawing window background, which used to be the default in AutoCAD many years ago. If you change the drawing window background to black, color 7 shows up white on the screen.

As you move the cursor around the color swatches, the **Index color:** note updates to show you the number of the color over which the cursor is hovering. Beside the **Index color:** note is the **Red, Green, Blue:** (RGB) note. This indicates the RGB numbers used to mix the highlighted color. When you pick a color, the **Index color:** note appears in the **Color:** text box. A preview of the newly selected color and a sample of the previously assigned color appear in the lower right of the dialog box. An easy way to explore the ACI numbering system is to pick a color swatch and see what number appears in the **Color:** text box.

After selecting a color, pick the **OK** button. The color you picked is now displayed as the color swatch for the highlighted layer name in the **Layer Properties Manager**. All objects drawn on this layer appear in the selected color by default.

Exercise 5-4
Complete the exercise on the Student CD.

Setting Layer Linetype

Different line thicknesses and linetypes are used to enhance the readability of drawings. The line conventions described earlier in this chapter can be applied selectively to objects by applying linetypes and thicknesses to individual layers. Each layer can be assigned a linetype that corresponds to a specific drawing requirement. AutoCAD provides standard linetypes that can be used to match the ASME standards or the standards for other drafting applications. You can also create your own custom linetypes. To achieve different line thicknesses, it is necessary to assign lineweights to layers.

The **Linetype** column of the list view of the **Layer Properties Manager** indicates the linetype applied to each layer. To change the linetype of an existing layer, pick the current linetype. This displays the **Select Linetype** dialog box, shown in Figure 5-13. The first time you use this dialog box, you will find only the default Continuous linetype listed in the **Loaded linetypes** list box. The Continuous linetype represents solid object lines with no breaks. AutoCAD maintains linetypes in external linetype definition files. Before any of these linetypes can be applied to a layer, they must be loaded into the **Select Linetype** dialog box.

Figure 5-13.
The **Select Linetype** dialog box allows you to load linetypes for use in the current drawing.

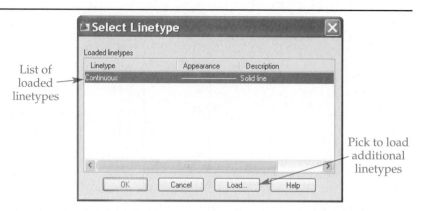

List of loaded linetypes

Pick to load additional linetypes

Figure 5-14.
The **Load or Reload Linetypes** dialog box displays linetypes available for loading.

Select file where linetype definitions are stored

Select linetypes to load into drawing

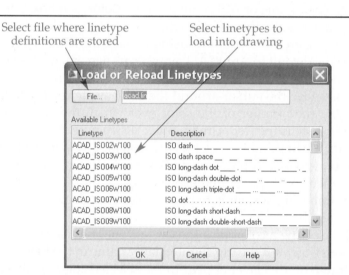

To add linetypes, pick the **Load...** button to display the **Load or Reload Linetypes** dialog box. See **Figure 5-14.** The linetypes available from the default acad.lin file are named and displayed in the **Available Linetypes** list. **Figure 5-15** shows each of the available linetypes. Use the scroll bars or up and down arrow keys to look at all the linetypes. Select the linetypes you want to load. Use the [Shift] key and pick to select linetypes between two picked linetypes. You can also use the [Ctrl] key and pick to select nonconsecutive linetypes. Quickly select all the linetypes by right-clicking and picking the **Select All** menu option, or deselect all linetypes by right-clicking and picking the **Clear All** menu option. Pick the **OK** button to return to the **Select Linetype** dialog box, where the linetypes you selected are now listed. See **Figure 5-16.** In the **Select Linetype** dialog box, pick the desired linetype, and then pick **OK**. The HIDDEN linetype selected in **Figure 5-16** is now the linetype assigned to the layer named Hidden, as shown in **Figure 5-17.**

> **NOTE**
>
> The acad.lin file is used by default. You can switch to the acadiso.lin file by picking the **File...** button in the **Load or Reload Linetypes** dialog box. This displays the **Select Linetype File** dialog box, where you can select the acadiso.lin file. The acad.lin and acadiso.lin files are identical, but the non-ISO linetype definitions are scaled up 25.4 times in the acadiso.lin file. The scale factor of 25.4 is used to convert from inches to millimeters. The ACAD ISO linetypes are for metric drawings.

Figure 5-15.
AutoCAD's default linetype library contains ACAD ISO, standard, and complex linetypes.

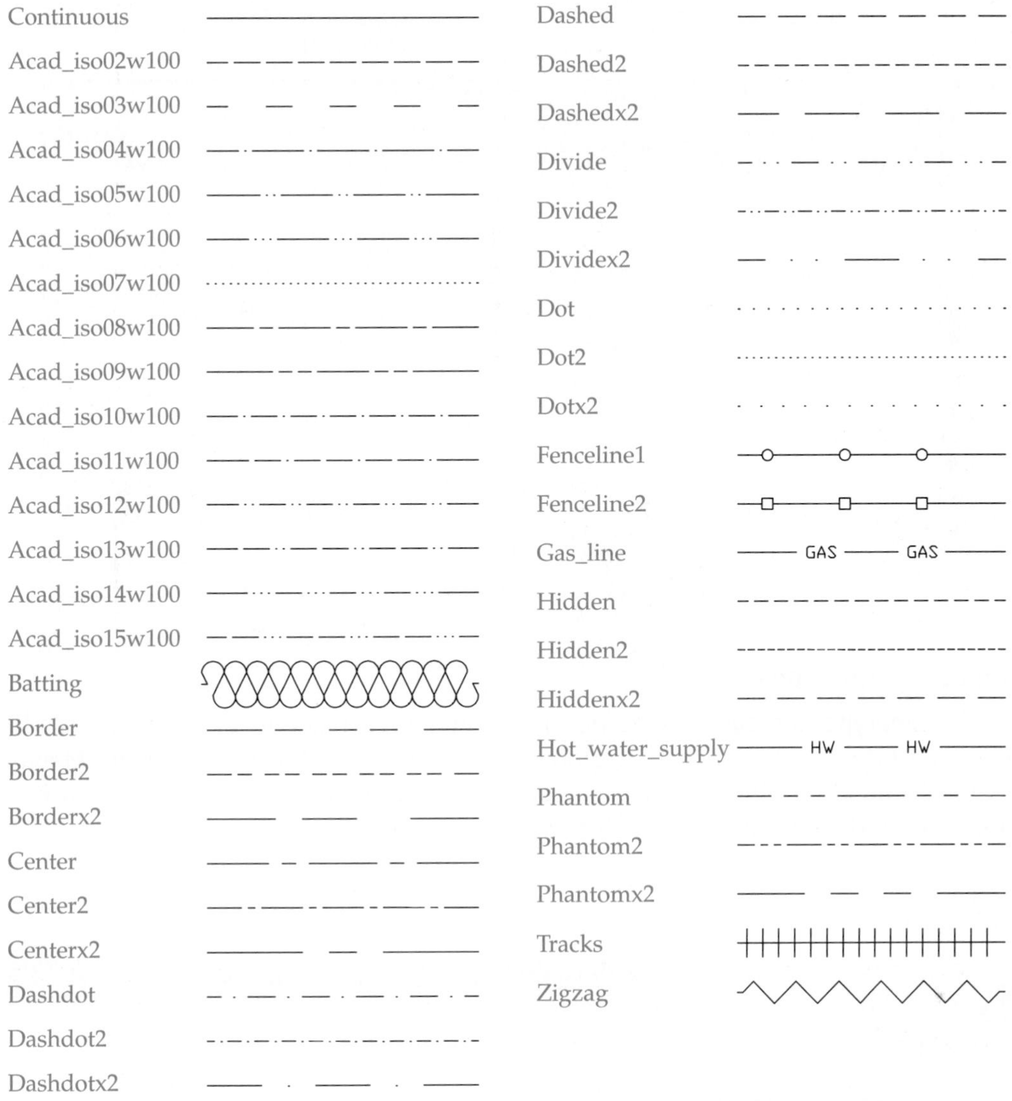
Continuous
Acad_iso02w100
Acad_iso03w100
Acad_iso04w100
Acad_iso05w100
Acad_iso06w100
Acad_iso07w100
Acad_iso08w100
Acad_iso09w100
Acad_iso10w100
Acad_iso11w100
Acad_iso12w100
Acad_iso13w100
Acad_iso14w100
Acad_iso15w100
Batting
Border
Border2
Borderx2
Center
Center2
Centerx2
Dashdot
Dashdot2
Dashdotx2
Dashed
Dashed2
Dashedx2
Divide
Divide2
Dividex2
Dot
Dot2
Dotx2
Fenceline1
Fenceline2
Gas_line
GAS
GAS
Hidden
Hidden2
Hiddenx2
Hot_water_supply
HW
HW
Phantom
Phantom2
Phantomx2
Tracks
Zigzag

Figure 5-16.
Linetypes loaded from the **Load or Reload Linetypes** dialog box are added to the **Loaded linetypes** list box.

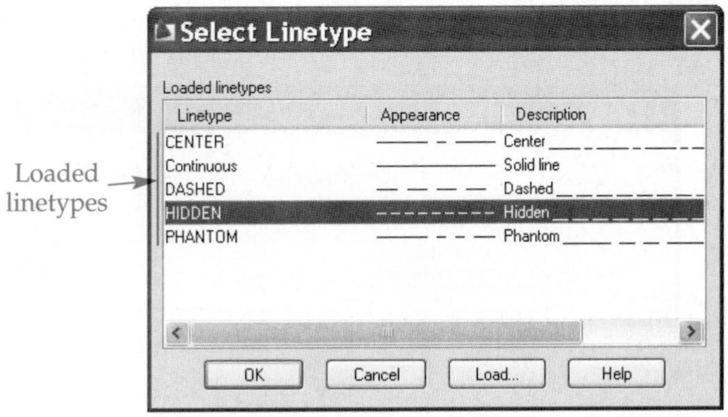
Loaded linetypes
Select Linetype
Loaded linetypes
Linetype
Appearance
Description
CENTER
Center
Continuous
Solid line
DASHED
Dashed
HIDDEN
Hidden
PHANTOM
Phantom
OK
Cancel
Load...
Help

Figure 5-17.
Objects drawn on the Hidden layer now have a HIDDEN linetype.

Linetype changed
to HIDDEN

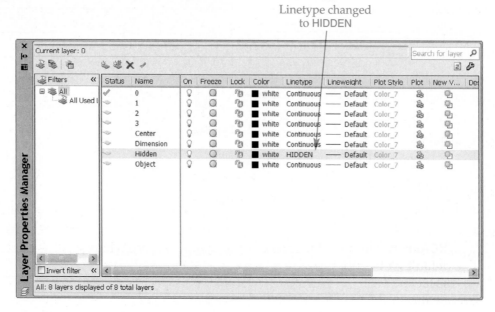

Managing linetypes

The **Linetype Manager** dialog box is a convenient place to load and access linetypes. See Figure 5-18. This dialog box is similar to the **Layer Properties Manager**. Picking the **Load...** button opens the **Load or Reload Linetypes** dialog box. Picking the **Delete** button deletes any selected linetypes that are not in use in the drawing.

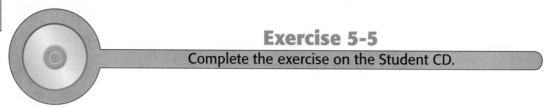

LINETYPE

Type
LINETYPE
LT

Menu Browser

Format
> Linetype

Exercise 5-5
Complete the exercise on the Student CD.

Figure 5-18.
The **Linetype Manager** dialog box is a useful tool for working with linetypes.

Sets selected
linetype current

Accesses the **Load or Reload
Linetype** dialog box

Deletes selected
linetype

List
filter

Linetypes in
drawing

Shows or
hides details

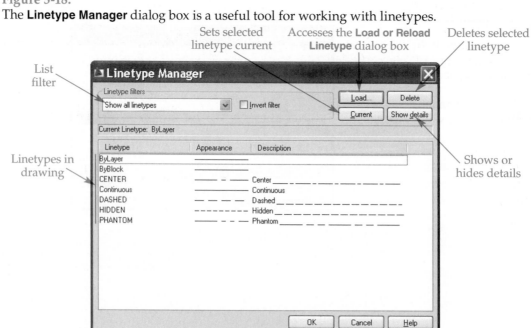

Figure 5-19.
The CENTER linetype at different linetype scales.

Scale Factor	Line
0.5	
1.0	
1.5	

Setting linetype scale

Linetype scale can be changed to increase or decrease the lengths of dashes and spaces in linetypes in order to make your drawing more closely match standard drafting practices. Changing the *global linetype scale* is the preferred method for adjusting linetype scale, though it is possible to change the linetype scale of individual objects.

The **LTSCALE** system variable can be used to make a global change to the linetype scale. The default global linetype scale factor is 1.0000. Any line with dashes initially assumes this factor. To change the linetype scale for the entire drawing, type LTSCALE. The current value is listed. Enter the new value and press [Enter]. The drawing regenerates and the global linetype scale is changed for all lines on the drawing. A value less than 1.0 makes the dashes and spaces smaller, and a value greater than 1.0 makes the dashes and spaces larger. See **Figure 5-19.** Experiment with different linetype scales until you achieve your desired results.

linetype scale: The lengths of dashes and spaces in linetypes.

global linetype scale: A linetype scale applied to every linetype in the current drawing.

CAUTION

Be careful when changing linetype scales to avoid making your drawing look odd and not in accordance with drafting standards.

Setting Layer Lineweight

Lineweight can also be assigned to a layer, defining whether objects drawn with that layer are thick or thin. Assigning lineweights to layers allows you to draw objects on specific layers to manage their lineweights. You can control the display of line thickness to match ASME or other standards related to your drafting application.

The **Lineweight** column of the list view in the **Layer Properties Manager** indicates the lineweight applied to each layer. To change the lineweight of an existing layer, pick the current lineweight. This displays the **Lineweight** dialog box, shown in **Figure 5-20.** Scroll through the **Lineweights:** list to select the desired lineweight. The **Lineweight** dialog box displays fixed lineweights available in AutoCAD. The Default lineweight is the lineweight initially assigned to a layer when it is created.

The area near the bottom of the **Lineweight** dialog box lists the original lineweight (the lineweight previously assigned to the layer) and the new lineweight (the new lineweight assigned to the layer). In **Figure 5-20,** the **Original:** and **New:** specifications are the same because the initial layer lineweight has not been changed from the default.

Type	
LINEWEIGHT	**LINEWEIGHT**
LWEIGHT	
LW	
Menu Browser	
Format	
> Lineweight	

lineweight: The assigned width of lines for display and plotting.

Figure 5-20.
The **Lineweight** dialog box is used to assign a lineweight to a layer.

Select lineweight from list

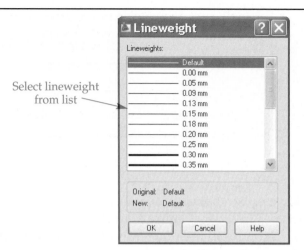

Lineweight settings

Menu Browser
Format
    > Lineweight

Current lineweights are set in the **Lineweight Settings** dialog box, shown in **Figure 5-21.** The **Lineweight Settings** dialog box can also be accessed by right-clicking the **Show/Hide Lineweight** button on the status bar and selecting the **Settings...** menu option. The **Units for Listing** area allows you to set the lineweight thickness to **Millimeters (mm)** or **Inches (in)**. The units are applied only to values in **Lineweight Settings** dialog box, allowing you to select lineweights based on a known unit of measurement.

Select a lineweight to make current from the **Lineweights** list. If lineweight is set to ByLayer, the object lineweight corresponds to the lineweight assigned to its layer. The Default option lineweight width is controlled by the Default list options. Settings other than ByLayer, ByBlock, or Default are used as overrides for lineweights of objects drawn with the selected option. The current lineweight is indicated in the **Current Lineweight** field.

Lineweight is shown on the screen when lineweight display is turned on. Check the **Display Lineweight** box to turn lineweight on. You can also toggle screen lineweights by picking the **Show/Hide Lineweight** button on the status bar.

When you select a lineweight default value from the **Default** drop-down list, this becomes the default lineweight for layers. The initial default setting is .010" or 0.25 mm.

PROFESSIONAL TIP

Set the default lineweight to the lineweight that is applied to most layers. Then use the Default lineweight option when assigning lineweight to those layers.

Figure 5-21.
The **Lineweight Settings** dialog box.

Select lineweight

Select units
Lineweight display
Default lineweight setting
Display scale

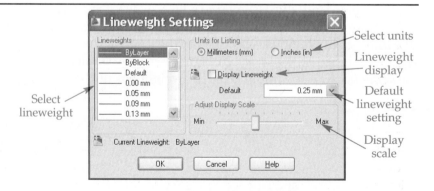

The **Adjust Display Scale** slider is used to adjust the lineweight display scale to improve the appearance of different lineweights. Adjusting the lineweight display scale toward the **Max** value can reduce AutoCAD performance. A setting near the middle of the scale or toward **Min** may be preferred.

Layers are meant to simplify the drafting process. They separate different details of the drawing and can reduce the complexity of what is displayed. Set object characteristics, including color, linetype, and lineweight using layers, and do not override these properties for individual objects. Also, once you establish layers, avoid resetting and mixing color, linetype, and lineweight properties. Doing so can mislead you and your colleagues when you try to find certain details.

Exercise 5-6
Complete the exercise on the Student CD.

Layer Plotting Properties

The **Plot Style** column lists the plot style assigned to each layer. By default, the plot style setting is disabled. Plot styles are described in Chapter 28.

Plot   No Plot

The **Plot** column displays icons to show whether the layer is plotted. Select the default printer icon to turn off plotting for a particular layer. The "no plot" icon is displayed when the layer is not available for plotting. The layer is still displayed and selectable, but it is not plotted.

Adding a Layer Description

The **Description** column provides an area to type a short description for each layer. To add or change a description, pick the description once to highlight it, pause for a moment, and then pick it again. When you pick the second time, the layer description becomes highlighted, allowing you to type a description. Layer description can also be defined by right-clicking and selecting the **Change Description** menu option.

Turning Layers On and Off

The **On** column shows whether a layer is on or off. The yellow light bulb, or **On** icon, means the layer is on. Objects on a layer that is turned on are displayed on-screen and can be selected and plotted. If you pick on the icon, the light bulb "turns off" (becomes gray), turning the layer off. Objects on a layer that is turned off are not displayed on-screen and are not plotted. Objects on layer that has been turned off can still be edited using advanced selection techniques and are regenerated when a drawing regeneration occurs.

On   Off

You can also turn a layer on and off using the **Layer Control** drop-down list in the **Layers** panel on the **Home** tab of the ribbon. Locate the layer you want to turn on or off and select the **On** or **Off** icon.

Freezing and Thawing Layers

Thawed   Frozen

The **Freeze** column shows whether a layer is thawed or frozen. Frozen layers are similar to turned-off layers. Objects on a layer that is frozen are not displayed and do not plot. Objects on a frozen layer, however, cannot be edited and are not regenerated when the drawing regenerates. Freezing layers containing objects that do not need to be referenced for current drawing tasks can greatly speed up system performance, while ensuring that the objects are not accidentally modified. The snowflake, or **Freeze**, icon is displayed when a layer is frozen. When a layer is thawed, objects on the layer are displayed on-screen, and they can be selected and regenerated. The sun, or **Thaw**, icon is displayed for thawed layers. Pick the **Freeze** or **Thaw** icon to toggle thawing and freezing.

New VP New VP
Freeze   Thaw

Icons in the **New VP Freeze** column control freezing or thawing of layers when a new viewport is created. Layouts and viewports are described in Chapters 28 and 29.

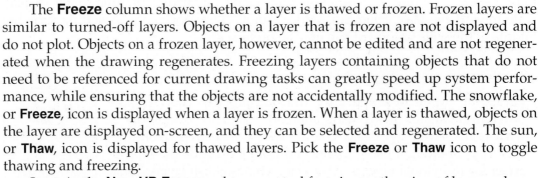

> **NOTE**
>
> You can also freeze or thaw a layer using the **Layer Control** drop-down list in the **Layers** panel of the **Home** tab on the ribbon. Locate the layer you want to freeze or thaw and select the **Freeze** or **Thaw** icon. The current layer cannot be frozen, and a layer that is frozen cannot be made current.

> **CAUTION**
>
> It is important to note that objects on frozen layers cannot be modified, but objects on layers that have been turned off can be modified. For example, if you turn off half your layers and use the **All** selection option with the **Erase** tool, even the objects on the turned-off layers are erased. The **Erase** tool does not, however, affect frozen layers.

Locking and Unlocking Layers

Lock   Unlock

The unlocked and locked padlock symbols (**Unlock** and **Lock** icons) located in the **Lock** column are for locking and unlocking layers. Layers are unlocked by default. Pick an **Unlock** icon to lock the layer. When you rest the crosshairs over an object on a locked layer, the lock icon appears.

A locked layer remains visible, and new objects can be added to it, but existing objects cannot be edited. Lock a layer whenever you want to see objects on-screen, but eliminate the possibility of selecting those objects. To quickly lock all layers except specific layers, select the layers you want to remain unlocked, and then right-click on the selection and pick the **Isolate selected layers** option.

> **NOTE**
>
> You can also lock or unlock a layer using the **Layer Control** drop-down list in the **Layers** panel on the **Home** tab of the ribbon. Locate the layer you want to lock or unlock and select the **Lock** or **Unlock** icon.

Locked layer fading

By default, all locked layers are faded, allowing unlocked layers to stand out. The quickest way to control locked layer fading is to use the options available in the expanded **Layers** panel on the **Home** tab of the ribbon. See **Figure 5-22**. Pick the **Locked**

Figure 5-22.
Locked layers are
faded by default.
Locked layer fading
can be enabled or
disabled and the
fade value can
be increased or
decreased.

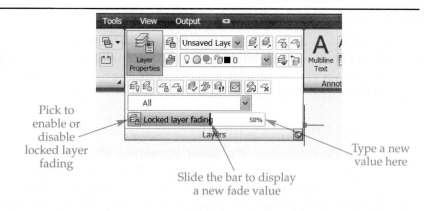

Pick to
enable or
disable
locked layer
fading

Type a new
value here

Slide the bar to display
a new fade value

layer fading button to allow or disable locked layer fading. When locked layer fading is allowed, use the **Locked Layer Fading** slider to increase or decrease fading, or type a new fading percentage. You can use a fade value between 0 and 90. A fade value of 0 fades the display of unisolated layers the least, while a fade value of 90 significantly fades unisolated layers. The default fade value is 50%. **Figure 5-23** shows the effect of locked layer fading on a drawing.

Renaming Layers

To change an existing layer name using the **Layer Properties Manager**, pick the name in the **Name** column once to highlight it, pause for a moment, and then pick it again. When you pick the second time, the layer name is highlighted, allowing you to type a new layer name. Layers can also be renamed by picking the name once to highlight it and then pressing the [F2] key, or by right-clicking and selecting the **Rename Layer** menu option. Layer 0 and layers associated with an external reference cannot be renamed.

Figure 5-23.
All of the layers in this drawing have been locked except A-WALL-FULL, which contains the walls. A—Locked layer fading is disabled. B—Locked layer fading is on and set to a fade value of 75.

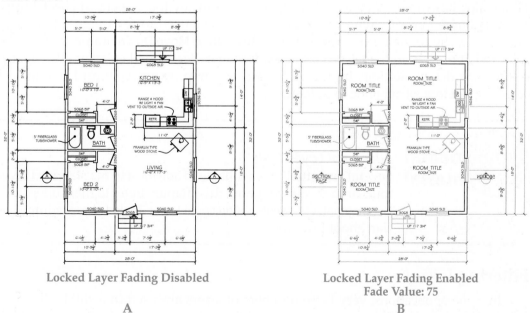

Locked Layer Fading Disabled

A

Locked Layer Fading Enabled
Fade Value: 75

B

Deleting Layers

To delete a layer using the **Layer Properties Manager**, select the layer and pick the **Delete Layer** button, or right-click on the layer and choose the **Delete Layer** option. You cannot delete or purge the 0 layer, the current layer, layers containing objects, or layers associated with an external reference.

Adjusting Property Columns

To resize a column in the **Layer Properties Manager**, move the cursor over the column edge to display the resize icon and drag the column to the desired width. The width of an individual column can be maximized to show the longest value in the column. Columns that list properties as icons are maximized to display the full column heading. To maximize the width of an individual column, right-click on the property column heading and select the **Maximize column** menu option. To maximize the width of all columns, right-click on any property column heading and select the **Maximize all columns** menu option.

The width of columns can be optimized to show the longest value in the column list for properties displayed as text, while reducing the width of columns that list properties as icons. To optimize the width of an individual column, right-click on the property column heading and select the **Optimize column** menu option. To optimize the width of all columns, right-click on any property column heading and select the **Optimize all columns** menu option.

By default, a vertical bar is displayed on the right side of the **Name** column. Any column left of the bar is "frozen". Frozen columns remain in position when you move the scroll bar near the bottom of the **Layer Properties Manager**. All columns to the right of the vertical bar can be scrolled using the horizontal scroll bar. To turn off the freeze function, right-click on any property column heading and select the **Unfreeze column** menu option. To freeze columns, right-click on a property column heading and select the **Freeze column** menu option to turn on the freeze function for every column left of the selected column.

You can hide columns in the **Layer Properties Manager** by right-clicking on any property column heading and deselecting the property column name from the menu. Another option is to right-click on any property column heading and select the **Customize...** menu option to display the **Customize Layer Columns** dialog box. This dialog box can be used to hide property columns by the associated check boxes. The **Customize Layer Columns** dialog box can also be used to rearrange columns by picking the column name and selecting the **Move Up** or **Move Down** button to move the column left or right in the **Layer Properties Manager**. Reset the display of all property columns to default settings by right-clicking on any property column heading and selecting **Restore all columns to defaults**.

 *Additional Layer Tools*
Several layer tools are available in addition to the standard layer tools described throughout this chapter. Refer to the Student CD: Supplemental Materials > Additional Layer Tools for more information about layer tools.

Filtering Layers

In some applications, very large numbers of layers are used in a single drawing. Displaying all layers at the same time in the list view pane can make it more difficult to work with the layers. The filter tree view pane in the **Layer Properties Manager** is

Figure 5-24.
Layer filters can be created and restored from the filter tree view of the **Layer Properties Manager**.

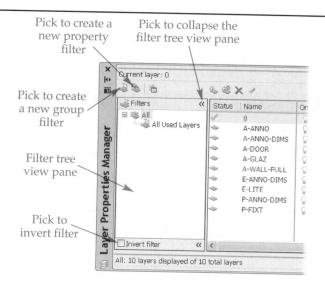

Pick to create a new property filter

Pick to collapse the filter tree view pane

Pick to create a new group filter

Filter tree view pane

Pick to invert filter

used to manage *layer filters* that can be applied to reduce the number of layers that appear in the list view. See **Figure 5-24.** Selecting the **All** node of the filter tree view displays all layers in the drawing. Layer filters are displayed in alphabetical order inside the **All** node. The **All Used Layers** filter is a default filter created by AutoCAD and cannot be removed or modified. Selecting the **All Used Layers** filter hides all the layers that have no objects on them.

layer filters: Filters that screen out, or filter, layers you do not want to display in the list view pane of the **Layer Properties Manager.**

NOTE

The filter tree view of the **Layer Properties Manager** can be collapsed by picking the **Collapse Layer filter tree** button. To display all filters and layers in the list view, right-click in the layer list area and select the **Show Filters in Layer List** menu option.

You can create two different types of layer filters: property filters and group filters. An example of using a *property filter* is filtering all layers that are turned on, or have a name beginning with the letter *A*, or both. The default **All Used Layers** filter is a property filter that filters layers according to layer status. An example of using a *group filter* is dragging and dropping all layers used to draw an electrical plan into a group filter. All of these layers can be selected through the group filter regardless of their individual properties.

property filter: A filter that screens layers according to a specific layer property.

group filter: A filter created by adding layers to the filter definition.

Creating a property filter

To create a property filter, pick the **New Property Filter** button to display the **Layer Filter Properties** dialog box. See **Figure 5-25.** Enter a name for the new filter in the **Filter name:** text box. The **Filter definition** area is where the properties are defined to hide the unwanted layers from the **Layer Properties Manager** and the **Layer Control** drop-down list. To create a definition, pick in any of the fields (empty boxes in the **Filter definition** area). The appropriate options become available for the selected layer setting. Options can be entered in the text edit box, selected from a drop-down list, or accessed using a dialog box. **Figure 5-26** describes each property filter definition option.

After you have defined a property filter, another row is added to the **Filter definition:** area. This allows you to create simple to advanced filters. **Figure 5-27** shows a filter named Floor Plan, in which two rows are used to filter out all the layers except the P-FIXT layer and layers beginning with the letter A. To save the filter, pick the **OK** button. The new filter now displays in the filter tree view area.

Figure 5-25.
New property filters are created in the **Layer Filter Properties** dialog box.

Edit the layer properties to define the layer filter

Enter name for filter

Layers included in the current filter settings

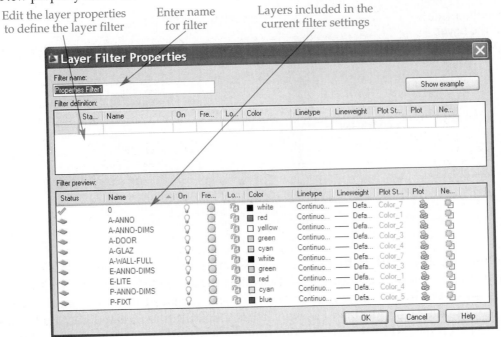

Figure 5-26.
Property filter definition options available in the **Layer Filter Properties** dialog box.

Option	Application
Status	Display the names of all layers, used layers only, or unused layers only. Pick the appropriate **In Use** or **Not In Use** icon.
Name	Type a layer name or a partial layer name using the * wildcard character. For example, if you want to see all the layers that start with an A, type a*.
On	Display only the names of layers that are on or only those that are off. Pick the **On** or **Off** icon.
Freeze	Display frozen layers only or thawed layers only. Pick the **Freeze** or **Thaw** icon.
Lock	Display locked layers only or unlocked layers only. Pick the **Lock** or **Unlock** icon.
Color	Filter according to color. Type a color number or name or pick the ... button to select a color.
Linetype	Filter according to linetype. Type a linetype name or pick the ... button to select a linetype.
Lineweight	Filter according to lineweight. Type a lineweight name or pick the ... button to select a lineweight.
Plot Style	Filter according to plot style. Type a plot style name or pick the ... button to select a plot style. This item is available only if the current drawing uses named plot style tables.
Plot	Display the names of layers that plot or the names of layers that do not plot. Pick the **Plot** or **No Plot** icon.
New VP Freeze	Display only frozen or only thawed layers applied when a new layout viewport is created. Pick the appropriate icon.

Figure 5-27.
Multiple rows in the **Filter definition:** area can be used to create a filter.

Layer filter definitions   Filter name

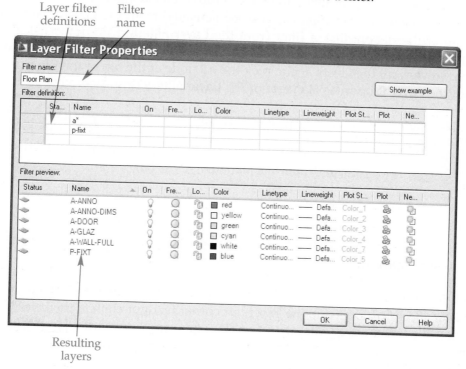

Resulting layers

Creating a group filter

To create a group filter, select the **New Group Filter** button. A group filter can also be created from outside the **Layer Properties Manager** using the **Layers** panel on the **Home** tab of the ribbon. In the expanded **Layers** panel, pick the **Layer Filters** drop-down list, right-click on the **All** filter and select the **New Group Filter...** menu option. A new group filter is created in the filter tree view. Select the **All** node at the top of the filter tree area to display all the layers in the drawing. Then, to add a layer to the group filter, select a layer in the layer list and drag and drop it onto the group filter name.

You can also add layers to a group filter by selecting the group filter, right-clicking, and choosing the **Add** option from the **Select Layers** cascading menu. This feature allows you to select objects on the layers you want to add to the group filter. After selecting the objects, right-click or press the [Enter] key to add the layers to the group filter.

Pick **Replace** from the **Select Layers** cascading menu to select objects on the layers to replace all other layers in the group filter. After selecting the objects, right-click or press the [Enter] key to add the layers to the group filter. The **Select Layers** menu option is also available by right-clicking in the **Layer Filters** drop-down list in the ribbon, **Home** tab, expanded **Layers** panel.

NOTE

A layer can be removed from a group filter by right-clicking on the layer in the layer list area of the **Layer Properties Manager** and choosing the **Remove From Group Filter** menu option.

Activating layer filters

To activate a layer filter using the **Layer Properties Manager**, select the filter from the filter tree view. A layer filter can also be activated from the **Layers** panel on the **Home** tab of the ribbon. Pick a filter from the **Layer Filters** drop-down list. When a layer filter is current, only those layers associated with the filter are shown in the layer list area. To view all the layers again, pick the **All** node at the top of the filter tree area in either the **Layer Properties Manager** or the **Layer Filters** drop-down list.

NOTE

A description of the active layer filter settings is provided in the lower **Layer Properties Manager** status bar.

Inverting layer filters

Layer filter settings can be inverted to display filtered layers. For example, selecting the **All Used Layers** filter shows only the layers that have objects on them. You can invert, or reverse, the **All Used Layers** filter to show all unused layers without creating an additional filter. To invert a layer filter using the **Layer Properties Manager**, pick the **Invert filter** check box located in the lower-left corner or right-click in the layer list area and select the **Invert Layer Filter** menu option. You can also invert a layer filter using the **Invert** option on the **Layer Filters** drop-down list in the expanded **Layers** panel on the **Home** tab of the ribbon.

Additional layer filter options

Other options associated with filters are accessible from a shortcut menu. To display the shortcut menu, right-click in the filter tree view or right-click in the **Layer Filters** drop-down list in the expanded **Layers** panel on the **Home** tab of the ribbon. Most of the options in the shortcut menu are the same for the filter types, but some options are available only for a certain filter. **Figure 5-28** describes filter options available and applied only to the layers associated with the filter.

Figure 5-28.
Additional layer filter options available from the shortcut menu.

Option	Function
Visibility	Changes the **On/Off** and **Thawed/Frozen** states of the unfiltered layers.
Lock	Locks or unlocks the unfiltered layers.
Viewport	Freezes or thaws the unfiltered layers in the current layout viewport.
Isolate Group	Freezes all layers except those associated with the filter and the current layer.
New Properties Filter	Opens the **Layer Filter Properties** dialog box.
New Group Filter	Creates a new group filter.
Convert to Group Filter	Converts a property filter to a group filter.
Rename	Renames the selected filter.
Delete	Deletes the selected filter.
Properties	Edits a property filter.
Select Layers	Provides options to add layers or replace layers in an existing group filter.

Filtering by searching

The **Layer Properties Manager** contains a search tool that can be used to filter layers in the list view without actually creating a filter. To use the search feature, type a layer name or a partial layer name using the * wildcard character in the **Search for layer** text box. For example, if you want to see all the layers that start with an A, type a*. As you type, layers that match the letters you enter are displayed. Adding additional letters narrows the search, with the most relevant or best matched layers listed first.

Exercise 5-7
Complete the exercise on the Student CD.

Layer States

Layer properties, such as on/off, frozen/thawed, plot/no plot, and locked/unlocked, determine whether objects drawn on a layer are displayed, plotted, and editable. Once a *layer state* is saved, you can readjust layer settings to meet your needs, with the option to restore a previously saved layer state at any time.

For example, a basic architectural drawing might use the layers shown in Figure 5-24. From this drawing file, three different drawings can be plotted: a floor plan, a plumbing plan, and an electrical plan. The following chart shows the layer settings for each of the three drawings:

> **layer state:** A saved setting, or state, of layer properties for all layers in the drawing.

Layer	Description	Floor Plan	Plumbing Plan	Electrical Plan
0		Off	Off	Off
A-ANNO	Floor Plan Notes	On	Frozen	Frozen
A-ANNO-DIMS	Floor Plan Dimensions	On	Frozen	Frozen
A-DOOR	Doors	On	Frozen	Locked
A-GLAZ	Windows	On	Frozen	Locked
A-WALL-FULL	Full Height Walls	On	Locked	Locked
E-ANNO-DIMS	Electrical Plan Dimensions	Frozen	Frozen	On
E-LITE	Electrical Plan Lights	Frozen	Frozen	On
P-ANNO-DIMS	Plumbing Plan Dimensions	Frozen	On	Frozen
P-FIXT	Plumbing Plan Fixtures	Locked	On	Locked

Each of the three groups of settings can be saved as an individual layer state. After the layer states are created, the settings can be brought back by restoring a layer state. This is easier than changing the settings for each layer individually.

Layer states can be saved using the **Layer States Manager**. See Figure 5-29. In addition to using the ribbon or menu browser, you can access the **Layer States Manager** by picking the **Layer States Manager** button from the **Layer Properties Manager** or right-clicking in the layer list view of the **Layer Properties Manager** and selecting the **Restore Layer State** menu option.

To create a new layer state, pick the **New...** button to display the **New Layer State to Save** dialog box. See Figure 5-30. Type a name for the layer state in the **New layer state name:** text box and enter a description. Pick the **OK** button to save the new layer state. Once you create a layer state, you can adjust layer properties as needed. Figure 5-31 describes the areas, options, and buttons available in the **Layer States Manager** to control layer states.

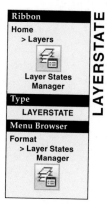

Ribbon
Home
  > Layers

Layer States Manager

Type
LAYERSTATE

Menu Browser

Format
  > Layer States Manager

LAYERSTATE

Figure 5-29.
The **Layer States Manager** allows you to save, restore, and manage layer settings.

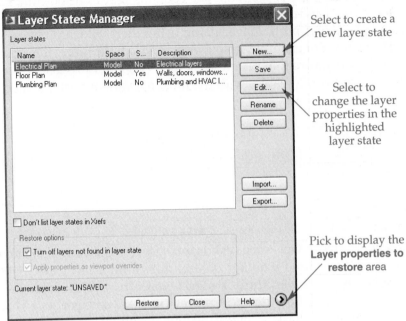

Select to create a new layer state

Select to change the layer properties in the highlighted layer state

Pick to display the **Layer properties to restore** area

Figure 5-30.
Creating a new layer state.

Enter the layer state name

Enter a description for the layer state

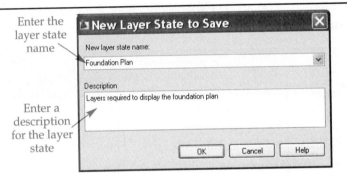

NOTE

To save a layer state outside the **Layer States Manager**, pick the **New Layer State...** option from the **Layer States** drop-down list in the **Layers** panel on the **Home** tab of the ribbon.

PROFESSIONAL TIP

If you have a drawing that does not contain any layers other than 0, importing a layer state file (.las) causes the layers from the layer state to be added to your drawing.

After you have created a layer state, you can restore layer properties to the settings saved in the layer state at any time. To activate a layer state quickly using the ribbon, select the layer state from the **Layer States** drop-down list in the **Layers** panel on the **Home** tab. You can also restore a layer state using the **Layer States Manager** by selecting the layer state from the list and picking the **Restore** button.

Figure 5-31.
Layer state options available in the **Layer States Manager**.

Item	Feature
Layer states	Displays saved layer states. The **Name** column provides the name of the layer state. The **Space** column indicates whether the layer state was saved in model space or paper space. The **Same as DWG** column indicates whether the layer state is the same as the current layer properties. The **Description** column lists the layer state description added when the layer state was saved.
Save	Pick to resave and override the selected layer state with the current layer properties.
Edit	Opens the **Edit Layer State** dialog box, where you can adjust the properties of each layer state without exiting the **Layer States Manager**.
Rename	Activates a text box that allows you to rename the current layer state.
Delete	Deletes the selected layer state.
Import	Opens the **Import layer state** dialog box, used to import an LAS file containing an existing layer state into the **Layer States Manager**.
Export	Opens the **Export layer state** dialog box, used to save a layer state as an LAS file. The file can be imported into other drawings, allowing you to share layer states between drawings containing identical layers.
Don't list layer states in Xrefs	Hides layer states associated with external reference drawings. External references are described in Chapter 32.
Restore options	Check the **Turn off layers not found in layer state** check box to turn off new layers or layers removed from a layer state when the layer state is restored. Check **Apply properties as viewport overrides** to apply layer viewport overrides when you are adjusting layer states within a layout.
Layer properties to restore	Check the layer properties that you want to restore when the layer state is restored. Pick the **Select All** button to pick all properties. Pick the **Clear All** button to deselect all properties.

Layer Settings

The **Layer Settings** dialog box provides several options for controlling layer display and function characteristics. Refer to the Student CD: Supplemental Materials > Layer Settings for more information about layer settings.

Reusing Drawing Content

In nearly every drafting discipline, individual drawings created as part of a given project are likely to share a number of common elements. All the drawings within a specific drafting project generally have the same set of standards. Drawing features, such as layer names and properties, text size and font used for annotation, dimensioning methods and appearances, drafting symbols, drawing layouts, and even drawing details, are often duplicated in many different drawings. These and other components of CAD drawings are referred to as *drawing content*. One of the most fundamental advantages of CAD systems is the ease with which content can be shared between drawings. Once a commonly used drawing feature has been defined, it can be used again as needed in any number of drawing applications.

drawing content: All of the objects, settings, and other components that make up a drawing.

The creation and use of drawing template files was covered in Chapter 2. Drawing templates represent one way to reuse drawing content that has already been defined. Creating your own customized drawing template files provides an effective way to start each new drawing using standard settings.

Drawing templates, however, provide only a starting point. During the course of a drawing project, you may need to add content to the current drawing that has been defined previously in another drawing. Some drawing projects require you to revise an existing drawing rather than start a completely new drawing. For other projects, you may need to duplicate the standards used in a drawing a client has supplied.

Introduction to DesignCenter

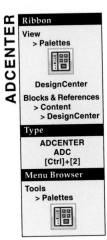

ADCENTER

Ribbon
View
> Palettes

DesignCenter
Blocks & References
> Content
> DesignCenter

Type
ADCENTER
ADC
[Ctrl]+[2]

Menu Browser
Tools
> Palettes

AutoCAD provides a powerful drawing content manager called **DesignCenter**. The **DesignCenter** palette allows you to reuse drawing content defined in previous drawings using a drag-and-drop operation. The main features of **DesignCenter** are shown in **Figure 5-32**. **DesignCenter** can be used to manage several types of drawing content, including layers, linetypes, blocks, dimension styles, layouts, table styles, text styles, and externally referenced drawings.

It is not necessary to open a drawing in AutoCAD in order to view or access its content. **DesignCenter** allows you to load content directly from any accessible drawing. You can also use **DesignCenter** to browse through existing drawing files and view their contents, or you can use its advanced search tools to look for specific drawing content.

Using DesignCenter to copy layers and linetypes

To copy content using **DesignCenter**, first use the tree view pane to select the drawing from which the content is to be copied. If the tree view is not already visible, toggle it on by picking the **Tree View Toggle** button in the **DesignCenter** toolbar. The first three tabs on the **DesignCenter** toolbar control the tree view display. Select the **Folders** tab to display the folders and files found on the hard drive and network. Pick the **Open Drawings** tab to list only drawings that are currently open. Select the **History** tab to list recently opened drawings.

Figure 5-32.
DesignCenter is used to copy content from one drawing to another.

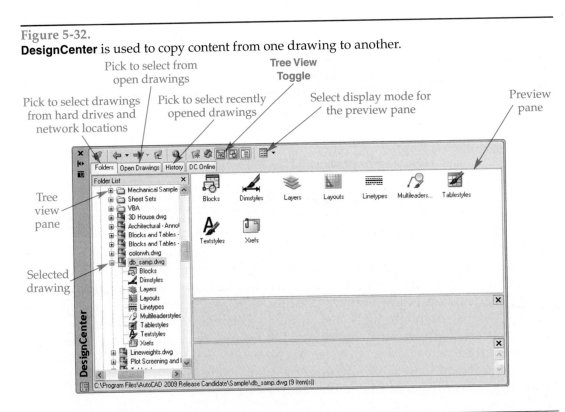

Figure 5-33.
Displaying the layers found in a drawing using **DesignCenter**.

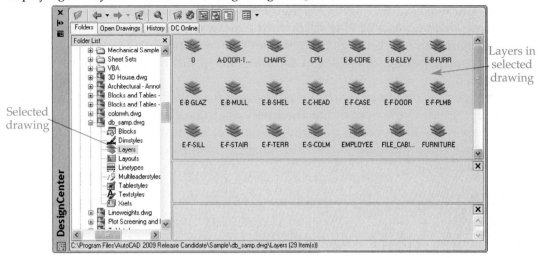

Pick the plus sign (+) next to a drawing icon to view the content categories for the drawing. Each category of drawing content is listed with a representative icon. Pick the **Layers** icon to load the preview pane with the layer content in the selected drawing. See **Figure 5-33.**

To use drag and drop to import layers into the current drawing, move the cursor over the desired icon in the preview pane in **DesignCenter**. Press and hold down the pick button, and then drag the cursor to the open drawing. See **Figure 5-34.** When you release the pick button, the selected content is added to your current drawing file.

Figure 5-34.
To copy layers shown in **DesignCenter** into the current drawing, select the layers to be copied and then drag and drop them into the drawing area of the current drawing.

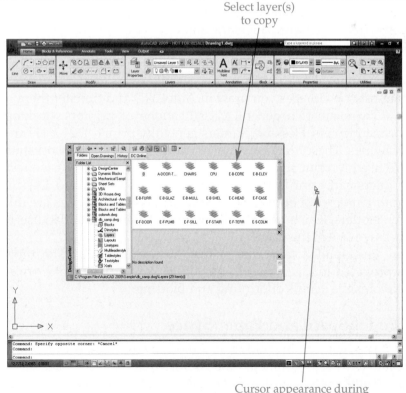

Layers can also be imported into the current drawing by selecting the desired icon(s) in the preview pane and right-clicking to open a shortcut menu. Pick the **Add Layer(s)** option to add the selected content to your current drawing.

If the name of a layer being loaded already exists in the destination drawing, that layer name and its settings are ignored. The existing settings for the layer are preserved, and a message is displayed at the tool line indicating that duplicate settings were ignored.

Linetypes can be copied using the same procedure used to copy layers. In the tree view, select the drawing containing the linetypes to be copied. Select the **Linetypes** icon to display the linetypes in the preview palette. Select the linetypes to be copied, and then use drag and drop or use the shortcut menu to add the linetypes to the current drawing.

Exercise 5-8
Complete the exercise on the Student CD.

Introduction to Printing and Plotting

hard copy: A physical drawing produced by a printer or plotter.

soft copy: The electronic data file of a drawing.

model: Any drawing composed of various objects, such as lines, circles, and text, and usually created at full size. However, this term is usually reserved for 3D drawings.

model space: The environment in AutoCAD where drawings and designs are created.

A drawing created with CAD can exist in two forms: *hard copy* and *soft copy*. A soft copy can only be displayed on the computer monitor, making it inconvenient to use for many manufacturing and construction purposes. If the power to the computer is turned off, the soft-copy drawing is not available. A hard-copy drawing is extremely versatile. It can be rolled up or folded and used on the shop floor or at a construction site. A hard-copy drawing can be checked and redlined without a computer or CAD software. Although CAD is the standard throughout the world for generating drawings, the hard-copy drawing is still a vital tool for communicating the design.

Hard-copy drawings are created by printers or plotters. These terms can be used interchangeably, although *plotter* typically refers to a large-format printer. Printers take the soft-copy images you draw in AutoCAD and transfer them onto paper.

There are two general classifications of printers: desktop printers and large-format printers. Desktop printers generally print 8 1/2″ × 11″ and sometimes 11″ × 17″ drawings. These are the printers common to computer workstations. Desktop printers are used to print small drawings and to print reduced-size test prints. Large-format printers can print larger drawings, such as C-size and D-size drawings. The most common types of both desktop and large-format printers are inkjet and laser printers. Pen plotters, which "draw" with actual ink pens, are still in use, but are not as common as they were in the past.

Prints and plots are made using the **Plot** dialog box. The information in this chapter is provided to give you only the basics, so you can make your first plot. Chapter 29 explores the details of printing and plotting.

Model Space and Paper Space

The first step in making an AutoCAD drawing is to create a *model*. The model is created in an environment called *model space*. Model space can be accessed by picking the **Model** button on the **Status** bar, or by using **Quick View Layouts** or **Quick View Drawings**. The **Quick View Layouts** tool is described in Chapter 28. See **Figure 5-35**. Model space can be accessed by picking the **Model** button on the status bar or by using **Quick View Layouts** or **Quick View Drawings**.

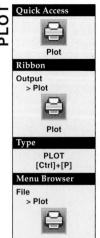

PLOT

Figure 5-35.
Model space is the environment in which drawings and designs are created.

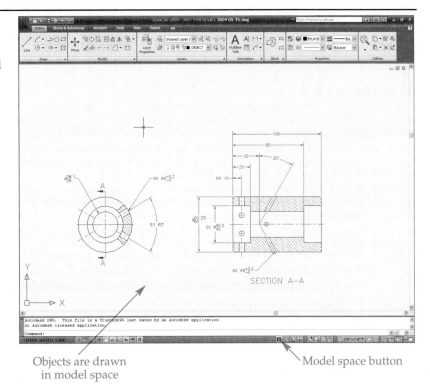

Objects are drawn in model space

Model space button

Once the drawing or model is completed, a *layout* can be created. A single drawing can have multiple layouts. Layouts are created in an environment called *paper space*. Paper space represents the sheet of paper used to lay out and plot a drawing or model. Paper space can be accessed by picking the **Layout** button on the status bar or by using **Quick View Layouts** or **Quick View Drawings**. See **Figure 5-36.**

Figure 5-36.
Paper space is the environment in which drawings and designs are laid out on paper for plotting.

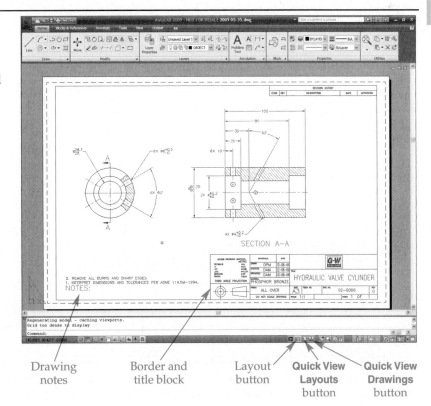

Drawing notes

Border and title block

Layout button

Quick View Layouts button

Quick View Drawings button

Drawings can be plotted from model space or from a layout. The following information describes plotting from model space only. Creating and plotting layouts is covered in Chapters 28 and 29.

Making a Plot

This section describes one of the many methods for creating a plot from model space. Refer to **Figure 5-37** as you read through the following plotting procedure:

1. Access the **Plot** dialog box. If the column on the far right of the dialog box shown in **Figure 5-37** is not displayed, pick the **More Options** button (**>**) in the lower-right corner.

2. Check the plot device and paper size specifications in the **Printer/plotter** and **Paper size** areas.

3. Select what is to be plotted in the **Plot area** section. The **Limits** option is displayed when you plot from model space. Select this option to plot everything inside the defined drawing limits. Pick the **Extents** option to plot the furthest extents of objects in the drawing. Select the **Display** option to plot the current screen display, exactly as it is shown when you plot. When you select the **Window** option, the **Page Setup** dialog box disappears temporarily so you can pick two opposite corners to define a window around the area you want to plot. Once the window is defined, a **Window...** button appears in the **Plot area** section. Pick the button to redefine the opposite corners of a window around the portion of the drawing you want to plot.

portrait: A vertical paper orientation.

landscape: A horizontal paper orientation.

4. Select an option in the **Drawing orientation** area. Choose **Portrait** to orient the drawing vertically (*portrait*) or **Landscape** to orient the drawing horizontally (*landscape*). The **Plot upside-down** option rotates the paper 180°.

Figure 5-37.
The **Plot** dialog box.

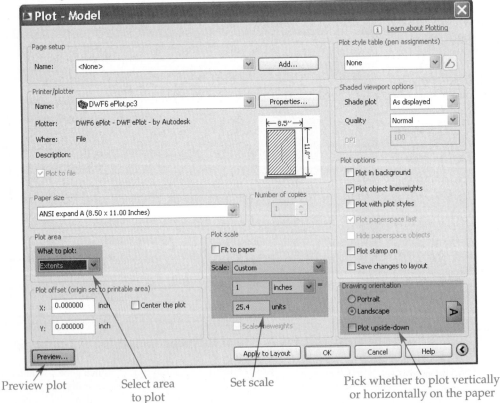

Preview plot   Select area to plot   Set scale   Pick whether to plot vertically or horizontally on the paper

5. Set the scale in the **Plot scale** area. Because you draw full-scale in AutoCAD, you typically need to scale drawings either up or down to fit the paper. Scale is measured as a ratio of either inches or millimeters to drawing units. Select a predefined scale from the **Scale:** drop-down list or enter your own values into the custom fields. Choose the **Fit to paper** check box to let AutoCAD automatically shrink or stretch the plot area to fill the paper.
6. If desired, use the **Plot offset (origin set to printable area)** area to set additional left and bottom margins around the plot or to center the plot.
7. Pick the **Preview...** button to display the sheet as it will look when it is plotted. See **Figure 5-38.** The cursor appears as a magnifying glass with + and – symbols. The plot preview image zooms if you hold the left mouse button and move the cursor. Press [Esc] to exit the preview.
8. Pick the **OK** button in the **Plot** dialog box to send the data to the plotting device.

Exercise 5-9
Complete the exercise on the Student CD.

Template Development Chapter 5 Lineweight, linetype, and layer definitions are important elements of most drawing templates. Refer to the Student CD for detailed instructions to add these elements to your mechanical, architectural, and civil drawing templates.

Figure 5-38.
A preview of the plot shows exactly how the drawing will appear on the paper.

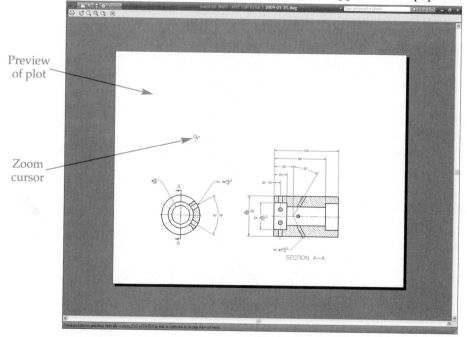

Chapter Test

1. Identify the following linetypes:

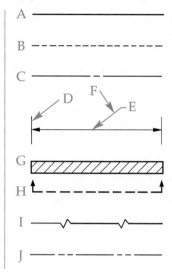

2. Identify three ways to access the **Layer Properties Manager**.
3. How can you tell if a layer is off, thawed, or unlocked by looking at the **Layer Properties Manager**?
4. Should you draw on layer 0? Explain.
5. How can several new layer names be entered consecutively without using the **New Layer** button in the **Layer Properties Manager**?
6. How do you make another layer current in the **Layer Properties Manager**?
7. How do you make another layer current using the ribbon?
8. How can you display the **Select Color** dialog box from the **Layer Properties Manager**?
9. List the seven standard color names and numbers.
10. How do you change a layer's linetype in the **Layer Properties Manager**?
11. What is the default linetype in AutoCAD?
12. What condition must exist before a linetype can be used in a layer?
13. Describe the basic procedure to change a layer's linetype to HIDDEN.
14. What is the function of the linetype scale?
15. Explain the effects of using a global linetype scale.
16. Why do you have to be careful when changing linetype scales?
17. What is the state of a layer *not* displayed on the screen and *not* calculated by the computer when the drawing is regenerated?
18. Explain the purpose of locking a layer.
19. Identify the following layer status icons:

A.   D.

B.   E.

C.   F.

20. Identify at least three layers that cannot be deleted from a drawing.
21. Describe the purpose of layer filters.
22. Name the two basic types of filters.
23. Which button in the **Layer Properties Manager** allows you to save layer settings so they can be restored at a later time?
24. In the tree view area of **DesignCenter**, how do you view the content categories of one of the listed open drawings?
25. How do you display all the available layers in a drawing using the **DesignCenter** preview pane?
26. Briefly explain how drag and drop works.
27. Define *hard copy* and *soft copy*.
28. Identify four ways to access the **Plot** dialog box.
29. Describe the difference between the **Display** and **Window** options in the **Plot area** section of the **Plot** dialog box.
30. Explain how to examine what a plot will look like before you actually print the drawing. What is the major advantage of doing a plot preview?

Drawing Problems

Before beginning these problems, set up template drawings with layer names, colors, linetypes, and lineweights for the type of drawing you are creating. Do not draw dimensions. Be sure to do preliminary planning for each drawing as described in this chapter.

▼ Basic

1. Draw the hex head bolt pattern shown below. Save the drawing as P5-1.

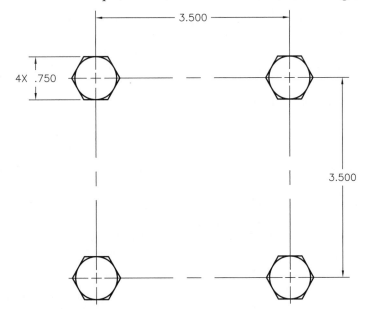

2. Create a 1/2″ hex nut with 3/4″ across the flats and a .422″ root diameter as shown. Save the drawing as P5-2.

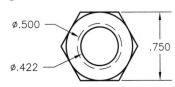

3. Draw the part shown below. Save the drawing as P5-3.

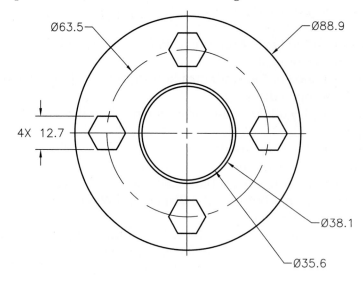

4. Draw the part shown below. Save the drawing as P5-4.

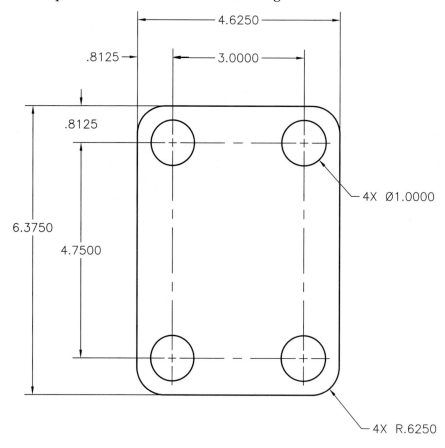

▼ Intermediate

5. Open P4-3, create a new layer for centerlines, and insert the centerlines. Save the drawing as P5-5.

6. Open P4-8, create a new layer for centerlines, and insert the centerlines. Save the drawing as P5-6.

▼ Advanced

7. Open P4-19, create a new layer for centerlines, and insert the centerlines. Change the global linetype scale to achieve an effect similar to the centerlines shown in Chapter 4. Save the drawing as P5-7.

8. Draw the plot plan shown below. Use the linetypes shown, which include Continuous, HIDDEN, PHANTOM, CENTER, FENCELINE2, and GAS_LINE. Make your drawing proportional to the example. Save the drawing as P5-8.

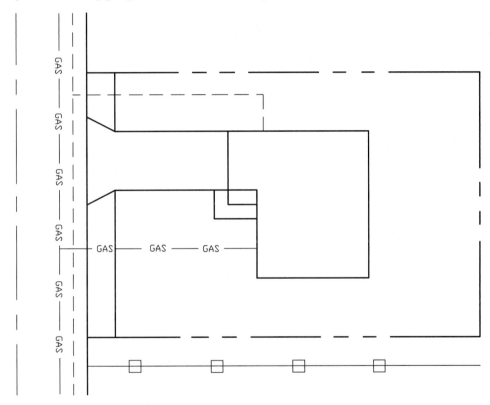

9. Draw the line chart shown below. Use the linetypes shown, which include Continuous, HIDDEN, PHANTOM, CENTER, FENCELINE1, and FENCELINE2. Make your drawing proportional to the given example. Save the drawing as P5-9.

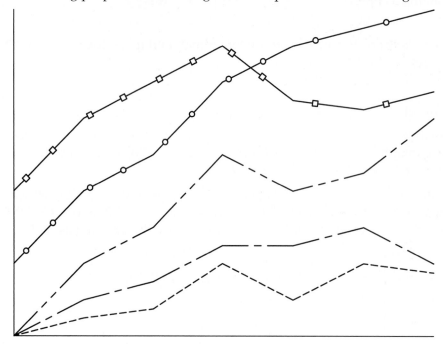

10. Create the controller integrated circuit diagram. Use a ruler or scale to keep the proportion as close as possible. Do not include the text. Save the drawing as P5-10.

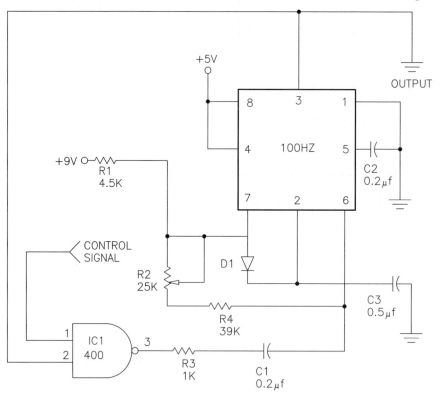

11. Draw a drift boat similar to the one shown below. Estimate dimensions. Save the drawing as P5-11.

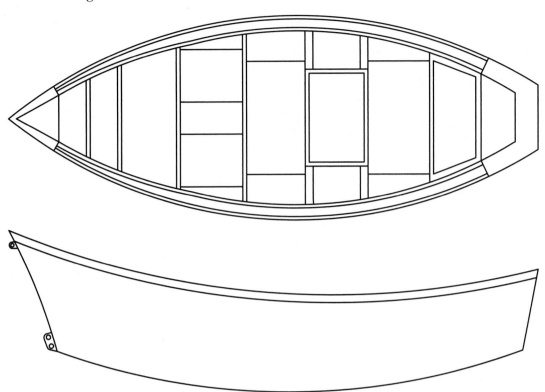

12. Draw the fishing boat shown. Save the drawing as P5-12.

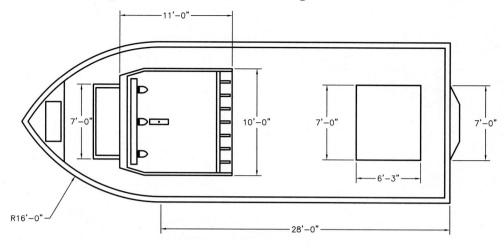

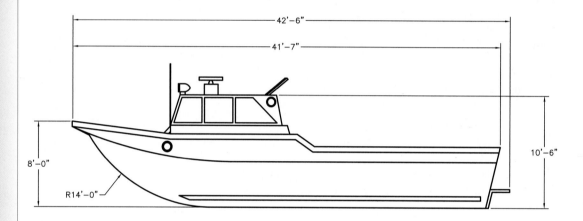

Display Options

Learning Objectives

After completing this chapter, you will be able to do the following:

✓ Magnify a small part of a drawing to work on details.
✓ Move the display window to reveal portions of the drawing outside the boundaries of the monitor.
✓ Use display tools transparently.
✓ Control display order.
✓ Create named views that can be recalled instantly.
✓ Create multiple viewports in the drawing window.
✓ Explain the difference between redrawing and regenerating the display.
✓ Toggle interface items on and off to maximize the drawing window.

You can view a specific portion of a drawing using AutoCAD display tools. The **ZOOM** tool magnifies objects so that you can see them more clearly. The portion of a zoomed drawing that is displayed on-screen can be changed using the **PAN** tool. Use the **View Manager** to create and name specific views of the drawing. When further drawing or editing operations are required, named views can be quickly and easily recalled. This chapter also describes the options for refreshing the screen.

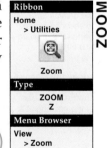

ZOOM	
Ribbon	
Home	
> Utilities	
	Zoom
Type	
	ZOOM
	Z
Menu Browser	
View	
> Zoom	

Zooming

Zooming gives you the ability to view drawing detail and draw extremely small items. The **ZOOM** tool provides several methods for getting close to your work. The option you choose is based on the portion of the drawing you want to display and whether you want to zoom in or zoom out. This chapter focuses on the ribbon and menu browser as the primary means of accessing **ZOOM** tool options. See Figure 6-1. When you select a zoom option from the ribbon or menu browser, all prompts are specific to the selected option. When using dynamic input or the command line to access zoom tools, you will need to enter specific options when prompted.

zooming: Making objects appear bigger (zoom in) or smaller (zoom out) on the screen without affecting their actual sizes.

Figure 6-1.
ZOOM tool options.
A—The **Zoom** flyout
button on ribbon.
B—The **Zoom**
submenu on the
menu browser.

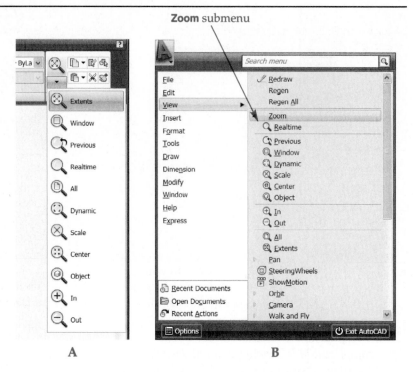

A

B

NOTE

The **ZOOM** tool can also be activated from various shortcut menus.

Realtime Zooming

When you access the **Realtime** zoom option, known as *realtime zooming*, the zoom cursor is displayed, which is a magnifying glass icon with a plus and minus. With the **ZOOM** tool active, press and hold the left mouse button and move the cursor up to *zoom in* and down to *zoom out*. When you achieve the display you want, release the mouse button. If the display needs further adjustment after the initial zoom, press and hold the left mouse button again and move the pointer to get the desired display. To exit realtime zooming, press the [Esc] key or the [Enter] key, or right-click and pick **Exit**.

If you right-click while the zoom cursor is active, a shortcut menu is displayed. This menu appears at the zoom cursor location and contains six viewing options. **Figure 6-2** briefly describes the purpose of each shortcut menu option. Most of these features are explained in detail throughout this chapter.

NOTE

Realtime zooming can also be activated by picking the **Zoom** button on the status bar.

PROFESSIONAL TIP

AutoCAD supports most mice that have a scroll wheel. This is a wheel between the two mouse buttons that usually scrolls the display up or down. Roll the wheel forward (away from you) to zoom in. Roll the wheel backward (toward you) to zoom out. This function also pans to the location of the crosshairs at the same time as zooming.

Figure 6-2.
Options on the shortcut menu that is displayed when you right-click while the zoom cursor is active.

Option	Cursor	Function
Pan		Activates the **Pan Realtime** option. Allows you to adjust the placement of the drawing on the screen.
Zoom		Starts the **Zoom Realtime** option. Often used to toggle back and forth between **Pan** and **Realtime** to adjust the view.
3D Orbit		Activates the **3D Orbit** tool for moving around a 3D object. A detailed explanation of 3D navigation tools is provided in *AutoCAD and Its Applications—Advanced.*
Zoom Window		Initiates the **Zoom Window** option. Unlike the typical zoom window, described later in this chapter, you must press and hold the pick button while dragging the window box to the opposite corner, then release the pick button.
Zoom Original	No cursor displayed	Restores the previous display before any realtime zooming or panning occurred. Useful if the modified display is not appropriate.
Zoom Extents	No cursor displayed	Activates the **Zoom Extents** option to zoom to the extents of the drawing geometry.

Other Useful Zoom Options

AutoCAD also provides other, older options for zooming. Depending on your drawing task, you may choose to use one or more of these options instead of the **Realtime** option or the navigation wheels described later in this chapter. For example, the **All** option zooms to the edges of the drawing limits. If objects are drawn beyond the limits, the **All** option zooms to the edges of your geometry. Always use this option after you change the drawing limits.

The **Extents** zoom option zooms to the extents, or edges, of objects in a drawing. If you have a mouse with a scroll wheel, double-click the wheel to quickly zoom to extents. The **Object** zoom option allows you to select an object or set of objects. The selection is zoomed and centered to fill the display area.

The **Window** zoom option allows you to pick opposite corners of a box. Objects in the box enlarge to fill the display. The **Window** option is the default if you pick a point on the screen upon entering the **ZOOM** tool at the keyboard.

The **Scale** zoom option allows you to zoom in or out according to a specific zoom, or magnification, scale factor. The Enter a scale factor (nX or nXP): prompt appears when you select the **Scale** option. The **nX** option scales the display relative to the current display. The **nXP** option is used in conjunction with model space and paper space. It scales a drawing in model space relative to paper space and is used primarily in the layout of scaled multiview drawings, found in Chapter 28.

NOTE

The **Previous, In, Out, Center,** and **Dynamic** options of the **ZOOM** tool are not described in this book. These options provide functions that can be achieved more easily using newer, more capable AutoCAD tools.

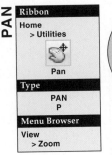

Ribbon

Home
> Utilities

Pan

Type

PAN
P

Menu Browser

View
> Zoom

Exercise 6-1
Complete the exercise on the Student CD.

Panning

panning: Moving a zoomed drawing around so that different parts of it are visible on-screen.

Panning is similar to looking through a camera lens and moving the camera across the drawing. The **PAN** tool is used for panning. **PAN** is often used in conjunction with the **ZOOM** tool to change the display.

NOTE
The **PAN** tool can also be activated by picking the **Pan** button on the status bar, or from various shortcut menus.

Panning Realtime

realtime panning: A panning operation in which you can see the drawing move on the screen as you pan.

When you first access the **PAN** tool, you are using the **Realtime** option, known as *realtime panning*. The **Realtime** option is the quickest and easiest method of adjusting the view around the objects on the screen. After starting the tool, press and hold the left mouse button and move the pan cursor in the direction you want to pan. A right-click displays the same shortcut menu available for realtime zooming. To exit realtime panning, press the [Esc] key or the [Enter] key, or right-click and pick **Exit**.

PROFESSIONAL TIP

If you have a mouse with a scroll wheel, press and hold the wheel button and move the mouse to perform a realtime pan.

NOTE

An alternative realtime panning method involves using drawing window scroll bars. To display the scroll bars, access the **Options** dialog box. Then, in the **Display** tab, **Window Elements** area, select the **Display scroll bars in drawing window** check box. However, real-time panning is more efficient than using the scroll bars.

Additional Panning Options

pan displacement: Picking two points in the drawing to move the viewing window so that objects originally appearing at the first point now appear at the second point.

AutoCAD provides additional panning tools that are available from the menu browser **View** > **Pan** submenu. Pick the **Point** option to specify a *pan displacement*. To use pan displacement, you pick two points. The drawing pans so that objects at the first point are relocated to the second point. The pan preset options—**Left**, **Right**, **Up**, and **Down**—pan the drawing in the selected direction by a set increment. Realtime panning is more efficient than pan displacement and pan presets.

Exercise 6-2

Complete the exercise on the Student CD.

Introduction to SteeringWheels

Type	
NAVSWHEEL	**NAVSWHEEL**
Menu Browser	
View	
> SteeringWheels	

AutoCAD **SteeringWheels** provide an alternative means of accessing and using certain view tools. Individual **SteeringWheels** are known as *navigation wheels*. Some navigation wheels and many of the tools available from navigation wheels are specifically used when preparing 3D models. The **ZOOM**, **CENTER**, **PAN**, and **REWIND** tools can be used for 2D drafting applications. All other **SteeringWheels** tools and options are covered in *AutoCAD and Its Applications—Advanced*.

NOTE

SteeringWheels can also be activated by picking the **SteeringWheel** button on the status bar and from various shortcut menus.

When you access **SteeringWheels** in model space, the **Full Navigation Wheel** is displayed by default, and the UCS icon changes to a 3D display. In layout views (paper space), the **2D Navigation Wheel** is shown. See **Figure 6-3**. Navigation wheels are displayed next to the cursor and are divided into *wedges*. Each wedge houses a navigation tool, similar to a tool button. Hover the cursor over a wedge to highlight the wedge. You can pick certain navigation wedges to activate a tool. Other wedges require that you hold down the left mouse button in order to use the tool.

wedges: The parts of a wheel that contain navigation tools.

Figure 6-3.
The **Full Navigation Wheel** is displayed by default when you access **SteeringWheels** in model space. The **2D Navigation Wheel** is shown in a layout.

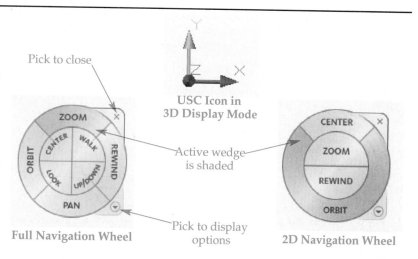

Pick to close

USC Icon in
3D Display Mode

Active wedge
is shaded

Full Navigation Wheel

Pick to display
options

2D Navigation Wheel

A navigation wheel remains on-screen until closed; allowing you to use multiple navigation tools. To close a navigation wheel, pick the **Close** button in the upper-right corner of the wheel, press the [Esc] key or the [Enter] key, or right-click and pick **Close Wheel**.

Zooming with the Navigation Wheel

The **ZOOM** navigation tool offers realtime zooming. Press and hold the left mouse button on the **ZOOM** wedge to display the pivot point icon and zoom navigation cursor. See Figure 6-4. The pivot point is the location where you pressed the **ZOOM** wedge. Move the zoom navigation cursor up to zoom in and down to zoom out. The pivot point icon also zooms in or out as a visual aid to zooming. When you achieve the display you want, release the left mouse button.

Using the Center Navigation Tool

The **CENTER** navigation tool centers the display screen at a picked point, without zooming. Press and hold the left mouse button on the **CENTER** wedge. The pivot point icon appears when you move the cursor over an object. Release the mouse button to pan so the location of the pivot point is relocated to the center of the drawing window when you release the mouse button. See Figure 6-5.

Panning with the Navigation Wheel

The **PAN** navigation tool uses realtime panning to adjust the view around the objects on the screen. Press and hold the left mouse button on the **PAN** wedge to display the pan navigation cursor. Move the pan navigation cursor in the direction you want to pan. Release the left mouse button when you achieve the desired display.

Figure 6-4.
To use the **ZOOM** navigation tool, move the cursor up to zoom in and down to zoom out.

The pivot point is located where you press and hold the **Zoom** wedge

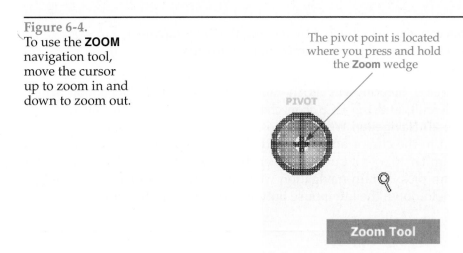

PIVOT

Zoom Tool

Figure 6-5.
To use the **CENTER** navigation tool, move the cursor over an object at the point you want to be centered in the drawing area and release the left mouse button.

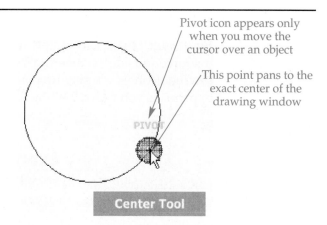

Pivot icon appears only when you move the cursor over an object

This point pans to the exact center of the drawing window

PIVOT

Center Tool

Rewinding

The **REWIND** navigation tool can be used to observe the effects view tools have made on the drawing display and to return the display to a previous appearance. For example, if you use the navigation wheel to zoom in, then pan, then zoom out, you can rewind through each action and return to the original display, the zoomed-in view, the panned display, and then back to the current zoomed-out view. By default, you can rewind through view actions created using most view tools. The activity does not have to be performed by a navigation wheel tool.

Pick the **REWIND** tool once to return to the previous display. Thumbnail images appear in frames as the previous view is restored. The orange-framed thumbnail surrounded by brackets indicates the display being restored and its location in the sequence of events. See **Figure 6-6.** You can repeatedly pick the **REWIND** button to cycle back through prior views. Another option is to press and hold the left mouse button on the **REWIND** wedge to display the framed view thumbnails. Then, while still holding the left mouse button, move the brackets left over the thumbnails to cycle through earlier displays. You can also move the brackets back to the right to return to later views. Release the left mouse button when you achieve the display you want.

Figure 6-6.
Use the **REWIND** navigation tool to step back through and restore previous display configurations.

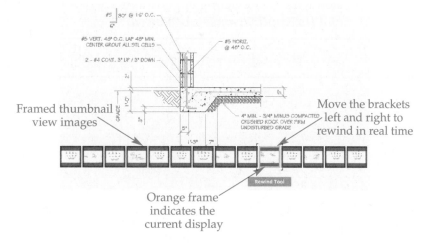

Framed thumbnail view images

Move the brackets left and right to rewind in real time

Rewind Tool

Orange frame indicates the current display

NOTE

By default, if you access and use a view tool, such as **ZOOM**, from a source outside of **SteeringWheels**, such as the menu browser, a rewind icon is shown in place of the thumbnail. A thumbnail appears as you move the brackets over the rewind icon.

Exercise 6-3

Complete the exercise on the Student CD.

SteeringWheel Options

A shortcut menu of options displays when you right-click while using a navigation wheel or when you pick the options button in the lower-right corner of a wheel. The options vary depending on the current work environment. Most of the options provide access to options and navigation wheels specifically for 3D modeling. The following options can be used for 2D drafting applications:

- **Mini Full Navigation Wheel.** Displays the **Full Navigation Wheel** in mini format. See Figure 6-7.
- **Full Navigation Wheel.** Displays the **Full Navigation Wheel** in the default big format.
- **Fit to Window.** Zooms and pans to show all objects centered in the drawing window.
- **SteeringWheel Settings....** Displays the **SteeringWheel Settings** dialog box.
- **Close Wheel.** Closes the navigation wheel.

SteeringWheels Settings

Various settings for the navigation wheels are defined using the **SteeringWheel Settings** dialog box. Refer to the Student CD: Supplemental Materials > SteeringWheels Settings for more information about options specific to 2D drafting. Settings associated with 3D modeling applications are described in *AutoCAD and Its Applications—Advanced*.

Figure 6-7.
The **Full Navigation Wheel** in mini mode.

Active wedge

Zoom

Name of active wedge appears below the wheel

Using Transparent Display Tools

To begin a new tool, you usually need to complete or cancel the current tool. Selecting a new tool usually cancels the tool in progress and then starts the new tool. However, some tools can be used as *transparent tools,* temporarily interrupting the active tool. After the transparent tool is completed, the tool that was interrupted is resumed. Therefore, it is not necessary to cancel the initial tool. Many display tools can be used transparently, including **PAN**, **ZOOM**, and **SteeringWheels**.

An example of when transparent commands are useful is drawing a line when one end of the line is somewhere off the screen. One option is to cancel the **LINE** tool, zoom out to see more of the drawing, and select **LINE** again. A more efficient method is to use **PAN** or **ZOOM** transparently with the **LINE** tool. To do so, begin the **LINE** tool and pick the first point. At the Specify next point: prompt, access the **PAN** or **ZOOM** tool. Any access method can be used, though right-clicking and selecting the **Pan** or **Zoom** menu option, or using the wheel mouse, is often quickest. Once the drawing is displayed correctly, pick the second point of the line. You can also activate tools transparently by typing an apostrophe (') before the tool name. For example, to enter the transparent **ZOOM** tool, type 'Z or 'ZOOM.

transparent tool: A tool that can be used while another tool is in progress.

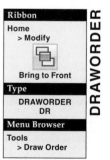

Controlling Draw Order

Drawings can have objects that overlap each other, but since most objects are made of thin lines, the overlap is difficult to see. Controlling the order of display is better illustrated with an object that has some width, such as a donut. See Figure 6-8. The bracket was drawn before the donuts. The donuts, and all other objects, can be moved above or below selected objects and to the front or back of all objects.

Use the **DRAWORDER** tool to change the order of objects in a drawing. You can also set draw order by picking an object to select it, right-clicking, and choosing **Draw Order** from the shortcut menu. See Figure 6-9. Select the **Above objects** option to move the selected object above the reference object. Select the **Under objects** option to move the selected object below the reference object. Select the **Front** option to place the selected object at the front of the drawing. Choose the **Back** option to place the selected object at the back of the drawing.

Ribbon
Home
> Modify

Bring to Front
Type
DRAWORDER
DR
Menu Browser
Tools
> Draw Order

DRAWORDER

Exercise 6-4

Complete the exercise on the Student CD.

Figure 6-8.
The order of objects can be changed to place any object under or above other objects.

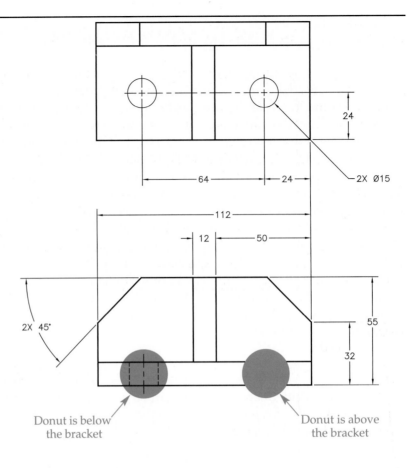

Donut is below the bracket

Donut is above the bracket

Figure 6-9.
The **Draw Order** flyout provides four options for rearranging the order of objects in a drawing.

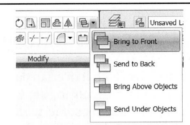

Creating Named Views

Using typical view tools such as **ZOOM** and **PAN** can be time-consuming on a large drawing with a number of separate details. Being able to specify a certain part of the drawing quickly is much easier. This is possible with the **View Manager**, which allows you to create named views of any area of the drawing. A view can be a portion of the drawing, such as the upper-left quadrant, or it can represent an enlarged area. After the view is created, you can instruct AutoCAD to display it at any time.

Access the **View Manager** to create and work with named views. The left side of the **View Manager** contains a list of view types, or nodes. See **Figure 6-10.** Each node, except **Current**, can be expanded to reveal any saved views. The **Current** node displays the properties of the current view. The **Model Views** node contains a list of saved model views. The **Layout Views** node contains a list of saved layout views. The **Preset Views** node lists all preset orthogonal and isometric views.

Picking one of the view nodes displays information about the view type. The right side of the **View Manager** contains buttons to control or modify the selected view or view type. These actions are also available in a shortcut menu when you right-click on the view or view type.

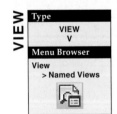

VIEW

Type	
	VIEW
	V
Menu Browser	
View	
> Named Views	

Figure 6-10.
The view nodes of the **View Manager** dialog box help organize saved and preset drawing views.

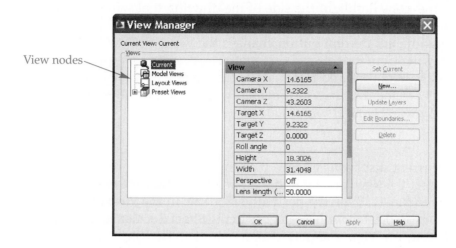

View nodes

Figure 6-11.
Select a named view to see its properties and a preview image.

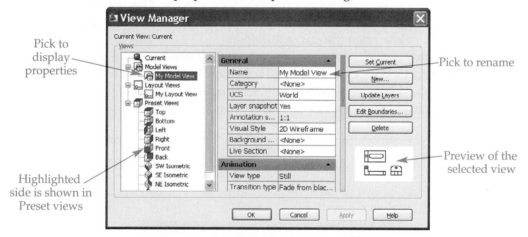

Pick to display properties

Highlighted side is shown in Preset views

Pick to rename

Preview of the selected view

Pick one of the view names to display information related to the current view in the middle area of the dialog box. See **Figure 6-11.** The first section, **General**, contains details such as the name of the view, layer settings saved with the view, and other specific view type settings. The **General** section is not visible while the **Current** node is selected. The **Animation** section sets the properties for animated drawings and slide shows. The settings in the **View** section include camera position, target position, and perspective status. The **Clipping** section controls front plane and back plane location and the clipping status. Some of these items are covered in more detail in this chapter; others are reserved for later chapters or *AutoCAD and Its Applications—Advanced,* where the information is more relevant.

NOTE

The lower-right corner of the **View Manager** shows a preview image of the selected view. This image is visible only when one of the named model or layout views is selected.

Preset Views

The **Preset Views** node is used to choose one of the ten preset views. Notice in Figure 6-11 that the icons highlight the side of the drawing that will be viewed. The orthogonal views include Top, Bottom, Front, Back, Left, and Right. Picking any of these icons and pressing the **Set Current** button changes the view in AutoCAD so you are looking at the drawing from the selected direction. The preset isometric views include Southwest, Southeast, Northeast, and Northwest. Selecting any of these icons displays a 3D (isometric) view of the drawing. Orthogonal and isometric views are covered in greater depth in *AutoCAD and Its Applications—Advanced.*

New Views

To save the current display as a view, pick the **New...** button or right-click on a view node and select the **New...** menu option to access the **New View/Shot Properties** dialog box. See Figure 6-12. Type the desired view name in the **View name:** edit box. If the named view is associated with a category in the **Sheet Set Manager**, the category can be selected from the **View category** drop-down list. The **Sheet Set Manager** is described in Chapter 33.

The **New View/Shot Properties** dialog box provides many options that are applicable to 3D modeling animations. When creating a basic 2D view, select **Still** from the **View Type** drop-down list, and focus on the settings in the **View Properties** tab. The **Current display** radio button is the default. Click **OK** to add the view name to the list. AutoCAD creates a view from the current display.

To use a window to define the view, pick the **Define window** radio button in the **New View** dialog box and then pick the **Define view window** button. Pick two points to define a window. After you select the second corner, the **New View** dialog box reappears. When you pick the **OK** button, the **View Manager** is updated to reflect the new view.

Figure 6-12.
In the **New View** dialog box, you can save the current display as a view or define a window to create a view.

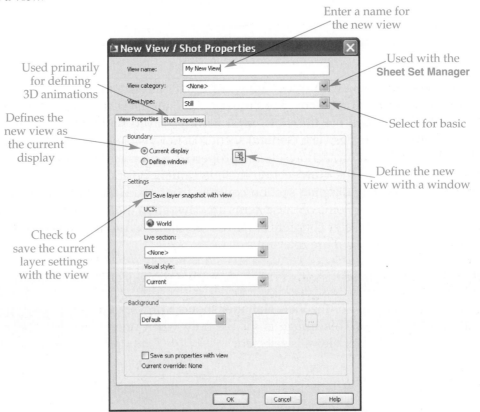

When you save a new view, you can save the current layer settings with it. These layer settings are recalled each time the view is set current. To do this, check the **Save layer snapshot with view** check box.

NOTE

It is possible to save a named UCS (user coordinate system) to a new view when it is created. The **UCS** tool is covered in depth in *AutoCAD and Its Applications—Advanced*.

Activating Views

To display one of the listed views, pick its name from the list in the **Views** area of the **View Manager** and pick the **Set Current** button. The name of the current view appears in the **Current View:** label above the **Views** area. Pick the **OK** button to display the selected view.

PROFESSIONAL TIP

Part of your project planning should include view names. A consistent naming system guarantees that all users know the view names without having to list them. The views can be set as part of the template drawings.

Exercise 6-5
Complete the exercise on the Student CD.

Tiled Viewports

The model space drawing window can be divided into viewports. These separations are called *tiled viewports*. Another type of viewport, *floating viewports*, are created in a layout. Tiled viewports are created in model space; floating viewports are created in paper space. Floating viewports and layouts are described in Chapter 28.

By default, the drawing window contains only one viewport. Additional viewports can be added. The edges of tiled viewports butt against one another like floor tile. Tiled viewports cannot overlap.

Viewports contain different views of the same drawing, displayed at the same time. Only one viewport can be active at any given time. The active viewport has a bold outline around its edges. See **Figure 6-13**.

Viewports in model space can be used for both 2D and 3D drawings. They are limited only by your imagination and need. Two-dimensional drawings, whether mechanical multiview, architectural construction details, or unscaled schematic drawings, lend themselves well to viewports. See *AutoCAD and Its Applications—Advanced* for examples of tiled viewports in 3D.

tiled viewports: Viewports created in model space.

floating viewports: Viewports created in paper space.

Figure 6-13.
An example of three tiled viewports in model space. All of the viewports contain the same objects, but the display in each viewport can be unique.

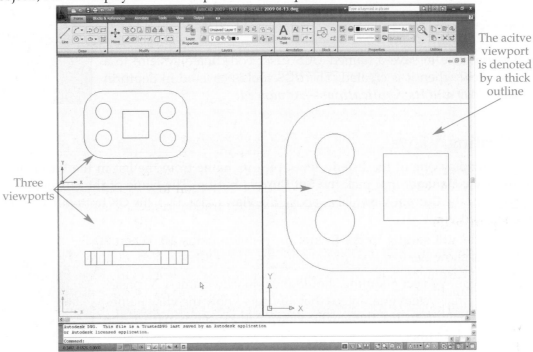

Three viewports

The acitve viewport is denoted by a thick outline

Creating Tiled Viewports

Viewports can be created using the **Viewports** dialog box. The **New Viewports** tab of this dialog box is shown in **Figure 6-14.** The **Standard viewports:** list contains many preset viewport configurations. The configuration name identifies the number of viewports and the arrangement or location of the largest viewport. Select a configuration to see a preview of the titled viewports in the **Preview** area on the right side of the **New Viewports** tab. Select *Active Model Configuration* to preview the current

Figure 6-14.
Specify the number and arrangement of tiled viewports in the **New Viewports** tab of the **Viewports** dialog box.

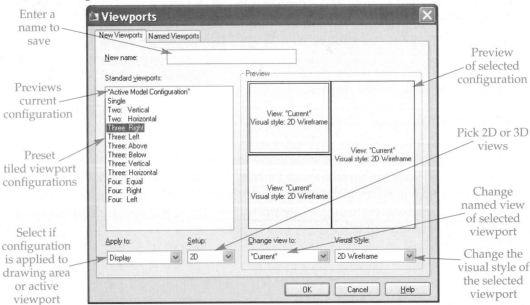

Enter a name to save

Previews current configuration

Preset tiled viewport configurations

Select if configuration is applied to drawing area or active viewport

Preview of selected configuration

Pick 2D or 3D views

Change named view of selected viewport

Change the visual style of the selected viewport

configuration. Pick the **OK** button to divide the drawing window into the selected viewport configuration.

> ### NOTE
>
> The same preset viewport configurations available from the **New Viewports** tab of the **Viewport** dialog box can be activated from the ***Active Viewport Configuration*** drop-down list in the **Viewports** panel on the **View** tab of the ribbon.

The additional options in the **Viewports** dialog box are useful when two or more viewports already exist. The **Apply to:** drop-down list allows you to specify whether the viewport configuration is applied to the entire drawing window or to the active viewport only. Select **Display** to apply the configuration to the entire drawing area. Select **Current Viewport** to apply the new configuration in the active viewport only. See **Figure 6-15.**

The default setting in the **Setup:** drop-down list is **2D**. When **2D** is selected, all viewports show the top view of the drawing. If the **3D** option is selected, the different viewports display various 3D views of the drawing. At least one viewport is set up with an isometric view. The other viewports have different views, such as a top view or side view. The viewport configuration is displayed in the **Preview** image. To change a view in a viewport, pick the viewport in the **Preview** image and then select the new viewpoint from the **Change view to:** drop-down list.

If none of the preset configurations is appropriate, you can create and save a unique viewport configuration. After you create the custom viewport configuration, enter a descriptive name in the **New name:** text box. When you pick the **OK** button, the new named viewport configuration is recorded and displayed in the **Named Viewports** tab the next time you access the **Viewports** dialog box. See **Figure 6-16.** Select a different named viewport configuration and pick **OK** to apply it to the drawing area. Named viewport configurations can be applied to the active viewport only.

Specific viewport configurations can also be selected from the **View > Viewports** menu in the menu browser. See **Figure 6-17.** The **1 Viewport** option replaces the current

Figure 6-15.
You can subdivide a viewport by choosing **Current Viewport in the Apply to:** drop-down list. Here, the top-left viewport was further subdivided using the **Two: Vertical** preset configuration.

Configuration applied to active viewport

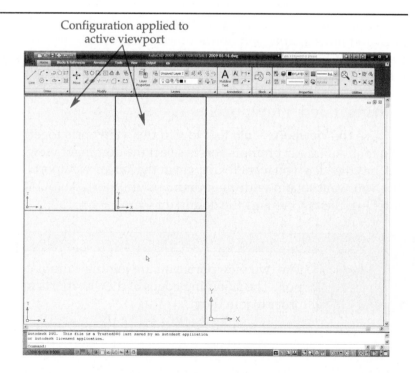

Figure 6-16.
The **Named Viewports** tab displays custom viewports.

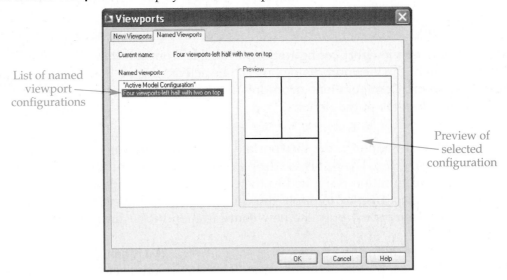

List of named viewport configurations

Preview of selected configuration

viewport configuration with a single viewport. When you select the **2 Viewports** option, you are prompted to select a vertical or horizontal arrangement. The arrangement you choose is applied to the active viewport only. This configuration does not replace the current viewport configuration. When you pick the **3 Viewports** you are prompted to select **Horizontal**, **Vertical**, **Above**, **Below**, **Left**, or **Right**. The arrangement you choose is applied to the active viewport only. This configuration does not replace the current viewport configuration. The **4 Viewports** option creates four equal viewports within the active viewport.

Working in Tiled Viewports

After you select the viewport configuration and return to the drawing area, move the pointing device around and notice that only the active viewport contains crosshairs. The cursor is an arrow in the other viewports. To make a different viewport active, move the cursor into it and pick.

As you draw in one viewport, the image is displayed in all viewports. Try drawing lines and other shapes and notice how the viewports are affected. Use a display tool, such as **ZOOM**, in the active viewport and notice the results. Only the active viewport reflects the use of the **ZOOM** tool.

Joining Tiled Viewports

Ribbon

View
> Viewports

Viewports, Join

Type

VIEWPORTS
VPORTS

Menu Browser

View
> Viewports
> Join

Use the **Viewports, Join** tool to join two viewports together. When you select the **Join** tool, AutoCAD prompts you to select the dominant viewport. Select the viewport that has the view you want to display in the joined viewport. Then select the viewport that you want to join with the dominant viewport. AutoCAD "glues" the two viewports together and retains the dominant view.

NOTE

The two viewports you are joining cannot create an L-shape viewport. The adjoining edges of the viewports must be the same size in order to join them.

Figure 6-17.
Some **Viewports**
options are available
from the **View**
menu in the menu
browser.

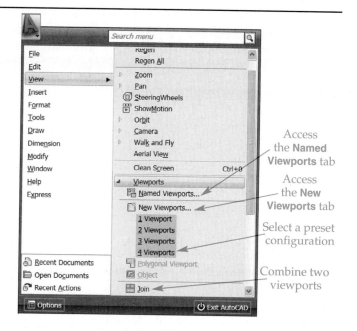

Access
the **Named
Viewports** tab

Access
the **New
Viewports** tab

Select a preset
configuration

Combine two
viewports

Exercise 6-6
Complete the exercise on the Student CD.

Redrawing and Regenerating the Screen

Redrawing refreshes the display of objects. *Regenerating* recalculates all object
coordinates and displays them based on the current zoom magnification. For example,
if curved objects appear as straight segments when you zoom in, you can regenerate
the display to smooth the curves. Each viewport is a separate virtual screen. As a
result, if you are using two or more viewports, you must decide whether you want to
redraw or regenerate a single viewport or all the viewports.

redrawing:
Refreshing the
display of objects on
the screen without
recalculating the
vectors.

regenerating:
Recalculating all
objects based on
the current zoom
magnification and
redisplaying them.

Tool	Function
REDRAW	Redraws the display of the current viewport only.
REGEN	Regenerates the display in the current viewport only.
REDRAWALL	Redraws the display of the entire drawing.
REGENALL	Regenerates the display of the entire drawing.

PROFESSIONAL TIP

AutoCAD does an automatic regeneration when you use a tool that
changes certain aspects of objects. This regeneration can take considerable time on large, complex drawings, and the regeneration may
not be necessary. If this is the case, use the **REGENAUTO** tool to turn
off automatic regenerations.

Figure 6-18.
Using the **Clean Screen** tool. A—Initial display with the **Properties** palette and **Layer Properties Manager** displayed. B—Display after using the **Clean Screen** tool.

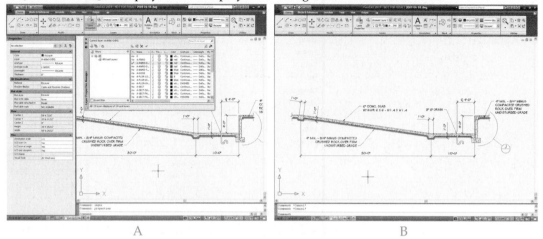

A   B

Clearing the Screen

The AutoCAD window can become crowded with multiple interface items, such as palettes, in the course of a drawing session. As the drawing area gets smaller, less of the drawing is visible. This can make drafting difficult. You can quickly maximize the size of the drawing area using the **Clean Screen** tool. This tool clears the AutoCAD window of all toolbars, palettes, and title bars. See Figure 6-18. A **Clean Screen** button is also available in the status bar. Accessing the **Clean Screen** tool toggles the clean screen display on and off.

PROFESSIONAL TIP

The **Clean Screen** tool can be helpful when you have multiple drawings displayed. Only the active drawing is displayed when the **Clean Screen** tool is used. This allows you to work more efficiently within one of the drawings.

 Supplemental Material

View Transitions and Resolution
Many display settings can be adjusted to control how display tools function and what you see on-screen. Common display settings include view transitions and view resolution. Refer to the Student CD: Supplemental Materials > View Transitions and Resolution for more information about these display settings.

 **Template Development**

Chapter 6

Drawing templates are easier to use if they show the entire drawing extents when they are first opened. Refer to the Student CD for detailed instructions to incorporate these elements into your mechanical, architectural, and civil drawing templates.

Chapter Test

Answer the following questions. Write your answers on a separate sheet of paper or complete the electronic chapter test on the Student CD.

1. During the drawing process, when should you use **ZOOM**?
2. Briefly explain how to use the **Realtime** zoom option.
3. What is the difference between the **Extents** and **All** zoom options?
4. What is the purpose of the **PAN** tool?
5. What is the difference between zooming and panning?
6. Which **SteeringWheels** navigation tools can be used in 2D drafting applications?
7. Explain how to use the **CENTER** tool on the **Full Navigation Wheel**.
8. What feature of the **Full Navigation Wheel** allows you to return to previous display settings?
9. How can you display a miniature version of the **Full Navigation Wheel**?
10. How is a transparent display command entered at the keyboard?
11. Name at least three display tools that can be used transparently.
12. Which tool changes the order in which objects are displayed in a drawing?
13. How can you obtain a list of existing views?
14. How do you create a named view of the current screen display?
15. How do you display an existing view?
16. What type of viewport is created in model space?
17. How can you specify whether a new viewport configuration applies to the entire drawing window or the active viewport?
18. Explain the procedures and conditions that need to exist for joining viewports.
19. What is the difference between the **REDRAW** and **REGEN** tools?
20. Which tool regenerates all of the viewports?

Drawing Problems

▼ Basic

1. Launch AutoCAD and perform the following tasks:
   A. Draw a circle.
   B. Use realtime zooming to zoom in and out on the circle.
   C. Use realtime panning to pan the screen display.
2. Create a freehand sketch of the full-size **Full Navigation Wheel**. Label each of the wedges.

▼ Intermediate

3. Create a freehand sketch of the clean-screen AutoCAD window. Label each of the screen areas. To the side of the sketch, write a short description of each screen area's function.
4. Open the drawing named 3D House.dwg found in the AutoCAD 2009\Sample folder. Perform the following display functions on the drawing:
   A. Zoom to the drawing extents.
   B. Create a view named Rendering.
   C. Replace the view with the Top view.
   D. Create a view named Plan using **Define Window** in the **New View** dialog box.
   E. Use realtime pan and realtime zoom to create a display of the dining room in the top-right area of the Plan view.
   F. Create a view of this display named Dining Room.
   G. Display the view named Rendering.
   H. Save the drawing as P6-4.

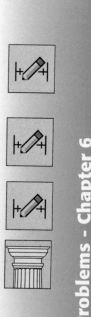

Drawing Problems - Chapter 6

Chapter 6   Display Options

▼ Advanced

5. Use the **Select Template** dialog box to load the Tutorial-iMfg.dwt template or another mechanical template you have access to that contains a border and title block. Do the following:
   A. Zoom into the title block area. Create and save a view named Title.
   B. Zoom to the extents of the drawing and create and save a view named All.
   C. Determine the areas of the drawing that will contain notes, parts list, and revisions. Zoom into these areas and create views with appropriate names, such as Notes, Partlist, and Revisions.
   D. Divide the drawing area into commonly used multiview sections. Save the views with descriptive names such as Top, Front, Rightside, and Leftside.
   E. Restore the view named All.
   F. Save the drawing as P6-5.

6. Use the **Select Template** dialog box to load the Tutorial-iArch.dwt template or another architectural drafting template you have access to that contains a border and title block. Do the following:
   A. Zoom into the title block area. Create and save a view named Title.
   B. Zoom to the extents of the drawing and create and save a view named All.
   C. Determine the area of the drawing that will contain notes, schedules, or revisions. Zoom into these areas and create views with appropriate names such as Notes, Schedules, and Revisions.
   D. Restore the view named All.
   E. Save the drawing as P6-6.

Drawing Problems - Chapter 6

Object Snaps and AutoTracking

Learning Objectives

After completing this chapter, you will be able to do the following:

- ✓ Set running object snap modes for continuous use.
- ✓ Use object snap overrides for single point selections.
- ✓ Select appropriate object snaps for various drawing tasks.
- ✓ Use the AutoSnap features to speed up point specifications.
- ✓ Use AutoTrack to locate points relative to other points in a drawing.

This chapter explains how the powerful object snap and AutoTrack™ tools are used in creating and editing drawings. Object snaps can be used to visually preview and confirm point locations prior to selection. AutoTrack offers two modes, *polar tracking* and *object snap tracking*, that use virtual construction lines to help locate points and position objects. In this chapter, you will learn how to take advantage of object snaps and AutoTrack when you create geometry.

Object Snap

Object snap is one of the most useful AutoCAD tools. It increases your drafting performance and accuracy through the concept of *snapping*. Object snap *modes* identify the object snap point. For example, the **Endpoint** object snap mode automatically selects the endpoint of an object, such as a line or arc. There are two methods of activating object snap modes: running object snaps and object snap overrides.

The AutoSnap™ feature is on by default and displays snap mode information while you draw using object snaps. AutoSnap uses visual signals that appear as *markers* displayed at the current selection point. **Figure 7-1** shows two examples of visual cues provided by AutoSnap. After a brief pause, a tooltip appears, indicating the object snap mode.

The table in **Figure 7-2** summarizes the object snap modes. Included with each mode is the marker that appears on-screen and the corresponding button, or menu graphic. Each object snap mode selects a different point on an object.

object snap: A tool that snaps to exact points, such as endpoints or midpoints, when you pick a point near these locations.

snapping: Picking a point near the intended position to have the crosshairs "snap" exactly to the specific point.

markers: Visual cues to confirm points for object snap.

Figure 7-1.
AutoSnap displays markers and related tooltips for object snap modes.

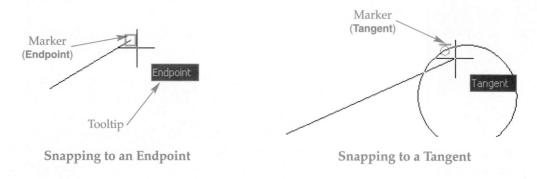

Snapping to an Endpoint   Snapping to a Tangent

Figure 7-2.
The object snap modes.

Object Snap Modes			
Mode	**Marker**	**Button**	**Description**
Endpoint	▢		Finds the nearest endpoint of a line, arc, polyline, elliptical arc, spline, ellipse, ray, solid, or multiline.
Midpoint	△		Finds the middle point of any object having two endpoints, such as a line, polyline, arc, elliptical arc, polyline arc, spline, ray, solid, xline, or multiline.
Center	○		Locates the center point of a radial object, including circles, arcs, ellipses, elliptical arcs, and radial solids.
Node	⊠		Picks a point object drawn with the **POINT**, **DIVIDE**, or **MEASURE** tool.
Quadrant	◇		Picks the closest of the four quadrant points that can be found on circles, arcs, elliptical arcs, ellipses, and radial solids. (Not all of these objects may have all four quadrants.)
Intersection	✕		Picks the closest intersection of two objects.
Extension	✛		Finds a point along the imaginary extension of an existing line, polyline, arc, polyline arc, elliptical arc, spline, ray, xline, solid, or multiline.
Insertion	⊐		Finds the insertion point of text objects and blocks.
Perpendicular	�		Finds a point that is perpendicular to an object from the previously picked point.
Tangent	⊙		Finds points of tangency between radial and linear objects.
Nearest	⧓		Locates the point on an object closest to the crosshairs.
Apparent Intersection	⊠		Selects a visual intersection between two objects that appear to intersect on screen in the current view, but may not actually intersect each other in 3D space.
Parallel	∥		Used to find any point along an imaginary line parallel to an existing line or polyline.
None			Temporarily turns running object snap off during the current selection.

Object snaps can be used with many drawing and editing tools for a variety of applications. Practice with the different object snap modes to find the ones that work best in various situations.

Running Object Snaps

Running object snaps are on by default and are often the quickest and most effective way to use object snap. By default, the **Endpoint**, **Center**, **Intersection**, and **Extension** running object snap modes are active. The quickest way to activate or deactivate running object snap modes is to right-click on the **Object Snap** or **Object Snap Tracking** button on the status bar to display the shortcut menu. Then select the running object snaps you want to turn on or off.

You can also set running object snap modes using the **Object Snap** tab in the **Drafting Settings** dialog box. See Figure 7-3. The **Drafting Settings** dialog box can be displayed from the keyboard or the menu browser or by right-clicking on any of the status bar toggle buttons and selecting the **Settings...** menu option. Select the desired running object snaps by picking the associated boxes or pick the **Select All** button to activate all object snaps. Pick the checked running object snaps to deactivate as needed, or pick the **Clear All** button to disable all running object snap modes.

To use running object snaps, move the crosshairs near the location on an existing object where the running object snap is intended to snap. When you see the appropriate marker, and if necessary, the tooltip, pick to locate the point at the exact position on the existing object. For example, with the **Endpoint** running object snap on, move the crosshairs toward the end of a line, arc, or spline. A small square marks the endpoint to be picked. Pick to locate the endpoint of the new object at the exact endpoint of the existing object. See Figure 7-4.

When you need to make several point specifications without the aid of running object snaps, you can toggle running object snaps off by picking the **Object Snap** button on the status bar or pressing the [F3] key. The advantage of this method is that you can make several picks and then restore the same running object snap modes. You can also turn off running object snaps by deselecting the **Object Snap On (F3)** check box in the **Object Snap** tab of the **Drafting Settings** dialog box.

running object snaps: Object snap modes that are set to run in the background during all drawing and editing procedures.

Type
DSETTINGS
DS
SE

Menu Browser
Tools
> Drafting
Settings...

Figure 7-3.
Running object snap modes can also be set in the Drafting Settings dialog box.

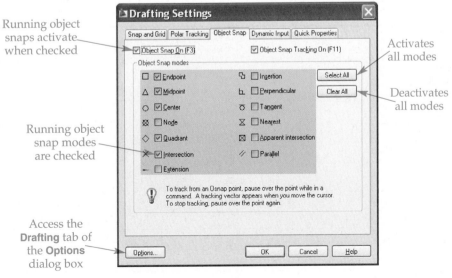

Running object snaps activate when checked

Activates all modes

Deactivates all modes

Running object snap modes are checked

Access the **Drafting** tab of the **Options** dialog box

Figure 7-4.
Using the **Endpoint** object snap. When snapping using running object spans be sure the correct snap marker and tooltip is displayed before you pick.

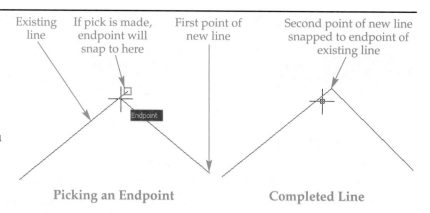

Existing line

If pick is made, endpoint will snap to here

First point of new line

Second point of new line snapped to endpoint of existing line

Picking an Endpoint

Completed Line

PROFESSIONAL TIP

You should activate only the running object snap modes that you use most often. Too many running objects snaps can make it difficult to snap to the appropriate location, especially on detailed drawings with several objects close together. Object snap modes that you use less often can be accessed using the object snap overrides explained next.

NOTE

By default, a keyboard entry overrides any currently running object snap modes. This can be changed in the **Priority for Coordinate Data Entry** area in the **User Preferences** tab of the **Options** dialog box.

Object Snap Overrides

object snap override: A method of entering a single object snap mode at the keyboard while a tool is in use. The selected object snap temporarily overrides the running object snap modes.

Enter an *object snap override* when you are prompted to select a point and the active running object snaps are conflicting with each other, or the desired snap is not running. Object snap overrides allow you to pick a location on an existing object that corresponds only to the selected object snap mode. After you select the point, the running object snap modes are reactivated.

After you access a tool, the preferred technique for activating an object snap override is to use the **Object Snap** shortcut menu. To use this method, press and hold the [Shift] key and then right-click to display the shortcut menu. See **Figure 7-5.** Select an

Figure 7-5.
The **Object Snap** shortcut menu provides quick access to object snap overrides.

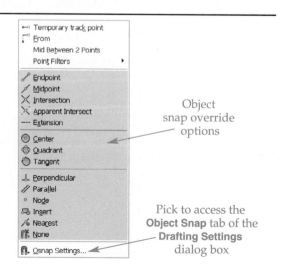

Object snap override options

Pick to access the **Object Snap** tab of the **Drafting Settings** dialog box

AutoCAD and Its Applications—Basics

object snap mode. Then move the crosshairs near the location on an existing object where the object snap is intended to snap. When you see the marker, pick to locate the point at the exact position on the existing object. This technique for accessing the **Object Snap** shortcut menu can be used regardless of the tool you use or whether you are about to pick the first point or an additional point.

By default, when you locate a start point using some tools, an alternative for selecting an object snap is to right-click without holding the [Shift] key. This option functions the same except that the **Object Snap** shortcut menu is available from the **Snap Overrides** cascading menu. Examples include selecting the center of a circle or an additional point using other tools, such as the second point of a line.

NOTE

Each object snap override can be activated by typing the first three letters of the name of the object snap. For example, you can enter END to activate the **Endpoint** object snap or CEN to activate the **Center** object snap.

PROFESSIONAL TIP

Remember that object snap modes are not tools. They are, however, used in conjunction with tools. If you activate an object snap mode when no tool is active, AutoCAD displays an error message.

Object Snap Modes

Object snap modes identify the object snap points used to accurately construct objects. Several object snap modes are available. Most object snap modes can be activated and used as either running object snaps or object snap overrides, while other modes are available only as object snap overrides.

Endpoint object snap

In many cases, you need to connect new geometry to the endpoint of an existing line, arc, or spline. To pick a point using the **Endpoint** object snap mode, move the crosshairs toward the endpoint of any line, arc, or spline. The endpoint marker appears at the endpoint to be picked. Pick to locate the point at the exact endpoint. Refer again to Figure 7-4.

Midpoint object snap

The **Midpoint** object snap mode finds and picks the midpoint of a line, polyline, or arc. To pick a point using the **Midpoint** object snap mode, position the crosshairs near the midpoint of the object. The midpoint marker appears at the midpoint to be picked. Pick to locate the point at the exact midpoint. See Figure 7-6.

Exercise 7-1

Complete the exercise on the Student CD.

Figure 7-6.
Using the **Midpoint** object snap.

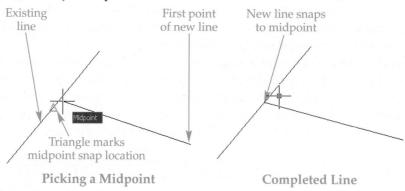

Picking a Midpoint   Completed Line

Center object snap

The **Center** object snap mode allows you to snap to the center point of a circle, donut, ellipse, elliptical arc, polyline arc, or arc. To pick a point using the **Center** object snap mode, be sure to move the crosshairs near the perimeter, not the center point, of the object. For example, when you locate the center of a large circle, the **Center** object snap mode will *not* locate the center if the crosshairs is not near the perimeter of the circle. When you see the center marker, pick to locate the point at the exact center. See Figure 7-7.

Quadrant object snap

quadrant: Quarter section of a circle, donut, or ellipse.

The **Quadrant** object snap mode finds the 0°, 90°, 180°, and 270° *quadrant* points on a circle, donut, ellipse, elliptical arc, polyline arc, or arc. To pick a point using the **Quadrant** object snap mode, move the crosshairs near the intended quadrant on the object. When you see the quadrant marker, pick to locate the point at the exact quadrant position. See Figure 7-8.

> **NOTE**
>
> Quadrant positions are unaffected by the current angle zero direction, but they always coincide with the current world coordinate system (WCS). The quadrant points of circles, donuts, and arcs are at the top, bottom, left, and right, regardless of the rotation of the object. The quadrant points of ellipses and elliptical arcs, however, rotate with the objects.

Figure 7-7.
Using the **Center** object snap.

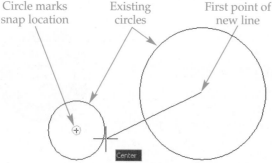
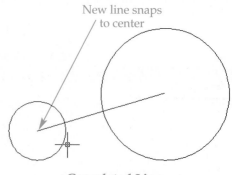

Picking a Center Point   Completed Line

Figure 7-8.
The four quadrant points of a circle can be selected with the **Quadrant** object snap.

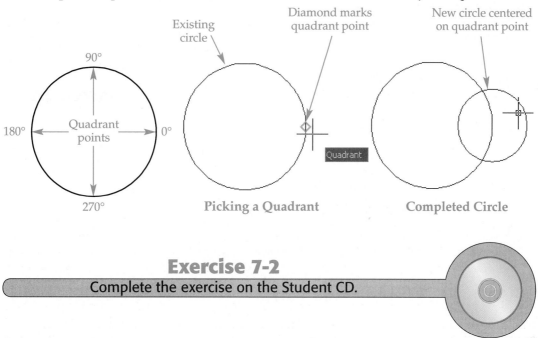

Picking a Quadrant   Completed Circle

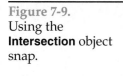

Exercise 7-2
Complete the exercise on the Student CD.

Intersection object snap

The **Intersection** object snap mode is used to snap to the intersection of two or more objects. To pick a point using the **Intersection** object snap mode, move the crosshairs near an intersection. When you see the intersection marker, pick to locate the point at the exact intersection. See Figure 7-9.

Apparent intersection object snap

Three-dimensional objects can display an *apparent intersection* when viewed from certain angles. Whether they actually intersect or not, the **Apparent Intersection** object snap returns the coordinate point where the objects appear to intersect in the current view. This is a valuable option when working with 3D drawings. Creating and editing 3D objects is described in *AutoCAD and Its Applications—Advanced*.

apparent intersection: The point where two objects created in 3D space appear to intersect in the current view.

Extension object snap

The **Extension** object snap mode is used to find any point along the imaginary extension of an existing line, polyline, or polyline arc. The **Extension** object snap differs from most other snaps because it requires *acquired points*. When an acquired point is found, a point symbol (+) marks the location. If the new object is to be created at the intersection of extensions from two objects, the crosshairs must be placed over the second object to locate its *tracking vector*. The last point, which is the actual snap point, can be placed anywhere along the tracking vector, including the intersection of two *extension paths*.

acquired point: A point found by moving the crosshairs over a point on an existing object to reference for use when picking a new point.

tracking vectors: Temporary lines that are displayed at specific angles, typically 0°, 90°, 180°, and 270°.

extension path: Dashed line or arc that extends from the acquired point to the current location of the crosshairs.

Figure 7-9.
Using the
Intersection object
snap.

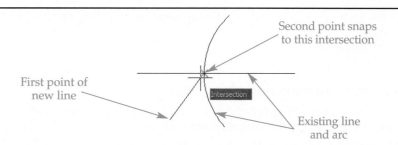

First point of new line

Second point snaps to this intersection

Existing line and arc

Figure 7-10.
The **Extension** object snap can be used to create a line from an extended intersection to an extended endpoint.

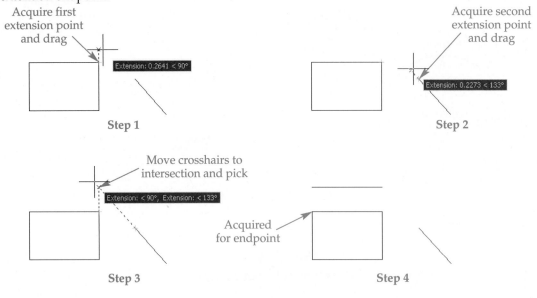

Figure 7-11.
Using the **Extension** object snap to create a line .8 unit away from a rectangle.

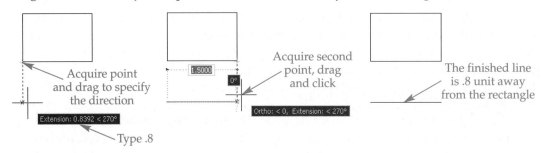

Figure 7-10 shows an example of how the **Extension** object snap mode is used to create a new line anywhere along the extension of an existing object. The first acquired point is found by moving the crosshairs directly over the upper-right corner of the rectangle. The tooltip for the extension is displayed, and the + symbol becomes visible at the end of the line (upper-right corner of the rectangle). The second acquired point is found in the same manner at the endpoint of the line on the right. Pick near the intersection of the two tracking vectors to locate the start point of the new line.

The **Extension** object snap can also be used to create the new line a specific distance away from the end of the old line. In Figure 7-11, the distance (.8) is typed while the first extension is displayed.

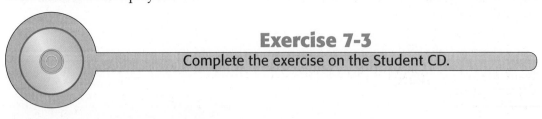

Exercise 7-3
Complete the exercise on the Student CD.

extended intersection: Object snap override in which the objects are selected one at a time and the intersection point is located automatically.

Extended intersection object snap

The *extended intersection* object snap is available only as an object snap override. When using **Extended Intersection**, you select the objects one at a time with the **Intersection** object snap, and the intersection point is automatically located. This is

AutoCAD and Its Applications—Basics

Figure 7-12.
Finding the extended intersection of two objects. A—Select the first object. B—When the second object is selected, the extended intersection becomes the snap point. C—The completed line.

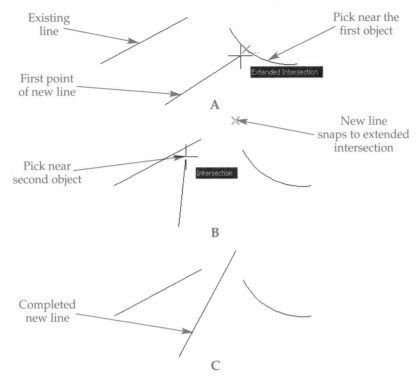

useful when two objects do not actually intersect and you need to access the point where these objects would intersect if they were extended.

To activate **Extended Intersection**, select the **Intersection** object snap override and pick an object (rather than an intersection). If the crosshairs is near an object, but not close to an actual intersection, the tooltip reads Extended Intersection, and the AutoSnap marker is followed by an ellipsis (...). **Figure 7-12** shows the use of **Extended Intersection** to find an intersection point between a line and an arc.

NOTE

If the intersection point is not in the currently visible screen area, the AutoSnap marker is not displayed when you select the second object. You can still confirm the point before picking by reading the tooltip, which confirms that the objects intersect somewhere beyond the currently visible area. If you select two objects that could not intersect, no AutoSnap marker or tooltip is displayed, and no intersection point is found if the pick is made.

Exercise 7-4
Complete the exercise on the Student CD.

Perpendicular object snap

In geometric construction, it is common to draw one object perpendicular to another. This is easily done using the **Perpendicular** object snap mode. This mode can be used with arcs, elliptical arcs, ellipses, splines, xlines, multilines, polylines, solids,

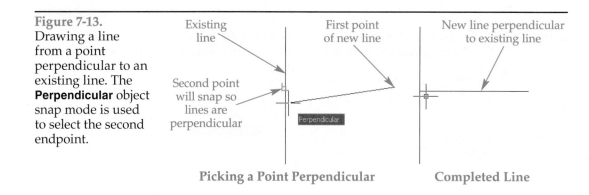

Figure 7-13.
Drawing a line from a point perpendicular to an existing line. The **Perpendicular** object snap mode is used to select the second endpoint.

Existing line

First point of new line

New line perpendicular to existing line

Second point will snap so lines are perpendicular

Perpendicular

Picking a Point Perpendicular

Completed Line

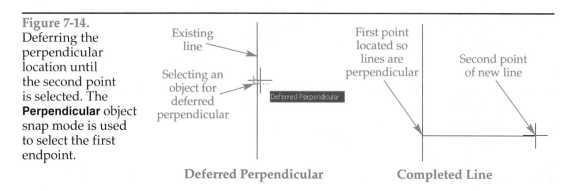

Figure 7-14.
Deferring the perpendicular location until the second point is selected. The **Perpendicular** object snap mode is used to select the first endpoint.

Existing line

First point located so lines are perpendicular

Second point of new line

Selecting an object for deferred perpendicular

Deferred Perpendicular

Deferred Perpendicular

Completed Line

traces, or circles. When you see the perpendicular marker, pick to locate the point exactly perpendicular to the existing object.

Figure 7-13 shows the **Perpendicular** object snap being used to locate the second point of a line perpendicular to a vertical line. In **Figure 7-14,** the object snap is used to start the line perpendicular to each object. The tooltip reads Deferred Perpendicular, and the AutoSnap marker is followed by an ellipsis (...). The second endpoint determines the location of the entire line in a *deferred perpendicular* condition.

deferred perpendicular:
Calculation of the perpendicular point is delayed until another point is picked.

NOTE

Perpendicularity is calculated from points picked and not as a relationship between objects. Also, perpendicularity is measured at the point of intersection. Therefore, it is possible to draw a line perpendicular to a circle or arc.

Exercise 7-5
Complete the exercise on the Student CD.

Tangent object snap

The **Tangent** object snap is used to align objects tangentially to an arc, circle, ellipse, elliptical arc, or spline. In **Figure 7-15,** the endpoint of a line is located using the **Tangent** object snap mode. The first point is selected normally. As the crosshairs is placed near the tangent point on the circle, the tangent marker appears, allowing you to pick the exact point of tangency.

When creating an object tangent to another object, you may need to pick multiple points to fix the tangency point. For example, the point at which a line is tangent to a circle

Figure 7-15.
Using the **Tangent** object snap.

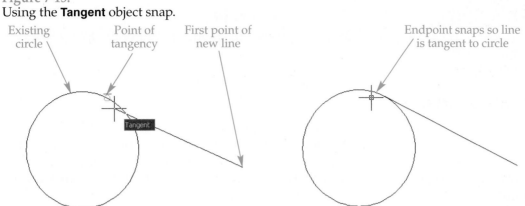

Existing circle — Point of tangency — First point of new line

Endpoint snaps so line is tangent to circle

Picking a Tangent Point

Completed Line

cannot be found without knowing the locations of both ends of the line. Until both points have been specified, the object snap specification is for *deferred tangency*. Once both endpoints are known, the tangency is calculated, and the object is drawn in the correct location. See Figure 7-16.

deferred tangency: Calculation of the point of tangency is delayed until both points have been picked.

Figure 7-16.
Drawing a line tangent to two circles.

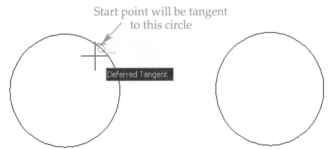

Start point will be tangent to this circle

First Tangent Point Deferred

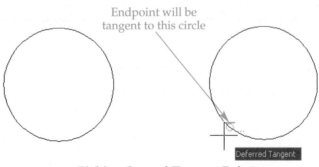

Endpoint will be tangent to this circle

Picking Second Tangent Point

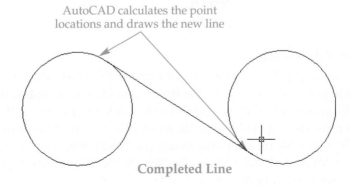

AutoCAD calculates the point locations and draws the new line

Completed Line

Exercise 7-6
Complete the exercise on the Student CD.

Parallel object snap

The process of drawing, moving, or copying objects that are not horizontal or vertical is improved with the **Parallel** object snap mode. This option is used to find any point along an imaginary line that is parallel to an existing line or polyline. The **Parallel** object snap is similar to the **Extension** object snap in that it uses an acquired point.

The acquired point is found by pausing the crosshairs over any point on the line to which the new object is to be parallel. When you see the parallel marker, you know the point has been acquired. Move the crosshairs in a direction parallel to the existing line to display the + symbol on the existing line. As you near a position parallel to the existing line, a parallel dashed line, known as the *parallel alignment path*, extends from the location of the crosshairs. When the parallel alignment path is displayed, the **Parallel** marker appears on the existing line. The last point, which is the actual snap point, can be placed anywhere along the parallel alignment path. See Figure 7-17.

parallel alignment path: A dashed line, parallel to the existing line, that extends from the location of the crosshairs when the **Parallel** object snap is in use.

Exercise 7-7
Complete the exercise on the Student CD.

Figure 7-17.
Using the **Parallel** object snap option to draw a line parallel to an existing line. A—Select the first endpoint for the new line, select the **Parallel** object snap, and then move the crosshairs near the existing line to acquire a point. B—After the parallel point is acquired, move the crosshairs near the location of the parallel line to display an extension path.

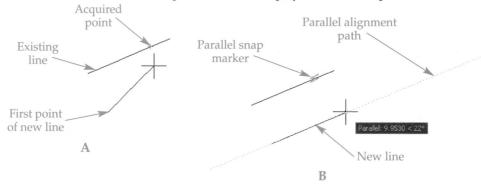

Node object snap

You can snap to point objects using the **Node** object snap mode. Point objects include points drawn using the **Point**, **Divide**, and **Measure** tools, as well as the extension line start points in dimensions. In order for object snap to find the point object, the point must be in a visible display mode. Controlling the point display mode is covered in Chapter 8. To pick a point using the **Node** object snap mode, move the crosshairs toward a point object. When you see the node marker, pick to locate the new point exactly on the point object.

AutoCAD and Its Applications—Basics

Nearest object snap

Use the **Nearest** mode to specify a point that is directly on an object, but cannot be located with any of the other object snap modes, or when the location of the intersection is not critical. To pick a point using the **Nearest** object snap mode, move the crosshairs over an existing object. When you see the nearest marker, pick to locate the point on the object closest to the crosshairs location.

Consider drawing a line object that is to end on another line. Trying to pick the point with the crosshairs is inaccurate because you are relying only on your screen and mouse resolution. The line you draw may fall short or extend past the line. Using **Nearest** ensures that the point is precisely on the object.

PROFESSIONAL TIP

Use object snap modes both when drawing and when editing. With practice, object snap use becomes second nature, greatly increasing your productivity and accuracy.

Exercise 7-8

Complete the exercise on the Student CD.

Temporary track point snap

Using **Temporary track point** is similar to using the **Extension** object snap mode. The main difference is that with **Temporary track point**, you actually pick points of reference, instead of acquiring points as with the **Extension** object snap mode. For example, temporary tracking can be used to place a circle at the center of a rectangle. See Figure 7-18. Though not necessary, temporary track points are usually selected using running object snaps or object snap overrides.

In Figure 7-18A a rectangle has been drawn. The **Circle, Radius** tool is then accessed to draw a circle in the center of the rectangle. At the Specify center point for circle or [3P/2P/Ttr (tan tan radius)]: prompt, the **Temporary tracking point** snap mode is selected. A **Midpoint** object snap mode is then used to pick the midpoint of one of the vertical lines. This establishes the Y coordinate of the rectangle's center. In Figure 7-18B the Specify center point for circle or [3P/2P/Ttr (tan tan radius)]: prompt appears again, the **Temporary tracking point** snap mode is selected, and a **Midpoint** object snap mode is used to pick the midpoint of one of the horizontal lines. This establishes the X coordinate of the rectangle's center. Finally, in Figure 7-18C, the point where the two tracking vectors intersect is selected, and a point is picked to define the radius of the circle.

Figure 7-18.
Using temporary tracking to locate the center of a rectangle. A—The midpoint of the left line is acquired. B—The midpoint of the bottom line is acquired. C—The center point of the circle is located at the intersection of the tracking vectors.

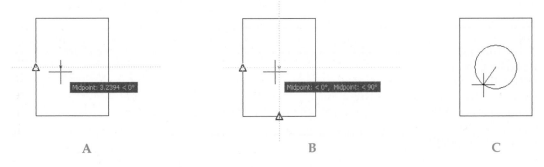

A   B   C

The direction in which you move the crosshairs once you establish a temporary tracking point determines whether the X or Y component is used. In the previous example, after picking the first tracking point, the crosshairs is moved horizontally. This means the Y axis value of the previous point is being used, and tracking is now ready for an X coordinate specification. After moving the crosshairs horizontally, you notice that movement is locked in a horizontal mode. If you need to move the crosshairs vertically, move it back to the previously picked point, and then move the crosshairs vertically. Use this method whenever you need to switch between horizontal and vertical movements.

Snap from

The **From** point object snap allows you to locate a point from a specified reference base point using a coordinate entry technique such as relative coordinate, polar coordinate, or direct distance entry. The example in Figure 7-19 shows the center point for a circle being established as a polar coordinate entry from the midpoint of an existing line.

In Figure 7-19, a line has been drawn. Access the **Circle, Radius** tool to draw a circle away from the line. At the Specify center point for circle or [3P/2P/Ttr (tan tan radius)]: prompt, select the **From** snap mode. Then use the **Midpoint** object snap mode to pick the midpoint of the line. At the <Offset>: prompt, enter the polar coordinate @2<45 to establish the center of the circle 2 units and at a 45° angle from the midpoint of the line. Picking a point to define the radius of the circle completes the operation.

Mid between 2 points snap

A point can be located at the midpoint of two picks by using the **Mid Between 2 Points** feature. This is different from the **Midpoint** object snap, which finds the midpoint of a selected object. **Mid Between 2 Points** picks the midpoint between any two points in the drawing area and can be used in conjunction with object snap modes. The example in Figure 7-20 locates the center of a circle between two line endpoints.

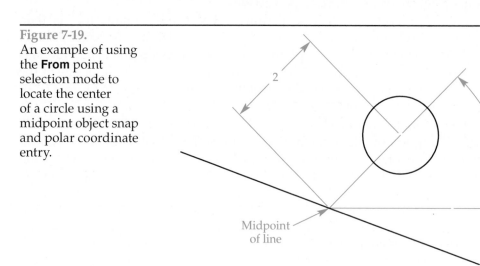

Figure 7-19.
An example of using the **From** point selection mode to locate the center of a circle using a midpoint object snap and polar coordinate entry.

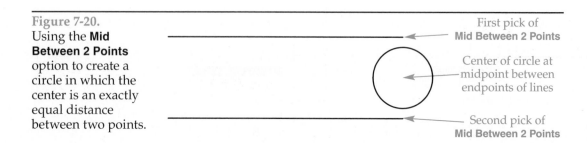

Figure 7-20.
Using the **Mid Between 2 Points** option to create a circle in which the center is an exactly equal distance between two points.

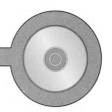

AutoTrack

Creating geometry that lines up with existing geometry is very common in drafting and design. AutoTrack makes this procedure straightforward and accurate by creating *alignment paths* and tracking vectors. The two AutoTrack modes are object snap tracking and polar tracking. All tools requiring a point selection can make use of AutoTrack.

alignment paths: Temporary lines and arcs that coincide with the position of existing objects.

Object Snap Tracking

Object snap tracking has two requirements: running object snaps must be active and the crosshairs must pause over the selected point long enough to acquire the point. Pick the **Object Snap Tracking** button on the status bar, press the [F11] function key, or use the **Object Snap Tracking On (F11)** check box in the **Object Snap** tab of the **Drafting Settings** dialog box to toggle object snap tracking on and off. Object snap tracking mode is only available for points selected by the currently active object snap modes. When running object snaps are active, all selected object snap modes are available for object snap tracking.

object snap tracking: Mode that provides horizontal and vertical alignment paths for locating points after a point is acquired with object snap.

In Figure 7-21, object snap tracking is used in conjunction with the **Perpendicular** and **Midpoint** running object snaps to draw a line that is 2 units long and perpendicular to the existing slanted line. The running object snap modes are set before the **Line** tool is accessed to draw the new line. Running object snaps and object snap tracking are active.

In Figure 7-22, object snap tracking is used to position a circle directly above the midpoint of a horizontal line and to the right of the midpoint of an angled line, with only the **Midpoint** running object snap active. Running object snaps and object snap tracking are active. After accessing the **Circle, Radius** tool, pause the crosshairs near the midpoint of the horizontal line to acquire it, and then pause the crosshairs near the midpoint of the angled line to acquire it. Move the crosshairs to the position as shown in the second step of Figure 7-22 until two tracking vectors appear. Pick to locate the center of the circle, and complete the operation by entering a radius.

Figure 7-21.
Using object snap tracking to draw a line. A—Select the midpoint of the existing line to locate the start point of the new line. B—Move the crosshairs slightly away from the existing line to display the perpendicular marker and the alignment path. C—The completed line, with the second endpoint identified using direct distance entry along the alignment path.

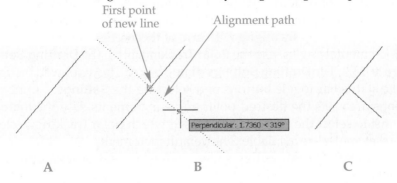

First point
of new line

Alignment path

Perpendicular: 1.7360 < 319°

A   B   C

Figure 7-22.
Object snap tracking is used to position this circle in line with the midpoints of each line.

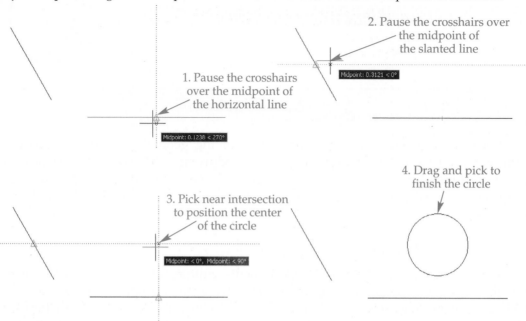

PROFESSIONAL TIP

Use object snap tracking whenever possible to complete tasks that require you to reference locations on existing objects. Often the combination of running object snaps and object snap tracking is the quickest way to construct geometry.

Exercise 7-10
Complete the exercise on the Student CD.

Polar Tracking

Polar tracking was introduced in Chapter 3. Pick the **Polar Tracking** button on the status bar, press the [F10] function key, or use the **Polar Tracking On (F10)** check box in the **Polar Tracking** tab of the **Drafting Settings** dialog box to toggle polar tracking on and off. When polar tracking mode is turned on, the crosshairs snaps to preset incremental angles if a point is being located relative to another point. For example, in the **LINE** tool, polar tracking is not active for the first point selection, but it is available for the second and subsequent point selections. Polar tracking vectors are displayed as dotted lines whenever the crosshairs aligns with any of these preset angles.

To set incremental angles, use the **Polar Tracking** tab in the **Drafting Settings** dialog box. See **Figure 7-23.** The **Drafting Settings** dialog box can be displayed by right-clicking on any of the status bar toggle buttons and selecting the **Settings...** option. The **Polar Angle Settings** area sets the desired polar angle increments. Use the **Increment angle** drop-down list to select the angle increments at which polar tracking vectors occur. A variety of preset angles are available. The default increment is 90, which provides angle increments every 90°. The 30° setting shown in **Figure 7-23** provides polar tracking in 30° increments.

Figure 7-23.
The **Polar Tracking** tab of the **Drafting Settings** dialog box.

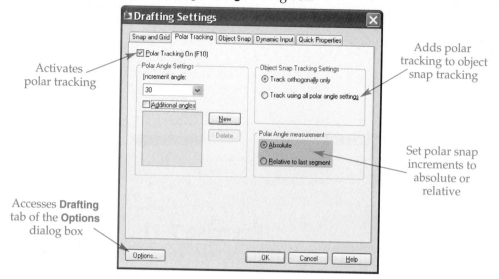

Activates polar tracking

Accesses **Drafting** tab of the **Options** dialog box

Adds polar tracking to object snap tracking

Set polar snap increments to absolute or relative

NOTE

The preset angle increments available in the **Polar Angle Settings** area of the **Drafting Settings** dialog box are also available in the shortcut menu displayed when you right-click on the **Polar Tracking** button on the status bar.

You can define specific polar tracking angles by picking the **New** button in the **Polar Angle Settings** area. Type a new angle value in the text box that appears in the **Additional angles** window. Pick the **New** button each time you want to add another angle. Additional angles are used together with the increment angle setting when you use polar tracking. Only the specific additional angle you enter is recognized, not each increment of the angle. Use the **Delete** button to remove angles from the list. Make the additional angle(s) inactive by unchecking the **Additional angles** check box.

The **Object Snap Tracking Settings** area sets the angles available with object snap tracking. If **Track orthogonally only** is selected, only horizontal and vertical alignment paths are active. If **Track using all polar angle settings** is selected, alignment paths are active for all polar snap angles.

The **Polar Angle measurement** setting determines whether the polar snap increments are constant or relative to the previous segment. If **Absolute** is selected, the polar snap angles are measured from the base angle of 0° set for the drawing. If **Relative to last segment** is selected, each increment angle is measured from a base angle established by the previously drawn segment.

Figure 7-24 shows how a parallelogram can be drawn with polar tracking active and set for 30° angle increments. Access the **LINE** tool and select the first point. Then move the crosshairs to the right while the polar alignment path indicates <0°. Enter a direct distance value. Move the crosshairs to the 60° polar alignment path and enter a direct distance value. Move the crosshairs to the 180° polar alignment path and enter a value. Finally, use polar tracking with an angle of 240° and a specified line distance, or use the **Close** option to finish the parallelogram.

NOTE

You cannot use polar tracking and **Ortho** at the same time. AutoCAD automatically turns **Ortho** off when polar tracking is on, and it turns polar tracking off when **Ortho** is on.

Figure 7-24.
Using polar tracking with 30° angle increments to draw a parallelogram. A—After the first side is drawn, the alignment path and direct distance entry are used to create the second side. B—A horizontal alignment path is used for the third side. C—The parallelogram is completed with the Close option.

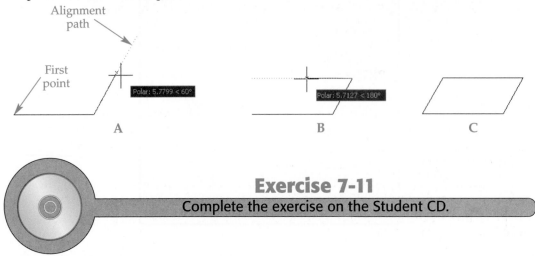

Alignment path

First point

Polar: 5.7799 < 60°

Polar: 5.7127 < 180°

A   B   C

Exercise 7-11
Complete the exercise on the Student CD.

Polar tracking with polar snaps

Polar tracking can also be used in conjunction with polar snaps. If polar snaps are used to draw the parallelogram in Figure 7-24, for example, there is no need to type the length of the line, because you set both the angle increment and a length increment. The desired angle and length increments are established in the **Snap and Grid** tab of the **Drafting Settings** dialog box. See Figure 7-25.

To activate polar snap, pick the **PolarSnap** button in the **Snap type & style** area of the dialog box. Picking this button activates the **Polar spacing** area and deactivates the **Snap** area. The length of the polar snap increment is set in the **Polar distance:** box. If the **Polar distance:** setting is 0, the polar snap distance will be the orthogonal snap distance. Figure 7-26 shows a parallelogram being drawn with 30° angle increments and length increments of .75. The lengths of the parallelogram sides are 1.5 and .75.

Figure 7-25.
The **Snap and Grid** tab of the **Drafting Settings** dialog box is used to set polar snap spacing.

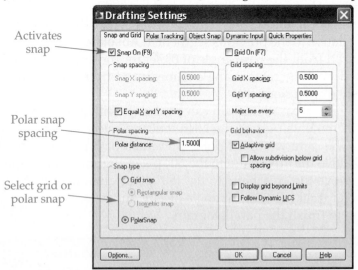

Activates snap

Polar snap spacing

Select grid or polar snap

Figure 7-26.
Drawing a parallelogram with polar snap.

A   B   C   D

Using polar tracking overrides

It takes some time to set up the polar tracking and the polar snap options, but it is worth the effort if you have several objects to draw that can take advantage of this feature. Use the polar tracking overrides to perform polar tracking when you need to define only one point. Polar tracking overrides work for the specified angle whether polar tracking is on or off. To activate a polar tracking override, type a less than symbol (<) followed by the desired angle when AutoCAD asks you to specify a point. For example, after you access the **LINE** tool and pick a first point, enter <30 to set a 30° override. Then move the crosshairs in the desired 30° direction and enter a distance, such as 1.5 to draw a 1.5-unit line.

Exercise 7-12
Complete the exercise on the Student CD.

Supplemental Material

AutoSnap and AutoTrack Options
The **Options** dialog box provides several options for controlling the appearance and function of AutoSnap and AutoTrack. Refer to the Student CD: Supplemental Materials > AutoSnap and AutoTrack Options for more information about options specific to these drawing tools.

Template Development
Chapter 7

You will find that you need different object snaps and polar tracking settings depending on the type of drawing you are creating. These settings can be specified in your drawing templates to save time and increase efficiency. Refer to the Student CD for detailed instructions to add these settings to your mechanical, architectural, and civil drawing templates.

Chapter Test

Answer the following questions. Write your answers on a separate sheet of paper or complete the electronic chapter test on the Student CD.

1. Define the term *object snap*.
2. What is an AutoSnap tooltip?
3. Name the following AutoSnap markers:

   A.   B.   C.

   D.   E.   F.

   G.   H.   I.

   J.   K.   L.

4. Define the term *running object snap*.
5. How do you activate the **Object Snap** shortcut menu?
6. How do you set running object snaps?
7. How do you access the **Drafting Settings** dialog box to change object snap settings?
8. If you are using running object snaps and want to make several point specifications without the aid of object snap, but want to continue the same running object snaps after making the desired point selections, what is the easiest way to turn off the running object snaps temporarily?
9. If you are using running object snaps and you want to make a single point selection without the effects of the running object snaps, what do you do?
10. Describe the object snap override.
11. Where are the four quadrant points on a circle?
12. What is the situation when the tooltip reads Extended Intersection?
13. What does it mean when the tooltip reads Deferred Perpendicular?
14. What conditions must exist for the tooltip to read Tangent?
15. What is a deferred tangency?
16. Give the tool and entries needed to draw a line tangent to an existing circle and perpendicular to an existing line:
    A. Tool: _____
    B. Specify first point: _____
    C. to _____
    D. Specify next point or [Undo]: _____
    E. to _____
17. Which object snaps depend on "acquired points" to function?
18. What two display features does AutoTrack use to help you line up new objects with existing geometry?
19. What are the two requirements to use object snap tracking?
20. When are polar tracking vectors displayed as dotted lines?

Drawing Problems

Load AutoCAD for each of the following problems, and use one of your templates or start a new drawing using your own variables.

▼ Basic

1. Draw the object below using the object snap modes. Do not draw the dimensions. Save the drawing as P7-1.

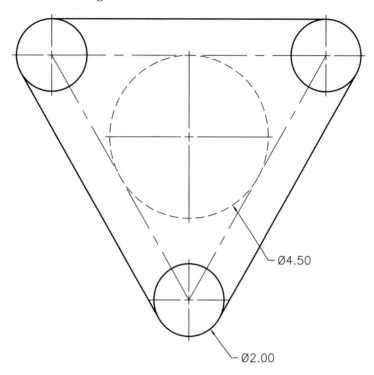

Ø4.50

Ø2.00

2. Draw the highlighted objects below, and then use the object snap modes indicated to draw the remaining objects. Save the drawing as P7-2.

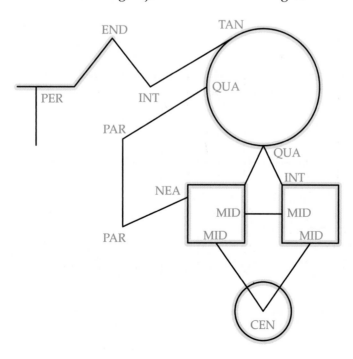

3. Draw the object below using the **Endpoint, Tangent, Perpendicular,** and **Quadrant** object snap modes. Save the drawing as P7-3.

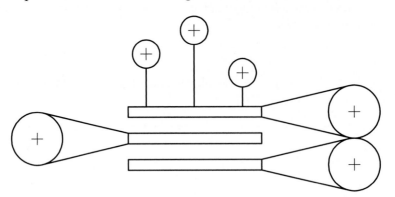

4. Draw the pipe separator shown below. Use object snaps and tracking to place the objects correctly. Do not dimension. Save the drawing as P7-4.

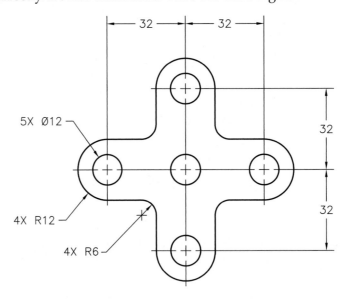

▼ **Intermediate**

5. Use the **Midpoint, Endpoint, Tangent, Perpendicular,** and **Quadrant** object snap modes to draw these electrical switch schematics. Do not draw the text. Save the drawing as P7-5.

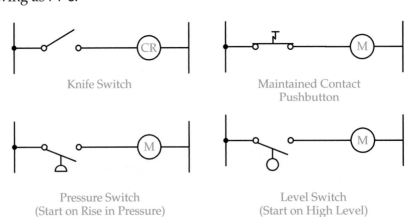

6. Draw the elbow shown. Save the drawing as P7-6.

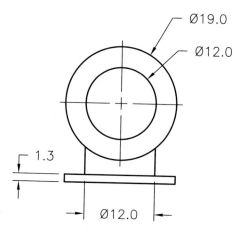

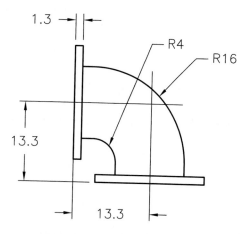

Ø19.0
Ø12.0
1.3
Ø12.0
1.3
R4
R16
13.3
13.3

7. Draw the elbow shown. Save the drawing as P7-7.

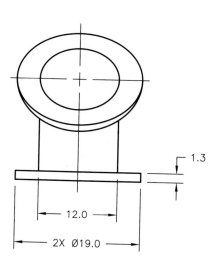

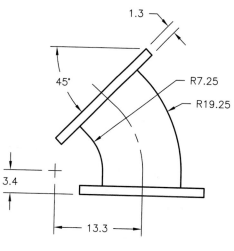

1.3
1.3
45°
R7.25
R19.25
3.4
13.3
12.0
2X Ø19.0

8. Draw the object shown. Do not draw dimensions. Save the drawing as P7-8.

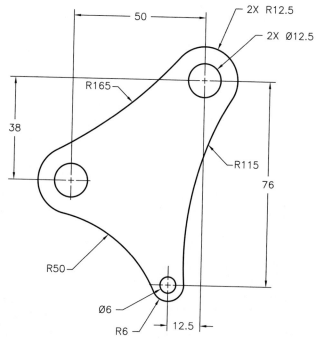

50
2X R12.5
2X Ø12.5
R165
38
R115
76
R50
Ø6
R6
12.5

9. Draw the object shown. Do not draw dimensions. Save the drawing as P7-9.

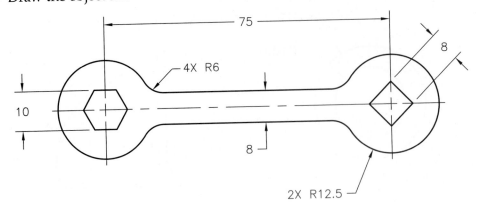

10. Draw the object shown. Do not draw dimensions. Save the drawing as P7-10.

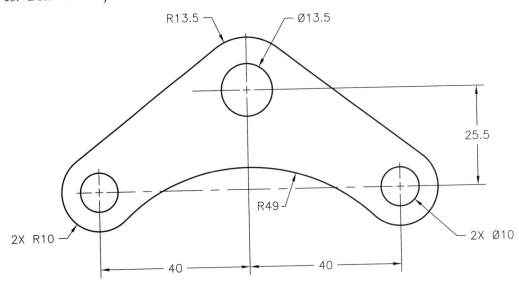

11. Use object snap modes to draw this elementary diagram. Do not draw the text. Save the drawing as P7-11.

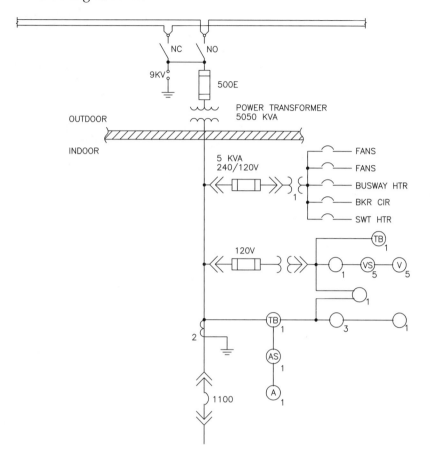

12. Draw the object shown. Do not draw dimensions. Save the drawing as P7-12.

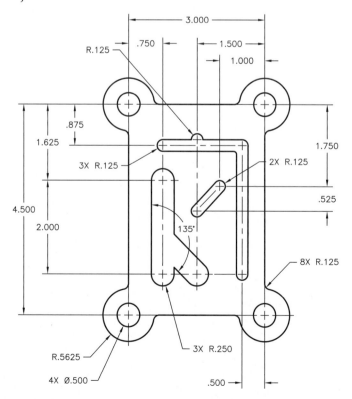

13. Design and draft a hammer similar to the one shown below using dimensions of your choice. Use the overall dimensions given as a basis for your design. Save the drawing as P7-13.

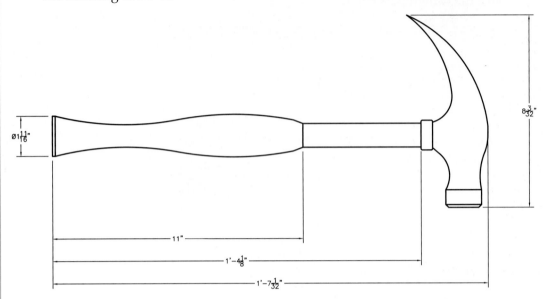

Construction Tools and Multiview Drawings

Learning Objectives

After completing this chapter, you will be able to do the following:

✓ Use the **OFFSET** tool to draw parallel lines and curves.
✓ Mark points on objects at equal lengths using the **DIVIDE** tool.
✓ Set designated increments on an existing object using the **MEASURE** tool.
✓ Create construction lines using the **XLINE** and **RAY** tools.
✓ Create orthographic multiview drawings and auxiliary views.

This chapter explains how to create parallel offset copies, divide objects, and place point objects. These skills, and the other geometry-creating skills you have acquired, can be applied to create multiview drawings.

Offsetting Parallel Lines and Curves

The **OFFSET** tool is one of the most common geometric construction tools. Use the **OFFSET** tool to form parallel lines and polylines. For example, existing lines or polylines can be offset to construct the thickness of architectural floor plan walls. Existing circles, arcs, and curves can be offset to form concentric objects. For example, the wall thickness of a pipe can be formed by offsetting a circle.

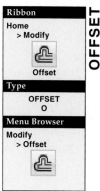

Specifying a Distance to Offset

Often the best way to use the **OFFSET** tool is to enter an offset value at the Specify offset distance or [Through/Erase/Layer] <*current*>: prompt. The last offset distance used is the default and is shown in brackets. For example, if you want to draw two parallel circles a distance of .1 unit apart, access the **OFFSET** tool, and at the Specify offset distance or [Through/Erase/Layer] <*current*>: prompt, enter a value of .1. Pick the circle you want to offset, and then pick the side of the circle on which the offset occurs. See Figure 8-1. The **OFFSET** tool remains active, allowing you to pick another object to offset using the same offset distance. When you are finished using the tool, press the [Enter] key, the [Esc] key or the space bar, or choose the **Exit** option.

If you do not know the offset value, but two reference points exist in the drawing area, you can pick a first point and then a second point instead of typing an offset value. The distance between these two points is used as the offset value.

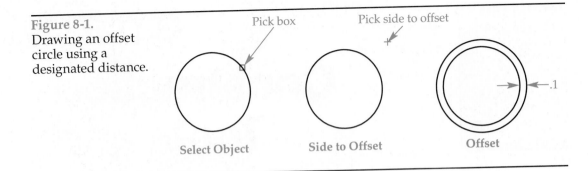

Figure 8-1.
Drawing an offset circle using a designated distance.

Pick box — Pick side to offset

Select Object　　　Side to Offset　　　Offset

.1

When the Select object to offset or [Exit/Undo] <*current*>: prompt first appears, the cursor turns into a pick box. After the object is picked, the cursor turns back into crosshairs. No other selection option (such as window or crossing selection) works with the **OFFSET** tool.

Another option is to pick a point through which the offset will be drawn. After you access the **OFFSET** tool, activate the **Through** option at the Specify offset distance or [Through/Erase/Layer] <*current*>: prompt instead of picking an object to offset. Pick the object you want to offset, and then pick the point through which the offset occurs. See Figure 8-2. The **OFFSET** tool remains active, allowing you to pick another object to offset using the **Through** option. Exit the **OFFSET** tool when you are finished.

Object snap modes can be used to assist in specifying the offset distance. For example, suppose you have a circle and a line and want to draw a concentric circle tangent to the line. For this example, access the **OFFSET** tool, and at the Specify offset distance or [Through/Erase/Layer] <*current*>: prompt, pick the existing circle using the **Quadrant** object snap. Then, at the Specify second point: prompt, pick the existing line using the **Perpendicular** object snap. Pick the circle to select for offsetting, and then pick between the circle and the line to define the side to offset. See Figure 8-3. The **OFFSET** tool remains active, allowing you to pick another object to offset using the new offset distance. Exit the **OFFSET** tool when you are finished.

Erasing the Original Object

When you offset an object, you may want to remove the original object. Instead of offsetting the object and then erasing the source object, you can use the **Erase** option of the **OFFSET** tool to erase the source object when it is offset. Initiate the **OFFSET** tool, enter the **Erase** option, and choose **Yes** at the Erase source object after offsetting? prompt to erase the source object. The **Yes** option remains as the default until it is changed to **No**. Be sure to change this option back to **No** if you do not want the source offset object to be erased the next time you use the **OFFSET** tool. Exit the **OFFSET** tool when you are finished.

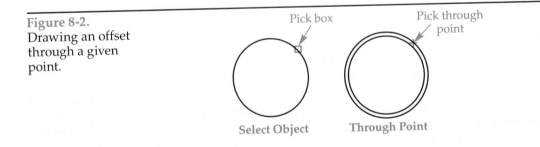

Figure 8-2.
Drawing an offset through a given point.

Pick box　　Pick through point

Select Object　　　Through Point

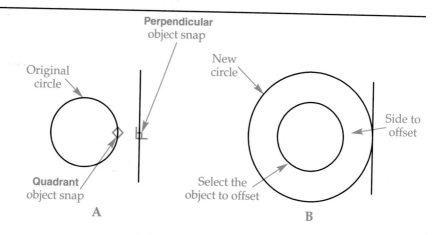

Figure 8-3.
Using the **OFFSET** tool to draw a concentric circle tangent to a line.

Original circle

Perpendicular object snap

New circle

Side to offset

Quadrant object snap

Select the object to offset

A

B

Changing the Layer of the Offset Object

The **Layer** option of the **OFFSET** tool allows you to place the offset object on the current layer. For example, if the offset source object is on the Electrical layer and the offset object needs to be placed on the Lighting layer, this can be done during the offset operation if Lighting is the current layer. After initiating the **OFFSET** tool, enter the **Layer** option and choose **Current** at the Enter layer option for offset objects prompt to create the offset object on the current layer. The **Current** option remains the default until it is changed to **Source**. Be sure to change this option back to **Source** if you want to have the offset object remain on the same layer as the offset source object. Exit the **OFFSET** tool when you are finished.

Offsetting Multiple Times

After the object to offset has been selected, the **Multiple** option can be used to offset an object more than once with the same distance between the objects without reselecting the object to offset. Initiate the **OFFSET** tool, specify the offset distance, and pick the source object. You can then select the **Multiple** option and begin picking to specify the offset direction. See **Figure 8-4.** Exit the **OFFSET** tool when you are finished.

Figure 8-4.
The **Multiple** option can be used to create multiple offsets with the same distance, without picking the source object again.

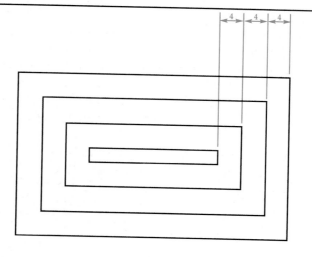

Exercise 8-1

Complete the exercise on the Student CD.

Drawing Points

Points are useful for identifying specific locations on a drawing and for marking positions on objects. You can draw points anywhere on the screen using the **POINT** tool. Once you access the **POINT** tool, you can pick or type coordinates to place points.

The **POINT** tool has two variations: **Single Point** and **Multiple Points**. To place a single point object and then exit the **POINT** tool, access the **POINT** tool using keyboard entry or select the **Single Point** option from the **Point** menu in the menu browser. To draw multiple points without exiting the **POINT** tool, use the **Multiple Points** button on the ribbon or the **Multiple Point** option from the **Point** submenu. Press [Esc] to exit the **POINT** tool.

Setting Point Style

The style and size of points are set using the **Point Style** dialog box. See **Figure 8-5**. By default, points are displayed as dots, which may not show up very well on-screen. Change the point style to make the points more visible. The **Point Style** dialog box contains twenty different point styles. The current point style is highlighted. To change the style, pick the graphic image of the desired style.

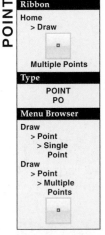

POINT	
Ribbon	
Home	
> Draw	
Multiple Points	
Type	
POINT	
PO	
Menu Browser	
Draw	
> Point	
> Single	
Point	
Draw	
> Point	
> Multiple	
Points	

DDTYPE	
Type	
DDTYPE	
Menu Browser	
Format	
> Point Style...	

Figure 8-5.
The **Point Style** dialog box. This is a quick way to select the point style and change the point size.

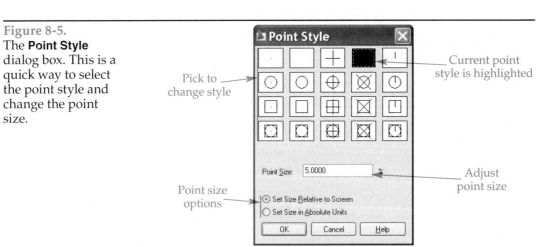

Pick to change style

Current point style is highlighted

Adjust point size

Point size options

Figure 8-6.
Points sized with the **Set Size Relative to Screen** setting change size as the drawing is zoomed. Points sized with the **Set Size in Absolute Units** setting remain a constant size.

Size Setting	Original Point Size	2X Zoom	.5 Zoom
Relative to Screen	⊠	⊠	⊠
Absolute Units	⊠	⊠	⊠

Setting Point Size

Set the point size by entering a value in the **Point Size:** text box of the **Point Style** dialog box. Pick the **Set Size Relative to Screen** button if you want the point size to change in relation to different screen magnifications (zooming in or out). Picking the **Set Size in Absolute Units** option button makes the points appear the same size no matter what screen magnification is used. See **Figure 8-6.**

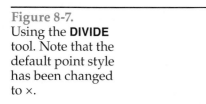

Exercise 8-2
Complete the exercise on the Student CD.

Marking an Object at Specified Increments

A line, circle, arc, or polyline can be divided into an equal number of segments using the **DIVIDE** tool. The **DIVIDE** tool does not break an object into multiple parts. It places point objects or blocks at equally spaced locations.

Access the **DIVIDE** tool and select the object you want to divide. Enter the number of segments to place the points and exit the **DIVIDE** tool. The point style determines the type of marks placed on the object. **Figure 8-7** shows an example of using the **DIVIDE** tool to place points at seven equal increments.

The **Block** option of the **DIVIDE** tool allows you to place a *block* at each division point. Select the **Block** option at the Enter the number of segments or [Block]: prompt to insert a block. AutoCAD asks if the block is to be aligned with the object. Blocks are described in detail in Chapters 26 and 27 of this textbook.

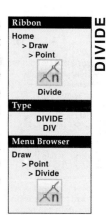

block: A previously drawn symbol or shape.

Figure 8-7.
Using the **DIVIDE** tool. Note that the default point style has been changed to ×.

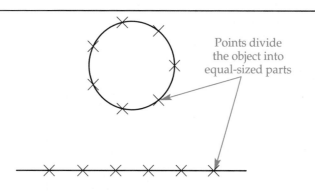

Points divide the object into equal-sized parts

Figure 8-8.
Using the **MEASURE** tool. Notice that the last segment may be shorter than the others, depending on the total length of the object.

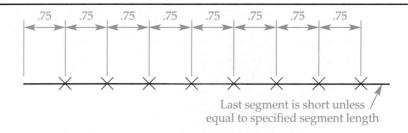

Last segment is short unless equal to specified segment length

MEASURE

Ribbon
Home
> Draw
> Point

Measure

Type
MEASURE
ME

Menu Browser
Draw
> Point
> Measure

Marking an Object at Specified Distances

While the **DIVIDE** tool divides an object into a specified number of increments, the **MEASURE** tool places marks a specified distance apart. Access the **MEASURE** tool to mark points on an object. Then pick the object and enter a value for the distance. The line shown in Figure 8-8 is measured with .75-unit segments. The point style determines the type of marks placed on the object.

Measuring begins at the end closest to where the object is picked. All increments are equal to the specified segment length, except the last segment, which may be shorter. Blocks can be inserted at the given distances using the **Block** option of the **MEASURE** tool.

Exercise 8-3
Complete the exercise on the Student CD.

Construction Lines and Rays

The tracking vectors and alignment paths available with the object snap and AutoTrack tools are examples of *construction lines*. These tools are very efficient for creating objects because vector and alignment "construction lines" appear only when needed. Sometimes, however, you may want construction lines to stay visible while you continue to create geometry. You can draw construction lines, or objects using any drawing tool, such as **LINE** or **ARC**. However, AutoCAD includes **XLINE** and **RAY** tools that are specifically designed for adding construction lines to help lay out a drawing. See Figure 8-9. An AutoCAD construction line, or *xline*, is drawn using the **XLINE** tool. A *ray* is drawn using the **RAY** tool.

construction lines: Lines commonly used to layout a drawing. AutoCAD provides two types of construction lines: xlines and rays.

xline: A line in AutoCAD that is infinite in both directions and is used to help build accurate geometry.

ray: An AutoCAD line object that is infinite in one direction only; considered semi-infinite.

Figure 8-9.
An example of a drawing laid out using construction lines.

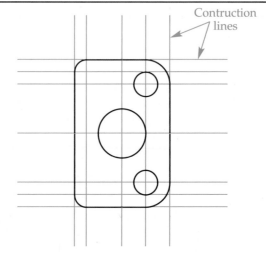

Contruction lines

Create construction geometry on a separate construction layer, named CONST or CONSTRUCTION, for example. The layer can be turned off or frozen when not needed, or construction objects drawn on the layer can be easily recognized and erased if necessary.

Using the Xline Tool

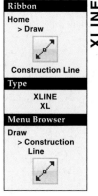

The **XLINE** tool is used to draw infinitely long construction lines, often called *xlines*. The basic xline is drawn by entering or selecting two points through which the construction line passes. After you pick the *root point*, you can select as many points as needed to create additional xlines. Xlines are created between every point and the root point. See Figure 8-10. When you are finished using the **XLINE** tool, right-click or press the [Enter] or [Esc] key or the space bar to exit the tool.

Xline options are available as alternatives to selecting two points to create the xline. After the first xline is drawn, the **XLINE** tool remains active, allowing you to create multiple xlines using the same option. The **Hor** option draws a horizontal construction line through a single specified point. The **Ver** option draws a vertical construction line through a specified point. Place as many horizontal or vertical construction lines as needed, and then exit the **XLINE** tool when you are finished.

Use the **Ang** option to draw a construction line at a specified angle through a selected point. Access the **XLINE** tool and activate the **Ang** option. Enter an angle and then pick a point through which the construction line is to be drawn. Another method is to select two points to define the angle. The **Reference** option of the **Ang** option allows you to use the angle of an existing line object as a reference angle for construction lines. This option is useful when you do not know the angle of the construction line, but you know the angle between an existing object and the construction line. See Figure 8-11.

The **Bisect** option draws a construction line that bisects a specified angle, using the vertex as the root point. This is a convenient option for use in some geometric constructions. See Figure 8-12.

The **Offset** option draws a construction line a specified distance from a selected line object. The **Offset** option of the **XLINE** tool functions much like the **OFFSET** tool. The difference is that the **Offset** option of the **XLINE** tool offsets an xline from the selected line, instead of the line itself. As with the **OFFSET** tool, you can specify an offset distance or use the **Through** option to pick a point through which to draw the construction line.

Ribbon
Home
> Draw
↗↙
Construction Line
Type
XLINE
XL
Menu Browser
Draw
> Construction
Line
↗↙

root point: The first point specified to create a construction line.

Figure 8-10.
Using the **XLINE** tool to draw an infinitely long construction line by picking two points through which the line passes.

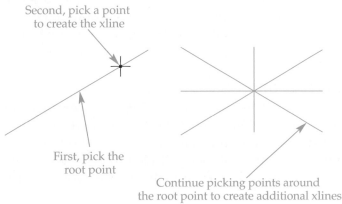

Second, pick a point to create the xline

First, pick the root point

Continue picking points around the root point to create additional xlines

---

Figure 8-11.
Using the **Reference** option of the **XLINE** tool, **Ang** option. A value of 90° is used in this example to make an xline perpendicular to the existing line.

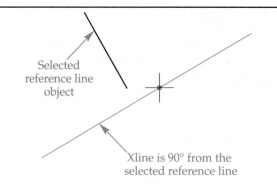

Selected reference line object

Xline is 90° from the selected reference line

Figure 8-12.
Using the **Bisect** option of the **XLINE** tool.

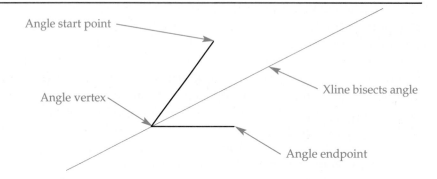

Angle start point

Xline bisects angle

Angle vertex

Angle endpoint

NOTE

Although xlines are infinite, they do not change the drawing extents. This means they have no effect on zooming operations.

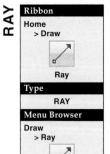

Exercise 8-4
Complete the exercise on the Student CD.

Using the Ray Tool

RAY

Ribbon
Home
> Draw

Ray

Type
RAY

Menu Browser
Draw
> Ray

The **RAY** tool is limited, compared to the **XLINE** tool. The **RAY** tool allows you to specify the point of origin and a point through which the ray passes. In this respect, the **RAY** tool works much like the default option of the **XLINE** tool. The ray, however, is infinite only in the direction of the second pick point.

Once you access the **RAY** tool, enter a coordinate or pick a point for the root point of the ray. Then pick a second point to create the ray. Continue defining points to create additional rays from the same root point. When you are finished using the **RAY** tool, right-click or press the [Enter] or [Esc] key or the space bar to exit.

Editing Construction Lines and Rays

Construction lines created using the **XLINE** and **RAY** tools are modified using standard editing tools, described in Chapters 12, 13, and 14. Xlines and rays change into a new object type when infinite ends are trimmed off. If one end of a construction line is trimmed off, it becomes a ray. If the infinite end of a ray is trimmed off, it becomes a normal line object. Therefore, in many cases, your construction lines can be modified to become part of the actual drawing. This approach can save a significant amount of time in many drawings.

Multiview Drawings

Each field of drafting has its own method to present views of a product. Architectural drafting uses plan views, exterior elevations, and sections. In electronics drafting, symbols are placed in a schematic diagram to show a circuit layout. In civil drafting, contour lines are used to show the topography of land. Mechanical drafting uses *multiview drawings*.

Multiview drawings are based on the standard ASME Y14.3M, *Multiview and Sectional View Drawings*. The views of a multiview drawing are created through **orthographic projection**. An imaginary **projection plane** is placed parallel to the object. Thus, the line of sight is perpendicular to the object. This results in views that appear two-dimensional. See **Figure 8-13.**

Six two-dimensional views show all sides of an object. The six views are the front, right side, left side, top, bottom, and rear. The views are placed in a standard arrangement so others can read the drawing. The front view is the central, or most important, view. Other views are placed around the front view. See **Figure 8-14.** Notice in this

multiview drawings: Presentation of views of drawings created through orthographic projection.

orthographic projection: Projecting object features onto an imaginary plane.

projection plane: The imaginary projection plane that is parallel to the object.

Figure 8-13.
Obtaining a front view with orthographic projection.

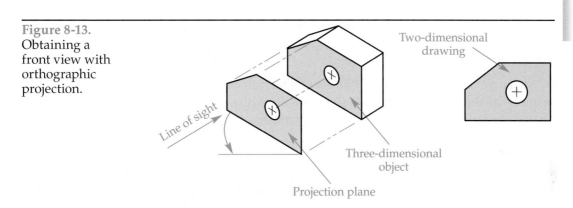

Figure 8-14.
Arrangement of the six orthographic views.

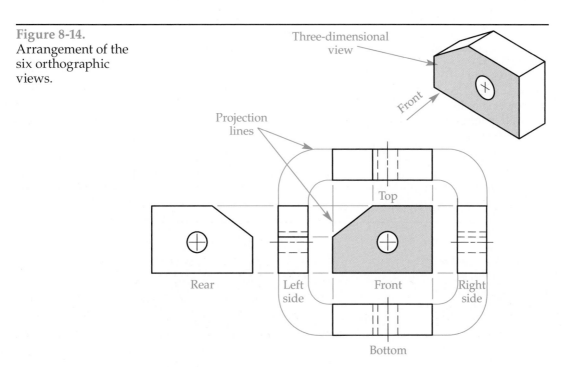

figure that the horizontal and vertical edges illustrated in the front view are aligned with the corresponding edges in the other views.

Selecting the Front View

The front view is usually the most descriptive view. The following rules should be considered when selecting the front view:

✓ Most descriptive
✓ Most natural position
✓ Most stable position
✓ Provides the longest dimension
✓ Contains the least number of hidden features

Choosing Additional Views

Additional views are selected relative to the front view. Very few products require all six views. The number of views needed depends on the complexity of the object. Use only enough views to completely describe the object. Drawing too many views is time-consuming and can clutter the drawing. In some cases, a single view is enough to describe the object. The object shown in **Figure 8-15** needs only two views. These two views completely describe the width, height, depth, and features of the object.

In some instances, an object can be fully described using one view. A thin part that has as uniform thickness, such as a gasket, can be drawn with one view. See **Figure 8-16.** The thickness is given as a note in the drawing or in the title block.

Auxiliary Views

In most cases, an object can be completely described using a combination of one or more of the six standard views. Sometimes, however, the multiview layout is not enough to properly identify some object surfaces. A *foreshortened* surface is typically described using an *auxiliary view.*

foreshortened: A surface at an angle to the line of sight. Foreshortened surfaces appear shorter than their true size and shape.

An auxiliary view is drawn by projecting lines perpendicular (90°) to a slanted surface. One projection line is often included on the drawing. It connects the auxiliary view to the view where the slanted surface appears as a line. The resulting auxiliary view shows the surface in true size and shape. For most applications, a *partial auxiliary view* is all that is needed. See **Figure 8-17.**

auxiliary view: View used to show a foreshortened surface in true size and shape. Foreshortened dimensions are not recommended.

partial auxiliary view: An auxiliary view that shows only a single inclined surface of an object, rather than the entire object.

Figure 8-15.
The views you choose to describe the object should show all height, width, and depth dimensions.

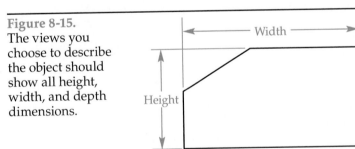

Figure 8-16.
A one-view drawing of a gasket. The thickness is uniform, so it can be given in a note.

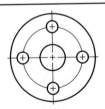

NOTE: THICKNESS 1.5mm

AutoCAD and Its Applications—Basics

Figure 8-17.
Auxiliary views show the true size and shape of an inclined surface.

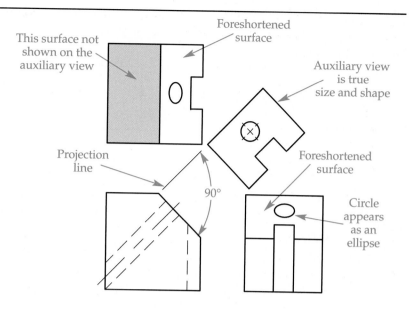

In some situations, there is not enough room on the drawing to project directly from the slanted surface. The auxiliary view is then placed elsewhere. See **Figure 8-18.** A *viewing-plane line* is drawn next to the view where the slanted surface appears as a line. It is terminated with bold arrowheads that point toward the slanted surface. Each end of the viewing-plane line is labeled with a letter. The letters relate the viewing-plane line with the proper auxiliary view. A title such as VIEW A-A is placed under the auxiliary view. When more than one auxiliary view is drawn, labels continue with B-B through Z-Z, if necessary. The letters *I*, *O*, and *Q* are not used because they can be confused with numbers. An auxiliary view drawn away from the standard view retains the same angle as if it is projected directly.

viewing-plane line: A thick dashed or phantom line identifying the viewing direction of a related view.

Figure 8-18.
Identifying an auxiliary view with a viewing-plane line. If there is not enough room, the view can be moved to a different location.

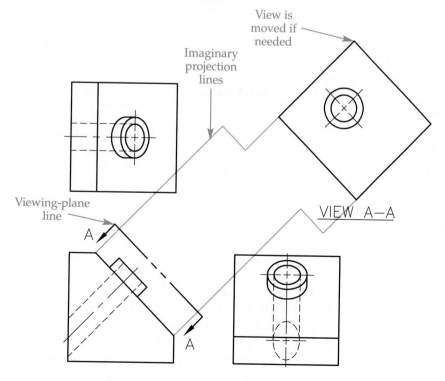

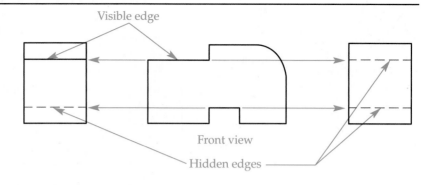

Figure 8-19.
Hidden features are shown with hidden lines.

Visible edge

Front view

Hidden edges

Figure 8-20.
Drawing centerlines.

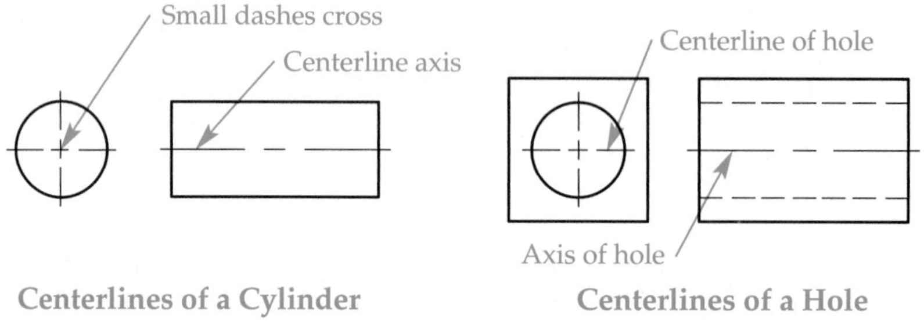

Small dashes cross

Centerline axis

Centerline of hole

Axis of hole

Centerlines of a Cylinder

Centerlines of a Hole

Showing Hidden Features

Hidden features are parts of the object that are not visible in the view at which you are looking. A visible edge appears as a solid object line. A hidden edge is shown with a hidden linetype, as described in Chapter 5. Notice in **Figure 8-19** how hidden features are shown as hidden lines. Hidden lines are thin to provide contrast with object lines.

Showing Symmetry and Circle Centers

As described in Chapter 5, the centerlines of symmetrical objects and the centers of circles are shown with centerlines. For example, in the circular view of a cylinder, centerlines cross to show the center of the cylinder. In the other view, the axis is drawn as a centerline. See **Figure 8-20.** The only place the small centerline dashes should cross is at the center of a circle.

Constructing Multiview Drawings

Multiview drawings can be constructed using a variety of techniques, depending on the objects needed, personal working preference, and the information you know about the size and shape of items. Often a combination of methods, including various coordinate point entries, object snaps, AutoTrack, and construction lines are used to produce drawings.

Figure 8-21 shows an example of how object snap tracking can be used to locate points for a new view by referencing points on existing views. In this example, a left side view is constructed from an existing front view using object snap tracking and a running **Endpoint** object snap mode. The completed left side view is provided for reference. Notice how the AutoTrack alignment path provides a temporary construction line. Polar tracking vectors offer a similar type of temporary construction line.

Figure 8-22 shows an example of how construction lines can be used to form three views. In this example, vertical and horizontal construction lines are offset to form a grid. The construction line intersections are used to locate line and arc endpoints and

Figure 8-21.
An example of
using object snap
tracking to construct
an additional view.
From and **Extension**
object snap
overrides could also
be used for similar
tasks.

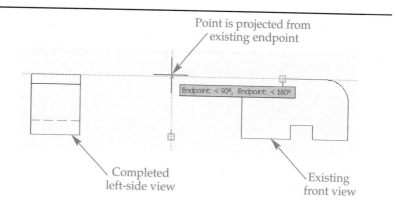

Point is projected from
existing endpoint

Endpoint: < 90°, Endpoint: < 180°

Completed
left-side view

Existing
front view

Figure 8-22.
An example of using a complete grid of construction lines to form a multiview drawing. The
rectangular outline of the right side, left side, and top views can be drawn quickly using the
RECTANGLE tool.

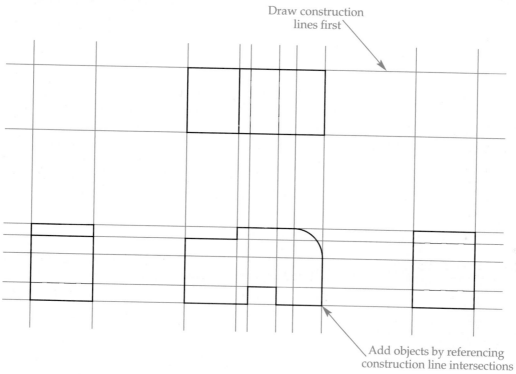

Draw construction
lines first

Add objects by referencing
construction line intersections

the center point of the arc. The **Intersection** object snap mode is used to quickly select
the intersecting construction lines. Notice that a single infinitely long construction line
can provide construction geometry for multiple views.

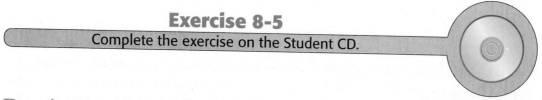

Exercise 8-5
Complete the exercise on the Student CD.

Drawing Auxiliary Views

Auxiliary views are constructed using the same tools and options used to draw any
of the six primary views. However, constructing auxiliary views presents unique chal-
lenges. Auxiliary view projection is created at 90° from an inclined surface to construct

Figure 8-23.
An example of using construction lines drawn perpendicular to the inclined surface on an existing view to construct an auxiliary view. The completed top and auxiliary views are shown for reference.

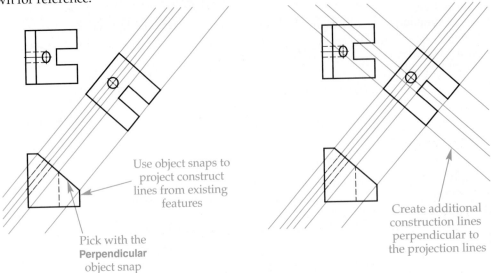

Use object snaps to project construct lines from existing features

Pick with the **Perpendicular** object snap

Create additional construction lines perpendicular to the projection lines

primary views. One of the most effective ways to draw a new auxiliary view, even without knowing or calculating the angle of the inclined surface, is to project construction lines from features on an existing view, perpendicular to the inclined surface.

Access the **XLINE** tool. When the Specify a point or [Hor/Ver/Ang/Bisect/Offset]: prompt appears, use the **Perpendicular** object snap mode to select the inclined surface. A construction line perpendicular to the inclined surface is now attached to the crosshairs. Use the appropriate object snap modes to select features on the existing view. Object snaps or additional perpendicular construction lines can then be used to complete the auxiliary view. See Figure 8-23.

NOTE

A construction line can also be made perpendicular to a line object using the **Reference** option of the **XLINE** tool's **Ang** option. Select the line object when prompted and enter an xline angle of 90.

Exercise 8-6
Complete the exercise on the Student CD.

Template Development

Chapter 8

Many drafters rely on points created by the **POINT, DIVIDE,** and **MEASURE** tools to construct geometry accurately. Point styles vary according to personal preference, but you can add your preferred style to your drawing templates. Refer to the Student CD for detailed instructions to add your preferred point style to your mechanical, architectural, and civil drawing.

AutoCAD and Its Applications—Basics

Chapter Test

1. List two ways to establish an offset distance using the OFFSET tool.
2. What option of the OFFSET tool is used to remove the source offset object?
3. How do you draw a single point, and how do you draw multiple points?
4. How do you access the Point Style dialog box?
5. If you use the DIVIDE tool and nothing appears to happen, what should you do?
6. How do you change the point size in the Point Style dialog box?
7. What tool is used to place point objects that divide a line into 24 equal parts?
8. What is the difference between the DIVIDE and MEASURE tools?
9. Why is it a good idea to put construction lines on their own layer?
10. Name the tool that allows you to draw AutoCAD construction lines.
11. Name the option that can be used to bisect an angle with a construction line.
12. What is the difference between the construction lines drawn with the tool identified in Question 10 and rays drawn with the RAY tool?
13. What ASME drafting standard applies to multiview drawings?
14. Provide at least four guidelines for selecting the front view of an orthographic multiview drawing.
15. How do you determine how many views of an object are necessary in a multiview drawing?
16. When can a part be shown with only one view?
17. When is an auxiliary view needed, and what does an auxiliary view show?
18. What is the angle of projection from the slanted surface into the auxiliary view?
19. List two methods of aligning the views in a multiview drawing.
20. Describe an effective method of constructing an auxiliary view even if you do not know the angle of the inclined surface.

Load AutoCAD for each of the following problems, and use one of your templates or start a new drawing using your own variables.

▼ Basic

1. Draw the front and side views of this offset support. Use object snap modes and tracking. Do not draw the dimensions. Save your drawing as P8-1.

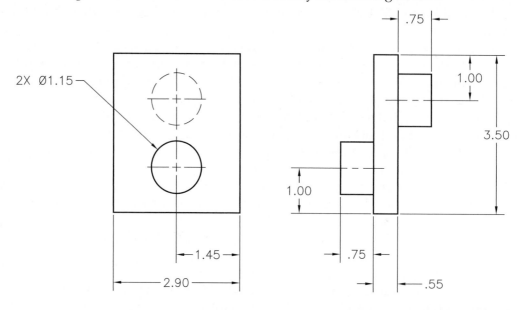

2. Draw the top and front views of this hitch bracket. Use object snap modes and tracking. Do not draw the dimensions. Save your drawing as P8-2.

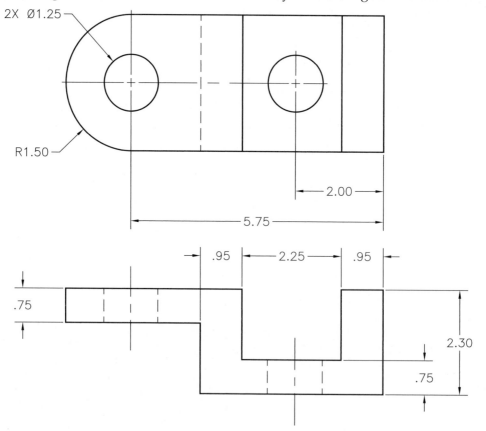

3. Draw this spring using the **Offset** tool for material thickness. Do not draw the dimensions. Save the drawing as P8-3.

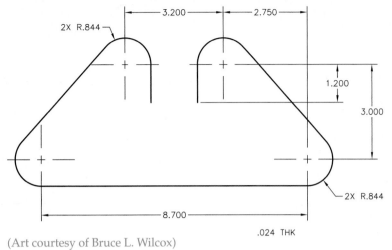

(Art courtesy of Bruce L. Wilcox)

4. Draw this sheet metal chassis. Do not draw the dimensions. Use object snap tracking and polar tracking to your advantage. Save the drawing as P8-4.

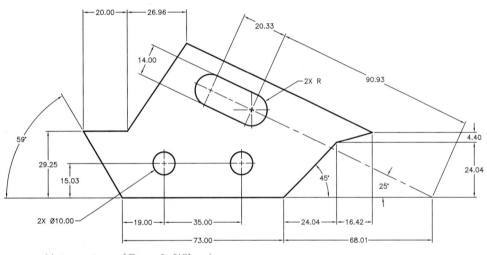

(Art courtesy of Bruce L. Wilcox)

▼ Intermediate

5. Use the **Offset** tool to draw the elevation of the desk shown. Center 1″ × 4″ rectangular drawer handles 2″ below the top of each drawer. The top of the legs begin 1″ from the edge of the bottom of the desk. Do not draw dimensions. Save the drawing as P8-5.

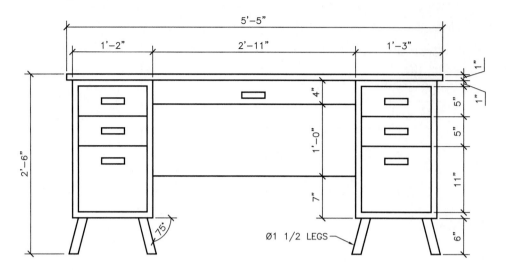

6. Draw this aluminum spacer. Use object snap modes and tracking. Do not draw the dimensions. Save the drawing as P8-6.

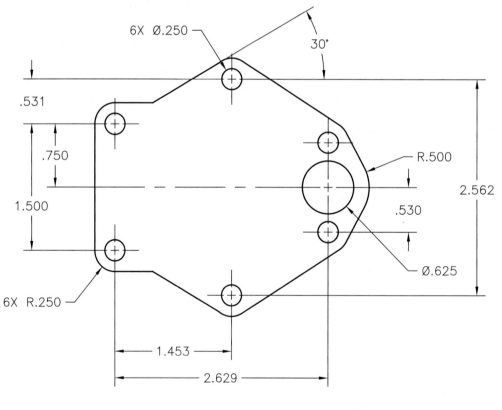

7. Draw this gasket. Do not draw the dimensions. Save the drawing as P8-7.

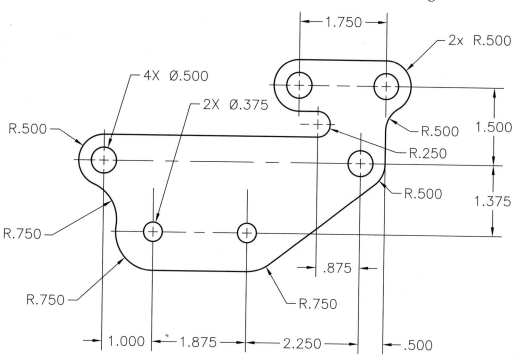

8. Draw this cup. Do not draw the dimensions. Save the drawing as P8-8.

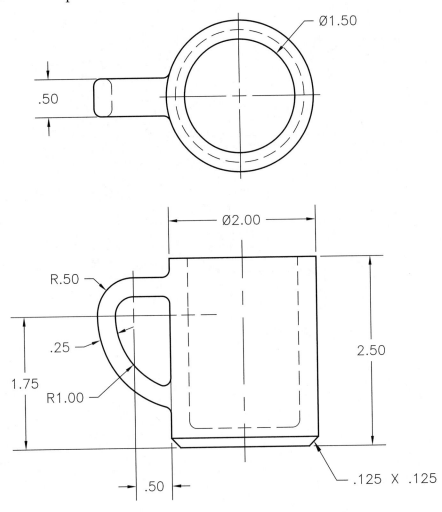

Ø1.50

.50

Ø2.00

R.50

.25

1.75

R1.00

2.50

.50

.125 X .125

FILLETS AND ROUNDS R.10

9. Draw this bushing. Do not draw the dimensions. Save the drawing as P8-9.

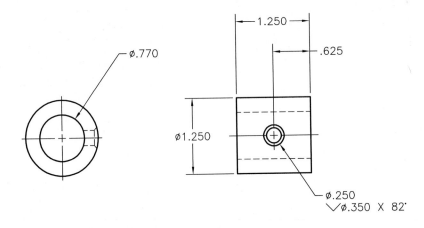

Ø.770

1.250

.625

Ø1.250

Ø.250
∨Ø.350 X 82°

10. Draw this wrench. Do not draw the dimensions. Save the drawing as **P8-10**.

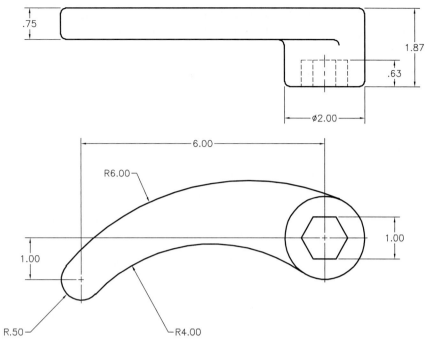

FILLETS AND ROUNDS = .125

11. Draw this support. Do not draw the dimensions. Save the drawing as **P8-11**.

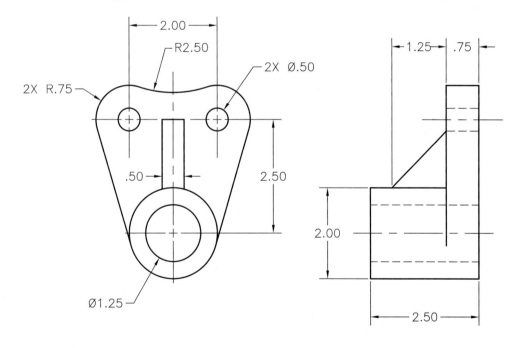

▼ Advanced

In Problems 12 through 17, draw the views needed to completely describe the objects. Use object snap modes, AutoTrack modes, and offsets as needed. Do not dimension. Save the drawings as P8-(problem number).

12.

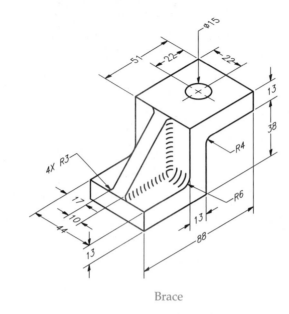

Brace

13.

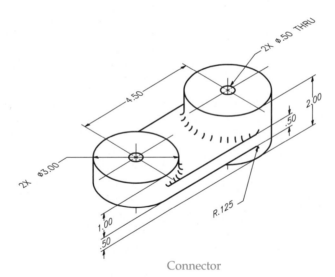

Connector

14.

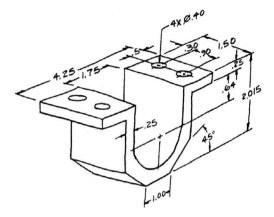

Journal Bracket (Engineer's Rough Sketch)

15.

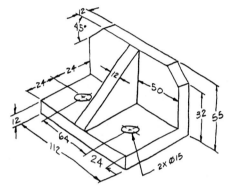

Angle Bracket (Engineer's Rough Sketch)
(Metric)

16.

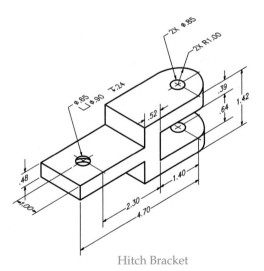

Hitch Bracket

Drawing Problems - Chapter 8

17. Draw the views of this pillow block, including the auxiliary view. Do not draw the dimensions. Save your drawing as **P8-17**.

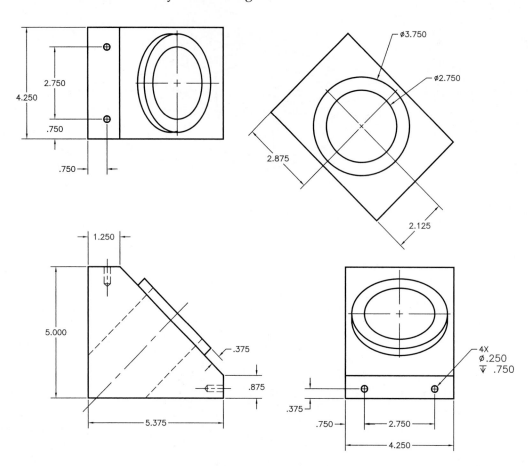

Text Styles and Multiline Text

Learning Objectives

After completing this chapter, you will be able to do the following:
- ✓ Describe and use proper text standards.
- ✓ Calculate drawing scale and text height.
- ✓ Develop and use text styles.
- ✓ Make multiple lines of text with the **MTEXT** tool.

Information on a drawing that cannot be described using objects and symbols is added using letters, numbers, words, and notes. Traditional hand lettering is a slow, time-consuming task. CAD programs significantly reduce the tedious nature of adding *text* to a drawing. Lettering with AutoCAD is fast and produces text that is consistent and easy to read.

> **text:** Lettering on a CAD drawing.

AutoCAD provides two basic systems for creating text. Multiline text is created with the **MTEXT** tool and is used to prepare a single text object that may consist of multiple lines of text, such as paragraphs or a list of general notes. Single-line text is created with the **TEXT** tool and is used to add single-line text objects. This chapter explains standards for proper text presentation based on ASME Y14.2M, *Line Conventions and Lettering* and describes how text is added to drawings using the **MTEXT** tool. The **TEXT** tool and other tools for working with text are covered in Chapter 10.

Text Standards and Composition

Industry and company standards dictate how text appears on a drawing. The ASME Y14.2M lettering standard recommends several text heights based on the particular function of the text on the drawing. The height of most text, such as dimensions and notes, is .12″ (3 mm). Taller text, used for titles and unique applications, is .24″ (6 mm) high. Many companies, especially those who produce architectural and civil drawings, depart from the ASME standard and use a minimum text height of .125″ (3 mm) and a text height of between .188″ and .25″ (5 mm to 6.5 mm) for taller text. Some companies specify a .188″, or 5/32″ (5 mm), lettering height for standard text. Regardless of the text height, all text should be consistent and easy to read.

Vertical text is standard on engineering drawings, although inclined text may be used, depending on company preference. See **Figure 9-1.** The recommended slant for

Figure 9-1.
Vertical and inclined text.

ABC.. abc.. 123..
ABC.. abc.. 123..

Figure 9-2.
Examples of fractional text for different unit formats.

Decimal Inch	Fractional Inch			Millimeter		
2.750 .25	$2\frac{3}{4}$ 2–3/4 2 3/4			2.5 3 0.7		

inclined text is 68° from horizontal. Text on a drawing is normally uppercase, but lowercase letters are used in some instances. Typically, the same style of text is used throughout a drawing, but in some cases, such as text on maps, a combination of text styles is used.

Numbers in dimensions and notes are the same height as standard text. When fractions are used in dimensions, the fraction bar should be placed horizontally between the numerator and denominator. AutoCAD provides methods for stacking text. However, many notes placed on drawings have fractions displayed with a diagonal fraction bar (/). A dash or space is usually placed between the whole number and the fraction. Examples of text for numbers and fractions in different unit formats are shown in **Figure 9-2.**

composition: The spacing, layout, and appearance of text.

AutoCAD text tools provide great control over text *composition*. Text can be laid out horizontally, as is typically the case when adding notes, or drawn at any angle according to specific requirements. AutoCAD automatically spaces letters and sets lines of text apart at an equal distance. This helps maintain the identity of individual notes.

PROFESSIONAL TIP

Text presentation is important on any drawing. Consider the following tips when adding text:
- Plan your drawing using rough sketches to allow room for text and notes.
- Arrange text to avoid crowding.
- Place related notes in groups to make the drawing easy to read.
- Place all general notes in a common location. Locate notes in the lower-left corner or above the title block when using ASME standards. Place notes in the upper-left corner when using military standards.
- Always use the spell checker.

Drawing Scale and Text Height

Ideally, you should determine drawing scale, scale factors, and text heights before you begin a drawing. These items are best incorporated as settings within your template drawing files, but they can be changed as needed. The scale factor of a drawing is important because this value is used to make sure the text is shown on-screen and

Figure 9-3.
An example of a portion of a floor plan drawn at full scale in model space. If text is drawn at full scale, as shown in A, the text is very small compared to the large objects. The text must be scaled, as shown in B, in order to be seen and plotted correctly.

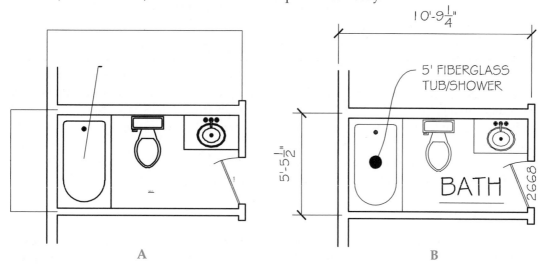

A   B

plotted at the proper height. To help understand the concept of drawing scale, look at the portion of a floor plan shown in **Figure 9-3.** Everything drawn in model space is drawn at full scale. This means that the bathtub, for example, is actually drawn 5′ long. However, at this scale, text size becomes an issue, because text that is drawn at full scale, 1/8″ high for example, is extremely small compared to the other full-scale objects. See **Figure 9-3A.** As a result, you must adjust the height of the text according to the drawing scale. See **Figure 9-3B.** You can calculate the scale factor manually and apply it to the text height, or you can allow AutoCAD to calculate it by using annotative text.

Scaling Text Manually

To manually adjust *text height* according to a specific drawing scale, you must calculate the drawing *scale factor*. The scale factor is then multiplied by the desired *paper text height* to get the model space text height.

Calculating the scale factor

Suppose, for example, that a drawing is to be plotted at a scale of 1/2″ = 1″. Since the scale factor is the reciprocal of the drawing scale, you can calculate it by dividing 1″ by 1/2″ (.5). 1 ÷ .5 = 2, so the scale factor in this case is 2.

Another example is an architectural drawing that is to be plotted at a scale of 1/4″ = 1′-0″. In this example you must first convert both values to the same units, typically inches. The scale is now 1/4″ = 12″ (because 12″ = 1′). Divide 12″ by 1/4″ (.25) to find a scale factor of 48 (12 ÷ .25 = 48).

A third example is a civil engineering drawing that has a scale of 1″ = 60′. This example also requires that you first convert both values to the same units, typically inches. The scale is now 1″ = 720″ (because 60 × 12 = 720). Divide 720″ by 1″ to find the scale factor of 720 (720 ÷ 1 = 720).

If your drawing is in millimeters with a scale of 1:1, the drawing can be converted to inches with the formula 1″ = 25.4 mm. Therefore, the scale factor is 25.4 (25.4 ÷ 1 = 25.4). When the metric drawing scale is 1:2, the scale factor for converting to inches is 1″ = 25.4 × 2, or 1″ = 50.8. The scale factor is 50.8.

text height: The specified height of text, which may be different from the plotting size for text scaled manually.

scale factor: The reciprocal of the drawing scale.

paper text height: The plotted text height.

Calculating text height

Once you have determined the scale factor, you can calculate the height of the AutoCAD text. In a drawing with a scale of 1″ = 1″, the scale factor equals 1. Therefore, the height of 1/8″ text in the drawing will be 1/8″ high, because the text height multiplied by a scale factor of 1 equals 1/8″.

However, if you are working on a civil engineering drawing with a scale of 1″ = 60′, for example, text drawn 1/8″ high appears as a dot. Remember, the drawing you are working on is 720 times larger than it is when plotted at the proper scale. Therefore, you must multiply the text height by the 720 scale factor to have text in correct proportion on the screen. Text height multiplied by scale factor equals the model space scaled text height. So, in this example, convert 1/8″ to fractional inches (.125″) and multiply: .125″× 720 = 90″. The proper text height in model space is 90″.

An architectural drawing with a scale of 1/4″ = 1′-0″ has a scale factor of 48. Text that is to be 1/8″ high when printed should be drawn 6″ high (1/8″ × 48 = 6″).

Annotative Text

annotative text:
Text that is scaled by AutoCAD according to the specified annotation scale.

annotation scale:
The drawing scale AutoCAD uses to calculate the height of annotative text.

AutoCAD scales *annotative text* according to the *annotation scale* you select, which eliminates the need for you to calculate the scale factor. When an annotation scale is selected, AutoCAD determines the scale factor and applies it automatically to annotative text, as well as any other annotative objects. For example, if you manually scale 1/8″ text for a drawing with a scale of 1/4″ = 1′-0″, or a scale factor of 48, you must draw the text using a text height of 6″ (1/8″ × 48 = 6″) in model space. When placing annotative text, using this example, you set an annotation scale of 1/4″ = 1′-0″. Then you draw the text using a paper text height of 1/8″ in model space. The 1/8″ high text is scaled to 6″ automatically because of the preset 1/4″ = 1′-0″ annotation scale.

Annotative text offers several advantages over manually scaled text, including the ability to control text scale based on annotation scale, not scale factor. Using annotative text is especially effective when drawing scale changes or when objects viewed at different scales are placed on a single sheet.

PROFESSIONAL TIP

If you anticipate preparing scaled drawings, you should use annotative text and other annotative objects instead of traditional manual scaling. However, scale factor does influence non-annotative items on a drawing and is still an important value to identify and use throughout the drawing process.

Setting annotation scale

Annotation scale should usually be set before you begin typing text so that the text height is automatically scaled. However, this is not always possible. It may be necessary to adjust the annotation scale throughout the drawing process, especially if multiple drawings with different scales are prepared for display on one sheet. This chapter approaches annotation scaling in model space only, using the process of selecting the desired annotation scale before typing text. When text at another scale is needed, pick the new annotation scale and then type the text.

When you access a text tool and an annotative text style is current, the **Select Annotation Scale** dialog box appears. This is a very convenient way to set annotation scale before typing. Text styles are described later in this chapter. The **Annotation Scale** flyout located on the status bar can also be used to adjust annotation scale. See Figure 9-4. Pick the desired annotation scale from the menu, remembering that the annotation scale is typically the same as the drawing scale.

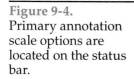

Figure 9-4.
Primary annotation
scale options are
located on the status
bar.

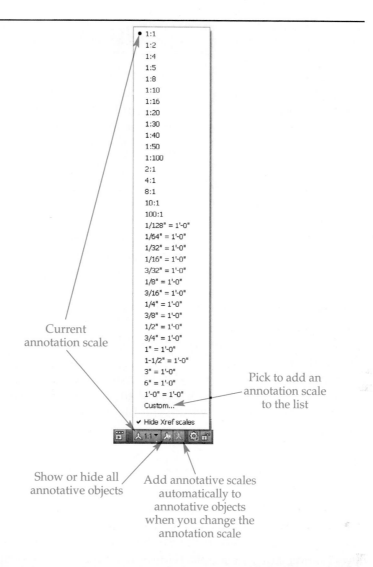

Current
annotation scale

Pick to add an
annotation scale
to the list

Show or hide all
annotative objects

Add annotative scales
automatically to
annotative objects
when you change the
annotation scale

NOTE

Many additional annotative object tools are described throughout this textbook. Some of these tools are more appropriate for working with layouts, as described in Chapter 28.

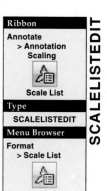

Editing annotation scales

If a certain scale is not available, or if you want to change existing scales, pick the **Annotation Scale** flyout in the status bar and choose the **Custom...** option to access the **Edit Scale List** dialog box. From this dialog box, you can move the highlighted scale up or down in the list by picking the **Move Up** or **Move Down** button. To remove the highlighted scale from the list, pick the **Delete** button.

Selecting **Edit...** opens the **Edit Scale** dialog box. Here you can change the name of the scale and adjust the scale by entering the paper and drawing units. For example, a scale of 1/4″ = 1′-0″ uses a paper units value of .25 or 1 and a drawing units value of 12 or 48.

To create a new annotation scale, pick the **Add...** button to display the **Add Scale** dialog box, which functions the same as the **Edit Scale** dialog box previously described. Pick the **Reset** button to restore the default annotation scale. When the annotation scale is set current, you are ready to type annotative text that is automatically created at the correct text height according to the drawing scale.

Ribbon
Annotate
> **Annotation**
Scaling

Scale List

Type
SCALELISTEDIT

Menu Browser
Format
> **Scale List**

SCALELISTEDIT

STYLE

Ribbon
Annotate
> Text
Text Style
Type
ST
Menu Browser
Format
>Text Style...

text style: A saved collection of settings for text height, width, oblique angle (slant), and other text effects.

AutoCAD *text styles* are used to set text characteristics. You may have several text styles, depending on the different characteristics needed for the text displayed in your drawing. Text characteristics can be manipulated independently of a text style. However, you should create a text style for each unique text requirement. For example, you may have a text style that is used for most applications, such as adding notes and dimensions, and a separate text style that uses different characteristics for adding text to a title block. Text styles should be added to drawing templates for repeated use.

Working with Text Styles

Text styles are created, modified, and deleted using the **Text Style** dialog box. See **Figure 9-5.** The **Styles** list box displays existing text styles. By default, Annotative and Standard text styles are available. Both use the Arial font, a 0° rotation angle, a width of 1, and a 0° oblique angle. The Annotative text style is preset to create annotative text, as indicated by the icon to the left of the style name. The Standard text style does not use the annotative function.

You can make a text style current by double-clicking the style name; right-clicking the name and selecting the **Current** option; or picking the name and selecting the **Current** button. Below the **Styles** list box is a drop-down list that can be used to filter the number of text styles displayed in the **Text Style** dialog box. Pick the **All Styles** option to show all text styles in the file or pick the **Styles in use** option to show only the current style and styles used in the drawing.

Creating New Text Styles

To create a new text style, first select an existing text style from the **Styles** list box to be used as a base for formatting the new text style. Then pick the **New...** button in the **Text Style** dialog box to open the **New Text Style** dialog box. See **Figure 9-6.** Notice that style1 is displayed in the **Style Name** text box. You can keep the default style1 or style2 name, but you should replace it with a more descriptive name. For example, to

Figure 9-5.
The **Text Style** dialog box is used to create, rename, delete, and set the characteristics of a text style.

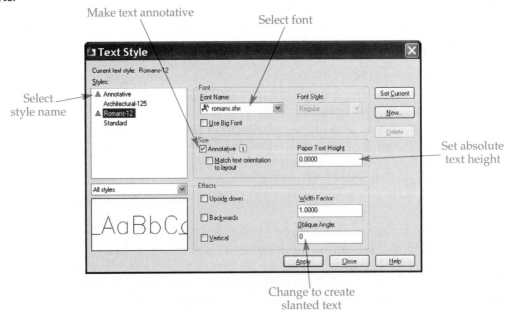

Figure 9-6.
Enter a descriptive name for the new text style in the **New Text Style** dialog box.

Default Style

New Style

create a text style for mechanical drawings that uses the Romans font and characters .12″ high, you should choose a style name that you can remember, such as ROMANS-12. A text style for architectural drawings that uses the Stylus BT font and characters .125″ high could be named ARCHITECTURAL-125.

Text style names can have up to 255 characters, including letters, numbers, dashes (–), underlines (_), and dollar signs ($). You can type uppercase or lowercase letters. After entering the text style name, pick the **OK** button. The new text style is displayed in the **Styles** list box of the **Text Style** dialog box, and you are ready to adjust text style characteristics.

PROFESSIONAL TIP

It is a good idea to record the names and details about the text styles you create and keep this information in a log for future reference.

Setting the Font Style

The **Font** area of the **Text Style** dialog box is where you select a *font* and the style of the selected font. Use the **Font Name** drop-down list to access the available fonts. Most available fonts, including the default Arial font, are TrueType fonts and are identified by the TrueType icon. TrueType fonts are *scaleable fonts* and have an outline. By default, TrueType fonts appear and are plotted filled. Examples of TrueType fonts are shown in **Figure 9-7.** The Stylus BT font is an excellent choice for the artistic appearance desired on architectural drawings.

Fonts that are linked to AutoCAD shape files have .shx file extensions and are identified by the AutoCAD compass icon. The Romans (roman simplex) font closely duplicates the single-stroke lettering that has long been the standard for most drafting. Examples of AutoCAD SHX fonts are shown in **Figure 9-8.**

The **Font Style** drop-down list is inactive unless the selected font has options available, such as bold or italic. None of the SHX fonts have additional options, but some of the TrueType fonts do. For example, the SansSerif font has Regular, Bold, BoldOblique, and Oblique options. Each option provides the font with a different appearance.

font: A letter face design.

scaleable fonts: Fonts that can be displayed or printed at any size while retaining proportional letter thickness.

Figure 9-7.
A few of the many TrueType fonts available.

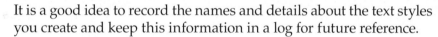

Swiss 721		Architect's Hand Lettered	
swiss (regular)	abcdABCD12345	stylus BT	abcdABCD12345
swissi (italic)	abcdABCD12345		
swissb (bold)	abcdABCD1234	Vineta (shadow)	
swissbi (bold italic)	abcdABCD12345	vinet (regular)	abcdABCD12345

Figure 9-8.
Examples of AutoCAD SHX fonts.

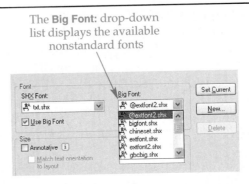

When you select an SHX font style in the **Text Style** dialog box, the **Use Big Font** check box is enabled. Pick the check box to activate *big fonts*. The **Big Font:** drop-down list is a supplement used to define many symbols not available in normal font files. See Figure 9-9.

Figure 9-9.
When you check the **Use Big Font** check box, the **Font Style:** drop-down list changes to display a list of available Big Fonts.

The **Big Font:** drop-down list displays the available nonstandard fonts

Big Fonts: Asian and other large-format fonts that have characters not present in normal font files.

CAUTION

A drawing that contains a significant amount of text, especially TrueType font text, can be taxing on system resources. Display changes may be slower and drawing regeneration time may increase.

AutoCAD Fonts

Additional standard fonts, characters, and TrueType fonts can be seen by experimenting with AutoCAD or referring to the reference material on the Student CD: Reference Materials > AutoCAD Fonts.

Text Style Height Options

The **Size** area of the **Text Style** dialog box contains options for defining text style height. Select the **Annotative** check box to set the text style as annotative. An annotative text style adjusts the height of text according to the selected annotation scale.

When the **Annotative** check box is checked, the **Match text orientation to layout** check box is available. Check this box to match the orientation of text in layout viewports with the layout orientation. Layouts are described in Chapter 28. The **Paper Text Height** text box is also available when the **Annotative** check box is checked. The default paper text height is 0.0000. This setting allows you to set the text height with the **TEXT** tool. If you set a value such as .125, the text height becomes fixed for this text style and you are not prompted for the text height. Setting a text height value other than zero saves time when you are creating several text items at the same height, but it also eliminates your flexibility.

When the **Annotative** check box is not selected, text must be scaled manually using the drawing scale factor. The **Height** text box presets the text height. The default is 0.0000. This setting allows you to set the text height with the **TEXT** tool. If you set a value, the text height becomes fixed for this text style and you are not prompted for the text height.

PROFESSIONAL TIP

It is recommended that a text height value of 0 be used for text styles used in dimensions. Dimension styles allow you to specify a text height value for the annotation text. If you specify a text height in the text style, this value overrides the dimension text height. Dimension styles are described in Chapter 18.

Adjusting Text Style Effects

The **Effects** area of the **Text Style** dialog box is used to set the text format. It contains options for printing text upside-down, backwards, and vertically. See **Figure 9-10**. The Vertical check box is inactive for all TrueType fonts. A check in this box makes SHX font text vertical. Text on drawings is normally placed horizontally, but vertical text can be used for special effects and graphic designs. Vertical text works best when the rotation angle is 270°.

The **Width Factor** text box provides a value that defines the text character width relative to its height. A width factor of 1 is the default. A width factor greater than 1 expands the characters, and a factor less than 1 compresses the characters. See **Figure 9-11**.

Figure 9-10.
Special effects for text styles can be set in the **Effects** area of the **Text Style** dialog box.

Upside-Down Text   Backwards Text   Vertical Text

Figure 9-11.
Examples of width factor settings for text.

Width Factor	Text
1	ABCDEFGHIJKLM
.5	ABCDEFGHIJKLMNOPQRSTUVWXY
1.5	ABCDEFGHI
2	ABCDEFG

Figure 9-12.
Examples of oblique
angle settings for
text.

Obliquing Angle	Text
0	ABCDEFGHIJKLM
15	*ABCDEFGHIJKLM*
–15	ABCDEFGHIJKLM

The **Oblique Angle** text box allows you to set the angle at which text is slanted. The 0 default draws characters vertically. A value greater than 0 slants the characters to the right, and a negative value slants the characters to the left. See **Figure 9-12.** Some fonts, such as italic, are already slanted.

PROFESSIONAL TIP

Some drafting companies, especially those in structural drafting, like to slant text 15° to the right. Also, water features named on maps often use text that is slanted to the right.

NOTE

The **Preview** area of the **Text Style** dialog box displays an example of the selected font and font effects. This is a very convenient way to see what the font looks like before using it in a new style.

Exercise 9-1
Complete the exercise on the Student CD.

Changing, Renaming, and Deleting Text Styles

You can change the current text style without affecting existing text objects. The changes are applied only to text added using the current style. If you change the font and orientation of an existing text style, all text items with that style are redrawn with the new values.

Existing text styles can be renamed in the **Text Style** dialog box. To rename a text style, slowly double-click the name or right-click on the name and select the **Rename** menu option.

To delete a text style, right-click on the name and select the **Delete** option, or pick the style and select the **Delete** button. AutoCAD does not allow you to delete a text style that has been used to create text objects in the drawing. If you want to delete a style that is in use, change the text objects in the drawing to a different style. You cannot delete or rename the Standard style.

Setting a Text Style Current

You can set a text style current using the **Text Style** dialog box by double-clicking the style in the **Styles** list box, right-clicking on the name and selecting the **Set current** option, or picking the style and selecting the **Set current** button. To quickly set a text

AutoCAD and Its Applications—Basics

Figure 9-13.
The fastest way to
set a style current
is to use the drop-
down list on the
ribbon.

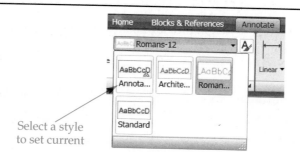

Select a style
to set current

style current without opening the **Text Style** dialog box, use the flyout located in the
Text panel on the **Annotate** tab of the ribbon. The name of the current text style is
displayed in the box. Pick the drop-down arrow to display the text style list, as shown
in Figure 9-13.

PROFESSIONAL TIP

You can import text styles from existing drawings using **DesignCenter**.
See Chapter 5 for more information about using **DesignCenter** to
import layers, linetypes, text styles, and other settings.

Creating Multiline Text

text boundary: An
imaginary box that
sets the location
and width for
multiline text.

The **MTEXT** tool is used to create multiline text objects. All the lines of multiline
text are part of the same object. When you access the **MTEXT** tool, AutoCAD asks you
to specify the first and opposite corners of the *text boundary*. When you pick the first
corner of the text boundary, the cursor changes to a box with grayed-out letters that
represent the current text height. Move the cursor to specify the desired size for your
paragraph and pick the opposite corner. See Figure 9-14.

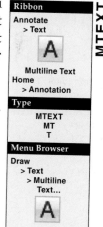

Figure 9-14.
The text boundary is a box within which your text will be placed. The arrow indicates the
direction of text flow.

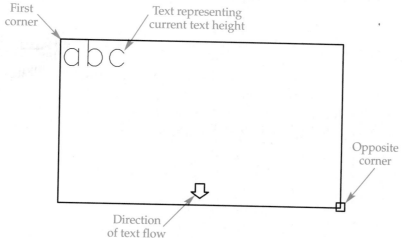

First
corner

Text representing
current text height

Opposite
corner

Direction
of text flow

Figure 9-15.
The **Multiline Text** tab on the ribbon provides many options for creating multiline text.

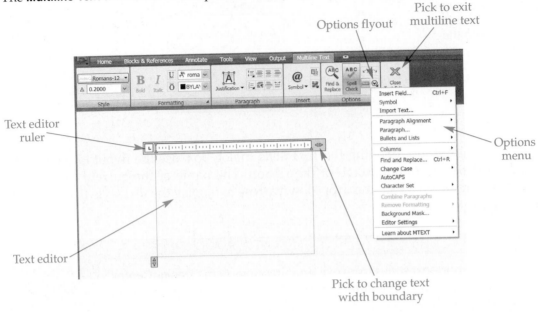

When you create the text boundary, an arrow in the boundary shows the direction of text flow. While the width of the boundary limits the width of the text paragraphs, it does not affect the possible height. The boundary height is automatically resized to fit the actual text typed. The direction of text flow indicates where the boundary will expand, if necessary. After you specify the text boundary, the **Multiline Text** contextual tab appears in the ribbon. See **Figure 9-15.**

The multiline text system functions much like a word processor. If you have ever used a software program such as Microsoft® Word, you will find similar controls and features when using multiline text. The **Multiline Text** tab of the ribbon provides tools for adjusting text typed into the *text editor*. A shortcut menu can be accessed by right-clicking anywhere outside of the ribbon. The menu and its options are displayed and explained in **Figure 9-16.** Most of the options given in the shortcut menu can also be accessed by picking the **Options** flyout from the **Options** panel of the **Multiline Text** tab. All of the options listed in the **Options** flyout menu are available in the text editor shortcut menu.

text editor: The part of the multiline or single-line text system where text is typed.

> **NOTE**
>
> If the ribbon has been closed, the **Text Formatting** toolbar appears after you specify the text boundary. This textbook focuses on using the **Multiline Text** contextual tab of the ribbon to add multiline text. The **Text Formatting** toolbar provides the same functions.

AutoCAD and Its Applications—Basics

Figure 9-16.
Display the text editor shortcut menu by right-clicking anywhere except on the ribbon while the text editor is active.

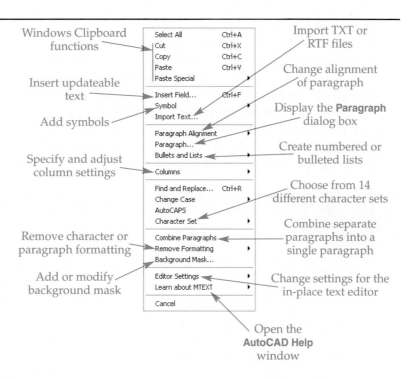

Windows Clipboard functions

Insert updateable text

Add symbols

Specify and adjust column settings

Remove character or paragraph formatting

Add or modify background mask

Import TXT or RTF files

Change alignment of paragraph

Display the **Paragraph** dialog box

Create numbered or bulleted lists

Choose from 14 different character sets

Combine separate paragraphs into a single paragraph

Change settings for the in-place text editor

Open the **AutoCAD Help** window

Using the Text Editor

The multiline text editor includes a ruler where indent and tab stops and indent and tab markers are located. A cursor is displayed within the text editor at the height set in the **Style** panel of the **Multiline Text** tab. The text editor is transparent by default so that you can see how the text you type appears on-screen in relation to other objects. The text editor can be made to appear opaque by selecting the **Opaque Background** option available from the **Editor Settings** cascading submenu of the shortcut menu or the **Options** flyout.

NOTE

Pick the **Ruler** button in the **Options** panel of the **Multiline Text** tab, or select the **Ruler** option from the **Editor Settings** cascading submenu on the shortcut menu or the **Multiline Text** tab **Options** flyout to turn the display of the paragraph ruler on or off. Use the **Undo** and **Redo** buttons, also found in the **Options** panel, to undo or redo text editor operations.

As you move the cursor into the text editor, it changes shape. If you have used other Windows text editors, you will recognize the familiar text cursor shape. If you begin typing where the text cursor is initially placed, your text begins in the upper-left corner of the text boundary. Pointing to a character position within the text and pressing the left mouse button places the cursor at that location. You can then begin typing or editing as needed.

Shortcut Keys

Most Windows-standard keystroke combinations work in AutoCAD's text editor. Refer to the Student CD: Reference Materials > Shortcut Keys for lists of keyboard entry tools. Keep printouts of these reference sheets handy while you learn AutoCAD.

To change the width of the text editor, drag one of the arrows at the end of the paragraph ruler. You can also change the width by right-clicking the text editor ruler or the arrows at the bottom of the text editor and selecting **Set Mtext Width...** from the shortcut menu. This displays the **Set Mtext Width** dialog box, where a new width for the paragraph can be specified. To change the height of the text editor, drag the arrows at the bottom of the text editor. You can also change the height by right-clicking the ruler or the arrows at the bottom of the text editor and selecting **Set Mtext Height...** from the shortcut menu. This displays the **Set Mtext Height** dialog box, where a new height for the paragraph can be specified.

PROFESSIONAL TIP

Change the width and height of the text editor to increase or decrease the number of lines of text. You should usually not press the [Enter] key to form lines of text, unless you are actually creating a new paragraph.

The procedure for selecting existing text is the same as in standard Windows text editors. Place the cursor at one end of the desired selection, press and hold the left mouse button, drag the cursor until the desired text is highlighted, and release the left mouse button. Any editing operations you perform affect the highlighted text. Another way to highlight text is to move the cursor to the word to be highlighted and double-click. To replace the highlighted text with entirely new text, either paste the new text from the Clipboard or begin typing. The selection is erased and the new text appears in its place. You can quickly select all text in the text editor by right-clicking inside the text editor and choosing the **Select All** menu option. The selected text highlight color can be changed by selecting the **Text Highlight Color...** option available from the **Editor Settings** cascading submenu of the shortcut menu or the **Options** flyout.

When you are finished typing text, exit the multiline text system by picking the **Close Text Editor** button in the **Close** panel of the **Multiline Text** tab or by picking outside of the text editor. You can also press the [Esc] key or right-click and select the Cancel menu option to exit, but you will be prompted to save changes. The easiest way to reopen the text editor to make changes to text content is to double-click on a multiline text object.

NOTE

The text editor displays text horizontally, right-side up, and forward. Any special effects such as vertical, backwards, or upside down take effect when you exit the text editor.

Exercise 9-2
Complete the exercise on the Student CD.

Style Settings

The **Style** panel of the **Multiline Text** tab includes options for changing the text style, annotative setting, and size. Activate text style options before typing, or select existing text in the text editor and then adjust the text style options to change the style of the selected text. A single multiline text object can use a combination of text style settings. Remember, however, that making changes to some style settings overrides the settings specified in the text style, which is often not appropriate.

The text style flyout provides access to existing text styles. This allows you to use a text style other than the current text style while typing. Use the **Annotative** button to override the current text style's annotative setting. If the current text style is annotative, the **Annotative** button is selected by default. The **Size** drop-down list is used to set the text height. If the current text style is annotative, or if you pick the **Annotative** button, the height you enter is the paper text height. If the current text style is not annotative, or if you deselect the **Annotative** button, the height you enter is the text height and must be multiplied by the scale factor.

Character Formatting

The **Formatting** panel of the **Multiline Text** tab includes options for adjusting text character formatting. Activate character format options before typing, or select existing text in the text editor and then adjust character format options to change the format of the selected text. A single multiline text object can use a combination of character text formatting options. Remember that making changes to character formatting overrides some of the settings specified in the text style and preset object properties, such as color. This practice is usually avoided.

Pick the **Bold** button to make text become bold. Select the **Italic** button to make text become italic. The **Bold** and **Italic** settings work only with some TrueType fonts. Pick the **Underline** button to underline text, and select the **Overline** button to place a line over text. The **Font** drop-down list allows you to override the text font. Multiline text color is set to ByLayer by default, but you can change the text color by picking one of the colors in the **Color** drop-down list. Though color should usually be defined as ByLayer, a single multiline text object can use a combination of text colors.

Additional character formatting options are available from the expanded **Formatting** panel. The **Oblique Angle** text box overrides the angle at which text is slanted. The value in the **Tracking** text box determines the amount of space between text characters. The default tracking value is 1, which results in normal spacing. The higher the value, the more space is added between characters. The lower the value, the tighter the spacing between characters. You can enter a value between 0.75 and 4.0. See **Figure 9-17**. The value in the **Width Factor** text box overrides the text character width.

> **NOTE**
>
>
> The **Character Set** cascading submenu, available from the shortcut menu or the **Options** flyout, displays a menu of code pages. A code page provides support for character sets used in different languages. Select a code page to apply it to the selected text.

Figure 9-17.
The **Tracking** option for multiline text determines the spacing between characters.

AutoCAD tracking
Normal Spacing

AutoCAD tracking
Tracking = 0.75

A u t o C A D   t r a c k i n g
Tracking = 2.0

Paragraph Formatting

justify: Align the margins or edges of text. For example, left-justified text is aligned along an imaginary left border.

Both the text boundary and the text within the boundary can be *justified.* The text boundary defines the size and location of the text editor and the extents of the text within the text editor. The text boundary can be arranged and located according to a specific justification, and the text within the boundary can be arranged independently of the text boundary justification. This provides great flexibility when determining the location and arrangement of text.

To justify the text boundary, select a justification option from the **Justification** flyout button of the **Paragraph** panel of the **Multiline Text** tab. Justification also determines the direction of text flow. Figure 9-18 displays the options for justifying the multiline text boundary vertically and horizontally.

paragraph alignment: The alignment of multiline text inside the text boundary.

Paragraph alignment occurs inside the text boundary. For example, when you apply a **Middle Center** text box justification, then set the paragraph alignment to **Left**, the text inside the boundary is aligned to the left edge of the text boundary, while the text boundary remains positioned according to the **Middle Center** justification. See Figure 9-19.

Figure 9-18.
Options for justifying the multiline text boundary.

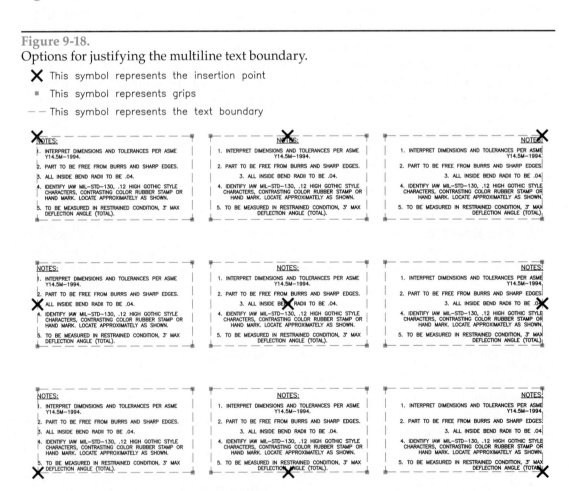

Figure 9-19.
Paragraph
alignment can
be adjusted
independently
of text boundary
justification.

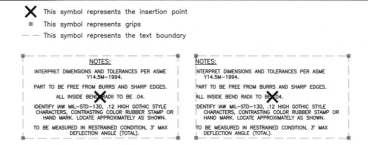

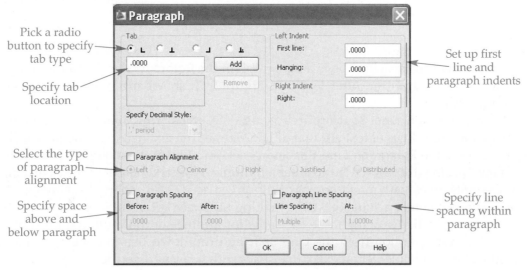

To adjust paragraph alignment, select one of the paragraph alignment buttons on the **Paragraph** panel, or pick one of the options from the **Paragraph Alignment** cascading submenu available from the shortcut menu or the **Options** flyout. Paragraph alignment can also be controlled using the **Paragraph** dialog box. See **Figure 9-20.** To display the **Paragraph** dialog box, pick the **Paragraph** button on the **Paragraph** panel or select the **Paragraph** option available from the shortcut menu or the **Options** flyout. To set paragraph alignment in the **Paragraph** dialog box, pick the **Paragraph Alignment** check box, then choose the appropriate paragraph alignment radio button. You can choose from five paragraph alignment options, as shown in **Figure 9-21.**

Tabs, indents, paragraph spacing, and paragraph line spacing can also be set in the **Paragraph** dialog box. The **Tab** area is used to set custom tab stops. Pick the tab type radio button, enter a value for the tab in the text box, and pick the **Add** button to add it to the list and insert the tab on the ruler. **Figure 9-22** shows and briefly describes each tab option. You can add as many custom tabs as necessary. Custom tabs can also be added to the ruler by picking the tab button on the far left side of the ruler until the desired tab symbol is displayed. Then pick a location on the ruler to insert the tab.

The **Left Indent** area is used to set the indentation for the first line of a paragraph of text as well as the remaining portion of a paragraph. Each time you start a new paragraph, the **First line** indent is used. As text wraps to the next line, the **Hanging** indent is used. The **Right Indent** area is used to set the indentation for the right side of a paragraph. As text is typed, the **Right** indent value, not the right edge of the text boundary, determines when the text wraps to the next line.

The **Paragraph Spacing** area is used to define the amount of space before and after paragraphs. To set paragraph line spacing, pick the **Paragraph Spacing** check

Figure 9-20.
The **Paragraph** dialog box.

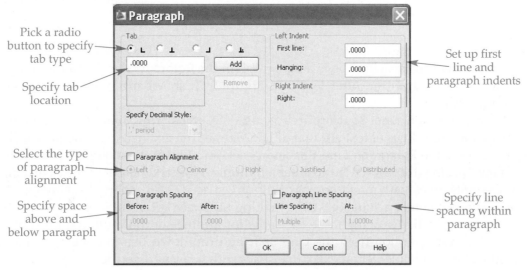

Figure 9-21.
Paragraph alignment options for multiline text. In each of these examples, the text boundary justification is set to Top Left.

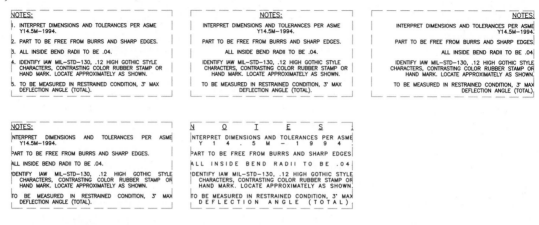

Figure 9-22.
Using custom tabs to position text in the text editor. When you press the [Tab] key, the cursor moves to the tab position. The type of tab then determines text behavior.

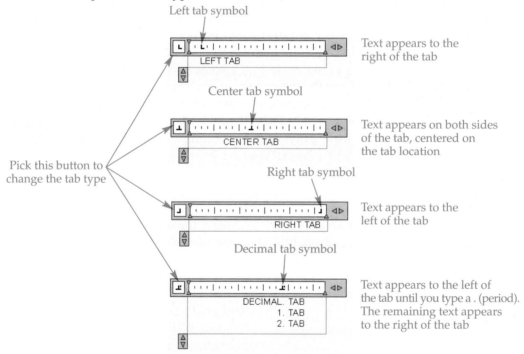

box. Then enter the spacing above a paragraph in the **Before** text box, and the spacing below a paragraph in the **After** text box. **Figure 9-23** shows examples of paragraph spacing settings.

line spacing: The vertical distance from the bottom of one line of text to the bottom of the next line.

The **Paragraph Line Spacing** area is used to adjust *line spacing*. Default line spacing for single lines of text is equal to 1.5625 times the text height. To adjust the line spacing, pick the **Paragraph Line Spacing** check box. Select the **Multiple** option from the **Line Spacing** drop-down list to enter a multiple of the text height in the **At** text box. For example, lines with a text height of .12" are spaced .1875" apart. To double-space lines, you could enter a value of 3.125x, making the space between lines of text .375".

To force the line spacing to be the same for all lines of the multiline text object, select the **Exactly** option from the **Line Spacing** drop-down list and enter a value in the **At** text box. If you enter an exact line spacing that is less than the text height, lines

Figure 9-23.
Examples of
paragraph spacing.
Each example uses a
text height of .1875″
and a first line left
indent of .5″.

Paragraph one typed
with no paragpah spacing.
Paragraph two typed with
no paragraph spacing

Paragraph one typed
with .25 before spacing and
no after spacing.

Paragraph two typed with
.25 before spacing and no
after spacing.

Paragraph one typed
with .125 before spacing
and .5 after spacing.

Paragraph two typed with
.125 before spacing and .5
after spacing.

of text are stacked on top of each other. To add spaces between lines automatically based on the height of the characters in the line, choose the **At Least** option from the **Line Spacing** drop-down list and enter a value in the **At** text box. The result is an equal spacing even between lines of text that have different heights.

Line spacing can also be set using the **Line Spacing** flyout button on the **Paragraph** panel of the **Multiline Text** tab. Select one of the available multiple options, pick the **More...** button to display the **Paragraph** dialog box, or choose the **Clear Line Spacing** option to apply an automatic spacing, similar to the **At Least** function.

NOTE

Multiple selected paragraphs can be combined to form a single paragraph using the **Combine Paragraphs** option available from the shortcut menu or the **Options** flyout.

PROFESSIONAL TIP

Quickly remove formatting from selected text using the **Remove Formatting** cascading submenu available from the shortcut menu or the **Options** flyout. Pick the **Remove Character Formatting** option to remove character formatting, such as bold, italic, or underline. Select the **Remove Paragraph Formatting** option to remove paragraph formatting, including lists. Pick the **Remove All Formatting** option to remove all character and paragraph formatting.

Exercise 9-4
Complete the exercise on the Student CD.

Creating Lists

Lists are commonly used to organize information. They provide a way to arrange related items in a logical order. Lists also help make lines of text more readable. General notes are usually provided in list format.

AutoCAD allows you to create lists as you enter text or to apply list formatting to existing text. The numbering or lettering adjusts automatically if items are added to or removed from a list. The **Allow Bullets and Lists** option must be selected in order to create a list. This option is active by default. Unchecking this option converts any list items in the text object to plain text characters and disables the other options in the menu.

Lists can also be set up to contain sublevel items. Sublevel items are designated with double numbers, letters, or bullets. Default tab settings are used unless you adjust the paragraph options. List tools are available from the **Numbering** flyout on the **Paragraph** panel of the **Multiline Text** tab or the **Bullets and Lists** cascading submenu available from the shortcut menu or the **Options** flyout. These tools are used to create numbered, bulleted, and alphabetical lists.

You can create an alphabetical list by choosing an option from the **Lettered** cascading submenu. Pick **Uppercase** to use uppercase lettering or choose **Lowercase** to use lowercase lettering. The **Uppercase** option is set by default. Numbered lists can be created by picking the **Numbered** option. To create a bulleted list in the default style, select the **Bulleted** option. This places a solid circle (the default bullet symbol) at the beginning of the line of text. When you start a new line of text, the next line is also bulleted.

Another method of creating lists is to set the **Allow Auto-list** option, which is active by default. When the **Allow Auto-list** option is turned on, AutoCAD detects characters that are frequently used to start a list and automatically assigns the first list item. For example, if a line of text begins with a number or letter and a period, AutoCAD assumes that you are starting a list and formats any additional lines of text to continue the list.

To create a numbered or lettered auto-list, you must include punctuation (such as a period, parenthesis, or colon) and press the [Tab] key after the number or letter that begins the first item. After you type the line of text and press the [Enter] key to start a new line, the next line uses the same formatting and the next consecutive number or letter. To end the list, press [Enter] twice. A numbered list is shown in **Figure 9-24.**

When creating a bulleted auto-list, you can use typical keyboard characters, such as a hyphen [-], tilde [~], bracket [>], or asterisk [*], at the beginning of a line. Another option is to insert a symbol at the beginning of a line. Then, to form the list, press the [Tab] key and type the line of text. When you press the [Enter] key, the line is formatted as a bulleted item and the next line uses the same bullet symbol and formatting. See **Figure 9-25.**

Figure 9-24.
Framing notes arranged in a numbered list.

FRAMING NOTES:
1. ALL FRAMING NOTES TO BE DFL #2 OR BETTER.
2. ALL HEATED WALLS @ HEATED LIVING AREA TO BE 2 X 6 @ 16" OC.
   FRAME ALL EXTERIOR NON-BEARING WALLS W/2 X 6 STUDS @ 24" OC.
3. USE 2 X 6 NAILER AT THE BOTTOM OF ALL 2-2 X 12 OR 4 X HEADERS
   @ EXTERIOR WALLS, BACK HEADER W/2" RIGID INSULATION.
4. BLOCK ALL WALLS OVER 10'-0" HIGH AT MID HEIGHT.

Figure 9-25.
In addition to the regular bullet symbol, other keyboard characters can be used for items in bulleted lists.

- An elevation of the beam with end views or sections
- Complete locational dimensions for holes, plates, and angles
- Length dimensions

Bulleted List with Bullet Symbols

~ Connection specifications
~ Cutouts
~ Miscellaneous notes for the fabricator

Bulleted List with Tilde Characters

AutoCAD and Its Applications—Basics

Picking the **Use Tab Delimiter Only** option limits unwanted list formatting by instructing AutoCAD to recognize only tabs when you are starting a list. If the **Use Tab Delimiter Only** option is unchecked, list formatting is applied when a space or tab follows the initial list item character.

Multiple lines of text can be converted to a list by selecting all of the lines of text and then picking a list formatting option. AutoCAD detects where the [Enter] key was used to start a new line of text and lists the lines in sequence. When you create a list in this manner, a tab is automatically placed after the number, letter, or symbol preceding the text. The size of the space can be adjusted by setting tabs and indents.

The following options are also available when creating lists:

- **Off.** Removes any list characters or bulleting from selected text.
- **Restart.** Renumbers or re-letters selected items in a new sequence. The numbering or lettering starts from the beginning (using 1 or A).
- **Continue.** Adds selected items to a list that exists above the currently selected item. The selected item is numbered to continue the previous list. Items below the selected item are also renumbered.

Exercise 9-5
Complete the exercise on the Student CD.

Stacking Text

When you enter a fraction in the **Text Editor**, the **AutoStack Properties** dialog box is displayed. See Figure 9-26. This dialog box allows you to activate AutoStacking, which causes the entered fraction to stack with a horizontal or diagonal fraction bar. You can also remove the leading space between a whole number and the fraction. This dialog box is displayed each time a fraction is entered. If you decide that you do not want this dialog box to pop up each time you create a fraction, you can pick the **Don't show this dialog again; always use these settings** check box.

Manual stacking

The **Stack** feature can be used to manually stack selected text vertically or diagonally. To use this feature to draw a vertically stacked fraction, place a forward slash between the top and bottom items. Then select the text and pick the **Stack** option from the shortcut menu or the **Options** flyout. To stack items as a *tolerance stack*, use

tolerance stack:
Text that is stacked vertically without a fraction bar.

Figure 9-26.
The **AutoStack Properties** dialog box.

Select style for fraction

Figure 9-27.
Different types of stack characters. ASME standards recommend that the text height of stacked fraction numerals be the same as the height of other dimension numerals.

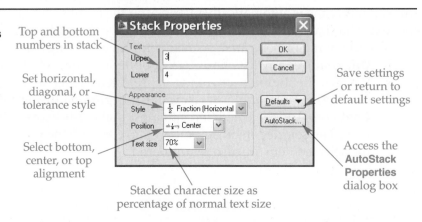

	Selected Text	Stacked Text
Vertical Fraction	1/2	$\frac{1}{2}$
Tolerance Stack	1^2	$\frac{1}{2}$
Diagonal Fraction	1#2	$\frac{1}{2}$

Figure 9-28.
The **Stack Properties** dialog box. Select 100% from the **Text size** drop-down list to conform to ASME standards.

Top and bottom numbers in stack

Set horizontal, diagonal, or tolerance style

Select bottom, center, or top alignment

Stacked character size as percentage of normal text size

Save settings or return to default settings

Access the **AutoStack Properties** dialog box

the caret (^) character between the top and bottom items. Typing a number sign (#) between selected numbers results in a diagonal fraction bar. See **Figure 9-27.**

Unstacking text

To unstack text that has been previously stacked, select the stacked text and pick the **Unstack** option from the shortcut menu or the **Options** flyout. The upper and lower values are placed on a single line with the appropriate character (^, #, or /) displayed between the numbers. The **Stack Properties** dialog box controls stacking settings. To access the dialog box, select the stacked text and pick the **Stack Properties** option from the shortcut menu or the **Options** flyout. The features of the **Stack Properties** dialog box are described in **Figure 9-28.**

Adding Symbols

A variety of common drafting symbols and other unique characters that are not found on a typical keyboard can be inserted into the text editor. Symbol characters can be inserted by selecting the **Symbol** flyout on the **Insert** panel of the **Multiline Text** tab or the **Symbol** cascading submenu available from the shortcut menu or the **Options** flyout. See **Figure 9-29.**

The **Symbol** menu allows the insertion of symbols at the text cursor location. The first two sections in the **Symbol** menu contain commonly used symbols. The third section contains the **Non-breaking Space** option, which keeps two separate words together on one line. Pick any of these symbols to insert them at the text cursor location and hide the **Symbol** menu. The **Other...** option opens the **Character Map** dialog box, shown in **Figure 9-30.** Use the following steps to insert a symbol from the **Character Map** dialog box:
1. Pick the desired symbols to display from the **Font:** drop-down list.
2. Pick the desired symbol and then pick the **Select** button. The selected symbol is displayed in the **Characters to copy:** box.
3. Pick the **Copy** button to copy the selected symbol or symbols to the Clipboard.
4. Pick the **Close** button to close the dialog box.

Figure 9-29.
The **Symbol** menu options.

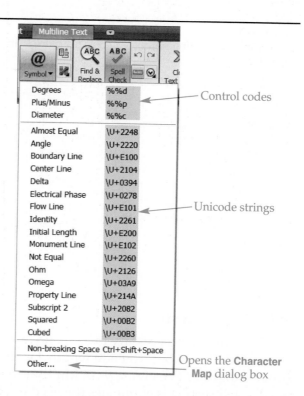

Control codes

Unicode strings

Opens the **Character Map** dialog box

Figure 9-30.
The **Character Map** dialog box.

Select font from drop-down list

Available symbols

Select to return to the **In-Place Text Editor**

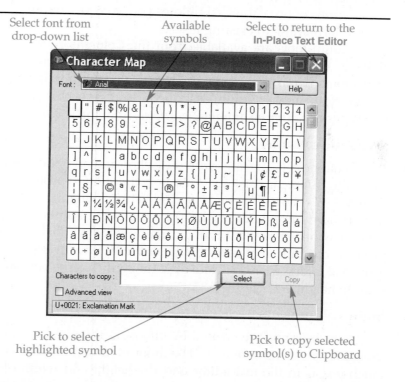

Pick to select highlighted symbol

Pick to copy selected symbol(s) to Clipboard

5. In the text editor, place the cursor where you want the symbols displayed.
6. Right-click to display the text editor shortcut menu. Pick the **Paste** option to paste the symbol at the cursor location.

Exercise 9-6

Complete the exercise on the Student CD.

Figure 9-31.
An example of drawing notes created as a single multiline text object and divided into three columns.

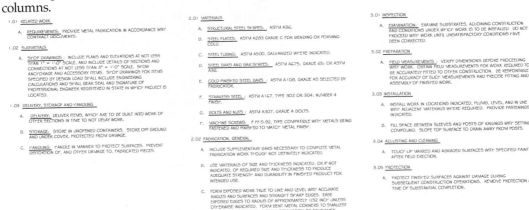

Forming Columns

Sometimes it is necessary to break up text into multiple sections, or columns. This is especially true when you add lengthy general notes or when information must be grouped together. See **Figure 9-31.** Multiline text columns are created in the text editor as a single object. This eliminates the need to create multiple text objects to form separate columns of text. AutoCAD allows you to create columns as you enter text or apply column formatting to existing text.

Column tools are available from the **Columns** flyout on the **Insert** panel of the **Multiline Text** tab, or from the **Columns** cascading submenu on the shortcut menu or the **Options** flyout. By default, the **No Columns** option is selected. This forms the text boundary, or single column, described throughout this chapter. You can create one of two types of columns: *dynamic columns* and *static columns*.

Dynamic columns

Dynamic columns are created by choosing an option from the **Dynamic Columns** cascading submenu. Pick the **Auto height** option to produce columns of equal height. **Figure 9-32** shows methods for adjusting dynamic columns using **Auto height**. Increasing column width or height reduces the number of columns, and decreasing column width or height produces more columns. Pick the **Manual height** option to produce columns that can be adjusted individually for height to produce distinct groups of information. Pick and drag the arrows at the bottom of each column to adjust column height. See **Figure 9-33.**

Static columns

Static columns are created by choosing the number of columns from the **Static Columns** cascading submenu. The amount of text in static columns depends on how much text is in the text editor and the height and width of the columns. However, the selected number of columns does not change even if text does not fill or extends past a column. **Figure 9-34** shows methods for adjusting static columns. Increasing column width or height rearranges the text in the specified number of columns, but the number of static columns does not change based on column width or height.

dynamic columns: Columns calculated automatically by AutoCAD according to the amount of text and the height and width of the columns.

static columns: Columns in which you divide the text into a specified number of columns.

Figure 9-32.

Controlling columns using the dynamic column **Auto Height** option. Notice how column text flows automatically from one column to the next.

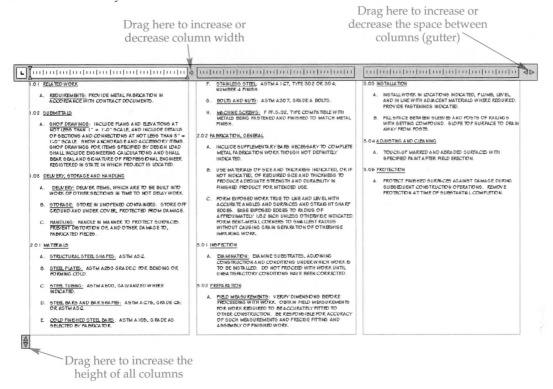

Drag here to increase or decrease column width

Drag here to increase or decrease the space between columns (gutter)

Drag here to increase the height of all columns

Figure 9-33.

Controlling the length of dynamic columns individually (manually).

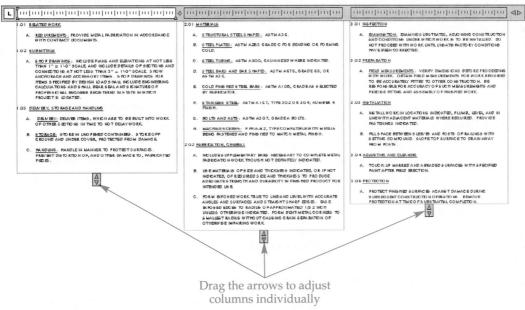

Drag the arrows to adjust columns individually

Figure 9-34.
Controlling static columns.

Drag here to increase or decrease column width

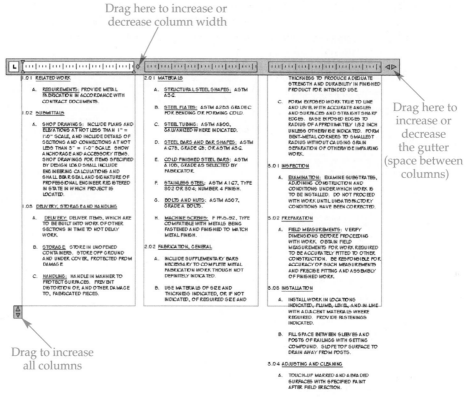

Drag here to increase or decrease the gutter (space between columns)

Drag to increase all columns

Column breaks and settings

The line of text at which a new column begins can be defined using the **Insert Column Break** option. To apply this technique, you must first define a dynamic or static column. Then place the cursor at a location in the text editor where you want a new column to start, such as the start of a paragraph. Pick the **Insert Column Break** option to form the break. The text is shifted to the next column at the location of the break. Continue applying column breaks as needed to separate sections of information.

The **Column Settings...** dialog box can be used as an alternative method for creating columns. To create dynamic columns, select the **Dynamic Columns** radio button, and then select either the **Auto height** or **Manual height** radio button. To create static columns, choose the **Static Columns** radio button and enter the number of static columns in the **Column Number** text box.

Additional controls become available depending on the selected column type radio button(s). Enter the number of static columns in the **Column Number** text box. The **Height** text box allows you to enter the height for all static or dynamic columns. The **Width** area allows you to set column width and the *gutter*. Enter the column width in the **Column** text box, and the gutter width in the **Gutter** text box. The **Total** text box is available only with static columns and is used to enter the total width of the text editor, which is the sum of the width of all columns and the gutter spacing between columns. To eliminate columns, pick the **No Columns** radio button.

gutter: The space between columns of text.

If you choose to remove columns using the **No Columns** option, any column breaks added using the **Insert Column Break** function remain set. Backspace to remove column breaks.

Exercise 9-7

Complete the exercise on the Student CD.

Using a Background Mask

Sometimes text has to be placed over existing objects in a drawing, such as graphic patterns, making the text hard to read. A *background mask* can solve this problem. To mask objects behind text, select **Background Mask...** from the shortcut menu or the **Options** flyout button. This displays the **Background Mask** dialog box. See Figure 9-35.

To apply the mask settings to the current multiline text object, check the **Use background mask** check box. The **Border offset factor:** text box sets how much of the underlying objects is masked out. This value, from 1 to 5, works with the text height value. If the border offset factor is set to 1, then the mask occurs directly within the boundary of the text. To offset the mask beyond the text boundary, use a value greater than 1. The formula is: border offset factor × text height = total masking distance from the bottom of the text. See Figure 9-36. The **Fill Color** area of the **Background Mask** dialog box allows you to apply color to the mask using the background color or a different color.

background mask: A mask that hides a portion of objects behind and around text so that the text is unobstructed.

Figure 9-35.
The **Background Mask** dialog box is used to specify settings for a text mask.

Determines how much of the background is masked

Sets mask color same as background color

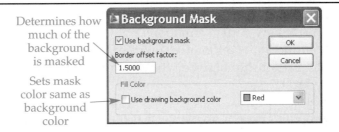

Figure 9-36.
The border offset factor determines the size of the background mask. The text in the figure is 1/8″ with different border offset factors.

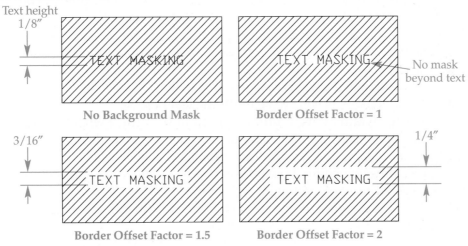

Importing Text

The **Import Text** option available from the shortcut menu or the **Options** flyout button allows you to import text from an existing text file directly into the text editor. The text file can be either a standard ASCII text file (TXT) or a rich text format (RTF) file. The imported text becomes a part of the current multiline text object.

The **Select File** dialog box is displayed when you access the **Import Text...** option. Select the text file to be imported and pick the **Open** button. The text is then inserted at the current cursor location.

Template Development
Chapter 9

Most drafting standards specify the style and size of text to be used on drawings. It is therefore a good idea to set up appropriate styles on your drawing templates. Refer to the Student CD for detailed instructions to add text styles to your mechanical, architectural, and civil drawing templates in compliance with ASME or related industry drafting standards.

Chapter Test

Answer the following questions. Write your answers on a separate sheet of paper or complete the electronic chapter test on the Student CD.

1. Which ASME standard contains guidelines for lettering?
2. What is text composition?
3. Determine the AutoCAD text height for text to be plotted .188″ high using a half (1″ = 2″) scale. (Show your calculations.)
4. Determine the AutoCAD text height for text to be plotted .188″ high using a scale of 1/4″ = 1′-0″. (Show your calculations.)
5. Explain the function of annotative text and give an example.
6. What is the relationship between the drawing scale and the annotation scale for annotative text?
7. Define *text style*.
8. Describe how to create a text style that has the name ROMANS-12_15, uses the romans.shx font, has a fixed height of .12, a text width of 1.25, and an oblique angle of 15.
9. Define *font*.
10. What are Big Fonts?
11. When setting text height in the **Text Style** dialog box, what value do you enter so text height can be altered each time the **TEXT** tool is used?
12. How would you specify text to display vertically on the screen?
13. What does a width factor of .5 do to text when compared to the default width factor of 1?
14. Explain how to make a text style current quickly.
15. Name the tool that lets you create multiline text objects.
16. How does the width of the multiline text boundary affect what you type?
17. What happens if the multiline text you are entering exceeds or is not as long as the boundary length that you initially establish?
18. In the multiline text editor, how do you open the text editor shortcut menu?
19. What is the purpose of tracking?
20. What is the difference between text boundary justification and paragraph alignment?

21. Define *line spacing*.
22. Explain the function of the **Allow Auto-list** option.
23. Explain how to convert multiple lines of text into a numbered list.
24. What happens when you enter a fraction for the first time in the multiline text editor, and what does this allow you to do?
25. How can you draw stacked fractions manually when using the **MTEXT** tool?
26. What happens when you pick the **Other...** option in the **Symbol** cascading menu of the text editor shortcut menu?
27. Briefly describe the difference between dynamic columns and static columns.
28. How can you insert a column break in static columns?
29. What text feature allows you to hide parts of objects behind and around text?
30. In what two formats can text be imported into the text editor?

Drawing Problems

▼ Basic

1. Use the **MTEXT** tool to type your name using a text style of your choosing and a text height of 1″. Print or plot your name as a name tag. Save the drawing as P9-1.

2. Use the **MTEXT** tool to type the definition of the following terms using a text style with the Romand font and a .12 text height. Save the drawing as P9-2.
   - scale factor
   - annotative text
   - annotation scale
   - text height
   - paper text height

3. Use the **MTEXT** tool to type the following text using a text style with the Stylus BT font and a .125 text height. The heading text height is .25. Save the drawing as P9-3.

KEY NOTES
1. SLOPING SURFACE
2. DIAGONAL SUPPORT STRUT
3. VENT- PROVIDE NEW CANT FLASHING
4. BRICK CHIMNEY- REMOVE TO BELOW DECK SURFACE

▼ Intermediate

4. Use the **MTEXT** tool to type the following text using a text style with the Romans font and a .12 text height. The heading text height is .24. Check your spelling. Save the drawing as P9-4.

NOTES:

1. INTERPRET ALL DIMENSIONS AND TOLERANCES PER ANSI Y14.4M-1994.
2. REMOVE ALL BURRS AND SHARP EDGES.
CASTING NOTES UNLESS OTHERWISE SPECIFIED:
1. .31 WALL THICKNESS
2. R.12 FILLETS
3. R.06 CORNERS
4. 1.5°-3.0° DRAFT
5. TOLERANCES
   ± 1° ANGULAR
   ± .03 TWO-PLACE DIMENSIONS
6. PROVIDE .12 THK MACHINING STOCK ON ALL MACHINED SURFACES.

5. Use the **MTEXT** tool to type the following text using a text style with the Stylus BT font and a .125 text height. The heading text height is .188. After typing the text exactly as shown, edit the text with the following changes:
   A. Change the \ in item 7 to 1/2.
   B. Change the [in item 8 to 1.
   C. Change the 1/2 in item 8 to 3/4.
   D. Change the ^ in item 10 to a degree symbol.
   E. Check your spelling after making the changes.
   F. Save as drawing P9-5.

COMMON FRAMING NOTES:
1. ALL FRAMING LUMBER TO BE DFL #2 OR BETTER.
2. ALL HEATED WALLS @ HEATED LIVING AREAS TO BE 2 X 6 @ 24" OC.
3. ALL EXTERIOR HEADERS TO BE 2-2 X 12 UNLESS NOTED, W/ 2" RIGID INSULATION BACKING UNLESS NOTED.
4. ALL SHEAR PANELS TO BE 1/2" CDX PLY W/8d @ 4" OC @ EDGE, HDRS, & BLOCKING AND 8d @ 8" OC @ FIELD UNLESS NOTED.
5. ALL METAL CONNECTORS TO BE SIMPSON CO. OR EQUAL.
6. ALL TRUSSES TO BE 24" OC. SUBMIT TRUSS CALCS TO BUILDING DEPT. PRIOR TO ERECTION.
7. PLYWOOD ROOF SHEATHING TO BE \ STD GRADE 32/16 PLY LAID PERP TO RAFTERS. NAIL W/8d @ 6" OC @ EDGES AND 12" OC @ FIELD.
8. PROVIDE [1/2" STD GRADE T&G PLY FLOOR SHEATHING LAID PERP TO FLOOR JOISTS. NAIL W/10d @ 6" OC @ EDGES AND BLOCKING AND 12" OC @ FIELD.
9. BLOCK ALL WALLS OVER 10'-0" HIGH AT MID.
10. LET-IN BRACES TO BE 1 X 4 DIAG BRACES @ 45^ FOR ALL INTERIOR LOAD-BEARING WALLS.

6. Draw the general caulking notes shown below. Save your drawing as P9-6.

CAULKING NOTES:

CAULKING REQUIREMENTS BASED ON 1992
OREGON RESIDENTIAL ENERGY CODE

1. SEAL THE EXTERIOR SHEATHING AT CORNERS, JOINTS, DOORS, WINDOWS, AND FOUNDATION SILL WITH SILICONE CAULK.
2. CAULK THE FOLLOWING OPENINGS W/ EXPANDED FOAM, BACKER RODS, OR SIMILAR:
   • ANY SPACE BETWEEN WINDOW AND DOOR FRAMES
   • BETWEEN ALL EXTERIOR WALL SOLE PLATES AND PLY SHEATHING
   • ON TOP OF RIM JOIST PRIOR TO PLYWOOD FLOOR APPLICATION
   • WALL SHEATHING TO TOP PLATE
   • JOINTS BETWEEN WALL AND FOUNDATION
   • JOINTS BETWEEN WALL AND ROOF
   • JOINTS BETWEEN WALL PANELS
   • AROUND OPENINGS

7. Draw the basic organizational chart shown below. Save your drawing as P9-7.

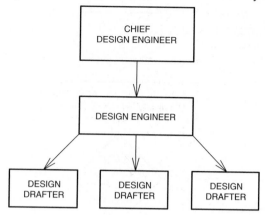

▼ Advanced

8. Draw the controller schematic shown below. Save your drawing as P9-8.

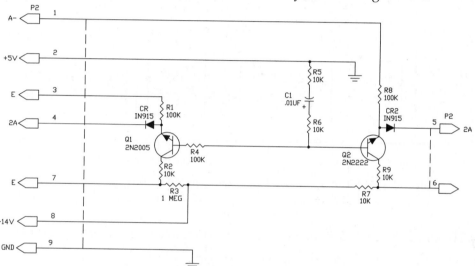

NOTES:

1. INTERPRET ELECTRICAL AND ELECTRONICS DIAGRAMS PER ANSI Y14.15.

2. UNLESS OTHERWISE SPECIFIED:

   RESISTANCE VALUES ARE IN OHMS.
   RESISTANCE TOLERANCE IS 5%.
   RESISTORS ARE 1/4 WATT.
   CAPACITANCE VALUES ARE IN MICROFARADS.
   CAPACITANCE TOLERANCE IS 10%.
   CAPACITOR VOLTAGE RATING IS 20V.
   INDUCTANCE VALUES ARE IN MICROHENRIES.

REFERENCE DESTINATIONS
LAST USED
R9
C1
CR2
Q2

9. Draw the electrical notes shown below. Save your drawing as P9-9.

ELECTRICAL NOTES:

1. ALL GARAGE AND EXTERIOR PLUGS AND LIGHT FIXTURES TO BE ON GFCI CIRCUIT.

2. ALL KITCHEN PLUGS AND LIGHT FIXTURES TO BE ON GFCI CIRCUIT.

3. PROVIDE A SEPARATE CIRCUIT FOR MICROWAVE OVEN.

4. PROVIDE A SEPARATE CIRCUIT FOR PERSONAL COMPUTER. VERIFY LOCATION WITH OWNER.

5. VERIFY ALL ELECTRICAL LOCATIONS W/ OWNER.

6. EXTERIOR SPOTLIGHTS TO BE ON PHOTOELECTRIC CELL W/ TIMER.

7. ALL RECESSED LIGHTS IN EXTERIOR CEILINGS TO BE INSULATION COVER RATED.

8. ELECTRICAL OUTLET PLATE GASKETS SHALL BE INSULATED ON RECEPTACLE, SWITCH, AND ANY OTHER BOXES IN EXTERIOR WALL.

9. PROVIDE THERMOSTATICALLY CONTROLLED FAN IN ATTIC WITH MANUAL OVERRIDE. VERIFY LOCATION WITH OWNER.

10. ALL FANS TO VENT TO OUTSIDE AIR. ALL FAN DUCTS TO HAVE AUTOMATIC DAMPERS.

11. HOT WATER TANKS TO BE INSULATED TO R-11 MINIMUM.

12. INSULATE ALL HOT WATER LINES TO R-4 MINIMUM. PROVIDE ALTERNATE BID TO INSULATE ALL PIPES FOR NOISE CONTROL.

13. PROVIDE 6 SQ. FT. OF VENT FOR COMBUSTION AIR TO OUTSIDE AIR FOR FIREPLACE CONNECTED DIRECTLY TO FIREBOX. PROVIDE FULLY CLOSABLE AIR INLET.

14. HEATING TO BE ELECTRIC HEAT PUMP. PROVIDE BID FOR SINGLE UNIT NEAR GARAGE OR FOR A UNIT EACH FLOOR (IN ATTIC).

15. INSULATE ALL HEATING DUCTS IN UNHEATED AREAS TO R-11. ALL HVAC DUCTS TO BE SEALED AT JOINTS AND CORNERS.

10. Draw the flow chart shown below. Save your drawing as P9-10.

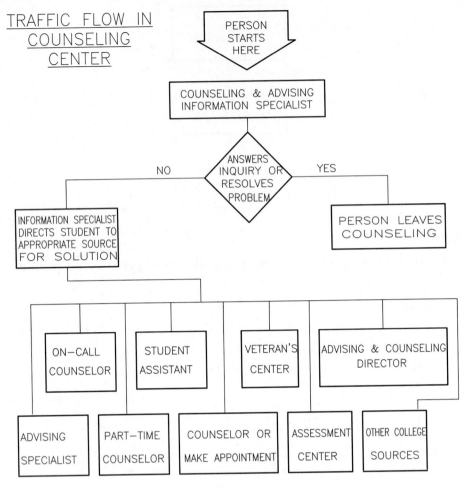

TRAFFIC FLOW IN COUNSELING CENTER

PERSON STARTS HERE

COUNSELING & ADVISING INFORMATION SPECIALIST

ANSWERS INQUIRY OR RESOLVES PROBLEM

NO   YES

INFORMATION SPECIALIST DIRECTS STUDENT TO APPROPRIATE SOURCE FOR SOLUTION

PERSON LEAVES COUNSELING

ON—CALL COUNSELOR

STUDENT ASSISTANT

VETERAN'S CENTER

ADVISING & COUNSELING DIRECTOR

ADVISING SPECIALIST

PART—TIME COUNSELOR

COUNSELOR OR MAKE APPOINTMENT

ASSESSMENT CENTER

OTHER COLLEGE SOURCES

11. Draw the electrical legend shown below. Save your drawing as P9-11.

ELECTRICAL LEGEND:

ϕ	110 VOLT DUPLEX CONVENIENCE OUTLET
ϕ GFCI	110 VOLT GROUND FAULT CIRCUIT INTERRUPT DUPLEX OUTLET
ϕ GFCI WP	110 VOLT WATERPROOF GFCI DUPLEX OUTLET
ϕ	110 VOLT SPLIT WIRED OUTLET
ϕ	220 VOLT OUTLET
ϕ	JUNCTION BOX
TV	CABLE TELEVISION OUTLET
ϕ	CLOCK OUTLET
	DOOR BELL
$	SINGLE POLE SWITCH
$^3	THREE-WAY SWITCH
o	CEILING-MOUNTED LIGHT
	WALL-MOUNTED LIGHT
	FLUORESCENT LIGHT
o	CIRCULAR RECESSED LIGHT
□	SQUARE RECESSED LIGHT
	LIGHT, FAN COMBINATION
	LIGHT, FAN, HEAT COMBINATION
● SD	CEILING-MOUNTED SMOKE DETECTOR
SD	WALL-MOUNTED SMOKE DETECTOR

Single-Line Text and Additional Text Tools

Learning Objectives

After completing this chapter, you will be able to do the following:

✓ Use the **TEXT** tool to create single-line text.
✓ Insert fields into text.
✓ Check your spelling.
✓ Edit existing text.
✓ Search for and replace text automatically.

In Chapter 9 you learned how to use the powerful **MTEXT** tool to create multiline text objects. This chapter describes how to use the **TEXT** tool to place single-line text. Each line of text created with the **TEXT** tool is a single text object. The **TEXT** tool is most useful for text items that require only one line. Whenever the text has more than one line or requires mixed fonts, sizes, colors, or other characteristics, multiline text should be used. This chapter also presents text editing functions and other valuable tools, including fields, methods for finding and replacing text, and spell checking.

Creating Single-Line Text

Single line text objects are created using the **TEXT** tool. When you enter the **TEXT** tool, the default option allows you to select a point on the screen where you want the text to begin. This point becomes the lower-left corner of the text, using default justification. Next you enter the text height. If the current text style is annotative, the height you enter is the paper text height. If the current text style is not annotative, the height you enter is the text height and must be multiplied by the scale factor.

The next prompt asks for the text's rotation angle. The default value is 0, which places the text horizontally. Other values rotate text in a counterclockwise direction. The text pivots about the start point as shown in **Figure 10-1**.

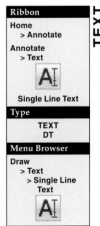

Ribbon
Home
  > Annotate
Annotate
  > Text

Single Line Text

Type
TEXT
DT

Menu Browser
Draw
  > Text
    > Single Line
      Text

TEXT

NOTE

If the default angle orientation or direction is changed, the text rotation is affected.

Figure 10-1.
Rotation angles for text. The start point is indicated here with a plus sign.

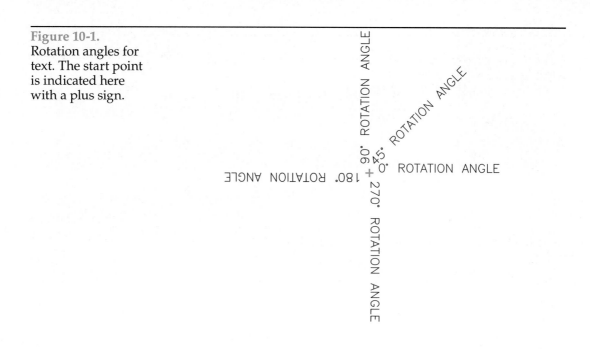

Figure 10-2.
Entering text with the **TEXT** tool.

After the text height and rotation angle are set, a text editor equal in height to the text height appears on-screen at the start point. As text is typed, the text editor increases in size to display the characters. See **Figure 10-2.** You can enter additional lines of text by pressing [Enter] at the end of each line. The text cursor automatically moves to the start point one line below the preceding line. Press [Enter] twice to exit the tool and keep what you have typed. You can cancel the tool at any time by pressing the [Esc] key. This action removes any incomplete lines of text.

A number of options for the **TEXT** tool are available by right-clicking to display a shortcut menu. These shortcut options function much like those for the **MTEXT** tool. Options for accessing help files and canceling the **TEXT** tool are also available from the shortcut menu.

Single-Line Text Justification

The **TEXT** tool offers a variety of justification options. Left justification is the default. To use a different justification option, use the **Justify** option to select it before you pick the start point of the text. Activate the **Justify** option at the Specify start point of text [Justify/Style]: prompt. Several text alignment options are available.

When the **Align** option is selected, AutoCAD automatically adjusts the text height to fit between the start point and endpoint. The height varies according to the distance between the points and the number of characters. The **Fit** option is similar to the **Align** option, except you can select the text height. AutoCAD adjusts character width to fit between the two given points, while keeping text height constant. **Figure 10-3** shows the effects of the **Align** and **Fit** options.

AutoCAD and Its Applications—Basics

Figure 10-3.
Examples of aligned and fit text. In aligned text, the text height is adjusted. In fit text, the text width is adjusted.

Text height varies between lines

AUTOCAD ALIGNED TEXT
WHEN USING ALIGNED TEXT
THE TEXT HEIGHT
IS ADJUSTED SO THAT THE TEXT
FITS BETWEEN
TWO PICKED POINTS

Align Option

AUTOCAD FIT TEXT
WHEN USING FIT TEXT
THE TEXT WIDTH
IS ADJUSTED SO THAT THE TEXT
HEIGHT REMAINS THE SAME
FOR EACH LINE

Text width varies between lines

Fit Option

PROFESSIONAL TIP

The **Align** and **Fit** options of the **TEXT** tool are not recommended because the text height or width are inconsistent from one line of text to another. Also, text height adjusted by the **Fit** option can cause one line of text to run into another.

The **Center** option allows you to select the center point for the baseline of the text. The **Middle** option allows you to center text both horizontally and vertically at a given point. The **Right** option justifies text at the lower-right corner. The letter height and rotation can also be changed when using these options. Figure 10-4 compares the **Center**, **Middle**, and **Right** options.

A number of text alignment options allow you to place text on a drawing in relation to the top, bottom, middle, left side, or right side of the text. These alignment options are shown in Figure 10-5.

Figure 10-4.
The **Center**, **Middle**, and **Right** text justification options.

AUTOCAD CENTERED TEXT

Center Option

AUTOCAD MIDDLE TEXT

Middle Option

AUTOCAD RIGHT–JUSTIFIED TEXT

Right Option

Figure 10-5.
Using the **TL**, **TC**, **TR**, **ML**, **MC**, **MR**, **BL**, **BC**, and **BR** text alignment options. Notice what the abbreviations stand for.

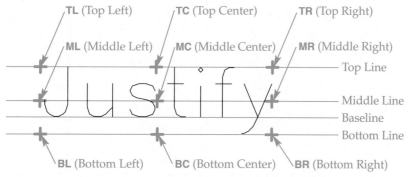

TL (Top Left)   TC (Top Center)   TR (Top Right)

ML (Middle Left)   MC (Middle Center)   MR (Middle Right)

Top Line

Middle Line

Baseline

Bottom Line

BL (Bottom Left)   BC (Bottom Center)   BR (Bottom Right)

Exercise 10-1

Complete the exercise on the Student CD.

Inserting Symbols

In order to insert a symbol with the **TEXT** tool, you must type a special code. For example, to add the note ∅2.75, type %%C2.75 in the text editor. In this example, %%C is the code used to add the diameter symbol. Many symbol codes and the symbols the codes create are shown in Figure 10-6. A single percent sign can be added normally. However, when a percent sign must precede another control code sequence, %%% can be used to force a single percent sign.

Drawing Underscored or Overscored Text

control code sequence: A key sequence beginning with %% that defines symbols in text created with the **TEXT** tool.

Text can be underscored (underlined) or overscored with the **TEXT** tool by typing a ***control code sequence*** in front of the line of text. Type %%O to overscore text and %%U to underscore text. To create the note UNDERSCORING TEXT, for example, type %%UUNDERSCORING TEXT. A line of text may require both underscoring and overscoring. To do this, use both control code sequences. For example, the control code sequence %%O%%ULINE OF TEXT produces LINE OF TEXT.

The %%O and %%U control codes are toggles that turn overscoring and underscoring on and off. Type %%U preceding a word or phrase to turn underscoring on. Type %%U after the desired word or phrase to turn underscoring off. Any text following the second %%U appears without underscoring. For example, DETAIL A HUB ASSEMBLY would be entered as %%UDETAIL A%%U HUB ASSEMBLY.

Figure 10-6.
Common control code sequences used to add symbols to single-line text.

Control Code or Unicode	Type of Symbol	Appearance
%%d	Degrees	°
%%p	Plus/Minus	±
%%c	Diameter	Ø
%%%	Percent	%
\U+2248	Almost Equal	≈
\U+2220	Angle	∠
\U+E100	Boundary Line	BL
\U+2104	Centerline	℄
\U+0394	Delta	Δ
\U+0278	Electrical Phase	ɸ
\U+E101	Flow Line	FL
\U+2261	Identity	≡
\U+E200	Initial Length	O→
\U+E102	Monument Line	ML
\U+2260	Not Equal	≠
\U+2126	Ohm	Ω
\U+03A9	Omega	Ω
\U+214A	Property Line	⅊
\U+2082	Subscript 2	$_2$
\U+00B2	Squared	^{2}
\U+00B3	Cubed	^{3}

Many drafters prefer to underline labels such as <u>SECTION A-A</u> or <u>DETAIL B</u>. Rather than draw line or polyline objects under the text, use **Middle** or **Center** justification modes and underscoring. The view labels are automatically underlined and centered under the views or details they identify.

Exercise 10-2
Complete the exercise on the Student CD.

Working with Fields

Fields display information related to a specific object, general drawing properties, or the current user or computer system. AutoCAD can update field information automatically. This makes fields useful tools for displaying information that may change throughout the course of a project. For example, you could insert the **Date** field into a title block. The field is then updated automatically with the current date throughout the life of the drawing file.

field: A special type of text object that can display a specific property value, setting, or characteristic.

Inserting Fields

Fields are created using the **Field** dialog box, shown in **Figure 10-7**, and can be inserted in both multiline and single-line text editors. To insert a field in an active multi-line text editor, pick the **Insert Field** button from the **Insert** panel of the **Multiline Text**

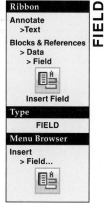

Figure 10-7.
Select fields using the **Field** dialog box.

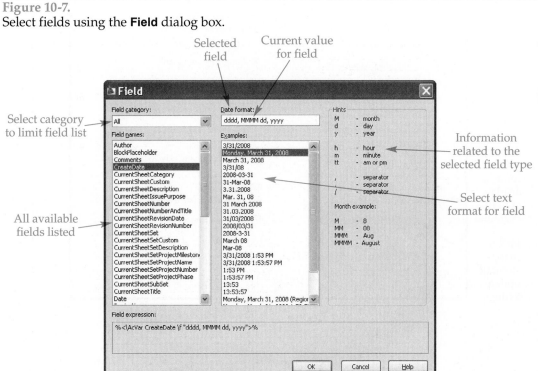

tab, pick the **Insert Field** option available from the shortcut menu or the **Options** flyout, or use the [Ctrl]+[F] key combination. To insert a field in an active single-line text editor, right-click and select **Insert Field...** from the shortcut menu or use the [Ctrl]+[F] key combination.

Many preset fields can be selected from the **Field** dialog box. Notice that the fields are separated into categories. When you select a category from the **Field category** drop-down list, only the fields within the category are displayed in the **Field names** list box. This makes it much easier to locate the desired field. Pick the field category, and then pick the field to be inserted from the **Field names** list box. You can also select from a list of formats to determine the display of the field. The **Format** list varies, depending on the selected field.

After you select the field and format, pick the **OK** button to insert the field. The field assumes the current text style. By default, the field text has a gray background. See **Figure 10-8.** This keeps you aware that the text is actually a field, so the value displayed may change. You can deactivate the background in the **Fields** area of the **User Preferences** tab of the **Options** dialog box. See **Figure 10-9.**

Figure 10-8.
A date and time field inserted into multiline text. The gray background identifies the text as a field.

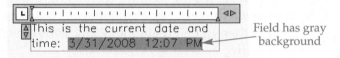

Field has gray background

Figure 10-9.
Control the background display for fields in the **User Preferences** tab of the **Options** dialog box.

Controls display of field background

Pick to change automatic update settings

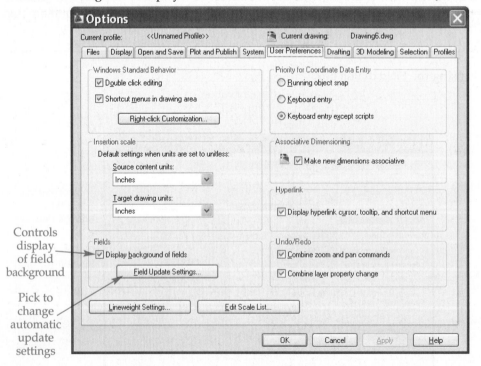

Updating Fields

After a field is inserted into a drawing, the value being displayed may change. For example, a field displaying the current date changes every day. A field displaying the file name changes if the file name changes. A field displaying the value of an object property changes if modifications to the object cause the property to change.

Updating can be completed automatically or manually. Automatic updating is set using the **Field Update Settings** dialog box. To access this dialog box, pick the **Field Update Settings...** button in the **Fields** area of the **User Preferences** tab of the **Options** dialog box. Whenever a selected event (such as saving or regenerating) occurs, all fields are automatically updated.

Update fields manually using the **Update Fields** tool. After picking the tool, select the fields to be updated. You can use the **All** selection option to update all fields in a single operation. You can also update a field within the text editor by right-clicking on the field and selecting the **Update Field** menu option.

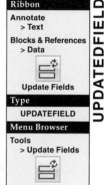

Editing Fields

To edit a field, you must first select the text object containing the field for editing. You can do this quickly by double-clicking on the text object. Then double-click the field to display the **Field** dialog box. You can also right-click in the field and pick **Edit Field...** from the shortcut menu. Use the **Field** dialog box to modify the field settings and pick **OK** to apply the changes.

You can also convert a field to standard text. When you convert a field, the currently displayed value becomes text, the association to the field is lost, and the value no longer updates. To convert a field to text, select the text for editing, right-click in the field, and pick the **Convert Field To Text** option.

NOTE

Fields can be used in conjunction with many AutoCAD tools, including inquiry tools, drawing properties, attributes, and sheet sets. Specific field applications are described where appropriate throughout this textbook.

Exercise 10-3
Complete the exercise on the Student CD.

Checking Your Spelling

AutoCAD provides tools for checking the spelling on your drawing. The quickest way to check your spelling is to use the **Spell Check** tool available in a current multi-line or single-line text editor. The **Spell Check** tool is active in multiline and single-line text editors by default. A red dashed line appears under a word that may be spelled incorrectly. Right-click on the underlined word to display options for adjusting the spelling. See **Figure 10-10.**

The first section at the top of the shortcut menu provides suggested replacements for the word. Pick the correct word to change the spelling in the text editor. If none of the initial suggestions are correct, you may be able to find the correct spelling from the **More Suggestions** cascading submenu.

Figure 10-10.
Quickly checking your spelling using the **Spell Check** tool. Spell checking in the multiline text editor is shown. The tool functions the same in the single-line text editor.

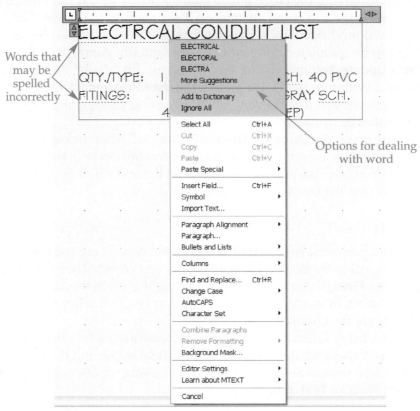

Words that may be spelled incorrectly

Options for dealing with word

If none of the spelling suggestions are appropriate, the word is either spelled correctly or is spelled so incorrectly that AutoCAD cannot recommend the right spelling. If the word is spelled correctly, pick the **Add to Dictionary** option to add the current word to the custom dictionary. You can add words with up to 63 characters. If you want to use the current spelling, recognized as incorrect by AutoCAD, but do not want to add the word to the dictionary, pick the **Ignore All** option. All words that match the currently found misspelled word in the active text editor are ignored and the underline is hidden. Common drafting words and abbreviations, such as the abbreviation for the word SCHEDULE (SCH.) in **Figure 10-10** can be added to the dictionary or ignored.

The **Spell Check** tool can be deactivated in multiline and single-line text editors by deselecting the **Check Spelling** option from the **Editor Settings** cascading submenu available from the shortcut menu or the **Multiline Text** tab **Options** flyout. The tool can also be turned off in an active multiline text editor by deselecting the **Spell Check** button on the **Options** panel of the **Multiline Text** tab.

Using the Spell Tool

Ribbon
Annotate
> Text

ABC
✓
Check Spelling

Type
SPELL
SP

Menu Browser
Tools
> Spelling

ABC
✓

An alternative method to check spelling is to use the **SPELL** tool to access the **Check Spelling** dialog box. See **Figure 10-11**. The **Check Spelling** dialog box is used to check spelling without activating a text editor. The tool checks multiline and single-line text objects.

To check spelling, you must first identify the portion of the drawing you want to spell-check by selecting an option from the **Where to Check** drop-down list. Pick the **Entire drawing** option to check the spelling of all text objects in the drawing file, including model space and all layouts, or choose the **Current space/layout** to check spelling only of text objects in the active layout or model space, if model space is active.

AutoCAD and Its Applications—Basics

Figure 10-11.
The **Check Spelling** dialog box.

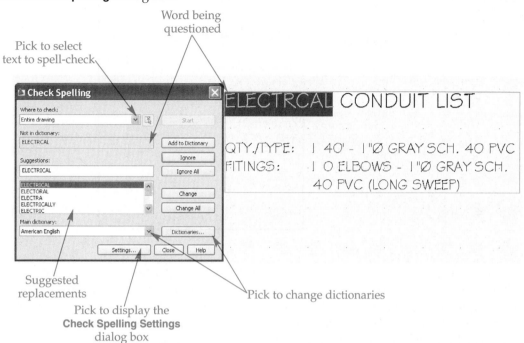

Word being questioned

Pick to select text to spell-check

Suggested replacements

Pick to display the **Check Spelling Settings** dialog box

Pick to change dictionaries

You can also choose to check the spelling of certain text objects by picking the **Selected objects** option. Then pick the **Select text objects** button to enter the drawing window and select all the text objects for which you want to check the spelling.

After you define where to check, pick the **Start** button to begin checking spelling. The first word that may be misspelled is highlighted in the drawing window and is active in the **Check Spelling** dialog box. **Figure 10-11** describes the options found in the **Check Spelling** dialog box.

PROFESSIONAL TIP

Before you check spelling, you may want to adjust some of the spell-checking preferences provided in the **Check Spelling Settings** dialog box. Access this dialog box by picking the **Settings...** button of the **Check Spelling** dialog box, or select the **Check Spelling Settings...** option from the **Editor Settings** cascading submenu available from the text editor shortcut menu or the **Multiline Text** tab **Options** flyout. The settings defined in the **Check Spelling Settings** dialog box apply to spelling checked using the **Spell Check** tool in an active text editor and while using the **Check Spelling** dialog box.

Changing Dictionaries

AutoCAD provides 19 dictionaries for spelling, including dictionaries for several non-English languages. Pick the **Dictionaries...** button of the **Check Spelling** dialog box, or select the **Dictionaries...** option from the **Editor Settings** cascading submenu available from the text editor shortcut menu or the **Multiline Text** tab **Options** flyout to access the **Dictionaries** dialog box. See **Figure 10-12.**

The **Main dictionary** list can be used to select one of the many language dictionaries to use as the current main dictionary. The main dictionary is protected; you cannot add definitions to it. The **Custom dictionary** list can be used to select the active

Figure 10-12.
The **Dictionaries**
dialog box.

Pick to select
main dictionary

Current
dictionary

Enter words to
add to custom
dictionary

Words defined
in custom
dictionary

Pick to import
words from a
word list or
different
dictionary

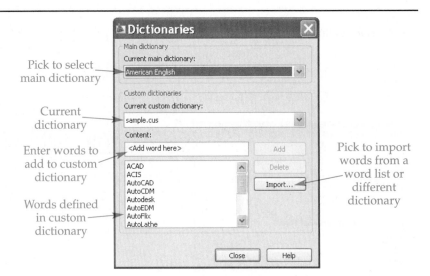

custom dictionary. The default custom dictionary is sample.cus. Type a word in the **Content** text box that you either want to add or delete from the custom dictionary. For example, ASME Y14.5M is custom text used in engineering drafting. Pick the **Add** button to accept the custom words in the text box, or pick the **Delete** button to remove the words from the custom dictionary. Custom dictionary entries may be up to 63 characters in length.

You can create and manage a custom dictionary by picking the **Manage Custom Dictionaries...** option from the drop-down list to access the **Manage Custom Dictionary** dialog box. Pick the **New** button to create a new custom dictionary by entering a new file name with a .cus extension. Words can be added or deleted and dictionaries can be combined using any standard text editor. If you use a word processor such as Microsoft® Word, be sure to save the file as *text only*, with no special text formatting or printer codes. Add an existing custom dictionary by picking the **Add** button, and choose the **Remove** button to delete a custom dictionary from the list. Existing custom dictionaries can also be added by picking the **Import...** button from the **Custom dictionary** area.

PROFESSIONAL TIP

You can create custom dictionaries for various disciplines. For example, common abbreviations and brand names for mechanical drawings might be added to a mech.cus file. A separate file named arch.cus might contain common architectural abbreviations and frequently used brand names.

Exercise 10-4
Complete the exercise on the Student CD.

Revising Text

AutoCAD provides several methods for reentering the text editor to make changes to text content. The easiest way to reopen the text editor is to double-click a multiline or single-line text object. Another technique to reenter the text editor is to use the **DDEDIT** tool. The **DDEDIT** tool can also be accessed by selecting a single-line text object, right-clicking, and selecting **Edit...** from the shortcut menu. The **DDEDIT** tool is a universal text editing tool that can be used to modify the content of most text objects, including multiline and single-line text.

Multiline text can also be edited using the **MTEDIT** tool. The **MTEDIT** tool can also be accessed by selecting a multiline text object, right-clicking, and selecting **Mtext Edit...** from the shortcut menu.

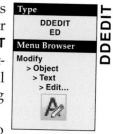

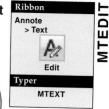

Exercise 10-5
Complete the exercise on the Student CD.

Changing Case

If you forget to type text using uppercase letters, you can quickly set all text to uppercase by selecting the text and picking the **UPPERCASE** option from the **Change Case** cascading submenu available from the text editor shortcut menu or the **Multiline Text** tab **Options** flyout. Select the **lowercase** option, also found in the **Change Case** cascading submenu, to change selected text to lowercase characters. The **AutoCAPS** option available from the text editor shortcut menu or the **Multiline Text** tab **Options** flyout turns on the [Caps Lock] on the keyboard when you open a multiline text editor. The caps lock is turned off when you exit the text editor so that text in other programs is not all uppercase.

Cutting, Copying, and Pasting Text

Clipboard functions allow you to cut, copy, or paste text to or from a text editor. Clipboard functions can be accessed quickly from the shortcut menu when a multiline or single-line text editor is active. Text can be pasted from any text-based application into the text editor. For example, you can copy text from an application such as Microsoft® Word, and then paste it into the text editor. The pasted text retains some of its properties. Likewise, text copied or cut from the text editor can be pasted into another text-based application.

AutoCAD provides three additional paste options for pasting text into the multiline text editor. These options are available from the **Paste Special** cascading submenu of the active text editor shortcut menu. Pick the **Paste without Character Formatting** option to paste text without applying preset character formatting such as bold, italic, or underline. Select the **Paste without Paragraph Formatting** option to paste text without applying current paragraph formatting, including lists. Pick the **Paste without Any Formatting** option to paste text without applying any current character and paragraph formatting.

Finding and Replacing Text

AutoCAD provides tools for searching for a piece of text in your drawing and replacing it with an alternative piece of text. You can search for and replace text in an active multiline or single-line text editor, or outside a text editor.

Figure 10-13.
Using the **Find and Replace** dialog box in an active text editor.

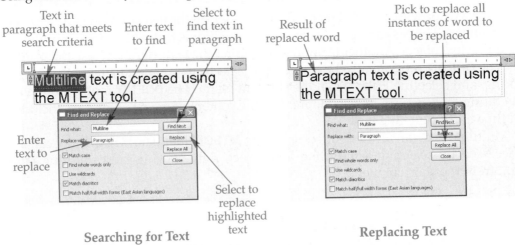

Searching for Text   Replacing Text

Using the Find and Replace tool

The **Find and Replace** tool can be activated in multiline and single-line text editors by selecting the **Find and Replace...** option available from the shortcut menu or the **Multiline Text** tab **Options** flyout. The tool can also be turned on in an active multiline text editor by selecting the **Find & Replace** button from the **Options** panel of the **Multiline Text** tab. The **Find and Replace** dialog box displays. See **Figure 10-13.**

Enter the text you are searching for in the **Find what:** text box. Enter the text that will be substituted in the **Replace with:** text box. Then pick the **Find Next** button to highlight the next instance of the search text. You can then pick the **Replace** or **Replace All** button to replace just the highlighted text or all words that match your search criteria. Check boxes are available to control which characters and words are recognized when finding and replacing text.

Using the Find tool

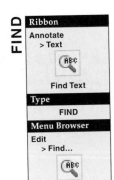

Use the **FIND** tool to find text throughout the entire drawing and replace it with a different piece of text. The tool is accessed when a text editor is not active and searches the entire drawing. AutoCAD displays the **Find and Replace** dialog box when you access the **FIND** tool. See **Figure 10-14.** Another method for accessing the **Find and Replace** dialog box is to enter the text string you want to find in the **Find Text** text box in the expanded **Text** panel on the **Annotation** tab of the ribbon, and press the [Enter] key.

The **Find and Replace** dialog box displayed when you access the **FIND** tool can be used to locate and replace text in multiple text objects. As a result, to find and replace text, you must first identify the portion of the drawing you want to search by selecting an option from the **Find Where** drop-down list. These options are similar to those described for the **Find Where** drop-down list in the **Check Spelling** dialog box.

The **Find and Replace** dialog box is much like the dialog box of the same name that appears when you find and replace text within a text editor. However, this version allows you to display the search results in a table within the dialog box. It also provides more search options. Pick the **More Options** button to display several check boxes used to control which characters and words are recognized when finding and replacing text.

Figure 10-14.
Using the version of the **Find and Replace** dialog box that appears when you use the **Find** tool.

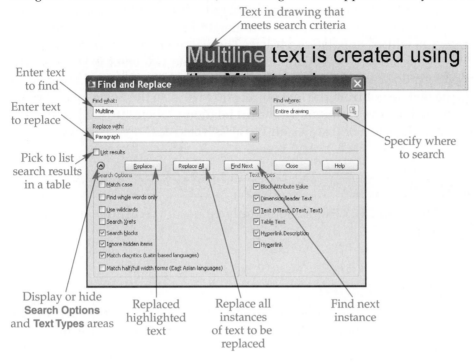

Text in drawing that meets search criteria

Enter text to find

Enter text to replace

Pick to list search results in a table

Specify where to search

Display or hide **Search Options** and **Text Types** areas

Replaced highlighted text

Replace all instances of text to be replaced

Find next instance

NOTE

The find and replace strings are saved with the drawing file and can be reused.

Scaling Text

One option for changing the height of text objects is to use the **SCALETEXT** tool. This tool allows you to scale text objects in relation to their individual insertion points or in relation to a single base point. The **SCALETEXT** tool works with single-line and multiline text objects. You can also select both types of text objects at the same time. After you access the **SCALETEXT** tool, select the text object(s) to be scaled. Then, at the Enter a base point option for scaling [Existing/Left/Center/Middle/Right/TL/TC/TR/ML/MC/MR/BL/BC/BR] <Existing>: prompt, specify the justification for the base point.

All the justification options except **Left** and **Existing** are shown in **Figure 10-4** and **Figure 10-5**. Using the **Left** option scales the text objects using their lower-left point as the base point. Using the **Existing** option scales the text objects using their existing justification setting as the base point. **Figure 10-15** shows text with different justification points being scaled using the **Existing** option. Notice how the text is scaled in relation to its own justification setting.

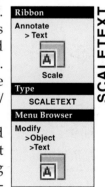

Ribbon

Annotate > Text

Scale

Type

SCALETEXT

Menu Browser

Modify >Object >Text

SCALETEXT

Figure 10-15.
The **Existing** option of the **SCALETEXT** tool scales text objects using their individual justification settings.

+BL Justification
MC Justification
TR Justification

Original Text

+BL Justification
MC Justification
TR Justification

Text Scaled Using Existing Base Point Option

After you specify the justification to be used as the base point, AutoCAD prompts for the scaling type. The **Specify new model height** option (default) is used to type a new value for the text height of non-annotative objects. If the selected text is annotative, the value you enter is ignored. The **Paper height** option is used to type a new value for the text height of annotative objects. The value entered here is the paper text height. If the selected text is non-annotative, the value you enter is ignored. The **Match object** option allows you to pick an existing text object. The selected text object's height adopts the text height from the text object you pick. Use the **Scale factor** option to scale text objects that have different heights in relation to their current heights. For example, using a scale factor of 2 scales all of the selected text objects to twice their current size.

> **NOTE**
>
> The **SCALETEXT** tool should only be used to scale non-annotative text.

Changing Text Justification

JUSTIFYTEXT

Ribbon
Annotate
> Text

Justify

Type
JUSTIFYTEXT

Menu Browser
Modify
>Object
>Text
>Justify

To change the justification point without moving the text, use the **JUSTIFYTEXT** tool. Pick the text for which you want to change justification, and enter the new justification option.

Exercise 10-6
Complete the exercise on the Student CD.

Express Tools
Chapter 10

The Express menu of the menu browser includes additional tools for improved functionality and productivity during the drawing processes. The following Express Tools represent the most useful text express tools. Refer to the Student CD for information on these tools.

Text Fit	**Arc-Aligned Text**
Text Mask	**Enclose Text with Object**
Unmask Text	**Change Text Case**
Convert Text to Mtext	

Chapter Test

Answer the following questions. Write your answers on a separate sheet of paper or complete the electronic chapter test on the Student CD.

1. List three ways to access the **TEXT** tool.
2. Give the control code sequence required to draw the following symbols when using the **TEXT** tool:
   A. 30°
   B. 1.375 ± .005
   C. Ø24
   D. <u>NOT FOR CONSTRUCTION</u>
3. Briefly discuss the function and purpose of fields.
4. What is different about the on-screen display of fields compared to that of text?
5. How can you access the **Field Update Settings** dialog box?
6. Explain how to convert a field to text.
7. What is the quickest way to check your spelling within a current text editor?
8. Identify three ways to access the AutoCAD spell checker.
9. How do you change the **Current word** if you do not think the word that is displayed in the **Suggestions:** text box of the **Check Spelling** dialog box is the correct word, but one of the words in the list of suggestions is the correct word?
10. How do you change the main dictionary for use in the **Check Spelling** dialog box?
11. What appears if you double-click on multiline text?
12. Identify the tool used to revise existing single-line text on the drawing by editing the text in place.
13. Name two tools that allow you to edit multiline text.
14. Name the tool that allows you to find a piece of text and replace it with an alternative piece of text in a single instance or for every instance in your drawing.
15. When using the **SCALETEXT** tool, which base point option would you select to keep the text object's current justification point?

Drawing Problems

1. Start AutoCAD, start a new drawing using one of your templates, and create text styles as needed. Use the **TEXT** tool to type the following information. Change the text style to represent each of the four fonts named. Use a .25 unit text height and 0° rotation angle. Save the drawing as P10-1.

   TXT–AUTOCAD'S DEFAULT TEXT FONT, WHICH IS AVAILABLE FOR USE WHEN YOU BEGIN A DRAWING.
   ROMANS–SMOOTHER THAN TXT FONT AND CLOSELY DUPLICATES THE SINGLE-STROKE LETTERING THAT HAS BEEN THE STANDARD FOR DRAFTING.
   ROMANC–A MULTISTROKE DECORATIVE FONT THAT IS GOOD FOR USE IN DRAWING TITLES.
   ITALICC–AN ORNAMENTAL FONT SLANTED TO THE RIGHT AND HAVING THE SAME LETTER DESIGN AS THE COMPLEX FONT.

2. Start AutoCAD, start a new drawing using one of your templates, and create text styles as needed. Change the options as noted in each line of text. Then use the **TEXT** tool to type the text, changing the text style to represent each of the fonts named. Use a .25 unit text height. Save the drawing as P10-2.

   TXT–EXPAND THE WIDTH BY THREE.
   MONOTXT–SLANT TO THE LEFT –30°.
   ROMANS–SLANT TO THE RIGHT 30°.
   ROMAND–BACKWARDS.
   ROMANC–VERTICAL.
   ITALICC–UNDERSCORED AND OVERSCORED.
   ROMANS–USE 16d NAILS @ 10″ OC.
   ROMANT–Ø32 (812.8).

3. Open P5-10 and add text to the circuit diagram. Use a text style with the Romans font. Create a layer for the text. Save the drawing as P10-3.

▼ Intermediate

4. Start AutoCAD and use the setup option of your choice. Create text styles with a .375 height and the following fonts: Arial, BankGothic Lt BT, CityBlueprint, Stylus BT, Swis721 BdOul BT, Vineta BT, and Wingdings. Use the **TEXT** tool to type the complete alphabet and numbers 1–10 for the text styles. Also, type all symbols available on the keyboard and the diameter, degree, and plus/minus symbols. Save the drawing as P10-4.

5. Create the window schedule shown below. Create the text using a text style with the Stylus BT font. Create a layer for the text. Draw the hexagonal symbols in the SYM column. Save the drawing as P10-5.

SYM.	SIZE	MODEL	ROUGH OPEN	QTY.
A	12 x 60	JOB BUILT	VERIFY	2
B	96 x 60	W4N5 CSM.	8'-0 3/4" x 5'-0 7/8"	1
C	48 x 60	W2N5 CSM.	4'-0 3/4" x 5'-0 7/8"	2
D	48 x 36	W2N3 CSM.	4'-0 3/4" x 3'-6 1/2"	2
E	42 x 42	2N3 CSM.	3'- 6 1/2" x 3'-6 1/2"	2
F	72 x 48	G64 SLDG.	6'-0 1/2" x 4'-0 1/2"	1
G	60 x 42	G536 SLDG.	5'-0 1/2" x 3'-6 1/2"	4
H	48 x 42	G436 SLDG.	4'-0 1/2" x 3'-6 1/2"	1
J	48 x 24	A41 AWN.	4'-0 1/2" x 2'-0 7/8"	3

WINDOW SCHEDULE

6. Create the door schedule shown below. Create the text using a text style with the Stylus BT font. Create a layer for the text. Draw the circle symbols in the SYM column. Save the drawing as P10-6.

DOOR SCHEDULE

SYM.	SIZE	TYPE	QTY.
1	36 x 80	S.C. R.P. METAL INSULATED	1
2	36 x 80	S.C. FLUSH METAL INSULATED	2
3	32 x 80	S.C. SELF CLOSING	2
4	32 x 80	HOLLOW CORE	5
5	30 x 80	HOLLOW CORE	5
6	30 x 80	POCKET SLDG.	2

7. Create the interior finish schedule shown below. Create the text using a text style with the Stylus BT font. Save the drawing as P10-7.

INTERIOR FINISH SCHEDULE

ROOM	FLOOR					WALLS				CEILING		
	VINYL	CARPET	TILE	HARDWOOD	CONCRETE	PAINT	PAPER	TEXTURE	SPRAY	SMOOTH	BROCADE	PAINT
ENTRY					●							
FOYER			●			●			●			●
KITCHEN			●				●			●		
DINING				●		●			●		●	●
FAMILY		●				●			●		●	●
LIVING		●				●		●			●	●
MSTR. BATH			●			●			●		●	
BATH #2			●			●			●		●	
MSTR. BED		●				●		●			●	●
BED #2		●				●			●		●	●
BED #3		●				●			●		●	●
UTILITY	●					●			●	●		●

8. Create the block diagram shown below. Create the text using a text style with the Romans font. Create a layer for the text. Save the drawing as P10-8.

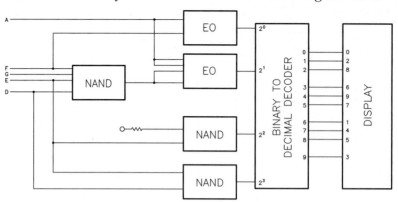

9. Create the block diagram shown below. Create the text using a text style with the Romans font. Do not include the arrowheads; you will create them in a later chapter. Create a layer for the text. Save the drawing as P10-9.

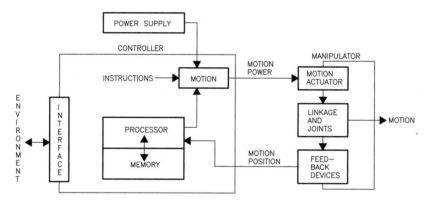

10. Draw the AND/OR schematic shown below. Save your drawing as P10-10.

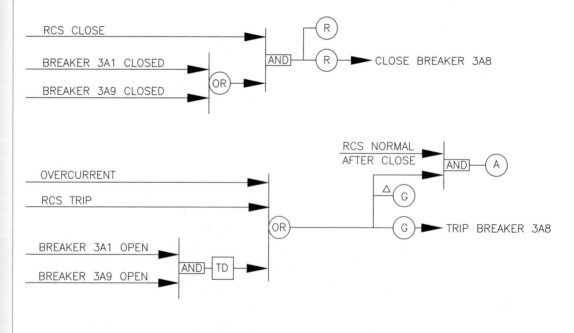

11. Draw the finish schedule shown below. Save your drawing as P10-11.

INTERIOR FINISH SCHEDULE

ROOM	CARPET	VINYL	TILE	HARDWOOD	PAINT	PAPER	TEXTURE	SPRAY	SMOOTH	BROCADE	PAINT
	FLOOR				WALLS				CEIL		
FOYER		•			•		•			•	•
KITCHEN		•				•			•	•	
DINING			•	•		•			•	•	
FAMILY	•					•			•	•	
LIVING	•					•			•	•	
MASTER BED	•					•			•		•
MASTER BATH			•			•		•	•		•
BATH 2			•			•		•	•		
BED 2	•					•			•	•	
BED 3	•					•			•	•	
UTILITY			•			•		•	•		•

▼ Advanced

12. Add title blocks, borders, and text styles to the template drawings you created in earlier chapters. Create a Border layer for the border lines and thick title block lines. Create a Title block layer for thin title block lines and text. Make three template drawings with borders and title blocks for your future drawings. Use the following guidelines:

A. Template 1 used for A-size, 8 1/2 × 11 drawings, named TITLEA–MECH.

B. Template 2 used for B-size, 11 × 17 drawings, named TITLEB–MECH.

C. Template 3 used for C-size, 17 × 22 drawings, named TITLEC–MECH.

D. Set the following values for the drawing aids:
   Units = three-place decimal
   Grid = .500
   Snap = .250

E. Draw a border 1/2" from the drawing limits.

F. Design a title block using created text styles. Place it in the lower-right corner of each drawing. The title block should contain the following information: Company or school name, address, date (field), drawn by, approved by, scale, title, drawing number, material, revision number. See the example below.

G. Record the information about each template in a log.

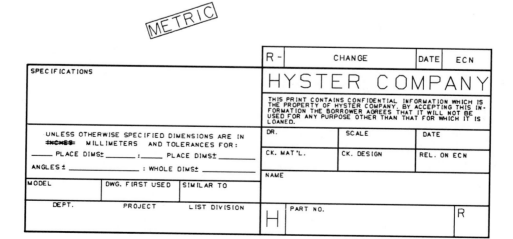

13. Start a new drawing using the C-size mechanical drawing template located on the Student CD. Draw a small parts list connected to the title block, similar to the one shown below.
   A. Enter PARTS LIST with a style containing a complex font.
   B. Enter the other information using text and the **TEXT** tool.
   C. Save the drawing as TITLEC-PARTS.
   D. Record the information about the template in a log.

3	HOLDING PINS	12
2	SIDE COVERS	3
1	MAIN HOUSING	1
KEY	DESCRIPTION	QTY

PARTS LIST

UNLESS OTHERWISE SPECIFIED
ALL DIMENSIONS IN

INCHES

AND TOLERANCES FOR:

1 PLACE DIMS: ±.1
2 PLACE DIMS: ±.01
3 PLACE DIMS: ±.005
ANGULAR: ±30'
FRACTIONAL: ±.1/32
FINISH: 125? in.

FIRST USED ON: | SIMILAR TO:

JANE'S
DESIGN

| DR: | SCALE: | DATE: | APPD: |
| JANE | FULL | XX–XX–XX | |

MATERIAL:
MILD STEEL

NAME:
XXX–XXXX

B | PART NO: 123–321 | REV: 0

14. Create an architectural template for a 17″ × 22″ or 22″ × 34″ sheet size with a title block along the right side similar to the one shown below. Use the same guidelines given for Problem 12. Save the drawing as ARCH. Record the information about the template in a log.

15. Draw title blocks with borders for your electrical, piping, and general drawings. Use the same guidelines provided in Problem 12. The title block can be similar to the one displayed with Problem 12, but the area for mechanical drafting tolerances is not required. Research sample title blocks to come up with your design. Save the drawings as templates named ELEC A, ELEC B, PIPE A, PIPE B, or use names related to the drawing type and sheet size.

16. Draw the engineering change notice form shown below. Save your drawing as P10-16.

Engineering Change Notice

ECN NO. _____

Disposition of production stock:
A =Alter or rework U=Use in production
T=Transfer to service stock   S=Scrap

Qty.	Drawing Size Part No.	R/N	Description	Change	Other Usage in Production	D/S
01						
02						
03						
04						
05						
06						
07						
08						
09						
10						
11						
12						
13						
14						
15						
16						
17						
18						

Reason:

_____

_____

_____

_____

Castings & forgings affected? ☐ Yes ☐ No	Design engineer:	Supervisor approval:	Release date:	Page

Working with Tables

Learning Objectives

After completing this chapter, you will be able to do the following:

✓ Create and modify table styles.
✓ Insert a table into a drawing.
✓ Edit a table.
✓ Insert formulas into table cells to perform calculations on numeric data.

Tables are commonly used in drafting to show bills of materials, door and window schedules, legends, and title block information. Review the tables and terminology shown in Figure 11-1. This will help you better understand tables and table information as you read this chapter.

table: An arrangement of rows and columns that organize data to make it easier to read.

Figure 11-1.
Tables in AutoCAD can be created with the title and header rows at the top or the bottom.

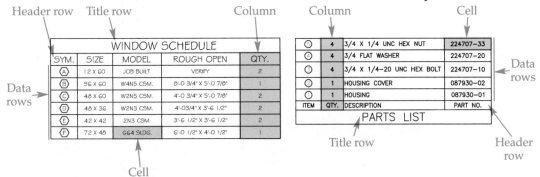

WINDOW SCHEDULE				
SYM.	SIZE	MODEL	ROUGH OPEN	QTY.
A	12 X 60	JOB BUILT	VERIFY	2
B	96 X 60	W4N5 CSM.	8'-0 3/4" X 5'-0 7/8"	1
C	48 X 60	W2N5 CSM.	4'-0 3/4" X 5'-0 7/8"	2
D	48 X 36	W2N3 CSM.	4'-03/4" X 3'-6 1/2"	2
E	42 X 42	2N3 CSM.	3'-6 1/2" X 3'-6 1/2"	2
F	72 X 48	G64 SLDG.	6'-0 1/2" X 4'-0 1/2"	1

⊙	4	3/4 X 1/4 UNC HEX NUT	224707-33
⊙	4	3/4 FLAT WASHER	224707-20
⊙	4	3/4 X 1/4-20 UNC HEX BOLT	224707-10
⊙	1	HOUSING COVER	087930-02
⊙	1	HOUSING	087930-01
ITEM	QTY.	DESCRIPTION	PART NO.
PARTS LIST			

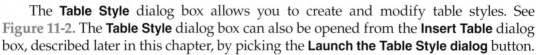

Table Styles

AutoCAD *table styles* are used to set table characteristics. You may have several table styles depending on the variety of tables you create and different characteristics needed. Table format options can be adjusted independently of a table style. However, you should create a table style for each unique table requirement. For example, you can have one table style for creating door and window schedules, and another table style with different characteristics for adding an interior finish schedule. In mechanical drafting, you might prepare a table style for parts lists and another table style for gear data tables. Table styles should be added to drawing templates for repeated use.

Working with Table Styles

The **Table Style** dialog box allows you to create and modify table styles. See **Figure 11-2**. The **Table Style** dialog box can also be opened from the **Insert Table** dialog box, described later in this chapter, by picking the **Launch the Table Style dialog** button.

The **Styles** list box displays existing table styles. By default, the Standard table style is available and current. When you insert a table into the drawing, it uses the formatting settings from the current table style. To set a style current, pick it once in the **Styles** list box and then select the **Set Current** button. A table style can also be set current by double-clicking the style in the **Styles** list box or right-clicking the style and selecting the **Set current** menu option.

Below the **Styles** list box is a drop-down list that can be used to filter the number of table styles displayed in the **Table Style** dialog box. Pick the **All Styles** options to show all table styles in the file, or pick the **Styles in use** option to show only the styles used in the drawing.

Creating New Table Styles

To create a new table style, first select an existing table style from the **Styles** list box. This style is used as a base for formatting the new table style. Then pick the **New…** button in the **Table Style** dialog box to open the **Create New Table Style** dialog box. See **Figure 11-3**. In the **New Style Name** text box, type a name for the new table style. The new table can be based on the formatting settings from a different existing table style by selecting the name of the table style from the **Start With** drop-down list.

Figure 11-2.
The **Table Style** dialog box.

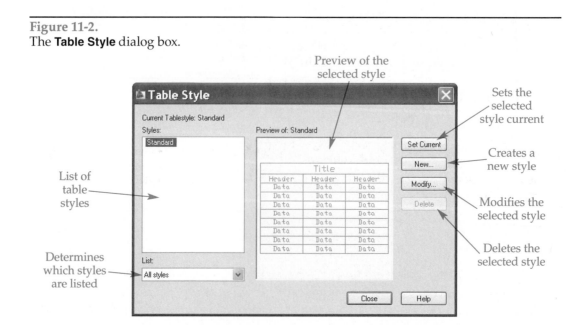

Figure 11-3.
In the **Create New Table Style** dialog box, specify the new table style's name and the existing style that will be copied as a basis for the new style.

Type in a name for the new table style

Displays the **New Table Style** dialog box

Copies settings from an existing style

Figure 11-4.
The formatting properties for a new style are specified in the **New Table Style** dialog box. The **Data** cell style is shown in the **Cell styles** area in this figure.

Pick to create a starting table style

Pick to remove the starting table reference

Select a cell style

Pick to create a new cell style

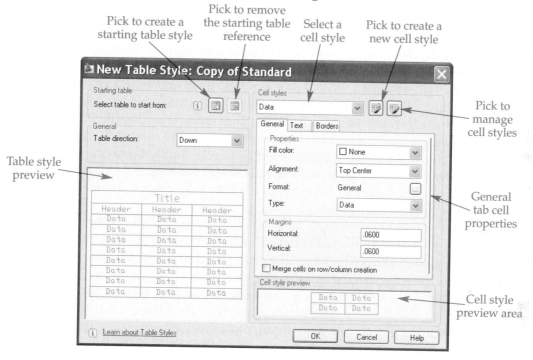

Table style preview

Pick to manage cell styles

General tab cell properties

Cell style preview area

The default new table style name is Copy of followed by the name of the selected existing style. You can keep the default name, but you should usually enter a more descriptive name, such as Parts List, Parts List No Heading, or Door Schedule. Table style names can have up to 255 characters, including letters, numbers, dashes (–), underlines (_), and dollar signs ($). You can type uppercase or lowercase letters. After entering the table style name, pick the **Continue** button to open the **New Table Style** dialog box and adjust table style characteristics. See **Figure 11-4.**

PROFESSIONAL TIP

It is a good idea to record the names and details about the table styles you create and keep this information in a log for future reference.

Adjusting Table Direction

The **Table direction** setting in the **General** area of the **New Table Style** dialog box determines the placement of the data rows. The two options are **Down** and **Up**. When the **Down** option is selected, the data rows are placed below the title and header rows.

When the **Up** option is selected, the data rows are placed above the title and header rows. The difference can be viewed in the preview window. Refer again to **Figure 11-1.**

Cell Styles

Three default cell styles are available in the **Cell Styles** area of the **New Table Style** dialog box: **Data**, **Header**, and **Title**. Cell styles allow data cell rows, the column header row, and the title row to have their own formatting properties. Picking a cell style from the drop-down list displays the properties for the corresponding element. In **Figure 11-4**, the **Data** cell style is selected. Cell formatting properties are set using the **General**, **Text**, and **Borders** tabs. The options in these tabs are the same for adjusting data, header, and title cell style types.

General tab settings

The **General** tab, shown in **Figure 11-4**, is used to set general table characteristics. The **Fill color** drop-down provides options for adjusting the color used to fill cells. The default setting is None, which does not fill cells with a color. The drawing window color determines the on-screen table display. You can fill cells with color to highlight or organize table information. Pick a color from the drop-down list to fill the cells with the selected color. The **Alignment** drop-down list is used to justify text within the cell.

Format shows the current cell format, which is General by default. Pick the ellipsis (...) button to access the **Table Cell Format** dialog box. See **Figure 11-5.** The **Data Type** area lists options for formatting the selected table cell: **Angle**, **Currency**, **Date**, **Decimal Number**, **General**, **Percentage**, **Point**, **Text**, and **Whole Number**. Selecting a format presents options for adjusting the format characteristics. Different options are available depending on the selected format.

Use the **Type** drop-down list to determine the type of data displayed in the cell. Pick **Data** from this drop-down list to define a data cell type. Choose **Label** if the cell is a label cell type, such as a column heading or the table title. The **Margins** area provides text boxes for setting the spacing between the cell content and the borders. This spacing applies to text and blocks. The values in the **Horizontal** and **Vertical** text boxes determine the spacing between the content and the cell border. The default setting is .06.

Pick the **Merge cells on row/column creation** check box to merge the row of cells together to form a single cell. This check box is selected by default for the **Title** cell style. The title cell provides an example of when you may want to merge cells.

Figure 11-5.
Many different data types are available to format a table cell.

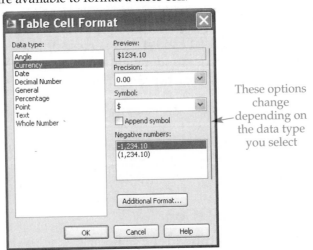

AutoCAD and Its Applications—Basics

Figure 11-6.
The **Text** tab in the **New Table Style** dialog box allows you to set text properties.

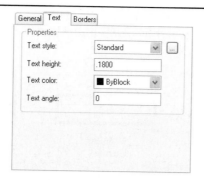

Figure 11-7.
In this table, a 90° text angle has been applied to the header cell style.

ROOM SCHEDULE					
NUMBER	NAME	LENGTH	WIDTH	HEIGHT	AREA
1	BEDROOM 1	11'-0"	10'-0"	9'-0"	110 SQ. FT.
2	BEDROOM 2	10'-0"	11'-0"	9'-0"	110 SQ. FT.
3	MASTER BEDROOM	12'-0"	14'-0"	9'-0"	168 SQ. FT.
4	LIVING ROOM	12'-0"	16'-0"	9'-0"	192 SQ. FT.
5	DINING ROOM	11'-0"	12'-0"	9'-0"	132 SQ. FT.
6	KITCHEN	11'-0"	10'-0"	9'-0"	110 SQ. FT.

Text tab settings

The **Text** tab, shown in **Figure 11-6,** is used to set text characteristics for the selected cell style. The **Text style** drop-down list displays all of the text styles that are defined in the current drawing. Select a style or pick the ellipsis (**...**) button to the right of the drop-down list to open the **Text Style** dialog box to create a new text style or modify an existing text style. Text styles are described in Chapter 9.

The **Text height** text box is used to specify the height of the text. The default setting for data row and column header cells is 0.1800. If a text height other than 0 has been set in the text style, this setting is grayed out. Use the **Text color** drop-down list to set the color of the text. The **Text angle** text box is used to define the rotation angle of text within the table cell. **Figure 11-7** shows an example of a 90° text angle applied to the **Header** cell style.

Borders tab settings

The **Borders** tab, shown in **Figure 11-8,** is used to control the border display and characteristics for the selected cell style. Use the **Lineweight** drop-down list to assign a unique lineweight to cell borders. The **Linetype** drop-down list allows you to assign a unique linetype to cell borders. As when creating layers, you must load linetypes if they are not currently loaded in the file in order to apply them to the cell border. The **Color** drop-down list is used to set the color of the cell borders.

Figure 11-8.
The **Borders** tab in the **New Table Style** dialog box allows you to set cell border properties.

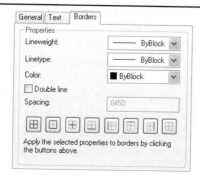

Figure 11-9.
Several border options are available for table cells. The settings shown are for data rows only.

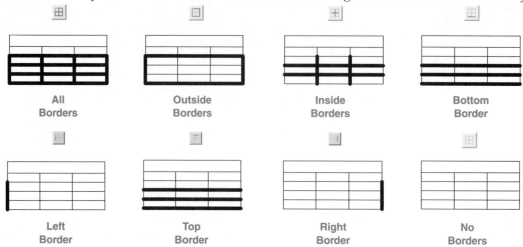

Pick the **Double line** check box to add another line around the default single line border style. When this check box is selected, the **Spacing** edit box becomes available, allowing you to enter the distance between the double lines. The default double line border spacing is 0.0450.

The **Border** buttons are used to control how the **Lineweight, Linetype, Color,** and **Double line** border properties are applied to the cell borders. From right to left, the options are: **All Borders, Outside Borders, Inside Borders, Bottom Border, Left Border, Top Border, Right Border,** and **No Borders.** Once you set the desired border properties, select or deselect these buttons according to how you want cell borders displayed. An example of each border style is shown in **Figure 11-9.**

> **NOTE**
>
> AutoCAD displays border lineweights on-screen only if lineweights are being displayed. Pick the **Show/Hide Lineweight** button on the status bar to display lineweights.

Creating cell styles

The default **Data, Header,** and **Title** cell styles are all that are needed for typical table applications. However, you can further increase the flexibility and options for creating tables by developing additional cell styles. For example, you can create a cell style called Data Yellow that is the same as the **Data** cell style but fills cells with a yellow color. Then when you draw a table, you can choose from either the **Data** or the **Data Yellow** cell style, depending on the application.

To create a new cell style, first select an existing cell style from the **Cell Styles** area drop-down list. This style will be used as a basis for formatting the new cell style. Then, pick the **Create new cell style...** button from the **Cell Styles** area, or select **Create new cell style...** from the **Cell Styles** area drop-down list. The **Create New Cell Style** dialog box is displayed. In the **New Style Name** text box, type a name for the new cell style. The new cell style can be based on the formatting settings of a different existing cell style by selecting the name of the cell style from the **Start With** drop-down list.

Cell styles are created, renamed, and deleted using the **Manage Cell Styles** dialog box, shown in **Figure 11-10.** To access this dialog box, pick the **Manage Cell Style dialog...** button from the **Cell Styles** area, or select **Manage cell styles...** from the **Cell Styles** area drop-down list.

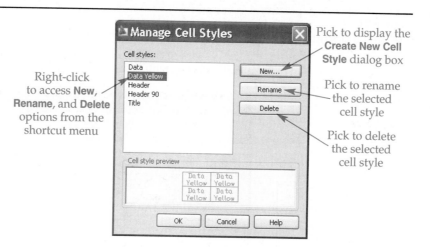

Right-click to access **New**, **Rename**, and **Delete** options from the shortcut menu

Pick to display the **Create New Cell Style** dialog box

Pick to rename the selected cell style

Pick to delete the selected cell style

NOTE

The **Preview** and **Cell style preview** areas of the **New Table Style** dialog box allow you to see how the selected table style characteristics appear in a table. This is a very convenient way to see what the table looks like before it is created.

Exercise 11-1
Complete the exercise on the Student CD.

Developing a Starting Table Style

One technique for creating a table is to base the new table on an existing table. This method is accomplished using a starting table style. A starting table style can be considered a table template that already contains all of the table style characteristics and the same table rows, columns, and data entries added to an existing table. Using a starting table style is much like copying a complete table and editing the table as needed. A starting table style can save a significant amount of time if you often prepare similar tables. For example, using a starting table style is effective if you already created a complete door schedule, and then want to add a very similar door schedule to a new drawing project that contains most of the same doors.

Before you can create a starting table style, an existing table must be available in the drawing. A starting table style references the characteristics of the selected reference table, including the number of columns and rows and the table direction. Other table style characteristics, such as text style, are set according to the selected base table style. As a result, it is usually most appropriate to create a new starting table style using a base table style that is the same as that used when the reference table was drawn. For example, if a door schedule was created using a table style named Door Schedule, you should base the new starting table style on the Door Schedule table style.

To create a starting table style, pick the **Select table to start from** button in the **Starting table** area. Then pick a border line of the table you want to reference to form the starting table style. The preview will display the selected table and the table style settings of the base table style. See **Figure 11-11.** You can modify the table direction and cell style options using the **General** and **Cell Styles** areas. Pick the **Remove Table** button to remove the table reference from the table style. A table is added to a drawing using a starting table style by picking the **Start from Table style** insertion option described later in this chapter.

Figure 11-11.
Creating a starting table style that references an existing table.

Pick to create a
starting table style

Pick to remove the
starting table reference

Select existing
table

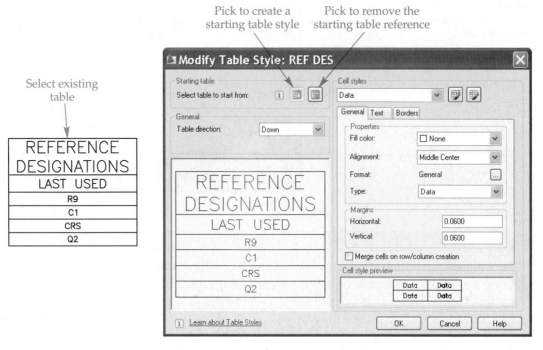

Changing, Renaming, and Deleting Table Styles

To change the characteristics of an existing table style, select the table style and pick the **Modify** button to access the **Modify Table Style** dialog box. The **Modify Table Style** dialog box is the same as the **New Table Style** dialog box. If you change the characteristics of an existing text style, all tables added using that style are redrawn with the new values.

Existing table styles can be renamed in the **Table Style** dialog box. To rename a table style, slowly double-click the name or right-click the name and select the **Rename** option. To delete a table style, right-click the name and select the **Delete** option, or pick the style and select the **Delete** button. AutoCAD will not allow you to delete a table style that has been used to create text objects in the drawing. If you want to delete the style, change the tables in the drawing to a different style. You cannot delete or rename the Standard style.

NOTE

Styles can also be renamed using the **Rename** dialog box. Select **Table styles** in the **Named Objects** list to rename the style.

Setting a Table Style Current

You can set a table style current using the **Table Style** dialog box by double-clicking the style in the **Styles** list box, right-clicking the style and selecting the **Set current** menu option, or picking the style and selecting the **Set current** button. To quickly set a table style current without opening the **Table Style** dialog box, use the **Table Style** drop-down list located in the **Annotate** panel on the **Home** tab or in the **Tables** panel on the **Annotate** tab of the ribbon. The name of the current table style is displayed in the box. Pick the box to display the table style list, as shown in **Figure 11-12**.

Figure 11-12.
The **Styles** drop-
down list is available
from the **Tables** panel
on the **Annotate** tab of
the ribbon.

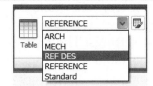

DesignCenter can be used to import table styles from existing drawing files into your current drawing file. Chapter 5 describes the process of using **DesignCenter** to reuse layers and other items. Apply the same techniques to reuse existing table styles.

Inserting Tables

The **TABLE** tool allows you to insert an empty table by specifying the number of rows and columns. After you insert the table, you can type text into the table cells. You can also insert blocks and fields into table cells. The **TABLE** tool also provides other methods for inserting tables, such as beginning a table using a starting table style, forming a table from data that has already been created in Microsoft® Excel, and creating a table by referencing AutoCAD data. Accessing the **TABLE** tool opens the **Insert Table** dialog box. See Figure 11-13.

Ribbon
Home
> Annotation
Annotate
> Tables
Table
Type
TABLE
TB
Menu Browser
Draw
> Table...

TABLE

Placing an Empty Table

An empty table is made by selecting the desired number of columns and data rows. Content is then typed in each cell, creating the table of information. Before placing a

Figure 11-13.
The **Insert Table** dialog box, shown with the **Start from empty table** insert option selected.

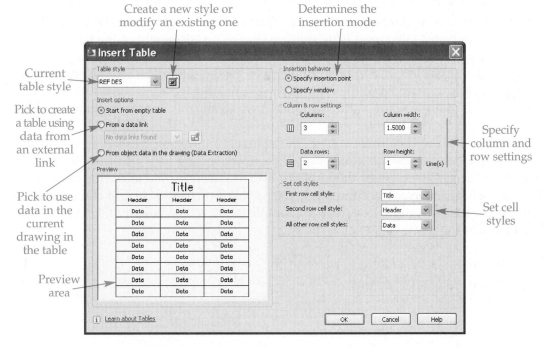

Create a new style or modify an existing one

Determines the insertion mode

Current table style

Pick to create a table using data from an external link

Pick to use data in the current drawing in the table

Preview area

Specify column and row settings

Set cell styles

table, select a table style from the **Table Style** drop-down list, or pick the ellipsis (...) button to create or modify a style. The preview area shows a preview of a table with the current table style settings. The preview area does not adjust to the column and row settings, but shows table style properties such as general, text style, and border settings. You cannot use a starting table style to form an empty table.

To place an empty table, pick the **Start from empty table** radio button from the **Insert options** area. The empty table insertion option is set in the **Insertion Behavior** area. Pick the **Specify insertion point** radio button to create a table using the values in the **Column & row settings** area, and then select a single point to place the table in the drawing.

The number in the **Columns** text box determines the total number of table columns. The **Column width** value specifies the initial width of all columns. You may want to enter a width larger than necessary in the **Column width** text box and then stretch the columns to size later. The number in the **Data rows** text box determines the total number of data table rows. The **Row height** value specifies the initial height of all rows based on the number of lines typed and the table style margin settings. After you make these settings and pick the **OK** button, AutoCAD prompts you to specify the insertion point of the table. A table created with three columns and five data rows using the **Insertion point** option is shown in Figure 11-14A.

NOTE

When you use the **Specify insertion point** option to place a table, the point at which the cursor is attached to the table is based on the table style direction.

Pick the **Specify window** radio button to create a table that fits into a designated area. The radio buttons that appear in the **Column & row settings** area control which column and row settings are active. To set a fixed number of columns, choose the **Columns** radio button. The **Column width** setting becomes unavailable and the table width you pick determines the column width. The alternative is to set a fixed column width by selecting the **Column width** radio button. The **Columns** setting becomes unavailable and the total number of table columns is determined based on the width of the table.

To set a fixed number of rows, pick the **Data rows** radio button. The row height is determined by the height of the table. The other option is to set a fixed row height by selecting the **Row height** radio button. The **Data rows** setting becomes unavailable and the total number of table rows is determined based on the height of the table.

After you make these settings and pick the **OK** button, AutoCAD prompts you to select the upper-left and lower-right corners for the table. The fixed **Column & row settings** values are used and the other settings are adjusted to fit the window. A table created with three columns and five data rows using the **Specify window** option is shown in Figure 11-14B.

The number of data rows you set in the **Insert Table** dialog box does not include the title and header rows. If you set the **Data Rows** setting to 1, for example, the table will have three rows because the top two rows are used for the table title and content headers. The default value for the row height is based on the text height and cell margin settings in the current table style. For example, enter a row height of 1 if you plan to have only a single line of text in each cell.

Figure 11-14.
Two ways to insert a table. A—Specifying a single insertion point. B—Windowing an area with two pick points.

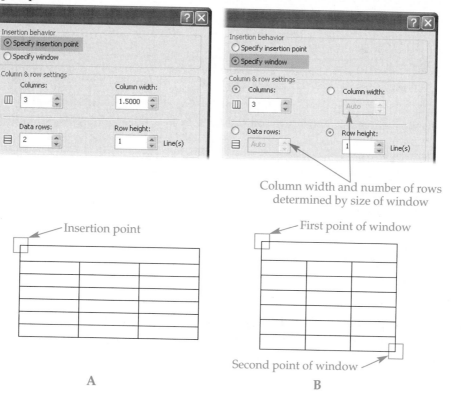

Column width and number of rows determined by size of window

Insertion point

First point of window

Second point of window

A   B

NOTE

After a table is inserted, it can be fully edited. Rows and columns can be added, so it is not critical that the exact number of columns and rows be entered before the table is created.

Exercise 11-2
Complete the exercise on the Student CD.

Entering Text into a Table

When a table is inserted, the **Multiline Text** tab of the ribbon appears by default, and the text cursor is placed in the top cell ready for typing. See **Figure 11-15.** The active cell is indicated by a dashed line around its border and a light gray background. The *table indicator* is used to identify individual cells in the table. This identification system is used to assign formulas to table cells for calculation purposes. Formulas are described later in this chapter. Before typing text in a cell, adjust the text settings in the **Multiline Text** tab of the ribbon, if needed. Remember, however, that making changes to some text characteristics overrides the settings specified in the text style or table style, which is often not appropriate.

Holding the [Alt] key and pressing [Enter] inserts a return within the cell. When you are finished entering the text in the active cell, press the [Tab] key to move to the

table indicator:
The grid of letters and numbers along the outer table border that identifies individual cells in a table.

Figure 11-15.
The **Multiline Text** tab of the ribbon is used by default to add and modify text table cell text. The active cell is indicated by a blinking cursor, a dashed border, and a light gray background.

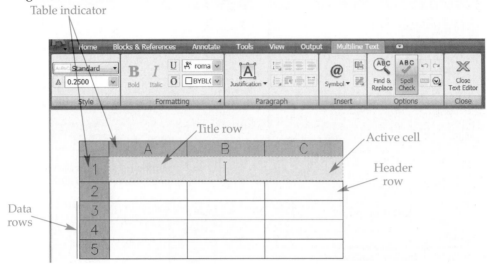

next cell. Holding the [Shift] key and pressing the [Tab] key moves the cursor backward (to the left or up) and makes the previous cell active. Pressing the [Enter] key makes the cell directly below the current cell active. The arrow keys on the keyboard can also be used to navigate through the cells in a table.

When you are finished typing text in the table, exit the multiline text system by picking the **Close Text Editor** button in the **Close** panel of the **Multiline Text** tab, or by picking outside of the table. You can also press the [Esc] key or right-click and select the **Cancel** option to exit, and you are prompted to save changes. The easiest way to reopen the text editor to make changes to text in a cell is to double-click on the cell. **Figure 11-16** shows a completed table.

> **NOTE**
>
> The options and settings available in the **Multiline Text** tab of the ribbon and shortcut menu function the same in table cells as they do in multiline text. Refer to Chapter 9 for more information about text formatting options.

Exercise 11-3
Complete the exercise on the Student CD.

Figure 11-16.
A completed parts list table.

1	PARTS LIST		
2	PART NUMBER	PART TYPE	QTY.
3	100−SCR−45	SCREW	18
4	202−BLT−32	BOLT	18
5	340−WSHR−06	WASHER	18

Figure 11-17.
The **Insert Table** dialog box can be used to create a new table using a starting table style.

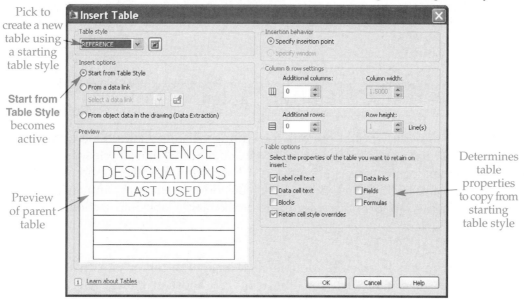

Pick to create a new table using a starting table style

Start from Table Style becomes active

Preview of parent table

Determines table properties to copy from starting table style

Using a Starting Table Style

If a predefined starting table style is available in your drawing, you can place a new table by referencing the starting table style. To create a table by referencing a starting table style, first select a starting table style from the **Table Style** drop-down list or select the ellipsis (…) button to create or modify a style. When you select a starting table style, the **Start from Table Style** radio button activates in the **Insert options** area. See Figure 11-17. The preview area shows a preview of the parent table with the current table style settings and table options.

The **Specify insertion point** insertion behavior option is the only method for inserting a table using a starting table style. However, you can add columns and rows to the table by entering or selecting values in the **Additional columns** and **Additional rows** text boxes. You can also specify which items from the parent table are included in the new table by selecting and deselecting the check boxes in the **Table options** area. For example, pick the **Data cell text** check box to create a new table that contains all the text entries added to the data cells of the parent table.

After you make these settings and pick the **OK** button, specify the insertion point of the table. The **Multiline Text** tab of the ribbon appears and the text cursor is placed in the top cell, ready to create new content or edit existing values. Exit the multiline text system when you finish typing text. A table created by referencing an existing starting table style with two additional rows is shown in Figure 11-18.

Figure 11-18.
You can create a new table quickly by referencing a starting table style.

Existing table style used to form a starting table style

REFERENCE DESIGNATIONS
LAST USED
R9
C1
CRS
Q2

In the new table, all table options are retained and two rows are added

REFERENCE DESIGNATIONS
LAST USED
R9
C1
CRS
Q2
T4
R6

Exercise 11-4
Complete the exercise on the Student CD.

Editing Tables

AutoCAD provides several options for editing existing tables. One option is to reenter the multiline text editor to edit the text in a table cell. For example, you may need to modify the text contents or change the text formatting. Another option is to make changes to the table layout. These changes include adding, removing, and resizing rows and columns, and wrapping table columns to break a large table into sections.

Editing Table Cell Text

To edit the text in a table cell, double-click inside the cell or pick inside the cell, right-click, and select **Edit Text** from the table cell shortcut menu. This makes the selected cell active and displays the **Multiline Text** tab of the ribbon. See **Figure 11-19.** When you are finished editing table text, exit the multiline text system by picking the **Close Text Editor** button in the **Close** panel of the **Multiline Text** tab, or picking outside of the table. You can also press the [Esc] key or right-click and select the **Cancel** option to exit, but you will be prompted to save changes.

Exercise 11-5
Complete the exercise on the Student CD.

Figure 11-19.
Double-clicking inside a cell opens the text formatting function, allowing you to make changes to the text.

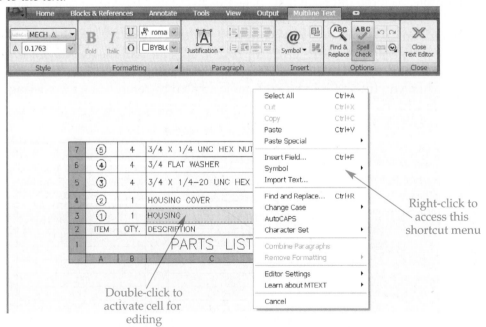

Picking Inside a Cell to Edit Table Layout

Several table layout settings can be accessed by picking (single-clicking) *inside* a cell to make the selected cell active and display the **Table** tab on the ribbon. See **Figure 11-20.** The highlighted cell includes *grips*. The **Table** tab of the ribbon contains options for adjusting table and individual cell layout. The same tools and options found in the **Table** tab of the ribbon, plus additional options, are available from a shortcut menu, as shown in **Figure 11-20.** To display the shortcut menu, select a cell and then right-click anywhere in the drawing window. The first section of the shortcut menu contains the Windows Clipboard functions. These options affect the entire contents of the cell. Selecting **Recent Input** displays a list of previously entered tools.

AutoCAD provides several ways to select multiple cells and apply changes to all the cells at once, as shown in **Figure 11-21.** One option is to pick in a cell and drag the window over the other cells. When you release the pick button, all of the cells touching the window become selected. Multiple cells can also be selected by picking a cell, holding down the [Shift] key, and then picking another cell. This process selects the picked cells and all of the cells between them. You can select entire columns or rows by picking the column or row number in the table indicator. To select the entire table, pick the corner of the table indicator.

> **grips:** Small boxes that appear at strategic points on an object, allowing you to edit the object directly.

NOTE

Make sure you pick completely inside of the cell. If you accidentally select one of the cell borders, the entire table becomes the selected object. Editing table layout by selecting a cell border is described later in this chapter.

Figure 11-20.
Several table layout modification options are available when you pick inside a cell.

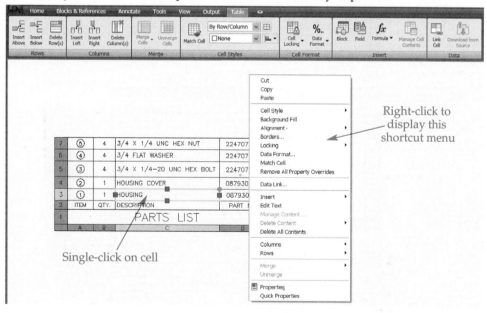

Figure 11-21.
Selecting multiple cells in a table for editing. A—Using the pick and drag method. B—Picking a range of cells using the [Shift] key. C—Selecting a row, column, or the entire table.

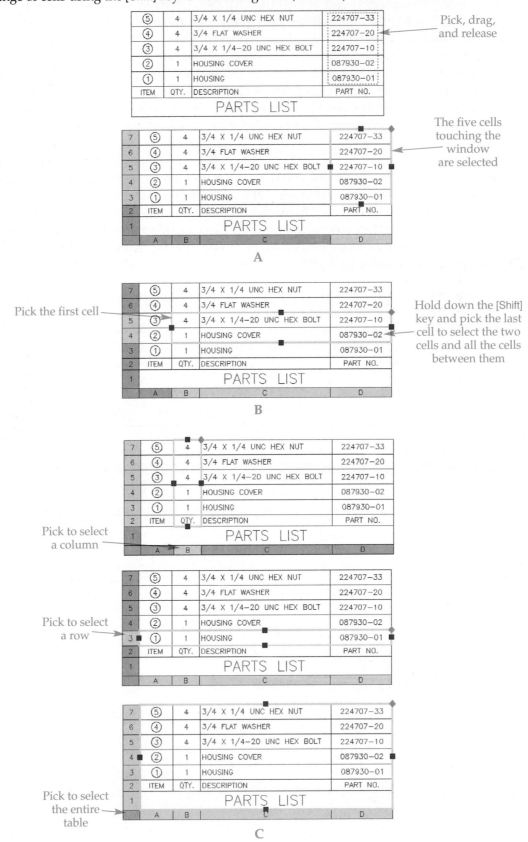

Quickly copying cell content

The most effective method for copying the content of one cell to multiple cells is to use the *auto-fill* function. To use auto-fill, pick inside the cell that contains the content you want to copy. The auto-fill grip is a diamond-shaped grip located in a corner of the cell. See Figure 11-22.

To use the auto-fill function, select the auto-fill grip, as shown in Figure 11-23A. Then, right-click directly on the auto-fill grip and select an option to define how to adjust the cell content of auto-fill copies. The **Fill Series** option fills cells with the cell content and any format overrides that have been applied. This option automatically increases or decreases values of certain data types, such as dates, as the fill occurs. See Figure 11-23B.

The **Fill Series Without Formatting** option fills cells with the content of the selected cell, but does not include any format overrides that have been added. The **Copy Cells** option copies the content and format overrides that have been applied to the selected cell. This option creates a static cell copy that does not adjust data values. See Figure 11-23C. The **Copy Cells Without Formatting** option copies cells with the content of the selected cell, but does not include any format overrides that have been added. The **Fill Formatting Only** option fills the cells only with format overrides that have been applied to the selected cell, allowing you to enter cell content manually.

After you choose the appropriate fill option, move the cursor to the last cell to which you want to copy the cell content and pick inside the cell. All cells between the first and last cell you picked are filled with the content of the active cell.

auto-fill: A table function that automatically fills selected cells based on the contents of a specified cell.

Figure 11-22.

Using the auto-fill function to copy cell content to multiple cells.

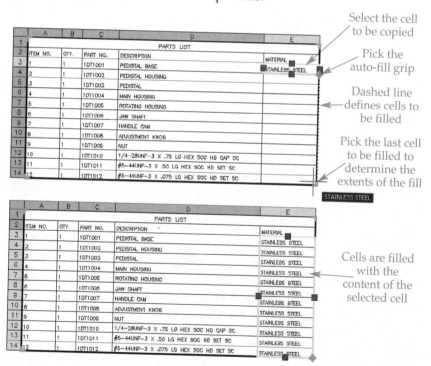

Figure 11-23.
Using the auto-fill options to control fill characteristics.

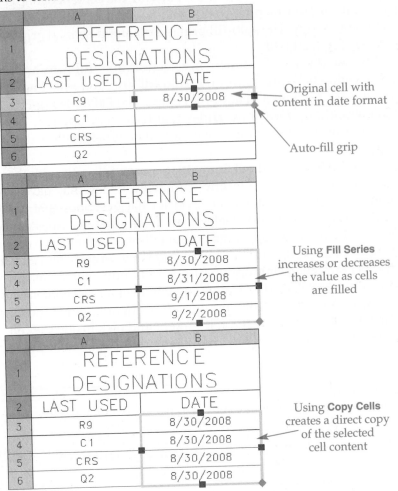

Original cell with content in date format

Auto-fill grip

Using **Fill Series** increases or decreases the value as cells are filled

Using **Copy Cells** creates a direct copy of the selected cell content

Modifying cell styles

Most cell style properties are defined according to the table style used to create the table. However, cell styles can be overridden for individual cells or groups of cells as needed. Cell style options are available from the **Cell Styles** panel of the ribbon and from the shortcut menu. Select a cell style from the **Cell Style** drop-down list to override the cell style used for the active cell. **Create New Cell Style...** and **Manage Cell Style...** options are also available. If you made changes to the active cell, you can save the changes as a new cell style that can be used to adjust the display of other cells or applied to a table style. To save the cell properties as a new cell style, right-click, pick the **Save as New Cell Style...** option from the **Cell Style** cascading submenu, and enter a name for the style in the **Save as New Cell Style** dialog box.

Pick the **Background Fill** drop-down list to change the cell background color. Select a cell alignment option from the **Alignment** flyout to override the justification of content within the selected cell. Cell content is located in relation to the cell borders. Pick the **Cell Borders** button to open the **Cell Border Properties** dialog box. This dialog box can be used to override cell border display properties and contains the same options found in the **Border** tab of the **Table Style** dialog box.

Select the **Match Cell** button to copy format settings from one cell to another. First select the cell that has the settings you want to copy. Then select the **Match Cell** button. AutoCAD prompts you to select a destination cell. Pick the cell to which you want to copy the settings. Select another cell or right-click to exit.

Adjusting cell format

Cell format options are available from the **Cell Format** panel of the ribbon and from the shortcut menu. The **Locking** flyout lists options for locking cells. Cells can be locked to protect them from unintended or inappropriate changes. The locked icon appears when you move the cursor over a locked cell. The **Unlocked** option unlocks the cell so that changes can be made to cell content and format. The **Content Locked** option locks only the content of the cell, still allowing changes to be made to the cell format. The **Format Locked** option locks only the cell format, allowing changes to be made to the content of the cell. The **Content and Format Locked** option locks cell content and format so that no changes can be made.

Data format is defined according to the table style used to create the table. However, format can be overridden for individual cells or groups of cells as needed. Override the data format of the cell(s) by picking an option from the **Data Format...** flyout, or choose the **Custom Table Cell Format...** option to open the **Table Cell Data Format** dialog box. This is the same dialog box available for adjusting table style data cell format.

PROFESSIONAL TIP

Most cell style and format properties are defined in the current table style. If you are making significant changes to cell properties, it is better to modify the table style or create a new style.

NOTE

Pick the **Remove All Property Overrides** option from the shortcut menu to restore the cell or cells to their original properties as defined in the selected table style.

Inserting blocks and fields

In addition to text, table cells can contain AutoCAD blocks, fields, and formulas. Formulas are described later in this chapter. Blocks are useful for creating a legend or for displaying images of parts in a parts list. The options for inserting a block in a table are briefly described here. For detailed information about blocks, refer to Chapters 26 and 27. Blocks, fields, and formulas can be inserted using the tools available from the **Insert** panel in the **Table** tab of the ribbon or from the **Insert** cascading submenu of shortcut menu.

Select the **Block...** button to insert a block into a table cell. This opens the **Insert a Block in a Table Cell** dialog box. **Figure 11-24** describes the options available in this dialog box. A cell can contain both text and blocks. Double-clicking a block in a cell opens the **Insert a Block in a Table Cell** dialog box. Double-clicking on text in a cell opens the **Text Formatting** function.

Pick the **Field...** button to open the **Field** dialog box, which is used to insert a field into a table cell. This is the same dialog box that is used to insert fields into single-line and multiline text. Fields can also be inserted into a cell using the multiline text editor. Refer to Chapter 10 for more information on inserting and using fields.

Figure 11-24.
Options in the **Insert a Block in a Table Cell** dialog box.

Feature	Description
Name	Used to choose the block from a drop-down list of the blocks stored in the current drawing.
Browse	Displays the **Select Drawing File** dialog box, where a drawing file can be selected and inserted into the table cell as a block.
AutoFit	Scales the block automatically to fit inside the cell.
Scale	Sets the block insertion scale. For example, a value of 2 inserts the block at twice its original size. A value of .5 inserts the block at half its created size. The **Scale** option is not available if the **AutoFit** check box is checked.
Rotation angle	Rotates the block to the specified angle.
Overall cell alignment	Determines the justification of the block in the cell and overrides the current cell alignment setting.

Adding and resizing columns and rows

Columns and rows can be added, deleted, and resized after a table is created. The following options are available from the **Columns** panel on the ribbon or the **Columns** cascading submenu in the shortcut menu:

- **Insert Left.** Adds a new column to the left of the selected cell.
- **Insert Right.** Adds a new column to the right of the selected cell.
- **Delete.** Deletes the entire column (or set of columns) containing the selected cell(s).
- **Size Equally.** Automatically sizes the selected columns to the same width. This option is only available when cells belonging to multiple columns are selected.

The following options are available from the **Rows** panel of the ribbon or the **Rows** cascading submenu of the table cell shortcut menu:

- **Insert Above.** Adds a new row above the selected cell.
- **Insert Below.** Adds a new row below the selected cell.
- **Delete.** Deletes the row (or set of rows) containing the selected cell(s).
- **Size Equally.** Automatically sizes the selected rows to the same height. This option is only available when cells belonging to multiple rows are selected.

NOTE

A quick way to insert a new row at the bottom of a table using a **Down** table direction is to position the cursor in the lower-right cell and press the [Tab] key. To insert a new row at the top of a table using an **Up** table direction, position the cursor in the upper-right cell and press the [Tab] key.

PROFESSIONAL TIP

The size of the columns and rows in a table can also be adjusted using grips. Grips are the boxes located in the middle of cell border lines. To resize a column or row, select a grip, move the mouse, and pick. Grips are described in detail in Chapter 14.

AutoCAD and Its Applications—Basics

Merging cells

You can combine adjacent cells by merging them. Merge tools are available from the **Merge** panel on the ribbon and from the **Merge** cascading submenu on the shortcut menu. To merge cells, first select multiple cells to be merged. Then select the appropriate merge option from the **Merge cells** flyout. Select the **All** option to merge all cells into one space. The **By Row** and **By Column** options allow you to merge cells in multiple rows or columns without removing the horizontal or vertical borders. Pick the **Unmerge Cells** button to separate merged cells back into individual cells.

NOTE

Selecting the **Delete All Contents** menu option deletes the contents in the selected cell. This is the same as selecting a cell and pressing the [Delete] key.

Exercise 11-6
Complete the exercise on the Student CD.

Picking a Cell Edge to Edit Table Layout

Additional methods for adjusting table layout are available when you pick the edge, or border, of a cell. This displays the table indicator grid, grips that can be used to adjust row height and column width, and the table break function. After picking a cell border, right-click anywhere in the drawing window to display the shortcut menu shown in **Figure 11-25**.

Figure 11-25.
Several additional table layout modification options are available when you pick any cell border.

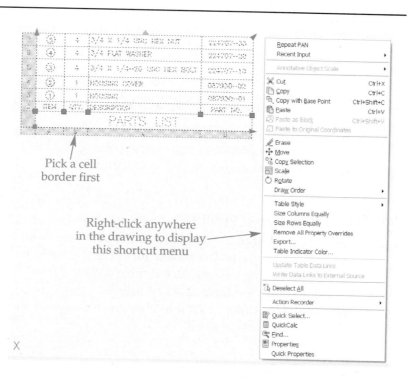

Pick a cell border first

Right-click anywhere in the drawing to display this shortcut menu

---

Adjusting table style

Select an existing table style from the **Table Style** cascading submenu of the shortcut menu to select a different table style for the selected table. Picking the **Set as Table in Current Table Style** option creates a starting table style based on the selected table and the current table style. This is an alternative technique for creating a starting table style without opening the **Table Style** dialog box. If the selected table was drawn using a starting table style, selecting the **Set as Table in Current Table Style** redefines the starting table. To save modifications made to the table as a new table style, pick the **Save as New Table Style...** option and enter a name for the style in the **Save as New Table Style** dialog box.

Resizing columns and rows

The size of the columns and rows in a table can also be adjusted using the grips boxes that appear when a table cell border is selected. Grips are the boxes and arrowheads located at the corners of columns and the table. To resize a column or row, select a grip box, move the cursor, and pick. The arrowhead grips can be used to increase or decrease row height and/or column width uniformly. Grips are described in detail in Chapter 14.

The **Size Columns Equally** option sizes all the columns in the table to the same width automatically. The total width of the table is divided evenly among the columns. The **Size Rows Equally** option sizes all the rows in the table to the same height. All rows increase in height to match the height of the tallest row in the table.

Using table breaks

Long tables may need to be divided into sections in order to fit the table on a sheet. Use the table break function to break a table into separate sections while maintaining a single table object. Table breaking is accessed by picking a cell edge. The table breaking grip is located midway between the sides of the table at the top or the bottom of the table, depending on the table direction. See **Figure 11-26.**

To break a table, first select the table breaking grip. Then move the cursor into the table to display a preview of the table sections and a dashed line with crosshairs. The crosshairs determines the location of the break. The closer to the table title and headers the crosshairs appears, the more sections are created, as shown in the table preview. When the preview of the table looks correct, pick the location to form the table breaks.

NOTE

After you add table breaks, several options become available from the **Properties** palette for adjusting the table sections. The **Properties** palette is covered in Chapter 14.

Additional table layout options

The following additional table options are available from the shortcut menu:

- **Remove All Property Overrides.** Restores the table to its original properties, defined according to the selected table style.
- **Export.** Exports the table as a CSV file.
- **Table Indicator Color....** Pick to change the color of the table indicator shown when you pick inside a cell.

Figure 11-26.
The procedure for breaking, or wrapping, a table into sections.

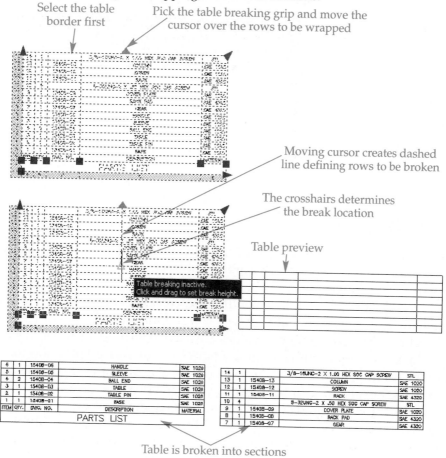

Select the table border first

Pick the table breaking grip and move the cursor over the rows to be wrapped

Moving cursor creates dashed line defining rows to be broken

The crosshairs determines the break location

Table preview

Table breaking inactive. Click and drag to set break height.

Table is broken into sections

Exercise 11-7
Complete the exercise on the Student CD.

Calculating Values in Tables

Performing calculations on data in tables using *formulas* is a common requirement. For example, in a parts list, you can add the number of parts and show the total. In a door or window schedule, a total count of the doors or windows is often calculated. In a room schedule, square footage is often calculated and listed for various areas. Formulas calculate operations based on numeric data in table cells. AutoCAD allows you to write formulas for sums, averages, counts, and other mathematical functions.

Table cells are identified in formulas by their column letter and row number. The table indicator grid appears when a table cell is being edited. This grid provides a numbering system for the cells. Columns are identified with letters, and rows are identified with numbers. For example, the cell located in Column A and Row 3 is identified as A3. This system of cell identification is illustrated in **Figure 11-27**. In the table shown, cell C6 is highlighted.

formulas:
Mathematical expressions that allow you to perform calculations within table cells.

Figure 11-27.
Table cells are
identified by
column letter and
row number. The
table indicator grid
provides a reference
for identifying each
cell individually.

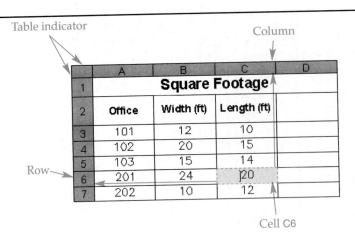

Creating Formulas

When you insert a formula into a cell, it evaluates values from other cells and displays the resulting value. Formulas are field objects. As with other types of fields, both the expression and the resulting value are displayed with a gray background. The value changes if values in the corresponding expression change. This enables you to update data in a table cell automatically when you update the data in other cells.

Table cells with existing numeric values are used in writing formulas. For example, you can add the values of all cells in a single column and display the total at the bottom of the column, in a new cell. You can define a formula that evaluates a range of continuous cells or cells that do not share a common border.

In a formula, the common symbols used for mathematical functions are entered as operators in the expression: + is used for addition, – for subtraction, * for multiplication, / for division, and ^ for exponentiation. Parentheses are used to enclose expressions for table cell formulas. To perform an operation correctly, you must enter the proper syntax in the table cell. The syntax uses the following conventions:

Entry	Description
=	The equal sign is used to begin an expression. This tells AutoCAD that you want to perform a calculation.
(	An open parenthesis is used to start the expression.
)	A closing parenthesis is used to close the expression.
(expression)	Write the expression by typing the cells to be evaluated and the desired operator symbol(s).

An example of a complete expression is =(C3+D4). This expression tells AutoCAD to add the value of C3 and the value of D4 and display the sum in the current cell. When identifying a cell in an expression, you must enter the letter before the number. For example, you cannot enter 3C to designate the cell identified as C3. If you enter an incorrect expression or an expression evaluating cells without numeric data, AutoCAD displays the pound character (#) to indicate the error.

NOTE

Parentheses are not needed in some expressions, but other expressions will not be calculated without them. It is good practice to use parentheses in all expressions.

Figure 11-28.
Entering a
multiplication
formula. A—The
expression is typed
in the table cell with
the correct syntax.
B—The resulting
value is displayed
after the expression
is calculated.

	A	B	C	D
1	Square Footage			
2	Office	Width (ft)	Length (ft)	Sq Ft
3	101	12	10	=(B3*C3) ←Expression
4	102	20	15	
5	103	15	14	
6	201	24	20	
7	202	10	12	

A

Square Footage			
Office	Width (ft)	Length (ft)	Sq Ft
101	12	10	120 ←Result
102	20	15	
103	15	14	
201	24	20	
202	10	12	

B

A formula can be added using the multiline text editor. An example of a multiplication formula is shown in Figure 11-28. The expression =(B3*C3) is entered in cell D3. The resulting value is shown after exiting the multiline text editor.

Grouped expressions can also be used in formulas. The expression sets are enclosed in parentheses. For example, the expression =(E1+F1)*E2 multiplies the sum of E1 and F1 by E2. Another example: =(E1+F1)*(E2+F2)/G6 multiplies the sum of E1 and F1 by the sum of E2 and F2 and divides the product by G6.

Creating sum, average, and count formulas

In addition to entering basic mathematical formulas in table cells manually, you can select from one of AutoCAD's formula types. These formulas can be used to calculate the sum, average, or count of a range of cells. To access the formula options, select a cell and choose an option from the **Formula** flyout on the ribbon, or pick **Formula** from the **Insert** cascading submenu of the shortcut menu to display a cascading menu with formula options. See Figure 11-29.

The **Sum** option allows you to add the values of a range of cells by specifying a selection window on-screen. AutoCAD prompts you to pick the first corner of a window defining the cell range. The range you specify can include cells from several columns and rows. Pick inside the top or bottom cell that you want to include in the calculation. Then move the cursor and pick inside the lowest or highest cell, making sure that all of the cells to be included in the formula are included in the window selection. See Figure 11-30. When the second point is selected, the expression is automatically entered into the cell. In the example shown, the square footage for each office is first calculated in the Sq Ft column on the right in Figure 11-30A. The values are then

Figure 11-29.
The **Formula** flyout
button of the ribbon
allows you to insert
a formula into a cell.

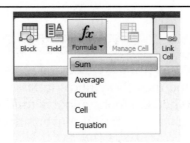

Figure 11-30.
Creating a sum
formula in a table
cell. A—Pick a cell
to hold the formula
and select a range of
cells for the formula
by windowing
around the cells.
B—After the second
point of the window
is picked, the
formula displays in
the cell.

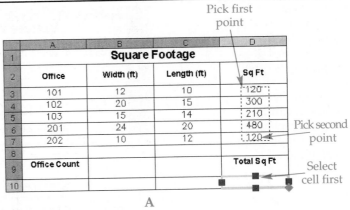

A

B

selected for a sum formula that calculates the total square footage of all of the offices, as shown in **Figure 11-30B.**

Notice in **Figure 11-30B** that the resulting expression is =Sum(D3:D7) This formula specifies that the selected cell is equal to the sum of cells D3 through D7. The colon symbol (:) is used to indicate the range of cells for the calculation.

The **Average** and **Count** options are similar to the **Sum** option. The **Average** option creates a formula that calculates the average value of the cells you select. The average is the sum of the selected cells divided by the number of cells selected. The **Count** option creates a formula that counts the number of selected cells. Only cells that contain a value are included in the count.

Sum, average, and count formulas can be typed directly into a cell without using the **Formula** flyout button or the **Insert** cascading menu. If you are calculating a value over a range of cells, use the colon symbol to designate the range. You can also write an expression that evaluates individual cells instead of a range. The cells do not have to share a common border. To write an expression using nonadjacent cells, use a comma to separate the cell names. For example, if cells D1, D3, and D6 need to be averaged, type =Average(D1,D3,D6). This formula calculates the average of the cell values for cells D1, D3, and D6.

A range of cells and individual cells can be included in the same expression. For example, if cells A1 through B10 need to be counted in addition to cells C4 and C6, enter =Count(A1:B10,C4,C6). Examples of sum, average, and count formulas are shown in **Figure 11-31.**

NOTE

When using architectural units in a drawing, you can type the foot (') and inch (") symbols in table cells for use in values and formulas. When the foot symbol is used for a cell value, a formula in another cell automatically converts the resulting value to inches and feet.

AutoCAD and Its Applications—Basics

Figure 11-31.
Sum, average, and
count formulas
and their resulting
values.

	A	B	C	D
1	Square Footage			
2	Office	Width (ft)	Length (ft)	Sq Ft
3	101	12	10	120
4	102	20	15	300
5	103	15	14	210
6	201	24	20	480
7	202	10	12	120
8				
9	Office Count	Average Sq Ft Per Room		Total Sq Ft
10	5	246.000000		1230

=Count(A3:A7)   =Average(D3:D7)   =Sum(D3:D7)

Other formula options

The **Formula** flyout button and **Insert** cascading submenu contain additional options for writing table formulas. The **Cell** option allows you to select a table cell from a different table and insert its contents in the current cell. The cell value can then be used in a new formula. When you select the **Cell** option, AutoCAD prompts you to select the cell. The value of the selected cell is then displayed in the current cell.

The **Equation** option is used to enter an expression manually. Selecting this option places an equal sign (=) in the current cell. You can then type the expression.

NOTE

You can use the **Field** tool to insert and edit table cell formulas. Selecting **Formula** from the **Field names** list in the **Field** dialog box displays option buttons for creating sum, average, and count formulas. You can also select a cell value from a different table as a starting point. Table cells are selected on-screen to define the formula. The **Formula** text box in the **Field** dialog box can be used to add to or edit the formula. Unit format options are also available.

Exercise 11-8
Complete the exercise on the Student CD.

Linking a Table to Excel Data
Existing data entered in a Microsoft® Excel spreadsheet or a CSV (comma separated) file can be used to create an AutoCAD table. Refer to the Student CD: Supplemental Materials > Linking a Table to Excel Data for detailed information about this process.

Extracting Table Data
Existing AutoCAD drawing information can be reused to create a table. Refer to the Student CD: Supplemental Materials > Extracting Table Data for detailed information about this process.

Template Development
Chapter 11

Adding a table style to your drawing templates helps ensure that your drawings have a uniform appearance and follow drafting industry standards. Refer to the Student CD for detailed instructions to add table styles to your mechanical, architectural, and civil drawing templates.

Chapter Test

Answer the following questions. Write your answers on a separate sheet of paper or complete the electronic chapter test on the Student CD.

1. What is the purpose of creating a table style?
2. Briefly describe the procedure for creating a table style based on an existing table style.
3. What does the **Alignment** setting in the **New Table Style** dialog box do?
4. Which setting would you adjust in the **New Table Style** dialog box to increase the spacing between the text and the top of the cell?
5. How can creating a new table using a starting table style save time?
6. How can you quickly make a table style current?
7. List three ways to open the **Insert Table** dialog box.
8. By default, what two types of rows are at the top of a table when it is inserted?
9. By default, what tab of the ribbon opens after a table has been inserted?
10. If you are finished typing in one cell and want to move to the next cell in the same row, what two keyboard keys can you use?
11. Describe the two ways to insert a table and explain how the methods differ.
12. List two ways to make a cell active for editing.
13. Explain how to insert a block into a table cell.
14. How do you insert a new row at the bottom of a table?
15. How are table cells identified in formulas?
16. Write the table cell formula that adds the value of C3 plus the value of D4.
17. What is the function of the colon symbol (:) in the formula =Sum(D3:D7)?
18. Write the table cell formula that averages the values of cells D1, D3, and D6.
19. What is the difference between a sum formula and a count formula?
20. Explain how to write a formula that calculates a function for cells that do not share common borders.

Drawing Problems

For each of the following problems, use one of your templates or start a new drawing using your own setup option.

▼ Basic

1. Create the parts list shown below. Make the measurements for the rows and columns approximately the same as in the given table. Save the drawing as P11-1.

KEY	QTY	NAME	DESCRIPTION	PART NO.
	1	CAPS	1/2–12UNC HEX NUT	210014–29
	1	CAPS	1/2 FLAT WASHER	320014–33
	2	CAPS	7/16 EXTERNAL SNAP RING	632043–43
	2	CAPS	1/4–20UNC WING NUT	255010–41
	2	CAPS	3/4 X 1/4–20UNC BOLT	803010–11

PARTS LIST

2. Create the table shown below. Make the measurements for the rows and columns approximately the same as in the given table. Save the drawing as P11-2.

REFERENCE DESIGNATIONS	
LAST USED	DATE
R9	8/30/2008
C1	8/31/2008
CRS	9/1/2008
Q2	9/2/2008

▼ Intermediate

3. Create the door schedule shown below. Make the measurements for the rows and columns approximately the same as in the given table. Save the drawing as P11-3.

DOOR SCHEDULE			
SYM.	SIZE	TYPE	QTY.
①	36x80	S.C. R.P. METAL INSULATED	1
②	36x80	S.C. FLUSH METAL INSULATED	2
③	32x80	S.C. SELF CLOSING	2
④	32x80	HOLLOW CORE	5
⑤	30x80	HOLLOW CORE	5
⑥	30x80	POCKET SLDG.	2

4. Create the window schedule shown below. Make the measurements for the rows and columns approximately the same as in the given table. Save the drawing as P11-4.

WINDOW SCHEDULE				
SYM.	SIZE	MODEL	ROUGH OPEN	QTY.
Ⓐ	12x60	JOB BUILT	VERIFY	2
Ⓑ	96x60	W4N5 CSM.	8'-0 3/4" x 5'-0 7/8"	1
Ⓒ	48x60	W2N5 CSM.	4'-0 3/4" x 5'-0 7/8"	2
Ⓓ	48x36	W2N3 CSM.	4'-0 3/4" x 3'-6 1/2"	2
Ⓔ	42x42	2N3 CSM.	3'-6 1/2" x 3'-6 1/2"	2
Ⓕ	72x48	G64 SLDG.	6'-0 1/2" x 4'-0 1/2"	1
Ⓖ	60x42	G536 SLDG.	5'-0 1/2" x 3'-6 1/2"	4
Ⓗ	48x42	G436 SLDG.	4'-0 1/2" x 3'-6 1/2"	1
Ⓙ	48x24	A41 AWN.	4'-0 1/2" x 2'-0 7/8"	3

5. Create the door schedule shown below. Make the measurements for the rows and columns approximately the same as in the given table. Save the drawing as P11-5.

DOOR SCHEDULE				DOOR SCHEDULE			
SYMBOL	SIZE	MODEL	QUANTITY	SYMBOL	SIZE	MODEL	QUANTITY
1	3'-0" X 6'-8"	S.C. R.P. METAL INSULATED	1	11	4'-0" X 6'-8"	BI-FOLD	1
2	3'-0" X 6'-8"	S.C.-FLUSH-METAL INSULATED	2	12	2'-0" X 6'-0"	SHATTER PROOF	1
3	2'-8" X 6'-8"	S.C.-SELF CLOSING	2	13	6'-0" X 6'-8"	WOOD FRAME-TEMP. SLDG GL.	1
4	2'-8" X 6'-8"	H.C.	5	14	9'-0" X 7'-0"	OVERHEAD GARAGE	2
5	2'-6" X 6'-8"	H.C.	3				
6	2'-6" X 6'-8"	POCKET	2				
7	2'-4" X 6'-8"	POCKET	1				
9	5'-0" X 6'-0"	BI-PASS	2				
10	3'-0" X 6'-8"	BI-FOLD	1				

6. Open P11-5 and make the following changes:
   - Change the DOOR SCHEDULE so that SYMBOL items 11, 12, 13, and 14 continue directly below SYMBOL items 1 through 10, with only one DOOR SCHEDULE heading at the top.
   - Change the following abbreviations to full words:
   - S.C.R.P. – SOLID CORE RAISED PANEL
   - S.C. – SOLID CORE
   - H.C. – HOLLOW CORE.

   Save the drawing as P11-6.

▼ Advanced

7. Create a parts list for a mechanical drawing with the content of your choice, or locate a drawing with a parts list and make a similar drawing. Save the drawing as P11-7.

8. Create a door and window schedule for an architectural drawing with the content of your choice, or locate a drawing with a door and window schedule and make a similar drawing. Save the drawing as P11-8.

9. Create a legend for a civil drawing with the content of your choice, or locate a drawing with a legend and make a similar drawing. Save the drawing as P11-9.

10. Create a parts list for a mechanical drawing with the content of your choice, or locate a drawing with a parts list and make a similar drawing. Save the drawing as P11-10.

11. Open P11-1 and make the following changes:
    - Change PARTS LIST to PURCHASE PARTS LIST.
    - Change Part Number 803010-11 as follows: Key: 7, Name: HEX HD, Description: $\frac{1}{4}$-20UNC-2 X $\frac{3}{4}$ BOLT.
    - Change Part Number 255010-41 as follows: Key: 11, Name: WING NUT, Description: $\frac{1}{4}$-20UNC.
    - Change Part Number 632043-43 as follows: Key: 15, Name: SNAP RING, Description: $\frac{\varnothing 7}{16}$ EXTERNAL.
    - Change Part Number 320014-33 as follows: Key: 19, Name: WASHER, Description: $\frac{\varnothing 1}{2}$ FLAT.
    - Change Part Number 210014-29 as follows: Key: 21, Name: NUT, Description: $\frac{1}{2}$-12UNC-2 HEX.

    Save the drawing as P11-11.

12. Create a table of your own design and use at least six of the applications of calculating values in tables described in this chapter. Save the drawing as P11-12.

13. Access the Student CD content for this chapter and create a table by linking to Microsoft® Excel data. To do this, create your own Excel spreadsheet or find an existing Excel spreadsheet containing the desired data. Link a table to the Excel data. Save the drawing as P11-13.

14. Access the Student CD content for this chapter and use the description to create a table the same as or similar to the given examples and then extract the table data into an AutoCAD drawing. Save the drawing as P11-14.

CHAPTER 12

Basic Object Editing Tools

Learning Objectives

After completing this chapter, you will be able to do the following:

✓ Use the **FILLET** tool to draw fillets, rounds, and other rounded corners.
✓ Place chamfers and angled corners with the **CHAMFER** tool.
✓ Separate objects using the **BREAK** tool.
✓ Combine objects using the **JOIN** tool.
✓ Use the **TRIM** and **EXTEND** tools to edit the length of objects.
✓ Modify the length, height, and width of objects using the **STRETCH** and **LENGTHEN** tools.
✓ Change the size of objects using the **SCALE** tool.

This chapter explains methods for changing objects using basic AutoCAD modification tools. You will learn various tools that can be used to increase drawing efficiency. The editing tools described in this chapter include many options. As you work through this chapter, experiment with each option to see which is the most effective in different situations.

Using the Fillet Tool

Fillets were introduced in Chapter 4 as a corner option for adding rounds to rectangles created with the **RECTANGLE** tool. AutoCAD refers to all rounded corners as fillets. The **FILLET** tool draws a rounded corner between intersecting and nonintersecting lines, circles, and arcs. See **Figure 12-1**.

fillet: A rounded corner.

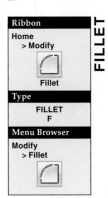

Ribbon
Home
> Modify
Fillet

Type
FILLET
F

Menu Browser
Modify
> Fillet

FILLET

Figure 12-1.
Using the **FILLET** tool.

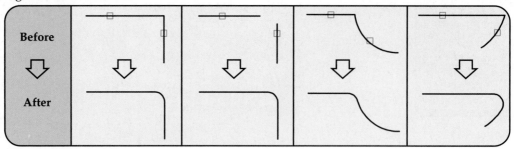

Setting the Fillet Radius

The size of a fillet is determined by the fillet radius. You must set this value before selecting the corner to be filleted. After initiating the **FILLET** tool, access the **Radius** option and enter the fillet radius dimension. You can then select the objects to be filleted. The fillet radius value you enter is stored as the new default radius setting, allowing you to quickly place additional fillets and rounds with the same radius.

> **NOTE**
>
> Only corners large enough to accept the fillet radius are eligible for filleting. If the specified fillet radius is too large, AutoCAD does not perform the fillet. Instead, a message, such as Distance is too large *Invalid*, is displayed.

Exercise 12-1
Complete the exercise on the Student CD.

Rounding the Corners of a Polyline

polyline: A series of lines and arcs that constitute a single object.

Fillets can be drawn at all corners of a closed *polyline* by selecting the **Polyline** option of the **FILLET** tool. The current fillet radius is used with this option. See **Figure 12-2.** AutoCAD tells you how many lines were filleted. If the polyline was drawn without using the **Close** option, the beginning corner is not filleted. Polylines are described further in Chapter 15.

Figure 12-2.
Using the **Polyline** option of the **FILLET** tool.

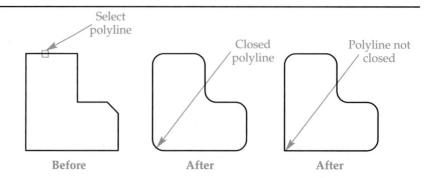

Figure 12-3.
Comparison of the **Trim** and **No trim** options of the **FILLET** tool.

Before Fillet	Fillet with Trim	Fillet with No Trim

Setting the Fillet Trim Mode

The **Trim** option controls whether or not the **FILLET** tool trims object segments that extend beyond the fillet radius point. When the **Trim** option is set to **Trim**, objects are trimmed. When the **Trim** option is set to **No Trim**, the filleted objects are not changed when the fillet is inserted, as shown in **Figure 12-3**.

PROFESSIONAL TIP

Objects can be filleted even when the corners do not meet. AutoCAD extends the lines as required to generate the specified fillet and complete the corner if the **Trim** option is set to **Trim**. If the **Trim** option is set to **No Trim**, AutoCAD does not extend the lines to complete the corner.

Filleting Square Corners

When the fillet radius is set to zero, you can use the **FILLET** tool to connect two lines. You can also create a zero-radius fillet without setting the radius to zero by holding down the [Shift] key when you pick the second line. This is a convenient way to connect objects at a corner.

Filleting Parallel Lines

You can use the **FILLET** tool to draw a radius between parallel lines. When parallel lines are selected, a radius is placed between the two lines. With the **Trim** option set to **Trim**, a longer line is trimmed to match the length of a shorter line. The radius of a fillet between parallel lines is always half the distance between the two lines, regardless of the radius setting. This is an effective method for creating a full radius, such as the end radii applied to a slot.

Making Multiple Fillets

To make several fillets without exiting the **FILLET** tool, select the **Multiple** option. The prompt for a first object repeats. When you have made all the fillets needed, press [Enter] or [Esc], or right-click and select the **Enter** option. When you use the **Multiple** mode, use the **Undo** option to discard the previous fillet.

Exercise 12-2

Complete the exercise on the Student CD.

Chapter 12 Basic Object Editing Tools

Figure 12-4.
Examples of chamfers.

.125 →
.125
.250 →
.125

"0" Chamfer   45° Chamfer   Unequal Chamfer

Using the Chamfer Tool

chamfer: In mechanical drafting, a small angled surface used to relieve a sharp corner.

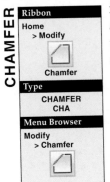

CHAMFER

Ribbon
Home
> Modify
Chamfer

Type
CHAMFER
CHA

Menu Browser
Modify
> Chamfer

Chamfers were introduced in Chapter 4 as a corner option for adding chamfers to rectangles created with the **RECTANGLE** tool. The **CHAMFER** tool draws an angled corner between intersecting and nonintersecting lines, polylines, xlines, and rays.

Chamfer size is determined based on the distance from the corner. A 45° chamfer is the same distance from the corner in each direction. See **Figure 12-4**. Chamfers are defined by two distances or by one distance and an angle. The defaults are zero units for the lengths and the angle. A value of .5 for both distances produces a 45° × .5 chamfered corner.

Setting the Chamfer Distances

The chamfer distances must be set before you can draw a chamfer. Chamfer distances are usually exact values, but you can pick two points to set each distance. To set the chamfer distance, initiate the **CHAMFER** tool, access the **Distance** option, and enter each chamfer distance. Now you are ready to select the two lines to be chamfered. The results of several chamfering operations are shown in **Figure 12-5**. The distances

Figure 12-5.
Using the **CHAMFER** tool.

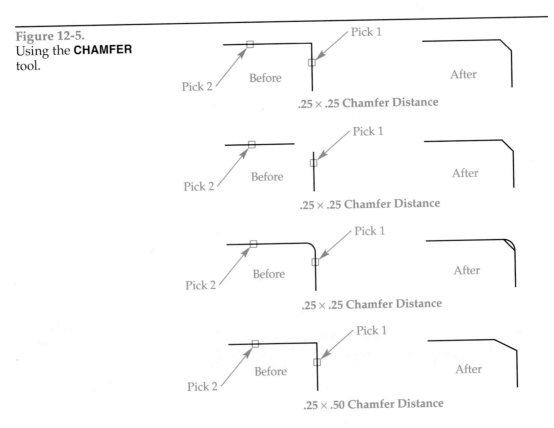

Pick 1
Pick 2
Before
After
.25 × .25 Chamfer Distance

Pick 1
Pick 2
Before
After
.25 × .25 Chamfer Distance

Pick 1
Pick 2
Before
After
.25 × .25 Chamfer Distance

Pick 1
Pick 2
Before
After
.25 × .50 Chamfer Distance

you set remain in effect until changed, allowing you to quickly place additional chamfers with the same distances.

Chamfering the Corners of a Polyline

All corners of a closed polyline can be chamfered using the **Polyline** option of the **CHAMFER** tool. To chamfer all the corners of a polyline, select the **Polyline** option and then select the polyline. The corners of the polyline are chamfered to the preset distance values. If the polyline was drawn without using the **Close** option, the beginning corner is not chamfered, as shown in **Figure 12-6.**

Setting the Chamfer Angle

Instead of setting two chamfer distances, you can set the chamfer distance for one line and set an angle to determine the chamfer to the second line using the **Angle** option of the **CHAMFER** tool. See **Figure 12-7.** After entering the distance and angle, select the two lines to be chamfered. The distance and angle you set remain in effect until changed, allowing you to quickly place additional chamfers with the same distance and angle.

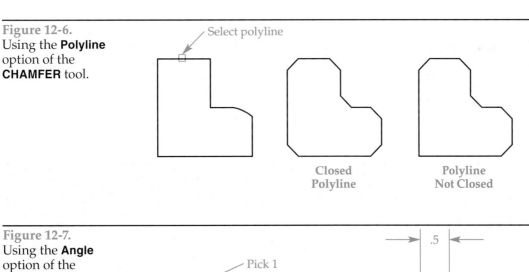

Figure 12-6.
Using the **Polyline** option of the **CHAMFER** tool.

Select polyline

Closed Polyline

Polyline Not Closed

Figure 12-7.
Using the **Angle** option of the **CHAMFER** tool with the chamfer length set at .5 and the angle set at 45°.

Pick 1

Pick 2

Before

.5

45°

After

Setting the Chamfer Method

When you set chamfer distances or a distance and an angle, AutoCAD maintains the setting until you change it. You can set the values for each method without affecting the other. Use the **Method** option if you want to toggle between drawing chamfers using the **Distance** and **Angle** options.

Setting the Chamfer Trim Mode

The **Trim** option controls whether the **CHAMFER** tool trims object segments that extend beyond the intersection. When the **Trim** option is set to **Trim**, objects are trimmed. When the **Trim** option is set to **No Trim**, the chamfered objects are not changed when the chamfer is inserted, as shown in **Figure 12-8**.

PROFESSIONAL TIP

Objects can be chamfered even when the corners do not meet. AutoCAD extends the lines as required to generate the specified chamfer and complete the corner if the **Trim** option is set to **Trim**. If the **Trim** option is set to **No Trim**, AutoCAD does not extend the lines to complete the corner.

Chamfering Square Corners

When the chamfer distances are set to zero, you can use the **CHAMFER** tool to connect two lines. You can also create a zero-distance chamfer without setting the distance to zero by holding the [Shift] key when you pick the second line. This is a convenient way to connect objects at a corner.

Figure 12-8.
Comparison of the **Trim** and **No trim** options of the **CHAMFER** tool.

Before Chamfer	Chamfer with Trim	Chamfer with No Trim

Making Multiple Chamfers

To make several chamfers without exiting the **CHAMFER** tool, select the **Multiple** option. The prompt for a first line repeats. When you have made all the chamfers needed, press [Enter] or [Esc], or right-click and select the **Enter** option. When you use the **Multiple** option, use the **Undo** option to discard the previous chamfer.

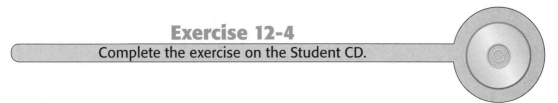

Exercise 12-4
Complete the exercise on the Student CD.

Breaking Objects

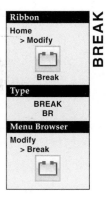

The **BREAK** tool is used to separate a single object into two objects. The break can remove a portion of an object or split the object at a single point. The **BREAK** tool requires you to select the object to be broken, the first break point, and the second break point. When you select the object, the point you pick is also used as the first break point by default. To select a different first break point, use the **First point** option at the Specify second break point or [First point]: prompt. After both break points are specified, the part of the object between the two points is deleted. See Figure 12-9.

If you select the same point for both the first and second break points, the **BREAK** tool splits the object into two pieces without removing a portion. This can be accomplished by entering @ at the Specify second break point or [First point]: prompt. The @ symbol repeats the coordinates of the previously selected point. You can also pick the **Break at Point** button on the expanded **Modify** panel on the **Home** tab of the ribbon to break an object at a single point with a single pick. Using the **BREAK** tool without removing a portion of the object is shown in Figure 12-10.

When breaking arcs or circles, always work in a counterclockwise direction. Otherwise, you may break the portion of the arc or circle you want to keep. If you want to break off the end of a line or an arc, pick the first point on the object. Pick the second point slightly beyond the end to be cut off. See Figure 12-11. When you pick a second point not on the object, AutoCAD selects the point on the object nearest the point you picked.

Figure 12-9.
Using the **BREAK** tool to break an object. The first pick can be used to select both the object and the first break point.

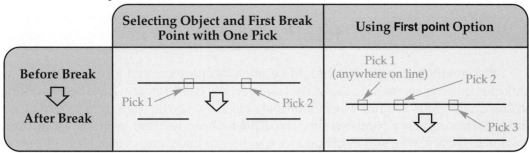

Figure 12-10.
Using the **BREAK** tool to break an object at a single point without removing any of the object. Select the same point as the first and second break points, or use the **Break at Point** button.

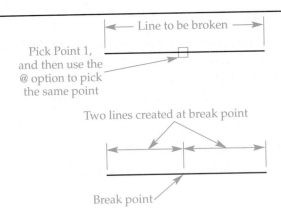

Line to be broken

Pick Point 1, and then use the @ option to pick the same point

Two lines created at break point

Break point

Figure 12-11.
Work counterclockwise when using the **BREAK** tool on circles and arcs.

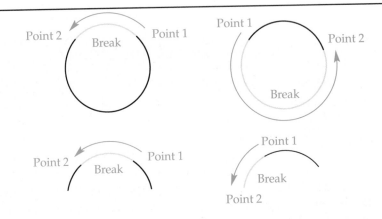

Point 2   Break   Point 1

Point 1   Point 2   Break

Point 2   Break   Point 1

Point 1   Break   Point 2

Exercise 12-5
Complete the exercise on the Student CD.

Joining Objects

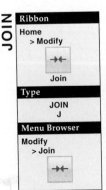

JOIN

Ribbon
Home
> Modify

Join

Type
JOIN
J

Menu Browser
Modify
> Join

Often multiple objects that should be one object are created as a result of using multiple drawing and editing tools. This is especially true after you have been working on the drawing for a while. These multiple objects make the drawing file size larger and the drawing more cumbersome. The **JOIN** tool can be used to quickly join lines, polylines, splines, arcs, and elliptical arcs together to make one object. Only objects of the same type can be joined together. For example, a line can be joined to another line, but a line cannot be joined to a polyline. Also, joined objects must be in the same 2D plane.

AutoCAD and Its Applications—Basics

Figure 12-12.
Lines must be collinear to be joined, but the lines can overlap and there can be gaps between them.

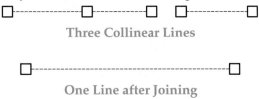

Three Collinear Lines

One Line after Joining

Joining Lines

Each type of object has different rules for joining. To join lines, the lines must be collinear. The lines can touch, have gaps between them, or be overlapping. See Figure 12-12.

Joining Polylines and Splines

To join polylines together, the polylines must have a common endpoint. No gaps can exist between the segments, and they cannot overlap. See Figure 12-13. The rules for joining splines together are the same as those for polylines. The splines must share a common endpoint.

Joining Arcs and Elliptical Arcs

Arcs that share the same center point and are on the same circular path can be joined. The arcs can be overlapping or have a gap between them. In Figure 12-14, two arcs with a gap have been joined together. When there is more than one gap between two arcs to be joined, using the **JOIN** tool may close a gap other than the one you desire. When closing arc gaps, make sure to pick the arcs in a counterclockwise direction.

Figure 12-13.
Only polylines that share an endpoint can be joined.

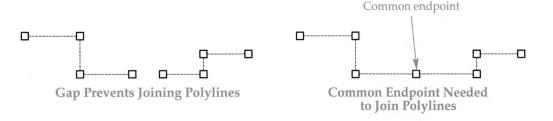

Gap Prevents Joining Polylines

Common endpoint

Common Endpoint Needed
to Join Polylines

Figure 12-14.
Arcs can have a gap or be overlapping, as shown on the left, but they must share the same circular path. On the right, the two arcs are shown after they have been joined.

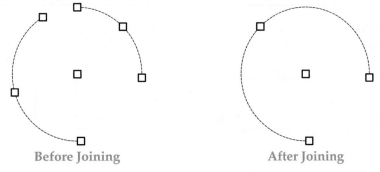

Before Joining

After Joining

Elliptical arcs are joined using the same rules as those for the arc. The elliptical arcs must be on the same elliptical path. They can, however, overlap or have gaps between them.

NOTE

Both arcs and elliptical arcs can be closed using the **JOIN** tool. When you use the **cLose** option on an arc, it becomes a circle. Using this option on an elliptical arc creates an ellipse.

Trimming Objects

cutting edge: An object such as a line, an arc, or text defining the point (edge) at which the object you are trimming will be cut.

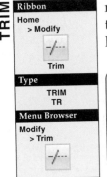

The **TRIM** tool cuts lines, polylines, circles, arcs, ellipses, splines, xlines, and rays that extend beyond a desired point of intersection. The **TRIM** tool requires you to pick a *cutting edge* and the object(s) to trim. If two corners of an object overrun, select two cutting edges and two objects.

Once you access the **TRIM** tool, pick as many cutting edges as necessary and then right-click or press the [Enter] key or space bar. Then pick the object(s) you want to trim to the cutting edge(s). When you are finished trimming, right-click or press the [Enter] key or space bar to exit the **TRIM** tool. See Figure 12-15.

NOTE

You can access the **EXTEND** tool while using the **TRIM** tool. After selecting the cutting edge, hold the [Shift] key while selecting an object to extend the object to the cutting edge. The **EXTEND** tool is described later in this chapter.

Trimming without Selecting a Cutting Edge

You can quickly trim objects back to the nearest intersection by right-clicking or pressing the [Enter] key or space bar at the first Select objects or <select all>: prompt instead of picking a cutting edge. Picking an object that intersects with another object trims the selected object to the first object. If multiple objects intersect the object to be trimmed, it is trimmed back to the first intersection. After trimming an object, you can select other objects to be trimmed without having to restart the tool. When you are done trimming, right-click or press the [Enter] key or space bar, or press the [Esc] key to exit the tool.

Figure 12-15.
Using the **TRIM** tool. Note the cutting edges.

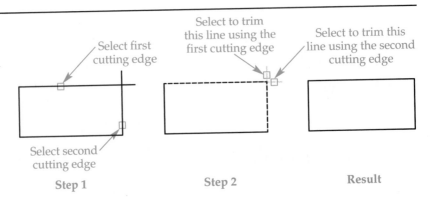

Select first cutting edge

Select second cutting edge

Select to trim this line using the first cutting edge

Select to trim this line using the second cutting edge

Step 1

Step 2

Result

Figure 12-16.
The only objects trimmed with the **Crossing** option are those that cross the edges of the crossing window. Automatic windowing accomplishes the same task.

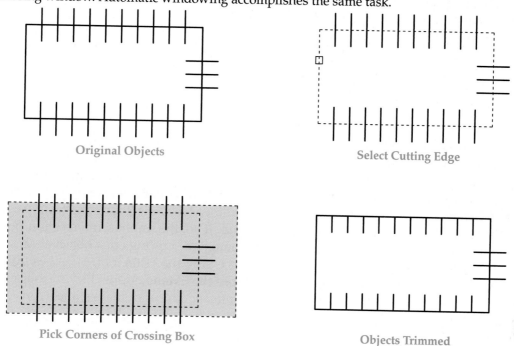

Original Objects

Select Cutting Edge

Pick Corners of Crossing Box

Objects Trimmed

Trim Selection Options

Often the quickest and most effective way to select multiple lines to trim is to use automatic windowing, as described in Chapter 3. However, the **TRIM** tool provides a **Crossing** option that forces a crossing selection, allowing you to select objects to be trimmed using a crossing box. After the objects have been selected as cutting edges, you are prompted to specify a first corner and a second corner. Any lines crossing any of the four lines that make up the crossing selection are trimmed back to the cutting edge. See Figure 12-16.

A **Fence** option is also available and can be used, especially if space does not allow for effective automatic windowing. The fence line can have multiple segments. Any lines crossing the fence line are trimmed to the nearest cutting edge. See Figure 12-17.

Figure 12-17.
The **Fence** option can be used to make selections around objects. In this case, the **RECTANGLE** tool was used to create the rectangle, so the cutting edge consists of the entire rectangle.

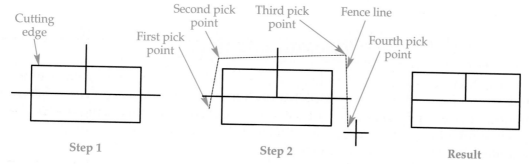

Step 1

Step 2

Result

Figure 12-18.
Trimming to an
implied intersection
when **Extend** mode
is active.

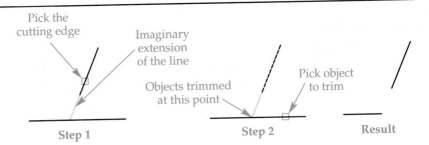

Pick the
cutting edge

Imaginary
extension
of the line

Pick object
to trim

Objects trimmed
at this point

Step 1   Step 2   Result

Trimming to an Implied Intersection

**implied
intersection:** The
point at which
objects would
meet if they were
extended.

Trimming to an *implied intersection* is possible using the **Edge** option of the **TRIM** tool. When you enter the **Edge** option, the choices are **Extend** and **No extend**. **No extend** is selected by default, and as a result, objects that do not intersect cannot be trimmed. When **Extend** is active, AutoCAD checks to see if the object selected as the cutting edge will extend to intersect the object to be trimmed. If so, the implied intersection point can be used to trim the object. This does not change the cutting edge object at all.

To trim to an implied intersection, after accessing the **TRIM** tool, pick the cutting edge(s). Then activate the **Edge** option and choose the **Extend** option. Pick the object(s) to trim. AutoCAD recognizes the implied intersection and makes the trim. See **Figure 12-18.**

Using the Erase Option

While you are trimming objects, you may have some unneeded objects left over. Construction lines are often used as trimming edges or boundaries and need to be erased after the trimming operation. While the **TRIM** tool is active, the **eRase** option can be used to delete objects. After the objects are deleted, the **TRIM** tool resumes.

Using the Undo Option

The **TRIM** tool has an **Undo** option that allows you to cancel the previous trimming without leaving the tool. This is useful when the result of a trim is not what you expected. To undo the previous trim, activate the **Undo** option immediately after performing an unwanted trim. The trimmed portion returns, and you can continue trimming other objects.

NOTE

The **TRIM** tool also provides a **Project** option, used for trimming 3D objects. Using AutoCAD for 3D drawing is explained in *AutoCAD and Its Applications—Advanced.*

---

boundary edge:
The edge to which
objects such as
lines, arcs, or text
are extended.

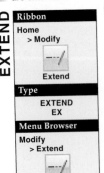

EXTEND

Ribbon
Home
> Modify

Extend

Type
EXTEND
EX

Menu Browser
Modify
> Extend

Extending Objects

The **EXTEND** tool is used to lengthen lines, elliptical arcs, rays, open polylines, and arcs to meet other objects. **EXTEND** does not work on closed polylines because an unconnected endpoint does not exist. The process of extending using the **EXTEND** tool is similar to trimming using the **TRIM** tool. The main difference is that you select *boundary edges*, rather than cutting edges.

Once you access the **EXTEND** tool, pick as many boundary edges as necessary, and then right-click or press the [Enter] key or space bar. Now, pick the object(s) you want to extend to the boundary edge(s). When you are finished extending, right-click or press the [Enter] key or space bar to exit the **EXTEND** tool. See **Figure 12-19.**

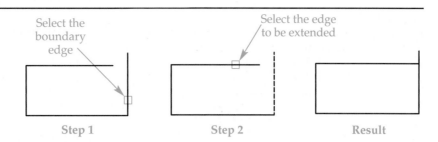

Figure 12-19.
Using the **EXTEND** tool. Note the boundary edges.

Select the boundary edge

Select the edge to be extended

Step 1

Step 2

Result

NOTE

You can access the **TRIM** tool while using the **EXTEND** tool. After selecting the boundary edge, hold the [Shift] key while selecting an object to trim the object at the boundary edge.

Extending without Selecting a Boundary Edge

You can quickly extend objects to the nearest object by right-clicking or pressing the [Enter] key or space bar at the first Select objects or <select all>: prompt, instead of picking a boundary edge. This selects all of the objects in the drawing as boundary edges. This method automatically extends selected objects to the nearest object in their path. After extending an object, you can select other objects to be extended or right-click, press the [Enter] key or space bar, or press the [Esc] key to exit the tool. Figure 12-20 illustrates how to combine the **EXTEND** and **TRIM** tools, without selecting a boundary edge, to insert a wall in a floor plan drawing. The same process can be used for a variety of applications.

Extend Selection Options

Like the **TRIM** tool, the **EXTEND** tool provides a **Crossing** option that forces a crossing selection, allowing you to select objects to be extended using a crossing box. After the objects have been selected as the boundary edges, you are prompted to specify a first corner and a second corner. Any lines crossing any of the four lines that make up the crossing selection are extended to the boundary edge. See Figure 12-21.

A **Fence** option is also available and can be used, especially if space does not allow for effective automatic windowing. The fence line can have multiple segments. Any lines crossing the fence line are extended to the nearest boundary edge. See Figure 12-22.

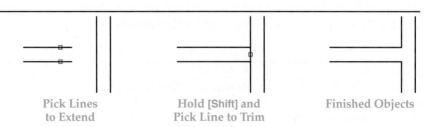

Figure 12-20.
To select all objects as boundary edges, press [Enter] instead of picking a boundary edge.

Pick Lines to Extend

Hold [Shift] and Pick Line to Trim

Finished Objects

Figure 12-21.
Selecting objects for extending with the **Crossing** option. Automatic windowing accomplishes the same task.

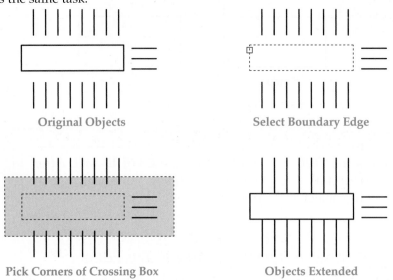

Original Objects

Select Boundary Edge

Pick Corners of Crossing Box

Objects Extended

Figure 12-22.
Multiple lines can be extended to a boundary edge using the **Fence** option.

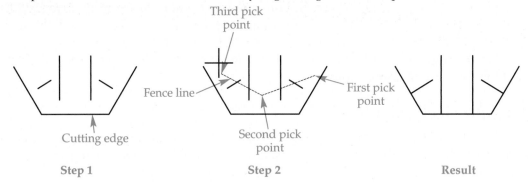

Step 1

Step 2

Result

Extending to an Implied Intersection

You can extend an object to an implied intersection when **Extend** mode is active. **Extend** mode is set using the **Edge** option. The **Edge** option setting affects both the **TRIM** and **EXTEND** tools. When **Extend** mode is active, the boundary edge object is checked to see if it intersects an object when it is extended. If so, the implied intersection point can be used as the boundary for the object to be extended, as shown in **Figure 12-23**. This does not change the boundary edge object at all.

Figure 12-23.
Extending to an implied intersection with **Extend** mode.

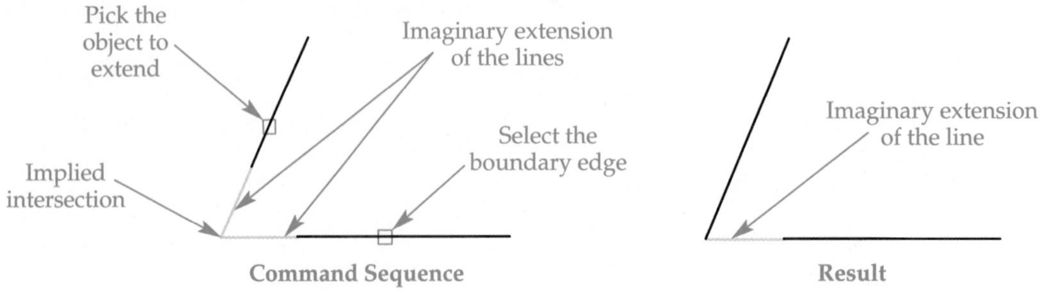

Command Sequence

Result

The **EXTEND** tool also provides **Undo** and **Project** options, which provide functions similar to those of the same options available with the **TRIM** tool.

Exercise 12-6
Complete the exercise on the Student CD.

Stretching Objects

The **STRETCH** tool is used to modify certain dimensions of an object while leaving other dimensions the same. In mechanical drafting, for example, a screw can be stretched to create a longer or shorter screw. In architectural design, room sizes may be stretched to increase or decrease the square footage.

Once you access the **STRETCH** tool, you must use a crossing selection or a crossing polygon to select only the objects that will be stretched. This is a very important requirement and is different from selection using other editing tools. See Figure 12-24. If you select the entire object, the **STRETCH** tool works like the **MOVE** tool. The **MOVE** tool is described in Chapter 13.

After selecting the objects to be stretched, you are asked to pick the *base point*. This is the point from which the objects will be stretched. Pick or enter a position for the base point. Though often the position of the base point is not critical, most drafters select a point on an object, the corner of a view, or the center of a circle. As you move the crosshairs, the object is stretched or compressed. When the displayed object is stretched to the desired position, enter or select a point to accept the stretch.

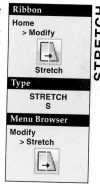

base point: The initial reference point AutoCAD uses when stretching, moving, copying, and scaling objects.

Figure 12-24.
Using the **STRETCH** tool.

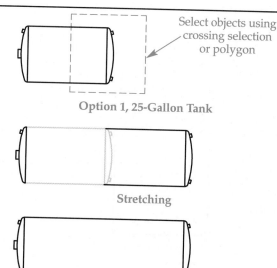

Select objects using crossing selection or polygon

Option 1, 25-Gallon Tank

Stretching

Option 2, 50-Gallon Tank

Using the Displacement Option

displacement:
The direction and distance in which an object is moved.

A selected object can be stretched relative to the origin, or 0,0,0 point, using the **Displacement** option. To stretch using a *displacement*, access the **STRETCH** tool and use a crossing selection or a crossing polygon to select only the objects to be stretched. Then select the **Displacement** option instead of defining the base point. At the Specify displacement <0,0,0>: prompt, enter an absolute coordinate to stretch the objects from the origin to the coordinate point. See Figure 12-25.

Using the First Point As Displacement

Another method for stretching an object is to use the first point as the displacement. This means the coordinates you use to select the base point are automatically used as the coordinates for the direction and distance for stretching the object. To apply this technique, access the **STRETCH** tool and use a crossing selection or a crossing polygon to select only the objects to be stretched. Then pick or enter the base point, and instead of defining the second point, right-click or press the [Enter] key or space bar to accept the <use first point as displacement> default. See Figure 12-26.

Figure 12-25.
Using the **Displacement** option of the **STRETCH** tool. A—An example of a 1 × 1 rectangle to be stretched. B—Stretching the rectangle using a (1,0) displacement.

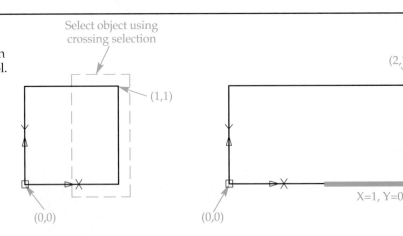

AutoCAD and Its Applications—Basics

Figure 12-26.
A—An example of a 1 × 1 rectangle to be stretched.
B—Stretching using the selected base point (1,1) as the displacement.

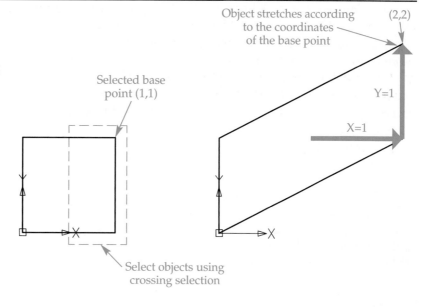

Selected base point (1,1)

Select objects using crossing selection

Object stretches according to the coordinates of the base point (2,2)

Y=1

X=1

Exercise 12-7
Complete the exercise on the Student CD.

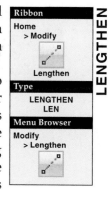

Using the Lengthen Tool

The **LENGTHEN** tool can be used to change the length of objects and the included angle of an arc. The **LENGTHEN** tool does not affect closed objects. For example, you can lengthen a line, a polyline, an arc, an elliptical arc, or a spline, but you cannot lengthen a closed ellipse, polygon, or circle. Only one object can be lengthened at a time.

Once you access the **LENGTHEN** tool, select the object for which you want to change the length. AutoCAD gives you the current length if the object is linear, or the included angle if the object is an arc. Choose one of the four lengthen options and follow the prompts. The **DElta** option allows you to specify a positive or negative change in length, measured from the endpoint of the selected object. The lengthening or shortening happens closest to the selection point and changes the length by the amount entered. See Figure 12-27. The **DElta** option has an **Angle** suboption that lets you change the included angle of an arc by a specified angle. See Figure 12-28.

Ribbon
Home
> Modify

Lengthen
Type
LENGTHEN
LEN
Menu Browser
Modify
> Lengthen

LENGTHEN

Figure 12-27.
Using the **DElta** option of the **LENGTHEN** tool with values of .75 and –.75.

Select the object closest to the end you want lengthened or shortened

Original Object

.75

Lengthened by an Increment of .75

–.75

Shortened by an Increment of –.75

The **Percent** option allows you to change the length of an object or the angle of an arc by a specified percentage. The original length is considered to be 100 percent. You can make the object shorter by specifying less than 100 percent or longer by specifying more than 100 percent. See Figure 12-29.

The **Total** option allows you to set the total length or angle of the object (the length or angle after the **LENGTHEN** operation). See Figure 12-30. The **DYnamic** option lets you drag the endpoint of the object to the desired length or angle using the crosshairs. See Figure 12-31. It is helpful to use dynamic input with polar tracking or Ortho mode or have the grid and snap set to usable increments when using this option.

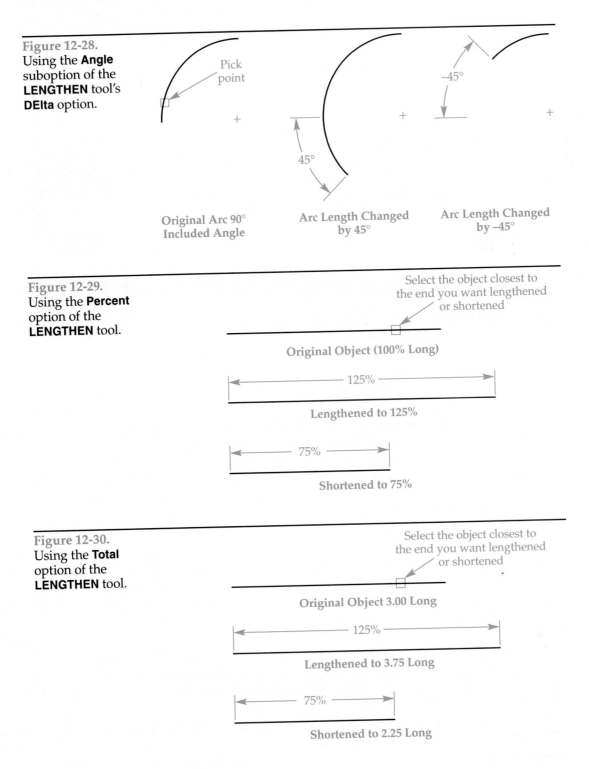

Figure 12-28.
Using the **Angle** suboption of the **LENGTHEN** tool's **DElta** option.

Pick point

−45°

45°

Original Arc 90° Included Angle

Arc Length Changed by 45°

Arc Length Changed by −45°

Figure 12-29.
Using the **Percent** option of the **LENGTHEN** tool.

Select the object closest to the end you want lengthened or shortened

Original Object (100% Long)

125%

Lengthened to 125%

75%

Shortened to 75%

Figure 12-30.
Using the **Total** option of the **LENGTHEN** tool.

Select the object closest to the end you want lengthened or shortened

Original Object 3.00 Long

125%

Lengthened to 3.75 Long

75%

Shortened to 2.25 Long

AutoCAD and Its Applications—Basics

Figure 12-31.
Using the **DYnamic** option of the **LENGTHEN** tool.

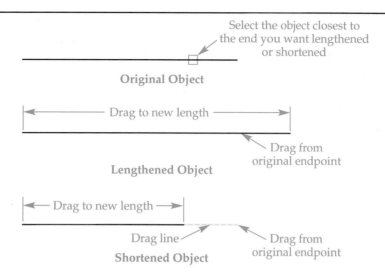

Select the object closest to the end you want lengthened or shortened

Original Object

Drag to new length

Lengthened Object

Drag from original endpoint

Drag to new length

Drag line

Shortened Object

Drag from original endpoint

NOTE

Only lines and arcs can be lengthened dynamically. The length of a spline can only be decreased. Splines are described in Chapter 16.

PROFESSIONAL TIP

You do not have to select the object before entering one of the **LENGTHEN** tool options, but doing so lets you know the current length and, if it is an arc, the angle of the object. This is especially helpful when you are using the **Total** option.

Exercise 12-8

Complete the exercise on the Student CD.

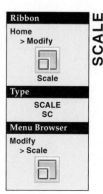

Using the Scale Tool

The **SCALE** tool is a convenient editing tool that can save hours of drafting time. This tool lets you change the size of a single object or an entire drawing. It enlarges or reduces the entire object proportionately. If associative dimensioning is used, the dimensions also change to reflect the new size. Associative dimensions are described in Chapter 21.

After you access the **SCALE** tool, pick a base point to define the point where the increase or decrease in size occurs. The selected objects move away from or toward the base point during the scale operation. The next step is to specify the scale factor. Enter a number to indicate the amount of enlargement or reduction. For example, if you want to make the selection twice the current size, type 2 at the Specify scale factor or [Copy/Reference] <current>: prompt, as shown in **Figure 12-32.** Examples of scale factors are presented in **Figure 12-33.**

Ribbon
Home
> Modify
Scale
Type
SCALE
SC
Menu Browser
Modify
> Scale

SCALE

Figure 12-32.
Using the **SCALE** tool. The base point does not move, but every other point in the object does.

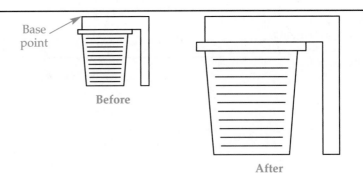

Base point

Before

After

Figure 12-33.
Scale factors and the resulting sizes.

Scale Factor	Resulting Size
10	10 times bigger
5	5 times bigger
2	2 times bigger
1	Equal to existing size
.75	3/4 of original size
.50	1/2 of original size
.25	1/4 of original size

Using the Reference Option

An object can also be scaled by specifying a new size in relation to an existing dimension. For example, suppose you have a shaft that is 2.50″ long, and you want to make it 3.00″ long. To do so, use the **Reference** option. Enter the current length at the Specify reference length: prompt, in this example 2.5. Next, enter the length you want the object to be, in this example 3. See Figure 12-34.

Creating a Copy While Scaling

If an object needs to be both copied and scaled, these changes can be made at the same time using the **SCALE** tool. The **Copy** option of the **SCALE** tool copies the selected object and scales it, leaving the original object unchanged.

NOTE

The **SCALE** tool changes all dimensions of an object proportionately. If you want to change only the width or length of an object, use the **STRETCH** or **LENGTHEN** tool.

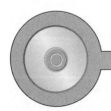

Exercise 12-9
Complete the exercise on the Student CD.

Figure 12-34.
Using the **Reference**
option of the **SCALE**
tool.

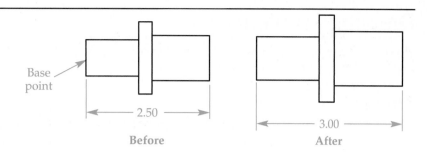

Base
point

2.50

Before

3.00

After

Chapter Test

Answer the following questions. Write your answers on a separate sheet of paper or complete the electronic chapter test on the Student CD.

1. How is the size of a fillet specified?
2. Explain how to set the radius of a fillet to .50.
3. Which option of the **CHAMFER** tool would you use to specify a .125 × .125 chamfer?
4. What is the purpose of the **mEthod** option in the **CHAMFER** tool?
5. Describe the difference between the **Trim** and **No trim** options when using the **CHAMFER** and **FILLET** tools.
6. How can you split an object in two without removing a portion?
7. In what direction should you pick points to break a portion out of a circle or an arc?
8. What tool can be used to combine two collinear lines into a single line object?
9. What two requirements must be met before two arcs can be joined?
10. Which tool performs the opposite function of the **EXTEND** tool?
11. Name the tool that trims an object to a cutting edge.
12. Name the tool associated with boundary edges.
13. Name the option in the **TRIM** and **EXTEND** tools that allows you to trim or extend to an implied intersection.
14. Which panel of the ribbon contains the **TRIM**, **EXTEND**, and **STRETCH** tools?
15. List two locations drafters normally choose as the base point when using the **STRETCH** tool.
16. Define the term *displacement*, as it relates to the **STRETCH** tool.
17. How do you cancel the **STRETCH** tool?
18. Identify the **LENGTHEN** tool option that corresponds to each of the following descriptions:
    A. Allows a positive or negative change in length from the endpoint.
    B. Changes a length or an arc angle by a percentage of the total.
    C. Sets the total length or angle to the value specified.
    D. Drags the endpoint of the object to the desired length or angle.
19. What tool would you use to reduce the size of an entire drawing by one-half?
20. Write the command aliases for the following tools:
    A. **CHAMFER**
    B. **FILLET**
    C. **BREAK**
    D. **TRIM**
    E. **EXTEND**
    F. **SCALE**
    G. **LENGTHEN**

Drawing Problems

Use your templates as appropriate for each of the following problems. Start a new drawing for each problem, unless indicated otherwise.

▼ Basic

1. Draw Object A using the **LINE** and **ARC** tools. Make sure the corners overrun and the arc is centered on the lines, but does not touch the lines. Use the **TRIM**, **EXTEND**, and **STRETCH** tools to make Object B. Save the drawing as P12-1.

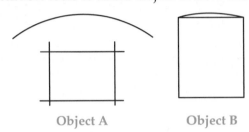

Object A   Object B

2. Open drawing P12-1 for further editing (Object A). Using the **STRETCH** tool, change the shape to create Object B. Save the drawing as P12-2.

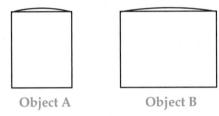

Object A   Object B

3. Refer to Figure 12-24 in this chapter. Draw the object shown in Option 1. Stretch the object to twice its length, as shown in Option 2. Stretch the object again to one and half times its length. *Hint:* use endpoint and midpoint object snap modes to stretch accurately. Save the drawing as P12-3.

4. Draw the object shown without dimensions. Use the **CHAMFER** tool to create the inclined surface. Save the drawing as P12-4.

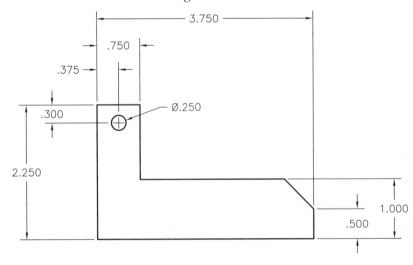

▼ Intermediate

5. Draw the object shown using the **ELLIPSE** and **LINE** tools. Use the **BREAK** or **TRIM** tool when drawing and editing the lower ellipse. Save the drawing as P12-5.

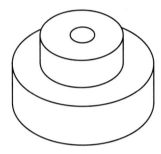

6. Open drawing P12-4 for further editing. Shorten the height of the object using the **STRETCH** tool, as shown below. Next, add to the object as indicated. Save the drawing as P12-6.

7. Use the **TRIM** and **OFFSET** tools to assist you in drawing this object. Do not draw centerlines or dimensions. Save the completed drawing as P12-7.

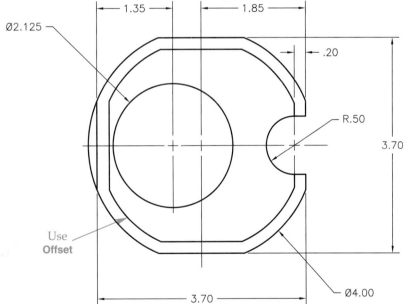

Drawing Problems - Chapter 12

8. Draw the following plate. Do not include dimensions in your drawing. Use the **FILLET** tool where appropriate. Save the drawing as P12-8.

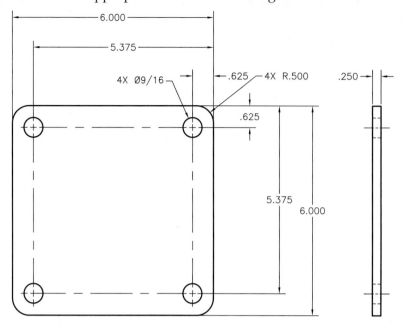

9. Draw the following toilet. Do not include dimensions. Use dimensions of your choice for objects not fully dimensioned. Save the drawing as P12-9.

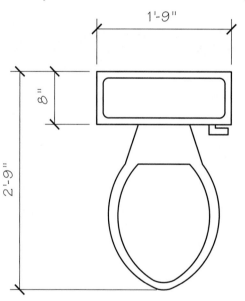

AutoCAD and Its Applications—Basics

▼ Advanced

10. Draw the following object without dimensions. Add rounds using the **FILLET** tool and chamfers using the **CHAMFER** tool. Use the trim mode setting to your advantage. Save the drawing as P12-10.

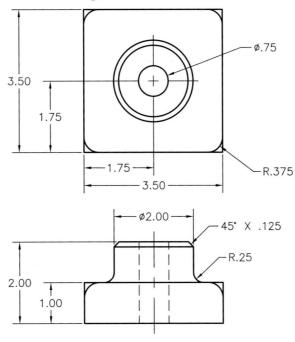

11. Draw the following bracket. Do not include dimensions in your drawing. Use the **FILLET** tool where appropriate. Save the drawing as P12-11.

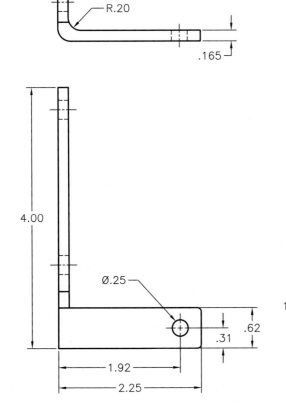

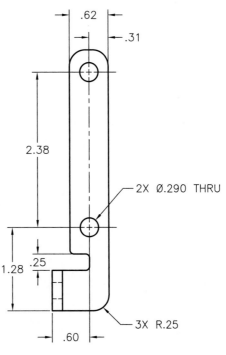

Drawing Problems - Chapter 12

12. Draw the beam wrap detail shown. Do not include leaders or notes. Use dimensions of your choice for objects not fully dimensioned. Save the drawing as P12-12.

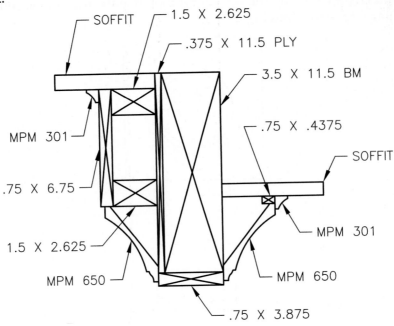

CHAPTER 13

Arranging and Patterning Objects

Learning Objectives

After completing this chapter, you will be able to do the following:

✓ Relocate objects using the **MOVE** tool.
✓ Change the angular positions of objects using the **ROTATE** tool.
✓ Use the **ALIGN** tool to simultaneously move and rotate objects.
✓ Make copies of existing objects using the **COPY** tool.
✓ Draw mirror images of objects using the **MIRROR** tool.
✓ Create patterns of objects using the **ARRAY** tool.

This chapter explains tools and methods for arranging and patterning objects using basic AutoCAD modification tools. These tools can be used to greatly increase drawing efficiency. You will learn how to move, rotate, copy, mirror, and pattern existing objects. The editing tools described in this chapter include many options. As you work through this chapter, experiment with each option to see which is the most effective in different situations.

Moving Objects

In many situations, you will find that a view or feature is not located where you want it. This problem is easy to fix with the **MOVE** tool. Using the **MOVE** tool is very similar to using the **STRETCH** tool. The difference is that when objects move, they remain the same size and shape. When you enter the **MOVE** tool, AutoCAD asks you to select the objects to be moved. Use any of the selection set options to select the objects. The next prompt requests the base point. The base point is the point from which the objects will be moved. Though the position of the base point is often not critical, most drafters select a point on an object, the corner of a view, or the center of a circle. The next prompt asks for the second point. This is the new position. All selected objects are moved the distance from the base point to the second point. See Figure 13-1.

Ribbon	MOVE
Home > Modify	
Move	
Type	
MOVE M	
Menu Browser	
Modify > Move	

Using the Displacement Option

A selected object can be moved relative to the origin, or 0,0,0 point, using the **Displacement** option. To move using a displacement, access the **MOVE** tool and select the objects you want to move. Then select the **Displacement** option instead of defining

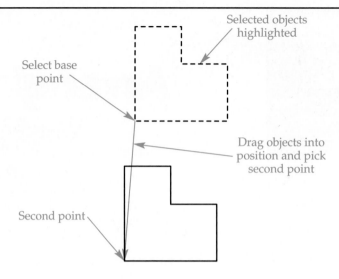

Figure 13-1.
Using the **MOVE** tool.

Selected objects highlighted

Select base point

Drag objects into position and pick second point

Second point

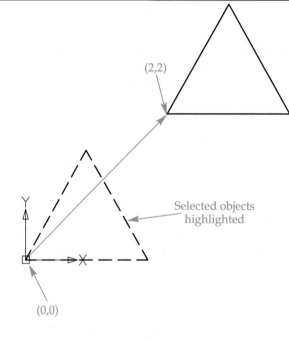

Figure 13-2.
Using the **Displacement** option of the **MOVE** tool to move objects. In this example, the origin is the base point and the absolute coordinate point (2,2) is the displacement.

(2,2)

Selected objects highlighted

Y

(0,0)

the base point. At the Specify displacement <0,0,0>: prompt, enter an absolute coordinate to move the objects from the origin to the coordinate point. See Figure 13-2.

Using the First Point As Displacement

Another method for moving an object is to use the first point as the displacement. This means the coordinates you use to select the base point are automatically used as the coordinates for the direction and distance for moving the object. To apply this technique, access the **MOVE** tool and select the objects you want to move. Then select the base point, and instead of defining the second point, right-click or press the [Enter] key or space bar to accept the <use first point as displacement> option. See Figure 13-3.

PROFESSIONAL TIP

Always use object snap modes to your best advantage with editing tools. For example, suppose you want to move an object to the center point of a circle. Use the **Center** object snap mode to select the center of the circle.

Figure 13-3.
Moving a circle using the selected base point, (1,1) in this example, as the displacement.

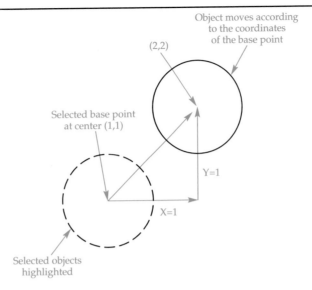

Object moves according to the coordinates of the base point

(2,2)

Selected base point at center (1,1)

Y=1

X=1

Selected objects highlighted

Exercise 13-1
Complete the exercise on the Student CD.

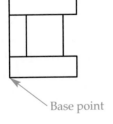

Rotating Objects

Ribbon
Home
> Modify

Rotate

Type
ROTATE
RO

Menu Browser
Modify
> Rotate

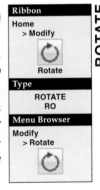

ROTATE

Design changes often require an object, feature, or view to be rotated. For example, the furniture in an office layout may have to be rotated for an interior design. AutoCAD allows you to revise the layout easily to obtain the final design using the **ROTATE** tool.

Once you access the **ROTATE** tool, select objects to rotate using any of the selection set options. After selecting the objects, pick a base point. The base point is the point, or axis, of rotation around which the objects rotate. Next, enter a rotation angle. A negative rotation angle revolves the object clockwise. A positive rotation angle revolves the object counterclockwise. See **Figure 13-4.**

Figure 13-4.
Rotation angles.

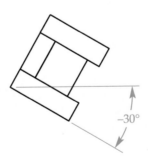

Base point

−30°

−30° Rotation

30°

30° Rotation

Figure 13-5.
Using the **Reference** option of the **ROTATE** tool. A—Entering reference angles. B—Selecting points on a reference line.

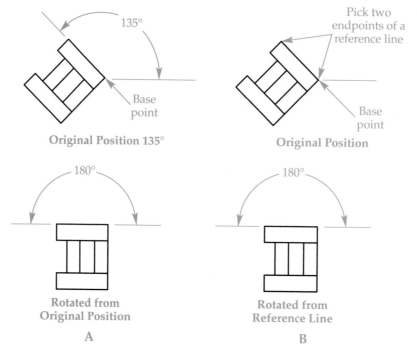

Using the Reference Option

Use the **Reference** option to rotate an object to a different angle based on the angle at which the object is currently rotated. The **Reference** option can be used in one of two ways. The first method is to define the existing angle and then the new angle. This method assumes that you know the angle at which the object is currently rotated. To use this technique, access the **ROTATE** tool, select the objects to rotate, and then pick the base point. Then select the **Reference** option instead of defining a rotation angle. Enter a reference angle, 135 for example, and then enter a new angle, such as 180. See Figure 13-5A.

The other method is to pick a reference line on the object and rotate the object in relationship to the reference line. This is the best choice when you do not know the angle at which the object is currently rotated. To use this technique, access the **ROTATE** tool, select the objects to rotate, and pick the base point. Then select the **Reference** option instead of defining a rotation angle. Pick the two endpoints of a reference line that forms the existing angle. Finally, enter the new angle. See Figure 13-5B.

Creating a Copy While Rotating

An object can be copied and rotated at the same time, leaving the original object in place. This can be done using the **Copy** option at the Specify rotation angle or [Copy/Reference] <*current*> prompt. When you specify the rotation angle, a new object is created and rotated, and the source object is left unchanged.

Exercise 13-2
Complete the exercise on the Student CD.

Aligning Objects

Use the **ALIGN** tool when you want to move and rotate an object at the same time. **ALIGN** is a 3D tool that can also be used for 2D drawings. After you access the **ALIGN** tool, select objects to rotate using any of the selection set options. Then, you must enter or select *source points* and *destination points*. Pick the first source point and then the first destination point. Next, pick the second source point, followed by the second destination point. For 2D applications, you only need two source points and two destination points. Right-click or press the [Enter] key or the space bar when the prompt requests the third source and destination points. See Figure 13-6.

The last prompt allows you to change the size of the object that is being moved. Choose the **Yes** option to scale the object if the distance between the source points is different from the distance between the destination points. Figure 13-7 illustrates using the **Scale** option of the **ALIGN** tool.

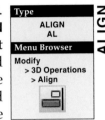

Type
ALIGN
AL
Menu Browser
Modify
> 3D Operations
> Align

source points: Points to define a reference line relative to the object's original position for an **ALIGN** operation.

destination points: Points to define the location of the reference line relative to the object's new location in an **ALIGN** operation.

Exercise 13-3
Complete the exercise on the Student CD.

Figure 13-6.
Using the **ALIGN** tool to move and rotate a kitchen cabinet layout against a wall.

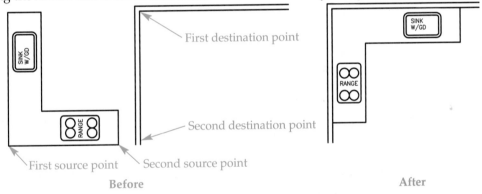

Before   **After**

Figure 13-7.
The **Scale** option of the **ALIGN** tool is used to change the size of an object while it is moved and rotated.

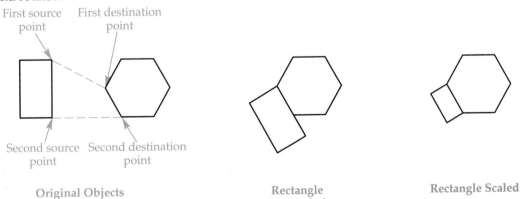

Original Objects   Rectangle Not Scaled   Rectangle Scaled

Figure 13-8.
Using the **COPY** tool.

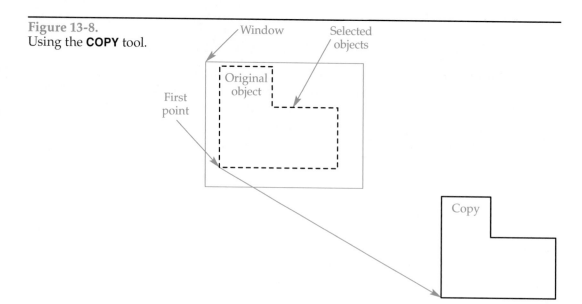

Copying Objects

COPY

Ribbon

Home
> Modify

Copy

Type

COPY
CO
CP

Menu Browser

Modify
> copy

The **COPY** tool is used to make a copy of an existing object or objects. Using the **COPY** tool is very similar to using the **MOVE** tool. However, when a second point is picked, the original object remains in place and a copy is drawn. See Figure 13-8. By default, you can continue creating copies of the selected objects. Press the [Enter] key or space bar or right-click and select the **Enter** option to exit the tool.

As with the **MOVE** tool, you can specify a base point and a second point, specify a displacement using the **Displacement** option, or define the first point as displacement. Each of these copying techniques functions the same when making copies as when moving objects. The difference is that the original object remains and a copy is created.

> **NOTE**
>
> By default, the **Multiple** copy mode is active, allowing you to create several copies of the same object using a single **COPY** operation by picking additional second points. To make a single copy of the selected objects and exit the tool after the copy is placed, enter the **mOde** option and activate the **Single** copy mode.

Exercise 13-4
Complete the exercise on the Student CD.

MIRROR

Ribbon

Home
> Modify

Mirror

Type

MIRROR
MI

Menu Browser

Modify
> Mirror

Mirroring Objects

The **MIRROR** tool is used to draw an object in a reflected, or mirrored, position. Mirroring a part is common in mechanical drafting to form the opposite component of a symmetrical assembly. Mirroring an entire drawing is common in architectural drafting, when a client wants a plan drawn in reverse. Once you enter the **MIRROR** tool, select the objects you want to mirror using any of the selection set options. Then

Figure 13-9.
When an object is reflected about a mirror line, the space between the object and the mirror line is also mirrored.

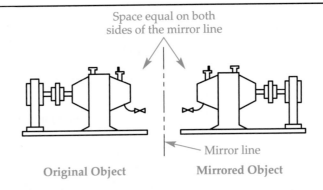

Space equal on both sides of the mirror line

Mirror line

Original Object

Mirrored Object

define a *mirror line*. The objects and any space between the objects and the mirror line are reflected. See Figure 13-9.

The mirror line can be placed at any angle. After you pick the first endpoint, a mirrored image appears and moves with the crosshairs. When you select the second mirror line endpoint, you have the option to delete the original objects. See Figure 13-10.

mirror line: The line of symmetry about which objects are mirrored.

Figure 13-10.
The **MIRROR** tool gives you the option to delete the old objects.

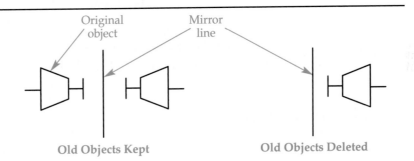

Original object

Mirror line

Old Objects Kept

Old Objects Deleted

NOTE

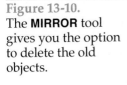

By default the **MIRRTEXT** system variable is set to **0**, which prevents text from being reversed with using the **MIRROR** tool. Enter a **MIRRTEXT** system variable value of **1** to mirror text in relation to the original object. See Figure 13-11. Backward text is generally not acceptable, although it is used for reverse imaging.

Exercise 13-5

Complete the exercise on the Student CD.

Figure 13-11.
The **MIRRTEXT** system variable options.

Mirror line

MIRRTEXT(1)

(1)TXƎTЯЯIM

MIRRTEXT(0)

MIRRTEXT(0)

Figure 13-12.
Examples of arrays.

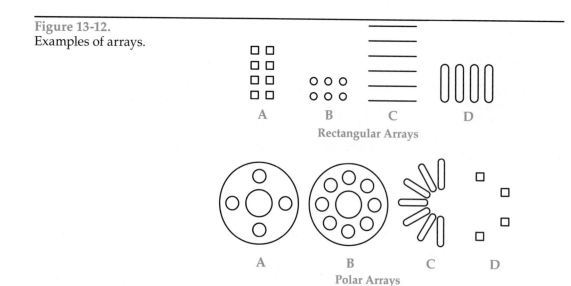

Rectangular Arrays

Polar Arrays

Patterning Objects with Array

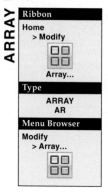

Some designs require a rectangular or circular pattern of the same object. For example, office desks are often arranged in rows. Suppose your design calls for four rows, each having four desks. You can create this design by drawing one desk and copying it fifteen times. This operation, however, is time-consuming. A quicker method is to create an *array*. There are two types of arrays: *rectangular* and *polar*. Some examples are shown in **Figure 13-12**.

Arrays are specified using the **ARRAY** tool, which displays the **Array** dialog box. See **Figure 13-13**. All input needed to create the array is specified in the **Array** dialog box. Use the **Rectangular Array** and **Polar Array** radio buttons to specify the type of array.

Figure 13-13.
The **Array** dialog box options for a rectangular array.

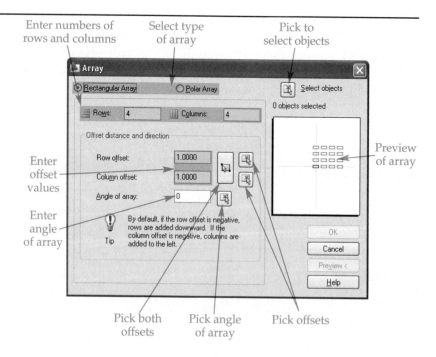

Enter numbers of rows and columns

Select type of array

Pick to select objects

Preview of array

Enter offset values

Enter angle of array

Pick both offsets

Pick angle of array

Pick offsets

Arranging Objects in a Rectangular Pattern

A rectangular array arranges objects in a specified number of rows and columns, with a specified amount of space between the rows and columns. The **Rectangular Array** radio button in the **Array** dialog box is selected by default. You can create an array that has a single row, a single column, or multiple rows and columns. Pick the **Select objects** button to return to the drawing area and select the objects to be arrayed. When you finish selecting objects, right-click or press the [Enter] key or space bar to return to the **Array** dialog box.

For example, suppose you want to create a rectangular pattern of a .5-unit square having four rows, four columns, and a .5 spacing between squares. Enter 4 in the **Rows:** and **Columns:** text boxes and 1.0000 in the **Row offset:** and **Column offset:** text boxes. See Figure 13-14. Notice that the distances do not refer to the space between the objects, but the distances between the same point on each object.

The distances can also be entered by picking points. Two methods are available. First, you can use the **Pick Row Offset** and **Pick Column Offset** buttons in the **Array** dialog box to specify each distance separately. In the second method, you can use the **Pick Both Offsets** button to specify both distances in one pick. Figure 13-15 illustrates the **Pick Both Offsets** method. You can use any point selection method—such as object snap modes, relative coordinates, or polar coordinates—to pick the second point.

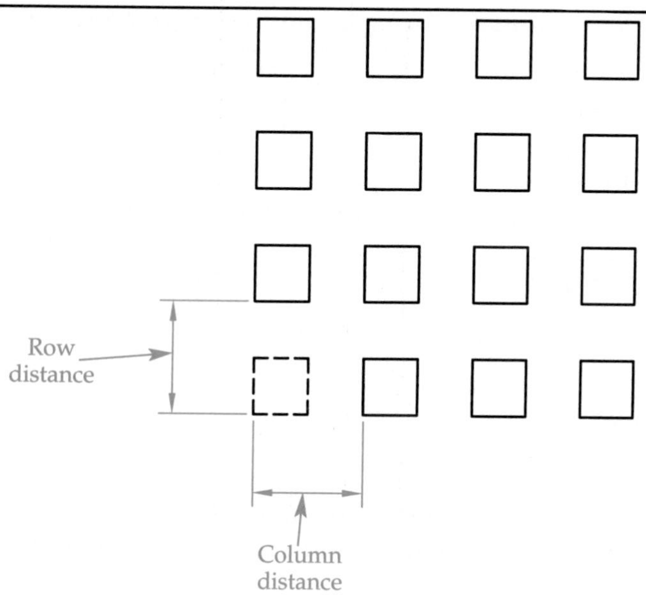

Figure 13-14.
The original object (in dashed lines) and the rectangular array. Note how the distances between rows and columns are determined.

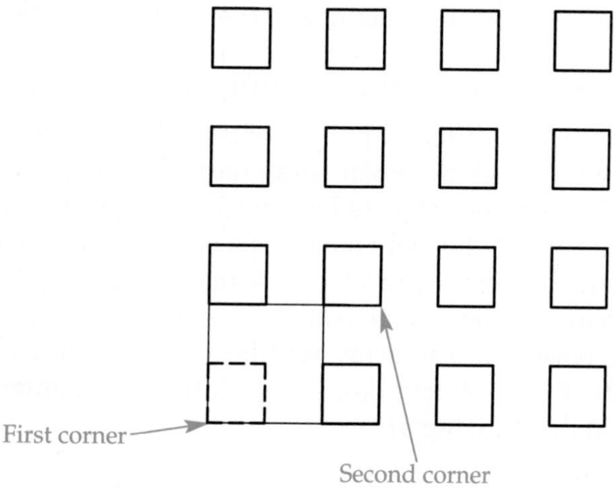

Figure 13-15.
The spacing of rows and columns in an array can be specified with a single point.

Figure 13-16.
Positive and negative offset distances determine the direction in which an array will grow.

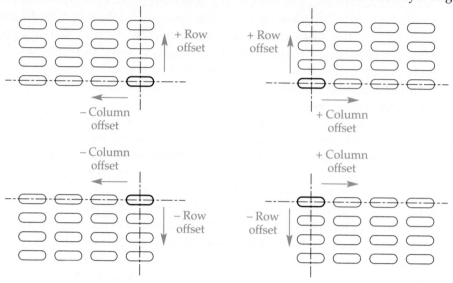

Figure 13-17.
Rectangular arrays can be set at an angle using the **Angle of array:** setting.

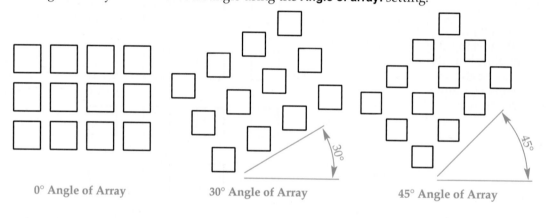

Figure 13-16 shows the four directions in which an array can grow. The direction is based on the use of positive and negative distance values for row and column offsets.

You can also create an angled rectangular array. Enter the angle in the **Angle of array:** text box or pick the **Pick Angle of Array** button to specify the angle with the crosshairs. The column and row alignments are rotated, not the objects. See Figure 13-17.

Arranging Objects around a Center Point

A polar array creates a circular pattern of the selected object around a center point. To create a polar array, pick the **Polar Array** radio button in the **Array** dialog box. See Figure 13-18. Pick the **Select objects** button to return to the drawing area and select the objects to be arrayed. When you have finished selecting objects, right-click or press the [Enter] key or space bar to return to the **Array** dialog box.

The next step in creating a polar array is to specify the center point. This is the point about which the objects in the array will be rotated. Enter the coordinates for the center point in the **X:** and **Y:** text boxes or pick the **Pick Center Point** button to select the center point in the drawing area.

Figure 13-18.
The **Array** dialog box options for a polar array.

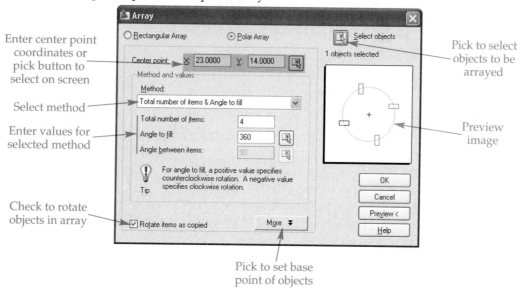

Enter center point coordinates or pick button to select on screen

Select method

Enter values for selected method

Check to rotate objects in array

Pick to select objects to be arrayed

Preview image

Pick to set base point of objects

After selecting the center point, you must specify the type of polar array to be created using the **Method:** drop-down list. The selected method determines which settings in the dialog box are available. Three methods are available:

- Total number of items & Angle to fill
- Total number of items & Angle between items
- Angle to fill & Angle between items

The **Total number of items:** setting is the total number of objects to be in the array, including the original object. If you do not know how many items will be in the array, use the Angle to fill & Angle between items method. The **Angle to fill:** setting can be positive or negative. To array the object in a counterclockwise direction, enter a positive angle. To array the object in a clockwise direction, enter a negative angle. Enter 360 to create a complete circular array. The **Angle between items:** setting specifies the angular distance between adjacent objects in the array. For example, if you want to create a circular pattern of five items spaced 18° apart, enter 5 in the **Total number of items:** text box and 18 in the **Angle between items:** text box.

You can have the objects rotated as they are copied around the center point by checking the **Rotate items as copied** check box. This keeps the same face of each object pointing toward the center point. If objects are not rotated as they are copied, they remain in the same orientation as the original object. See **Figure 13-19.**

Figure 13-19.
Rotating objects in a polar array. A—The square is rotated as it is arrayed. B—The square is not rotated as it is arrayed.

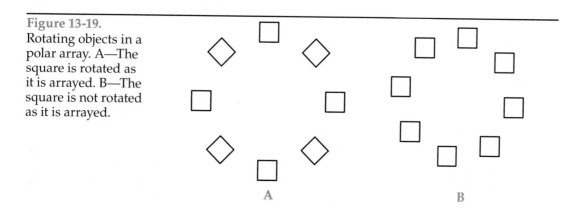

A

B

When AutoCAD creates a polar array, the base point of the object is rotated and remains at a constant distance from the center point. The default base point varies for different types of objects, as shown in the following table:

Object Type	Default Base Point
Arc, circle, ellipse	Center
Rectangle, polygon	First corner
Line, polyline, donut	Start point
Block, text	Insertion point

If the default base point does not produce the desired array, you can select a different base point for the selected object. Pick the **More** button in the **Array** dialog box to display the **Object base point** area. Deactivate the **Set to object's default** check box. Enter a new base point in the text boxes or pick the button to select a base point on screen.

Exercise 13-6
Complete the exercise on the Student CD.

Chapter Test

Answer the following questions. Write your answers on a separate sheet of paper or complete the electronic chapter test on the Student CD.

1. List two locations drafters normally choose as the base point when using the **MOVE** tool.
2. How would you go about rotating an object 45° clockwise?
3. Briefly describe the two methods of using the **Reference** option of the **ROTATE** tool.
4. Name the tool that can be used to move and rotate an object simultaneously.
5. How many points must you select to align an object in a 2D drawing?
6. Which tab and panel of the ribbon contains the **MOVE** and **COPY** tools?
7. Explain the difference between the **MOVE** and **COPY** tools.
8. Briefly explain how to make several copies of the same object.
9. What tool allows you to draw a reverse image of an existing object?
10. What is the difference between polar and rectangular arrays?
11. What four values should you know before you create a rectangular array?
12. Suppose an object is 1.5″ (38 mm) wide and you want to create a rectangular array with .75″ (19 mm) spacing between objects. What should you specify for the distance between columns?
13. How do you specify a clockwise polar array rotation?
14. What values should you know before you create a polar array?
15. Give the keyboard shortcuts for the following tools:
    A. **MOVE**
    B. **COPY**
    C. **MIRROR**
    D. **ROTATE**
    E. **ALIGN**
    F. **ARRAY**

Drawing Problems

Use your templates as appropriate for each of the following problems. Start a new drawing for each problem, unless indicated otherwise.

▼ Basic

1. Open P12-1. Rotate the object 90 degrees to the right and mirror the object to the left. Use the vertical base of the object as the mirror line. Your final drawing should look like the example below. Save the drawing as P13-1.

2. Open drawing P12-2. Make two copies of the object to the right of the original object. Scale the first copy 1.5 times size of the original object. Scale the second copy 2 times the size of the original object. Move the objects so they are approximately centered in your drawing area. Move the objects as needed to align the bases of all objects and provide an equal amount of space between the objects. Save the drawing as P13-2.

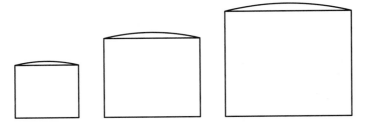

3. Draw Objects A, B, and C at the sizes shown below, but do not include the dimensions. Make a copy of Object A two units up. Make four copies of Object B three units up, center to center. Make three copies of Object C three units up, center to center. Save the drawing as P13-3.

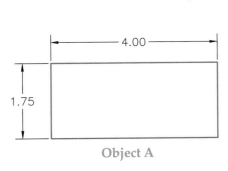

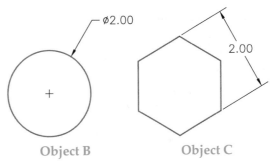

Object A   Object B   Object C

4. Open P12-4. Draw a mirror image as Object B. Now, remove the original view and move the new view so that Point 2 is at the original Point 1 location. Save the drawing as P13-4.

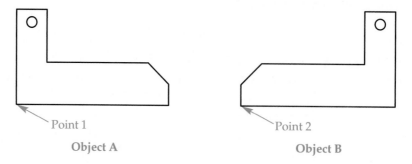

Object A   Object B

▼ Intermediate

5. Draw the object shown below without dimensions. The object is symmetrical; therefore, draw only one half. Mirror the other half into place. Use the **CHAMFER** and **FILLET** tools to your best advantage. All fillets and rounds are .125. Use the **JOIN** tool where necessary. Save the drawing as P13-5.

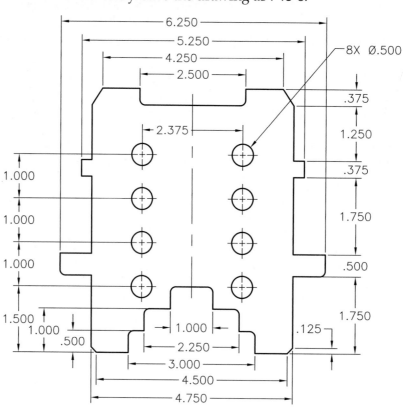

Drawing Problems - Chapter 13

6. Draw the object shown below without dimensions. Mirror the right half into place. Use the **CHAMFER** and **FILLET** tools to your best advantage. Save the drawing as P13-6.

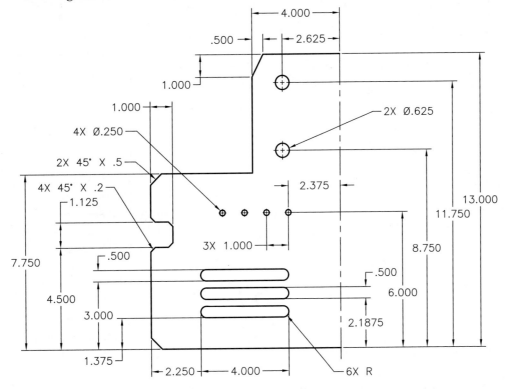

7. Redraw the objects shown below. Mirror the drawing, but make sure the text remains readable. Delete the original image during the mirroring process. Save the drawing as P13-7.

2b1
TRANSFER

5a2 4a1 8a1
LTS.HTRS.FANS

2b1

1b1
RESET

11b1
BYPASS

8. Draw this timer schematic. Save the drawing as P13-8.

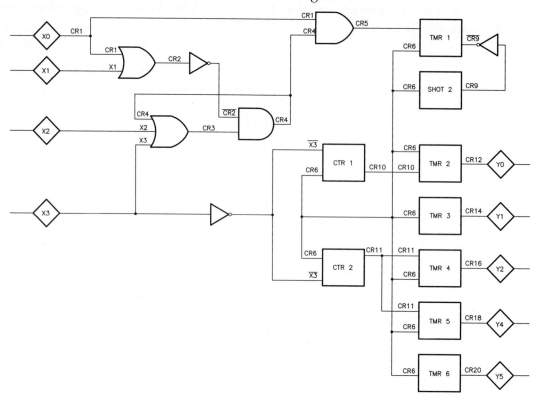

9. Use tracking and object snaps to draw the object shown below based on these instructions:
   A. Draw the outline of the object first, followed by the ten ∅.500 holes (A).
   B. The holes labeled B are located vertically halfway between the centers of the holes labeled A. They have a diameter one-quarter the size of the holes labeled A.
   C. The holes labeled C are located vertically halfway between the holes labeled A and B. Their diameter is three-quarters of the diameter of the holes labeled B.
   D. The holes labeled D are located horizontally halfway between the centers of the holes labeled A. These holes have the same diameter as the holes labeled B.
   E. Draw the rectangles around the circles as shown.
   F. Do not draw dimensions, notes, or labels.
   G. Save the drawing as P13-9.

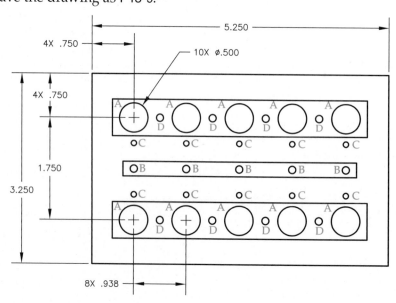

10. Draw the portion of the gasket shown on the left. Do not include dimensions. Use the **MIRROR** tool to complete the gasket as shown on the right. Save the drawing as P13-10.

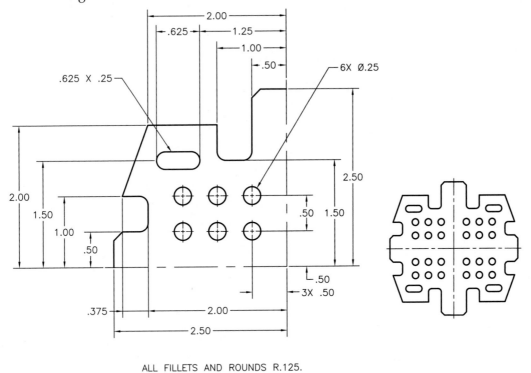

ALL FILLETS AND ROUNDS R.125.
CHAMFERS 45° X .125

11. Draw the padded bench. Do not dimension. Use the **COPY** and **ARRAY** tools as needed. Save the drawing as P13-11.

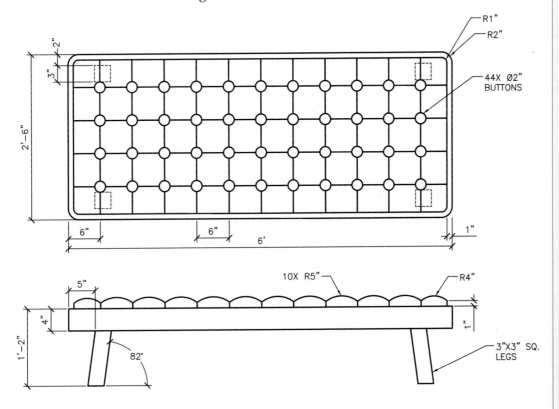

12. Draw the handwheel shown below. Do not dimension. Use the **ARRAY** tool to draw the spokes. Save the drawing as P13-12.

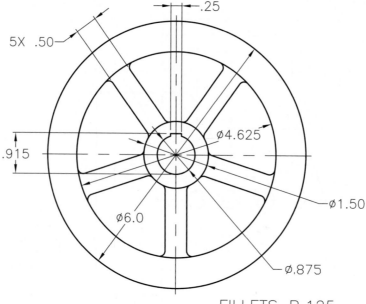

FILLETS R.125

13. Draw the control diagram. Draw one branch (including text) and use the **COPY** tool to your advantage. Use text editing tools as needed. Save the drawing as P13-13. (Design and drawing by EC Company, Portland, Oregon)

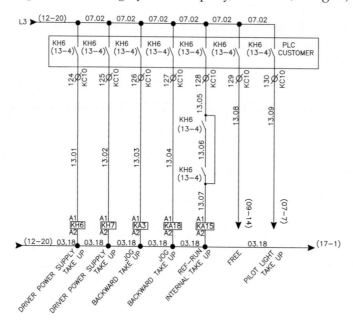

▼ Advanced

14. You have been given an engineer's sketches and notes to construct a drawing of a sprocket. Create a front and side view of the sprocket using the **ARRAY** tool. Place the drawing on one of your templates. Do not add dimensions. Save the drawing as P13-14.

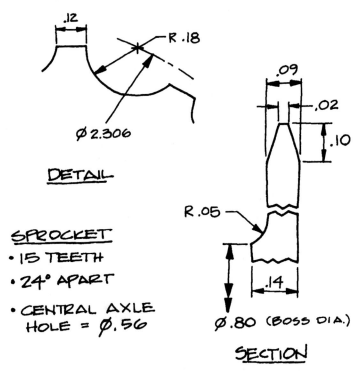

15. Draw the following object views using the dimensions given. Use **ARRAY** to construct the hole and tooth arrangements. Use one of your templates for the drawing. Do not add dimensions. Save the drawing as P13-15.

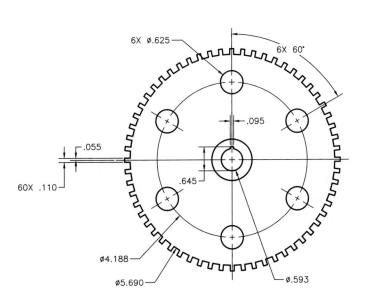

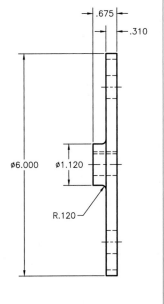

16. Draw this refrigeration system schematic. Save the drawing as P13-16.

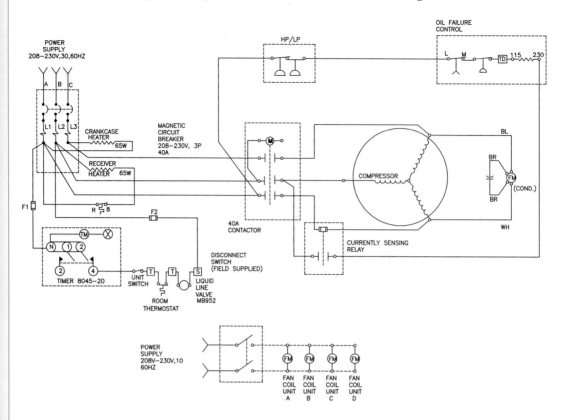

17. The following structural sketch shows a steel column arrangement on a concrete floor slab for a new building. The *I*-shaped symbols represent the steel columns. The columns are arranged in "bay lines" and "column lines." The column lines are numbered *1*, *2*, and *3*. The bay lines are labeled *A* through *G*. The width of a bay is 24'-0". Line balloons, or tags, identify the bay and column lines. Draw the arrangement, using **ARRAY** for the steel column symbols and the tags. Do not dimension the drawing. The following guidelines will help you:
   A. Begin a new drawing using an architectural template.
   B. Select architectural units and set up the drawing to print on a 36 × 24 sheet size. Determine the scale required for the floor plan to fit on this sheet size and specify the drawing limits accordingly.
   C. Draw the steel column symbol to the dimensions given.
   D. Set the grid spacing at 2'-0" (24").
   E. Set the snap spacing at 12".
   F. Draw all other objects.
   G. Place text inside the balloon tags. Set the running object snap mode to **Center** and justify the text to **Middle**. Make the text height 6".
   H. Place a title block on the drawing.
   I. Save the drawing as P13-17.

AutoCAD and Its Applications—Basics

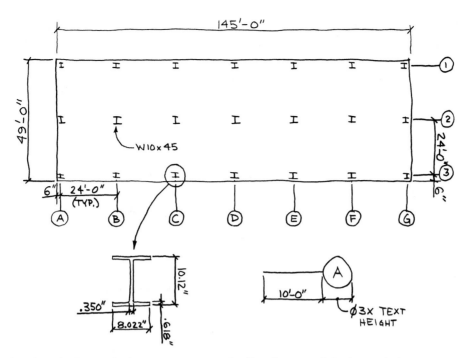

18. The sketch shown below is a proposed office layout of desks and chairs. One desk is shown with the layout of a chair, keyboard, monitor, and tower-mounted computer (drawn with dotted lines). All of the desk workstations should have the same configuration. The exact sizes and locations of the doors and windows are not important for this problem. Use the following guidelines to complete this problem:
    A. Begin a new drawing.
    B. Choose architectural units.
    C. Set up the drawing to print on a C-size sheet, and be sure to create the drawing in model space.
    D. Use the appropriate drawing and editing tools to complete this problem quickly and efficiently.
    E. Draw the desk and computer hardware to the dimensions given.
    F. Do not dimension the drawing.
    G. Save the drawing as P13-18.

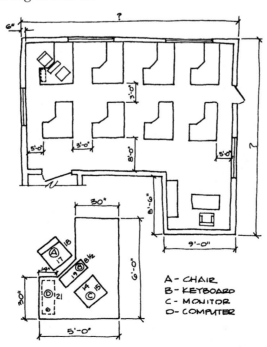

19. Draw the front elevation of this house. Create the features proportional to the given drawing. Use the **ARRAY** and **TRIM** tools to place the siding and porch rails evenly. Save the drawing as P13-19.

Using Grips, Properties, and Quick Select

Learning Objectives

After completing this chapter, you will be able to do the following:

✓ Use grips to stretch, copy, move, rotate, scale, and mirror objects.
✓ Edit objects using the **Quick Properties** panel and the **Properties** palette.
✓ Use the **MATCHPROP** tool to match object properties.
✓ Edit between drawings.
✓ Create selection sets using the **Quick Select** dialog box.

You have already learned how to use tools that let you perform a variety of drawing and editing activities with AutoCAD. These tools give you a great deal of flexibility and increase productivity. Typically, when using tools such as **ERASE**, **FILLET**, **MOVE**, and **COPY,** you access a tool first and then follow prompts that require you to select the object to be edited. This chapter describes the process of editing objects and changing object properties by selecting an object first and then performing editing operations. This chapter also explains tools for selecting objects using selection set filters.

Using Grips

Grips are small boxes that appear at strategic points on an object when you select the object while no tool is active. For example, the grips appear at the endpoints and midpoint of a straight line and at the center and quadrant points of a circle. Figure 14-1 shows the locations of grips on several different types of objects.

To activate grips, move the crosshairs pick box to the desired object and pick. The object is highlighted, and grips are displayed as *unselected grips*. Unselected grips are considered *warm* and appear as blue (Color 150) filled-in squares or arrows by default. Move the crosshairs over a warm grip and pause to change the color of the grip to pink (Color 11). Notice that the crosshairs snap to grips. Pausing over a warm grip and letting it change color ensures that you select the correct grip, especially when multiple grips are close together. Pick the highlighted grip to activate it.

A *selected grip* is considered *hot*, and appears as a red (Color 12) filled-in square or arrow by default. A hot grip can be used to perform a **STRETCH**, **COPY**, **MOVE**, **ROTATE**, **SCALE**, or **MIRROR** operation. If more than one object is selected, displaying warm grips, what you do with the hot grips affects all of the selected objects. Objects having warm and hot grips are highlighted and are part of the current selection set.

grips: Small boxes that appear at strategic points on an object, allowing you to edit the object's size and other properties.

unselected grips: Grips that have not yet been picked to perform an operation.

warm grips: Unselected grips.

selected grip: A grip that has been picked to perform an operation.

hot grip: A selected grip.

Figure 14-1.
Grips are placed at strategic locations on objects.

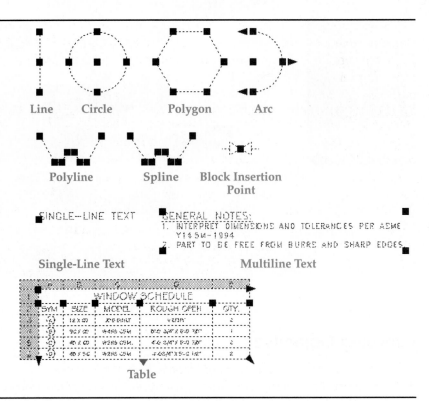

To remove highlighted objects from a selection, hold down the [Shift] key and pick the objects to be removed. The [Shift] key is also used to add or remove hot grips. To make a second grip hot, hold the [Shift] key down while selecting both the first and second grip. To add more grips to the hot grip selection set, continue to hold the [Shift] key down and select additional grips. With the [Shift] key held down, selecting a hot (red) grip returns it to the warm (blue) stage. **Figure 14-2** shows two circles being modified at the same time using hot grips.

Figure 14-2.
You can modify multiple objects simultaneously by using the [Shift] key to select additional grips to make them hot.

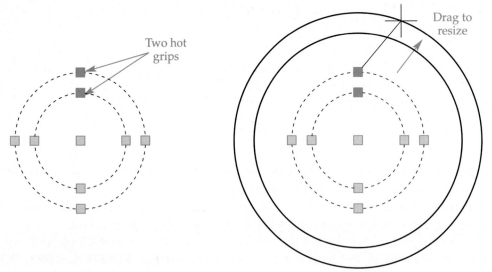

Return objects to the selection set by picking them again. Remove all hot grips from the selection set by pressing the [Esc] key to cancel. Press [Esc] again to remove all grips from the selection set. You can also right-click and select **Deselect All** from the shortcut menu to remove all grips.

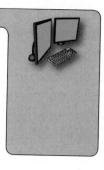

noun/verb selection: Performing tasks in AutoCAD by selecting the object(s) before entering a tool.

verb/noun selection: Performing tasks in AutoCAD by entering a tool before selecting objects.

Grip Tools

Grips provide access to the **STRETCH, MOVE, ROTATE, SCALE,** and **MIRROR** tools. In addition, the **Copy** option of the **MOVE** function and sometimes, depending on the hot grip, the **STRETCH** function, imitate the **COPY** tool. Grip tools are not selected using traditional ribbon buttons or menu browser options. Instead, select a grip to make the grip hot and activate the grip tools. The first tool is **STRETCH**, as indicated by the ** STRETCH ** Specify stretch point or [Base point/Copy/Undo/eXit]: prompt. You can use the **STRETCH** tool at this prompt or select another grip tool. Press the [Enter] key or the space bar or right-click and select the **Enter** option to cycle through additional tool options:

```
** STRETCH **
Specify stretch point or [Base point/Copy/Undo/eXit]: ↵
** MOVE **
Specify move point or [Base point/Copy/Undo/eXit]: ↵
** ROTATE **
Specify rotation angle or [Base point/Copy/Undo/Reference/eXit]: ↵
** SCALE **
Specify scale factor or [Base point/Copy/Undo/Reference/eXit]: ↵
** MIRROR **
Specify second point or [Base point/Copy/Undo/eXit]: ↵
** STRETCH **
Specify stretch point or [Base point/Copy/Undo/eXit]:
```

As an alternative to cycling through the tool options, you can right-click to access a grips shortcut menu, which is available only after a hot grip has been activated. The shortcut menu allows you to access the five grip editing options without using the keyboard. A third option to activate a tool is to enter the first two characters of the desired tool. Type MO for **MOVE**, MI for **MIRROR**, RO for **ROTATE**, SC for **SCALE**, and ST for **STRETCH**.

Stretching Objects

The **STRETCH** tool is initially active when you make a grip hot. The process of stretching using grips is similar to stretching using the traditional **STRETCH** tool. The main difference is that the hot grip acts as the base point for the stretch. Move the cross-hairs to make the selected object stretch, as shown in **Figure 14-3.** If you pick the middle grip of a line or an arc, the center grip of a circle, or the insertion point grip of a block, single-line text, multiline text, or table, the object moves instead of stretching.

Figure 14-3.
Using the **STRETCH** grip tool. Note the selected grip in each case.

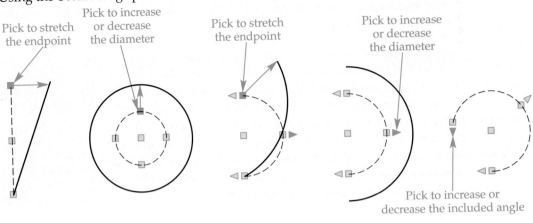

Figure 14-4 shows two methods to stretch features of an object. Step 1 in Figure 14-4A stretches the first corner, and Step 2 stretches the second corner. Alternatively, you can combine the two operations by holding down the [Shift] key as you pick the two grips, as shown in Figure 14-4B.

Use the **Base point** option to select a base point anywhere in the drawing to use instead of the hot grip base point. Use the **Copy** option to activate the copy function of the **STRETCH** tool. Depending on the hot grip, the **Copy** option either allows you to produce a copy of the entire selected object, similar to the traditional **COPY** tool, or a stretched copy of the selected object. Activate the **Undo** option to undo the previous operation. Choose the **eXit** option to exit the tool. You can also use the [Esc] key to cancel the tool. When you exit the tool, the hot grip is gone, but the warm grips remain. Pressing [Esc] twice removes the selected and unselected grips.

Grid snaps, coordinate entry techniques, polar tracking, object snaps, and object snap tracking can all be used with any of the grip editing tools to improve accuracy. Remember to use these functions as you edit your drawings. Dynamic input is especially effective with the **STRETCH** grip tool. Figure 14-5 shows an example of how the dimensional input feature of dynamic input can be used to quickly modify the size of

Figure 14-4.
Stretching an object. A—Select corners to stretch individually. B—Select several hot grips by holding down the [Shift] key.

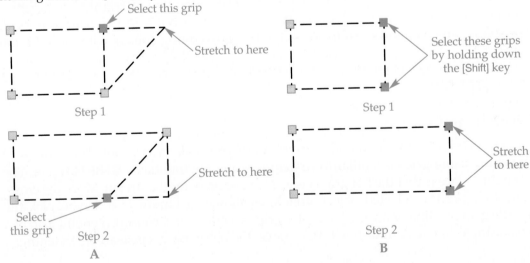

Figure 14-5.
Using the dimensional input feature of dynamic input with the **STRETCH** grip tool.

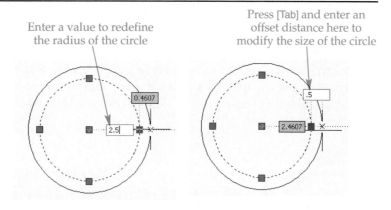

Enter a value to redefine the radius of the circle

Press [Tab] and enter an offset distance here to modify the size of the circle

a circle or to offset a circle a specific distance while using the **STRETCH** grip tool. In this example, enter the new radius of the circle in the distance input field, or press the [Tab] key to enter an offset in the other distance input field. This is just one example of how dynamic input can be using in combination with grips. Similar operations can be used with most objects.

Exercise 14-1
Complete the exercise on the Student CD.

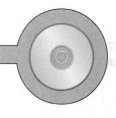

Moving Objects

To move an object with grips, select the object, pick a grip to use as the base point, and then right-click and choose the **Move** menu option or cycle through the tools until you get to the **MOVE** function. Move the object to a new point by entering or picking the new location. See **Figure 14-6.** Use grid snaps, coordinate entry techniques, polar tracking, object snaps, or object snap tracking to move the object accurately. The **Undo** and **eXit** options function the same when using the **MOVE** tool as when using the **STRETCH** tool.

Exercise 14-2
Complete the exercise on the Student CD.

Figure 14-6.
When you specify the **MOVE** tool, the selected grip becomes the base point for the move.

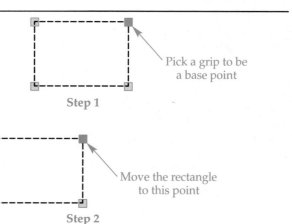

Pick a grip to be a base point

Step 1

Move the rectangle to this point

Step 2

Copying Objects

The **Copy** option is included in each of the grip editing tools. If you pick a grip that moves the entire object when using the **STRETCH** tool, and then activate the **Copy** option, the stretch functions as a copy. However, the **Copy** option in the **MOVE** tool is the true form of the **COPY** tool, allowing you to copy from any selected grip. The hot grip acts as the copy base point. Create as many copies of the selected object as needed, and then exit the tool.

Exercise 14-3
Complete the exercise on the Student CD.

Rotating Objects

To rotate an object using grips, select the object, pick a grip to use as the base point, and then right-click and choose the **Rotate** option, or cycle through the tools until you get to the **ROTATE** function. Then enter a rotation angle. Typically, the rotation angle is input at the keyboard, though other point entry methods can be used to rotate the object accurately. The **Undo** and **eXit** options function the same when using the **ROTATE** tool as when using the **STRETCH** tool.

The **Reference** option can be used when the object is already rotated at a known angle and you want to rotate it to a new angle. The selected base point remains in the same place when the object is rotated. The reference angle is the current angle. If you know the value of the current angle, enter the value at the prompt. Otherwise, pick two points on the reference line to identify the existing angle. Enter a value for the new angle or pick a point. Figure 14-7 shows the **ROTATE** options.

Exercise 14-4
Complete the exercise on the Student CD.

Figure 14-7.
The rotation angle and **Reference** options of the **ROTATE** grip tool.

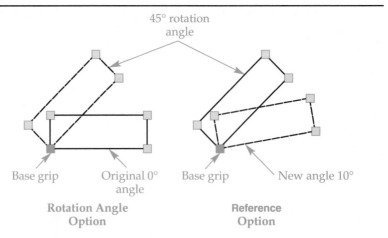

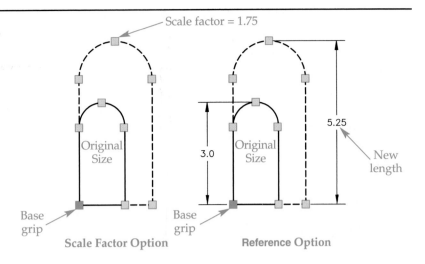

Figure 14-8.
When using the **SCALE** tool with grips, you can enter a scale factor or use the **Reference** option.

Scale factor = 1.75

5.25 — New length

3.0

Original Size

Original Size

Base grip

Base grip

Scale Factor Option

Reference Option

Scaling Objects

To scale an object with grips, select the object, pick a grip to use as the base point, and then right-click and choose the **Scale** option, or cycle through the tools until you get to the **SCALE** function. Then enter a scale factor or pick a point to increase or decrease the size of the object. The **Undo** and **eXit** options function the same when using the **SCALE** tool as when using the **STRETCH** tool.

The **Reference** option can be used if you know the current length and the desired length. The selected base point remains in the same place when the object is scaled. The reference length is the current length. If you know the value of the current length, enter the value at the prompt. Otherwise, pick two points on the reference line to identify the existing length. Enter a value or pick a point to define the new length. Figure 14-8 shows the **SCALE** options.

Exercise 14-5
Complete the exercise on the Student CD.

Mirroring Objects

To mirror an object with grips, select the object, pick a grip to use as the base point, and then right-click and choose the **Mirror** option, or cycle through the tools until you get to the **MIRROR** function. Then pick another grip or any point on the screen as the second point of the mirror line. See Figure 14-9. Unlike the standard **MIRROR** tool, the

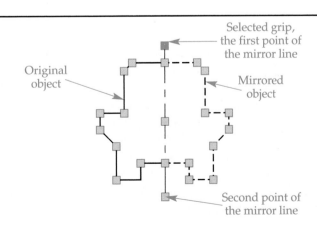

Figure 14-9.
When you use grips to access the **MIRROR** tool, the selected grip becomes the first point of the mirror line, and the original object is automatically deleted.

Selected grip, the first point of the mirror line

Original object

Mirrored object

Second point of the mirror line

grips version of the **MIRROR** tool does not give you the immediate option to delete the old objects. The old objects are deleted automatically. To keep the original object while mirroring, use the **Copy** option of the **MIRROR** tool. The **Undo** and **eXit** options function the same when using the **MIRROR** tool as when using the **STRETCH** tool.

Exercise 14-6
Complete the exercise on the Student CD.

Adjusting Object Properties

Every drawing object has specific properties. Some objects, such as lines, have few properties, while other objects, such as multiline text or tables, contain many properties. Properties include geometry characteristics, such as the location of the endpoint of a line in X,Y,Z space, the diameter of a circle, or the area of a rectangle. Layer is another property associated with all objects. The layer on which an object is drawn defines other object properties, including color, linetype, and lineweight. Most objects also include object-specific properties. For example, text objects have text properties, and tables have column, row, and cell properties. Properties are defined when an object is created and can be modified to edit the drawing.

Object properties can be edited using modification tools or a variety of other methods, depending on the property. For example, the layer property of an object can be adjusted using layer tools. The multiline text editor can be used to adjust the properties of an existing multiline text object. Another technique to view and make changes to object properties is to use the **Quick Properties** panel or the **Properties** palette.

PROFESSIONAL TIP

Use the **Quick Properties** panel or the **Properties** palette whenever you want to adjust object properties, but especially when you want to modify a particular property or set of properties for multiple objects at once.

Using the Quick Properties Panel

The **Quick Properties** panel is displayed by default whenever you pick an object. See Figure 14-10. The **Quick Properties** panel always floats and cannot be docked. By default, the panel appears above and to the right of the crosshairs. The drop-down list at the top of the **Quick Properties** panel indicates the type of object selected. Properties associated with the selected object are shown below the drop-down list in rows.

If you pick a circle, for example, rows of circle properties are listed. When multiple objects are selected, you can use the **Quick Properties** panel to modify all of the objects, or you can pick only one of the selected objects from the drop-down list to be modified. See Figure 14-11. Select All (*n*) to change the properties of all selected objects. Only properties shared by all selected objects are displayed when All (*n*) is selected. To modify only one type of object, select the appropriate object type.

The **Quick Properties** panel lists the most common properties associated with the selected objects. You should recognize most of the properties, because these are the same values you used to create the objects. By default, three properties are shown, unless the selected objects contain fewer properties. If more properties are available, hover over the **Quick Properties** bar on the left side of the panel to expand the list.

AutoCAD and Its Applications—Basics

Figure 14-10.
The **Quick Properties** panel can be used to modify some object properties. A—The initial display of the **Quick Properties** panel for the **LINE** tool. B—The expanded list of properties.

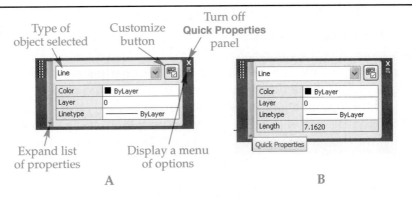

Type of object selected

Customize button

Turn off **Quick Properties** panel

Expand list of properties

Display a menu of options

A

B

Figure 14-11.
The **Quick Properties** panel with three objects selected. You can edit the objects individually or all together by selecting All (3).

Total number of objects selected

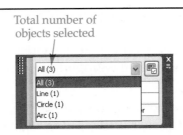

To change a property, pick the property or its current value. The way you change a value depends on the selected property. A text box opens when you select certain properties, such as the **Radius** property shown when you select an arc or circle or the **Text height** property available when you select a single-line or multiline text object. Enter a new value in the text box to change the value of the property. Most text boxes display a calculator icon on the right side that opens the **QuickCalc** tool for calculating values. **QuickCalc** is covered in Chapter 17. Other properties, such as the **Layer** property, display a drop-down arrow with a list of values from which to choose. A pick button is available for geometric properties, such as the **Center X** and **Center Y** properties shown when you select a circle. Select the button to pick a new coordinate location. An **...** (ellipsis) button, when available, opens a dialog box related to the property.

Press the [Esc] key when you are finished using the **Quick Properties** panel. If you pick the **Close** button in the upper-right corner of the panel, the **Quick Properties** tool is turned off. The **Quick Properties** tool can also be turned on and off by picking the **Quick Properties** button on the status bar or typing the [Ctrl]+[Shift]+[P] key combination.

Exercise 14-7
Complete the exercise on the Student CD.

Supplemental Material

Quick Properties Panel Options
Options for adjusting the display and function of the **Quick Properties** panel are available from a menu displayed when you pick the **Options** button on the **Quick Properties** panel, or from the **Quick Properties** tab of the **Drafting Settings** dialog box. Refer to the Student CD: Supplemental Materials > Quick Properties Panel Options for detailed information on adjusting **Quick Properties** panel options.

Using the Properties Palette

PROPERTIES

Ribbon
View
> Palettes

Properties

Type
PROPERTIES
PROPS
CH
MO

Menu Browser
Tools
> Palettes

The **Quick Properties** panel provides a quick way to view and modify the most common properties associated with a selected object or objects. The **Properties** palette provides the same function as the **Quick Properties** panel, but it allows you to view and adjust all of the properties related to the selected objects.

The **Properties** palette is shown in Figure 14-12. It can be docked, locked, and resized in the drawing area. You can access tools and continue to work in AutoCAD while the **Properties** palette is displayed. To close the palette, pick the **X** in the top-left corner, select **Close** from the options menu, or use the [Ctrl]+[1] key combination.

> **NOTE**
>
> If an object has already been selected, you can access the **Properties** palette by right-clicking and selecting **Properties** from the shortcut menu. You can also double-click many objects to select the object and open the **Properties** palette automatically.

The **Properties** palette is divided into categories. The five categories—**General**, **3D Visualization**, **Plot style**, **View**, and **Misc**—list the current settings for the drawing. Underneath each category are rows of object properties. For example, in Figure 14-12, the Color row in the **General** category displays the current color. The color property in this example is ByLayer.

The upper-right portion of the **Properties** palette contains three buttons. Pick the **Quick Select** button to access the **Quick Select** dialog box, where you can create object selection sets. This dialog box is described later in this chapter. Picking the **Select Objects** button deselects the currently selected objects and changes the crosshairs to a pick box. The third button toggles the value of the **PICKADD** system variable, which determines whether you need to hold down the [Shift] key when adding objects to a selection set.

Figure 14-12.
The **Properties** palette can be used to modify the properties of an object.

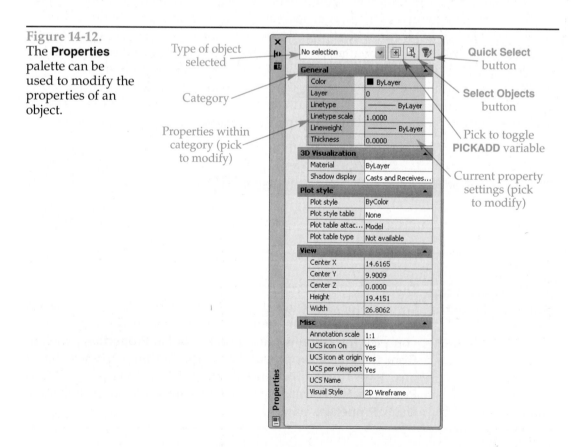

Figure 14-13.
The Properties
palette with four
objects selected. You
can edit the objects
individually or all
together by selecting
All (4).

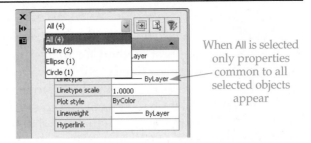

When All is selected
only properties
common to all
selected objects
appear

In order to modify an object using the **Properties** palette, the palette must be open and an object must be selected. For example, if a circle and a line are drawn and you need to modify the circle, either double-click the circle or pick the circle to make the grips appear and then open the **Properties** palette. Working with properties in the **Properties** palette is very similar working with properties in the **Quick Properties** panel. When objects are selected, the drop-down list at the top of the **Properties** palette indicates the type of object selected. The categories and property rows update to display properties associated with the selected objects.

If you pick a circle, for example, rows of circle properties are listed. When multiple objects are selected, you can use the **Properties** palette to modify all of the objects, or you can pick only one of the selected objects from the drop-down list to be modified. This drop-down list works exactly like the one in the **Quick Properties** panel. See Figure 14-13.

You will recognize many of the properties listed in the **Properties** palette, because these are the same values you used to create the object. However, the **Properties** palette lists all properties related to the object, and as a result you may not recognize some of the properties. For example, the **3D Visualization** category and any properties related to the Z axis are for use in 3D applications. These properties and any other properties that you are not familiar with should not be adjusted for basic drawing applications.

Change properties using the **Properties** dialog box the same way you change properties using the **Quick Properties** palette. Use the appropriate text box, drop-down list, or button to modify the value. When all the changes to the object have been made, press the [Esc] button on the keyboard to clear the grips and remove the object from the **Properties** palette. The object is now displayed in the drawing window with the desired changes.

When all the changes to the object have been made, press the [Esc] button on the keyboard to clear the grips and remove the object from the **Properties** palette. The object is now displayed in the drawing window with the desired changes.

General Properties

All objects have a **General** category in the **Properties** palette. Refer again to Figure 14-12. The **General** category allows you to modify properties such as color, layer, linetype, linetype scale, plot style, lineweight, and thickness. The **Quick Properties** panel also lists certain general properties.

NOTE

The layer of a selected object can also be changed by selecting a layer from the **Layer Control** drop-down list of the **Layers** panel of the ribbon. Color, linetype, plot style, and lineweight, can also be adjusted by selecting from the appropriate control drop-down list of the **Properties** panel of the ribbon.

CAUTION

Colors, linetypes, and lineweights should be set as ByLayer. This is the best method for managing these settings. Changing color, linetype, or lineweight to a value other than ByLayer overrides logical properties, making the property an *absolute value*. Therefore, if the color of an object is set to red, for example, it appears red regardless of the layer on which it is drawn. For most applications, linetype scale should be set globally so the linetype scale of all objects is constant. Adjusting the linetype scale of individual objects can create nonstandard drawings and make it difficult to adjust linetype scale globally. For most applications you should not override color, linetype, linetype scale, plot style, lineweight, or thickness.

absolute value: In property settings, a value set directly instead of being referenced by layer or a block. The current layer settings are ignored when an absolute value is set.

Geometry Properties

One of the most common categories in the **Properties** palette is **Geometry**. See **Figure 14-14.** Although most objects have a **Geometry** category, the properties within the category vary depending on the type of object. The **Quick Properties** panel also lists certain geometry properties. Typically, three properties allow you to change the absolute coordinates for the object by specifying the X, Y, and Z coordinates. When you select one of these properties, a pick button is displayed. The button allows you to pick a point in the drawing for the new location. In addition to choosing a point with the pick button, you can change the value of the coordinate in a text box or use the calculator button to calculate a new location.

An example of the properties displayed when a circle is selected is shown in **Figure 14-15.** The **Geometry** category displays the current location of the center of the circle by showing three properties: **Center X**, **Center Y**, and **Center Z**. To choose a new center location for the circle, select the appropriate property. Pick a new point or type or calculate the coordinate values. Other properties can also be modified for the circle, such as the radius, diameter, circumference, and area. By changing any of these values, you are modifying the size of the circle.

Figure 14-14.
The **Properties** palette with a Line object selected. Only three categories can be modified for the line object.

Type of object selected

General properties

Start point and endpoint coordinates

These values cannot be directly modified, but change if endpoints are modified

Line		
General		
Color	■ ByLayer	
Layer	0	
Linetype	——— ByLayer	
Linetype scale	1.0000	
Plot style	ByColor	
Lineweight	——— ByLayer	
Hyperlink		
Thickness	0.0000	
3D Visualization		
Material	ByLayer	
Geometry		
Start X	16.5842	
Start Y	7.6946	
Start Z	0.0000	
End X	20.9738	
End Y	12.5358	
End Z	0.0000	
Delta X	4.3895	
Delta Y	4.8412	
Delta Z	0.0000	
Length	6.5349	
Angle	48	

Figure 14-15.
The **Properties** palette with a Circle object selected for editing.

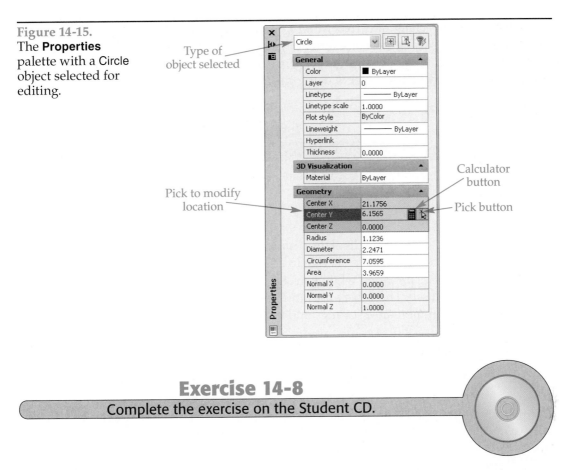

Type of object selected

Calculator button

Pick to modify location

Pick button

Exercise 14-8
Complete the exercise on the Student CD.

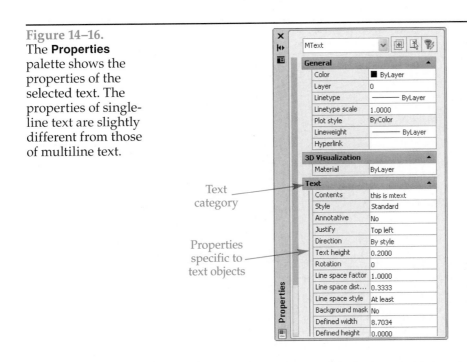

Text Properties

The **Text** category, which is displayed when single-line or multiline text is selected, contains properties such as text style and justification. **Figure 14-16** shows text properties associated with multiline text. The **Quick Properties** panel also lists certain text specific properties. These properties can be adjusted using traditional techniques, such as reentering the text editor to modify the text. However, the **Properties** palette provides a convenient way to modify a variety of text properties without reentering the

Figure 14–16.
The **Properties** palette shows the properties of the selected text. The properties of single-line text are slightly different from those of multiline text.

Text category

Properties specific to text objects

text editor. It is especially effective when you want to adjust a particular property for multiple selected text objects. For example, you can change the annotative setting of all text in the drawing using the **Annotative** property row, or reset the height of multiple single-line or multiline text objects using the **Height** property row.

Exercise 14-9
Complete the exercise on the Student CD.

Table Properties

The **Properties** dialog box displays certain table properties depending on whether you select inside a cell or pick a cell edge to edit table layout. See Figure 14-17. The **Cell** and **Content** categories provided when you select inside a cell are used to adjust the properties of the selected cell. The **Table** and **Table Breaks** categories shown when you select a cell edge include common table settings and table break properties.

NOTE

The **Quick Properties** panel also lists certain table properties.

PROFESSIONAL TIP

If the height of rows is taller than desired, or if rows are no longer equal height, enter a very small value in the **Table height** row of the **Table** category to return all rows to the smallest height possible based on the margin spacing between cell content and cell borders.

Figure 14-17.
Table properties. A—The properties displayed when you select inside a cell to edit table layout. B—The properties displayed when you pick a cell edge to edit table layout.

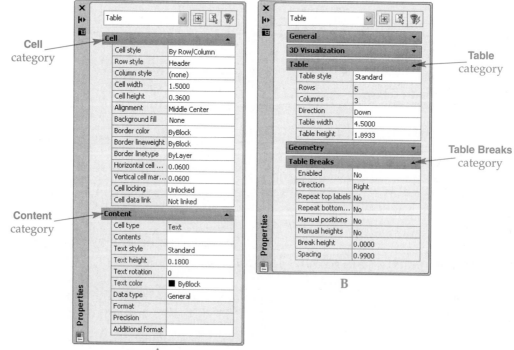

After you add table breaks, several useful options become available in the **Table Breaks** category of the **Properties** palette for adjusting the table sections. The **Enabled** option toggles between the broken and unbroken table display. Table breaking is enabled and displays **Yes** when a break is created. To return the table to its unbroken display, pick **No**. The **Direction** option defines direction of flow, or wrap, when a table is broken. Picking **Right** wraps the table to the right and is the default value; selecting **Left** wraps the table to the left; and picking **Up** wraps the table above.

The **Repeat top labels** option of the **Table Breaks** category repeats cells that use a **Label** cell type at the beginning of each table section. Typically, the title cell and header cells use a **Label** cell type. Choose **Yes** to add the title and header cells to the wrapped table sections. The **Repeat bottom labels** option repeats cells that use a **Label** cell type at the end of each table section. The **Manual positions** option allows you to move table sections independently while maintaining the table as a single object. When **No** is selected, table sections move as a group.

The **Manual height** option of the **Table Breaks** category adds a table breaking grip to each table section. This allows you to adjust the number of rows in each table section independently and add additional breaks in each section. When **No** is selected, the table breaking grip is provided at the original table section only and controls the number of breaks. The **Break height** text box is used to define the height of each table section. The number of sections is calculated based on the selected height. The **Spacing** text box is used to define the spacing between table sections. A value of 0 places the sections together.

Exercise 14-10
Complete the exercise on the Student CD.

Matching Properties

Ribbon

Home
> Properties

Match Properties

Type

MATCHPROP
PAINTER
MA

Menu Browser

Modify
> Match
Properties

MATCHPROP

The **MATCHPROP** tool allows you to copy properties quickly from one object to one or more other objects. This can be done in the same drawing or between drawings. When you first access the **MATCHPROP** tool, AutoCAD prompts you for the source object. The source object is the object with the properties you want to copy to another object or series of objects. After you select the source object, AutoCAD displays the properties it will paint to the destination object. The next prompt allows you to pick the objects you want to receive the properties of the source object. Most selection techniques, including the pick box, window, crossing, and ALL selection methods, can be used to pick the destination object(s).

To change the properties to be painted, select the **Settings** option before picking the destination object(s). The **Property Settings** dialog box appears, showing the types of properties that can be painted. See **Figure 14-18**. The **Basic Properties** area lists the general properties of the selected object. The **Special Properties** area contains check boxes that allow you to paint over a variety of additional properties related to object styles. Properties are replaced in the destination object if the corresponding **Property Settings** dialog box check boxes are active. If you do not want a specific property to be copied, deselect the appropriate check box. For example, if you want to paint only the layer property and text style of one text object to another text object, uncheck all boxes except the **Layer** and **Text** property check boxes.

Figure 14-18.
The **Property Settings** dialog box for the **MATCHPROP** tool. Select the properties to paint onto a new object.

Properties to be painted to other objects →

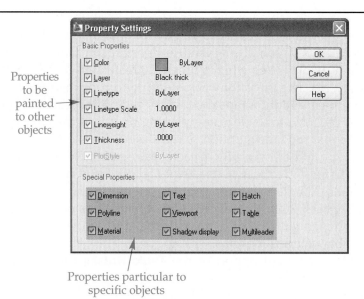

Properties particular to specific objects

Exercise 14-11

Complete the exercise on the Student CD.

Editing between Drawings

The advantages of using AutoCAD include the ability to edit in more than one drawing at a time and to edit between open drawings. For example, you can copy objects from one drawing to another drawing. You can also refer to a drawing to obtain information, such as a distance, while working in a different drawing.

Figure 14-19 shows two drawings (the drawings created during Exercises 14-8 and 14-11) opened and tiled horizontally. The Windows *copy and paste* function is used to copy an object from one drawing to another. To use this feature in AutoCAD, the object you intend to copy must be selected with grips. For example, if you want to copy the pentagon from drawing EX14-11 to drawing EX14-8, first select the pentagon. Then right-click to display the shortcut menu shown in **Figure 14-20**.

copy and paste: A Windows function that allows an object to be copied and then pasted in another location or file.

The shortcut menu has two options that allow you to copy to the Windows Clipboard. The **Copy** option copies selected objects from AutoCAD onto the Windows Clipboard to be used in another application or AutoCAD drawing. The **Copy with Base Point** option also copies the selected objects to the Clipboard, but it allows you to specify a base point to position the copied object when it is pasted. When you use this option, AutoCAD prompts you to select a base point. Select a logical base point, such as a corner or center point of the object.

After you select one of the copy options, make the second drawing active by picking in it or by using the [Tab]+[Ctrl] key combination. Right-click to display the shortcut menu shown in **Figure 14-21**. Notice that the copy options remain available, but three paste options are now available below the copy options. The paste options are only available if there is something on the Clipboard. The **Paste** option pastes any information on the Clipboard into the current drawing. If the **Copy with Base Point** option was used to place objects in the Clipboard, the objects being pasted are attached to the crosshairs at the specified base point.

Figure 14-19.
Multiple drawings can be tiled to make editing between drawings easier.

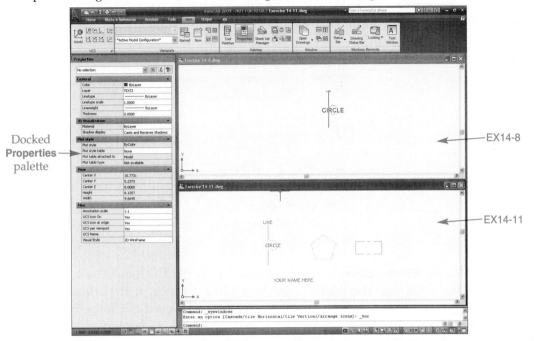

Docked **Properties** palette

EX14-8

EX14-11

Figure 14-20.
Two copy options appear on the shortcut menu.

Copy options

Repeat SYSWINDOWS		
Polyline Edit		
Annotative Object Scale	▶	
Cut	Ctrl+X	
Copy	Ctrl+C	
Copy with Base Point	Ctrl+Shift+C	
Paste	Ctrl+V	
Paste as Block	Ctrl+Shift+V	
Paste to Original Coordinates		
Erase		
Move		
Copy Selection		
Scale		
Rotate		
Draw Order	▶	
Deselect All		
Action Recorder	▶	
Quick Select...		
QuickCalc		
Find...		
Properties		
✓ Quick Properties		

Figure 14-21.
Choose one of the
three paste options
from the shortcut
menu.

Paste
options

Repeat ZOOM	
Recent Input	▶
✂ Cut	Ctrl+X
📋 Copy	Ctrl+C
📋 Copy with Base Point	Ctrl+Shift+C
📋 Paste	Ctrl+V
📋 Paste as Block	Ctrl+Shift+V
📋 Paste to Original Coordinates	
↩ Undo Pan and Zoom	
↪ Redo	Ctrl+Y
Pan	
🔍 Zoom	
SteeringWheels	
Action Recorder	▶
Quick Select...	
QuickCalc	
Find...	
Options...	

The **Paste as Block** option "joins" all objects on the Clipboard when they are pasted into the drawing. The pasted objects act like a block in that they are single objects grouped together to form one object. Blocks are covered in Chapters 26 and 27. Use the **EXPLODE** tool to break up the block so that the objects act individually again. The **Paste to Original Coordinates** option pastes the objects from the Clipboard to the same coordinates at which they were located in the original drawing.

NOTE

You can also copy and paste between documents using the Windows-standard [Ctrl]+[C] and [Ctrl]+[V] keyboard shortcuts.

PROFESSIONAL TIP

You may find it more convenient to use the **MATCHPROP** tool to match properties between drawings. To use the **MATCHPROP** tool between drawings, select the source object from one drawing and the destination object from another.

Exercise 14-12
Complete the exercise on the Student CD.

QSELECT

Ribbon
Home
> Utilities

Quick Select

Type
QSELECT

Menu Browser
Tools
> Quick Select...

Using Quick Select

When creating complex drawings, you often need to perform the same editing operation on many objects. For example, assume you have designed a complex metal part with more than 40 holes for 1/8″ bolts. A design change occurs, and you are notified that 3/16″ bolts will be used instead of 1/8″ bolts. Therefore, the hole size must also change. You could select and modify each circle individually, but it would be more efficient to create a selection set of all the circles and then modify them all at the same time. The **Quick Select** dialog box is the most common tool for creating selection sets by specifying object types and property values for selection. See Figure 14-22.

Figure 14-22.
Selection sets can be defined in the **Quick Select** dialog box.

Select specific object type or multiple

Pick to select objects with pick box

Specify operator to be used to define selected objects using property value

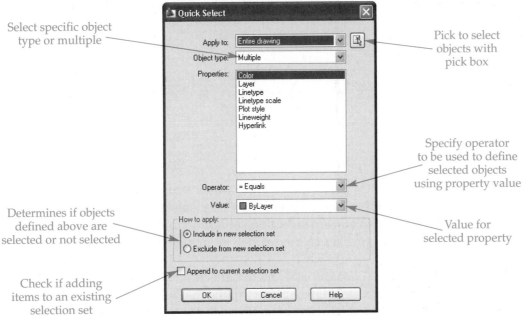

Determines if objects defined above are selected or not selected

Value for selected property

Check if adding items to an existing selection set

NOTE

You can also access the **Quick Select** dialog box by right-clicking in the drawing area and choosing the **Quick Select...** shortcut menu option or by picking the **Quick Select** button of the **Properties** palette.

With the **Quick Select** dialog box, you can quickly create a selection set based on the filtering criteria you specify. A selection set can be defined in several ways using the **Quick Select** dialog box. One method is to specify an object type (such as text, line, or circle) to be selected throughout the drawing. Another option is to specify a property (such as a color or layer) that objects must possess in order to be selected. A third option is to pick the **Select objects** button and select the objects on-screen. Once the selection criteria are defined using one of these techniques, you can use the radio buttons in the **How to apply:** area to include or exclude the defined objects.

Look at **Figure 14-23** as you follow this example that uses the **Quick Select** tool:

1. Open the **Quick Select** dialog box.
2. In the **Apply to:** drop-down list, select **Entire drawing**. (If you access the **Quick Select** dialog box after a selection set is defined, a **Current selection** option allows you to create a subset of the existing set.)
3. In the **Object type:** drop-down list, select **Multiple**. This allows you to select any object type. The drop-down list contains all the object types in the drawing.
4. In the **Properties:** list, select **Color**. The items in the **Properties:** list vary depending on what is specified in the **Object type:** drop-down list.
5. In the **Operator:** drop-down list, select **= Equals**.
6. The **Value:** drop-down list contains values corresponding to the entry in the **Properties:** drop-down list. In this case, color values are listed. Select the color of the right-hand objects in **Figure 14-23A**.
7. Under the **How to apply:** area, pick the **Include in new selection set** radio button.
8. Pick the **OK** button.

AutoCAD selects all objects with the color specified in the **Value:** drop-down list, as shown in **Figure 14-23B**.

Figure 14-23.
Creating selection sets with the **Quick Select** dialog box. A—Objects in drawing. B—Selection set containing objects with the display color specified. C—Circle object added to initial selection set.

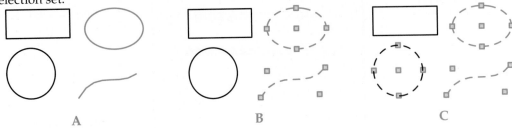

A   B   C

Once a set of objects has been selected, the **Quick Select** dialog box can be used to refine the selection set. Use the **Exclude from new selection set** option to exclude objects, or use the **Append to current selection set** option to add objects. The following procedure refines the selection set created above to include any circles in the drawing that have a black color.

1. While the initial set of objects is selected, right-click in the drawing area and select **Quick Select…** from the shortcut menu to open the **Quick Select** dialog box.
2. Check the **Append to current selection set** check box at the bottom of the dialog box. AutoCAD automatically selects the **Entire drawing** option in the **Apply to:** drop-down list.
3. Select **Circle** in the **Object type:** drop-down list, **Color** in the **Properties:** drop-down list, **= Equals** in the **Operator:** drop-down list, and **Black** (or **ByLayer**, as appropriate) in the **Value:** drop-down list.
4. In the **How to apply:** area, pick the **Include in new selection set** radio button.
5. Pick the **OK** button. The selection now appears as shown in **Figure 14-23C**.

PROFESSIONAL TIP

Use the **Quick Properties** panel or the **Properties** palette to adjust properties of items selected using the **Quick Select** dialog box.

Object Selection Filters

The **Object Selection Filter** dialog box can also be used to select multiple objects according to object characteristics. The **Object Selection Filter** dialog box provides some additional options that are not found in the **Quick Select** dialog box, such as saving selection set filters. Refer to the Student CD: Supplemental Materials > Object Selection Filters for detailed information on this process.

Creating Object Groups

Multiple objects can be grouped together to create a named selection set. This is another, though somewhat cumbersome, method for selecting multiple objects. Refer to the Student CD: Supplemental Materials > Creating Object Groups for detailed information on creating objects groups and using the **Object Grouping** dialog box.

 **Express Tools**

Chapter 14

The **Express** menu on the menu browser includes additional tools for improved functionality and productivity during the drawing process. The following Express Tools apply to creating selection sets. Refer to the Student CD: Express Tools > Chapter 14 for information about these tools.

Get Selection Set

Fast Select

 # Chapter Test

Answer the following questions. Write your answers on a separate sheet of paper or complete the electronic chapter test on the Student CD.

1. Name the editing tools that can be accessed automatically using grips.
2. How can you select a grip tool other than the default **STRETCH**?
3. What is the purpose of the **Base Point** option in the grip tools?
4. Explain the function of the **Undo** option in the grip tools.
5. What happens when you choose the **eXit** option from the grips shortcut menu?
6. Which option of the **ROTATE** grip tool option would you use to rotate an object from an existing 60° angle to a new 25° angle?
7. What scale factor would you use to scale an object to become three-quarters of its original size?
8. Describe the options for editing object properties.
9. Where does the **Quick Properties** panel appear by default when an object is selected?
10. By default, how many properties are shown in the **Quick Properties** panel?
11. Describe three items that might be displayed when you pick a property from a **Quick Properties** panel or **Properties** palette row.
12. Identify at least two ways to access the **Properties** palette.
13. Explain how you would change the radius of a circle from 1.375 to 1.875 using the **Properties** palette.
14. How can you change the linetype of an object using the **Properties** palette?
15. What does it mean when color, linetype, and lineweight are specified as ByLayer?
16. What tool is used to change the properties of objects to match the properties of a different object?
17. Briefly discuss how the Windows copy and paste function works to copy an object from one drawing to another.
18. Name the option that joins a group of objects as a block when they are pasted.
19. When you use the option described in Question 18, how do you separate the objects back into individual objects?
20. Identify four ways to open the **Quick Select** dialog box.

Drawing Problems

Use templates as appropriate for each of the following problems. Use grips and the associated editing tools or other editing techniques described in this chapter.

▼ Basic

1. Draw the objects labeled A. Then use the **STRETCH** tool to make them look like the objects labeled B. Do not include dimensions. Save the drawing as P14-1.

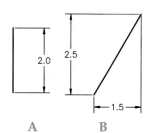 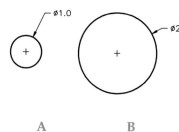 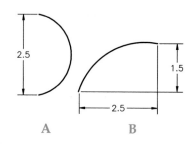

2. Draw the object labeled A. Using the **Copy** option of the **MOVE** tool, copy the object to the position labeled B. Edit Object A so it resembles Object C. Edit Object B so it looks like Object D. Do not include dimensions. Save the drawing as P14-2.

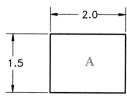

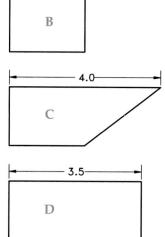

3. Draw the object labeled A. Copy the object, without rotating it, to a position below, as indicated by the dashed lines. Rotate the object 45°. Copy the rotated object labeled B to a position below, as indicated by the dashed lines. Use the **Reference** option to rotate the object labeled C to 25°, as shown. Do not include dimensions. Save the drawing as P14-3.

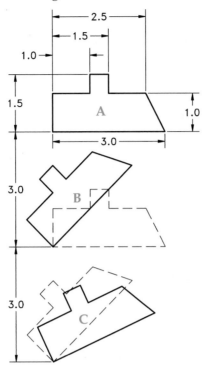

▼ Intermediate

4. Draw the individual objects (vertical line, horizontal line, circle, arc, and C shape) in A using the dimensions given. Use grips and the editing tools to create the object shown in B. Do not include dimensions. Save the drawing as P14-4.

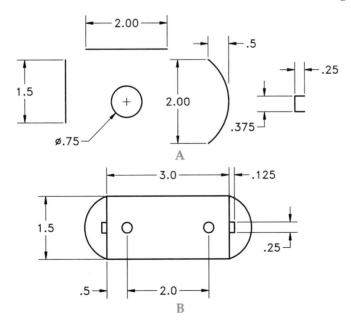

Drawing Problems - Chapter 14

5. Use the completed drawing from Problem 14-4. Erase everything except the completed object and move it to a position similar to that shown in A. Copy the object two times to positions B and C. Use the **SCALE** grip tool to scale the object in position B to 50 percent of its original size. Use the **Reference** option of the **SCALE** tool to enlarge the object in position C from the existing 3.0 length to a 4.5 length, as shown in C. Do not include dimensions. Save as P14-5.

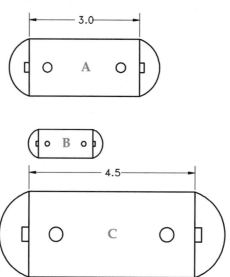

6. Draw the dimensioned partial object shown in A. Do not include dimensions. Mirror the drawing to complete the four quadrants, as shown in B. Change the color of the horizontal and vertical parting lines to Red and the linetype to CENTER. Save the drawing as P14-6.

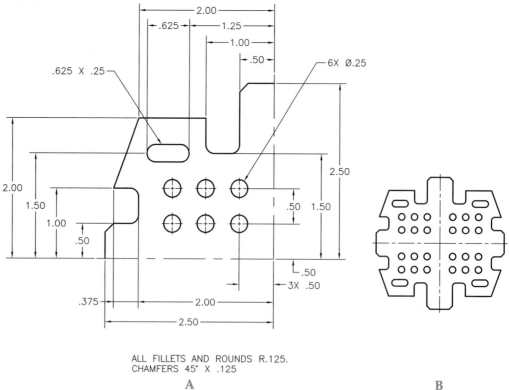

ALL FILLETS AND ROUNDS R.125.
CHAMFERS 45° X .125

A   B

7. Load the final drawing you created in Problem 14-6. Use the **Properties** palette to change the diameters of the circles from .25 to .125. Change the linetype of the slots to PHANTOM. Be sure the linetype scale allows the linetypes to be displayed. Save the drawing as P14-7.

8. Use the editing tools described in this chapter to assist you in drawing the following object. Draw the object within the boundaries of the given dimensions. All other dimensions are flexible. Do not include dimensions in the drawing. Save the drawing as P14-8.

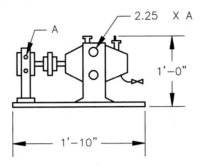

9. Draw the gasket half shown below. Do not include dimensions. Mirror the drawing to complete the other half of the gasket. Save the drawing as P14-9.

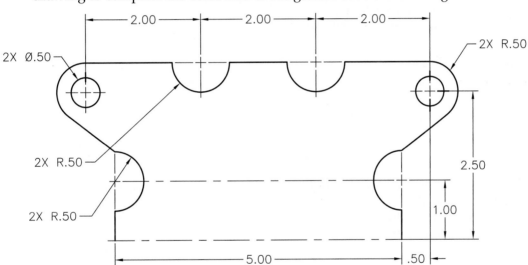

▼ Advanced

10. Draw the following object within the boundaries of the given dimensions. All other dimensions are flexible. Do not include dimensions. After drawing the object, create a page for a vendor catalog, as follows:
    - All labels should be ROMAND text, centered directly below the view. Use a text height of .125".
    - Label the drawing ONE-GALLON TANK WITH HORIZONTAL VALVE.
    - Keep the valve the same scale as the original drawing in each copy.
    - Copy the original tank to a new location and scale it so it is 2 times its original size. Rotate the valve 45°. Label this tank TWO-GALLON TANK WITH 45° VALVE.
    - Copy the original tank to another location and scale it to 2.5 times the size of the original. Rotate the valve 90°. Label this tank TWO-AND-ONE-HALF GALLON TANK WITH 90° VALVE.
    - Copy the two-gallon tank to a new position and scale it so it is 2 times this size. Rotate the valve to 22°30'. Label this tank FOUR-GALLON TANK WITH 22°30' VALVE.
    - Left-justify this note at the bottom of the page: Combinations of tank size and valve orientation are available upon request.
    - Use the **Properties** palette to change all tank labels to ROMANC, .25" high.
    - Change the note at the bottom of the sheet to ROMANS, centered on the sheet, using uppercase letters.
    - Save the drawing as P14-10.

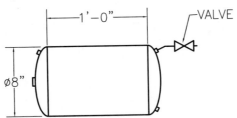

11. Create the interior finish schedule shown below using the **TABLE** tool. Make the measurements for the rows and columns approximately the same as in the given table. Use the **Properties** palette to assist you in constructing the schedule. Save the drawing as P14-11.

INTERIOR FINISH SCHEDULE

ROOM	FLOOR					WALLS				CEILING		
	VINYL	CARPET	TILE	HARDWOOD	CONCRETE	PAINT	PAPER	TEXTURE	SPRAY	SMOOTH	BROCADE	PAINT
ENTRY					•							
FOYER			•			•		•				•
KITCHEN			•					•		•		•
DINING				•		•			•	•		•
FAMILY		•				•			•	•		•
LIVING		•				•	•			•		•
MSTR. BATH			•			•			•		•	•
BATH #2			•			•		•	•		•	•
MSTR. BED		•				•	•		•		•	•
BED #2		•				•			•	•	•	•
BED #3		•				•			•	•	•	•
UTILITY	•					•			•	•	•	•

Drawing Problems – Chapter 14

CHAPTER 15

Polylines

Learning Objectives

After completing this chapter, you will be able to do the following:
- ✓ Use the **PLINE** tool to draw straight and curved polylines.
- ✓ Use the **REVCLOUD** tool to mark up drawings.
- ✓ Edit existing polylines with the **PEDIT** tool.
- ✓ Use the **EXPLODE** tool to change polylines into individual line and arc segments.
- ✓ Create a polyline boundary.

The term *polyline* is composed of the word parts *poly-* and *line*. *Poly-* means "many." Polylines provide more flexibility than lines. They can be used to create a single object composed of arcs and straight lines of varying thickness. This chapter explains how to use the **PLINE** tool to draw polylines and the **PEDIT** tool to edit polylines. You will also learn to create revision cloud polyline objects using the **Revision Cloud** tool.

polyline: A single object made up of one or more line and/or arc segments.

Drawing Polylines

Polylines are drawn using the **PLINE** tool. When using the default polyline settings, the process of drawing polyline segments is identical to the process of creating line segments using the **LINE** tool. The difference is that once drawn, all segments of a polyline are treated as a single object. The **PLINE** tool also offers additional options not found with the **LINE** tool. It can be used to draw a variety of special shapes, including thick and tapered lines and polyline arcs.

The default polyline settings create a polyline with a constant width of 0. A polyline drawn using a constant width of 0 is similar to a standard line and accepts the lineweight applied to the layer on which the polyline is drawn. If this is acceptable, select the endpoint of the line segment. If you draw additional line segments, the endpoint of the first line segment automatically becomes the starting point of the next line segment. When you are finished drawing line segments, press [Enter], [Esc] or the space bar or right-click and select the **Enter** menu option.

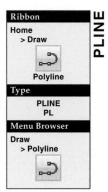

Ribbon
Home
> Draw

Polyline

Type
PLINE
PL

Menu Browser
Draw
> Polyline

PLINE

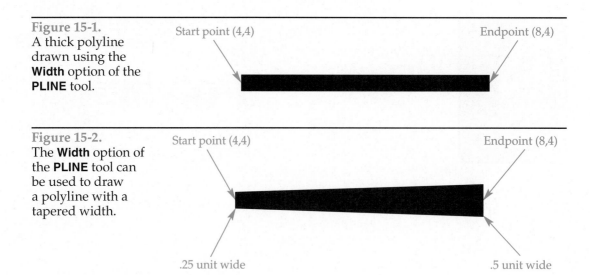

Figure 15-1.
A thick polyline drawn using the **Width** option of the **PLINE** tool.

Start point (4,4)   Endpoint (8,4)

Figure 15-2.
The **Width** option of the **PLINE** tool can be used to draw a polyline with a tapered width.

Start point (4,4)   Endpoint (8,4)

.25 unit wide   .5 unit wide

Setting the Polyline Width

To change the width of a line segment, access the **PLINE** tool, select the first point, and then use the **Width** option. When the **Width** option is selected, AutoCAD prompts you to specify the starting and ending widths of the line. The starting width value becomes the default setting for the ending width. Therefore, to draw a line segment with constant width, right-click or press [Enter] or the space bar at the second prompt. After the widths are specified, the rubberband line from the first point reflects the width settings. Figure 15-1 shows a 4″ polyline with starting and ending widths of .25″. Notice that the starting and ending points of the line are located at the center of the line segment's width. Using a starting or ending width value other than 0 overrides the lineweight applied to the layer on which the polyline is drawn.

To create a tapered line segment, enter different values for the starting and ending widths. In the example shown in Figure 15-2, the starting width is .25 units, and the ending width is .5 units. One special use of a tapered polyline is the creation of arrowheads. To draw an arrowhead, use the **Width** option of the **PLINE** tool, specify 0 as the starting width, and then use any desired ending width.

Using the Halfwidth Option

The **Halfwidth** option of the **PLINE** tool allows you to specify the width of the polyline from the center to one side, as opposed to the total width of the polyline defined using the **Halfwidth** option. After accessing the **PLINE** tool, pick the first point of the polyline, and then enter the **Halfwidth** option. Specify starting and ending values. Notice that the polyline in Figure 15-3 is twice as wide as the polyline in Figure 15-2, even though the same values are entered.

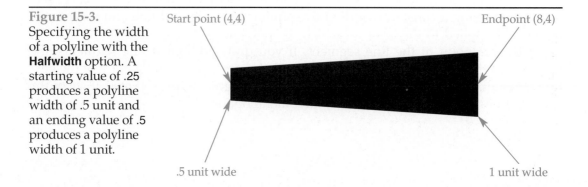

Figure 15-3.
Specifying the width of a polyline with the **Halfwidth** option. A starting value of .25 produces a polyline width of .5 unit and an ending value of .5 produces a polyline width of 1 unit.

Start point (4,4)   Endpoint (8,4)

.5 unit wide   1 unit wide

You can display wide polylines as filled objects or as an outline only. These functions are controlled by the **Apply solid fill** setting in the **Display performance** area of the **Display** tab in the **Options** dialog box. This setting can also be changed by typing FILL or FILLMODE.

Using the Length Option

The **Length** option of the **PLINE** tool allows you to draw a polyline parallel to the previous polyline or line. After drawing a polyline, reissue the **PLINE** tool and pick a start point. Enter the **Length** option and give the desired length. The second polyline is drawn parallel to the previous polyline with the length you specified.

Exercise 15-1
Complete the exercise on the Student CD.

Undoing Previously Drawn Polyline Segments

To remove the last segment of a polyline without leaving the **PLINE** tool, use the **Undo** option. This removes the previously drawn segment and allows you to continue from the previous endpoint. You can use the **Undo** option repeatedly to continue deleting polyline segments until the entire object is gone. You cannot, however, specify a new first point for the polyline using this option.

Exercise 15-2
Complete the exercise on the Student CD.

Drawing Polyline Arcs

The **Arc** option of the **PLINE** tool is similar to the **ARC** tool, except that the **Width** and **Halfwidth** options of the **PLINE** tool can be used to set an arc width. The arc width can range from 0 to the radius of the arc. A polyline arc can also be drawn with different starting and ending widths using the **Width** option. See Figure 15-4. The **Width** and **Arc** options can be entered in either order.

By default, a polyline arc continued from a previous line or polyline is tangent to the last object drawn. The center of the arc is determined automatically, but you can pick a new center. You can also specify settings with one of the **Arc** suboptions of the **PLINE** tool, including: **Angle**, **CEnter**, **Direction**, **Radius**, **Second pt** (second point), and **CLose**. The polyline arc suboptions are very similar to the **ARC** tool options.

Figure 15-4.
A polyline arc with
different starting
and ending widths.

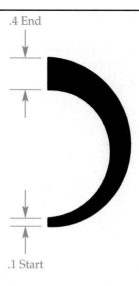

.4 End

.1 Start

Figure 15-5.
Drawing a polyline
arc with a 60°
included angle.

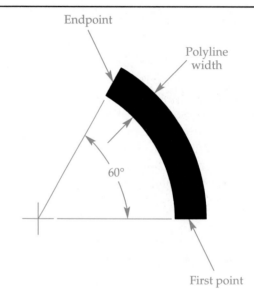

Endpoint

Polyline
width

60°

First point

Specifying the Included Angle

The **Angle** suboption of the **PLINE Arc** option specifies an included angle for a polyline arc. The angle value is based on the number of degrees in a circle. For example, a value of 180 draws a half circle, and 270 draws three quarters of a circle. The values 0 and 360 cannot be entered. A negative value draws the arc in a clockwise direction. Figure 15-5 shows a polyline arc with an included angle of 60°.

Specifying a New Center Point

When a polyline arc is drawn as a continuation of a polyline segment, the center point of the arc is calculated automatically. If the polyline arc does not continue from another object or if the center point AutoCAD calculated is not suitable, use the **CEnter** suboption to specify a new center point for the arc. When you access the **CEnter** suboption and pick the center point, the radius of the arc is set as the distance from the center point to the start point. You can then choose from three methods to complete the polyline arc: pick the endpoint of the arc, use the **Angle** option to specify the included angle, or use the **Length** option to specify the chord length of the arc.

Using the Direction Suboption

The **Direction** suboption alters the bearing of the arc. By default, a polyline arc is created tangent to the last polyline, arc, or line drawn. The **Direction** suboption is used to change this setting. You can also use **Direction** when you are drawing an unconnected polyline arc. It functions much like the **Direction** option of the **ARC** tool.

After selecting the **Direction** suboption of the **PLINE Arc** option, specify the tangent direction for the start point of the arc. You can enter a numeric angle value, or you can pick a point to define the angle relative to the start point.

Drawing a Polyline Arc by Radius

Polyline arcs can be drawn by giving the arc's radius. Enter the **Radius** suboption of the **PLINE Arc** option, specify the radius, and then specify the second endpoint for the arc.

Specifying a Three-Point Polyline Arc

A three-point polyline arc can be drawn using the **Second pt** suboption. After entering the **Second pt** suboption, AutoCAD prompts you to pick the second point and endpoint of the arc.

Using the Close Suboption

The **CLose** suboption saves drafting time by automatically adding the last segment to close a polygonal shape. Using the **CLose** suboption of the **PLINE Arc** option closes the shape with a polyline arc segment, rather than a straight line segment. See Figure 15-6.

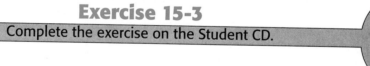

Exercise 15-3
Complete the exercise on the Student CD.

Figure 15-6.
Using the **CLose** suboption to close a polygonal shape.

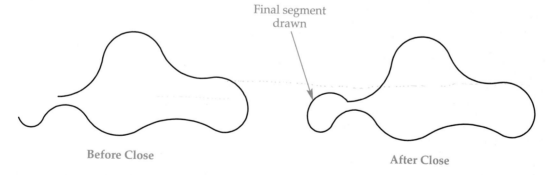

Final segment drawn

Before Close

After Close

Creating Revision Clouds

A *revision cloud* is a polyline of sequential arcs forming a cloud-shaped object. Figure 15-7 shows a cloud with a leader and note attached. Revision clouds are typically used by people who review drawings and mark notes and changes. The revision cloud points the drafter to a specific portion of the drawing that may need to be edited.

Revision clouds are drawn using the **REVCLOUD** tool. Drawing a revision cloud is somewhat different than drawing most other objects, because a single pick is all that is required. To begin drawing the revision cloud, pick a start point in the drawing. After you pick the start point, the prompt tells you to guide the crosshairs along the cloud path. Move the crosshairs around the objects to be enclosed until you come close to the start point. AutoCAD then closes the cloud automatically and exits the tool.

Defining the Arc Length

The size of the arcs in a revision cloud can be set by entering the **Arc length** option of the **REVCLOUD** tool. This value measures the length of an arc from its start point to its end point. You can change the arc length to any desired value. Access the **Arc length** option before picking the start point for the revision cloud. AutoCAD prompts for the minimum arc length and then for the maximum arc length. Enter the minimum and maximum arc lengths to return to the Specify start point: prompt. Specifying different minimum and maximum values causes the revision cloud to have an uneven, hand-drawn look.

Figure 15-7.
A revision cloud can be used to identify areas of a drawing that have been modified.

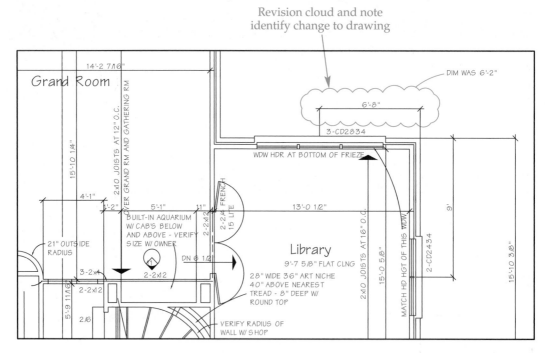

Figure 15-8.
Revision clouds can be created in two different styles: the **Normal** style and the **Calligraphy** style.

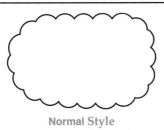

Normal Style

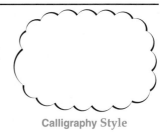

Calligraphy Style

Converting Objects into Revision Clouds

Circles, closed polylines, ellipses, polygons, and rectangles can be converted to revision clouds by selecting the **Object** option of the **REVCLOUD** tool. Access the **Object** option instead of picking the start point for the revision cloud. Then pick the object to convert to a revision cloud. Enter the **No** option at the Reverse direction: prompt, or use the **Yes** option to reverse the direction of the cloud arcs.

Changing Revision Cloud Style

The **Style** option of the **REVCLOUD** tool offers two style choices: **Normal** and **Calligraphy**. The default style is **Normal**, in which the arcs are a consistent width. In the **Calligraphy** style, the start and end widths of the individual arcs are different, creating a more stylish revision cloud. See **Figure 15-8.**

NOTE

The **WIPEOUT** tool is used to clear a portion of the drawing, without erasing objects. This tool is used for applications similar to those for **REVCLOUD**, most often for redlining, or marking up, a drawing. A wipeout can be created by picking points or converting an existing closed polyline object into a wipeout. You also have the option of turning the display of the frame, or boundary, on or off. If text is required in addition to the wipeout, however, it is more convenient to use the **Background mask** function of the **MTEXT** tool.

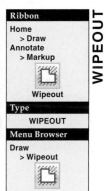

WIPEOUT

Ribbon
Home
> Draw
Annotate
> Markup

Wipeout

Type
WIPEOUT

Menu Browser
Draw
> Wipeout

Exercise 15-4
Complete the exercise on the Student CD.

Editing Polyline Objects

AutoCAD combines all polyline segments constructed during a single **PLINE** tool operation to form a single object. The entire polyline object is edited using the **PEDIT** tool. There is no default option for the **PEDIT** tool; you must select one of the options. When you pick a wide polyline to edit, you must select the edge of a polyline segment rather than the center. If you want to edit more than one polyline, activate the **Multiple** option before selecting.

If the object you select is a line or arc object, AutoCAD issues a prompt that gives you the option to turn it into a polyline. If you select the **Yes** option, the object is converted to a polyline and the **PEDIT** tool continues normally. Circles drawn with the **CIRCLE** tool cannot be changed to polylines for editing purposes. Polyline circle

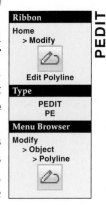

PEDIT

Ribbon
Home
> Modify

Edit Polyline

Type
PEDIT
PE

Menu Browser
Modify
> Object
> Polyline

Figure 15-9.
Open and closed
polylines.

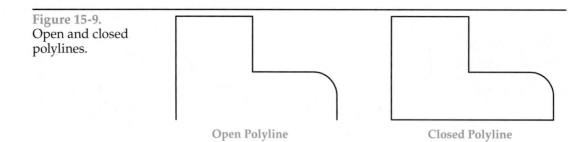

Open Polyline   Closed Polyline

segments can be created by using the **Arc** option of the **PLINE** tool and drawing two 180° arcs, or a complete polyline circle can be drawn using the **DONUT** tool.

NOTE

You can also access the **PEDIT** tool by selecting a polyline, right-clicking, and choosing the **Polyline Edit** shortcut menu option.

Opening and Closing a Polyline

The **Open** and **Close** options of the **PEDIT** tool allow you to close an open polyline or open a closed polyline. See Figure 15-9. The **Open** option is only available if the polyline was closed using the **Close** option of the **PLINE** tool. It is not displayed if the polyline was closed by drawing the final segment manually. Instead, the **Close** option is displayed. If you select an open polyline, the **Close** option is displayed instead of the **Open** option. Enter the **Close** option to close the polyline.

Joining Other Objects to Polylines

Connected polylines, lines, and arcs can be joined to create a single polyline using the **Join** option of the **PEDIT** tool. The **Join** option works only if the polyline and other existing objects meet *exactly*. They cannot cross, nor can there be any spaces or breaks between the objects. See Figure 15-10.

Select each object to be joined or group the objects with one of the selection set options. The original polyline can be included in the selection set, but it does not need to be. See Figure 15-11. If you select lines and arcs to join, AutoCAD automatically converts these objects to polylines.

PROFESSIONAL TIP

Once items have been joined into a continuous polyline, the polyline can be closed using the **Close** option of the **PEDIT** tool.

Figure 15-10.
Features that can
and cannot be
joined using the **Join**
option of the **PEDIT**
tool.

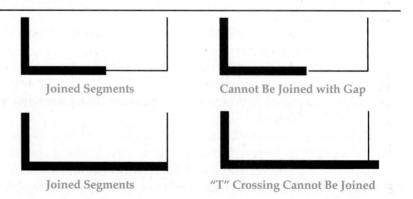

Joined Segments   Cannot Be Joined with Gap

Joined Segments   "T" Crossing Cannot Be Joined

Figure 15-11.
Joining a polyline
to other connected
lines and arcs.

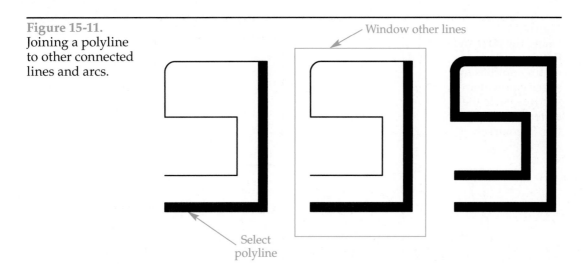

Window other lines

Select
polyline

Figure 15-12.
Changing the width
of a polyline.

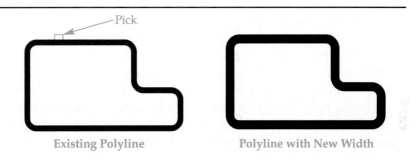

Pick

Existing Polyline

Polyline with New Width

Changing the Width of a Polyline

The **Width** option of the **PEDIT** tool allows you to assign a new width to a polyline. The width of the original polyline can be constant, or it can vary. *All* segments will be changed, however, to the constant width you specify. See Figure 15-12. The width of donuts can be changed using this procedure as well.

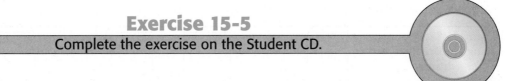

Exercise 15-5
Complete the exercise on the Student CD.

Editing a Polyline Vertex or Point of Tangency

The **Edit vertex** option of the **PEDIT** tool is used to edit a *polyline vertex* and a *point of tangency*. When you enter the **Edit vertex** option, an "X" marker appears on-screen at the first polyline vertex or point of tangency. The **Edit vertex** option contains several suboptions, described throughout this chapter.

Only the point identified by the "X" marker is affected by editing functions. In Figure 15-13, the marker is moved clockwise through the points using the **Next** option and counterclockwise using the **Previous** option. If you edit the vertices of a polyline and nothing appears to happen, use the **Regen** option to regenerate the polyline. Select the **eXit** option to return to the **PEDIT** tool prompt.

polyline vertex:
The point at which
two straight polyline
segments meet.

point of tangency:
The point at which
a polyline arc meets
another polyline arc
or a straight polyline
segment.

Making breaks in a polyline

You can break a polyline into two separate polylines with the **Break** option of the **PEDIT Edit vertex** option. Enter the **Edit vertex** option, use the **Next** or **Previous** option to

Figure 15-13.

Figure 15-13.
Using the **Next** and
Previous vertex
editing options to
specify polyline
vertices. Note the
different positions of
the "X" marker.

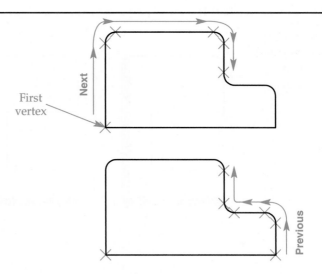

First
vertex

Next

Previous

move the "X" marker to the first vertex where the polyline is to be broken, and then enter
the **Break** option. A marker is placed at the first break point. After moving to the second
vertex of the break, enter the **Go** option. The **Go** option instructs AutoCAD to remove the
portion of the polyline between the two points. You can also break the polyline without
removing a segment by specifying **Go** without moving to a second vertex.

Figure 15-14 shows an example of breaking a polyline that was drawn clockwise.
In this example, the **Edit vertex** option is entered and the **Next** option is used to move
the marker to Point 1. The **Break** option is then issued at Point 1. The **Previous** option is
now used to specify Point 2. The **Previous** option is used again to specify Point 3, and
again to specify Point 4. Then the **Go** option is issued to break the polylines between
Points 1 and 4.

Inserting a new vertex in a polyline

A new vertex can be added to a polyline using the **Insert** editing option. The new
vertex can be inserted on an existing polyline segment, but does not need to be. First, use
the **Next** or **Previous** option to locate the vertex next to where you want the new vertex.
Select the **Insert** option and pick the new vertex location. See Figure 15-15.

Figure 15-14.
Using the **Break**
vertex editing
option to break a
polyline and remove
a portion.

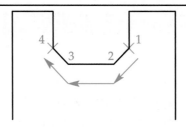

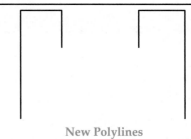

Break Points Specified

New Polylines

Figure 15-15.
Using the **Insert**
vertex editing option
to add a new vertex
to a polyline.

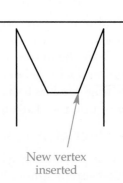

New vertex
location

New vertex
inserted

Figure 15-16.
Using the **Move**
vertex editing option
to move a polyline
vertex to a new
location.

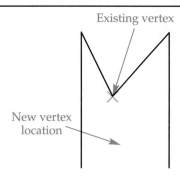
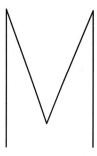

Moving a polyline vertex

The **Move** vertex editing option enables you to move a polyline vertex to a new location. The "X" marker must first be placed on the vertex you want to move. Enter the **Move** option and specify the new vertex location. See **Figure 15-16**.

Straightening polyline segments or arcs

The **Straighten** vertex editing option allows you to straighten polyline segments or arcs between two points. Position the "X" marker at one end of the polyline segment to be straightened and enter the **Straighten** option. The **Straighten** option has four suboptions: **Next**, **Previous**, **Go**, and **Exit**. Use the **Next** and **Previous** options to position the "X" marker at the end of the segment to be straightened. Then enter the **Go** option to straighten the polyline segment. If the "X" marker is not moved before the **Go** option is issued, AutoCAD straightens the segment from the marked point to the next vertex. This provides a quick way to straighten an arc. See **Figure 15-17**.

Changing polyline segment widths

The **Width** vertex editing option is used to change the starting and ending widths of an individual polyline segment. To change a segment width, move the "X" marker to the beginning vertex of the segment to be altered. Enter the **Width** option and specify the new width.

The default starting width value is the current width of the segment to be changed. The default ending width value is the same as the revised starting width. If nothing appears to happen to the segment when you specify the ending width and press [Enter], use the **Regen** option to have AutoCAD regenerate the polyline. See **Figure 15-18**.

Figure 15-17.
The **Straighten**
vertex editing option
is used to straighten
polyline segments
and arcs.

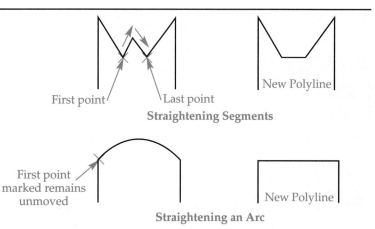

Figure 15-18.
Changing the
width of a polyline
segment with the
Width vertex editing
option. Use the
Regen option to
display the change.

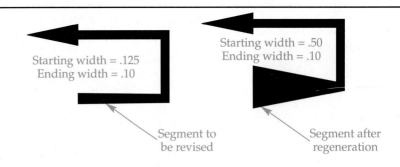

Starting width = .125
Ending width = .10

Starting width = .50
Ending width = .10

Segment to
be revised

Segment after
regeneration

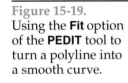

Exercise 15-6

Complete the exercise on the Student CD.

Fitting a Curve to a Polyline

In some situations, you may need to convert a polyline into a series of smooth curves.
One example of this is a graph. A graph may show a series of plotted points as a smooth
curve rather than straight segments. This process is called *curve fitting* and is accomplished using the **Fit** option and the **Tangent** vertex editing option of the **PEDIT** tool.
The **Fit** option creates a *fit curve* by constructing pairs of arcs that pass through control
points. You can specify the control points, or you can use the vertices of the polyline.

Prior to curve fitting, each vertex can be given a tangent direction. AutoCAD then
fits the curve based on the tangent directions you set. You do not have to enter tangent
directions, however. Specifying tangent directions is a way to edit vertices when the
Fit option of the **PEDIT** tool does not produce the best results.

The **Tangent** vertex editing option is used to edit tangent directions. After entering
the **PEDIT** tool and the **Edit vertex** option, move the "X" marker to the first vertex to be
changed. Enter the **Tangent** option and specify a tangent direction in degrees or pick
a point in the expected direction. An arrow placed at the vertex then indicates the
direction you chose.

Continue by moving the marker to each vertex you want to change, entering the
Tangent option for each vertex and selecting a tangent direction. When the tangent
directions have been specified for all vertices to be changed, enter the **Fit** option of the
PEDIT tool to create the curve.

You can also enter the **PEDIT** tool, select a polyline, and enter the **Fit** option without
adjusting tangencies. The polyline shown in **Figure 15-19** was made into a smooth

curve fitting:
Converting a
polyline into a series
of smooth curves.

fit curve: A curve
that passes through
all of its control
points.

Figure 15-19.
Using the **Fit** option
of the **PEDIT** tool to
turn a polyline into
a smooth curve.

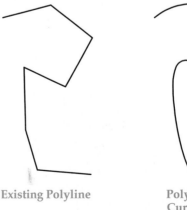

Existing Polyline

Polyline after
Curve Fitting

curve using the **Fit** option. If the resulting curve does not look correct, enter the **Edit vertex** option. Make changes using the various vertex editing options, as necessary.

Using the Spline Option

When you edit a polyline with the **Fit** option of the **PEDIT** tool, the resulting curve passes through each polyline vertex. The **Spline** option of the **PEDIT** tool also smoothes the corners of a straight-segment polyline. This option, however, produces different results. It creates a *spline curve* that passes through the first and last control points or vertices only. The curve *pulls* toward the other vertices, but does not necessarily pass through them. See **Figure 15-20.**

The **Spline** option creates a curve that approximates a true B-spline. B-splines are described in detail in Chapter 16. You can choose between two types of calculations to create the curve—*cubic* and *quadratic*. Like a cubic curve, a quadratic curve passes through the first and last control points. The remainder of the curve is tangent to the polyline segments between the intermediate control points, as shown in **Figure 15-21.**

The **SPLINETYPE** system variable determines whether AutoCAD draws cubic or quadratic curves. The default setting is 6. At this setting, the **Spline** option of the **PEDIT** tool draws a cubic curve. If the **SPLINETYPE** system variable is set to 5, a quadratic curve is generated. The only valid values for **SPLINETYPE** are 5 and 6.

The number of line segments used to construct spline curves can be set by entering a value in the **Segments in a polyline curve** text box in the **Display resolution** area of the **Display** tab of the **Options** dialog box. The default value is 8, which creates a fairly smooth spline curve with moderate regeneration time. If you decrease the value,

spline curve: A curve that passes through the first and last control points and is influenced by the other control points.

cubic curve: A very smooth curve created by the **PEDIT Spline** option when **SPLINETYPE** is set at 6.

quadratic curve: A curve created by the **PEDIT Spline** option when **SPLINETYPE** is set at 5.

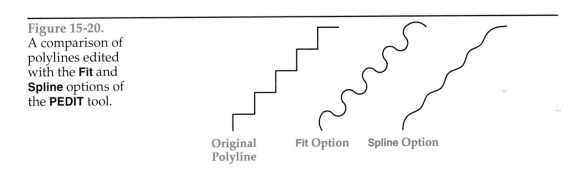

Figure 15-20.
A comparison of polylines edited with the **Fit** and **Spline** options of the **PEDIT** tool.

Original Polyline   Fit Option   Spline Option

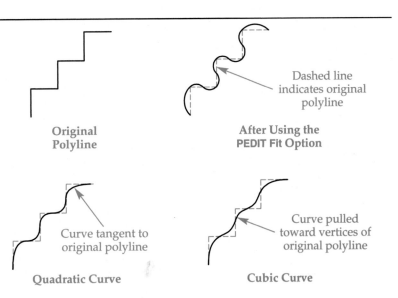

Figure 15-21.
The **SPLINETYPE** system variable controls whether a quadratic or cubic curve is drawn with the **Spline** option.

Original Polyline

After Using the PEDIT Fit Option
Dashed line indicates original polyline

Quadratic Curve
Curve tangent to original polyline

Cubic Curve
Curve pulled toward vertices of original polyline

Figure 15-22.
A comparison of curves drawn with different display resolution settings.

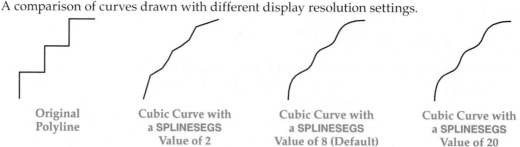

| Original Polyline | Cubic Curve with a SPLINESEGS Value of 2 | Cubic Curve with a SPLINESEGS Value of 8 (Default) | Cubic Curve with a SPLINESEGS Value of 20 |

the resulting spline curve is less smooth. The resulting spline curve is smoother if you increase the value, but the regeneration time and drawing file size increase. See Figure 15-22.

NOTE

Both the **Fit** option and the **Spline** option of the **PEDIT** tool create approximations of a B-spline curve. To create a true B-spline curve, use AutoCAD's **SPLINE** tool instead. The **SPLINE** tool is described in Chapter 16.

Exercise 15-7
Complete the exercise on the Student CD.

Straightening All Polyline Segments

The **Decurve** option of the **PEDIT** tool returns a polyline that has been edited with the **Fit** or **Spline** options to its original form. The information entered for tangent directions is kept, however, for future reference. You can also use the **Decurve** option to straighten the curved segments of a polyline. See Figure 15-23.

PROFESSIONAL TIP

If you make a mistake while editing a polyline, remember that the **PEDIT** tool includes an **Undo** option. Using the **Undo** option more than once allows you to step backward through each operation.

Figure 15-23.
The **Decurve** option of the **PEDIT** tool is used to straighten the curved segments of a polyline.

| Original Polyline | Polyline after Using the **Decurve** Option |

Exercise 15-8
Complete the exercise on the Student CD.

Changing the Appearance of Polyline Linetypes

The **Ltype gen** (linetype generation) option of the **PEDIT** tool determines how linetypes other than Continuous appear in relation to the vertices of a polyline. For example, when a Center linetype is used and the **Ltype gen** option is disabled, the polyline has a long dash at each vertex. When the **Ltype gen** option is activated, the polyline is generated with a constant pattern in relation to the polyline as a whole. See Figure 15-24.

Exploding Polylines

The **EXPLODE** tool allows you to change a polyline into a series of individual segments. Once you access the **EXPLODE** tool, pick the objects you want to explode. You can then edit each segment individually. The resulting segments are not, however, polylines; they become lines and arcs. The resulting line or arc is redrawn along the centerline of the original polyline. The **EXPLODE** tool also removes all width characteristics and tangency information. If you explode a wide polyline, AutoCAD reminds you of this fact. See Figure 15-25.

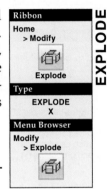

Figure 15-24.
A comparison of polylines and splined polylines with the **Ltype gen** option of the **PEDIT** tool on and off.

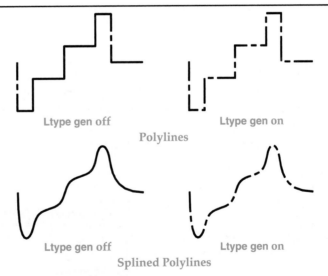

Ltype gen off   Ltype gen on

Polylines

Ltype gen off   Ltype gen on

Splined Polylines

Figure 15-25.
Exploding a wide polyline causes it to lose width information.

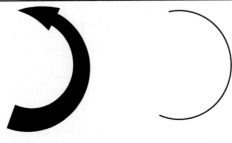

Original Polyline   Exploded Polyline

Exercise 15-9
Complete the exercise on the Student CD.

Creating a Polyline Boundary

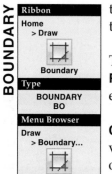

region: A closed 2D area that can have physical properties such as centroids and products of inertia.

boundary set: The part of the drawing AutoCAD evaluates to define a boundary.

island: A closed area inside a boundary.

When you draw an object with the **LINE** tool, each line segment is a single object. You can create a polyline boundary from line segments that form a closed area using the **BOUNDARY** tool. The **Boundary Creation** dialog box is displayed when you access the **BOUNDARY** tool. See Figure 15-26.

The **Object type:** drop-down list contains two options—**Polyline** and **Region**. The **Polyline** option is the default and creates a polyline around the area. If you select **Region**, AutoCAD creates a *region* that can be used for area calculations, shading, extruding a solid model, or other purposes.

In the **Boundary set** drop-down list, the **Current viewport** setting is active. The **Current viewport** option defines the *boundary set* from everything visible in the current viewport, even if it is not in the current display. The **New** button, located to the right of the drop-down list, allows you to define a different boundary set. When you pick this button, the **Boundary Creation** dialog box closes and the Select objects: prompt appears. You can then select the objects you want to use to create a boundary set. After you are done, right-click or press [Enter] or the space bar. The **Boundary Creation** dialog box returns with **Existing set** active in the **Boundary set** drop-down list. This means the boundary set is defined from the objects you selected.

The **Island detection** setting specifies whether *islands* within the boundary are used as boundary objects. See Figure 15-27. When **Island detection** is checked, islands within a boundary are detected and become separate boundaries.

The only other active feature in the **Boundary Creation** dialog box is the **Pick Points** button, which is located in the upper-left corner. When you pick this button, the **Boundary Creation** dialog box closes and the Pick internal point: prompt appears. If the point you pick is inside a closed polygon, the boundary is highlighted, as shown in Figure 15-28. The **Boundary Definition Error** alert box appears if the point you pick is not within a closed polygon. Pick **OK** and try again.

Figure 15-26.
The **Boundary Creation** dialog box.

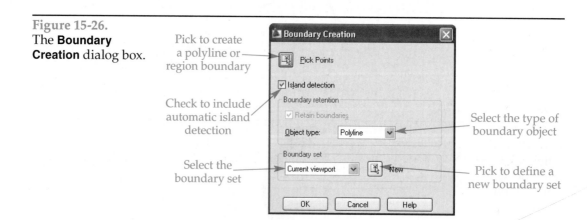

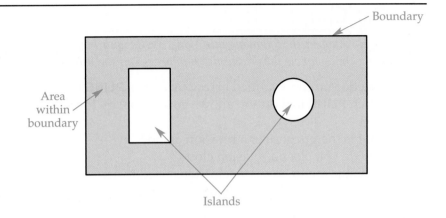

Figure 15-27.
When you define a boundary set, you can include or exclude islands.

Boundary

Area within boundary

Islands

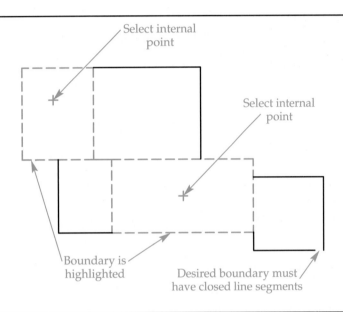

Figure 15-28.
When you select a point inside a closed polygon, the boundary is highlighted.

Select internal point

Select internal point

Boundary is highlighted

Desired boundary must have closed line segments

Unlike an object created with the **Join** option of the **PEDIT** tool, a polyline boundary created with the **BOUNDARY** tool does not replace the original objects from which it was created. The polyline traces over the defining objects with a polyline. The separate objects still exist underneath the newly created boundary. To avoid duplicate geometry, move the boundary to another location on the screen, erase the original defining objects, and then move the boundary back to its original position.

PROFESSIONAL TIP

Area calculations can be simplified by using the **BOUNDARY** tool or joining objects with the **Join** option of the **PEDIT** tool before issuing the **AREA** tool. The **AREA** tool is covered in Chapter 17. If you want to retain the original separate objects, explode the polyline after the area calculation if you used the **Join** option of the **PEDIT** tool. Erase the polyline boundary after the calculation if you used the **BOUNDARY** tool.

Chapter Test

Answer the following questions. Write your answers on a separate sheet of paper or complete the electronic chapter test on the Student CD.

1. How do you draw a filled arrow using the **PLINE** tool?
2. Which **PLINE** tool option allows you to specify the width from the center to one side?
3. What is the purpose of a revision cloud?
4. How do you close a revision cloud?
5. Name the menu browser selections used to access the polyline editing options.
6. Which two **PEDIT** tool options allow you to open a closed polyline and close an open polyline?
7. Name the tool and option required to turn three connected lines into a single polyline.
8. When you enter the **Edit vertex** option of the **PEDIT** tool, where does AutoCAD place the "X" marker?
9. How do you move the "X" marker to edit a different polyline vertex?
10. Name the **Edit vertex** option of the **PEDIT** tool that relates to each definition below.
    A. Moves the "X" marker to the next position.
    B. Moves a polyline vertex to a new location.
    C. Breaks a polyline at a point or between two points.
    D. Generates the revised version of a polyline.
    E. Specifies a tangent direction.
    F. Adds a new polyline vertex.
    G. Returns to the **PEDIT** tool prompt.
11. Which **PEDIT** tool option and suboption allow you to change the starting and ending widths of a polyline?
12. Why might it appear that nothing happens when you change the starting and ending widths of a polyline?
13. Name the **PEDIT** tool option and suboption used for curve fitting.
14. Can you use the **Fit** option of the **PEDIT** tool without using the **Tangent** vertex editing suboption first? Explain.
15. Explain the difference between a fit curve and a spline curve.
16. Compare a quadratic curve, cubic curve, and fit curve.
17. Which **SPLINETYPE** system variable setting allows you to draw a quadratic curve?
18. Explain how you can adjust the way polyline linetypes are generated using the **PEDIT** tool.
19. Which tool removes all width characteristics and tangency information from a polyline?
20. Name the tool used to create a polyline boundary.

Drawing Problems

▼ Basic

1. Use the **PLINE** tool to draw the following object with a .032 line width. Do not draw dimensions. Save the drawing as P15-1.

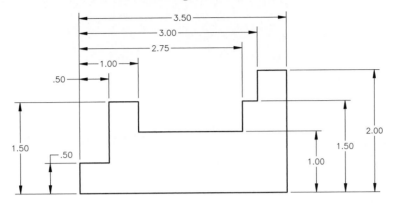

2. Use the **PLINE** tool to draw the following object with a .032 line width. Do not draw dimensions. Save the drawing as P15-2.

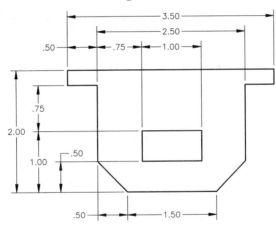

3. Use the **PLINE** tool to draw the following object with a .032 line width. Do not draw dimensions.
   A. Deactivate solid fills and use the **REGEN** tool, and reactivate solid fills and reissue the **REGEN** tool.
   B. Observe the difference with solid fills enabled.
   C. Save the drawing as P15-3.

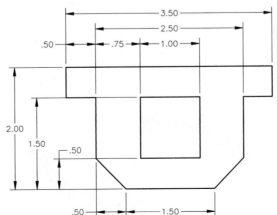

4. Use the **PLINE** tool to draw the filled rectangle shown below. Do not draw dimensions. Save the drawing as P15-4.

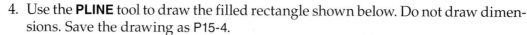
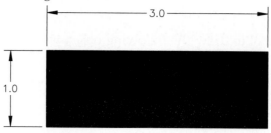

5. Draw the objects shown below. Do not draw dimensions. Save the drawing as P15-5.

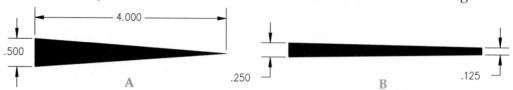

6. Draw the object shown below. Do not draw dimensions. Set decimal units, .25 grid spacing, .0625 snap spacing, and limits of 11,8.5. Save the drawing as P15-6.

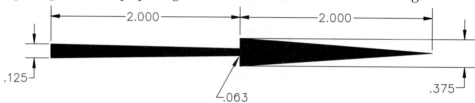

7. Open P10-9 and add the arrowheads. Draw one arrowhead using the **PLINE** tool, and then use the necessary editing tools to place the rest. Refer to the original problem. Save the drawing as P15-7.

▼ Intermediate

8. Draw the single polyline shown below. Use the **Arc**, **Width**, and **Close** options of the **PLINE** tool to complete the shape. Set the polyline width to 0, except at the points indicated. Save the drawing as P15-8.

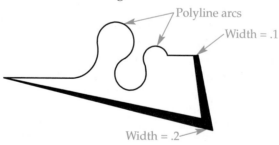

Polyline arcs
Width = .1
Width = .2

9. Draw the two curved arrows shown below using the **Arc** and **Width** options of the **PLINE** tool. The arrowheads should have a starting width of 1.4 and an ending width of 0. The body of each arrow should have a beginning width of .8 and an ending width of .4. Save the drawing as P15-9.

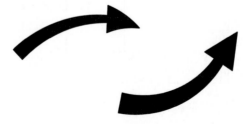

10. Open drawing P15-8 and make a copy of the original object to edit. Use the **PEDIT** tool to change the object drawn into a rectangle. Use the **Decurve** and **Width** options and the **Straighten, Insert,** and **Move** vertex editing options of the **PEDIT** tool. Save the completed drawing as P15-10.

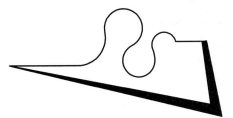

11. Open drawing P15-9 and make the following changes. Save the drawing as P15-11.
    A. Combine the two polylines using the **Join** option of the **PEDIT** tool.
    B. Change the beginning width of the left arrow to 1.0 and the ending width to .2.
    C. Draw a polyline .062 wide, similar to Line A, as shown.

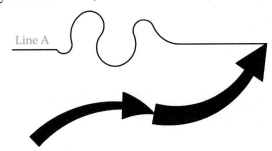

Line A

12. Draw a polyline .032 wide, using the following absolute coordinates.

Point	Coordinates	Point	Coordinates	Point	Coordinates
1	1,1	5	3,3	9	5,5
2	2,1	6	4,3	10	6,5
3	2,2	7	4,4	11	6,6
4	3,2	8	5,4	12	7,6

Copy the polyline three times so there are four polylines. Use the **Fit** option of the **PEDIT** tool to smooth the first copy. Use the **Spline** option of the **PEDIT** tool to turn the second copy into a quadratic curve. Make the third copy into a cubic curve. Use the **Decurve** option of the **PEDIT** tool to return one of the three copies to its original form. Save the drawing as P15-12.

13. Use the **PLINE** tool to draw a patio plan similar to the one shown in Example A below. Draw the house walls 6″ wide. Copy the drawing three times and use the **PEDIT** tool to create the remaining designs shown. Use the **Fit** option for Example B, a quadratic spline for Example C, and a cubic spline for Example D. Change the **SPLINETYPE** system variable as required. Save the drawing as P15-13.

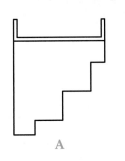

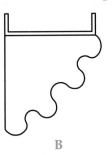

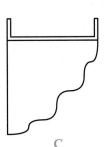

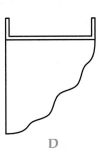

A   B   C   D

14. Open drawing P15-13 and create four new patio designs. This time, use grips to edit the polylines and create designs similar to Examples A, B, C, and D below. Save the drawing as P15-14.

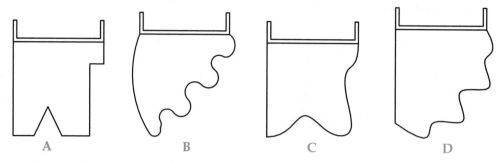

▼ Advanced

15. Draw the flow chart shown below. Use polylines to draw the connecting lines, arrows, and diamonds. Use AutoCAD's grid and snap to locate points. Save the drawing as P15-15.

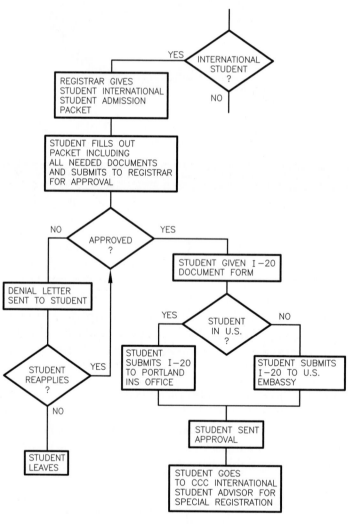

16. Draw the flow chart shown below. Use polylines to draw the connecting lines, arrows, and diamonds. Use AutoCAD's grid and snap to locate points. Save the drawing as P15-16.

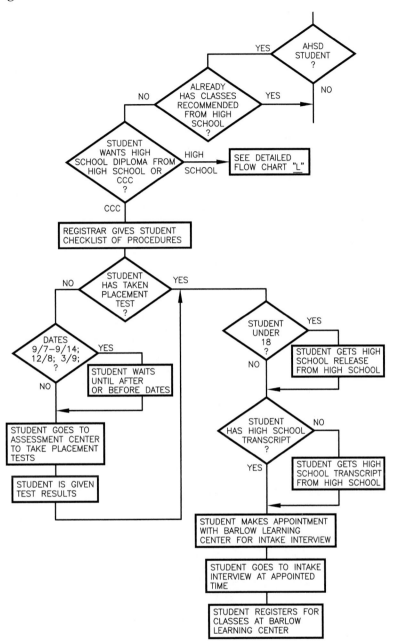

17. Draw the following roof plan. Do not dimension. Save the drawing as P15-17.

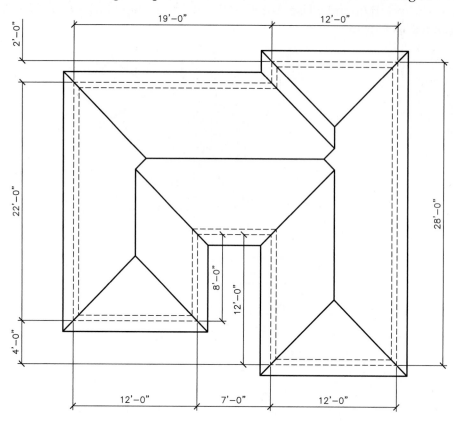

Learning Objectives

After completing this chapter, you will be able to do the following:
- ✓ Draw true spline curves using the **SPLINE** tool.
- ✓ Edit splines with the **SPLINEDIT** tool.
- ✓ Use the **MLINE** tool to draw multilines.
- ✓ Create multiline styles with the **MLSTYLE** tool.
- ✓ Edit multiline intersections, corners, and vertices.

This chapter explores drawing and editing AutoCAD splines and multilines. The **SPLINE** tool is used to create true splines. Splines can be edited using the **SPLINEDIT** tool. Multilines are drawn using the **MLINE** tool, and its options and are modified using the **MLEDIT** tool.

Drawing True Splines

The **SPLINE** tool is used to create a special type of curve called a *nonuniform rational B-spline (NURBS) curve,* or spline. A spline created by fitting a spline curve to a polyline is a linear approximation of a true spline and is not as accurate as a spline drawn using the **SPLINE** tool. An additional advantage of spline objects over smoothed polylines is that splines use less disk space.

To create a spline, access the **SPLINE** tool and specify control points using any standard coordinate entry method. For example, the spline shown in Figure 16-1 uses absolute coordinate values of 2,2 for the first point, 4,4 for the second point, and 6,2 for the last point. After you specify all spline control points, press [Enter] or the space bar or right-click and select the **Enter** menu option to end the point entry process. To complete the spline, enter values at the Specify start tangent: and Specify end tangent: prompts. Specifying the start and end tangents changes the direction in which the spline curve begins and ends. Press [Enter] or the space bar or right-click and select the **Enter** option at the tangent prompts to accept the default direction, as calculated by AutoCAD, for the specified curve.

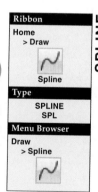

SPLINE

Ribbon
Home
 > Draw

Spline

Type
SPLINE
SPL
Menu Browser
Draw
 > Spline

**nonuniform
rational B-spline
(NURBS) curve:** A
true (mathematically
correct) spline.

Figure 16-1.
A spline drawn
with the **SPLINE**
tool. AutoCAD's
default start and end
tangents were used
for this spline.

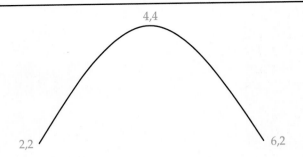

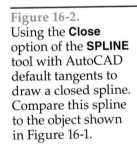

If you specify only two points for a spline curve and accept Auto-
CAD's default start and end tangents, an object that looks like a line
is created, but the object is a spline.

Drawing Closed Splines

The **Close** option of the **SPLINE** tool is used to draw closed splines by connecting
the last point to the first point. See Figure 16-2. After closing a spline, you are prompted
to specify the tangent direction. Press [Enter] or the space bar or right-click and select
the **Enter** option to accept the default calculated by AutoCAD.

Specifying the Spline Tangents

The previous **SPLINE** tool examples use the default AutoCAD tangent directions.
You can set tangent directions by entering values at the prompts that appear after
you pick spline points. The tangency is based on the tangent direction of the selected
point. The results of specifying vertical and horizontal tangent directions are shown
in Figure 16-3.

Figure 16-2.
Using the **Close**
option of the **SPLINE**
tool with AutoCAD
default tangents to
draw a closed spline.
Compare this spline
to the object shown
in Figure 16-1.

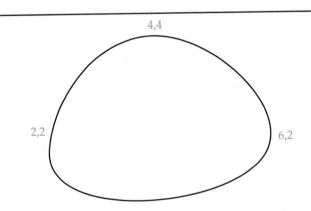

Figure 16-3.
These splines were
drawn through the
same points, but they
have different start
and end tangent
directions. The
arrows indicate the
tangent directions.

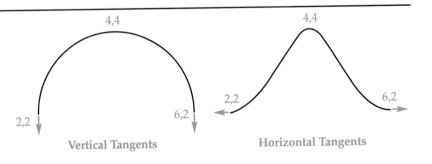

Vertical Tangents   Horizontal Tangents

Converting a Spline-Fitted Polyline to a Spline

A spline-fitted polyline object can be converted to a spline object using the **Object** option of the **SPLINE** tool. Once you access the **SPLINE** tool, activate the **Object** option instead of defining control points. Then pick a spline-fitted polyline object, created using the **PEDIT** tool, to convert the polyline into a spline.

Exercise 16-1

Complete the exercise on the Student CD.

Ribbon
Home > Modify
Edit Spline
Type
SPLINEDIT SPE
Menu Browser
Modify > Object > Spline
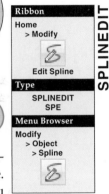

SPLINEDIT

Editing Splines

The **SPLINEDIT** tool is used to edit spline objects. Several editing options are available. You can add, move, or delete control points to alter the shape of an existing curve. You can also open or close a spline and change the start and end tangents. Once you access the **SPLINEDIT** tool and pick a spline, the control points are identified by grips, as shown in **Figure 16-4.** You must then select one of the six **SPLINEDIT** options.

Editing Fit Data

The **Fit data** option of the **SPLINEDIT** tool is used to edit spline *fit points*. The **Fit data** option has several suboptions. Use the **eXit** suboption of the **Fit data** option to return to the **SPLINEDIT** tool option prompt. **Figure 16-5** provides examples of using fit data options.

fit points: Spline control points.

The **Add** suboption of the **Fit data** option adds new fit points to a spline definition. A new fit point can be located by picking a point or entering coordinates. Fit points appear as unselected grips. When a fit point is selected, it becomes highlighted along with the next fit point on the spline. You can then add a fit point between the two

Figure 16-4.
The control points for a spline are displayed as grips.

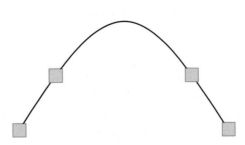

Figure 16-5.
Examples of using the **Fit data** options of the **SPLINEDIT** tool to edit a spline. Compare the original spline to each of the edited objects.

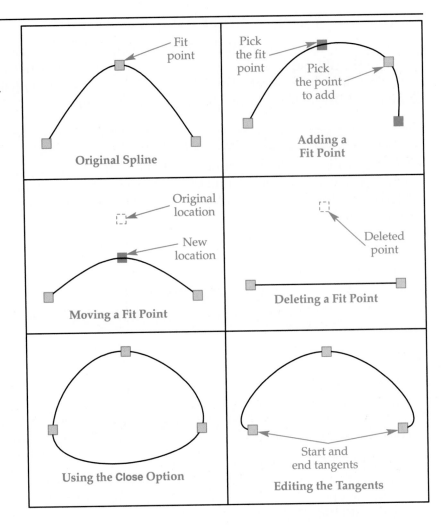

highlighted points. If you select the endpoint of the spline, only the endpoint becomes highlighted. If you select the start point, choose the **After** or **Before** option to insert the new fit point before or after the existing point. When a fit point is added, the spline curve updates according to the new point.

The **Add** suboption of the **Fit data** option functions in a running mode. This means you can continue to add points as needed. Press [Enter] or the space bar or right-click and select the **Enter** option at a Specify new point <exit>: prompt to select other existing fit points and add points anywhere on the spline.

If the selected spline is open, the **Close** suboption of the **Fit data** option is available. If the spline is closed, the **Open** suboption is offered. These options allow you to open a closed spline or close an open spline.

The **Delete** suboption of the **Fit data** option deletes fit points as needed. However, at least two fit points must remain to define the spline. Like the **Add** suboption, the **Delete** suboption operates in a running mode, allowing as many deletions as needed. The spline curve updates to reflect changes made by deleting the point.

The **Move** suboption of the **Fit data** option allows fit points to be moved as necessary. When you enter the **Move** suboption, the start point of the spline is highlighted. You can specify a different location by picking a new point. You can also specify other fit points to move. Pick the **Specify new location** option to move the currently highlighted point to a specified location. Select the **Next** option to highlight the next fit point. This option is activated by pressing [Enter]. Select the **Previous** option to highlight the previous fit point. Pick the **Select point** option to select a different fit point to move. Pick the **eXit** option to return to the **Fit data** option prompt.

The **Purge** suboption of the **Fit data** option lets you remove fit point data from a spline. After you use this option, the resulting spline is not as easy to edit. In very large drawings in which many complex splines have been created, purging fit point data reduces the file size by simplifying spline definitions. After a spline is purged, the **Fit data** option is no longer displayed by the **SPLINEDIT** tool for the purged spline.

The **Tangents** suboption of the **Fit data** option allows you to edit the start and end tangents for an open spline and the start tangent for a closed spline. The tangency is based on the direction of the selected point. You can also use the **System default** option to set the tangency values to the AutoCAD defaults.

Fit tolerance values can be adjusted using the **toLerance** suboption of the **Fit data** option. The results are immediate, so the fit tolerance can be adjusted as necessary to produce different results.

Opening or Closing a Spline

The **Open** and **Close** options of the **SPLINEDIT** tool are alternately displayed, depending on the current status of the spline object being edited. If the spline is open, the **Close** option is displayed. The **Open** option is displayed if the spline is closed. Use the available option to open or close an existing spline.

Moving a Vertex

The **Move vertex** option of the **SPLINEDIT** tool allows you to move the fit points of a spline. When you access this option, you can specify a new location for a selected fit point. The options displayed are identical to those used with the **Move** suboption of the **Fit data** option. You can pick a new location for the highlighted fit point, or you can enter a suboption. The following **Move vertex** suboptions are available:

- **Specify new location.** Moves the currently highlighted point to a specified location.
- **Next.** Highlights the next fit point.
- **Previous.** Highlights the previous fit point.
- **Select point.** Picks a different fit point to move; provides an alternative to cycling through points with the **Next** or **Previous** suboptions.
- **eXit.** Returns to the **SPLINEDIT** prompt.

Exercise 16-2
Complete the exercise on the Student CD.

Smoothing or Reshaping a Spline Section

The **Refine** option of the **SPLINEDIT** tool allows fine-tuning of the spline curve. Fit points can be added to help smooth or reshape a section of the spline. The **Add control point** suboption of the **Refine** option specifies new fit points on a spline as needed.

The **Elevate order** suboption of the **Refine** option causes more control points to appear on the curve for greater control and spline *order* refinement. For example, a cubic spline has an order of 4. In **Figure 16-6,** the order of the spline is elevated from 4 to 6. The order setting can be from 4 to 26, but it cannot be adjusted downward. For example, if the order is set to 24, the only remaining settings are 25 and 26.

order: In a spline, the degree of the spline polynomial + 1.

The **Weight** suboption of the **Refine** option changes the weight of a control point. When all control points have the same weight, they exert the same amount of pull on the spline. When a weight value is reduced for a control point, the spline is not pulled as close to the point as before. Likewise, when a weight value is increased, the control point exerts more pull on the spline. Refer again to **Figure 16-6.** The default setting

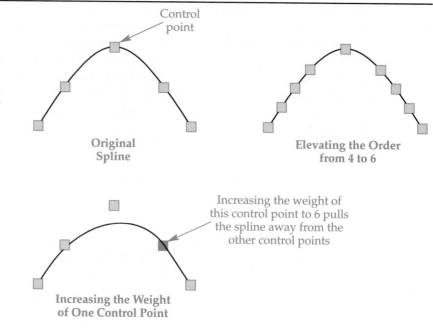

Figure 16-6.
The effects of elevating the order of a spline and increasing the weight of an individual control point.

Control point

Original Spline

Elevating the Order from 4 to 6

Increasing the weight of this control point to 6 pulls the spline away from the other control points

Increasing the Weight of One Control Point

of 1.0000 can be adjusted, but the weight setting must be positive. The control point selection suboptions of the **Weight** option are the same as those used with the **Move vertex** option of the **SPLINEDIT** tool. You can specify a new weight for the highlighted control point using the **Enter new weight** option.

Reversing the Order of Spline Control Points

The **rEverse** option of the **SPLINEDIT** tool allows you to reverse the listed order of the spline control points. This makes the previous start point the new endpoint and the previous endpoint the new start point. Using this option affects the various control point selection options.

Undoing Splinedit Changes

The **Undo** option of the **SPLINEDIT** tool undoes the previous change made to the spline. You can use this option to undo changes back to the beginning of the current **SPLINEDIT** tool sequence.

Exercise 16-3
Complete the exercise on the Student CD.

multiline: A single object consisting of up to 16 parallel line elements.

elements: The individual lines that make up a multiline.

Drawing Multilines

Multilines are combinations of parallel lines consisting of up to 16 individual lines called *elements*. The **MLINE** tool is used to draw multilines. The prompts and options for the **MLINE** tool are similar to those for the **LINE** tool. You can use the **Close** option at the last prompt to close a polygon. Select the **Undo** option during the tool sequence to undo the previously drawn multiline segment.

Figure 16-7.
Multilines drawn using each of the three justification options. The definition points (represented by plus symbols) are picked in a counterclockwise rotation.

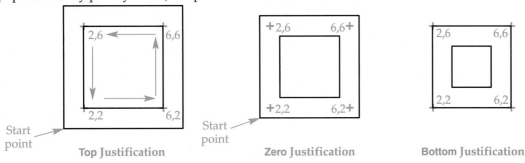

| Top Justification | Zero Justification | Bottom Justification |

> **NOTE**
>
> A multiline configuration, or style, is set using the **MLSTYLE** tool. The default multiline style has two elements and is called STANDARD. The STANDARD multiline style consists of two open-ended parallel lines. Multiline styles are described later in this chapter.

Multiline Justification

Multiline justification determines how multiline elements are offset from their *definition points*. Justification is based on counterclockwise movement and can be specified only once during a **MLINE** tool sequence. The **Justification** options are **Top** (default), **Zero**, and **Bottom**.

To change the justification, choose the **Justification** option at the first prompt displayed after you enter the **MLINE** tool. Then select the desired justification option. The results of the three different **Justification** options using identical point entries are shown in Figure 16-7.

definition points:
The points you pick or coordinates you enter to specify multilines.

> **PROFESSIONAL TIP**
>
> As shown in Figure 16-7, the multiline **Justification** options control the direction of the offsets for elements of the current style. The multiline segments in these examples are drawn in a counterclockwise direction. Unexpected results can sometimes occur when you use the **MLINE** tool, depending on the justification and drawing direction.

Exercise 16-4
Complete the exercise on the Student CD.

Adjusting Multiline Scale

The **Scale** option of the **MLINE** tool defines the offset distance between multiline elements. Scale is a multiplier applied to the offset distance specified in the multiline style. The default scale setting of 1 sets the distance between multiline elements equal to 1 times the offset distance. For example, the default STANDARD multiline style

Figure 16-8.
Multiline scale
settings.

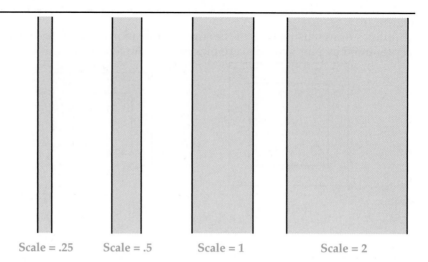

| Scale = .25 | Scale = .5 | Scale = 1 | Scale = 2 |

creates two parallel lines 1 unit apart. When the multiline scale is set to 1, the distance between the lines is 1 ($1 \times 1 = 1$). If the multiline scale is specified as 2, however, the distance between the two lines is 2 ($1 \times 2 = 2$). Multilines drawn with different scale settings are shown in Figure 16-8.

Exercise 16-5
Complete the exercise on the Student CD.

Creating Multiline Styles

Type
MLSTYLE
Menu Browser
Format
> Multiline Style...

MLSTYLE

Access the **MLSTYLE** tool to display the **Multiline Style** dialog box dialog. See Figure 16-9. The **Multiline Style** dialog box is used to define, edit, and save multiline styles. You can save styles to an external file so they can be used in other drawings. The **Preview of:** area in the lower part of the **Multiline Style** dialog box displays a representation of the selected multiline style.

Figure 16-9.
The **Multiline Style** dialog box is used to define, edit, and save multiline styles.

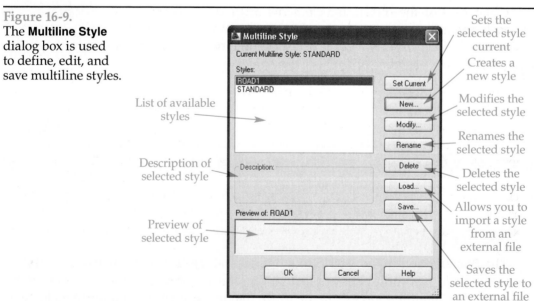

Sets the selected style current

Creates a new style

List of available styles

Modifies the selected style

Renames the selected style

Description of selected style

Deletes the selected style

Allows you to import a style from an external file

Preview of selected style

Saves the selected style to an external file

Figure 16-10.
To create a new multiline style, specify a name and existing multiline style settings in the **Create New Multiline Style** dialog box.

Type in a name for the new style

Select an existing style to use its properties for the new style

Figure 16-11.
The options in the **New Multiline Style** dialog box control the settings for a new multiline.

Description of the style

Caps area controls multiline capping

Determines the fill setting for the multiline style

Option for displaying joints

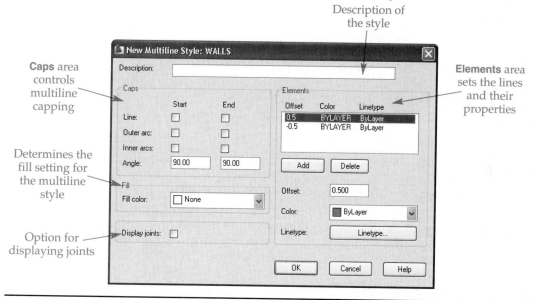

Elements area sets the lines and their properties

To create a new multiline style, pick the **New...** button to display the **Create New Multiline Style** dialog box. See **Figure 16-10.** In the **New Style Name:** text box, enter a name for the new multiline style. The properties from an existing style can be used for the new style by selecting the existing style from the **Start With:** drop-down list. After you enter the new style name, pick the **Continue** button to open the **New Multiline Style** dialog box, used to define the appearance of the multiline. See **Figure 16-11.** The optional **Description:** field can be used to enter a brief description of the multiline style.

Using caps, fill, and joints

The settings in the **Caps** area of the **New Multiline Style** dialog box control the placement of *caps* on multilines. Using the check boxes, you can set caps at the start point, endpoint, or both. Several examples of cap options are shown in **Figure 16-12.**

Caps can be drawn as straight lines or arcs. Arcs can be set to connect the ends of the outermost elements only, pairs of inner elements, or both the outer and inner elements. The multiline style must contain at least two multiline elements for outer arcs to be drawn. Arcs are drawn tangent to the elements they connect. You can also change the angle of the caps relative to the direction of the multiline elements by entering values in the **Angle:** text boxes. There is a text box for the start points and another for the endpoints, so you can set the styles independently.

The **Fill color:** setting in the **Fill** area allows you to create a solid multiline. When the **Fill color:** setting is **None**, the multiline is not filled. To specify the fill color, select a color from the **Fill color:** drop-down list. Multilines drawn with and without a fill are shown in **Figure 16-13.**

caps: Short lines connecting the elements of a multiline at the start point and endpoint.

Figure 16-12.
Various cap options for multilines.

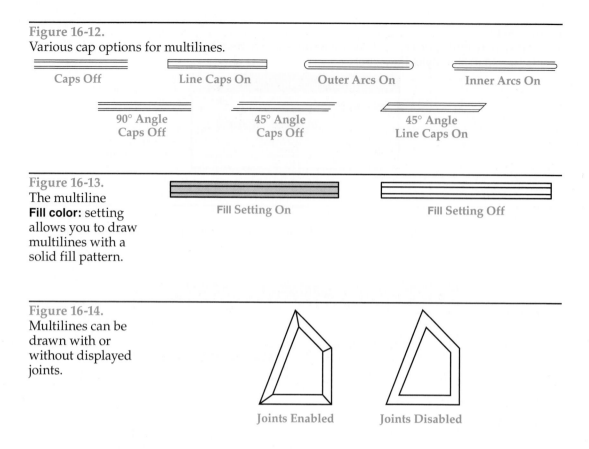

Caps Off   Line Caps On   Outer Arcs On   Inner Arcs On

90° Angle
Caps Off   45° Angle
Caps Off   45° Angle
Line Caps On

Figure 16-13.
The multiline
Fill color: setting
allows you to draw
multilines with a
solid fill pattern.

Fill Setting On   Fill Setting Off

Figure 16-14.
Multilines can be
drawn with or
without displayed
joints.

Joints Enabled   Joints Disabled

joints (miters):
Lines connecting
the vertices of
adjacent multiline
elements.

When **Display joints:** is checked, *joints* are displayed on the multiline. Joints are also referred to as *miters*. Multilines drawn with and without joints are shown in Figure 16-14.

Setting element properties

The **Elements** area of the **New Multiline Style** dialog box allows you to add or delete elements (lines) from the multiline style and specify the properties of each element. The options in this area change properties such as linetype, color, and offset. After you set element properties, pick **OK** to apply them to the new multiline style. The new style is then added to the **Multiline Style** dialog box.

Changing the Multiline Style

To use a saved multiline style as the current multiline style, access the **STyle** option of the **MLINE** tool and enter the style name. Before you can access a new multiline style, however, you must create and save it using the **Multiline Style** dialog box.

If you forget the name of the desired multiline style, you can enter ? at the Enter mline style name or [?]: prompt. The text window opens, listing the currently loaded multiline styles. See Figure 16-15. Type the name of the style you want to use.

If you try to specify a multiline style that is not loaded, the **Load multiline style from file** dialog box is displayed. You can look for the desired multiline style in the acad.mln file library, or you can pick the **Tools** button and then **Find...** to open the **Find:** dialog box.

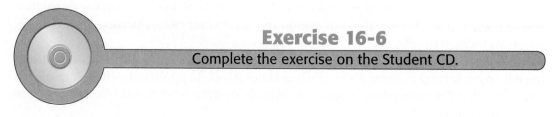

Exercise 16-6
Complete the exercise on the Student CD.

Figure 16-15.
A list of loaded
multiline styles can
be displayed in the
text window.

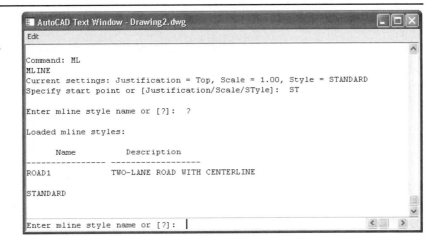

```
AutoCAD Text Window - Drawing2.dwg
Edit

Command: ML
MLINE
Current settings: Justification = Top, Scale = 1.00, Style = STANDARD
Specify start point or [Justification/Scale/STyle]:  ST

Enter mline style name or [?]:  ?

Loaded mline styles:

      Name            Description
---------------- ------------------
ROAD1            TWO-LANE ROAD WITH CENTERLINE

STANDARD

Enter mline style name or [?]:
```

Editing Multilines

The **MLEDIT** tool allows limited editing operations for multiline objects using the **Multilines Edit Tools** dialog box. See Figure 16-16. This dialog box contains four columns. Each column contains three buttons of related tool options. The image on each button gives you an example of what to expect when using the editing option. When you pick a button, the dialog box closes and AutoCAD prompts you to continue with the tool.

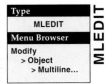

Type	
MLEDIT	
Menu Browser	
Modify	
> Object	
> Multiline...	

MLEDIT

Editing Intersections

The first (left) column in the **Multilines Edit Tools** dialog box displays three different types of multiline intersections. Pick a button to create the type of intersection shown. The effects of the cross options are shown in Figure 16-17.

When you pick the **Closed Cross** button, the first multiline you select is called the *background*, and the second multiline is called the *foreground*. A closed cross intersection is created by trimming the background, while the foreground remains unchanged. The trimming is apparent, not actual. The line visibility of the background multiline is changed, but it is still a single multiline.

Select the **Open Cross** button to trim all the elements of the first multiline and only the outer elements of the second multiline. The tool sequence is the same as that

background: The first multiline you select to create a closed cross intersection.

foreground: The second multiline you select to create a closed cross intersection.

Figure 16-16.
The **Multilines Edit Tools** dialog box has twelve different options for editing multilines.

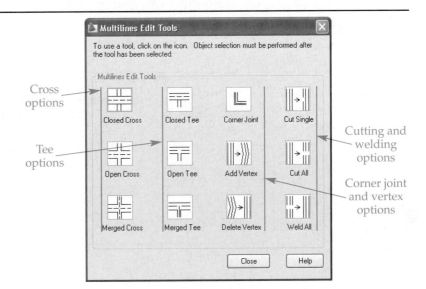

Figure 16-17.
Creating closed
cross, open cross,
and merged cross
intersections with
the **MLEDIT** tool.

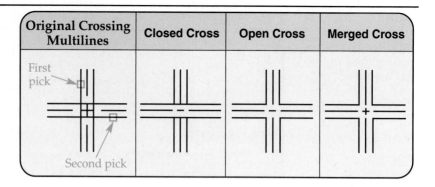

used for the **Closed Cross** option. The **Merged Cross** button allows you to trim the outer elements of both multilines. The inner elements are not changed.

Exercise 16-7
Complete the exercise on the Student CD.

Editing Tees

The buttons in the second column of the **Multilines Edit Tools** dialog box are used to edit multiline tees. The results of using the tee options are illustrated in Figure 16-18. Pick the **Closed Tee** button to trim or extend the first selected multiline to its intersection with the second multiline. Select the **Open Tee** button to trim the elements where a trimmed or extended multiline intersects another multiline. The first pick specifies the multiline to trim or extend, and the second pick specifies the intersecting multiline. The intersecting multiline is trimmed and left open where the two multilines join.

Pick the **Merged Tee** button to trim the intersecting multiline after the first multiline is trimmed or extended. The inner elements, however, remain joined. This creates an open appearance with the outer elements, while merging the inner elements.

Exercise 16-8
Complete the exercise on the Student CD.

Figure 16-18.
Using the tee options
of the **MLEDIT** tool to
edit multiline tees.

Editing Corner Joints and Multiline Vertices

The buttons in the third column of the **Multilines Edit Tools** dialog box provide options for creating corner joints and editing multiline vertices. Pick the **Corner Joint** button to create a corner joint between two multilines. The first multiline is trimmed or extended to its intersection with the second multiline, as shown in Figure 16-19.

Select the **Add Vertex** button to add a vertex to an existing multiline at the location you pick. See Figure 16-20. The tool sequence differs slightly from the sequences used with the other **MLEDIT** options. After you select the **Add Vertex** option, AutoCAD prompts you to pick a location for the vertex.

Pick the **Delete Vertex** button to remove a vertex from an existing multiline. The vertex closest to the location you pick is deleted. Refer again to Figure 16-20. The tool sequence is the same as for the **Add Vertex** option.

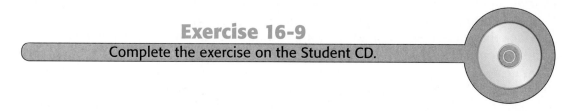

Exercise 16-9
Complete the exercise on the Student CD.

Figure 16-19.
A corner joint can be created between two multilines using the **Corner Joint** option of the **MLEDIT** tool.

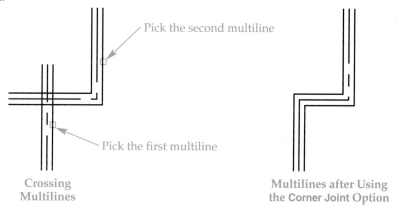

Pick the second multiline

Pick the first multiline

Crossing
Multilines

Multilines after Using
the Corner Joint Option

Figure 16-20.
The **Add Vertex** and **Delete Vertex** options of the **MLEDIT** tool are used to edit multiline vertices.

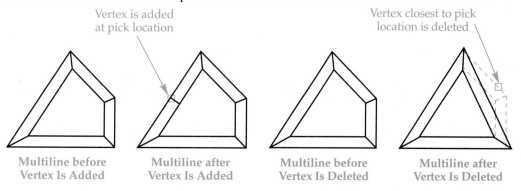

Vertex is added
at pick location

Vertex closest to pick
location is deleted

Multiline before
Vertex Is Added

Multiline after
Vertex Is Added

Multiline before
Vertex Is Deleted

Multiline after
Vertex Is Deleted

Figure 16-21

Figure 16-21
The **MLEDIT** cutting
options allow you to
cut single multiline
elements or entire
multilines between
two specified points.

Original Multiline	Cut Single	Cut All
	Pick points	

Cutting and Welding Multilines

The fourth column of buttons in the **Multilines Edit Tools** dialog box is used for *cutting* a portion out of a single multiline element or the entire multiline. The spaces between multiline elements can also be connected, or *welded*.

cutting: The process of deleting a portion of a multiline element or an entire multiline.

welding: The process of connecting the spaces between multiline elements.

Pick the **Cut Single** button to cut a single multiline element between two specified points. See **Figure 16-21.** Cutting affects only the visibility of elements and does not separate a multiline object. The multiline is still a single object. After you select the **Cut Single** option, AutoCAD prompts you to pick the cutting points.

Select the **Cut All** button to cut all elements of a multiline between specified points. Refer again to **Figure 16-21.** The multiline is still a single object, even though it appears to be separated. Pick the **Weld All** button and select a point on each side of the cut multiline to repair all cuts in the multiline. The multiline is restored to its precut condition.

PROFESSIONAL TIP

Multiline objects can be converted to individual line segments with the **EXPLODE** tool. This tool is explained in Chapters 15 and 26.

Exercise 16-10
Complete the exercise on the Student CD.

Chapter Test

Answer the following questions. Write your answers on a separate sheet of paper or complete the electronic chapter test on the Student CD.

1. Name the tool that can be used to create a true spline.
2. How do you accept the AutoCAD defaults for the start and end tangents of a spline?
3. Name the **SPLINE** tool option that allows you to turn a spline-fitted polyline into a true spline.
4. Name the tool that allows you to edit splines.
5. What is the purpose of the **Add** suboption of the **Fit data** option of the **SPLINEDIT** tool?
6. What is the minimum number of fit points for a spline?
7. Name the **SPLINEDIT** option that allows you to move the fit points in a spline.

8. Which suboption of the **SPLINEDIT Fit data** option allows you to reduce file size, but also makes the resulting spline harder to edit?

9. What is the purpose of the **Refine** option of the **SPLINEDIT** tool?

10. Identify the **Refine** suboption of the **SPLINEDIT** tool that lets you increase, but not decrease, the number of control points appearing on a spline curve.

11. Name the **Refine** suboption of the **SPLINEDIT** tool that controls the pull exerted by a control point on a spline.

12. How many operations can you undo inside the **SPLINEDIT** tool with the **Undo** option?

13. Name the **MLINE** tool option that establishes how the resulting lines are offset based on the definition points provided.

14. Briefly describe the effect of the **Scale** option of the **MLINE** tool.

15. How do you access the **Multiline Style** dialog box?

16. What are multiline caps?

17. What is another term for multiline joints?

18. Name the tool and entries needed to draw a multiline with zero justification and the saved style ROAD1.
    A. Command: _____
    B. Current settings: Justification = *current*, Scale = *current*, Style = *current*
        Specify start point or [Justification/Scale/STyle]: _____
    C. Enter mline style name or [?]: _____
    D. Current settings: Justification = *current*, Scale = *current*, Style = ROAD1
        Specify start point or [Justification/Scale/STyle]: _____
    E. Enter justification type [Top/Zero/Bottom] <*current*>: _____
    F. Current settings: Justification = Zero, Scale = *current*, Style = ROAD1
        Specify start point or [Justification/Scale/STyle]: _____
    G. Specify next point: _____
    H. Specify next point or [Undo]: _____

19. What is displayed when you enter the **MLEDIT** tool?

20. How do you access one of the **MLEDIT** options?

21. List the three options used for editing multiline intersections with the **MLEDIT** tool.

22. Name the **MLEDIT** option in which the intersecting multiline is trimmed and left open after the first multiline is trimmed or extended to its intersection with the intersecting multiline.

23. What term describes the operation used to repair a portion of a multiline that has been cut?

24. Which **MLEDIT** option lets you remove a portion from an individual multiline element?

25. Which **MLEDIT** option removes all the elements of a multiline between two specified points?

Start a new drawing for each of the following problems. Specify your own units, limits, and other settings to suit each problem.

▼ Basic

1. Draw the objects shown using the **MLINE** tool. Use the justification options indicated with each illustration. Set the limits to 11,8.5; grid spacing to .50; snap spacing to .25; and the offset for the multiline elements to .125. Do not add text or dimensions. Save the drawing as P16-1.

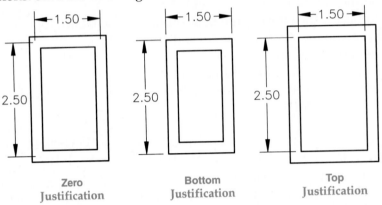

2. Draw the partial floor plan using the multiline tools. Carefully observe how the dimensions correlate with the multiline elements to determine your justification settings. Also, use the appropriate cap and multiline editing options. Use architectural units. Set the limits to 88",68"; grid spacing to 24"; and snap spacing to 12". Make all walls 6" thick. Do not add dimensions. Save the drawing as P16-2.

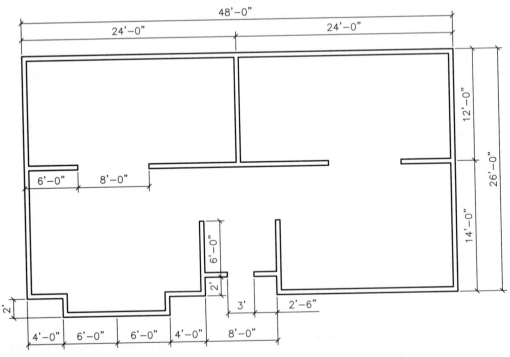

3. Draw the proposed subdivision map using the multiline tools. The roads are 30′ wide. Use a centerline linetype for the center of each road. Adjust the linetype scale as needed. Do not include dimensions. Save the drawing as P16-3.

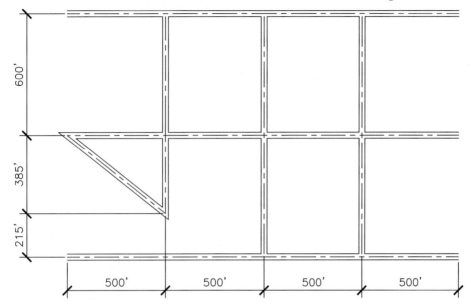

4. Draw the proposed electrical circuit using the multiline tools. Establish a line offset proportional to the given layout. Use a phantom linetype for the center of each run. Do not draw the grid, which is provided as a drawing aid. Save the drawing as P16-4.

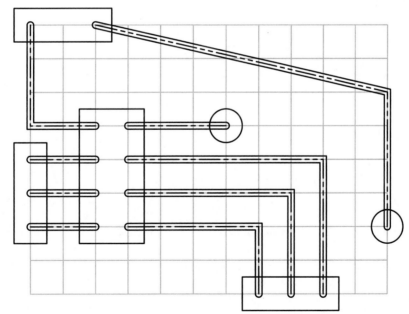

5. Use the **SPLINE** tool to draw the curve for the cam displacement diagram below. Use the following guidelines and the given drawing to complete this problem:
   A. The total rise equals 2.000.
   B. The total displacement can be any length.
   C. Divide the total displacement into 30° increments.
   D. Draw a half circle divided into 6 equal parts on one end.
   E. Draw a horizontal line from each division of the half circle to the other end of the diagram.
   F. Draw the displacement curve with the **SPLINE** tool by picking points where the horizontal and vertical lines cross.
   G. Label the displacement increments along the horizontal scale as shown. Save the drawing as P16-5.

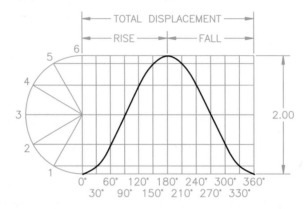

6. Draw a spline similar to the original spline shown below. Copy the spline seven times to create a layout similar to the one given. Perform the **SPLINEDIT** operations identified under each of the seven copies. Save the drawing as P16-6.

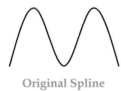
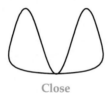

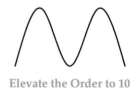

Original Spline   Close   Move a Control Point   Elevate the Order to 10

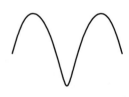

Add Two Control Points   Delete a Control Point   Edit the Tangents   Increase the Weight of a Control Point to 4

Drawing Problems – Chapter 16

▼ Advanced

7. Draw the partial floor plan using multilines for the walls. Do not dimension the floor plan. Save the drawing as P16-7.

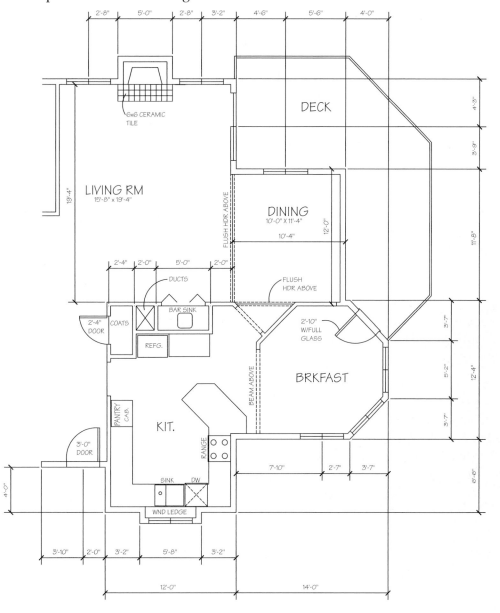

8. Use **SPLINE** and other tools, such as **ELLIPSE**, **MIRROR**, and **OFFSET**, to design an architectural door knocker similar to the one shown. Use an appropriate text tool and font to place your initials in the center. Save the drawing as P16-8.

Drawing Problems – Chapter 16

9. Draw the map shown below, using **SPLINE** to create the curved shapes. Try to make the shapes as similar to those on the map as possible. Save the drawing as P16-9.

CATFISHING ANCHOR LOCATIONS

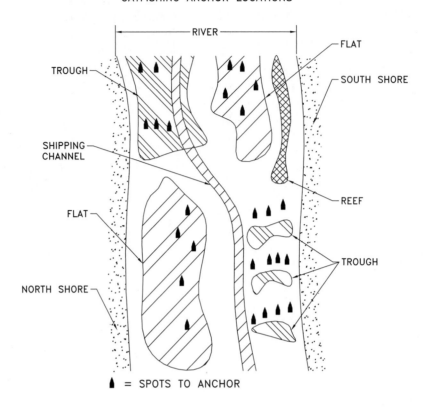

▲ = SPOTS TO ANCHOR

10. Draw the three views of a sports car, using **SPLINE** to create the curved shapes. Save the drawing as P16-10.

CHAPTER 17

Obtaining Drawing Information

Learning Objectives

After completing this chapter, you will be able to do the following:

✓ Identify a point location.
✓ Find the distance between two points.
✓ Use the **AREA** tool to calculate the area of an object by adding and subtracting objects.
✓ Display object properties in a drawing using fields.
✓ List data related to a single point, an object, a group of objects, or an entire drawing.
✓ Determine the amount of time spent in a drawing session.
✓ Determine the status of drawing parameters.
✓ Perform basic and advanced mathematical calculations using the **QuickCalc** calculator.

When working on a drawing, you often need to access information about the drawing, such as point locations, object distances, and areas. This chapter explains how to retrieve this data. You will also learn how to access other drawing information, such as object properties and how much time you have spent on a drawing. This chapter also describes how to use the **QuickCalc** calculator to calculate values while you are working.

NOTE

The **Region/Mass Properties** tool provides data related to the properties of a 2D region or 3D solid. This tool is described in *AutoCAD and Its Applications—Advanced*.

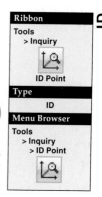

ID

Ribbon
Tools
 > Inquiry

ID Point

Type
ID

Menu Browser
Tools
 > Inquiry
 > ID Point

Identifying Point Locations

The **ID** tool displays the coordinate location of a single point in the drawing, such as the endpoint of a line or the center of a circle. The tool can be used transparently within other tools. Once you access the **ID** tool, use any coordinate entry or selection method to enter or pick the point to be identified. Typically, object snap modes are used for accuracy. If dynamic input is on, the X,Y,Z coordinates of the point appear next to the crosshairs until you move the crosshairs. The coordinates are also displayed in the **Command** window.

blip: Small cross that may be displayed when a point is picked on the screen.

In combination with AutoCAD's *blip* mode, the **ID** tool can help you identify where a coordinate is on the screen. Suppose you want to see where the point 8.75,6.44 is located. Access the **ID** tool and enter 8.75,6.44 at the Specify point: prompt. AutoCAD responds by placing a blip at that exact location.

> **NOTE**
>
> The **BLIPMODE** system variable is off by default. In order to use this feature, you must turn **BLIPMODE** on.

Finding the Distance between Two Points

DIST

Ribbon
Tools
> Inquiry
Distance
Type
DIST
DI
Menu Browser
Tools
> Inquiry
> Distance

The **DIST** (distance) tool is used to find the distance between two points. This tool can be used transparently within other tools. Once you access the **DIST** tool, use any coordinate entry or selection method to enter or pick the first point, followed by the second point. As with the **ID** tool, you should use object snap modes to pick locations accurately.

The **DIST** tool provides the distance between the points, angle in the XY plane, angle from the XY plane, and delta X, Y, and Z values. See Figure 17-1. In a 2D drawing, the angle from the XY plane and delta Z values are always 0. If dynamic input is on, distance information appears next to the crosshairs until you move the crosshairs. The same information is also displayed in the **Command** window.

Figure 17-1.
The data provided by the **DIST** tool.

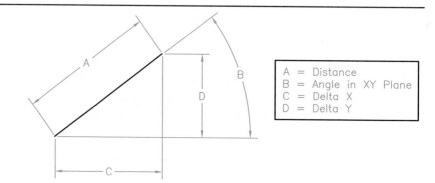

A = Distance
B = Angle in XY Plane
C = Delta X
D = Delta Y

Identifying Object Area

Use the **AREA** tool to find the area of an object. Like the **DIST** tool, this tool can be used transparently within other tools. Once you access the **AREA** tool, use any coordinate entry or selection method to select all of the vertices of an object. See Figure 17-2. Use object snap modes to pick the vertices accurately.

The **AREA** tool provides the area between and perimeter defined by the selected points. If dynamic input is on, the area and perimeter appears next to the crosshairs until you move the crosshairs. The same information is also displayed in the **Command** window.

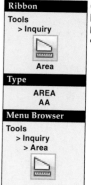

Ribbon
Tools
> Inquiry
Area
Type
AREA
AA
Menu Browser
Tools
> Inquiry
> Area

AREA

PROFESSIONAL TIP

AutoCAD gives you the area inside three or more points picked on the screen, even if the three points are not connected by lines. The perimeter of the selected points is also given.

Using the Object Option

The area of a line, polyline, circle, spline, or rectangle can be found using the **Object** option of the **AREA** tool. Once you access the **AREA** tool, activate the **Object** option instead of picking object vertices. Then select the object to display its area. The area of the object and a second value appear next to the crosshairs, if dynamic input is on, and at the **Command** window. The second value returned by the **Object** option varies, depending on the type of object selected, as shown in the following table:

Object	Values Returned
Line	Selected value does not have an area (no value given)
Polyline	Area and length or perimeter
Circle	Area and circumference
Spline	Area and length or perimeter
Rectangle	Area and perimeter

Figure 17-2.
Pick all vertices to find the area of an object drawn with the **LINE** tool.

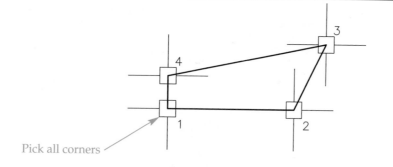

Pick all corners

Adding and Subtracting Areas

Using the **Add** option of the **AREA** tool, you can pick multiple objects or areas. As you add objects or areas, a running total of the area is automatically calculated. The **Subtract** option allows you to remove objects or areas from the selection set. Once either of these options is selected, the **AREA** tool remains in effect until canceled.

An example of using the **Add** and **Subtract** options of the **AREA** tool in the same operation is shown in Figure 17-3. In this example, the **Add** option of the **AREA** tool is selected to enter the **Add** mode. Then the **Object** option is selected and the rectangle is picked. The area and perimeter of the rectangle are displayed, along with a total area, because **Add** mode is active. Right-click or press the [Enter] key or space bar at the (ADD mode) select objects: prompt to continue. Now choose the **Subtract** option to enter **Subtract** mode. Select the **Object** option, and pick the first circle to subtract from the area of the rectangle. Pick the second circle to subtract the area of the second circle. The area and circumference of each circle is given when the circle is selected, along with the total area of the rectangle minus the total area of the subtracted objects.

The total area of the rectangle in Figure 17-3, after subtracting the areas of the two holes, is 12.4292. This information is provided at the **Command** window. Press the [Enter] key twice or press the [Esc] key to exit the tool.

PROFESSIONAL TIP

Calculating area, circumference, and perimeter values of shapes drawn with the **LINE** tool can be time-consuming. You must pick each vertex on the object. If you need to calculate areas, it is best to create lines and arcs with the **PLINE** or **SPLINE** tool. Use the **Object** option of the **AREA** tool when adding or subtracting objects.

Figure 17-3.
To calculate the area of a rectangle drawn with the **RECTANGLE** tool, first select the outer boundary of the rectangle using the **Add** option of the **AREA** tool. Select the inner boundaries (the circles) using the **Subtract** option. This will calculate the area of the object.

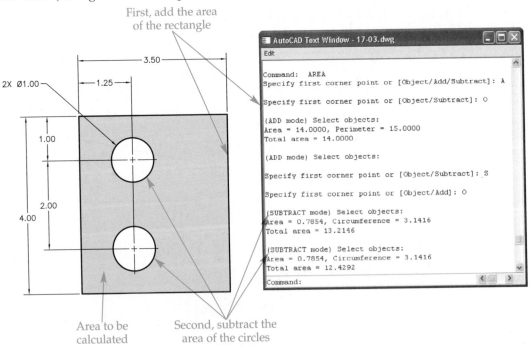

First, add the area of the rectangle

Area to be calculated

Second, subtract the area of the circles

AutoCAD and Its Applications—Basics

Displaying Information with Fields

You can list some object properties and drawing information using *fields*. Fields were introduced in Chapter 10. Each object type, such as a line, circle, or polyline, has different properties that can be displayed in a field. For example, using fields, you can place text next to a circle listing its area and circumference.

To display an object property value using a field, access the **Field** dialog box. To insert a field in an active multiline text editor, pick the **Insert Field** button from the **Insert** panel of the **Multiline Text** tab, pick the **Insert Field** option available from the shortcut menu or the **Options** flyout, or use the [Ctrl]+[F] key combination. To insert a field in an active single-line text editor, right-click and select **Insert Field...** from the shortcut menu, or use the [Ctrl]+[F] key combination.

In the **Field** dialog box, pick Objects from the **Field category:** drop-down list, and then pick Object in the **Field names:** list box. See Figure 17-4. Pick the **Select object** button to return to the drawing window and pick an object. When you select an object, the **Field** dialog box reappears with the available properties listed. See Figure 17-5. Pick the property, select the format, and pick the **OK** button to insert the field. Once the field is created, whenever the object is modified, the value displayed in the field can be updated to reflect the new value. In addition to object property settings such as layer, linetype, lineweight, and plot style, many inquiry properties can be included in a field. The table in Figure 17-6 lists some of the inquiry data that can be displayed in fields for various object types.

field: Text object that displays a property, setting, or value for an object, drawing, or computer system.

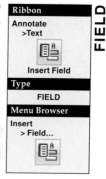

Figure 17-4.
Pick the Object field to add a property for a specific object to a field. Pick the **Select object** button to select the object.

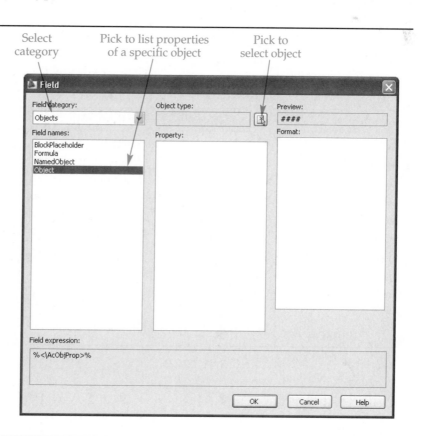

Select category — Pick to list properties of a specific object — Pick to select object

Figure 17-5.
After you pick the object, properties specific to the object type are listed. Select the property and format for the field.

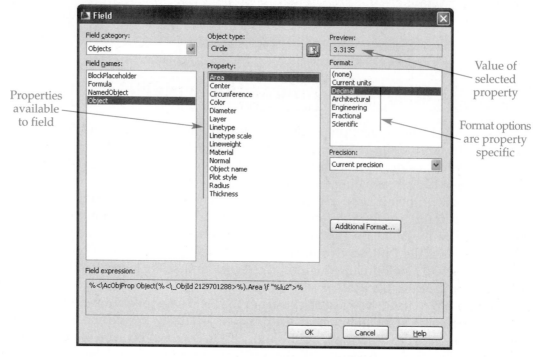

Properties available to field

Value of selected property

Format options are property specific

Figure 17-6.
This table is a partial listing of inquiry properties available for various object types.

Object Properties Available for Display in Fields			
Line Object	**Circle Object**	**Polyline Object**	**Rectangle Object**
Length	Area	Area	Area
Angle	Circumference	Length	Length
Delta	Diameter		
Start	Radius		
End	Center		
Arc Object	**Ellipse Object**	**Spline Object**	**Region Object**
Area	Area	Area	Area
Arc length	Center	Degree	Perimeter
Radius	Major axis	Start tangent	
Center	Minor axis	End tangent	
Total angle	Major radius		
Start	Minor radius		
End	Radius ratio		
Start angle	Start		
End angle	End		
	Start angle		
	End angle		

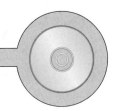

Listing Drawing Data

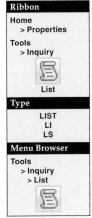

The **LIST** tool displays data about any AutoCAD object. Line lengths, circle and arc locations and radii, polyline widths, and object layers are just a few of the items you can identify with the **LIST** tool. Access the **LIST** tool, select the objects you want to list, and right-click or press the [Enter] key or space bar. The data for each object you picked is displayed in the **Command** window and in the text window.

Figure 17-7A shows an example of the text window displayed when a line is picked. The Delta X and Delta Y values indicate the horizontal and vertical distances between the *from point* and *to point* of the line. These two values, along with the length and angle, provide you with four measurements for a single line. See Figure 17-7B.

Figure 17-8 shows an example of the text window displayed when multiple objects are selected. In this example, single-line text, multiline text, a circle, and a rectangle have all been selected at the same time to list properties. When multiple objects are selected and all of the information does not fit in the window, AutoCAD prompts you to press the [Enter] key to proceed to additional object information.

Figure 17-7.
A—An example of the text window displayed when you use the **LIST** tool to list the properties of a line. B—The various data and measurements of a line provided by the **LIST** tool.

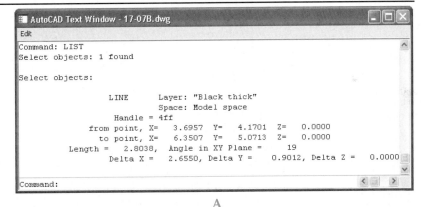

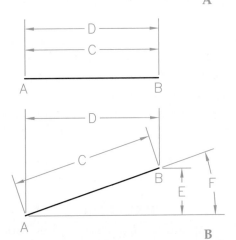

Figure 17-8.
An example of the text window displayed when you use the **LIST** tool to list the properties of single-line text, multiline text, a circle, and a rectangle.

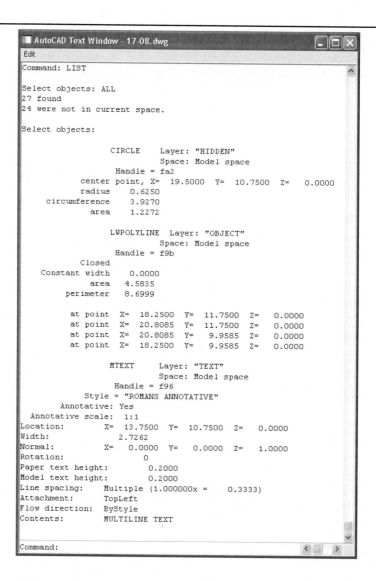

```
AutoCAD Text Window - 17-08.dwg
Edit

Command: LIST

Select objects: ALL
27 found
24 were not in current space.

Select objects:

                CIRCLE     Layer: "HIDDEN"
                           Space: Model space
                 Handle = fa2
         center point, X=  19.5000  Y=  10.7500  Z=    0.0000
            radius    0.6250
      circumference    3.9270
             area    1.2272

                LWPOLYLINE  Layer: "OBJECT"
                            Space: Model space
                 Handle = f9b
         Closed
  Constant width    0.0000
             area    4.5835
        perimeter    8.6999

        at point  X=  18.2500  Y=  11.7500  Z=   0.0000
        at point  X=  20.8085  Y=  11.7500  Z=   0.0000
        at point  X=  20.8085  Y=   9.9585  Z=   0.0000
        at point  X=  18.2500  Y=   9.9585  Z=   0.0000

                MTEXT      Layer: "TEXT"
                           Space: Model space
                 Handle = f96
             Style = "ROMANS ANNOTATIVE"
         Annotative: Yes
    Annotative scale:  1:1
  Location:       X=  13.7500  Y=  10.7500  Z=   0.0000
  Width:            2.7262
  Normal:         X=   0.0000  Y=   0.0000  Z=   1.0000
  Rotation:          0
  Paper text height:      0.2000
  Model text height:      0.2000
  Line spacing:     Multiple (1.000000x =     0.3333)
  Attachment:       TopLeft
  Flow direction:   ByStyle
  Contents:         MULTILINE TEXT

Command:
```

NOTE

The **DBLIST** (database list) tool lists all data for every object in the current drawing. To use this tool, type DBLIST at the keyboard. The information is provided in the same format used by the **LIST** tool, although the text window does not appear automatically.

PROFESSIONAL TIP

The **LIST** tool is the most powerful inquiry tool in AutoCAD. It provides all the information you need about an object. Also, the **LIST** tool reports the area and perimeter of polylines so you do not need to use the **AREA** tool. The **LIST** tool also reports an object's color and linetype, unless both are BYLAYER.

Exercise 17-3

Complete the exercise on the Student CD.

Figure 17-9.
An example of
the text window
displayed when
the **TIME** tool is
accessed.

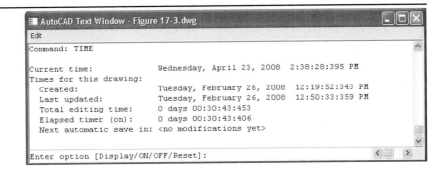

AutoCAD Text Window - Figure 17-3.dwg

Edit

```
Command: TIME

Current time:              Wednesday, April 23, 2008  2:38:28:395 PM
Times for this drawing:
  Created:                 Tuesday, February 26, 2008  12:19:52:343 PM
  Last updated:            Tuesday, February 26, 2008  12:50:33:359 PM
  Total editing time:      0 days 00:30:43:453
  Elapsed timer (on):      0 days 00:30:43:406
  Next automatic save in:  <no modifications yet>
```

Enter option [Display/ON/OFF/Reset]:

Checking the Time

The **TIME** tool allows you to display the current time, time related to your drawing, and time related to the current drawing session. When you access the **TIME** tool, time information is displayed in the **Command** window and in the text window. Figure 17-9 shows an example of the text window displayed when the **TIME** tool is accessed.

You should keep a few concepts in mind when you check the text window display after issuing the **TIME** tool. First, the drawing creation time starts when you begin a new drawing, not when a new drawing is first saved. Second, the **SAVE** tool affects the Last updated: time. If you exit AutoCAD and do not save the drawing, however, all time in that session is discarded. Finally, you can time a specific drawing task by using the **Reset** option of the **TIME** tool to reset the elapsed timer. When you enter the drawing area, the timer is on by default. If you want to stop the timer, enter the OFF option. If the timer is off, enter ON to start it again.

When the **TIME** tool is issued, the times shown in the text window are static. This means that none of the times are being updated. You can request an update by using the **Display** option.

TIME

Ribbon
Tools
> Inquiry
Time

Type
TIME

Menu Browser
Tools
> Inquiry
> Time

NOTE

The Windows operating system maintains the date and time settings for the computer. You can change these settings in the Windows Control Panel. To access the Control Panel, pick Settings and then Control Panel from the start menu.

Exercise 17-4
Complete the exercise on the Student CD.

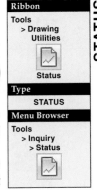

Reviewing the Drawing Status

While working on a drawing, you may forget some of the drawing parameters, such as the limits, grid spacing, or snap values. All of the information about a drawing can be displayed using the **STATUS** tool.

When you access the **STATUS** tool, drawing information is displayed in the **Command** window and in the text window. Figure 17-10 shows an example of the text

STATUS

Ribbon
Tools
> Drawing
Utilities

Status

Type
STATUS

Menu Browser
Tools
> Inquiry
> Status

Figure 17-10.
The drawing information listed by the **STATUS** tool is shown in the text window.

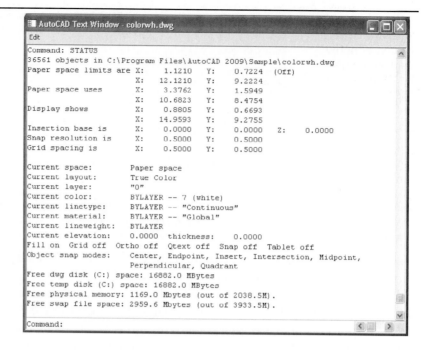

```
AutoCAD Text Window - colorwh.dwg
Edit
Command: STATUS
36561 objects in C:\Program Files\AutoCAD 2009\Sample\colorwh.dwg
Paper space limits are X:      1.1210   Y:      0.7224   (Off)
                       X:     12.1210   Y:      9.2224
Paper space uses       X:      3.3762   Y:      1.5949
                       X:     10.6823   Y:      8.4754
Display shows          X:      0.8805   Y:      0.6693
                       X:     14.9593   Y:      9.2755
Insertion base is      X:      0.0000   Y:      0.0000   Z:      0.0000
Snap resolution is     X:      0.5000   Y:      0.5000
Grid spacing is        X:      0.5000   Y:      0.5000

Current space:          Paper space
Current layout:         True Color
Current layer:          "0"
Current color:          BYLAYER -- 7 (white)
Current linetype:       BYLAYER -- "Continuous"
Current material:       BYLAYER -- "Global"
Current lineweight:     BYLAYER
Current elevation:      0.0000   thickness:      0.0000
Fill on  Grid off  Ortho off  Qtext off  Snap off  Tablet off
Object snap modes:      Center, Endpoint, Insert, Intersection, Midpoint,
                        Perpendicular, Quadrant
Free dwg disk (C:) space: 16882.0 MBytes
Free temp disk (C:) space: 16882.0 MBytes
Free physical memory: 1169.0 MBytes (out of 2038.5M).
Free swap file space: 2959.6 MBytes (out of 3933.5M).

Command:
```

window displayed when the **STATUS** tool is accessed. Press the [Enter] key if necessary to proceed to additional status information.

The number of objects in a drawing refers to the total number of objects—both erased and existing. Free dwg disk (C:) space: represents the space left on the drive containing your drawing file. Drawing aid settings are shown, along with the current settings for layer, linetype, and color. When you finish reviewing the information, press [F2] to close the text window. You can also switch to the drawing window without closing the text window by picking anywhere inside the drawing window or using the Windows [Alt]+[Tab] feature.

Using QuickCalc

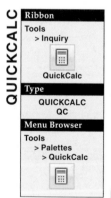

QUICKCALC

Ribbon
Tools
> Inquiry

QuickCalc

Type
QUICKCALC
QC

Menu Browser
Tools
> Palettes
> QuickCalc

Most drafting projects require you to make calculations. For example, when working from a sketch with missing dimensions, you may need to calculate a distance or angle, or you may need to double-check dimensions. Often these calculations are made using a handheld calculator. An alternative is to use **QuickCalc**, which is a palette containing a basic calculator, a scientific calculator, a units converter, and a variables feature. See Figure 17-11. You can use **QuickCalc** like a basic calculator, or you can use it while drafting by pasting values to the command line while a tool is active. The **QuickCalc** palette consists of a built-in toolbar, calculation and history areas, and calculation tools.

> **NOTE**
>
> You can also access the **QuickCalc** palette by right-clicking in the drawing window and selecting the **QuickCalc** menu option.

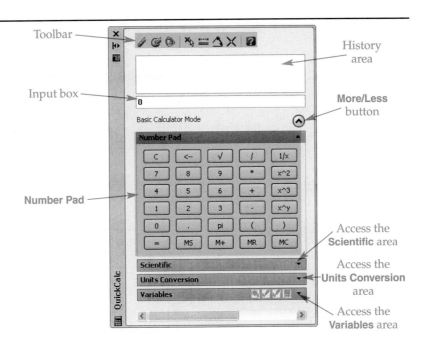

Figure 17-11.
All of the areas of the **QuickCalc** window can be used to perform calculations.

Toolbar

Input box

Number Pad

History area

More/Less button

Access the **Scientific** area

Access the **Units Conversion** area

Access the **Variables** area

Entering Expressions

The basic mathematical functions used in numeric expressions include addition, subtraction, multiplication, division, and exponential notation. Grouped expressions can be entered by using parentheses to break up the expressions that need to be calculated separately. For example, to calculate the result of 6 + 2 and then multiply the result by 4, enter (6+2)*4. If you do not add the parentheses, the result will be wrong. The symbols used for the basic mathematical operators are shown in the following table:

Symbol	Function	Example
+	Addition	3+26
–	Subtraction	270–15.3
*	Multiplication	4*156
/	Division	256/16
^	Exponent	22.6^3
( )	Grouped expressions	2*(16+2^3)

Expressions can be typed directly into the input box using the numbers and symbols on the keyboard. After typing the expression, press [Enter] to have the expression evaluated. Expressions can also be entered by picking the numbers and symbols with the cursor in the **Number Pad**. Picking a number or symbol places that item into the input box. After entering the expression, pick the equal (=) button on the number pad to have the expression evaluated. The **Number Pad** offers some options that are not available from the keyboard. These options are displayed in **Figure 17-12.**

When an expression is evaluated, the result is displayed in the input box and the expression is moved to the history area. **Figure 17-13** displays the **QuickCalc** palette after calculating 96.27 + 23.58. When using only the input box of **QuickCalc**, you can hide the additional sections to save valuable drawing space. To do this, pick the **More/Less** button below the input box. See **Figure 17-13.** When the **QuickCalc** palette displays all of the areas, the button is an up arrow and its tooltip reads **Less**. To display the areas after they have been hidden, pick the button again.

Figure 17-12.
The basic **Number Pad** area contains additional options that cannot be accessed using the keyboard.

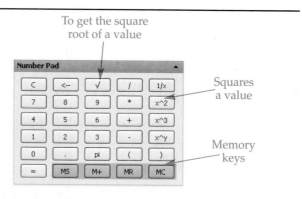

To get the square root of a value

Squares a value

Memory keys

Figure 17-13.
A—Type an expression into the input box.
B—After typing the expression, press the [Enter] key to have the expression evaluated. The expression and result are stored in the history area.

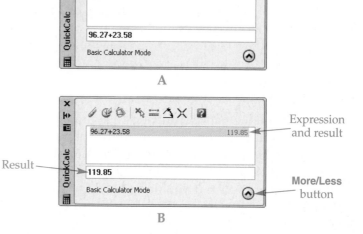

A

Result

Expression and result

More/Less button

B

NOTE

If you move the cursor outside of the **QuickCalc** palette, the drawing area automatically becomes active. To make **QuickCalc** active, pick anywhere inside the **QuickCalc** palette.

PROFESSIONAL TIP

If you make a mistake in the input box, you do not need to clear the input box and start over again. Use the left and right arrow keyboard keys to move through the field. Right-clicking in the input box displays the shortcut options for copying and pasting text.

Clearing the Input and History Areas

After pressing the [Enter] key or picking the equal (=) button to evaluate an expression, you can type a new expression without having to clear the last result. AutoCAD automatically starts a new expression. The input box can be cleared manually when needed by either placing the cursor in the input box and using the [Backspace] or [Delete] key from the keyboard, or by picking the **Clear** button from the **QuickCalc** toolbar. The history area can be cleared by picking the **Clear History** button. See Figure 17-14.

Figure 17-14.
The input box and
history areas can
be cleared using
the buttons on the
QuickCalc toolbar.

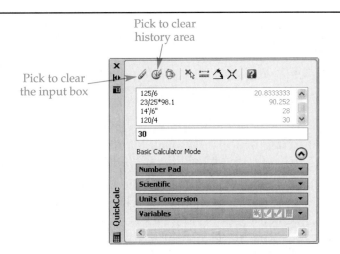

Pick to clear
history area

Pick to clear
the input box

125/6	20.8333333
23/25*98.1	90.252
14'/6"	28
120/4	30

30

Basic Calculator Mode

Number Pad

Scientific

Units Conversion

Variables

QuickCalc

CAUTION

If you enter an expression that cannot be evaluated, AutoCAD
displays an **Error in Expression** dialog box. Pick the **OK** button,
correct the error, and try it again.

Advanced Calculations

Trigonometry functions, some geometry functions, and exponential functions can
be found in the **Scientific** area of **QuickCalc**. See Figure 17-15. To use one of the expressions, type a value in the input box, pick the appropriate expression button, and press
[Enter] or pick the equal (=) button. When you pick the expression button, the input box
value is displayed in parentheses after the expression. For example, to get the *sine* of
14, clear the input box, type 14 in the input box, and pick the **sin** button. The input box
now reads sin(14). Press the [Enter] key or pick the equal (=) button to get the result.

NOTE

The expression button can be picked first, but it puts a default value
of 0 in parentheses. You can then place the cursor in the input box
to type a different number in the parentheses if needed.

Figure 17-15.
The scientific expressions available in **QuickCalc**.

	Sine	Cosine	Tangent	Base–10 Log	Base–10 Exponent
A	Sine	Cosine	Tangent	Base–10 Log	Base–10 Exponent
B	Arcsine	Arccosine	Arctangent	Natural Log	Natural Exponent
C	Convert Radians to Degrees	Convert Degrees to Radians	Absolute Value	Round	Truncate
	1	2	3	4	5

Figure 17-16.
Picking the current
unit type activates
the field and
displays the drop-
down list button.

Drop-down
list button

Converting Units

The **Units Conversion** area allows you to convert one unit type to another. The unit types available are **Length, Area**, **Volume**, and **Angular**. For example, to use the unit converter to convert 23 centimeters to inches, pick in the **Units type** field to display the drop-down list. See **Figure 17-16.** Pick the drop-down list button to display the different unit types and select Length. Activate the **Convert from** field and select Centimeters from the drop-down list. Activate the **Convert to** field and select Inches from the drop-down list. Type 23 in the **Value to convert** field and press the [Enter] or pick the equal (=) button. The **Converted value** field displays the converted units.

The converted value can be passed to the input box for use in an expression by picking the **Return Conversion to Calculator Input Area** button. See **Figure 17-17.** If the button is not visible, pick once on the converted units in the **Converted value** field.

Using Variables

variable: Text item
that represents
another value and
can be accessed
later as needed.

constant:
Expression or value
that stays the same.

function:
Expression that
asks for user input
to get values that
can be passed to
the expression.

If you use an expression or value frequently, you can save it as a *variable* so you do not have to type it every time. The **Variables** area of **QuickCalc** includes two types of predefined variables: *constant* and *function*. In the **Variables** area, variables can be created, edited, deleted, and passed to the input box. See **Figure 17-18.**

To create a new variable, select the **New Variable...** button. This opens the **Variable Definition** dialog box shown in **Figure 17-19.** Type a name for the variable in the **Name:** field. Select a group for the variable to reside in the **Group with:** field. In the **Value or expression:** field, type the value or the expression for the variable. Give a description for the variable in the **Description** field. Pick the **OK** button to save the variable and display it in the **Variables** area.

Select the **Edit Variable** button to open the **Variable Definition** dialog box with the information for the selected variable. If no variable is selected, this button is grayed out. Pick the **Delete** button to delete the selected variable. Pick the **Return Variable to Input Area** button to pass the selected variable to the input box. The variable can also be passed to the input box by double-clicking the variable name.

Figure 17-17.
After a value has
been converted, it
can be passed to the
input box.

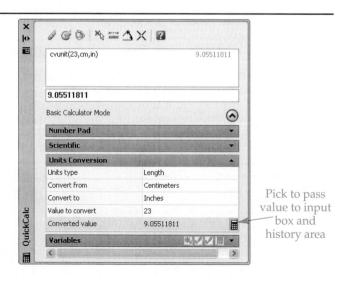

Pick to pass
value to input
box and
history area

AutoCAD and Its Applications—Basics

Figure 17-18.
The **Variables** area of **QuickCalc** allows you to store values and expressions for later use.

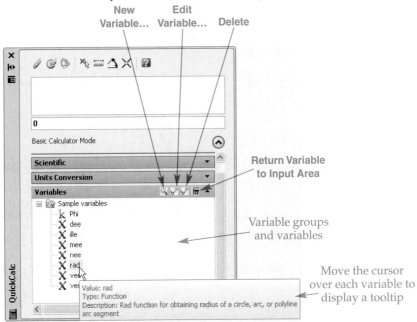

Variable tools can also be accessed by right-clicking in the **Variable** area to display the shortcut menu. Two additional options are available from this shortcut menu. Pick the **New Category** option to create a new category for saving variables. Select the **Rename** option to rename the selected variable. You can also rename a variable by selecting it, pausing, and then selecting it again to activate the name for editing.

PROFESSIONAL TIP

The predefined variables and their functions are explained in the AutoCAD help file. To view these, pick the **Help** button on the **QuickCalc** built-in toolbar to open the **AutoCAD Help** window. On the **Quick Reference** tab of the page, pick the **Variables Area** link and then scroll down to the bottom of the page.

Figure 17-19.
New variables can be defined in the **Variable Definition** dialog box.

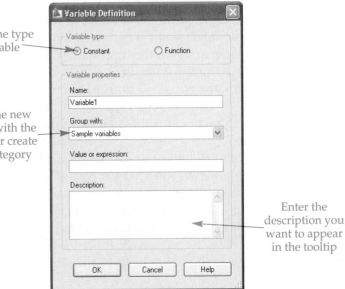

Figure 17-20.
Values can be passed
from **QuickCalc** to
AutoCAD, and they
can be retrieved
from AutoCAD and
passed to **QuickCalc**.

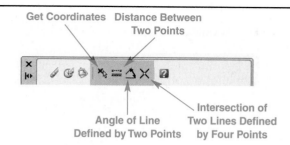

Get Coordinates   Distance Between
Two Points

Angle of Line   Intersection of
Defined by Two Points   Two Lines Defined
by Four Points

Using Drawing Values

Values can be obtained from the drawing and passed to the **QuickCalc** input box using tools available from the built-in **QuickCalc** toolbar. When you select any of the buttons shown in Figure 17-20, the **QuickCalc** palette is temporarily hidden so that you can select points from the drawing window.

Pick the **Get Coordinates** button to select a point from the drawing window and place the X,Y,Z coordinates of the selected point in the input box. Pick the **Distance Between Two Points** button and select two points from the drawing area to display the distance between them in the input box. Select the **Angle of Line Defined by Two Points** button and pick two points on a line to calculate the angle of the line and display it in the input box. Select the **Intersection of Two Lines Defined by Four Points** button to find the intersection of two lines by picking points on the two lines. The X,Y,Z coordinates of the intersection is placed in the input box.

Using QuickCalc with Tools

The previous information focuses on using the **QuickCalc** palette to calculate unknown values while drafting, much like using a handheld calculator or the Windows Calculator. **QuickCalc** can also be used while a tool is active to *pass* a calculated value to the command line as a response to a prompt. **QuickCalc** functions differently depending on whether the **QuickCalc** palette is already displayed when you access a tool or you access a tool and then activate **QuickCalc**. There are a few alternatives for using **QuickCalc** while a tool is active. The following information focuses on two basic options.

If the **QuickCalc** palette is already displayed when you access a tool, when the prompt requesting an unknown value appears, calculate the value using the **QuickCalc** palette and then press the **Paste value to command line** button to pass the value to the command line. For example, to draw a line a distance of 14'8" + 26'3" horizontally from a start point, ensure that the **QuickCalc** palette is displayed, and then access the **LINE** tool and pick a start point. Then use polar tracking or **Ortho** mode to move the crosshairs to the right or left of the first selected point so the line is at 0°. At the Specify next point or [Undo]: prompt, enter 14'8" + 26'3" in the **QuickCalc** palette input box and press [Enter] or pick the equal (=) button. The result is 40'11". Pick the **Paste value to command line** button to make the value 40'11" appear at the command line. Press the [Enter] key or the space bar or right-click and select the **Enter** option to draw the 40'11" line.

If the **QuickCalc** palette is not displayed while a tool is active, you can still calculate and use a value. When the prompt requesting an unknown value appears, access **QuickCalc** by typing 'QUICKCALC, right-clicking and selecting the **QuickCalc** menu option. You can also access **QuickCalc** from the menu browser. A **QuickCalc** *window*, which is not the same as the **QuickCalc** palette, opens in command calculation mode. See Figure 17-21. Use the necessary tools to evaluate an expression. Then pick the **Apply** button to pass the value back to the command line, and close the **QuickCalc** window.

Figure 17-21.
When the **QuickCalc** window is opened while a tool is active, the tool is displayed and the **Apply** and **Close** buttons are available at the bottom of the window.

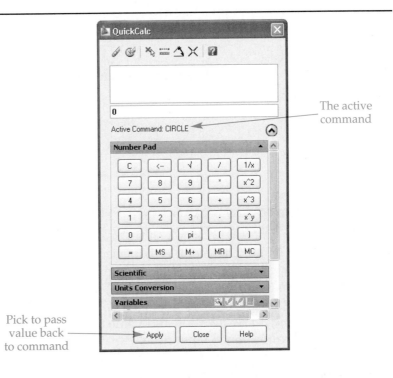

The active command

Pick to pass value back to command

Using QuickCalc with Object Properties

QuickCalc can also be used to calculate expressions for an object in the **Properties** palette. When the **Properties** palette is open, pick a field that contains a numeric value to display the calculator icon. In **Figure 17-22**, a circle is selected, and the **Radius** field in the **Properties** palette is active. Pick the calculator icon to open the **QuickCalc** window, again not the same item as the **QuickCalc** palette, in property calculation mode. Expressions and values are used in the same manner as when using **QuickCalc** at any other time. When the expression is evaluated in the input box, pick the **Apply** button to pass the value to the property field in the **Properties** palette. The object automatically updates based on the new value.

Figure 17-22.
The calculator icon is displayed when you select a numeric field in the **Properties** palette.

Selected object

Active field

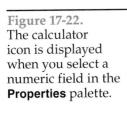

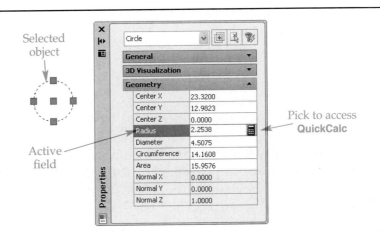

Pick to access **QuickCalc**

Figure 17-23.
The history area
shortcut menu
contains additional
functions and
settings.

Shortcut
menu

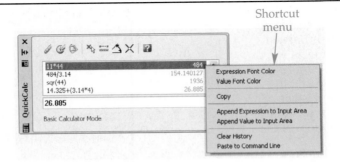

Additional QuickCalc Options

The history area contains some settings and features that can only be accessed from the shortcut menu. This menu is displayed when you right-click anywhere in the history area. See **Figure 17-23.** The following options are available:

- **Expression Font Color.** Allows you to change the color of the expression font.
- **Value Font Color.** Allows you to change the color of the value font.
- **Copy.** Copies the expression and value to the Windows clipboard.
- **Append Expression to Input Area.** Passes the expression to the input box.
- **Append Value to Input Area.** Passes the value to the input box.
- **Clear History.** Clears the history area.
- **Paste to Command Line.** Passes the value to the Command: prompt.

As with other palettes, picking the **Properties** button on the **QuickCalc** palette displays the **Properties** menu. The options allow you to change the settings for the palette's appearance, including its ability to be docked, hidden, or made transparent. The settings for these properties are explained in Chapter 1.

Chapter Test

Answer the following questions. Write your answers on a separate sheet of paper or complete the electronic chapter test on the Student CD.

1. What are the two purposes of the **ID** tool?
2. What types of information are provided by the **DIST** tool?
3. What information is provided by the **AREA** tool?
4. To add the areas of several objects when using the **AREA** tool, when do you select the **Add** option?
5. Explain how picking a polyline when using the **AREA** tool is different from picking an object drawn with the **LINE** tool.
6. What term is used to describe a text object that displays a set property, setting, or value for an object?
7. What is the purpose of the **LIST** tool?
8. Describe the meanings of *delta X* and *delta Y*.
9. What is the function of the **DBLIST** tool?
10. What tool, other than **AREA**, provides the area and perimeter of an object?
11. What information is provided by the **TIME** tool?
12. When does the drawing creation time start?
13. Which inquiry tool is used to list drawing aid settings for the current drawing?
14. List at least three ways to open the **QuickCalc** palette.
15. Name the four sections of the **QuickCalc** palette.

16. Give the proper symbol to use for the following math functions:
    A. Addition
    B. Subtraction
    C. Multiplication
    D. Division
    E. Exponent
    F. Grouped expressions
17. Under which section of the **QuickCalc** palette can the square root function be found?
18. Under which section of the **QuickCalc** palette can the arccosine function be found?
19. When using one of the scientific functions, which should you do first: pick the scientific function button or type in the value to be used in the input box?
20. Name the four types of units that can be converted using **QuickCalc**.
21. What term describes a text item that represents another value and can be accessed later as needed?
22. Which tool button is used to pass the value in the **QuickCalc** input box to the command line?
23. Name three ways to start **QuickCalc** while in the middle of a command.
24. When using **QuickCalc** while a tool is active, how do you pass the value to the command line?
25. When the **Properties** palette is open, what do you need to do first to see the calculator icon so that **QuickCalc** can be used?

Drawing Problems

Start a new drawing for each of the following problems. Specify your own units, limits, and other settings to suit each problem.

▼ Basic

1. Use **QuickCalc** to calculate the result of the following equations.
    A. $27.375 + 15.875$
    B. $16.0625 - 7.1250$
    C. $5 \times 17'\text{-}8''$
    D. $48'\text{-}0'' \div 16$
    E. $(12.625 + 3.063) + (18.250 - 4.375) - (2.625 - 1.188)$
    F. 7.25^2

2. Convert 4.625″ to millimeters.

3. Convert 26 mm to inches.

4. Convert 65 miles to kilometers.

5. Convert 5 gallons to liters.

6. Find the square root of 360.

7. Calculate 3.25 squared.

▼ Intermediate

8. Show the calculation and answer that would be used with the **LINE** tool to make an 8″ line .006 in./in. longer in a pattern to allow for shrinkage in the final casting. Show only the expression and answer.

9. Solve for the deflection of a structural member. The formula is written as $PL^3/48EI$, where P = pounds of force, L = length of beam, E = Modulus of Elasticity, and I = moment of inertia. The values to be used are P = 4000 lbs, L = 240″, and E = 1,000,000 lbs/in². The value for I is the result of the beam (width × height³)/12, where width = 6.75″ and height = 13.5″.

10. Calculate the coordinate located at 4,4,0 + 3<30.

11. Calculate the coordinate located at (3 + 5,1 + 1.25,0) + (2.375,1.625,0).

12. Draw the object shown below using the dimensions given. Check the time when you start the drawing. Draw all the features using the **PLINE** and **CIRCLE** tools. Use the **Object**, **Add**, and **Subtract** options of the **AREA** tool to calculate the following measurements:

A. The area and perimeter of Object A.
B. The area and perimeter of area B. The slot ends are full radius.
C. The area and circumference of one of the circles.
D. The area of Object A, minus the area of Object B.
E. The area of Object A, minus the areas of the other three features.

Enter the **TIME** tool and note the editing time spent on your drawing. Save the drawing as P17-12.

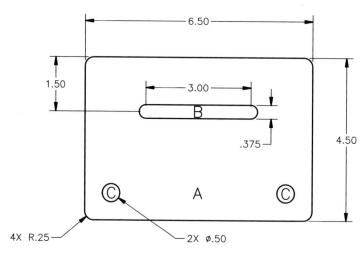

13. Draw the deck shown below using the **PLINE** tool. Using the **POLYGON** tool, draw the hot tub. Use the following guidelines to complete this problem:
    A. Specify architectural units for your drawing. Use 1/2" fractions and decimal degrees. Leave the remaining settings for the drawing units at the default values.
    B. Set the limits to 100',80' and use the **All** option of the **ZOOM** tool.
    C. Set the grid spacing to 2' and the snap spacing to 1'.
    D. Calculate the measurements listed below.
        a. The area and perimeter of the deck.
        b. The area and perimeter of the hot tub.
        c. The area of the deck minus the area of the hot tub.
        d. The distance between Point C and Point D.
        e. The distance between Point E and Point C.
        f. The coordinates of Points C, D, and F.
    E. Enter the **DBLIST** tool and check the information listed for your drawing.
    F. Enter the **TIME** tool and note the total editing time spent on your drawing.
    G. Save the drawing as P17-13.

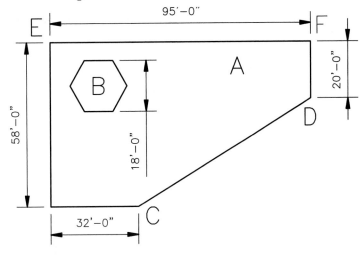

14. The drawing shown below is a side view of a pyramid. The pyramid has four sides. Create an auxiliary view showing the true size of a pyramid face. Save the drawing as P17-14. Using inquiry techniques, calculate the following:
    A. The area of one side.
    B. The perimeter of one side.
    C. The area of all four sides.
    D. The area of the base.
    E. The true length (distance) from the midpoint of the base on one side to the apex.

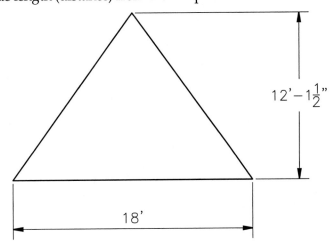

Drawing Problems - Chapter 17

▼ Advanced

15. Given the following right triangle, make the required trigonometry calculations.
    A. Length of side c (hypotenuse).
    B. Sine of angle *A*.
    C. Sine of angle *B*.
    D. Cosine of angle *A*.
    E. Tangent of angle *A*.
    F. Tangent of angle *B*.

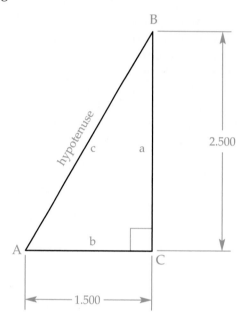

16. The drawing below is a view of the gable end of a house. Draw the house using the dimensions given, and draw the windows as single lines only (the location of the windows is not important). The spacing between each of the second-floor windows is 3". The width of this end of the house is 16'-6". The length of the roof is 40'. You may want to use the **PLINE** tool to assist in creating specific shapes in this drawing, except as noted above. Save the drawing as P17-16. Calculate the following:

A. The total area of the roof.
B. The diagonal distance from one corner of the roof to the other.
C. The area of the first-floor window.
D. The total area of all second-floor windows, including the 3" spaces between each of them.
E. Siding will cover the house. What is the total area of siding for this end?

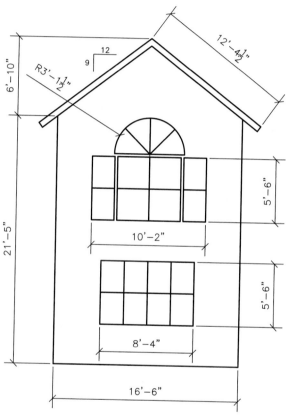

17. Draw the property plat shown below. Label property line bearings and distances only if required by your instructor. Calculate the area of the property plat in square feet and convert to acres. Save the drawing as P17-17.

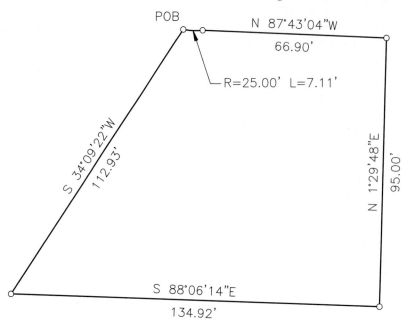

18. Draw the subdivision plat shown below. Label the drawing as shown. Calculate the acreage of each lot and record each value as a label inside the corresponding lot (for example, .249 AC). Save the drawing as P17-18.

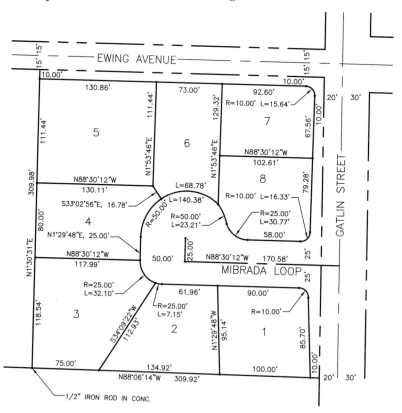

Dimension Standards and Styles

Learning Objectives

After completing this chapter, you will be able to do the following:

✓ Describe common dimension standards and practices.
✓ Manage dimension scales using manual and annotative methods.
✓ Create dimension styles.
✓ Manage dimension styles.

A *dimension* can consist of numerical values, lines, symbols, and notes. Typical dimensioning features and applications are shown in Figure 18-1. AutoCAD dimensioning functions provide significant dimensioning flexibility. Dimension styles control the height, width, style, and spacing of dimension components. Dimension tools allow you to dimension the size and location of most features and objects.

dimension: A description of the size, shape, or location of features on an object or structure.

This textbook provides comprehensive coverage of the elements of AutoCAD dimensioning. This chapter describes fundamental dimension standards and practices and dimension styles. Chapter 19 explains the process of adding linear and angular dimensions. Chapter 20 covers techniques for dimensioning features and provides information on alternate dimensioning practices. Chapter 21 covers editing procedures for dimensions. Chapter 22 covers dimensioning applications with tolerances. Chapter 23 introduces geometric dimensioning and tolerancing practices.

Dimension Standards and Practices

Dimensions communicate information about the drawing. Each drafting field, such as mechanical, architectural, civil, and electronics, uses a different type of dimensioning technique. It is important for a drafter to place dimensions in accordance with industry and company standards. Dimensioning standards are used so that an object designed in one place can be manufactured or built accurately somewhere else.

The standard emphasized in this textbook is ASME Y14.5M-1994, *Dimensioning and Tolerancing*. The *M* in Y14.5M means the standard is written with metric numeric values for dimensions. ASME Y14.5M-1994 is published by the American Society of Mechanical Engineers (ASME). This textbook describes the correct application of both inch and metric dimensioning.

Dimensioning practices often depend on product requirements, manufacturing accuracy, standards, and tradition. Dimensional information includes size dimensions,

Figure 18-1.
Dimensions describe size and location of objects and features. Follow accepted conventions when dimensioning.

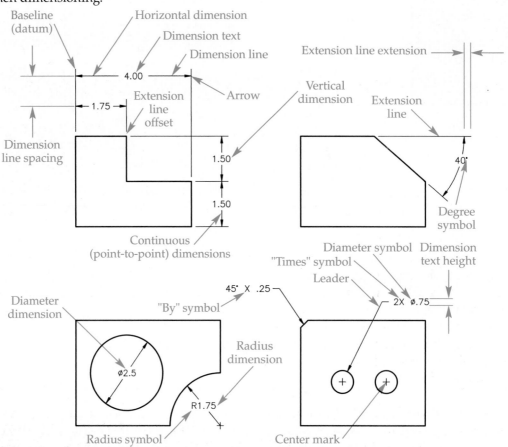

location dimensions, and notes. You will learn appropriate dimensioning practices in this chapter and throughout this textbook.

Unidirectional Dimensioning

unidirectional dimensioning:
A dimensioning system in which all dimensions and numbers are placed horizontally on the drawing.

Unidirectional dimensioning is typically used in mechanical drafting. The term *unidirectional* means "in one direction." In this type of dimensioning, all dimensions are read from the bottom of the sheet. Unidirectional dimensions normally have arrowheads on the ends of dimension lines. The dimension number is usually centered in a break near the center of the dimension line. See **Figure 18-2.**

Figure 18-2.
In unidirectional dimensions, all dimension numbers and notes are placed horizontally on the drawing.

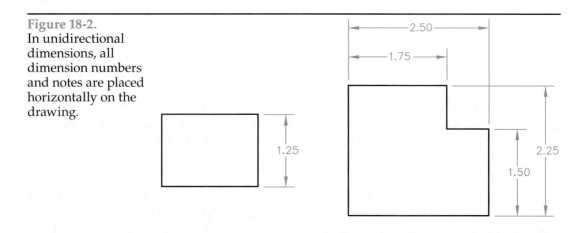

Figure 18-3.
An example
of aligned
dimensioning
in architectural
drafting. Notice
the tick marks
used instead of
arrowheads and the
placement of the
dimensions above
the dimension line.

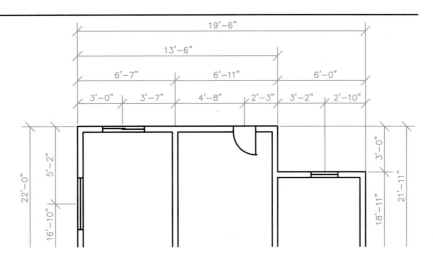

Aligned Dimensioning

Aligned dimensions are typically placed on architectural and structural drawings. Dimension text for horizontal aligned dimensions reads horizontally. Dimension text for vertical aligned dimensions is placed so it reads from the right side of the sheet. Text for dimensions placed at an angle reads at the same angle as the dimension line. Notes are usually placed so they read horizontally.

Aligned dimension lines are often terminated using tick marks, dots, or arrowheads. In architectural drafting, the dimension number is generally placed above the dimension line and tick marks are used as terminators. See Figure 18-3.

aligned dimensioning: A dimensioning system in which the dimension numbers line up with the dimension lines.

Size and Location Dimensions

Size dimensions provide the size of physical features. Size dimensioning practices depend on the methods used to dimension different geometric *features*. See Figure 18-4. *Location dimensions* are used to locate features on an object. Holes and arcs are dimensioned to their centers in the view in which they appear circular. Rectangular features are dimensioned to their edges. See Figure 18-5. An example of location dimensions used in architectural drafting is the dimensioning of windows and doors, usually to their centers, on a floor plan. The *rectangular coordinate system* and the *polar coordinate system* are the two basic systems used for creating location dimensions. See Figure 18-6.

size dimensions: Dimensions that provide the size of physical features.

feature: Any physical portion of a part or object, such as a surface, hole, window, or door.

location dimensions: Dimensions used to locate features on an object without specifying the size of the feature.

rectangular coordinate system: A system for locating dimensions from surfaces, centerlines, or center planes using linear dimensions.

polar coordinate system: A coordinate system in which angular dimensions locate features from surfaces, centerlines, or center planes.

Figure 18-4.
Size dimensions.

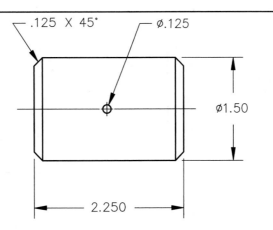

Figure 18-5.
Location dimensions are used to locate circular and rectangular features.

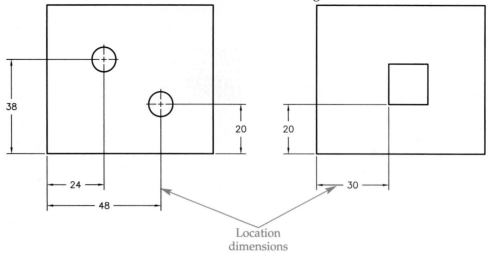

Location
dimensions

Figure 18-6.
A—Rectangular coordinate location dimensions. B—Polar coordinate location dimensions.

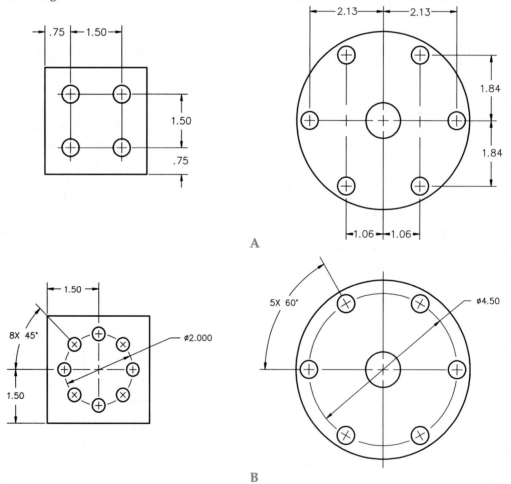

A

B

Figure 18-7.
A—An example of a
specific note. B—An
example of general
notes.

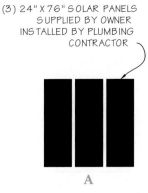

(3) 24" X 76" SOLAR PANELS
SUPPLIED BY OWNER
INSTALLED BY PLUMBING
CONTRACTOR

A

GENERAL NOTES:

1.   PROVIDE SCREENED VENTS @ EA. 3RD. JOIST SPACE @ ALL ATTIC EAVES.
2.   PROVIDE SCREENED ROOF VENTS @ 10'-0" O.C. (1/300 VENT TO ATTIC SPACE).
3.   USE 1/2" CCX PLY. @ ALL EXPOSED EAVES.
4.   USE 300# COMPOSITION SHINGLES OVER 15# FELT.

B

Notes

One method for describing feature size, location, or other information is through the use of *specific notes* and *general notes*. Specific notes are attached to the feature being dimensioned using a leader line. General notes are placed in the lower-left corner, upper-left corner, or above or next to the title block, depending on sheet size and industry, company, or school practice. See Figure 18-7.

specific notes:
Notes that relate to individual or specific features on the drawing.

general notes:
Notes that apply to the entire drawing.

Dimensioning Features and Objects

In mechanical drafting, flat surfaces are dimensioned by giving measurements for each feature. If an overall dimension is provided, you can omit one of the dimensions. The overall dimension controls the omitted dimension. In architectural drafting, it is common to place all dimensions without omitting any of them. Providing all dimensions on an architectural drawing can help make construction easier. See Figure 18-8.

Dimensioning Cylindrical Shapes

Both the diameter and the length of a cylindrical shape can be dimensioned in the view in which the cylinder appears rectangular. See Figure 18-9. The diameter symbol next to the dimension indicates that the part is a cylinder. This allows the view in which the cylinder appears as a circle to be omitted.

Dimensioning Square and Rectangular Features

Square and rectangular features are usually dimensioned in the views in which the length and height are shown. The square symbol can be used preceding the dimension for the square feature, eliminating the need for an additional view. See Figure 18-10.

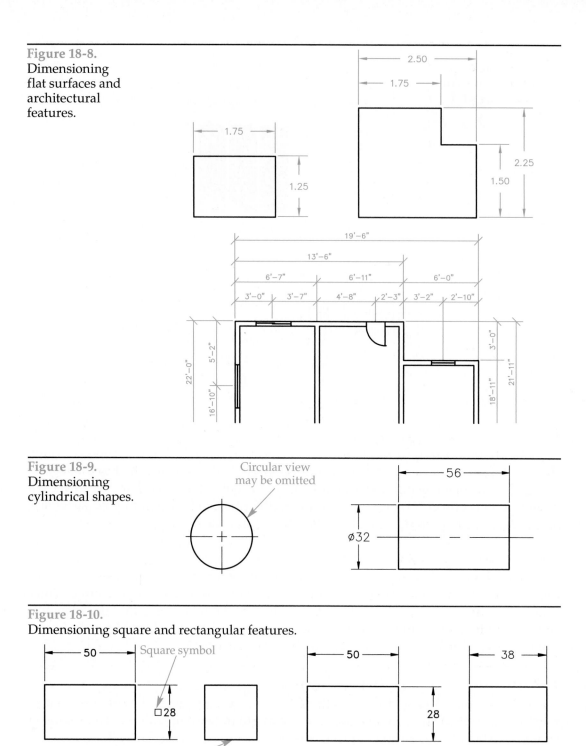

Figure 18-8.
Dimensioning flat surfaces and architectural features.

Figure 18-9.
Dimensioning cylindrical shapes.

Circular view may be omitted

Figure 18-10.
Dimensioning square and rectangular features.

Square symbol

□28

Square view may be omitted

Dimensioning Cones and Regular Polygons

There are two ways to dimension a conical shape. One method is to dimension the length and the diameters at both ends. Another method is to dimension the taper angle and the length. Regular polygons that have an even number of sides are dimensioned by giving the distance across the flats and the length. See **Figure 18-11.**

Figure 18-11.
Dimensioning cones and hexagonal cylinders.

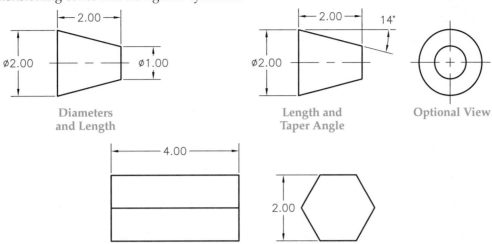

Diameters
and Length

Length and
Taper Angle

Optional View

Drawing Scale and Dimensions

Ideally, you should determine the drawing scale, scale factors, and size of dimension characteristics before you begin a drawing. They are best incorporated as settings within your template drawing files, but they can be changed as needed. The scale factor of a drawing is important because this value is used to ensure that dimension characteristics, such as the height of dimension text, is shown on-screen and plotted at the proper size.

To understand the concept of drawing scale, look at the portion of a floor plan shown in **Figure 18-12.** Everything drawn in model space is drawn at full-scale. This means that the bathtub, for example, is actually drawn 5′ long. However, this becomes an issue when you add dimensions, because dimension characteristics drawn at full scale (for example, 1/8″-high dimension text) are extremely small compared to the other full-scale objects. See **Figure 18-12A.** To display the text properly, you must adjust the size of dimension characteristics according to the drawing scale, as shown in **Figure 18-12B.** You can calculate the scale factor manually and apply it to dimensions, or you can use annotative dimensions and allow AutoCAD to calculate the scale factor.

Figure 18-12.
An example of a portion of a floor plan drawn at full scale in model space. If dimensions are drawn at full scale, as shown in A, the dimensions are very small compared to the large objects. The dimensions must be scaled, as shown in B in order to be seen and plotted correctly.

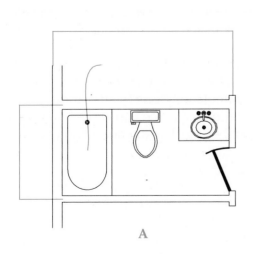

A

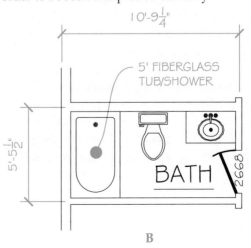

B

Scaling Dimensions Manually

To adjust the size of dimension features manually according to a specific drawing scale, you must first calculate the drawing scale factor. Then multiply the scale factor by the desired plotted dimension size to get the model space dimension size. This calculation can be applied to each dimension automatically by entering the scale factor in the **Fit** tab of the **New** (or **Modify**) **Dimension Style** dialog box, described later in this chapter. Refer to Chapter 9 for information on determining the drawing scale factor.

Annotative Dimensions

AutoCAD scales annotative dimensions according to the annotation scale you select, which eliminates the need for you to calculate the scale factor. When you select an annotation scale, AutoCAD determines the scale factor and automatically applies it to annotative objects, including annotative dimensions. For example, if you scale dimensions manually at a drawing scale of 1/4″ = 1′-0″, or a scale factor of 48, you must enter 48 in the **Fit** tab of the **New** (or **Modify**) **Dimension Style** dialog box. If you place annotative dimensions, you set an annotation scale of 1/4″ = 1′-0″. Then, when annotative dimensions are added, AutoCAD scales them automatically according to the 1/4″ = 1′-0″ annotation scale.

Annotative dimensions offer several advantages over manually scaled dimensions, including the ability to control the scale of dimension features based on annotation scale, not scale factor. Using annotative dimensions is especially effective when drawing scale changes or when objects viewed at different scales are placed on a single sheet.

PROFESSIONAL TIP

If you anticipate preparing scaled drawings, you should use annotative dimensions and other annotative objects instead of traditional manual scaling. However, scale factor does influence other, non-annotative items on a drawing and is still an important value to identify and use throughout the drawing process.

Setting annotation scale

You should usually set the annotation scale before you begin adding dimensions, so that the dimension characteristics are automatically scaled. However, this is not always possible. It may be necessary to adjust the annotation scale throughout the drawing process, especially if multiple drawings at different scales are prepared on one sheet. Dimensioning chapters in this textbook approach annotation scaling in model space only, by first selecting the desired annotation scale and then placing dimensions. When dimensions at another scale are to be added, pick the new annotation scale, and then place the dimension.

When you access a dimension tool and an annotative dimension style is current, the **Select Annotation Scale** dialog box appears. This is a very convenient way to set annotation scale before adding dimensions. The **Annotation Scale** flyout button located on the status bar can also be used to adjust annotation scale. See **Figure 18-13.** Pick the desired annotation scale from the menu, remembering that the annotation scale is typically the same as the drawing scale.

Figure 18-13.
Annotation scale
options can be found
on the status bar.

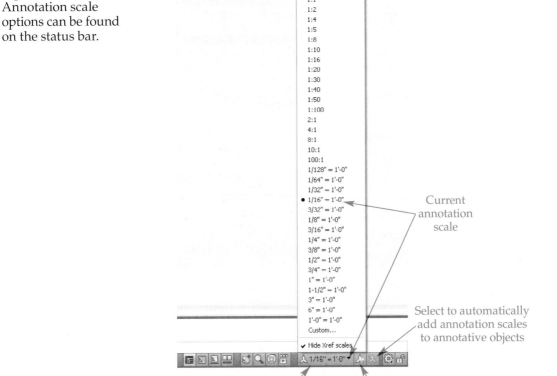

1:1
1:2
1:4
1:5
1:8
1:10
1:16
1:20
1:30
1:40
1:50
1:100
2:1
4:1
8:1
10:1
100:1
1/128" = 1'-0"
1/64" = 1'-0"
1/32" = 1'-0"
• 1/16" = 1'-0"
3/32" = 1'-0"
1/8" = 1'-0"
3/16" = 1'-0"
1/4" = 1'-0"
3/8" = 1'-0"
1/2" = 1'-0"
3/4" = 1'-0"
1" = 1'-0"
1-1/2" = 1'-0"
3" = 1'-0"
6" = 1'-0"
1'-0" = 1'-0"
Custom...

✓ Hide Xref scales

Current
annotation
scale

Select to automatically
add annotation scales
to annotative objects

Pick this flyout
button to select an
annotation scale

Select to show all
annotative objects

Editing annotation scales

If a certain scale is not available, or if you want to change existing scales, pick the **Annotation Scale** flyout in the status bar and choose the **Custom...** option to access the **Edit Scale List** dialog box. See **Figure 18-14.** This dialog box can be used to move the highlighted scale up or down in the list by picking the **Move Up** or **Move Down** button. To remove the highlighted scale from the list, pick the **Delete** button, or to modify it, pick the **Edit...** button. Selecting **Edit...** opens the **Edit Scale** dialog box. Here you can change the name of the scale and adjust the scale by entering the paper and drawing units. For example, a scale of 1/4" = 1'-0" uses a paper units value of .25 or 1 and a drawing units value of 12 or 48.

To create a new annotation scale, pick the **Add...** button in the **Edit Scale List** dialog box to display the **Add Scale** dialog box, which functions the same as the **Edit Scale** dialog box previously described. Pick the **Reset** button to restore the default annotation scale. Once the annotation scale is set current, you are ready to place dimensions that are created at the correct size automatically according to the drawing scale.

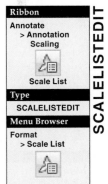

SCALELISTEDIT

Ribbon
Annotate > Annotation Scaling
Scale List
Type
SCALELISTEDIT
Menu Browser
Format > Scale List

NOTE

Many additional annotative object tools are described throughout this textbook. Some of these tools are more appropriate when working with layouts, as described in Chapter 31.

Figure 18-14.
The **Edit Scale List** dialog box is used to modify the display of the annotation scale list and to add annotation scales.

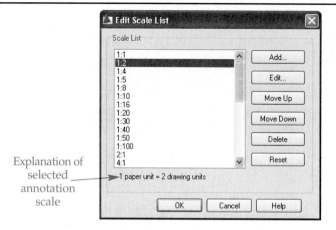

Explanation of selected annotation scale

Dimension Styles

dimension style: A saved configuration of settings for the size and appearance of dimensions.

The appearance of dimensions, from the size and the style of the text to the display of the dimension line, is controlled by many different settings. *Dimension styles* are saved configurations of these settings. You might think of dimension styles as dimensioning standards. Dimension styles are usually established for a specific type of drafting field or application. You can customize dimension styles to correspond to drafting standards such as ASME/ANSI, International Organization for Standardization (ISO), military (MIL), architectural, structural, or civil standards, or your own school or company standards.

A dimension style is created by changing dimension settings as needed to achieve the desired appearance for the drafting application. For example, a dimension style used for mechanical drafting may use unidirectional dimensions, the Romans text font placed in a break in the dimension line, and dimension lines terminated with arrowheads. Refer again to Figure 18-2. A dimension style for architectural drafting may use aligned dimensions, the Stylus BT text font placed above the dimension line, and dimension lines terminated with slashes, as shown in Figure 18-3.

Some drawings only require a single dimension style because AutoCAD has the ability to control all dimension characteristics using one dimension style. However, you may need multiple dimension styles depending on the variety of dimensions displayed in your drawing and different dimension characteristics. Dimension characteristics can be overridden for individual dimensions. However, you should generally create a dimension style for each unique dimensioning requirement. Dimension styles should be added to drawing templates for repeated use.

Working with Dimension Styles

Dimension styles are created and modified using the **Dimension Style Manager** dialog box. See Figure 18-15. The **Styles:** list box displays the dimension styles defined in the current drawing. The default dimension style is a nonannotative style named Standard. It is provided along with a predefined annotative dimension style named Annotative. You can make a dimension style current by double-clicking the style name, right-clicking on the name and selecting the **Set current** option, or picking the name and selecting the **Current** button. When a dimension style is current, all new dimensions are created in that style.

The selection in the **List:** drop-down list controls whether all styles or only the styles in use are displayed in the **Styles:** list box. If the current drawing contains external reference drawings (xrefs), the **Don't list styles in Xrefs** box can be checked to eliminate xref-dependent dimension styles from the **Styles:** list box. This is often

---

DIMSTYLE

Ribbon
Home
> Annotation
Annotate
> Dimensions

Dimension Style

Type
DIMSTYLE
DIMSTY
DDIM
DST
D

Menu Browser
Format
> Dimension Style...

Figure 18-15.
The **Dimension Style Manager** dialog box. The non-annotative dimension style Standard and the annotative dimension style Annotative are available by default.

Current dimension style

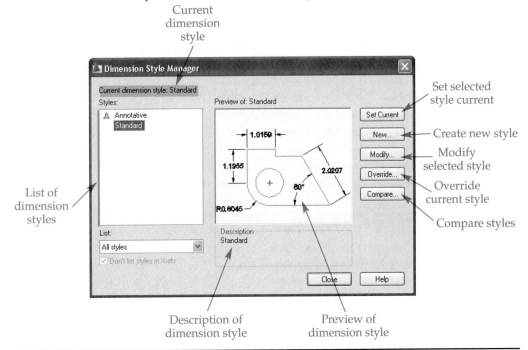

Set selected style current

Create new style

Modify selected style

Override current style

Compare styles

List of dimension styles

Description of dimension style

Preview of dimension style

valuable because xref dimension styles cannot be set current, and they cannot be used to create new dimensions. External references are described in Chapter 32.

The **Description** area and **Preview of:** image provide information about the selected dimension style. If you change any of the default dimension settings without first creating a new dimension style, the changes are automatically stored in a dimension style override.

Creating New Dimension Styles

To create a new dimension style, first select an existing dimension style from the **Styles:** list box that will be used as a base for formatting the new dimension style. Then pick the **New...** button in the **Dimension Style Manager**. This opens the **Create New Dimension Style** dialog box. See **Figure 18-16.**

Enter a descriptive name for the new dimension style, such as Architectural or Mechanical, in the **New Style Name** text box. The **Start With** drop-down list saves time by basing the settings for a new style on an existing dimension style. Pick the **Annotative**

Figure 18-16.
The **Create New Dimension Style** dialog box.

Enter name of new style

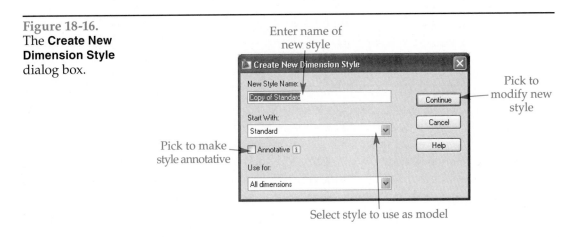

Pick to modify new style

Pick to make style annotative

Select style to use as model

check box to make the dimension style annotative. The dimension style can also be made annotative by selecting the **Annotative** check box in the **Fit** tab of the **New** (or **Modify**) **Dimension Style** dialog box, described later in this chapter.

The Use for drop-down list specifies the dimensions to which the new style will be applied. Use the All dimensions option to create a new dimension style. If you select the Linear dimensions, Angular dimensions, Radius dimensions, Diameter dimensions, Ordinate dimensions, or Leaders and Tolerances option, you create a "substyle" of the dimension style specified in the Start With: text box.

Pick the **Continue** button to access the **New Dimension Style** dialog box, shown in **Figure 18-17**, which is used to adjust dimension style characteristics. The **Lines**, **Symbols and Arrows**, **Text**, **Fit**, **Primary Units**, **Alternate Units**, and **Tolerances** tabs access the settings used for changing the way dimensions are displayed. These tabs are described in the next sections. After completing the information in all tabs, pick the **OK** button to return to the **Dimension Style Manager** dialog box.

> **NOTE**
>
> The preview image shown in the upper-right corner of each **New** (or **Modify**) **Dimension Style** dialog box tab displays a representation of the dimension style. It changes according to the selections you make.

Figure 18-17.
The **Lines** tab of the **New Dimension Style** dialog box.

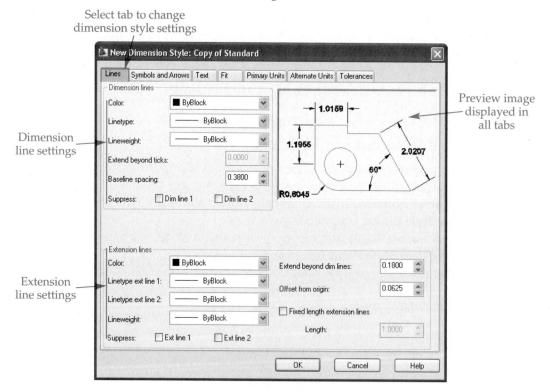

The values of dimension style settings are stored in AutoCAD system variables called *dimension variables*. Changing the values of dimension variables by entering the variable name on the tool line is not a recommended method for setting or changing dimension style settings. Changes made in this manner can introduce inconsistencies with other dimensions. Changes to dimensions are best made by redefining styles or performing style overrides. Dimension variables have limited practical uses and are more likely to be used in advanced applications such as scripting and customizing. For a listing of dimension variables, see the *Reference Materials* section on the Student CD.

dimension variables: System variables that store the values of dimension style settings.

Using the Lines Tab

The **Lines** tab of the **New** (or **Modify**) **Dimension Style** dialog box controls all settings for the display of the dimension and extension lines. Refer again to **Figure 18-17**.

Dimension line settings

The **Dimension lines** area of the **Lines** tab is used to change the format of the dimension line. **Color**, **Linetype**, and **Lineweight** drop-down lists are available for changing the dimension line color, linetype, and lineweight. By default, color, linetype, and lineweight are set to ByBlock. All *associative dimensions* are created as block objects. Associative dimensions are described in detail in Chapter 21. The ByBlock setting means that the color, linetype, and lineweight assigned to the created block are used for the component objects of the block. Blocks are explained in Chapters 26 and 27.

associative dimension: Dimension in which all elements are connected to the object being dimensioned; updates when the associated object is changed.

If the current dimension line color, linetype, or lineweight is set to ByLayer when the dimension block is created, then it comes in with a ByLayer setting. The component objects of the block then take on the color, linetype, and lineweight of the layer on which the dimension is created. If the current object color, linetype, or lineweight is an absolute value, such as a Blue color, a Continuous linetype, or a 0.05mm lineweight, then the component objects of the block take on that specific value regardless of the layer on which the dimension is created.

The **Extend beyond ticks** text box is inactive unless you use tick marks instead of arrowheads. Architectural tick marks or oblique arrowheads are often used for dimensions on architectural drawings. In this style of dimensioning, the dimension lines often cross extension lines. The extension represents how far the dimension line extends beyond the extension line. See **Figure 18-18**. The 0.00 default is used to draw dimensions that do not extend past the extension lines.

Figure 18-18.
Using the **Extend beyond ticks** setting to allow the dimension line to extend past the extension line. With the default value of 0, the dimension line does not extend.

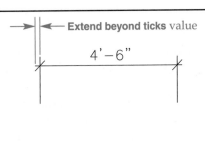

Extend beyond ticks value

4'–6"

Figure 18-19.
The **Baseline spacing** setting controls the spacing between dimension lines.

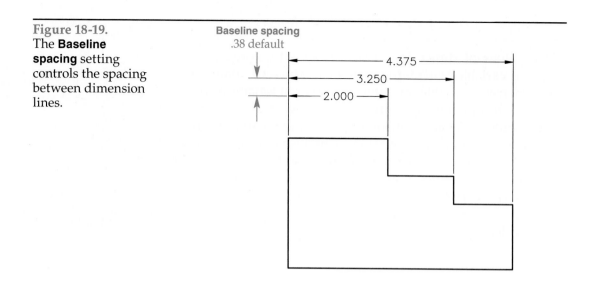

Figure 18-20.
Using the **Dim line 1** and **Dim line 2** dimensioning settings. "Off" is equivalent to an unchecked **Suppress** check box in the **Lines** tab.

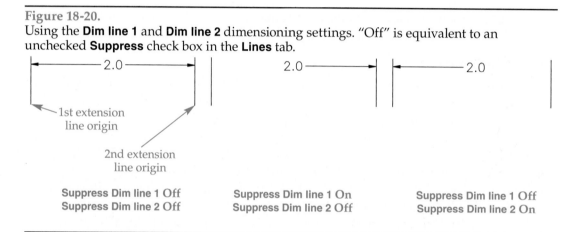

The **Baseline spacing** text box allows you to change the spacing between the dimension lines of baseline dimensions created with the **DIMBASELINE** tool. The default spacing is .38 units, which is too close for most drawings. See Figure 18-19. Try other values to help make the drawing easy to read. The ASME minimum dimension line spacing for baseline dimensioning is .375 (10mm). A value of .5 (12mm) or .75 (19mm) is usually more appropriate.

The **Suppress** feature has two toggles that prevent the display of the first, second, or both dimension lines and their arrowheads. The **Dim line 1** and **Dim line 2** check boxes refer to the first and second points picked when a dimension is created. Both dimension lines are displayed by default. The results of using these options are shown in Figure 18-20.

Extension line settings

The **Extension lines** area of the **Lines** tab is used to change the format of the extension lines. **Color**, **Linetype ext line 1**, **Linetype ext line 2**, and **Lineweight** drop-down lists are available for changing the extension line color, linetype, and lineweight. The default values are ByBlock. The **Linetype ext line 1** drop-down list is used to specify the linetype to be used for the first extension line, which is determined by the first point picked when the dimension is created. The **Linetype ext line 2** drop-down list is used to define the linetype of the second extension line.

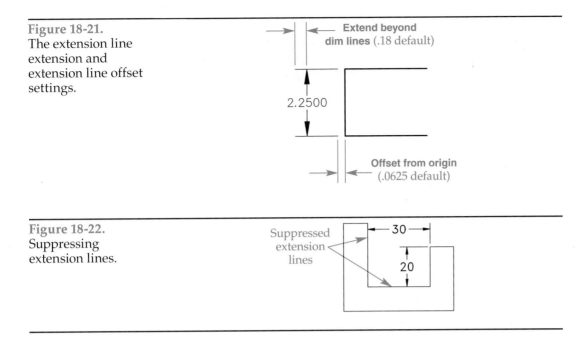

Figure 18-21.
The extension line extension and extension line offset settings.

Extend beyond
dim lines (.18 default)

2.2500

Offset from origin
(.0625 default)

Figure 18-22.
Suppressing extension lines.

Suppressed extension lines

30

20

The **Extend beyond dim lines** option is used to set the distance the extension line runs past the last dimension line. See **Figure 18-21.** The default value is .18; an extension line extension of .125 (3mm) is recommended by ASME standards. The **Offset from origin** option is used to change the distance between the object and the beginning of the extension line. Most applications require this small offset. The default is .0625. ASME standards recommend an extension line offset distance of .063 (1.5mm). When an extension line meets a centerline, however, use a setting of 0.0 to prevent a gap.

The **Fixed length extension lines** check box sets a given length for extension lines. When checked, the **Length** text box becomes active. The value in the **Length** text box is used to set a restricted length for the extension lines. The length is measured from the dimension line toward the extension line origin.

The **Suppress** feature suppresses the first, second, or both extension lines using the **Ext line 1** and **Ext line 2** check boxes. Extension lines are displayed by default. An extension line might be suppressed, for example, if it coincides with an object line. See **Figure 18-22.**

Using the Symbols and Arrows Tab

The settings in the **Symbols and Arrows** tab are used to control the appearance of arrowheads, center marks, and other symbol components of dimensions. See **Figure 18-23.**

Arrowhead settings

The **Arrowheads** area provides several different arrowhead options and controls the arrowhead size. Use the appropriate drop-down list to select the arrowhead to be used for the **First**, **Second**, and **Leader** arrowheads. The default arrowhead is closed filled, which is recommended by ASME standards, although closed blank, closed, or open arrowheads are sometimes used. A small dot is used on a leader pointing to a surface. Other arrowhead styles are shown in **Figure 18-24.** If you pick a new arrowhead in the **First:** drop-down list, AutoCAD automatically makes the same selection for the **Second:** drop-down list.

Notice that **Figure 18-24** does not contain an example of a user arrow. This option is used to access an arrowhead of your own design. For this to work, you must first design an arrowhead and save it as a block. Blocks are described in Chapters 26 and 27. When

Figure 18-23.
The **Symbols and Arrows** tab of the **New Dimension Style** dialog box.

Select tab to specify arrow style

Arrowhead properties

Center mark properties

Dimension break size

Arc length dimension settings

Jog symbol angle setting

Jog text height setting

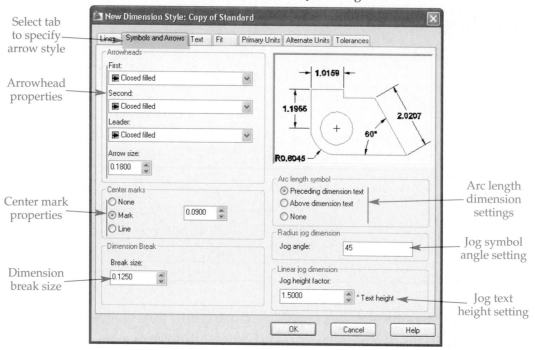

Figure 18-24.
Examples of dimensions drawn using the options found in the **Arrowheads** drop-down lists.

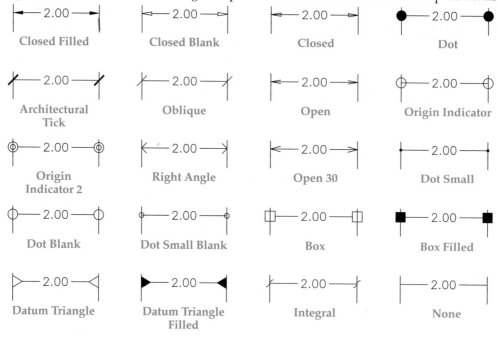

you pick **User Arrow...** in an **Arrowheads** drop-down list, the **Select Custom Arrow Block** dialog box is displayed. Type the name of your custom arrow block in the **Select from Drawing Blocks:** text box or pick a block from the drop-down list and then pick **OK** to specify the arrow for the style.

When you select the oblique or architectural tick arrowhead, the **Extend beyond ticks:** text box in the **Lines** tab is activated. This allows you to enter a value for a

Figure 18-25.
The default arrow
size is .18. ASME
standards specify an
arrowhead size of
.125″.

dimension line projection beyond the extension line. The default value is zero, but some architectural companies like to project the dimension line past the extension line. Refer again to **Figure 18-18.**

The **Arrow size:** text box allows you to change the size of arrowheads. The default value is .18. An arrowhead size of .125″ is common on mechanical drawings. **Figure 18-25** shows the arrowhead size value.

Center mark settings

The **Center marks** area allows you to select the way center marks are placed in circles and arcs when using circular feature dimensioning tools. Fillets and rounds generally have no center marks. The **None** option provides for no center marks to be placed in circles and arcs. The **Mark** option places center marks without centerlines. The **Line** option places center marks and centerlines. The **Size:** text box in the **Center marks** area is used to change the size of the center mark and centerline. The size defines half the length of a centerline dash and the distance that the centerline extends past the object. The default size is .09. The results of drawing center marks and centerlines are shown in **Figure 18-26.**

Adjusting break size

The **Dimension Break** area controls the amount of extension line removed when you use the **DIMBREAK** tool. Enter or select a value in the **Break size:** text box to specify the total length of the break. **Figure 18-27** shows an example of a 3-mm extension line break. The default size is .125. ASME standards do not recommend breaking extension lines.

Figure 18-26.
Arcs and circles
displayed with
center marks and
centerlines.

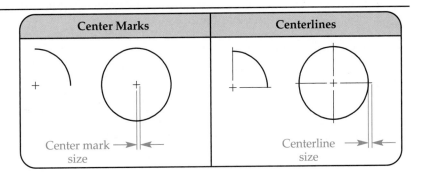

Center Marks	Centerlines

Figure 18-27.
Use the **Break size**
setting to specify the
length of the break
created using the
DIMBREAK tool.

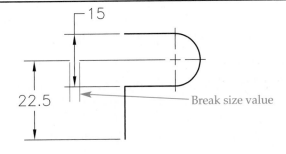

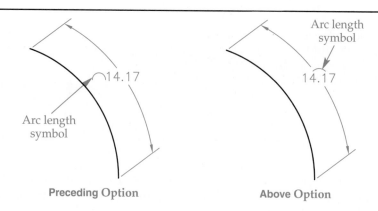

Figure 18-28.
The arc length symbol can be placed in front of or above the arc dimension text.

Arc length symbol

Arc length symbol

Preceding Option

Above Option

Adding an arc length symbol

The **Arc Length Symbol** area controls the placement of the arc length symbol when you are using the **DIMARC** tool. The default **Preceding dimension text** option places the symbol in front of the dimension value. If **Above dimension text** is selected, the arc length symbol is placed over the length value. See **Figure 18-28.** To suppress the symbol so that it does not show, use the **None** option.

Adjusting jog angle

The **Jog angle** setting in the **Radius jog dimension** area controls the appearance of the break line used for the jog symbol when you are using the **DIMJOGGED** tool. This value sets the incline formed by the line connecting the extension line and dimension line. The default angle is 45°.

Setting jog height

The **Jog height factor** setting in the **Linear jog dimension** area controls the size of the break symbol created using the **DIMJOGLINE** tool. This value sets the height of the break symbol based on a multiple of the text height. For example, the default value of 1.5 creates a break symbol that is .18″ tall if the text height is .12″. The default angle is 45°.

NOTE

The **DIMJOGGED** and **DIMJOGLINE** tools are described in more detail in Chapter 20.

Exercise 18-1
Complete the exercise on the Student CD.

Using the Text Tab

Changes can be made to dimension text by picking the **Text** tab in the **New** (or **Modify**) **Dimension Style** dialog box. See **Figure 18-29.**

Text appearance settings

The **Text appearance** area is used to set the dimension text style, color, height, and frame. The dimension text style uses the Standard text style by default. Text styles must be loaded in the current drawing before they are available for use in dimension text. Pick the desired text style from the **Text style** drop-down list. If the style has not yet

Figure 18-29.
The **Text** tab of the **New Dimension Style** dialog box.

Select tab to set up dimension text

Set appearance of the text

Set location of text relative to dimension line

Set alignment of text relative to dimension line

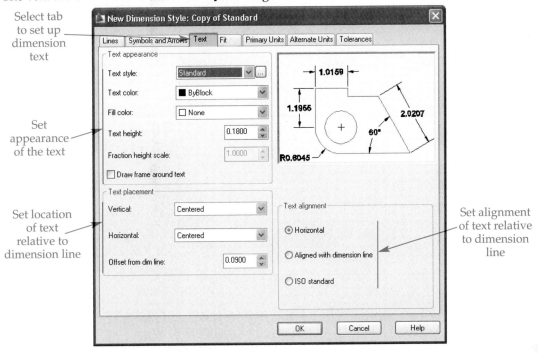

been loaded, pick the ellipsis (…) button next to the drop-down list to launch the **Text Style** dialog box and load the desired style. The default text color is ByBlock, but it can be changed using the **Text color** drop-down list.

Use the **Text height** text box to specify the height of dimension text. Dimension text height is commonly the same as the text height for items found on the rest of the drawing except for titles, which are larger. AutoCAD's default dimension text height is .18, which is an acceptable standard. Many companies use a text height of .125. The ASME standard recommends text height between .12 and .18. The text height for titles and labels is usually between .18 and .24.

The **Fraction height scale** setting controls the height of fractions for architectural and fractional unit dimensions. The value in the **Fraction height scale** box is multiplied by the text height value to determine the height of the fraction. A value of 1.0 creates fractions that are the same text height as regular (nonfractional) text, which is the normally accepted standard. A value less than 1.0 makes the fraction smaller than the regular text height.

Select the **Draw frame around text** check box to draw a rectangle around the dimension text. The distance between the text and the frame is determined by the setting for the **Offset from dim line** value, explained later in this section.

Text placement settings

The **Text placement** area is used to place the text relative to the dimension line. See **Figure 18-30.** The **Vertical:** drop-down list provides vertical justification options. Pick the **Centered** option to place dimension text centered in a gap provided in the dimension line. This is the dimensioning practice most commonly used in mechanical drafting and many other fields. This option is the default.

Figure 18-30.
Dimension text justification options. A—Vertical justification options, with the horizontal Centered justification. B—Horizontal justification options, with the vertical Centered justification.

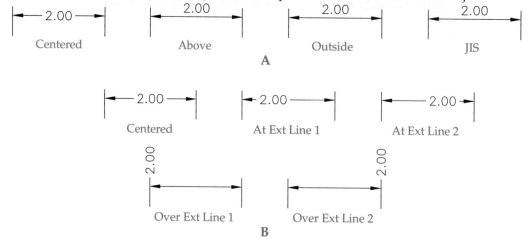

Select the **Above** option to place the dimension text horizontally and above horizontal dimension lines. For vertical and angled dimension lines, the text is placed in a gap provided in the dimension line. This option is generally used for architectural drafting and building construction. Architectural drafting commonly uses aligned dimensioning, in which the dimension text is aligned with the dimension lines and all text reads from either the bottom or the right side of the sheet.

Pick the **Outside** option to place the dimension text outside the dimension line and either above or below a horizontal dimension line or to the right or left of a vertical dimension line. The direction you move the cursor determines the above/below and left/right placement. Choose the **JIS** option to align the text according to the Japanese Industrial Standard.

The **Horizontal:** drop-down list provides options for controlling the horizontal placement of dimension text. Pick the **Centered** option to place dimension text centered between the extension lines. This option is the AutoCAD default. Select the **At Ext Line 1** option to locate the text next to the extension line placed first, or choose the **At Ext Line 2** option to locate the text next to the extension line placed second. Pick the **Over Ext Line 1** to place the text aligned with and over the first extension line, or select the **Over Ext Line 2** option to place the text aligned with and over the second extension line. Placing text aligned with and over an extension line is not common practice.

The **Offset from dim line:** text box sets the gap between the dimension line and the dimension text. This setting also controls the distance between the leader shoulder and the text and the space between the basic dimension box and the text. Basic dimensions are used in geometric tolerancing and are explained in Chapters 22 and 23. The default gap is .09. The gap should be set to half the text height. **Figure 18-31** shows the gap in linear and leader dimensions.

Figure 18-31.
The gap (offset) used for text in a linear dimension and a leader dimension.

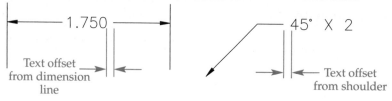

Text alignment settings

The **Text alignment** area allows you to control the alignment of dimension text. Use this area to specify unidirectional dimensions or aligned dimensions. The **Horizontal** option draws the unidirectional dimensions commonly used for mechanical manufacturing drafting applications. The **Aligned with dimension line** option creates aligned dimensions, which are typically used for architectural dimensioning. The **ISO Standard** option creates aligned dimensions when the text falls between the extension lines and horizontal dimensions when the text falls outside the extension lines.

Using the Fit Tab

The **Fit** tab in the **New** (or **Modify**) **Dimension Style** dialog box is used to establish dimension *fit format*. See **Figure 18-32**.

Fit options

The **Fit options** area controls how text and arrows should behave if they do not fit between the two extension lines. These effects are most obvious on dimensions when space is limited. Watch the preview image change as you try each of the fit options. This will help you understand how each option acts.

The **Either text or arrows (best fit)** radio button is selected by default and places text and dimension lines with arrowheads inside extension lines if space is available. Dimension lines with arrowheads are placed outside of extension lines if space is limited. Everything is placed outside of extension lines if there is not enough space between extension lines.

Pick the **Arrows** radio button to place the text, dimension line, and arrowheads inside the extension lines if there is enough space. The text is placed outside if there is enough space for only the arrowheads and dimension line inside the extension lines. Everything is placed outside if there is not enough room for anything inside.

fit format: The arrangement of dimension text and arrowheads on a drawing.

Figure 18-32.
The **Fit** tab of the **New Dimension Style** dialog box.

Select tab to set up fit options

Description of selected option

Text and arrows fit options

Placement of grip-edited dimension text

Pick to make style annotative

Set scale for dimension features

User control options

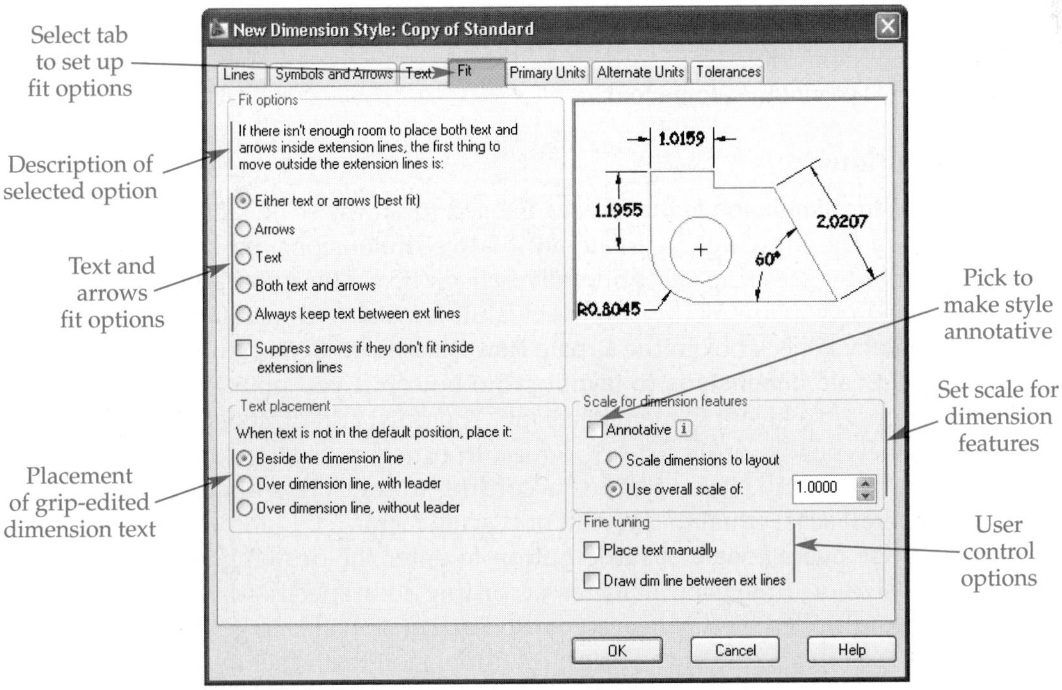

Select the **Text** radio button to place the text, dimension line, and arrowheads inside the extension lines if there is enough space for everything. If there is enough space for only the text inside the extension lines, then the dimension lines and arrowheads are placed outside. Everything is placed outside if there is not enough room for the text inside.

When you pick the **Both text and arrows** radio button, the text, dimension line, and arrowheads are placed inside the extension lines if there is enough space. Everything is placed outside the extension lines if there is not enough space inside.

Select the **Always keep text between ext lines** radio button to always place the dimension text between the extension lines. This may cause problems when there is limited space between extension lines.

Pick the **Suppress arrows if they don't fit inside extension lines** radio button to remove the arrowheads if they do not fit inside the extension lines. Use this option with caution because it can create dimensions that violate standards.

Text placement settings

Sometimes it becomes necessary to move the dimension text from its default position. The text can be moved by grip editing the text portion of the dimension. The options in the **Text placement** area instruct AutoCAD how to handle these grip-editing situations.

Select the **Beside the dimension line** radio button to restrict dimension text movement. When the dimension text is grip edited and moved, the text is constrained to move with the dimension line and can only be placed within the same plane as the dimension line. If you pick the **Over dimension line, with leader** radio button, when the dimension text is grip edited and moved, the text can be moved in any direction away from the dimension line. A leader line is created that connects the text to the dimension line. Choose the **Over dimension line, without leader** radio button to be able to move the dimension text in any direction away from the dimension line without a connecting leader.

PROFESSIONAL TIP

To return the dimension text to its default position, select the dimension, right-click to display the shortcut menu, and select **Dim Text position > Home text**.

Text scale options

The **Scale for dimension features** area is used to set the scale factor for all dimension features in the drawing. To create annotative dimensions, make the dimension style annotative by selecting the **Annotative** check box. The **Annotative** check box is already selected if you are modifying the default Annotative dimension style or if you pick the **Annotative** check box in the **Create New Dimension Style** dialog box.

Select the **Scale dimensions to layout** radio button if you plan to dimension in a floating viewport in a layout (paper space) tab. You must add dimensions to the model in a floating viewport in order for this option to function. Scaling dimensions to the layout allows the overall scale to adjust according to the active floating viewport by setting the overall scale equal to the viewport scale factor.

Pick the **Use overall scale of** radio button to enter the drawing scale factor used to adjust the size of dimension features according to a specific drawing scale. The scale factor is multiplied by the desired plotted dimension size to get the model space dimension size. For example, if the height of dimension text is set to .12 and the value for the overall scale is set to 2 for a half scale drawing, then the dimension text can be measured within the drawing to be .24 units ($2 \times .12 = .24$). If the drawing is plotted with a plot scale of 1:2 (half), the size of the dimension text on the paper measures .12 units.

PROFESSIONAL TIP

Dimensions can be drawn in either model space or layout (paper) space. Model space dimensions must be scaled by the drawing scale factor to achieve the correct feature sizes, such as text height and arrow size. Associative paper space dimensions automatically adjust to model modifications and do not need to be scaled. Also, if you dimension in paper space, you can dimension the model differently in two viewports. However, paper space dimensions are not visible when you are working in model space, so you must be careful not to move a model space object into a paper space dimension. Avoid using nonassociative paper space dimensions.

Fine tuning settings

The **Fine tuning** area provides you with maximum flexibility in controlling the placement of dimension text. The **Place text manually** option gives you control over text placement and dimension line length outside extension lines. You can place the text where you want it, such as to the side within the extension lines or outside of the extension lines.

The **Draw dim line between ext lines** option forces AutoCAD to place the dimension line inside the extension lines, even when the text and arrowheads are outside. The default application is to place the dimension line and arrowheads outside the extension lines. See Figure 18-33. Forcing the dimension line inside the extension lines is not an ASME standard, but it is preferred by some companies.

Exercise 18-2
Complete the exercise on the Student CD.

Using the Primary Units Tab

The **Primary Units** tab of the **New** (or **Modify**) **Dimension Style** dialog box is used to set units for linear and angular dimensions. See Figure 18-34.

Figure 18-33.
The effect of the **Draw dim line between ext lines** option in the **Fine tuning** area of the **Fit** tab.

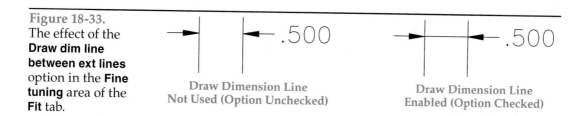

Draw Dimension Line
Not Used (Option Unchecked)

Draw Dimension Line
Enabled (Option Checked)

Figure 18-34.
The **Primary Units** tab of the **Modify Dimension Style** dialog box.

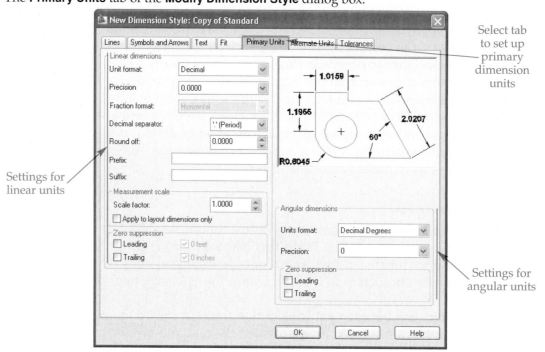

Select tab to set up primary dimension units

Settings for linear units

Settings for angular units

Linear dimension settings

The **Linear dimensions** area is used to specify settings for linear dimensions. Use the **Unit format** drop-down list to set the type of units for dimension text. The default selection is **Decimal** units. Definitions and examples of the different types of units are provided in Chapter 2.

The **Precision** drop-down list allows you to decide how many zeros follow the decimal place when decimal units are selected. Precision settings in mechanical drafting depend on the accuracy required to manufacture specific features. Some features require greater precision than others, generally due to fits between mating parts. For example, a precision setting of 0.00 represents less exactness than a setting of 0.0000. This is explained in further detail in Chapter 22. The default precision is 0.0000; the 0.00 and 0.000 settings are also common in mechanical drafting. When fractional units are selected, the precision values specify the smallest desired fractional denominator. The default is 1/16″ but you can choose other options ranging from 1/256″ to 1/2″; 0″ displays no fractional values. A variety of dimension precisions may be found on the same drawing.

The **Fraction format** drop-down list is only available if the unit format is **Architectural** or **Fractional**. The options for controlling the display of fractions are **Diagonal**, **Horizontal**, and **Not Stacked**.

Use the **Decimal separator** drop-down list to specify commas, periods, or spaces as separators for decimal numbers. The '.' **(Period)** option is the default. The **Decimal separator** option is not available if the unit format is **Architectural** or **Fractional**.

The **Round off** text box specifies the accuracy of rounding for dimension numbers. The default is zero, which means that no rounding takes place and all dimensions are placed exactly as measured. If you enter a value of .1, all dimensions are rounded to the closest .1 unit. For example, an actual measurement of 1.188 is rounded to 1.2.

Add a *prefix* to a dimension by entering a value in the **Prefix** text box. A typical application for a prefix is SR3.5, where SR means "spherical radius." When a prefix is used on a diameter or radius dimension, the prefix replaces the ⌀ or R symbol. Add a *suffix* to a dimension by entering a value in the **Suffix** text box. A typical application

prefixes: Special notes or applications placed in front of the dimension text.

suffixes: Special notes or applications placed after the dimension text.

AutoCAD and Its Applications—Basics

for a suffix is 3.5 MAX, where MAX is the abbreviation for "maximum." The abbreviation in can also be used when one or more inch dimensions are placed on a metric dimensioned drawing. Conversely, a suffix of mm can be used on one or more millimeter dimensions placed on an inch drawing.

The **Measurement scale** area in the **Linear dimensions** area of the **Primary Units** tab is used to set the scale factor of linear dimensions. Set the value in the **Scale factor:** text box. If a value of 1 is set, dimension values are displayed the same as they are measured. If the setting is 2, dimension values are twice as much as the measured amount. For example, an actual measurement of 2 inches is displayed as 2 with a scale factor of 1, but the same measurement is displayed as 4 when the scale factor is 2. Placing a check in the **Apply to layout dimensions only** check box makes the linear scale factor active only for dimensions created in paper space.

The **Zero suppression** area in the **Linear dimensions** area of the **Primary Units** tab provides four check boxes used to suppress leading and trailing zeros in the primary units. The **Leading** option is unchecked by default, which leaves a zero on decimal units less than 1, such as 0.5. This option is used to place metric dimensions as recommended by the ASME standard. Check this box to remove the 0 on decimal units less than 1, as recommended by the ASME standard for inch dimensioning. The result is a decimal dimension such as .5. This option is not available for architectural units.

The **Trailing** option is unchecked by default, which leaves zeros after the decimal point based on the precision setting. This is usually off for inch dimensioning because the trailing zeros often control tolerances for manufacturing processes. Check this box for metric dimensions to conform to the ASME standard. This option is not available for architectural units.

The **0 feet** option is checked by default. It removes the zero in dimensions given in feet and inches when there are zero feet. For example, when this option is unchecked, a dimension may read 0'-11". When **0 feet** is checked, however, the dimension reads 11". This option is only available for architectural and engineering units.

The **0 inches** option is also checked by default. It removes the zero when the inch part of dimensions displayed in feet and inches is less than one inch, such as 12'-7/8". If this option is not checked, the same dimension reads 12'-0 7/8". Also, this option removes the zero from a dimension with no inch value; for example, 12' is used instead of 12'-0". This option is only available for architectural and engineering units.

Angular dimension settings

The **Angular dimensions** area is used to set the type of angular units for dimensioning. Angular units are described in the section of Chapter 2 that explains the **Drawing Units** dialog box. (The **Drawing Units** dialog box does not control the type of units used for dimensioning.)

Set the dimension units by selecting an option from the **Units format** drop-down list. The default setting is **Decimal Degrees**. The other options are **Degrees Minutes Seconds**, **Gradians**, and **Radians**. The **Precision** drop-down list is used to set the desired precision of the angular dimension value.

The **Zero suppression** area has check boxes for the **Leading** and **Trailing** suppression options. These options are used to keep or remove leading or trailing zeros on the angular dimension.

Using the Alternate Units Tab

alternate units (dual dimensioning units): Dimensions in which measurements in one system, such as inches, are followed by bracketed measurements in another system, such as millimeters.

The **Alternate Units** tab of the **New** (or **Modify**) **Dimension Style** dialog box is used to set *alternate units,* or *dual dimensioning units.* See Figure 18-35. Dual dimensioning practices are no longer a recommended ASME standard. ASME recommends that drawings be dimensioned using inch or metric units only. However, alternate units can be used in many other applications.

The **Alternate Units** tab has many of the same settings found in the **Primary Units** tab. However, the **Display alternate units** check box must be checked in order to activate the settings. The **Multiplier for alt units** setting is multiplied by the primary unit to establish the value for the alternate unit. The default is 25.4 because an inch value is multiplied by 25.4 to convert it to millimeters. The **Placement** area controls the location of the alternate-unit dimension. You can choose to place the alternate-unit dimension after the primary value or below the primary value.

> **NOTE**
>
> The final tab in the **New Dimension Style** dialog box, **Tolerances**, is described in Chapter 22.

Exercise 18-3
Complete the exercise on the Student CD.

Figure 18-35.
The **Alternate Units** tab of the **Modify Dimension Style** dialog box.

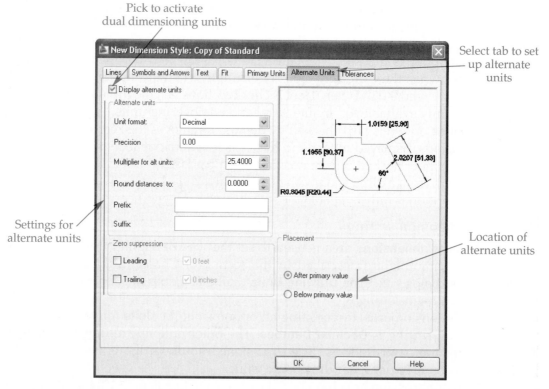

Pick to activate dual dimensioning units

Select tab to set up alternate units

Settings for alternate units

Location of alternate units

Making Your Own Dimension Styles

Creating and recording dimension styles is part of your AutoCAD management responsibility. You should carefully evaluate the items in the dimensions for the type of drawings you do. During this process, be sure to check school, company, or national standards carefully to verify the accuracy of your plan. Then make a list of features and values for the dimensioning settings you use based on what you have learned in this chapter. When you are ready, use the **Dimension Style Manager** dialog box options to establish dimension styles named to suit your drafting practices.

Figure 18-36 provides possible settings for three dimension styles. One list is for mechanical drafting using inch measurements, another is for mechanical drafting using metric units, and the last is for architectural drafting applications. For settings not listed here, use the AutoCAD defaults.

Figure 18-36.
This chart shows dimension settings for typical mechanical and architectural drawings.

Setting	Mechanical (Inch)	Mechanical (Metric)	Architectural
Dimension line spacing	.50	12	1/2″
Extension line extension	.063	3	1/8″
Extension line offset	.0625	1.5	3/32″
Arrowhead options	Closed filled, closed, or open	Closed filled, closed, or open	Architectural tick, dot, closed filled, oblique, or right angle
Arrowhead size	.125	3	1/8″
Center	Line	Line	Mark
Center size	.25	6	1/4″
Text placement	Manually	Manually	Manually
Vertical justification	Centered	Centered	Above
Text alignment	Horizontal	Horizontal	Aligned with dimension line
Primary units	Decimal (default)	Decimal (default)	Architectural
Dimension precision	0.000	0.000	1/16″
Zero suppression (metric)	Leading off Trailing on	Leading off Trailing on	Leading off Trailing on
Zero suppression (inch)	Leading on Trailing off	Leading on Trailing off	Leading on Trailing off
Angles	Decimal degrees (default)	Decimal degrees (default)	Decimal degrees
Tolerances	By application	By application	None
Text style	RomanS	RomanS	Stylus BT
Text height	.12	3	1/8″
Text gap	.063	1.5	1/16″

Exercise 18-4

Complete the exercise on the Student CD.

Changing Dimension Styles

You can change the current dimension style without affecting existing dimensions. The changes are applied only to dimensions added using the current style. Use the **Dimension Style Manager** to change existing dimension styles. Pick the **Modify** button to open the **Modify Dimension Style** dialog box, which allows you to make changes to the style highlighted in the **Styles** list.

Pick the **Override** button to open the **Override Current Style** dialog box, used to *override* a dimension style. Including a text prefix for just a few of the dimensions on a drawing is an example of an override. The **Override** button is only available for the current style. Once an override is created, it is made current and is displayed as a branch, called the *child*, of the *parent* style from which it is created. The override settings are lost when any other style, including the parent, is set current.

Sometimes it is useful to view the details of two styles to determine their differences. Select the **Compare...** button to display the **Compare Dimension Styles** dialog box. You can compare two styles by selecting the name of one style from the **Compare:** drop-down list and the name of the other in the **With:** drop-down list. The differences between the selected styles are displayed in the dialog box.

override: A temporary change to the current style settings; the process of changing a current style temporarily.

child: A style override.

parent: The dimension style from which a style override is created.

NOTE

The **New Dimension Style**, **Modify Dimension Style**, and **Override Current Style** dialog boxes have the same tabs.

Renaming and Deleting Dimension Styles

Existing dimension styles can be renamed in the **Dimension Style Manager**. To rename a dimension style, slowly double-click the name or right-click the name and select the **Rename** option.

NOTE

Styles can also be renamed using the **Rename** dialog box. You can access this dialog box by selecting **Format > Rename...** in the menu browser or by typing RENAME. Select **Dimension styles** in the **Named Objects** list to rename the style.

To delete a dimension style using the **Dimension Style Manager**, right-click the name and select the **Delete** option. If you try to delete a dimension style that has been used to create dimensions in the drawing, AutoCAD displays the message The dimension style "name" is in use and can't be deleted. This means that there are dimensions in the drawing that reference this style. If you want to delete the style, change the dimensions in the drawing to a different style.

Setting a Dimension Style Current

You can set a dimension style current using the **Dimension Style Manager** by double-clicking the style in the **Styles** list box, right-clicking on the name and selecting the **Set current** option, or picking the style and selecting the **Set current** button. To quickly set a dimension style current without opening the **Dimension Style Manager**, use the **Dimension Style** drop-down list located in the **Annotation** panel on the **Home** tab and the **Dimensions** panel on the **Annotate** tab of the ribbon. The name of the current dimension style is displayed in the box.

PROFESSIONAL TIP

You can import dimension styles from existing drawings using **DesignCenter**. See Chapter 5 for more information about using **DesignCenter** to import file content.

Exercise 18-5

Complete the exercise on the Student CD.

Template Development

Chapter 18

Dimension styles require time and effort to set up properly. By adding dimension styles to your drawing templates, you can avoid having to repeat this process each time you begin a new drawing. Refer to the Student CD for detailed instructions to add dimension styles to your mechanical, architectural, and civil drawing templates.

Chapter Test

Answer the following questions. Write your answers on a separate sheet of paper or complete the electronic chapter test on the Student CD.

1. What does the *M* mean in the title of the standard ASME Y14.5M-1994?
2. List at least three factors that influence a company's dimensioning practices.
3. Define the term *general notes*.
4. Name two basic coordinate systems that are used to create location dimensions.
5. Briefly discuss the difference between placing specific and general notes on a drawing.
6. Explain how to dimension a cylinder using only one view.
7. Describe two ways to dimension a cone.
8. When is the best time to determine the drawing scale and scale factors for a drawing?
9. Explain how to add a scale to the **Annotation Scale** flyout in the status bar.
10. Define *dimension style*.
11. Name the dialog box that is used to create dimension styles.
12. Identify at least three ways to access the dialog box identified in Question 3.
13. Name the dialog box tab used to control the appearance of dimension lines and extension lines.
14. Name at least four arrowhead types that are available in the **Symbols and Arrows** tab for common use on architectural drawings.
15. Name the dialog box tab used to control the dimensioning settings that display the dimension text.
16. What has to happen before a text style can be accessed for use in dimension text?
17. What is ASME's recommended height for dimension numbers and notes on drawings?
18. Name the dialog box tab used to control dimensioning settings that adjust the location of dimension lines, dimension text, arrowheads, and leader lines.
19. How can you delete a dimension style from a drawing?
20. How do you set a dimension style current?

Drawing Problems

Start a new drawing for each of the following problems. Specify your own units, limits, and other settings to suit each problem.

▼ Basic

1. Start AutoCAD, start a new drawing using one of your templates, and create a RomanS text style using the romans font. Create the Mechanical (Inch) dimension style shown in **Figure 18-36**. Use the default AutoCAD settings for the dimension style settings not listed. Save the drawing as P18-1.

2. Start AutoCAD, start a new drawing using one of your templates, and create a RomanS text style using the romans font. Create the Mechanical (Metric) dimension style shown in **Figure 18-36**. Use the default AutoCAD settings for the dimension style settings not listed. Save the drawing as P18-2.

3. Start AutoCAD, start a new drawing using one of your templates, and create a Stylus BT text style using the Stylus BT font. Create the Architectural dimension style shown in **Figure 18-36**. Use the default AutoCAD settings for the dimension style settings not listed. Save the drawing as P18-3.

4. Write a short report explaining the difference between unidirectional and aligned dimensioning. Use a word processor and include sketches giving examples of each method.

5. Write a short report explaining the difference between size and location dimensions. Use a word processor and include sketches giving examples of each method.

6. Write a short report discussing the basic difference between dimensioning for mechanical drafting (drafting for manufacturing) and architectural drafting. Use a word processor and include sketches giving examples of each method.

7. Make sketches showing the standard practice for dimensioning a cylindrical object, a square object, and a conical object.

8. Make sketches showing the standard practice for dimensioning angles. Make one sketch showing coordinate dimensioning and another showing angular dimensioning.

▼ Intermediate

9. Find a copy of the ASME Y14.5M, *Dimensioning and Tolerancing* standard and write a report of approximately 350 words explaining the importance and basic content of this standard.

10. Interview your drafting instructor or supervisor and determine what dimension standards exist at your school or company. Write them down and keep them with you as you learn AutoCAD. Make notes as you progress through this textbook on how you use these standards. Also note how the standards could be changed to better match the capabilities of AutoCAD.

▼ Advanced

11. Create a freehand sketch of **Figure 18-1.** Label each of the dimension items. To the side of the sketch, write a short description of each item.

12. Research civil drafting and create a template establishing the dimension styles for a civil drawing.

13. Visit at least three local manufacturing companies where design drafting work is done as part of their business. Write a report with drawing examples identifying the standards used at each company.

14. Find a local manufacturing company where design drafting work is done as part of their business. Write a report with drawing examples identifying the standards used at the company.

15. Find and visit two local companies, one architectural and one civil, where design drafting work is done as part of their business. Write a report with drawing examples identifying the standards used at each company.

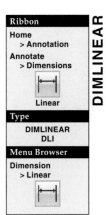

CHAPTER 19

Linear and Angular Dimensioning

Learning Objectives

After completing this chapter, you will be able to do the following:

- ✓ Add linear dimensions to a drawing.
- ✓ Add angular dimensions to a drawing.
- ✓ Draw datum and chain dimensions.
- ✓ Add dimensions for multiple items using the **QDIM** tool.

A variety of dimensions are often needed to fully describe the size and shape of features and objects on a drawing. Two of the most common types of dimensions are linear and angular dimensions. This chapter covers the process of adding linear and angular dimensions to a drawing using a variety of AutoCAD dimensioning tools. You will also learn how to add a break symbol to a dimension line and use the **QDIM** tool.

When you dimension objects with AutoCAD, the objects are automatically measured exactly as you have drawn them. This makes it important for you to draw objects and features accurately. Use object snap modes to your best advantage when dimensioning.

Placing Linear Dimensions

Linear means "straight." In most cases, linear dimensions measure straight distances, such as horizontal, vertical, or slanted surfaces. The **DIMLINEAR** tool allows you to measure the length of an object and place the dimension line, extension lines, dimension text, and arrowheads. Once the **DIMLINEAR** tool is initiated, you are asked to pick the origin of the first extension line. Then you are asked for the origin of the second extension line. The points you pick are the extension line origins. See **Figure 19-1.** Use object snap modes to pick directly on the corners of the object where the extension lines begin.

The **DIMLINEAR** tool allows you to generate horizontal, vertical, or rotated dimensions. After you select the object or points of origin for dimensioning, the Specify dimension line location or [Mtext/Text/Angle/Horizontal/Vertical/Rotated] prompt appears. The **Specify dimension line location** option is default. To use this option, drag the dimension line to a desired location and pick. See **Figure 19-2.** This is where preliminary

Ribbon

Home
 > Annotation
Annotate
 > Dimensions

⊢⊣

Linear

Type

DIMLINEAR
DLI

Menu Browser

Dimension
 > Linear

⊢⊣

DIMLINEAR

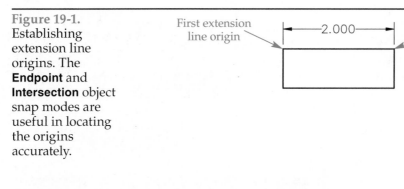

Figure 19-1.
Establishing extension line origins. The **Endpoint** and **Intersection** object snap modes are useful in locating the origins accurately.

First extension line origin

Second extension line origin

2.000

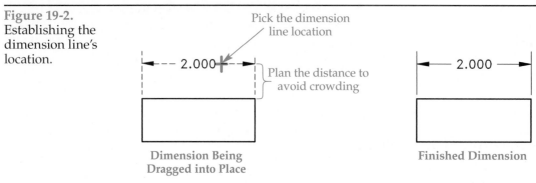

Figure 19-2.
Establishing the dimension line's location.

Pick the dimension line location

2.000

Plan the distance to avoid crowding

Dimension Being Dragged into Place

2.000

Finished Dimension

plan sheets and sketches help you determine proper distances to avoid crowding. The extension lines, dimension line, dimension text, and arrowheads are drawn automatically when you pick the location.

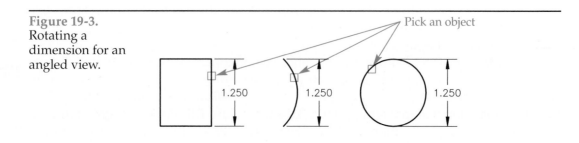

Exercise 19-1
Complete the exercise on the Student CD.

Selecting an Object to Dimension

In the previous section, individual linear dimension extension line origins were picked to establish the extents of the dimension. An alternative method for defining extension line origins involves picking a single line, circle, or arc to dimension. This function also works with the **DIMALIGNED** and **QDIM** tools, described later in this chapter. You can use this option whenever you see the Specify first extension line origin or <select object>: prompt. Press [Enter], the space bar, or right-click and then pick the object being dimensioned. When you select a line or arc, AutoCAD begins the extension lines from the endpoints. If you pick a circle, the extension lines are drawn from the closest quadrant and its opposite quadrant. See **Figure 19-3**.

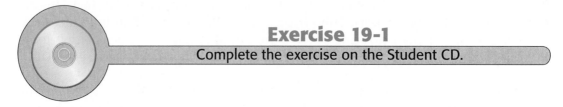

Figure 19-3.
Rotating a dimension for an angled view.

Pick an object

1.250

1.250

1.250

AutoCAD and Its Applications—Basics

Dimlinear Options

Select the **Mtext** option to access the multiline text editor. See **Figure 19-4.** Here you can add information or override the associative dimension value or text formatting. See Chapter 9 for a complete description of the multiline text editor. The highlighted value represents the current dimension value. Edit the dimension text and pick **OK**. For example, the ASME standard recommends that a reference dimension be displayed enclosed in parentheses. Type open and closed parentheses around the value to create a reference dimension.

The **Text** option allows you to use the single-line text editor to change dimension text. However, the **Text** and **Mtext** options both create multiline text objects. The current dimension value is shown in brackets. Pressing [Enter] accepts the current value. If you need to modify the text, type the new text. For example, you can type parentheses around the value to create a reference dimension.

The **Angle** option allows you to change the dimension text angle. This option can be used to create rotated dimensions or to adjust the dimension text to a desired angle. Enter the desired angle at the Specify angle of dimension text: prompt.

The **Horizontal** option sets the dimension being created to a horizontal distance only. This may be helpful when you are dimensioning the horizontal distance of a slanted surface. The **Mtext, Text**, and **Angle** options are available again in case you want to change the dimension text value or angle. The **Vertical** option sets the dimension being created to a vertical distance only. This may be helpful when you are dimensioning the vertical distance of a slanted surface. As with the **Horizontal** option, the **Mtext, Text**, and **Angle** options are available.

The **Rotated** option allows you to specify an angle for the dimension line. A practical application is dimensioning to angled surfaces and auxiliary views. This technique is different from other dimensioning tools because you are asked to provide a dimension line angle. See **Figure 19-5.** At the Specify angle of dimension line <0>: prompt, enter a value or pick two points on the line to be dimensioned.

Figure 19-4.
AutoCAD can determine the extension line origins automatically if you select a line, arc, or circle.

Multiline Text tab of the ribbon appears

Represents the dimension calculated by AutoCAD

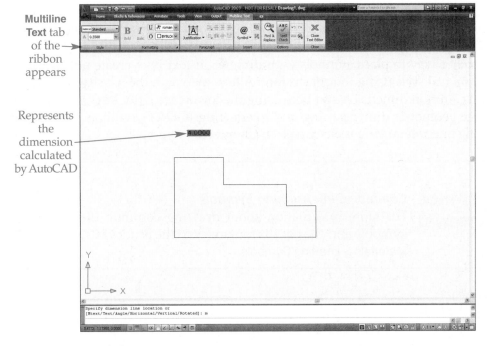

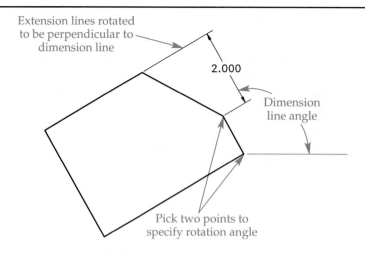

Figure 19-5.
When you use the **Mtext** option, the **Multiline Text** tab of the ribbon appears, and AutoCAD's calculated dimension value appears in a text box for editing.

Extension lines rotated to be perpendicular to dimension line

2.000

Dimension line angle

Pick two points to specify rotation angle

Exercise 19-2
Complete the exercise on the Student CD.

Including Symbols with Dimension Text

After you select a feature to dimension, AutoCAD responds with the measurement dimension text. In some cases, such as when you are dimensioning radii and diameters, AutoCAD automatically places the radius (R) or diameter (∅) symbol before the dimension value. However, in other cases, this is not automatic. The recommended ASME standard for a diameter dimension is to place the diameter symbol (∅) before the number. This can be done using the **Mtext** option of the dimensioning tools. When the multiline text editor appears, place the cursor at the location where you want the symbol, and insert the **Diameter** symbol from the **Symbol** flyout. After you close the text editor, the tool continues and you are asked to pick the dimension line location. Other symbols are also available from the **Symbol** flyout.

Another method to insert symbols is to use the **Text** option of the dimensioning tools. When the single-line text editor appears, place the cursor at the location where you want the symbol and use control codes to place symbols.

Still another way to place symbols with dimension text is to create a dimension style that has a text style using the gdt.shx font. A text style with the gdt.shx font allows you to place common dimension symbols using the lowercase letter keys. This font is used to place geometric dimensioning and tolerancing (GD&T) symbols. Geometric dimensioning and tolerancing is discussed in Chapter 23.

Common Dimensioning Symbols
For more information about drawing common dimensioning symbols and the gdt.shx font, refer to the Student CD: Reference Materials > Drafting Symbols.

Dimensioning in AutoCAD should be performed as accurately and neatly as possible. You can achieve consistently professional results by using the following guidelines:

- Never truncate, or round off, decimal values when entering locations, distances, or angles. For example, enter .4375 for 7/16 rather than .44.
- Set the precision to the most common precision level in the drawing before adding dimensions. Most drawings have varying levels of precision for specific drawing features, so adjust the precision as needed for each dimension.
- Always use precision drawing aids, such as object snaps, to ensure the accuracy of dimensions.
- Never type a different dimension value from what appears in the <> brackets. If a dimension needs to change, revise the drawing or dimensioning settings accordingly. The ability to change the text is provided so a different text format can be specified and so that prefixes and suffixes can be added to the dimension.

Exercise 19-3
Complete the exercise on the Student CD.

Dimensioning Angled Surfaces and Auxiliary Views

When you dimension a surface drawn at an angle, it may be necessary to align the dimension line with the surface. For example, auxiliary views are normally placed at an angle. In order to dimension these features properly, use the **DIMALIGNED** tool or the **Rotated** option of the **DIMLINEAR** tool.

The results of the **DIMALIGNED** tool are shown in **Figure 19-6.** Notice the difference between the aligned dimension in this figure and the rotated dimension in **Figure 19-5.**

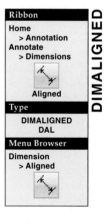

Figure 19-6.
The **DIMALIGNED** tool allows you to place dimension lines parallel to angled features.

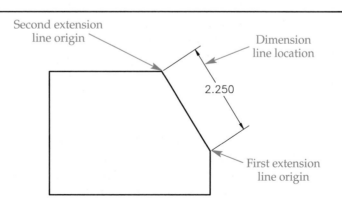

Exercise 19-4
Complete the exercise on the Student CD.

Dimensioning Long Objects

conventional break (break): A notation used to "cut out" part of a long object that has a constant shape to make the object fit better on the drawing sheet.

When you create a drawing of a long part that has a constant shape, the view may not fit on the desired sheet size, or it may look strange compared to the rest of the drawing. To overcome this problem, a *conventional break* (or *break*) is used to shorten the view. For many long parts, the use of a conventional break is required to display views or increase the view scale without increasing the sheet size. Dimensions added to conventional breaks still describe the actual length of the product in its unbroken form. A break symbol is often added to the dimension line to indicate that the drawing view has been broken and that the feature is longer than it appears in the drawing view. See Figure 19-7.

The **DIMJOGLINE** tool can be used to add a break symbol to dimension lines created using the **DIMLINEAR** or **DIMALIGNED** tools. Once you access the **DIMJOGLINE** tool, pick a linear or aligned dimension line. Then pick a point to place the break symbol as shown in Figure 19-7. An alternative to selecting the location of the break symbol is to press the [Enter] key to accept the default location. You can move the break after the symbol is placed by using grip editing or by reusing the **DIMJOGLINE** tool to select a different location. To remove the break symbol, access the **DIMJOGLINE** tool and select the **Remove** option.

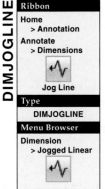

DIMJOGLINE

Ribbon
Home > Annotation
Annotate > Dimensions
Jog Line
Type
DIMJOGLINE
Menu Browser
Dimension > Jogged Linear

NOTE
A single break symbol can be added to a dimension line.

Exercise 19-5
Complete the exercise on the Student CD.

Figure 19-7.
Using the **DIMJOGLINE** tool to place a dimension line break symbol.

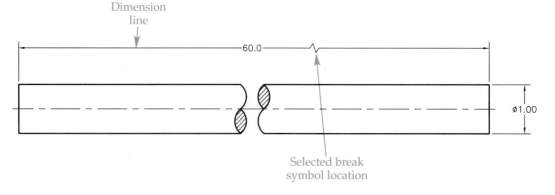

Dimension line

60.0

ø1.00

Selected break symbol location

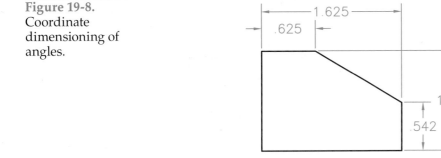

Figure 19-8.
Coordinate
dimensioning of
angles.

Dimensioning Angles

Coordinate and angular dimensioning are both accepted methods for dimensioning angles. *Coordinate dimensioning* is shown in Figure 19-8. This can be accomplished with the **DIMLINEAR** tool.

Angular dimensioning is shown in Figure 19-9. You can dimension the angle between any two nonparallel lines. The intersection of the lines is the angle's *vertex*. AutoCAD automatically draws extension lines if they are needed. The **DIMANGULAR** tool is used for the angular method.

Once you access the **DIMANGULAR** tool, pick the first leg of the angle to be dimensioned, and then pick the second leg of the angle. The last prompt asks you to pick the dimension line arc location. If there is enough space, AutoCAD places the dimension text, dimension line arc, and arrowheads inside the extension lines. If there is not enough room between extension lines for the arrowheads and text, AutoCAD automatically places the arrowheads outside and the text inside the extension lines. If space is very tight, AutoCAD may place the dimension line arc and arrowheads inside and the text outside, or even place everything outside of the extension lines. See Figure 19-10.

coordinate dimensioning:
A method of dimensioning angles in which dimensions locate the corner of the angle.

angular dimensioning:
A method of dimensioning angles in which one corner of an angle is located with a dimension and the value of the angle is provided in degrees.

vertex: The point at which the two lines forming an angle meet.

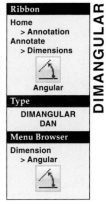

Ribbon	
Home	
> Annotation	
Annotate	
> Dimensions	

Type	
DIMANGULAR	
DAN	

Menu Browser	
Dimension	
> Angular	

DIMANGULAR

PROFESSIONAL TIP

Four possible dimensions (two different angles) can be created with an angular dimension. These options can be previewed by moving the dimension to a different location around an imaginary circle. Use the **Quadrant** option of the **DIMANGULAR** tool to isolate a specific quadrant of the imaginary circle and force the dimension to produce the value found in the selected quadrant.

Figure 19-9.
Two examples of
drawing angular
dimensions.

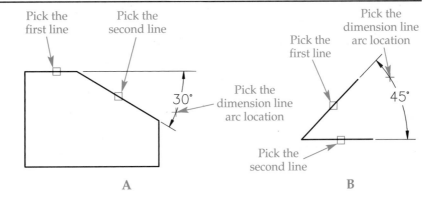

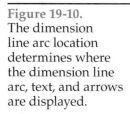

Figure 19-10.
The dimension line arc location determines where the dimension line arc, text, and arrows are displayed.

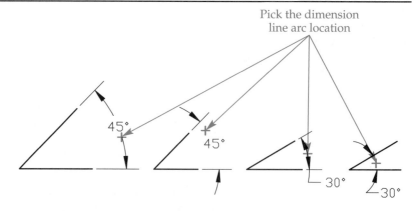

Pick the dimension line arc location

45° 45° 30° 30°

Figure 19-11.
Placing angular dimensions on arcs.

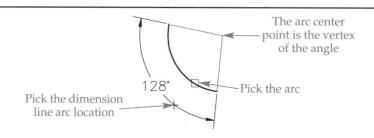

The arc center point is the vertex of the angle

Pick the arc

128°

Pick the dimension line arc location

Placing Angular Dimensions on Arcs

The **DIMANGULAR** tool can be used to dimension the included angle of an arc. The center point of the arc becomes the angle vertex, and the two arc endpoints are the origin points for the extension lines. See **Figure 19-11.**

Placing Angular Dimensions on Circles

The **DIMANGULAR** tool can also be used to dimension a portion of a circle. The center point of the circle becomes the angle vertex and two picked points are the origin points for the extension lines. See **Figure 19-12.** The point you pick on the circle is the endpoint of the first extension line. You are then asked for the second angle endpoint, which is the endpoint of the second extension line.

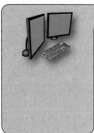

PROFESSIONAL TIP

Using angular dimensioning for circles increases the number of possible solutions for a given dimensioning requirement, but the actual uses are limited. One application is dimensioning an angle from a quadrant point to a particular feature without having to first draw a line to dimension. Another benefit of this option is the ability to specify angles that exceed 180°.

Figure 19-12.
Placing angular dimensions on circles.

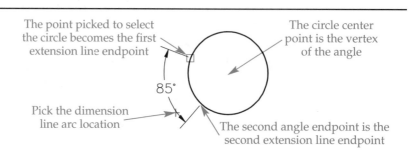

The point picked to select the circle becomes the first extension line endpoint

The circle center point is the vertex of the angle

85°

Pick the dimension line arc location

The second angle endpoint is the second extension line endpoint

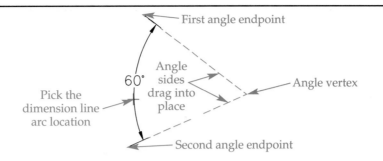

Figure 19-13.
Placing angular dimensions using three points.

First angle endpoint

Angle sides drag into place

60°

Angle vertex

Pick the dimension line arc location

Second angle endpoint

Angular Dimensioning through Three Points

You can also establish an angular dimension through three points. The points are the angle vertex and two angle line endpoints. See **Figure 19-13.** To do this, press [Enter], the space bar, or right-click after the first prompt, pick the vertex, and then pick the two endpoints. This method also dimensions angles over 180°.

Exercise 19-6
Complete the exercise on the Student CD.

Datum and Chain Dimensioning

Datum dimensioning is commonly used in mechanical drafting because each dimension is independent of the others, and references a *datum*. This achieves more accuracy in manufacturing. **Figure 19-14** shows an object dimensioned with surface datums.

datum dimensioning: A method of dimensioning in which several dimensions originate from a common surface, centerline, or center plane.

datum: Theoretically perfect surface, plane, point, or axis from which measurements can be taken.

Figure 19-14.
Datum dimensioning.

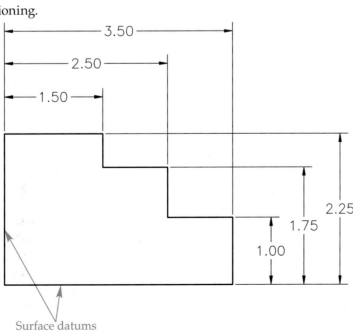

3.50

2.50

1.50

2.25

1.75

1.00

Surface datums

Figure 19-15.
Chain dimensioning. The example on the right is most common, though either technique is acceptable depending on the design and dimensioning requirement.

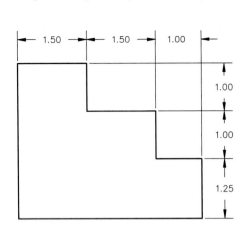
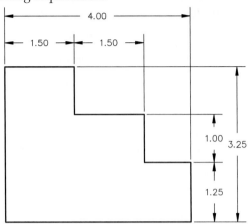

chain dimensioning (point-to-point dimensioning): A method of dimensioning in which dimensions are placed in a line from one feature to the next.

Chain dimensioning, also called *point-to-point dimensioning*, dimensioning is sometimes used in mechanical drafting. However, this method provides less accuracy than datum dimensioning because each dimension is dependent on other dimensions in the chain. In mechanical drafting, it is common to leave one dimension out and provide an overall dimension that controls the missing value. Architectural drafting uses chain dimensioning in most applications. Architectural drafting practices usually show dimensions all the way across features plus an overall dimension. **Figure 19-15** shows two examples of chain dimensioning.

Adding Datum Dimensions

baseline dimensioning: AutoCAD's term for datum dimensioning.

AutoCAD refers to datum dimensioning as *baseline dimensioning*. Datum dimensioning is controlled by the **DIMBASELINE** tool. The **DIMBASELINE** tool allows you to select several points to define a series of datum dimensions. Baseline dimensions can be created with linear, angular, and ordinate dimensions. Ordinate dimensions are described in Chapter 20.

When you access the **DIMBASELINE** tool, AutoCAD asks you to specify a second extension line origin. This is because a baseline dimension is a continuation of an existing dimension. Therefore, a dimension must exist before you can use the tool. AutoCAD automatically selects the most recently drawn dimension as the base dimension unless you specify a different one. As you continue to add datum dimensions, AutoCAD automatically places the extension lines, dimension lines, arrowheads, and text.

To use baseline dimensions, create the first dimension using the **DIMLINEAR** tool. Then access the **DIMBASELINE** tool and pick the next second extension line origin. Then pick the next second line extension origin. Continue picking extension line origins until all features are dimensioned. Press [Enter] or the space bar or right-click twice, once at the Specify a second extension line origin or: prompt, and once at the Select base dimension: prompt, to create the dimensions and exit the tool. Notice that as additional extension line origins are picked, AutoCAD automatically places the dimension text; you do not specify a location. **Figure 19-16** shows an example of using the **DIMBASELINE** tool to pick two additional extension line origins, after a linear dimension has been added.

If you want to add datum dimensions to an existing dimension other than the most recently drawn dimension, use the **Select** option by pressing [Enter] or the space bar or right-clicking and selecting the **Enter** menu option at the first prompt. At the Select base dimension: prompt, pick the dimension to serve as the base. The extension

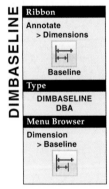

Figure 19-16.
Using the
DIMBASELINE
tool. AutoCAD
automatically places
the extension lines,
dimension lines,
arrowheads, and
text.

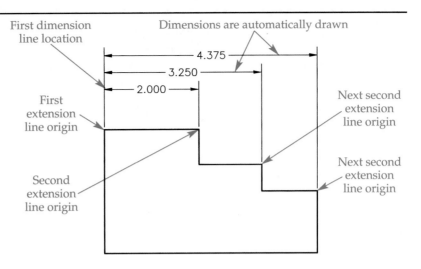

line nearest the point where you select the dimension is used as the baseline point. Then select the new second extension line origins as described earlier.

You can also draw baseline dimensions to angular features. First, draw an angular dimension. Then enter the **DIMBASELINE** tool. **Figure 19-17** shows angular baseline dimensions. As with linear dimensions, you can pick an existing angular dimension other than the one most recently drawn.

Adding Chain Dimensions

AutoCAD refers to chain dimensioning as *continued* dimensioning. Chain dimensioning is controlled by the **DIMCONTINUE** tool, which allows you to select several points to define a series of chain dimensions. Chain dimensioning is shown in **Figure 19-18**.

The **DIMBASELINE** and **DIMCONTINUE** tools are used in the same manner. When creating chain dimensions, you will see the same prompts and options you see while creating datum dimensions. Like datum dimensions, continued dimensions can be created with linear, angular, and ordinate dimensions.

continued dimensioning: AutoCAD's term for chain dimensioning.

Figure 19-17.
Using the
DIMBASELINE
tool to add datum
dimensions to
angular features.

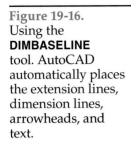

Figure 19-18.
Using the
DIMCONTINUE
tool to create chain
dimensions.

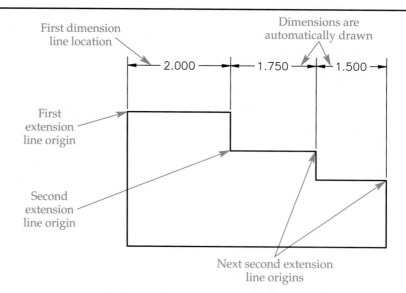

First dimension
line location

Dimensions are
automatically drawn

2.000 ── 1.750 ── 1.500

First
extension
line origin

Second
extension
line origin

Next second extension
line origins

NOTE

Use the **Undo** option in the **DIMBASELINE** and **DIMCONTINUE** tools
to undo previously drawn dimensions.

PROFESSIONAL TIP

You do not have to use **DIMBASELINE** or **DIMCONTINUE** immediately
after you create a dimension that is to be used as a base or chain. You
can come back later and use the **Select** option to pick the dimension
you want to use to draw datum or chain dimensions.

Exercise 19-7
Complete the exercise on the Student CD.

Using Qdim to Dimension

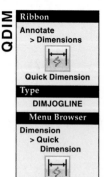

Ribbon
Annotate
> Dimensions

Quick Dimension
Type
DIMJOGLINE
Menu Browser
Dimension
> Quick
Dimension

The **QDIM**, or quick dimension, tool makes chain and datum dimensioning easier
by eliminating the need to define the exact points being dimensioned. Often, the points
that need to be selected for dimensioning are the endpoints of lines or the center points
of arcs. AutoCAD automates the process of point selection in the **QDIM** tool by finding
those points for you.

The type of geometry selected affects the **QDIM** output. If a single polyline is
selected, **QDIM** attempts to draw linear dimensions to every vertex of the polyline.
If a single arc or circle is selected, **QDIM** draws a radius or diameter dimension. If
multiple objects are selected, linear dimensions are drawn to the vertex of every line
or polyline and to the center of every arc or circle. In each case, AutoCAD finds the
points automatically.

Figure 19-19.
The **QDIM** tool can dimension multiple features or objects at the same time.

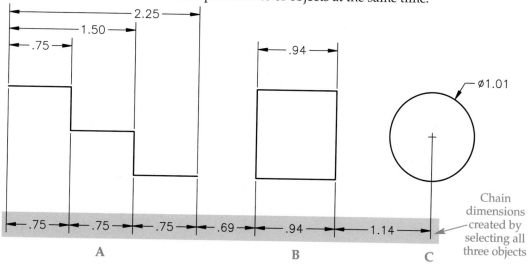

Once you access the **QDIM** tool, pick several lines, polylines, arcs, and/or circles and press [Enter] or the space bar, or right-click. Then pick a position for the dimension lines to create the dimensions and exit the tool. **Figure 19-19** shows examples of different types of objects being dimensioned with the **QDIM** tool. The upper dimensions are created by selecting each object separately. The lower dimensions are created by selecting all of the objects at once.

The **Continuous** option creates chain dimensions. The **Baseline** option creates datum dimensions. The **Staggered** option creates staggered (noncontinuous) dimensions. The **Ordinate**, **Radius**, and **Diameter** options provide methods of adding ordinate, radius, and diameter dimensions. These dimensions are described in Chapter 20. In **Figure 19-19A,** the **QDIM** tool was accessed and the polyline was selected. Then the **Baseline** option was activated and a position for the dimension line was selected above the polyline to create the dimension and exit the tool. The dimensions at the bottom of **Figure 19-19** were created using the **Continuous** option of the **QDIM** tool and selecting all three objects.

The **datumPoint** option can be used to change the datum point for datum or chain dimensions. The **Settings** option allows you to set the object snap mode for establishing the extension line origins to **Endpoint** or **Intersection**.

NOTE

The **QDIM** tool can also be used as a way to edit any existing associative dimension. Editing dimensions and a description of the **Edit** option of the **QDIM** tool are described in Chapter 21.

Chapter Test

Answer the following questions. Write your answers on a separate sheet of paper or complete the electronic chapter test on the Student CD.

1. Name the two **DIMLINEAR** options that allow you to change dimension text.
2. Name the two dimensioning tools that provide linear dimensions for angled surfaces.
3. Which tool allows you to place a break symbol in a dimension line?
4. Describe a way to specify an angle in degrees if the angle is greater than 180°.
5. What is the purpose of AutoCAD's gdt.shx font?
6. Name the tool used to dimension angles in degrees.
7. Which type of dimensioning is generally preferred for manufacturing because of its accuracy?
8. Give two examples of symbols that are automatically placed with dimensions.
9. What is AutoCAD's term for datum dimensioning?
10. How do you place a datum dimension from the origin of the previously drawn dimension?
11. How do you place a datum dimension from the origin of a dimension that was drawn during a previous drawing session?
12. What is the conventional term for the type of dimensioning AutoCAD refers to as continuous dimensioning?
13. Which type of dimensions are created when you select multiple objects in the **QDIM** tool?
14. Which tool other than **DIMBASELINE** is used to create baseline dimensions?
15. Name at least three modes of dimensioning available through the **QDIM** tool.

Drawing Problems

Use one of your templates for each problem. Set limits, units, dimension styles, and other parameters as needed. Use the following general guidelines.

A. Use dimension styles that match the type of drawing as described in this chapter.
B. Use object snap modes to your best advantage.
C. Apply dimensions accurately using ASME or other related industry/architectural standards. Dimensions are in inches, or feet and inches, unless otherwise specified.
D. Set separate layers for dimensions and other features.
E. For mechanical drawings, place the following general notes 1/2" from the lower-left corner:

> NOTES:
> 1. INTERPRET DIMENSIONS AND TOLERANCES PER ASME Y14.5M-1994.
> 2. REMOVE ALL BURRS AND SHARP EDGES.
> 3. UNLESS OTHERWISE SPECIFIED, ALL DIMENSIONS ARE IN INCHES
>   (or MILLIMETERS as applicable).

▼ Basic

1. Open a new drawing using a mechanical template and save it as P19-1. Then open P3-6 and copy one instance of Object A and Object B to the new drawing. Dimension the two objects. Save the drawing.

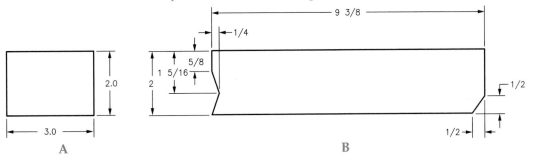

A   B

2. Open P3-4 and finish the drawing by adding the dimensions. Use datum dimensioning. Save the drawing as P19-2.

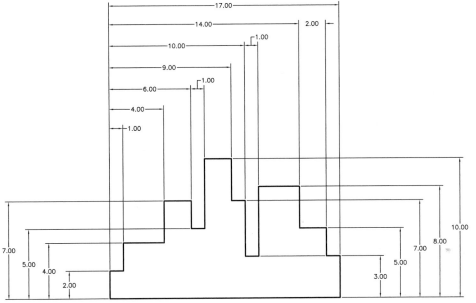

3. Open P3-7 and finish the drawing by dimensioning both objects. Save the drawing as P19-3.

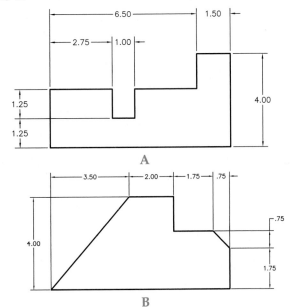

A

B

Drawing Problems - Chapter 19

4. Open P3-10 and finish the drawing by adding dimensions. Save the drawing as P19-4.

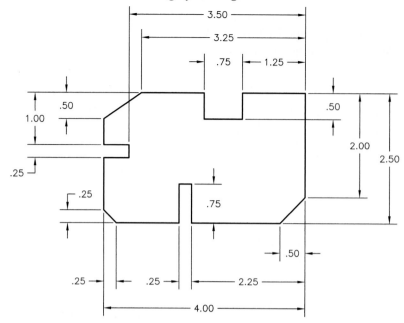

5. Open P3-11 and finish the drawing by adding dimensions. Note that this is a metric drawing. Save the drawing as P19-5.

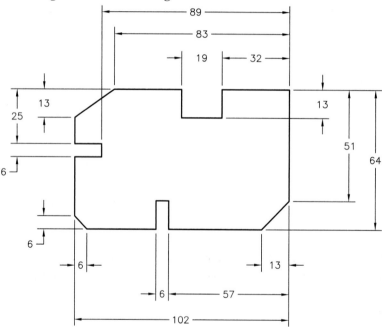

6. Open P3-8 and finish the drawing by adding dimensions. Save the drawing as P19-6.

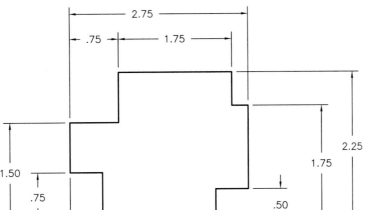

7. Open P3-9 and finish the drawing by adding dimensions. Save the drawing as P19-7.

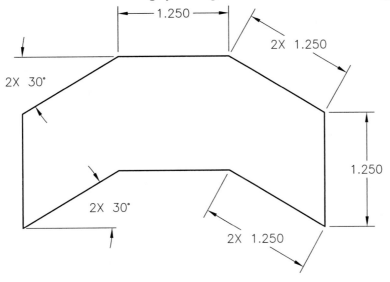

8. Write a report explaining the difference between datum and chain dimensioning. Use a word processor and include sketches giving examples of each method.

9. Create the views of a shaft and dimension as shown. Save the drawing as P19-9.

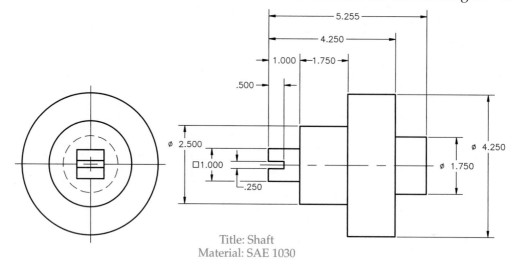

Title: Shaft
Material: SAE 1030

10. Open P3-12 and finish the drawing by adding dimensions. Save the drawing as P19-10.

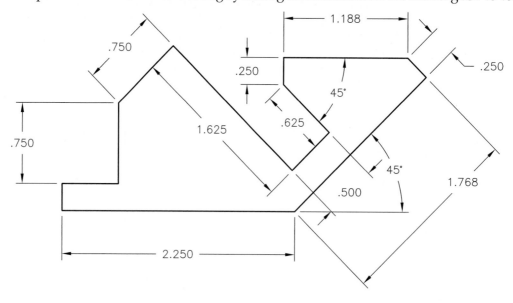

11. Open a new drawing using an architectural template. Create the partial floor plan shown below and dimension as shown. Save the drawing as P19-11.

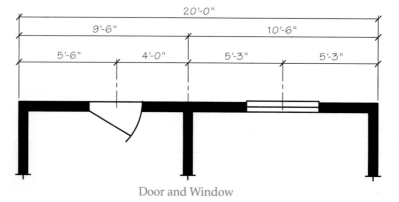

Door and Window

12. Open a new drawing using an architectural template. Create the partial floor plan and dimension as shown. Save the drawing as P19-12.

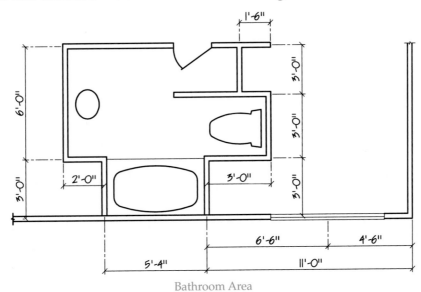

Bathroom Area

13. Open a new drawing using a mechanical template. Create the object and dimension as shown. Save the drawing as P19-13.

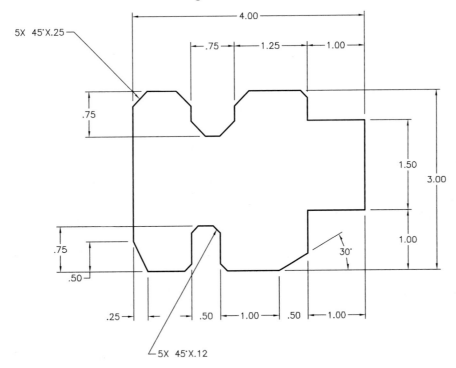

14. Open a new drawing using a mechanical template. Create the object and dimension as shown. Save the drawing as P19-14.

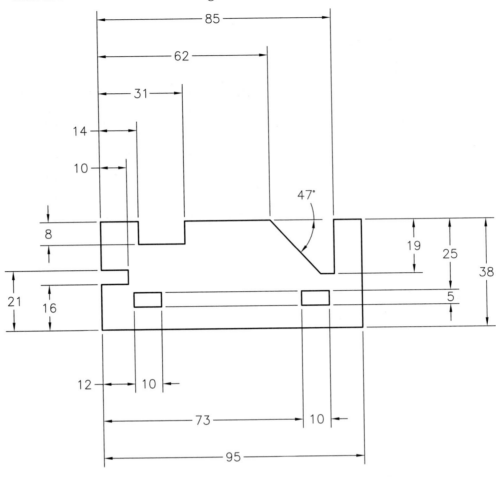

▼ **Advanced**

15. Open P3-3, as shown below, and make one copy of the object at a new location to the right of the original object. Dimension the object on the left using datum dimensioning. Dimension the object on the right using chain dimensioning. Save the drawing as P19-15.

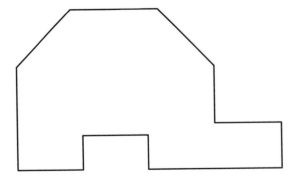

16. Open P8-5 and finish the drawing by adding the dimensions for all features. Save the drawing as P19-16.

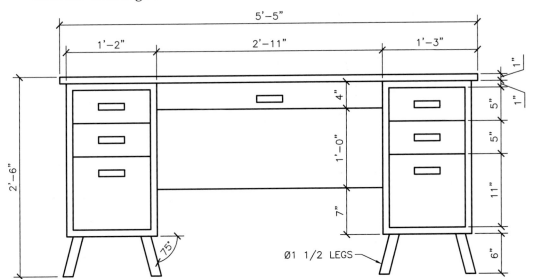

17. Draw this floor plan. Size the windows and doors to your own specifications. Save the drawing as P19-17.

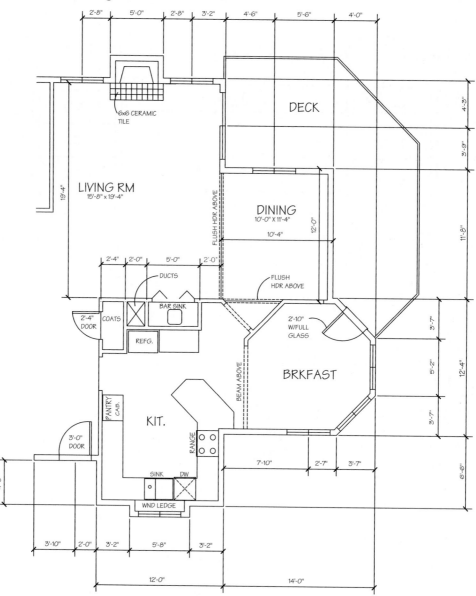

Dimensioning Features and Alternate Practices

Learning Objectives

After completing this chapter, you will be able to do the following:

✓ Add diameter and radius dimensions to a drawing.
✓ Create and use multileader styles.
✓ Prepare thread symbols and notes.
✓ Use alternate dimensioning practices.
✓ Dimension objects with arrowless dimensions.

Most objects or parts to be manufactured contain holes, slots, or other features. The size and location of these features must be described for manufacturing. This chapter describes dimensioning practices for object features and also introduces alternate dimensioning practices that are sometimes used in mechanical drawings.

Dimensioning Circles

Circles are normally dimensioned by giving the diameter. The ASME standard for dimensioning arcs is to give the radius. However, AutoCAD allows you to dimension either a circle or an arc with a diameter dimension using the **DIMDIAMETER** tool.

When you access the **DIMDIAMETER** tool, you are prompted to select an arc or circle. Once you select an arc or circle, a leader line and diameter dimension value attach to the crosshairs. Drag the leader to the desired location and length, and pick the location to place the dimension. The resulting leader points to the center of the circle or arc, as recommended by the ASME standard. See Figure 20-1.

The **DIMDIAMETER** tool also has the **Mtext**, **Text**, and **Angle** options that were introduced earlier. Use the **Mtext** or **Text** option to add information to or change the text value. Use the **Angle** option to change the angle of the text, though this practice is not common.

Ribbon
Home
> Annotation
Annotate
> Dimensions
◯
Diameter
Type
DIMDIAMETER
DDI
Menu Browser
Dimension
> Diameter
◯

DIMDIAMETER

Exercise 20-1
Complete the exercise on the Student CD.

Figure 20-1.
Using the
DIMDIAMETER tool.

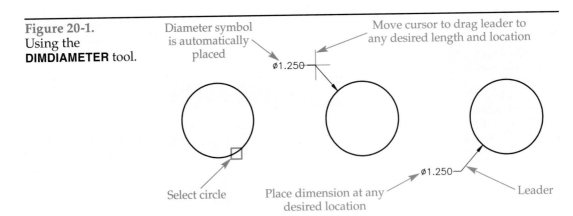

Diameter symbol
is automatically
placed

ø1.250

Move cursor to drag leader to
any desired length and location

Select circle

Place dimension at any
desired location

ø1.250

Leader

Figure 20-2.
Dimensioning holes.

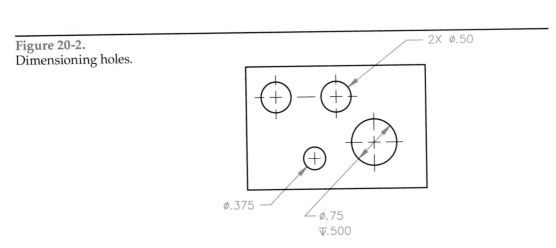

2X ø.50

ø.375

ø.75

▽.500

Dimensioning Holes

Holes are dimensioned in the view in which they appear as circles. Give location dimensions to the center and a leader showing the diameter. Leader lines can be drawn using the **DIMDIAMETER** tool, as previously described. The center mark type and size are controlled by the dimension style. Multiple holes of the same size can be noted with one hole dimension by preceding the dimension with the number of occurrences followed by X. In **Figure 20-2,** the 2X ⌀.50 dimension is an example of this practice. Use the **Mtext** or **Text** option of the **DIMDIAMETER** tool to create this dimension.

PROFESSIONAL TIP

The ASME standard recommends a small space between the object and the extension line. This happens when the **Offset from origin** setting in the dimension style is set to its default or some other desired positive value. This is very useful *except* when you are dimensioning to centerlines for the location of holes. When you pick the endpoint of the centerline, a positive value leaves a space between the centerline and the beginning of the extension line. This is not a preferred practice. Change the **Offset from origin** setting to 0 to remove the gap. Be sure to change back to the positive setting when dimensioning other objects.

Figure 20-3.
Dimension notes for machining processes. The symbols can be inserted as blocks or with lowercase letters when the gdt.shx font is used.

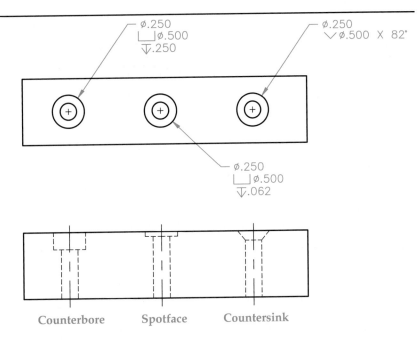

Counterbore   Spotface   Countersink

Dimensioning for Manufacturing Processes

Counterbore, spotface, and *countersink* manufacturing processes are examples of features dimensioned using symbols. These processes are dimensioned in the circular view, like holes, with a leader providing machining information in a note. See **Figure 20-3.** The **Mtext** option of the **DIMDIAMETER** tool provides a convenient method for dimensioning manufacturing processes. Many symbols are available by using the gdt.shx font. Custom symbols can be drawn as blocks. Blocks are described in Chapters 26 and 27.

Dimensioning Repetitive Features

For *repetitive features,* the number of repetitions is followed by an X, a space, and the size dimension. The dimension is then connected to the feature with a leader. Use the **Mtext** or **Text** option available with several dimensioning tools to dimension repetitive features. **Figure 20-4** shows how the **Mtext** or **Text** option is used with the **DIMANGULAR, DIMLINEAR,** and **DIMDIAMETER** tools to dimension repetitive features. The 8X note shown was created using the **MLEADER** tool, described later in this chapter.

counterbore: A larger-diameter hole machined at one end of a smaller hole that provides a place for the head of a bolt.

spotface: A larger-diameter hole machined at one end of a smaller hole that provides a smooth, recessed surface for a washer; similar to a counterbore, except not as deep.

countersink: A cone-shaped recess at one end of a hole that provides a mating surface for a screw head of the same shape.

repetitive features: Many features having the same shape and size.

Figure 20-4.
Dimensioning repetitive features (shown in color).

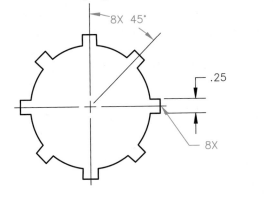

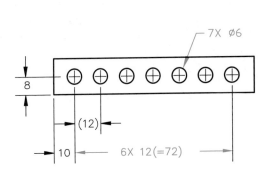

Dimensioning Arcs

DIMRADIUS

Ribbon
Home
> Annotation
Annotate
> Dimensions

Radius

Type
DIMRADIUS
DRA

Menu Browser
Dimension
> Radius

The standard for dimensioning arcs is a radius dimension, which is placed with the **DIMRADIUS** tool. When you access the **DIMRADIUS** tool, you are prompted to select an arc or circle. Once you pick an arc or circle, a leader line and radius dimension value attach to the crosshairs. Drag the leader to the desired location and length, and pick the location to place the dimension. The resulting leader points to the center of the arc or circle, as recommended by the ASME standard. See Figure 20-5.

As with the **DIMDIAMETER** tool, you can use the **Mtext** or **Text** option to add information to or change the dimension text. You can also use the **Angle** option to change the angle of the text value, though this practice is not common.

Dimensioning Arc Length

DIMARC

Ribbon
Home
> Annotation
Annotate
> Dimensions

Arc Length

Type
DIMARC
DAR

Menu Browser
Dimension
> Arc Length

The length of an arc can be dimensioned using the **DIMARC** tool. The length measures the distance along the arc segment. When you access the **DIMARC** tool, you are prompted to select an arc or polyline arc segment. Once you select the arc, the arc length symbol and dimension value attach to the crosshairs. To place the dimension, move the text to the desired location and pick. By default, the symbol is placed before the text. The ASME standard recommends placing the symbol over the text, as shown in Figure 20-6. The **New Dimension Style** dialog box controls the symbol placements.

Before placing the arc length dimension, you can add information to or change the dimension text with the **Mtext** or **Text** option, or you can use the **Angle** option to change the angle of the text. Use the **Partial** option if you do not want to dimension the length of the entire arc. Choosing this option prompts you to select a first point on the arc and a second point. The length between these two points is dimensioned. When the arc is greater than 90°, the **Leader** option is also available. This allows you to add a leader pointing to the arc being dimensioned.

Figure 20-5.
Using the **DIMRADIUS** tool to dimension arcs.

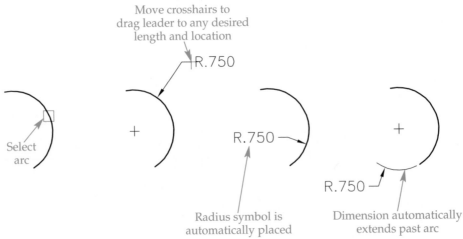

Figure 20-6.
Using the **DIMARC**
tool to dimension
the length of an arc.

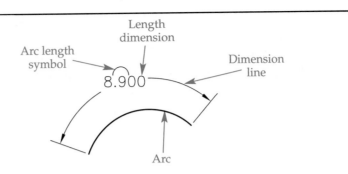

Figure 20-6.
Using the **DIMARC**
tool to dimension
the length of an arc.

Figure 20-7.
Using the
DIMJOGGED tool
to place a radius
dimension for a
large arc.

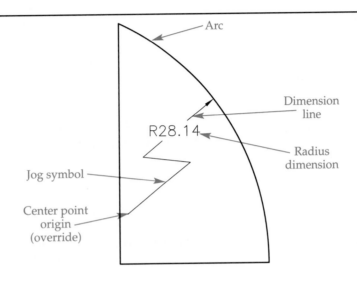

Dimensioning Large Circles and Arcs

When a circle or arc is so large that its center point cannot be displayed on the layout, use the **DIMJOGGED** tool to create the dimension. This tool allows you to draw a radius dimension by selecting a center point origin and placing a break symbol on the dimension line. After accessing the **DIMJOGGED** tool, pick an arc or circle. Then pick a point for the origin of the center location. This is the point that represents, or overrides, the actual center of the arc or circle. Select a location for the dimension line and pick a location to place the break symbol. See **Figure 20-7.** The components of the dimension can be moved by grip editing after the dimension has been placed.

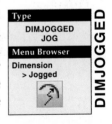

Dimensioning Fillets and Rounds

Fillets and *rounds* can be dimensioned individually as arcs, using the **DIMRADIUS** tool, or in a general note. See **Figure 20-8.** On mechanical drawings, it is common to include a general note such as ALL FILLETS AND ROUNDS R.125 UNLESS OTHERWISE SPECIFIED on the drawing.

fillets: Small inside arcs designed to strengthen inside corners.

rounds: Small arcs on outside corners used to relieve sharp corners.

Figure 20-8.
Dimensioning fillets
and rounds.

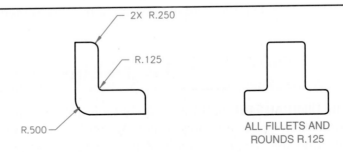

Figure 20-9.
Dimensioning curves that do not have a constant radius.

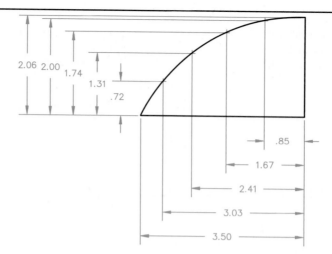

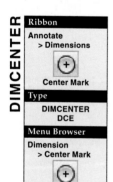

Exercise 20-3
Complete the exercise on the Student CD.

Dimensioning Curves

When possible, curves are dimensioned as arcs. When they are not in the shape of a constant-radius arc, they should be dimensioned to points along the curve using the **DIMLINEAR** tool. See Figure 20-9.

Adding Center Dashes or Centerlines

When small circles or arcs are dimensioned, the **DIMDIAMETER** and **DIMRADIUS** tools automatically add center dashes, if the current dimension style allows. If the dimension of a large circle crosses through the center, the dashes are left out. However, you can add center dashes and centerlines manually with the **DIMCENTER** tool.

DIMCENTER can be used to place either center marks or centerlines depending on the settings in the current dimension style, and the desired application. The ASME standard basically refers to AutoCAD center marks as the center dashes of centerlines. Typically, center marks are applied to circular objects that are too small to receive centerlines. Center marks are also used with arrowless dimensioning practice, regardless of circular object size, as described later in this chapter.

Once you access the **DIMCENTER** tool, you are prompted to pick an arc or circle. When you pick the object, center marks appear. The size of the center marks and the length that the centerlines extend outside the circle or arc is controlled by the **Center marks** area in the **Symbols and Arrows** tab of the **New Dimension Style** dialog box.

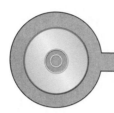

DIMCENTER

Ribbon
Annotate
> Dimensions

Center Mark

Type
DIMCENTER
DCE

Menu Browser
Dimension
> Center Mark

Leader Lines

leader: A line that connects note text to a specific feature or location on a drawing.

annotation: Text on a drawing, such as a note or dimension.

The **DIMDIAMETER** and **DIMRADIUS** tools automatically place *leader lines* when you dimension circles and arcs. AutoCAD multileaders allow you to begin and end a leader line at a specific location. Multileaders consist of single or multiple lines of *annotations*, including symbols, with the leader. Multileaders are typically used for adding specific notes, staggering a leader line to go around other drawing features, drawing multiple leaders and custom leaders, adding curved leaders for architectural applications, and aligning and combining specific notes.

The **MLEADER** tool is used to create multileaders. Multileader characteristics, such as leader format, annotation style, and arrowhead size, are controlled by multileader styles. Multiple-segment leaders can also be created, and separate leaders can be aligned and grouped. Adding and removing multiple leader lines and aligning leaders is described in Chapter 21.

Multileader Styles

The appearance of leaders created using multileader tools, from the size and style of leader text to the display of the leader line, is controlled by several different settings. *Multileader styles* are created by changing multileader settings as needed to achieve the desired appearance for your drafting application. This process is very similar to developing a dimension style.

In mechanical drafting, properly drawn leaders have one straight segment extending from the feature to a horizontal *shoulder* that is 1/8"–1/4" (3 mm–6 mm) long. While most other fields also use straight leaders, AutoCAD provides the option of drawing curved leaders, which are often used in architectural drafting. See Figure 20-10.

multileader styles: Saved configurations for the appearance of leaders.

shoulder: A short horizontal line usually added to the end of straight leader lines.

Working with Multileader Styles

Multileader styles are created using the **Multileader Style Manager** dialog box. See Figure 20-11. The **Styles:** list box displays the multileader styles defined in the current drawing. The default multileader style is a non-annotative style named Standard, which is provided along with an annotative multileader style named Annotative. You can make a multileader style current by double-clicking the style name; right-clicking on the name and selecting the **Set current** option; or picking the name and selecting the **Set Current** button. When a multileader style is current, all new multileaders are

Ribbon
Home
> Annotation
Annotate
> Multileaders
Multileader Style
Type
MLEADERSTYLE
MLS
Menu Browser
Format
> Multileader Style...

MLEADERSTYLE

Figure 20-10.
Multileader styles control the display of leaders created using the **MLEADER** tool.

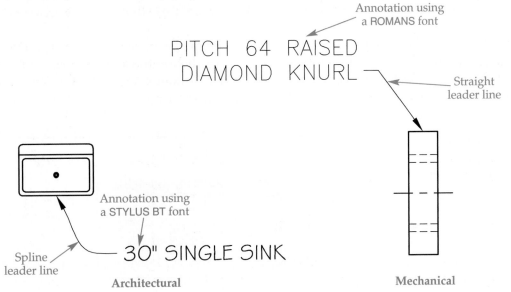

Figure 20-11.
The **Multileader Style Manager** dialog box. The Standard multileader style is the AutoCAD default.

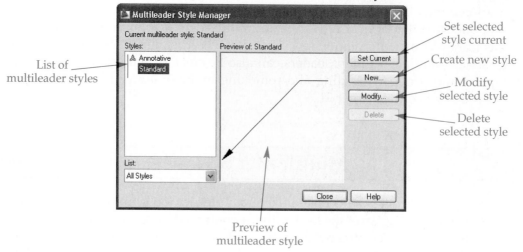

List of multileader styles

Set selected style current

Create new style

Modify selected style

Delete selected style

Preview of multileader style

created in that style. The selection in the **List:** drop-down list controls whether all styles or only the styles in use are displayed in the **Styles:** box.

The **Preview of:** image displays the characteristics of the selected multileader style. If you change any of AutoCAD's default multileader settings without first creating a new multileader style, the changes are automatically stored in a multileader style override.

Creating a New Multileader Style

To create a new multileader style, first select an existing multileader style from the **Styles:** list box to use as a base for formatting the new multileader style. Then pick the **New...** button in the **Multileader Style Manager**. This opens the **Create New Multileader Style** dialog box. See **Figure 20-12.**

Enter a descriptive name for the new multileader style, such as Architectural, Mechanical, Straight, or Spline, in the **New Style Name** text box. The **Start With:** drop-down list helps save time by basing the settings for a new style on an existing multileader style. Pick the **Annotative** check box to make the multileader style annotative. The multileader style can also be made annotative later by selecting the **Annotative** check box in the **Leader Structure** tab of the **Modify Multileader Style** dialog box, described later in this chapter.

After you make your selections, pick the **Continue** button to open the **Modify Multileader Style** dialog box, where you can adjust the multileader style's characteristics. See **Figure 20-13.** The **Leader Format**, **Leader Structure**, and **Content** tabs access the settings used for changing the way multileaders are displayed. These tabs are

Figure 20-12.
The **Create New Multileader Style** dialog box.

Name new style

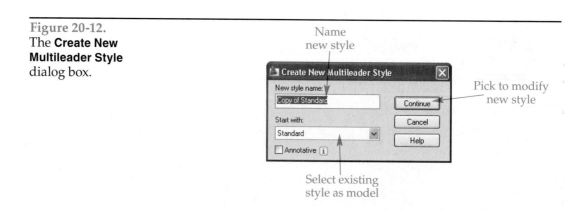

Pick to modify new style

Select existing style as model

AutoCAD and Its Applications—Basics

Figure 20-13.
The **Leader Format** tab of the **Modify Multileader Style** dialog box.

Preview image is
displayed in all tabs

General
multileader
format
settings

Multileader
arrowhead
settings

Multileader
break size
setting

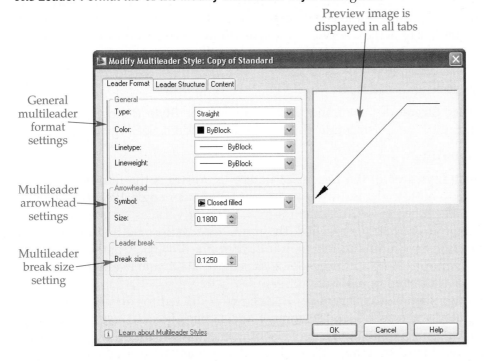

described in the next sections. After completing the information in all tabs, pick the **OK** button to return to the **Multileader Style Manager** dialog box.

NOTE

The preview in the upper-right corner of the **Modify Multileader Style** dialog box tab displays a representation of the multileader style and changes to reflect the selections you make.

Leader Format Settings

The **Leader Format** tab of the **Modify Multileader Style** dialog box controls leader line settings. Refer again to **Figure 20-13**.

General leader format settings

The **General** area contains a **Type** drop-down list that is used to specify the leader line shape. The **Straight** option produces leaders with straight-line segments. The **Spline** option produces the curved leader lines that are often used in architectural drafting. Pick the **None** option to create a multileader style that does not use a leader line, but can be associated with other multileaders using the **MLEADERALIGN** and **MLEADERCOLLECT** tools, which are described in Chapter 21.

Color, **Linetype**, and **Lineweight** drop-down lists are available for changing the multileader color, linetype, and lineweight. These options function the same for multileaders as the options available for adjusting dimension line style.

Arrowhead settings

The **Arrowhead** area provides several different arrowhead options and controls the arrowhead size. Select the arrowhead style from the **Symbol:** drop-down list. The arrowhead symbol options are the same as those for dimension style arrowheads. The **Size:** text box allows you to change the size of the leader arrowhead. The default value is .18. An arrowhead size of .125″ (3 mm) is used on most drawings.

Adjusting break size

The **Leader Break** area controls the amount of leader line removed by the **DIMBREAK** tool. Enter or select a value in the **Break size:** text box to specify the total length of the break. The default size is .125. ASME standards do not recommend breaking leader lines.

Leader Structure Settings

The **Leader Structure** tab of the **Modify Multileader Style** dialog box contains settings that control the construction and size of multileaders. See **Figure 20-14.**

Setting constraints

The **Constraints** area of the **Leader Structure** tab restricts the number of points requested when a multileader is drawn and defines the leader angle. Pick the **Maximum leader points** check box to set the maximum number of vertices on the leader line. After the maximum number is reached, the multileader is formed automatically. To use fewer than the maximum number of points, press the [Enter] key at the Specify next point: prompt while creating a multileader. Deselect the **Maximum leader points** check box to allow an unlimited number of vertices.

The first two segments of the leader line can be restricted to certain angles using the **First segment angle** and **Second segment angle** check boxes. Deselect the check boxes to draw leader lines at any angle. Select the check boxes and pick a value from the drop-down list to restrict the angle of the leader segment according to the selected value. The **Ortho** mode setting overrides the angle constraints, so it is advisable to turn **Ortho** mode off while using this tool.

PROFESSIONAL TIP

The ASME standard for leaders recommends that leader lines not have angles less than 15° or greater than 75° from horizontal. Use the **First segment angle** and **Second segment angle** settings to help maintain this standard.

Figure 20-14.
The **Leader Structure** tab of the **Modify Multileader Style** dialog box.

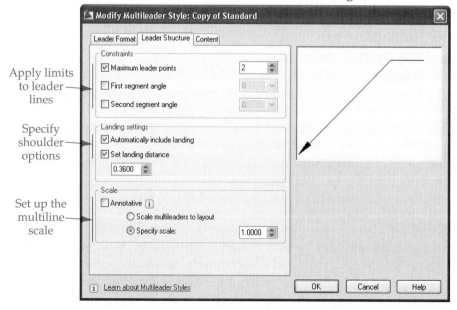

Landing settings

The **Landing settings** area of the **Leader Structure** tab controls the display and size of the *landing* and is only available with straight multileader styles. Select the **Automatically include landing** check box to display a shoulder automatically when the second point of a leader line has been selected. This is the preferred method of creating straight leader lines. Deselect the check box to create leaders without shoulders, or to draw the shoulders manually as the third leader point. When the **Automatically include landing** check box is selected, the **Set landing distance** check box becomes available for selection. Pick the **Set landing distance** check box to define a specific shoulder length, typically 1/8"–1/4" (3 mm–6 mm), in the text box. Deselect the text box to be prompted for the shoulder length when you place a multileader.

Scale options

The **Scale** area of the **Leader Structure** tab is used to set the scale factor for all multileaders in the drawing. To create annotative multileaders, first make the multileader style annotative by selecting the **Annotative** check box. If you picked the **Annotative** check box in the **Create New Multileader Style** dialog box, the **Annotative** check box is already selected.

Select the **Scale dimensions to layout** radio button if you are adding multileaders in a floating viewport in paper space. You must add multileaders to the model in a floating viewport in order for this option to function. Scaling multileaders to the layout allows the overall scale to adjust according to the active floating viewport by setting the overall scale equal to the viewport scale factor. Pick the **Use overall scale of** radio button to enter the drawing scale factor that will be used to adjust the size of multileaders according to a specific drawing scale. The scale factor is multiplied by the plotted dimension size to get the model space dimension size.

Content Settings

The **Content** tab of the **Modify Multileader Style** dialog box, shown in Figure 20-15, controls the display of text or a block with the leader line. Use the **Multileader type:**

Figure 20-15.
The **Content** tab of the **Modify Multileader Style** dialog box with the **Mtext** multileader type selected.

Select the multileader type

Set up multileader text options

Specify how the multileader attaches to mtext

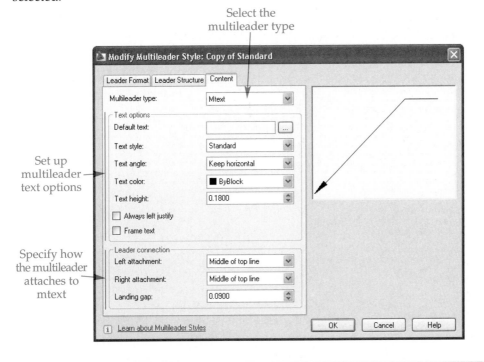

Figure 20-16.
Examples of each multileader content type.

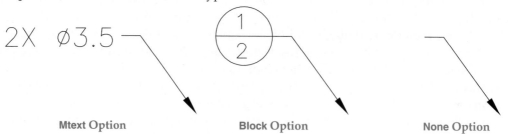

Mtext Option   Block Option   None Option

drop-down list to select the type of object to be inserted and attached to the end of the leader line or shoulder. The options include **Mtext**, **Block**, and **None**. See **Figure 20-16**.

Attaching Mtext

Pick the **Mtext** option from the **Multileader type:** drop-down list to attach a multiline text object to the leader. The **Mtext** option is selected in **Figure 20-15**. The **Text options** area of the **Content** tab is displayed when **Mtext** is selected as the content type.

The **Default text** option allows you to use the same text automatically for all multileaders. This is useful when the same note or symbol is required in many places throughout a drawing. Pick the ellipses (...) button to return to the drawing window and use the multiline text editor to enter text that will be used each time the leader is drawn. Pick the **OK** button to return to the **Modify Multileader Style** dialog box.

Multileaders use the Standard text style by default. Text styles must be defined or loaded in the current drawing before they are available for use in multileader text. Once loaded, a multileader text style can be selected from the **Text style** drop-down list.

Select an option from the **Text angle** drop-down list to control the angle at which text is placed in reference to the angle of the leader line or shoulder. **Figure 20-17** shows the effects of applying each text angle option to the same multileader. Use the **Text color** drop-down list to select a color for the text. The multileader text color default is ByBlock. Define the text height by entering a value in the **Text height** text box. Multileader text height is usually the same as dimension text height.

Figure 20-17.
Text angle options available for mtext.

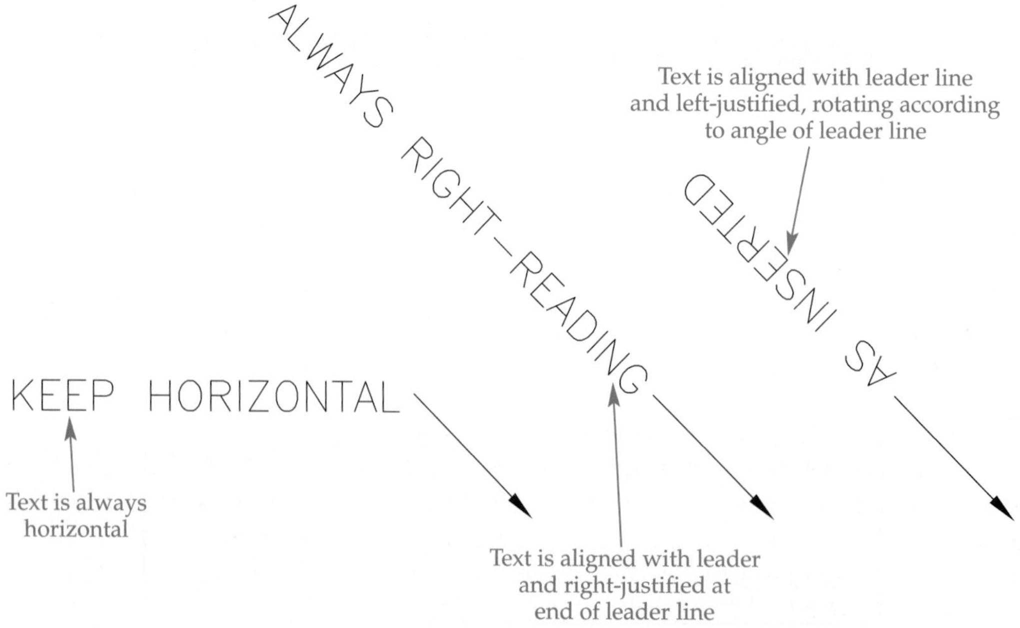

ALWAYS RIGHT-READING

Text is aligned with leader line
and left-justified, rotating according
to angle of leader line

AS INSERTED

KEEP HORIZONTAL

Text is always
horizontal

Text is aligned with leader
and right-justified at
end of leader line

Figure 20-18.
Placement of mtext is controlled by the options in the **Content** tab of the **Modify Multileader Style** dialog box. The shaded examples are the recommended ASME standards.

	Top of Top Line	Middle of Top Line	Middle of Multiline Text	Middle of Bottom Line	Bottom of Bottom Line
Text on Left Side	⌀.250 ⌴⌀.500 ▽.062	⌀.250 ⌴⌀.500 ▽.062	⌀.250 ⌴⌀.500 ▽.062	⌀.250 ⌴⌀.500 ▽.062	⌀.250 ⌴⌀.500 ▽.062
Text on Right Side	⌀.250 ⌴⌀.500 ▽.062	⌀.250 ⌴⌀.500 ▽.062	⌀.250 ⌴⌀.500 ▽.062	⌀.250 ⌴⌀.500 ▽.062	⌀.250 ⌴⌀.500 ▽.062

The **Always left justify** option forces the multiline text to be left-justified, regardless of the direction of the leader line. Pick the **Frame text** check box to create a box around the multiline text box. The default properties of the frame are controlled by the settings of the current multileader style.

The **Leader connection** area of the **Content** tab is also displayed when the **Mtext** type is selected. This area contains options that determine how the mtext object is positioned relative to the endpoint of the leader line shoulder. Use the **Left attachment:** drop-down list to define where multiple lines of text are positioned when the leader is on the left side of the text. Use the **Right attachment:** drop-down list to define where multiple lines of text are positioned when the leader is on the right side of the text. These options are shown in **Figure 20-18**. The **Underline bottom line** option causes a line to be drawn along the bottom of the multiline text box. The **Underline all text** option underlines each line of leader text. The **Leading gap** text box is used to specify the space between the leader line or shoulder and the text. The default is .09, but .063 is standard.

PROFESSIONAL TIP

Common drafting practice is to use the **Middle of bottom line** option for left-sided text and the **Middle of top line** option for right-sided text. These are the default settings.

Inserting a symbol

Pick the **Block** option from the **Multileader type:** drop-down list to insert a specified *block* at the end of the leader. Blocks are explained in detail in Chapters 26 and 27. The **Block** area of the **Content** tab is displayed when the **Block** option is selected. See **Figure 20-19.**

A variety of block symbols that contain attributes are available by default from the **Source block:** drop-down list. You also have the option of using your own saved block by picking the **User Block...** option. The **Select Custom Content Block** dialog box is displayed when you pick the **User Block...** option. Pick a block from the **Select from Drawing Blocks:** drop-down list and then pick **OK.**

Use the **Attachment:** drop-down list to specify how the block is attached to the leader line. Pick the **Insertion point** option to attach the block to the leader according to the block insertion point, or base point. Choose the **Center extents** option to attach the block directly to the leader, aligned to the block's center, even if the block insertion point is not on the block itself. See **Figure 20-20.**

Figure 20-19.
The **Content** tab of the **Modify Multileader Style** dialog box with the **Block** multileader type selected.

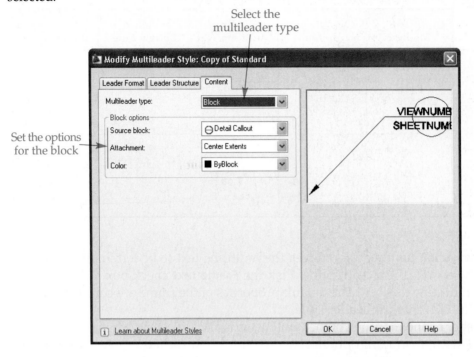

Select the multileader type

Set the options for the block

Figure 20-20.
Adjusting multileader block attachment.

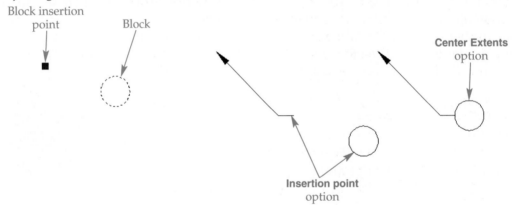

Block insertion point

Block

Center Extents option

Insertion point option

The block color default is ByBlock. Use the **Color** drop-down list to select a color for the block. If the color you want is not in the drop-down list, pick **Select Color...** to select a color from the **Select Color** dialog box.

Using no content

Select the **None** option from the **Multileader type:** drop-down list to end the leader with no annotation. The **None** option can be used whenever there is a need to create only a leader, without text or a symbol attached to the leader line or shoulder.

NOTE

Leaders can be added to existing multileaders using the **Add Leader** tool. This eliminates the need to create a separate multileader style that uses the **None** multileader type for most applications.

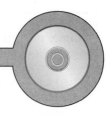

Modifying Multileader Styles

You can change the current multileader style without affecting existing multileaders. The changes are applied only to multileaders added using the current style. Use the **Multileader Style Manager** to change existing multileader styles. Select the **Modify** button to reopen the **Modify Multileader Style** dialog box, which allows you to make changes to the style highlighted in the **Styles:** list box.

You can rename existing multileader styles in the **Multileader Style Manager**. Either slowly pick the style name twice or right-click the name and select the **Rename** option. To delete a multileader style, right-click on the name and select the **Delete** option, or pick the style and select the **Delete** button. The current multileader style and multileader styles that have been used to create leaders in the drawing cannot be deleted, so the **Delete** option is not available for these styles. If you want to delete a style that is current or in use, make a different style current, or change the leaders in the drawing to a different style.

Setting a Multileader Style Current

You can set a multileader style current using the **Multileader Style Manager** by double-clicking the style in the **Styles** list box, right-clicking on the name and selecting the **Set current** option, or picking the style and selecting the **Set Current** button. To set a multileader style current without opening the **Multileader Style Manager**, use the **Multileader Style** drop-down list located in the **Annotation** panel on the **Home** tab or the **Multileaders** panel on the **Annotate** tab of the ribbon.

PROFESSIONAL TIP

You can import multileader styles from existing drawings using **DesignCenter**. See Chapter 5 for more information about using **DesignCenter** to import file content.

Placing Multileaders

Once you develop a multileader style and make the style current, you are ready to insert a leader. Leaders are drawn using the **MLEADER** tool. Additional tools are available for adding and removing multiple leader lines, arranging multiple leaders, and combining leader content.

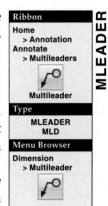

Ribbon
Home > Annotation
Annotate > Multileaders
Multileader
Type
MLEADER MLD
Menu Browser
Dimension > Multileader

MLEADER

Inserting a Multileader

How you place a leader depends on the multileader style settings you select. In general, there are three methods for inserting a multileader, depending on what portion of the leader is selected first. Review the components of a leader, shown in Figure 20-21, before reading the options for creating a multileader.

The first option for inserting a leader is **Specify leader arrowhead location**. To use this option, first select the location at which you want the arrowhead to point. Then choose where the leader ends and the shoulder begins. If the **Mtext** option is active, enter leader text using the multiline text editor.

Figure 20-21.
Examples of leaders created using the **MLEADER** tool. A — An architectural leader created using a spline leader line, the **Specify leader arrowhead location** option, and three leader points. B — A mechanical leader created using a straight leader line, the **leader Landing first** option, and two leader points.

A

B

The second method uses the **leader Landing first** option. To use this technique, first select where the leader ends and the shoulder begins. Then choose the location where the arrowhead points. If the **Mtext** option is active, enter leader text using the multiline text editor.

The third method involves picking the **Content first** option. To use this technique, first define the leader content. If the **Mtext** option is active, type text using the multiline text editor. Then you can select the location where the arrowhead points.

Select **Options** to access a list of options that can be used to override the current multileader style characteristics. These options are the same as those found in the **Modify Multileader Style** dialog box.

NOTE

The **QLEADER** and **LEADER** tools can be used to create leader lines and specific notes similar to those drawn using multileaders. However, these tools provide fewer options for controlling the display of leaders.

Exercise 20-5
Complete the exercise on the Student CD.

Dimensioning Chamfers

chamfer: An angled surface used to relieve sharp corners.

Chamfers of 45° are dimensioned either with a leader giving the angle and linear dimension, or with two linear dimensions. This can be accomplished using the **MLEADER** tool. See Figure 20-22. Chamfers other than 45° must have either the angle and a linear dimension or two linear dimensions placed on the view. See Figure 20-23. The **DIMLINEAR** and **DIMANGULAR** tools are used for this purpose.

AutoCAD and Its Applications—Basics

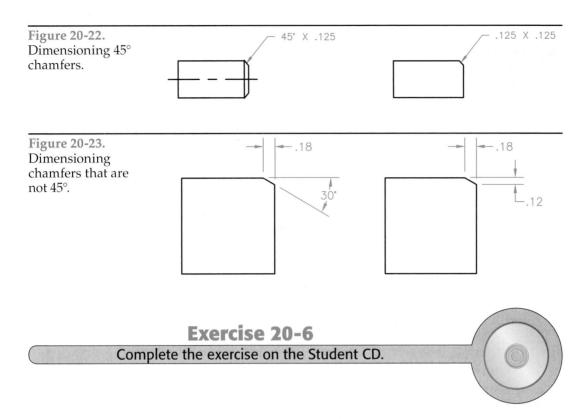

Figure 20-22.
Dimensioning 45°
chamfers.

45° X .125

.125 X .125

Figure 20-23.
Dimensioning
chamfers that are
not 45°.

.18

30°

.18

.12

Exercise 20-6
Complete the exercise on the Student CD.

Thread Drawings and Notes

The parts of a screw thread are shown in **Figure 20-24.** Threads are commonly shown on a drawing with a simplified representation. Thread depth is shown with a hidden line. This method is used for both external and internal threads. See **Figure 20-25.** A chamfer is often placed on the external thread. This makes it easier to engage the mating thread.

The objects show the reader that a thread exists, but the thread note gives exact specifications. The thread note is typically connected to the thread with a leader. See

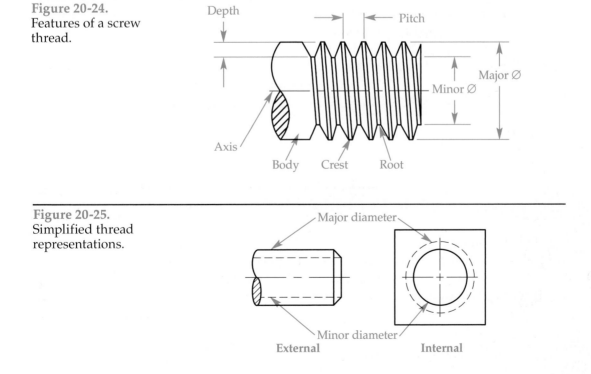

Figure 20-24.
Features of a screw
thread.

Depth

Pitch

Major ⌀

Minor ⌀

Axis

Body   Crest   Root

Figure 20-25.
Simplified thread
representations.

Major diameter

Minor diameter

External   **Internal**

Figure 20-26.
Displaying the thread note with a leader.

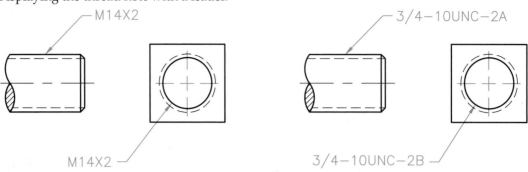

Figure 20-26. The most common thread forms are the Unified and metric screw threads. The thread note for Unified screw threads must be specified in the following format:

3/4 -	10UNC -	2A
(1)	(2) (3)	(4) (5)

(1) Major diameter of thread. Given as a fraction or number.
(2) Number of threads per inch.
(3) Thread series. UNC = Unified National Coarse. UNF = Unified National Fine.
(4) Class of fit. 1 = large tolerance. 2 = general purpose tolerance. 3 = tight tolerance.
(5) Thread type. A = external thread. B = internal thread.

The thread note for metric threads is specified in the following format:

M	14 X 2
(1)	(2) (3)

(1) M = metric thread.
(2) Major diameter in millimeters.
(3) Pitch in millimeters.

There are too many Unified and metric screw threads to describe in detail here. Refer to the ***Machinery's Handbook***, published by Industrial Press Inc., or a comprehensive mechanical drafting text for more information.

Exercise 20-7
Complete the exercise on the Student CD.

Alternate Dimensioning Practices

Dimension lines are often omitted on drawings in industries in which computer-controlled machining processes are used or unconventional dimensioning practices are required because of product features. Arrowless, tabular, and chart dimensioning are three types of dimensioning in which dimension lines are omitted.

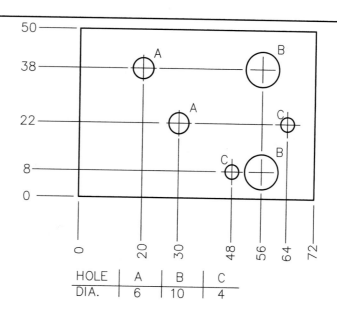

Figure 20-27.
Arrowless
dimensioning.

HOLE	A	B	C
DIA.	6	10	4

Arrowless Dimensioning

    Arrowless dimensioning is becoming popular in mechanical drafting. It is also used in electronics drafting, especially for chassis layout. Each dimension in arrowless dimensioning represents a measurement originating from a *datum*. Holes or other features are labeled with identification letters. Sizes for these features are given in a table placed on the drawing. See **Figure 20-27.**

Tabular Dimensioning

    In *tabular dimensioning,* each feature is labeled with a letter or number that correlates to a table. The table gives the location of features from the X and Y axes. See **Figure 20-28.** It also provides the depth of features from a Z axis, when appropriate.

arrowless dimensioning: Type of dimensioning that includes only extension lines and text aligned with the extension lines.

datum: The 0 dimension, baseline, or common point from which all measurements are made in arrowless dimensioning.

tabular dimensioning: A form of arrowless dimensioning in which dimensions are shown in a table.

Figure 20-28.
Tabular dimensioning. (Doug Major)

HOLE	QTY.	DESCRIP.	X	Y	Z
A1	1	⌀7	64	38	18
B1	1	⌀5	5	38	THRU
B2	1	⌀5	72	38	THRU
B3	1	⌀5	64	11	THRU
B4	1	⌀5	79	11	THRU
C1	1	⌀4	19	38	THRU
C2	1	⌀4	48	38	THRU
C3	1	⌀4	5	21	THRU
C4	1	⌀4	30	21	THRU
C5	1	⌀4	72	21	THRU
C6	1	⌀4	19	11	THRU
D1	1	⌀2.5	48	6	THRU

UNLESS OTHERWISE SPECIFIED
■ — MILLIMETERS
AND TOLERANCES FOR:
1 PLACE DIMS: ± .1
2 PLACE DIMS: ± .01
3 PLACE DIMS: ± .005
ANGULAR: ± 30'
FRACTIONAL: ± 1/32
FINISH: 3.2 ?m

✱ MAJOR DESIGN ✱

| DR: D. MAJOR | SCALE: 1.5:1 | DATE: 27FEB | APPD: |

MTRL:
STAINLESS STEEL
NAME:
MOUNTING BASE
B | PART NO: 10099 | REV: 0

NOTES:
1. INTERPRET DIMENSIONS AND TOLERANCES PER ASME Y14.5M—1994.
2. REMOVE ALL BURRS AND SHARP EDGES.

Figure 20-29.
Chart dimensioning.

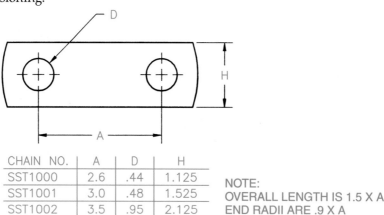

CHAIN NO.	A	D	H
SST1000	2.6	.44	1.125
SST1001	3.0	.48	1.525
SST1002	3.5	.95	2.125

NOTE:
OVERALL LENGTH IS 1.5 X A
END RADII ARE .9 X A

Chart Dimensioning

chart dimensioning:
A type of dimensioning in which the variable dimensions are shown with letters that correlate to a chart where the possible dimensions are given.

Chart dimensioning may take the form of unidirectional, aligned, arrowless, or tabular dimensioning. It provides flexibility when dimensions change as requirements of the product change. See **Figure 20-29.**

Creating Arrowless Dimensions

ordinate dimensioning:
AutoCAD's term for arrowless dimensioning.

AutoCAD refers to arrowless dimensioning as *ordinate dimensioning*. Ordinate dimensions are drawn using the **DIMORDINATE** tool. In order to create ordinate dimensions accurately, you must move the default origin (0,0,0 coordinate) to the object datum. This involves understanding the world coordinate system (WCS) and user coordinate system (UCS). Once you establish the datum by temporarily moving the origin, use the **DIMORDINATE** tool to place arrowless dimensions.

WCS and UCS

The origin (0,0,0 coordinate) of the WCS has been in the lower-left corner of the drawing window for the drawings you have created throughout this textbook. In most cases, this is appropriate. However, when you use arrowless dimensioning on a drawing, it is best to have the dimensions originate from a primary datum, which is often a corner of the object. Depending on how the object is drawn, this point may or may not align with the WCS origin.

The WCS is fixed; a UCS, on the other hand, can be moved to any orientation. User coordinate systems are described in detail in *AutoCAD and Its Applications—Advanced*. In general, a UCS allows you to set your own coordinate system.

Measurements made with the **DIMORDINATE** tool originate from the current UCS origin. By default, this is the 0,0 origin. You can move the UCS origin to the corner of an object or an appropriate datum feature by selecting **Tools** > **Move UCS** from the menu browser. You are then prompted to specify a new origin point. Use an object snap mode to select the corner of the object or the appropriate datum feature. See **Figure 20-30.**

When you finish drawing arrowless dimensions from a datum, you can leave the UCS origin at the datum or move it back to the WCS origin. To return to the WCS, select **Tools** > **New UCS** > **World** from the menu browser.

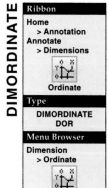

DIMORDINATE

Ribbon
Home
> Annotation
Annotate
> Dimensions

Ordinate

Type
DIMORDINATE
DOR

Menu Browser
Dimension
> Ordinate

Figure 20-30.
Move the UCS origin to the appropriate datum location.

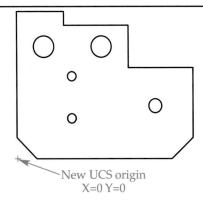

New UCS origin
X=0 Y=0

Using the Dimordinate Tool

When you use the **DIMORDINATE** tool, AutoCAD automatically places an extension line and a dimension at the location you pick. The dimension is measured as an X or Y coordinate distance.

Since you are working in the XY plane, it is often best to use vertical and horizontal polar tracking or turn **Ortho** mode on. Also, if the drawing includes circles, use the **DIMCENTER** tool to place center marks in the circles. See **Figure 20-31.** This makes the drawing conform to ASME standards and provides something to pick when you dimension the circle locations.

Now you are ready to start placing ordinate dimensions. Access the **DIMORDINATE** tool. When the Specify feature location: prompt appears, move the crosshairs to the point or feature to be dimensioned. If the feature is the corner of the object, pick the corner. If the feature is a circle, pick the *end* of the center mark, not the center of the object. This leaves the required space between the center mark and the extension line. See **Figure 20-32.** Zoom in if needed and use the object snap modes. The next prompt asks for the leader endpoint. This actually refers to the extension line endpoint, so pick the endpoint of the extension line.

Figure 20-31.
Add center marks to circles in the drawing.

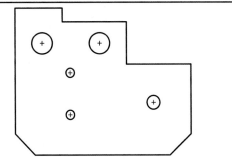

Figure 20-32.
Pick the endpoints of center marks to establish the correct offset, or develop a specific dimension style with an extension line origin offset of 0 for placing dimensions from center marks.

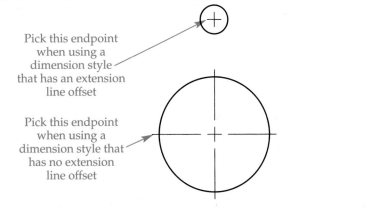

Pick this endpoint when using a dimension style that has an extension line offset

Pick this endpoint when using a dimension style that has no extension line offset

If the X axis or Y axis distance between the feature and the extension line endpoint is large, the axis AutoCAD uses for the dimension by default may not be the desired axis. When this happens, use the **Xdatum** or **Ydatum** option to specify the axis from which the dimension originates. The **Mtext**, **Text**, and **Angle** options are identical to the options available with other dimensioning tools. Pick the leader endpoint to complete the tool.

Figure 20-33A shows the ordinate dimensions placed on the object. Notice that the dimension text is aligned with the extension lines. Aligned dimensioning is standard with ordinate dimensioning. Finally, complete the drawing by adding any missing lines, such as centerlines or fold lines. Identify the holes with letters and create a corre-lated dimensioning table. See Figure 20-33B.

Figure 20-33.
A—Placing ordinate dimensions.
B—Completing the drawing.

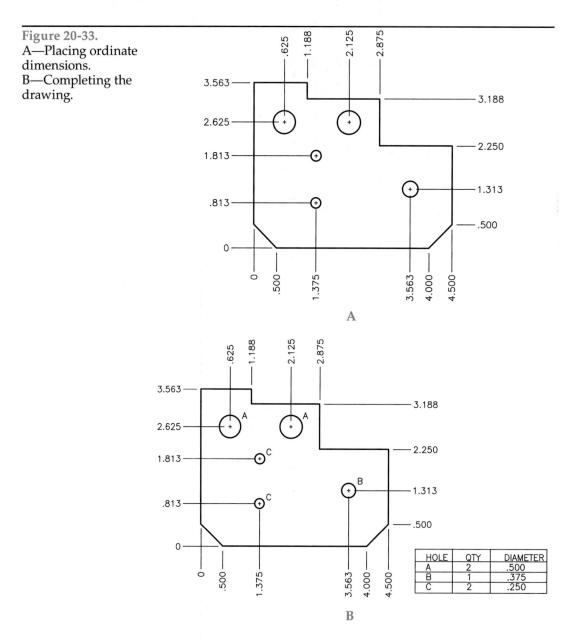

PROFESSIONAL TIP

Most ordinate dimensioning tasks work best with polar tracking or **Ortho** mode on. However, when the extension line is too close to an adjacent dimension, it is best to stagger the extension line as shown in the following illustration. With **Ortho** mode off, the extension line is automatically staggered when you pick the offset second extension line point, as shown here.

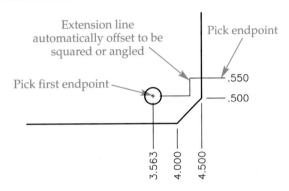

Extension line automatically offset to be squared or angled

Pick endpoint

Pick first endpoint

.550

.500

3.563   4.000   4.500

Exercise 20-8

Complete the exercise on the Student CD.

Template Development

Chapter 20

Like dimension styles, multileader styles require effort to set up properly. By adding multileader styles to your drawing templates, you can avoid having to repeat this process each time you begin a new drawing. Refer to the Student CD for detailed instructions to add multileader styles to your mechanical, architectural, and civil drawing templates.

Chapter Test

Answer the following questions. Write your answers on a separate sheet of paper or complete the electronic chapter test on the Student CD.

1. Which tool provides diameter dimensions for circles?
2. Which tool provides radius dimensions for arcs?
3. Explain how to add a center mark to a circle without using the **DIMDIAMETER** or **DIMRADIUS** tool.
4. List at least three common uses for multileaders.
5. What is the proper length for the shoulder of a leader in mechanical drafting?
6. What is the most common size for leader arrowheads?
7. What angle constraints should you use for leaders to maintain the ASME standard?
8. How do you make a multileader style current?
9. Describe the three different ways you can place a multileader.
10. Describe two ways to dimension a 45° chamfer.

---

11. Identify the elements of this Unified screw thread note: 1/2-13UNC-2B.
    A. 1/2
    B. 13
    C. UNC
    D. 2
    E. B
12. Identify the elements of this metric screw thread note: M 14 X 2.
    A. M
    B. 14
    C. 2
13. Define the term *arrowless dimensioning.*
14. What term does AutoCAD use to refer to arrowless dimensioning?
15. What is the importance of the user coordinate system (UCS) when drawing arrowless dimensions?

Drawing Problems

Use one of your templates for each problem. Set limits, units, dimension styles, and other parameters as needed. Use the following general guidelines.

A. Use dimension styles and multileader styles that match the type of drawing as described in this chapter and Chapters 18 and 19.
B. Use object snap modes to your best advantage.
C. Apply dimensions accurately using ASME or other related industry/architectural standards. Dimensions are in inches, or feet and inches, unless otherwise specified.
D. Set separate layers for dimensions and other features.
E. For mechanical drawings, place the following general notes 1/2″ from the lower-left corner:

   NOTES:

   1. INTERPRET DIMENSIONS AND TOLERANCES PER ASME Y14.5M-1994.

   2. REMOVE ALL BURRS AND SHARP EDGES.

   3. UNLESS OTHERWISE SPECIFIED, ALL DIMENSIONS ARE IN INCHES (or MILLIMETERS as applicable).

▼ Basic

1.

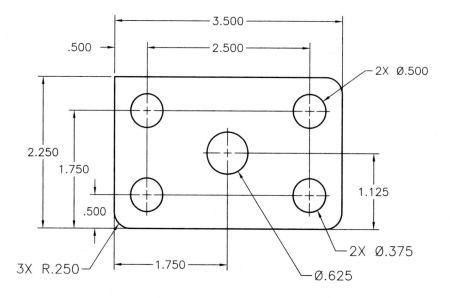

2.

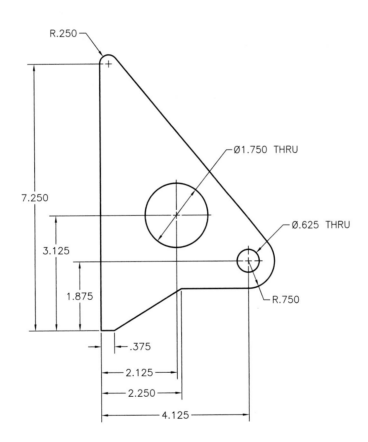

6.000
5.375
.625
4X Ø9/16
4X R.500
.625
5.375
6.000
.500

3.

R.250
7.250
Ø1.750 THRU
Ø.625 THRU
3.125
1.875
R.750
.375
2.125
2.250
4.125

4.

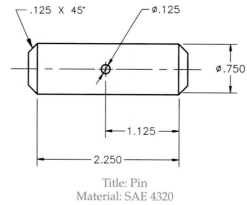

Title: Pin
Material: SAE 4320

5.

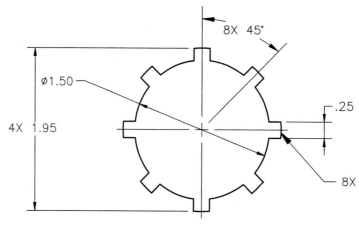

Title: Spline
Material: MS .125 THK

AutoCAD and Its Applications—Basics

6.

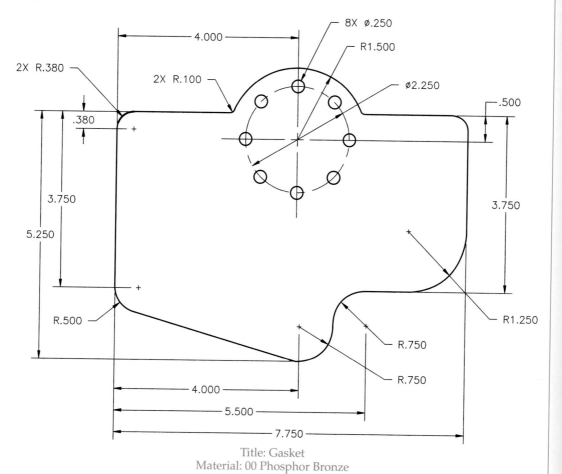

Title: Gasket
Material: 00 Phosphor Bronze

7.

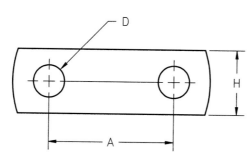

CHAIN NO.	A	D	H
SST1000	2.6	.44	1.125
SST1001	3.0	.48	1.525
SST1002	3.5	.95	2.125

Note:
Overall Length is 1.5XA
end radii are .9XA

Title: Chain Link
Material: Steel

8.

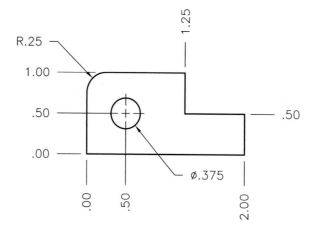

9.

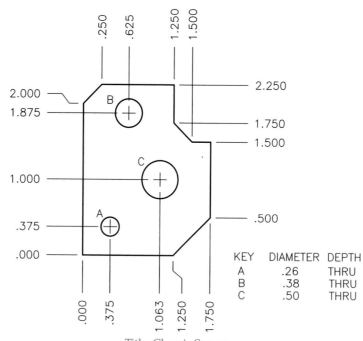

Title: Chassis Spacer
Material: .008 Aluminum

KEY	DIAMETER	DEPTH
A	.26	THRU
B	.38	THRU
C	.50	THRU

10.

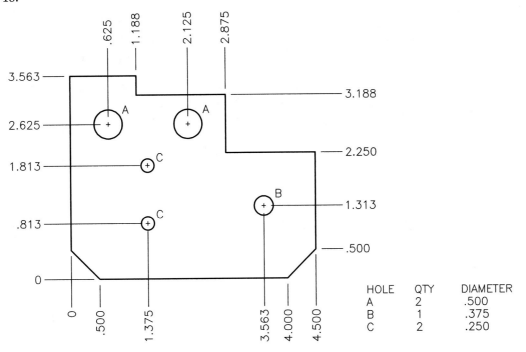

HOLE	QTY	DIAMETER
A	2	.500
B	1	.375
C	2	.250

Title: Chassis
Material: Aluminum .100 THK

11.

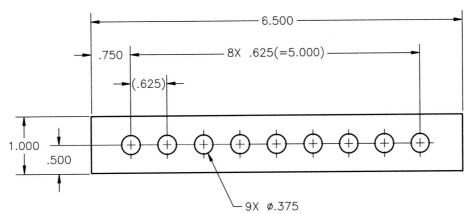

9X ⌀.375

▼ Intermediate

12. Convert the given drawing to a drawing with the holes located using arrowless dimensioning based on the X and Y coordinates given in the table. Place a table above your title block with Hole (identification), Quantity, Description, and Depth (Z axis).

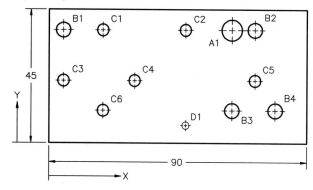

HOLE	QTY	DESC	X	Y	Z
A1	1	⌀7	64	38	18
B1	1	⌀5	5	38	THRU
B2	1	⌀5	72	38	THRU
B3	1	⌀5	64	11	THRU
B4	1	⌀5	79	11	THRU
C1	1	⌀4	19	38	THRU
C2	1	⌀4	48	38	THRU
C3	1	⌀4	5	21	THRU
C4	1	⌀4	30	21	THRU
C5	1	⌀4	72	21	THRU
C6	1	⌀4	19	11	THRU
D1	1	⌀2.5	48	6	THRU

Title: Base
Material: Bronze

For Problems 13-15, use the isometric drawing provided to create a multiview orthographic drawing for the part. Include only the views necessary to fully describe the object. Dimension according to the ASME standards described in this chapter using a dimension style appropriate for mechanical drafting.

13.

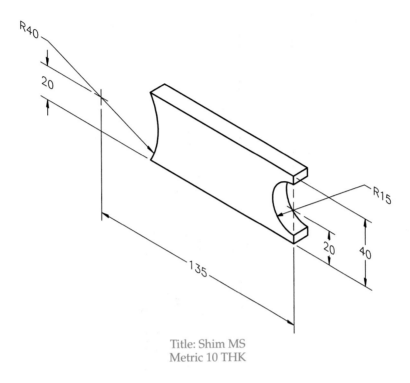

Title: Shim MS
Metric 10 THK

14. Half of the object is removed for clarity. The entire object should be drawn.

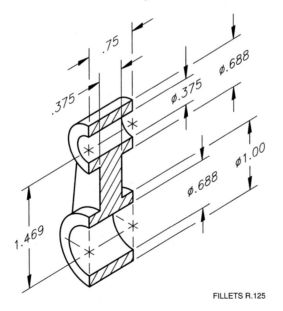

FILLETS R.125

Title: Shaft Support
Material: Cast Iron (CI)

15. Half of the object is removed for clarity. The entire object should be drawn.

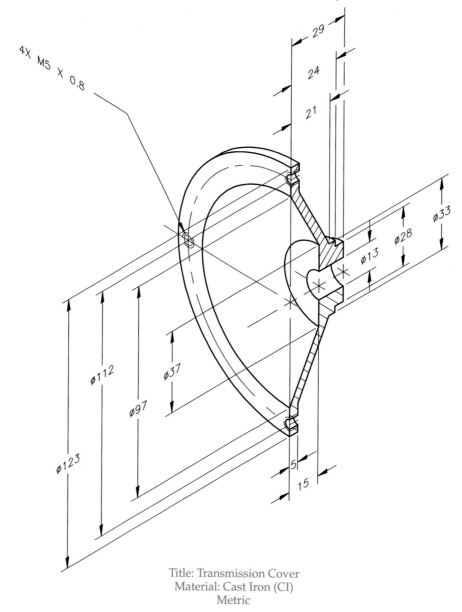

4X M5 X 0.8

29

24

21

ø33

ø28

ø13

ø112

ø37

ø97

ø123

5

15

Title: Transmission Cover
Material: Cast Iron (CI)
Metric

16.

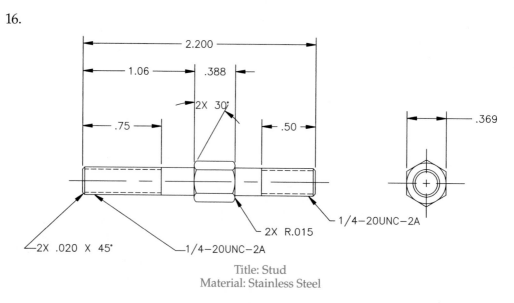

2.200

1.06

.388

2X 30°

.75

.50

.369

2X .020 X 45°

1/4-20UNC-2A

2X R.015

1/4-20UNC-2A

Title: Stud
Material: Stainless Steel

17.

HOLE LAYOUT

KEY	SIZE	DEPTH	NO. REQD
A	⌀.250	THRU	6
B	⌀.125	THRU	4
C	⌀.375	THRU	4
D	R.125	THRU	2

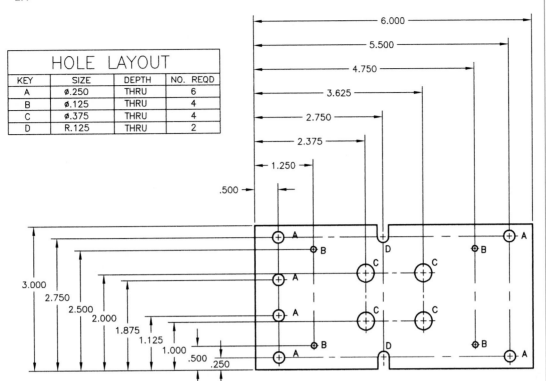

Title: Chassis Base (datum dimensioning)
Material: 12 gage Aluminum

18.

HOLE LAYOUT

KEY	SIZE	DEPTH	NO. REQD
A	⌀.250	THRU	6
B	⌀.125	THRU	4
C	⌀.375	THRU	4
D	R.125	THRU	2

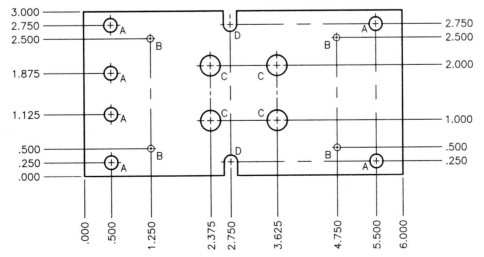

Title: Chassis Base (arrowless dimensioning)
Material: 12 gage Aluminum

HOLE LAYOUT

KEY	X	Y	SIZE	TOL
A1	.500	2.750	⌀.250	±.002
A2	.500	1.875	⌀.250	±.002
A3	.500	1.125	⌀.250	±.002
A4	.500	.250	⌀.250	±.002
A5	5.500	2.750	⌀.250	±.002
A6	5.500	.250	⌀.250	±.002
B1	1.250	2.500	⌀.125	±.001
B2	1.250	.500	⌀.125	±.001
B3	4.750	2.500	⌀.125	±.001
B4	4.750	.500	⌀.125	±.001
C1	2.375	2.000	⌀.375	±.005
C2	2.375	1.000	⌀.375	±.005
C3	3.625	2.000	⌀.375	±.005
C4	3.625	1.000	⌀.375	±.005
D1	2.750	2.750	R.125	±.002
D2	2.750	.250	R.125	±.002

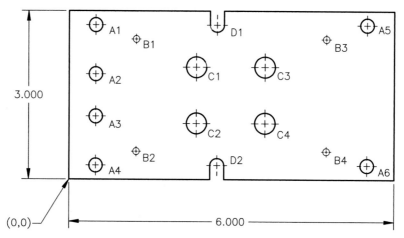

Title: Chassis Base (arrowless tabular dimensioning)
Material: 12 gage Aluminum

20.

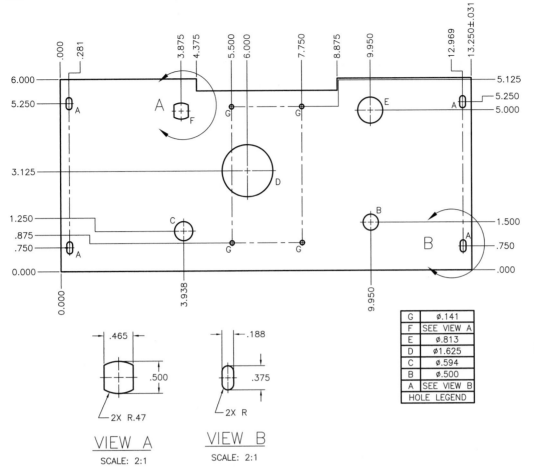

VIEW A
SCALE: 2:1

VIEW B
SCALE: 2:1

G	ø.141
F	SEE VIEW A
E	ø.813
D	ø1.625
C	ø.594
B	ø.500
A	SEE VIEW B
HOLE LEGEND	

21.

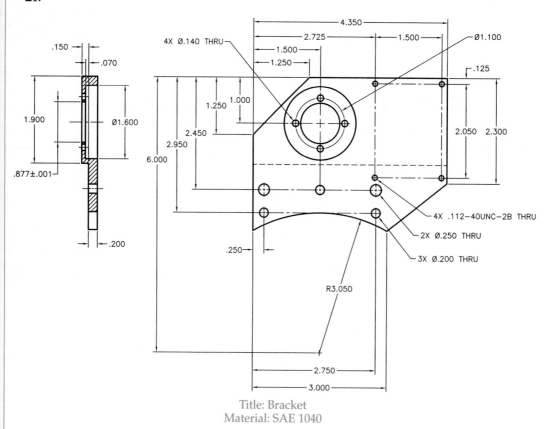

Title: Bracket
Material: SAE 1040

22.

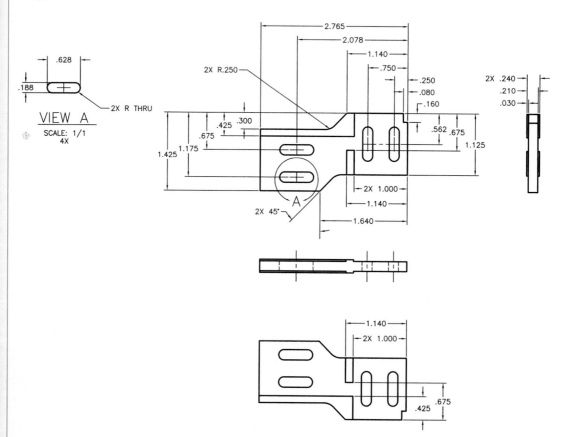

VIEW A
SCALE: 1/1
4X

For Problems 23 and 24, use the isometric drawing provided to create a multiview orthographic drawing for the part. Include only the views necessary to fully describe the object. Dimension according to the ASME standards described in this chapter using a dimension style appropriate for mechanical drafting.

23.

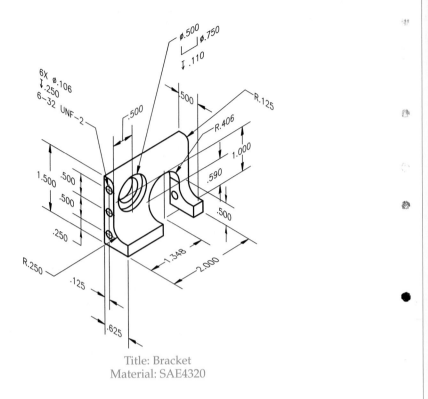

Title: Bracket
Material: SAE4320

24. Carefully evaluate the given problem before beginning. Many given dimensions are provided to the inside surfaces of the bracket. This application is incorrect. Calculate the dimensions as needed to place datum dimensioning from the surfaces labeled A and B. Do not place the A and B on your final drawing.

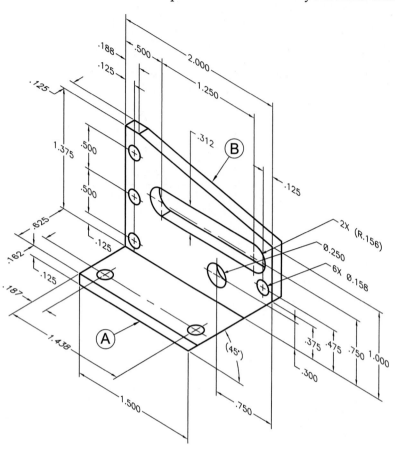

CHAPTER 21

Editing Dimensions

Learning Objectives

After completing this chapter, you will be able to do the following:

✓ Edit individual elements of associative dimensions.
✓ Make changes to and control the appearance of existing dimensions and dimension text.
✓ Update dimensions to reflect the current dimension style.
✓ Override dimension style settings.
✓ Apply the properties of one dimension to other dimensions using **MATCHPROP**.
✓ Change dimension line spacing and alignment.
✓ Break dimension, extension, and leader lines.
✓ Create inspection dimensions.
✓ Edit existing multileaders.

The tools used to edit dimensions vary from basic erasing techniques to specific dimension object editing tools. You will often find it necessary to edit the placement of dimension text, a text value, or the settings in a dimension style. This chapter describes a variety of useful techniques for editing dimensions.

Editing Associative Dimensions

An *associative dimension* is made up of a group of individual elements that are treated as a single object. When an associative dimension is selected for editing, the entire group of elements is highlighted. If you use the **ERASE** tool, for example, you can pick the dimension as a single object and erase all of its elements at once.

One benefit of associative dimensioning is that it permits existing dimensions to be updated as an object is edited. This means when a dimensioned object is edited, the dimension value automatically changes to match the edit. The automatic update is applied only if you accepted the default text value during the original dimension placement. This provides you with an important advantage when editing an associatively dimensioned drawing. Any changes to objects are automatically transferred to the dimensions.

associative dimension: Dimension that updates automatically when the associated object is changed.

Activating Associative Dimensions

Dimensions are associative by default. Associative dimensions should be used whenever possible. To set associative dimensioning, open the **Options** dialog box and select the **User Preferences** tab. Then check or uncheck the **Make new dimensions associative** option in the **Associative Dimensioning** area. When the **Make new dimensions associative** option is checked, the components that make up a dimension are grouped and the dimension is associated with the object. If the object is stretched, trimmed, or extended, the dimension updates automatically. See Figure 21-1. An associative dimension also updates when you use grips or the **MOVE**, **MIRROR**, **ROTATE**, or **SCALE** tools.

NOTE

Associative dimensions created in paper space but attached to model space objects also automatically update when the object is edited.

nonassociative dimension:
Dimension made up of separate elements; does not update when the dimensioned object is changed.

Nonassociative dimensions can be converted to associative dimensions using the **DIMREASSOCIATE** tool. Once you access the **DIMREASSOCIATE** tool, you are prompted to select the dimensions to be associated. Then an X marker appears at the first extension line endpoint. Select the point on an object with which to associate this extension line. Then select the associated point for the second extension line.

Use the **Next** option to advance to the next definition point. You can also use the **Select object** option to select an object with which to associate the dimension. The extension line endpoints are then automatically associated with the object endpoints.

To disassociate a dimension from an object, access the **DIMDISASSOCIATE** tool and then select the dimension. The dimension objects are still grouped together, but the dimension will not be associated with an object.

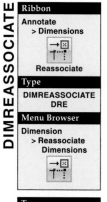

DIMREASSOCIATE

Ribbon
Annotate > Dimensions
Reassociate
Type
DIMREASSOCIATE DRE
Menu Browser
Dimension > Reassociate Dimensions

Type
DIMDISASSOCIATE

Figure 21-1.
The original drawing was created with associative dimensions. When the drawing was revised to change the rectangle dimensions and the circle diameter, the dimensions automatically updated to reflect the new object geometry.

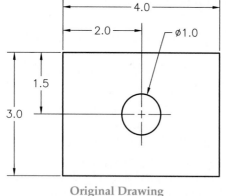

Original Drawing

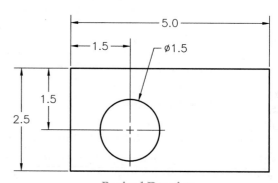

Revised Drawing

Dimension Definition Points

When a dimension location is redefined, the revised position is based on the *definition points*, or *defpoints*. If you select an object for editing and want to include the dimensions in the edit, you must include the definition points of the dimension in the selection set.

Definition points are displayed with the dimension and are located on the Defpoints layer. This layer is automatically created by AutoCAD. Normally, the Defpoints layer does not plot. The definition points are plotted only if the Defpoints layer is renamed and the layer is set to plot. The definition points are displayed when the dimensioning layer is on, even if the Defpoints layer is turned off. Use the **Node** object snap to snap to a definition point.

definition points (defpoints): The points used to specify the dimension location and the center point of the dimension text.

Exercise 21-1
Complete the exercise on the Student CD.

CAUTION

An associative dimension is treated as one object even though it consists of extension lines, a dimension line, arrowheads, and text. To edit the individual parts of a dimension, you must first explode the dimension using the **EXPLODE** tool. You should rarely, if ever, have to explode dimensions. Exploded dimensions lose their layer assignments and their association to the related features and dimension styles.

PROFESSIONAL TIP

One way to edit individual dimension properties without exploding them is to use the **Properties** palette to create a dimension style override.

Editing Dimension Text Values

The **DDEDIT** tool can be used to edit existing dimension text. For example, you can add a prefix or suffix to the text or edit the dimension text format. This is useful when you want to alter dimension text without creating a new dimension. For example, a linear dimension does not automatically place a diameter symbol with the text value, yet you need a diameter symbol to dimension linear diameters. Using the **DDEDIT** tool is one way to place this symbol on the dimension after the dimension has already been placed in the drawing.

When you access the **DDEDIT** tool, the Select an annotation object or [Undo]: prompt is displayed. When you select a dimension to edit, the multiline text editor is displayed and the dimension value is highlighted in blue. See **Figure 21-2.** The cursor is located at the beginning of the text string, so you can add a symbol in front of the value without moving the cursor. **Figure 21-3** shows an example of adding a diameter symbol in front of an existing dimension value. You can move to the end of the value by pressing the right arrow key on the keyboard.

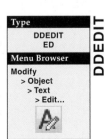

Type
DDEDIT
ED
Menu Browser
Modify
> Object
> Text
> Edit...

DDEDIT

Figure 21-2.
The **DDEDIT** tool allows you to edit dimension text using the **Multiline Text** tab on the ribbon.

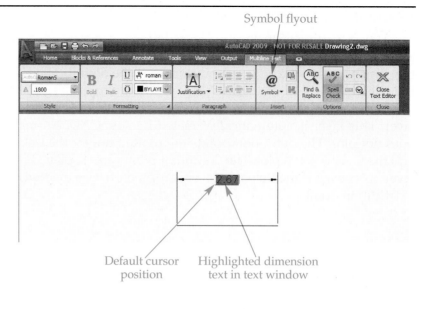

Default cursor position
Highlighted dimension text in text window

Figure 21-3.
Using the **DDEDIT** tool to add a diameter symbol to an existing dimension.

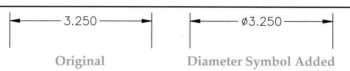

Original
Diameter Symbol Added

Picking once on the dimension value highlights the value for editing, as indicated by a different highlight color. The entire dimension value is selected, and typing new text replaces the existing text. To change back to the initial selection mode, pick to the left of the text value or press the left arrow key on the keyboard. You can also pick to the right of the text value or press the right arrow key on the keyboard. The highlight color turns back to blue, indicating that the dimension value is not discarded, but that the new text or symbol is added to it.

CAUTION

You can replace the highlighted text representing the dimension value with numeric values. However, if the dimension is later stretched, trimmed, or extended, the dimension text value will not change. Therefore, leave the default value intact whenever possible.

Exercise 21-2
Complete the exercise on the Student CD.

Editing Dimension Text Placement

Proper dimensioning practice requires dimensions that are clear and easy to read. This sometimes involves moving the text of adjacent dimensions. For example, in Figure 21-4, one of the dimensions has been moved to a new location to separate the text elements.

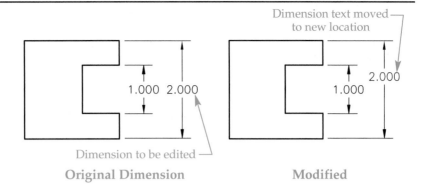

Figure 21-4.
Staggering dimension text for improved readability.

Dimension text moved to new location

2.000
1.000

1.000 2.000

Dimension to be edited

Original Dimension   **Modified**

Using Grips

Using grips is the quickest way to adjust dimension text position. This method requires no tool entry. Pick the dimension, pick the dimension text grip, and drag the text to the new location. If the dimension is associative, the text of the selected dimension automatically drags with the crosshairs. This allows you to relocate the text with your pointing device. If you pick a point, AutoCAD automatically moves the text and reestablishes the break in the dimension line.

Using the Dimtedit Tool

The **DIMTEDIT** tool can also be used to change the placement and orientation of existing associative dimension text. After entering the **DIMTEDIT** tool, select the dimension to be altered. If the dimension is associative, drag the dimension text to a new location and pick to move the text automatically and reestablish the break in the dimension line.

The **DIMTEDIT** tool also provides options for relocating dimension text to a specific location and for rotating the text. These options are offered at the Specify new location for dimension text or [Left/Right/Center/Home/Angle]: prompt. However, it is usually quicker to select the appropriate button from the **Dimensions** panel on the **Annotation** tab of the ribbon or select the menu option from the **Dimension** > **Align Text** submenu on the menu browser. The following options are available:

- **Restore Default Text Position (Home).** Moves relocated text back to its original position.
- **Text Angle (Angle).** Rotates text about its middle point to the rotation angle you specify.
- **Left Justify (Left).** Moves horizontal text to the left and vertical text down.
- **Center Justify (Center).** Centers the dimension text on the dimension line.
- **Right Justify (Right).** Moves horizontal text to the right and vertical text up.

The result of using each **DIMTEDIT** tool option is shown in Figure 21-5.

PROFESSIONAL TIP

When you create new dimensions, you can place dimension text more easily by activating the **Place text manually** check box in the **Fit** tab of the **New** (or **Modify**) **Dimension Style** dialog box.

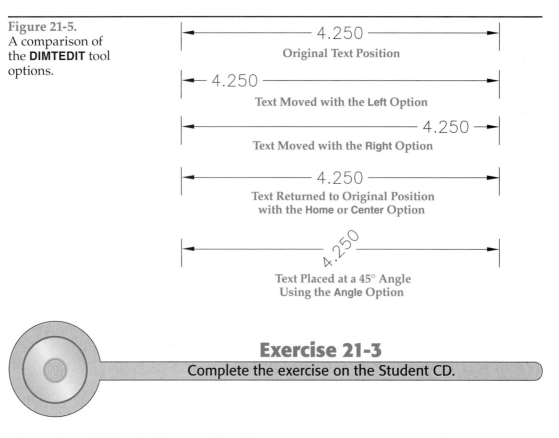

Figure 21-5.
A comparison of the **DIMTEDIT** tool options.

4.250
Original Text Position

4.250
Text Moved with the **Left** Option

4.250
Text Moved with the **Right** Option

4.250
Text Returned to Original Position
with the **Home** or **Center** Option

4.250
Text Placed at a 45° Angle
Using the **Angle** Option

Exercise 21-3

Complete the exercise on the Student CD.

Creating Oblique Extension Lines

The **DIMEDIT** tool can be used to edit the placement and orientation of an existing associative dimension. Most of the tool options are similar to those available with other dimension editing tools. However, the **Oblique** option is unique to the **DIMEDIT** tool and allows you to change the angle of the extension lines of an existing dimension.

After entering the **DIMEDIT** tool, select the dimension to be altered. Then select from the options offered at the Enter type of dimension editing [Home/New/Rotate/Oblique]: prompt. If you know you want to use the **Oblique** option, the quickest way to access the tool, without first activating the **DIMEDIT** tool, is through the ribbon or menu browser.

The **Home** option functions the same as the **Home** option of the **DIMTEDIT** tool. The **New** option is similar to using the **DDEDIT** tool to edit dimension text values. When you enter the **New** option, the multiline text editor is displayed with a 0.0000 (depending on the precision) value highlighted. The highlighted 0.0000 value represents the associated dimension value. Replace or add to the 0.0000 value. Then pick the **OK** button and select the dimension to make the change. The **Rotate** option functions the same as the **Angle** option of the **DIMTEDIT** tool.

Use the **Oblique** option of the **DIMEDIT** tool to create oblique extension lines. For example, the curve shown on the left in **Figure 21-6A** is dimensioned using linear dimensions. The extension lines of two of the linear dimensions have been made oblique, as shown on the right curve, to adjust the placement of dimensions when space is limited. Another example is shown in **Figure 21-6B**. In this example, oblique extension lines are used to orient the extension lines properly with the angle of the stairs in a stair section. Notice how the associated values and orientation of the dimension lines in these examples do not change.

To create oblique extension lines, first dimension the object using the **DIMLINEAR** tool as appropriate, even if dimensions are crowded or overlap. Then, access the **Oblique** option of the **DIMEDIT** tool and pick the dimensions to be redrawn at an oblique angle. Next, you are asked for the obliquing angle. Careful planning is needed to make sure

DIMEDIT

Ribbon
Annotate > Dimensions
⊢H⊣
Oblique

Type
DIMEDIT

Menu Browser
Dimension > Oblique...
⊢H⊣

AutoCAD and Its Applications—Basics

Figure 21-6.
Drawing
dimensions with
oblique extension
lines.

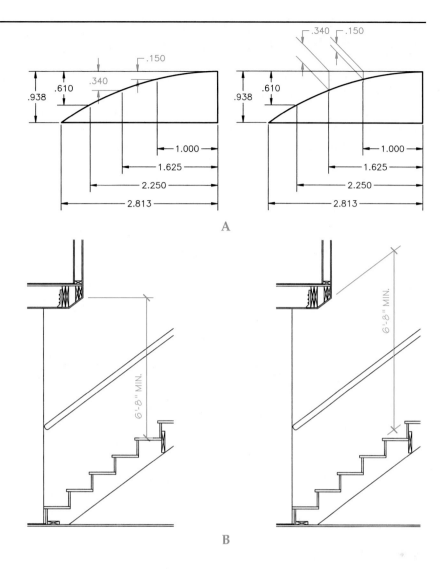

A

B

you enter the correct obliquing angle. Obliquing angles originate from 0° East and revolve counterclockwise. Enter a specific value or pick two points to define the obliquing angle.

NOTE

The **Oblique** option of the **DIMEDIT** tool can also be used to dimension oblique and isometric drawings. These types of drawings are described in Chapter 25.

Exercise 21-4
Complete the exercise on the Student CD.

Editing Dimensions with the Qdim Tool

The **QDIM** tool can be used to place a new dimension in a drawing, as described in Chapter 19. However, the **QDIM** tool can also be used to perform several dimension editing operations. You can change the arrangement of existing dimensions, add a dimension, or remove an existing dimension.

The **Continuous** option allows you to change a selected group of dimensions to chain dimensions. In chain, or continuous, dimensioning the dimensions are placed next to each other in a line, or end to end. This is described in Chapter 19. An example of continuous dimensioning is shown in Figure 21-7A.

The **Baseline** option allows you to create a series of baseline dimensions from existing dimensions. In baseline dimensioning, all dimensions originate from common features. Baseline dimensions are shown in Figure 21-7B. In this example, the **Baseline** option has been used to change the dimensioning arrangement from continuous to baseline.

The **Edit** option allows you to add dimensions to, or remove dimensions from, a selected group and then automatically reorder the group. You can use the **Add** suboption of the **Edit** option to add a dimension. Use the **Remove** suboption to remove a dimension. For example, to add the dimension shown in Figure 21-7C to the baseline dimensions, access the **QDIM** tool. Select all of the dimensions in the group to change and right-click or press [Enter] or the space bar. Access the **Edit** option and then the **Add** option. Then pick the location or feature for which the dimension is to be added and right-click or press [Enter] or the space bar at the Indicate dimension point to add, or [Remove/eXit] <eXit>: prompt. Finally, pick a location for the baseline dimension arrangement.

The dimensions are automatically realigned after you pick a location for the arrangement. You do not have to pick all of the dimensions in the group. However, if you do not pick the entire group, you must select the location carefully. The spacing for the edited dimension and the dimensions in the group that were not selected may not be consistent.

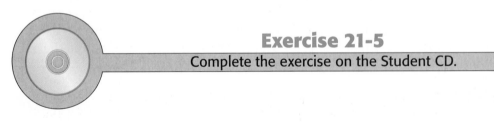

Exercise 21-5
Complete the exercise on the Student CD.

Figure 21-7.
The **QDIM** tool can be used to change existing dimension arrangements and add or remove dimensions.

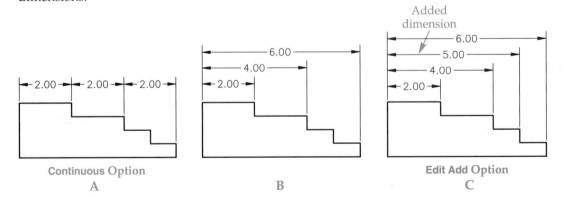

Figure 21-8.
Select a dimension
and then right-
click to access this
shortcut menu.

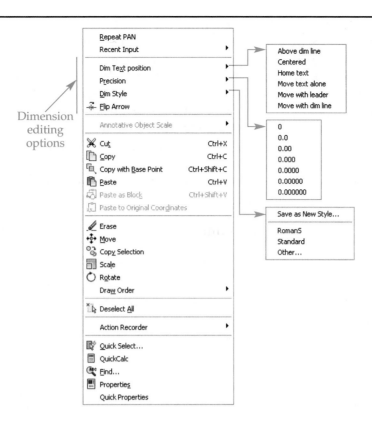

Dimension
editing
options

Dimension Shortcut Menu Options

When you select a dimension and right-click, a shortcut menu is displayed. See **Figure 21-8.** The options in the **Dim Text position** cascading menu automatically move the dimension text according to the option you select. The options in the **Precision** cascading menu allow you to adjust the number of decimal places displayed in a dimension text value. The **Dim Style** cascading menu allows you to create a new dimension style based on the properties of the selected dimension. You can also change the dimension style of the dimension.

The **Flip Arrow** option allows you to flip the direction of a dimension arrowhead to the opposite side of the extension line or object that it is touching. For example, if the arrowheads and the dimension value are crowded inside the extension lines, the arrowheads can be flipped to the outside of the extension lines quickly to make the dimension easier to read. When this option is used with a dimension that has a first and second arrowhead, only one of the arrowheads is flipped at a time. This allows you to control the arrowheads independently. The arrowhead that is flipped is the one that is closer to the point you picked when you selected the dimension (not the right-click point).

Changing the Dimension Style

Chapter 18 describes the process of making changes to an existing dimension style using the **Modify Dimension Style** dialog box. When you make changes to a dimension style, any dimensions drawn using the dimension style automatically adjust according to the new dimension style settings.

If your drawing contains a number of dimension styles, you may need to change the style of an existing dimension to a different style. One option, as previously described, is to right-click on the dimension(s) you want to change, and pick a different dimension style from the **Dim Style** cascading menu. A second method involves picking the dimension(s) you want to change and selecting a different dimension style from the **Dimension Style** drop-down list located on the **Home** and **Annotation** tabs of the ribbon. A third option is to select the dimension(s) you want to change and select a new dimension style from the **Quick Properties** panel or the **Properties** palette.

Another technique for changing the dimension style of an existing dimension is to use the **Update** dimension tool. Before you access the **Update** dimension tool, be sure the current dimension style is the dimension style you want to apply to existing dimensions. Then, access the **Update** dimension tool and pick the dimension(s) you want to change to the current style.

Ribbon

Annotate
> Dimensions

Update

Menu Browser

Dimension
> Update

Overriding Existing Dimension Style Settings

Generally, it is appropriate to set up one or more dimension styles to perform specific tasks relating to your dimensioning practices. However, in some situations, a few dimensions require settings that are not covered by your basic styles. These situations may be too few to merit creating a new style. For example, assume you have the value for **Offset from origin** set at .063, which conforms to ASME standards. However, three dimensions in your final drawing require a 0 **Offset from origin** setting. For these dimensions, you can perform a *dimension style override*.

dimension style override: A temporary alteration of settings for the dimension style that does not actually modify the style.

Dimension Style Overrides for Existing Dimensions

The **Properties** palette is the most effective tool to use for overriding the dimension style settings of existing dimensions. The **Properties** palette is covered in Chapter 14. The dimension properties listed in the **Properties** palette are divided into eight categories. See Figure 21-9. To change an existing property or value, access the proper category and pick the property to highlight it. You can then change the corresponding value.

The changes made in the **Properties** palette are overrides to the dimension style for the selected dimension. The changes do not alter the original dimension style. Also, the changes are not applied to new dimensions.

Dimension Style Overrides for New Dimensions

To override the dimension style for dimensions you are about to create, open the **Dimension Style Manager**. Then select the dimension style that you are going to override from the **Styles** list. Pick the **Override...** button to display the **Override Current Style** dialog box. This dialog box has the same features as the **New** (or **Modify**) **Dimension Style** dialog box. Make any changes to the style and pick the **OK** button. The style you overrode now has a branch under it labeled **<style overrides>**, which is set as the current style. Close the **Dimension Style Manager** and draw the needed dimensions.

To clear the overrides, return to the **Dimension Style Manager** and set any other style current. However, this discards the overrides. If you want to incorporate the overrides into the style that was overridden, right-click on the **<style overrides>** name and select **Save to current style** from the shortcut menu. To save the changes to a new style, pick the **New...** button. Then select **<style overrides>** in the **Start With** drop-down list in the **Create New Dimension Style** dialog box. In the **New Dimension Style** dialog box, pick **OK** to save the overrides as a new style.

Figure 21-9.
The **Properties** palette can be used to edit dimension properties and create a dimension style override.

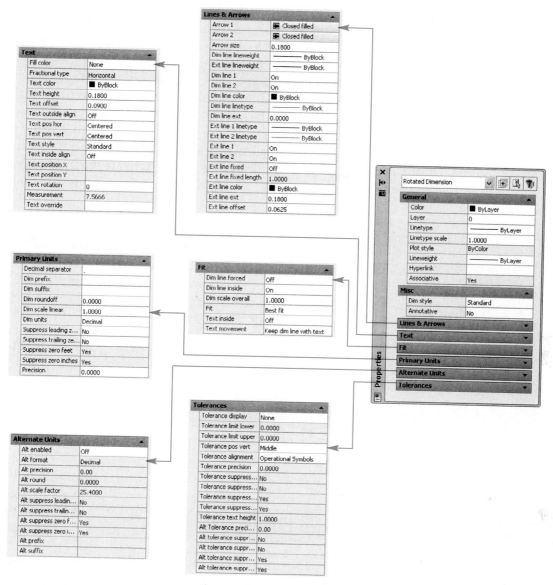

Carefully evaluate the dimensioning requirements in a drawing before performing a style override. It may be better to create a new style. For example, if a number of the dimensions in the current drawing require the same overrides, generating a new dimension style is a good idea. If only one or two dimensions need the same changes, performing an override may be more productive.

Exercise 21-6
Complete the exercise on the Student CD.

Using the Matchprop Tool

MATCHPROP

Ribbon
Home
> Properties

Match Properties

Type
MATCHPROP

Menu Browser
Modify
>Match
Properties

The **MATCHPROP** tool allows you to select the properties of one dimension and apply those properties to one or more existing dimensions. This tool is covered in Chapter 14. Once you access the **MATCHPROP** tool, pick the source dimension that has the desired properties and then pick the dimensions to change. Press [Enter] to update all of the destination dimensions to reflect the properties of the source dimension.

For the **MATCHPROP** tool to work with dimensions, the **Dimension** setting must be active. You can check this after you select the source object. When the Current active settings: prompt appears, Dim should appear with the other settings. If this setting does not appear when you are prompted to select a destination object, type S for the **Settings** option. This displays the **Property Settings** dialog box. Activate the **Dimension** check box in the **Special Properties** area and pick **OK**. Then select the destination dimensions.

PROFESSIONAL TIP

The style of the source dimension is applied to the destination dimensions. If the dimension style of the source dimension has been overridden, the "base" style is applied along with the dimension style override. Reapplying the "base" style removes the overrides.

Exercise 21-7
Complete the exercise on the Student CD.

Using the Dimspace Tool

The amount of space between a drawing feature and the first dimension line, and the space between dimension lines, varies depending on the drawing and industry or company standard. ASME standards recommend a minimum spacing of .375″ (10mm) from a drawing feature to the first dimension line and a minimum spacing of .25″ (6mm) between dimension lines. A minimum spacing of 3/8″ is common for architectural drawings. These minimum recommendations are generally less than desired by actual company or school standards.

Typically, the spacing between dimension lines is equal, and chain dimensions are aligned. See Figure 21-10. As a result, it is important to determine the correct location and spacing of dimension lines. However, dimension line spacing and alignment can be adjusted after dimensions are added. This is a common requirement when there is a need to increase or decrease the space between dimension lines, such as when the scale of the drawing changes or when dimensions are spaced unequally or misaligned.

The **STRETCH** and **DIMTEDIT** tools or grips can be used to adjust the location and alignment of dimension lines individually. You must determine the exact location or amount of stretch applied to each dimension line before using these tools. An alternative method is to use the **DIMSPACE** tool, which can be used to adjust the space equally between dimension lines or align dimension lines.

Figure 21-10.
Correct drafting practice requires dimension lines to be equally spaced and aligned for readability.

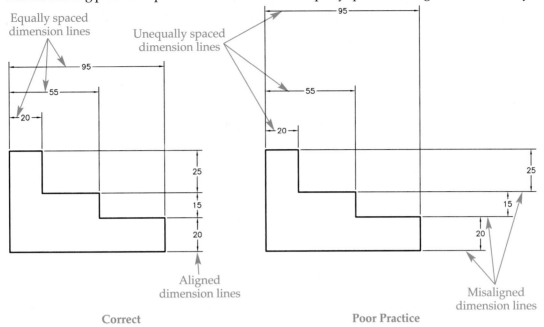

Correct   Poor Practice

When you access the **DIMSPACE** tool, you are prompted to select the *base dimension* and then to pick the dimensions to space. Select each dimension to space or align and press [Enter]. The Enter value or [Auto]: prompt appears. Enter a value to space the dimension lines equally. For example, enter .5 to space the selected dimension lines .5″ apart. Enter a value of 0 to align the dimensions. See Figure 21-11. Use the **Auto** option to space dimension lines using a value that is twice the height of the dimension text.

base dimension: The dimension line that remains in the same location, with which other dimension lines are spaced or aligned.

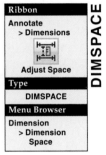

Ribbon
Annotate > Dimensions
Adjust Space
Type
DIMSPACE
Menu Browser
Dimension > Dimension Space

DIMSPACE

NOTE

The **DIMSPACE** tool can be used to space and align both linear dimensions and angular dimensions.

Figure 21-11.
Using the **DIMSPACE** tool to space and align dimension lines correctly.

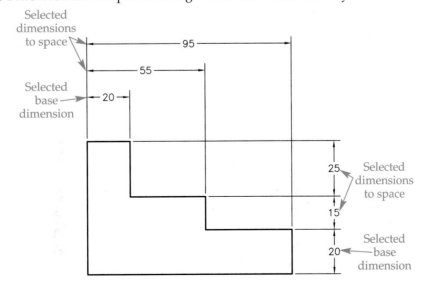

Using the Dimbreak Tool

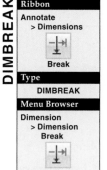

DIMBREAK

Ribbon
Annotate
> Dimensions
Break

Type
DIMBREAK

Menu Browser
Dimension
> Dimension
Break

Drafting standards state that when dimension, extension, or leader lines cross a drawing feature or another dimension, the line is not broken at the intersection. See **Figure 21-12.** However, the **DIMBREAK** tool can be used to create breaks if desired.

When you access the **DIMBREAK** tool, you are prompted to select the dimension to break. This is the dimension that contains the dimension, extension, or leader line that you want to break across an object. Another option is to use **Multiple** to select more than one dimension. If you pick a single dimension to break, the Select object to break dimension or [Auto/Restore/Manual]: prompt is displayed. If you use the **Multiple** option to select multiple dimensions, you must press [Enter] after the dimensions are selected to display the Enter and option [Break/Restore]: prompt.

The **Auto** option of the **DIMBREAK** tool is set by default, and breaks the dimension, extension, or leader line at the selected object. The size of the break is defined by the **Dimension Break** setting of the current dimension style. You can pick additional objects if necessary to break the dimension at other locations. See **Figure 21-13.** Use the **Manual** option to define the size of the break by selecting two points along the dimension, extension, or leader line, instead of using the break size set in the current dimension style. Activate the **Restore** option to remove an existing break created using the **DIMBREAK** tool.

When you use the **Multiple** option to select multiple dimensions, the **Break** and **Restore** options are available. Select the **Break** option to break the selected dimension, extension, or leader lines everywhere they intersect another object. Use the **Restore** option to remove any existing breaks that have been added to the selected dimensions using the **DIMBREAK** tool.

Figure 21-12.
Drafting standards state that when dimension, extension, or leader lines cross a drawing feature or another dimension, the line is not broken at the intersection.

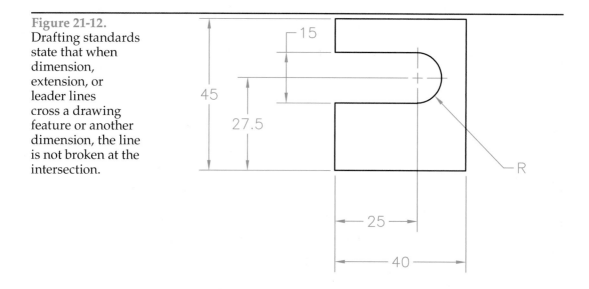

Figure 21-13.
Use the **DIMBREAK** tool to break dimension, extension, or leader lines when they cross an object. **Caution:** This example violates ASME standards and is for reference only. Extension and leader lines do not break over object lines, but drafters commonly prefer to break an extension line when it crosses a dimension line.

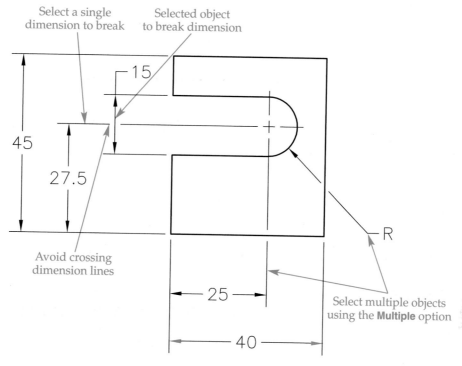

Select a single dimension to break

Selected object to break dimension

Avoid crossing dimension lines

Select multiple objects using the **Multiple** option

Exercise 21-9
Complete the exercise on the Student CD.

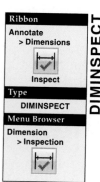

Creating Inspection Dimensions

Inspections and tests occur throughout the design and manufacture of a product. These tests are done to ensure the correct size and location of product features. In some cases, size and location dimensions include information about how frequently the dimension should be tested for consistency and tolerance during the manufacturing of a product. See Figure 21-14. This information can be added to most existing dimensions using the **DIMINSPECT** tool.

Accessing the **DIMINSPECT** tool displays the **Inspection Dimension** dialog box. See Figure 21-15. To create an inspection dimension, pick the **Select dimensions** button and choose the dimensions to which you want to add inspection information. You can select multiple dimensions, though the same inspection specifications will be added to each. Next, define the shape of the inspection dimension frame by picking the appropriate radio button in the **Shape** area. The inspection dimension contains the inspection label, the dimension value, and the inspection rate. Frames around the values are omitted when the **None** shape option is selected.

To include a label, pick the **Label** check box and type the label in the text box. The label is located on the left side of the inspection dimension and identifies the specific dimension. The inspection dimension shown in Figure 21-14 is labeled A. The

Ribbon
Annotate
> Dimensions
Inspect

Type
DIMINSPECT

Menu Browser
Dimension
> Inspection

DIMINSPECT

Figure 21-14.
An example of an inspection dimension added to a part drawing. This example shows an angular shape with a label, dimension, and inspection rate frame.

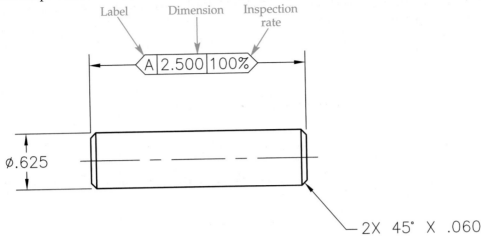

Label   Dimension   Inspection rate

⟨A|2.500|100%⟩

⌀.625

2X 45° X .060

Figure 21-15.
The **Inspection Dimension** dialog box is used to add inspection information to existing dimensions.

Pick to select existing dimensions to add inspection information

Pick to remove inspection information from the selected dimensions

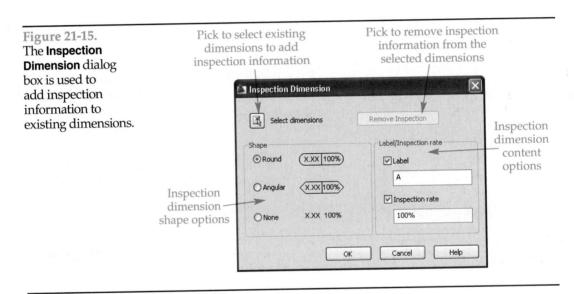

Inspection dimension shape options

Inspection dimension content options

dimension frame houses the dimension value specified when the dimension is created. The length of the part shown in **Figure 21-14** is 2.500 and the dimension was created using the **DIMLINEAR** tool. The **Inspection rate** check box is selected by default and allows you to describe how often the dimension should be tested by entering a value in the text box. The inspection rate for the dimension shown in **Figure 21-14** is 100%. This rate can have different meanings depending on the application. In this example, the inspection rate of 100% means that the length of the part must be checked for tolerance every time the part is added to an assembly.

To remove an inspection dimension, first access the **DIMINSPECT** tool. Then pick the **Select dimensions** button in the **Inspection Dimension** dialog box and choose the dimensions that contain the inspection information you want to remove. Press [Enter] to return to the **Inspection Dimension** dialog box, and pick the **Remove Inspection** button to return the dimension to its condition prior to adding the inspection content.

Editing Multileaders

AutoCAD provides tools to add leader lines to or remove them from existing multileaders. The **MLEADERALIGN** tool allows you to space and align leaders in an easy-to-read pattern. The **MLEADERCOLLECT** tool allows separate multileaders to be grouped together using a single leader line.

Adding and Removing Multiple Leader Lines

Additional leader lines can be added to an existing multileader using the **Add Leader** tool. Multiple leaders are not a recommended ASME standard, but they are used for some applications, such as welding symbols. See **Figure 21-16.**

Once you access the **Add Leader** tool, pick the existing multileader to which you want to add a leader line. Then select the location for the additional leader line arrowhead. You can place as many additional leader lines as needed without accessing the tool again. When you are finished, press [Enter] or [Esc] to draw the leader lines and exit the tool. When a leader line is added to a multileader using the **Add Leader** tool, all the leader lines become one object.

Use the **Remove Leader** tool to remove unneeded multiple leader lines. Once you access the **Remove Leader** tool, pick the existing leader lines you want to remove and press [Enter] or [Esc] to delete the selected leader lines.

Ribbon
Home
> Annotation
Annotate
> Multileaders

Add Leader

Menu Browser
Modify
> Object
> Multileader
> Add Leader

Ribbon
Home
> Annotation
Annotate
> Leaders

Remove Leader

Menu Browser
Modify
> Object
> Multileader
> Remove Leader

NOTE

The **MLEADEREDIT** tool can also be used to add and remove multileader lines.

Figure 21-16.
Applications of multiple leader lines. A—Do not use multiple leader lines in mechanical applications. B—Multiple leader lines are often used in welding applications.

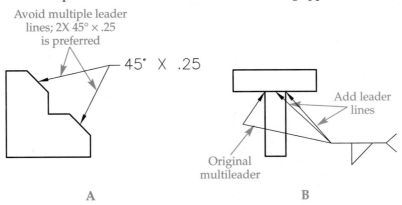

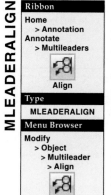

Exercise 21-11
Complete the exercise on the Student CD.

Aligning Multileaders

An advantage of using multileaders is the ability to space and align leaders in an easy-to-read pattern. It is good practice to determine the correct location and spacing of the leaders before you add them. However, leader spacing and alignment can be adjusted after leaders are added. This is a common requirement when there is a need to increase or decrease the space between leader lines, such as when the scale of the drawing changes, when leaders are spaced unequally, or when leaders are misaligned. See Figure 21-17.

The **STRETCH** tool or grips can be used to adjust the location and alignment of leaders individually. You must determine the exact location of or amount of stretch to be applied to each leader before using these tools. An alternative method is to use the **MLEADERALIGN** tool, which can be used to align and adjust the space between leaders.

When you access the **MLEADERALIGN** tool, you are prompted to select the leaders you want to space and align. You can use the **MLEADERALIGN** tool to adjust the location of a single leader in reference to another leader, but for most applications, several leaders should be selected. Select each leader to space or align and press [Enter]. The default multileader alignment is set to **Use current spacing**. When you are prompted to select the multileader to align to, select the **Options** option to change the multileader alignment. The following sections describe each option.

Figure 21-17.
Leaders that are equally spaced and aligned improve drawing readability.

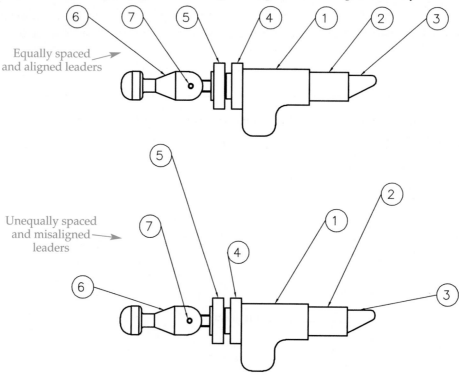

Figure 21-18.
Using the **Distribute** option to align and equally space leaders. In this example, horizontally aligned points are used.

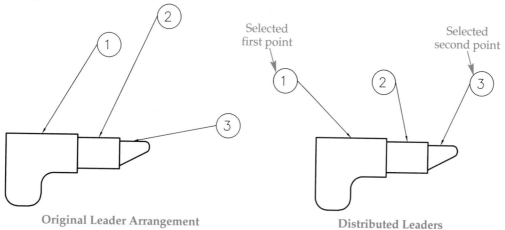

Original Leader Arrangement

Distributed Leaders

Using the distribute option

Select the **Distribute** option to align and distribute, or divide, the selected leaders equally between two points. When you select the **Distribute** option, you are prompted to specify the first point. The first point you pick identifies the location of one of the leaders and determines the area from which the rest of the selected leaders are distributed. Next, you are prompted to specify the second point. The second point you pick identifies the location of each additional leader. The leaders are aligned with the first point and are equally divided among the distance between the first and second points. See Figure 21-18.

Making leader segments parallel

Use the **make leader segments Parallel** option to make all the selected leader lines parallel to one of the selected leader lines. When you select the **make leader segments Parallel** option, you are prompted to select the multileader to align to. This is an existing leader that you want to keep in the same location and at the same angle. All other leaders become parallel to this selection. The length of each leader line, except for the leader aligned to, increases or decreases in order to become parallel with the first leader. See Figure 21-19.

Figure 21-19.
Using the **make leader segments Parallel** option to make leader lines parallel to each other.

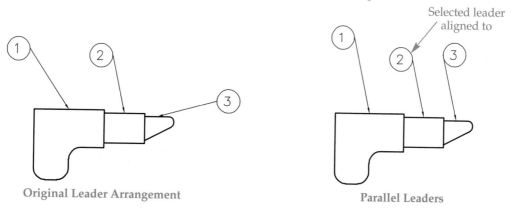

Original Leader Arrangement

Parallel Leaders

Figure 21-20.
Using the **Specify spacing** option to align and equally space leaders.

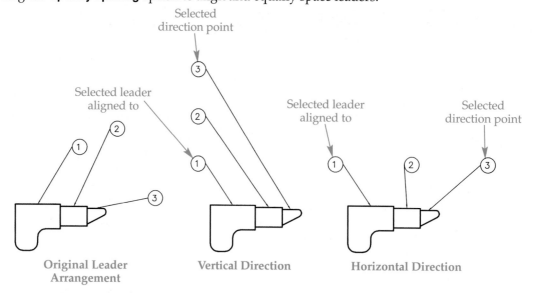

Specify the leader spacing

Choose the **Specify spacing** option to align and equally space the selected leaders according to distance between each leader. The spacing is the distance, or clear space, between the extents of each leader's content. After you enter the spacing, you are prompted to select the multileader to align to. All other leaders are aligned with and spaced from this selection. Finally, specify the direction of the leader arrangement by entering or picking a point. See Figure 21-20.

Using the current leader spacing

Select the **Use current spacing** option to align and space the selected leaders equally according to the distance between one of the selected leaders and the next closest leader. When you select the **Use current spacing** option, you are prompted to select the multileader to align to. All other leaders will be aligned with and spaced from this selection. Then specify the direction of the leader arrangement by entering or picking a point. See Figure 21-21.

Figure 21-21.
Using the **Use current spacing** option to align and equally space leaders.

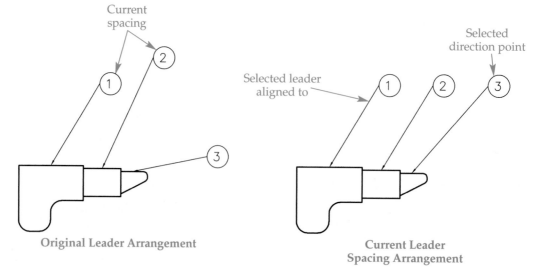

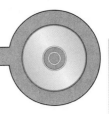

Exercise 21-12
Complete the exercise on the Student CD.

Grouping Multileaders

Separate multileaders created using a **Block** multileader content style can be grouped together using a single leader line. This practice is common when adding *balloons* to assembly drawings. *Grouped balloons* can be used for closely related clusters of assembly components, such as a bolt, washer, and nut. See Figure 21-22. Use the **MLEADERCOLLECT** tool to group multiple existing leaders together using a single leader line.

When you access the **MLEADERCOLLECT** tool, you are prompted to select the leaders you want to space and align. The order in which you select the leaders determines how the leaders are grouped. Select leaders in a sequential order, ending with the leader that has the leader line you want to keep. The options illustrated in Figure 21-23 become available after the leaders have been selected.

Select the **Horizontal** option to align the grouped leader content horizontally or the **Vertical** option to align the grouped leader content vertically. Pick a point to locate the grouped leader. Select the **Wrap** option to wrap the grouped leader content to additional lines as needed when the number of items exceeds a specified width or quantity. Enter the width at the Specify width prompt, or use the **Number** option to enter a quantity not to exceed before the grouped leaders are wrapped. Then pick a point to locate the grouped leader.

Ribbon
Home > Annotation
Annotate > Multileaders
Collect
Type
MLEADERCOLLECT
Menu Browser
Modify > Object > Multileader > Collect

MLEADERCOLLECT

Figure 21-22.
Grouped balloons can be used for closely related features.

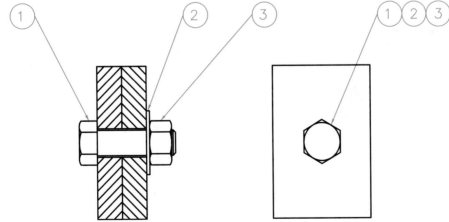

Figure 21-23.
Examples of options for grouping leaders using the **MLEADERCOLLECT** tool.

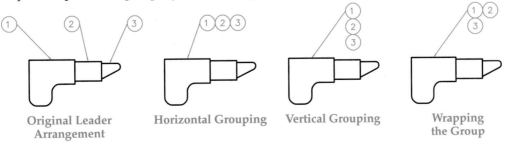

Original Leader Arrangement   Horizontal Grouping   Vertical Grouping   Wrapping the Group

Chapter Test

Answer the following questions. Write your answers on a separate sheet of paper or complete the electronic chapter test on the Student CD.

1. Define *associative dimension*.
2. Why is it important to have associative dimensions for editing objects?
3. Which **Options** dialog box setting controls associative dimensioning?
4. Which tool is used to convert nonassociative dimensions to associative dimensions?
5. Which tool is used to convert associative dimensions to nonassociative dimensions?
6. What are definition points?
7. Explain how to add a diameter symbol to a dimension text value using the **DDEDIT** tool.
8. Name the tool that allows you to control the placement and orientation of an existing associative dimension text value.
9. Name two applications in which you might need to create oblique extension lines.
10. Which tool and option can you use to add a new baseline dimension to an existing set of baseline dimensions?
11. Which four tool options related to dimension editing are available in the shortcut menu accessed when a dimension is selected?
12. Name three methods of changing the dimension style of a dimension.
13. How does the **Dimension Update** tool affect selected dimensions?
14. When you use the **Properties** palette to edit a dimension, what is the effect on the dimension style?
15. How do you access the **Property Settings** dialog box?
16. Which tool can be used to adjust the space equally between dimension lines or align dimension lines without requiring you to determine the exact location or amount of stretch needed?
17. What two options are available when you use the **Multiple** option of the **DIMBREAK** tool?
18. What tool is used to add information about how frequently the dimension should be tested for consistency and tolerance during the manufacturing of a product?
19. Name an application in which leaders with multiple leader lines are commonly used.
20. Identify the four options available to change the multileader alignment.

Drawing Problems

▼ **Basic**

1. Open P19-9 and edit as follows.
   A. Erase the front (circular) view.
   B. Stretch the vertical dimensions to provide more space between dimension lines. Be sure the space you create is the same between all vertical dimensions.
   C. Stagger the existing vertical dimension text numbers if they are not staggered as shown in the original problem.
   D. Erase the 1.750 horizontal dimension and then stretch the 5.255 and 4.250 dimensions to make room for a new datum dimension from the baseline to where the 1.750 dimension was located. This should result in a new baseline dimension that equals 2.750. Be sure all horizontal dimension lines are equally spaced.
   E. Save the drawing as P21-1.

2. Open P20-1 and edit as follows.
   A. Stretch the total length from 3.500 to 4.000, leaving the holes the same distance from the edges.
   B. Fillet the upper-left corner. Modify the 3X R.250 dimension accordingly.
   C. Save the drawing as P21-2.

3. Open P19-12 and edit as follows.
   A. Make the bathroom 8'-0" wide by stretching the walls and vanity that are currently 6'-0" wide to 8'-0". Do this without increasing the size of the water closet compartment. Provide two equally spaced oval sinks where there is currently one.
   B. Save the drawing as P21-3.

4. Open P20-18 and edit as follows.
   A. Lengthen the part .250 on each side for a new overall dimension of 6.500.
   B. Change the width of the part from 3.000 to 3.500 by widening an equal amount on each side.
   C. Save the drawing as P21-4.

5. Open P20-16 and edit as follows.
   A. Shorten the .75 thread on the left side to .50.
   B. Shorten the .388 hexagon length to .300.
   C. Save the drawing as P21-5.

6. Draw the shim as shown at A. Then edit the .150 and .340 values using oblique dimensions as shown at B. Use ASME standards and provide the general notes given with the Chapter 20 problems. Save the drawing as P21-6.

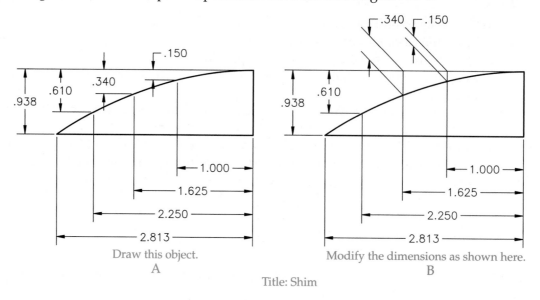

Draw this object.
A

Modify the dimensions as shown here.
B

Title: Shim

▼ Intermediate

7. Open P20-4 and edit as follows.
   A. Use the existing drawing as the model and make four copies.
   B. Leave the original drawing as it is and edit the other four pins in the following manner, keeping the Ø.125 hole exactly in the center of each pin.
   C. Give one pin a total length of 1.500.
   D. Create the next pin with a total length of 2.000.
   E. Edit the third pin to a length of 2.500.
   F. Change the last pin to a length of 3.000.
   G. Organize the pins on your drawing in a vertical row ranging in length from the smallest to the largest. You may need to change the drawing limits.
   H. Save the drawing as P21-7.

8. Open P20-5 and edit as follows.
   A. Modify the spline to have twelve projections, rather than eight.
   B. Change the angular dimension, linear dimension, and 8X dimension to reflect the modification.
   C. Save the drawing as P21-8.

9. Open P20-11 and edit as follows.
   A. Stretch the total length from 6.500 to 7.750.
   B. Add two more holes that continue the equally spaced pattern of .625 apart.
   C. Change the 8X .625(=5.00) dimension to read 10X .625(=6.250).
   D. Save the drawing as P21-9.

▼ Advanced

10. Draw the stairs cross section using the dimensions and notes provided. Use oblique dimensions where necessary. Establish the missing information using your own specifications. Save the drawing as P21-10.

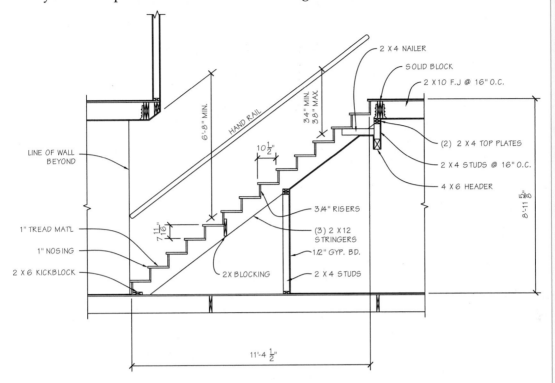

11. Use a word processor to write a report of at least 250 words explaining the importance of associative dimensioning. Site at least three examples from actual industry applications. Show at least four drawings illustrating your report.

12. Open P16-7 and save it as P21-12A. If you have not yet created the floor plan, create it now. Dimension the drawing as shown below, ignoring the revisions. Save the dimensioned drawing. Then use **SAVEAS** to create a copy named P21-12B. In P21-12B, make the client-requested revisions to the floor plan, as shown. Make sure the dimensions reflect the changes you have made. Save the revised drawing.

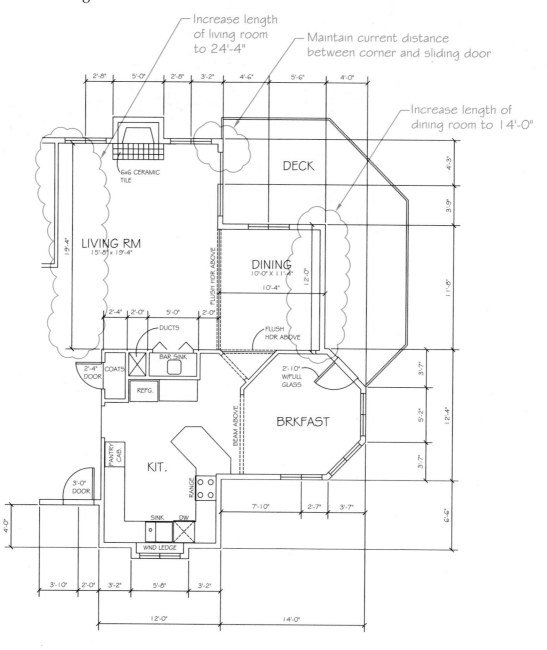

Learning Objectives

After completing this chapter, you will be able to do the following:

✓ Define and use dimensioning and tolerancing terminology.
✓ Set the precision for dimensions and tolerances.
✓ Set up the primary units for use with inch or metric dimensions.
✓ Create and use dimension styles with various tolerance settings.

Chapter 18 introduced the creation of dimension styles and explained how to set the specifications for dimension geometry, fit format, primary units, alternate units, and text. This chapter describes the basics of tolerancing and explains how to prepare dimensions with tolerances for mechanical manufacturing drawings.

Tolerancing Fundamentals

A *tolerance* can be applied directly to the dimension, indicated by a general note, or identified in the drawing title block. See Figure 22-1. The dimension stated as 12.50±.25 in Figure 22-2 is in a style known as *plus-minus dimensioning*. The tolerance of this dimension is the difference between the maximum and minimum *limits*. This tolerance style can be used when the variance is the same in the positive and negative directions. In this case, the upper limit is 12.75 (12.50 +.25 = 12.75), and the lower limit is 12.25 (12.50 – .25 = 12.25). To find the tolerance, subtract the lower limit from the upper limit. The tolerance in this example is .50 (12.75 – 12.25).

The *specified dimension* of the feature shown in Figure 22-2 is 12.50. A tolerance on a drawing may be calculated and shown using *limits dimensioning*. Many schools and companies prefer this method because calculations are not required. Additional tolerance methods are also common, depending on the design requirement. Examples of equal and unequal *bilateral tolerances* are shown in Figure 22-3. An example of a *unilateral tolerance* is shown in Figure 22-4.

---

tolerance: Total amount by which a specific dimension is permitted to vary.

plus-minus dimensioning: A tolerance style in which the positive and negative variance is equal and is preceded by a ± symbol.

limits: The largest and smallest numerical values the feature can have.

specified dimension: The part of the dimension from which the limits are calculated.

limits dimensioning: Method in which the upper and lower limits are given, instead of the specified dimension and specific tolerance.

bilateral tolerance: A tolerance style that permits variance in both the positive and negative directions from the specified dimension.

unilateral tolerance: Permits a variation in only one direction from the specified dimension.

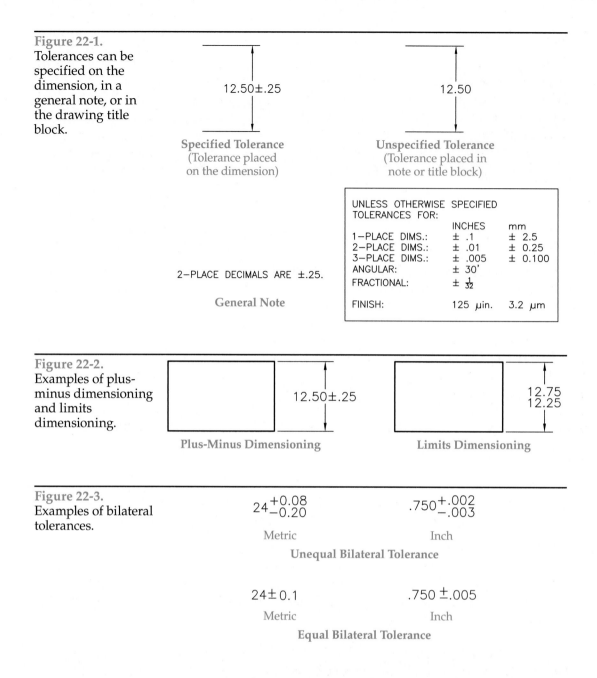

Figure 22-1.
Tolerances can be specified on the dimension, in a general note, or in the drawing title block.

12.50±.25

Specified Tolerance
(Tolerance placed on the dimension)

12.50

Unspecified Tolerance
(Tolerance placed in note or title block)

2–PLACE DECIMALS ARE ±.25.

General Note

```
UNLESS OTHERWISE SPECIFIED
TOLERANCES FOR:
                        INCHES      mm
1–PLACE DIMS.:          ± .1        ± 2.5
2–PLACE DIMS.:          ± .01       ± 0.25
3–PLACE DIMS.:          ± .005      ± 0.100
ANGULAR:                ± 30'
FRACTIONAL:             ± 1/32

FINISH:                 125 μin.    3.2 μm
```

Figure 22-2.
Examples of plus-minus dimensioning and limits dimensioning.

12.50±.25

Plus-Minus Dimensioning

12.75
12.25

Limits Dimensioning

Figure 22-3.
Examples of bilateral tolerances.

$24^{+0.08}_{-0.20}$

Metric

$.750^{+.002}_{-.003}$

Inch

Unequal Bilateral Tolerance

24 ± 0.1

Metric

$.750\pm.005$

Inch

Equal Bilateral Tolerance

Assigning Decimal Places

The ASME Y14.5M *Dimensioning and Tolerancing* standard has separate recommendations for the display of decimal places in inch and metric dimensions. Examples of decimal dimension values in inches and metric units are shown in **Figure 22-3** and **Figure 22-4**.

Figure 22-4.
A unilateral tolerance allows variation in only one direction from the specified dimension.

$24_{-0.2}^{\ \ 0}$

$24^{+0.2}_{\ \ 0}$

Metric

$.625^{+.000}_{-.004}$

$.625^{+.004}_{-.000}$

Inch

Inch Dimensioning

A specified inch dimension is expressed to the same number of decimal places as its tolerance. Zeros are added to the right of the decimal point if needed. For example, the inch dimension .250±.005 has an additional zero added to the .25 to match the three-decimal tolerance. Similarly, the dimensions 2.000±.005 and 2.500±.005 both have zeros added to match the tolerance.

Both values in a plus-minus tolerance for an inch dimension have the same number of decimal places. Zeros are added to fill in where needed. For example:

$$\begin{matrix} +.005 \\ -.010 \end{matrix} \quad not \quad \begin{matrix} +.005 \\ -.01 \end{matrix}$$

Metric Dimensioning

The decimal point and zeros are omitted from the dimension when a metric dimension is a whole number. For example, the metric dimension 12 has no decimal point followed by a zero. This rule is true unless tolerance values are displayed. When a metric dimension includes a decimal portion, the last digit to the right of the decimal point is not followed by a zero. For example, the metric dimension 12.5 has no zero to the right of the 5. This rule is true unless tolerance values are displayed.

Both values in a bilateral tolerance for a metric dimension have the same number of decimal places. Zeros are added to fill in where needed. Zeros are not added after the specified dimension to match the tolerance. For example, both 24±0.25 and 24.5±0.25 are correct. Some companies prefer to add zeros after the specified dimension to match the tolerance, however, in which case 24.00±0.25 and 24.50±0.25 are both correct.

Setting Primary Units

The appearance of dimensions, including dimension values, is controlled by dimension styles. Chapter 18 describes the process of creating and editing dimension styles. The initial phase of dimensioning with tolerances involves setting the appropriate values for the primary units. The **Primary Units** tab of the **New** (or **Modify**) **Dimension Style** dialog box is used to set the type of units and precision of the dimension. See Figure 22-5.

In the **Linear dimensions** area of the **Primary Units** tab, the **Precision** drop-down list allows you to specify the number of zeros displayed after the decimal point of the specified dimension. The ASME standard recommends that the precision for the dimension and the tolerance be the same for inch dimensions, but it may be different for metric values, as previously described.

The **Zero suppression** settings control the display of zeros before and after the decimal point. For metric dimensions, the **Leading** options should be off, and the **Trailing** options should be on. For inch dimensions, the **Leading** options should be on, and the **Trailing** options should be off.

Figure 22-5.
Settings for the unit format and precision of linear dimensions are located in the **Primary Units** tab.

Set the precision for specified dimensions

Set the zero suppression

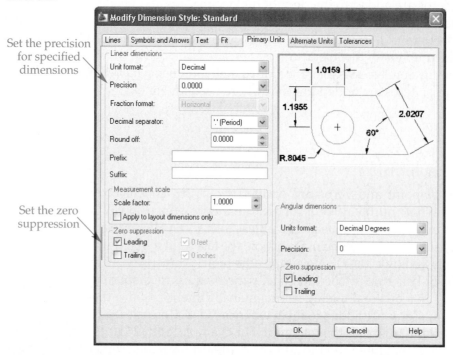

Setting Tolerance Methods

The **Tolerances** tab of the **New** (or **Modify**) **Dimension Style** dialog box is used to apply a tolerance method to your drawing. See **Figure 22-6.** The default option in the **Method:** drop-down list is None. This means no tolerance method, or specific tolerance,

Figure 22-6.
The **Tolerances** tab contains formatting settings for tolerance dimensions.

Select a tolerance method

Set the precision for tolerance dimensions

Settings should match the **Zero suppression** linear dimension settings in the **Primary Units** tab

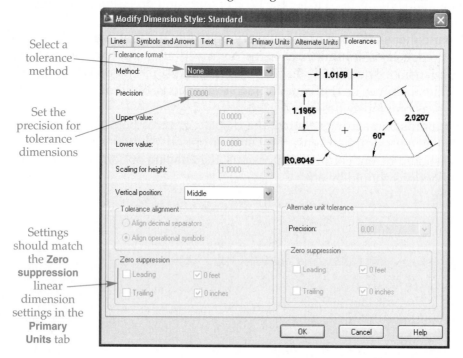

Figure 22-7.
A tolerance
dimensioning
method can be
selected from the
options in the
Method: drop-down
list, located in the
Tolerance format area
of the **Tolerances** tab.

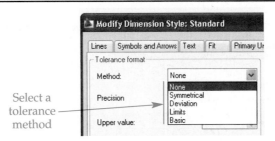

Select a
tolerance
method

is used with your dimensions. As a result, most of the options in the **Tolerances** tab are disabled. If you pick a tolerance method from the drop-down list, the resulting image in the tab reflects the selected method. The drop-down list options are shown in Figure 22-7.

Symmetrical Tolerance Method

A *symmetrical tolerance* is created by selecting the **Symmetrical** option from the **Method:** drop-down list. Use this option to draw dimension text that displays an equal bilateral tolerance in the plus-minus format. When the **Symmetrical** option is selected, the **Upper value:** text box, **Scaling for height:** text box, and **Vertical position:** drop-down list are enabled. The preview image displays an equal bilateral tolerance. See Figure 22-8. You can enter a tolerance value in the **Upper value:** text box. Although it is disabled, you can see that the value in the **Lower value:** text box matches the value in the **Upper value:** text box.

symmetrical tolerance: AutoCAD's term for an equal bilateral tolerance.

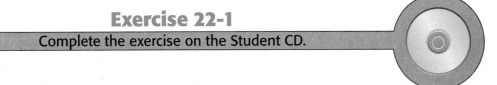

Exercise 22-1

Complete the exercise on the Student CD.

Figure 22-8.
Setting the **Symmetrical** tolerance method option current, with an equal bilateral tolerance value of .005.

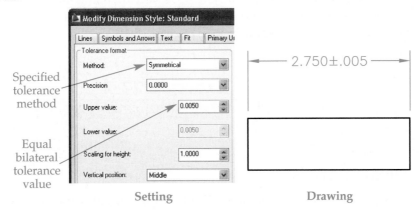

Specified tolerance method

Equal bilateral tolerance value

Setting   Drawing

Figure 22-9.
Setting the **Deviation** tolerance method option current, with unequal bilateral tolerance values.

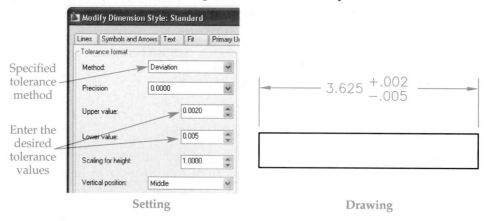

Specified tolerance method

Enter the desired tolerance values

Setting   Drawing

Figure 22-10.
When a unilateral tolerance is specified, AutoCAD automatically places the plus or minus symbol in front of the zero tolerance, if English units are used. The symbol is omitted with metric units.

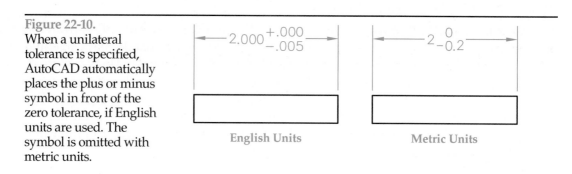

English Units   Metric Units

Deviation Tolerance Method

deviation tolerance:
AutoCAD's term for an unequal bilateral tolerance.

A *deviation tolerance* is created by picking the **Deviation** option from the **Method:** drop-down list. A deviation tolerance deviates (varies) from the specified dimension with two different values. After selecting the **Deviation** option, the **Upper value:** and **Lower value:** text boxes are enabled so you can enter the desired upper and lower tolerance values. See Figure 22-9. The preview image in the tab changes to match a representation of an unequal bilateral tolerance.

The deviation option can also be used to draw a unilateral tolerance by entering 0 for either the **Upper value:** or **Lower value:** setting. If you are using inch units, AutoCAD includes the plus or minus sign before the zero tolerance. When metric units are used, the sign is omitted for the zero tolerance. See Figure 22-10.

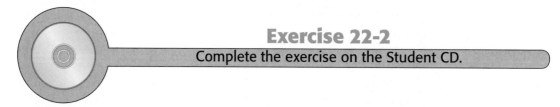

Exercise 22-2
Complete the exercise on the Student CD.

Limits Tolerance Method

In limits dimensioning, the tolerance limits are given, and no calculations from the specified dimension are required (unlike plus-minus dimensioning). The limits tolerance method can be set by picking **Limits** in the **Method:** drop-down list. When this option is set, the **Upper value:** and **Lower value:** text boxes are enabled. You can then enter the desired upper and lower tolerance values to be added and subtracted from the specified dimension. The upper and lower values you enter can be the same or different. See Figure 22-11.

Figure 22-11.
Selecting the limits tolerance method and setting limit values.

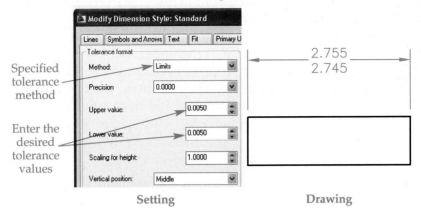

Specified tolerance method

Enter the desired tolerance values

Setting   Drawing

Exercise 22-3
Complete the exercise on the Student CD.

Basic Tolerance Method

The basic tolerance method is used to draw *basic dimensions*. The basic tolerance method can be set by picking **Basic** in the **Method:** drop-down list. With this setting, the **Upper value:** and **Lower value:** options in the **Tolerance format** area are disabled because a basic dimension has no tolerance. A basic dimension is distinguished from other dimensions by a rectangle placed around the dimension number, as shown in Figure 22-12.

basic dimension:
A theoretically perfect dimension used in geometric dimensioning and tolerancing.

Figure 22-12.
The basic tolerance method is used for basic dimensioning. The dimension text for a basic dimension is placed inside a rectangle.

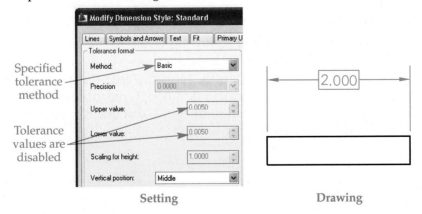

Specified tolerance method

Tolerance values are disabled

Setting   Drawing

Picking the **Draw frame around text** check box in the **Text** tab of the **New** (or **Modify**) **Dimension Style** dialog box also activates the basic tolerance method. Choose a tolerance method based on the characteristics of the tolerance. If the upper and lower variance is equal, choose the **Symmetrical** option to create an equal bilateral tolerance. If the upper and lower variance differs, use the **Deviation** option. Use the **Limits** option to show only the minimum and maximum allowed values.

Tolerance Precision and Zero Suppression

After a tolerance method is specified in the **Method:** drop-down list of the **Tolerances** tab, you can set the precision of the tolerance. By default, when you set the primary unit precision on the **Primary Units** tab, AutoCAD automatically makes the tolerance precision in the **Tolerances** tab the same unit precision. If the setting does not reflect the level of precision you want, change it using the **Precision** drop-down list in the **Tolerance format** area.

A tolerance method must be selected before the **Zero suppression** tolerance format options can be specified. The suppression settings for linear dimensions in the **Tolerances** tab should be the same as the **Zero suppression** tolerance format settings in the **Primary Units** tab. AutoCAD does not automatically match the tolerance setting to the primary units setting.

When you are drawing inch tolerance dimensions, you should activate the **Leading** check box in the **Zero suppression** area of the **Tolerances** tab. The same option should be activated for linear dimensions in the **Primary Units** tab. You can then properly draw inch tolerance dimensions without placing the zero before the decimal point, as recommended by ASME standards. These settings allow you to draw a tolerance dimension such as .625±.005.

When you are drawing metric tolerance dimensions, deactivate the **Leading** check box in the **Zero suppression** area of the **Tolerances** tab. Deactivate the same option for linear dimensions in the **Primary Units** tab. This allows you to place a metric tolerance dimension with the zero before the decimal point, as recommended by ASME standards, for example, a dimension such as 12±0.2.

Tolerance Justification

Use the options in the **Vertical position:** drop-down list in the **Tolerance format** area of the **Tolerances** tab to control the alignment, or justification, of deviation tolerance dimensions. The **Middle** option centers the tolerance with the specified dimension and is the default. This is also the recommended ASME practice. The other justification options are **Top** and **Bottom**. Deviation tolerance dimensions displaying each of the justification options are shown in Figure 22-13.

Figure 22-13.
Examples of the tolerance justification options for deviation tolerance dimensions.

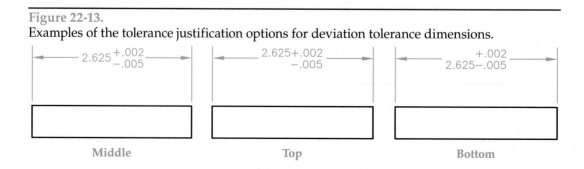

| Middle | Top | Bottom |

The options in the **Tolerance alignment** area become available for selection when you use a deviation or limits tolerance method. The selected option controls the left and right tolerance justification. When you are using a deviation tolerance method, pick the **Align decimal separators** radio button to vertically align the upper and lower tolerance value decimal points. Select the **Align operational symbols** radio button to vertically align the upper and lower tolerance plus and minus symbols. See Figure 22-14. When you are using the limits tolerance method, pick the **Align decimal separators** radio button to vertically align the upper and lower limit decimal points. Select the **Align operational symbols** radio button to left-justify the upper and lower limits. See Figure 22-15.

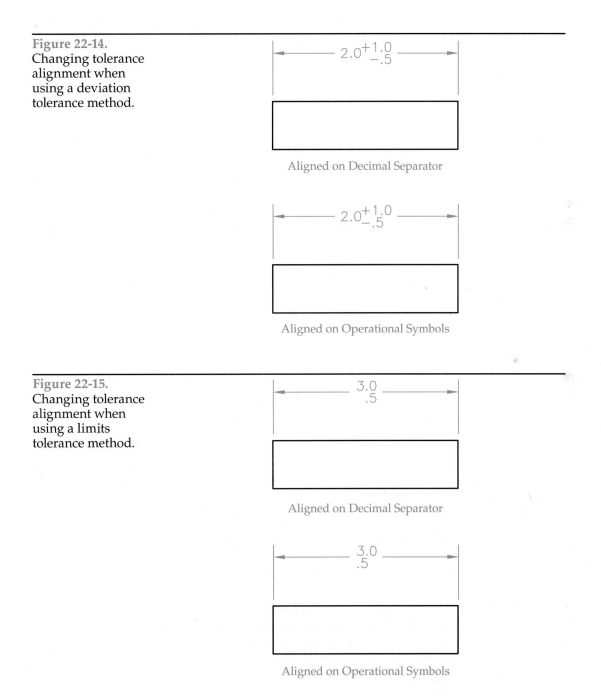

Figure 22-14.
Changing tolerance alignment when using a deviation tolerance method.

$2.0^{+1.0}_{-.5}$

Aligned on Decimal Separator

$2.0^{+1.0}_{-.5}$

Aligned on Operational Symbols

Figure 22-15.
Changing tolerance alignment when using a limits tolerance method.

3.0
.5

Aligned on Decimal Separator

3.0
.5

Aligned on Operational Symbols

Figure 22-16.
Using different scale settings for the text height of tolerance dimensions.

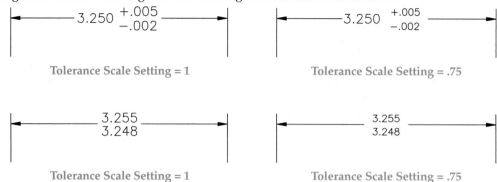

Tolerance Scale Setting = 1   Tolerance Scale Setting = .75

Tolerance Scale Setting = 1   Tolerance Scale Setting = .75

Tolerance Height

You can set the text height of the tolerance dimension in relation to the text height of the specified dimension using the **Scaling for height:** text box in the **Tolerance format** area of the **Tolerances** tab. The default of 1.0000 makes the tolerance dimension text the same height as the specified dimension text. This is the recommended ASME standard. If you want the tolerance dimension height to be three-quarters as high as the specified dimension height, for example, type .75 in the **Scaling for height:** text box. Some companies prefer this practice to keep the tolerance part of the dimension from taking up additional space. Examples of tolerance dimensions with different text heights are shown in Figure 22-16.

Exercise 22-4
Complete the exercise on the Student CD.

Chapter Test

Answer the following questions. Write your answers on a separate sheet of paper or complete the electronic chapter test on the Student CD.

1. Define the term *tolerance*.
2. What are the limits of the tolerance dimension 3.625±.005?
3. Give an example of an equal bilateral tolerance in inches and in metric units.
4. Give an example of an unequal bilateral tolerance in inches and in metric units.
5. Give an example of a unilateral tolerance in inches and in metric units.
6. What happens to the preview image in the **Tolerances** tab when a tolerance method option is picked from the **Method:** drop-down list?
7. What is the purpose of the **Symmetrical** tolerance method option?
8. What is the purpose of the **Deviation** tolerance method option?
9. What is the purpose of the **Limits** tolerance method option?
10. How do you set the number of zeros displayed after the decimal point for a tolerance dimension?
11. Which **Zero suppression** settings should you specify for linear and tolerance dimensions when you are using metric units?

12. Which **Zero suppression** settings should you specify for linear and tolerance dimensions when you are using inch units?
13. Name the tolerance dimension justification option recommended by the ASME standards.
14. Explain the result of setting the **Scaling for height:** option to 1 in the **Tolerances** tab.
15. What setting would you use for the **Scaling for height:** option if you wanted the tolerance dimension height to be three-quarters of the specified dimension height?

Drawing Problems

Set the limits, units, dimension style options, and other parameters as needed for the following problems. Use the guidelines given below.

A. Draw and dimension the necessary views for the following drawings to exact size. These problems are presented in 3D. Draw the proper 2D views for each.
B. Apply dimensions accurately using ASME standards. Create dimension styles that suit the specific needs of each drawing. For example, save different dimension styles for metric and inch dimensions.
C. Create separate layers for the views and dimensions.
D. Plot the drawings with 0.6 mm object lines and 0.3 mm thin lines.
E. Place the following general notes in the lower-left corner of each drawing.
NOTES:
1. INTERPRET DIMENSIONS AND TOLERANCES PER ASME Y14.5M-1994.
2. REMOVE ALL BURRS AND SHARP EDGES.
3. UNLESS OTHERWISE SPECIFIED, ALL DIMENSIONS ARE IN MILLIMETERS (or INCHES as applicable).
F. Save the drawings as P19-1 through P19-7.

▼ Basic

1.

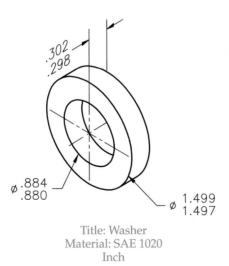

Title: Washer
Material: SAE 1020
Inch

2.

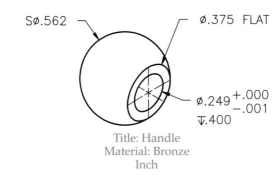

SØ.562   Ø.375 FLAT

$Ø.249 {}^{+.000}_{-.001}$

▽.400

Title: Handle
Material: Bronze
Inch

3.

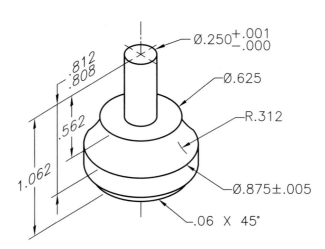

$Ø.250 {}^{+.001}_{-.000}$

$^{.812}_{.808}$

.562

.625

R.312

1.062

Ø.625

Ø.875±.005

.06 X 45°

ALL OTHER THREE PLACE DECIMALS ±.010

4.

4X Ø6.0±0.2

$76.0 {}^{0}_{-0.4}$

$16 {}^{0}_{-0.4}$

8

$Ø66 {}^{0}_{-0.4}$

Ø36

Title: Spacer
Material: Cold Rolled Steel
Metric

5.

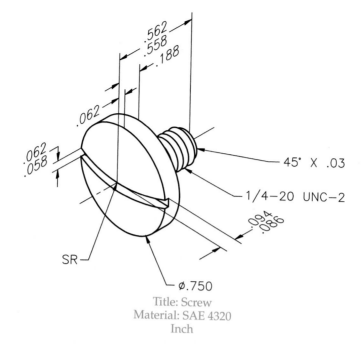

.562
.558
.188
.062
.062
.058

45° X .03

1/4−20 UNC−2

.094
.086

SR

Ø.750

Title: Screw
Material: SAE 4320
Inch

6. This object is shown as a section for clarity. Do not draw a section.

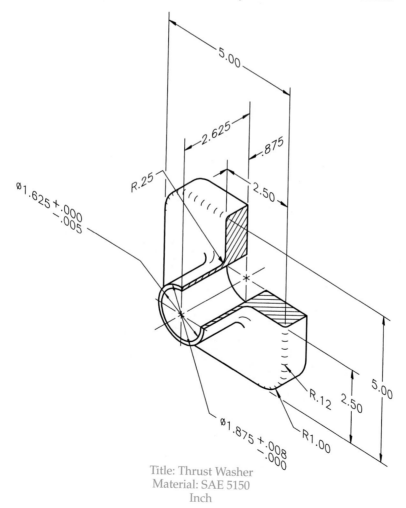

5.00

2.625

.875

2.50

R.25

Ø1.625 +.000
−.005

5.00

2.50

R.12

Ø1.875 +.008
−.000

R1.00

Title: Thrust Washer
Material: SAE 5150
Inch

7.

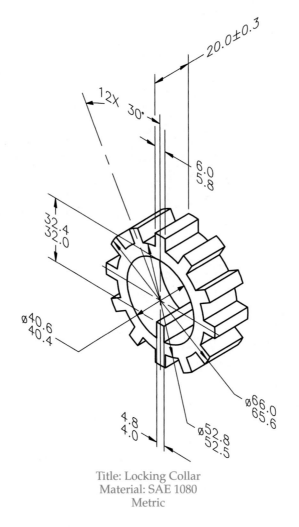

Title: Locking Collar
Material: SAE 1080
Metric

8. Draw the vise clamp shown below. Save the drawing as P19-8.

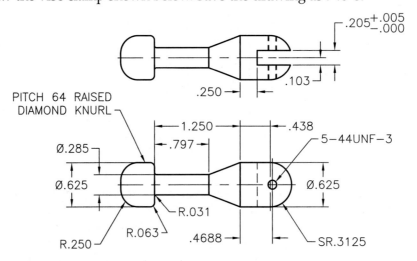

Learning Objectives

After completing this chapter, you will be able to do the following:

✓ Identify symbols used in geometric dimensioning and tolerancing (GD&T).
✓ Use the **TOLERANCE** and **QLEADER** tools to create geometric tolerancing symbols.
✓ Draw and edit feature control frames.
✓ Draw and edit datum feature symbols.
✓ Place basic dimensions on a drawing.

This chapter is an introduction to geometric dimensioning and tolerancing (GD&T) principles, or *geometric tolerancing*, as adopted by the American National Standards Institute (ANSI) and published by the American Society of Mechanical Engineers (ASME) for engineering and related document practices. The standard is ASME Y14.5M-1994, *Dimensioning and Tolerancing*.

The drafting applications covered in this chapter use the AutoCAD geometric tolerancing capabilities and additional recommendations to comply with the ASME Y14.5M-1994 standard. This chapter is only an introduction to GD&T. For complete coverage of GD&T, refer to *Geometric Dimensioning and Tolerancing*, published by Goodheart-Willcox Co., Inc. Before beginning this chapter, you should have a solid understanding of dimensioning and tolerancing standards and AutoCAD dimensioning applications, as presented in previous chapters.

geometric tolerancing: A general term that refers to tolerances used to control the form, profile, orientation, runout, and location of features on an object.

Dimensioning Symbols

The use of *symbols* aids in clarity and drawing presentation and reduces the time required to create a drawing. Symbols must be clearly drawn to the required size and shape so they communicate the desired information uniformly. ASME Y14.5M recommends the use of symbols because symbols are read the same way at every company and in any country. In an international economy, it is important to have effective communication on engineering drawings. Symbols make this communication process uniform. ASME Y14.5M also states that the adoption of dimensioning symbols does not prevent the use of equivalent terms or abbreviations in situations where symbols are considered inappropriate.

symbols: Graphic representations of specific information that would be difficult and time-consuming to convey in note form.

Geometric Characteristic Symbols

geometric characteristic symbols: Symbols that are used to provide specific controls related to the form of an object, orientation of features, outlines of features, relationship of features to an axis, or location of features.

Geometric characteristic symbols are the symbols used in GD&T. They identify specific controls that go beyond basic size and location dimensioning for mechanical manufacturing. The five basic types of geometric characteristic symbols are form, profile, location, orientation, and runout. See **Figure 23-1.**

Material Condition Symbols

material condition symbols (modifying symbols): Symbols used to modify the geometric tolerance in relation to the produced size or location of the feature.

Material condition symbols, often referred to as *modifying symbols,* are used only in geometric dimensioning applications. The symbols used to indicate maximum material condition (MMC) and least material condition (LMC) are shown in **Figure 23-2.**

Figure 23-1.
Geometric characteristic symbols recommended by ASME Y14.5M-1994.

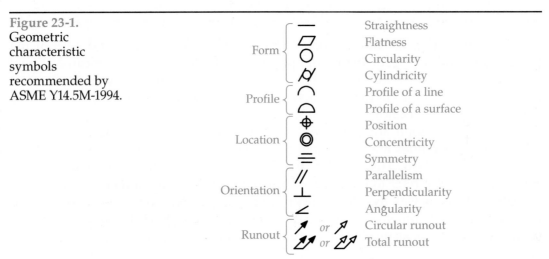

Figure 23-2.
Material condition symbols.
(h = text height)

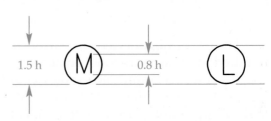

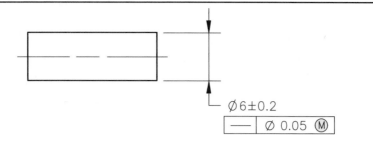

Figure 23-3.
This drawing shows how maximum material condition (MMC) is applied to a feature. The symbol for MMC is shown highlighted.

	Possible produced sizes	Maximum out-of-straightness
MMC	6.20	0.05
	6.10	0.15
	6.00	0.25
	5.90	0.35
LMC	5.80	0.45

Maximum material condition (MMC) control

If the material condition control is *maximum material condition (MMC)*, the symbol for MMC must be placed in the feature control frame. Feature control frames are shown when applicable, and are further described later in this chapter. See **Figure 23-3.** When the MMC application is used, the specified geometric tolerance is held at the MMC *produced size*. See the table in **Figure 23-3.** As the produced size varies from MMC, the geometric tolerance increases, equal to the change. The maximum geometric tolerance is at the LMC produced size.

Least material condition (LMC) control

If the material condition control is *least material condition (LMC)*, the symbol for LMC must be placed in the feature control frame. When this application is used, the specified geometric tolerance is held at the LMC produced size. As the produced size varies from LMC, the geometric tolerance increases, equal to the change. The maximum geometric tolerance is at the MMC produced size.

Surface control, regardless of feature size (RFS)

When no material condition symbol follows the geometric tolerance in a feature control frame, the material condition is assumed to be *regardless of feature size (RFS)*. When a feature control frame is connected to a feature surface with a leader or an extension line, it is referred to as a *surface control*. See **Figure 23-4.** The geometric characteristic symbol shown in **Figure 23-4** is straightness, but the format is the same for any characteristic.

Notice in the table in **Figure 23-4** that the possible sizes range from 6.20 (MMC) to 5.80 (LMC). With surface control, *perfect form* is required at MMC. The geometric tolerance at MMC is zero, as shown in the chart. As the produced size varies from MMC in the chart, the geometric tolerance increases, until it equals the amount specified in the feature control frame.

Axis control, regardless of feature size

Axis control is indicated when the feature control frame is shown with a diameter dimension. See **Figure 23-5.** Regardless of feature size (RFS) is assumed. With axis control, perfect form is not required at MMC. Therefore, the specified geometric tolerance stays the same at every produced size. See the table in **Figure 23-5.**

maximum material condition (MMC): The maximum allowable produced size.

produced size: The actual size of the feature when measured after manufacture.

least material condition (LMC): The minimum allowable produced size.

regardless of feature size (RFS): A material condition in which the geometric tolerances remain the same, regardless of the actual produced size.

surface control: A feature control frame that is connected to a feature surface with a leader or extension line.

perfect form: A manufactured feature at which geometric tolerance is perfect or 0.

axis control: A control that specifies how far out-of-true an axis can be; indicated when the feature control frame is shown with a diameter dimension.

Figure 23-4.
Surface control, regardless of feature size (RFS). In ASME Y14.5M-1994, there is no symbol for regardless of feature size (RFS). RFS is assumed unless otherwise specified. The actual meaning of the geometric tolerance is shown in the table.

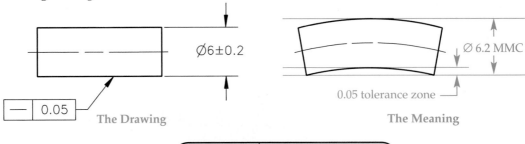

	Possible produced sizes	Maximum out-of-straightness
MMC	6.20	* 0
	6.10	0.05
	6.00	0.05
	5.90	0.05
LMC	5.80	0.05

* Perfect form required

Figure 23-5.
Axis control, regardless of feature size (RFS). The actual meaning of the geometric tolerance is shown in the table.

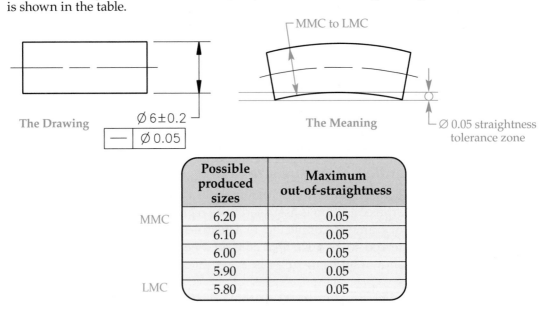

	Possible produced sizes	Maximum out-of-straightness
MMC	6.20	0.05
	6.10	0.05
	6.00	0.05
	5.90	0.05
LMC	5.80	0.05

Feature Control Frames

feature control frame: The rectangular frame that contains the geometric characteristic, geometric tolerance, material condition, and datum reference (if any) for an individual feature.

The *feature control frame* is divided into compartments. The geometric characteristic symbol is placed in the first compartment, followed by the geometric tolerance. Where applicable, the geometric tolerance is preceded by the diameter symbol, which describes the shape of the tolerance zone, and is followed by a material condition symbol (if other than RFS). See **Figure 23-6.**

Figure 23-6.
Feature control frames contain the geometric characteristic symbol, geometric tolerance, and diameter symbol (as applicable). Note that the geometric tolerance is expressed as a total, not a plus-minus value.

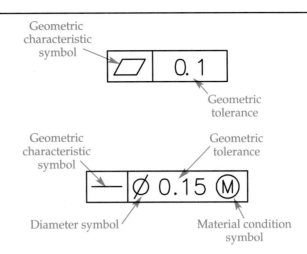

Figure 23-7.
Examples of datum references indicated in feature control frames.

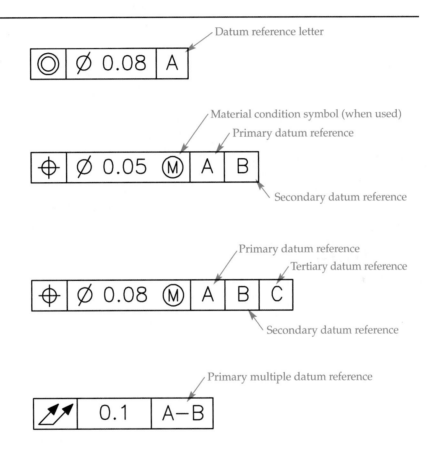

When a geometric tolerance is related to one or more *datums*, the datum reference letters are placed in compartments following the geometric tolerance. When a *multiple datum reference* is established, the datum reference letters are separated by a dash and placed in a single compartment after the geometric tolerance. Several feature control frames with datum references are shown in **Figure 23-7.**

Elements in a feature control frame are displayed in a specific order. See **Figure 23-8.** Notice that the datum reference letters can be followed by a material condition symbol where applicable.

datum: A theoretically perfect surface, plane, point, or axis.

multiple datum reference: A reference that is established by two datum features, such as an axis established by two datum diameters.

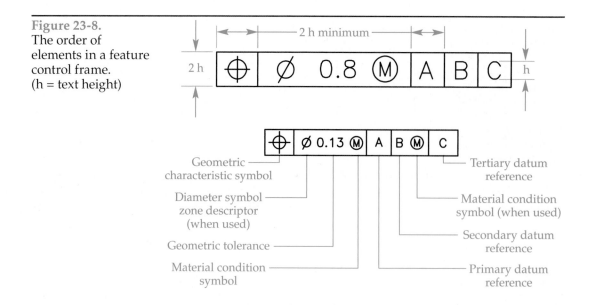

Figure 23-8.
The order of elements in a feature control frame. (h = text height)

Geometric characteristic symbol

Diameter symbol zone descriptor (when used)

Geometric tolerance

Material condition symbol

Tertiary datum reference

Material condition symbol (when used)

Secondary datum reference

Primary datum reference

Basic Dimensions

A *basic dimension* provides the basis from which permissible variations are established by tolerances on other dimensions, in notes, or in feature control frames. A basic dimension tells you where the *geometric tolerance zone* or *datum target* is located. Basic dimensions are shown on a drawing with a rectangle placed around the dimension text. See **Figure 23-9.** A general note can also be used to identify basic dimensions in some applications. For example, the note UNTOLERANCED DIMENSIONS LOCATING TRUE POSITION ARE BASIC indicates the use of basic dimensions. The basic dimension rectangle is a signal to the reader to look for a geometric tolerance in a feature control frame related to the features being dimensioned.

Figure 23-9.
Basic dimensions are identified by a rectangle drawn around the text. (h = text height)

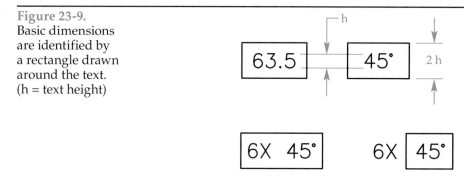

The number of times or places may be applied to a basic dimension by placement inside or outside of the basic dimension symbol.

Other symbols commonly used in GD&T are shown in Figure 23-10. The *free state symbol* describes the distortion of a part after the removal of forces applied during manufacture. The free state symbol is placed in the feature control frame after the geometric tolerance and the material condition (if any), if the feature must meet the tolerance specified while in free state.

The tangent plane symbol is placed after the geometric tolerance in the feature control frame when it is necessary to control a feature surface by contacting points of tangency. The projected tolerance zone symbol is placed in the feature control frame to inform the reader that the geometric tolerance zone is projected away from the primary datum. The between symbol is used with profile geometric tolerances to identify where the profile tolerance is applied.

The statistical tolerance symbol indicates that a tolerance is based on *statistical tolerancing*, which is based on the requirements of *statistical process control (SPC)*. The statistical tolerancing symbol is placed after the dimension or geometric tolerance that requires SPC. See Figure 23-11. When the feature can be manufactured by either SPC or conventional means, both the statistical tolerance with the statistical tolerance symbol and the conventional tolerance must be shown. An appropriate general note should accompany the drawing. Either of the following two notes is acceptable:

free state symbol: A symbol that specifies the distortion of a manufactured part after the forces of manufacture have been removed.

statistical tolerancing: The assignment of tolerances to related dimensions based on the requirements of statistical process control.

statistical process control (SPC): A method of monitoring and adjusting a manufacturing process based on statistical signals.

Figure 23-10.
Additional recommended dimensioning symbols.
(h = text height)

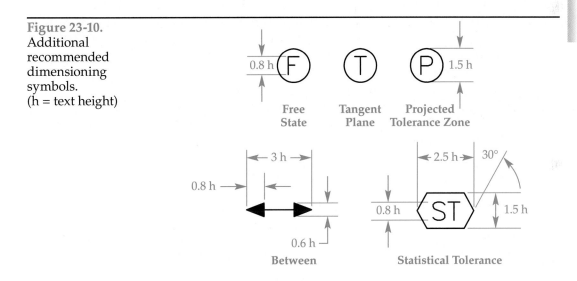

Figure 23-11.
Different ways to apply a statistical tolerance. The statistical tolerance symbol is shown here highlighted.

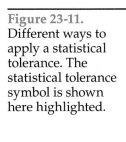

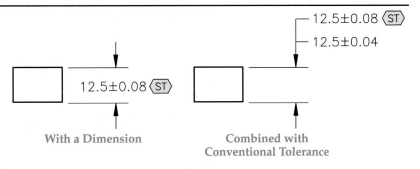

- FEATURES IDENTIFIED AS STATISTICAL TOLERANCED SHALL BE PRODUCED WITH STATISTICAL PROCESS CONTROL.

- FEATURES IDENTIFIED AS STATISTICAL TOLERANCED SHALL BE PRODUCED WITH STATISTICAL PROCESS CONTROL OR THE MORE RESTRICTIVE ARITHMETIC LIMITS.

Datum Feature Symbols

As previously described, datums refer to theoretically perfect surfaces, planes, points, or axes. In this introduction to datum-related symbols, the datum is assumed. In GD&T, datums are identified with a *datum feature symbol*.

Each datum feature requiring identification must have its own identification letter. Any letter of the alphabet can be used to identify a datum, except *I*, *O*, or *Q*. These letters are not used because they can be confused with the numbers *1* or *0*. When the number of datums on a drawing exceeds 23, double letters are used, starting with *AA* through *AZ* and then continuing with *BA* through *BZ*. Datum feature symbols can be repeated only as necessary for clarity.

Figure 23-12 shows examples of datum feature symbols recommended by ASME Y14.5M-1994. The leader line tipped with a datum terminator is used to connect the datum feature to the datum identification. When a surface is used to establish a datum plane on a part, the datum feature symbol is placed on the edge view of the surface or on an extension line in the view where the surface appears as a line. See Figure 23-13.

When the datum is an axis, the datum feature symbol can be added using one of the following methods. See Figure 23-14.

- Placed on the outside surface of a cylindrical feature.
- Centered on the opposite side of the dimension line arrowhead.
- Replace the dimension line and arrowhead when the dimension line is placed outside the extension lines.
- Placed on a leader line shoulder.
- Placed below and attached to the center of a feature control frame.

Figure 23-12.
The datum feature symbol, based on ASME Y14.5M-1994. (h = text height)

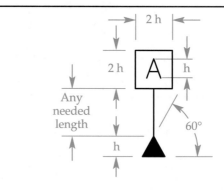

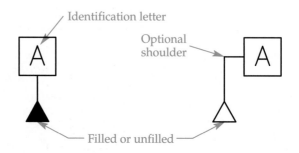

AutoCAD and Its Applications—Basics

Figure 23-13.
Datum feature symbols used to identify datum planes.

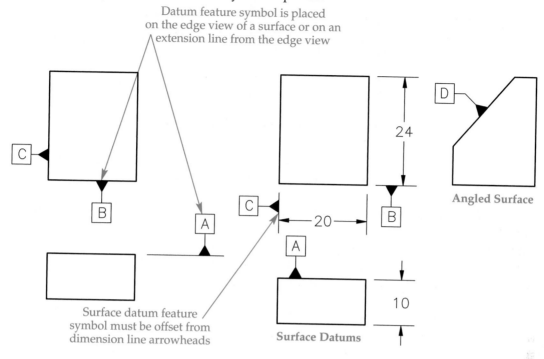

Datum feature symbol is placed on the edge view of a surface or on an extension line from the edge view

Surface datum feature symbol must be offset from dimension line arrowheads

Angled Surface

Surface Datums

Figure 23-14.
Methods of using the datum feature symbol to represent a datum axis.

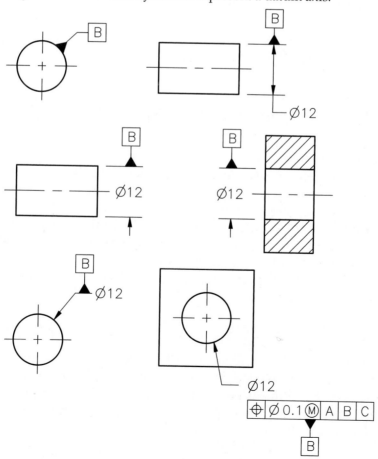

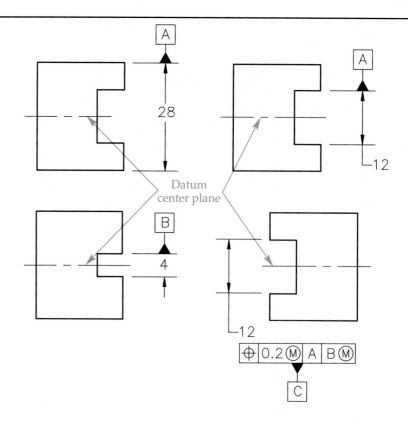

Figure 23-15. Placing datum center plane symbols.

Elements on a rectangular symmetrical part or feature can be located and dimensioned in relationship to a datum center plane. Datum center plane symbols are shown in Figure 23-15. Axis and center plane datum feature symbols must align with, or replace, the dimension line arrowhead, or the datum feature symbol must be placed on the feature, leader shoulder, or feature control frame.

GD&T with AutoCAD

AutoCAD allows you to add certain GD&T symbols to your drawings using the **TOLERANCE**, **QLEADER**, and **MLEADER** tools. The **TOLERANCE** tool launches the **Geometric Tolerance** dialog box, which is the primary method for adding feature control frames and datum target symbols.

GD&T symbols can also be connected to a leader using a combination of the **TOLERANCE** and **MLEADER** tools. The **MLEADER** tool has replaced the **QLEADER** tool as the primary method for placing leaders. However, the **QLEADER** tool continues to provide a quick and effective option for producing GD&T symbols that are automatically attached to a leader. These tools are described in the following sections.

PROFESSIONAL TIP

Draw GD&T symbols on a dimensioning layer so the symbols and text can be plotted as lines that have the same thickness as extension and dimension lines (.01″ or 0.3 mm). The suggested text font is romans.shx. These practices correspond with the standard ASME Y14.2M-1992, *Line Conventions and Lettering*.

Using the Tolerance Tool

Ribbon

Annotate
> Dimensions

[⊕.1]

Tolerance

Type

TOLERANCE
TOL

Menu Browser

Dimension
> Tolerance

[⊕.1]

TOLERANCE

The **TOLERANCE** tool provides options for creating feature control frames and datum target symbols. The **Geometric Tolerance** dialog box is displayed when you access the **TOLERANCE** tool. See **Figure 23-16.** The **Geometric Tolerance** dialog box is divided into areas containing compartments that relate to the components found in a feature control frame. Each area contains two levels that can be used to create a feature control frame.

The first, or upper, level is used to make a single feature control frame. The lower level is used to create a double feature control frame. Double feature control frames are described later in this chapter. The dialog box also provides options for displaying a diameter symbol and a modifying symbol. In addition, the **Geometric Tolerance** dialog box allows you to display a projected tolerance zone symbol and value and part of the datum feature symbol.

Selecting a Geometric Characteristic Symbol

Geometric characteristic symbols can be accessed in the **Sym** area located at the far left of the **Geometric Tolerance** dialog box. This area has two boxes that can be used to display one or two geometric characteristic symbols.

Picking one of the boxes in the **Sym** area opens the **Symbol** dialog box. See **Figure 23-17.** Pick a symbol to display it in the **Sym** box you selected. After making a selection, the **Geometric Tolerance** dialog box returns. You can pick the same box again to select a different symbol if necessary. To remove a previously selected symbol, pick the blank image in the lower-right corner of the **Symbol** dialog box.

Tolerance 1 Area

The **Tolerance 1** area of the **Geometric Tolerance** dialog box allows you to enter the first geometric tolerance value used in the feature control frame. If you are drawing a single feature control frame, enter the desired value in the upper text box. If you are drawing a double feature control frame, also enter a value in the lower text box.

Figure 23-16.
The **Geometric Tolerance** dialog box is used to draw geometric dimensioning and tolerancing (GD&T) symbols and feature control frames.

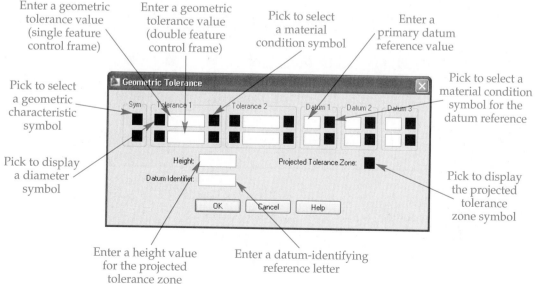

Enter a geometric tolerance value (single feature control frame)

Enter a geometric tolerance value (double feature control frame)

Pick to select a material condition symbol

Enter a primary datum reference value

Pick to select a geometric characteristic symbol

Pick to select a material condition symbol for the datum reference

Pick to display a diameter symbol

Pick to display the projected tolerance zone symbol

Enter a height value for the projected tolerance zone

Enter a datum-identifying reference letter

Figure 23-17.
The **Symbol** dialog box is used to select a geometric characteristic symbol for use in a feature control frame.

Pick the desired symbol

Pick to remove a symbol from the **Sym** area

Figure 23-18.
The **Material Condition** dialog box. Notice that the symbol for regardless of feature size (RFS) is available. This symbol is not used in ASME Y14.5M-1994, but you may need it when editing older drawings.

Old RFS symbol

Pick the desired symbol

Pick to remove a selected symbol

You can add a diameter symbol by picking the box to the left of the text box. Pick the diameter box again to remove the diameter symbol.

The box to the right of the text box is used to place a material condition symbol. When you pick this, the **Material Condition** dialog box appears. See **Figure 23-18.** Pick the desired symbol to display it in the box you selected. To remove a material condition symbol, pick the blank tile in the **Material Condition** image tile menu. The RFS symbol in **Figure 23-18** was used in ANSI Y14.5M-1982. The symbol is not used in ASME Y14.5M-1994 because RFS is assumed unless otherwise specified.

In **Figure 23-19,** a position symbol is shown in the **Sym** image tile, and 0.5 is entered as the tolerance value in the upper text box in the **Tolerance 1** area. The tolerance value is preceded by a diameter symbol and followed by an MMC symbol. Remember that a zero precedes metric decimals, but not inch decimals.

Figure 23-19.
The **Geometric Tolerance** dialog box with a diameter symbol, geometric tolerance value, and maximum material condition (MMC) symbol added to the **Tolerance 1** area.

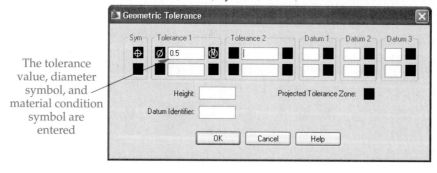

The tolerance value, diameter symbol, and material condition symbol are entered

Tolerance 2 Area

The **Tolerance 2** area of the **Geometric Tolerance** dialog box is used for the addition of a second geometric tolerance to the feature control frame. This is not a common application, but it may be used in some cases when restrictions are placed on the geometric tolerance specified in the first compartment. For example, a second geometric tolerance value of 0.8 MAX means that the specification given in the first compartment is maintained, but it cannot exceed 0.8.

Datum Areas

The **Datum 1** area of the **Geometric Tolerance** dialog box is used to establish the information needed for the primary datum reference compartment. Like the **Tolerance** areas, this area offers two levels of text boxes to create single or double feature control frames. You can also specify a material condition symbol for the datum reference by picking the box to the right of the corresponding text box to open the **Material Condition** dialog box. The **Datum 2** and **Datum 3** areas are used to specify the secondary and tertiary datum reference information. Refer to **Figure 23-8** to see how the datum reference and related material condition symbols are placed in the feature control frame.

Projected Tolerance Zone Box and Height Text Box

The **Projected Tolerance Zone:** box can be picked to display a projected tolerance zone symbol in the feature control frame. The **Height:** text box specifies the height of a projected tolerance zone. The projected tolerance zone symbol and the height value are used together when a projected tolerance zone is applied to the drawing. The use of a projected tolerance zone in a drawing is described later in this chapter.

Datum Identifier Text Box

The **Datum Identifier:** text box is used to enter a datum-identifying reference letter to be used as part of the datum feature symbol. An uppercase letter should be entered.

Completing the Tool

After you enter all the desired information in the **Geometric Tolerance** dialog box, pick **OK** and pick a point to place the tolerance in the drawing. The feature control frame for the given example is shown in **Figure 23-20.**

> **NOTE**
>
> The height of the feature control frame is automatically set to twice the height of the text. Text on engineering drawings is generally drawn at a height of .12″ (3 mm), which makes the feature control frame height .24″ (6 mm). This complies with the ASME Y14.5M standard.

Exercise 23-1

Complete the exercise on the Student CD.

Figure 23-20.
In this example, primary, secondary, and tertiary datum reference values have been added and are shown highlighted, along with the geometric tolerance value. The feature control frame created by the values specified in the dialog box is shown below.

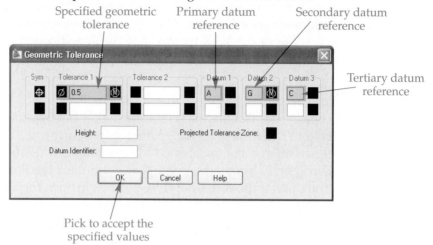

Feature Control Frame

Attaching Feature Control Frames to Leaders

In many cases, leader lines are connected to feature control frames in order to identify toleranced features. The **QLEADER** tool allows you to draw leader lines and access the **Geometric Tolerance** dialog box used to create feature control frames in one operation. This is the most effective technique for creating a feature control frame that is automatically attached and associated with a leader. However, other GD&T symbols, such as datum feature symbols, can be created more effectively using different methods. These options are described later in this chapter.

Using the Mleader Tool

The **MLEADER** tool is used to create leaders, but it does not have an option to create a feature control frame at the same time. As a result, you must draw the leader separately using the **MLEADER** tool and the feature control frame using the **TOLERANCE** tool. Apply the **None** multileader content type when using this method. The leader can be drawn before or after the symbol. See **Figure 23-21.**

Using the Qleader Tool

The **QLEADER** tool allows you to place a leader and attach a feature control frame in one operation. Some of the leader line characteristics, such as the arrowhead size, are controlled by the dimension style settings. Other features, such as the leader format and annotation style, are controlled by the **Settings** option in the **QLEADER** tool.

When you enter the **QLEADER** tool, use the **Settings** option to open the **Leader Settings** dialog box. See **Figure 23-22.** Select the **Annotation** tab if it is not displayed. Then pick the **Tolerance** radio button to display the **Geometric Tolerance** dialog box for creation of a feature control frame after the leader line is drawn.

Figure 23-21.
Use the **MLEADER** tool to create a leader before drawing the feature control frame using the **TOLERANCE** tool, or add the leader to an existing feature control frame.

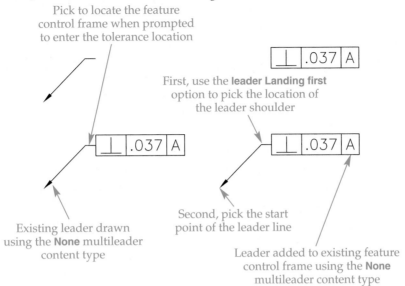

Pick to locate the feature control frame when prompted to enter the tolerance location

First, use the **leader Landing first** option to pick the location of the leader shoulder

Existing leader drawn using the **None** multileader content type

Second, pick the start point of the leader line

Leader added to existing feature control frame using the **None** multileader content type

Next, select the **Leader Line & Arrow** tab of the **Leader Settings** dialog box. Pick the **Straight** radio button to create a leader with straight-line segments. When adding a feature control frame to a leader line, you should set the maximum number of vertices in the **Maximum** text box of the **Number of Points** area to 2. When you set the maximum number of leader points to 2, you select the start and endpoints of the leader line. Then the **QLEADER** tool stops drawing the leader, automatically places the leader shoulder, and displays the **Geometric Tolerance** dialog box.

The **Arrowhead** area of the **Leader Line & Arrow** tab uses the default value assigned to leaders within the current dimension style. To change the appearance of the arrowhead, pick the drop-down list and select a terminator from the full range of choices.

The first two segments of the leader line can be restricted to certain angles. These angles are set in the **Angle Constraints** area of the **Leader Line & Arrow** tab. The options for each segment are **Any angle**, **Horizontal**, **90°**, **45°**, **30°**, and **15°**. The **Ortho** mode setting overrides the angle constraints, so it is advisable to turn **Ortho** mode off while using this tool.

Figure 23-22.
The **Leader Settings** dialog box. Activate the **Tolerance** radio button to place a feature control frame with the **QLEADER** tool.

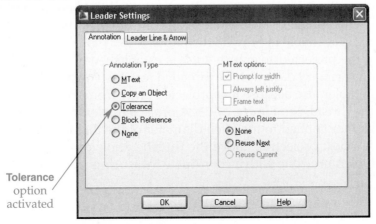

Tolerance option activated

Figure 23-23.
When you complete the **QLEADER** tool, the feature control frame is connected to the leader line.

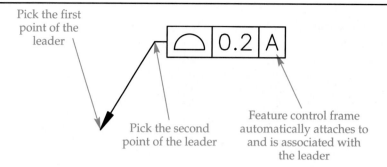

Pick the first point of the leader

Pick the second point of the leader

Feature control frame automatically attaches to and is associated with the leader

Pick the **OK** button to exit the **Leader Settings** dialog box. When asked to specify the first leader point, pick the leader start point. Then pick the next leader point. If the maximum number of leader points is set to 2, the **Geometric Tolerance** dialog box is displayed. Otherwise, press [Enter] to end the leader line and display the **Geometric Tolerance** dialog box. Specify the desired settings and values for the feature control frame. Pick the **OK** button. The feature control frame is connected to the leader line in your drawing, as shown in **Figure 23-23.**

NOTE

The **LEADER** tool can also be used to draw GD&T symbols that are automatically attached to leaders. However, this tool does not provide the same convenience and ability to comply with drafting standards as the **QLEADER** tool.

Exercise 23-2
Complete the exercise on the Student CD.

Introduction to Projected Tolerance Zones

positional tolerance: A tolerance that is used to define a zone in which the center, axis, or center plane of a feature is permitted to vary from true position.

true position: A theoretically exact location of a feature.

projected tolerance zone: A positional tolerance zone established at true position projecting a specified distance away from the primary datum.

In some situations where *positional tolerance* is used to control variance from *true position*, it may be necessary to control perpendicularity and position next to the part using a *projected tolerance zone*. See **Figure 23-24.** The normal positional tolerance extends through the thickness of the part. This application, however, can cause an interference between the location of a thread or press-fit object and its mating part. This is because the actual angle of a threaded hole controls the attitude of the fixed fastener. No clearance is available to provide flexibility.

For this reason, the projected tolerance zone is established at true position and extends away from the primary datum at the threaded feature. The projected tolerance zone provides a larger tolerance because it is projected away from the primary datum, rather than within the thread. See **Figure 23-25.** A projected tolerance is also easier to inspect than the tolerance applied to the pitch diameter of the thread. This is because a thread gauge with a post projecting above the threaded hole can easily be used to verify the projected tolerance zone with a coordinate measuring machine (CMM).

Figure 23-24.
Positional tolerance defines a zone of tolerance around the true position of a feature.

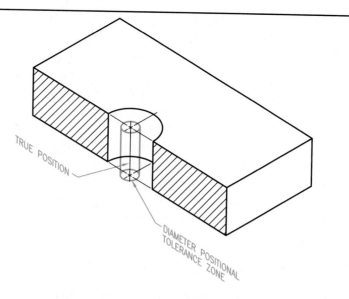

Figure 23-25.
A projected tolerance zone representation with the length of the projected tolerance zone given in the feature control frame. The projected tolerance zone symbol is shown highlighted.

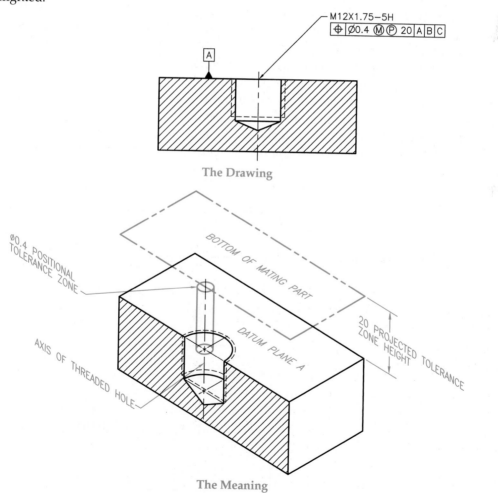

Representing a Projected Tolerance Zone

One method for displaying the projected tolerance zone is to place the projected tolerance zone symbol and height in the feature control frame after the geometric tolerance and related material condition symbol. The related thread specification is then connected to the section view of the thread symbol. With this method, the projected tolerance zone is assumed to extend away from the threaded hole at the primary datum. Refer again to Figure 23-25.

To provide additional clarification, the projected tolerance zone can be shown using a chain line in the view where the related datum appears as an edge and the minimum height of the projection is dimensioned. See Figure 23-26. The projected tolerance zone symbol is shown alone in the feature control frame after the geometric tolerance and material condition symbol (if any). The meaning is the same as previously described.

Drawing the Projected Tolerance Zone

AutoCAD specifies projected tolerance zones according to the 1982 standard. When following this standard, enter the desired geometric tolerance, diameter symbol, material condition symbol, and datum reference in the **Geometric Tolerance** dialog box, as previously described. Pick the **Projected Tolerance Zone:** box to display the projected tolerance zone symbol and enter the height in the **Height:** text box. See Figure 23-27. Place the feature control frame in the desired location in the drawing. Notice that AutoCAD displays the projected tolerance zone height in a separate compartment below the feature control frame, in accordance with ANSI Y14.5M-1982.

To specify a projected tolerance zone according to the 1994 standard, create a feature control frame with any modifier letters and the letter P after the tolerance value. The height of the projected tolerance zone is typed after the P. Leave one space between each letter and the height value. See Figure 23-28. Then use the **CIRCLE** tool to draw a circle around the modifier and the letter P. You can use the **BLOCK** tool, described in Chapters 26 and 27, to group the feature control frame and circles so they can be selected as a single object.

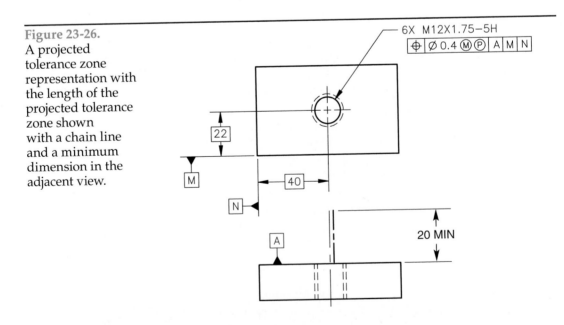

Figure 23-26.
A projected tolerance zone representation with the length of the projected tolerance zone shown with a chain line and a minimum dimension in the adjacent view.

Figure 23-27.
To add projected tolerance zone specifications to the feature control frame, enter the projected tolerance zone height and symbol in the **Geometric Tolerance** dialog box.

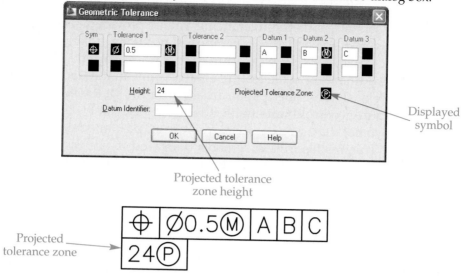

Projected tolerance zone height

Displayed symbol

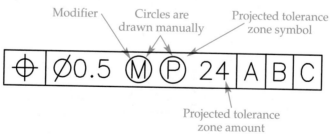

Projected tolerance zone

Feature Control Frame

Figure 23-28.
Specifying a projected tolerance zone in accordance with ASME Y14.5M-1994.

Type letters for modifier and projected tolerance zone

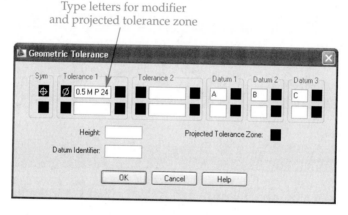

Modifier

Circles are drawn manually

Projected tolerance zone symbol

Projected tolerance zone amount

Feature Control Frame

Exercise 23-3
Complete the exercise on the Student CD.

Drawing a Double Feature Control Frame

Several GD&T applications require that the feature control frame be doubled in height, with two sets of geometric tolerancing values provided. These applications include unit straightness and flatness, composite positional tolerance, and coaxial positional tolerance. To draw a double feature control frame, use the **TOLERANCE** tool to create the desired first level of the feature control frame in the **Geometric Tolerance** dialog box as previously described. You can also use the **QLEADER** tool if you are connecting the feature control frame to a leader line. Pick the lower box in the **Sym** area. When the **Symbol** dialog box is displayed again, pick another geometric characteristic symbol. This results in two symbols displayed in the **Sym** area. Continue specifying the needed information in the lower-level **Tolerance** and **Datum** compartments. See **Figure 23-29**.

composite frame:
A double feature control frame in which one geometric symbol displayed in a single compartment.

A *composite frame* is created when the symbols in the two **Sym** boxes are the same. Some situations require the same geometric characteristic symbol twice, one in the upper frame and another in the lower frame. These are two single-segment feature control frames. To create this type, draw two separate feature control frames and block them. If you are drawing a double feature control frame with different geometric characteristic symbols for a combination control, the feature control frame must have two separate compartments. See **Figure 23-30**.

Figure 23-29.
Specifying information for a double feature control frame in the **Geometric Tolerance** dialog box.

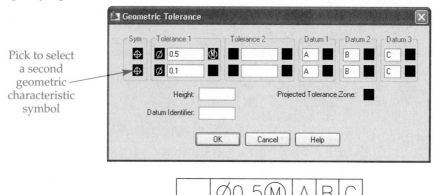

Pick to select a second geometric characteristic symbol

Figure 23-30.
If the same geometric characteristic symbol is entered in both **Symbol** boxes of the **Geometric Tolerance** dialog box, only one symbol is shown in the first compartment of the feature control frame. Create two separate feature control frames to display the same symbol in both frames. If two different symbols are used, they are displayed in separate compartments.

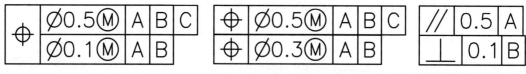

Same Symbol for Both Control Frames   **Create Separate Single Control Frames to Repeat Symbol**   **Double Feature Control Frame with Different Symbols**

Exercise 23-4
Complete the exercise on the Student CD.

Drawing Datum Feature Symbols

Datum feature symbols can be added using the **TOLERANCE** and **QLEADER** tools. Usually, however, you must use a combination of **TOLERANCE** and **MLEADER** or **QLEADER** tools to draw an appropriate datum feature symbol. The method used to draw a datum feature symbol depends on the feature the symbol identifies. When you use the **Geometric Tolerance** dialog box to specify a datum feature symbol, enter the datum reference letter in the **Datum Identifier:** text box. See Figure 23-31.

Options for Drawing Datum Feature Symbols

The datum feature symbols shown in Figure 23-32 can be drawn using the **TOLERANCE** and **MLEADER** or **QLEADER** tools. One option is to use the **TOLERANCE** tool first to place the datum identifier and then add a leader that connects the feature to the identifier. The other option is to draw a leader first and then use the **TOLERANCE** tool to add the datum identifier. This usually requires you to move the datum identifier to the correct location using object snaps. Both methods are shown in Figure 23-33.

When you use the **MLEADER** tool to add the leader, create a separate multileader style with a **Datum triangle filled** arrowhead symbol, set the maximum leader points to 2, do not include a landing, and use the **None** multileader content type. When you use the **QLEADER** tool to add the leader, create a dimension style that uses the **Datum triangle filled** leader, use the **None** annotation type, and set the maximum leader points to 2.

PROFESSIONAL TIP

When a datum feature symbol requires a shoulder, add the shoulder manually by picking a third point. This avoids shifting the angle of the leader line.

Figure 23-31.
Using the **Geometric Tolerance** dialog box to enter a datum-identifying reference letter. This letter is used to create the datum feature symbol.

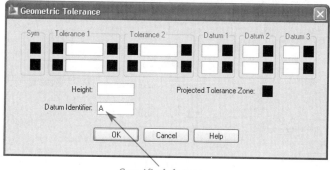

Specified datum
reference letter

Figure 23-32.
Examples of datum feature symbols created using a combination of **TOLERANCE** and **MLEADER** or **QLEADER** tools.

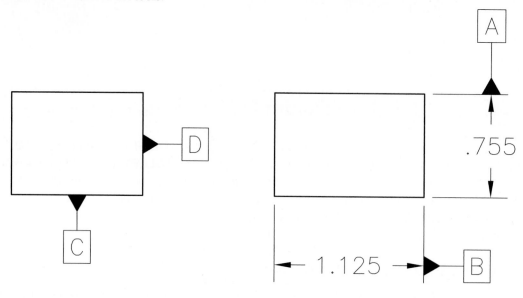

Figure 23-33.
Use the **MLEADER** or **QLEADER** tools to add a leader before a feature control frame is drawn using the **TOLERANCE** tool, or add the leader to an existing feature control frame.

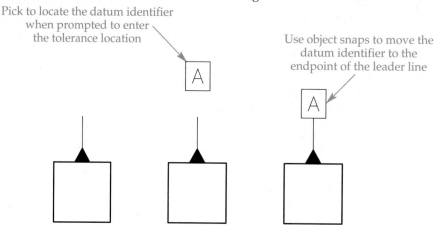

Pick to locate the datum identifier when prompted to enter the tolerance location

Use object snaps to move the datum identifier to the endpoint of the leader line

Datum identifier added to existing (vertical) leader

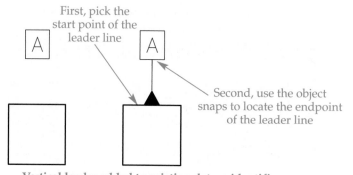

First, pick the start point of the leader line

Second, use the object snaps to locate the endpoint of the leader line

Vertical leader added to existing datum identifier

Figure 23-34.
Use the **Tolerance** annotation option of the **QLEADER** tool to add a datum feature symbol to an angled surface.

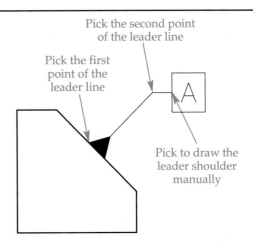

Pick the second point of the leader line

Pick the first point of the leader line

Pick to draw the leader shoulder manually

A

Adding Datum Feature Symbols to Angled Surfaces

You must follow specific steps in order to add a datum feature symbol to an angled surface, as shown in **Figure 23-34.** One option is to use the **QLEADER** tool. Before adding the leader, create a dimension style that uses the **Datum triangle filled** leader. Then enter the **QLEADER** tool and use the **Settings** option to open the **Leader Settings** dialog box. Select the **Annotation** tab if it is not displayed and pick the **Tolerance** radio button. Select the **Leader Line & Arrow** tab of the **Leader Settings** dialog box and pick the **Straight** radio button. When adding a datum feature to a leader line, you should set the maximum number of vertices in the **Maximum** text box of the **Number of Points** area to 3. This allows you to construct the leader shoulder manually. If you let AutoCAD form the leader shoulder automatically, it will shift the angle of the leader line.

Select the **OK** button to exit the **Leader Settings** dialog box. Pick the leader start point and then the next leader point. The second point must create a line segment that is perpendicular to the angled surface. Pick the third point to define the length of the leader shoulder. If the maximum number of leader points was set to 3, the **Geometric Tolerance** dialog box is displayed. Otherwise, press [Enter] to end the leader line and display the **Geometric Tolerance** dialog box. Specify a value in the **Datum identifier** text box and pick the **OK** button.

PROFESSIONAL TIP

Another option for placing GD&T symbols is to create your own blocks with attributes. Blocks can be inserted into the drawing and the attribute data can be adjusted as needed. Blocks can also be added to multileader lines using the Block multileader content type. Chapters 26 and 27 provides a detailed description of how to create blocks.

Exercise 23-5
Complete the exercise on the Student CD.

Drawing Basic Dimensions

A basic dimension is shown in **Figure 23-35.** Basic dimensions can be drawn automatically by setting a basic tolerance in the **Tolerances** tab of the **Modify Dimension Style** dialog box, as described in Chapter 22. It is recommended that you establish a

---

Figure 23-35.
A basic dimension.

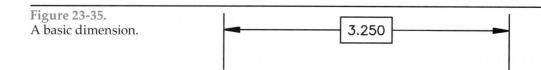

separate dimension style for basic dimensions because not all of the dimensions on a drawing will be basic.

The height of the basic dimension rectangle is twice the height of the text, as shown in Figure 23-9. Text on engineering drawings is generally drawn at a height of .12" (3 mm), which makes the basic dimension rectangle height .24" (6 mm). As a result, the distance from the text to the basic dimension rectangle should be equal to half the text height. For example, if the height of the drawing text is .12", the space between the text and the basic dimension rectangle should be .06" to result in a .24" high frame. The distance from the text to the basic dimension rectangle is controlled by the **Offset from dim line:** setting in the **Text** tab of the **New** (or **Modify**) **Dimension Style** dialog box. The setting also controls the gap between the dimension line and the dimension text for linear dimensions.

NOTE

Picking the **Draw frame around text** check box in the **Text** tab of the **New** (or **Modify**) **Dimension Style** dialog box also activates the basic tolerance method.

Exercise 23-6

Complete the exercise on the Student CD.

Editing Feature Control Frames

A feature control frame acts as one object. When you pick any location on the frame, the entire object is selected. You can edit feature control frames using editing tools such as **ERASE**, **COPY**, **MOVE**, **ROTATE**, and **SCALE**. The **STRETCH** tool only allows you to move a feature control frame. This effect is similar to the results of using the **STRETCH** tool with text objects.

You can edit the values inside a feature control frame using the **DDEDIT** tool. When you enter this tool and select the desired frame, the **Geometric Tolerance** dialog box is displayed with all the current values. After you make the desired changes, pick **OK** to update the feature control frame.

You can also use the **DDEDIT** tool to edit basic dimensions. When you select a basic dimension for editing, the text editor is displayed. You can then edit the basic dimension as you would any other dimension.

DDEDIT

Type
DDEDIT
ED
Menu Browser
Modify
> Object
> Text
> Edit...

NOTE

If you double-click on a dimension object, AutoCAD opens the **Properties** palette.

AutoCAD and Its Applications—Basics

Sample GD&T Applications

This chapter is intended to give you a general overview of GD&T applications and basic instructions on how to draw GD&T symbols using AutoCAD. If you are in the manufacturing industry, you may have considerable use for GD&T. The support information presented in this chapter may be a review, or it may inspire you to learn more about this topic. The drawings in Figure 23-36 are intended to show you some common GD&T applications using the dimensioning and geometric characteristic symbols available in AutoCAD.

Figure 23-36.
Examples of typical geometric dimensioning and tolerancing (GD&T) applications using various dimensioning and geometric characteristic symbols.

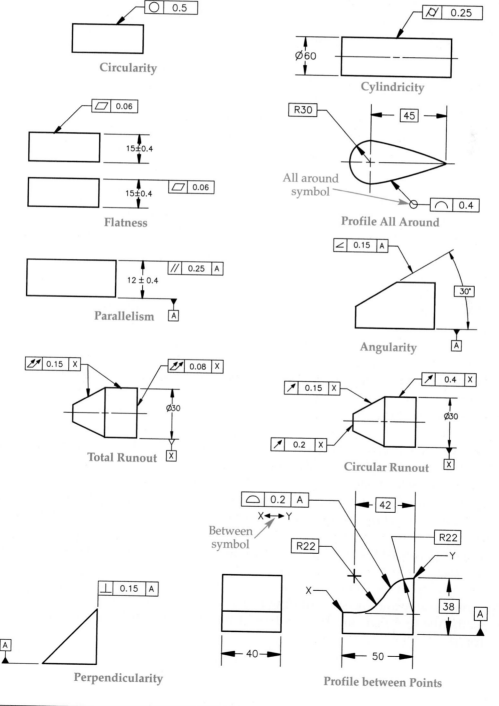

Chapter Test

Answer the following questions. Write your answers on a separate sheet of paper or complete the electronic chapter test on the Student CD.

1. Name the current standard for dimensioning and tolerancing adopted by the American National Standards Institute (ANSI) and published by the American Society of Mechanical Engineers (ASME).

2. Identify each of the following geometric characteristic symbols:

   A. —   H. ◎

   B. ▱   I. ≡

   C. ○   J. //

   D. ⌀   K. ⊥

   E. ⌒   L. ∠

   F. ⌓   M. ↗

   G. ⊕   N. ⤧

3. Identify the parts of the feature control frame shown below.

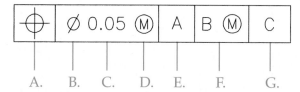

4. Name three tools that can be used to add GD&T symbols to your drawing.

5. Identify the dialog box that contains settings used to create a feature control frame.

6. How do you access the **Symbol** dialog box, in which a geometric characteristic symbol can be selected?

7. How do you remove a geometric characteristic symbol from one of the image tiles in the **Sym** area of the **Geometric Tolerance** dialog box?

8. Identify the tool that provides you with the ability to place a leader and attach a feature control frame in one operation.

9. Describe the procedure used to draw a feature control frame connected to a leader line.

10. Describe how to place a projected tolerance zone symbol and height value with the feature control frame, based on ANSI Y14.5M-1982.

11. Explain how to create a double feature control frame.

12. Describe how to draw a datum feature symbol without an attached feature control frame. How do you add a leader line with a filled datum triangle to the symbol?

13. Which AutoCAD setting allows you to draw basic dimensions? How is it accessed?

14. Identify the AutoCAD setting that controls the space between the text in a feature control frame and the surrounding frame.

15. Name the tool that can be used to edit the existing values in a feature control frame.

Drawing Problems

Create dimension styles that will assist you with the following problems. Draw fully dimensioned multiview drawings. The required number of views depends on the problem and is to be determined by you. Apply geometric tolerancing as described in this chapter. Modify the available AutoCAD drawing applications to comply with ASME Y14.5M-1994 standards. The problems are presented in accordance with ASME Y14.5M-1994.

Note: Some of the drawing problems refer to drawings created in drawing problems from previous chapters. If you have not yet created those drawings, you will need to do so before working these problems.

▼ Basic

1. Draw the following object. Untoleranced dimensions are ±0.3. Save the drawing as P23-1.

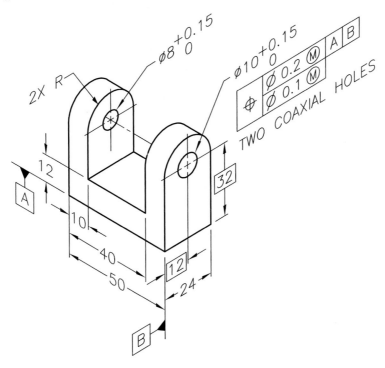

2. Open drawing P22-6. Edit the drawing by adding the geometric tolerancing applications shown below. Untoleranced dimensions are ±.02 for two-place decimal precision and ±.005 for three-place decimal precision. Save the drawing as P23-2.

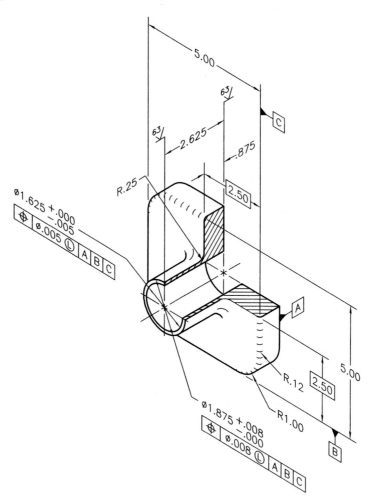

3. Open drawing P22-4. Edit the drawing by adding the geometric tolerancing applications shown below. Untoleranced dimensions are ±0.5. Save the drawing as P23-3.

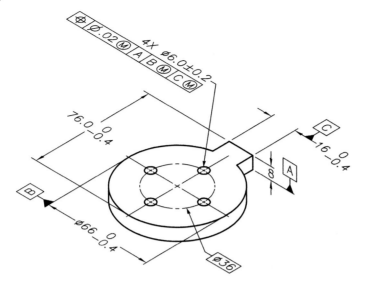

▼ Intermediate

4. Open drawing P22-7. Edit the drawing by adding the geometric tolerancing applications shown below. Save the drawing as P23-4.

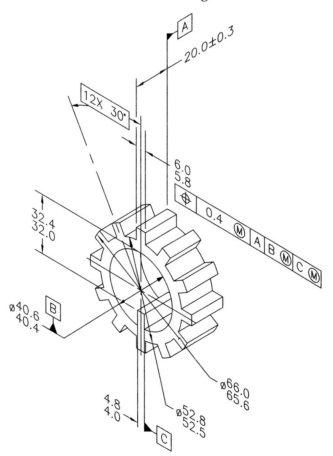

5. Draw the following object as previously instructed. The problem is shown with a full section for clarity. You do not need to draw a section. Untoleranced dimensions are ±.010. Save the drawing as P23-5.

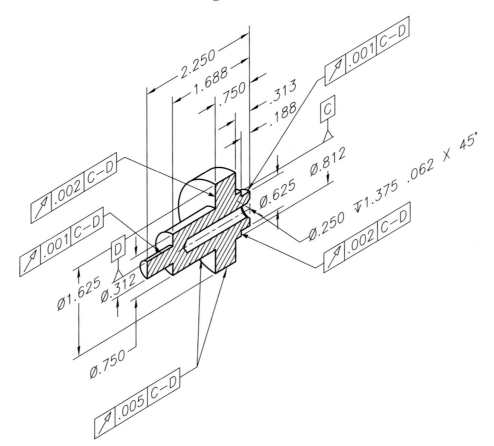

6. Open drawing P20-21. Edit the drawing by adding the geometric tolerancing applications shown below. Save the drawing as P23-6.

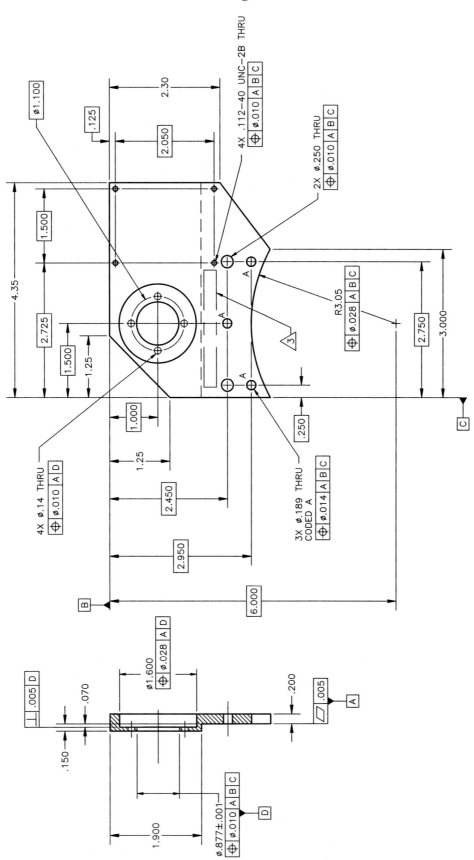

7. Draw the following object as previously instructed. The problem is shown with a half section for clarity. You do not need to draw a section. Untoleranced dimensions are ±.010. Save the drawing as P23-7.

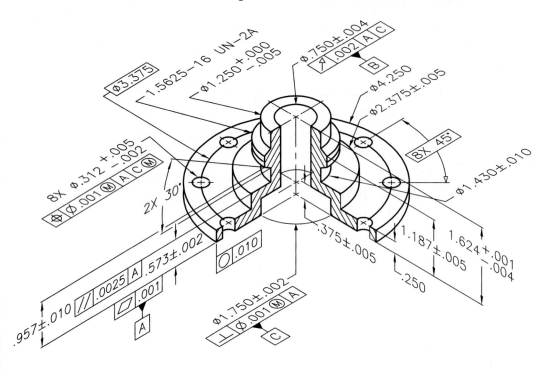

Section Views and Graphic Patterns

Learning Objectives

After completing this chapter, you will be able to do the following:

- ✓ Identify sectioning techniques.
- ✓ Add graphic patterns using the **BHATCH** tool.
- ✓ Insert hatch patterns into drawings using **DesignCenter** and tool palettes.
- ✓ Edit existing hatch patterns with the **HATCHEDIT** tool.
- ✓ Use the **SOLID** tool.

Many drawings use repetitive symbols or objects, known as *graphic patterns*, to describe specific information. For example, the front elevation of the house shown in **Figure 24-1** contains patterns of lines that create graphic representations of siding, brick, and roof materials. AutoCAD includes tools, such as **BHATCH** and **SOLID**, that can be used to draw graphic patterns quickly. One of the most common graphic patterns is a group of section lines added to a section view.

graphic pattern:
The patterned arrangement of the objects in a symbol.

Figure 24-1.
Graphic patterns are used to describe patterns of information on a drawing, such as the siding, brick, and roof materials added to the front elevation of a house.

Section Views

In mechanical drafting, internal features in drawings appear as hidden lines. It is poor practice to dimension to hidden lines, but these features must be dimensioned. Therefore, *section views*, or *sections*, are used to clarify the hidden features. Section views are used in conjunction with multiview drawings to completely describe the exterior and interior features of an object. See **Figure 24-2.**

When sections are drawn, a *cutting-plane line* is placed in one of the views to show where the cut was made. The cutting-plane line is drawn with a thick dashed or phantom line in accordance with ASME Y14.2M, *Line Conventions and Lettering*. The arrows on the cutting-plane line indicate the line of sight when looking at the section view.

Cutting-plane lines are often labeled with letters that relate to the proper section view. A title, such as SECTION A-A, is placed under the view. When more than one section view is drawn, labels continue with B-B through Z-Z. The letters *I*, *O*, and *Q* are not used because they may be confused with numbers.

Labeling section views is necessary for drawings with multiple sections. When only one section view is present and its location is obvious, a label is not needed. *Section lines* are used in the section view to show where material has been cut away.

Sectioning is also used in other drafting fields, such as architectural and structural drafting. Cross sections through buildings show the construction methods and materials. See **Figure 24-3.** The cutting-plane lines used in these fields are often composed of letter and number symbols. This helps coordinate the large number of sections found in a set of architectural drawings.

Section Lines

Section line symbols are placed in the section view to show where material has been cut away. Section lines are placed at 45° unless another angle is required to satisfy the next two rules. Avoid section lines placed at angles greater than 75° or less than 15° from horizontal. Section lines should not be drawn parallel or perpendicular to any other adjacent lines on the drawing. Also, section lines should not cross object lines.

Section lines may be drawn using different patterns to represent the specific type of material. Equally spaced section lines represent a general application. See **Figure 24-2.** This is adequate in most situations. Additional patterns are not necessary if the type

section view (section): A view that shows internal features as if a portion of the object has been cut away.

cutting-plane line: The line that cuts through the object to expose internal features.

section lines: Lines that show where material has been cut away.

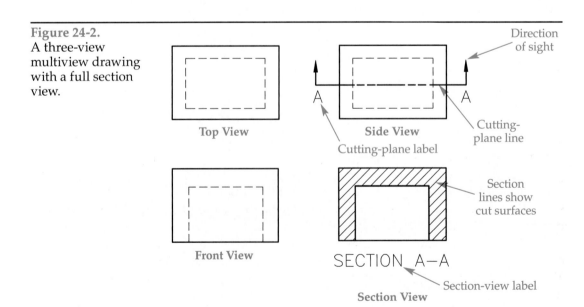

Figure 24-2.
A three-view multiview drawing with a full section view.

Top View

Side View

Front View

Direction of sight

Cutting-plane label

Cutting-plane line

Section lines show cut surfaces

SECTION A—A

Section-view label

Section View

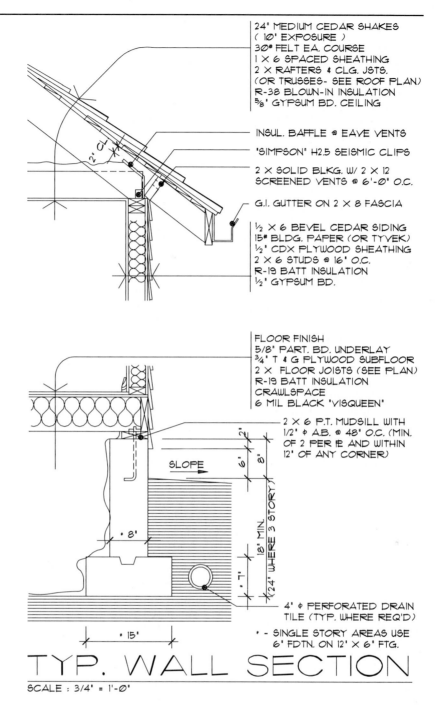

Figure 24-3.
An architectural
section view. (Alan
Mascord Design
Associates)

24" MEDIUM CEDAR SHAKES
(10" EXPOSURE)
30# FELT EA. COURSE
1 X 6 SPACED SHEATHING
2 X RAFTERS & CLG. JSTS.
(OR TRUSSES- SEE ROOF PLAN)
R-38 BLOWN-IN INSULATION
⅝" GYPSUM BD. CEILING

INSUL. BAFFLE @ EAVE VENTS

'SIMPSON' H2.5 SEISMIC CLIPS

2 X SOLID BLKG. W/ 2 X 12
SCREENED VENTS @ 6'-Ø" O.C.

G.I. GUTTER ON 2 X 8 FASCIA

½ X 6 BEVEL CEDAR SIDING
15# BLDG. PAPER (OR TYVEK)
½" CDX PLYWOOD SHEATHING
2 X 6 STUDS @ 16" O.C.
R-19 BATT INSULATION
½" GYPSUM BD.

FLOOR FINISH
5/8" PART. BD. UNDERLAY
¾" T & G PLYWOOD SUBFLOOR
2 X FLOOR JOISTS (SEE PLAN)
R-19 BATT INSULATION
CRAWLSPACE
6 MIL BLACK 'VISQUEEN'

2 X 6 P.T. MUDSILL WITH
1/2" ⌀ A.B. @ 48" O.C. (MIN.
OF 2 PER ⅊ AND WITHIN
12" OF ANY CORNER)

SLOPE

4' ⌀ PERFORATED DRAIN
TILE (TYP. WHERE REQ'D)

* - SINGLE STORY AREAS USE
6' FDTN. ON 12" X 6' FTG.

TYP. WALL SECTION
SCALE : 3/4' = 1'-Ø'

of material is clearly indicated in the title block. Different section line material symbols are needed when connected parts of different materials are sectioned.

AutoCAD provides standard section line symbols, known as *hatch patterns*. These symbols are defined in the acad.pat file. The AutoCAD pattern labeled ANSI31 is the general section line symbol and is the default pattern in a new drawing. It is also used when representing cast iron in a section. The ANSI32 symbol is used for sectioning steel. When you change to a different hatch pattern, the new pattern becomes the default in the current drawing until it is changed.

When very thin objects are sectioned, the material may be completely blackened or shaded to clarify features. To do this, use AutoCAD's Solid hatch pattern. The ASME Y14.2M standard recommends that very thin sections be drawn without section lines or solid fills.

hatch patterns:
AutoCAD's standard
section line
symbols.

Types of Sections

Many types of sections are available, depending on the application. The section used depends on the detail to be sectioned. For example, one object may require that the section be taken completely through the object. Another may only need to remove a small portion to expose the interior features.

An example of a *full section* is shown in **Figure 24-2**. In this type of section, the cutting plane passes completely through the object along the center plane, as shown by the cutting-plane line. *Offset sections* are the same as full sections, except the cutting plane is staggered. This allows you to cut through features that are not in a straight line. See **Figure 24-4**.

An example of a *half section* is shown in **Figure 24-5**. The term *half* is used because half of the view appears in section and the other half is shown as an exterior view. Half sections are commonly used on symmetrical objects. A centerline is used to separate the sectioned part of the view from the unsectioned portion. Hidden lines are normally omitted from the unsectioned side.

Figure 24-6 provides an example of an *aligned section*. The cutting plane cuts through the feature to be sectioned. It is then rotated to align with the center plane before projecting into the section view. Using an offset section for this application would distort the image.

An example of a *revolved section* is shown in **Figure 24-7**. The section may be revolved in place within the object, or part of the view may be broken away. This type of section makes dimensioning easier.

Removed sections serve much the same function as revolved sections. A cutting-plane line shows where the section has been taken. When multiple removed sections are taken, the cutting-plane lines and related views are labeled. Drawing only the ends of the cutting-plane lines simplifies the views. See **Figure 24-8**. *Broken-out sections* are used to clarify a hidden feature. See **Figure 24-9**.

full sections: Sections in which half the object is removed.

offset sections: Sections that have a staggered cutting plane.

half sections: Sections that show one-quarter of the object removed.

aligned sections: Sections used when a feature is out of alignment with the center plane.

revolved sections: Sections that clarify the contour of objects that have the same shape throughout their length.

removed sections: Section views that are removed from the regular view; similar to revolved sections.

broken-out sections: Sections that show only a small portion of the object removed.

Figure 24-4.
An offset section.

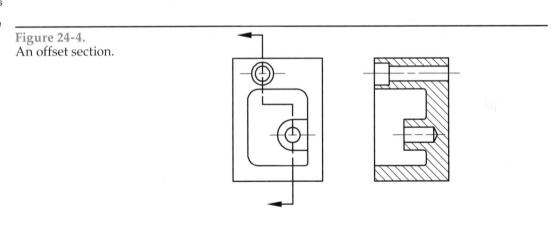

Figure 24-5.
A half section.

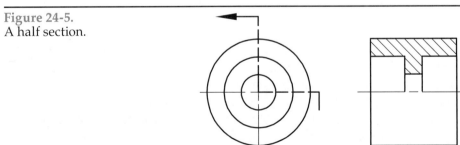

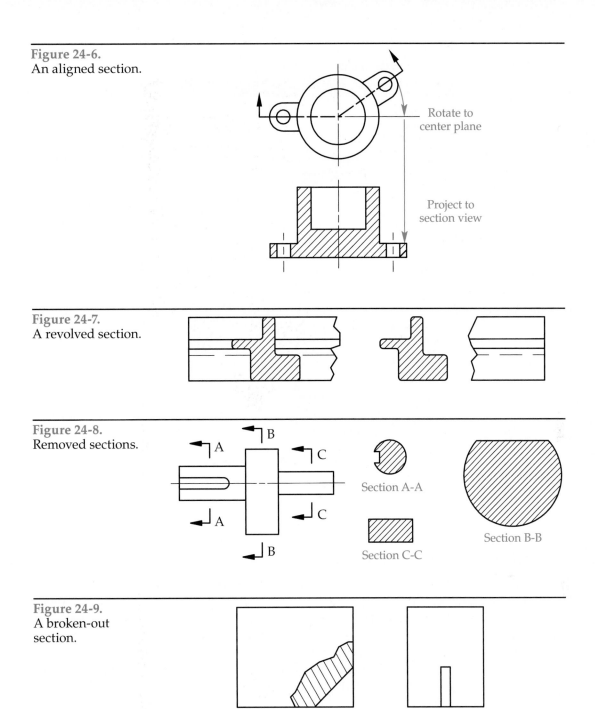

Figure 24-6.
An aligned section.

Rotate to center plane

Project to section view

Figure 24-7.
A revolved section.

Figure 24-8.
Removed sections.

A

B

A

C

C

B

Section A-A

Section C-C

Section B-B

Figure 24-9.
A broken-out section.

Drawing Hatch Patterns Using the Bhatch Tool

AutoCAD hatch patterns are not limited to sectioning. Hatch patterns are typically added as shading on a technical illustration or an architectural elevation, as shown in **Figure 24-1.** They can also be used as artistic patterns in a variety of applications, such as graphic layout for an advertisement or promotion.

The **BHATCH** tool simplifies the hatching process by automatically hatching a selected enclosed area. Hatch patterns are selected and applied using the **Hatch and Gradient** dialog box. The **Hatch and Gradient** dialog box is divided into **Hatch** and **Gradient** tabs. The **Hatch** tab is separated into different areas that control the hatch settings. See **Figure 24-10.**

Ribbon
Home
> Draw

Hatch

Type

BHATCH
HATCH
BH
H

Menu Browser

Draw
> Hatch...

BHATCH

Figure 24-10.
The **Hatch** tab of the **Hatch and Gradient** dialog box.

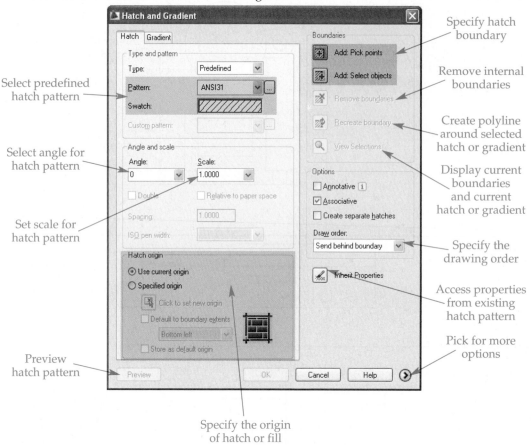

Select predefined
hatch pattern

Select angle for
hatch pattern

Set scale for
hatch pattern

Preview
hatch pattern

Specify hatch
boundary

Remove internal
boundaries

Create polyline
around selected
hatch or gradient

Display current
boundaries
and current
hatch or gradient

Specify the
drawing order

Access properties
from existing
hatch pattern

Pick for more
options

Specify the origin
of hatch or fill

Selecting a Hatch Pattern

The hatch pattern is selected in the **Type and pattern** area on the **Hatch** tab of the **Hatch and Gradient** dialog box. Hatch pattern categories are available in the **Type:** drop-down list. The **Predefined** category contains predefined AutoCAD patterns stored in the acad.pat and acadiso.pat files. The **User defined** category creates a pattern of lines based on the current linetype in your drawing. You can control the angle and spacing of the lines. The **Custom** category allows you to specify a pattern defined in any custom PAT file you have added to the AutoCAD search path.

Predefined hatch patterns

AutoCAD has many predefined hatch patterns. To select a predefined hatch pattern, select **Predefined** in the **Type:** drop-down list and then select the predefined pattern. You can select the pattern from the **Pattern:** drop-down list or you can pick the ellipsis (**...**) button next to the **Pattern:** drop-down arrow to display the **Hatch Pattern Palette** dialog box. See **Figure 24-11.**

The **Hatch Pattern Palette** dialog box provides sample images of the predefined hatch patterns. The hatch patterns are divided among the four tabs: **ANSI, ISO, Other Predefined**, and **Custom**. Select the desired pattern from the appropriate tab and pick the **OK** button to return to the **Hatch and Gradient** dialog box. The selected pattern is displayed in the **Swatch:** preview box and listed in the **Pattern:** text box. You can also access the **Hatch Pattern Palette** dialog box by picking the image displayed in the **Swatch:** preview box.

Figure 24-11.
The **Hatch Pattern Palette** dialog box can be used to select a predefined or custom hatch pattern.

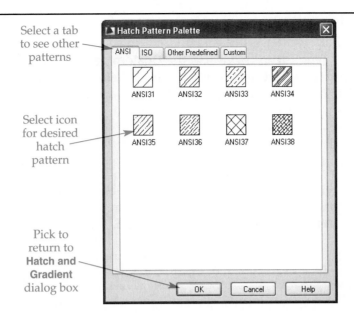

Select a tab to see other patterns

Select icon for desired hatch pattern

Pick to return to **Hatch and Gradient** dialog box

You can control the angle and scale of any predefined pattern with the **Angle:** and **Scale:** drop-down lists located in the **Angle and scale** area. For predefined ISO patterns, you can also control the ISO pen width using the **ISO pen width:** drop-down list.

User defined hatch patterns

A user defined hatch pattern is a pattern of lines drawn using the current line-type. These patterns can only be used in the current drawing. The angle for the pattern relative to the X axis is set in the **Angle:** text box and the spacing between the lines is set in the **Spacing:** text box. Both of these options are located in the **Angle and scale** area of the **Hatch and Gradient** dialog box.

You can also specify double hatch lines by selecting the **Double** check box. This check box is only available when User defined is selected in the **Type:** drop-down list. **Figure 24-12** shows examples of user defined hatch patterns.

Figure 24-12.
Examples of user defined hatch patterns with different hatch angles and spacing.

Angle	0°	45°	0°	45°
Spacing	.125	.125	.250	.250
Single Hatch				
Double Hatch				

Custom hatch patterns

Custom hatch patterns are created and then saved in PAT files. When you select Custom in the **Type:** drop-down list, the **Custom pattern:** drop-down list is enabled. Select a pattern from the **Custom pattern:** drop-down list, or pick the ellipsis (**...**) button to select the pattern from the **Custom** tab of the **Hatch Pattern Palette** dialog box. You can set the angle and scale of custom hatch patterns, just as you can with predefined hatch patterns.

Setting the Hatch Pattern Scale

Predefined and custom hatch patterns can be scaled by entering or selecting a value using the **Scale:** text box. The pattern scale default is 1. If the drawn pattern is too small or too large, enter a new scale. **Figure 24-13** shows examples of different scales.

PROFESSIONAL TIP

Use a smaller hatch scale for small objects and a larger hatch scale for larger objects. This makes your section lines look appropriate for the drawing scale. Often you must use your best judgment when selecting a hatch scale.

The drawing scale factor is an important consideration when you select the hatch pattern scale. You must enter an appropriate hatch scale in order to make sure the hatch pattern is shown on-screen and plotted at the proper size. To understand the concept of hatch scale, look at the section view shown in **Figure 24-14.** In this example, the section line spacing should be the same distance apart regardless of drawing scale. The section lines on the drawing displayed at a scale of 1:1 are shown correctly. The section lines drawn using the same hatch scale are too close when the drawing is

Figure 24-13.
Hatch pattern scale factors.

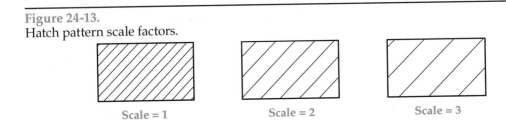

Scale = 1   Scale = 2   Scale = 3

Figure 24-14.
The hatch pattern scale may appear incorrect as the drawing scale changes.

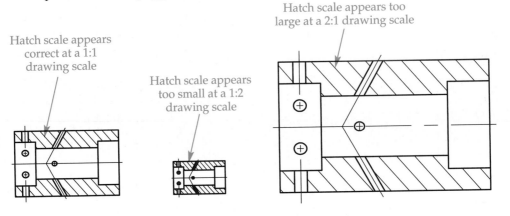

Hatch scale appears correct at a 1:1 drawing scale

Hatch scale appears too small at a 1:2 drawing scale

Hatch scale appears too large at a 2:1 drawing scale

displayed at a scale of 1:2, and are too far apart when the drawing is displayed at a scale of 2:1. To overcome this issue, you must adjust the hatch pattern scale according to the drawing scale. This involves finding the scale factor. You can calculate the scale factor manually and apply it to hatch patterns, or you can allow AutoCAD to calculate it by using annotative hatch patterns.

Scaling hatch patterns manually

To manually adjust hatch scale according to a specific drawing scale, you must calculate the drawing scale factor. Then multiply the scale factor by the desired plotted hatch scale to get the model space hatch scale. Enter this value in the **Scale:** text box. **Figure 24-15** shows examples of adjusting hatch scale according to drawing scale. Refer to Chapter 9 for information on determining the drawing scale factor.

Annotative hatch patterns

Pick the **Annotative** check box in the **Options** area to make the hatch pattern annotative. Annotative hatch patterns are scaled by AutoCAD according to the annotation scale you select, which is the same as the drawing scale, eliminating the need for you to calculate the scale factor and multiply the scale factor by the hatch scale. When you select an annotation scale from the **Annotation Scale** flyout button located on the status bar, AutoCAD determines the scale factor and automatically applies it to annotative hatch patterns, or any annotative object. The result is a hatch pattern that is displayed at the proper scale regardless of the drawing scale, much like the example shown in **Figure 24-15,** but without requiring you to change the hatch scale between different drawing scales. For example, if you enter a value in the **Scale:** text box that is appropriate for an annotation scale of 1/4″ = 1′-0″, and then change the annotation scale to 1″ = 1′-0″, the displayed scale of the hatch pattern relative to the drawing scale does not change. It looks the same on the 1/4″ = 1′-0″ scale drawing as it does on the 1″ = 1′-0″ scale drawing.

NOTE

When displayed in a floating viewport, annotative hatch patterns remain planar to the layout, even if the drawing view is rotated using 3D view tools or twisted into a position that is nonplanar to the layout using the **TWist** option of the **DVIEW** tool. See Chapters 28 and 29 for more information about floating viewports.

Figure 24-15.
The hatch pattern scale may require adjusting, depending on the drawing scale.

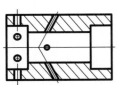

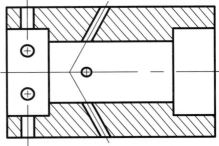

Drawing Scale: 1:1
Drawing Scale Factor: 1
Hatch Scale: 1

Drawing Scale: 1:2
Drawing Scale Factor: 2
Hatch Scale: 2

Drawing Scale: 2:1
Drawing Scale Factor: .5
Hatch Scale: .5

Scaling hatch patterns relative to paper space

The **Relative to paper space** check box in the **Angle and scale** area is used to scale the hatch pattern relative to the scale of the active viewport. You must enter a floating layout viewport in order to select the **Relative to paper space** check box. The hatch scale automatically adjusts according to the viewport scale. For example, a floating viewport scale set to 4:1 uses a scale factor of .25 (1 ÷ 4 = .25). If you enter a hatch scale of 1, the hatch scale is automatically drawn at a scale of .25 (1 × .25 = .25).

Setting the Hatch Origin Point

When creating hatch patterns, you sometimes want lines on the hatch pattern to line up with an existing object. This could be the case when using one of the brick hatch patterns, for example. In the **Hatch origin** area of the **Hatch and Gradient** dialog box, the default setting is **Use current origin**. This refers to the current UCS origin, which is used as the defining point for how the hatch pattern is created and how it repeats itself. To specify a different origin point, select **Specified origin**. See Figure 24-16.

When the **Specified origin** option is selected, the other settings become available. Picking the **Click to set new origin** button temporarily hides the **Hatch and Gradient** dialog box so a different origin can be selected in the drawing window. For example, if you want a hatch pattern to start in the lower-left corner of a rectangle, use the **Endpoint** object snap to select the corner of the rectangle. In Figure 24-17A, the **Use current origin** setting is used. In Figure 24-17B, notice how it seems that the hatch pattern starts perfectly from the lower-left corner of the rectangle. This is because this corner was picked to be the origin point. After you select a point for the origin, the **Hatch and Gradient** dialog box is displayed again.

The hatch origin point can be aligned with specific points on the hatch boundary. To use this setting, check the **Default to boundary extents** box. When this is checked, the drop-down list below it becomes available. The options in the drop-down list are **Bottom left**, **Bottom right**, **Top right**, **Top left**, and **Center**. The hatch origin is defined at

Figure 24-16.
The **Specified origin** setting in the **Hatch origin** area of the **Hatch** tab activates the other hatch origin settings.

Pick to specify a different origin point

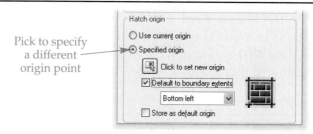

Figure 24-17.
A—The **Use current origin** setting is used. B—The **Specified origin** option is selected and the **Click to set new origin** button is used to select the lower-left corner of the rectangle.

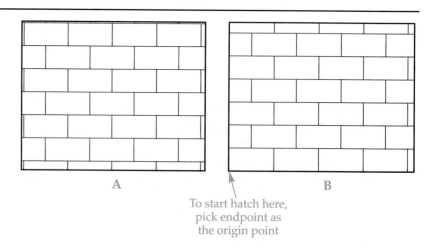

A

B

To start hatch here, pick endpoint as the origin point

the selected point on the boundary. The custom origin point can be saved by checking **Store as default origin**.

Selecting Areas to Hatch

Using the **Add: Pick points** button is the easiest method of defining an area to be hatched. When you pick the button, the drawing returns. Pick a point within the region to be hatched, and AutoCAD automatically defines the boundary around the selected point. More than one internal point can be selected. When you are finished selecting points, press [Enter] or the space bar, or right-click and pick the **Enter** option to return to the **Hatch and Gradient** dialog box. Then pick the **OK** button to apply the hatch. See **Figure 24-18**.

NOTE

At the Select internal point: prompt, you can type U or UNDO to undo the last selection, in case you picked the wrong area. You can also undo the hatch pattern by typing U after the pattern is drawn. However, to save time, you can preview the hatch before applying it.

Use the **Add: Select objects** button to define the hatch boundary if you have items that you want to hatch by picking the object, rather than picking inside the object. See **Figure 24-19**. These items can be circles, polygons, or closed polylines. This method works especially well if the object to be hatched is crossed by other objects, such as the graph lines that cross the bars in **Figure 24-20**. Picking a point inside the bar results in the hatch displayed in **Figure 24-20A**. You can pick inside each individual area

Figure 24-18.
Defining the hatch boundary by picking a point.

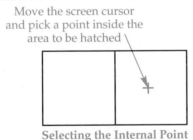

Move the screen cursor and pick a point inside the area to be hatched

Selecting the Internal Point   The Result

Figure 24-19.
Selecting objects to be hatched.

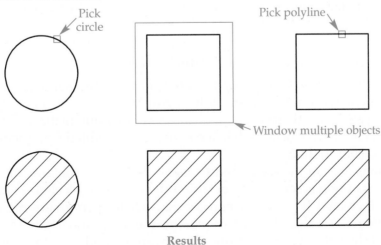

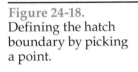

Pick circle

Pick polyline

Window multiple objects

Results

Figure 24-20.
A—Applying a hatch pattern to objects that cross each other using the **Add: Pick points** button.
B—Applying a hatch pattern to a closed polygon using the **Add: Select objects** button.

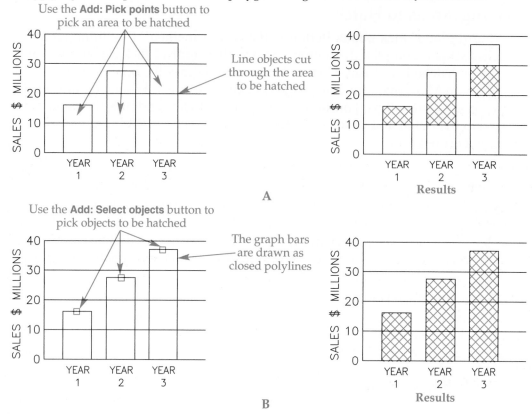

of each bar, but this can be time-consuming. If the bars were drawn using a closed polyline, all you have to do is use the **Add: Select objects** button to pick each bar. See **Figure 24-20B.**

The **Add: Select objects** button can also be used to pick an object inside an area to be hatched to exclude it from the hatch pattern. An example of this is the text shown inside the hatch area in **Figure 24-21.**

The **Remove boundaries** button is active after either points or objects have been selected. Picking this button returns you to the drawing screen and allows you to select objects to remove their boundaries from the hatch area. Once the objects have been selected, press [Enter] or the space bar, or right-click and pick the **Enter** option to display the **Hatch and Gradient** dialog box. Boundaries can also be removed by using the **remove Boundaries** option at the Command: prompt while using the **Add: Pick points** button or the **Add: Select objects** button.

Specifying the Hatch Pattern Composition

associative hatch patterns: Patterns that update automatically when the boundary is edited.

nonassociative hatch pattern: A pattern that is independent of its boundaries, and does not automatically update when the boundary is changed.

The **BHATCH** tool creates *associative hatch patterns* by default, but it can be set to create *nonassociative hatch patterns*. If the boundary of an associative hatch pattern is stretched, scaled, or otherwise edited, the new area automatically fills with the original hatch pattern. Associative hatch patterns can be edited using the **HATCHEDIT** tool, described later in this chapter.

The **Options** area of the **Hatch and Gradient** dialog box contains the **Associative** check box. This option is selected by default. When it is not selected, a nonassociative hatch pattern is created. If you pick a nonassociative hatch pattern to scale, for example, only the boundary is scaled; the pattern remains the same. You need to select both the boundary and the pattern before editing if you want to modify both.

Figure 24-21.
Using the **Add:**
Select objects
button to exclude
an object from the
hatch pattern.

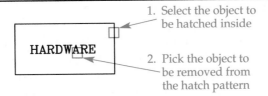

1. Select the object to
   be hatched inside

2. Pick the object to
   be removed from
   the hatch pattern

Results

To create multiple hatch patterns, you can select multiple areas and objects during a single procedure. By default, these hatch patterns are a single object. This means if you select one hatch pattern, they are all selected. Editing the properties of one of the hatch patterns edits all of them. This may not always be the result that you want. When you check the **Create separate hatches** check box in the **Options** area before applying the hatch patterns, individual hatch patterns are created for each boundary.

Defining the Drawing Order

A hatch pattern can be displayed in front of or behind other objects when it is placed in the drawing. The **Draw order** options in the **Options** area of the **Hatch and Gradient** dialog box control the order of display when the hatch pattern overlaps another object. The **Send behind boundary** option is selected by default and makes the hatch pattern appear behind the boundary that defines the hatch pattern area.

Select the **Bring in front of boundary** option to make the hatch pattern appear on top of the boundary that defines the hatch pattern area. Select the **Do not assign** option to have no drawing order setting assigned to the hatch pattern.

Use the **Send to back** option to send the hatch pattern behind all other objects in the drawing. Any objects that are in the hatching area appear as if they are on top of the hatch pattern. Use the **Bring to front** option to bring the hatch pattern in front of, or on top of, all other objects in the drawing. Any objects that are in the hatching area appear as if they are behind the hatch pattern.

If the draw order setting needs to be changed after the hatch pattern is created, use the **DRAWORDER** tool. You can also select the hatch pattern, right-click, and then select the appropriate shortcut menu option from the **Draw Order** cascading menu.

Selecting an Existing Pattern

You can specify the hatch pattern by selecting an identical hatch pattern from the drawing. Picking the **Inherit Properties** button allows you to select a previously drawn hatch pattern and use it for the current hatch pattern settings. Once you select the **Inherit Properties** button, pick the desired associative hatch pattern. Then pick a point inside the new area to be hatched to apply the pattern.

After picking the internal point desired, press [Enter] or the space bar, or right-click and pick the **Enter** option to return to the **Hatch and Gradient** dialog box. The dialog box displays the settings of the selected pattern. At the Pick internal point or [Select objects/remove Boundaries]: prompt, access the **Select objects** option to select additional objects for the hatch pattern. Use the **remove Boundaries** option to remove objects from the current selection set being hatched.

Previewing the Hatch

Use preview tools to be sure the hatch pattern and hatch boundary settings are correct before applying a hatch pattern to the selected area. The **View Selections** button is available after you pick objects to be hatched. Pick this button to display the drawing with the hatch boundaries highlighted. When you are finished reviewing the boundaries, press [Enter] or right-click to return to the **Hatch and Gradient** dialog box.

Pick the **Preview** button, located in the lower-left corner of the **Hatch and Gradient** dialog box, to look at the hatch pattern before you apply it to the drawing. This allows you to see if any changes need to be made before the hatch is drawn. When you use this option, AutoCAD temporarily places the hatch pattern on your drawing. Press [Enter] or right-click to accept the results. To make changes after previewing the hatch, press [Esc] or the space bar to return to the **Hatch and Gradient** dialog box. Change the hatch pattern, scale, or rotation angle as needed and preview the hatch again. When you are satisfied with the preview of the hatch, pick the **OK** button in the **Hatch and Gradient** dialog box to apply it to the drawing.

Hatching Objects with Islands

islands: Boundaries inside another boundary.

AutoCAD can either ignore *islands* and hatch through them or consider them islands and hatch around them. See **Figure 24-22**. When you use the **Add: Pick points** button to hatch an internal area, islands are left unhatched by default, as shown in **Figure 24-22B**. However, if you want islands to be hatched, use the **remove Boundaries** option or pick the **Remove boundaries** button in the **Hatch and Gradient** dialog box after selecting the internal point. Then, pick the islands you want to remove and press [Enter] or the space bar, or right-click and pick the **Enter** option to return to the dialog box. The island objects are now hatched. See **Figure 24-22C**.

The island detection style and method is set in the **Islands** area of the **Hatch and Gradient** dialog box. By default, this area is hidden. Expand the dialog box to show this area by picking the **More Options** button in the lower-right corner of the dialog box. See **Figure 24-10.** This area of the **Hatch and Gradient** dialog box can be hidden again by picking the **Less Options** button in the lower-right corner. The **Islands** area is shown in **Figure 24-23.** If no islands exist, specifying an island detection style has no effect.

Island display style options are illustrated by the images in the dialog box. Pick the **Normal** radio button to hatch inward from the outer boundary. If AutoCAD encounters an island, it turns off hatching until it encounters another island. Then the hatching is reactivated. Every other closed boundary is hatched with this option. Select the **Outer** radio button to hatch inward from the outer boundary. AutoCAD turns hatching off when it encounters an island and does not turn it back on. AutoCAD hatches only the outermost level of the structure and leaves the internal structure blank. Choose the **Ignore** radio button to ignore all islands and hatch everything within the selected boundary.

Figure 24-22.
A—Original objects. B—Using the **Add: Pick points** button to hatch an internal area leaves islands unhatched. C—After picking an internal point, use the **Remove boundaries** button and pick the islands. This allows the islands to be hatched.

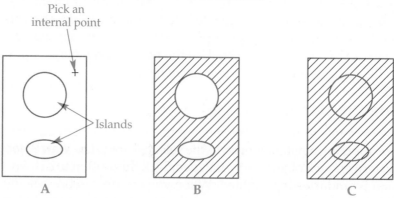

Figure 24-23.
The **Islands** area of the **Hatch and Gradient** dialog box is displayed by picking the **More Options** button. The **Boundary retention** and **Boundary set** areas of the **Hatch and Gradient** dialog box provide options to improve hatching efficiency.

Island detection style

Pick to limit area of drawing considered for hatching

Pick to hide right column of dialog box

PROFESSIONAL TIP

Pick the **Outer** island display style to ensure that islands are not unintentionally hatched.

Exercise 24-1

Complete the exercise on the Student CD.

Improving Boundary Hatching Speed

You can improve the hatching speed and resolve other hatching problems using options in the expanded **Hatch and Gradient** dialog box. Refer to Figure 24-23. The drop-down list in the **Boundary set** area specifies what is evaluated when hatching. The default setting is Current viewport. You can define a boundary area to limit what AutoCAD evaluates when hatching by picking the **New** button. At the Select objects: prompt, use a window to select the features of the object to be hatched. See Figure 24-24.

Figure 24-24.
The boundary set
limits the area that
AutoCAD evaluates
during a hatching
operation.

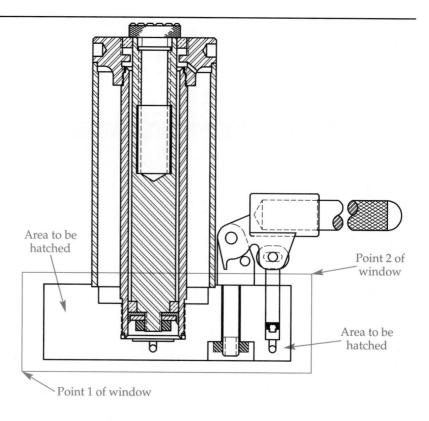

Area to be
hatched

Point 2 of
window

Area to be
hatched

Point 1 of window

After you select the object(s), the **Hatch and Gradient** dialog box returns, and the drop-down list in the **Boundary set** area displays Existing set. The drawing with the new hatch pattern applied is shown in **Figure 24-25.** You can make as many boundary sets as necessary. The last boundary made remains current until another is created.

The **Retain boundaries** check box in the **Boundary retention** area can be selected as soon as a boundary set is made. When you pick an internal area to be hatched, AutoCAD automatically creates a temporary boundary around the area. If the **Retain boundaries** check box is unchecked, the temporary boundaries are automatically

Figure 24-25.
Results of hatching
the drawing in
Figure 24-24 after
selecting a
boundary set.

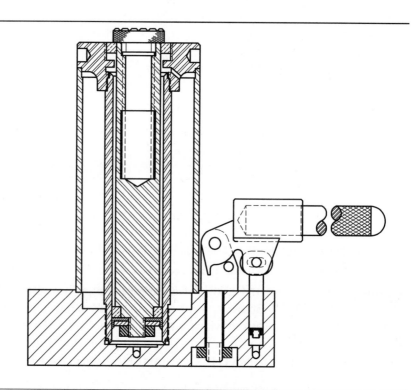

Figure 24-26.
A boundary can be saved as either a polyline or a region. These options are only available if the **Retain boundaries** option is checked.

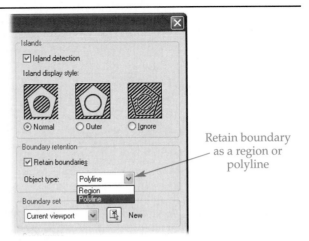

Retain boundary as a region or polyline

removed when the hatch is complete. If you select the **Retain boundaries** check box, the hatch boundaries are kept when the hatch is completed. When the **Retain boundaries** check box is checked, the **Object type:** drop-down list is enabled. See **Figure 24-26.** If the default Polyline option is selected, the boundary is a polyline object around the hatch area. If the Region option is selected, the hatch boundary is the hatched *region*.

region: A closed two-dimensional area.

PROFESSIONAL TIP

A number of techniques can help you save time when hatching, especially with large and complex drawings. These include:

- Zoom in on the area to be hatched to make it easier for you to define the boundary. When you zoom into an area to be hatched, the hatch process is faster because AutoCAD does not have to search the entire drawing to find the hatch boundaries.
- Preview the hatch before you apply it. This allows you to make last-minute adjustments easily.
- Turn off layers that contain lines or text that might interfere with your ability to define hatch boundaries accurately.
- Create boundary sets of small areas within a complex drawing to help save time.

Hatching Unenclosed Areas and Correcting Boundary Errors

The **BHATCH** tool works well unless you have an error in the hatch boundary or pick a point outside a boundary area to be hatched. The most common error is a gap in the boundary. See **Figure 24-27.** This can be very small and difficult to detect, and it happens when you do not close the geometry. However, AutoCAD is quick to let you know by displaying the **Boundary Definition Error** alert box. See **Figure 24-28.** This alert notifies you that the area cannot be hatched unless you close the boundary or specify a *gap tolerance* value.

The gap tolerance can be set in the **Gap Tolerance** area of the **Hatch and Gradient** dialog box. See **Figure 24-29.** The value in the **Tolerance:** text box is set to 0 by default. Setting a different value allows you to hatch an unenclosed boundary. AutoCAD ignores any gaps in the boundary equal to or smaller than the gap tolerance when applying the hatch. Before generating the hatch, AutoCAD issues a warning to remind you that the boundary is not closed.

gap tolerance: The amount of gap allowed between segments of a boundary when hatching.

Figure 24-27.
The **ZOOM** tool can be used to find the source of a hatching error.

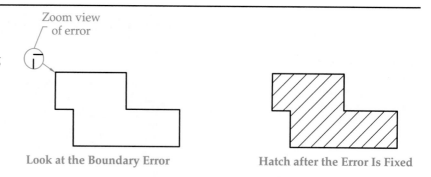

Zoom view of error

Look at the Boundary Error

Hatch after the Error Is Fixed

Figure 24-28.
The **Boundary Definition Error** alert box is displayed if problems occur in your hatching operation.

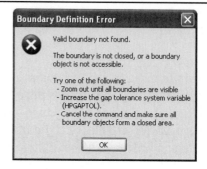

Boundary Definition Error

Valid boundary not found.

The boundary is not closed, or a boundary object is not accessible.

Try one of the following:
- Zoom out until all boundaries are visible
- Increase the gap tolerance system variable (HPGAPTOL).
- Cancel the command and make sure all boundary objects form a closed area.

OK

Figure 24-29.
The **Tolerance** setting controls whether hatching can be applied to open boundaries.

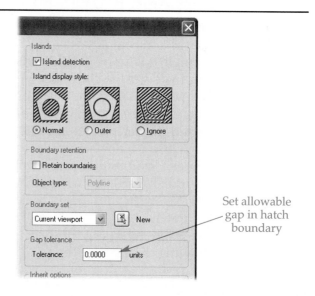

Set allowable gap in hatch boundary

PROFESSIONAL TIP

When you are creating an associative hatch, it is best to specify only one internal point per hatch block placement. If you specify more than one internal point in the same operation, AutoCAD creates one hatch object from all points picked. This can cause unexpected results when you are trying to edit what appears to be a separate hatch object.

Defining Inherit Options

The **Inherit Properties** button allows you to use the settings from an existing hatch pattern in the drawing by selecting it. This button was described earlier in this chapter. When this button is used, the **Inherit options** area in the **Hatch and Gradient** dialog box controls the hatch origin. See **Figure 24-30**.

AutoCAD and Its Applications—Basics

Figure 24-30.
The **Inherit options** area of the **Hatch and Gradient** dialog box is displayed by picking the **More Options** button.

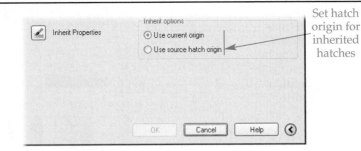

Set hatch origin for inherited hatches

The default option is **Use current origin**. When this option is selected, the hatch being created uses the origin point setting specified in the **Hatch origin** area on the **Hatch** tab in the **Hatch and Gradient** dialog box. Selecting the **Use source hatch origin** option causes the hatch being created to use the origin point of the hatch that was selected with the **Inherit Properties** button.

Creating Solid Hatch Patterns

As described earlier in this chapter, solid hatches can be created with the Solid predefined hatch pattern. See **Figure 24-31.** This is a quick way to fill a closed object solid. The Solid pattern can be accessed from the **Pattern:** drop-down list in the **Hatch and Gradient** dialog box or the **Other Predefined** tab in the **Hatch Pattern Palette** dialog box.

More advanced types of fills can be applied to closed objects using the *gradient fill* hatching options available with the **BHATCH** tool. Gradient fills can be used to simulate color-shaded objects. Nine different gradient fill patterns are available in the **Gradient** tab of the **Hatch and Gradient** dialog box. See **Figure 24-32.** Gradient fills are based on linear sweep, spherical, radial, and curved shading. They create the appearance of a lit surface with a gradual transition from an area of highlight to a filled area. When two colors are used, a transition from light to dark between the colors is simulated.

gradient fill: A shading transition between the tones of one color or two separate colors.

The options in the **Gradient** tab of the **Hatch and Gradient** dialog box include settings for one or two fill colors, gradient configuration, and fill angle. The **One color** radio button is selected by default and is used to specify a fill that has a smooth transition between the darker shades and lighter tints of one color. To select a color, pick the ellipsis (...) button next to the color swatch to access the **Select Color** dialog box. When the **One color** option is active, the **Shade** and **Tint** slider appears. Use the slider to specify the *tint* or *shade* of a color used for a one-color gradient fill.

tint: A specific color mixed with white.

Pick the **Two color** radio button to specify a fill using a smooth transition between two colors. A color swatch with an ellipsis (...) button is displayed for each color. Picking the **Centered** check box applies a symmetrical configuration. If this option is not selected, the gradient fill is shifted to simulate the projection of a light source from the left of the object. Use the **Angle** drop-down list to specify the angle of the gradient fill. The default angle is 0°. The fill can be rotated by selecting a different angle from the drop-down list. The specified angle is relative to the current UCS and is independent of the angle setting for hatch patterns.

shade: A specific color mixed with gray or black.

Figure 24-31.
Using the Solid hatch pattern to make a basic solid hatch object.

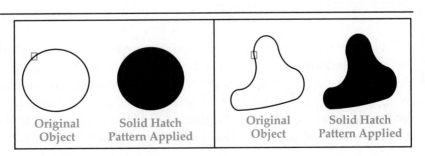

Original Object   Solid Hatch Pattern Applied   Original Object   Solid Hatch Pattern Applied

Figure 24-32.
The **Gradient** tab of the **Hatch and Gradient** dialog box contains options for creating gradient fill hatch patterns.

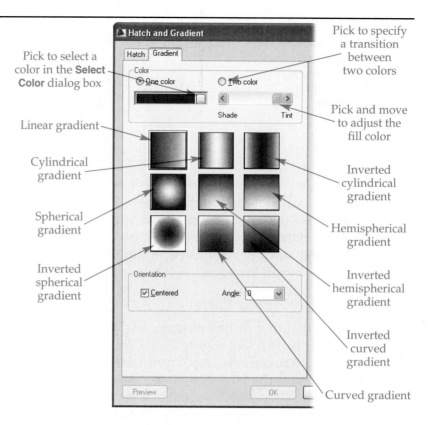

Pick to select a color in the **Select Color** dialog box

Pick to specify a transition between two colors

Pick and move to adjust the fill color

Linear gradient

Cylindrical gradient

Spherical gradient

Inverted spherical gradient

Inverted cylindrical gradient

Hemispherical gradient

Inverted hemispherical gradient

Inverted curved gradient

Curved gradient

> **NOTE**
>
>
>
> As with other types of hatch patterns, gradient fills are associative by default. They can also be edited in the same way as other hatch patterns with the **HATCHEDIT** tool.

Using DesignCenter to Insert Hatch Patterns

Hatch patterns can be inserted using **DesignCenter**. To add a hatch pattern from **DesignCenter**, you need to select a PAT file. Once the PAT file is selected, the hatch patterns it contains are displayed in the preview pane. See **Figure 24-33.**

> **NOTE**
>
> AutoCAD includes two PAT files: acad.pat and acadiso.pat. Both are located in Program Files/AutoCAD 2009/UserDataCache/Support. To verify the location of AutoCAD support files, access the **Files** tab in the **Options** dialog box and check the path listed under the Support File Search Path.

ADCENTER

Ribbon
View
> Palettes

DesignCenter

Type
ADCENTER
ADC

Menu Browser
Tools
> Palettes
> DesignCenter

Usually the quickest and most effective technique for transferring a hatch pattern from **DesignCenter** into the active drawing is to use a drag-and-drop operation. To use this method, pick the hatch pattern from **DesignCenter** and hold down the pick button. When you move the cursor into the active drawing, a hatch pattern symbol is displayed under the cursor, as shown in **Figure 24-34A.** Place the cursor in the area to be hatched and release the pick button. The hatch is applied automatically. See **Figure 24-34B.**

Figure 24-33.
Pick a PAT file in **DesignCenter** to display the available hatch patterns in the preview palette.

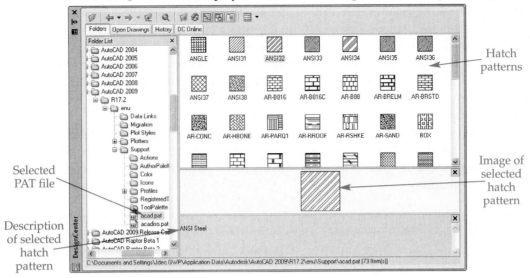

Hatch patterns

Selected PAT file

Description of selected hatch pattern

Image of selected hatch pattern

Figure 24-34.
When a hatch pattern is selected in the preview pane, a preview image appears. A—The hatch pattern symbol appears under the cursor during the drag-and-drop and paste operations. B—Pick a point to apply the hatch pattern.

Selected hatch pattern

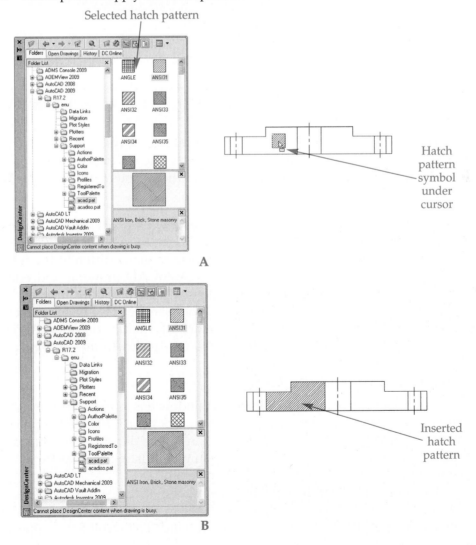

Hatch pattern symbol under cursor

A

Inserted hatch pattern

B

A similar operation to drag and drop is copy and paste. Right-click the hatch pattern in **DesignCenter** and pick **Copy** from the shortcut menu. Move the cursor into the active drawing, right-click, and select **Paste** from the shortcut menu. The hatch pattern symbol is displayed beneath the crosshairs. Pick in the area to be hatched to apply the hatch pattern.

Another option is to use **DesignCenter** in combination with the **Hatch and Gradient** dialog box. Right-click a hatch pattern in **DesignCenter** and select **BHATCH...** from the shortcut menu to access the **Hatch and Gradient** dialog box. The selected hatch pattern is displayed automatically.

When hatch patterns are inserted from **DesignCenter**, the angle, scale, and island detection settings match the settings of the previous hatch pattern. Use the **HATCHEDIT** tool to change these settings after inserting the hatch pattern. Hatch editing is described later in this chapter.

> **NOTE**
>
> If you drag and drop or paste a hatch pattern into an area that is not a closed boundary, AutoCAD displays the Valid hatch boundary not found message.

Exercise 24-2
Complete the exercise on the Student CD.

Using Tool Palettes to Insert Hatch Patterns

The **Tool Palettes** window provides a number of ways to manage frequently used blocks, hatch patterns, and other types of objects, such as gradients, images, tables, and external reference files. This section describes the various features in the **Tool Palettes** window. See Figure 24-35.

> **NOTE**
>
> Tool palettes can be used to store many different types of drawing content and tools, such as AutoCAD drawing and editing tools, customized tools, user-defined macros, script files, and AutoLISP routines. The **Command Tools Samples** tool palette contains examples of custom tools. For more information on AutoCAD customization, refer to *AutoCAD and Its Applications—Advanced*.

Locating and Viewing Content

tool palette: Special type of palette containing tabs that help organize tools and other features.

Each *tool palette* in the **Tool Palettes** window has its own tab along the side of the window. To view the content in a tool palette, pick the related tab to open it. If the **Tool Palettes** window contains more palettes than can be displayed on-screen, pick on the edge of the lowest tab to display a selection menu listing the palette tabs. Locate the name of the tab to access the related tool palette.

The tool palette can be navigated using one of two scroll methods. If all of the content of a selected tool palette does not fit in the window, the remainder can be viewed by using the scroll bar or the scroll hand. The scroll hand appears when the

Figure 24-35.
The **Tool Palettes**
window can be used
to access and insert
hatch patterns.

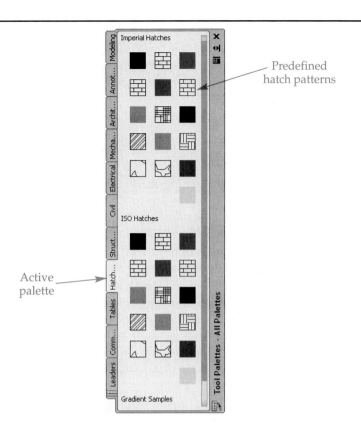

Predefined
hatch patterns

Active
palette

cursor is placed in an empty area in the tool palette. Picking and dragging scrolls the
tool palette up and down.

> **NOTE**
>
> By default, the tools in each tool palette are represented by icons.
> Several tool palette view options are available, including the ability
> to display a tool as an image of your choice. For more informa-
> tion on adjusting tool palette display, refer to *AutoCAD and Its
> Applications—Advanced.*

Insert Hatch Patterns

Inserting hatch patterns with the **Tool Palettes** window is similar to inserting them
with **DesignCenter**. To drag and drop a hatch pattern from the **Tool Palettes** window,
access the tool palette in which the pattern resides. Then, either pick the pattern and
drag the image into the drawing while holding down the mouse button, or place the
cursor over the hatch pattern image and pick once. When you move the cursor into
the drawing area, the hatch pattern is attached to the crosshairs. The location where
the crosshairs and the hatch pattern are connected is defined by the insertion point of the
hatch pattern. Drag the pattern image to the desired boundary area and pick.

After the hatch pattern is inserted, you can make modifications with the **HATCHEDIT**
tool. Hatch editing is described later in this chapter.

> **NOTE**
>
> Tool palettes can be added to the **Tool Palettes** window and
> tools can be added to tool palettes. For more information on
> creating and modifying tool palettes, refer to *AutoCAD and Its
> Applications—Advanced.*

Editing Hatch Patterns

You can edit hatch boundaries and hatch patterns with grips and editing tools such as **ERASE**, **COPY**, **MOVE**, **ROTATE**, **SCALE**, and **TRIM**. If a hatch pattern is associative, changes made to the hatch boundary are automatically applied to the associated hatch pattern. As explained earlier, a hatch pattern is associative if the **Associative** option in the **Options** area of the **Hatch and Gradient** dialog box is active.

A convenient way to edit a hatch pattern is to use the **HATCHEDIT** tool. A quick method to access the **HATCHEDIT** tool is to double-click the hatch pattern you want to edit. When you select a hatch pattern or patterns to edit, the **Hatch Edit** dialog box is displayed. See Figure 24-36. The **Hatch Edit** dialog box has the same features as the **Hatch and Gradient** dialog box, except the **Recreate boundary** button in the **Boundaries** area is available.

The **Recreate boundary** button can be used to create a new boundary for the hatch pattern. It essentially redraws a new boundary on top of the existing boundary. If the current boundary is made up of several different lines, this tool can be used to draw the boundary very quickly as one object. When you pick the **Recreate boundary** button, the **Hatch Edit** dialog box is temporarily hidden. You must decide if the boundary type

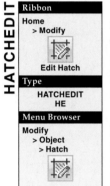

Figure 24-36.
The **Hatch Edit** dialog box is used to edit hatch patterns. Notice that only the options related to hatch characteristics are available.

Pick to recreate boundary

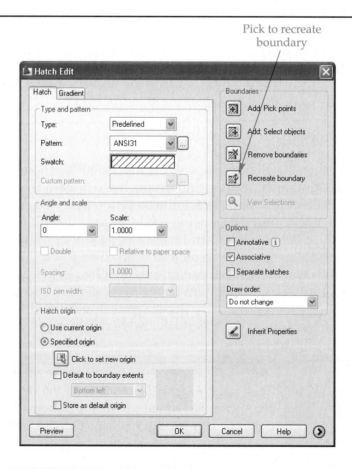

will be a region or a polyline by selecting the appropriate option. The next query asks if you want the hatch pattern to be associated with the new boundary. The **Hatch Edit** dialog box then displays again.

The other features in the **Hatch Edit** dialog box work the same as they do in the **Hatch and Gradient** dialog box. You can change the pattern type, scale, or angle; remove the associative qualities; or set the inherit properties of an existing hatch pattern. You can also preview the edited hatch before applying it to your drawing.

Exercise 24-4
Complete the exercise on the Student CD.

Editing Associative Hatch Patterns

When you edit an object with an associative hatch pattern, the hatch pattern changes to match the edit. For example, when the object in Figure 24-37A is stretched, the hatch pattern matches the new object. When the island in Figure 24-37B is erased, the hatch pattern is automatically revised to fill the area where the island was located. As long as the original boundary is being edited, the associative hatch will update.

Drawing a new object and associating it with an existing hatch pattern creates a new island. See Figure 24-38. In this example, a rectangle has been drawn and needs to be added to the hatch boundary to create an island. After a rectangle is drawn, double-click the hatch pattern to open the **Hatch Edit** dialog box. Picking the **Add: Select objects** button hides the dialog box and allows you to pick the rectangle. Press [Enter] and the **OK** button to finish. The rectangle is now an associated island.

Figure 24-37.
A—Editing objects with associative hatch patterns. B—The hatch pattern changes to match the edit.

Original

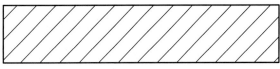
Object Stretched

A

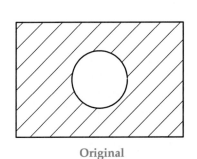
Original

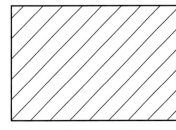
Circle Erased

B

Figure 24-38.
Objects can be added to a hatch pattern boundary after the pattern is created.

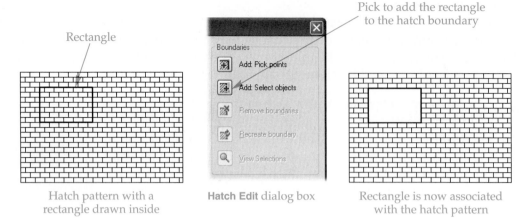

Rectangle

Pick to add the rectangle to the hatch boundary

Hatch pattern with a rectangle drawn inside

Hatch Edit dialog box

Rectangle is now associated with the hatch pattern

Exercise 24-5
Complete the exercise on the Student CD.

Using the Solid Tool

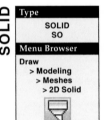

Type	
SOLID	
SO	
Menu Browser	
Draw	
> Modeling	
> Meshes	
> 2D Solid	

Solid fills are usually best added using the Solid predefined hatch pattern of the **BHATCH** tool. However, the **SOLID** tool can be used to draw basic solid filled shapes without first creating a boundary. When you access the **SOLID** tool, you are prompted to select points. Figure 24-39 shows examples of solid fills created according to specific point selection sequences.

When using the **SOLID** tool, you are prompted for another third point after the first four. This prompt allows you to fill in additional parts of the same object, if needed. AutoCAD assumes that the third and fourth points of the previous solid are now points one and two for the next solid. The additional points you select fill in the object in a triangular fashion. Continue picking points, or press [Enter] to stop.

Exercise 24-6
Complete the exercise on the Student CD.

Express Tools
Chapter 24

The Express menu of the menu browser includes additional tools for improved functionality and productivity during the drawing processes. The following Express Tool is a hatch express tool. Refer to the Student CD for information on this tool.

Super Hatch

Figure 24-39.
Using the **SOLID** tool. Select the points in the orders shown. The **SOLID** tool allows you to enter a second "third point" (Point 5 in the example with five selected points) after you enter the fourth point.

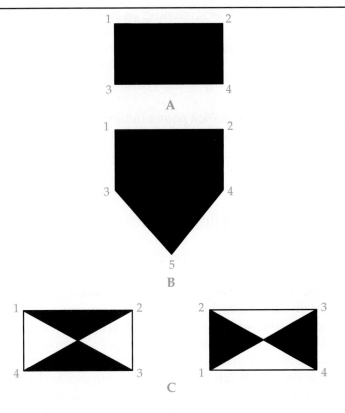

Chapter Test

Answer the following questions. Write your answers on a separate sheet of paper or complete the electronic chapter test on the Student CD.

1. AutoCAD's standard section line symbols are called _____.
2. Which AutoCAD hatch pattern is used as a general section line symbol?

For Questions 3–8, name the type of section identified in each of the following statements:

3. Half of the object is removed; the cutting-plane line generally cuts completely through along the center plane.
4. The cutting-plane line cuts through one-quarter of the object; used primarily on symmetrical objects.
5. The cutting-plane line is staggered through features that do not lie in a straight line.
6. The section is turned in place to clarify the contour of the object.
7. The section is rotated and located away from the object. The location of the section is normally identified with a cutting-plane line.
8. A small portion of the view is removed to clarify an internal feature.
9. Identify two ways to select a predefined hatch pattern in the **Hatch and Gradient** dialog box.
10. Explain the purpose and function of the ellipsis (**...**) buttons in the **Hatch and Gradient** dialog box.
11. How do you change the hatch angle in the **Hatch and Gradient** dialog box?
12. Explain how to set a hatch scale in the **Hatch and Gradient** dialog box.
13. Describe the fundamental difference between using the **Add: Pick points** and the **Add: Select objects** buttons in the **Hatch and Gradient** dialog box.
14. How do you hatch an object with text inside without hatching the text?
15. Define *associative hatch pattern*.

16. What is the result of stretching an object that is hatched with an associative hatch pattern?
17. Explain how to use an existing hatch pattern on a drawing as the pattern for your next hatch.
18. Describe the purpose of the **Preview** button found in the **Hatch and Gradient** dialog box.
19. If you use the **Add: Pick points** button inside the **Hatch and Gradient** dialog box to hatch an area, how do you hatch around an island inside the area to be hatched?
20. Explain the three island detection style options.
21. How do you limit AutoCAD hatch evaluation to a specific area of the drawing?
22. What is the purpose of the **Gap Tolerance** setting in the **Hatch and Gradient** dialog box?
23. What are gradient fill hatch patterns? How are they created with the **BHATCH** tool?
24. Name the two files that contain hatch patterns that can be copied from **DesignCenter**.
25. Explain how to use drag and drop to insert a hatch pattern from **DesignCenter** into an active drawing.
26. Explain two ways to use drag and drop for inserting a hatch pattern from a tool palette into the drawing.
27. Name the tool that may be used to edit existing associative hatch patterns.
28. How does the **Hatch Edit** dialog box compare to the **Hatch and Gradient** dialog box?
29. What happens if you erase an island inside an associative hatch pattern?
30. In addition to the **BHATCH** tool, what tool can be used to fill an object with a solid color?

Drawing Problems

Draw the following problems using tools described in this chapter and in previous chapters. Use an appropriate template for each problem. Use text styles that correlate with the problem content. Place dimensions and notes when needed. Make your drawings proportional to the given problems when dimensions are not given. Save each of the drawings as P24-*(problem number).*

▼ Basic

1.

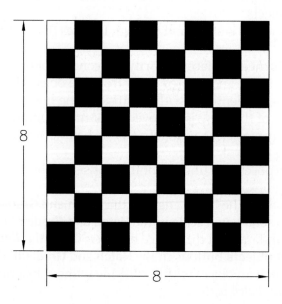

2.

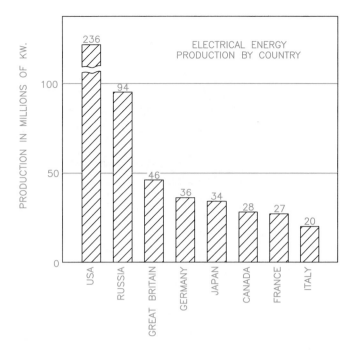

PRODUCTION IN MILLIONS OF KW.

ELECTRICAL ENERGY
PRODUCTION BY COUNTRY

236
94
46
36
34
28
27
20

USA RUSSIA GREAT BRITAIN GERMANY JAPAN CANADA FRANCE ITALY

3.

COMPONENT LAYOUT

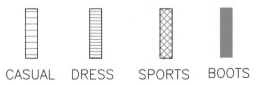

Dynamic corrector — Static corrector

CRT

Cathode
Filament

Aperture flooding
Beam centering
Focus coil
Deflection yoke
Anode connection

4.

SOLOMAN SHOE COMPANY

PERCENT OF TOTAL SALES EACH DIVISION

CASUAL   DRESS   SPORTS   BOOTS

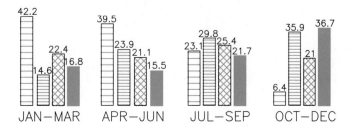

42.2
14.6
22.4
16.8
JAN—MAR

39.5
23.9
21.1
15.5
APR—JUN

23.1
29.8
25.4
21.7
JUL—SEP

6.4
35.9
21
36.7
OCT—DEC

Drawing Problems - Chapter 24

5.

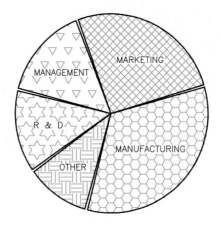

DIAL TECHNOLOGIES
EXPENSE BUDGET
FISCAL YEAR

MARKETING

MANAGEMENT

R & D

OTHER

MANUFACTURING

6.

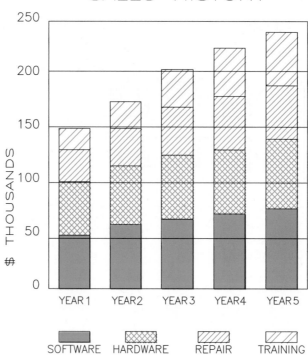

SALES HISTORY

250

200

150

$ THOUSANDS

100

50

0

YEAR 1   YEAR2   YEAR 3   YEAR4   YEAR 5

SOFTWARE   HARDWARE   REPAIR   TRAINING

For Problems 7-13, use the following guidelines:

A. Use an appropriate template with a mechanical drawing title block.
B. Create separate layers for views, dimensions, and section lines.
C. Place the following general notes 1/2" from the lower-left corner.
   NOTES:
   1. INTERPRET DIMENSIONS AND TOLERANCES PER ASME Y14.5M-1994
   2. REMOVE ALL BURRS AND SHARP EDGES

▼ Intermediate

7. Draw and dimension these views, which include aligned and broken-out sections. Add the following notes: FINISH ALL OVER 1.63 mm UNLESS OTHERWISE SPECIFIED and ALL DIMENSIONS ARE IN MILLIMETERS. All arc and circle contours are tangent. Estimate any dimensions not given. Save the drawing as P24-7.

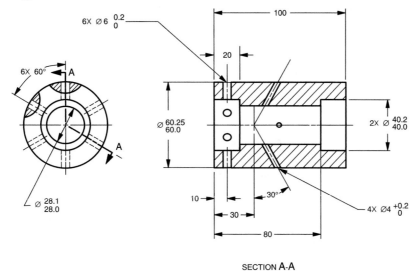

SECTION A-A

Name: Nozzle
Material: Phosphor Bronze

8. Draw and dimension the given views. Save the drawing as P24-8.

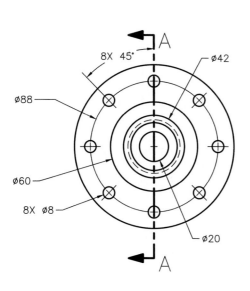

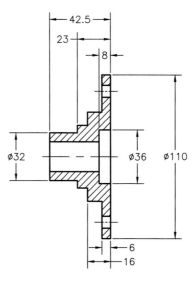

SECTION A—A

Name: Hub
Material: Cast Iron

9. Given the engineer's rough sketch, draw and dimension the given views, including the aligned section shown on the right. Add the following notes: FINISH ALL OVER 1.63 mm UNLESS OTHERWISE SPECIFIED and ALL DIMENSIONS ARE IN MILLIMETERS. Save the drawing as P24-9.

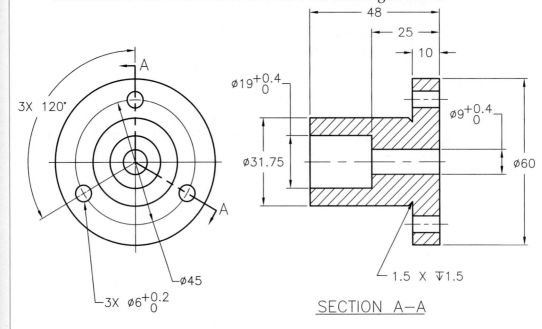

10. Draw and dimension the views of the chain guide as shown. Save the drawing as P24-10.

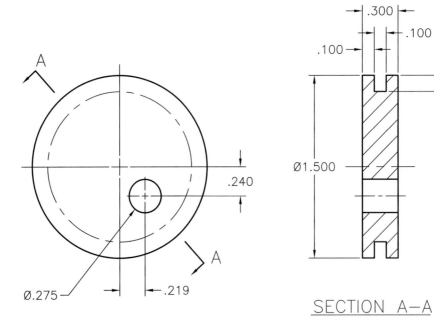

Drawing Problems - Chapter 24

11. Draw and dimension the views of the sleeve and notes as shown. Save the drawing as P24-11.

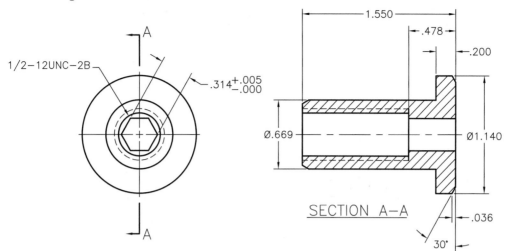

1/2−12UNC−2B

.314 +.005 / −.000

1.550
.478
.200
Ø.669
Ø1.140

SECTION A−A

.036
30°

4. PAINT ACE GLOSS BLACK ALL OVER.
3. CASE HARDEN 45−50 ROCKWELL.
2. REMOVE ALL BURRS AND SHARP EDGES.
1. INTERPRET ALL DIMENSIONS AND
   TOLERANCES PER ASME Y14.5M−1994.

▼ Advanced

12. Draw and dimension the given views. Add the following notes: OIL QUENCH 40-45C, CASE HARDEN .020 DEEP, and 59-60 ROCKWELL C SCALE. Save the drawing as P24-12.

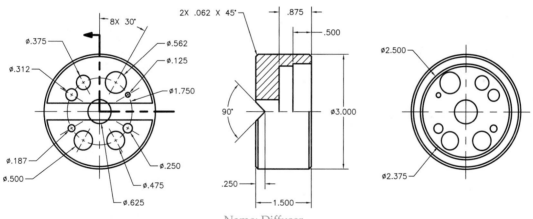

8X 30°
Ø.375
Ø.312
Ø.187
Ø.500
Ø.562
Ø.125
Ø1.750
Ø.250
Ø.475
Ø.625

2X .062 X 45°
.875
.500
90°
Ø3.000
.250
1.500

Ø2.500
Ø2.375

Name: Diffuser
Material: AISI 1018

13. Draw and dimension the views of the tow hook as shown. Save the drawing as P24-13.

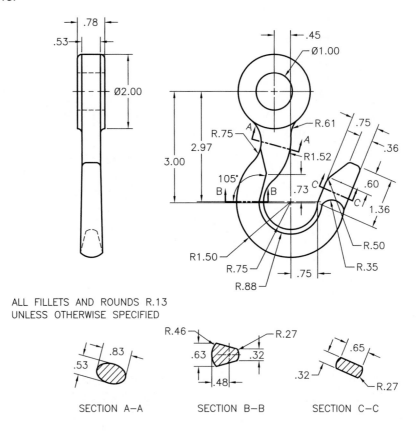

ALL FILLETS AND ROUNDS R.13
UNLESS OTHERWISE SPECIFIED

SECTION A–A   SECTION B–B   SECTION C–C

Draw the following problems using tools described in this chapter and in previous chapters. Use an appropriate template for each problem. Use text styles that correlate with the problem content. Place dimensions and notes when needed. Make your drawings proportional to the given problems when dimensions are not given. Save each of the drawings as P24-*(problem number).*

14.

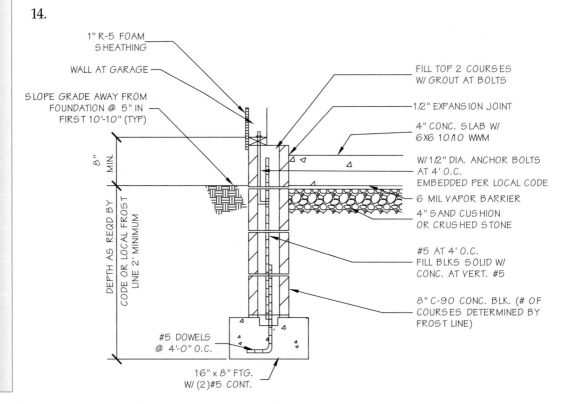

15.

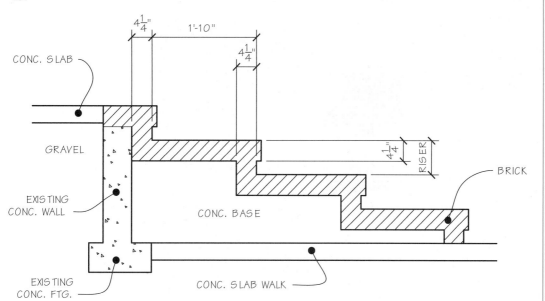

CONC. SLAB

GRAVEL

EXISTING
CONC. WALL

EXISTING
CONC. FTG.

$4\frac{1}{4}$" 1'-10" $4\frac{1}{4}$"

$4\frac{1}{4}$" RISER

BRICK

CONC. BASE

CONC. SLAB WALK

16.

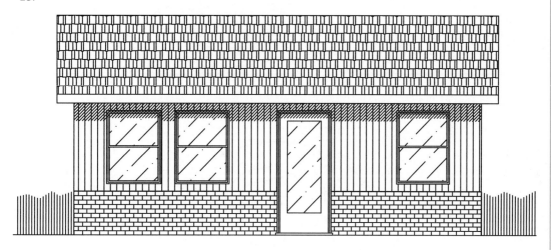

17.

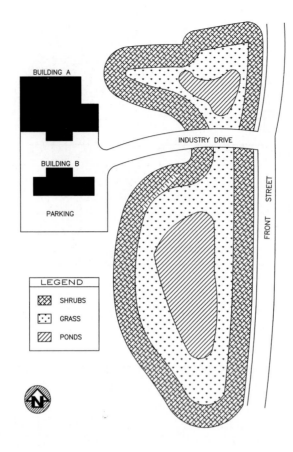

BUILDING A

BUILDING B

PARKING

INDUSTRY DRIVE

FRONT STREET

LEGEND

SHRUBS

GRASS

PONDS

N

18.

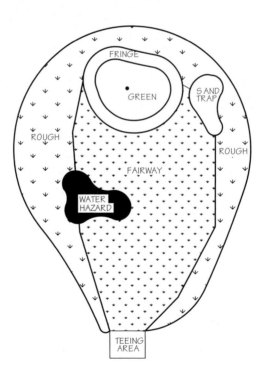

FRINGE

GREEN

SAND TRAP

ROUGH

ROUGH

FAIRWAY

WATER HAZARD

TEEING AREA

19.

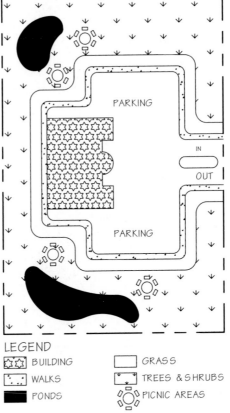

LEGEND

⬡⬡ BUILDING	▭ GRASS
⋮⋮ WALKS	⊻ TREES & SHRUBS
⬛ PONDS	⬡ PICNIC AREAS

20.

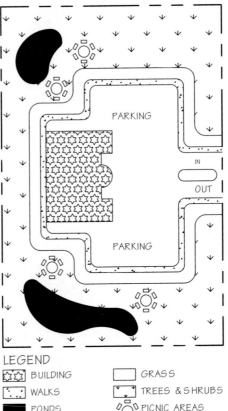

TOP OF FALLS
1ST CASCADE

680ft.
640
560
480
400
320
240

20'
75'
35'
120'
460'
140'
70'

SCALE 1:480

PROFILE OF MULTNOMAH FALLS
&
GEOLOGIC INFORMATION

20' COLLONADE OF AN 80—FOOT THICK FLOW, NOTCHED BY MULTNOMAH CREEK.

75' PILLOW LAVA

35' A GLASSY FLOW, WITH WELL—FORMED ENTABLATURE AND COLLONADE.

120' CONSISTING OF TWO TIERS OF HACKLY—JOINTED BASALT, WITH NO COLLONADE.

140' ENTABLATURE WITH THIN COLUMNS, TOPPED BY A VESICULAR ZONE.

70' OF ENTABLATURE BENEATH THE LOWER FALLS.

BRIEF DESCRIPTION OF TERMS.
COLONNADE: THE LOWER PORTION OF A LAVA FLOW OF COLUMNAR—JOINTED BASALT.
ENTABLATURE: THE UPPER MASSIVE OF A LAVA FLOW OF HACKLY—JOINTED BASALT.

* INFORMATION TAKEN FROM:
"THE MAGNIFICENT GATEWAY"
AUTHOR: JOHN ELIOT ALLEN
PAGES: 89—91

21.

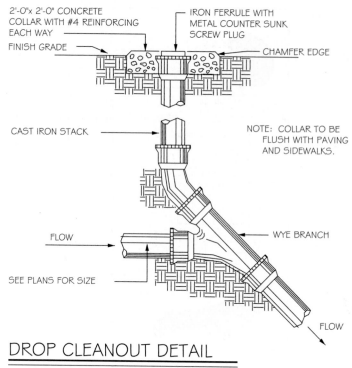

2'-0"x 2'-0" CONCRETE
COLLAR WITH #4 REINFORCING
EACH WAY

IRON FERRULE WITH
METAL COUNTER SUNK
SCREW PLUG

FINISH GRADE

CHAMFER EDGE

CAST IRON STACK

NOTE: COLLAR TO BE
FLUSH WITH PAVING
AND SIDEWALKS.

FLOW

WYE BRANCH

SEE PLANS FOR SIZE

FLOW

DROP CLEANOUT DETAIL

SCALE: NONE

CHAPTER 25

Basic Pictorial Drawings

Learning Objectives

After completing this chapter, you will be able to do the following:

✓ Describe the three basic types of pictorial drawings.
✓ Construct accurate isometric drawings.
✓ Dimension isometric drawings.

Being able to visualize and draw three-dimensional shapes is a skill that every drafter, designer, and engineer should possess. This is especially important in 3D modeling. However, there is a distinct difference between drawing a view that *looks* three-dimensional and creating a *true* 3D model.

A 3D model can be rotated on the display screen and viewed from any angle. The computer calculates the points, lines, and surfaces of the objects in space. For information on 3D modeling, viewing and visualization techniques, see *AutoCAD and Its Applications—Advanced*. This chapter is provided as background information on the classic drawing techniques used in pictorial drawing. The focus of this chapter is creating views that *look* three-dimensional using some special AutoCAD functions and two-dimensional coordinates and objects.

Pictorial Drawing Overview

The word *pictorial* means "like a picture." It refers to any form of 2D drawing that illustrates height, width, and depth. Several forms of pictorial drawings are used in industry today. The least realistic is oblique. However, this is the simplest type. The most realistic, but also the most complex, is perspective. The realism and complexity of isometric drawing falls midway between the two.

pictorial: A 2D drawing that is similar to a picture.

Oblique Drawings

An *oblique drawing* shows objects with one or more parallel faces at their true shape and size. A scale is selected for the orthographic, or front, faces. Then an angle for the depth (receding axis) is chosen. The three types of oblique drawings are cavalier, cabinet, and general. See **Figure 25-1.** These types vary in the scale of the receding axis. The receding axis is drawn at full scale for a cavalier view and at half scale for a cabinet view. The general oblique is normally drawn with a 3/4 scale for the receding axis.

oblique drawing: A drawing that shows objects with one or more parallel faces having true shape and size.

Figure 25-1.
The scale of the receding axis differs in the three types of oblique drawings.

Cavalier   Cabinet   General

Axonometric Drawings

The general term for drawings that display three dimensions on a two-dimensional surface such as a drawing sheet is *axonometric drawings*. The three types of axonometric drawings are isometric, dimetric, and trimetric.

Isometric drawings are more realistic than oblique drawings. The entire object appears as if it is tilted toward the viewer. The word *isometric* means "equal measure." This equal measure refers to the angle between the three axes (120°) after the object has been tilted. The tilt angle is 35°16′. This is shown in **Figure 25-2.** The 120° angle corresponds to an angle of 30° from horizontal. In the construction of isometric drawings, lines that are parallel in the orthogonal views must be parallel in the isometric view.

The most appealing aspect of isometric drawing is that all three axis lines can be measured using the same scale. This saves time, while still producing a pleasing pictorial of the object.

Dimetric and trimetric drawings are closely related to isometric drawing. These forms of pictorial drawing differ from isometric in the scales used to measure the three axes. *Dimetric* drawing uses two different scales and *trimetric* uses three scales. Using different scales is an attempt to create *foreshortening*. This means the lengths of the sides appear to recede. The relationship between isometric, dimetric, and trimetric drawings is illustrated in **Figure 25-3.**

axonometric drawings: Drawings in which a 3D object is rotated for display on a 2D drawing sheet so all three dimensions can be seen.

isometric drawings: Drawings in which the three axes are equally spaced at 120°.

dimetric: An axonometric drawing in which two different scales are used to measure the three axes.

trimetric: An axonometric drawing in which three different scales are used to measure the three axes.

foreshortening: Property of a drawing in which objects appear to recede in the distance.

Figure 25-2.
An object is tilted 35°16′ to achieve an isometric view having 120° between the three axes. Notice the highlighted face in each view.

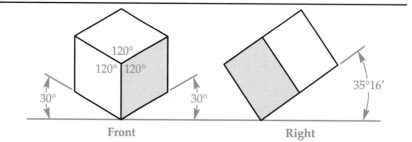

Front   Right

Figure 25-3.
Isometric, dimetric, and trimetric drawings differ in the scales used to draw the three axes. In the isometric shown here, all three sides are drawn at full scale, or 1. You can see how the dimetric and trimetric scales vary.

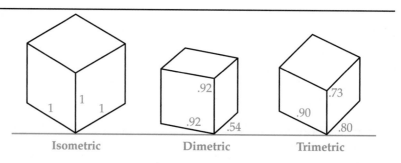

Isometric   Dimetric   Trimetric

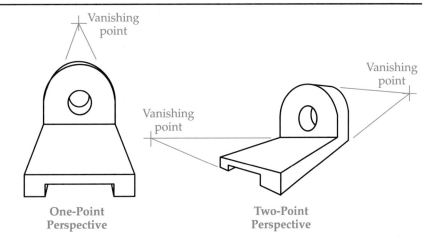

One-Point Perspective

Two-Point Perspective

Perspective Drawing

The most realistic form of pictorial drawing is a *perspective drawing*. The eye naturally sees objects in perspective. Look down a long hall and notice that the wall and floor lines seem to converge in the distance at an imaginary point. That point is called the *vanishing point*. The most common types of perspective drawing are one-point and two-point perspectives. These forms of pictorial drawing are often used in architecture. They are also used in the automotive and aircraft industries. Examples of one-point and two-point perspectives are shown in **Figure 25-4.** A perspective of a true 3D model can be produced in AutoCAD using the **ViewCube**. See *AutoCAD and Its Applications—Advanced* for complete coverage of **ViewCube**.

perspective drawing: The most realistic form of pictorial drawing, in which receding objects meet at one or more vanishing points on the horizon.

vanishing point: The point at which objects seem to converge in the distance at an imaginary point.

Isometric Drawing

The most common method of pictorial drawing used in industry is isometric. Isometric drawings provide a single view showing three sides that can be measured using the same scale. An isometric view has no perspective and may appear somewhat distorted. Two of the isometric axes are drawn at 30° to horizontal, while the third is drawn at 90°. See **Figure 25-5.**

The three axes shown in **Figure 25-5** represent the width, height, and depth of the object. Lines that appear horizontal in an orthographic view are placed at a 30° angle. Lines that are vertical in an orthographic view are placed vertically. These lines are parallel to the axes. Any line parallel to an axis can be measured and is called an *isometric line*. Lines that are not parallel to the axes are called *nonisometric lines* and cannot be measured. Note the two nonisometric lines in **Figure 25-5.**

isometric line: Any line that is parallel to an axis in an isometric drawing.

nonisometric lines: Lines that are not parallel to the axes in an isometric drawing.

Figure 25-5.
Layout of the isometric axes.

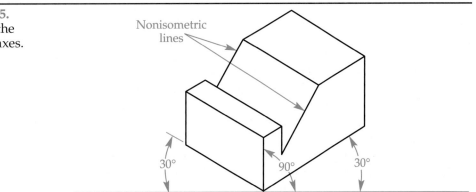

Nonisometric lines

30°   90°   30°

Figure 25-6.
Proper isometric circle (ellipse) orientation on isometric planes. The minor axis always aligns with the axis centerline.

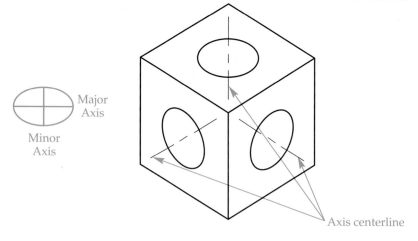

Circles appear as ellipses in an isometric drawing. Circular features shown on isometric objects must be oriented properly or they appear distorted. The correct orientation of isometric circles on the three principal planes is shown in Figure 25-6. The small diameter (minor axis) of the ellipse must always align on the axis of the circular feature. Notice that the centerline axes of the holes in Figure 25-6 are parallel to one of the isometric planes.

A basic rule to remember about isometric drawing is that lines that are parallel in an orthogonal view must be parallel in the isometric view. AutoCAD's **ISOPLANE** tool makes that task, and the positioning of ellipses, easy.

PROFESSIONAL TIP

If you are ever in doubt about the proper orientation of an ellipse in an isometric drawing, remember that the minor axis of the ellipse must always be aligned on the centerline axis of the circular feature. This is shown clearly in Figure 25-6.

Settings for Isometric Drawing

You can quickly set your isometric variables in the **Snap and Grid** tab of the **Drafting Settings** dialog box. See Figure 25-7. This dialog box can also be accessed by right-clicking the **Snap Mode** or **Grid Display** status bar button and then selecting **Settings...** from the shortcut menu.

To activate the isometric snap grid, pick the **Isometric snap** radio button in the **Snap type** area. Notice that the **Snap X spacing** and **Grid X spacing** text boxes are now grayed out. Since X spacing relates to horizontal measurements, it is not used in **Isometric snap** mode. You can only set the Y spacing for grid and snap in isometric. Be sure to check the **Snap On (F9)** and **Grid On (F7)** check boxes if you want **Snap** and **Grid** modes to be activated. Pick the **OK** button to display the grid dots on the screen in an isometric orientation, as shown in Figure 25-8. If the grid dots are not visible, turn the grid on.

Notice that the crosshairs appear angled. This aids you in drawing lines at the proper isometric angles. Try drawing a four-sided surface using the **LINE** tool. Draw the surface so it appears to be the left side of a box in an isometric layout. See Figure 25-9. To draw nonparallel surfaces, you can change the angle of the crosshairs to make your task easier, as discussed in the next section.

To turn off the **Isometric snap** mode, pick the **Rectangular snap** radio button in the **Snap type** area. The **Isometric snap** mode is turned off and you are returned to the drawing area when you pick the **OK** button.

AutoCAD and Its Applications—Basics

Figure 25-7.
The **Drafting Settings** dialog box allows you to make settings needed for isometric drawing.

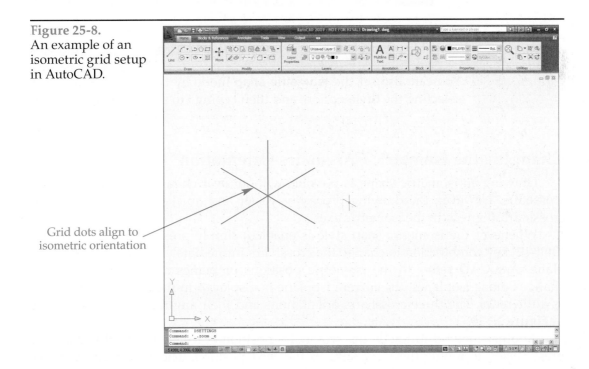

Pick to activate isometric snap grid

Figure 25-8.
An example of an isometric grid setup in AutoCAD.

Grid dots align to isometric orientation

Figure 25-9.
A four-sided object drawn with the **LINE** tool can be used as the left side of an isometric box.

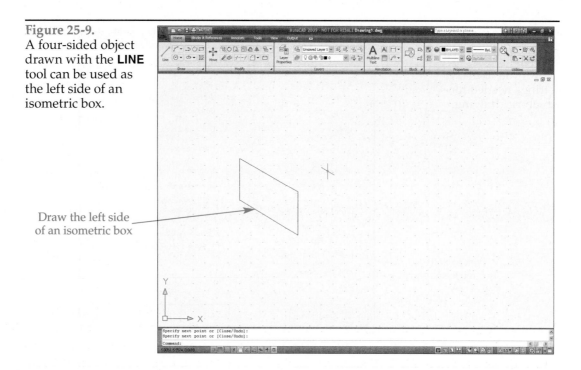

Draw the left side of an isometric box

NOTE

You can also set the **Isometric snap** mode by typing SNAP or SN, selecting the **Style** option, and then typing I to select **Isometric**.

Changing the Isometric Crosshairs Orientation

Drawing an isometric shape is possible without ever changing the angle of the crosshairs. However, the drawing process is easier and quicker if the angle of the crosshairs aligns with the isometric axes.

Whenever the isometric snap style is enabled, simply press the [F5] key or the [Ctrl]+[E] key combination to change the crosshairs immediately to the next isometric plane. AutoCAD refers to the isometric positions or planes as *isoplanes*. As you change among isoplanes, the current isoplane is displayed in the command window as a reference. The three crosshairs orientations and their angular values are shown in **Figure 25-10.**

isoplanes: The three isometric positions or planes.

Another method to toggle the crosshairs position is to use the **ISOPLANE** tool. Press [Enter] to toggle the crosshairs to the next position. The command window displays the new isoplane setting. You can toggle immediately to the next position by pressing [Enter] to repeat the **ISOPLANE** tool and pressing [Enter] again. To specify the

Figure 25-10.
You can toggle among the three isometric crosshairs positions using the [F5] function key, the [Ctrl]+[E] key combination, or the **ISOPLANE** tool.

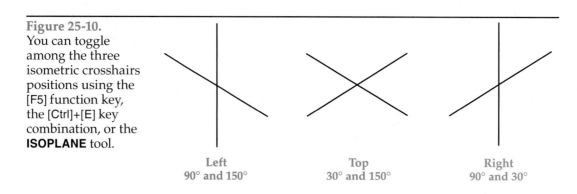

Left
90° and 150°

Top
30° and 150°

Right
90° and 30°

plane of orientation, type the first letter of that position. The **ISOPLANE** tool can also be used transparently.

The crosshairs are always in one of the isoplane positions when **Isometric snap** mode is in effect. An exception occurs in display or editing tools when a multiple selection set method, such as a window, is used. In these cases, the crosshairs change to the normal vertical and horizontal positions. When the display or editing tool is closed, the crosshairs reverts to its former isoplane orientation.

Exercise 25-1
Complete the exercise on the Student CD.

Isometric Ellipses

Placing an isometric ellipse on an object is easy with AutoCAD because of the **Isocircle** option of the **ELLIPSE** tool. An ellipse is positioned automatically on the current isoplane. To use the **ELLIPSE** tool, first make sure you are in **Isometric snap** mode. Once the **ELLIPSE** tool is initiated, type I for the **Isocircle** option. Then pick the center point and set the radius or diameter. Note that the **Isocircle** option only appears when you are in **Isometric snap** mode.

Button
ELLIPSE
EL

Always check the isoplane position before placing an ellipse (isocircle) on your drawing. You can dynamically view the three positions that an ellipse can take. Use the **ELLIPSE** tool, enter the **Isocircle** option, pick a center point, and toggle the crosshairs orientation. See **Figure 25-11.** The ellipse rotates each time you toggle the crosshairs.

The isometric ellipse (isocircle) is a true ellipse. When an ellipse is selected, grips are displayed at the center and four quadrant points. See **Figure 25-12.** However, do not use grips to resize or otherwise adjust an isometric ellipse. As soon as you resize an isometric ellipse in this manner, its angular value is changed and it is no longer isometric. You can use the center grip to move the ellipse. Also, if you rotate an isometric ellipse while **Ortho** mode is on, it will not appear in a proper isometric plane. You *can* rotate an isometric ellipse from one isometric plane to another, but you must enter a value of 120°.

Figure 25-11.
The orientation of an isometric ellipse is determined by the current isometric plane.

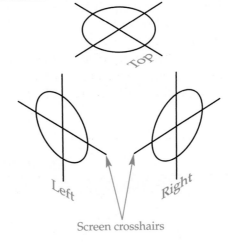

Figure 25-12.
An isometric ellipse
has grips at its four
quadrant points and
center.

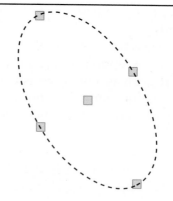

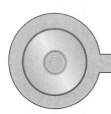

Exercise 25-2
Complete the exercise on the Student CD.

Constructing Isometric Arcs

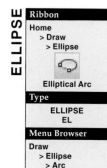

The **ELLIPSE** tool can also be used to draw an isometric arc of any included angle. To construct an isometric arc, use the **Arc** option of the **ELLIPSE** tool while in **Isometric snap** mode. Once the **ELLIPSE** tool is initiated, type A to initiate the **Arc** option, pick the **Isocircle** option, and then pick the center of the arc. Pick values for the radius, start angle, and end angle.

A common application of isometric arcs is drawing fillets and rounds. Once a round is created in isometric, the edge (corner) of the object sits back from its original, unfilleted position. See **Figure 25-13A**. You can draw the complete object first and then trim away the excess after locating the fillets. You can also draw the isometric arcs and then the connecting lines. Either way, the center point of the ellipse is a critical feature and should be located first. The left-hand arc in **Figure 25-13A** was drawn first and copied to the back position. Use **Ortho** mode to help quickly draw 90° arcs.

The next step is to move the original edge to its new position, which is tangent to the isometric arcs. You can do this by snapping the endpoint of the line to the quadrant point of the arc. See **Figure 25-13B**. Notice the grips on the line and on the arc. The endpoint of the line is snapped to the quadrant grip on the arc. The final step is to trim away the excess lines and arc segment. The completed feature is shown in **Figure 25-13C**.

Rounded edges, when viewed straight on, cannot be shown as complete-edge lines that extend to the ends of the object. Instead, a good technique to use is a broken line in the original location of the edge. This is clearly shown on the right-hand edge in **Figure 25-13C**.

Exercise 25-3
Complete the exercise on the Student CD.

Figure 25-13.
Fillets and rounds can be drawn with the **Arc** option of the **ELLIPSE** tool. A broken line is used to represent an edge that is viewed straight on.

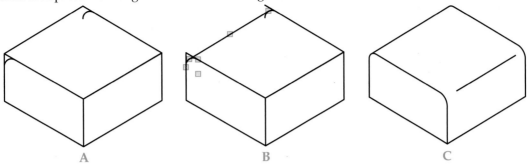

A   B   C

Creating Isometric Text Styles

Text placed in an isometric drawing should appear to be parallel to one of the isometric planes. Text should align with the plane to which it applies. Text may be located on the object or positioned away from it as a note. Drafters and artists occasionally neglect this aspect of pictorial drawing and it shows on the final product.

Properly placing text on an isometric drawing involves creating new text styles. Figure 25-14 illustrates possible orientations of text on an isometric drawing. These examples were created using only two text styles. The text styles have an obliquing angle of either 30° or −30°. The labels in Figure 25-14 refer to the following table. The angle in the figure indicates the rotation angle entered when using one of the text tools. For example, ISO-2 90 means that the ISO-2 style was used and the text was rotated 90°. This technique can be applied to any font.

Name	Font	Obliquing Angle
ISO-1	Romans	30°
ISO-2	Romans	−30°

Exercise 25-4

Complete the exercise on the Student CD.

Figure 25-14.
Isometric text applications. The text shown here indicates which style and angle were used.

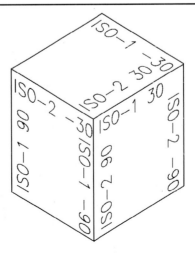

Isometric Dimensioning

An important aspect of dimensioning in isometric is to place dimension lines, text, and arrowheads on the proper plane. Remember these guidelines:

- Extension lines should always extend in the plane being dimensioned.
- The heel of the arrowhead should always be parallel to the extension line.
- Strokes of the text that would normally be vertical should always be parallel with the extension lines or dimension lines.

These techniques are shown on the dimensioned isometric part in **Figure 25-15.** AutoCAD does not automatically dimension isometric objects. You must first create isometric arrowheads and text styles. Then, manually draw the dimension lines and text as they should appear in each of the three isometric planes. This is time-consuming when compared to dimensioning normal 2D drawings.

You have already learned how to create isometric text styles. These can be set up in an isometric template drawing if you draw isometrics often. Examples of arrows for the three isometric planes are shown in **Figure 25-16.**

Figure 25-15.
A dimensioned isometric part. Note the text and arrowhead orientation in relation to the extension lines.

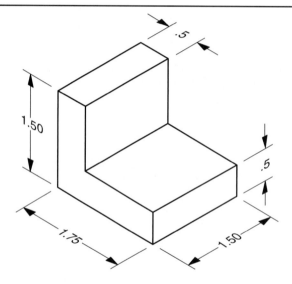

Figure 25-16.
Examples of arrowheads in each of the three isometric planes.

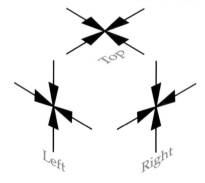

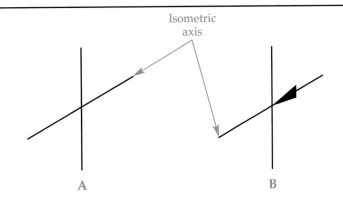

Figure 25-17. Creating isometric arrowheads. A—Draw the two isometric axes for arrowhead placement. B—Draw the first arrowhead on one of the axis lines. Then mirror the arrowhead to create the others.

Isometric axis

A   B

Isometric Arrowheads

You can draw isometric arrowheads and fill them in with a solid hatch pattern. A variable-width polyline cannot be used because the heel of the arrowhead will not be parallel to the extension lines.

You do not need to draw every arrowhead individually. First, draw two isometric axes, as shown in **Figure 25-17A**. Then draw one arrowhead like the one shown in **Figure 25-17B**. Use the **MIRROR** tool to create additional arrows. As you create new arrows, move them to their proper plane.

You can save each arrowhead as a block in your isometric template or prototype. Use block names that are easy to remember. Blocks are discussed in Chapters 26 and 27.

Oblique Dimensioning

AutoCAD has a way to dimension isometric and oblique lines semiautomatically. First, draw the dimensions using any of the linear dimensioning tools. The object in **Figure 25-18A** was dimensioned using the **DIMALIGNED** and **DIMLINEAR** tools. Then use the **Oblique** option of the **DIMEDIT** tool to rotate the extension lines. See **Figure 25-18B**.

To use the **Oblique** option, you can access the **DIMEDIT** tool and then type O for **Oblique**. When prompted, select the dimension and enter the obliquing angle.

This technique creates suitable dimensions for an isometric drawing and is quicker than the method previously discussed. However, this method does not rotate the arrows to align the arrowhead heels with the extension lines. It also does not draw the dimension text aligned in the plane of the dimension. Therefore, this method does not produce technically correct dimensions.

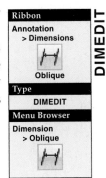

Ribbon
Annotation > Dimensions
Oblique
Type
DIMEDIT
Menu Browser
Dimension > Oblique

DIMEDIT

Figure 25-18.
Using the **Oblique** option of the **DIMEDIT** tool, you can create semiautomatic isometric dimensions by editing existing dimensions.

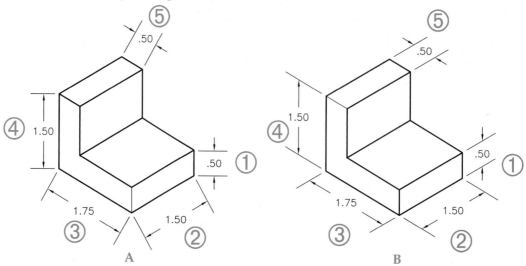

Dimension	Obliquing Angle
1	30°
2	–30°
3	30°
4	–30°
5	30°

Chapter Test

Answer the following questions. Write your answers on a separate sheet of paper or complete the electronic chapter test on the Student CD.

1. The simplest form of pictorial drawing is _____.
2. How does isometric drawing differ from oblique drawing?
3. How do dimetric and trimetric drawings differ from isometric drawings?
4. The most realistic form of pictorial drawing is _____.
5. What must be set in the **Drafting Settings** dialog box to turn on **Isometric snap** mode and set a snap spacing of .2?
6. What function does the **ISOPLANE** tool perform?
7. Name the tool and option used to draw an isometric circle.
8. What factor determines the orientation of an isometric ellipse?
9. Where are grips located on a circle drawn in isometric?
10. Can grips be used to resize an isometric circle correctly? Explain your answer.
11. How are isometric arcs drawn?
12. How can you create text that can be used on an isometric drawing?
13. How can you create isometric arrowheads?
14. What technique does AutoCAD provide for semiautomatically dimensioning isometric objects?
15. Why does the technique in Question 14 not produce technically correct dimensions?

Drawing Problems

▼ Basic

Create an isometric template drawing. Items that should be set in the template include grid spacing, snap spacing, ortho setting, and text size. Save the template as isoproto.dwt. *Use the template to construct the isometric drawings in Problems 1–10. Save the drawing problems as* P25-*(problem number).*

1.

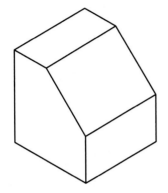

2.

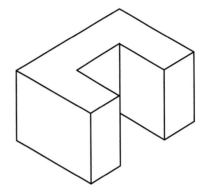

3.

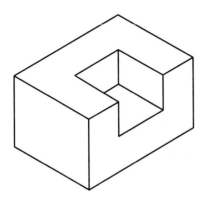

4.

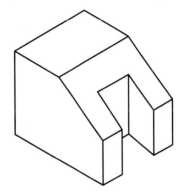

5.

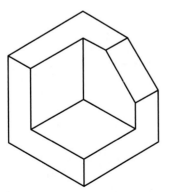

6.

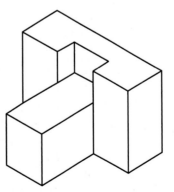

7.

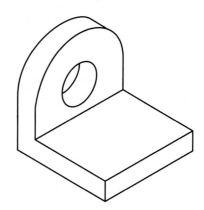

8.

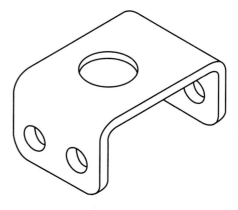

9.

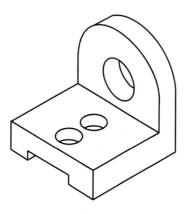

10.

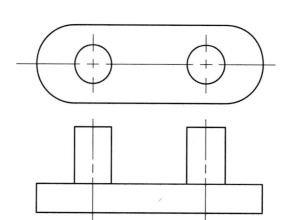

▼ Intermediate

For Problems 11–14, create isometric drawings using the views shown. Measure the drawings to obtain the dimensions.

11.

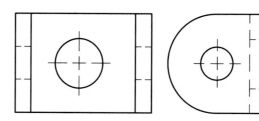

12.

13.

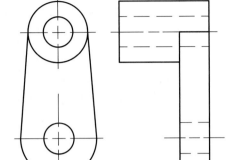

14.

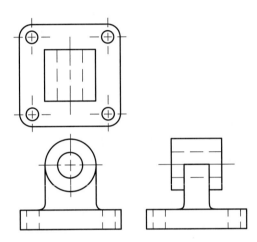

15. Construct a set of isometric arrowheads to use when dimensioning isometric drawings. Load your isometric template drawing. Create arrowheads for each of the three isometric planes. Name them with the first letter indicating the plane: T for top, L for left, and R for right. Also, number them clockwise from the top. See the example below for the right isometric plane. Do not include the labels in your drawing. Save the template again when finished.

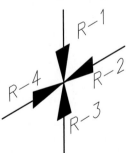

16. Create a set of isometric text styles like those shown in **Figure 25-14.** Load your template drawing and make a complete set in one font. Make additional sets in other fonts if you wish. Enter a text height of 0 so you can specify the height when placing the text. Save the template when finished.

---

17. Begin a new drawing using your isometric template. Select one of the following problems from this chapter and dimension it: Problem 5, 7, 8, or 9. When adding dimensions, be sure to use the proper arrowhead and text style for the plane on which you are working. Save the drawing as P25-17.

▼ Advanced

18. Create an isometric drawing of the switch plate shown below. Select a view that best displays the features of the object. Do not include dimensions. Save the drawing as P25-18.

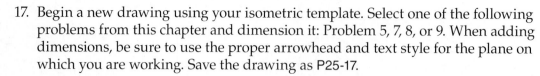

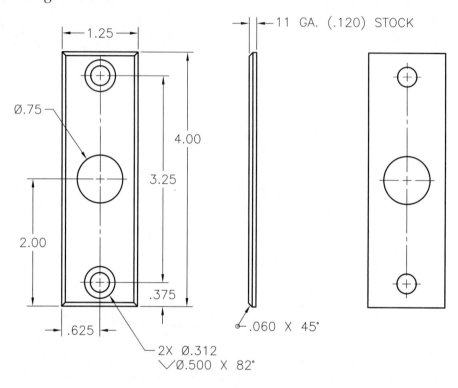

19. Create an isometric drawing of the retainer shown below. Select a view that best displays the features of the object. Do not include dimensions. Save the drawing as P25-19.

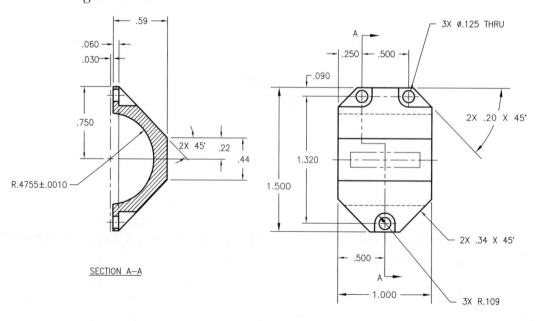

SECTION A—A

Learning Objectives

After completing this chapter, you will be able to do the following:

✓ Create and save blocks.
✓ Insert blocks into a drawing.
✓ Edit a block and update it in a drawing.
✓ Create blocks as drawing files.
✓ Construct and use a symbol library of blocks.
✓ Purge blocks from a drawing file.

One of the greatest benefits of using AutoCAD is the capability to create and use *blocks*. A block created with the **BLOCK** tool is stored within a drawing as a *block definition*. The block can be inserted into the drawing in which it was defined as many times as needed. A *wblock* created with the **WBLOCK** tool is saved as a separate drawing file and can be inserted as many times as needed into *any* drawing. Both types of blocks can be scaled and rotated as they are inserted to meet the drawing requirements, and both types can be shared between drawings.

block: A user-created symbol that has been saved and stored in a drawing for future use.

block definition: Information about a block that is stored within the drawing file.

wblock: A block definition that is saved as a separate drawing file.

Constructing Blocks

A block can be any shape, group of objects, symbol, view, or drawing. Before constructing a block, review the drawing you are working on. This is where a sketch of your drawing can be useful. Look for any shapes, components, notes, and assemblies that are used more than once. These features can be drawn once and then saved as blocks for multiple use.

Selecting a Layer

Before you begin drawing block components, you should identify the appropriate layer on which to create the objects. It is critical that you understand how layers and object properties are applied when you create and insert blocks.

The preferred method of block creation and usage is to draw all block objects on the 0 layer. If the objects used for a block are originally created on the 0 layer, the block assumes, or inherits, the properties of the layer on which it is inserted. If the objects have been drawn on a different layer, place all the objects on layer 0 before creating the block.

The second method for using layers is to create block objects using a layer or layers other than the 0 layer. If the objects for the block are originally created on a layer other than the 0 layer, the objects belong to the layer on which the block is inserted, but they retain the properties of the layer or layers on which the objects were created. This method can often cause confusion because a group of objects (a block) belongs to one layer, but has the properties of a different layer. As a result, you should usually draw objects for a block on the 0 layer.

To create a block that assumes the current color and linetype when it is inserted into a drawing, regardless of the current layer, set the absolute color and linetype before drawing the objects. If the block should assume the current color when it is inserted into a drawing, set the object color to ByBlock, by selecting ByBlock in the **Color** drop-down list on the **Properties** panel on the **Home** tab of the ribbon, or by picking the **ByBlock** button in the **Select Color** dialog box. If the block should assume the current linetype when it is inserted into a drawing, set the object linetype to ByBlock, by selecting ByBlock in the **Linetype** drop-down list of the **Properties** panel on the **Home** tab of the ribbon, or by picking the ByBlock linetype option using the **Linetype Manager** dialog box.

Drawing Block Components

insertion base point: The point on a block that attaches to the crosshairs for insertion into the drawing.

Draw a block as you would any other drawing geometry. When you finish drawing the object, determine the best location for the *insertion base point*. When you insert the block into a drawing, the insertion base point attaches to the crosshairs for placement. Several examples of commonly used blocks are shown in **Figure 26-1** with their insertion points highlighted.

> **PROFESSIONAL TIP**
>
> Multiple features that are identical except for scale can be created from a single block. In these cases, the base block should be drawn to fit inside a one-unit square. It does not matter if the object is measured in feet, inches, or millimeters. This makes it easy to scale the block later when you insert it into a drawing.

Figure 26-1.
Common drafting symbols and their insertion points for placement on drawings. The insertion points are shown here as colored dots.

Electrical Symbols

Architectural Symbols

Mechanical Symbols

AutoCAD and Its Applications—Basics

Creating Blocks

When you draw a shape or symbol, you have not yet created a block. Use the **BLOCK** tool to save your object as a block. The **Block Definition** dialog box is displayed when you access the **BLOCK** tool. See **Figure 26-2**. Use the **Block Definition** dialog box to name and describe the block, enter or select a block insertion base point, select existing drawing objects to make up the block, and adjust block definition options.

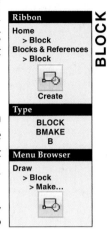

Naming and describing the block

Enter a descriptive name for the block in the **Name:** text box of the **Block Definition** dialog box. For example, a vacuum pump might be named PUMP or a certain size door might be named DOOR_3068. The block name cannot exceed 255 characters. It can include numbers, letters, and spaces, as well as the dollar sign ($), hyphen (-), and underscore (_).

A block name is often descriptive enough to identify the correct block. However, you can enter a textual description of the block in the **Description:** text box to help identify the block for easy reference. For example, the PUMP block might include the description This is a vacuum pump symbol, or the DOOR_3068 block might include the description This is 3' wide by 6'-8" tall interior single-swing door.

Defining the block insertion base point

The **Base point** area of the **Block Definition** dialog box is used to define the block insertion base point. You can enter the coordinates for the insertion base point by typing values in the **X:**, **Y:**, and **Z:** text boxes, or you can select the insertion base point directly from the drawing.

Choose the **Pick point** button to return to the drawing and select an insertion base point. The **Block Definition** dialog box reappears once the insertion base point is selected. An alternative technique is to choose the **Specify On-screen** check box. When selected, this option allows you to pick an insertion base point from the drawing after you pick the **OK** button to exit the **Block Definition** dialog box. This method can save

---

Figure 26-2.
Blocks are created using the **Block Definition** dialog box.

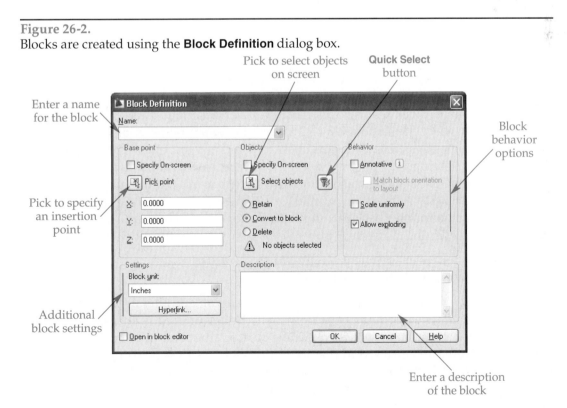

---

time by picking the insertion base point without using the **Pick point** button and reentering the **Block Definition** dialog box.

Selecting block objects

The **Objects** area of the **Block Definition** dialog box contains options for selected objects for the block definition. Pick the **Select objects** button to return to the drawing and select objects that will make up the block. Press [Enter], the space bar, or right-click when you are finished to redisplay the **Block Definition** dialog box. The number of selected objects is shown in the **Objects** area and an image of the selection is displayed next to the **Name:** drop-down list. To create a selection set, use the **QuickSelect** button to define a filter for your selection set. The **Quick Select** dialog box is described in Chapter 14.

An alternative method for selecting objects is to choose the **Specify On-screen** check box. When selected, this option allows you to pick objects from the drawing after you pick the **OK** button to exit the **Block Definition** dialog box. This method can save time by selecting objects without using the **Select objects** button and reentering the **Block Definition** dialog box.

The **Objects** area is also used to specify whether to retain, convert, or delete the selected existing objects. Pick the **Retain** radio button to keep the selected objects in the current drawing (in their original state). Select the **Convert to block** radio button to replace the selected objects with the block you are creating. Choose the **Delete** radio button to remove the selected objects after the block is defined.

PROFESSIONAL TIP

If you select the **Delete** option and then decide that you want to keep the original geometry in the drawing after you have defined the block, enter the **OOPS** tool. This returns the original objects to the screen and keeps the block definition, whereas using the **UNDO** tool removes the block definition from the drawing.

Block scale settings

To make the block annotative, pick the **Annotative** check box in the **Behavior** area. AutoCAD scales blocks that you define as annotative according to the annotation scale you select. This is the same as the drawing scale, which eliminates the need to calculate the scale factor. Block scaling options are further described later in this chapter.

When you select the **Annotative** check box, the **Match block orientation to layout** check box becomes available. Pick this check box to keep annotative blocks planar to the layout in a floating viewport, even if the drawing view is rotated, as it might be if you rotate the UCS. Selecting this option also prohibits you from using the **ROTATE** tool to rotate a block.

If the **Scale uniformly** check box in the **Behavior** area is checked, you do not have the option of specifying different X and Y scale factors when the block is inserted into a drawing.

Additional block definition settings

The **Block Definition** dialog box contains several additional block definition options. If the **Allow exploding** check box in the **Behavior** area is checked, the block can be exploded. If the box is not checked, the block cannot be exploded either when it is inserted or after it is inserted in the drawing. Select a unit type from the **Block unit** drop-down list in the **Settings** area to specify the insertion units of the block. Pick the **Hyperlink...** button to access the **Insert Hyperlink** dialog box to insert a hyperlink in the block. If the **Open in block editor** check box is checked, the new block is immediately opened in the **Block Definition Editor** after the block is created. The **Block Definition Editor** is described later in this chapter.

NOTE

To verify that the block was saved properly, reopen the **Block Definition** dialog box. Pick the **Name:** drop-down list button to display a list of all blocks in the current drawing. The block names are organized in numerical and alphabetical order.

PROFESSIONAL TIP

Blocks can be used to create other blocks. Suppose you design a complex part or view that will be used repeatedly. You can insert existing blocks into the view and then save the entire object as a block. This is called *nesting*. The top-level block must be given a name that is different from any nested block. Proper planning and knowledge of all existing blocks can speed up the drawing process and the creation of complex parts.

nesting: Creating a block that includes other blocks.

Exercise 26-1
Complete the exercise on the Student CD.

Inserting Blocks

Once a block has been created, there are several options for inserting the block in a drawing. Blocks are normally inserted on specific layers, so set the proper layer *before* inserting the block. You should also determine the proper size and rotation angle for the block before insertion.

Once a block has been inserted into a drawing, it is referred to as a ***block reference***. Any named objects, such as blocks and layers, are referred to as ***dependent symbols***. AutoCAD automatically updates dependent symbols in a drawing the next time the drawing is opened.

block reference: A specific instance of a block inserted into a drawing.

dependent symbols: Named objects in a drawing that has been inserted or referenced into another drawing.

Using the Insert Tool

The **INSERT** tool is one of the most common methods for inserting blocks and wblocks, described later in this chapter, in a drawing. The **Insert** dialog box is displayed when you access the **INSERT** tool. See **Figure 26-3.**

Selecting the block to insert

Pick the **Name:** drop-down list button to show the blocks defined in the current drawing. Then select the name of the block you want to insert. You can also type the name of the block in the **Name:** text box. Pick the **Browse...** button to display the **Select Drawing File** dialog box in which you can select a drawing file (wblock) for insertion into the current drawing. This process is described later in this chapter.

Figure 26-3.
The **Insert** dialog box allows you to select and prepare a block for insertion. Select the block you want to insert from the drop-down list or enter the block name in the **Name:** text box.

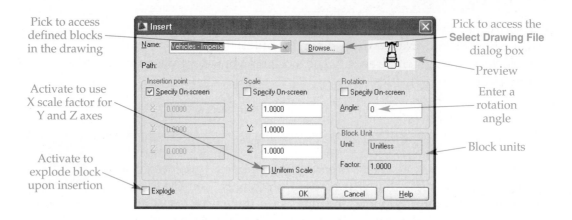

Pick to access
defined blocks
in the drawing

Activate to use
X scale factor for
Y and Z axes

Activate to
explode block
upon insertion

Pick to access the
Select Drawing File
dialog box

Preview

Enter a
rotation
angle

Block units

Defining the block insertion point

INSERT

Ribbon

Home
> Block
Blocks & References
> Block

Insert

Type

DDINSERT
INSERT
I

Menu Browser

Insert
> Block...

The **Insertion point** area of the **Insert** dialog box contains options for specifying where the block is to be inserted. If the **Specify On-screen** check box is selected, the block is inserted dynamically when you pick **OK** and you must pick an insertion point on screen. If you want to insert the block using absolute coordinates, disable the check box and enter the coordinates in the **X:**, **Y:**, and **Z:** text boxes.

Scaling blocks

The **Scale** area of the **Insert** dialog box allows you to specify scale values for the block in relation to the X, Y, and Z axes. By default, the **Specify On-screen** check box is deselected, allowing you to enter scale values in the **X:**, **Y:**, and **Z:** text boxes. If you want to be prompted for the scale when inserting the block, select the **Specify On-screen** check box.

If you activate the **Uniform Scale** check box, you can specify a scale value for the X axis. The same value is then used for the Y and Z axes when the block is inserted. If the block was created with the **Scale uniformly** check box checked in the **Block Definition** dialog box, only the **X** value is active. The Y and Z coordinates also use this value so the block is uniform.

It is possible to create a mirror image of a block by entering a negative value for the scale factor. For example, entering –1 for both the X scale factor and the Y scale factor mirrors the block to the opposite quadrant of the original orientation specified and retains the original size. Different mirroring techniques are shown in Figure 26-4.

A block that is scaled during insertion can be classified as a real block, schematic block, or unit block. Examples of *real blocks* include a bolt, a bathtub, a pipe fitting, or the car shown in Figure 26-5A. Examples of *schematic blocks* include notes, detail bubbles, or section symbols. See Figure 26-5B. Annotative blocks are typically classified as schematic blocks. When you insert an annotative schematic block, AutoCAD automatically determines the block scale based on the annotation scale. When you insert a non-annotative schematic block, you must specify the scale factor.

real block: A block originally drawn at a 1:1 scale and then inserted using 1 for both the X and Y scale factors.

schematic block: A block originally drawn at a 1:1 scale and then inserted using the drawing scale factor for both the X and Y scale values.

NOTE

For most applications, annotative blocks should be inserted at a scale of 1 in order for the annotation scale to be applied correctly. Entering a scale other than 1 adjusts the scale of the block by multiplying the scale value by the annotative scale factor.

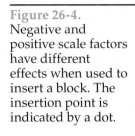

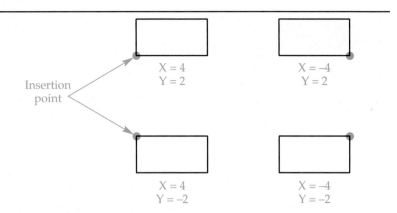

Insertion point

X = 4
Y = 2

X = –4
Y = 2

X = 4
Y = –2

X = –4
Y = –2

There are three different types of ***unit blocks***. One example of a ***1D unit block*** is a 1-unit (1″, for example) line object that is turned into a block. A ***2D unit block*** is any blocked object that can fit inside a 1-unit × 1-unit (1″ × 1″ for example) square. A ***3D unit block*** is any blocked object that can fit inside a 1-unit (1″ for example) cube. To use a unit block, insert the block and determine the individual scale factors for each axis. For example, a 1D unit block could be inserted at a scale of 4, which would turn the line into a 4″ line, when using inch units. A 2D unit block could be assigned different scale factors for the X and Y axes, such as 4 for the X axis and 12 for the Y axis, to create the 4″ × 12″ beam shown in Figure 26-5C. A 3D unit block could be inserted at different scales for the X, Y, and Z axes.

Rotating blocks

The **Rotation** area of the **Insert** dialog box allows you to insert the block at a specified angle. By default, the **Specify On-screen** check box is disabled and the block is inserted at an angle of zero. If you want to use a different angle, enter a value in the **Angle:** text box. If you want to be prompted for the rotation angle when you insert the block, check the **Specify On-screen** check box.

unit block: A 1D, 2D, or 3D block drawn to fit in a 1-unit, 1-unit-square, or 1-unit-cubed area so that it can be scaled easily.

1D unit block: A 1-unit, one-dimensional object, such as a straight line segment, that has been saved as a block.

2D unit block: A 2D object that fits into a 1-unit × 1-unit square and has been saved as a block.

3D unit block: A 3D object that fits into a 1-unit × 1-unit × 1-unit cube and has been saved as a block.

NOTE

Blocks defined using the **Match block orientation to layout** option cannot be rotated.

Figure 26-5.
A—Real blocks, such as this car, are drawn at a one-to-one scale and inserted using a scale factor of 1 for both the X and Y axes. B—A schematic block is inserted using the scale factor of the drawing for the X and Y axes. C—A 2D unit block can be inserted at different scales for the X and Y axes.

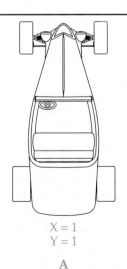

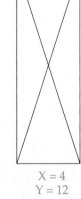

GENERAL NOTE: THIS IS AN EXAMPLE OF A SCHEMATIC BLOCK THAT HAS BEEN INSERTED BY THE SCALE FACTOR.

A1

X = 48
Y = 48

X = 1
Y = 1

X = 4
Y = 12

A

B

C

A block's rotation angle can be based on the current UCS. If you want to insert a block at a specific angle based on the current UCS or an existing UCS, be sure the proper UCS is active. Then insert the block and use a rotation angle of zero. If you decide to change the UCS later, any inserted blocks retain their original angle.

Additional block insertion items

The **Insert** dialog box contains additional block insertion options. When a block is created, it is saved as a single object, no matter how many objects were used to create the block. Select the **Explode** check box if you want to explode the block into its original objects for editing purposes. If you explode the block on insertion, it assumes its original properties, such as its original layer, color, and linetype. If **Allow exploding** was unchecked when the block was created, the **Explode** check box in the **Insert** dialog box is inactive. The **Block Unit** area displays read-only information about the selected block. The **Unit:** display box indicates the units for the block. The **Factor:** display box indicates the scale factor.

Working with specify on-screen prompts

When you pick the **OK** button, prompts appear for any values defined as **Specify On-screen** in the **Insert** dialog box. If you are specifying the insertion point on-screen, the Specify insertion point or [Basepoint/Scale/X/Y/Z/Rotate/PScale/PX/PY/PZ/PRotate]: prompt appears. Enter or select a point to insert the block, or select an option.

If you select one of the options, the new value overrides any setting in the **Insert** dialog box. The options allow you to specify a different base point, enter a value for the overall scale, enter independent scale factors for the X, Y, and Z axes, enter a rotation angle, and preview the scale of the X, Y, and Z axes or the rotation angle before entering actual values. If you are specifying the X scale factor on screen, the Enter X scale factor, specify opposite corner, or [Corner/XYZ] <1>: prompt appears. Pick a point or enter a value for the scale.

Moving the cursor scales the block dynamically as it is dragged. If you want to scale the block visually, pick a point when the object appears to be at the correct size. You can also use the **Corner** option to scale the block dynamically.

The Enter Y scale factor <use X scale factor>: prompt appears if you enter an X scale factor, or press [Enter], the space bar, or right-click to accept the default scale value. Enter a value, or press [Enter], the space bar, or right-click to accept the same scale specified for the X axis.

The X and Y scale factors allow you to stretch or compress the block to suit your needs. See **Figure 26-6.** This is why it is a good idea to draw blocks to fit inside a one-unit square. It makes the block easy to scale because you can enter the exact number of units for the X and Y dimensions. For example, if you want the block to be three units long and two units high enter 3 at the Enter X scale factor, specify opposite corner, or [Corner/XYZ] <1>: prompt, and enter 2 at the Enter Y scale factor <use X scale factor>: prompt.

The insertion base point that was specified when the block was created may not always be the best point when inserting the block. Instead of inserting the block and then moving it, you can use the **Basepoint** option to specify a different base point before inserting the block. To use this option, select the **Basepoint** option when prompted to specify the insertion point. The block is then temporarily placed on the screen. When you pick the new base point for the block, the block is reattached to the crosshairs at that point. A message appears indicating that the tool is resuming and you are prompted to specify the insertion point.

AutoCAD and Its Applications—Basics

Figure 26-6.
A comparison of
different X and
Y scale factors used
for inserting a 2D
unit block.

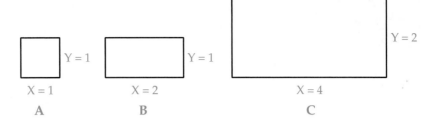

X = 1   X = 2   X = 4
Y = 1   Y = 1   Y = 2
  A   B   C

Exercise 26-2

Complete the exercise on the Student CD.

Inserting Multiple Arranged Copies of a Block

The features of the **INSERT** and **ARRAY** tools are combined using the **MINSERT**
tool. This method of inserting and arraying blocks saves time and disk space when
creating multiple arranged copies of a block.

Button
MINSERT

An example of an application using the **MINSERT** tool is shown in Figure 26-7.
To follow this example, draw a 4′ × 3′ rectangle (you must use architectural units) and
save it as a block named DESK. Now, access the **MINSERT** tool and name the block. Pick
a point as the insertion point and then accept the X scale factor of 1, the Y scale factor
of use X scale factor, and the rotation angle of 0. The arrangement is to be three rows
and four columns. In order to make the horizontal spacing between desks 2′, and the
vertical spacing 4′, you must consider the size of the desk when entering the distance
between rows and columns. Enter 7′ (3′ desk depth × 4′ space between desks) at the
Enter distance between rows of specify unit cell: prompt. Enter 6′ (4′ desk width × 2′ space
between desks) at the Specify distance between columns: prompt.

The complete pattern takes on the characteristics of a block, except that an array
created with the **MINSERT** tool cannot be exploded. Since the array cannot be exploded,
you must use the **Properties** palette to modify the number of rows and columns, change
the spacing between objects, or change the layer, color, or linetype properties. If the
initial block is rotated, all arrayed objects are also rotated about their insertion points.
If the arrayed objects are rotated about the insertion point while using the **MINSERT**
tool, all objects are aligned on that point.

Figure 26-7.
Creating an
arrangement of
desks using the
MINSERT tool.

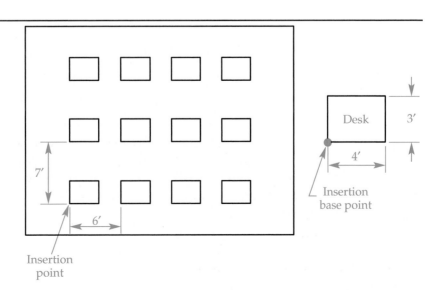

As an alternative to the previous example, if you were working with different desk sizes, a 2D unit block may serve your purposes better than an exact size block. To create a 5′ × 3′-6″ (60″ × 42″) desk, for example, insert a one-unit-square block using either the **INSERT** or **MINSERT** tool, and enter 60 for the X scale factor and 42 for the Y scale factor.

Exercise 26-3
Complete the exercise on the Student CD.

Inserting Entire Drawings

The **INSERT** tool can also be used to insert an entire drawing file into the current drawing. To do so, access the **INSERT** tool. Pick the **Browse...** button in the **Insert** dialog box to access the **Select Drawing File** dialog box, and select a drawing file to insert.

When one drawing is inserted into another, the inserted drawing becomes a block reference. As a block, it may be moved to a new location with a single pick. The drawing is inserted on the current layer, but it does not inherit the color, linetype, or thickness properties of that layer. You can explode the inserted drawing back to its original objects if desired. Once exploded, the drawing objects revert to their original layers. A drawing that is inserted brings any existing block definitions, layers, linetypes, text styles, and dimension styles into the current drawing.

By default, every drawing has an insertion base point of 0,0,0 when you insert it into another drawing. If you want to change the insertion base point of the drawing, use the **BASE** tool. Once you access the BASE tool, select a new insertion base point. Save the drawing before inserting it into another drawing.

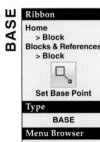

BASE

Ribbon
Home
> Block
Blocks & References
> Block
[icon]
Set Base Point
Type
BASE
Menu Browser
Draw
> Block
> Base
[icon]

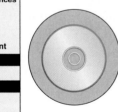

Exercise 26-4
Complete the exercise on the Student CD.

Creating a Block from a Drawing File

You can create a block from any existing drawing. This allows you to avoid redrawing the object as a block, thus saving time. Remember, if something has already been drawn, try to use it as a block rather than redrawing it.

For example, to define a block named BOLT from an existing drawing named fastener.dwg, enter the **INSERT** tool. Use the **Browse...** button to select the fastener.dwg file. The selected file is displayed in the **Name:** text box. Use this text box to change the name from fastener to BOLT and pick **OK**. You can then insert the file into the drawing or press the [Esc] key to exit the tool. A block named BOLT has now been created from the file and can be used as desired.

Using DesignCenter to Insert Blocks

DesignCenter can be used to insert blocks or entire drawings into your current drawing. The **Folders** tab of the **DesignCenter** shows the hierarchy of files and folders on your computer, including network drives. The **Open Drawings** tab displays all of the drawing files open in the current AutoCAD session. The **History** tab displays the files most recently accessed in **DesignCenter**. The **DC Online** tab gives you access to drawing content that can be downloaded from the Internet. See **Figure 26-8**.

To view the blocks defined in a drawing, select the **Blocks** branch in the tree view or double-click on the **Blocks** icon in the content area. Once you find the desired block, drag and drop, copy and paste, or use the **Insert** dialog box to insert the block into the current drawing.

To use the drag-and-drop method, move the cursor over the block in the content area, press and hold down the pick button, and drag the cursor to the drawing editor. Release the pick button to insert the block into the drawing where the cursor is located. The block is inserted based on the type of block units specified when the block was created. For example, if the original block was a 1×1 square and the block units were specified as feet when the block was created, then the block will be a $12'' \times 12''$ square when it is inserted from **DesignCenter**.

A similar operation to drag and drop is copy and paste. Right-click on the block in **DesignCenter** and pick **Copy** from the shortcut menu. Move the cursor into the active drawing, right-click, and select **Paste** from the shortcut menu. The block is attached to the cursor. Enter or select a point to insert the block.

Another option is to use **DesignCenter** in combination with the **Insert** dialog box. Right-click on a block in **DesignCenter** and select **Insert Block...** from the shortcut menu to access the **Insert** dialog box. The selected block is displayed automatically. This option allows you to scale, rotate, or explode the block during insertion.

Figure 26-8.
DesignCenter Online provides many sources for blocks and other drawing content.

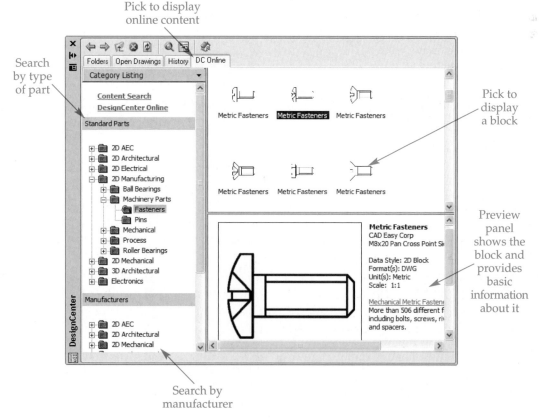

To insert an entire drawing using **DesignCenter**, select the folder in the tree view that contains the drawing. Any drawings in the selected folder appear in the content area. Drag and drop or copy and paste the desired drawing into the current drawing. You can also right-click a drawing icon in the content area and select **Insert as Block...** from the shortcut menu.

Using Tool Palettes to Insert Blocks

The **Tool Palettes** window provides another quick way to access blocks for insertion into a drawing. See **Figure 26-9.** This feature is similar to **DesignCenter** in that blocks can be previewed before inserting them. The window is divided into *tool palettes*, each indicated by a tab along the side of the window. Blocks located in a tool palette are known as *block insertion tools*.

tool palettes: Collections of related blocks, hatches, tools, and other tools arranged in a visual palette format for quick selection.

block insertion tools: Blocks located on a tool palette.

NOTE

Tool palettes can be used to store many different types of drawing content and tools, such as AutoCAD drawing and editing tools, customized tools, user-defined macros, script files, and AutoLISP routines. Examples of custom tools are provided in the **Command Tools Samples** tool palette. For more information on AutoCAD customization, refer to *AutoCAD and Its Applications—Advanced*.

To insert a block from the **Tool Palettes** window, select the tool palette tab in which the block resides and locate the block. Use the scroll bar on the side of the window to move up or down in the tool palette, if needed. When you locate the block, place the cursor over the block icon. If the block contains a description, the description appears next to the cursor. You can use the drag-and-drop method to insert the block, or you can pick once on the block icon and then move the cursor into the drawing area and

Figure 26-9.
The **Tool Palettes** window. Blocks may be inserted into the current drawing from a selected tab.

Active tab (palette)

Blocks available in palette

Additional palette tabs

Scroll down to access more tools

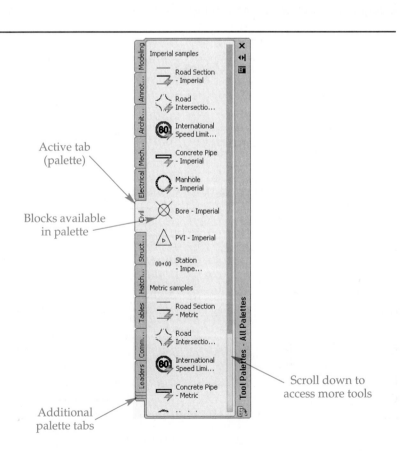

AutoCAD and Its Applications—Basics

pick again to place the block. With either method, the block is attached to the crosshairs once the cursor is moved into the drawing area. The block is connected to the crosshairs at the insertion point of the block.

When inserting a block with the "pick-pick" method, you can access scaling and rotation options for the block before picking an insertion point. Use the **Scale** option to scale the block along the XYZ axes or use the **Rotate** option to specify a rotation angle for the block. Blocks inserted from tool palettes are automatically scaled based on a ratio of the current drawing scale to the scale used in the original block definition.

> **NOTE**
>
> Tool palettes can be added to the **Tool Palettes** window, and tools can be added to tool palettes. For more information on creating and modifying tool palettes, refer to *AutoCAD and Its Applications—Advanced*.

Exercise 26-5
Complete the exercise on the Student CD.

Editing Blocks

There are two forms of block editing. One form involves modifying a block inserted in a drawing using tools such as **MOVE**, **COPY**, **ROTATE**, or **MIRROR**. When using grip editing, the grip box is positioned at the insertion base point of the block. The **Properties** palette and **Quick Properties** panel can also be used to make limited changes to inserted blocks. Remember, once a block has been inserted, it is treated as a single object.

The second type of block editing involves redefining the block by changing the separate objects within the block, or editing the block definition. Blocks can be redefined using the **Block Editor** or exploded and then recreated. These techniques are described later in this chapter.

Changing Block Properties to ByLayer

If block component properties, such as color and linetype, were originally set to values other than ByLayer, the objects belong to the selected layer, but they retain the properties of the layer on which the objects were created. To solve this problem, you can edit the block definition or use the **SETBYLAYER** tool to accomplish the same task without editing the block definition.

Once you access the **SETBYLAYER** tool, the Select objects or [Settings]: prompt is displayed. Enter the **Settings** option to display the **SetByLayer Settings** dialog box. Select the check boxes that correspond to the object properties that you want to convert to ByLayer. Pick **OK** to exit the **SetByLayer Settings** dialog box.

Next, select the objects whose properties you want to set to ByLayer. When you have finished selecting objects, press [Enter], the space bar, or right-click to display the Change ByBlock to ByLayer? prompt. Select the **Yes** option to change all object properties currently set to ByBlock to ByLayer. Pick the **No** option to change all object properties

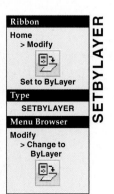

Ribbon
Home
> Modify

Set to ByLayer

Type
SETBYLAYER

Menu Browser
Modify
> Change to
ByLayer

SETBYLAYER

currently set to values other than ByBlock to ByLayer. AutoCAD then asks if you want to include blocks. If the selected object is a block, choosing **Yes** converts the properties of all references of the same block in the drawing to ByLayer. If you pick **No**, only the properties of the selected block are set to ByLayer. All other references of the same block remain unchanged.

Using the Block Editor

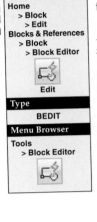

BEDIT

Ribbon
Home
> Block
> Edit
Blocks & References
> Block
> Block Editor

Edit

Type
BEDIT

Menu Browser
Tools
> Block Editor

You can edit a block definition in-place using the **BEDIT** tool. When you activate the **BEDIT** tool, the **Edit Block Definition** dialog box appears. See **Figure 26-10**.

To edit an existing block, select the name of the block from the list of blocks. A preview and the description of the selected block are shown. You can create a new block by typing a name for the new block in the **Block to create or edit** field. Then pick the **OK** button to open the selected block (or new block) in the **Block Editor**. See **Figure 26-11**.

The **Block Editor** consists of the **Block Editor** tab of the ribbon, the **Block Authoring Palettes** window, and the drawing area in block edit mode. The **Block Editor** tab of the ribbon is highlighted and is always shown regardless of the selected tab. If a block was selected for editing, it is displayed in the drawing area, with the UCS icon positioned at the block insertion base point. If a new block name was entered, the drawing area is empty so the new block can be created. All other objects in the drawing are hidden.

Use drawing and editing tools to create or modify the block. Some tools are not available in the **Block Editor**. The tools in the panels of the **Block Editor** tab of the ribbon are used to create blocks and block geometry. **Figure 26-12** describes some of the basic tools available in the **Block Editor** tab. Many of the tools and options found on the **Block Editor** tab relate to dynamic blocks and are described in Chapter 27. Other options are described when appropriate. When you finish editing, close the **Block Editor**. To exit block editing mode and return to the drawing, pick the **Close Block Editor** button on the **Close** panel of the **Block Editor** tab of the ribbon, or type BCLOSE. If changes have not been saved, a dialog box appears asking if you want to

Figure 26-10
The **Edit Block Definition** dialog box.

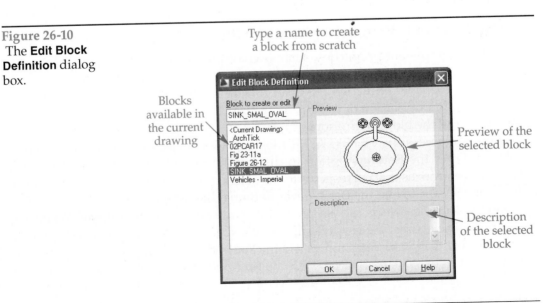

Type a name to create a block from scratch

Blocks available in the current drawing

Preview of the selected block

Description of the selected block

AutoCAD and Its Applications—Basics

Figure 26-11.
In block editing mode, the **Block Editor** tab of the ribbon and the **Block Authoring Palettes** window are available.

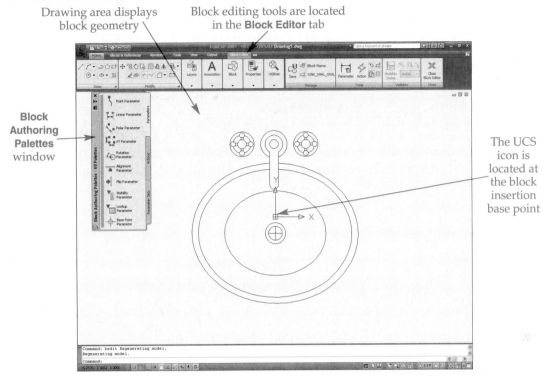

Drawing area displays block geometry

Block editing tools are located in the **Block Editor** tab

Block Authoring Palettes window

The UCS icon is located at the block insertion base point

save changes. Pick **Yes** to save the changes, **No** to discard the changes, or **Cancel** to return to block editing mode.

PROFESSIONAL TIP

A block can be opened directly in the **Block Editor** by right-clicking the block in the drawing and selecting **Block Editor** from the shortcut menu. A block can also be opened directly in the **Block Editor** when it is created by checking the **Open in block editor** check box in the **Block Definition** dialog box.

Figure 26-12.
The **Block Editor** tab of the ribbon contains several block editing tools and options. The basic editing features are described in this table.

Button	Description
Save	Saves the changes and updates the block definition.
	Opens the **Save Block As** dialog box, used to save the block as a new block, using a different name.
	Opens the **Edit Block Definition** dialog box, which is the same dialog box displayed when entering block editing mode. You can select a different block to edit or specify the name of a new one to create from scratch.
	Toggles the **Block Authoring Palettes** window off and on.
Close Block Editor	Closes the **Block Editor**.

Adding a block description within the block editor

You can add a description to a block in the **Block Definition** dialog box when the block is created. This description can be changed in the **Block Editor**. To modify a description, open the **Block Editor** and open the **Properties** palette with no objects selected. Make changes to the description using the **Description** property in the **Block** category. Pick the **Save Block Definition** button and the **Close Block Editor** button to return to the drawing.

NOTE

Blocks can also be edited "in-place" using the **REFEDIT** tool. In-place editing using the **REFEDIT** tool is described in Chapter 32, as it applies to external references. The same techniques can be used to edit blocks.

Exercise 26-6

Complete the exercise on the Student CD.

Exploding and Redefining a Block

EXPLODE

Ribbon
Home
> Modify

Explode

Type
EXPLODE
X

Menu Browser
Modify
> Explode

As previously described, you can explode a block as it is inserted using the **Insert** dialog box. This is useful when you want to edit the individual objects of the block. You can also use the **EXPLODE** tool after the block is inserted to break it apart into its individual objects. The **EXPLODE** tool can be used to break apart any existing block, polyline, or dimension. Once you access the **EXPLODE** tool, select the objects to explode and press [Enter] or the space bar or right-click to create the explosion.

When a block is exploded, its component objects can be edited individually. To see if the **EXPLODE** tool worked properly, select any object that was formerly part of the block. Only that object should be highlighted. If so, the block was exploded properly.

NOTE

The block cannot be exploded if a block was created with **Allow exploding** unchecked in the **Block Definition** dialog box. If you try to use the **EXPLODE** tool on a block like this, the message 1 could not be exploded appears on the command line.

You can redefine a block using the **EXPLODE** and **BLOCK** tools together. To redefine an existing block, follow this procedure:

1. Insert the block to be redefined anywhere in your drawing.
2. Make sure you know where the insertion point of the block is located.
3. Explode the block using the **EXPLODE** tool.
4. Edit the components of the block as needed.
5. Recreate the block definition using the **BLOCK** tool.
6. Give the block the same name and insertion point as it originally had.
7. Select the objects to be included in the block.
8. Pick **OK** in the **Block Definition** dialog box to save the block. When a message from AutoCAD appears asking if you want to redefine the block, pick **Yes**.

A common mistake is to forget to use the **EXPLODE** tool before redefining the block. When you try to create the block again with the same name, an alert box indicating the block references itself is displayed. This means you are trying to create a block that already exists. When you press the **OK** button, the alert box disappears and the **Block Definition** dialog box is redisplayed. Press the **Cancel** button, explode the block to be redefined, and try again.

Exercise 26-7
Complete the exercise on the Student CD.

Understanding the Circular Reference Error

When you try to redefine a block that already exists using the same name, a *circular reference error* occurs. AutoCAD informs you that the block references itself or that it has not been modified. The concept of a block referencing itself may be a little difficult to grasp at first without fully understanding how AutoCAD works with blocks. A block can be composed of many objects, including other blocks. When you use the **BLOCK** tool to incorporate an existing block into a new block, AutoCAD makes a list of all the objects that compose the new block. This means AutoCAD refers to any existing block definitions that are selected to be part of the new block. If you select an instance, or reference, of the block being redefined as a component object for the new definition, a problem occurs. The new block refers to a block of the same name, or references itself. Figure 26-13 illustrates the process of correctly, Figure 26-13A, and incorrectly, Figure 26-13B, redefining a block to avoid a circular reference error. The block in this example is named BOX.

circular reference error: An error that occurs when a block definition references itself.

Figure 26-13.
A—The correct procedure for redefining a block. B—Redefining a block that has not first been exploded creates an invalid circular reference.

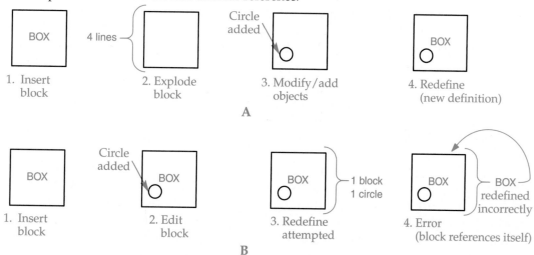

Figure 26-14.
The **Rename** dialog box allows you to change the name of blocks and other named objects.

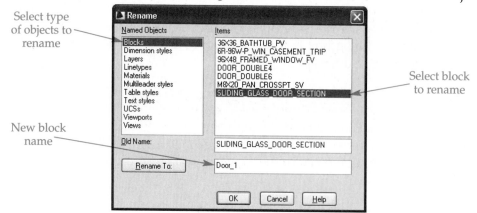

Select type of objects to rename

Select block to rename

New block name

Renaming Blocks

Blocks can be renamed without editing using the **RENAME** tool. The **Rename** dialog box is shown when you access the **RENAME** tool. See Figure 26-14.

To change the name of a block named Plate to Flange, as shown in Figure 26-14, select Blocks from the **Named Objects** list. A list of block names defined in the current drawing appears in the **Items** list. Highlight plate in the list. When this name appears in the **Old Name:** text box, type the new block name Flange in the **Rename To:** text box. When you pick the **Rename To:** button, the new block name appears in the **Items** list. Pick **OK** to exit the **Rename** dialog box.

Creating Blocks as Drawing Files

Blocks created with the **BLOCK** tool are stored in the drawing in which they are made. The **WBLOCK** (write block) tool allows you to create a drawing (DWG) file from a block. You can also use the **WBLOCK** tool to create a global block from any object. It does not have to be previously saved as a block. The resulting drawing file can then be inserted as a block into any drawing. The **Write Block** dialog box is displayed when you access the **WBLOCK** tool. See Figure 26-15.

Creating a New Wblock

One method of using the **WBLOCK** tool is to create a drawing file from existing objects that have not been made into a block. To use this technique, pick the **Objects** radio button, which is selected by default, in the **Source** area of the **Write Block** dialog box. See Figure 26-15. The process of creating a wblock from existing, non-block objects is similar to the process of creating a block using the **BLOCK** tool. Enter or select an insertion base point using options in the **Base point** area, and define which objects are used and the disposition of the objects using options in the **Objects** area. The **Base point** and **Objects** areas function the same as those found in the **Block Definition** dialog box.

In contrast to a block, a wblock is saved to disk as a drawing file, *not* as a block in the current drawing. Enter a path and file name for the block in the **File name and path:** text box or pick the ellipsis (**...**) button next to the text box to display the **Browse for Drawing File** dialog box. Navigate to the folder where you want to save the file, confirm the name of the file in the **File name:** text box, and pick the **Save** button. The **Write Block** dialog box is redisplayed with the path and file name shown in the **File name**

Figure 26-15.
Using the **Write Block** dialog box to create a wblock from selected objects without first defining a block.

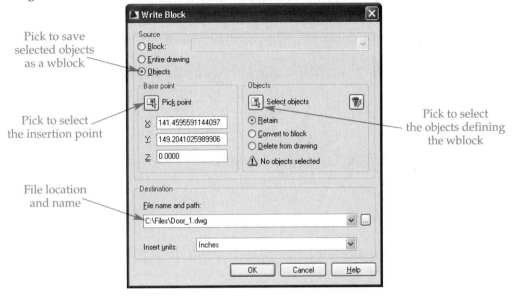

and path: text box. Finally, select the type of units that **DesignCenter** uses to insert the block in the **Insert units:** drop-down list. This is also located in the **Destination** area. When you are finished, pick **OK**. The objects are saved as a wblock in the folder you specified. Now, you can use the **INSERT** tool in any drawing to insert the block.

Saving an Existing Block as a Wblock

A wblock can also be created from an existing block. To use this technique, pick the **Block** radio button in the **Source** area of the **Write Block** dialog box. See **Figure 26-16.** Then, select the block you want to save as a wblock from the drop-down list. Once the block is selected, use the options in the **Destination** area, as previously described, to create the wblock.

Figure 26-16.
Using the **Write Block** dialog box to create a wblock from an existing block.

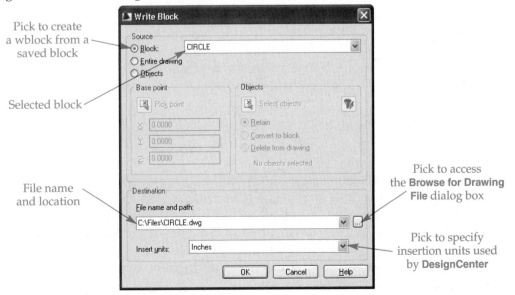

Storing a Drawing as a Wblock

An entire drawing can also be stored as a wblock. To do this, pick the **Entire drawing** radio button in the **Source** area of the **Write Block** dialog box. Once the **Entire drawing** radio button is selected, use the options in the **Destination** area, as previously described, to create the wblock. In this case, the whole drawing is saved to disk as if you had used the **SAVE** tool. However, all unused blocks are deleted from the drawing. If the drawing contains any unused blocks, this method may reduce the size of a drawing considerably.

Exercise 26-8
Complete the exercise on the Student CD.

Revising an Inserted Drawing

You may find that you need to revise a drawing file that has been used in other drawings. If this happens, you can quickly update any drawing in which the revised drawing is used. For example, if a drawing file named pump was modified after being used several times in a drawing, use the **INSERT** tool and access the original drawing file with the **Select Drawing File** dialog box. Then activate the **Specify On-screen** check box in the **Insertion point** area and pick **OK**. When a message from AutoCAD appears and asks if you want to redefine the block, pick **Yes**. All of the pump references are automatically updated. Next, press the [Esc] key. By canceling the tool, no new insertions of the pump drawing are made.

PROFESSIONAL TIP

If you work on projects in which inserted drawings may be revised, it is far more productive to use reference drawings instead of inserted drawing files. Reference drawings are used with the **XREF** tool, which is described in Chapter 32. All referenced drawings are automatically updated when a drawing file that contains the externally referenced material is loaded into AutoCAD.

Symbol Libraries

symbol library: A collection of related blocks, shapes, views, symbols, or other content.

As you become proficient with AutoCAD, you will want to start constructing *symbol libraries*. Arranging a storage system for frequently used symbols increases productivity and saves time. First, you need to establish how the symbols are stored (as blocks or drawing files) and determine where they will be stored for insertion into different drawings.

Creating a Symbol Library

The two basic options for creating a symbol library are to save all of the blocks within a single drawing or to save each block to a separate file (wblock). If you decide to have one drawing that contains all of the blocks, each person in the office or classroom must have access to that drawing. If individual drawing files (wblocks) are used, each student or employee must have access to the files.

Once you have created a set of related block definitions, you can arrange the blocks in a symbol library. Each block should be identified with a name and insertion point

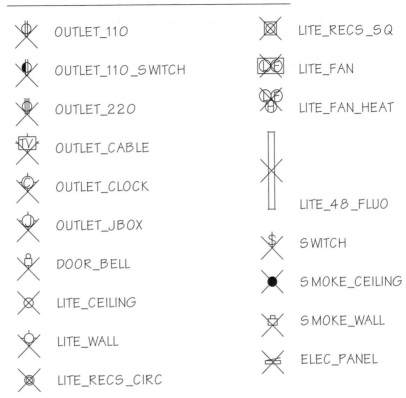

Figure 26-17.
A printed copy of electrical blocks stored in a symbol library. The "X" symbols indicate insertion points and are not part of the block.

ELECTRICAL SYMBOLS

OUTLET_110

OUTLET_110_SWITCH

OUTLET_220

OUTLET_CABLE

OUTLET_CLOCK

OUTLET_JBOX

DOOR_BELL

LITE_CEILING

LITE_WALL

LITE_RECS_CIRC

LITE_RECS_SQ

LITE_FAN

LITE_FAN_HEAT

LITE_48_FLUO

SWITCH

SMOKE_CEILING

SMOKE_WALL

ELEC_PANEL

location. Whether the blocks are being stored in a single drawing file or as individual files, several guidelines can be used to create the symbol library:

- Assign one person to create the symbols for each specialty.
- Follow school or company standards for blocks and symbols.
- When saving multiple blocks in a drawing file, save one group of symbols per drawing file.
- When using wblocks, give the drawing files meaningful names so they can be assigned to separate folders on the hard drive.
- Provide all users with a hard copy of the symbol library showing each symbol, its insertion point, where it is located, and any other necessary information. See **Figure 26-17.**
- If a network is not in use, place the symbol library file(s) on each workstation in the classroom or office.
- Keep backup copies of all files in a secure place.
- When symbols are revised, update all files containing the edited symbols.
- Inform all users of any changes to saved symbols.

Storing Symbol Drawings

The local or network hard drive is one of the best places to store a symbol library. It is easy to access, quick, and more convenient to use than portable media. Removable media, such as a removable hard drive, USB flash drive, or CDs can be used for backup purposes if a network drive with an automatic backup function is not available. In the absence of a network or modem, removable media can also be used to transport files from one workstation to another.

There are several methods of storing symbols on the hard drive. Symbols can be saved as wblocks and organized within folders. It is recommended to store symbols

Figure 26-18.
An efficient way to store blocks saved as drawing files is to set up a Blocks folder containing folders for each type of block on the hard drive.

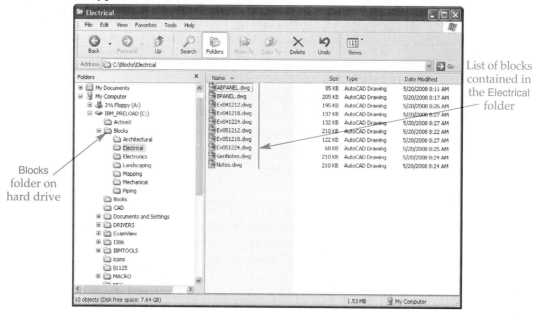

Blocks folder on hard drive

List of blocks contained in the Electrical folder

outside of the AutoCAD folder. This will keep the system folder uncluttered and allow you to differentiate which folders and files were originally installed with AutoCAD. A good idea is to create a \Blocks folder for storing your blocks, as shown in Figure 26-18.

If multiple symbols are saved within a drawing, they can be inserted using **DesignCenter** or the **Tool Palettes** window. When using this system, several drawing files may be used to group similar symbols. For example, you may want to create several different symbol libraries based on the following types of symbols: electronic, electrical, piping, mechanical, structural, architectural, landscaping, and mapping. Limit the symbols in a drawing to a reasonable number so the symbols can be found relatively easily. If there are too many blocks in a drawing, it may be difficult to locate the desired symbol.

Drawing files saved on the hard drive should be arranged in a logical manner. All workstations in the classroom or office should have folders with the same names. One person should be assigned to update and copy symbol libraries to all workstations. Drawing files should be copied onto each workstation from a master CD or network drive. The master and backup versions of the symbol libraries should be kept in separate locations.

purge: Delete unused named objects from a drawing file.

PURGE

Ribbon
Tools
> Drawing
Utilities

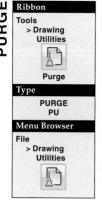

Purge

Type
PURGE
PU

Menu Browser
File
> Drawing
Utilities

Purging Named Objects

A block is one example of a named object. In many drawing sessions, not all of the named objects defined within a drawing are used. For example, your drawing may contain several layers, text styles, and blocks that are not used. Since these objects increase the drawing file size, it is good practice to delete or *purge* the unused objects from the drawing, using the **PURGE** tool. The **Purge** dialog box is displayed when you access the **PURGE** tool. See Figure 26-19.

Select the appropriate radio button at the top of the dialog box to view content that can be purged or to view content that cannot be purged. Before purging, select the **Confirm each item to be purged** check box to have an opportunity to review each item before it is deleted. If you want to purge nested items, check the **Purge nested items** check box.

Figure 26-19.
The **Purge** dialog box.

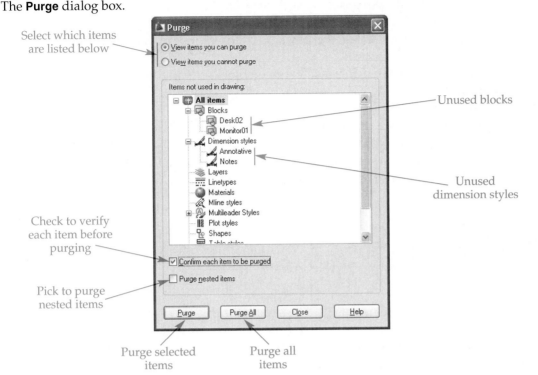

Select which items
are listed below

Unused blocks

Unused
dimension styles

Check to verify
each item before
purging

Pick to purge
nested items

Purge selected
items

Purge all
items

If you want to purge only some items, use the tree view to locate and highlight the items, and then pick the **Purge** button. If you want to purge all unused items, pick the **Purge All** button. Purging may cause other named objects to become unreferenced. Thus, you may need to purge more than once to completely purge the drawing of unused named objects.

Chapter Test

Answer the following questions. Write your answers on a separate sheet of paper or complete the electronic chapter test on the Student CD.

1. Which color and linetype settings should you use if you want a block to assume the current color and linetype when it is inserted into a drawing?
2. Why would you draw blocks on layer 0?
3. What properties do blocks drawn on a layer other than layer 0 assume when inserted?
4. A block name cannot exceed _____ characters.
5. How can you access a listing of all blocks in the current drawing?
6. Define the term *nesting* in relation to blocks.
7. How do you preset block insertion variables using the **Insert** dialog box?
8. Describe the effect of entering negative scale factors when inserting a block.
9. What type of block is a one-unit line object?
10. Name a limitation of an array pattern created with the **MINSERT** tool.
11. What is the purpose of the **BASE** tool?
12. What are the three ways you can insert a block into a drawing from **DesignCenter**?
13. What tool allows you to change a block's layer without editing the block definition?

14. Identify the tool that allows you to break an inserted block into its individual objects for editing purposes.
15. Suppose you have found that a block was incorrectly drawn. Unfortunately, you have already inserted the block 30 times. How can you edit all of the blocks quickly?
16. What is the primary difference between blocks created with the **BLOCK** and **WBLOCK** tools?
17. Define *symbol library*.
18. Name an advantage of having a symbol library of blocks in a single drawing, rather than using wblocks.
19. Explain two ways to remove all unused blocks from a drawing.
20. What is the purpose of the **PURGE** tool?

Drawing Problems

▼ Basic

1. Open P13-17 from Chapter 13. The sketch for this drawing is shown below. Erase all copies of the symbols that were made, leaving the original objects intact. These include the steel column symbols and the bay and column line tags. Then, do the following:
   A. Make blocks of the steel column symbol and the tag symbols.
   B. Use the **MINSERT** tool or the **ARRAY** tool to place the symbols in the drawing.
   C. Dimension the drawing as shown in the sketch.
   D. Save the drawing as P26-1.

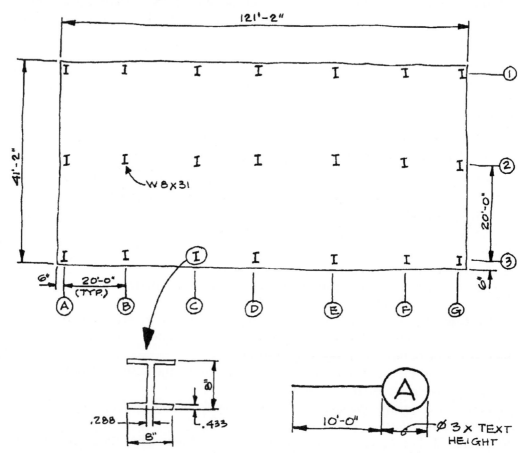

2. Open P13-18 from Chapter 13. The sketch for this drawing is shown below. Erase all of the desk workstations except one. Then do the following:
   A. Create a block of the workstation.
   B. Insert the block into the drawing using the **MINSERT** tool.
   C. Dimension one of the workstations as shown in the sketch.
   D. Save the drawing as P26-2.

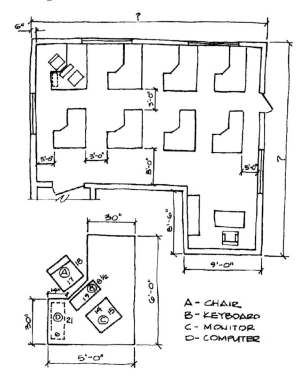

A - CHAIR
B - KEYBOARD
C - MONITOR
D - COMPUTER

3. Do this problem only if you have completed Problem 26-7 first. Open P26-7. Modify the NAND gates to become XNOR gates, as shown below, by modifying the block definition. Save the drawing as P26-3.

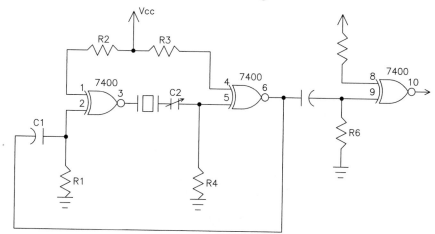

▼ Intermediate

Problems 4–6 represent a variety of diagrams created using symbols as blocks. Create each drawing as shown (the drawings are not drawn to scale). The symbols should first be created as blocks or wblocks and then saved in a symbol library using one of the methods described in this chapter. Place a border and title block on each drawing. Save the drawings as P26-4, P26-5, *and so on.*

4.

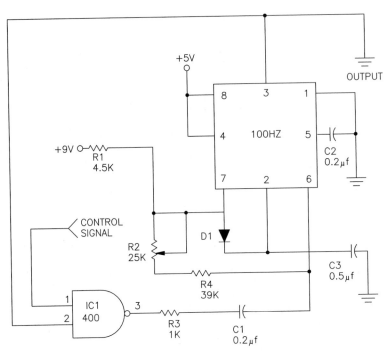

Integrated Circuit for Clock

5.

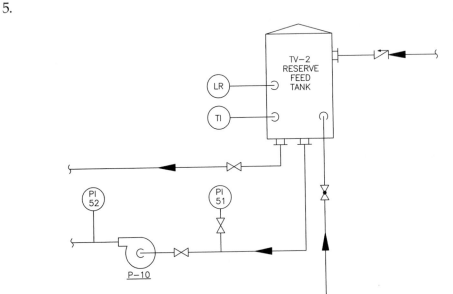

Piping Flow Diagram

AutoCAD and Its Applications—Basics

6.

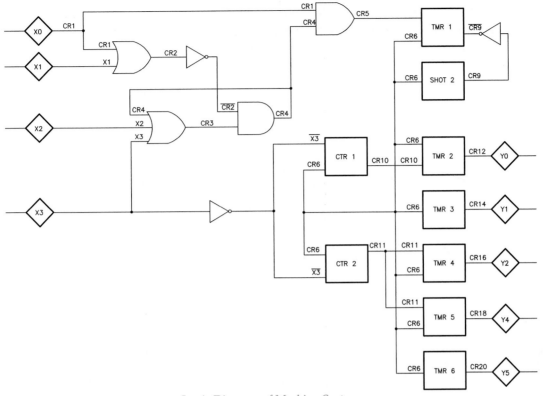

Logic Diagram of Marking System

7. Draw the digital logic circuit shown. Create each type of component in the circuit as a block. Save the drawing as P26-7.

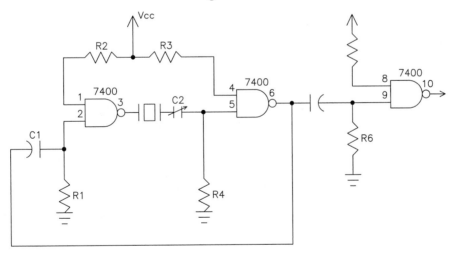

Problems 8–12 are presented as engineering sketches. They are schematic drawings created using symbols and are not drawn to scale. The symbols should first be drawn as blocks and then saved in a symbol library. Place a border and title block on each of the drawings.

8. The rough sketch shown below is a logic diagram of a portion of a computer's internal components. Create the drawing on a C-size sheet. Save the drawing as P26-8.

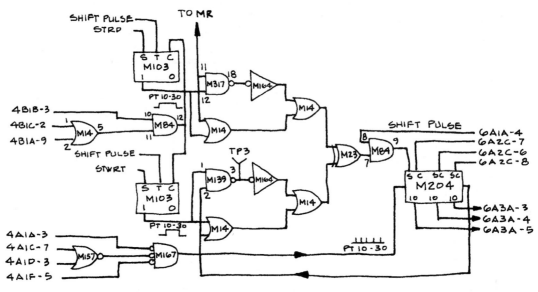

9. The rough sketch shown below is a piping flow diagram of a cooling water system. Create the drawing on a B-size sheet. Look closely at this drawing before you begin. Using blocks and the correct editing tools, it may be easier to complete than you think. Draw the thick flow lines with polylines. Save the drawing as P26-9.

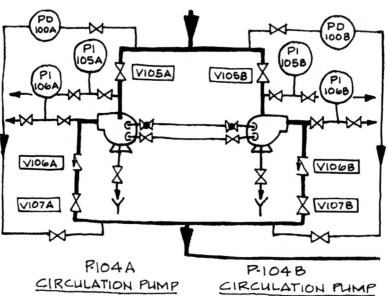

10. The rough sketch shown below is the general arrangement of a basement floor plan for a new building. The engineer has shown one example of each type of equipment. Use the following instructions to complete the drawing:

A. Create the drawing on a C-size sheet.
B. All text should be 1/8″ high, except the text for the bay and column line tags, which should be 3/16″ high. The diameter of the line balloons for the bay and column lines should be twice the diameter of the text height.
C. The column and bay line steel symbols represent wide-flange structural shapes and should be 8″ wide × 12″ high.
D. The PUMP and CHILLER installations (except PUMP #4 and PUMP #5) should be drawn per the dimensions given for PUMP #1 and CHILLER #1. Use the dimensions shown for the other PUMP units.
E. TANK #2 and PUMP #5 (P-5) should be drawn per the dimensions given for TANK #1 and PUMP #4.
F. Tanks T-3, T-4, T-5, and T-6 are all the same size and are aligned 12′ from column line A.
G. Plan this drawing carefully and create as many blocks as necessary to increase your productivity. Dimension the drawing as shown, and provide location dimensions for all equipment not shown in the engineer's sketch.
H. Save the drawing as P26-10.

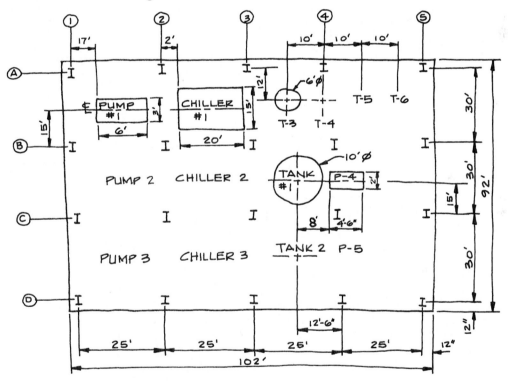

11. The drawing saved as P26-10 must be revised. The engineer has provided you with a sketch of the necessary revisions. It is up to you to alter the drawing as quickly and efficiently as possible. The dimensions shown on the sketch below *do not* need to be added to the drawing; they are provided for construction purposes only. Revise P26-10 so all chillers and the four tanks reflect the changes. Save the drawing as P26-11.

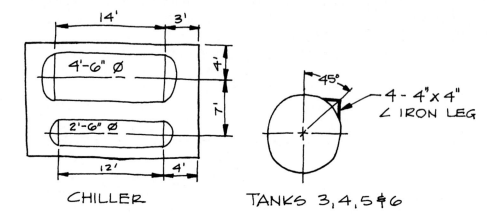

CHILLER   TANKS 3, 4, 5 & 6

12. The rough sketch of a piping flow diagram shown below is part of an industrial effluent treatment system. Draw it on a C-size sheet. Eliminate as many bends in the flow lines as possible. Place arrowheads at all flow line intersections and bends. The flow lines should not run through any valves or equipment. Use polylines for the thick flow lines. Save the drawing as P26-12.

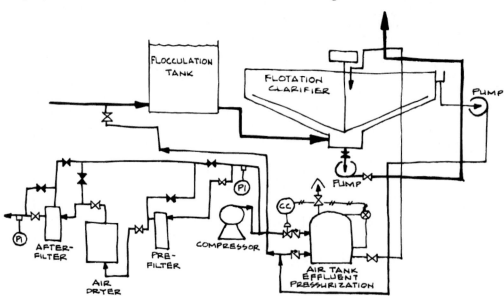

13. Create computer, plotter, and printer/copier blocks and then draw the network diagram. Save the drawing as P26-13.

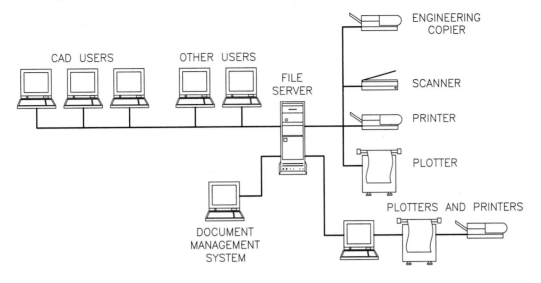

14. Draw the piping diagram shown, creating blocks for each type of fitting. Save the drawing as P26-14.

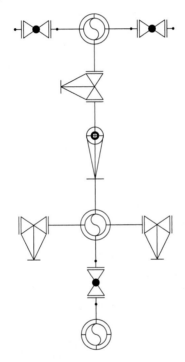

15. Create component blocks based on the dimensions shown. Then use the blocks to draw the schematic below. Save the drawing as P26-15.

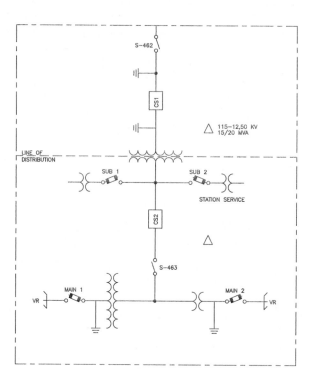

16. Create a symbol library for one of the drafting disciplines listed below and save it as a template or drawing file. Then, after checking with your instructor, draw a problem using the library. If you save the symbol library as a template, start the problem with the template. If you save it as a drawing file, start a new drawing and insert the symbol library into it. Specialty areas you might create symbols for include:
    • Mechanical (machine features, fasteners, tolerance symbols)
    • Architectural (doors, windows, fixtures)
    • Structural (steel shapes, bolts, standard footings)
    • Industrial piping (fittings, valves)
    • Piping flow diagrams (tanks, valves, pumps)
    • Electrical schematics (resistors, capacitors, switches)
    • Electrical one-line (transformers, switches)
    • Electronics (IC chips, test points, components)
    • Logic diagrams (AND gates, NAND gates, buffers)
    • Mapping, civil (survey markers, piping)
    • Geometric tolerancing (feature control frames)
    Save the drawing as P26-16 or choose an appropriate file name, such as ARCH-PRO or ELEC-PRO. Display the symbol library created in this problem and print a hard copy. Put the printed copy in your notebook as a reference.

AutoCAD and Its Applications—Basics

Creating and Using Dynamic Blocks

Learning Objectives

After completing this chapter, you will be able to do the following:

✓ Explain the function of dynamic blocks.
✓ Assign dynamic properties to blocks.
✓ Modify dynamic blocks with the **Multiplier** and **Offset** options.
✓ Use parameter sets.
✓ Modify parameters and actions.

A normal block typically represents a very specific item, such as a 1″ long bolt. If the same style of bolt is available in three other lengths, then three additional blocks should be created. Another option is to create a single *dynamic block* that is adjusted according to each unique bolt length. Creating and using dynamic blocks can increase productivity and reduce the size of symbol libraries, making them more manageable. This chapter describes how to create and use dynamic blocks.

dynamic block:
A block to which parameters and actions have been assigned.

Introduction to Dynamic Blocks

A dynamic block is a normal block that is edited to change the size and/or shape of objects within the block, without drawing additional blocks, and without affecting other instances of the same block. **Figure 27-1** shows an example of a dynamic block of a single-swing door symbol. In this example, the dynamic properties of the block allow you to create many different single-swing door symbols, according to the door size, wall thickness, the side of the wall where the door swings, door swing angle representation, wall angle, and exterior or interior usage. All of these characteristics are assigned to a single dynamic block.

A dynamic block is created by adding a *parameter(s)* to block geometry. Most parameters are then assigned an *action(s)*. A dynamic block can contain multiple parameters, and a single parameter can be assigned multiple actions. The dynamic block of the single-swing door symbol in **Figure 27-1,** for example, contains several parameters that are used to control door characteristics, or variables.

A dynamic block is inserted into a drawing the same as a normal block. The difference is that a dynamic block can be modified, either during or after insertion, to create unique instances of the symbol. As you learn to create and use dynamic blocks,

parameter: A value that defines custom properties such as positions, distances, and angles for objects in a dynamic block.

action: A definition that controls how the parameters of a dynamic block behave.

Figure 27-1.
A—An example of a single swing door symbol dynamic block. B—The dynamic block can be used to create many unique single swing door symbols, without creating new blocks or affecting other instances of the same block.

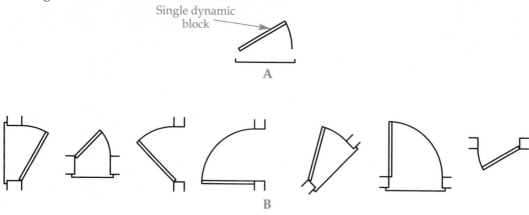

you will notice that many actions function as editing tools with which you are already familiar, allowing operations such as stretch, move, scale, array, and rotate.

An example of a bolt symbol created as a dynamic block is shown in **Figure 27-2A.** The block is selected for modification in the same manner as when grip editing. The shaft objects of the bolt symbol have been assigned a linear parameter with a stretch action as indicated by the *parameter grips*. To increase the length of the bolt symbol, the right-hand linear parameter grip is selected and dragged, or stretched, to the right. See **Figure 27-2B.**

parameter grips:
Special grips that allow you to change the parameters of a dynamic block.

PROFESSIONAL TIP

AutoCAD includes several files of dynamic block symbols, found in the following path: Program Files/AutoCAD 2009/ Sample/ Dynamic Blocks. Dynamic blocks are also available from the **Tool Palettes** window. Explore these sample symbols as you learn to create and use dynamic blocks.

Figure 27-2.
A linear parameter and stretch action have been assigned to the shaft objects in this block of a bolt. A—Selecting the block displays the linear grips. B—Selecting a linear grip and dragging it stretches the shaft of the bolt.

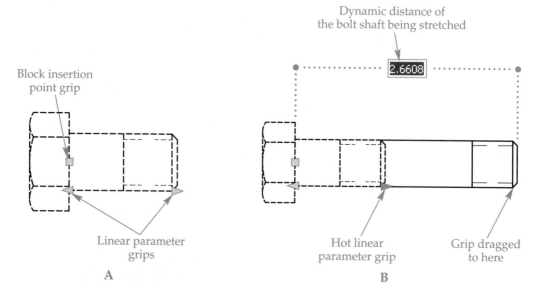

Assigning Dynamic Properties

Dynamic blocks are constructed using the same techniques as normal blocks. The difference is dynamic properties are added to define a block as dynamic. Dynamic properties are added to object geometry using the **Block Editor**, which is accessed using the **BEDIT** tool. The process of editing a block using the **Block Editor** was introduced in Chapter 26. The **Edit Block Definition** dialog box appears when you access the **BEDIT** tool. See **Figure 27-3**.

Dynamic blocks can be created from scratch, based on predawn objects, or an existing block can be edited to include dynamic properties. To create a dynamic block from scratch, directly in the **Block Editor**, type a name for the new block in the **Block to create or edit** field. To use existing drawing geometry that has not been made into a block, and if no other objects are in the drawing, pick the **Current Drawing** option. Enter a name for the block something other than the default **Current Drawing** name. To add dynamic properties to a block loaded in the current drawing, select the name of the block from the list of blocks. A preview and the description of the selected block are shown. Pick the **OK** button to open the new (or selected block) in the **Block Editor**. See **Figure 27-4**. Refer to Chapter 26 for more information about basic **Block Editor** options.

Ribbon

Home
> Block
Blocks & References
> Block
> Block Editor

Edit

Type

BEDIT

Menu Browser

Tools
> Block Editor

BEDIT

NOTE

An existing block can be opened directly in the **Block Editor** by right-clicking the block in the drawing and selecting **Block Editor** from the shortcut menu. A block can also be opened in the **Block Editor** when it is created using the **Block** tool, by checking the **Open in block editor** check box in the **Block Definition** dialog box.

The **Block Authoring Palettes** window and the **Block Editor** tab of the ribbon provide tools and options for assigning dynamic block properties. The quickest method to access a parameter is to select an option from the **Parameters** tab in the **Block Authoring Palettes** window. See **Figure 27-5A**. You can also insert a parameter by picking the **Parameters** button from the **Tools** panel in the **Block Editor** tab on the ribbon, or by typing BPARAMETER. You must then select a specific parameter option.

The quickest way to access an action is to select an option from the **Actions** tab in the **Block Authoring Palettes** window. See **Figure 27-5B**. You can also assign an action

---

Figure 27-3.
The **Edit Block Definition** dialog box.

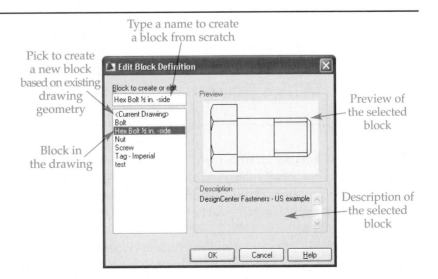

Type a name to create a block from scratch

Pick to create a new block based on existing drawing geometry

Block in the drawing

Preview of the selected block

Description of the selected block

Figure 27-4.
In block editing mode, the **Block Editor** tab of the ribbon and the **Block Authoring Palettes** window are available.

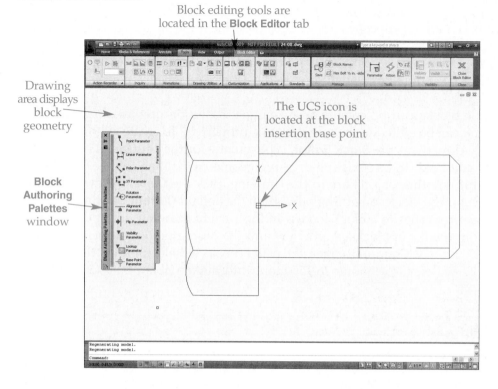

Block editing tools are located in the **Block Editor** tab

Drawing area displays block geometry

The UCS icon is located at the block insertion base point

Block Authoring Palettes window

Figure 27-5.
The available parameters and actions can be accessed from the **Block Authoring Palettes** window.

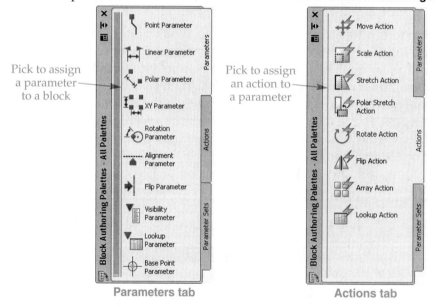

Pick to assign a parameter to a block

Pick to assign an action to a parameter

Parameters tab

Actions tab

by picking the **Actions** button from the **Tools** panel in the **Block Editor** tab on the ribbon, or by typing BACTION. You must then select a specific action option. Actions can be assigned to certain parameters, such as point parameters, by double-clicking on the parameter, and selecting an action option. Only certain actions can be assigned to a given parameter.

Once you add a parameter(s) to a block and assign an action(s) to the parameter(s), you are ready to save and use the dynamic block. To save the block, pick the **Save** button on the **Manage** panel in the **Block Editor** tab on the ribbon, or type BSAVE. An AutoCAD alert appears stating that saving the edits to the block updates any block references in the drawing. Pick the **Yes** button to save the edits. To exit the **Block Editor**, pick the **Close** button on the **Close** panel in the **Block Editor** tab on the ribbon, or type BCLOSE.

> **NOTE**
>
> Dynamic blocks can become very complex with the addition of many dynamic properties. A single dynamic block can potentially take the place of a very large symbol library. This chapter focuses on basic dynamic block applications, fundamental use of parameters, and the process of assigning a single action to a parameter.

Point Parameters

A *point parameter* creates a position property, and can be assigned move and stretch actions. For example, a point parameter with a move action can be assigned to a door tag that is part of a door block so the tag can be moved independently of the door. Point parameters can also be added to provide multiple insertion point options. For example, add point parameters to the ends of a weld symbol reference line to create two possible insertion point options.

point parameter: A parameter that defines an XY coordinate location in the drawing.

Figure 27-6 provides an example of how to insert a point parameter. When you access the **Point Parameter** option, the Specify parameter location or [Name/Label/Chain/Description/Palette]: prompt appears. The point parameter location defines the grip point and the X and Y coordinates. This is the parameter grip that appears when the block is selected in the drawing. Selecting and moving the parameter grip carries out the action that is assigned to the parameter. In the **Figure 27-6** example, the center of the door tag is selected as the position for the parameter. The position of the parameter can be moved after initial placement if necessary. The yellow alert icon shown in **Figure 27-6** indicates that no action has been assigned to the parameter.

Once you select the point parameter position, pick a location for the *parameter label*, away from block objects. All parameters include and require you to locate a parameter label. The label appears only in block editing mode. By default, the label for a point parameter is Position. You can change the parameter label text to a more descriptive label when you create the parameter by using the **Label** option before specifying the parameter location. After the parameter is created, you can change the label text using the **Properties** palette. The location of the label can be moved after initial placement, if necessary.

parameter label: A label that indicates the purpose of a parameter.

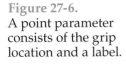
Figure 27-6.
A point parameter consists of the grip location and a label.

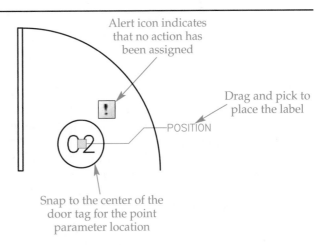

Alert icon indicates that no action has been assigned

Drag and pick to place the label

POSITION

Snap to the center of the door tag for the point parameter location

---

Chapter 27 Creating and Using Dynamic Blocks

Other options are available before you specify the parameter location, in addition to the **Label** option previously described. These options can also be modified in the **Properties** palette after the label has been inserted. The **Name** option allows you to specify a name for the parameter. The **Chain** option determines whether the parameter can be affected by a chain action. Chain actions are described in more detail later in this chapter. The **Description** option allows you to type a description for the parameter. A description is longer than the name or label and is used to explain more fully the purpose of the parameter. The description you enter displays as a tooltip when the dynamic block is used. The **Palette** option determines whether the label text is displayed in the **Properties** palette when the block is selected in the drawing.

PROFESSIONAL TIP

Change the name of a parameter label to a more descriptive name. Naming labels helps you organize parameters and recognize the parameter during editing. This is especially important when adding multiple parameters to a block.

Exercise 27-1
Complete the exercise on the Student CD.

Assigning a move action to a point parameter

The process of assigning an action is slightly different depending on the method used to access the action. If you pick the **Action** button from the **Tools** panel in the **Block Editor** tab on the ribbon, or type BACTION, you must first select the parameter, followed by specifying the action type. If you pick the action from the **Block Authoring Palettes** window, the action type is already selected and you are prompted to pick the parameter. Finally, if you double-click the parameter, the parameter is already selected, but you must choose the action type.

move action: An action used to move a block object independently of other objects in the same block.

Figure 27-7 illustrates the process of adding a *move action* to the door symbol example described in the previous section. First, access the **Move Action** option and pick the point parameter if not already selected. Then, when prompted to select objects, select all of the objects that make up the door tag. These are the objects that are movable when the block is edited. Once the objects to move are selected, press [Enter] or the space bar, or right-click. Then, pick a point near the parameter label to place the action icon. Save the block and exit the **Block Editor**. The dynamic block is now ready to use.

Figure 27-7.
Assigning a move action to a point parameter.

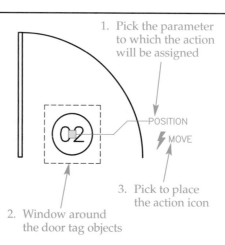

1. Pick the parameter to which the action will be assigned

2. Window around the door tag objects

3. Pick to place the action icon

Using a move action dynamically

In Figure 27-8A, the door block has been inserted and is selected for editing. The point parameter grip is displayed as a light blue square and is shown in the center of the door tag. The insertion point that was specified when the block was created is displayed as a standard unselected grip, and in this example is shown in the lower-left corner of the block. To move the objects composing the door tag within the block, select the point parameter grip to make it active, and move the door tag objects to a new location. See Figure 27-8B. Pick a point in the drawing area to specify a new location for the door tag. See Figure 27-8C.

Figure 27-8.
Dynamically moving an action assigned to a point parameter. A—When the block is selected to display grips, the point parameter grip is shown as a light blue square. B—Select the point parameter grip and move it. C—The door tag is at a new location, but it is still part of the block.

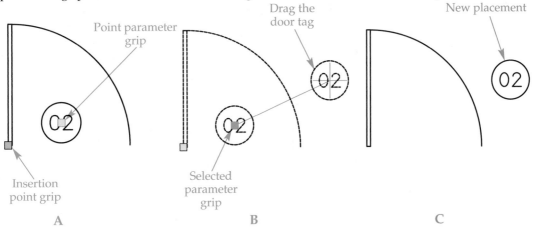

Linear Parameters

linear parameter:
A parameter that creates a measurement reference between two points.

A *linear parameter* creates a distance property, and can be assigned move, scale, stretch, and array actions. Think of a linear parameter as a linear dimension with a dimension value that can be changed to adjust the size and shape of objects. For example, a linear parameter with a stretch action can be assigned to a block of a bolt so that the bolt shaft can be made longer or shorter. A second linear parameter and stretch action can be assigned to the bolt head to control the bolt head diameter.

Figure 27-9 provides an example of how to insert a linear parameter. When you access the **Linear Parameter** option, the Specify start point or [Name/Label/Chain/Description/Base/Palette/Value set]: prompt appears. In the Figure 27-9 example, the **Label** option is used to name the linear parameter Shaft Length. The default label for a linear parameter is Distance. The name can also be changed after the parameter is inserted using the **Properties** palette.

The Specify start point or [Name/Label/Chain/Description/Base/Palette/Value set]: prompt reappears after renaming the parameter. Pick the endpoint of the lower edge of the shaft that is connected to the bolt head. Next, using polar tracking or the extension object snap, pick the point where the edge of the shaft would meet the end if extended. The start and endpoints of a linear parameter define the location of the parameter grips that appear when the block is selected in the drawing. Selecting a parameter grip and moving it carries out the action that is assigned to the parameter, changing the distance between the selected points. Once you select the linear parameter start and endpoints, pick a location for the parameter label, away from block objects.

A linear parameter has the same **Name**, **Label**, **Chain**, **Description**, and **Palette** options available when placing a point parameter. Two additional options are also available. The **Base** option allows either the start point or the midpoint of the linear parameter to be used as the base for the action. The **Value set** option allows specific values to be defined for the action. Both options are fully described later in the chapter.

Figure 27-9.
Defining a linear parameter.

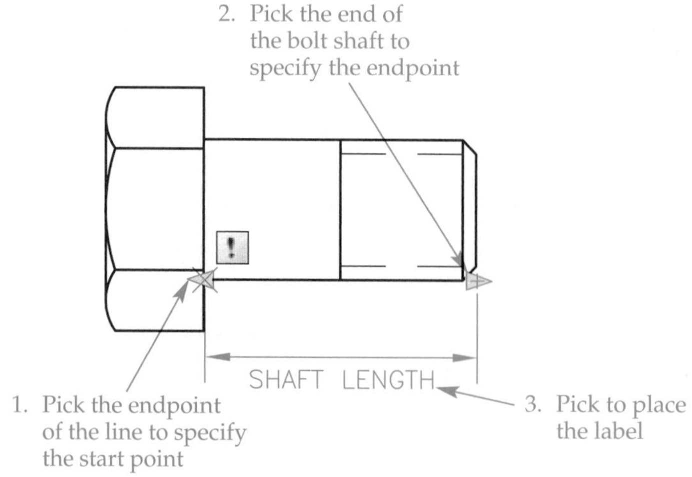

1. Pick the endpoint of the line to specify the start point

2. Pick the end of the bolt shaft to specify the endpoint

3. Pick to place the label

SHAFT LENGTH

Assigning a stretch action to a linear parameter

Figure 27-10 illustrates the process of adding a *stretch action* to the bolt symbol example described in the previous section. First, access the **Stretch Action** option and pick the linear parameter if it is not already selected. You must then specify a parameter point to associate with the action.

By default, a linear parameter has two parameter grips—one at the first pick point and another at the second pick point. These are the grips to select in the drawing to carry out the action assigned to the parameter. When a parameter has more than one parameter grip, AutoCAD needs to know the grip (parameter point) to which the action is associated. Move the crosshairs close to the parameter point that the action is associated with to display the appropriate red snap marker, and pick to select the parameter point. An alternative is to choose the **sTart point** option to select the first point that was picked when creating the linear parameter or use the **Second point** option to select the second point.

Next, create a crossing window by picking a point to the upper-right of the end of the bolt shaft followed by picking a point near the lower-middle of the shaft, making sure all the shaft objects are selected. See **Figure 27-10A.** Once the crossing window is created, pick the objects to be stretched. You do not need to use another crossing window, because one was defined in the previous operation. However, crossing selection is often quicker. See **Figure 27-10B.** Once the objects to stretch are selected, press [Enter] or the space bar, or right-click. Then, pick a point near the parameter label to place the action icon. See **Figure 27-10C.** Save the block and exit the **Block Editor**. The dynamic block is now ready to use.

stretch action:
An action used to change the size and shape of block objects with a stretch operation.

Figure 27-10.
Assigning a stretch action to a linear parameter. A—Specify the parameter, parameter grip, and create a crossing window. B—Use a crossing window to specify the objects that will be affected by the stretch action. C—Pick near the parameter point to place the action icon.

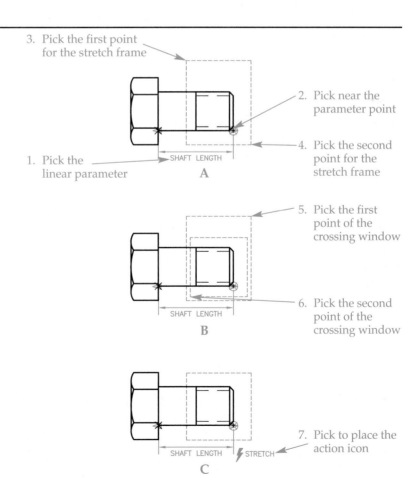

Figure 27-11.
Selecting the block
in the drawing
displays the
parameter grips.

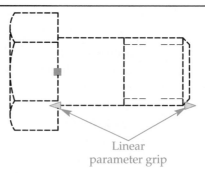

Linear
parameter grip

Using a stretch action dynamically

Figure 27-11 shows the bolt block inserted with the default shaft length, and selected for editing. Linear parameter grips are displayed as light blue arrows. The insertion point specified when the block was created is displayed as a standard unselected grip, and in this example is shown in the middle of the left edge of the bolt head.

The stretch action is assigned to the grip at the far end of the bolt shaft. To increase the length, select the parameter grip at the end of the shaft and drag it to the new length. Use any point entry method to define the length of the bolt shaft. If dynamic input is enabled, the distance of the shaft is dynamically updated in the distance field as you stretch the shaft. You can specify an exact length by entering a value in the distance field. The **Properties** palette can also be used to define the distance.

PROFESSIONAL TIP

The distance field displayed when dynamic input is enabled is a special property of the linear parameter. This feature allows you to enter an exact distance or length. Therefore, to get the best results when using the linear parameter, it is important that the first and second parameter points be inserted at the correct locations. The distances can also be specified using the appropriate property row of the **Properties** palette. Other parameters display similar fields and property rows.

Exercise 27-3

Complete the exercise on the Student CD.

Stretching objects symmetrically

The **Base** option of a parameter can be used to specify a midpoint for the stretch action. This enables block objects to maintain symmetry when modified. The **Base** option can be specified before the first point of the linear parameter is picked or set later in the **Properties** palette.

Figure 27-12 shows an example of a linear parameter with a stretch action assigned to the objects composing the bolt head. In this example, the **Linear Parameter** option is activated and the **Base** option is selected. The **Midpoint** suboption is then selected, followed by the **Label** option, which is used to name the linear parameter Head Diameter. The Specify start point or [Name/Label/Chain/Description/Base/Palette/Value set]: prompt reappears after you rename the parameter. Pick the upper-right corner of the bolt head to specify the start point, followed by picking the lower-left corner of the bolt head to

732   AutoCAD and Its Applications—Basics

Figure 27-12.
The base point of a linear parameter is displayed as an X. When the **Midpoint** option is used, the base point is in the center between the two parameter grips.

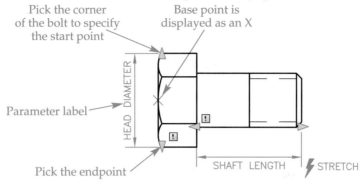

specify the endpoint. The midpoint is automatically calculated based on the start and endpoints. Once you select the linear parameter start and endpoints, pick a location for the parameter label, away from block objects.

Now assign a stretch action to the parameter for each side of the bolt head. **Figure 27-13** shows the process of assigning a stretch action to one side of the bolt head. First, access the **Stretch Action** option and pick the Head Diameter linear parameter if it is not already selected. Next, pick the upper linear parameter point. Now, create a crossing window by picking a point above and to the left of the bolt head, followed by picking a point just above the midpoint and within the shaft, as shown in **Figure 27-13A.** Once the crossing window is created, pick the objects that will stretch. See **Figure 27-13B.** Once the objects to stretch are selected, press [Enter] or the space bar, or right-click. Then, pick a point near the parameter label to place the action icon.

Repeat the previous sequence to assign a second stretch action to the parameter. Associate it with the lower parameter point and specify the objects as the lower objects of the bolt head. Save the block and exit the **Block Editor**. The dynamic block is now ready to use. Once inserted, the block can be edited by dragging one of the Head Diameter parameter grips to increase or decrease the opposite side of the bolt head the same length. You can also enter a head diameter using dynamic input or the **Properties** palette. See **Figure 27-14.**

Figure 27-13.
Assigning a stretch action to one side of the bolt head. A—Create a crossing window around the top of the bolt head. B—Use a window to select the objects to be included in the stretch.

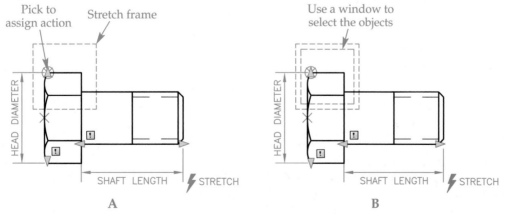

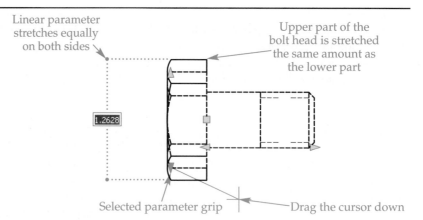

Figure 27-14.
Dynamically stretching the bolt head. Note that the head is stretched symmetrically.

Linear parameter stretches equally on both sides

Upper part of the bolt head is stretched the same amount as the lower part

1.2628

Selected parameter grip

Drag the cursor down

Assigning a scale action to a linear parameter

A linear parameter can also be assigned a *scale action.* For example, a block of a countertop consists of the countertop and a sink. The dimensions of the countertop remain static, while different size sinks can be used. Instead of creating a different block for each countertop/sink combination, you can create one dynamic block by adding a linear parameter with a scale action to the objects that make up the sink. This allows the sink to be scaled to the correct size as needed.

Figure 27-15 shows an example of a linear parameter with a scale action assigned to the objects composing the sink. In this example, the **Linear Parameter** option is activated and the **Base** option is selected. The **Midpoint** suboption is then selected, followed by the **Label** option, which is used to name the linear parameter Sink Length. The Specify start point or [Name/Label/Chain/Description/Base/Palette/Value set]: prompt reappears after renaming the parameter. Pick the quadrant on one side of the sink to specify the start point, followed by picking the opposite sink quadrant to specify the endpoint. The midpoint is automatically calculated based on the start and endpoints. Once you select the linear parameter start and endpoints, pick a location for the parameter label, away from block objects.

Now assign a scale action to the parameter. First, access the **Scale Action** option and pick the Sink Length linear parameter if it is not already selected. Next, select the linear parameter and all the objects that make up the sink. Once the objects to scale are selected, press [Enter] or the space bar, or right-click.

When using a scale action, it is critical to scale objects relative to the correct location, or base point. If the base point is not in the correct location, undesirable results are produced. At the Specify action location or [Base type]: prompt, select the **Base type** option. The default option is **Dependent**, which scales the objects relative to the base point of the associated parameter. To specify a different location, use the **Independent**

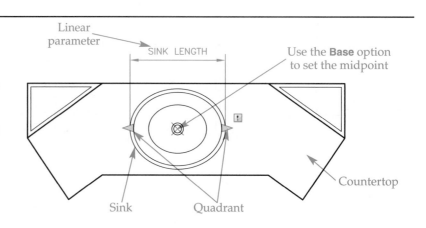

Figure 27-15.
A linear parameter is inserted into the block of a sink and countertop. The base point is specified as the center of the sink so it will stretch symmetrically.

Linear parameter

SINK LENGTH

Use the **Base** option to set the midpoint

Sink

Quadrant

Countertop

option. For the sink, it is important that the objects be scaled relative to the exact center of the sink. This keeps the sink centered within the countertop. At the Enter base point type [Dependent/Independent]: prompt, choose the **Independent** option followed by picking the center of the sink. Finally, pick a point near the parameter label to place the action icon. Save the block and exit the **Block Editor**. The dynamic block is now ready to use.

Using a scale action dynamically

Figure 27-16 shows the countertop block inserted with the default sink length, and selected for editing. Select either of the linear parameter grips and drag the cursor to dynamically scale the sink objects. Since the center of the sink was selected as the base point, the sink objects are scaled relative to the center. In **Figure 27-16,** the right-hand grip is selected and dragged to the right to increase the size of the sink. Enter or select a point to resize the sink. Dynamic input or the **Properties** palette can also be used change the size.

Exercise 27-4
Complete the exercise on the Student CD.

Figure 27-16.
Scaling the sink dynamically. The scale action is not applied to the countertop.

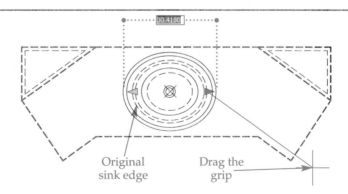

Original sink edge

Drag the grip

Polar Parameters

A *polar parameter* includes two parameter points with a distance property and an angle property. A polar parameter can be assigned move, scale, stretch, polar stretch, and array actions. **Figure 27-17** shows a block consisting of a large circle containing a smaller circle. In this example, a polar parameter with a move action is inserted into the block allowing the smaller circle to be moved a specified distance and angle without affecting the larger circle.

Figure 27-17 provides an example of how to insert a polar parameter. When you access the **Polar Parameter** option, the Specify base point or [Name/Label/Chain/Description/Palette/Value set]: prompt appears. Pick the center of the large circle as the base point. Then, pick the center of the small circle to specify the endpoint, followed by picking a location for the parameter label, away from block objects.

Assigning a move action to a polar parameter

Assigning a move action to a point parameter was described earlier in this chapter. **Figure 27-18** illustrates the process of assigning a move action to the polar parameter created in the previous section. First, access the **Move Action** option and pick the polar parameter if not already selected. Then, select the parameter point in the center of the small circle to associate the move action with this parameter grip. When prompted to select objects, select the small circle as the object to be included in the move action, and press [Enter] or the space bar, or right-click to accept the selection. Finally, pick a point near the parameter label to place the action icon. Save the block and exit the **Block Editor**. The dynamic block is now ready to use.

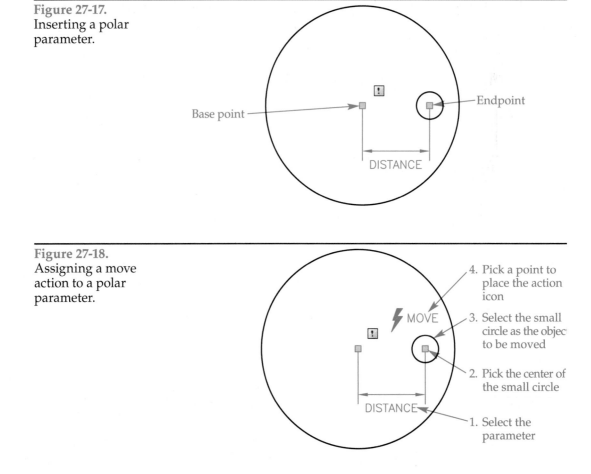

Figure 27-17.
Inserting a polar parameter.

Base point

Endpoint

DISTANCE

Figure 27-18.
Assigning a move action to a polar parameter.

MOVE

DISTANCE

4. Pick a point to place the action icon

3. Select the small circle as the object to be moved

2. Pick the center of the small circle

1. Select the parameter

Figure 27-19.
Moving an object
with a polar
parameter displays
the distance and the
angle from the base
point if dynamic
input is enabled.

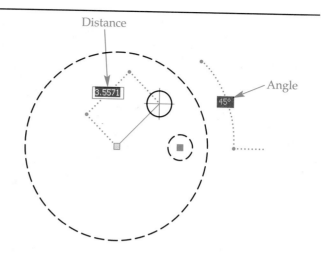

Distance

3.5571

Angle

45°

Using a move action dynamically

Figure 27-19 shows the dynamic block created in the previous sections inserted with the default small circle location, and selected for editing. Select the parameter grip in the center of the small circle and drag it. Pick a point to place the small circle at a new location, or use a coordinate entry method to define the exact distance and angle. For example, to move the small circle three inches away from the center of the large circle at 45°, type @3<45 and press [Enter]. Dynamic input or the **Properties** palette can also be used to move the objects.

> **NOTE**
>
> In the previous example, the parameter grip for the base point can also be moved by selecting it and dragging. No action or objects are assigned to the base point grip, so only the grip itself is moved. However, this affects the distance and angle to the endpoint.

Exercise 27-5

Complete the exercise on the Student CD.

Rotation Parameters

A *rotation parameter* creates an angle property, and can only be assigned a rotate action. Figure 27-20 shows an example of a speedometer block in which the needle pointer should be able to rotate around the circumference of the dial. A rotation parameter with an associated rotation action can be used to allow the modification.

Figure 27-21 provides an example of how to insert a rotation parameter. When you access the **Rotation Parameter** option, the Specify base point or [Name/Label/Chain/Description/Palette/Value set]: prompt appears. Pick the center of the needle's circular base. Then, pick a point to define a circle on which the rotation parameter is placed. Next, pick the arrow tip to place the parameter grip, or enter 90 (90°) to place the parameter grip in line with the needle. Finally, pick a location for the parameter label, away from block objects.

As shown in Figure 27-21, an angle of 90° places the parameter grip in line with the arrow. By default, the base angle for a drawing is at 0° to the east. The **Base angle** option allows you to specify a base angle that is different from the current drawing base angle.

rotation parameter: A parameter that allows objects in a block to be rotated independently of the block.

Figure 27-20.
The needle can be rotated to indicate different speeds on this speedometer by assigning a rotation parameter with a rotate action to the needle.

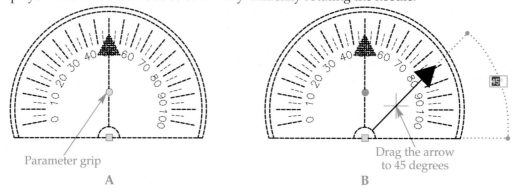

Figure 27-21.
Inserting a rotation parameter into the speedometer block. A—The parameter grip is displayed when the block is selected. B—Dynamically rotating the needle.

Assigning a rotate action to a rotation parameter

A *rotate action* is assigned to a rotation parameter. To assign a rotate action to the previous speedometer example, access the **Rotate Action** option and pick the rotation parameter if not already selected. Then, select the rotation parameter and all of the objects that make up the arrow, and press [Enter] or the space bar, or right-click to accept the selection. Then pick a point near the parameter label to place the action icon. The **Base type** option can be used to define a different rotational base point. By default, the rotation point is the base point of the rotation parameter. Save the block and exit the **Block Editor**. The dynamic block is now ready to use.

Using a rotate action dynamically

Figure 27-21A shows the dynamic block created in the previous sections inserted with the default needle rotation, and selected for editing. Select the parameter grip and drag to rotate the needle objects around the base point. Dynamic input or the **Properties** palette can also be used to adjust the rotation angle. In Figure 27-21B, the needle is dragged until a dynamic input value of 45° is displayed.

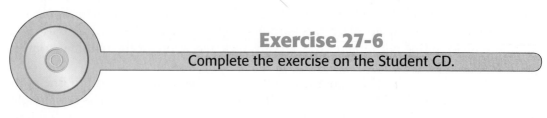

Exercise 27-6
Complete the exercise on the Student CD.

Alignment Parameters

An *alignment parameter* creates an alignment property. When a dynamic block with an alignment parameter is moved near another object in the drawing, the block automatically rotates to align with that object based on the angle and alignment line defined in the block. This parameter saves time by eliminating the need to determine an angle of rotation and then rotate the block. An alignment parameter affects the entire block, not individual components. Therefore, no actions are assigned to this parameter.

Figure 27-22 provides an example of how to insert an alignment parameter into a gate valve symbol. By inserting an alignment parameter into the block, the gate valve can be moved near any pipe line and it automatically rotates to align with the pipe. When you access the **Alignment Parameter** option, the prompt Specify base point of alignment or [Name]: appears. Pick the point in the center of the valve to locate the parameter grip and define the first point in the angle of the alignment line.

Once the base point is selected, the Specify alignment direction or alignment type [Type]: prompt appears. Use the **Type** option to specify the type of alignment. These options do not affect how the block is aligned; they determine the direction of the alignment grip. When set to perpendicular, the grip points perpendicular to the alignment line. When set to tangent, the grip points tangent to the alignment line. For the gate valve example, the **Type** option is selected followed by the **Tangent** option.

After specifying the base point, and if necessary the alignment type, drag the pointer in the direction that is desired for the angle and pick. The endpoint of the symbol is selected as shown in Figure 27-22. The angle between the first point and the second point defines the alignment line.

The parameter grip for an alignment parameter looks like a small square with a triangle on one side. See Figure 27-22. When the parameter has been assigned to the block, the triangle on the parameter grip points in the direction of alignment. This "arrow" points perpendicular to or tangent to the object in the drawing to which the block is being aligned. Save the block and exit the **Block Editor**. The dynamic block is now ready to use.

Using an alignment parameter dynamically

Figure 27-23 shows the dynamic block created in the previous sections inserted with the default orientation, and selected for editing. Select the parameter grip and drag the block near another object. The block is automatically aligned to the object. The rotation is determined by the alignment path, the type of alignment, and the angle of the other object. In **Figure 27-23,** the gate valve block is dragged near the pipe line.

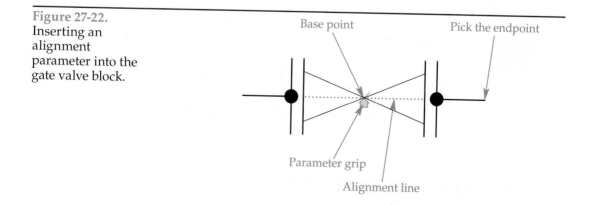

Figure 27-22.
Inserting an alignment parameter into the gate valve block.

Base point

Pick the endpoint

Parameter grip

Alignment line

Figure 27-23.
When the gate valve block is dragged near the angled line, the block automatically aligns
with the line.

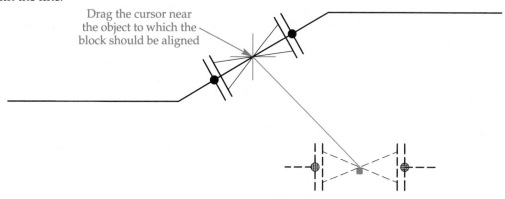

Drag the cursor near
the object to which the
block should be aligned

NOTE

When you manipulate a block with an alignment parameter, the
Nearest object snap is temporarily turned on, if it is not already on.

Exercise 27-7

Complete the exercise on the Student CD.

Flip Parameters

flip parameter:
A parameter that
mirrors selected
objects within a
block.

A *flip parameter* creates a flip state, and can only be assigned a flip action. For
example, flip parameters with flip actions can be assigned to a door symbol so the
door can be placed on either side of a wall, and used for interior or exterior applications. Another example is using a flip parameter to control the side of a reference line
where a weld symbol is placed for arrow side or other side applications.

Figure 27-24 provides an example of how to insert a flip parameter. When you
access the **Flip Parameter** option, the Specify base point of reflection line or [Name/Label/
Description/Palette]: prompt appears. Pick the base point shown in **Figure 27-24A** to
place the parameter grip. Then pick the endpoint of the swing arc. Select a location for
the parameter label away from block objects to complete the operation.

PROFESSIONAL TIP

During editing, a block with a flip parameter is mirrored about the
reflection line. You must place the reflection line in the correct location so the flip creates a symmetrical, or mirrored, copy. This typically
requires the refection line to be coincident with the block insertion
point.

Assigning a flip action to a flip parameter

flip action: An
action used to flip
the entire block.

A *flip action* is assigned to a flip parameter. To assign a flip action to the previous
door example, access the **Flip Action** option and pick the rotation parameter if not
already selected. Then, select the rotation parameter and all of the objects that make
up the door block, and press [Enter] or the space bar, or right-click to accept the selec-

Figure 27-24.
A—Inserting a flip parameter. B—Moving the parameter so the block will correctly flip about the centerline of a wall.

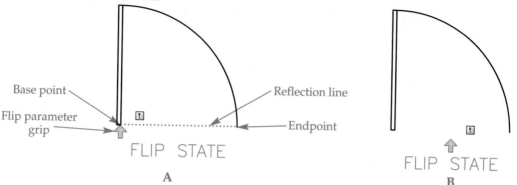

tion. Then pick a point near the parameter label to place the action icon. Save the block and exit the **Block Editor**. The dynamic block is now ready to use.

Using a flip action dynamically

Figure 27-25A shows the dynamic block created in the previous sections inserted with the default door flip side, and selected for editing. A pick on the parameter grip flips the objects to the other side of the reflection line, as shown in **Figure 27-25B**. Unlike other parameters and actions described to this point, dragging is not required. A single pick initiates the action.

PROFESSIONAL TIP

Add another flip parameter with a flip action to the door described in the previous section, so the door can also be flipped from side to side. In this way, one block takes the place of four blocks to accommodate different door positions.

Figure 27-25.
A—The flip parameter grip is displayed when the block is selected. B—Picking the flip parameter grip flips the block about the reflection line. Since all of the objects within the block were selected for the action, the entire block is flipped.

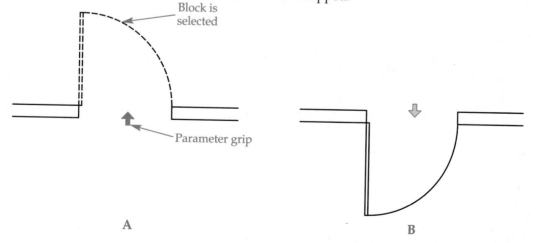

XY Parameters

An *XY parameter* creates horizontal and vertical distance properties, and can be assigned move, scale, stretch, and array actions. Four parameter grips are inserted with the XY parameter—one at each corner of a 2D box defined by the parameter. The XY parameter can be used for a variety of applications depending on the assigned action(s).

Figure 27-26 provides an example of how to insert an XY parameter. When you access the **XY Parameter** option, the Specify base point or [Name/Label/Chain/Description/Palette/Value set]: prompt appears. Pick the base point. The base point is the "origin" for the X and Y distances. Next, pick a point to specify the XY grip, or endpoint. Grips are then automatically created on the X and Y axis aligned with the base point.

Assigning an array action to an XY parameter

An *array action* is one type of action that can be assigned to an XY parameter. The block of architectural glass block shown in **Figure 27-26** is an example of using an XY parameter with an array action. In this example, adjusting (arraying) the block dynamically allows you to create an architectural feature of glass blocks of any size, without using a separate array operation.

To assign an array action to the glass block example, access the **Array Action** option and pick the XY parameter if not already selected. Then, select the objects to be included in the array, and press [Enter] or the space bar, or right-click to accept the selection. At the Enter the distance between rows or specify unit cell: prompt, enter a value for the distance between rows or pick two points to set the row and column values. At the Enter the distance between columns: prompt, enter a value for the distance between columns. This prompt does not appear if you selected two points to define the row and column values.

In the example of the glass block, be sure to allow for a grout joint when setting the row and column distance. Before assigning the action, you may want to draw a construction point offset from the block by the width of the grout joint. Then you can pick two points to define the row and column values. Be sure to erase the construction point before saving the block. Otherwise, the point is included in the block definition.

Finally, pick a point near the parameter label to place the action icon. Save the block and exit the **Block Editor**. The dynamic block is now ready to use.

Figure 27-26.
Inserting an XY parameter into a block of architectural glass block. The XY parameter consists of X and Y distance properties and four grips.

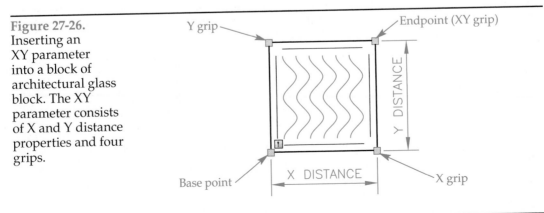

Figure 27-27.
Dynamically creating an array of architectural glass block. The block has an XY parameter and array action. The pattern of rows and columns is created by dragging the XY parameter. Notice the grout lines between the glass blocks. By properly defining the dynamic block, these lines are added automatically.

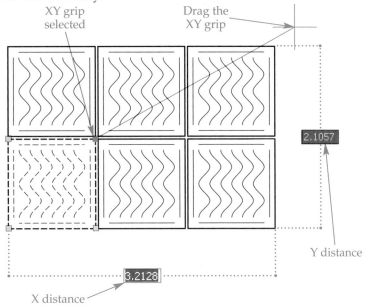

Using an array action dynamically

Figure 27-27 shows the dynamic block created in the previous sections inserted, and selected for editing. There are four parameter grips and the block insertion point grip, which can coincide with one of the parameter grips. Select any of the parameter grips and drag to array the objects. Dynamic input or the **Properties** palette can also be used to adjust the X and Y distances. Notice that the grout lines are added because the action was properly defined. The resulting array remains a single block.

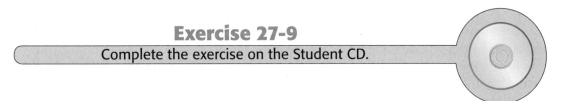

Exercise 27-9
Complete the exercise on the Student CD.

Visibility Parameters

A *visibility parameter* allows *visibility states* to be assigned to objects within a block. Selecting the visibility parameter grip on a block displays a list of the visibility states created for the block. Selecting one of the visibility states changes the block to view assigned to the visibility state. No action is associated with a visibility parameter.

An example of a visibility parameter is shown in **Figure 27-28.** The four different valves shown in **Figure 27-28A** are created from a single block. When the block is defined, all of the objects representing the different variations need to be drawn. Draw the objects in reference to, or on top of, the other objects within the block. See **Figure 27-28B.** Then assign a visibility parameter and define the visibility states.

Once you access the **Visibility Parameter** option, the Specify parameter location or [Name/Label/Description/Palette]: prompt appears. Unless you choose one of the options, the only step involved in creating a visibility parameter is to pick the location of the

visibility parameter: A parameter that allows multiple different views to be assigned to objects within a block.

visibility states: Views created by selecting block objects to display or hide.

Figure 27-28.
A—All four of these different valves can be created from one block by using a visibility parameter. B—All of the objects composing all four valves are shown together.

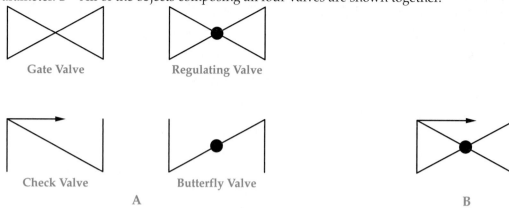

Gate Valve   Regulating Valve

Check Valve   Butterfly Valve

A

B

parameter label. The parameter grip is placed at the point you pick for the parameter location. Picking this grip in the drawing displays a shortcut menu that contains a list of the visibility states. A visibility parameter is associated with an entire block, so there is no prompt to select objects. A dynamic block can only contain one visibility parameter.

Creating visibility states

BVSTATE

Ribbon
Block Editor
> Visibility

Visibility States

Type
BVSTATE

Once a visibility parameter has been assigned to a block, the visibility tools in the **Visibility** panel of the **Block Editor** tab on the ribbon are enabled. See **Figure 27-29.** Use the **BVSTATE** tool to create a visibility state using the **Visibility States** dialog box. See **Figure 27-30A.**

Pick the **New...** button to open the **New Visibility State** dialog box. See **Figure 27-30B.** In the **Visibility state name:** text box, name the new visibility state. For the valve block example shown in **Figure 27-28,** an appropriate name could be GATE VALVE, REGULATING VALVE, CHECK VALVE, or BUTTERFLY VALVE, depending on which valve the visibility state represents. Each of these visibility states are eventually created.

In the **Visibility options for new states** area, select the option that is appropriate for the new state. Pick the **Hide all existing objects in new state** radio button to make all of the objects in the block invisible when the new visibility state is created. This allows you to turn on (display) only the objects that you want to be visible in the visibility state. Pick the **Show all existing objects in new state** radio button to make all of the objects in the block visible when the new visibility state is created. This allows you to turn off (hide) any objects that you want to be invisible for the state. Select the **Leave visibility of existing objects unchanged in new state** radio button to display only the currently visible objects when the new visibility state is created.

Figure 27-29.
The visibility tools are found in the **Visibility** panel of the **Block Editor** tab on the ribbon.

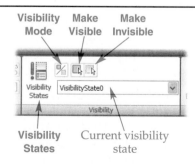

Visibility Mode   Make Visible   Make Invisible

Visibility States

Current visibility state

Visibility States

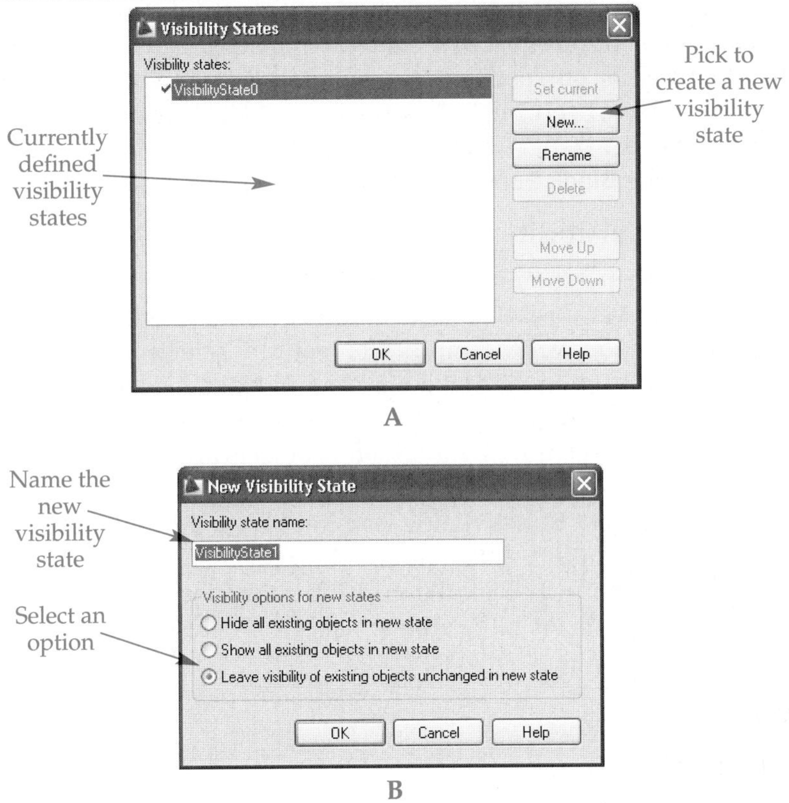

Figure 27-30.
A—Manage
visibility states
using the **Visibility
States** dialog box.
B—Create new
visibility states
using the **New
Visibility State**
dialog box.

Pick to
create a new
visibility
state

Currently
defined
visibility
states

Name the
new
visibility
state

Select an
option

A

B

Once you enter a name and select the appropriate visibility option, pick the **OK** button to create the new visibility state. The new state is added to the list in the **Visibility States** dialog box and made current, as indicated by the check mark next to the name. Pick the **OK** button in the **Visibility States** dialog box to return to block editing mode.

Now, using the **Make Visible** and **Make Invisible** tools, display only the objects that should be visible in the state. Pick the **Make Visible** button to select objects to be made visible. Invisible objects are temporarily displayed as semitransparent so they can be selected. Select the **Make Invisible** button to select objects to be made invisible. For example, to make a visibility state to depict the gate valve shown in **Figure 27-28A** from the valve block shown in **Figure 27-31A,** use the **Make Invisible** tool to turn off the filled circle and the arrow. See **Figure 27-31B**. The changes are automatically saved to the visibility state. Pick the **Visibility Mode** button to toggle the visibility mode on and off. When on, the objects that are currently invisible are displayed as semitransparent. When off, only the visible objects are shown. The visibility mode can also be toggled on and off by typing BVMODE.

Figure 27-31.
A—The VALVE
block with all of
the objects visible.
B—The VALVE block
after the arrow
and filled circle
are hidden (made
invisible) to create
the GATE VALVE
visibility state.

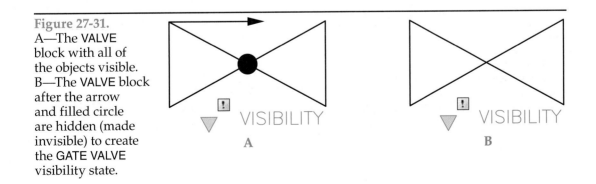

Repeat the process to create additional visibility states for the block. For the valve block, a total of four visibility states are needed. The **Current visibility state** drop-down list displays the current visibility state. Picking the button displays all of the visibility states that have been created for the block. Selecting one of the states in the drop-down list makes it current. When all the visibility states have been created, save the block and close the **Block Editor**. The dynamic block is now ready to use.

Modifying visibility states

Like other dynamic block properties, visibility states are modified in the **Block Editor**. However, visibility states require some special consideration when modified. Set the state you want to modify current by selecting it in the **Current visibility state** drop-down list. Use the **Make Visible** and **Make Invisible** tools to change the visibility of objects as needed. New objects can also be drawn in block editing mode using normal AutoCAD drawing tools. New objects are automatically hidden in all visibility states other than the current state.

The **Visibility States** dialog box can be used to rename, delete, and rearrange the order of the visibility states in the shortcut menu presented when you pick the visibility parameter grip. Pick the visibility state you want to rename, delete, or move up or down from the **Visibility states:** list box. Then select the appropriate button to make the desired change.

The order in which states appear in the **Visibility States** dialog box is the same order in which they appear in the shortcut menu displayed when the grip is selected in the drawing. The state at the top of the list is the default view for the block.

PROFESSIONAL TIP

If you add new objects when modifying a state, be sure any other parameters/actions applied to the block are updated to include the new objects, if needed.

Using a visibility parameter dynamically

Figure 27-32A shows the dynamic block created in the previous sections inserted, and selected for editing. The visibility grip appears as a horizontal line with a triangle below it. Select the grip to display a shortcut menu containing the visibility states created for the block. The current visibility state has a check mark next to its name. To switch to a different view of the block, select the name of the visibility state in the list. See Figure 27-32B. The **Properties** palette can also be used to change the visibility state.

Exercise 27-10
Complete the exercise on the Student CD.

Figure 27-32.
A—Picking the visibility parameter grip displays the available visibility states shortcut menu. The current state is checked. B—Selecting a different visibility state from the shortcut menu changes the appearance of the block.

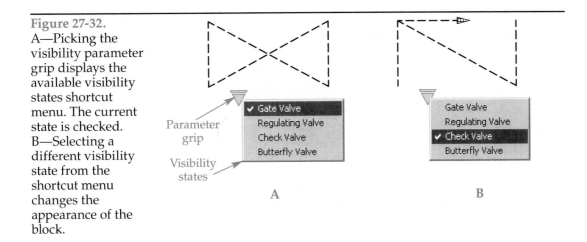

Parameter grip

Visibility states

A

B

Lookup Parameters

A *lookup parameter* creates a lookup property and is used together with a *lookup action*. For example, **Figure 27-33** shows three symbols created from a single block by adjusting the rotation parameter of the middle line. The specified rotation angles are 0, 10, and 20 degrees. The length of the start and end lines automatically adjust to match the rotation of the middle line. In this example, by selecting one of three options, three unique parameters with associated actions change automatically to create different symbols.

Once you access the **Lookup Parameter** option, the Specify parameter location or [Name/Label/Description/Palette]: prompt appears. Unless you choose one of the options, the only step involved in creating a lookup parameter is to pick the location of the parameter label. The parameter grip is placed at the point you pick for the parameter location. Picking this grip in the drawing displays a shortcut menu that contains a list of the custom groups. A lookup parameter is associated with an entire block, so there is no prompt to select objects.

lookup parameter: A parameter that allows tabular properties to be used with existing parameter values.

lookup action: An action used to select a preset group of parameter values to carry out the actions with stored values.

Example lookup parameter block

Figure 27-34 shows the block, in the **Block Editor**, described earlier and used to create the three symbols shown in **Figure 27-33.** To create this block the geometry of the 0° symbol is drawn. Then in the **Block Editor**, a linear parameter, labeled Start Line, is inserted. To create this parameter, select the start point as the bottom of the start line, and the endpoint as the top of the start line. Then assign a stretch action to the parameter. The action is associated with the top parameter grip and a crossing window is drawn around the top of the start line. The start line is selected as the object.

Another linear parameter, labeled End Line, is inserted. To create this parameter, select the start point as the bottom of the end line, and the endpoint as the top of the end line. Then assign a stretch action to the parameter. The action is associated with

Figure 27-33.
A lookup parameter was used to create these three views of the same block. Notice how the geometry is changed.

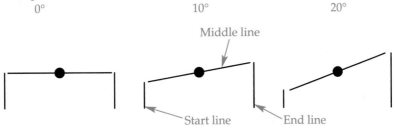

0°   10°   20°

Middle line

Start line   End line

Figure 27-34.
The **Property Lookup Table** dialog box.

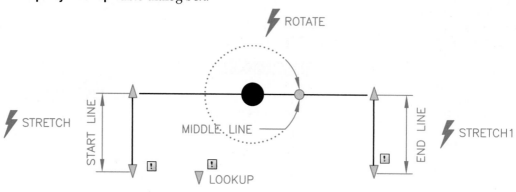

the top parameter grip and a crossing window is drawn around the top of the end line. The end line is selected as the object.

A rotation parameter, labeled Middle Line, is then inserted. To create this parameter, specify the base point as the center of the circle. Then select the right endpoint of the middle line to set the radius, and specify the default rotation angle as 0. Now assign a rotation action to the parameter. Pick the center of the circle as the rotation base point, and select the middle line as the object.

The next phase of block development is to insert a lookup parameter, and assign a lookup action to the parameter. Once the lookup parameter and associated lookup action are in place, you can create a lookup table that references the existing linear and rotation parameters.

Assigning a lookup action to a lookup parameter

To assign a lookup action, access the **Lookup Action** option and pick a lookup parameter if not already selected. Then pick a point near the parameter to place the lookup action icon. After specifying the lookup action location, the **Property Lookup Table** dialog box appears. See **Figure 27-35.** This dialog box is used to create a lookup table, as described in the next sections.

Figure 27-35.
The block with linear parameters and stretch actions assigned to the start and end lines and a rotation parameter and rotate action assigned to the middle line.

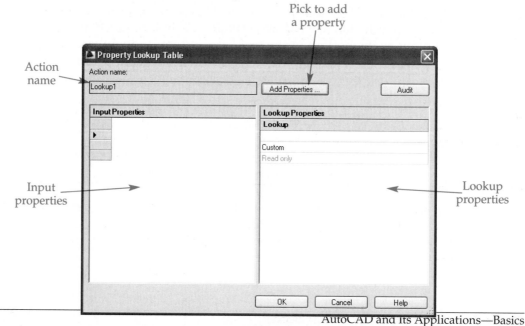

Figure 27-36.
Parameter
properties are listed
in the **Add Parameter
Properties** dialog
box.

Select a
property
to add

Select the
type of
property

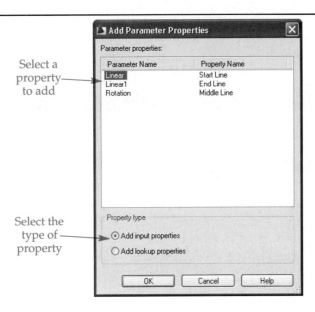

Creating a lookup table

A lookup table is used to group parameter properties into custom named lookup records. The **Property Lookup Table** dialog box is used to create and edit a lookup table, and appears when you add a lookup action to a lookup parameter. The **Action name:** display box indicates the name of the lookup action associated with the table.

To add a parameter property to the table, pick the **Add Properties...** button to open the **Add Parameter Properties** dialog box. See **Figure 27-36.** The parameters that have been assigned to the block appear in the **Parameter properties:** list. Notice that the property name is the parameter label. Only parameters containing property values are displayed in the **Parameter properties:** list. The lookup, alignment, and base point parameters do not contain property values.

The **Property type** area determines which type of property parameters are shown in the list. By default, the **Add input properties** radio button is active, which displays the available input property parameters. To display the available lookup property parameters, select the **Add lookup properties** radio button.

To add a parameter property to the lookup table, select the property in the **Parameter properties:** list and pick the **OK** button. A new column is then added to the **Input Properties** area of the **Property Lookup Table** dialog box. The **Input Properties** area allows you to specify a value for parameters that have been added to the table. The name of the parameter property is the column header. See **Figure 27-37.** To add values for the parameter, type the value in each cell in the column. Add a custom name for each row (record) on the same row in the **Lookup** column in the **Lookup Properties** area. This area displays the name that appears in the shortcut menu when the lookup parameter grip is selected in the drawing.

For the example valve block described in the previous sections, add the Middle Line, Start Line, and End Line parameter properties to the table. Then, complete the lookup table as shown in **Figure 27-37.** Start with the Middle Line values. Press [Enter] after typing the value to add a new blank row below it. Then add the remaining values. Pick in a cell and type the value. Press [Enter], pick in a different cell, or use the tab or arrow keys to navigate through the table.

The row (record) that contains the <Unmatched> value, which is named Custom in the **Lookup** column, is used when the current parameter values of the block do not match any of the records in the table. You cannot add any values to the row, but you can change the name of **Custom.**

Figure 27-37.
A lookup table with multiple parameters and values added.

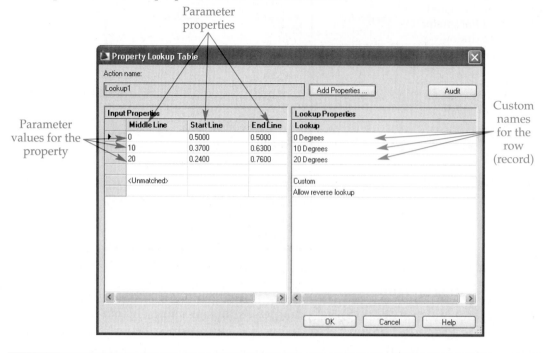

Parameter
properties

Parameter
values for the
property

Custom
names
for the
row
(record)

Picking in the cell at the bottom of the **Lookup** column, which currently indicates Read only, displays a drop-down list containing two options. The default Read only setting means that the lookup parameter grip is not displayed when the block is selected in the drawing. To have the lookup parameter grip displayed, select Allow reverse lookup from the drop-down list. See **Figure 27-38.** This can only be selected if all names in the lookup table are unique.

After you add all of the properties to the table and assign values to each, pick the **Audit** button in the **Property Lookup Table** dialog box to check each row (record) in the table to make sure it is unique. Any errors are reported. If no errors are found, as

Figure 27-38.
The field at the bottom of the **Lookup** column determines whether the lookup parameter grip is displayed when the block is selected in the drawing.

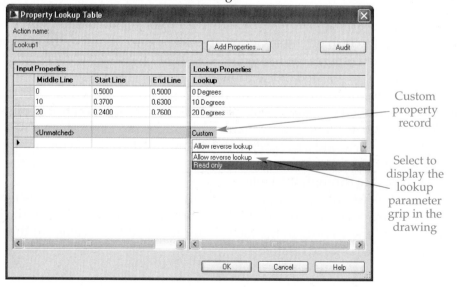

Custom
property
record

Select to
display the
lookup
parameter
grip in the
drawing

indicated by a message box, pick the **OK** button to return to the **Block Editor**. Save the block and close the **Block Editor**. The dynamic block is now ready to use.

Modifying a lookup table

To modify a lookup table, open the block in the **Block Editor** and double-click on the lookup action icon to display the **Property Lookup Table** dialog box. Edits can be made to values and properties in the same way as they were created. Additional options can be accessed by right-clicking on a column heading or on a row to display a shortcut menu.

Right-click on a column heading to access a menu with options for adjusting columns. Pick the **Sort** option to sort the records (rows) by the selected column's values. Picking **Sort** a second time reverses the order of the sort. Pick the **Maximize all headings** option to adjust the widths of all columns to the size of the column headings. Choose the **Maximize all data cells** option to adjust the widths of all columns to the values in the columns. Select the **Size columns equally** option to adjust the widths of all columns so they are equal. Pick the **Delete property column** option to delete the column corresponding to the heading you right-clicked to display the shortcut menu. Select the **Clear contents** option to delete all the values entered in the column corresponding to the heading you right-clicked to display the shortcut menu.

Right-click on a row to access a menu with options for adjusting rows. Pick the **Insert row** option to insert a new row above the row you right-clicked. Select the **Delete row** option to delete the row you right-clicked. The **Clear contents** option deletes all of the values entered in the row you right-clicked. Pick the **Move up** option to move the row you right-clicked up by one row, or select the **Move down** option to move the row you right-clicked down by one row. Select the **Range syntax examples** option to display in the online documentation examples of how values can be entered into a lookup table.

Using a lookup action dynamically

Figure 27-39 shows the dynamic block created in the previous sections inserted, and selected for editing. Since Allow reverse lookup was selected in the lookup table, the lookup parameter grip is displayed along with the other parameter grips. Pick the lookup parameter grip to display a shortcut menu containing a list of custom named lookup records. The entries in this shortcut menu match the entries in the **Lookup** column of the **Property Lookup Table** dialog box. See Figure 27-39. Pick one of the entries in the shortcut menu to change the geometry in the block based on the parameter values in the lookup table.

Other parameters assigned to the block, linear and rotation in the case of the example block, can still be changed independently. When you change any of the parameters, the lookup parameter becomes Custom, because the current parameter values do not match one of the records in the lookup table.

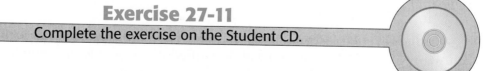

Exercise 27-11
Complete the exercise on the Student CD.

Figure 27-39.
The lookup parameter grip is displayed when the block is selected. The list of available lookup records is displayed when the lookup parameter grip is selected.

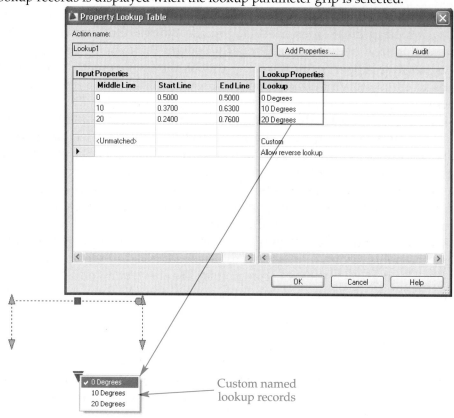

Custom named lookup records

Base Point Parameters

The **Block Editor** origin (0,0,0 point) determines the default location of the block insertion base point. Typically, blocks constructed in the **Block Editor** are created in reference to the origin, using the origin as the desired location of the base point. The base point you choose when creating a block using the **BLOCK** tool, is attached to the origin when the block is opened in the **Block Editor**. A *base point parameter* can be inserted anytime you want to "override" the default origin base point.

base point parameter: A parameter that defines an alternate base point for a block.

When you access the **Base Point Parameter** option, the Specify parameter location: prompt appears. Pick a point to place the base point parameter. The parameter is displayed as a circle with crosshairs. After the block has been saved, the location of the base point parameter becomes the new base point for the block. No actions can be assigned to a base point parameter. However, the parameter can be included in the selection set for actions.

Parameter Value Sets

value set: A set of allowed values for a parameter.

A *value set* is typically assigned in order to ensure that only applicable values are used when a block is dynamically modified. For example, if a window style is only available in widths of 36″, 42″, 48″, 54″, and 60″, then a value set can be created for a linear parameter to limit selection options to these sizes. Next, a stretch action can be applied to the parameter. Then, when the block is dynamically modified, the values specified in the value set are the only values that can be used for the width. See Figure 27-40.

A value set can be used with linear, polar, XY, and rotation parameters. The **Value set** option is available at the first prompt after selecting one of the parameters to insert.

When you choose the **Value set** option, the Enter distance value set type [None/List/Increment]: prompt appears.

The **List** option allows you to create a list of possible sizes. After selecting the **List** option, type all of the valid values for the parameter separated by commas. Using the previous example of the window, enter 36,42,48,54,60. Then press [Enter] or the space bar, or right-click to return to the initial parameter prompt and add the parameter as if a value set is not being used. After the parameter is inserted and the value set specified, the valid values for the parameter appear as tick marks.

The **Increment** option allows you to specify an incremental value to be used by the parameter. A minimum and maximum value are also set to provide a limit for the increments. In the example of the window, the **Value set** option is used again to set 6" width increments. This time choose the **Increment** option. Type 6 for the distance increment, 36 for the minimum distance, and 60 for the maximum distance. The distance increment is the incremental value to be used. The minimum distance is the lowest value that can be used; the maximum distance is the highest value. Once the maximum distance is entered, initial parameter prompt returns.

After the value set and parameter are created, you must assign an action to the parameter. For the window block in Figure 27-40, a stretch action is assigned to the linear parameter. This allows the window to be stretched to the valid widths specified in the value set. Save the block and close the **Block Editor**. The dynamic block is now ready to use.

Using a value set with a parameter

Insert the dynamic block and select it to display grips. To use the value set with the window example, pick the linear parameter grip. Tick marks appear, indicating the positions of valid values. As you drag the grip, the modified block snaps to the nearest tick mark. If dynamic input is enabled, you can also enter a value in the input field. If you type a value that is not in the value set, the nearest valid value is used. The **Properties** palette can also be used to select value set options. These options are available from the **Value Set** category.

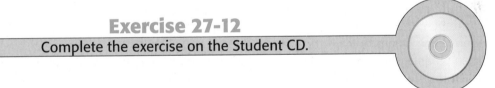

Exercise 27-12
Complete the exercise on the Student CD.

Figure 27-40.
When a value set is used, tick marks appear at locations corresponding to the values in the value set. The block can only be stretched to one of these tick marks.

Block is stretched to the 48" size

Window block is created at a width of 36"

Tick marks show the value set parameter values

Figure 27-41.

A—A block of
a table with six
chairs. B—Using a
chain action with
a linear parameter,
you can array the
chairs automatically
when the table is
stretched.

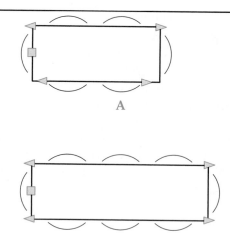

A

B

Assigning a Chain Action to a Parameter

chain action: An
action that triggers
another action
when a parameter is
modified.

A *chain action* limits the number of edits that have to be performed by allowing one action to trigger other actions at the same time. In the example shown in Figure 27-41, when the table is stretched, the chairs along the table are arrayed to match the new table length. This is accomplished in one step by using a chain action.

Point, linear, polar, XY, and rotation parameters can be part of a chain action. The **Chain** option is available at the first prompt after selecting one of the parameters to insert. When you choose the **Chain** option, the Evaluate associated actions when parameter is edited by another action? [Yes/No]: prompt appears. The default setting is **No**, which means that the action for the parameter cannot be affected by another action. To create a chain action on a parameter, the **Chain** option must be set to **Yes**.

Creating a chain action

Figure 27-42 shows the block, in the **Block Editor**, described earlier and used to create the symbol shown in Figure 27-41. To create this block the geometry of the default table and chair arrangement is drawn. Then in the **Block Editor,** a linear parameter, labeled Chair Array, is inserted. Before picking the start point and endpoint, choose the **Chain** option and select the Yes option at the Evaluate associated actions when parameter is edited by another action? [Yes/No]: prompt. To create this parameter, select the start point and the endpoint shown in Figure 27-42A. Then assign an array action to the parameter. The chairs on the top and bottom of the table are selected as the objects to array. At the Enter the distance between rows or specify unit cell: prompt, use object snaps to snap to the endpoint of one of the chairs and then snap to the same endpoint on the chair next to the first chair.

Another linear parameter, labeled Table Stretch, is inserted. To create this parameter, select the start point and endpoint shown in Figure 27-42B. Then assign a stretch action to the parameter. The action is associated with the endpoint parameter grip of the Table Stretch parameter. A crossing window is drawn around the right end of the table and the right parameter grip for the Chair Array parameter. See Figure 27-42C. The table, the chair at the right end of the table, and the Chair Array parameter are selected as the objects. Save the block and close the **Block Editor**. The dynamic block is now ready to use.

Figure 27-42.
A—Inserting a linear parameter to be used with an array action for the chairs. B—Inserting a linear parameter that will be used to stretch the table. C—Assigning a stretch action to the linear parameter. When you specify the crossing window, be sure the CHAIR ARRAY parameter grip is within the frame.

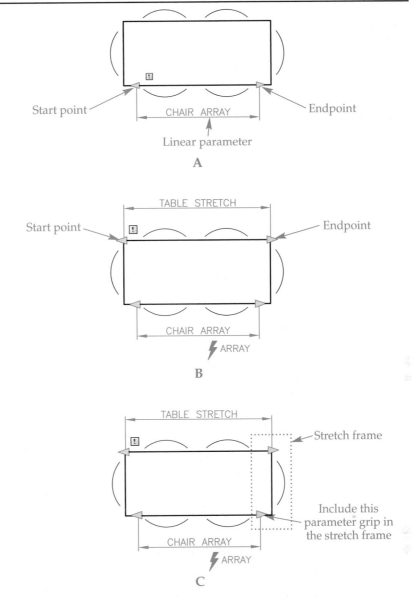

Using a chain action

Figure 27-43 shows the dynamic block created in the previous sections inserted, and selected for editing. Select the right Table Stretch parameter grip, and drag the grip to the right to stretch the table and array the chairs. Pick a point to create the new table length with the chairs arrayed automatically.

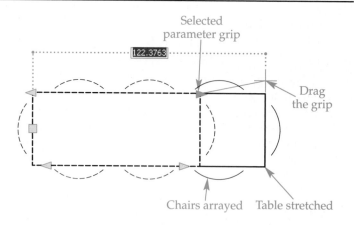

Figure 27-43.
As you drag the
parameter grip,
the table stretches
and the chairs are
arrayed.

Selected
parameter grip

122.3763

Drag
the grip

Chairs arrayed   Table stretched

Action Multiplier and Offset Options

When you insert a move, stretch, or polar stretch action, the Specify action location or [Multiplier/Offset]: prompt appears after you select the objects to which the action applies. If you choose the **Multiplier** option, AutoCAD prompts you to enter a distance multiplier. The value you enter in the parameter property when you edit the parameter grip is multiplied by the value entered. For example, if you enter 2 as the distance multiplier when creating a move action and specify a value of 4 units to move the parameter grip in the drawing, the object actually moves 8 units.

If you use the **Offset** option, AutoCAD prompts you to enter an offset angle. This angle is used to increase or decrease the parameter grip angle. For example, if an offset angle value of 45 is specified when a move action is created and a parameter grip is moved at an angle of 10° in the drawing, the object actually moves to an angle of 55°.

Using Parameter Sets

The **Parameter Sets** tab of the **Block Authoring Palettes** window contains commonly used parameters and actions paired as sets. These are the same parameters and actions found in the **Parameters** tab and the **Actions** tab. When you choose a set, you are prompted for the normal parameter settings. When you specify the parameter point, the action is automatically associated with the parameter.

The action is created without any objects associated with it, which is indicated by the yellow alert icon. If the parameter set contains an action that needs to have objects associated to it, as most do, double-click anywhere on the action icon. AutoCAD prompts you for the missing item(s). Depending on the type of action, the prompts may differ.

The **BACTIONSET** tool can also be used to associate objects to an action. To use this tool, type BACTIONSET. AutoCAD prompts you to select the action and then the objects.

Modifying Parameters and Actions

The location of existing parameters and actions can be edited in the **Block Editor** with grip editing. To modify the location of a parameter grip, open the block in the **Block Editor** and select the parameter. The parameter grips and the location grip for

AutoCAD and Its Applications—Basics

the parameter label appear. Use normal grip editing procedures to move a grip to a different location.

Existing parameter and action settings are edited using the **Properties** palette. In the **Block Editor**, open the **Properties** palette and select a parameter or action to modify. The settings in the **Properties** palette change depending on the type of parameter or action that is selected.

Any parameter or action can be deleted using the **ERASE** tool in the **Block Editor**. Select the parameter or action when prompted by the tool. A parameter or action can also be deleted by selecting it and pressing the [Delete] key.

Exercise 27-13
Complete the exercise on the Student CD.

Chapter Test

Answer the following questions. Write your answers on a separate sheet of paper or complete the electronic chapter test on the Student CD.

1. Define *dynamic block*.
2. Compare and contrast dynamic blocks and normal blocks.
3. Define *parameter*.
4. Define *action*.
5. List the parameters that can be inserted into a block.
6. Briefly describe AutoCAD's **Block Editor**.
7. What does a point parameter do? Identify the actions that can be assigned to a point parameter.
8. Describe the shape and default color of a point parameter grip.
9. What does a linear parameter do? Identify the actions that can be assigned to a linear parameter.
10. Describe the shape and default color of a linear parameter grip.
11. What does a stretch action do?
12. Compare and contrast a polar parameter and a linear parameter. Identify the actions that can be assigned to a polar parameter.
13. What does a rotation parameter do? Identify the actions that can be assigned to a rotation parameter.
14. What does an alignment parameter do? Identify the actions that can be assigned to an alignment parameter.
15. Give an example of where an alignment parameter may be used on a block.
16. What is the basic function of the flip parameter?
17. List the function of each grip of an XY parameter. Identify the actions that can be assigned to an XY parameter.
18. How are visibility states defined and used on a dynamic block?
19. Explain how a lookup parameter differs from a visibility parameter.
20. What does a base point parameter do?
21. What is a value set? Give an example of its use.
22. Name the two types of value sets.
23. Define *chain action*. Identify the parameters that can be part of a chain action.
24. Explain how the **Multiplier** and **Offset** options can be used.
25. What are parameter sets? Explain how they are used.

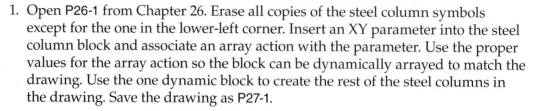

▼ Basic

1. Open **P26-1** from Chapter 26. Erase all copies of the steel column symbols except for the one in the lower-left corner. Insert an XY parameter into the steel column block and associate an array action with the parameter. Use the proper values for the array action so the block can be dynamically arrayed to match the drawing. Use the one dynamic block to create the rest of the steel columns in the drawing. Save the drawing as **P27-1**.

2. Create a block named **WIRE ROLL** as shown below. Do not include the dimensions. Insert a linear parameter on the entire length of the roll. Use a value set with the following values: 36″, 42″, 48″, and 54″. Assign a stretch action to the parameter and associate the action with either parameter grip. Create a crossing window that will allow the length of the role to be stretched. Select all of the objects on one end and the length lines as the objects to be stretched. Insert the **WIRE ROLL** block four times into a drawing and stretch each block to use a different value set length. Save the drawing as **P27-2**.

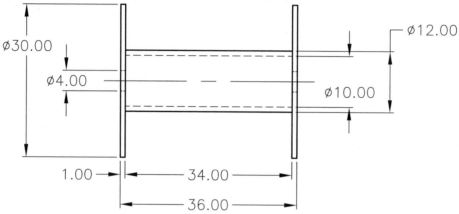

3. Create a block named **90D ELBOW** as shown below on the left. Do not include the dimensions. Insert two flip parameters and two flip actions. One of the flip parameter/action combinations is to flip the elbow horizontally. The second flip parameter/action combination is to flip the elbow vertically. Use the dynamic block to create the drawing shown below on the right. Save the drawing as **P27-3**.

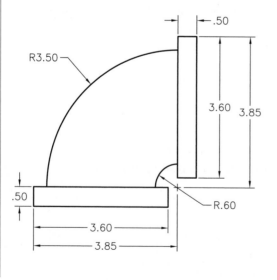

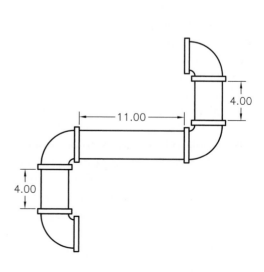

4. Create a block of the 48″ window shown below on the left. Do not include the dimensions. Insert an alignment parameter so the length of the window can be aligned with a wall. Then, draw the walls shown below on the right. Insert the window block as needed. Use the alignment parameter to align the window to the walls. Windows are centered on wall segments unless dimensioned. Save the drawing as P27-4.

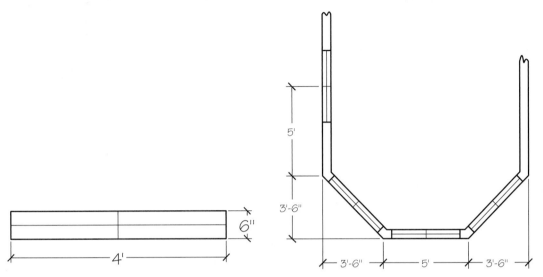

5. Create a block named **CONTROL VALVE** as shown below on the left. Include the label in the block. Insert a point parameter and assign a move action to it. Select the two lines of text as the objects to which the action applies. Insert the **CONTROL VALVE** block into the drawing three times. Use the point parameter to move the text to match the three positions shown below. Save the drawing as P27-5.

CONTROL VALVE
PART #336HR

 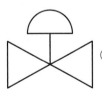

CONTROL VALVE
PART #336HR

CONTROL VALVE
PART #336HR

▼ Intermediate

6. Create a single block that can be used to represent each of the three door blocks shown below. Name the block 30 INCH DOOR; do not include labels. Create an appropriately named visibility state for each view: 90 OPEN, 60 OPEN, and 30 OPEN. Insert the 30 INCH DOOR block into the drawing three times. Set each block to a different visibility state. Save the drawing as P27-6.

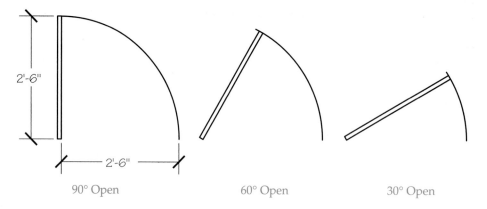

2'-6"

2'-6"

90° Open   60° Open   30° Open

7. Create a block named FLANGE as shown below. Do not include dimensions. Insert a rotation parameter specifying the center of the flange as the base point. Assign a rotate action to the parameter, selecting the six Ø.2 circles as the objects to which the action applies. Insert the FLANGE block into the drawing twice. Use the rotation parameter to create the two configurations shown below. Save the drawing as P27-7.

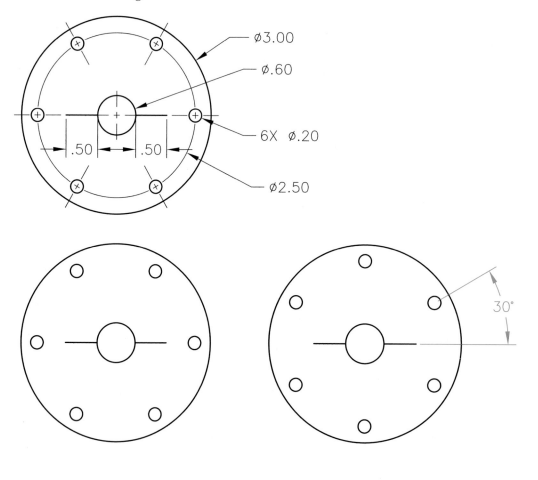

Ø3.00

Ø.60

6X Ø.20

Ø2.50

.50   .50

30°

8. Open P27-7. Save the drawing as P27-8. Open the FLANGE block in the **Block Editor** and use the **Properties** palette to give the following settings to the rotation parameter:
   A. **Angle label**—BOLT HOLES
   B. **Angle description**—ROTATION OF BOLT HOLE PATTERN
   C. **Ang type**—INCREMENT
   D. **Ang increment**—30
   E. Save the changes and exit the **Block Editor**. Save the drawing.

▼ Advanced

9. The drawing below shows a fan with an enlarged view of the motor. This fan can have one of three motors of different sizes. Create the fan as a dynamic block.
   A. Draw all the objects. Do not dimension the drawing or draw the enlarged view.
   B. Create a block named FAN consisting of the objects shown in the enlarged view.
   C. Open the block in the **Block Editor** and insert a linear parameter along the top of the motor (the 1.50″ dimension). Use a value set with the following values: 1.5, 1.75, and 2.
   D. Assign a scale action to the linear parameter. Select all of the objects that make up the motor as the objects to which the action applies. Use an independent base point type and specify the base point as the lower-left corner of the motor (the implied intersection).
   E. Save the block and exit the **Block Editor**.
   F. Insert the block three times into the drawing. Use the linear parameter grip to scale the motor to the three different sizes, as shown below on the right.
   G. Save the drawing as P27-9.

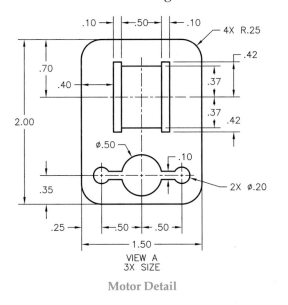

VIEW A
3X SIZE

Motor Detail

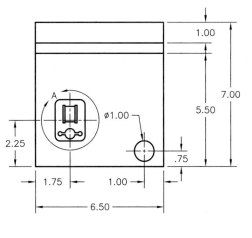

Fan

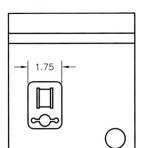

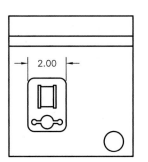

Drawing Problems - Chapter 27

10. The bolt shown in the drawing below is available in four different lengths. As the length increases, the size of the bolt head increases for added strength. Create a dynamic block that will allow the length of the shaft and the size of the bolt head to be changed in a single operation.

  A. Draw the objects composing the bolt and create a block named BOLT. Do not include dimensions.

  B. Insert a linear parameter along the length of the shaft from the bottom of the bolt head to the end of the shaft. Label it SHAFT LENGTH.

  C. Assign a stretch action to the SHAFT LENGTH parameter. Associate the action with the parameter grip at the end of the shaft. Create a crossing window around the end of the shaft that includes the threads. Select the end of the shaft, threads, and edges of the shaft.

  D. Insert a linear parameter along the depth of the bolt head (the .3″ dimension). Label it HEAD THICKNESS.

  E. Assign a scale action to the HEAD THICKNESS parameter and select the objects that compose the bolt head. Use an independent base point type and specify the midpoint of the vertical line where the shaft meets the bolt head.

  F. Insert a lookup parameter and then assign a lookup action to it.

  G. Add the SHAFT LENGTH and the HEAD THICKNESS parameters to the lookup table. Complete the table with the following properties:

Shaft Length	Head Thickness	Lookup
1	0.3	1″ Length
1.5	0.333	1.5″ Length
2	0.366	2″ Length
2.5	0.4	2.5″ Length

  H. Set the table to allow reverse lookup, save the block, and exit the **Block Editor**.

  I. Insert the block four times into the drawing. Specify a different lookup property for each block.

  J. Save the drawing as P27-10.

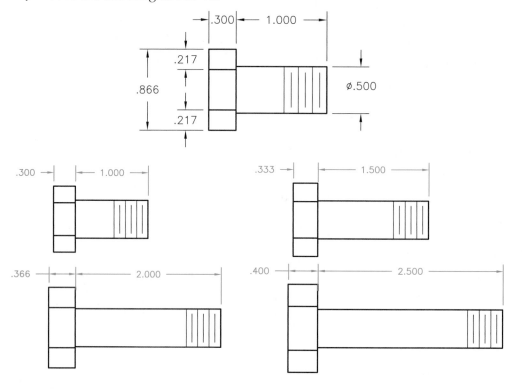

Drawing Problems – Chapter 27

Working with Layouts

Learning Objectives

After completing this chapter, you will be able to do the following:

✓ Describe the purpose for and proper use of layouts.
✓ Begin to prepare layouts for plotting.
✓ Manage layouts.
✓ Use the **Page Setup Manager** to define plot settings.
✓ Use plot styles and plot style tables.

Once you create an AutoCAD drawing, you may want to print or plot the drawing on a sheet of paper. Drawings are plotted for a variety of reasons. For example, it is typically easier for a construction crew in the field or workers in a machine shop to refer to a print than to use a computer to view the drawing file.

Chapter 5 introduced printing and plotting and described the process of plotting from model space. Model space is usually plotted to make a quick hard copy of model space objects for reference. Ordinarily, however, drawings are created in model space and then laid out for plotting in paper space. This chapter describes the initial stages of plotting a layout. Chapter 29 describes finalizing layouts and making plots.

Introduction to Layouts

The first step in making an AutoCAD drawing is to create a *model* in *model space*. See **Figure 28-1A.** Model space is usually active by default. You have been using model space throughout this textbook to create objects and dimensioned drawing views. Once a model is complete, a *layout* is used in *paper space* to prepare the final drawing for plotting.

An AutoCAD layout represents the sheet of paper used to lay out and plot a drawing or model. A layout may include the following items:

- Floating viewport(s)
- Border
- Title block
- Revision block
- General notes
- Bill of materials or parts list
- Page setup information

model: A 2D or 3D drawing composed of various objects, such as lines, circles, and text, and usually created at full size.

model space: The environment in AutoCAD in which drawings and designs are created.

layout: A specific arrangement of views or drawings for plotting or printing on paper.

paper space: The environment in AutoCAD where layouts are created.

Figure 28-1B shows an example of a final drawing ready to be plotted.

A major element of the layout system is the *floating viewport*. Consider a layout to be a virtual sheet of paper and a floating viewport as a hole cut into the paper to show objects drawn in model space. In **Figure 28-1B**, a single viewport is used to expose objects drawn in model space. The floating viewport in this example is created on a layer that is turned off so the viewport is not displayed on-screen or plotted. Floating viewports are covered in Chapter 29.

A single drawing can have multiple layouts. Each layout represents a different paper space, or plot, definition. Each layout can include multiple floating viewports to provide additional or alternate drawing views, prepared at different scales if necessary. Layouts with floating viewports offer you the ability to construct properly scaled drawings and use a single drawing file to prepare several unique final drawings and

Figure 28-1.
A—Drawings and designs are created in model space.
B—Drawings and designs are finalized and laid out on paper for plotting in paper space.

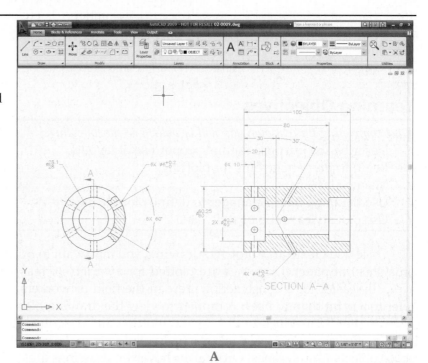

A

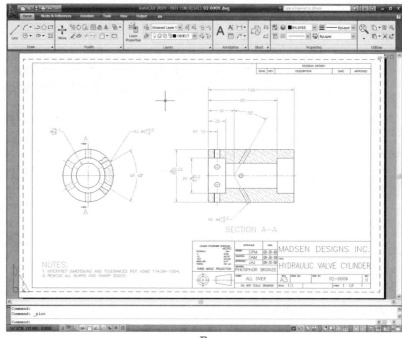

B

AutoCAD and Its Applications—Basics

drawing views. For example, an architectural drawing file might include several details that are too large to place on a single sheet of paper. Multiple layouts, and if necessary different scaled floating viewports, can be used to prepare as many sheets as needed to plot all details found in the drawing.

Working with Layouts

Before preparing a layout for plotting, you should be familiar with tools and options for displaying and managing layouts. The status bar provides the most convenient tools for managing layouts. See Figure 28-2. Pick the **Model** button to activate model space. This button has been selected throughout this textbook as you have learned to create drawing geometry and add dimensions and annotations. You can also activate model space by typing MODEL.

Pick the **Layout** button to exit model space and enter paper space. If the file contains multiple layouts, none of which has been previously accessed, the top-level layout is displayed when you pick the **Layout** button. If a different layout has been opened previously, this layout appears when you pick the **Layout** button.

Figure 28-1A shows an example of dimensioned views drawn in model space. AutoCAD's predefined acad.dwt drawing template has been used in this example. As a result, when the **Layout** button is selected, a layout named **Layout1** appears. See Figure 28-3. The layout is displayed using default settings based on an 8.5″ × 11″ sheet of paper in a landscape (horizontal) orientation. The white rectangle you see on the grey background is a representation of the sheet. Dashed lines mark the sheet *margins*. A large, rectangular floating viewport reveals model space objects. The acad.dwt drawing template file includes an additional layout named **Layout2**.

margin: The extent of the printable area; objects drawn past the dashed line do not print.

NOTE

Look at the user coordinate system (UCS) icon to confirm whether you are in model space or paper space. When you enter a layout, the UCS icon changes from two arrows to a triangle that indicates the X and Y coordinate directions.

Use the **Model** and **Layout** buttons on the status bar to move back and forth quickly between the most often used layout and model space. Other layouts can be accessed conveniently using the **Quick View Layouts** and **Quick View Drawings** tools, also available from the status bar. These tools offer additional options for controlling layouts and provide the ability to reenter model space.

Figure 28-2.
The status bar provides convenient tools for displaying model space and displaying and managing layouts.

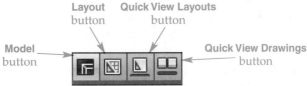

Layout button · Quick View Layouts button · Model button · Quick View Drawings button

---

Figure 28-3.
Layout1 is displayed when the **Layout** button on status bar is selected. This layout is provided in the acad.dwt file.

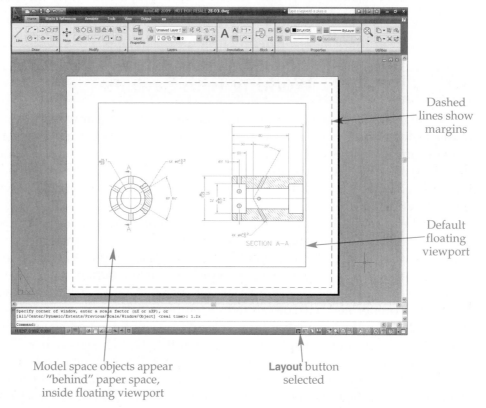

Dashed lines show margins

Default floating viewport

Model space objects appear "behind" paper space, inside floating viewport

Layout button selected

NOTE

Several settings that affect the display of layouts are contained in the **Layout elements** area of the **Display** tab in the **Options** dialog box. Use the default settings until you are comfortable working with layouts.

Exercise 28-1
Complete the exercise on the Student CD.

Using the Quick View Layouts Tool

The **Quick View Layouts** tool is used to display and adjust layouts in the current drawing file. The quickest way to access the **Quick View Layouts** tool is to pick the **Quick View Layouts** button on the status bar. The visual display of this tool allows you to select and display the appropriate layout and control existing layouts without actually changing layouts or entering paper space.

The **Quick View Layouts** tool is similar to the **Quick View Drawings** tool, described in Chapter 2. When accessed, the **Quick View Layouts** tool appears in the lower center of the AutoCAD window. See **Figure 28-4.** The **Model** thumbnail image is displayed on the left, followed by a thumbnail image of each layout in the current drawing with the layout name below each image. Layouts are arranged in the order they are created,

Figure 28-4.
The **Quick View Layouts** tool offers an effective visual method for changing between model space and paper space and provides options for managing layouts.

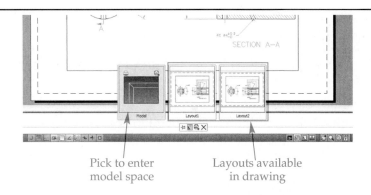

Pick to enter model space

Layouts available in drawing

Figure 28-5.
Hover over a thumbnail to display **Plot...** and **Publish...** buttons.

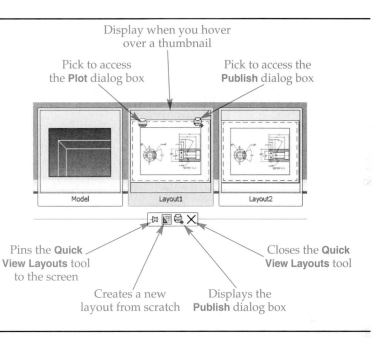

Display when you hover over a thumbnail

Pick to access the **Plot** dialog box

Pick to access the **Publish** dialog box

Pins the **Quick View Layouts** tool to the screen

Creates a new layout from scratch

Displays the **Publish** dialog box

Closes the **Quick View Layouts** tool

from left to right. Hover the cursor over a thumbnail image to highlight the image and show additional options. See **Figure 28-5.** Pick a layout thumbnail to enter paper space with the selected layout current, or pick the **Model** thumbnail to reenter model space.

> **NOTE**
>
> Layouts are represented by an icon until you enter the layout for the first time (initialize the layout). The icon then changes to a thumbnail image of the layout.

The **Quick View Layouts** tool provides a small toolbar below the thumbnail images, as shown in **Figure 28-5.** By default, the **Quick View Layouts** tool disappears when you pick a thumbnail to switch layouts or enter model space. To keep the tool on-screen after you select a thumbnail, pick the **Pin Quick View Layouts** button on the left side of the toolbar. Pick the **New Layout** button to create a new layout from scratch. Creating new layouts is described later in this chapter. Pick the **Publish...** button to access the **Publish** dialog box, covered in Chapter 33. Select the **Close** button to exit the **Quick View Layouts** tool.

Right-click on a thumbnail image to access a shortcut menu of options used for controlling layouts. Pick the **Activate Model Tab** option to enter model space. Select the **Activate Previous Layout** option to make the previously current layout current. Pick the **Select All Layouts** option to select all layouts in the current drawing. This is a valuable option for selecting all layouts for editing purposes, such as deleting, or for publishing. In addition to these basic functions, the shortcut menu is the primary resource for adding layouts and moving, renaming, and deleting existing layouts. Options available from the shortcut menu are described when applicable throughout this textbook.

Using the Quick View Drawings Tool

The **Quick View Drawings** tool was introduced in Chapter 2 as a means of working with multiple open documents. It provides the same features for working with layouts as the **Quick View Layouts** tool, but **Quick View Drawings** allows you to manage the layouts found in all open drawings. Use this tool to increase productivity when you are working between existing drawings. The quickest way to access the **Quick View Drawings** tool is to pick the **Quick View Drawings** button on the status bar. Refer to Chapter 2 for more information on the basic features of the **Quick View Drawings** tool, including information about using the tool to work with multiple open documents.

After opening the **Quick View Drawings** tool, hover the cursor over the drawing file you want to control. The model and layout thumbnail images appear above the highlighted drawing. Move the cursor over the model or a layout thumbnail to enlarge the display. See Figure 28-6. Pick a layout thumbnail to switch to the highlighted file and enter paper space with the selected layout active, or pick the **Model** thumbnail to switch to the highlighted file in model space. Right-click on a thumbnail to access the same shortcut menu displayed when you right-click on a thumbnail using the **Quick View Layouts** tool. Right-clicking on the thumbnail makes the associated file current.

Figure 28-6.
The **Quick View Drawings** tool can also be used to manage layouts located in other open files. Hover over a file thumbnail to display model and layout thumbnails for the file.

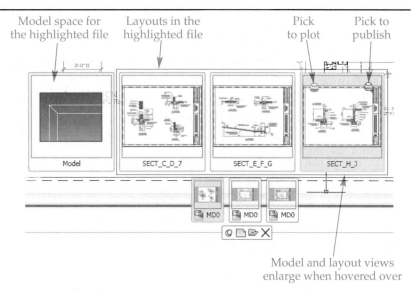

Model space for the highlighted file   Layouts in the highlighted file   Pick to plot   Pick to publish

Model   SECT_C_D_7   SECT_E_F_G   SECT_H_J

Model and layout views enlarge when hovered over

Adding Layouts

There are several ways to add new layouts to a drawing. You can create a new layout from scratch or use the **Create Layout** wizard. Usually, however, it is best to reference an existing layout that is already set up, if available. You can insert an existing layout from a different DWG, DWT, or DXF file into the current file, or create a copy of a layout from the current file.

Starting from scratch

To create a new layout from scratch, right-click on a thumbnail image in the **Quick View Layouts** or **Quick View Drawings** display, or right-click on the **Quick View Layouts** button on the status bar and pick the **New Layout** option. A new layout appears on the far right of the list of layouts. The settings applied to the new layout differ depending on the template file used to create the original file. For example, when you add a new layout to a drawing started from the acad.dwt drawing template file, the new layout is named **Layout3** and includes an 8.5" × 11" sheet of paper, a landscape (horizontal) orientation, and a large floating viewport. The layout is named according to the names of other existing layouts. The acad.dwt drawing template file already includes layouts named **Layout1** and **Layout2**.

Using the Create Layout wizard

Use the **Create Layout** wizard to build a layout from scratch using values and options you enter in the wizard. The pages of the wizard guide you through the process of developing the layout. They provide options for naming the new layout and selecting a printer, paper size, drawing units, paper orientation, title block, and viewport configuration.

Type
LAYOUTWIZARD
Menu Browser
Insert
> Layout
>Create Layout
Wizard
>Tools
> Wizards
> Create
Layout...

LAYOUTWIZARD

Using a template

To create a new layout from a layout stored in an existing DWG, DWT, or DXF file, right-click on a thumbnail image in the **Quick View Layouts** or **Quick View Drawings** display, or right-click on the **Quick View Layouts** button on the status bar, and pick the **From Template...** option. When you select this option, the **Select Template From File** dialog box appears. See **Figure 28-7A.** The Template folder in the path set by the AutoCAD Drawing Template File Location is selected by default.

Select the file containing the layout(s) you want to add to the current drawing and pick the **Open** button. The **Insert Layout(s)** dialog box appears. See **Figure 28-7B.** This dialog box lists all layouts in the selected file. Highlight the layout(s) you want to copy and pick the **OK** button.

Figure 28-7.
Adding a layout
using an existing
layout stored
in a different
drawing, drawing
template, or DXF
file. A—Select the
file containing the
layout. B—Highlight
the layout(s) to be
added to the current
drawing.

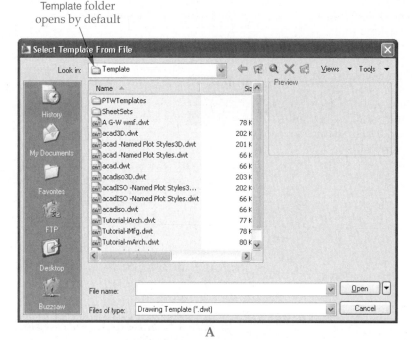

Template folder
opens by default

A

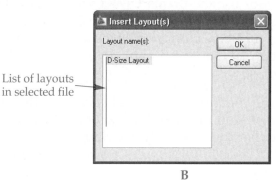

List of layouts
in selected file

B

Using DesignCenter

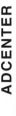
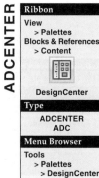

ADCENTER

Ribbon
View
> Palettes
Blocks & References
> Content

DesignCenter

Type
ADCENTER
ADC

Menu Browser
Tools
> Palettes
> DesignCenter

DesignCenter can also be used to insert existing layouts into the current drawing. The **Folders** tab of the **DesignCenter** shows the hierarchy of files and folders on your computer, including network drives. The **Open Drawings** tab displays all of the drawing files open in the current AutoCAD session. The **History** tab displays the files most recently accessed in **DesignCenter**. The **DC Online** tab gives you access to drawing content that can be downloaded from the Internet.

To view the layouts defined in a drawing, select the **Layouts** branch in the tree view or double-click on the **Layouts** icon in the content area. See **Figure 28-8.** Select the layout(s) to be copied from the content area and then drag and drop to insert the layouts in the current drawing, or use the **Add Layout(s)** or **Copy** and **Paste** options from the shortcut menu.

Copying and moving layouts

To use the **Quick View Layouts** or **Quick View Drawings** to create a copy of a layout located in the current file, right-click on the thumbnail image of the layout you want to copy, or make the layout you want to copy current and right-click on the **Quick View Layouts** button on the status bar. Then pick the **Move or Copy...** option to display the **Move or Copy** dialog box. See **Figure 28-9.** Select the **Create a copy** check box and pick the layout that you want to appear to the right of the new layout, or pick (move to end) to place the copy at the far right, past all other layouts. By default, the new layout is automatically

Figure 28-8.
Layouts can be shared between drawings using **DesignCenter**.

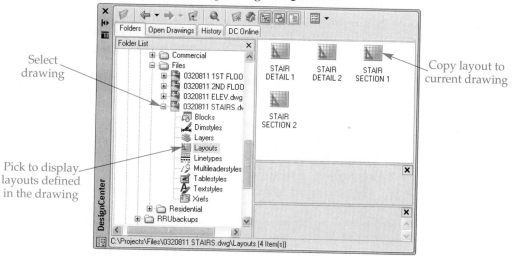

Select drawing

Pick to display layouts defined in the drawing

Copy layout to current drawing

Figure 25-9.
The **Move or Copy** dialog box allows you to reorganize layouts and copy layouts within a drawing.

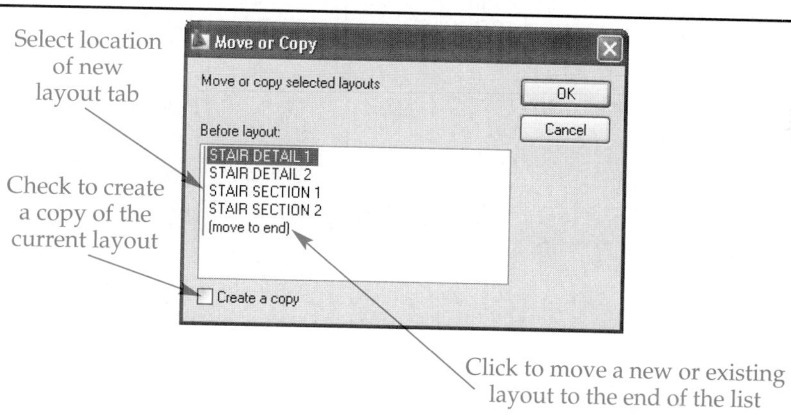

Select location of new layout tab

Check to create a copy of the current layout

Click to move a new or existing layout to the end of the list

assigned the name of the current or selected layout plus a number in parentheses. Use the **Rename** option, described later in this chapter, to rename the layout.

As the name implies, the **Move or Copy** dialog box is also used to move layouts. When you add and rename layouts, the layouts do not automatically rearrange into a predetermined order. Layouts should be organized in an appropriate order to reduce confusion and aid in the publishing process, described in Chapter 33. A layout is moved using the **Move or Copy** dialog box in the same way as a layout is copied, except that you do not select the **Create a copy** check box.

Renaming Layouts

Layouts are easier to recognize and use when they have descriptive names. To rename a layout, right-click on the layout thumbnail image you want to rename in the **Quick View Layouts** or **Quick View Drawings** display. Pick the **Rename** option, or double-click slowly on the current name. The layout name becomes highlighted. Type the new name to be applied to the layout and press [Enter].

Deleting Layouts

To delete an unused layout from the drawing, right-click on the thumbnail image of the layout you want to remove in the **Quick View Layouts** or **Quick View Drawings** display, and pick the **Delete** option. An alert message warns you that the layout will be permanently deleted. Pick the **OK** button to delete the layout.

Exporting a Layout to Model Space

The **EXPORTLAYOUT** tool is used to save the layout display as a separate DWG file. This tool produces a "snapshot" of the current layout display that can be used for applications when it is necessary to combine model space and paper space objects, such as when you want to export a file as an image (model space and paper space do not export together as an image).

The quickest way to access the **EXPORTLAYOUT** tool is to right-click on the thumbnail image of the layout you want to export in the **Quick View Layouts** or **Quick View Drawings** display. Pick the **Export Layout to Model…** option to display the **Export Layout to Model Space** dialog box. This dialog box functions much like the **Save As** dialog box. Pick a location for the file and use the default file name, or enter a different name and pick the **SAVE** button. Everything shown in the layout, including objects drawn in model space, are converted to model space and are saved as a new file.

> **CAUTION**
>
> The **EXPORTLAYOUT** tool eliminates the relationship between model space and paper space. It should only be used when it is necessary to export model space and paper space together as a single unit.

Exercise 28-2
Complete the exercise on the Student CD.

Initial Layout Setup

Preparing a layout for plotting involves creating and modifying floating viewports, adjusting plot settings, and adding layout content such as symbols, a border, and a title block. This chapter focuses on the process of preparing layouts for plotting using the **Page Setup Manager**. When you complete this initial phase, you will be better prepared to add content to layouts and create and manage floating viewports, as described in Chapter 29.

page setup: A saved collection of settings required to create a finished plot of a drawing.

Most settings that determine how a drawing is plotted are established in a *page setup*. These settings include printer selection, paper size and orientation, the plot area and offset, plot scale, plot style, and other settings. In Chapter 5 you were introduced to these settings as they are found in the **Plot** dialog box. The same settings can be defined using the **Page Setup** dialog box, accessed from the **Page Setup Manager**. The **Page Setup** and **Plot** dialog boxes are very similar, except that the **Plot** dialog box provides a few additional plot options that are specific to creating a print.

The **Page Setup Manager** and related **Page Setup** dialog box are used to create and modify saved page setups that control how layouts appear on-screen and plot. This is where initial layout setup occurs. The **Plot** dialog box is then used to create the actual plot using the saved page setup.

> **PROFESSIONAL TIP**
>
> Layout setup usually involves several steps. Once a layout is set up, only a few steps are required to produce a plot. Add fully defined layouts to your drawing templates for convenient future use.

AutoCAD and Its Applications—Basics

Working with Page Setups

A well-defined page setup decreases the amount of time required to prepare a drawing for plotting. Access the **PAGESETUP** tool to create page setups using the **Page Setup Manager**. See Figure 28-10.

The **Page Setup Manager** is also available by right-clicking on a layout in the **Quick View Layouts** or **Quick View Drawings** display, or directly on the **Quick View Layouts** button of the status bar, and selecting the **Page Setup Manager...** menu option. The **Page setups** area of the **Page Setup Manager** contains a **Page Setups** list box that lists available page setups, as well as buttons to add and modify page setups. Information about the highlighted page setup is provided in the **Selected page setup details** area.

When you access the **Page Setup Manager** in model space, *Model* is displayed in the **Page Setups** list box by default. When you access the **Page Setup Manager** in paper space, the current layout is displayed in the **Page Setups** list box by default. When you are preparing a layout for plotting, check to be sure that you are in paper space and the appropriate layout is current.

Each layout can have a unique page setup. The page setup tied to the current layout is recognized by asterisks (*) before and after the layout name. Additional page setups can be created and used instead of the page setup associated with the layout.

Pick the **New...** button to create a new page setup using the **New Page Setup** dialog box. See Figure 28-11. Type a name for the new page setup and choose an option from the **Start with:** list box. When you pick the **OK** button to create the page setup, the **Page Setup** dialog box appears. The **Page Setup** dialog box is described later in this chapter.

Create a new page setup whenever you want to use different plot characteristics without overriding plot settings or spending time making page setup changes. For example, you can create two page setups to provide the option of plotting to two different printers or plotters. Pick the **Import...** button to use existing page setups from a DWG, DWT, or DXF file.

Figure 25-10.
Use the **Page Setup Manager** to modify existing page setups and to create and import page setups.

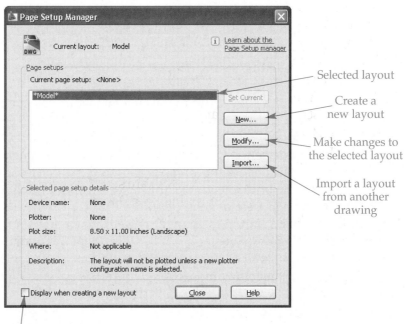

Selected layout

Create a new layout

Make changes to the selected layout

Import a layout from another drawing

When checked, the **Page Setup Manager** opens when a new layout is created

Figure 25-11.
The **New Page Setup** dialog box appears when you create a new page setup. Selecting None in the **Start with:** list box does not select a printer. **Default** selects the computer's default printer.

New page setup name

Select a layout to copy its settings

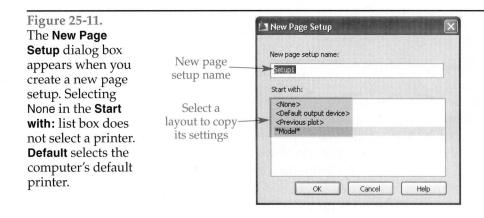

Figure 25-12.
The **Page Setup** dialog box is used to adjust the plot settings for the selected page setup. This is where the initial phase of layout setup begins.

Current layout

Page setup name

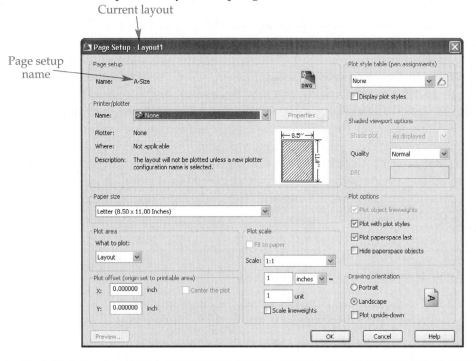

To attach a different page setup to the current layout, select a page setup from the list, and pick the **Set Current** button, or right-click on the page setup and choose the **Set Current** menu option. The layout can now plot according to the selected page setup. When you make a different page setup current, the selected page setup overrides the layout page setup. The page setup name is shown in parentheses next to the name of the layout. To rename or delete an existing page setup, right-click on the page setup and pick the **Rename** or **Delete** menu option.

Select the **Modify…** button to change the settings of an existing page setup using the **Page Setup** dialog box. See **Figure 28-12.** The **Page Setup** dialog box defines page setup characteristics. These settings control layout appearance and plot function. Each area, as described in the following sections, controls a specific plot setting.

plot device (output device): The printer, plotter, or alternative plotting system to which the drawing is sent. Also called an *output device*.

Selecting a Plot Device

The **Printer/plotter** area of the **Page Setup** dialog box, shown in **Figure 28-13**, is used to select the appropriate *plot device* and adjust the plot device configuration

Figure 25-13.
The **Printer/plotter** area of the **Page Setup** dialog box.

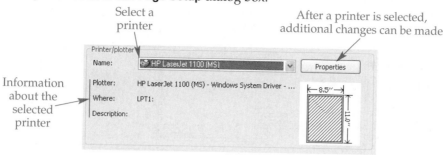

Select a printer

After a printer is selected, additional changes can be made

Information about the selected printer

if necessary. Information about the current plot device is displayed. By default, no plot device is selected, as indicated by the None setting. If a plot device is configured (installed and ready to use), select the plot device you want to plot to from the **Name:** drop-down list.

Plotter Configuration

For more information about managing and configuring plot devices, refer to the Student CD: Supplemental Materials > Plotter Configuration.

Choosing a Sheet Size

The **Paper size** area of the **Page Setup** dialog box, shown in **Figure 28-14,** controls the sheet size. Drafters often think of the drawing size as *sheet size*. Sheet size takes into account the size of the drawing and additional space for dimensions, notes, and clear space between the drawing and border lines. The sheet size also includes space for the title block, the revision block, zoning, and an area for general notes.

sheet size: The size of the paper you use to lay out and plot the final drawing.

The sheet size determines the size of the virtual sheet of paper displayed in a layout, as well as the actual sheet size you plan to use when plotting. Select the appropriate sheet size from the drop-down list in the **Paper size** area.

Standard sheet sizes

American Society of Mechanical Engineers (ASME) and American National Standards Institute (ANSI) standard sheet sizes and formats are specified in the documents ASME Y14.1, *Decimal Inch Drawing Sheet Size and Format,* and ASME Y14.1M, *Metric Drawing Sheet Size and Format.* ASME Y14.1 lists sheet size specifications in inches, as follows:

Figure 25-14.
The **Paper size** area is used to define the sheet size applied to the layout, which corresponds to the sheet size on which you plan to plot.

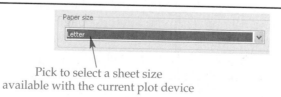

Pick to select a sheet size available with the current plot device

Figure 28-15.
A—Standard drawing sheet sizes (ASME Y14.1). B—Standard metric drawing sheet sizes
(ASME Y14.1M).

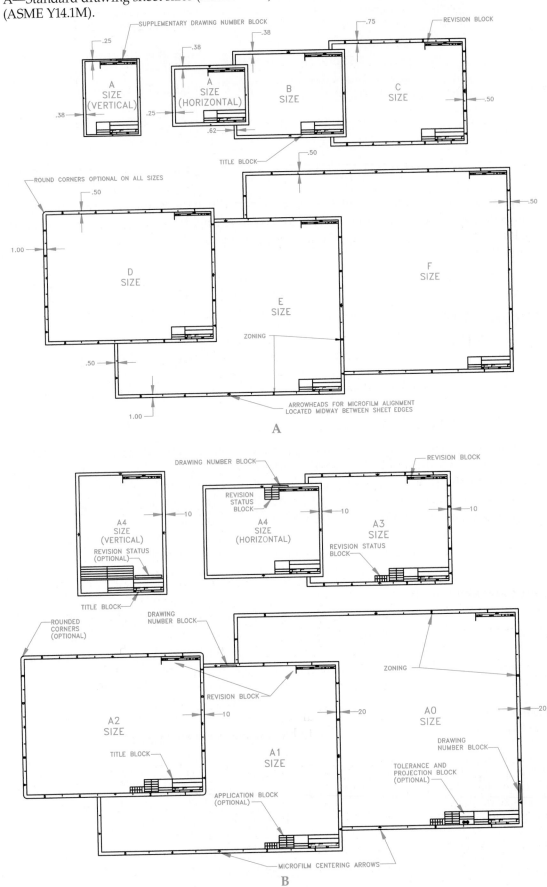

Size Designation	Size (in inches)	
	Vertical	Horizontal
A	8 1/2	11 (horizontal format)
	11	8 1/2 (vertical format)
B	11	17
C	17	22
D	22	34
E	34	44
F	28	40
Sizes G, H, J, and K are roll sizes.		

ASME Y14.1M provides sheet size specifications in metric units. Standard metric drawing sheet sizes are designated as follows:

Size Designation	Size (in millimeters)	
	Vertical	Horizontal
A0	841	1189
A1	594	841
A2	420	594
A3	297	420
A4	210	297

Longer lengths are referred to as elongated and extra-elongated drawing sizes. These are available in multiples of the short side of the sheet size. Figure 28-15 shows standard ASME/ANSI sheet sizes. When verbally stating sheet size values, the horizontal measurement is generally followed by the vertical measurement. For example, a C-size sheet is described as 22 (horizontal) × 17 (vertical).

Specifying the Drawing Orientation

The **Drawing orientation** area of the **Page Setup** dialog box controls the plot rotation. Landscape orientation is the most common engineering drawing orientation and is set by default in most AutoCAD-supplied templates. Portrait orientation is the standard for most written documents printed on 8.5″ × 11″ paper.

Pick the **Plot upside-down** check box to produce variations of the standard landscape and portrait orientations. See Figure 28-16. When you select an upside-down orientation, it may help to consider landscape format to be a rotation angle of 0° and portrait format to be a rotation angle of 90°. Therefore, an upside-down landscape format rotates the drawing 180° and an upside-down portrait orientation rotates the drawing 270°. Use the preview image to help select the appropriate orientation.

PROFESSIONAL TIP

The way in which a sheet feeds into a printer or plotter can affect the sheet size and drawing orientation you select. Sheets of paper, especially large sheets, often feed into a plotter with the short side of the sheet entering first. This may require you to use a sheet size that orients the sheet in a portrait format, for example D-Size 22x34 instead of D-Size 34x22, while still using a landscape drawing orientation.

Chapter 28   Working with Layouts

Figure 28-16.
The **Drawing
orientation** area
contains options
for adjusting the
drawing angle of
rotation.

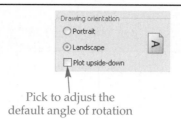

Pick to adjust the
default angle of rotation

Exercise 28-3
Complete the exercise on the Student CD.

Choosing the Plot Area

The **Plot area** section of the **Page Setup** dialog box, shown in **Figure 28-17**, allows you to choose the portion of the drawing to be plotted. Select an option from the **What to plot:** drop-down list. The **Layout** option is available when you plot a layout. When this option is selected, everything inside the margins of the layout is plotted. Plotting the layout using the **Layout** option is the default and most common setting for plotting a layout. Other plot area options are used primarily when plotting model space or when it is necessary to adjust the area plotted in paper space.

The **View** option is available when named views exist in the drawing. The option also appears only if a named view was created in the model space or paper space environment associated with the current page setup. When you pick the **View** option, an additional drop-down list appears in the **Plot area** section, allowing you to select a specific view to define as the plot area. Named views are described in Chapter 6. Refer to Chapter 5 for information about other **Plot area** options.

Defining the Plot Offset

The **Plot offset** area of the **Page Setup** dialog box, shown in **Figure 28-18**, controls how far the drawing is offset from the plot origin. The plot origin can be defined as the lower-left corner of the printable area or the lower-left corner of the sheet, depending on the radio button selected in the **Specify plot offset relative to** area in the **Plot and Publish** tab of the **Options** dialog box.

Figure 28-17.
Use the **Plot area** section to define what portion of the drawing is plotted.

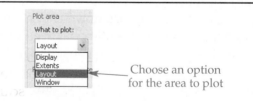

Choose an option
for the area to plot

Figure 28-18.
The **Plot offset** area controls how far the drawing is offset from the lower-left corner of the printable area or layout border.

Enter offset from
lower-left corner

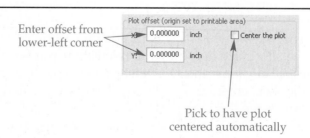

Pick to have plot
centered automatically

When the default **Printable area** radio button is selected in the **Options** dialog box, the **Plot offset (origin set to printable area)** title appears. The values you enter in the **X:** and **Y:** text boxes define the offset from the printable area. Use the default values of 0.000 to locate the plot origin at the lower-left corner of the printable area, which corresponds to the lower-left corner of the layout margin (dashed rectangle). To move the drawing away from the default printable area origin, change the values in the text boxes. For example, to move the drawing one unit to the right and two units above the lower-left corner of the margin, enter 1 in the **X:** text box and 2 in the **Y:** text box. Negative values can also be used.

When the **Edge of paper** radio button is selected in the **Options** dialog box, the **Plot offset (origin set to layout border)** title appears. When this option is active, the values you enter in the **X:** and **Y:** text boxes define the offset from the edge of the sheet. Use the default values of 0.000 to locate the plot origin at the lower-left corner of the sheet. To move the drawing away from the sheet origin, change the values in the text boxes.

When you select any of the options from the **What to plot:** drop-down list in the **Plot area** section, except the **Layout** option, the **Center the plot** check box is enabled. Pick this check box to shift the plot origin automatically as needed to center the selected plot area in the printable area.

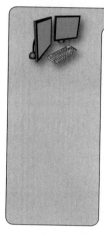

PROFESSIONAL TIP

If your drawing is not centered on the sheet when you plot using the **Layout** area option, open the **Options** dialog box and select the **Plot and Publish** tab. Pick the **Edge of paper** radio button in the **Specify plot offset relative to** area. Then use values of 0.000 in the X and Y offset text boxes in the **Page Setup** dialog box to locate the plot origin at the lower-left corner of the sheet. Depending on the specific plot configuration, you may also need to pick the **Plot upside-down** check box in the **Drawing orientation** area of the **Page Setup** dialog box to locate the origin exactly at the lower-left corner of the sheet. Alternatively, resolve the issue by changing the plot offset to the X and Y values of the lower-left corner of the printable area.

Selecting a Plot Scale

Objects should always be drawn at their actual size, or full scale, in model space, regardless of the size of the objects. For example, if you are drawing a small machine part and the length of a line in the drawing is 2 mm, the line should actually be drawn 2 mm long in model space. Alternatively, if you are drawing a building and the length of a line in the drawing is 80′, the line should actually be drawn 80′ long in model space. For layout and printing purposes, most drawings must therefore be scaled to fit properly on a sheet, according to a specific *drawing scale*.

When you scale a drawing, you increase or decrease the *displayed* size of drawing objects. This is done using a properly scaled floating viewport in a layout. The procedure for scaling floating viewports is described in Chapter 29. When setting up a layout for plotting, remember that the layout is also at full scale. The difference between model space and paper space is that objects in model space can be very large or very small, while objects in paper space always correspond to sheet size. In order for objects on the layout and in model space to appear correctly when plotted, a layout must be plotted at full scale, or 1:1.

The **Plot scale** area of the **Page Setup** dialog box is used to specify the plot scale. See **Figure 28-19**. The **Scale:** drop-down list provides several predefined decimal and architectural scales, as well as a **Custom** option. For most applications, when setting up a layout for plotting, the plot scale is set to 1:1. This ensures that the layout and scaled

drawing scale: The ratio between the actual size of objects in the drawing and the size at which the objects are plotted on a sheet of paper.

Figure 28-19.
Use the **Plot scale** area to adjust the scale at which the drawing is plotted. The plot scale is typically set to 1:1 to plot a layout even though the drawing scale may not be 1:1.

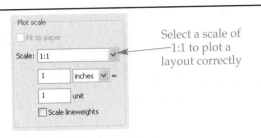

Select a scale of 1:1 to plot a layout correctly

floating viewports plot correctly. If you choose a scale other than 1:1, the layout is not plotted to scale.

NOTE

When preparing to plot in model space, you may choose to select a scale other than 1:1. For example, to plot an architectural floor plan, you might want to set the plot scale to 1/4″ = 1′-0″. If the desired scale is not available, enter values in the text boxes below the predefined scales drop-down list and select the correct unit of measure from the drop-down list. The **Custom** option automatically displays when you enter values. For example, 1 inch = 600 units is a custom scale entry used to plot at a scale of 1″ = 50′ (50′ x 12″ = 600). Refer to Chapter 9 for more information about drawing scale and scale factors.

Pick the **Fit to paper** check box if you want AutoCAD to adjust the plot scale automatically to fit on the selected sheet. This is useful if you are not concerned about plotting to scale, such as when creating a quick "check copy" of your work on a sheet that is too small to plot at the appropriate scale. Select the **Scale lineweights** check box to scale (increase or decrease the weight of) lines when the plot scale changes.

PROFESSIONAL TIP

In the rare event that you need to plot an inch drawing on a metric sheet, use a custom scale of 1 inch = 25.4 unit. Conversely, use a custom scale of 25.4 mm = 1 unit to plot a metric drawing on an inch sheet.

Exercise 28-4

Complete the exercise on the Student CD.

Using Plot Styles

The appearance of objects on-screen is controlled by object properties. By default, what you see on-screen is what is plotted. For example, if you draw objects on a layer that uses the color Red, Continuous linetype, and 0.60 mm lineweight, the objects are displayed and plotted red, continuous, and thick, assuming you show lineweights on-screen and use a color plotter. If this situation is desirable, you are ready to continue with the page setup and plotting process.

However, if you want to define exactly how objects are plotted, regardless of what is displayed on-screen, you must assign *plot styles* to objects. Use plot styles to maintain object properties in the drawing, but plot objects according to specific plotting properties. For example, all of the objects in a drawing are often plotted as dark as possible, which requires all objects use the color Black when plotted. In this example, plot styles allow you to plot all objects black without making them black on-screen. Plot styles are also used when it is necessary to plot objects using shades of gray instead of color, or to plot objects lighter or darker than they are displayed on-screen.

plot styles: Properties, including color, linetype, lineweight, line end treatment, and fill style, that are applied to objects for plotting purposes only.

Plot style tables

Plot styles are contained in *plot style tables*. You can choose to use either a *color-dependent plot style table* or a *named plot style table*. When you use a color-dependent plot style table, objects are plotted according to the color of the object. Color-dependent plot style tables contain 256 preset plot styles—one for each AutoCAD Color Index (ACI) color. Each color-dependent plot style is linked to an index color. Plot style properties control how objects of a certain color are treated when plotted. For example, the plot style Color 1, which is Red, defines how all red objects on-screen are plotted. If plot style Color 1 is assigned a Black plot color, all objects drawn using a Red color are plotted black, even though the objects are red on-screen.

plot style table: A configuration, saved as a separate file, which groups plot styles and provides complete control over plot style settings.

color-dependent plot style table: A file that contains plot style settings used to assign plot values to object color.

When you use a named plot style table, drawing objects are plotted according to named plot style values, which can be assigned to a layer or object. Any layer or object assigned a named plot style is plotted using the settings specified for that plot style. For example, say you create a layer named OBJECT that uses the color Red, and you create a plot style named BLACK that uses the color Black. Then you assign the BLACK plot style to the OBJECT layer. Objects drawn on the OBJECT layer plot using the BLACK plot style and plot black in color, even though the objects are red on-screen.

named plot style table: A file that contains plot style settings used to assign plot values to objects or layers.

Ideally, you should decide which plot style table is appropriate for your application before you begin drawing. The templates created in the Template Development feature of this textbook, for example, assume that drawings are plotted so that all objects appear dark, or black, with different object linetypes and lineweights. Either a color-dependent plot style table or a named plot style table can be used to create this effect. Default AutoCAD plot style behavior is set to use color-dependent plot style tables. For basic applications, it is usually best to use color-dependent plot style tables, because they are used by default and do not require you to assign named plot styles to layers or objects.

Configuring plot style table type

You must choose a plot style table type (color-dependent or named) to apply to new drawings *before* you start a new drawing file, unless you use a template that already is assigned a plot style table type. The plot style table type used by default when you create new drawings is configured in the **Options** dialog box. Pick the **Plot Style Table Settings...** button in the **Plot and Publish** tab of the **Options** dialog box. This opens the **Plot Style Table Settings** dialog box. See Figure 28-20.

When you create a new drawing, you can control the type of plot style tables that are available by selecting the appropriate radio button in the **Default plot style behavior for new drawings** area. To use a named plot style table, pick the **Use named plot styles** radio button *before* you start a new drawing file. Select a specific plot style table to use as the default for new drawings from the **Default plot style table:** drop-down list in the **Current plot style table settings** area. When the **Use named plot styles** radio button is selected, the **Default plot style for layer 0:** and **Default plot style for objects:** options are enabled.

Figure 28-20.
Use the **Plot and Publish** tab of the **Options** dialog box to set up default plot style modes and tables for new drawings.

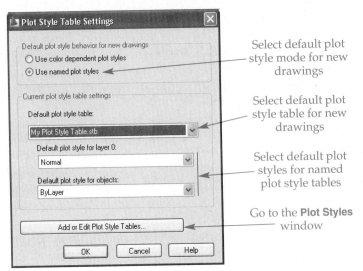

Select default plot style mode for new drawings

Select default plot style table for new drawings

Select default plot styles for named plot style tables

Go to the **Plot Styles** window

> **NOTE**
>
> When you use a template to create a new drawing, the plot style settings defined in the template override the settings you specify in the **Plot Style Table Settings** dialog box. For example, if the template is configured to use named plot style tables, you can only select a named plot style table to apply to the plot, even if the **Use color dependent plot styles** radio button is selected in the **Plot Style Table Settings** dialog box.

STYLESMANAGER

Ribbon
Output
> Plot

Plot Style Manager

Type
STYLESMANAGER

Menu Browser
File
> Plot Style Manager

Pick the **Add or Edit Plot Style Tables...** button to open the **Plot Styles** window. See **Figure 28-21**. The **Plot Styles** window lists all available color-dependent and named plot style tables that are saved in the Plot Style Table Search Path, as defined in the expanded **Printer Support File Path** option in the **Files** tab of the **Options** dialog box. Color-dependent plot style table files (CTB files) are identified by the .ctb extension. Named plot style table files (STB files) have an .stb extension. Double-click on **Add-A-Plot Style Table Wizard** to create a new plot style table, or double-click on an existing plot style table file to edit the file.

Creating and Editing Plot Style Tables
The plot style tables supplied with AutoCAD are appropriate for many plotting applications. However, if you decide the supplied plot style tables do not meet your needs, you can create new plot style tables and edit plot style properties. Refer to the Student CD: Supplemental Materials > Creating and Editing Plot Style Tables for detailed information on creating and editing plot style tables.

Selecting a plot style table

Use the **Plot style table (pen assignments)** area of the **Page Setup** dialog box, shown in **Figure 28-22,** to activate and manage plot style tables. Select a plot style table to use from the drop-down list. The **None** option is default and can be used instead of selecting a specific color-dependent or named plot style table. Select **None** to plot exactly what is shown on-screen, without using plot styles, assuming you use a color plotter to plot objects with color.

Predefined plot style tables are also available. These plot style table files are found in the **Plot Styles** window. Only color-dependent or named plot style tables are listed, depending on the plot style tables assigned to the current drawing. The most often used color-dependent plot style tables are:

- Monochrome.ctb—plots the drawing in monochrome (black and white).
- Grayscale.ctb—plots the drawing using shades of gray.
- One of the screening files—plots the drawing using faded, or screened, colors.

When you are using named plot style tables, it is common to select one of the following:

- Autodesk-Color.stb—provides access to named plot styles for plotting the drawing using solid and faded colors.
- Monochrome.stb—references a named plot style for plotting the drawing in monochrome.
- Autodesk-MONO.stb—provides access to named plot styles that can be used to plot objects monochrome, in color, and in faded monochrome.

Figure 28-21.
The **Plot Styles** window lists all available plot style files and can be used to create and edit plot style tables.

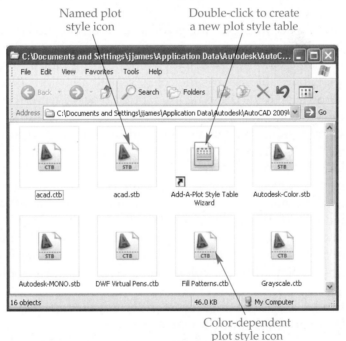

Figure 28-22.
Use the **Plot style table (pen assignments)** area to select, create, and edit plot style tables.

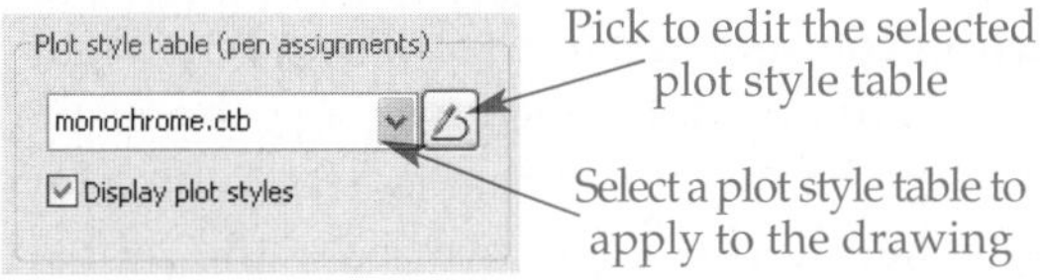

Exercise 28-5

Complete the exercise on the Student CD.

Applying plot styles

Once you select a plot style table from the drop-down list in the **Plot style table (pen assignments)** area of the **Page Setup** dialog box, the plot styles contained in the selected plot style table are ready to be assigned to objects in the drawing. When you select a color-dependent plot style table, the plot styles are automatically applied to objects in the drawing according to the color of the objects. No additional steps are required to apply color-dependent plot styles to objects. The property values set for the plot styles override the on-screen display values during plotting. For example, the monochrome.ctb plot style table assigns the color Black to all colors. When you use this plot style table, all objects in the drawing are plotted black, even if the objects display different colors on-screen.

When you select a named plot style table, the named plot styles contained in the table are available for use and can be applied to layers or to individual objects. Any layer or object assigned a named style is plotted using the settings specified for that style. Named plot style tables contain as many named plot styles as have been created. For example, the monochrome.stb plot style table contains the default Normal plot style and a style named Style 1. When you apply the Normal plot style to layers or objects, objects plot exactly as they appear on-screen. Style 1 assigns the color Black to all layers or objects that use Style 1 for plotting. In order to plot all objects in the drawing black, even if the objects display different colors on-screen, you must apply Style 1 to all layers.

Named plot styles are assigned to layers in the **Layer Properties Manager** palette. See Figure 28-23. Identify the layer to which you want to assign a named plot style and select the default plot style, such as **Normal,** from the **Plot Style** column. The **Select Plot Style** dialog box appears. See Figure 28-24. Select a named style to assign it to the highlighted layer. Any object drawn on a layer assigned to a named plot style plots using the settings in the named plot style.

Named plot styles can also be assigned to individual objects. If a plot style is attached to an object that is drawn on a layer assigned a named plot style, the plot style attached to the object overrides the plot style settings assigned to the layer. Plot styles can be assigned to objects using the **Properties** palette or the **Plot Style Control** drop-down list in the **Properties** panel on the **Home** tab of the ribbon. See Figure 28-25.

AutoCAD and Its Applications—Basics

NOTE

If the current drawing is set to use a named plot style table, the default plot style for all layers is Normal. The default plot style for all objects is ByLayer. Objects plotted with these settings keep their original properties.

Exercise 28-6

Complete the exercise on the Student CD.

Figure 28-23.
Named plot styles are assigned to layers using the **Layer Properties Manager** palette.

Pick plot style name for layer to select a different plot style

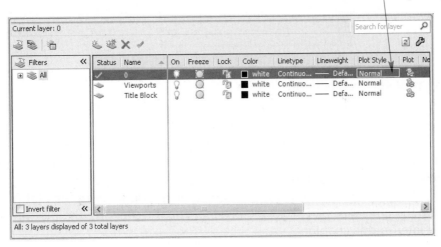

Figure 28-24.
Use the **Select Plot Style** dialog box to select a plot style to assign to a layer.

Pick plot style for layer from list of plot styles in plot style table

Current plot style table

Access **Plot Style Table Editor** dialog box

Identifies current layout tab

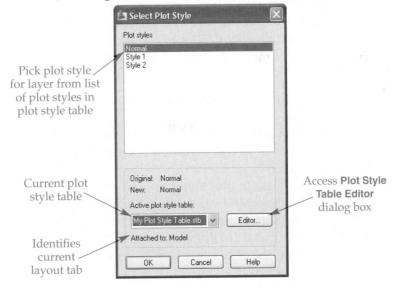

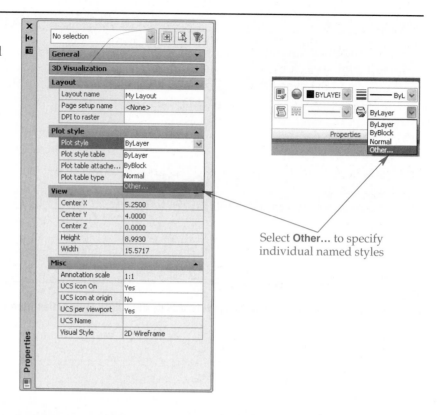

Figure 28-25.
A plot style can be assigned individual objects using the **Properties** palette or the **Plot Style Control** drop-down list in the ribbon.

Select **Other...** to specify individual named styles

Viewing plot style effects on-screen

To display plot style effects on-screen, pick the **Display plot styles** check box in the **Plot style table** area in the **Page Setup** dialog box. Objects on-screen appear as they will plot. Typically, it is not appropriate to work with objects displayed as they will plot, especially if you print in monochrome. In this example, the color assigned to a layer appears black, which defeats the purpose of assigning unique colors to layers. A better practice is to use the preview feature of the **Page Setup** or **Plot** dialog box to preview the effects of plot styles before plotting. Previewing the plot on-screen is described later in this chapter.

Shaded Viewport Options

The settings that control viewport shading are found in the **Shaded viewport options** area of the **Page Setup** dialog box. These options set the type and quality of shading for a plot and apply to plotting 3D models from a shaded or rendered viewport. 3D models are explained in *AutoCAD and Its Applications—Advanced*.

Other Plotting Options

The **Plot options** area of the **Page Setup** dialog box contains additional plot options that affect how specific items are plotted. If you plan to plot objects using a plot style table, make sure the **Plot with plot styles** check box is selected. The main purpose of this check box is to toggle the use of plot styles on and off. This allows you to create a plot quickly with or without using plot styles.

When you deselect the **Plot with plot styles** check box, the **Plot object lineweights** check box is enabled, and it is selected by default. When it is selected, all objects with a lineweight greater than 0 are plotted using the assigned lineweight. Deselect the check box to plot all objects using a 0, or thin, lineweight.

Pick the **Plot paperspace last** check box to plot paper space objects after model space objects. This option ensures that objects in paper space that overlap objects in model space are plotted on top of model space objects. The **Plot paperspace last** check box is disabled when you plot in model space, because no paper space objects are found in model space. Select the **Hide paperspace objects** check box to remove hidden lines from 3D objects created in paper space. This option is only available when you are plotting from a layout tab and affects only objects drawn in paper space. It does not affect any 3D objects in a viewport.

Completing Page Setup

Once you select all appropriate page setup options, pick the **Preview** button in the lower-left corner of the **Page Setup** dialog box to preview the effects of the page setup. The **Page Setup** dialog box is temporarily hidden and you enter preview mode. What you see on-screen is the exact plot appearance, assuming you use a color plotter to make color prints.

The **Realtime Zoom** tool is activated automatically in the preview window. Additional view tools are available from the toolbar near the top of the window or from a shortcut menu. Use these tools to help confirm that the plot settings are correct. When you finish previewing the plot, press [Esc] or [Enter], or right-click and select the **Exit** option. Selecting **Exit** returns to the **Page Setup** dialog box so you can make any needed changes. Pick the **OK** button to exit the **Page Setup** dialog box, and pick **Close** button to exit the **Page Setup Manager**.

Exercise 28-7
Complete the exercise on the Student CD.

Template Development
Chapter 28

The layouts you use in your drawing files depend on the types of drawings you create and the paper size you use. Because layouts take time and thought to prepare, you should add commonly used layouts to your drawing templates. Refer to the Student CD for detailed instructions to set up appropriate layouts for your mechanical, architectural, and civil drawing templates.

Chapter Test

Answer the following questions. Write your answers on a separate sheet of paper or complete the electronic chapter test on the Student CD.

1. What is a model?
2. Define *model space.*
3. How is a layout used?
4. Define *paper space.*
5. What is a floating viewport?
6. If you pick the **Layout** button to enter paper space and the file contains multiple layouts, none of which has been previously accessed, which layout is displayed by default? Which layout is displayed if a different layout has already been opened?
7. How do you move back and forth quickly between the most often used layout and model space?
8. Briefly describe the function of the **Quick View Layouts** tool.
9. Define *page setup.*
10. Briefly describe the basic function of the **Page Setup Manager** and the related **Page Setup** dialog box.
11. Briefly describe the function of the **Plot** dialog box and when it is used in relation to the **Page Setup Manager** and **Page Setup** dialog box.
12. Identify the importance of a well-defined page setup.
13. How can you identify the page setup that is tied to the current layout?
14. What is a plot device?
15. Define *sheet size.*
16. Which ANSI standards specify sheet sizes?
17. What factors should you consider when you select a sheet size for a drawing?
18. What is the plot offset of a layout?
19. Define *drawing scale.*
20. What are plot styles?
21. Briefly explain the purpose of a plot style table.
22. How are plot styles assigned in a color-dependent plot style?
23. Briefly explain the function of a named plot style table.
24. How can you be certain that your page setup options will produce the desired plot?
25. What is the purpose of the dashed rectangle that appears on the default layout?

Drawing Problems

Note: Some of the following problems refer to drawings or templates created in previous chapters. If you have not yet created those drawings, you will need to do so before working these problems.

▼ Basic

1. Use a word processor to list five items commonly found in a layout. Provide a brief description of each item.

2. Follow the instructions in the Template Development portion of the Student CD to add and set up layouts for the MECHANICAL-INCH template file.

3. Follow the instructions in the Template Development portion of the Student CD to add and set up layouts for the MECHANICAL-METRIC template file.

4. Follow the instructions in the Template Development portion of the Student CD to add and set up layouts for the ARCHITECTURAL-US template file.

5. Follow the instructions in the Template Development portion of the Student CD to add and set up layouts for the ARCHITECTURAL-METRIC template file.

6. Follow the instructions in the Template Development portion of the Student CD to add and set up layouts for the CIVIL-US template file.

7. Follow the instructions in the Template Development portion of the Student CD to add and set up layouts for the CIVIL-METRIC template file.

▼ Intermediate

8. Start a new drawing using the acad.dwt template. Create a plot style table named Black35mm.cbt that will plot all colors in the AutoCAD drawing in black ink on the paper, with a lineweight of 0.35 mm. (*Hint:* To make the same change to a property of all the plot styles, select the first plot style in the list, in this case Color 1, then scroll to the end of the list, hold down the shift key and select the last plot style in the list, in this case Color 255).

9. Start a new drawing using the acad -Named Plot Styles.dwt template. Create a plot style table named BlackShades.stb. Create the following plot styles:
   - Black100% with color set to black, all other properties set to their default values.
   - Black50% with color set to black, screening set to 50, all other properties to their default values.
   - Black25% with color set to black, screening set to 25, all other properties to their default values.
   Save the drawing as P28-9.

10. Open the P8-14 file you created in Problem P8-14. Save a copy of P8-14 as P28-10. Delete the default **Layout2**. Create a new B-size sheet layout according to the following steps:
    A. Rename the default **Layout1** to **B-SIZE**.
    B. Select the **B-SIZE** layout and access the **Page Setup Manager**.
    C. Modify the **B-SIZE** page setup according to the following settings:
       • **Printer/Plotter:** Select a printer or plotter that can plot a B-size sheet
       • **Paper size:** Select the appropriate B-size sheet (varies with printer or plotter)
       • **Plot area:** Layout
       • **Plot offset:** 0,0
       • **Plot scale:** 1:1 (1 inch = 1 unit)
       • **Plot style table:** monochrome.ctb
       • **Plot with plot styles**
       • **Plot paperspace last**
       • Do not check **Hide paperspace objects**
       • **Drawing orientation:** Select the appropriate orientation (varies with printer or plotter)
       Resave P28-10.

11. Open the P8-15 file you created in Problem 8-15. Save a copy of P8-15 as P28-11. Delete the default **Layout2**. Create a new A2-size sheet layout according to the following steps:
    A. Rename the default **Layout1** to **A2-SIZE**.
    B. Select the **A2-SIZE** layout and access the **Page Setup Manager**.
    C. Modify the **A2-SIZE** page setup according to the following settings:
       • **Printer/Plotter:** Select a printer or plotter that can plot an A2-size sheet
       • **Paper size:** Select the appropriate A2-size sheet (varies with printer or plotter)
       • **Plot area:** Layout
       • **Plot offset:** 0,0
       • **Plot scale:** 1:1 (1 mm = 1 unit)
       • **Plot style table:** monochrome.ctb
       • **Plot with plot styles**
       • **Plot paperspace last**
       • Do not check **Hide paperspace objects**
       • **Drawing orientation:** Select the appropriate orientation (varies with printer or plotter)
       Resave P28-11.

12. Open the P8-16 file you created in Problem 8-16. Save a copy of P8-16 as P28-12. Delete the default **Layout2**. Create a new B-size sheet layout according to the following steps:
    A. Rename the default **Layout1** to **B-SIZE**.
    B. Select the **B-SIZE** layout and access the **Page Setup Manager**.
    C. Modify the **B-SIZE** page setup according to the following settings:
       • **Printer/Plotter:** Select a printer or plotter that can plot a B-size sheet
       • **Paper size:** Select the appropriate B-size sheet (varies with printer or plotter)
       • **Plot area:** Layout
       • **Plot offset:** 0,0
       • **Plot scale:** 1:1 (1 inch = 1 unit)
       • **Plot style table:** monochrome.ctb
       • **Plot with plot styles**
       • **Plot paperspace last**

- Do not check **Hide paperspace objects**
- **Drawing orientation:** Select the appropriate orientation (varies with printer or plotter)

Resave P28-12.

▼ Advanced

13. Draw the wood beam details using the dimensions and notes provided. Establish the missing information using your own specifications, or determine the correct size of items not dimensioned. Prepare a single layout for plotting on a C-size sheet, using the monochrome.ctb plot style. Delete all other layouts. Save the drawing as P28-13.

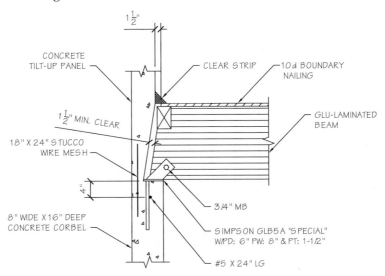

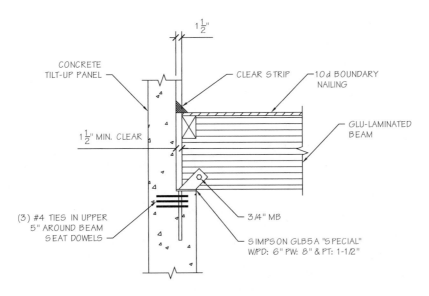

14. Use a word processor to write a report of approximately 250 words explaining the difference between model space and paper space and describing the importance of using layouts. Cite at least three examples from actual industry applications of using layouts to prepare a multi-sheet drawing. Use at least four drawings to illustrate your report.

CHAPTER 29

Plotting Layouts

Learning Objectives

After completing this chapter, you will be able to do the following:

✓ Work in the layout environment.
✓ Use floating viewports.
✓ Preview and plot layouts.

In Chapter 28, you learned the initial steps required to create a print of your drawing from a layout. These steps include managing layouts and creating and modifying page setups. This chapter explores the additional steps used to complete layout setup, including adding content to the layout and placing and using floating viewports. You will also use the **Plot** tool to send the layout to a printer or plotter.

Layout Content

Model space is used to create drawing views and add dimensions and annotations directly to views. Layouts are reserved for adding items such as a border, title block, revision block, general notes, and a bill of materials or parts list. This provides more flexibility for laying out and scaling drawing views. Consider the objects you add to a layout to be *sheet* content and the objects placed in model space to be *drawing* content. A complete drawing is created when sheet and drawing content are brought together. See Figure 29-1.

Drawing in Paper Space

A layout is a representation of a flat piece of paper. As a result, paper space is a 2D drawing environment. Most 2D AutoCAD drawing and editing tools and options described throughout this textbook function the same in paper space as in model space. Some tools, however, are specific to, or most often used in, either model space or paper space. For example, the **Full Navigation Wheel** appears by default when you access the **SteeringWheel** view tool in model space. The **2D Navigation Wheel** appears in paper space and is specific to 2D drafting.

Figure 29-1.
An example of
dimensioned
drawing views
created in model
space; a border, title
block, revision block,
and general notes
created in paper
space; and all items
brought together
to form the final
drawing.

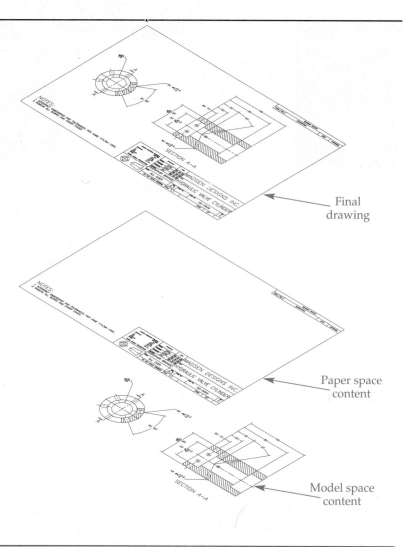

Final
drawing

Paper space
content

Model space
content

NOTE

Although paper space is a 2D environment, 3D models created in model space can be displayed in floating viewports in paper space.

Layout content such as general notes and view titles can be added as multiline or single-line text. A bill of materials, parts list, or similar type of tabular information is placed using the **TABLE** tool or construed using blocks. Most other items, such as the border, title block, and revision block, are best created as blocks that are inserted into the layout. In Chapter 30, you will use attributes to automate the process of assigning information to title blocks, revision blocks, and parts lists.

As in model space, geometry drawn on a layout is created at full scale. One difference between model space and paper space is that objects in model space may be very large or very small, while paper space objects always correspond to the sheet size. All layout content is drawn using the actual size you want the objects to appear on the plotted sheet.

When you draw in paper space, use layers appropriate for the layout and the objects added to the layout. You may want to create a single layer named SHEET, for example, on which you draw all layout content. Another option might be to use layers specific to layout items, such as a BORDER layer to draw or insert the border and a TITLE layer to draw or insert the title block. A layer named VPORT is typically assigned to floating viewports so the viewport boundary can be turned off, frozen, or set to "no plot" before plotting. Floating viewports are explained later in this chapter.

NOTE

The layer that is current when you first access a layout is assigned to the default floating viewport boundary. If you use the default viewport, it may be necessary to change the layer on which it is drawn.

The Layout Origin

Drawing and editing in paper space is most often done on the sheet, which is the white rectangle you see on the grey background. However, it is possible, and necessary in some applications, to create objects off the sheet. When you are drawing and editing on a layout, remember that the origin, or (0,0) point, is controlled by the X and Y values you enter in the **Plot offset** area of the **Page Setup** dialog box. For example, if you draw a line with a start point of (1,1), the line begins 1 unit to the left and 1 unit up from the plot origin. The default origin is located at the lower-left corner of the printable area. See **Figure 29-2.** Refer to Chapter 28 for more information on plot origin and the **Plot offset** area of the **Page Setup** dialog box.

Layout content is often drawn in reference to the edge of the sheet. For example, a border might be positioned 1/2″ inside of the sheet edge. In this situation, it is usually best to define the layout origin as the lower-left corner of the sheet. The best option is to select the **Edge of paper** radio button in the **Specify plot offset relative to** area in the **Publish and Plot** tab of the **Options** dialog box. In the **Plot offset** area of the **Page Setup** dialog box, use values of 0.000 in the X and Y offset text boxes to locate the plot origin at the lower-left corner of the sheet. This is an excellent way to center the drawing on the sheet.

NOTE

Depending on the specific plot configuration, you may need to pick the **Plot upside-down** check box in the **Drawing orientation** area of the **Page Setup** dialog box in addition to using the **Edge of paper** offset option. Draw an object to see if (0,0) is actually located exactly at the lower-left corner of the sheet. If not, pick the **Plot upside-down** check box to solve the problem.

PROFESSIONAL TIP

Defining the plot offset relative to the edge of the paper has the benefit of maintaining the plot offset location from the sheet edge even when a different plotter or plot configuration is used, as long as you use the same sheet size.

Figure 29-2.
The default location of the plot origin is often not appropriate, because all point entry is in reference to the lower-left corner of the printable area. Change the location of the plot origin to define the lower-left corner of the sheet at the (0,0) point when drawing.

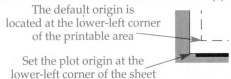

The default origin is located at the lower-left corner of the printable area

Set the plot origin at the lower-left corner of the sheet

A second option is to select the **Printable area** radio button in the **Specify plot offset relative to** area in the **Publish and Plot** tab of the **Options** dialog box. Then identify the values of the lower-right corner of the printable area. This information is available in the **Device and Document Settings** tab of the plotter's **Configuration Editor**. Next, in the **Plot offset** area of the **Page Setup** dialog box, change the X and Y plot offset values to the values of the lower-left corner of the printable area. The values you enter must be negative. The origin is offset from the printable area, which means if you use a different plotter or plot configuration, the printable area can change, causing the offset to shift.

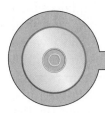

Exercise 29-1
Complete the exercise on the Student CD.

Using Floating Viewports

As described in Chapter 28, floating viewports are used in layouts to display items drawn in model space. The primary advantage of using the layout/floating viewport system is the ability to prepare scaled drawings without increasing or decreasing the actual size of drawing views or sheet content. You can also create multiple viewports on a single layout to show uniquely scaled drawing views. For example, a single sheet might contain a floor plan drawn at a 1/4″ = 1′-0″ scale, an eave detail drawn at a 3/4″ = 1′-0″ scale, and a foundation detail drawn at a 3/4″ = 1′-0″ scale. See Figure 29-3.

A floating viewport boundary is the portion of the viewport that you see. Everything inside the viewport is "showing through" from model space. Tools such as **MOVE**, **ERASE**, **STRETCH**, and **COPY** are used in paper space to modify the viewport boundary. Display tools such as **VIEW**, **PAN**, and **ZOOM** are used to modify the display of model space objects in the floating viewport. Additional options are available for adjusting how objects appear, according to the layers on which objects are drawn. This allows you to define how the drawing appears within the viewport. As you work through the following sections describing floating viewports, be sure a layout tab is selected.

PROFESSIONAL TIP

By default, when you first select a layout and enter paper space, a rectangular floating viewport appears around objects in model space. As part of layout setup, you may want to use the **ERASE** tool to erase the default viewport and draw a new viewport (or several viewports). Erasing the default viewport, or erasing everything in the layout, does not erase objects in model space.

Creating Floating Viewports

A variety of techniques can be used to create new floating viewports in paper space. The **Viewports** dialog box provides options for creating one to four new viewports according to a specific viewport configuration. The **MVIEW** tool is a text-based method for creating new viewports. The **MVIEW** tool provides the same options found in the

Figure 29-3.
An example of a layout, ready to plot, that includes three floating viewports used to display drawing views at different scales. The layer on which the viewport is drawn is turned off before plotting.

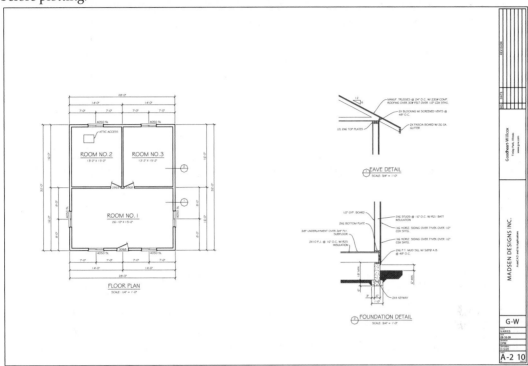

Viewports dialog box, plus additional viewport definition options. Many of the methods for creating new viewports can also be accessed directly from the **Viewports** panel on the **View** tab of the ribbon or by selecting **View** > **Viewports** in the menu browser.

Using the Viewports dialog box

The **Viewports** dialog box, shown in Figure 29-4, is explained in Chapter 6 as it relates to creating tiled viewports in model space. The **Viewports** dialog box looks and functions the same in paper space as in model space, with just a few differences. One difference is that the **Apply to:** drop-down list in the **New Viewports** tab in model space is replaced by the **Viewport spacing:** text box in paper space. This text box is available only when you select a standard viewport configuration that places two or more viewports, as shown in Figure 29-4. Enter or select a value to define the space between multiple viewports.

Another difference is that when you pick the **OK** button to create floating viewports, the viewports do not automatically appear, as in model space. Instead, you are prompted to select a first and second corner to define the area in which the viewport configuration appears. See Figure 29-5. If you use the **Fit** option, AutoCAD fits the viewport(s) into the printable area without requiring you to pick points. Refer to Chapter 6 for more information about the **Viewports** dialog box.

Ribbon
View
> Viewports

New

Type
VIEWPORTS
VPORTS

Menu Browser
View
> Viewports
> New
Viewports...

VIEWPORTS

NOTE

New floating viewports can also be created by selecting a specific configuration from the menu browser. Select **View** > **Viewports** and then select the **1 Viewport**, **2 Viewports**, **3 Viewports**, or **4 Viewports** option and follow the prompts to create the appropriate configuration.

Figure 29-4.
The **Viewports** dialog box with the **New Viewports** tab selected. The **Viewport Spacing:** setting is available when paper space is active.

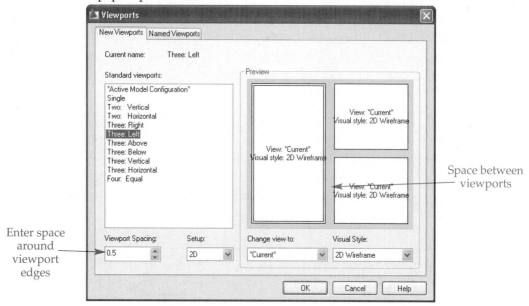

Enter space around viewport edges

Space between viewports

Figure 29-5.
Enter or select two points on the layout to specify the area filled by the viewport configuration.

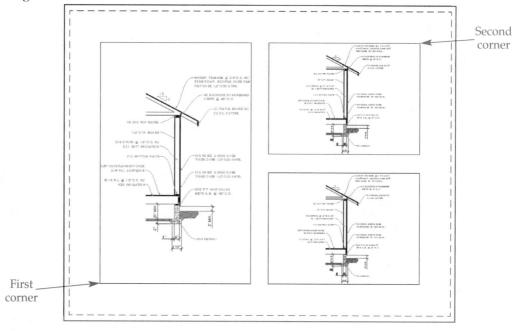

Second corner

First corner

Exercise 29-2
Complete the exercise on the Student CD.

Using the Mview tool

Floating viewports can also be created using the **MVIEW** tool. Once you access the **MVIEW** tool, you can create a single viewport by selecting opposite corners of the viewport, or press [Enter] or the space bar, or right-click and choose **Enter** to activate the **Fit** option. The **Fit** option creates a viewport that fills the printable area.

The **2**, **3**, and **4** options provide preset viewport configurations similar to those available from the **Viewports** dialog box or the **View** > **Viewports** menu on the menu browser. The **Fit** suboption is offered when you are creating multiple viewports. The **Shadeplot** option includes the same options available from the **Visual Style** drop-down list in the **Viewports** dialog box. Use of the **Shadeplot** option is explained in *AutoCAD and Its Applications—Advanced.*

The **Restore** option is used to convert a saved viewport configuration into individual floating viewports. Typically, this option is used to convert tiled viewports into floating viewports. For example, if model space displays two tiled viewports, use the **Restore** option to create two floating viewports. See **Figure 29-6.**

Button
MVIEW
MV

MVIEW

Figure 29-6.
A—A **Two: Horizontal** tiled viewport configuration in model space. B—The model space tiled viewports converted to floating viewports using the **Restore** option of the **MVIEW** tool.

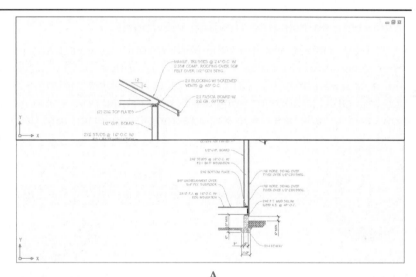

A

B

When you access the **Restore** option, you are prompted to enter the viewport configuration name. In the previous example, you would select the **Active** option to use the two tiled viewports from model space. This is the active model space viewport configuration. Next, select opposite corners of the viewport, or press [Enter] or the space bar, or right-click and choose **Enter** to activate the **Fit** option. The same model space tiled viewport configuration is now displayed in paper space as floating viewports.

Forming polygonal floating viewports

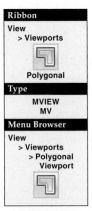

Ribbon
View
> Viewports

Polygonal

Type
MVIEW
MV

Menu Browser
View
> Viewports
> Polygonal
Viewport

The most common shape for a floating viewport is rectangular. This shape is suitable for many applications. However, the **Polygonal** option of the **MVIEW** tool can be used to form a floating viewport outline using a polyline. This option can be accessed directly from the ribbon or menu browser.

Forming a polygonal floating viewport is exactly like drawing a polyline, except the **Halfwidth** and **Width** options are not available for drawing a polygonal viewport. The viewport shape can be any closed shape composed of lines and arcs. Figure 29-7 shows an example of a polygonal floating viewport used to define the maximum drawing view area 1/2" in from the border and title block.

Converting objects into floating viewports

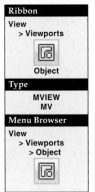

Ribbon
View
> Viewports

Object

Type
MVIEW
MV

Menu Browser
View
> Viewports
> Object

Use the **Object** option of the **MVIEW** tool to convert any closed object drawn in paper space into a floating viewport. This option can be accessed directly from the ribbon or menu browser. After you select the **Object** option, select any closed shape, such as a circle, ellipse, or polygon, to convert the object into a viewport. Figure 29-8 shows an example of a circle and a rectangle converted into floating viewports.

Exercise 29-3
Complete the exercise on the Student CD.

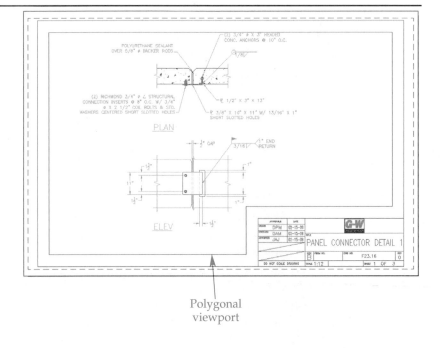

Figure 29-7.
An example of a polygonal floating viewport. The layer on which the viewport is drawn will be turned off or frozen before plotting.

Polygonal
viewport

Figure 29-8.
Any closed object can be converted into a floating viewport. The layer on which these viewports are drawn will be left on for plotting.

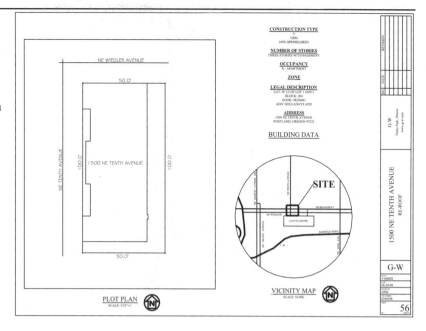

Adjusting the Floating Viewport Boundary

For purposes of adjusting a floating viewport boundary, you should consider the boundary as an object. For example, treat rectangular viewports like rectangles, polygonal viewports like closed polyline objects, circular viewports like circles, and elliptical viewports like ellipses. Use grips or tools such as **MOVE**, **ERASE**, **STRETCH**, and **COPY** as needed to modify the size, shape, and location of floating viewports. When you adjust a floating viewport, the "hole" cut through the sheet changes.

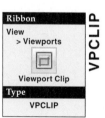

Exercise 29-4
Complete the exercise on the Student CD.

Clipping viewports

The **VPCLIP** tool can be used to redefine the boundary of an existing viewport. To access the tool from a shortcut menu, select a viewport and then right-click and pick the **Viewport Clip** option. A floating viewport can be clipped to an existing closed object that you must draw before accessing the tool, or it can be clipped to a polygonal shape that you create while using the tool.

After you access the **VPCLIP** tool, select the viewport you want to clip. Then select an existing closed shape, such as a circle, ellipse, or polygon, to recreate the viewport in the shape of the selected object. See **Figure 29-9.** An alternative, once you select the existing closed shape, is to use the **Polygonal** option to redefine the viewport according to a polygonal shape. This option functions the same as the **Polygonal** option of the **MVIEW** tool, except the existing viewport is transformed into the new shape.

A clipped floating viewport is recognized as clipped. A **Delete** option is offered when you access the **VPCLIP** tool and select a clipped viewport. Use the **Delete** option to remove the clipped definition and convert the shape into a rectangle sized to fit the extents of the original clipping object or polygonal shape.

Figure 29-9.
An example of clipping a viewport to an existing rectangle. The original viewport is removed and the rectangle is converted into a viewport.

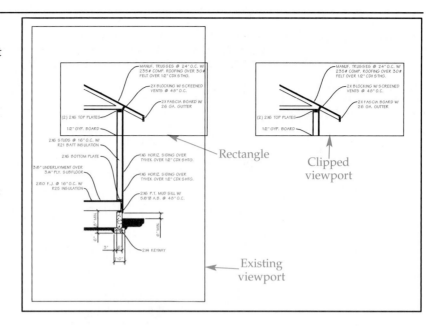

Rectangle

Clipped viewport

Existing viewport

Activating and Deactivating Floating Viewports

An active floating viewport allows you to work on model space objects while you are in paper space. This allows you to adjust the display of the model space drawing that is shown in the viewport. The process of activating and adjusting a viewport is repeated for every floating viewport in the layout to achieve the final drawing.

To activate a floating viewport, double-click inside the viewport area or type MSPACE or MS. If the layout contains a single viewport, the viewport appears highlighted, indicating that it is current. The layout space UCS icon is removed, and the model space UCS icon displays in the corner of the viewport, because you are now working directly in model space, through the paper space viewport. If the layout includes multiple floating viewports, all the viewports display the model space UCS icon. The active and highlighted viewport is the viewport you double-click on, or the newest viewport if you use the MSPACE tool. See Figure 29-10. To make a different viewport active, pick once inside the viewport.

After you adjust the display of all floating viewports, you must re-enter paper space to plot and continue working with the layout. To activate paper space, double-click outside the viewport area, or type PSPACE or PS. The layout space UCS icon reappears, and the model space UCS icon is removed from the corner of the viewports.

Figure 29-10.
The currently active viewport appears highlighted. An active floating viewport allows you to work in model space while AutoCAD displays paper space.

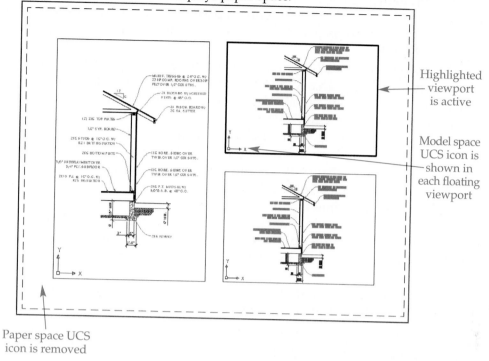

Highlighted viewport is active

Model space UCS icon is shown in each floating viewport

Paper space UCS icon is removed

Scaling a Floating Viewport

The scale you assign to a floating viewport is the same as the drawing scale. The quickest way to set viewport scale is to activate a viewport or pick a viewport boundary while in paper space, but *do not* activate the viewport. Then, select the appropriate scale from the **Viewport Scale** flyout button located on the status bar. **Figure 29-11**

Figure 29-11.
Using the **Viewport Scale** flyout button on the status bar to set the drawing scale.

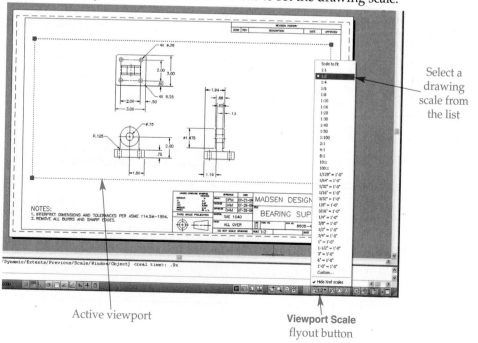

Select a drawing scale from the list

Active viewport

Viewport Scale flyout button

shows an example of selecting 1:2 from the **Viewport Scale** flyout button to scale the active viewport 1:2, or half scale.

The **Properties** palette can also be used to control viewport scale. In order to use this method, you must be in paper space. Pick the viewport you want to scale and access the **Properties** palette. Then select the **Standard scale** drop-down list and choose a viewport scale.

If a scale is not available from the **Viewport Scale** or **Standard scale** list, choose the **Custom...** option to access the **Edit Scale List** dialog box. See **Figure 29-12A**. The **Edit Scale List** dialog box can also be accessed by picking **Format > Scale List...** from the menu browser. The **Edit Scale List...** button on the **User Preferences** tab of the **Options** dialog box also opens the **Edit Scale List** dialog box. To create a new annotation scale, pick the **Add...** button in the **Edit Scale List** dialog box to display the **Add Scale** dialog box. See **Figure 29-12B**. Enter the name of the new scale and the new paper and drawing units. For example, a scale of 1/4″ = 1′-0″ requires a paper units value of .25 or 1 and a drawing units value of 12 or 48.

The **Edit Scale List** dialog box is used to move the highlighted scale up or down in the list by picking the **Move Up** or **Move Down** button. You can remove the highlighted scale from the list by picking the **Delete** button, or you can modify it by picking the **Edit...** button. Select the **Edit...** button to open the **Edit Scale** dialog box. This dialog box functions just like the **Add Scale** dialog box. Pick the **Reset** button to restore the default scale set, eliminating new scales and changes.

NOTE

Setting viewport scale is a zoom function that increases or decreases the *displayed* size of the drawing in the viewport. The **XP** option of the **ZOOM** tool can be used to specify the scale of the active viewport.

Figure 29-12.
A—Use the **Edit Scale List** dialog box to add, modify, and arrange viewport (and annotation) scales. B—Create a new scale using the **Add scale** dialog box.

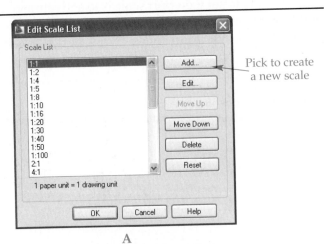

Pick to create a new scale

A

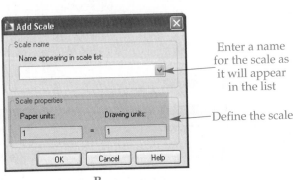

Enter a name for the scale as it will appear in the list

Define the scale

B

AutoCAD and Its Applications—Basics

If you use an option of the **ZOOM** tool other than a specific XP value to adjust the drawing inside an active floating viewport, the drawing looses the correct scale. Once the viewport scale is set, do not zoom in or out. Lock the viewport, as described later in this chapter, to help ensure that the drawing remains properly scaled.

Scaling annotations

Information on a drawing that cannot be described using drawing features and symbols is added as annotation. Objects are drawn at full scale in model space. As a result, annotation and other objects, such as hatch patterns, are scaled so they appear on-screen and are plotted correctly. Use annotative object tools to automate the process of scaling these objects. Scaled viewports and annotative objects function together to properly scale drawings and increase multiview drawing flexibility. Annotative objects should typically be used in place of traditional annotation scaling practices. Annotative objects are covered in Chapter 31.

Controlling linetype scale

As described in Chapter 5, the **LTSCALE** system variable is used to make a global change to the linetype scale to increase or decrease the lengths of the dashes and spaces found in some linetypes. The **LTSCALE** value is usually modified to make linetypes match standard drafting practices. However, depending on the size of objects in model space and the resulting floating viewport scale, an **LTSCALE** value in model space may not be appropriate for paper space.

For example, an **LTSCALE** value of .5 is appropriate for a U.S. customary mechanical drawing plotted at full scale. In this example, an **LTSCALE** value of .5 is applied to model space and paper space because both environments function at full scale. If the drawing is scaled to 2:1, a linetype scale of .25 (scale factor of 1/2 × **LTSCALE** value of .5 = .25) is needed in model space and paper space in order for lines to appear correctly in both environments. Fortunately, by default AutoCAD calculates the appropriate linetype scale display in model space and paper space according to the **LTSCALE** setting.

The **CELTSCALE**, **PSLTSCALE**, and **MSLTSCALE** system variables control how the **LTSCALE** system variable is applied, or not applied, to linetypes in model space and paper space. The **CELTSCALE**, **PSLTSCALE**, and **MSLTSCALE** system variables are set to 1 by default, and should be set to 1 in order for the **LTSCALE** value to be applied correctly in model space and paper space. All linetypes will then appear with the same lengths of dashes and dots regardless of the floating viewport scale, and no matter whether you are in paper space or model space.

Using the previous example, lines will appear correctly in model space and at a scale of 1:1 and 2:1 in paper space. However, when you scale a floating viewport or change the annotation scale in model space, you must remember to use the **REGEN** tool to regenerate the display. Otherwise, the linetype scale will not update according to the new scale. The **MSLTSCALE** system variable is associated with the selected annotation scale and is further described in Chapter 31.

Adjusting the View

When a floating viewport is first created, AutoCAD performs a **ZOOM Extents** of the drawing shown in the viewport. This allows you to view everything in model space through the viewport. The **Scale to fit viewport scale** option accomplishes the same task. When you scale a viewport, AutoCAD adjusts the view from the center of the viewport. This is often the appropriate display. However, if you change the size or shape of the viewport, if the view should not be centered, or if you want to display a

Figure 29-13.
This drawing shows examples of when it is appropriate to show all model space objects, and when it is necessary to display only a portion of model space. Use the **PAN** tool to adjust the position of model space objects in the floating viewport.

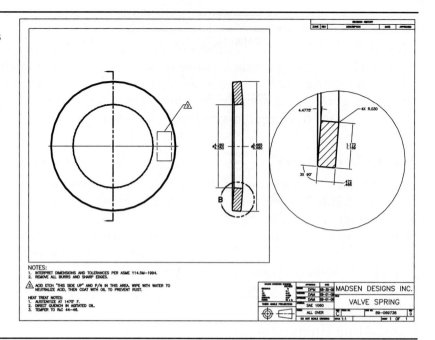

specific portion of the drawing, you must adjust the view. Use the **PAN** tool while in an active viewport to redefine the location of the view.

Viewport edges can "cut off" the drawing once the viewport is correctly scaled. This may be acceptable if you want to display a portion of a view. However, if you want to display the entire view, increase the size of the viewport boundary, or select a different scale to reduce the displayed size of the view to fit the viewport. If it is not appropriate to increase the size of the viewport or decrease the scale, use a larger sheet size. **Figure 29-13** shows a drawing with two viewports. One shows everything in model space, the other "cuts off" model space objects and displays them at a higher zoom level to create a detail.

Locking and Unlocking Floating Viewports

Once the drawing is adjusted in the viewport to reflect the proper scale and view, the viewport can be locked so the scale or view orientation does not accidentally change. This allows you to use display tools such as **ZOOM** and **PAN** to aid in working with objects in model space without changing the scale or position of the view. The quickest way to lock or unlock a viewport is to activate a viewport or pick a viewport boundary while in paper space and then pick the **Lock/Unlock Viewport** button located on the status bar.

Other methods can also be used to lock or unlock a viewport. One option is to select a viewport in paper space and right-click. From the **Display Locked** cascading submenu, select **Yes** to lock the viewport or select **No** to unlock the viewport. Another option is to select a viewport in paper space and access the **Properties** palette. From the **Display Locked** drop-down list, select **Yes** to lock the viewport or select **No** to unlock the viewport. You can also use the **Lock** option of the **MVIEW** tool. Follow the prompts to select the viewport(s) you want to lock or unlock.

Exercise 29-5
Complete the exercise on the Student CD.

Figure 29-14.
Use the **Layer Properties Manager** to control the display of layers in floating viewports.

Controls freezing in new viewports   Controls freezing in the active viewports   Layer property overrides

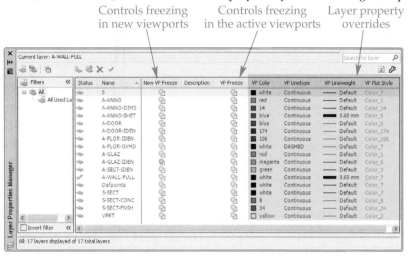

Controlling Layer Display

In Chapter 5, you learned the importance of the AutoCAD layer system and how to use layers in model space. Layers function the same in paper space as in model space. The **On**, **Freeze**, **Color**, **Linetype**, **Lineweight**, **Plot Style**, and **Plot** settings described throughout this textbook are *global layer settings*. **On**, **Freeze**, and **Plot** are global layer states. **Color**, **Linetype**, **Lineweight**, and **Plot Style** are global layer properties. Changing a global layer setting affects objects drawn in model space and paper space. For example, if you change the color of a layer in model space and lock the layer, all objects drawn on that layer in paper space also change color and become locked.

AutoCAD provides the option to freeze layers in a floating viewport and apply *layer property overrides*. These features expand the function of the layer system and improve your ability to reuse drawing content.

Layer display in floating viewports is best controlled using the **LAYER** tool, which opens the **Layer Properties Manager** palette. See **Figure 29-14.** This is the same palette you have used to manage layers throughout this textbook. The **NEW VP Freeze, VP Freeze, VP Color, VP Linetype, VP Lineweight,** and **VP Plot Style** columns control layer display options for floating viewports. Except for the **NEW VP Freeze** column, these columns appear only in layout mode. You probably need to use the scroll bar at the bottom of the palette to see the columns. The options can be applied to layout content, such as the viewport boundary. However, layer settings are most often applied to an active floating viewport. As you work through the following sections describing how to control layer display in floating viewports, be sure the floating viewport to which you want to apply the settings is active.

global layer settings: Layer settings applied to both model space and paper space.

layer property overrides: Color, Linetype, Lineweight, and Plot Style properties that are applied to specific viewports.

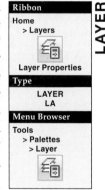

Ribbon
Home
> Layers
Layer Properties

Type
LAYER
LA

Menu Browser
Tools
> Palettes
> Layer

LAYER

NOTE

The **VPLAYER** tool is a text-based tool that can also be used to control layer display in floating viewports. The **Layer Properties Manager** palette is faster and easier to use than the **VPLAYER** tool.

Freezing and thawing

Layers can be frozen in the active viewport to create unique views using a single drawing. For example, **Figure 29-15A** shows the model space display of a floor plan with electrical plan content added directly to the floor plan using electrical plan layers. **Figure 29-15B** shows two layouts in the same drawing file. One layout creates a floor

---

Figure 29-15.
A—An example of "overlapping" layers in model space. B—Layers are frozen in separate layouts to create unique drawing views.

A

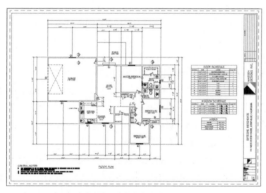 

Floor Plan Layout
Created by freezing electrical layers
in the floating viewport

Electrical Plan Layout
Created by freezing floor plan
layers in the floating viewport

B

plan with no electrical information, and the other layout creates an electrical plan without specific floor plan content.

In this example, many objects, such as doors, walls, and windows are drawn on layers that maintain the global **Thaw** setting. As a result, these objects are shown in model space and both floating viewports. Layers are frozen in specific viewports (**VP Freeze**) to create two different drawings. This example shows viewport layer freezing in two different viewports, each viewport in a different layout, but the same concept can be applied to multiple viewports in the same layout.

The **VP Freeze** column of the **Layer Properties Manager** palette controls freezing and thawing layers in the current viewport. Pick the **VP Thaw** (sun and viewport)

VP   VP
Freeze   Thaw

icon or the **VP Freeze** (snowflake and viewport) icon to toggle freezing and thawing in the current viewport. Using the **VP Freeze** icon freezes only the layers in a floating viewport, whereas the **Freeze** icon freezes layers globally in all floating viewports. A layer can be frozen or thawed in all layout viewports, including those created before picking the **VP Freeze** icon or **VP Thaw** icon, by right-clicking and picking the **VP Freeze Layer in All Viewports** or **VP Thaw Layer in All Viewports** option.

New VP New VP
Freeze   Thaw

The **New VP Freeze** column of the **Layer Properties Manager** palette controls freezing and thawing of layers in *newly created* floating viewports. Pick the **VP Thaw** (sun and viewport) icon or the **VP Freeze** (snowflake and viewport) icon to toggle freezing and thawing in any new floating viewport. This feature has no effect on the active viewport. Use the **New VP Freeze** option if you do not want specific layers to display in any new floating viewports.

Exercise 29-6
Complete the exercise on the Student CD.

Layer property overrides

Use layer property overrides to create unique views without changing individual object properties, creating separate drawing files, or readjusting global layer properties. For example, **Figure 29-16A** shows the model space display of a hopper and conveyer system. The hopper and conveyer are drawn on unique layers. **Figure 29-16B** shows a layout with two floating viewports. The viewport on the left shows the hopper and conveyer with global layer settings applied, as shown in model space. The viewport on the right shows the hopper with a layer color override and the conveyer with a layer color and linetype override. In this example, layer property overrides are used to create a view that clearly shows the two separate components. Phantom lines are used to highlight the conveyer as the mechanism.

The **VP Color**, **VP Linetype**, **VP Lineweight**, and **VP Plot Style** columns in the **Layer Properties Manager** palette control the property overrides assigned to layers. The **VP Plot Style** column is enabled only when a named plot style is being used. Layer property overrides only apply to floating viewports in paper space. When you enter model space, layers that contain layer property overrides are not uniquely identified.

The process of overriding a layer property is just like that for changing a global value. For example, to override the color assigned to a layer, pick the color swatch and choose a color from the **Select Color** dialog box. The difference is that layer property

Figure 29-16.
A—A hopper and conveyer drawn in model space. B—Using property overrides to create a unique layout view.

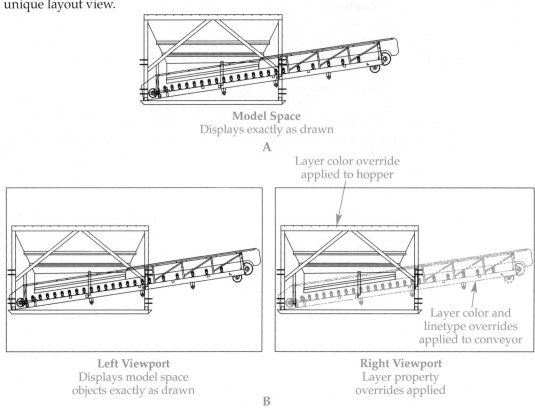

Model Space
Displays exactly as drawn
A

Layer color override
applied to hopper

Layer color and
linetype overrides
applied to conveyor

Left Viewport
Displays model space
objects exactly as drawn

Right Viewport
Layer property
overrides applied

B

overrides are applied only to specific layers in an active floating viewport. Object properties do not change from **Bylayer**, and the model space display does not change.

When viewed in paper space, the **Properties** palette, **Layer Properties Manager** palette, and **Layer Control** drop-down list on the ribbon indicate which layers include layer property overrides. See **Figure 29-17.** Layers that contain layer property overrides are identified in the **Layer Properties Manager** palette with a sheet and viewport icon in the status column. The layer name, global properties affected by the overrides, and the property overrides are highlighted. The **Viewport Overrides** filter is used to quickly display and manage only those layers that include layer property overrides. Layer property overrides can also be saved in a layer state.

Layers that contain layer property overrides are identified in the **Properties** palette with a highlighted layer name. Properties that are affected by the override are also highlighted and are defined as **Bylayer (VP)**. In the **Layer Control** drop-down list on the ribbon, layers that include layer property overrides are highlighted.

NOTE

The **Viewport Overrides** icon appears in the status bar when you activate a floating viewport or assign layer property overrides to the active viewport.

If you no longer want to apply layer property overrides, you must remove the overrides from the layer. Changing a property back to the original, or global, value does not remove the override. Right-click on a layer that contains layer property overrides in the **Layer Properties Manager** palette and pick **Remove Viewport Layer Overrides for** to access a cascading submenu of options for removing layer property overrides.

Figure 29-17.

Layer property overrides are displayed in the **Properties Manager** palette, **Layer Properties Manager** palette, and **Layer Control** drop-down list on the ribbon.

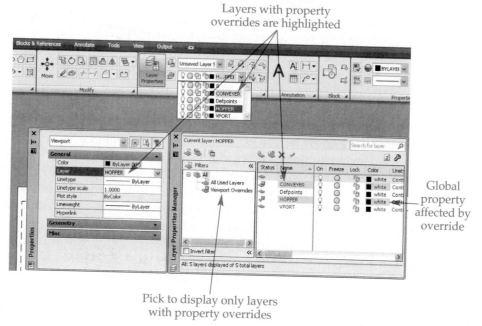

Layers with property overrides are highlighted

Global property affected by override

Pick to display only layers with property overrides

To remove layer property overrides from the layer you right-clicked on, pick the **Selected Layers** option and then the **In Current Viewport Only** or **In All Viewports** option to remove layer property overrides from the current viewport or from all viewports that include overrides.

NOTE

The **Layer** option of the **MVIEW** tool and the **Reset** option of the **VPLAYER** tool can also be used to remove layer property overrides.

Exercise 29-7
Complete the exercise on the Student CD.

Turning Off Floating Viewport Objects

By default, object display in floating viewports is turned on, allowing you to view model space through the viewport. Objects in the floating viewport can be hidden without removing the viewport. This is convenient if, for example, you do not want to plot a certain view, but still want to have access to the viewport.

One option to toggle the display of objects in the viewport on and off is to select a viewport while in paper space and right-click. From the **Display Viewport Objects** cascading menu, select **No** to hide objects or select **Yes** to display objects. Another option is to select a viewport while in paper space and access the **Properties** palette. From the **On** drop-down list, select **Yes** to show objects or select **No** to hide objects. You can also use the **ON** and **OFF** options of the **MVIEW** tool. Follow the prompts to select the viewport(s) in which you want to display or hide objects.

Maximizing Floating Viewports

When you activate a floating viewport, you are working in model space from within the paper space display. The primary function of activating a floating viewport is to adjust the display of model space to prepare a final drawing. Typically, you should avoid working inside an active viewport to make changes to model space objects. There are two options for making significant changes to model space items. One option is to re-enter model space. It is usually best to enter model space when you want to view all objects drawn in model space, even those that are drawn using a layer that is frozen or has property overrides assigned in the floating viewport.

A second option is to maximize a floating viewport. To maximize a viewport, pick the **Maximize Viewport** button on the status bar or select a viewport, right-click, and choose the **Maximize Viewport** option. When you maximize a viewport, you fill the entire drawing window with the selected floating viewport. See **Figure 29-18.** This allows you to work more effectively than when much of the window is covered with layout content, such as a border and title block. In addition, a maximized viewport displays objects exactly as they appear, in the floating viewport. Layers frozen in the viewport and layer property overrides are applied. Typically, you should maximize a floating viewport when you want to use view tools such as **ZOOM** and **PAN** and make changes to objects in model space, while remaining in paper space.

If the drawing includes multiple viewports, use the **Maximize Previous Viewport** and **Maximize Next Viewport** buttons on the status bar to change to other floating viewports in a maximized display. To redisplay the entire layout, pick the **Minimize Viewport** button on the status bar; right-click and choose the **Minimize Viewport** menu option; or type **VPMIN**.

Figure 29-18.
Maximize a floating viewport to work in a model-space-like environment, but with layout characteristics, such as layers frozen in the viewport and layer property overrides.

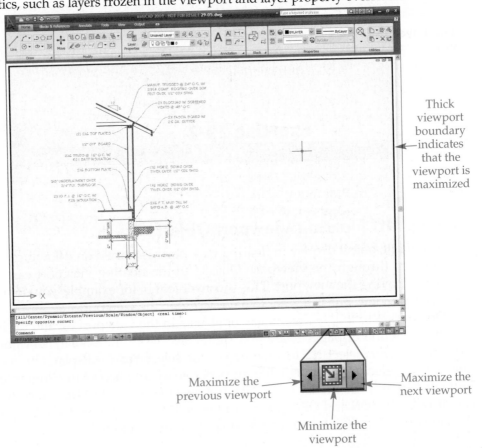

Thick viewport boundary indicates that the viewport is maximized

Maximize the previous viewport

Maximize the next viewport

Minimize the viewport

NOTE

NOTE

Floating viewports can be maximized even if a viewport is not active.

PROFESSIONAL TIP

If you do not want to see floating viewport boundaries on the plotted sheet, remember to freeze or turn off the layer on which the floating viewport is drawn before you plot.

Exercise 29-8

Complete the exercise on the Student CD.

Plotting

After you prepare a layout for plotting, you are ready to plot. If you developed an appropriate page setup and layout, the process of creating the actual print should be almost automatic. Select the layout you want to plot and access the **PLOT** tool. The **Plot** dialog box appears with the name of the layout displayed on the title bar. See **Figure 29-19**.

NOTE

You can also access the **Plot** dialog box by picking the **Plot...** button or selecting from the shortcut menu available from the **Model** or a layout thumbnail image in the **Quick View Layouts** or **Quick View Drawings** tool display.

The **Page Setup** and **Plot** dialog boxes are very similar, except the **Plot** dialog box provides a few additional plot options that are specific to actually creating a print. All the settings in the **Plot** dialog box correspond to those in the **Page Setup** dialog box. Pick the **>**, or **More Options**, button in the lower-right corner of the **Plot** dialog box to toggle the display of additional dialog box areas. **Figure 29-19** shows the entire **Plot** dialog box. Enter or select a number in the text box found in the **Number of copies** area to specify how many copies of the layout to plot. Other plot settings are found in the **Plot options** area. Pick the **Plot in background** check box to continue working in AutoCAD while your computer processes the plot.

Most of the **Plot** dialog box settings are the same as those found in the **Page Setup** dialog box. Changing plot settings in the **Plot** dialog box is an effective way to override the page setup for a unique plotting requirement. The settings you make in the **Plot** dialog box are set back to those defined in the page setup after the plot is sent to the printer or plotter, unless you save changes. This is a convenient way to make a plot using slightly modified plot settings without creating a new page setup. For example, you can make a quick "check print" by selecting a small plotter, using an A- or B-size sheet and scaling the plot to fit the paper. By default, once the print is made, settings

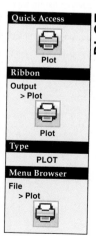

Figure 29-19.
Use the **Plot** dialog box to finalize the layout and send the drawing to the printer, plotter, or file.

Select a different page setup from the list

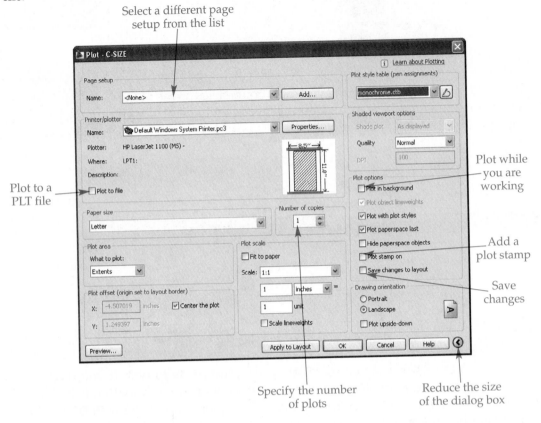

Plot to a PLT file

Plot while you are working

Add a plot stamp

Save changes

Specify the number of plots

Reduce the size of the dialog box

return to those originally assigned in the page setup, allowing you to quickly plot the final drawing using the appropriate printer, sheet size, and scale (1:1).

Adding a Plot Stamp

plot stamp: Text added only to the hard copy that includes information such as the drawing name or the date and time the drawing was printed.

Pick the **Plot stamp on** check box in the **Plot options** area of the **Plot** dialog box to add a *plot stamp* to the drawing. When the check box is selected, the **Plot Stamp Settings...** button appears. Pick the button to display the **Plot Stamp** dialog box. See **Figure 29-20.**

Pick the check boxes located in the **Plot stamp fields** area to identify the information to be included in the plot stamp. To create additional plot stamp items, pick the **Add/Edit** button in the **User defined fields** area, and use the **User Defined Fields** dialog box to add, edit and delete custom fields. For example, you can add a field for the client name, project name, or contractor who uses the drawing. Select the fields from the drop-down lists in the **User defined fields** area.

The **Preview** area provides a preview of the location and orientation of the plot stamp. The preview does not show the actual plot stamp text. Plot stamp settings are saved in a plot stamp parameter (PSS) file. Pick the **Save As** button to save the current settings as a new PSS file, or pick the **Load** button to access and use an existing PSS file.

Figure 29-20.
Use the **Plot Stamp** dialog box to specify the information included in the plot stamp. Plot stamp information can be saved as a PSS file.

Select items to be included in plot stamp

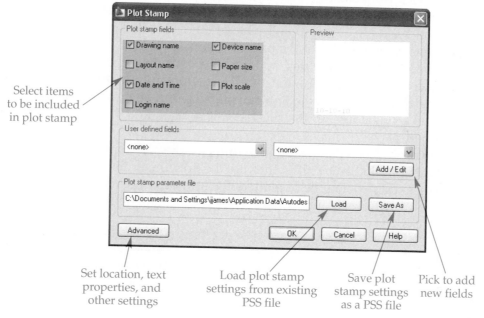

Set location, text properties, and other settings

Load plot stamp settings from existing PSS file

Save plot stamp settings as a PSS file

Pick to add new fields

NOTE

The log file settings are independent of the plot stamp settings. You can produce a log file without creating a plot stamp or have a plot stamp without producing a log file.

Pick the **Advanced** button to display the **Advanced Options** dialog box. See Figure 29-21. The **Advanced Options** dialog box is used to specify additional plot stamp settings. The **Location and offset** area includes options to define the position of

Figure 29-21.
The **Advanced Options** dialog box is used to define the plot stamp location, orientation, text font and size, and units.

Pick corner where stamp is located

Set plot stamp orientation

Select font

Offset distances

Enter text height

Pick where offsets are measured from

Units for text height and offsets

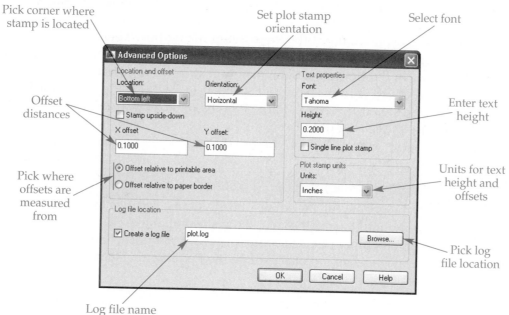

Log file name

Pick log file location

the plot stamp. Select the corner where the plot stamp begins from the **Location** drop-down list. If you want the plot stamp to print upside-down, pick the **Stamp upside-down** check box. Pick **Horizontal** or **Vertical** from the **Orientation** drop-down list to specify the orientation of the plot stamp. Use the **X Offset** and **Y Offset** text boxes to set the offset distances for the plot stamp and pick whether the distances are measured from the edge of the printable area or the paper border.

The **Text properties** area provides options for controlling the plot stamp text characteristics. Use the **Font** drop-down list to select a font and the **Height** text box to specify the text height. Pick the **Single line plot stamp** check box if you want the plot stamp contained to a single line. If this check box is not checked, the plot stamp will be printed on two lines.

Use the **Units** drop-down list to select the units for the plot stamp offset and text height. The plot stamp units can be different from the drawing units. Select the **Log file location** check box to create a log file of plotted items. Specify the name of the log file in the text box. Pick the **Browse...** button to specify the location of the log file.

NOTE

Plot stamp settings can also be configured by picking the **Plot Stamp Settings...** button on the **Plot and Publish** tab of the **Options** dialog box.

Saving Changes to the Layout

Original settings in the **Plot** dialog box are based on the page setup assigned to the layout. If you make changes in the **Plot** dialog box and want to save changes to the layout page setup for future plots, pick the **Save changes to layout** check box in the **Plot options** area. Changes can also be saved by picking the **Apply to Layout** button. If the **Save changes to layout** check box is not selected and/or you do not pick the **Apply to Layout** button, changes made in the **Plot** dialog box are discarded, and the original page setup is used the next time you open the **Plot** dialog box.

Page Setup Options

In Chapter 28, you learned the process of creating page setups using the **Page Setup Manager** and **Page Setup** dialog boxes. A page setup can also be defined using the **Plot** dialog box. To apply this technique, access the **Plot** dialog box and make changes to plot settings, just as you would in the **Page Setup** dialog box. Then select the **Add...** button in the **Page setup** area to display the **Add Page Setup** dialog box. Enter a name for the page setup in the **New page setup name:** text box. All current settings in the **Plot** dialog box are saved with the new page setup. Select a page setup from the **Name:** drop-down list to restore the settings in the **Plot** dialog box. Pick the **<Previous plot>** option to reference the setting used to create the last plot, or pick the **Import...** button to import a page setup from a DWG, DWT, or DXF file.

NOTE

When using the **Plot** dialog box to define settings for a page setup, you should name the page setup *after* you make changes to settings. If you name the page setup and want to make changes later, such as changes to a plot style, use the **Page Setup Manager** dialog box instead.

Previewing the Plot

The final step before plotting is to preview the plot. The plot preview shows you exactly what your plot *should* look like, based on plot and layout settings. You should always preview the plot before sending the information to the plot device. This allows you to check the drawing for errors, view the effects of plot settings, and eliminate unnecessary plots.

To preview the plot, pick the **Preview** button in the lower-left corner of the **Plot** dialog box. The **Plot** dialog box is temporarily hidden, and you enter preview mode. See **Figure 29-22.** What you see on-screen is exactly what will plot, assuming you use a color plotter to make color prints and load the correct sheet size in the plot device.

The **Realtime Zoom** tool is activated automatically. Additional view tools are available from the toolbar near the top of the window or from a shortcut menu. Use these tools to help confirm that the plot settings are correct. When you finish previewing the plot and are ready to plot, pick the **Plot** button on the toolbar, or right-click and select the **Plot** menu option. To exit the preview without plotting, pick the **Close** button on the toolbar, press [Esc] or [Enter], or right-click and select the **Exit** option. The **Plot** dialog box returns so that you can make any needed changes. Pick the **OK** button to send the plot to the plot device and close the **Plot** dialog box.

NOTE

A plot device other than **None** must be selected in order to activate the **Preview...** button.

Exercise 29-9

Complete the exercise on the Student CD.

Figure 29-22.
Previewing a plot is an excellent way to confirm that the plot will be correct before sending the information to the plot device.

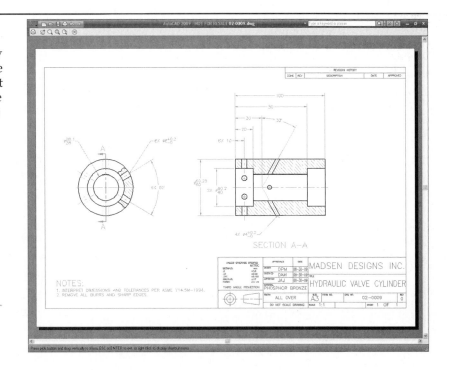

Plotting to a File

If a plot device is not available, but you are ready to plot, an alternative is to plot to a file. A plot file is saved with a PLT extension. The file stores all the drawing geometry, plot styles, and plot settings assigned to the drawing. A PLT file can be plotted using a *plot spooler*. In offices or schools with only one printer or plotter, a plot spooler can be attached to the printer or plotter. This device usually allows you to take a PLT file from a storage disk and copy it to the plot spooler, which in turn plots the drawing.

plot spooler: A disk drive with memory that allows you to plot files.

To plot to a file, open the **Plot** dialog box, select the plot device from the **Name:** drop-down list, and check the **Plot to file** check box. The location where the plot file is saved is set in the **Plot and Publish** tab of the **Options** dialog box. To specify the path, pick the ellipsis (**...**) button for the **Select default location for all plot-to-file operations** dialog box.

NOTE

"Electronic plots" are created as DWF and DWFx files. Creating electronic plot sets and using DWF and DWFx files are explained in *AutoCAD and Its Applications—Advanced.*

Supplemental Material

Additional Plotting Options

The **Plot and Publish** tab of the **Options** dialog box contains general plotting settings. Some options are described when applicable throughout this textbook. Several additional options are also available. Refer to the Student CD: Supplemental Materials > Additional Plotting Options for detailed information on this process.

Chapter Test

Answer the following questions. Write your answers on a separate sheet of paper or complete the electronic chapter test on the Student CD.

1. Name the two types of content that are brought together to create a complete drawing.
2. What tools can be used to modify the boundary of a floating viewport?
3. What **MVIEW** tool can form a floating viewport outline using a polyline?
4. What **MVIEW** tool can be used to convert any closed object drawn in paper space into a floating viewport?
5. How do you activate a floating viewport?
6. How can you tell that a viewport is activated in paper space?
7. How do you reactivate paper space after activating a floating viewport for editing?
8. How does the scale you assign to a floating viewport compare with the drawing scale?
9. To what value should the **CELTSCALE**, **PSLTSCALE**, and **MSLTSCALE** system variables be set so that the **LTSCALE** value will be applied correctly in model space and paper space?
10. Viewport edges may "cut off" the drawing when the viewport is correctly scaled. List three things you can do if you want to display the entire view.
11. Why should you lock a viewport after you have adjusted the drawing in the viewport to reflect the proper scale and view?
12. By default, floating viewport object display is turned on, allowing you to view model space through the viewport. Give an example of why you would want to hide objects in the floating viewport without removing the viewport.
13. What is a plot stamp?
14. If you make changes to the page setup using the **Plot** dialog box, how can you save these changes to the page setup so that they can be used for future plots?
15. Give at least two reasons why you should always preview the plot before sending the information to the plot device.

Drawing Problems

Note: Some of the following problems refer to drawings or templates created in previous chapters. If you have not yet created those drawings, you will need to do so before working these problems.

▼ Basic

1. Open the P28-10 file you created in Problem 28-10. Save a copy of P28-10 as P29-1. Make the **B-SIZE** layout current. Create a new layer named **VPORT**. Delete the default floating viewport and create a single floating viewport .5" in from the edges of the sheet on the **VPORT** layer. Scale model space in the viewport to 1:1. Plot the layout, leaving the **VPORT** layer on and thawed. Resave the problem.

2. Open the P28-11 file you created in Problem 28-11. Save a copy of P28-11 as P29-2. Activate the **A2-SIZE** layout. Create a new layer named **VPORT**. Delete the default floating viewport and create a single floating viewport 10 mm from the edges of the sheet on the **VPORT** layer. Scale model space in the viewport to 1:1. Plot the layout, leaving the **VPORT** layer on and thawed. Resave the problem.

3. Open the P28-12 file you created in Problem 28-12. Save a copy of P28-12 as P29-3. Activate the **B-SIZE** layout. Create a new layer named **VPORT**. Delete the default floating viewport and create a single floating viewport .5″ from the edges of the sheet on the **VPORT** layer. Scale model space in the viewport to 1:1. Plot the layout, leaving the **VPORT** layer on and thawed. Resave the problem.

▼ Intermediate

4. Open the P28-13 file you created in Problem 28-13. Save a copy of P28-13 as P29-4. Create a floating viewport and scale model space in the viewport using an appropriate scale. Plot the layout, leaving the **VPORT** layer on and thawed. Resave the problem.

5. Open the P8-1 file you created in Problem 8-1. Save a copy of P8-1 as P29-5. Delete the default **Layout2**. Create a new A-size sheet layout according to the following steps:
   A. Rename the default **Layout1** to **A-SIZE**.
   B. Select the **A-SIZE** layout and access the **Page Setup Manager**.
   C. Modify the **A-SIZE** page setup according to the following settings:
      • **Printer/Plotter:** Select a printer or plotter that can plot an A-size sheet
      • **Paper size:** Select the appropriate A-size sheet (varies with printer or plotter)
      • **Plot area:** Layout
      • **Plot offset:** 0,0
      • **Plot scale:** 1:1 (1 in. = 1 unit)
      • **Plot style table:** monochrome.ctb
      • **Plot with plot styles**
      • **Plot paper space last**
      • Do not check **Hide paper space objects**
      • **Drawing orientation:** Select the appropriate orientation (varies with printer or plotter)
   D. Create a new layer named **VPORT**.
   E. Delete the default floating viewport and create a single floating viewport .5″ from the edges of the sheet on the **VPORT** layer.
   F. Scale model space in the viewport to 1:2. Plot the layout, leaving the **VPORT** layer on and thawed.
   Resave the problem.

6. Open the P8-7 file created in Problem 8-7. Save a copy of P8-7 as P29-6. Create layouts and floating viewports as need to plot the drawing at an appropriate scale.

▼ Advanced

7. Open P29-7 from the Student CD supplied with this textbook. Create a layout, plot style, and page setup so it can be plotted as follows: Using color-dependent plot styles, have the equipment (shown in color in the diagram) plot with a line-weight of 0.8 mm and 80% screening on an A-size sheet oriented horizontally. Plotted text height should be 1/8". Plot in paper space at 1:1. Save the drawing as P29-7.

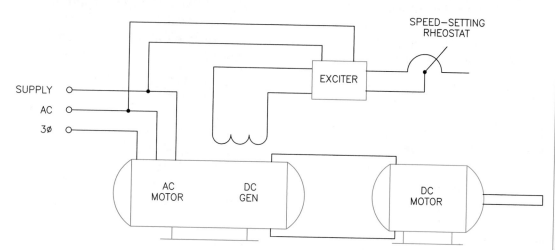

8. Open P29-8 from the Student CD supplied with this textbook. Create four layouts with the names and displays as follows:
   - The **Entire Schematic** layout plots the entire schematic on a B-size sheet.
   - The **3 Wire Control** layout plots only the 3 Wire Control diagram on an A-size sheet, horizontally oriented.
   - The **Motor** layout plots the motor symbol and connections in the lower center of the schematic on an A-size sheet, oriented vertically.
   - The **Schematic** layout plots schematic without the 3 Wire Control and motor components on an A-size sheet, oriented horizontally.

Set up the layouts so they can be plotted with a text height of 1/8″. Plot in paper space at a scale of 1:1. Save the drawing as P29-8.

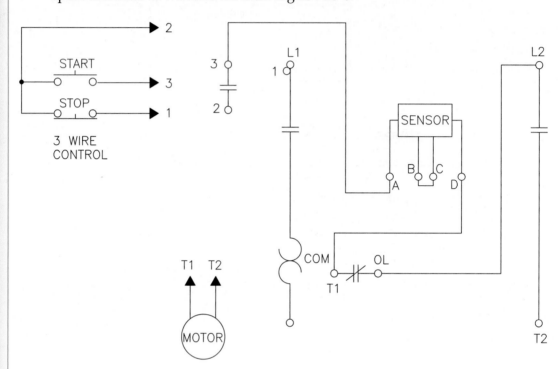

Using Attributes

Learning Objectives

After completing this chapter, you will be able to do the following:

- ✓ Define attributes.
- ✓ Create and insert blocks that contain attributes.
- ✓ Edit attribute values and definitions in existing blocks.
- ✓ Create title blocks, revision blocks, and parts lists with attributes.
- ✓ Display attribute values in fields.

Blocks often include text or numerical information. For example, a door identification symbol contains a letter or number that links the door with information in a door schedule. Text added to a block is static, which means it cannot be changed unless you edit the block. An alternative is to assign *attributes* to the block. Adding an attribute to the door identification symbol example allows you to use any letter or number with the symbol when you insert or edit the block, without creating additional block definitions. Several blocks with attributes are shown in Figure 30-1.

Attributes significantly increase the usefulness of blocks. In addition to being used as text, attribute information can be *extracted* from the drawing. Extracted attribute data can be used for a variety of applications, including parts lists and bills of materials.

attributes: Text or numerical values assigned to blocks.

extracted: Gathered from the drawing file database and displayed either in the drawing or in an external document.

Defining Attributes

Attributes are created during the initial phase of block development, along with any objects to be included in the block definition. Before assigning attributes to a block, you must determine the text information needed for the block. Often the name of the object is the first attribute. This could be followed by other attribute items, such as the manufacturer, type, size, price, and weight of an item. For example, a valve symbol for a piping flow diagram might list all of the product-related data along with the symbol. The number of attributes you can create is limited only by the project requirements.

The **ATTDEF** tool displays the **Attribute Definition** dialog box, which is used to assign attributes. See Figure 30-2. The **Attribute Definition** dialog box is divided into four main areas. Each area allows you to set specific aspects of an attribute.

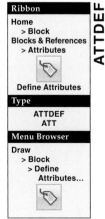

Ribbon
Home
> Block
Blocks & References
> Attributes

Define Attributes
Type
ATTDEF
ATT
Menu Browser
Draw
> Block
> Define
Attributes...

ATTDEF

Figure 30-1.
Examples of blocks with defined attributes.

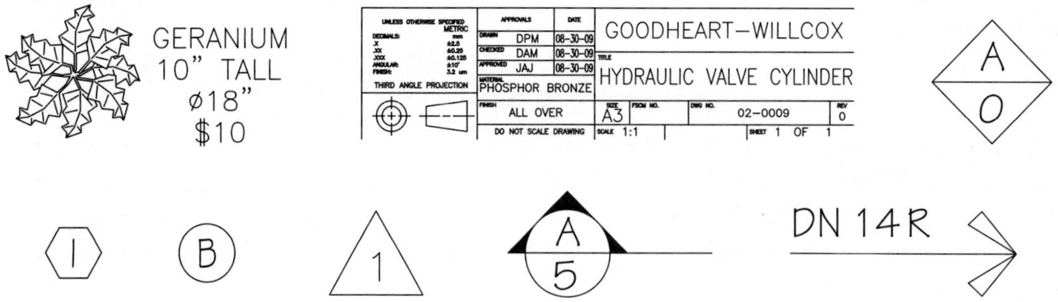

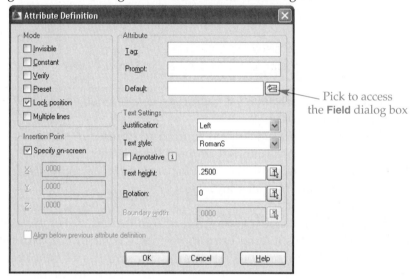

Figure 30-2.
Attributes can be assigned to blocks using the **Attribute Definition** dialog box.

Setting Attribute Modes

The **Mode** area of the **Attribute Definition** dialog box is used to set attribute modes. If the **Invisible** check box is selected, the attribute is not displayed when the block is inserted. Otherwise, the attribute is shown with the inserted block. Select the **Invisible** option if you want to include attribute data in the block that can be referenced and extracted, but you do not want the information to appear on the screen or drawing.

Pick the **Constant** check box if the value of the attribute should always be the same. All insertions of the block display the same value for the attribute; you are not prompted for a new value. Leave the **Constant** check box deselected to use different attribute values for multiple insertions of the block. Pick the **Verify** check box if you want a prompt to ask you whether the specified attribute value is correct when the block is inserted. Choose the **Preset** check box to have the attribute assume preset values during block insertion. This option disables the attribute prompt. Leave this check box unchecked to display the normal prompt.

Select the **Lock position** check box if you do not want to have the option of moving the attribute independently of the block after it has been inserted. The **Lock position** check box is also used for an attribute that will be part of a dynamic block. This check box must be checked for the attribute to be included as part of the action selection set when you assign an action to a dynamic block. If it is unchecked, the attribute is filtered out when the action is assigned to the dynamic block. Dynamic blocks are covered in Chapter 27.

The **Attribute Definition** dialog box can be used to create single-line or multiple-line attributes. Pick the **Multiple lines** check box to activate options for creating a multiple-line attribute. Deselect the check box to create a single-line attribute.

Using the Attribute Area

The **Attribute** area of the **Attribute Definition** dialog box lets you assign a tag, prompt, and default value to the attribute using the appropriate text box. The text boxes can contain up to 256 characters. If the first character in an entry is a space, start the string with a backslash (\). If the first character is a backslash, begin the entry with two backslashes (\\).

Use the **Tag** text box to enter the name, or tag, of the attribute. For example, the tag for a size attribute for a valve block could be SIZE. You must enter a tag in order to create an attribute. Any characters can be used *except* spaces. All text is displayed in uppercase.

Enter a statement in the **Prompt** text box that AutoCAD will use to prompt you when the block is inserted or edited. For example, if SIZE is specified as the attribute tag, What is the valve size? or Enter valve size: might be entered as the prompt. The prompts can be left blank. If the **Constant** attribute mode is selected, this option is disabled.

The entry in the **Default** text box is used as a default attribute value when the block is inserted. You might enter a message regarding the type of information needed, such as 10 SPACES MAX or NUMBERS ONLY. If the **Multiple lines** attribute mode is deselected, the default value can be entered directly in the text box. Use the **Insert field** button to include a field in the default value. If the **Multiple lines** attribute mode is selected, the ellipsis (...) button is displayed. Pick the ellipsis button to enter the drawing area and place multiline text. This process is very similar to adding multiline text to your drawing using the **MTEXT** tool. Figure 30-3 displays the **In-Place Text Editor** used for adding a multiple line attribute. Multiline text is covered in Chapter 9. The default value can also be left blank.

NOTE

The abbreviated **Text Formatting** toolbar shown in Figure 30-3 is provided by default. To display the complete **Text Formatting** toolbar, set the **ATTIPE** system variable to 1. The **ATTIPE** system variable is set to 0 by default.

Figure 30-3.
You can define multiple-line attributes directly on-screen. An abbreviated version of the **Text Formatting** toolbar is provided by default.

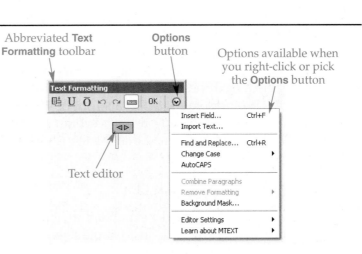

Adjusting Attribute Text Options

The **Text Options** area of the **Attribute Definition** dialog box allows you to specify attribute text settings. Many of these options function like the text settings for single-line and multiline text, as described in Chapter 9. Use the **Justification** drop-down list to select a justification for the attribute text. The default option is Left. In single-line attributes, the text itself is justified. In the **Multiple lines** attribute mode, the text boundary is justified.

Use the **Text Style** drop-down list to select a text style for the attribute from the styles defined in the current drawing. Pick the **Annotative** check box to make the attribute text height annotative. AutoCAD scales annotative attributes according to the selected annotation scale, which is the same as the drawing scale. This eliminates the need for you to calculate the scale factor.

Specify the height of the attribute text in the **Height** text box or pick the **Text Height** button to the right of the text box to return temporarily to the drawing area and pick two points to indicate the text height. Once you pick the points, the dialog box returns and the corresponding height is shown in the text box. Enter an angular value in the **Rotation** text box to specify a rotation angle for the attribute text or pick the **Rotation** button to the right of the text box and specify a rotation by picking two points in the drawing area.

The **Boundary width** option is available only when the **Multiple lines** attribute mode is selected. Enter a width for the multiple-line attribute boundary in the **Boundary width** text box, or pick the **Boundary width** button to the right of the text box and specify a text boundary width by picking two points in the drawing area.

Defining the Attribute Insertion Point

The **Insertion Point** area of the **Attribute Definition** dialog box provides options for defining the location of the attribute. You can enter coordinates in the text boxes if the **Specify On-screen** check box is unchecked. If the check box is checked, you must select the attribute location on-screen after picking the **OK** button to place the attribute and close the **Attribute Definition** dialog box.

If the drawing contains at least one attribute, the **Align below previous attribute definition** check box is enabled. Checking it places the new attribute directly below the most recently created attribute using the justification of that attribute. If the drawing does not contain any attributes, this check box is disabled. When this check box is checked, the **Text Options** and **Insertion Point** areas become inactive. This is an effective technique for placing a group of different attributes in the same block.

Placing the Attribute

After all elements of the attribute are defined, pick **OK** to close the **Attribute Definition** dialog box. The attribute tag appears on-screen automatically if coordinates are specified, or if the **Align below previous attribute definition** option is used. If not, AutoCAD prompts you to select a location. When the block is inserted, you are prompted for information based on the attribute definition. If the attribute mode is set to **Invisible**, do not be concerned that the tag is visible; this is the only time the tag appears.

Editing Attribute Properties

The **Properties** palette provides expanded attribute editing capabilities. **Figure 30-4** shows the **Properties** palette with an attribute selected. You can change the color, linetype, or layer of the selected attribute in the **General** section. The attribute tag, prompt, and default value entries are listed in the **Text** section. You can select **Tag**, **Prompt**, or **Value** to change the corresponding values. If the value contains a field, it appears

Figure 30-4.
The **Properties**
palette can be used
to modify attributes.

Selected
object to edit

Pick to change
the attribute tag

Pick to change
an attribute mode
setting

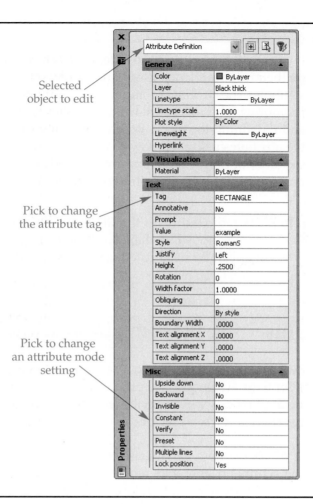

Attribute Definition		
General		▲
Color	■ ByLayer	
Layer	Black thick	
Linetype	———— ByLayer	
Linetype scale	1.0000	
Plot style	ByColor	
Lineweight	———— ByLayer	
Hyperlink		
3D Visualization		▲
Material	ByLayer	
Text		▲
Tag	RECTANGLE	
Annotative	No	
Prompt		
Value	example	
Style	RomanS	
Justify	Left	
Height	.2500	
Rotation	0	
Width factor	1.0000	
Obliquing	0	
Direction	By style	
Boundary Width	.0000	
Text alignment X	.0000	
Text alignment Y	.0000	
Text alignment Z	.0000	
Misc		▲
Upside down	No	
Backward	No	
Invisible	No	
Constant	No	
Verify	No	
Preset	No	
Multiple lines	No	
Lock position	Yes	

as normal text in the **Properties** palette. If you modify the field text, it is automatically converted to text. The **Text** section also contains options to change the attribute text settings. You can change the insertion point of the text attribute in the **Geometry** section by using the **Position** options to enter new coordinates. Additional text options are available in the **Misc** section.

PROFESSIONAL TIP

Perhaps the most powerful feature of the **Properties** palette for editing attributes is the ability to change the original attribute modes. **Invisible**, **Constant**, **Verify**, and **Preset** modes can be activated and deactivated in the **Misc** category of the **Properties** palette.

Creating Blocks with Attributes

Once attributes are created, use the **BLOCK** or **WBLOCK** tool to define the block. Blocks are described in Chapters 26 and 27. When creating the block, be sure to select all of the objects and attributes that go with the block. The order in which you select the attribute definitions is the order in which you are prompted or the order in which the attributes appear in the **Edit Attributes** dialog box.

If the **Convert to Block** radio button in the **Block Definition** dialog box is selected, the **Edit Attributes** dialog box appears when you create the block. See **Figure 30-5.** This is the dialog box that can be used to adjust attribute values when the block is inserted.

Inserting Blocks with Attributes

Use the **INSERT** tool or another block insertion tool, such as **DesignCenter,** to insert a block that contains attributes. The process of inserting a block with attributes is the same as inserting a block without attributes. The only difference is that after you define the block insertion point, scale factors, and rotation angle, you are prompted for attribute values.

By default, the **ATTDIA** system variable is set to 0, which displays single-line attribute prompts at the command line or dynamic input cursor, and multiple-line attribute prompts using the AutoCAD text window. A better method of entering attribute values is to set the **ATTDIA** system variable to 1 before inserting blocks to enable the **Edit Attribute** dialog box. This dialog box appears after you enter the insertion point, scale, and rotation angle, allowing you to answer each of the attribute prompts. Type single-line attribute values directly in the text boxes. To define multiple-line attributes, select the ellipses (**…**) button next to the text boxes, which allows you to enter values on-screen. If a value includes a field, you can right-click the field to edit it or convert it to text.

The **Edit Attributes** dialog box can list up to eight attributes. If the block has more than eight attributes, pick the **Next** button at the bottom of the dialog box to display the next page of attributes. When you finish entering values for the attributes, pick the **OK** button to close the dialog box. The inserted block now appears on-screen with any visible attributes.

Figure 30-5.
The **Edit Attributes** dialog box allows you to enter attribute definitions when a block is inserted.

Accept or change the existing attributes

Pick to display the next page of attributes

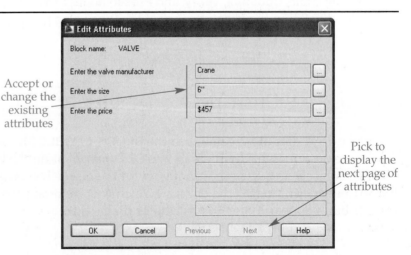

Exercise 30-1

Complete the exercise on the Student CD.

Attribute Prompt Suppression

Some drawings may use blocks with attributes that always retain their default values. In this case, there is no need to be prompted for the attribute values when you insert the block. You can turn off the attribute prompts by setting the **ATTREQ** system variable to 0. After making this setting, try inserting the VALVE block created in Exercise 30-1. Notice that none of the attribute prompts appear. To display attribute prompts again, change the setting back to 1. The **ATTREQ** system variable setting is saved with the drawing.

PROFESSIONAL TIP

Part of your project and drawing planning should involve setting system variables such as **ATTREQ**. Setting **ATTREQ** to 0 before using blocks can save time in the drawing process. Always remember to set **ATTREQ** back to 1 when you want to use the prompts instead of accepting defaults. When anticipated attribute prompts are not issued, you should check the current **ATTREQ** setting and adjust it if necessary.

Controlling Attribute Display

Attributes are intended to contain valuable information about the blocks in a drawing. Some attributes are used only to generate parts lists or bills of materials and to speed accounting. These types of attributes are not displayed on-screen or during plotting. Use the **ATTDISP** tool to control the display of attributes on-screen.

Use the **Normal** option to display attributes exactly as they were created. This is the default setting. Use the **ON** option to display *all* attributes, including those defined with the **Invisible** mode. Apply the **OFF** option to suppress the display of all attributes.

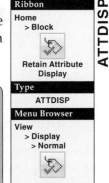

PROFESSIONAL TIP

After attributes have been created, defined with blocks, and checked for accuracy, hide them with the **OFF** option of the **ATTDISP** tool. If attributes are left on, they clutter the screen and lengthen regeneration time. In a drawing in which attributes should be visible but are not, check the current setting of **ATTDISP** and adjust it if necessary.

Changing Attribute Values

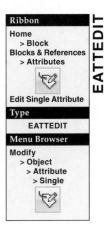

You can edit attributes before they are included in a block using the **Properties** palette. Once a block with attributes has been created and inserted, different tools are used to edit the inserted attributes. Inserted attribute values within a single block can be modified using the **EATTEDIT** tool. When you access this tool, you are prompted to select a block. Pick the block containing the attributes you want to modify to display the **Enhanced Attribute Editor**. See **Figure 30-6**.

Figure 30-6.
Select the attribute to be modified and change its value in the **Attribute** tab of the **Enhanced Attribute Editor**.

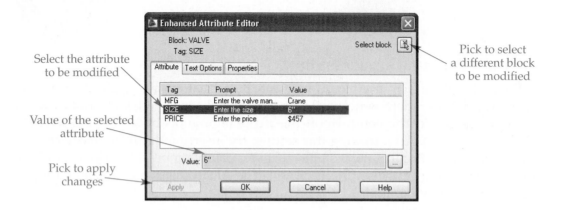

Select the attribute to be modified

Value of the selected attribute

Pick to apply changes

Pick to select a different block to be modified

The **Enhanced Attribute Editor** contains three tabs. The **Attribute** tab is displayed by default with the attributes in the selected block listed in the window. Pick the attribute to be modified and enter a new value in the **Value:** text box. If the attribute was created as a multiple-line attribute, the ellipsis (**...**) button is available for selection, allowing you to modify text on-screen. Pick the **Apply** button after adjusting the value.

NOTE

You can also edit multiple-line attribute values without accessing the **Enhanced Attribute Editor** by using the **ATTIPEDIT** tool.

To select a different block to modify, pick the **Select block** button in the dialog box. The dialog box closes temporarily to allow you to select a different block in the drawing. The dialog box then reappears and displays the attributes for the selected block.

Other properties of the selected attribute are modified using the other tabs in the **Enhanced Attribute Editor** dialog box. The **Text Options** tab allows you to modify the text properties of the attribute. See Figure 30-7A. The **Properties** tab contains settings for the object properties of the attribute. See Figure 30-7B. After editing the attribute values and properties, pick the **Apply** button to have the changes reflected on-screen. Pick the **OK** button to close the dialog box.

Exercise 30-2
Complete the exercise on the Student CD.

Figure 30-7.

A—The **Text Options** tab provides options in addition to those set in the **Attribute Definition** dialog box. B—The **Properties** tab can be used to modify an attribute's object properties.

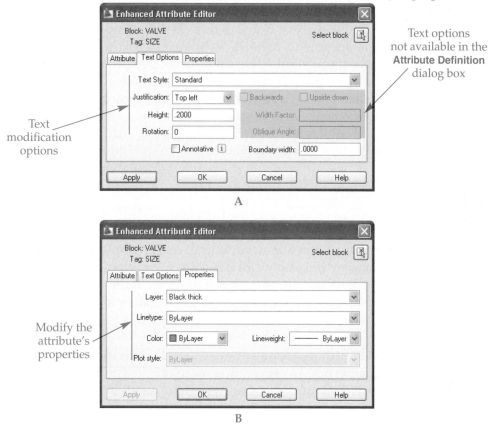

Text modification options

Text options not available in the **Attribute Definition** dialog box

A

Modify the attribute's properties

B

Using the Find Tool to Edit Attributes

One of the quickest ways to edit attributes is to use the **FIND** tool. With no tool active, right-click in the drawing area and select **Find...** from the shortcut menu. The **Find and Replace** dialog box is displayed. You can then search the entire drawing or a selected group of objects for an attribute. The **Find and Replace** dialog box is described in detail in Chapter 10.

Editing Attribute Values and Properties Globally

The **Enhanced Attribute Editor** allows you to edit attribute values by selecting blocks one at a time. The **-ATTEDIT** tool is used to edit several block attributes at once or to edit attributes individually by answering prompts.

When you access the **-ATTEDIT** tool, a prompt asks if you want to edit attributes individually. Use the default **Yes** option to select specific blocks with attributes you want to edit. Use the **No** option to change the same attribute on several insertions of the same block. This is known as *global attribute editing*.

If you choose the **Yes** option, the following prompts appear immediately: Enter block name specification <*>:, Enter attribute tag specification <*>:, and Enter attribute value specification <*>:. To selectively edit attribute values, respond to each prompt with the correct name or value. You are then prompted to select one or more attributes. If you receive the message "0 found" after selecting attributes, you picked an attribute that was not specified correctly. It is often quicker to press [Enter] at each of the three specification prompts and then pick the attribute to edit. Select an option and follow the prompts to edit the attribute(s).

global attribute editing: Editing or changing all insertions, or instances, of the same block in a single operation.

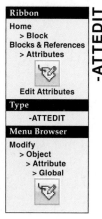

Ribbon
Home
> Block
Blocks & References
> Attributes

Edit Attributes

Type
-ATTEDIT

Menu Browser
Modify
> Object
> Attribute
> Global

-ATTEDIT

If you choose the **No** option, the Edit only attributes visible on screen? prompt appears. Select Yes to edit all visible attributes or No to edit all attributes, including those that are invisible. The same three prompts previously described for individual block editing now appear.

In **Figure 30-8A,** the VALVE block from Exercise 30-1 was inserted three times with the manufacturer's name specified as CRANE. In this example, the name was supposed to be POWELL. To change the attribute for each insertion, enter the **-ATTEDIT** tool and specify global editing. Then, press [Enter] at each of the three specification prompts. When the **Select Attributes** prompt appears, pick CRANE on each of the VALVE blocks and press [Enter] when complete. At the Enter string to change: prompt enter CRANE, and at the Enter new string: prompt, enter POWELL. The CRANE attributes on the selected blocks are changed to the new value POWELL, as shown in **Figure 30-8B.**

PROFESSIONAL TIP

Use care when assigning the **Constant** mode to attribute definitions. The **-ATTEDIT** tool displays 0 found if you attempt to edit a block attribute with a **Constant** mode setting. Assign the **Constant** mode only to attributes you know will not change.

NOTE

The **-ATTEDIT** tool can also be used to edit individual attribute values and properties. However, it is more efficient to use the **Enhanced Attribute Editor** for changing individual attributes.

Exercise 30-3
Complete the exercise on the Student CD.

Figure 30-8.
Using the global editing technique with the **-ATTEDIT** tool allows you to change the same attribute on several block insertions.

GATE
CRANE
6"

GATE
CRANE
6"

GATE
CRANE
6"

Existing Blocks

A

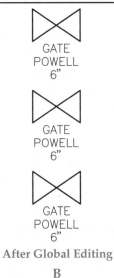

GATE
POWELL
6"

GATE
POWELL
6"

GATE
POWELL
6"

After Global Editing

B

Changing Attribute Definitions

Before saving an attribute within a block, you can modify the tag, prompt, and default value using the **Properties** palette. However, once an attribute is saved in a block definition, you must use the **Block Attribute Manager** to change the attribute definition. See Figure 30-9.

The **Block Attribute Manager** lists the attributes for the selected block. To select a block, choose it from the **Block:** drop-down list or pick the **Select block** button to return to the drawing area and pick the block. By default, the tag, prompt, default value, and modes for each attribute are listed.

The attribute list reflects the order in which prompts appear when a block is inserted. Use the **Move Up** and **Move Down** buttons to change the order of the selected attribute within the list. To delete an attribute, pick the **Remove** button.

Select the attribute properties listed in the **Block Attribute Manager** by picking the **Settings...** button to open the **Block Attribute Settings** dialog box. See Figure 30-10. Check the properties to list in the **Display in list** area. When the **Emphasize duplicate tags** check box is selected, attributes with identical tags are highlighted in red. To apply the changes you make in the **Block Attribute Manager** to existing blocks, check the **Apply changes to existing references** check box. Pick the **OK** button to return to the **Block Attribute Manager**.

To modify an attribute definition, select the attribute in the **Block Attribute Manager** and pick the **Edit...** button. The **Edit Attribute** dialog box is displayed. See Figure 30-11. The **Attribute** tab of this dialog box allows you to modify the modes, tag, prompt, and default value.

The **Text Options** and **Properties** tabs of the **Edit Attribute** dialog box are identical to the tabs found in the **Enhanced Attribute Editor** and allow you to modify the object properties of the attributes. If the **Auto preview changes** check box at the bottom of the dialog box is checked, changes to attributes are displayed in the drawing area immediately.

After modifying the attribute definition in the **Edit Attribute** dialog box, pick the **OK** button to return to the **Block Attribute Manager**. Then pick the **OK** button in the **Block Attribute Manager** to return to the drawing. When attributes within a block are modified, future insertions of the block reflect the changes. Existing blocks are updated only if the **Apply changes to existing references** check box in the **Settings** dialog box is checked. If this option is not selected, the existing blocks retain the original attribute definitions.

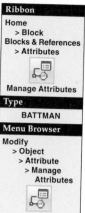

Ribbon
Home
> Block
Blocks & References
> Attributes

Manage Attributes
Type
BATTMAN
Menu Browser
Modify
> Object
> Attribute
> Manage Attributes

BATTMAN

Figure 30-9.
Use the **Block Attribute Manager** to change attribute definitions, delete attributes, and change the order of attribute prompts.

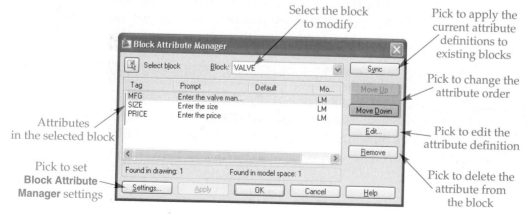

Figure 30-10.
The **Block Attribute Settings** dialog box controls the types of attributes displayed in the **Block Attribute Manager**.

Select the attribute properties to list in the **Block Attribute Manager**

Identifies duplicate tags

Updates existing blocks

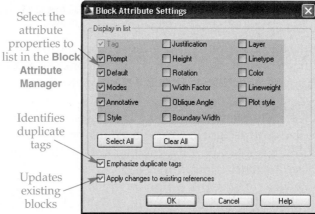

Figure 30-11.
Use the **Edit Attribute** dialog box to modify attribute definitions and properties.

Use these tabs to modify attribute properties

Select modes

Modify attribute definition

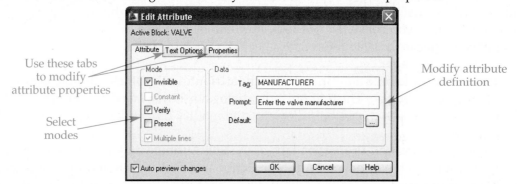

NOTE

The **Block Attribute Manager** modifies attribute *definitions*, not attribute *values*. Attribute values can be modified with the **Enhanced Attribute Editor**.

Redefining a Block and Its Attributes

You may encounter a situation in which an existing block and its associated attributes must be revised. You may need to delete existing attributes, add new attributes, or revise the geometry of the block itself. The **BEDIT** and **REFEDIT** tools are best used for this application. The **BEDIT** tool is described in Chapter 26, and the **REFEDIT** tool is covered in Chapter 32. Both tools allow you to make changes to a block definition, including attributes assigned to the block, without exploding the block.

NOTE

The **ATTREDEF** tool can also be used to redefine a block and its attributes. However, the **ATTREDEF** tool is text-based, and the block must first be exploded. Use **BEDIT** or **REFEDIT** tool to edit the block.

Automating Drafting Documentation

Attributes are powerful tools for assigning textual information to blocks. Attributes can also be used to automate any detailing or documentation task that requires a great deal of text. Such tasks include the creation of title block information, revision block data, and a parts list or bill of materials. Filling out these items is usually one of the more time-consuming tasks associated with drafting documentation. The task can be efficiently automated by assigning attributes to a block.

Creating Title Blocks

To create an automated title block, first draw the title block objects and add text that does not change, such as titles. Format the title block in accordance with industry or company standards. Use the correct layer(s), typically the 0 layer, and be sure to include your company or school logo in the title block. If you work in an industry that produces items for the federal government, also include the applicable Federal Supply Code for Manufacturers (FSCM) in the title block. A title block drawn in accordance with the ASME Y14.1 *Decimal Inch Drawing Sheet Size and Format* standard is shown in **Figure 30-12.**

NOTE

The FSCM is a five-digit numerical code identifier applicable to any organization that produces items used by the federal government. It also applies to government activities that are responsible for the development of certain specifications, drawings, or standards that control the design of items.

Next, define attributes for each area of the title block. As you create attributes, determine the appropriate text height and justification for each definition. Attributes should be defined for the drawing title, drawing number, drafter, checker, dates, drawing scale, sheet size, material, finish, revision letter, and tolerance information. See **Figure 30-13.** Approval attributes can be created with a prompt such as ENTER INITIALS OR SEEK SIGNATURE, providing the flexibility to type initials or leave the cell blank for written initials. The same practice can be applied to date attributes. Include any other information that may be specific to your organization or application. Assign default values to the attributes wherever possible. For example, if your organization consistently specifies the same overall tolerances on drawing dimensions, the tolerance attributes should be assigned default values.

Figure 30-12.
A title block must comply with applicable standards. This title block complies with the ASME Y14.1, *Decimal Inch Drawing Sheet Size and Format* standard.

UNLESS OTHERWISE SPECIFIED INCHES	APPROVALS	DATE			
DECIMALS: in .X .XX .XXX ANGULAR: FINISH:	DRAWN				
	CHECKED		TITLE		
	APPROVED				
THIRD ANGLE PROJECTION	MATERIAL				
	FINISH		SIZE · FSCM NO. · DWG NO.		REV
	DO NOT SCALE DRAWING		SCALE	SHEET	OF

Figure 30-13.
Define attributes for each area of the title block.

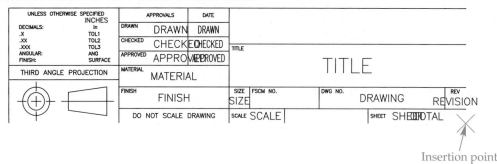

Insertion point

PROFESSIONAL TIP

The size of each area within the title block limits the number of characters displayed in a line of text. You may want to include a reminder about the maximum number of characters in the attribute prompt. For example, the prompt could read Enter drawing name (15 characters max). Each time a block or drawing containing the attribute is used, the prompt displays the reminder.

After you define each attribute in the title block, use the **BLOCK** tool to create a block of the defined attributes within the current file, or use the **WBLOCK** tool to save the drawing as a file to disk. Regardless of the method used, attributes allow you to enter title block data quickly and accurately without the use of text tools. Figure 30-14 shows the completed title block after insertion of the attribute block created in Figure 30-13.

Using the Block method

The **BLOCK** tool uses the **Block Definition** dialog box to create a block with associated attributes. When you select the objects for the block, be sure to include the defined attributes. For the insertion base point, pick a corner of the title block that is convenient to use each time the block is inserted. The point indicated in Figure 30-13 is an appropriate location for the insertion base point for this particular title block. Use the **Delete** option in the **Block Definition** dialog box to remove the selected objects from the drawing. Finally, create the block.

The drawing file now contains a title block with attributes. Insert the block in the current file as needed, or use **DesignCenter** to add the block to other drawings. When you insert the title block, enter the appropriate attribute information at the text prompt or in the **Edit Attributes** dialog box, depending on the current **ATTDIA** settings. If you are creating a template, insert the block at the appropriate location and save the file as a drawing template when template development is complete. Edit the values in an existing title block using the **Enhanced Attribute Editor**.

Figure 30-14.
The title block after insertion of the attributes. Dates and approvals are added when the drawing is complete.

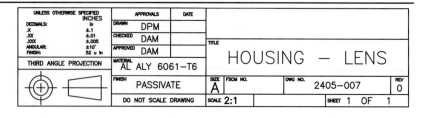

Using the Wblock method

The **WBLOCK** tool saves a drawing file to disk so it can be inserted into any drawing that is currently open. Drawings used in this manner should be given descriptive names. An A-size title block, for example, could be named TITLE_A or FORMAT_A.

Creating Revision Blocks

It is almost certain that a detail drawing will require revision at some time. Typical changes include design improvements and the correction of drafting errors. The first time a drawing is revised, it is usually assigned the revision letter *A*. If necessary, revision letters continue with *B* through *Y*, but the letters *I, O, Q, S, X,* and *Z* are not used because they might be confused with numbers.

Drawing layout formats include an area with columns specifically designated to record all drawing changes. This area is normally located at the upper-right corner of the drawing sheet and is commonly called the ***revision block***. A column for ***zones*** is included only if applicable. Although A-size and B-size title blocks may include zones, they are rarely needed.

Often, a table is used to create a revision block. Tables are described in Chapter 10. An alternative is to use blocks and attributes to document revisions. The process is similar to creating a title block, as previously explained. However, a revision block requires two separate blocks. The first block consists of lines and text and no attributes. It is used to form the title and heading rows. See **Figure 30-15A**. The second block includes attributes and is inserted whenever there is a revision. See **Figure 30-15B**.

Format the revision block according to industry or company standards, and use the correct layer, typically the 0 layer. As you create attributes, determine the appropriate text height and justification for each definition. Attributes should be defined for the zone (if necessary), revision letter, description, date, and approval. An APPROVED attribute can be given a prompt such as ENTER INITIALS OR SEEK SIGNATURE, providing the flexibility to type initials or leave the cell blank for written initials. The same practice can be applied to the date attribute.

Use the **BLOCK** or **WBLOCK** tool to create the blocks. If you create the blocks as wblocks, use descriptive names such as REVBLK or REV. **Figure 30-16** shows an example of revision information added by inserting the two blocks created in **Figure 30-15** in the upper-left inside corner of the border.

revision block: A block that provides space for the revision letter, a description of the change, the date, and approvals.

zones: A system of letters and numbers used on large drawings to help direct the print reader's attention to the correction location on the drawing.

Figure 30-15.
A revision block can be created using two separate blocks. A—The first block forms the title and heading rows. B—The second block includes attributes and is added each time an engineering change is employed. The revision block shown complies with the ASME Y14.1, *Decimal Inch Drawing Sheet Size and Format* standard.

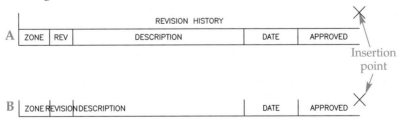

Figure 30-16.
The completed revision block after two blocks are inserted.

REVISION HISTORY				
ZONE	REV	DESCRIPTION	DATE	APPROVED
C3	A	ADDED .125 CHAMFER	08–30–10	

Figure 30-17.
A parts list can be created using two separate blocks. A—The first block forms the title (if used) and heading rows. B—The second block includes attributes and is inserted as many times as necessary to define each assembly component. The revision block shown complies with the ASME Y14.1, *Decimal Inch Drawing Sheet Size and Format* standard.

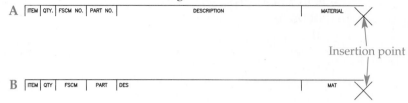

Creating Parts Lists

Assembly drawings require a parts list, or bill of materials, that provides information about each component of the assembly or subassembly. This information includes the quantity, FSCM (when necessary), part number, description, and item number for each component. In some organizations, the parts list is generated as a separate document, usually in an 8-1/2″ × 11″ format. At other companies, it is common practice to include the parts list on the face of the assembly drawing. If the parts list is added to the assembly drawing, it is usually placed directly above the title block, depending on industry and company standards. Parts lists provide another example of how attributes can be used to automate the documentation process.

A table is typically used to create a parts list, though blocks and attributes can also be used. The process is very similar to creating a revision block, as previously explained. The first block consists of lines and text, no attributes, and is used to add the title (if used) and heading rows. See **Figure 30-17A**. The second block includes attributes and is inserted as many times as necessary to document each assembly component. See **Figure 30-17B**.

Format the parts list according to industry or company standards, and use the correct layer, typically the 0 layer. As you create attributes, select the appropriate text height and justification for each definition. Attributes should be defined for the item number, quantity, FSCM (when necessary), part number, item description, and material specification.

Use the **BLOCK** or **WBLOCK** tool to create the blocks. If you save the blocks as wblocks, use a descriptive name such as PL for parts list or BOM for bill of materials. **Figure 30-18** shows an example of the beginning of a parts list developed by inserting the two blocks created in **Figure 30-17** above the title block.

Figure 30-18.
The beginning of a completed parts list after two blocks are inserted.

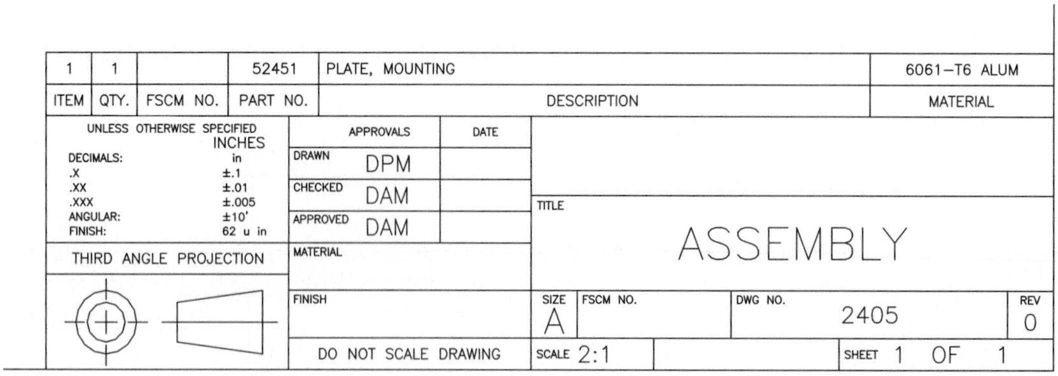

Using Fields to Reference Attributes

Use fields to display the value of an attribute in a location away from the block. To display an attribute value in a field, access the **Field** dialog box from within the **MTEXT** or **TEXT** tool, from the ribbon or menu browser, or by typing FIELD. In the **Field** dialog box, pick **Objects** from the **Field category:** drop-down list and then pick **Object** in the **Field names:** list box. Next, pick the **Select object** button to return to the drawing window and select the block containing the attribute.

When you select the block, the **Field** dialog box reappears with the available properties (attributes) listed. Pick the desired attribute tag to display the corresponding value in the **Preview:** box. Select the format and pick **OK** to insert the field in the text object.

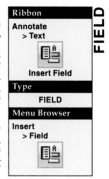

Collecting Attribute Information

Existing AutoCAD drawing information, including attributes, can be reused to create an AutoCAD table or exported to an external file. Refer to the Student CD: Supplemental Materials > Collecting Attribute Information for a detailed explanation on this process.

Chapter 30

A variety of useful layout content containing attributes can be added to your drawing template layout. Refer to the Student CD for detailed instructions to add a border, title block, and revision block to your drawing templates.

Chapter Test

Answer the following questions. Write your answers on a separate sheet of paper or complete the electronic chapter test on the Student CD.

1. What is an attribute?
2. Explain the purpose of the **ATTDEF** tool.
3. Define the function of the following attribute modes:
   A. **Invisible**
   B. **Constant**
   C. **Verify**
   D. **Preset**
4. What is the purpose of the **Default** text box in the **Attribute Definition** dialog box?
5. How can you edit attributes before they are included within a block?
6. How can you change an existing attribute from visible to invisible?
7. If you select a block's attributes using the **Window** or **Crossing** selection method as the attributes are created, in what order will you be prompted for the attribute values?
8. What purpose does the **ATTREQ** system variable serve?
9. List the three options for attribute display.
10. Explain how to change the value of an inserted attribute.

11. What is meant by *global attribute editing*?
12. After a block with attributes has been saved, what method can you use to change the order of prompts when the block is inserted?
13. What three detailing or documentation tasks can be automated using attributes?
14. What section of an assembly drawing provides information about each component of the assembly or subassembly?
15. What allows you to display the value of an attribute in a location away from the block?

Drawing Problems

Note: Some of the drawing problems refer to Template Development activities from previous chapters. These activities are located on the Student CD. If you have not been building these templates throughout this textbook, create the templates now.

▼ Basic

1. Start a new drawing. Draw the structural steel wide flange shape shown below using the dimensions given. Do not dimension the drawing. Create attributes for the drawing using the information given. Make a block of the drawing and name it W12 X 40. Insert the block once to test the attributes. Save the drawing as P30-1.

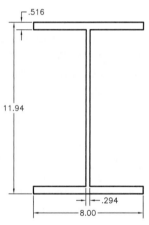

Attributes			
	Steel	W12 × 40	Visible
	Mfr.	Ryerson	Invisible
	Price	$.30/lb	Invisible
	Weight	40 lbs/ft	Invisible
	Length	10′	Invisible
	Code	03116WF	Invisible

2. Follow the instructions in the Template Development portion of the Student CD to complete the MECHANICAL-INCH template file.

3. Follow the instructions in the Template Development portion of the Student CD to complete the MECHANICAL-METRIC template file.

4. Follow the instructions in the Template Development portion of the Student CD to complete the ARCHITECTURAL-US template file.

5. Follow the instructions in the Template Development portion of the Student CD to complete the ARCHITECTURAL-METRIC template file.

6. Follow the instructions in the Template Development portion of the Student CD to complete the CIVIL-US template file.

7. Follow the instructions in the Template Development portion of the Student CD to complete the CIVIL-METRIC template file.

▼ Intermediate

8. Open the drawing from Problem 1 (P30-1) and construct the floor plan shown using the dimensions given. Dimension the drawing. Insert the block W12 X 40 six times as shown. Required attribute data are given in the chart below the drawing. Enter the appropriate information for the attributes as you are prompted. Note that the steel columns labeled 3 and 6 require slightly different attribute data. You can speed the drawing process by using **ARRAY** or **COPY**. Save the drawing as P30-8.

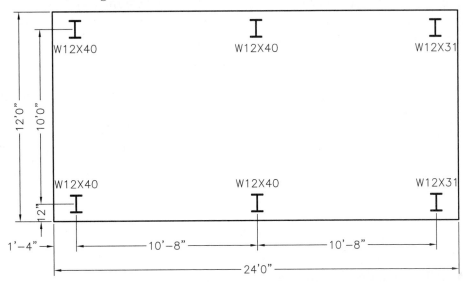

	Steel	Mfr.	Price	Weight	Length	Code
Blocks ①, ②, ④, & ⑤	W12 × 40	Ryerson	$.30/lb	40 lbs/ft	10′	03116WF
Blocks ③ & ⑥	W12 × 31	Ryerson	$.30/lb	31 lbs/ft	8.5′	03125WF

9. Open the drawing you created in Problem 30-1 (P30-1) and save it as P30-9. Edit the W12 X 40 block in the newly saved drawing according to the following information.

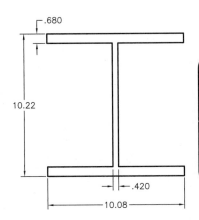

Attributes			
	Steel	W10 × 60	Visible
	Mfr.	Ryerson	Invisible
	Price	$.25/lb	Invisible
	Weight	60 lbs/ft	Invisible
	Length	10′	Invisible
	Code	02457WF	Invisible

Drawing Problems – Chapter 30

10. Open the drawing from Problem 8 (P30-8). Create a tab-separated extraction file for the blocks in the drawing. Extract the following information for each block:
    * Block name
    * Steel
    * Manufacturer
    * Price
    * Weight
    * Length
    * Code
    Save the file as P30-9.txt.

11. Open the drawing from Problem 8 (P30-8). Create a table from the block attribute data and insert it into the drawing. Save the drawing as P30-10

12. Select a drawing from Chapter 26 and create a bill of materials for it using the **Data Extraction** wizard. Use the comma-separated format to display the file. Display the file in Windows Notepad.

13. Create a drawing of the computer workstation layout in the classroom or office in which you are working. Provide attribute definitions for all of the items listed here.
    * Workstation ID number
    * Computer brand name
    * Model number
    * Processor chip
    * Amount of RAM
    * Hard disk capacity
    * Video graphics card brand and model
    * CD-ROM/DVD-ROM speed
    * Date purchased
    * Price
    * Vendor's phone number
    * Other data as you see fit
    Generate and extract file for all of the computers in the drawing.

CHAPTER 31

Annotative Objects

Learning Objectives

After completing this chapter, you will be able to do the following:

✓ Explain the differences between manual and annotative object scaling.
✓ Define objects as annotative.
✓ Create and use annotative objects in model space.
✓ Display annotative objects in scaled layout viewports.
✓ Adjust the scale of annotations according to a new drawing scale.
✓ Use annotative objects to help prepare multiview drawings.

Annotation and similar items, such as dimension objects and hatch patterns, are scaled so that information appears on-screen and is plotted correctly relative to full-scale objects. AutoCAD provides annotative tools to automate this process. Annotative tools also provide additional flexibility when you are working with layouts to create multiview drawings. This chapter describes the tools and options for creating and using *annotative objects*.

annotation: Letters, numbers, words, and notes used to describe information on a drawing.

annotative objects: AutoCAD objects that can be made to adapt automatically to the current drawing scale.

> ## Introduction to Annotative Objects

Objects are always drawn at full scale in model space. For example, if you are drawing a small machine part and the length of the part is 2 mm, the line should actually be drawn 2 mm long in model space. Another example is when you are drawing a building and the length of the building is 80′; the line should actually be drawn 80′ long in model space. These examples describe drawing objects that are too small or too large to be laid out or plotted at full scale, and as a result must be scaled to fit properly on a sheet.

When you *scale* a drawing, you increase or decrease the *displayed* size of drawing objects. This is done using a properly scaled floating viewport in a layout. Scaling a drawing greatly affects the display of items added to drawing objects in model space, such as annotations, because these items should be the same size on a plotted sheet relative to other objects, regardless of the displayed size, or scale, of the rest of the drawing. See Figure 31-1.

scale: The ratio between the actual size of drawing objects and the size at which the objects are plotted on a sheet of paper. Also the process of enlarging or reducing objects to fit properly on a sheet of paper.

Figure 31-1.
The drawing features in this example are so large they must be scaled in order to fit on a standard size sheet. The annotations are scaled according to the plotted size of the drawing; otherwise, they would be so small they could not be seen.

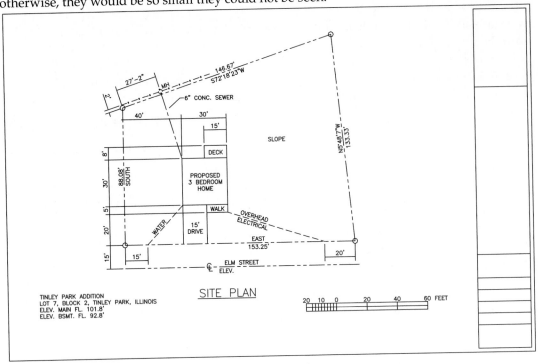

Traditionally, annotations, hatches, and other objects are scaled manually, which means you determine the scale factor of the drawing scale and then multiply the scale factor by the plotted size of the objects. In contrast, AutoCAD scales annotative objects automatically according to the annotation scale you select, which is the same as the drawing scale. This eliminates the need for you to calculate the scale factor and manually adjust the size of objects according to the drawing scale.

PROFESSIONAL TIP

You should use annotative objects instead of traditional manual scaling even if you do not anticipate using a drawing scale other than 1:1.

Defining Annotative Objects

Annotative objects include single-line and multiline text, dimensions, leaders and multileaders, GD&T symbols created using the **TOLERANCE** tool, hatch patterns, blocks, and attributes. The method used to define objects as annotative varies depending on the object type. Objects can be made annotative when they are first created or converted from non-annotative to annotative.

AutoCAD and Its Applications—Basics

Creating New Annotative Objects

Single-line and multiline text is defined as annotative when it is drawn using an annotative text style. To make a text style annotative, pick the **Annotative** check box in the **Size** area of the **Text Style** dialog box. See **Figure 31-2.** For most applications, a drawing should contain at least one annotative and one non-annotative text style. An example of text that is typically not annotative is text added directly to a layout. Recall that layouts are printed at a scale of 1:1.

Dimensions are annotative if they are created using an annotative dimension style. To make a dimension style annotative, pick the **Annotative** check box in the **Fit** tab of the **New** (or **Modify**) **Dimension Style** dialog box. See **Figure 31-3.** Leaders and

Figure 31-2.
Single-line and multiline text objects are annotative if they are drawn using an annotative text style.

Pick to make the text style annotative

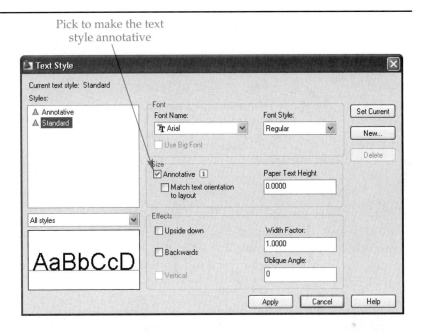

Figure 31-3.
Dimensions, leaders, and GD&T symbols created using the **TOLERANCE** tool are annotative if they are drawn using an annotative dimension style.

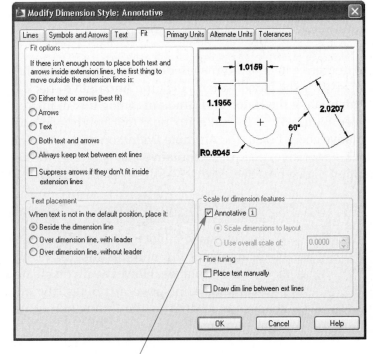

Pick to make the dimension style annotative

Figure 31-4.
Multileaders are
annotative if they
are drawn using
an annotative
multileader style.

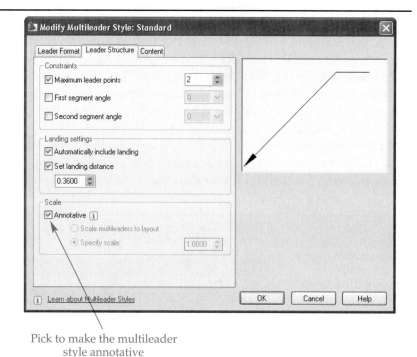

Pick to make the multileader
style annotative

GD&T symbols created using the **TOLERANCE** tool are also defined as annotative when they are drawn using an annotative dimension style. Multileaders are defined as annotative when they are drawn using an annotative multileader style. To make a multileader style annotative, pick the **Annotative** check box in the **Leader Structure** tab of the **Modify Multileader Style** dialog box. See **Figure 31-4**.

NOTE

When you create an annotative multileader using the block multi-leader type, the block automatically becomes annotative, even if the block is not set as annotative.

Annotative hatch patterns are defined when you set the hatch scale as annotative when creating the hatch pattern. Pick the **Annotative** check box in the **Options** area on the **Hatch** tab of the **Hatch and Gradient** dialog box to make the hatch pattern annotative. See **Figure 31-5**. To make attribute text height and spacing annotative, pick the **Annotative** check box in the **Attribute Definition** dialog box. See **Figure 31-6A.** To make a block annotative, pick the **Annotative** check box in the **Behavior** area of the **Block Definition** dialog box. See **Figure 31-6B**.

NOTE

When you make a block annotative, any attributes included in the block automatically become annotative, even if the attributes are not set as annotative. However, if you create a non-annotative block that contains annotative attributes, the annotative attribute scale changes according to the annotation scale, while the size of the block remains fixed.

Figure 31-5.
Set the hatch
pattern scale to be
annotative when
you create the hatch
pattern.

Pick to make the hatch
scale anotative

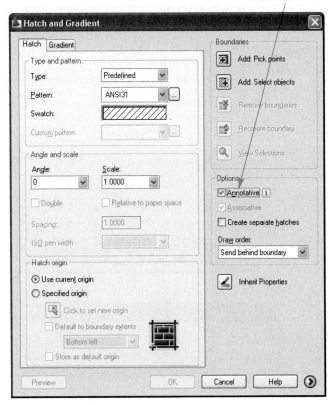

Making Existing Objects Annotative

You should specify objects as annotative when you first create them in model space. However, any of the objects described in the previous section that were originally drawn as non-annotative can be given annotative status. The appropriate style controls the annotative status of single-line and multiline text, dimensions, leaders and multileaders, and GD&T symbols created using the **TOLERANCE** tool. As a result, changing the style in which the original object was drawn to an annotative style makes the object annotative. Existing hatch patterns, blocks, and attributes must be edited or recreated in order to be defined as annotative.

One method that is used to make existing objects annotative is to override the non-annotative status of an object using the **Properties** palette. This technique is most effective when you want to make a limited number of objects annotative. The location of the annotative properties in the **Properties** palette varies depending on the selected object. The **Annotative** and **Annotative scale** properties are common to all annotative objects. The **Annotative** property can be used to make non-annotative objects annotative by selecting **Yes** from the drop-down list. To make annotative objects non-annotative, pick the **No** from the **Annotative** drop-down list.

CAUTION

Use caution when overriding an object to annotative status. Annotative objects such as text should originally be drawn in or changed to an annotative text style for most applications.

Figure 31-6.
Set blocks and attributes as annotative when you create them.

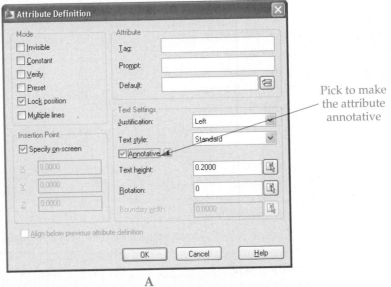

Pick to make
the attribute
annotative

A

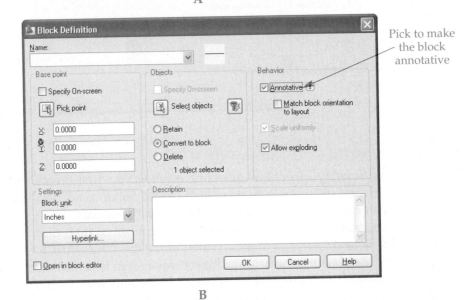

Pick to make
the block
annotative

B

NOTE

The **MATCHPROP** tool can be used to select the properties of annotative objects and apply those properties to existing objects, making the objects annotative.

Exercise 31-1

Complete the exercise on the Student CD.

AutoCAD and Its Applications—Basics

Using annotative objects reduces the need to determine the drawing scale factor. However, you must still identify the appropriate drawing scale. The drawing scale is the same as the *annotation scale*. Ideally, drawing scale should be determined during template development and incorporated into the settings in your template files. If drawing scale is not applied to settings in your templates, you should identify the scale before beginning a drawing, or at least before you begin placing annotations.

annotation scale: The scale AutoCAD uses to calculate the scale factor that is applied to annotative objects.

Setting Annotation Scale

Annotation scale should be set before you begin adding annotations, so that annotations are scaled automatically. However, it may be necessary to adjust the annotation scale throughout the drawing process, especially if the drawing scale changes or if multiple drawings with different scales are prepared on one sheet. You should approach scaling annotations in model space by first selecting an annotation scale and then placing annotative objects. When annotations at another scale are to be drawn, pick the new annotation scale before placing the annotative objects.

The **Annotation Scale** flyout button on the model space status bar is the primary tool for adjusting annotation scale. See Figure 31-7. Pick the desired annotation scale from the menu. The annotation scale can also be set in the **Properties** palette by selecting the annotation scale from the **Annotation Scale** option in the **Misc** category. This option is available when no objects are selected.

Figure 31-7.
Annotation scale options are located on the status bar. If you display the drawing status bar, the **Annotation Scale** button moves from the application status bar to the drawing status bar.

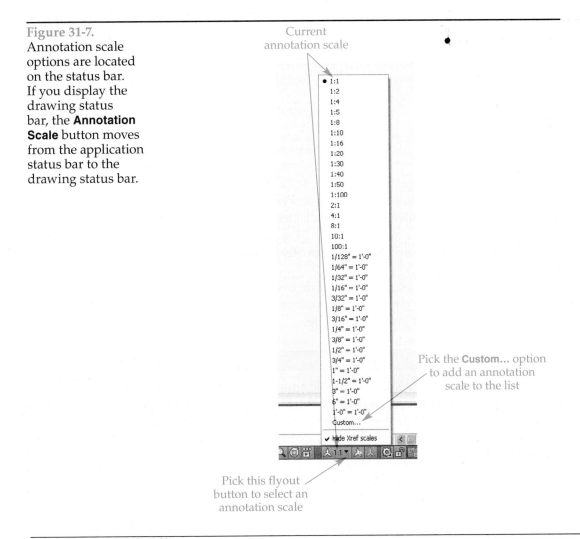

Current annotation scale

Pick the **Custom...** option to add an annotation scale to the list

Pick this flyout button to select an annotation scale

If a scale is not available from the **Annotation Scale** menu, choose the **Custom...** option to access the **Edit Scale List** dialog box. The **Edit Scale List** dialog box can also be accessed by picking **Format > Scale List...** from the menu browser, or from the **Options** dialog box > **User Preferences** tab > **Edit Scale List...** button. The **Edit Scale List** dialog box is the same dialog box used to edit floating viewport scales and is fully described in Chapter 29.

NOTE

Annotation scale sets the drawing scale in model space for controlling annotative objects. Viewport scale sets the drawing scale in a layout floating viewport to define the drawing scale. Both scales should be the same and should match the drawing scale.

Controlling Model Space Linetype Scale

As described in Chapter 29, the **CELTSCALE**, **PSLTSCALE**, and **MSLTSCALE** system variables control how the **LTSCALE** system variable is applied to linetypes in model space and paper space. Leave the **CELTSCALE**, **PSLTSCALE**, and **MSLTSCALE** system variables at their default setting of 1 to apply the **LTSCALE** value correctly according to the current annotation scale. However, when you change the annotation scale, you must remember to use the **REGEN** tool to regenerate the display. Otherwise, the linetype scale will not update according to the new scale.

PROFESSIONAL TIP

When you open a drawing in AutoCAD 2009 that was created in an AutoCAD version earlier than AutoCAD 2008, the **MSLTSCALE** system variable is set to 0. Change the value to 1 to take advantage of annotative linetype scaling.

Drawing Annotative Text

Annotative text is created using the same tools as non-annotative text. The difference is the value you enter for text height. When you create annotative multiline text, ensure that the **Annotative** button is selected and enter the paper text height, such as 1/4″, in the **Size** text box. See **Figure 31-8.** The text scale, which includes spacing, width, and paragraph settings, automatically adjusts according to the current annotation scale.

When drawing annotative single-line text, after you pick the start point, you are prompted to specify the paper height, such as 1/4″. The text scale automatically adjusts according to the current annotation scale.

NOTE

The **Properties** palette contains specific annotative text properties in addition to those displayed for all annotative objects. For example, the **Paper text height** property can be used to enter a paper text height. The **Model text height** property is provided for reference and identifies the height of the text after the scale factor is automatically applied.

Figure 31-8.
Creating annotative multiline text. Multiline text could potentially contain both annotative and non-annotative text.

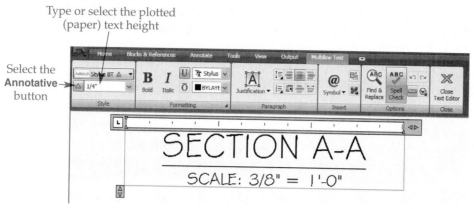

Drawing Annotative Dimensions

Annotative dimensions, leaders, GD&T symbols created using the **TOLERANCE** tool, and multileaders are drawn using the same tools as non-annotative dimensions. Once you activate an annotative dimension or multileader style and select the appropriate annotation scale, the process of placing correctly scaled dimensions is automatic.

However, you must still determine the correct dimension and text location and spacing from objects when you add dimensions and text to scaled drawings. This involves multiplying the scale factor by the plotted spacing. For example, if your first dimension line should be 3/4″ from an object when plotted and your drawing is scaled to 1/4″ = 1′-0″, the correct spacing in model space is 36″ from the object (a scale factor of 48 × 3/4″ = 36″).

Adding Annotative Hatch Patterns

The difference between adding annotative and non-annotative hatch patterns is the way in which the hatch scale is affected by the drawing scale. When you create annotative hatch patterns, the scale you enter in the **Scale:** text box produces the same results regardless of the annotation scale you select. For example, if you enter a value in the **Scale:** text box that is appropriate for an annotation scale of 1/4″ = 1′-0″, and then change the annotation scale to 1″ = 1′-0″, the displayed scale of the hatch pattern does not change relative to the drawing display. It looks the same on the 1/4″ = 1′-0″ scaled drawing as on the 1″ = 1′-0″ scaled drawing.

In contrast, when you create non-annotative hatch patterns, if you enter a value in the **Scale:** text box that is appropriate for a drawing scaled to 1/4″ = 1′-0″ and then change the drawing scale to 1″ = 1′-0″, the displayed scale of the hatch pattern increases. It looks four times as large on the 1″ = 1′-0″scaled drawing as on the 1/4″ = 1′-0″ scaled drawing.

Placing Annotative Blocks and Attributes

Annotative blocks are typically used for annotation purposes and can be classified as *schematic blocks*. When you insert an annotative schematic block, AutoCAD determines the block scale based on the current annotation scale, eliminating the need for you to enter a scale factor. For most applications, annotative blocks should be inserted at a scale of 1 in order for the annotation scale to be applied correctly. Entering a scale other than 1 adjusts the scale of the block by multiplying the block scale by the annotation scale.

schematic block:
A block that is originally drawn at a 1:1 scale.

Exercise 31-2

Complete the exercise on the Student CD.

Displaying Annotative Objects in Layouts

Once you create drawing features and symbols and add annotative objects according to the appropriate annotation scale, you are ready to display and plot your drawing using a paper space layout. Refer to Chapter 28 to review the process of using layouts and accessing paper space.

Scaling a Floating Viewport

A drawing is scaled in an active floating viewport. Refer to Chapter 29 to review the process of using and scaling floating viewports. Figure 31-9 shows an example of a drawing scaled to 3/8″ = 1′-0″. The drawing features were drawn at full scale in model

Figure 31-9.
A drawing is scaled in a floating paper space viewport. Picking the **Viewport Scale** flyout button is one of the easiest ways to set the viewport scale.

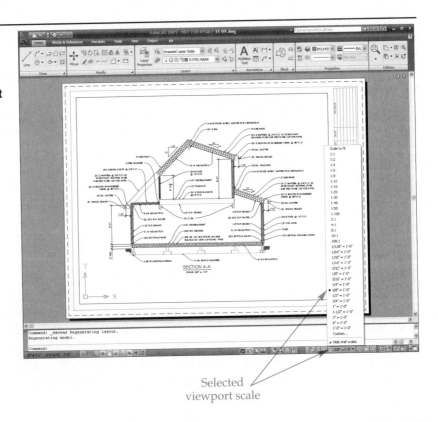

Selected viewport scale

space. The annotation scale in model space was then set to 3/8″ = 1′-0″, and annotative text, dimensions, multileaders, hatch patterns, and blocks were added. The annotative objects were automatically scaled according to the 3/8″ = 1′-0″ annotation scale.

In the example shown in Figure 31-9, the viewport scale and the annotation scale are the same, which is typical when scaling annotative objects. If you select a different viewport scale from the **Viewport Scale** flyout button, the annotation scale automatically adjusts according to the viewport scale. However, if you adjust the viewport scale by zooming, for example, the annotation scale does not change. The viewport scale and the annotation scale must match in order for your drawing and annotative objects to be scaled correctly.

The **Properties** palette can also be used to control viewport and annotation scale. In order to use this method, you must be in paper space to access the viewport properties. In the **Properties** palette, select **Standard scale** from the list, pick the drop-down arrow, and choose a viewport scale. The annotation scale is adjusted using the **Annotation scale** option. See Figure 31-10.

PROFESSIONAL TIP

Lock the viewport display to avoid zooming and disassociating the viewport scale from the annotation scale. Refer to Chapter 29 for more information on locking and unlocking floating viewports.

Figure 31-10.
The **Properties** palette can also be used to set the viewport and annotation scale.

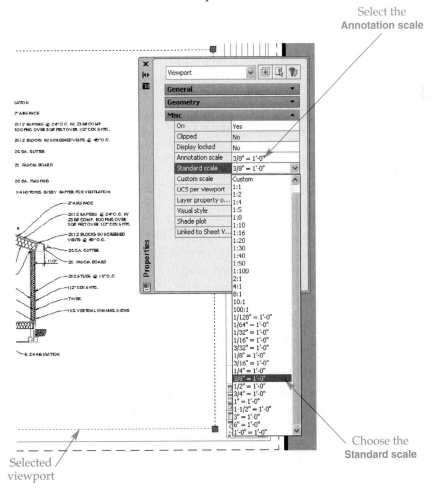

Select the
Annotation scale

Choose the
Standard scale

Selected
viewport

Exercise 31-3
Complete the exercise on the Student CD.

Changing Drawing Scale

No matter how much you plan a drawing, drawing scale can change throughout the drawing process for a variety of reasons. If it is necessary to use a smaller sheet, drawing scale may need to be reduced. If drawing features are redesigned and become larger, or if additional detail must be shown on the drawing, the drawing scale may need to be increased.

Changing the drawing scale affects the size and position of your annotations. A major advantage of using annotative objects is the ease in which annotation scale is adjusted according to different drawing scales. When adjusting drawing scale, remember that the annotation scale is the same as the drawing scale.

You can change annotation scale in model space by selecting a new annotation scale from the **Annotation Scale** flyout button. To change the annotation scale in an active viewport in a layout, adjust the viewport scale by selecting the drawing scale from the **Viewport Scale** flyout button. Again, the viewport and annotation scale should be set to the same scale for most applications.

Using the Annoupdate Tool

When you create single-line text using a non-annotative text style, and then change the style to be annotative, text drawn using the style becomes annotative. However, the properties of the annotative text remain set according to the non-annotative text style. When you create annotative text using an annotative text style, and then change the style to be non-annotative, text drawn in the style becomes non-annotative. However, the properties of the non-annotative text remain set according to the annotative style.

Type
ANNOUPDATE

Use the **ANNOUPDATE** tool to update text properties to reflect the current properties of the text style in which the text is drawn. When prompted to select objects, pick the text you want to update to the current modified text style. After making your selections, press [Enter] to exit the tool and update the text.

Introduction to Scale Representations

So far, the content of this chapter has assumed that a drawing has been developed using a single annotation scale. In order for the scale of annotative objects to change when the drawing scale changes, annotative objects must support the new scale. This involves assigning new annotation scales to annotative objects. If annotative objects do not support the new scale, the annotative object scale does not change, and can actually cause the objects to become invisible. The following example helps to describe this concept.

Figure 31-11A shows an example of a drawing scaled to 3/8″ = 1′-0″ and placed on an architectural C-size sheet. The annotation scale in this example is set to 3/8″ = 1′-0″, so the annotative objects are automatically scaled according to a 3/8″ = 1′-0″ drawing scale. In order to change the scale of the drawing to 1/2″ = 1′-0″ to display additional detail, you must ensure that the annotative objects support a scale of 1/2″ = 1′-0″.

annotative object representation:
Display of an annotative object at an annotation scale that the object supports.

Once the annotation scale of 1/2″ = 1′-0″ is added to the annotative objects, you can change the annotation scale or the viewport scale to 1/2″ = 1′-0″, and the annotative objects are automatically scaled correctly. See **Figure 31-11B.** The annotative objects in this example support two annotation scales: 3/8″ = 1′-0″ and 1/2″ = 1′-0″. As a result, two *annotative object representations* can be displayed.

Figure 31-11.

A—A drawing created using an annotation scale of 3/8″ = 1′-0″ on an architectural C-size sheet. The annotative objects are automatically drawn at the correct scale. B—The same drawing, modified to an annotation scale of 1/2″ = 1′-0″ and placed on an architectural D-size sheet. An annotation scale of 1/2″ = 1′-0″ has been added to all the annotative objects, allowing the objects to adapt to the new scale automatically.

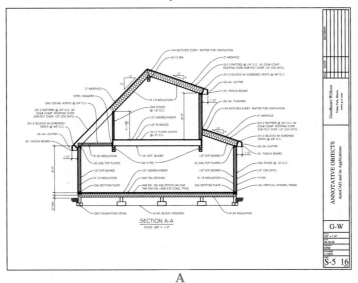

A

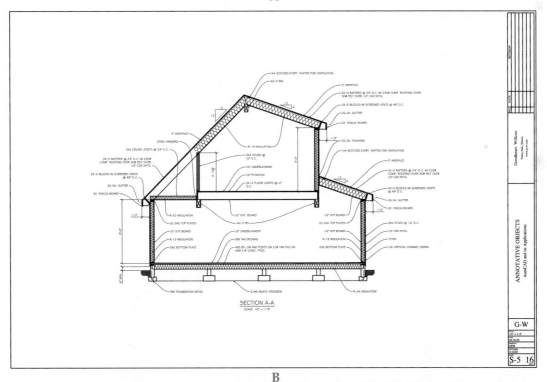

B

NOTE

Annotative objects display an icon when you hover the crosshairs over the objects. Objects that support a single annotation scale display the annotative icon shown in **Figure 31-12A.** Annotative objects that support more than one annotation scale display the annotative icon shown in **Figure 31-12B.** These icons are displayed only if you have the selection preview options selected in the **Selection** tab of the **Options** dialog box.

Figure 31-12.
Examples of
annotative objects
that support single
and multiple
annotation scales.

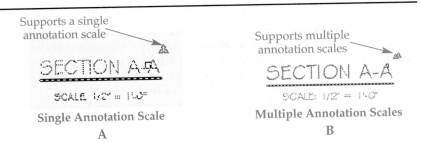

Supports a single
annotation scale

SECTION A-A

SCALE 1/2" = 1'-0"

Single Annotation Scale
A

Supports multiple
annotation scales

SECTION A-A

SCALE: 1/2" = 1'-0"

Multiple Annotation Scales
B

Understanding Annotation Visibility

Before changing the current annotation scale, you should understand its effects on annotative object visibility. If annotative objects do not support an annotation scale, the annotative object scale does not change. Additionally, annotative objects can be made to disappear when an annotation scale that the objects do not support is made current. For example, if annotative objects only support an annotation scale of 3/8" = 1'-0", when an annotation scale of 1/2" = 1'-0" is set current, the annotative object scale remains set at 3/8" = 1'-0", and the objects become invisible.

The easiest way to turn on and off annotative object visibility according to the current annotation scale is to pick the **Annotation Visibility** button on the status bar. See **Figure 31-13.** This is most effective when you are adding and deleting annotation

Figure 31-13.
A—The annotative objects in this example only support a 3/8" = 1'-0" annotation scale. However, with **ANNOALLVISIBLE** turned on, all annotative objects are shown, even with the annotation scale set to 1/2" = 1'-0". B—The **Annotation Visibility** button on the status bar controls this feature. If you display the drawing status bar, the **Annotation Visibility** button moves from the application status bar to the drawing status bar.

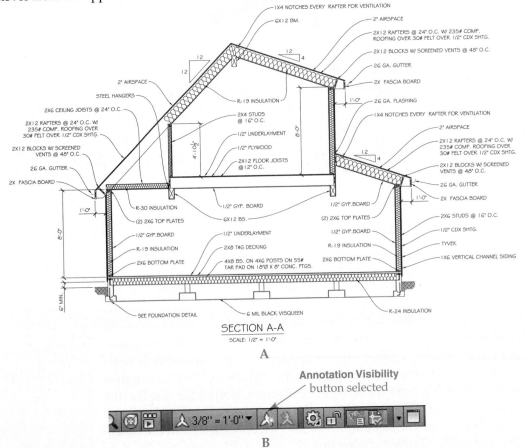

Annotation Visibility
button selected

B

AutoCAD and Its Applications—Basics

Figure 31-14.
When **ANNOALLVISIBLE** is turned off, only those annotative objects that support the current annotation scale are shown. The annotative objects in this example are not shown because they only support a 3/8″ = 1′-0″ annotation scale, and the current annotation scale is 1/2″ = 1′-0″.

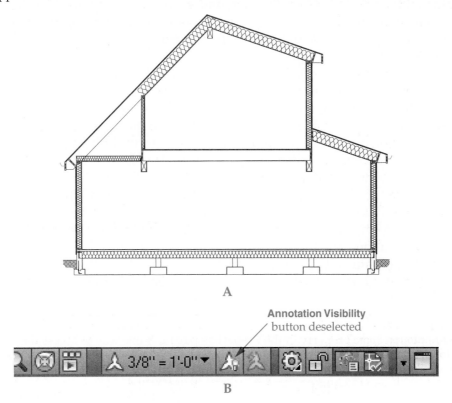

A

Annotation Visibility
button deselected

B

scales to or from annotative objects. If multiple annotation scales have been added to the annotative objects, the annotative object representation is shown, based on the current scale.

Deselect the **Annotation Visibility** button to display only the annotative objects that support the current annotation scale. When this option is used, any annotative objects that are not supported by the current annotation scale become invisible. See Figure 31-14. This is most effective when you want to annotate a drawing, or a portion of a drawing, using a different annotation scale and you do not want to see annotative object representations specific to a different annotation scale. Turning off the visibility of annotative objects that do not support the current annotation scale is also extremely effective when preparing multiview drawings because it eliminates the need to create separate layers for objects displayed at different scales. This process is described later in this chapter.

Adding and Deleting Annotation Scales

One method for assigning additional annotation scales to annotative objects is to add the scales to selected objects. This method can be used whenever the drawing scale changes, but it is especially effective when you only want to add annotation scales to specific objects, such as when creating multiview drawings. Examples that demonstrate this function are described later in this chapter. You can add annotation scales to selected objects using the **Properties** palette or annotation scaling tools.

The annotation scale can be deleted from annotative objects if an annotation scale is no longer used, should not be displayed in a specific view, or is making it difficult to work with annotative objects. When an annotation scale is deleted from annotative objects, the scale is no longer applied. You can delete annotation scales from selected objects using the **Properties** palette or annotation scaling tools.

Using the Properties palette

The **Properties** palette can be used to add annotation scales to selected annotative objects. The location of the annotative properties in the **Properties** palette varies depending on the selected object. The **Annotative scale** property displays the annotation scale currently applied to the selected annotative object and contains an ellipsis button (...) that opens the **Annotation Object Scale** dialog box when selected. See Figure 31-15.

The **Object Scale List** shows all of the annotation scales associated with the selected annotative object. A scale must be listed in order for the scale to be applied to the annotative object. If a different annotation scale is selected, and that scale is not displayed in the **Object Scale List**, annotative objects do not adapt to the new annotation scale, and you have the option of turning off the annotative objects' visibility. Using the previous example, 1/2″ = 1′-0″ must be listed in the **Object Scale List** in order for the annotative objects to adapt to the new annotation scale of 1/2″ = 1′-0″.

Pick the **Add...** button to add a scale to the **Object Scale List**. This opens the **Add Scales to Object** dialog box. Highlight scales in the **Scale List** and pick the **OK** button to add the scales to the **Object Scale List**. Once a scale is added to the **Object Scale List**, picking an annotation scale that corresponds to any of the listed scales automatically scales the selected annotative object. To remove a scale from the **Object Scale List**, highlight the scale you want to remove and pick the **Delete** button.

Figure 31-15.
A—The **Annotation scale** property in the **Properties** palette is one way to access the **Annotation Object Scale** dialog box. B—This dialog box can be used to add and delete annotation scales to and from annotative objects.

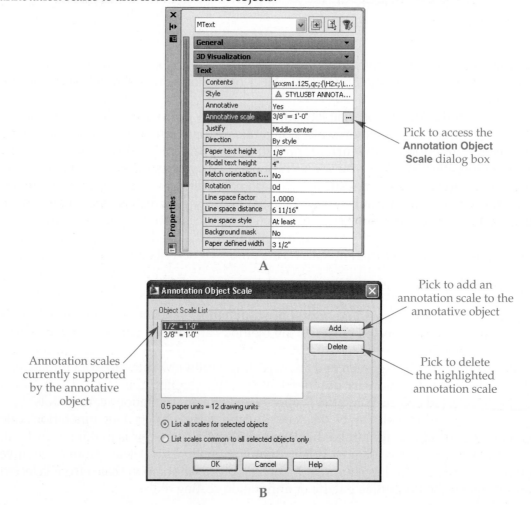

Pick to access the **Annotation Object Scale** dialog box

A

Pick to add an annotation scale to the annotative object

Annotation scales currently supported by the annotative object

Pick to delete the highlighted annotation scale

B

If multiple annotative objects are selected, it may be helpful to display only the annotative scales that are common to the selected objects. This can be done by selecting the **List scales common to all selected objects only** radio button. To show all the annotation scales associated with any of the selected objects, even if some of the objects do not support the listed scales, pick the **List all scales for selected objects** radio button. Picking this option is helpful when you want to delete a scale that is listed but that is only applied to certain objects.

NOTE

If a desired scale is not available in the **Add Scales to Object** dialog box, you must close the **Annotation Object Scale** dialog box and access the **Edit Scale List** dialog box to add a new scale to the list of available scales.

Using the Objectscale tool

The **OBJECTSCALE** tool can also be used to add and delete annotation scales supported by annotative objects. A quick way to access the **OBJECTSCALE** tool is to select an annotative object and then right-click and pick the **Add/Delete Scale...** option from the **Annotative Objects Scales** cascading menu of the shortcut menu. If you activate the **OBJECTSCALE** tool by right-clicking on objects, the **Annotation Object Scale** dialog box is displayed and annotation scales can be added to or deleted from the selected objects. If you access the tool before selecting objects, all annotative objects are displayed, even those objects that do not support the current annotation scale. Select the annotative objects to modify and press [Enter] to display the **Annotation Object Scale** dialog box.

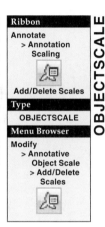

Automatically Adding Annotation Scales

Another technique for assigning additional annotation scales to annotative objects is to add a selected annotation scale automatically to all annotative objects in the drawing. This eliminates the need to add annotation scales to individual annotative objects and quickly produces newly scaled drawings.

The ability to add an annotation scale to all existing annotative objects is controlled by the **ANNOAUTOSCALE** system variable. You can enter 1, –1, 2, –2, 3, –3, 4, or –4, depending on the desired effect. Figure 31-16A describes each option. Once the initial value is entered, the easiest way to toggle this system variable on and off is to pick the button on the status bar, shown in Figure 31-16B.

CAUTION

Use caution when adding annotation scales automatically. Due to the effectiveness and transparency of the tool, annotation scales are often added to annotative objects unintentionally. Though scales can later be deleted, this causes additional work and confusion.

Exercise 31-4
Complete the exercise on the Student CD.

Figure 31-16.
A—Options of the **ANNOAUTOSCALE** system variable. B—Once the initial **ANNOAUTOSCALE** system variable is entered, use the button on the status bar to toggle **ANNOAUTOSCALE** on and off. If you display the drawing status bar, the **ANNOAUTOSCALE** button moves from the application status bar to the drawing status bar.

Value	Mode	Description
1	On	Adds the selected annotation scale to annotative objects, not including those drawn on a layer that is turned off, frozen, locked, or frozen in a viewport.
–1	Off	1 behavior is used when **ANNOAUTOSCALE** is turned back on.
2	On	Adds the selected annotation scale to annotative objects, not including those drawn on a layer that is turned off, frozen, or frozen in a viewport.
–2	Off	2 behavior is used when **ANNOAUTOSCALE** is turned back on.
3	On	Adds the selected annotation scale to annotative objects, not including those drawn on a layer that is locked.
–3	Off	3 behavior is used when **ANNOAUTOSCALE** is turned back on.
4	On	Adds the selected annotation scale to all annotative objects regardless of the status of the layer on which the annotative object is drawn. 4 is the AutoCAD default setting when toggled on.
–4	Off	4 behavior is used when **ANNOAUTOSCALE** is turned back on. –4 is the AutoCAD default setting when toggled off.

A

Pick to toggle the
ANNOAUTOSCALE system
variable on or off

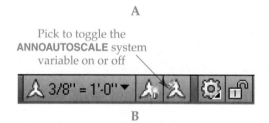

B

Preparing Multiview Drawings

Mechanical drawings and architectural construction drawings often contain sections and details drawn at different scales. Using annotative objects offers several advantages, especially when objects in model space are viewed at different scales in layouts. Several views are created in model space in a single file. A different annotation scale is applied to each drawing view that contains annotative objects, reducing the need to calculate multiple drawing scale factors. Additionally, by adjusting the annotative scale representation's visibility and position, you can prepare differently scaled multiview drawings, while eliminating the need to use separate, scale-specific layers and annotations.

Creating Differently Scaled Drawings

The concepts described in this chapter can be applied to developing multiview drawings, with each view displayed at a specific scale. By adjusting the annotation scale, you can draw annotative objects at different scales while maintaining the appropriate scale of previously drawn annotative objects.

Figure 31-17A shows an example of two different drawing views, both drawn at full scale in model space. The full section in **Figure 31-17A** is scaled to 3/8″ = 1′-0″. To prepare this view, the annotation scale in model space is set to 3/8″ = 1′-0″, and

Figure 31-17.
Two different drawing views drawn at full scale in model space. The full section uses an annotation scale of 3/8″ = 1′-0″, and the stair section uses an annotation scale of 1/2″ = 1′-0″. A—Annotation visibility is on. B—Annotation visibility is off.

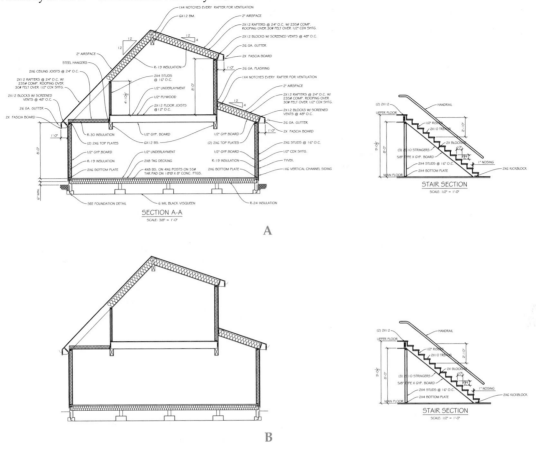

annotative text, dimensions, multileaders, hatch patterns, and blocks are added. The annotative objects are automatically scaled according to the 3/8″ = 1′-0″ annotation scale. The stair section in this example is scaled to 1/2″ = 1′-0″. To prepare this view, the annotation scale in model space is changed from 3/8″ = 1′-0″ to 1/2″ = 1′-0″. Then annotative text, dimensions, and multileaders are added. The annotative objects are automatically scaled according to the 1/2″ = 1′-0″ annotation scale. If you look closely, you can see the different scales applied to the drawing views.

With annotation visibility on, as shown in Figure 31-17A, you can see all annotative objects, and observe the effects of using different scales. With annotation visibility off, as shown in Figure 31-17B, only annotative objects that support the current annotation scale, which is 1/2″ = 1′-0″ in this example, can be seen.

The next step is to display and plot the drawing using multiple paper space viewports. Figure 31-18 shows an architectural D-size sheet layout with two floating viewports. One viewport is used to display the full section at a viewport scale of 3/8″ = 1′-0″. The other viewport is used to display the stair section at a viewport scale of 1/2″ = 1′-0″.

Exercise 31-5
Complete the exercise on the Student CD.

Figure 31-18.
Using viewports with different scales to create a multiview drawing.

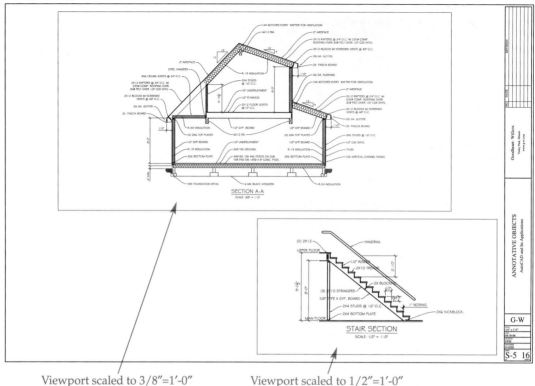

Viewport scaled to 3/8″=1′-0″   Viewport scaled to 1/2″=1′-0″

Reusing Annotative Objects

Often the same drawing features are shown at different scales. For example, you may want to plot a drawing on a large sheet using a large scale, and plot the same drawing on a smaller sheet using a smaller scale. Alternatively, you may want to enlarge a portion of an existing view and add annotations to the view enlargement. Traditionally, these processes involve creating scale-specific layers and then drawing copies of annotations on the layers that are appropriate for the drawing scale. The layers that do not match the scale of the floating layout viewport are then frozen.

Using annotative objects significantly improves the ability to reuse existing drawing features. You can use annotation visibility to hide annotative objects not supported by the current annotation scale. You can also adjust the position of scale representations according to the appropriate annotation scale. These options give you the ability to include differently scaled annotative objects on the same drawing sheet without creating copies of the objects and without using scale-specific layers.

Using invisible scale representations

If annotative objects do not support an annotation scale, the annotative objects disappear when the annotation scale that the objects do not support is made current. This is a valuable technique for displaying certain items at a specific scale. Annotative object visibility can be turned on and off by picking the **Annotation Visibility** button on the status bar.

The following example shows how adjusting the visibility of annotative objects that only support the current annotation scale can be used to create an additional view from existing drawing features. In this example, an annotation scale of 3/4″ = 1′-0″ is used to create a foundation detail. To begin constructing the foundation detail, the 3/4″ = 1′-0″ annotation scale is added to the existing earth hatch pattern so it can be shown on the full section and the foundation detail. See **Figure 31-19.** Next, with the

Figure 31-19.
The earth hatch pattern can be reused by adding the 3/4″ = 1′-0″ foundation detail scale to the annotative hatch pattern.

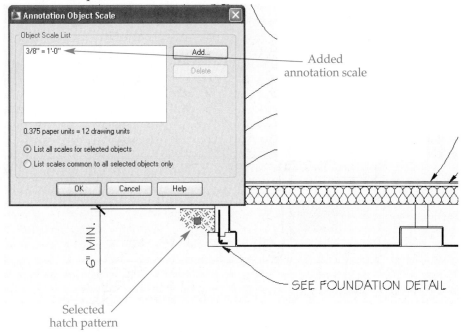

Added annotation scale

6″ MIN.

SEE FOUNDATION DETAIL

Selected hatch pattern

current annotation scale set to 3/4″ = 1′-0″, annotative text, dimensions, multileaders, and hatch patterns are added to the foundation detail. See **Figure 31-20.** These objects only support the 3/4″ = 1′-0″ annotation scale, so they can be made invisible on the full section, which is scaled to 3/8″ = 1′-0″.

PROFESSIONAL TIP

If objects already support an annotation scale, but you do not want to display those annotations at the current scale, delete the annotation scale from the objects.

Adjusting scale representation position

A major benefit of using annotative objects is the ability to reuse objects for differently scaled drawing views. The previous example of adding a 3/4″ = 1′-0″ annotation scale to the earth hatch pattern highlights this concept. Additionally, the location and spacing of annotative objects on one scale are often not appropriate for another scale. To overcome this issue, you can reposition each scale representation.

In the foundation detail example, some of the existing 3/8″ = 1′-0″ scaled full section dimensions and multileaders are to be reused in the foundation detail. The first step is to add a 3/4″ = 1′-0″ annotation scale to the objects. Next, with **ANNOALLVISIBLE** turned off, as shown in **Figure 31-21,** you can see the resulting position of the selected objects, which is initially the same location as the 3/8″ = 1′-0″ objects. The only difference is that now the 3/8″ = 1′-0″ objects also support a 3/4″ = 1′-0″ scale.

Adjust the position of annotation scale representations using grip editing methods. When you select annotative objects that support more than one annotation scale, all scale representations are shown by default. See **Figure 31-22.** An annotative object is a single object, but it can contain several scale representations. Grips are attached to the scale representation that corresponds to the current annotation scale. Using grips to edit scale representations is similar to editing the object used to create the scale

Figure 31-20.
Adding annotative text, dimensions, multileaders, and hatch patterns using a 3/4″ = 1′-0″ annotation scale.

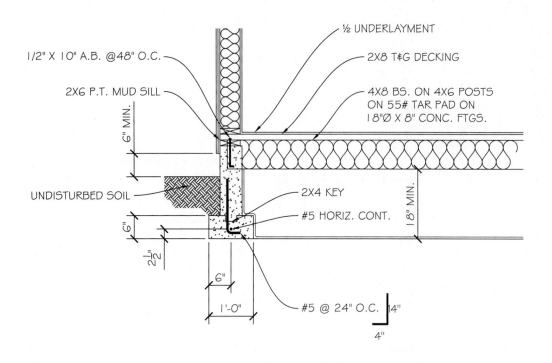

½ UNDERLAYMENT

2X8 T&G DECKING

4X8 BS. ON 4X6 POSTS
ON 55# TAR PAD ON
18″Ø X 8″ CONC. FTGS.

1/2″ X 10″ A.B. @48″ O.C.

2X6 P.T. MUD SILL

6″ MIN.

UNDISTURBED SOIL

2X4 KEY

#5 HORIZ. CONT.

18″ MIN.

6″

2½″

6″

1′-0″

#5 @ 24″ O.C.

4″

4″

Figure 31-21.
A—Some of the existing 3/8″ = 1′-0″ scaled objects can be reused to create another drawing

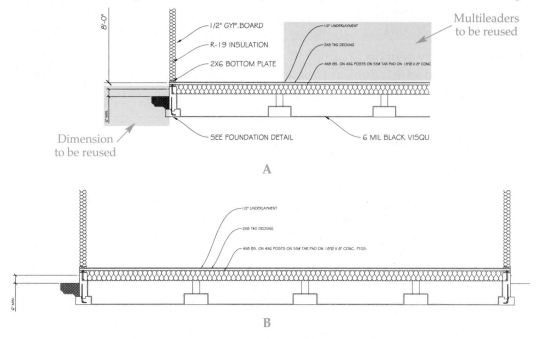

8′-0″

1/2″ GYP. BOARD

R-19 INSULATION

2X6 BOTTOM PLATE

Multileaders
to be reused

½″ UNDERLAYMENT

2X8 T&G DECKING

4X8 BS. ON 4X6 POSTS ON 55# TAR PAD ON 18″Ø X 8″ CONC

6″ MIN.

Dimension
to be reused

SEE FOUNDATION DETAIL

6 MIL BLACK VISQU

A

½″ UNDERLAYMENT

2X8 T&G DECKING

4X8 BS. ON 4X6 POSTS ON 55# TAR PAD ON 18″Ø X 8″ CONC. FTGS.

6″ MIN.

B

Figure 31-22.
The position of annotation scale representations can be adjusted using grip editing techniques. When you select annotative objects that support more than one annotation scale, all scale representations are shown by default.

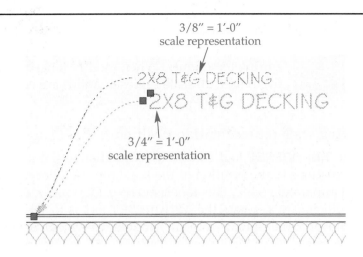

3/8″ = 1′-0″
scale representation

2X8 T&G DECKING
2X8 T&G DECKING

3/4″ = 1′-0″
scale representation

representation. The difference when editing a scale representation is that you are adjusting a scaled "copy" of the object. **Figure 31-23** shows the effects of editing the position of dimension and multileader scale representations on the foundation detail. The representations are selected to help demonstrate the effects of editing scale representation position. Notice that all elements of the scale representation can be edited to produce the desired annotations at the appropriate location.

PROFESSIONAL TIP

Use the **DIMSPACE** and **MLEADERALIGN** tools to quickly adjust the dimension spacing and multileader alignment after the drawing scale changes.

The display of selected scale representations is controlled by the **SELECTIONANNODISPLAY** system variable, which is set to 1 by default. As a result, all scale representations are shown and appear dimmed when you pick an annotative object that supports multiple annotation scales. See **Figure 31-22**. However, if the selected object supports several annotation scales, the display can be confusing. Set the **SELECTIONANNODISPLAY** system variable to 0 in order to display only the scale representation that corresponds to the current annotation scale.

Figure 31-23.
Editing the position of scale representations is much like creating scaled copies of existing annotations.

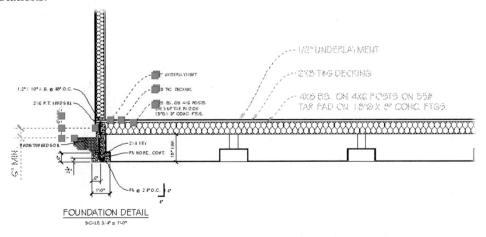

FOUNDATION DETAIL
SCALE 3/4" = 1'-0"

Resetting scale representation position

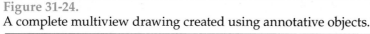

The **ANNORESET** tool can be used to change the position of all selected scale representations to the position of the scale representation that is set according to the current annotation scale. This tool removes all unique scale representation positions.

A quick way to access the **ANNORESET** tool is to select annotative objects, right-click and pick the option from the **Annotative Object Scale** cascading menu of the shortcut menu. If you activate the **ANNORESET** tool by right-clicking on objects, the position of the selected objects is reset. If you access the tool before selecting objects, pick the annotative objects. After making your selections, press [Enter] to exit the tool and reset the scale representation positions.

Completing a Multiview Drawing

The last step to creating the multiview drawing is to display and plot the drawing using multiple paper space viewports. Figure 31-24 shows an architectural D-size sheet layout with three floating viewports. One viewport is used to display the full section at a viewport scale of 3/8″ = 1′-0″. A second viewport is used to display the stair section at a viewport scale of 1/2″ = 1′-0″. A third viewport is used to display the foundation detail at a viewport scale of 3/4″ = 1′-0″.

Figure 31-24.
A complete multiview drawing created using annotative objects.

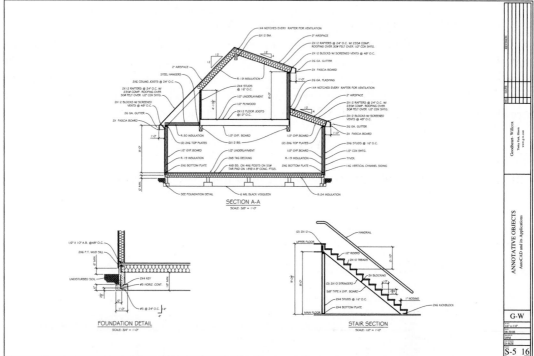

Sidebar (left margin):

ANNORESET

Ribbon
Annotate
> Annotation
Scaling

Synchronize
Multiple-scale
Positions

Type
ANNORESET

Menu Browser
Modify
> Annotative
Object Scale
> Synchronize
Multiple-
scale
Positions

PROFESSIONAL TIP

When drawings using annotative objects are saved to earlier versions of AutoCAD that do not support annotative objects, scale representations can be converted to non-annotative objects, but automatically placed on unique layers. To use this function, select **Tools > Options... > Open and Save** tab > **Maintain visual fidelity for annotative objects** check box.

Exercise 31-6
Complete the exercise on the Student CD.

Chapter Test

Answer the following questions. Write your answers on a separate sheet of paper or complete the electronic chapter test on the Student CD.

1. What are annotative objects? Identify at least four types of objects that can be made annotative.
2. Explain the practical differences between manual and annotative object scaling.
3. Which **MSLTSCALE** system variable setting should you use so you do not have to calculate the drawing scale factor when entering an **LTSCALE** value?
4. How do you set the text scale, including spacing, width, and paragraph settings to adjust automatically according to the current annotation scale?
5. Calculate the correct spacing in model space if your first dimension line should be 3/4″ from an object when plotted, and your drawing is scaled to 1/4″ = 1′-0″.
6. Identify an important relationship between the viewport scale and the annotation scale.
7. Name the tool used to update text properties according to the current properties of the text style on which the text is drawn.
8. What is an annotative object representation?
9. Briefly describe the result of setting the **ANNOAUTOSCALE** system variable to a value of 4.
10. Briefly discuss the effect of turning annotation visibility on and off.

▼ Basic

1. Open P24-9.dwg and save it as P31-1. Convert all the non-annotative objects to annotative objects. Resave the drawing.

2. Open P26-10.dwg and save it as P31-2. Convert all of the non-annotative objects to annotative objects. Resave the drawing.

▼ Intermediate

3. Create the section view and side view shown. Use annotative objects to prepare a full-scale drawing of the part. Change the annotation scale to 2:1 and adjust the scale representations as needed according to the new scale. Save the drawing as P31-3.

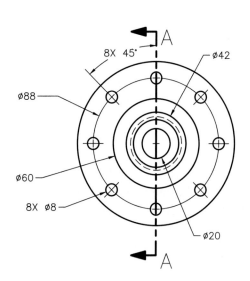

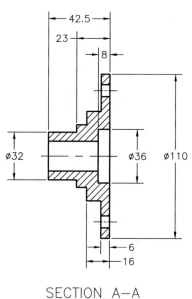

SECTION A–A

Name: Hub
Material: Cast Iron

4. Create the section view and side views shown. Use annotative objects to prepare a full-scale drawing of the part. Change the annotation scale to 2:1 and adjust the scale representations as needed according to the new scale. Save the drawing as P31-4.

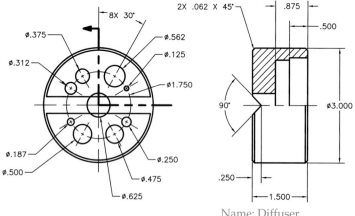

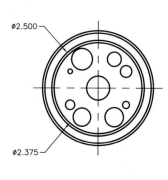

Name: Diffuser
Material: AISI 1018

5. Draw the fan shown at full scale in model space. Use annotative objects to prepare a full-scale view of the fan as shown and a view enlargement of the motor. You should not have to create a copy of the motor or develop scale specific layers. Save the drawing as P31-5.

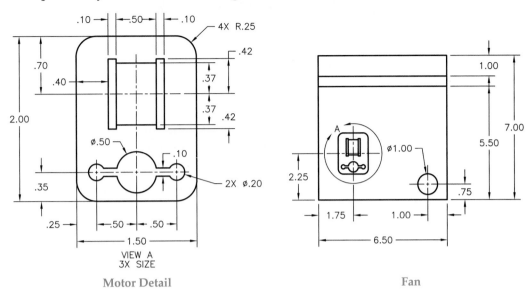

Motor Detail

Fan

▼ Advanced

6. Draw the floor plan shown at full scale in model space. Use annotative objects to prepare a 1/4" = 1'-0" view. Change the annotation scale to 1/8" = 1'-0" and adjust the scale representations as needed according to the new scale. Save the drawing as P31-6.

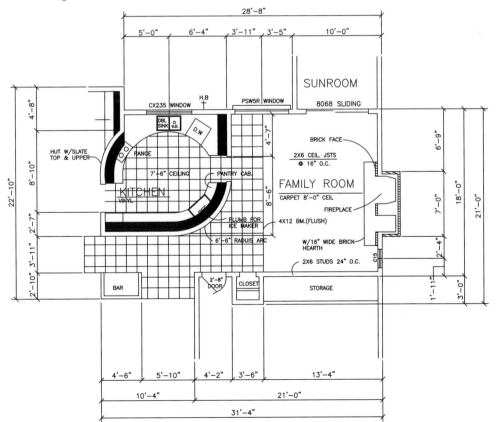

7. Draw the part shown at full scale in model space. Use annotative objects to prepare a full-scale view and a view enlargement of the part as shown. You should not have to create a copy of the part or develop scale specific layers. Save the drawing as P31-7.

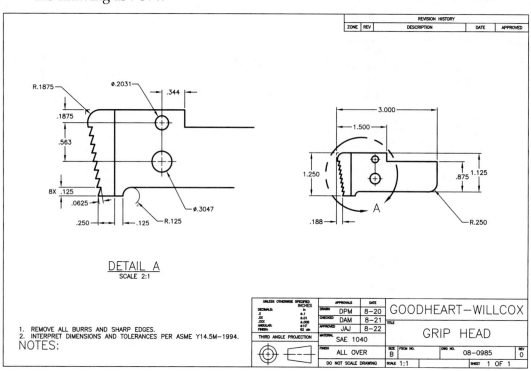

Drawing Problems - Chapter 31

CHAPTER 32

Using External References

Learning Objectives

After completing this chapter, you will be able to do the following:

✓ Explain the function of external references.
✓ Attach an existing drawing to the current drawing.
✓ Use **DesignCenter** and tool palettes to attach external references.
✓ Bind external references and selected dependent objects to a drawing.
✓ Edit external references in the current drawing.

External references (xrefs) expand on the concept of reusing existing content. This is a major benefit of designing and drafting with AutoCAD. Xrefs are excellent for applications in which existing base drawings, complex symbols, images, and details are shared by several users, are used often, or are used to develop new drawings. This chapter introduces the various applications for xrefs and explains how to use xref drawings.

> **external reference (xref):** A DWG, DWF, raster image, or DNG file that is incorporated into a drawing for reference only.

Introduction to Xrefs

AutoCAD allows you to reference existing drawing (DWG), design web format (DWF), raster image, and digital negative (DNG) files into the *host drawing*, also known as the *master drawing*. Using an xref is similar to inserting an entire drawing as a block. However, unlike blocks, which are actually located in each file after they are inserted, an externally referenced file's geometry is not added to the host drawing. File data is displayed on-screen for reference only. The result is useable information, but a much smaller host file size than would occur if the objects were inserted as a block or copied and pasted.

> **host (master) drawing:** The drawing into which xrefs are incorporated.

In addition to reducing drawing file size, one of the greatest benefits of using xrefs is that whenever the host drawing is opened, the latest versions of the xrefs can be displayed. If the original xref files are modified between the time you revise the host drawing and the next time you open and plot the drawing, all revisions are reflected. This is because AutoCAD reloads each xref whenever the host drawing is loaded. This allows several people in a class or office to reference the same file, with the assurance that any revisions to the reference file are displayed in any drawing where the xref is used.

Types of Xref Files

Files that can be referenced into a current drawing include existing DWG, DWF, raster image, and DNG files. DWF files are AutoCAD drawing files or other application files that are compressed for publication and viewing on the Web. A DWF file is usually referenced into a drawing in order to share information from the Web or from an application other than AutoCAD.

Raster image and DNG files are referenced into a drawing whenever there is a need to add an image to a drawing, such as for a company logo in a title block. Externally referencing an image into a drawing is an excellent technique, because the large file size often associated with a raster image is not reproduced in the current drawing. External reference DWF, image, and DNG files are explained in *AutoCAD and Its Applications—Advanced*.

Xref Applications

DWG files are the most common externally referenced files. In general, you can use xref drawings whenever you want to use existing drawing information to develop another drawing. There are countless applications for xref drawings in every drafting field. The following sections provide typical xref drawing applications. As you work with AutoCAD, you may discover a variety of uses for xref drawings.

Reference existing geometry

One of the most common applications for xref drawings is to reference existing geometry into the current drawing to use as a pattern or source of needed information. For example, a floor plan includes size and shape information that can be used to prepare additional plans, elevations, sections, and details. Figure 32-1 shows an example of referencing a floor plan file into a new drawing to use as an outline for drawing a roof plan (roof plan file). In this example, a floor plan xref is attached to the roof plan file to serve as an outline for creating the roof plan.

Figure 32-2 shows an example of the roof plan file created in Figure 32-1 attached to an elevation file as an xref and then used to project an elevation. The roof plan xref includes a *nested* floor plan xref. In this example, the elevation file references the roof plan. The roof plan in turn references the floor plan.

nested xrefs: Xrefs contained within other xrefs.

Create a multiview drawing

Commonly used drawings such as sections and details can be created as separate drawing files and then attached as xrefs to a host drawing. This method is similar to the use of blocks. By using floating viewports and controlling the display of layers within floating viewports, you can create a multiview layout. A multiview drawing can be prepared entirely from existing xref drawings or from a combination of objects created "in place" and attached xrefs.

Figure 32-3A shows an example of several stock details referenced into the model space environment of a new drawing. Floating viewports are used to arrange the details in a layout. See Figure 32-3B. When a detail is modified, in the original drawing file, all xrefs of the detail can be updated in the files in which the detail is used.

Figure 32-1.
An example of using a floor plan xref drawing as a pattern, or outline, to draw a roof plan.

**Floor Plan Xref
Drawing**

Roof Plan Added

Final Roof Plan Geometry
with floor plan xref
layers turned off

Figure 32-2.
Using a roof plan
xref drawing that
contains a nested
floor plan xref
drawing as a pattern
for projecting
geometry needed to
create an elevation.
Projection lines are
drawn using the
XLINE tool and are
shown for reference.

Roof plan xref
includes the nested
floor plan xref

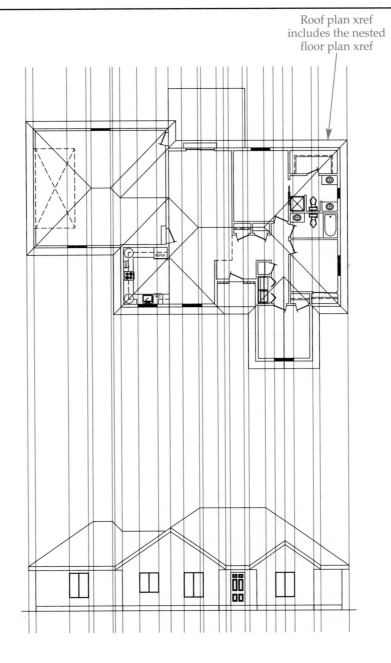

Figure 32-3.
A—Frequently used drawing views can be xrefed into model space, reducing the size of the file and providing the ability to easily change instances of the view used in multiple drawings. B—Xrefed views are arranged in floating viewports like other model space objects.

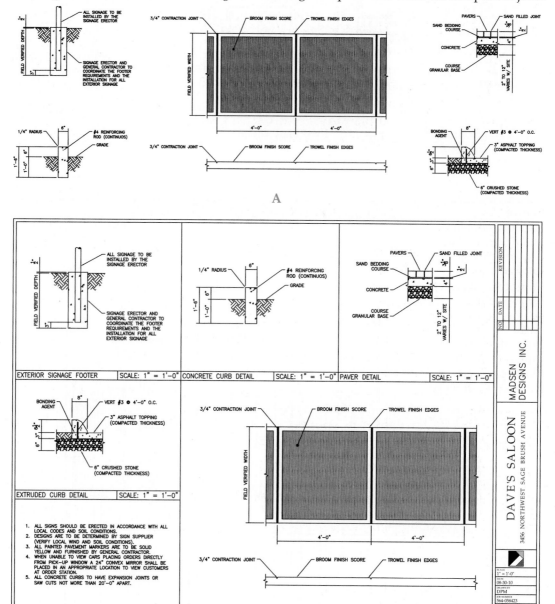

Add layout content

The previous section focused on using xref drawings to add content to model space in order to create a multiview drawing. The same concept can be applied to adding layout content. Layout content, such as a title block or a long list of general notes, typically uses a standard format. If the format requires modification, such as adding a new note to a list of general notes, you can make changes to the xref drawing and easily update each host file that references the xref. The general notes shown in **Figure 32-3B** are added to the layout as an xref.

Arrange sheet views

When working with sheet sets, you can use external references to arrange sheet views in layouts. Sheet sets are described in Chapter 33.

PROFESSIONAL TIP

Blocks, wblocks, and even copied and pasted non-block objects can be used in a manner similar to xref drawings. However, xrefs are much easier to manage, provide greater flexibility, and can be updated in all host drawings. You should always use xref drawings to control file size if you plan to use the drawing in multiple host drawings, and if the design might change.

Preparing Xref and Host Drawings

Before you begin placing xref drawings, you should prepare the xref and host drawing files for xref insertion. When you place an xref drawing, everything you see in model space is inserted into the host file as a single item. Layout content is not xrefed. The default insertion base point for an xref file is the model space origin, or 0,0,0 point. This is the point attached to the crosshairs or located at the specified insertion point when you insert the xref into the host drawing. If it is critical that xref objects coincide with the 0,0,0 point for insertion, move all objects in model space as needed.

The **BASE** tool can also be used to change the insertion base point of the drawing. Access the **BASE** tool, and then select a new insertion base point. Save the drawing before using it as an external reference to another drawing.

Little preparation should be necessary to prepare the host file to accept an xref, if you use an appropriate template. The host file should include a unique layer (named XREF, for example) on which to place xrefs. As you will learn, layers in an xrefed drawing file remain intact when you add the xref to the current drawing. Therefore, properties and states that you assign to the XREF layer have no effect on xref objects. The main purpose of the XREF layer is to contain the xref on a specific layer. Set the XREF layer current and proceed to placing the xref drawing.

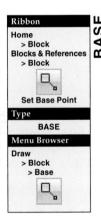

Placing External Reference Drawings

If you know you want to place an xref *drawing*, use the **XATTACH** tool to automate the process. An xref can also be placed using the **External References** palette. See **Figure 32-4.** The **External References** palette is a complete external reference management tool. To place an xref drawing using the **External References** palette, pick the **Attach DWG** button from the **Attach** flyout, or right-click on the **File References** pane and select the **Attach DWG...** menu option.

The **Select Reference File** dialog box appears when you use the **XATTACH** tool or choose the **Attach DWG** option from the **External References** palette. Use the **Select Reference File** dialog box to locate the drawing file you want to add to the current file as an xref. Then pick the **Open** button to display the **External Reference** dialog box. See **Figure 32-5.**

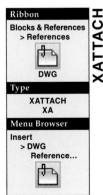

The **External Reference** dialog box is used to indicate how and where the reference is to be placed in the current drawing. The name and path of the selected xref are shown in the upper-left corner of the dialog box. If an external reference already exists in the current drawing, you can place another copy of it by choosing the existing drawing file you want to attach again from the **Name:** drop-down. To place a different xref drawing, pick the **Browse...** button and select the new file in the **Select Reference File** dialog box.

Figure 32-4.
The **External References** palette provides access to all options for externally referenced files.

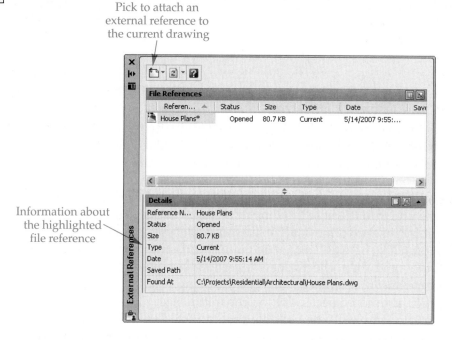

Pick to attach an external reference to the current drawing

Information about the highlighted file reference

Figure 32-5.
The **External Reference** dialog box is used to specify how an external reference is placed in the current drawing.

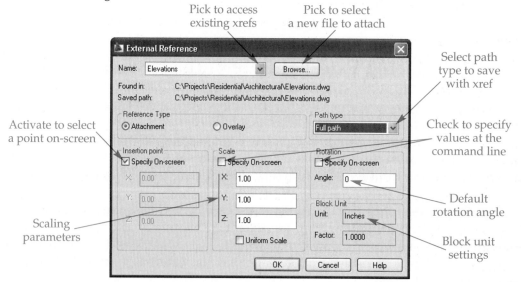

Pick to access existing xrefs

Pick to select a new file to attach

Select path type to save with xref

Activate to select a point on-screen

Check to specify values at the command line

Scaling parameters

Default rotation angle

Block unit settings

Attachment vs. Overlay

When inserting an xref drawing, you can select whether to place the xref as an *attachment* or an *overlay* by selecting the **Attachment** or **Overlay** radio button in the **Reference Type** area of the **External Reference** dialog box. Xrefs are attached for most applications. An xref is most often overlaid in order to share content with others in a design drafting team, typically while working in a networked environment. In this situation, drawings can be overlaid without referencing nested xrefs.

As previously described, nesting occurs when an xref file contains, or references, another xref file. An attached xref is known as the *parent xref*. When an xref is attached, any nested xrefs that it contains are brought into the host drawing. When an xref is overlaid, nested xrefs are not carried into the host drawing. Furthermore, if you overlay an xref in a host drawing and then attach the host drawing to another drawing, the overlaid xref does not appear, even though the host drawing attaches.

For example, you should typically attach a floor plan xref to a host file to create a foundation plan. You can then attach the foundation plan xref to a host file to draw a section. Attaching the foundation plan brings the foundation and floor plan geometry into the section file for reference. If a member of your design team wants to use your section or is working on a drawing that already has the floor and/or foundation plan attached, she or he can overlay the section xref into a drawing without bringing in the floor plan and foundation plan.

attachment: An xref that is linked or referenced into the current drawing.

overlay: An xref that is displayed an xref without being attach to the current drawing.

parent xref: An xref that contains one or more other xrefs.

> **NOTE**
>
> Xref reference type can be changed after insertion. You can change an overlay to an attachment or an attachment to an overlay. Managing xrefs is described later in this chapter.

Selecting the Path type

Use the **Path type** drop-down list in the **Path Type** area of the **External Reference** dialog box to set how AutoCAD stores the path to the xref file. This path is used to find the xref file when you open the host file. The path is displayed under the xref name in the **Saved path:** listing in the **External Reference** dialog box, and later appears in the **External References** palette. See Figure 32-6.

The **Full path** option is an *absolute path* and is active by default. When using this option, xref drawings must be located in the same drive and folder specified in the saved path. The host drawing can be moved to any location, but the xref drawings must remain in the saved path. This option is acceptable if it is unlikely the host and xref drawings will be copied or moved to another computer, drive, or folder.

absolute path: A path to a file defined by the file's location on the computer system.

If you share your drawings with a client or eventually archive the drawings, the **Relative path** option is often more appropriate. This option saves a *relative path*, and cannot be used if the xref file is on a local or network drive other than the drive that stores the host file. If the host drawing and xref files are located in a single folder and subfolders, this folder can be copied to any location without losing the connection between files. For example, the folder can be copied from the C: drive of one computer to the D: drive of another computer, to a folder on a CD, or to an archive server. If these types of transfers are performed with the **Full path** option, you need to open the host drawing after copying and redefine the saved paths for all xref files.

relative path: A path to a file defined according to its location relative to the host drawing.

You can also choose not to save the path to the xref file by selecting the **No Path** option. When using this option, the xref file can only be found and loaded if the path to the file is included in one of the Support File Search Path locations or if the xref file is in the same folder as the host file. The Support File Search Path locations are specified in the **Files** tab of the **Options** dialog box.

Figure 32-6.
An xref file attached to the current drawing can be referenced with a full path, a relative path, or no path. The type of path used is displayed in the **Save Path** column in the **External References** palette.

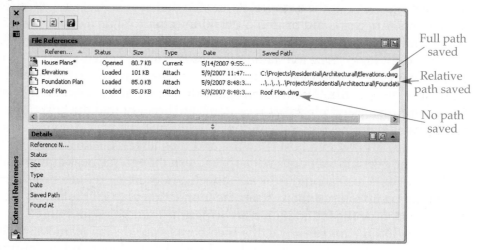

NOTE
AutoCAD also searches for xref files in all paths of the current project name. These paths are listed under the Project Files Search Path in the **Files** tab of the **Options** dialog box. You can create a new project as follows:
1. Pick Project Files Search Path to highlight it, and then pick the **Add...** button.
2. Enter a project name if desired.
3. Pick the plus sign icon (+), and then pick the word Empty.
4. Pick the **Browse...** button and locate the folder that is to become part of the project search path. Then pick **OK**.
5. Complete the project search path definition by entering the **PROJECTNAME** system variable and specifying the same name that is used in the **Options** dialog box.

Additional Xref Placement Options

The lower portion of the **External Reference** dialog box contains options for xref insertion location, scaling, rotation angle, and block unit settings. The text boxes in the **Insertion point** area allow you to enter 2D or 3D coordinates for insertion of the xref if the **Specify On-screen** check box is not checked. Activate the **Specify On-screen** check box if you want to specify the insertion location on-screen.

Scale factors for the xref can be set in the **Scale** area. By default, the X, Y, and Z scale factors are set to 1. You can enter new values in the corresponding text boxes or activate the **Specify On-screen** check box to display scaling prompts when the xref is inserted. Checking the **Uniform Scale** check box tells AutoCAD to use the X scale factor for the Y and Z scale factors.

The rotation angle for the inserted xref is 0 by default. You can specify a different rotation angle in the **Angle:** text box, or activate the **Specify On-screen** check box to be prompted for the rotation angle. The **Block Unit** area displays the unit and scale factor stored with the selected drawing file.

Inserting the Xref

After defining all xref information in the **External Reference** dialog box, you are ready to insert the xref into the current drawing. Pick the **OK** button. If the **Specify On-screen** check box in the **Insertion point** area was selected, the xref is attached to the crosshairs and you are prompted for the insertion point. You can use any valid point specification option, including object snap modes.

The insertion options for attaching an xref are essentially the same as those used to insert a block. Both tools function in a similar manner, but the internal workings and results are different. Remember that externally referenced files are not added to the current drawing file's database, as are inserted blocks. Therefore, using external references helps keep your drawing file size to a minimum.

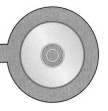

Exercise 32-1
Complete the exercise on the Student CD.

Placing Xrefs with DesignCenter and Tool Palettes

External references can be added to a drawing quickly using **DesignCenter** or the **Tool Palettes** window. Inserting blocks using these features is described in Chapter 26. Similar procedures are used for attaching xrefs.

To place an xref into the current drawing using **DesignCenter**, first use the **Tree View** area to locate the folder containing the drawing to be attached. Then display the drawing files located in the selected folder in the **Content** area. Right-click on the drawing file in the **Content** area and select the **Attach as Xref...** menu option. Another method is to drag and drop the drawing into the current drawing area using the *right mouse button*. When you release the button, select the **Attach as Xref...** menu option. The **External Reference** dialog box appears. Enter the appropriate values and pick **OK** to place the xref.

In order to use the **Tool Palettes** window to place an xref, you must first add an xref or drawing file to a tool palette. To add an xref to a tool palette, drag an existing xref from the current drawing or an xref from the **Content** area of **DesignCenter** into the **Tool Palettes** window. The xref can then be attached, by default, to the current drawing from the palette using drag and drop.

Xref files in tool palettes are identified with an external reference icon. If a drawing file, not an xref, is added to a tool palette from the current drawing or **DesignCenter**, it is designated as a block tool. To convert the block tool to an xref tool, right-click on the image in the **Tool Palettes** window and select **Properties...** to display the **Tool Properties** dialog box. Then change the **Insert as** field status from Block to Xref using the **Insert as** drop-down list. The **Reference type** row controls whether the xref is inserted as an attachment or an overlay.

Working with Xref Objects

An xref is inserted as a single object. You can use editing tools such as **MOVE** and **COPY** to modify the xref as needed. However, there are some significant differences between xrefs and other objects. For example, if you erase an xref, the xref definition remains in the file, similar to an erased block. You must detach an xref to remove it from the file.

Dependent Objects

Another important distinction between xrefs and other objects involves the concept of *dependent objects*. When an xref is placed in a drawing, any named objects, such as layers and blocks, found in the xref file are brought into the host file with the xref as dependent objects, even if the objects are not used in the xref file. Dependent objects are only displayed in the host drawing. The actual object definitions are stored in the xref drawing.

Dependent objects are renamed when an xref is attached to a drawing so that the xref file name precedes the actual object name. The names are separated by a vertical bar symbol (|). For example, a layer named A-walls within an xref drawing file named Room comes into the host drawing as Room|A-walls. See **Figure 32-7.** The name distinguishes the xref-dependent layer name from the same layer name that may exist in the host drawing. This also makes it easier to manage layers when several xrefs are attached to the host drawing, because the layers from each reference file are prefixed with unique file names. Xref-dependent layers cannot be renamed.

When an xref is attached, dependent objects such as layers are added to the host drawing only in order to support the display of the objects in the xref file. The **Layer Control** drop-down list on the ribbon displays xref-dependent layers grayed out. This indicates that the layers cannot be set current or used to draw objects. However, xref layers can be turned off, frozen, or locked. You can also change the colors and linetypes of xref layers. Changing a display property of an xref layer only affects the layer in the host drawing and does not modify the actual xref file(s). To assign a different color or linetype to an xref-dependent layer, access the **Layer Properties Manager** dialog box, select the layer, and change its color or linetype.

NOTE

An xref filter available in the **Layer Properties Manager** palette can be used to display and manage dependent layers. Dependent layers can also be saved in a layer state.

Figure 32-7.
Xref-dependent layer names in the host drawing are preceded by the xref drawing name and the vertical bar symbol (|).

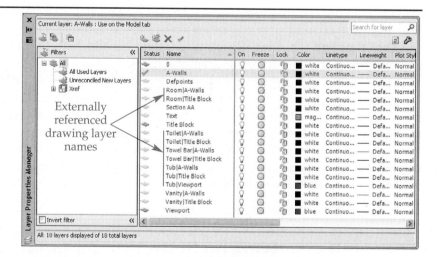

Externally referenced drawing layer names

AutoCAD and Its Applications—Basics

PROFESSIONAL TIP

When you attach a drawing as an xref, the reference file comes into the host drawing with the same layer colors and linetypes used in the original file. If you reference a drawing to check the relationship of objects between two drawings, it is a good idea to change the xref layer colors to make it easier to differentiate between the content of the host drawing and the xref drawing. Changing xref layer colors affects only the display in the current drawing and not the original reference file.

Exercise 32-2
Complete the exercise on the Student CD.

Managing Xrefs

The **External References** palette is the primary tool for managing and accessing current information about xrefs that have been attached to or overlaid on a drawing. The **External References** palette displays an upper **File References** pane and a lower **Details** pane. See Figure 32-8. The **File References** pane can be displayed in either list view or tree view.

Figure 32-8.
The **External References** palette is used to view and manage referenced files. The **File References** pane is shown in **List View** mode and **Details** pane is shown in **Details** mode.

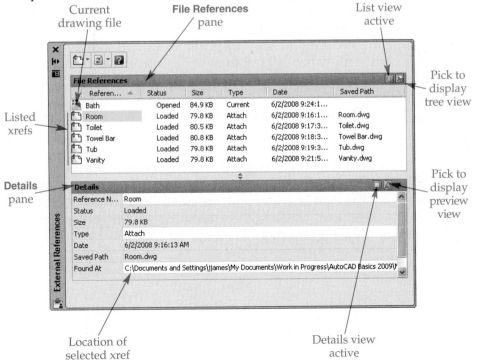

List View Display

The list view display mode shown in Figure 32-8 is active by default and can be set by picking the **List View** button or pressing the [F3] key. The labeled columns displayed in list view provide information about xrefs and are used to manage them.

The **Reference Name** column displays the current drawing file name followed by the names of all existing xrefs in alphabetical or chronological order. The current drawing is indicated with the standard AutoCAD drawing file icon, and xrefs appear as a sheet of paper with a paper clip. The **Status** column describes the status of each xref. The xref status can be:

- **Loaded.** The xref is attached to the drawing.
- **Unloaded.** The xref is attached but not displayed or regenerated.
- **Unreferenced.** The xref has nested xrefs that are not found or are unresolved. An unreferenced xref is not displayed.
- **Not Found.** The xref file is not found in the specified search paths.
- **Unresolved.** The xref file is missing or cannot be found.
- **Orphaned.** The parent of the nested xref cannot be found.

The **Size** column lists the file size for each xref. The **Type** column indicates whether the xref is attached or referenced as an overlay. The **Date** column indicates the last modification date for the file being referenced.

The **Saved Path** column lists the path name saved with the xref. If only a file name appears here, the path has not been saved. AutoCAD uses prefixes to describe the relative paths to xref files. In Figure 32-6, the path to the FPlans reference file is preceded by the characters .\. The period (.) represents the folder containing the host drawing. From that folder, AutoCAD looks in the Architectural folder, where the FPlans drawing is found. A similar specification is used for the Elevation reference file in Figure 32-9. In this instance, the Elevation file is found in the same folder as the host drawing. The specification for the Wall reference file is preceded by the characters ..\. The double period instructs AutoCAD to move up one folder level from the current location. The double period can be repeated to move up multiple folder levels. For example, the Panel reference file in Figure 32-9 is found by moving up two folder levels from the folder of the host drawing and then opening the Symbols folder.

NOTE

The path saved to the xref is one of several locations searched by AutoCAD when a host drawing is opened and an xref must be loaded. AutoCAD searches path locations for loading xref files in the following order:

1. The path associated with the xref (the full path or a relative path)
2. The current folder of the host drawing
3. The project paths specified in the Project Files Search Path
4. The support paths specified in the Support File Search Path
5. The Start in: folder path specified for the AutoCAD application shortcut, which is accessed using the **Properties** option in the desktop icon shortcut menu.

Figure 32-9.
Relationship between the symbols in the **Saved Path** list and file locations within the folder structure.

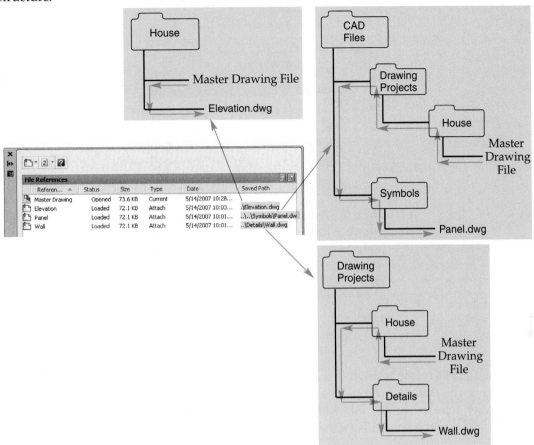

PROFESSIONAL TIP

In the list view display mode, the column widths can be adjusted as necessary to view complete information. To adjust the width of a column, move the cursor to the edge of the button at the top of the column until the cursor changes to a horizontal resizing cursor. Press and hold the left mouse button and drag the column to the desired width. The column width adjustments you make are used for subsequent displays of the dialog box. If the columns extend beyond the width of the dialog box window, a horizontal scroll bar appears at the bottom of the list.

Tree View Display

To see a list of externally referenced files in the **File References** pane, and to show nesting levels, pick the **Tree View** button or press the [F4] key. See Figure 32-10. Nesting levels are shown in a format similar to the arrangement of folders. The xref icon can take on different appearances, depending on the status of the xref. An xref whose status is unloaded or not found has a grayed-out icon. An upward arrow shown with the icon means the xref has just been reloaded, and a downward arrow means the xref has just been unloaded.

The **Details** pane can be displayed in either **Preview** mode or **Details** mode. To display an image of the xref selected in the **File References** pane, pick the **Preview** button on the **Details** pane. See Figure 32-10.

Figure 32-10.
The **File References** pane in **Tree View** mode shows nested xref levels. The **Details** pane in **Preview** mode shows a thumbnail preview of the selected xref.

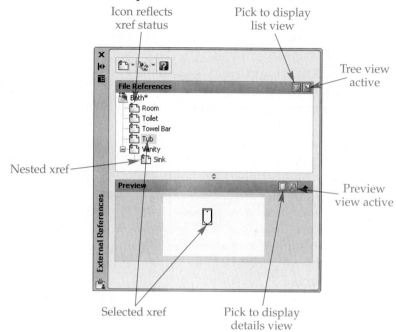

The **Details** mode, shown in **Figure 32-8,** is active by default and can be activated by picking the **Details** button. The information listed in the **Details** pane corresponds to the xref selected in the **File References** pane. The rows displayed in **Detail** mode are the same as the columns found in the **List View** mode of the **File References** pane. However, in the **Details** pane, you can modify the reference name by entering a new name in the **Reference Name** text box. You can also adjust the reference type from an attachment to an overlay or from an overlay to an attachment by picking the appropriate option from the **Type** drop-down list. In addition, the **Details** pane contains a **Found At** row that can be used to update the location of an xref path.

Detaching, Reloading, and Unloading Xrefs

detach: Remove an xref from a host drawing.

Each time you open a host drawing containing an attached xref, the xref is also loaded and appears on-screen. This association remains permanent until it is removed or detached. Erasing an xref does not detach it from the host drawing. To *detach* an xref, right-click the reference name in the **File References** pane of the **External References** palette and pick the **Detach** shortcut menu option. When you detach an externally referenced file, all instances of the xref are removed from the current drawing, along with all referenced data. All xrefs nested within the detached file are also removed.

reload: Update an xref in the host drawing file.

In some situations, you may need to update, or *reload,* an xref file in the host drawing. For example, if an externally referenced file is edited while the host drawing is open, the updated version may be different from the version you see. To update the xref, right-click the reference name in the **File References** pane of the **External References** palette and pick the **Reload** shortcut menu option, or pick the **Reload All References** button from the flyout to reload all unloaded xrefs. Reloading xrefs forces AutoCAD to read and display the most recently saved version of each xref drawing.

unload: Suppress the display of an xref without removing it from the host drawing.

To *unload* an xref, right-click on the reference name in the **File References** pane of the **External References** palette and pick the **Unload** shortcut menu option. When an xref is unloaded, it is not displayed or regenerated, and AutoCAD's performance increases. To display the xref again, right-click the reference name in the **File References** pane of the **External References** palette and pick the **Reload** shortcut menu option, or pick the **Reload All References** button from the flyout to reload all unloaded xrefs.

Updating the Xref Path

A file path saved with an externally referenced file is displayed in the **Saved Path** column of the **File References** pane and the **Saved Path** row of the **Details** pane in the **External References** palette. If an xref file is not found in the **Saved Path** location when the host drawing is opened, AutoCAD searches along the *library path*, which includes the current drawing folder and the Support File Search Path locations set in the **Files** tab of the **Options** dialog box. If a file with a matching name is found, it is resolved. In such a case, the **Saved Path** location differs from where the file was actually found.

You can check this in the **External References** palette by comparing the path listed in the **Saved Path** column of the **File References** pane and **Saved Path** row of the **Details** pane with the listing in the **Found At** row of the **Details** pane. To update the **Saved Path** location, select the path in the **Found At** edit box and pick the **Browse...** button to the right of the edit box to access the **Select new path** dialog box. Use this dialog box to locate the new folder and select the desired file. Then pick the **Open** button to update the path.

When a referenced drawing is moved and the new location is not on the library path, its status is indicated as Not Found. To find the xref file and update the **Saved Path** location, select the path in the **Found At** edit box and pick the **Browse...** button to the right of the edit box to access the **Select new path** dialog box. Use this dialog box to locate the new folder and select the desired file. Then pick the **Open** button to update the path.

> **library path:** The path AutoCAD searches by default to find an xref file, including the current folder and locations set in the **Options** dialog box.

The Manage Xrefs Icon

When changes are made to parent drawings for xrefs used in a host drawing, a notification appears in the AutoCAD status bar tray. This tray is located in the lower-right corner of the drawing window. Changes are indicated by the appearance of the **Manage Xrefs** icon, a balloon message, or both. Notifications in the status bar tray for xref changes and other system updates are controlled by options in the **Tray Settings** dialog box. This dialog box is accessed by selecting **Tray Settings...** from the status bar shortcut menu. If the **Display icons from services** check box is selected in the **Tray Settings** dialog box, the **Manage Xrefs** icon is displayed in the status bar tray when an xref is attached to the current drawing. If an xref in the current file has been modified since the file was opened, the **Manage Xrefs** icon appears with an exclamation sign over it. Pick the **Manage Xrefs** icon, or right-click on the **Manage Xrefs** icon and select the **External References...** shortcut menu option to open the **External References** palette so the xref file can be reloaded.

When the **Display notifications from services** check box is selected in the **Tray Settings** dialog box, a balloon message notification appears with the name of the modified xref file. See **Figure 32-11A**. You can then pick on the xref file name in the balloon message to reload the file. In the example shown, a Towel Bar xref has been added to the Room parent xref drawing. The xref is then reloaded in the current drawing named Bath. See **Figure 32-11B**. Xrefs can also be reloaded by right-clicking on the **Manage Xrefs** icon and selecting **Reload DWG Xrefs** from the shortcut menu.

Exercise 32-3

Complete the exercise on the Student CD.

Figure 32-11.
The **Manage Xrefs** icon in the AutoCAD status bar tray provides a notification when an xref file has been modified and saved. A—A balloon message is displayed with an exclamation point over the icon. B—Reloading the xref file updates the current drawing and changes the appearance of the icon.

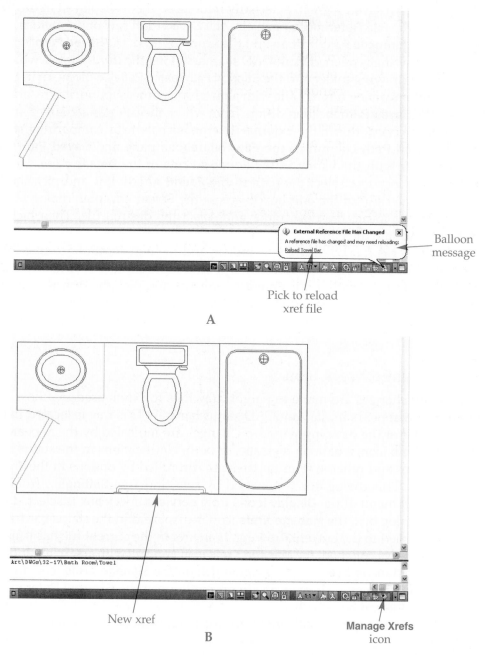

Clipping an Xref

In some cases, it may be necessary to display only a specific portion of an xref drawing. To accommodate this need, AutoCAD allows you to create a boundary that displays an xref *subregion*. All geometry that falls outside the boundary is invisible, and objects that are partially within the subregion appear to be trimmed at the boundary. Although clipped objects appear trimmed, the xref file is not changed in any way. Clipping is applied to a selected instance of an xref, and not to the actual xref definition.

subregion: The displayed portion of a clipped xref.

The **XCLIP** tool is used to create and modify clipping boundaries. A quick way to access the **XCLIP** tool is to select an object that is part of the xref file, then right-click and select the **Clip Xref** shortcut menu option. Once you access the **XCLIP** tool, if the xref is not already selected, pick an object that is part of the xref to be clipped. Then press [Enter] to accept the default **New boundary** option and select the clipping boundary.

When you select the **New boundary** option, you are prompted to specify the clipping boundary. Use the default **Rectangular** option to create a rectangular boundary. Then pick the corners of the rectangular boundary. An example of using the **XCLIP** tool and a rectangular boundary is illustrated in Figure 32-12. Note that the geometry outside the clipping boundary is no longer displayed after the tool is completed.

If you do not want to create a rectangular clipping boundary, select the **New boundary** option and then choose one of the other boundary options. Use the **Select polyline** option to select an existing polyline object as a boundary definition. The border can consist only of straight line segments, so any arc segments in the selected polyline are treated as straight line segments. If the polyline is not closed, the start and end points of the boundary are connected. The **Polygonal** option allows you to draw an irregular polygon as a boundary. This option is similar to the **WPolygon** selection option and allows a flexible boundary definition.

An **Invert clip** option is also available when you choose the **New boundary** option. Pick the **Invert clip** option to invert the portion of the selected xrefs that is clipped. By default, the portion of the xrefs outside of the clipping boundary is no longer displayed. Inverting the clip displays only the portion of the xref outside of the boundary.

Figure 32-12.
A clipping boundary is used to clip selected areas of an xref. A—Using the **Rectangular** boundary selection option. B—The clipped xref.

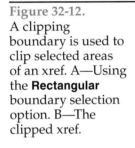

Rectangular
clipping boundary

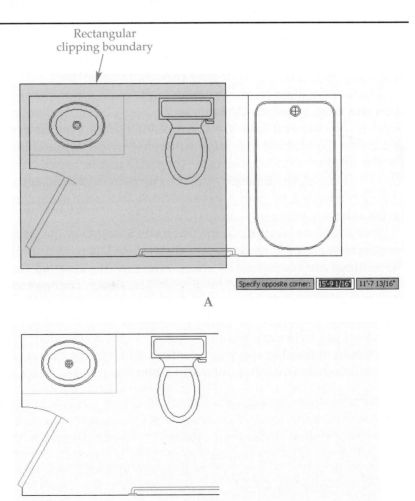

Specify opposite corner: 15'-9 1/16" 11'-7 13/16"

A

B

XCLIPFRAME

Type
XCLIPFRAME

Menu Browser

Modify
> Object
> External
Reference
> Frame

A clipped xref can be edited just like an unclipped xref. Additionally, the clipping boundary moves with the xref. Note that nested xrefs are clipped according to the clipping boundary for the parent xref.

The clipping boundary, or frame, is invisible by default. Use the **XCLIPFRAME** system variable to toggle the display of the clipping boundary frame. Set the value of **XCLIPFRAME** to 1 to turn on the frame.

The other options of the **XCLIP** tool can be used after a boundary is defined. The **ON** and **OFF** options turn the clipping feature on or off as needed. The **Clipdepth** option is used to define front and back clipping planes. The front and back clipping planes define the portion of a 3D drawing that is displayed. Clipping 3D models is described in *AutoCAD and Its Applications—Advanced*. Use the **Delete** option to remove an existing clipping boundary, returning the xref to its unclipped display. Use the **generate Polyline** option to create and display a polyline object at the clip boundary to frame the clipped portion.

Exercise 32-4

Complete the exercise on the Student CD.

Using Demand Loading and Xref Editing Controls

demand loading: Loading only the part of an xref file necessary to regenerate the host drawing.

Demand loading controls how much of an external reference file is loaded when it is attached to the host drawing. This improves performance and saves disk space because the entire xref file is not loaded. For example, any data on frozen layers, as well as any data outside of clipping regions, is not loaded.

Demand loading is enabled by default. To check or change the setting, open the **Open and Save** tab of the **Options** dialog box. The three demand loading options are found in the **Demand load Xrefs:** drop-down list in the **External References (Xrefs)** area. Select the **Enabled with copy** option to turn on demand loading. Other users can edit the original drawing because AutoCAD uses a copy of the referenced drawing. You can also pick the **Enabled** option to turn on demand loading. While the drawing is being referenced, the xref file is kept open and other users cannot edit the file. Select the **Disabled** option to turn off demand loading.

Two additional settings in the **Open and Save** tab of the **Options** dialog box control the effects of changes made to xref-dependent layers and in-place reference editing. The settings are controlled by check boxes in the **External References (Xrefs)** area. Both check boxes are selected by default. The **Retain changes to Xref layers** check box allows you to keep all changes made to the properties and states of xref-dependent layers. Any changes to layers take precedence over the layer settings in the xref file. The edited properties are retained even if an xref is reloaded. The **Allow other users to Refedit current drawing** check box controls whether the current drawing can be edited in place by others while it is open and when it is referenced by another file.

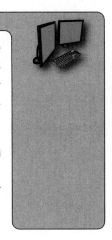

PROFESSIONAL TIP

If a drawing will be used as an external reference, it is good practice to save the file with *spatial indexes* and *layer indexes*. These lists help improve AutoCAD's performance when you reference drawings with frozen layers and clipping boundaries. Create spatial and layer indexes using the following procedure:

1. Access the **Save Drawing As** dialog box.
2. Pick **Options...** from the **Tools** flyout button and select the **DWG Options** tab of the **Saveas Options** dialog box.
3. Select the type of index required from the **Index type:** drop-down list.
4. Pick the **OK** button and save the drawing.

spatial index: A list of objects ordered according to their locations in 3D space.

layer index: A list of objects ordered according to the layers on which they reside.

Binding an Xref

An externally referenced file can be made a permanent part of the host drawing as if it had been placed with the **INSERT** tool. This is called *binding* an xref. Binding is useful when you need to send the full drawing file to another location or user, such as a plotting service or a client. To bind an xref using the **External References** palette, right-click on the reference name and pick the **Bind...** shortcut menu option. This displays the **Bind Xrefs** dialog box, which contains **Bind** and **Insert** radio buttons.

binding: Converting an xref to a permanently inserted block in the host drawing.

Using the Insert and Bind Options

The **Insert** option converts the xref into a normal block, as if you had used the **INSERT** tool to place the file. In addition, the drawing is entered into the block definition table and all named objects, such as layers, blocks, and styles, are incorporated into the host drawing as named in the xref. For example, if an xref file named PLATE is bound and it contains a layer named OBJECT, the xref-dependent layer PLATE|OBJECT becomes the locally defined layer OBJECT. All other xref-dependent objects are stripped of the xref name, and they assume the properties of the locally defined objects with the same name. The **Insert** binding option provides the best results for most purposes.

The **Bind** option also converts the xref into a normal block. However, the xref name is kept with the names of all dependent objects, and the vertical line in each of the names is replaced with two dollar signs with a number in between. For example, an xref layer named Title|Notes is renamed Title\$0\$Notes when the xref is bound using the **Bind** option. The number inside the dollar signs is automatically incremented if a local object definition with the same name exists. For example, if Title\$0\$Notes already exists in the drawing, the layer is renamed to Title\$1\$Notes. In this manner, unique names are created for all xref-dependent object definitions that are bound. Any of the named objects can be renamed using the **RENAME** tool.

Binding Specific Dependent Objects

Binding an xref allows you to make all dependent objects in an xref file a permanent part of the host drawing. Dependent objects include named items such as blocks, dimension styles, layers, linetypes, and text styles. Before binding, you cannot directly use any dependent objects from a referenced drawing in the host drawing. For example, a layer that exists only in an xref drawing cannot be made current in the host drawing. The same applies for text styles.

In some cases, you may only need to incorporate one or more specific named objects, such as a layer or block, from an xref into the host drawing, instead of binding

Figure 32-13.
The **Xbind** dialog box is used to bind xref-dependent objects individually to the host drawing.

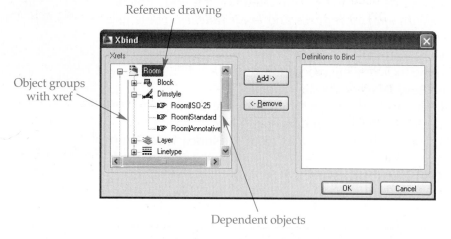

Reference drawing

Object groups with xref

Dependent objects

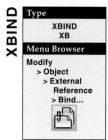

XBIND

Type	
XBIND	
XB	
Menu Browser	

Modify
> Object
>> External
>> Reference
>> Bind...

the entire xref. If you only need selected items, it can be counterproductive to bind an entire drawing. Instead, you can use the **XBIND** tool to bind only the named objects you select. The **Xbind** dialog box appears when you access the **XBIND** tool. See Figure 32-13. This dialog box allows you to select individual xref-dependent objects for binding.

The xrefs shown are indicated by the AutoCAD drawing file icons. To select an individually named object from a group, you must first expand the group listing by clicking on the plus sign next to the corresponding icon. To select an object for binding, highlight it and pick the **Add** button. The names of all objects selected and added are displayed in the **Definitions to Bind** list. When all desired objects are selected, pick the **OK** button. A message displayed on the command line indicates how many objects of each type were bound.

Individual objects that are bound using the **XBIND** tool are renamed in the same manner as objects that are bound using the **Bind** option in the **Bind Xrefs** dialog box. In addition to being renamed, a bound layer can also be assigned a linetype that was not previously defined in the host drawing. An automatic bind is performed, so the required linetype definition can be referenced by the new layer. A new linetype name, such as xref1$0$hidden, is created for the linetype. In similar manner, a previously undefined block may be automatically bound to the host drawing because of binding nested blocks. Bound objects can be renamed using the **RENAME** tool.

Exercise 32-5
Complete the exercise on the Student CD.

Editing Xref Drawings

reference editing:
Editing reference drawings from within the host file.

Xref drawings can be edited in place, within the host drawing, by *reference editing*. Any changes can then be saved to the original drawing from within the host drawing. Alternatively, the xref can be opened in a new drawing window and edited directly.

Editing Xrefs in Place

The **REFEDIT** tool is used to edit externally referenced drawings in place. A quick way to access the **REFEDIT** tool is to select an object that is part of the xref file in the drawing area, then right-click and select the **Edit Xref In-place** menu option.

Once you access the **REFEDIT** tool, pick an object that is part of the xref to be edited, if the xref is not already selected. The **Reference Edit** dialog box is displayed with the **Identify Reference** tab active. See **Figure 32-14.** A preview of the selected xref is shown in the **Preview** panel, and the name of the file is highlighted. In the example shown, the Room reference drawing has been selected. Notice how nested blocks, like the Bath Tub 26 x 60 in. block found in the Tub reference, are listed under their parent xref.

In the **Path:** area, the **Automatically select all nested objects** radio button is selected by default. Using this option makes all the xref objects available for editing. If you want to edit only certain xref objects, pick the **Prompt to select nested objects** radio button. When this option is selected, the Select nested objects: prompt is displayed after you pick the **OK** button. This prompt asks you to pick objects that belong to the previously selected xref. Pick all lines and any other geometry of the object to be edited, and then press [Enter]. The nested objects that you select make up the *working set*. If multiple instances of the same xref are displayed, be sure to pick objects from the one you originally selected.

working set:
Nested objects selected for editing during a **REFEDIT** operation.

Additional options for reference editing are available in the **Settings** tab of the **Reference Edit** dialog box. The **Create unique layer, style, and block names** option controls the naming of selected layers and objects that are *extracted*, or temporarily removed from the drawing for editing purposes. If this check box is selected, layer and object names are given the prefix n, with n representing an incremental number. This is similar to the renaming method used when you bind an xref.

extracted:
Temporarily removed from the drawing for editing purposes.

The **Display attribute definitions for editing** option is available only if a block object is selected in the **Identify Reference** tab of the **Reference Edit** dialog box. Checking this option allows you to edit any attribute definitions included in the reference. Attributes are covered in detail in Chapter 30.

To prevent accidental changes to objects that do not belong to the working set, you can check the **Lock objects not in working set** option. This makes all objects outside of the working set unavailable for selection in reference editing mode.

If the selected xref file contains other references, the **Reference name:** area lists all nested xrefs and blocks in tree view. In the example given, Toilet, Tub, Vanity, and Towel Bar are nested xrefs in the Room xref. If you pick the drawing file icon next to Vanity, for example, in the tree view, an image preview is displayed and the selected xref is highlighted in the drawing window. See **Figure 32-15.**

Figure 32-14.
The **Reference Edit** dialog box lists the name of the selected reference drawing and displays an image preview.

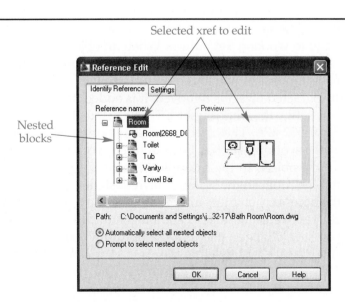

Figure 32-15.
The **Preview** panel displays the Vanity nested xref after it is selected in the tree view.

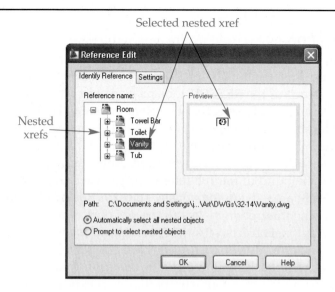

Selected nested xref

Nested xrefs

Figure 32-16.
The **Refedit** tab and panel appear when you select a nested xref to edit.

Xref and Block, Add to Working Set

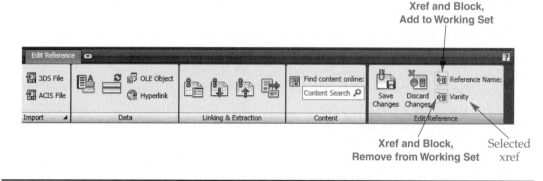

Xref and Block, Remove from Working Set

Selected xref

When you finish adjusting settings, pick the **OK** button to begin editing the xref file and display the **Edit Reference** tab and **Edit Reference** panel of the ribbon. See **Figure 32-16.** Use the tools in the **Edit Reference** panel to add objects to the working set, remove objects from the working set, and save or discard changes to the original xref file.

Any object that is drawn during the in-place edit is automatically added to the working set. Additional existing objects can be added to the working set using the **Xref and Block, Add to Working Set** button. When an object is added to the working set, it is extracted, or removed, from the host drawing. The **Xref and Block, Remove from Working Set** button allows you to remove selected objects from the working set. When a previously extracted object is removed, it is added back to the host drawing.

After you define the working set, all unselected objects are faded, or grayed out, as shown in **Figure 32-17A.** The objects in the working set appear in the normal display mode. Once the working set has been defined, you can use any drawing or editing tools to alter the object. In the example given in **Figure 32-17A,** the vanity has been selected from the room so the sink can be redesigned and a faucet added.

Once the necessary changes are made, pick the **Save Changes** button. If you want to exit the reference editing session without saving changes, pick the **Discard Changes** button. If you save changes, pick the **OK** button when AutoCAD asks if you want to continue with the save and redefine the xref. All instances of the xref are updated. See **Figure 32-17B.**

Figure 32-17.
Reference editing.
A—Objects in the
drawing that are
not a part of the
working set are
grayed out during
the reference editing
session. B—All
instances of the xref
are immediately
updated after
reference editing.

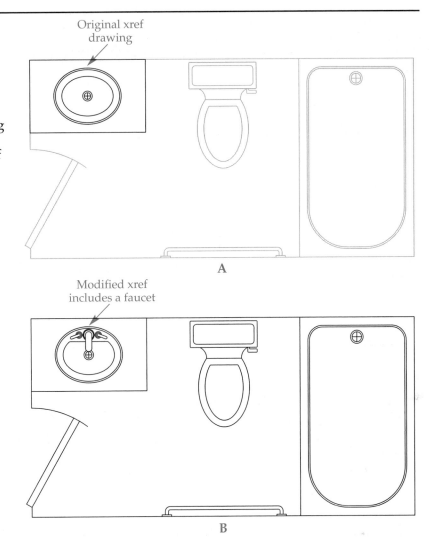

Original xref
drawing

A

Modified xref
includes a faucet

B

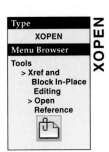

NOTE

In-place reference editing is best suited for minor revisions. Major
revisions to the xref file should be done in the original drawing.

CAUTION

All reference edits made using reference editing are saved back to
the original drawing file and affect any host drawing that references the file when the host is opened. For this reason, it is critically
important that external references be edited only with the permis-
sion of your instructor or supervisor.

Opening an Xref File

Type
XOPEN
Menu Browser
Tools
> Xref and
Block In-Place
Editing
> Open
Reference

XOPEN

The **XOPEN** tool provides an alternative to using the **REFEDIT** tool. **XOPEN** allows
you to open an xref from within the host drawing in a new drawing window. A quick
way to access the **XOPEN** tool is to select an object that is part of the xref file in the
drawing area, then right-click and select the **Open Xref** menu option. This is essentially
the same procedure as using the **OPEN** tool, but faster.

Once you access the **XOPEN** tool, pick an object that is part of the xref to be opened,
if the xref is not already selected. The xref drawing file opens in a different drawing

window. After you make changes and save the xref file, you must reload the xref file in the host drawing file. Use the **External References** palette or the **Manage Xrefs** icon in the status bar to reload the modified xref file. This ensures that the host file you are working in is up-to-date.

NOTE

You can also open an xref in the **External References** palette by right-clicking the xref name and selecting the **Open** shortcut menu option.

Exercise 32-6

Complete the exercise on the Student CD.

Chapter Test

Answer the following questions. Write your answers on a separate sheet of paper or complete the electronic chapter test on the Student CD.

1. What three types of files can be referenced into an AutoCAD drawing?
2. What effect does the use of referenced drawings have on drawing file size?
3. When are xrefs updated in the master drawing?
4. List at least three common applications for xrefs.
5. On what layer should you insert xrefs into a drawing?
6. Which tool is used to attach an xref drawing to the current file?
7. What is the difference between an overlaid xref and an attached xref?
8. What is a nested xref?
9. What is the difference between an absolute path and a relative path?
10. Describe the process of placing an xref using **DesignCenter**.
11. What must you do before you can use a tool palette to place an xref?
12. If you attach an xref file named FPLAN to the current drawing, and FPLAN contains a layer called ELECTRICAL, what name will appear for this layer in the **Layer Properties Manager**?
13. What is the purpose of the **Detach** option in the **External References** palette?
14. What could you do to suppress an xref temporarily without detaching it from the master drawing?
15. Which tool allows you to display only a specific portion of an externally referenced drawing?
16. What are spatial and layer indexes, and what function do they perform?
17. Why would you want to bind a dependent object to a master drawing?
18. What does the layer name WALL0NOTES mean?
19. What tool is used to edit external references in place?
20. What tool allows you to open a parent xref drawing into a new AutoCAD drawing window by selecting the xref in the master drawing?

Drawing Problems

Note: Some of the following problems refer to drawings created in previous chapters. If you have not yet created those drawings, you will need to do so before working these problems.

▼ Basic

1. Attach a dimensioned problem from Chapter 19 into a new drawing as an xref. Save the drawing as P32-1.

2. Attach a dimensioned problem from Chapter 20 into a new drawing as an xref. Save the drawing as P32-2.

3. Attach a dimensioned problem from Chapter 22 into a new drawing as an xref. Save the drawing as P32-3.

▼ Intermediate

4. Attach the EX29-9.dwg file used in Exercise 29-9 into a new drawing as an xref. Copy the xref three times. Use the **XCLIP** tool to create a clipping boundary on each view. Apply an inverted rectangular clip to the original xref, a polyline boundary on the first copy, and a polygonal boundary on the second copy. Save the drawing as P32-4.

5. Attach the EX29-9.dwg file used in Exercise 29-9 into a new drawing as an xref. Bind the xref to the new drawing. Rename the layers to the names assigned to the original EX29-9 (xref) file. Explode the block created by binding the xref. Save the drawing as P32-5.

6. Create the multi-detail drawing shown according to the following information:
   - Use the MECHANICAL-INCH.dwt drawing template file available on the Student CD.
   - Set drawing units to fractional.
   - Xref the following files into model space: Detail-Item 1.dwg, Detail-Item 2.dwg, Detail-Item 3.dwg, Detail-Item 4.dwg, Detail-Item 5.dwg, and Detail-Item 6.dwg. These files are available on the Student CD.
   - Use six floating viewports on the **C-SIZE** layout to arrange and scale the details. Use a 1:2 scale.
   - Plot the drawing.

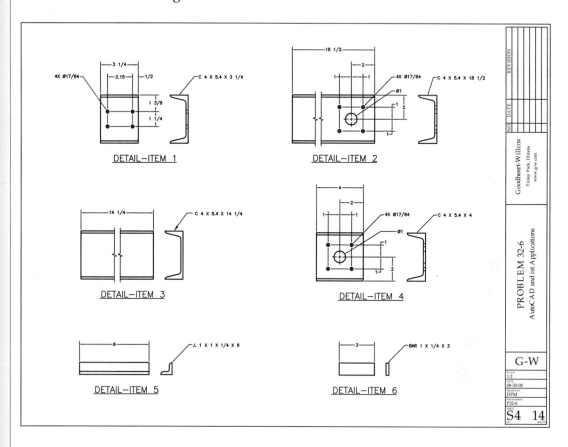

▼ **Advanced**

7. Design and draw a basic residential floor plan using an appropriate template. Save the file as P32-7FLOOR. Xref the P32-7FLOOR file into a new file as an attachment. Use the xref to help draw a roof plan. Save the roof plan file as P32-7ROOF.

8. Xref the P32-8ROOF file into a new file as an attachment. Use the xref to help draw front and rear elevations. Save the elevation file as P32-8.

9. Use a word processor to write a report of approximately 250 words explaining the purpose of external references. Include a brief description of the types of files that can be referenced. Cite at least three examples from actual industry applications of using external references to help prepare drawings. Use at least four sketches to illustrate your report.

CHAPTER 33

Creating and Using Sheet Sets

Learning Objectives

After completing this chapter, you will be able to do the following:

✓ Identify and describe the functions of the **Sheet Set Manager**.
✓ Create sheet sets and subsets.
✓ Add sheets and sheet views to a sheet set.
✓ Plot or publish a set of sheets.
✓ Insert callout blocks and view labels into sheet views.
✓ Set up custom properties for a sheet set.
✓ Create a sheet list table.
✓ Archive a set of electronic files for a sheet set.

As a project develops, a set of drawings is used to build the design. Typically, information from a number of sources, such as clients and vendors, influence the design and drawing process. Effectively organizing and distributing drawings during the course of a design project is critical to delivering accurate drawings in an orderly and timely manner. *Sheet sets* help simplify the management of a project that contains multiple drawings and views. This chapter describes how to use sheet sets to structure different drawing layouts into groups of files for reviewing, plotting, and publishing purposes.

sheet set: A collection of drawing sheets for a project.

NOTE

Sheet sets combine many AutoCAD features to automate and organize the entire drawing set for a project. To understand and effectively apply sheet sets, you must understand content described throughout this textbook, including templates, views, fields, blocks, layouts, attributes, and external references. If you encounter difficulties in understanding an aspect of sheet sets, it may be helpful to review the underlying concept being applied.

Introduction to Sheet Sets

In AutoCAD, *sheets* are created in layouts in a drawing file and can have additional project-specific properties. All of the sheets in a sheet set can use a single

sheet: A printed drawing or electronic layout produced for a project.

Figure 33-1.
The **Sheet Set Manager** palette contains the **Sheet List, Sheet Views**, and **Model Views** tabs. The **Sheet Set Control** drop-down list contains options for creating and opening a sheet set.

Auto-hide

Properties

Pick to create a sheet set

Title bar

Sheet Set Control drop-down list

Current tab

Open...
Recent ▶
New Sheet Set...
Open...

Sheet Set Manager

Sheet List

Sheet Views

Model Views

---

fields: Special text objects that display values that can be updated automatically.

template. The template can contain a title block with attributes containing *fields*. The field values may include items such as project name and sheet number. Thus, if the project name changes during the course of the project, the field is modified in the template, and the change is automatically applied to all sheets within the set. If a new sheet is inserted into a sheet set, the sheet numbers and all sheet references update automatically. This automation saves a great deal of time and improves the accuracy of the set of drawings.

Once a sheet set is complete, you can easily print, publish, and archive the entire set in a single operation. This is very efficient. For example, it is far easier to plot a sheet set containing twenty sheets than to open and plot twenty separate drawings.

Sheet sets are created, organized, and accessed using the **Sheet Set Manager** palette. The **Sheet Set Manager** palette is initially divided into three tabs. The **Sheet Set Control** drop-down list at the top of the **Sheet Set Manager** is used to open and create sheet sets. See **Figure 33-1.** The buttons next to the drop-down list control and manage the items listed in the **Sheet Set Manager**. These buttons vary depending on the currently selected tab. Like other palettes, the **Sheet Set Manager** can be resized, docked, and set to auto-hide. The **Sheet Set Manager** also makes use of extensive tooltips that describe and allow you to preview items in the palette.

SHEETSET

Quick Access

Sheet Set Manager

Ribbon

View
> Palettes

Sheet Set Manager

Type

SHEETSET
SSM

Menu Browser

Tools
> Palettes
> Sheet Set Manager

NOTE

When no drawing is open, the **Sheet Set Manager** button appears in the **Quick Access** toolbar, and a **Sheet Set Manager** option is available from the menu browser by selecting **File** > **Sheet Set Manager**. Use either option to access the **Sheet Set Manager** without opening a drawing.

Creating Sheet Sets

Sheet sets are created with the **Create Sheet Set** wizard. See **Figure 33-2.** This wizard is accessed from within the **Sheet Set Manager** by picking **New Sheet Set...** from the **Sheet Set Control** drop-down list. Sheet sets can be created from an example sheet set or from existing drawing files.

Figure 33-2.
Select **An example
sheet set** on the
Begin page to use
an AutoCAD sheet
set or another
existing sheet set as
a template.

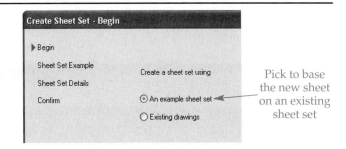

Pick to base
the new sheet
on an existing
sheet set

Creating a Sheet Set from an Example Sheet Set

An example sheet set uses an existing sheet set as a model, similar to a template, for developing a new sheet set. The example sheet set is modified as needed to fit the needs of the new sheet set. AutoCAD provides several example sheet sets based on different drafting disciplines. You are not limited to the examples provided—you can use any existing sheet set as an example sheet set. To create a new sheet set from an example sheet set, access the **Create Sheet Set** wizard, and at the **Begin** page, pick the **An example sheet set** radio button.

Pick the **Next** button to display the **Sheet Set Example** page. See Figure 33-3. Sheet set information is saved in a sheet set data file (DST). When you create a sheet set from an example sheet set, you start from an existing DST file. By default, the **Select a sheet to use as an example** radio button is selected, and a list box displays all DST files in the default Template folder. Pick a sheet set from the list box, or select the **Browse to another sheet set to use as an example** radio button and then select the ellipsis (...) button and use the dialog box to locate a DST file in another folder. After selecting the DST file for the example sheet set, pick the **Next** button to display the **Sheet Set Details** page. See Figure 33-4.

The **Sheet Set Details** page allows you to modify the existing sheet set data and create settings for your new project. Enter the name, or title, of the sheet set in the **Name of new sheet set** text box. This is typically the project number or a short description of the project. If desired, type a description for the sheet set in the **Description (optional)** area. The **Store sheet set data file (.dst) here** text box determines where the sheet set file is saved on the hard drive. Pick the ellipsis (...) button and select a folder in the dialog box to redefine the default sheet set file location.

Figure 33-3.
Use the **Sheet Set Example** page to select an example sheet set.

List of sheet sets
in **Template** folder

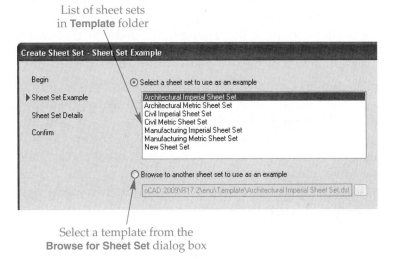

Select a template from the
Browse for Sheet Set dialog box

Figure 33-4.
Enter a name, description, and file path location for the new sheet set on the **Sheet Set Details** page.

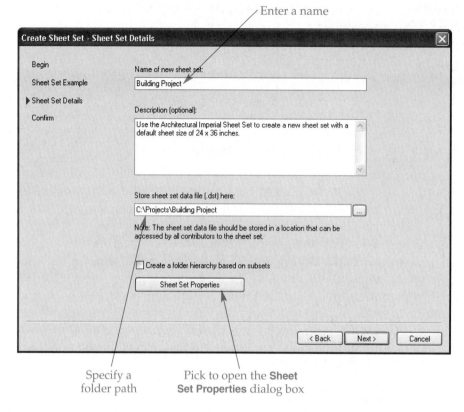

Enter a name

Specify a folder path

Pick to open the **Sheet Set Properties** dialog box

Pick the **Sheet Set Properties** button to open the **Sheet Set Properties** dialog box. See Figure 33-5. The **Sheet Set** category includes basic sheet set properties. The **Name** field contains the sheet set name entered in the **Name of new sheet set** text box of the **Sheet Set Details** page. The **Sheet set data file** field shows the location of the DST file, specified in the **Store sheet set data file (.dst) here** text box of the **Sheet Set Details** page. The **Description** field contains the description of the sheet set entered in the **Description** area of the **Sheet Set Details** page. The **Model view** field specifies the folder(s) containing drawing files that are used for the sheet set. The **Label block for views** field specifies the block used to label views. The **Callout blocks** field specifies blocks available for use as callout blocks. The **Page setup overrides file** field specifies the location of an AutoCAD template file (DWT file) containing a page setup to be used to override the existing sheet layout settings. All of these settings except the **Sheet set data file** option can be changed by picking in the text box to activate it. When file locations are required, the ellipsis (**...**) button appears. Pick this button to navigate to the location you want to specify.

The properties in the **Project Control** category allow you to store and update information based on the current project. The properties in the **Sheet Creation** category determine the location of the drawing files for new sheets and the template used to create them. When a new sheet is added to a sheet set, AutoCAD creates a new drawing file based on the template and layout specified in the **Sheet creation template** setting. The folder path in the **Sheet storage location** field determines where the new file is saved. It is important to specify the correct location so you know where the files are being saved.

When selecting the **Sheet creation template** value, you must specify both a template file and a layout. To modify this setting, pick in the text box and then pick the ellipsis (**...**) button. This displays the **Select Layout as Sheet Template** dialog box. See Figure 33-6.

All layouts in the selected template are displayed in the list box. Select the layout and then pick the **OK** button.

If the value in the **Prompt for template** field is set to **No**, the template layout specified in the **Sheet creation template** field is automatically used when a new sheet is created. This is the default setting. If the field value is set to **Yes**, you can select a different layout when creating a new sheet. Information specific to the project is set up in the **Sheet Set Custom Properties** section. This topic is described later in this chapter.

Once all the values in the **Sheet Set Properties** dialog box are set, pick the **OK** button. This returns you to the **Sheet Set Details** page. Pick the **Next** button to continue creating the new sheet set. The **Sheet Set Preview** area on the **Confirm** page displays all of the information associated with the sheet set. See Figure 33-7. In the example

Figure 33-5.
The main properties of a sheet set are stored in the **Sheet Set Properties** dialog box.

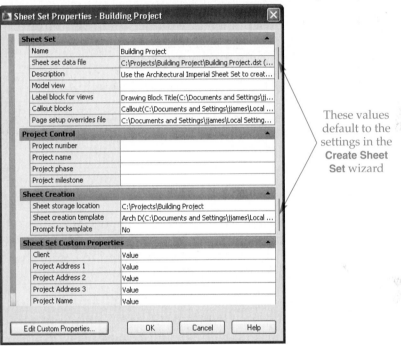

These values default to the settings in the **Create Sheet Set** wizard

Figure 33-6.
An existing layout is used as a template for new sheets in a sheet set.

Pick to select a different template file

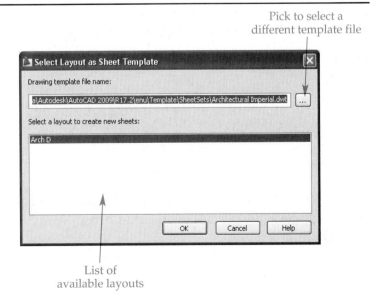

List of available layouts

Figure 33-7.
Use the **Confirm** page to preview settings before creating the sheet set.

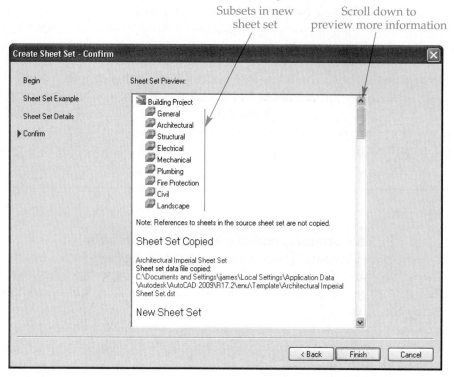

Subsets in new sheet set

Scroll down to preview more information

shown, a sheet set named Building Project has been created. This sheet set contains a number of *subsets* related to the project, such as General and Architectural. After the sheet set is created, sheets can be added to each subset. After reviewing the information on the **Confirm** page, pick the **Finish** button to create the sheet set. If a setting needs to be changed, use the **Back** button.

PROFESSIONAL TIP

The information in the **Sheet Set Preview** area can be copied to a word processing program to be saved or printed. To do this, highlight all of the text and then use the [Ctrl]+[C] key combination. Open a new document in the word processing program and use the [Ctrl]+[V] key combination to paste the text into the document.

When you pick the **Finish** button, the sheet set data file is saved to the specified location. The sheet set can then be opened in the **Sheet Set Manager**. Since a sheet set is not associated with a particular drawing file, any sheet set can be opened, regardless of the open drawing file.

Exercise 33-1

Complete the exercise on the Student CD.

Creating a Sheet Set from Existing Drawing Files

Existing drawings can also be used to create a sheet set. Layouts are imported from drawing files to create sheets. Each layout in the drawings becomes a separate sheet. When you create a sheet set in this manner, organize all the files used in the project in a structured hierarchy of folders. To simplify access to the different layout tabs, it is recommended that you place only one layout in each drawing file. To ensure that all sheets have the same layout settings, create a sheet creation template as well. The template is specified in the **Sheet Set Properties** dialog box.

To create a new sheet set from an existing drawing project, access the **Create Sheet Set** wizard, and at the **Begin** page, select the **Existing drawings** radio button and pick the **Next** button. On the **Sheet Set Details** page, specify a name and description for the sheet set and the location where the data file will be saved. Pick the **Sheet Set Properties** button to specify the sheet set properties. Pick the **Next** button to display the **Choose Layouts** page. See Figure 33-8.

The **Choose Layouts** page is used to specify the drawings and layouts to be added to the sheet set. Pick the **Browse...** button to select the folder(s) containing the drawing files with the desired layouts. The selected folder, the drawing files it contains, and all layouts within those drawings are displayed. When you first open a folder in the **Choose Layouts** page, all of the drawing files with layouts in that folder are added for selection. Each item has a check box next to it. The layouts that are checked are added to the new sheet set. If a layout should not be part of the new sheet set, uncheck the box next to it. In Figure 33-8, the boxes next to Furniture.dwg and its layouts have been unchecked, so they are not included in the sheet set. Unchecking a drawing file automatically unchecks all of the layouts in the file. If the folder is unchecked, all of the layouts in the drawing files are unchecked. More folders can be added to the **Choose Layouts** page by using the **Browse for Folder** dialog box.

Figure 33-8.
Existing layouts can be imported to a new sheet set from the **Choose Layouts** page.

Pick to select folders

Pick to set sheet naming and organization options

Folder containing drawing files with layouts

Unchecked layouts will not be part of the new sheet set

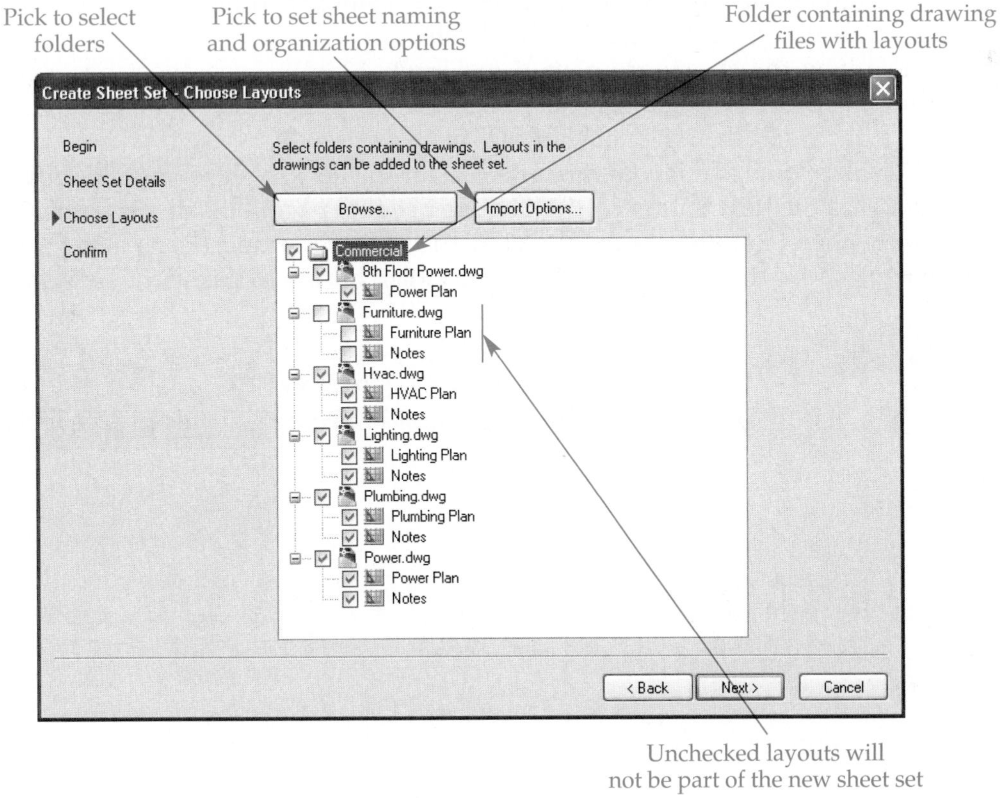

Figure 33-9.
Naming conventions for sheets and folder structuring options are specified in the **Import Options** dialog box.

Check to include drawing file name with layout name for new sheets

Check to create subsets from folders

Check to omit top folder name from subset structure

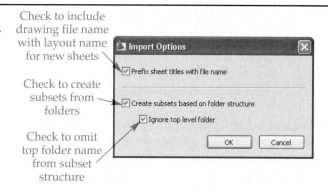

When a sheet set is created using existing layouts, the name for a new sheet can be the same as the layout name, or it can be the drawing file name combined with the layout name. Sheet naming options are accessed by picking the **Import Options...** button to display the **Import Options** dialog box. See Figure 33-9. If the **Prefix sheet titles with file name** check box is checked, the layouts that become sheets are named with the drawing file name and the name of the layout. For example, if a layout named First Floor Electrical is imported from the drawing file Electrical Plan.dwg, the sheet that is created is named Electrical Plan – First Floor Electrical. To have the sheets take on only the layout name, uncheck the **Prefix sheet titles with file name** check box.

An imported sheet set can be organized so that the folders are grouped into subsets. If the **Create subsets based on folder structure** option is checked in the **Import Options** dialog box, all of the folder names added to the sheet set become subsets. The layouts in the folders are added under each subset. The **Ignore top level folder** option determines whether a subset is created for the folder name at the top level. Figure 33-10A shows the **Choose Layouts** page with layouts imported from the Residential folder for the Residential Project sheet set. This sheet set has been created with the **Create subsets based on folder structure** option checked in the **Import Options** dialog box. The result of this configuration is shown in the **Sheet Set Manager** in Figure 33-10B. Creating subsets for sheet sets helps organize the sheets.

Notice how the sheets are named in Figure 33-10B. Each sheet has a number preceding its name. By default, a sheet is displayed in the **Sheet Set Manager** with its number, a dash, and then the name of the sheet.

When all folders and layouts are selected for the new sheet set and all settings are specified, pick the **Next** button on the **Choose Layouts** page. This displays the **Confirm** page. In the **Sheet Set Preview** area, review the sheet set properties. If a setting needs to be changed, use the **Back** button. Pick the **Finish** button to create the new sheet set.

Exercise 33-2
Complete the exercise on the Student CD.

Figure 33-10.
Creating a sheet set named Residential Project with subsets. A—Layouts are imported from the Architectural and Structural subfolders in the Residential folder. The subfolders are designated as subsets for the new sheet set. B—The subsets are shown in the **Sheet Set Manager**.

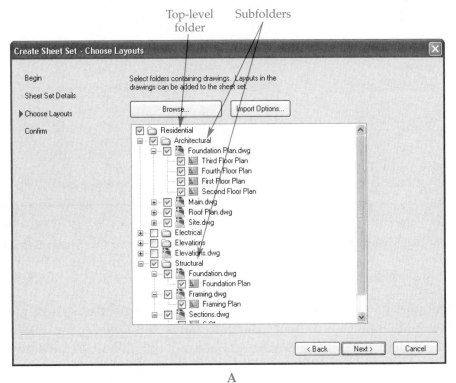

A

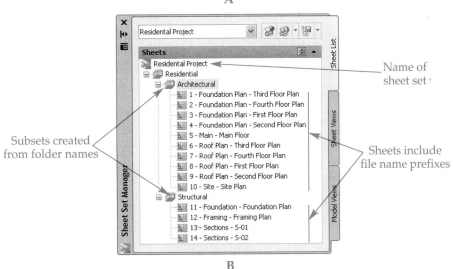

B

Working with Sheet Sets

Sheet sets are displayed and edited using the **Sheet Set Manager**. Open an existing sheet set from within the **Sheet Set Manager** by picking a sheet set from the **Sheet Set Control** drop-down list. See Figure 33-11. The top portion of the drop-down list displays sheet sets that have been opened in the current AutoCAD session. When AutoCAD is closed, this area is cleared. Select **Recent** to display a list of the most recently opened sheet sets. Select **Open…** to display the **Open Sheet Set** dialog box. Then navigate to a sheet set data file (DST file) and open it in the **Sheet Set Manager**.

Figure 33-11.
The **Sheet Set Control** drop-down list displays sheet sets that are currently open. Picking **Open...** allows you to browse for a sheet set that is not in the list.

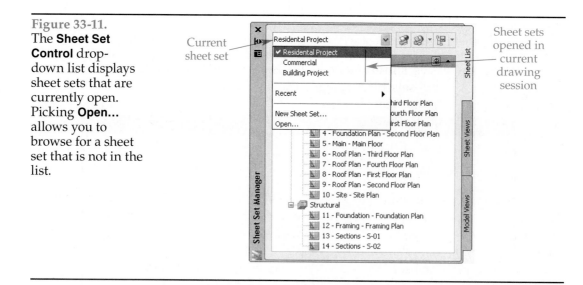

Current sheet set

Sheet sets opened in current drawing session

Sheets in a sheet set are managed in the **Sheet List** tab of the **Sheet Set Manager**. Sheet views are managed in the **Sheet Views** tab, and drawing files with layouts are managed in the **Model Views** tab. Almost all of the options for working with sheet sets are available from shortcut menus. Right-clicking on a sheet set displays the shortcut menu shown in **Figure 33-12**. Many of the menu options are described when applicable throughout this chapter. The **Close Sheet Set** option removes the sheet set from the **Sheet Set Manager**. Pick the **Resave All Sheets** option to update the drawing files that are part of the current sheet set. All of the files need to be closed first. An open drawing file cannot be updated.

NOTE

To update changes to the sheet list manually, pick the **Refresh Sheet Status** button. See **Figure 33-12**.

Figure 33-12.
This shortcut menu is displayed by right-clicking on a sheet set name in the **Sheet List** tab.

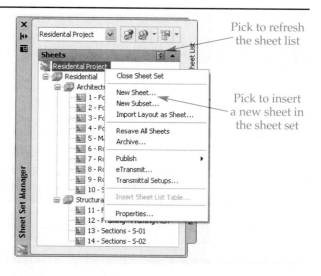

Pick to refresh the sheet list

Pick to insert a new sheet in the sheet set

Working with Subsets

Creating subsets is similar to creating subfolders under a top-level folder in Windows Explorer. Subsets help manage the contents of the sheet set. For example, create a subset named Architectural to store all architectural sheets for a project, a subset named Electrical to store all electrical sheets, and a subset named Plumbing to store all plumbing sheets.

subsets: Groups of layouts based on folder hierarchy.

Creating a New Subset

To create a new subset, right-click on the sheet set name or an existing subset in the **Sheet Set Manager** and select the **New Subset...** option. This opens the **Subset Properties** dialog box. See **Figure 33-13.** Type the name of the new subset in the **Subset name** text box. For example, if a subset is being created for all of the electrical sheets in a sheet set, name the subset Electrical. When a new sheet is added to the subset using a template, the sheet is saved to the hard drive as a drawing file. To create a new folder for the subset, select the **Create folders relative to parent subset storage location** check box. The folder structure mimics the subset structure. The **Store new sheet DWG files in** setting determines the path to which new sheets are saved. The default value is the location specified when the sheet set was initially created.

Each subset can also have its own template and layout for new sheets. This is specified in the **Sheet creation template for subset** setting. For example, if the electrical sheets use their own title block and notes, a template sheet with these settings should be used. The procedure for specifying the template and layout for a subset is identical to the procedure used to select the sheet set properties.

Modifying a Subset

After a subset is created, you can modify its settings by right-clicking on the subset and selecting the **Properties...** menu option. This displays the **Subset Properties** dialog box. The **Rename Subset...** shortcut menu option also opens the **Subset Properties** dialog box. To delete a subset, right-click on the subset and select the **Remove Subset** menu option. This option is unavailable if the subset contains sheets.

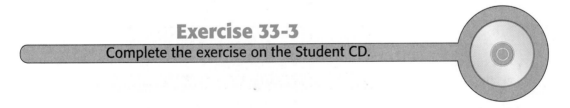

Exercise 33-3
Complete the exercise on the Student CD.

Figure 33-13.
Settings for a new subset are made in the **Subset Properties** dialog box.

Enter a name for the new subset

Path to which new sheets will be saved

Template layout for new sheets

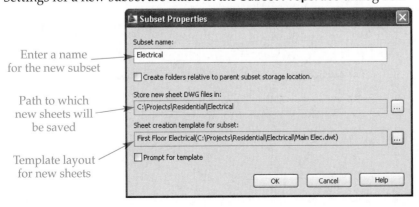

Working with Sheets

One of the most useful features of the **Sheet Set Manager** is the ability to open a sheet quickly for review or modification. To open a sheet, double-click on the sheet or right-click on the sheet and select the **Open** option. The drawing file that contains the referenced layout tab opens and the layout is set current.

> **NOTE**
>
> When files are opened from the **Sheet Set Manager**, they are added to the open files list. Use **Quick View Drawings** or the drawing window control features of the ribbon or the menu browser to view all of the open files. However, opening many files can affect the performance of AutoCAD. Save and close files that are no longer needed.

Adding a Sheet Using a Template

A new sheet can be added to a sheet set by using the template layout sheet or by importing an existing layout. In order to add a sheet using the template layout sheet, a template must be specified in the **Sheet creation template** setting of the **Sheet Set** properties. To add a sheet using the template, right-click on the sheet set name or the subset where the sheet needs to be added, and select the **New Sheet...** option. If a template layout is not specified, an alert appears and you are directed to pick a template layout using the **Select Layout as Sheet Template** dialog box. If a template layout was previously defined, or after you select the template layout, the **New Sheet** dialog box appears. See Figure 33-14.

Type the sheet number in the **Number** text box and the sheet name in the **Sheet title** text box. A new drawing file is created. The sheet title becomes the name of the layout in the drawing file. Enter the name for the file in the **File name** text box. By default, this is the sheet number and title. The **Folder path** field shows where the drawing file will be saved. This path is specified in the **Subset Properties** or **Sheet Set Properties** dialog box.

Figure 33-14.
When you create a new sheet from a template, the sheet is defined in the **New Sheet** dialog box.

Enter a sheet number

Enter a sheet name (layout name)

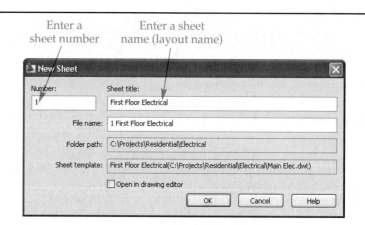

Figure 33-15.
Existing layouts can be added as sheets to a sheet set from the **Import Layouts as Sheets** dialog box.

Pick to select drawing file

Uncheck to exclude a layout from being imported

Adding an Existing Layout as a Sheet

An existing drawing layout can be added to a sheet set directly from an open drawing or using the **Sheet Set Manager**. To add an existing layout to a sheet set using the **Sheet Set Manager**, right-click on the sheet set name or the subset in which the sheet needs to be added, and select the **Import Layout as Sheet...** menu option. This displays the **Import Layouts as Sheets** dialog box. See **Figure 33-15.** Pick the **Browse for Drawings** button to select a drawing file. The layouts from the drawing file are shown in the list box. The **Status** field indicates whether the layout can be imported into the sheet set. If a layout is already part of a sheet set, it cannot be imported. By default, all of the layouts in the drawing are checked in the list. Uncheck the box to exclude a layout from being imported as a sheet. If the **Prefix sheet titles with file name** check box is checked, the name of the file is included in the sheet title. To import the sheets, pick the **Import Checked** button.

Use the **Quick View Layouts** or **Quick View Drawings** tool to add an existing layout to a sheet set directly from an open drawing. Right-click on the layout thumbnail image you want to import and select the **Import Layout as Sheet...** menu option. This displays the **Import Layouts as Sheets** dialog box previously described, with the selected layout listed automatically. The drawing must be saved and the layout must be set up for the **Import Layout as Sheet...** shortcut menu item to be available.

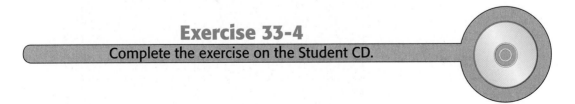

Exercise 33-4
Complete the exercise on the Student CD.

Modifying Sheet Properties

The properties of a sheet, such as the name, number, and description, are modified by right-clicking on the sheet name in the **Sheet Set Manager** to display the shortcut menu. The sheet name and number can be changed by selecting **Rename & Renumber...** from this menu. This displays the **Rename & Renumber Sheet** dialog box, which is similar to the **New Sheet** dialog box. If the sheet is one of several in a subset, picking the **Next** button moves to the next sheet in the subset.

The **Sheet Properties** dialog box also allows you to change the sheet name and number, along with the description and the publish option. To open the **Sheet Properties** dialog box, right-click on the sheet name and select the **Properties...** menu option. See Figure 33-16. Type a description of the sheet in the **Description** text box. The **Include for publish** option determines whether the sheet is included when the sheet set is published or plotted. The default value is **Yes**.

The **Expected layout** and **Found layout** text boxes display the file path where the sheet was originally saved and the file path where the sheet was found. If the paths are different, update the **Expected layout** field by picking the ellipsis (...) button. To delete a sheet from a sheet set, select the **Remove Sheet** menu option. This does not delete the drawing file from the hard drive; it only removes the sheet from the sheet set.

NOTE

If the hard drive location of a drawing file is modified and the drawing file has layouts that are associated with a sheet set, the association is broken. You must re-import the layouts into the sheet set or update the specified path to the drawing file in the **Sheet Properties** dialog box.

Figure 33-16.
The properties of a sheet can be modified in the **Sheet Properties** dialog box.

Determines whether the sheet is published or included in plot

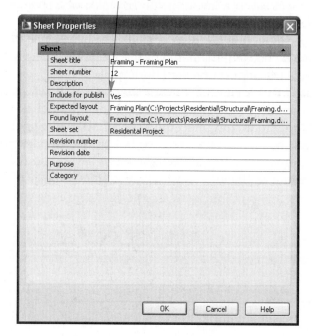

Sheet	
Sheet title	Framing - Framing Plan
Sheet number	12
Description	
Include for publish	Yes
Expected layout	Framing Plan(C:\Projects\Residential\Structural\Framing.d...
Found layout	Framing Plan(C:\Projects\Residential\Structural\Framing.d...
Sheet set	Residental Project
Revision number	
Revision date	
Purpose	
Category	

Publishing a Sheet Set

Sheet sets can be *published* by creating drawing web format (DWF) files or DWFx files, which are supported by Windows Vista. DWF and DWFx files are compressed, vector-based files that can be viewed with the Autodesk Design Review software that can be installed with AutoCAD. A sheet set can also be published by sending it to a plotter. For more information about outputting DWF and DWFx files, refer to *AutoCAD and Its Applications—Advanced*.

publishing: Creating electronic files for distribution or plotting.

Using the Publish Shortcut Menu

An entire sheet set can be published to a DWF or DWFx file or plotted using the options in the **Publish** shortcut menu in the **Sheet Set Manager**. To access the **Publish** shortcut menu, pick the **Publish** button on the **Sheet Set Manager** toolbar or select **Publish** from the shortcut menu. See Figure 33-17.

> **NOTE**
>
> A sheet set, a subset, or individual sheets can be selected for publishing. Select the appropriate items using the [Shift] and [Ctrl] keys in the **Sheet Set Manager**.

The **Publish to DWF** and **Publish to DWFx** options are used to create a DWF or DWFx file from the sheet set or the selected sheets. In the **Select DWF File** dialog box, specify a name and location for the file. The file is created with each sheet on a separate page in a multi-sheet file. Use the **Publish to Plotter** option to plot the sheet set or selected sheets to the default plotter or printer using the plot settings from each layout. Pick the **Publish using Page Setup Override** option to display page setups available for use as overrides. Selecting a page setup from the list forces the sheet to use the selected page setup settings instead of the plot settings that are saved with the layout. This option is unavailable if a page setup override has not been specified for the sheet set or subset.

The **Publish in Reverse Order** option publishes sheets in the opposite order from the order displayed in the **Sheet Set Manager**. On some printers, publishing a sheet set

Figure 33-17.
The **Publish** shortcut menu options are used to prepare a sheet set for publishing or plotting.

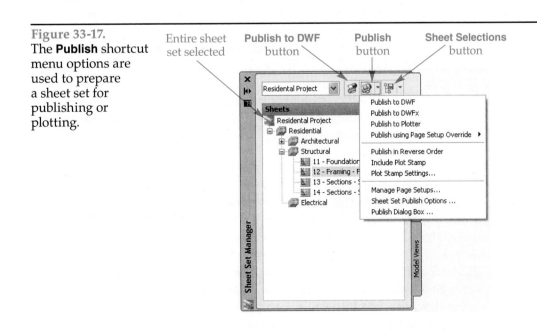

Figure 33-18.
Sheet selection sets can be created from selected sheets or subsets in a sheet set. They are accessed from the **Sheet Selections** shortcut menu.

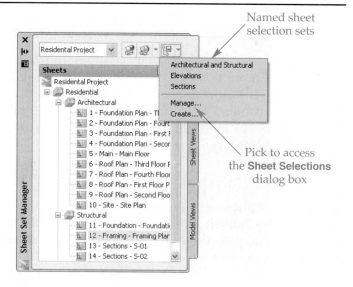

in reverse order is helpful when you are plotting sheets so that the last sheet is on the bottom of the stack, at the end of the entire set. Select the **Include Plot Stamp** option to place the plot stamp information for the layout on the sheet when it is plotted. Select the **Plot Stamp Settings** option to open the **Plot Stamp** dialog box to specify the plot stamp settings. The **Manage Page Setups** option opens the **Page Setup Manager**, allowing you to create a new page setup or modify an existing one. The **Sheet Set Publish Options** option displays the **Sheet Set Publish Options** dialog box. This displays the available settings for creating a DWF or DWFx file. The **Publish Dialog Box** option opens the **Publish** dialog box. All of the sheets in the current sheet set or the sheet selection are listed.

Creating Sheet Selection Sets

During the course of a project, the same set of sheets may need to be published many times. A selection of sheets can be saved so that the sheets can be accessed again quickly for publishing. To save a sheet selection set, select the sheets to be included in the set. If necessary, select a subset to include all of the sheets in a subset. Then pick the **Sheet Selections** button on the **Sheet Set Manager** toolbar and select the **Create…** option. In the **New Sheet Selection** dialog box, enter a name for the selection set and pick the **OK** button. The new selection set appears when you pick the **Sheet Selections** button. In Figure 33-18, three different sheet selection sets are shown. When a selection set is selected from the shortcut menu, the sheets are automatically highlighted in the **Sheet Set Manager**.

To rename or delete a sheet selection set, pick **Manage…** from the **Sheet Selections** shortcut menu. In the **Sheet Selections** dialog box, select the sheet selection set and then pick the **Rename** or **Delete** button.

Using Sheet Views

sheet view: A referenced portion of a drawing set, such as an elevation, a section, or a detail.

Sheets can contain *sheet views*. Sheet views can be automatically labeled, placed on separate sheets, and referenced to each other using blocks with attributes containing fields. These sheet view field values update automatically to reflect changes in sheet numbering. Use the **Sheet Views** tab of the **Sheet Set Manager** to group views by category and open views for viewing and editing. Special tools in the **Sheet Set Manager** are used to identify views with numbers, labels, and callout blocks.

AutoCAD and Its Applications—Basics

Adding a View Category

View categories are used to organize views in the **Sheet Views** tab. View categories are similar to the subsets created in the **Sheet List** tab. To create a new view category, make the **Sheet Views** tab current and ensure that the **View by category** button is selected. See **Figure 33-19**. Pick the **New View Category** button or right-click on the sheet set name and select **New View Category...** from the shortcut menu to open the **View Category** dialog box. See **Figure 33-20**. In the **Category name** text box, enter a name for the category. For example, if you are going to add four elevation views to the new category, it could be named Elevations.

The **View Category** dialog box lists all of the available callout blocks for the current view category. Check the box next to the callout block to make it available for all of the views that are added to this category. If a block is not in the list, use the **Add Blocks...** button to select it from a drawing file. Once the necessary callout blocks are selected, pick the **OK** button to create the new category. Callout blocks are described later in this chapter.

Figure 33-19.
View categories are created in the **Sheet Views** tab of the **Sheet Set Manager**.

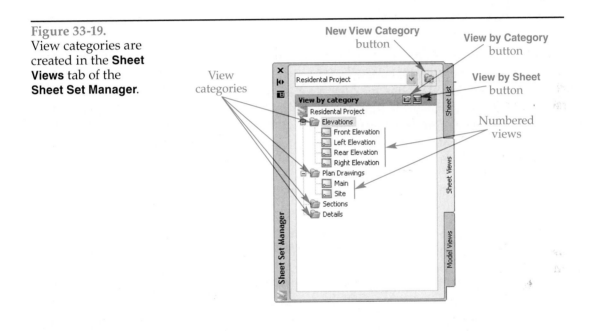

Figure 33-20.
The **View Category** dialog box is used to name the category and select callout blocks for use with views.

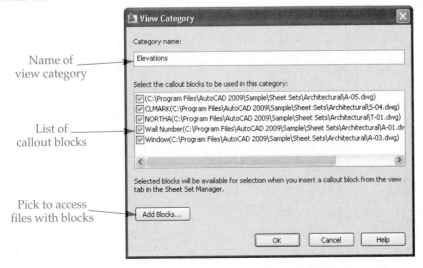

Modifying a View Category

View category properties are modified by right-clicking on the category name in the **Sheet Set Manager** and selecting the **Rename...** or **Properties...** menu option. Selecting either of these options opens the **View Category** dialog box. The category name can be changed and different callout blocks can be added to the category. To delete a category, right-click on the category name and select the **Remove Category** option. The **Remove Category** option is unavailable if there are views in the category. The views must be removed before the category can be deleted.

Creating Sheet Views in an Existing Sheet

New views can be added to sheets and organized within sheet sets from the **Sheet Set Manager**. Use the following procedure to add a view to an existing sheet set:

1. Open the desired sheet set and add a category for the view if it has not already been created.
2. To add a view to a sheet, the sheet has to be a part of the sheet set. If the sheet has not been added to the sheet set, add it now.
3. Open the drawing file and set the layout tab current where the new view will be created.
4. Use display tools to orient the view as needed and then use the **VIEW** tool to access the **View Manager**.
5. In the **View Manager**, pick the **New...** button to open the **New View** dialog box.
6. Select the category that you want the view to be a part of from the **View category** drop-down list. See **Figure 33-21**.
7. Specify the rest of the view settings and pick the **OK** button to save the view.

Figure 33-21.
The **View Category** drop-down list displays the available view categories for the view being defined.

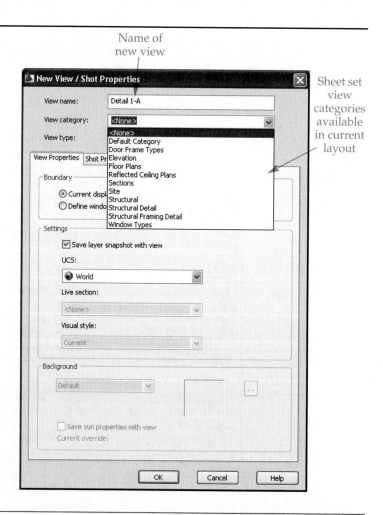

Name of new view

Sheet set view categories available in current layout

The newly saved view now appears in the **Sheet Set Manager** under the view category that was selected in the **New View** dialog box.

Once a view is added to a sheet set, it can be displayed from the **Sheet Set Manager** by double-clicking on the view name or by right-clicking on the name and selecting the **Display** option. If the drawing file is already open, the view is set current. If the drawing file is not open, the file is opened so that the view can be set current.

The view list can be displayed by category or by sheet. Refer to Figure 33-19. The **View by category** button displays all of the categories. The views are accessed by expanding the category and then the sheet. Pick the **View by sheet** button to display the sheet name. Expand the sheet name to display the saved views within the sheet.

Creating Sheet Views from Resource Drawings

Sheet views can be created from *resource drawings* listed in the **Model Views** tab. The sheet view can be the entire model space drawing or a model space view. When a model space view or drawing is inserted into a sheet, the resource drawing becomes an external reference of the sheet drawing.

Folders containing reference drawings are listed in the **Model Views** tab, as shown in Figure 33-22. To add a new folder, double-click on the Add New Location entry or pick the **Add New Location** button and select a folder. You cannot select specific drawing files—you must select the folder containing the drawing. Only drawings listed in the **Model Views** tab can be inserted into a sheet to create a new sheet view. If the drawing you want to use is not listed, you must add the folder containing the drawing to the resource drawing list.

The folder and all of the drawing files that are in it are now listed in the **Locations** list area. The model space views saved in the drawing are listed under the drawing file. The options available for a drawing file are located in the drawing file shortcut menu. To display the menu, right-click on a drawing file.

Pick the **Open** option to open the drawing file and set model space current. Double-clicking on the drawing file also opens the file. Select the **Open read-only** option to open the drawing file as read-only so that changes cannot be made to the file. The

resource drawings: Drawing files that contain model space views that are referenced to be used as sheet views.

Figure 33-22.
Sheet views can be created by inserting model space views and drawings from the **Model Views** tab. To see a thumbnail and details, hover the cursor over the drawing or view.

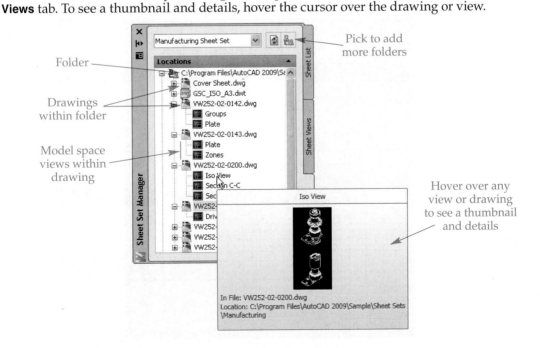

Place on Sheet option inserts the file into the current sheet as a sheet view. AutoCAD prompts you to specify an insertion point and creates a viewport automatically in the sheet. The **See Model Space Views** option expands the list of model space views in the drawing. This is the same as picking the + sign next to the drawing file. Select the **eTransmit** option to open the **Create Transmittal** dialog box so the selected file and its associated files can be packaged together.

If a model space view has been saved in the drawing, it is listed under the drawing file name. You can insert the model space view as a sheet view in a sheet. To do so, right-click on the model space view name and select the **Place on Sheet** option. Pick an insertion point in the sheet.

When you insert a model space view or drawing into a sheet, AutoCAD creates a viewport and an external reference to the selected drawing. AutoCAD assigns a scale for the viewport, or you can right-click before selecting the insertion point and select the scale for the sheet view. The scale is stored as the **ViewportScale** property of the **SheetView** field and is often displayed in the view label block.

When sheet views are created from resource drawings, an entry is added to the **Sheet Views**. If you insert a model space view, the view name is added to the **Sheet Views** tab. If you insert a drawing, the drawing name is added to the **Sheet Views** tab. To delete a location from a sheet set, right-click on the location and select the **Remove Location** menu option.

Naming and Numbering Sheet Views

Most projects contain several elevations, sections, or details. These items are typically numbered within the drawing set for easier reference. For example, the drawing set may include a foundation plan and a sheet with foundation details. On the foundation detail sheet, each detail is identified by a unique number. The foundation plan includes references to these numbers.

To change the name or number of a sheet view, right-click on the sheet view name in the **Sheet Views** tab of the **Sheet Set Manager** and select the **Rename & Renumber...** menu option. The **Rename & Renumber View** dialog box is displayed. See Figure 33-23. Enter a number for the view in the **Number** text box. The name of the view is modified in the **View title** text box. Pick the **Next** button to move to the next view in the view category. Pick the **OK** button when you are finished. The view number is displayed in front of the view name in the **Sheet Set Manager**.

Exercise 33-5
Complete the exercise on the Student CD.

Figure 33-23.
A view can be numbered in the **Rename & Renumber View** dialog box.

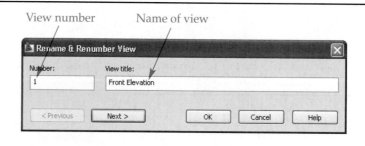

Working with Sheet View Blocks

The elevations, sections, details, and other drawings shown in sheet views are often located on one sheet and referenced on a different sheet. When using sheet views, you can insert blocks to identify the sheet view name, number, and scale on both the sheet with the sheet view and the sheet that refers to the sheet views. Typically, two types of blocks are used: callout blocks and view label blocks. Using sheet view blocks can greatly automate the process of adding drawing titles and labels.

Using callout blocks

A *callout block* refers to a sheet view. For example, when a section line is drawn through a building, a callout block is placed at the end of the section line. The callout block indicates the sheet or location where the section view is found and provides information about the viewing direction. A callout block can also be used on a foundation plan, for example, to identify an area addressed by a detail drawing. The callout block is typically located on a different sheet from the sheet view it references.

Several styles of callout blocks are available from AutoCAD to use for different types of sheet views. See **Figure 33-24.** The upper value in a callout block is typically the sheet view number, and the lower value is the drawing on which the sheet view appears. In the default callout blocks, the upper value is an attribute containing the **ViewNumber** property of the **SheetView** field. See **Figure 33-25.** This lists the sheet view number specified for the sheet view. The lower value is the **SheetNumber** property of the **SheetSet** value. This lists the sheet number of the sheet containing the sheet view.

> **callout block:** A block inserted to indicate a reference to another sheet.

Figure 33-24.
Callout blocks provide reference information for views and sheets. A—Elements of an elevation symbol. B—Examples of commonly used callout blocks.

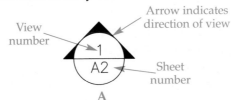

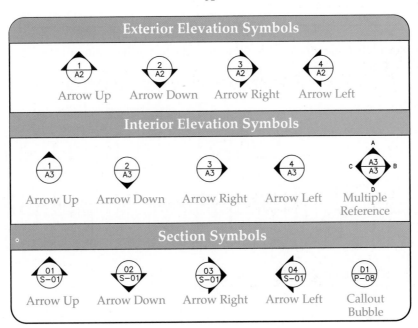

Figure 33-25.
The **ViewNumber** property displays the sheet view number. This field property is used in callout blocks.

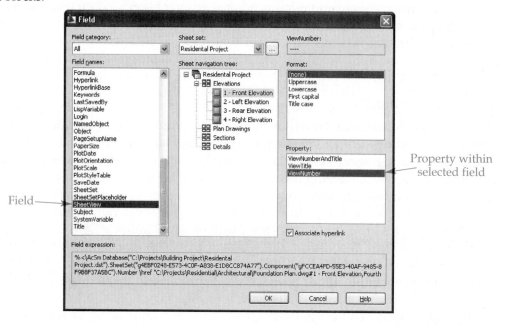

Because fields are used in the sheet view blocks, the values displayed are automatically updated if there are changes in the sheet set. For instance, if a new sheet is added in the middle of a sheet set, all later sheets need to be renumbered. The sheet view block values update automatically as the sheet numbers change.

Using view label blocks

View label blocks are placed below the sheet view. See Figure 33-26. Like callout blocks, view label blocks include attributes containing fields that automatically update to reflect changes to the sheet set or sheet views. View label blocks typically include three properties of the **SheetView** fields: **ViewNumber**, **ViewTitle**, and **Viewport Scale.**

> **view label block:** A block that contains view information such as the view name, number, and scale.

Figure 33-26.
View labels normally appear below the view on a sheet, and indicate information such as the view name, number, and scale.

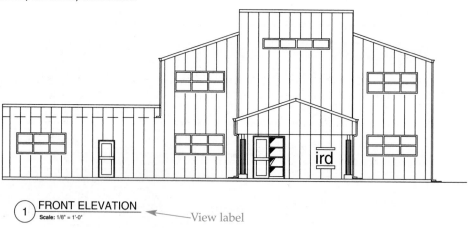

Using block hyperlinks

The callout and view label blocks used in the AutoCAD sample sheet sets also include hyperlink fields, or *hyperlinks.* You can pick the hyperlink on a callout block to instantly access the referenced detail, section, or elevation. This greatly simplifies the process of accessing sheet views.

hyperlinks: Links in a document connected to related information in other documents or on the Internet.

Associating callout and view label blocks

To insert a callout or view label block from the **Sheet Set Manager**, the block first needs to be available to the sheet set in which the view is defined. These blocks are specified in the **Sheet Set Properties** dialog box. To access this dialog box, right-click on the sheet set name in the **Sheet Set Manager** and select the **Properties...** option. The available blocks are specified in the **Callout blocks** text box and **Label block for views** text box. The name of each block is listed, followed by the path to the drawing file where the block is saved.

PROFESSIONAL TIP

A sheet set or view category can have multiple callout blocks available, but only one view label block.

To add a callout block to a sheet set, pick in the **Callout blocks** text box and then pick the ellipsis (...) button to open the **List of Blocks** dialog box. See Figure 33-27. Pick the **Add...** button to display the **Select Block** dialog box. In this dialog box, pick the ellipsis (...) button to select the drawing file that contains the block. Then select the block from the block list area of the **Select Block** dialog box. If the drawing file consists of only the objects that make up the drawing file, use the **Select the drawing file as a block** option. To delete a block from the block list, select it in the **List of Blocks** dialog box and pick the **Delete** button.

Specifying a view title block is similar to specifying a callout block. However, there can be only one view title block specified for the sheet set, so the **List of Blocks** dialog box is not displayed.

Each view category can be assigned its own callout blocks. This way, only the blocks that are needed for the views in a category are available. For example, a category named Section may only need a section callout bubble, while a category named Elevation may need ten different types of elevation symbols. To modify the callout blocks available for a view category, right-click on the category name and select the **Properties...** menu option to open the **View Category** dialog box.

Figure 33-27.
All callout blocks available to a sheet set are listed in the **List of Blocks** dialog box.

Pick to access **Select Block** dialog box

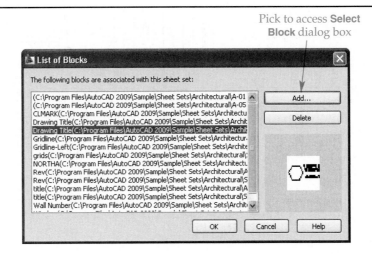

By default, the callout blocks and view title block assigned to a sheet set are displayed in the block list area. To make a block available to the view category, check the box next to the block. See **Figure 33-20.** This makes the block available to all of the views in the view category. To add new blocks to the view category, pick the **Add Blocks…** button to access the **Select Block** dialog box.

Inserting callout and view label blocks

To insert a callout block, open the sheet where the reference is to be placed. In the **Sheet Views** tab of the **Sheet Set Manager**, right-click on the sheet view name and select the block from the **Place Callout Block** cascading menu. See **Figure 33-28A.** Then, specify an insertion point for the block. Follow prompts to scale and rotate the block as needed. When you insert the block, AutoCAD gives the block the same sheet view number and sheet number as the reference view and sheet. See **Figure 33-28B.** If the reference information changes, AutoCAD automatically renumbers the block.

Figure 33-28.
Placing callout blocks in a view. A—Right-click on the reference view name and select **Place Callout Block** to display a shortcut menu with all of the callout blocks available. B—Callout blocks are placed in the 1-Main Floor Plan view in the A-01 sheet to reference the section view named 1-Section in the A-05 sheet.

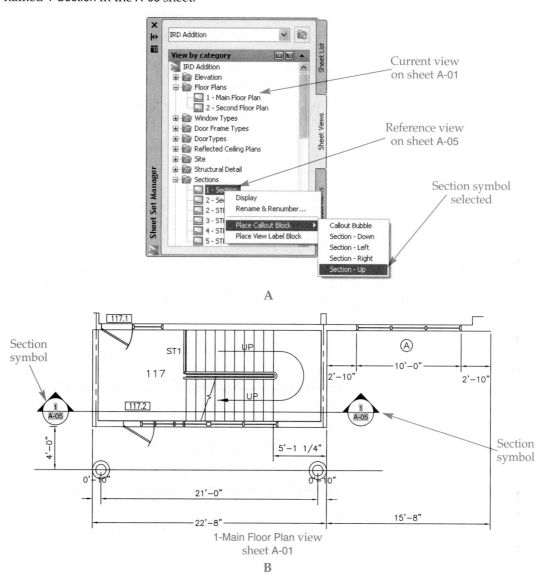

The process of inserting a view label block is similar to that for inserting a callout block. In the **Sheet Set Manager**, right-click on the sheet view name and select the **Place View Label Block** menu option. Follow prompts to specify an insertion point, scale, and rotation angle. When the block is inserted, the label appears with the view name and number. If the view name or number is changed in the sheet set, AutoCAD automatically updates the information.

Exercise 33-6
Complete the exercise on the Student CD.

Sheet Set Fields

Fields are valuable features for sheet sets. As the project develops, field text on sheets can be set to display up-to-date information when changes occur. For example, title block items such as the number of sheets, drawing number, the project number, and the date the sheet was plotted can be created as fields to automate the process of making changes to the values.

Fields are created using the **Field** dialog box and can be inserted in both multiline and single-line text editors. To insert a field in an active multiline text editor, pick the **Insert Field** button from the **Insert** panel of the **Multiline Text** tab or pick the **Insert Field** option available from the shortcut menu or the **Options** flyout. To insert a field in an active single-line text editor, right-click and select **Insert Field...** from the shortcut menu.

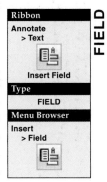

Specifying Fields for Sheet Sets

AutoCAD provides specific field types for use with sheet sets. Select **SheetSet** from the **Field category:** drop-down list to display a list of predefined field types in the **Field names:** list box. See Figure 33-29. These fields are inserted to display values that are defined in the sheet, sheet view, or sheet set, such as the sheet title, number, or description. Some of the fields also have several properties. Select one of the field types or properties to display the related value in the **Field** dialog box. For example, selecting the **CurrentSheetNumber** field allows you to insert a field that displays the sheet number of the current sheet. If the sheet is renumbered at a later date, the field changes to display the most current information.

Select the **SheetSet** field to display the **Sheet navigation tree**, which provides options for inserting many values. If you select the sheet set at the top of the tree, a set of properties related to the entire set appears in the **Property** list box. These properties include settings that can be applied to all sheets in the set, such as project information and client information. These settings do not change from sheet to sheet; they are the same on all sheets. When these field properties are included in the sheet set title block, all sheets display the same values.

Pick a sheet in the **Sheet navigation tree** to display properties related to the individual sheet. These properties include **SheetTitle**, **SheetNumber**, **Drawn By**, and **Checked By** settings. When these field properties are included in the sheet set template title block, each sheet can display a unique value. If a new sheet is added to a sheet set, the fields automatically update.

Figure 33-29.
Select **SheetSet** in the **Field category:** list in the **Field** dialog box to display the many fields related to sheet sets.

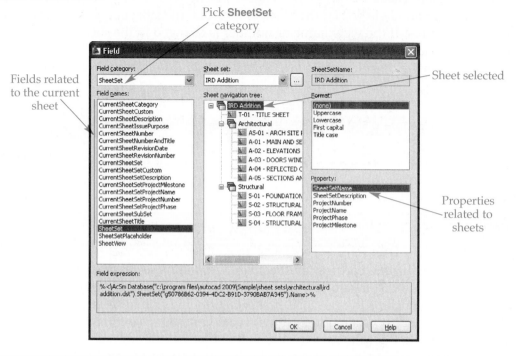

Pick **SheetSet** category

Sheet selected

Fields related to the current sheet

Properties related to sheets

Select the **SheetSetPlaceholder** field to insert a field that acts as a *placeholder.* Choose a placeholder from the **Placeholder type:** list box to assign a temporary value to the associated field, such as SheetNumber. Placeholders are used to insert temporary field values in user-defined callout blocks and view labels. When defined with attributes in a callout block, placeholders update to display the correct values automatically when the block is inserted onto a sheet from the **Sheet Set Manager.**

Like the **SheetSet** field, the **SheetView** field has many options. Select the **SheetView** field to display the **Sheet navigation tree** with a view list for the sheet set. If you pick the sheet set name in the **Sheet navigation tree**, the sheet set properties are displayed. These properties are identical to those displayed with the **SheetSet** field. If you pick a sheet view name in the **Sheet navigation tree**, sheet view properties are displayed. These properties are specific to a sheet view and include **ViewTitle**, **ViewNumber**, and **ViewScale**. These field properties are used in callout and view label blocks.

Using Custom Properties

Select the **CurrentSheetCustom** or **CurrentSheetSetCustom** field to insert a field that is linked to a custom property defined for a sheet or sheet set. Information about the sheet set or a specific sheet is stored electronically with fields and custom properties. This information can then be viewed from the **Sheet Set Manager.** The data can also be inserted into the drawing using the **Field** tool, which creates a link between the text data and the custom field data. The data can then be modified in the **Sheet Set Manager** and the linked data is updated in the drawing files.

Figure 33-30.
Information can be attached to a sheet set in the **Custom Properties** dialog box.

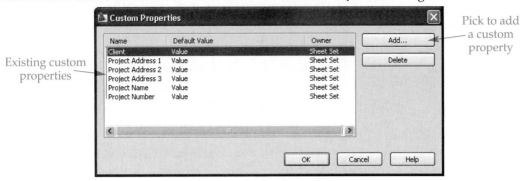

Existing custom properties

Pick to add a custom property

Figure 33-31.
Enter the information for the custom property in the **Add Custom Property** dialog box.

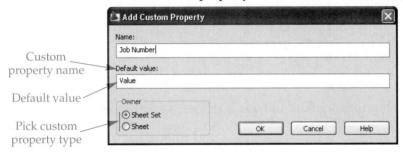

Custom property name

Default value

Pick custom property type

Adding a custom property field

Custom properties are managed in the **Sheet Set Properties** dialog box. To add a custom property field to a sheet set, right-click on the sheet set name in the **Sheet Set Manager** and select the **Properties...** menu option. In the **Sheet Set Properties** dialog box, pick the **Edit Custom Properties...** button to open the **Custom Properties** dialog box. See Figure 33-30.

To add a custom property field to the sheet set, pick the **Add...** button. This displays the **Add Custom Property** dialog box. See Figure 33-31. Enter a name for the custom property in the **Name** field. Examples of a custom property include Job Number, Client Name, Checked By, and Date. If the data for the custom property is usually the same value, enter it in the **Default value** field. For example, if the custom property is Checked by, and most of the sheets in this project are checked by ST, then ST could be entered as the default value. The **Owner** area has two options: **Sheet Set** and **Sheet**. If the custom property is associated with the entire project, select **Sheet Set**. If the custom property is assigned to each individual sheet, select **Sheet**. When you select **Sheet**, the custom property is available in the **Sheet Properties** dialog box and the data is attached to each individual sheet. Pick the **OK** button to add the custom property to the sheet set.

Entering custom property data

To modify or enter information into a custom property field for a sheet set, open the **Sheet Set Properties** dialog box and modify the value. If custom properties have been added for a sheet, the individual sheets display the custom property fields. To modify or enter information into a sheet custom property field, right-click on the sheet and select the **Properties...** menu option. Custom properties are listed under the **Sheet Custom Properties** heading of the **Sheet Properties** dialog box. See Figure 33-32.

Figure 33-32.
Custom properties
for individual sheets
are available in the
Sheet Properties
dialog box after they
have been added to
the sheet set.

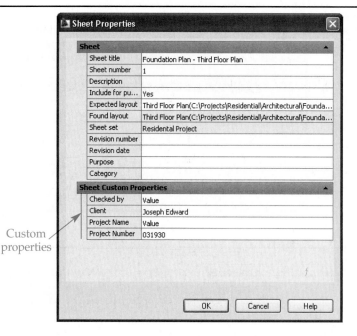

<table>
<tr><td colspan="2">**Sheet Properties**</td></tr>
</table>

Sheet	
Sheet title	Foundation Plan - Third Floor Plan
Sheet number	1
Description	
Include for pu...	Yes
Expected layout	Third Floor Plan(C:\Projects\Residential\Architectural\Founda...
Found layout	Third Floor Plan(C:\Projects\Residential\Architectural\Founda...
Sheet set	Residental Project
Revision number	
Revision date	
Purpose	
Category	

Sheet Custom Properties	
Checked by	Value
Client	Joseph Edward
Project Name	Value
Project Number	031930

Custom
properties

OK   Cancel   Help

Deleting a custom property

To delete a custom property field that is no longer needed, right-click on the sheet set and select **Properties...** to open the **Sheet Set Properties** dialog box. Then pick the **Edit Custom Properties...** button. In the **Custom Properties** dialog box, select the custom property to remove and pick the **Delete** button.

NOTE

If a sheet set is created from an example sheet set, any custom properties from the example sheet set are added to the new sheet set.

Exercise 33-7
Complete the exercise on the Student CD.

Creating a Sheet List Table

sheet list: A list of all the pages in a sheet set and the type of information that can be found on each sheet.

One of the first pages of a sheet set typically includes a *sheet list*. A sheet list displays all of the pages in the sheet set and what type of information can be found on the sheet. A sheet list can be created as a table object using information from the sheet properties. The information in the table is directly linked to the sheet properties, so if the sheet information is updated in the **Sheet Set Manager**, the sheet list table updates automatically.

Inserting a Sheet List Table

A sheet list table can only be inserted into a drawing from the **Sheet Set Manager**. To insert a sheet list table, open the **Sheet Set Manager** and open the sheet where the table will be inserted. Right-click on the sheet set name and select the **Insert Sheet List Table...** menu option. This opens the **Insert Sheet List Table** dialog box shown in Figure 33-33.

Figure 33-33.
Properties for the sheet list table are set up in the **Insert Sheet List Table** dialog box.

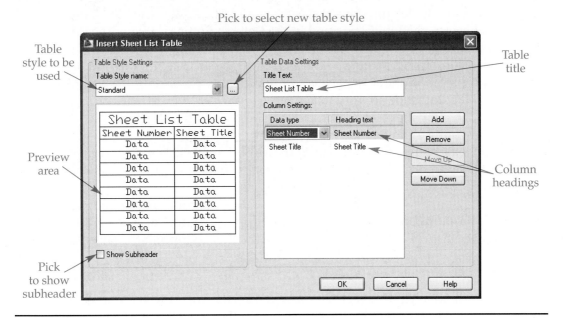

A preset table style for the sheet list can be selected from the **Table Style name** drop-down list. A preview of the table is displayed in the preview area. The **Show Subheader** check box determines whether the table includes a subheader row.

The information displayed in the table is set in the **Table Data Settings** area. Enter the title for the sheet list into the **Title Text** text box. Specify the information the table contains in the **Column Settings** area. Pick the **OK** button to insert the table. You are then prompted to specify the insertion point for the table. **Figure 33-34** shows a sheet list table that uses the sheet number and sheet description fields.

NOTE

A sheet list table can only be inserted into a layout tab of a drawing file that is a part of the sheet set. The **Insert Sheet List Table...** options are unavailable if the drawing file is not part of the sheet set or if model space is current.

Figure 33-34.
A sheet list table displays information about each sheet in the sheet set.

SHEET INDEX	
Sheet Number	Sheet Description
T–01	SHEET INDEX, VICINITY MAP, BUILDING CODE ANALYSIS
Architectural	
AS–01	ARCHITECTURAL SITE PLAN, NOTES
A–01	MAIN FLOOR PLAN, SECOND FLOOR PLAN, WALL TYPE NOTES
A–02	EXTERIOR ELEVATIONS
A–03	DOOR & FRAME SCHEDULE, ROOM FINISH SCHEDULE, DOOR, DOOR FRAME & WINDOW TYPES
A–04	MAIN & SECOND FLOOR REFLECTED CEILING PLANS
A–05	STAIR SECTIONS AND DETAILS
Structural	
S–01	FOUNDATION PLAN, PILE SCHEDULE, PILE TYPICAL DETAIL
S–02	STRUCTURAL SECTIONS AND DETAILS
S–03	FLOOR FRAMING PLAN AND SECTIONS
S–04	STRUCTURAL SECTIONS

Modifying the Column Heading Data

A sheet list table can include various types of information from the drawing file and the sheet set. By default, the Sheet Number and Sheet Title fields are included. The sheet list table information is specified in the **Column Settings** area of the **Insert Sheet List Table** dialog box.

A new column can be added to the sheet list table by picking the **Add** button. The new column is placed under the last column in the list. To specify the data type, pick the name in the **Data type** column to activate the drop-down list. Pick the drop-down list button to display the information that can be used in the sheet list table. Select the type of data you want to include. Then type the heading for the sheet list column in the **Heading text** column. The data types that are available in the drop-down list come from sheet set properties and drawing properties. To add a different data type to the list, you need to add a custom property to the sheet set.

To delete a data column from the list, select the data column and pick the **Remove** button. Use the **Move Up** and **Move Down** buttons to reposition the order of the columns. The column at the top of the list is inserted as the first column in the sheet list table.

Editing a Sheet List Table

The information in the sheet list table is directly linked to the data source field. For example, if the sheet numbers are modified in the **Sheet Set Manager**, the sheet list table can be updated to reflect those changes. To do this, select the sheet list table in the drawing file, right-click, and select the **Update Sheet List Table** option.

To modify the properties for the table, select the table, right-click, and select the **Edit Sheet List Table Settings...** option. This opens the **Edit Sheet List Table Settings** dialog box. After making the changes, pick the **OK** button to update the sheet list table.

NOTE

A sheet list table can be modified using the same techniques used for any other table. For example, text can be modified and columns and rows can be added. When the **Update Sheet List Table** tool is used on the modified table, a warning dialog box is displayed stating that any manual modifications are discarded.

Using Sheet List Table Hyperlinks

If the **Sheet Number** or **Sheet Title** columns are included in the sheet list table, hyperlinks are automatically assigned to the data. To open a sheet using a hyperlink, hover the crosshairs over a sheet number or sheet title until the hyperlink icon and tooltip appear. The tooltip displays the message CTRL + click to follow link. Hold the [Ctrl] key and pick the hyperlink to open the selected sheet. This is another way to open a sheet quickly.

Exercise 33-8
Complete the exercise on the Student CD.

Archiving a Sheet Set

At different periods throughout a project, you may want to *archive* the drawing set. For example, when a set of drawings in a project is presented to the client for the first time, the client may want to make some changes. It may be wise to archive the files for future reference, before the modifications are made. Archive copies all of the drawing files and their related files to a single location. Related files include external references, font files, plot style table files, and template files.

archiving:
Gathering and storing all of the electronic drawing files related to a project.

Setting Up an Archive

To archive a sheet set, right-click on the sheet set name and select **Archive...** from the shortcut menu, or type ARCHIVE. The **Archive a Sheet Set** dialog box opens. See Figure 33-35. The **Sheets** tab displays all of the subsets and sheets in the sheet set. Check the sheets to be archived. The drawing files and their related files are listed in the **Files Tree** tab. Pick the + sign next to a file to display its related files.

A file that is not part of the sheet set can be included in the archive by picking the **Add a File** button on the **Files Tree** tab. See Figure 33-36. This opens the **Add File**

Figure 33-35.
The files to be archived and the archive settings are specified from the **Archive a Sheet Set** dialog box.

File display tabs

List of files to be archived

Enter any notes about the archive

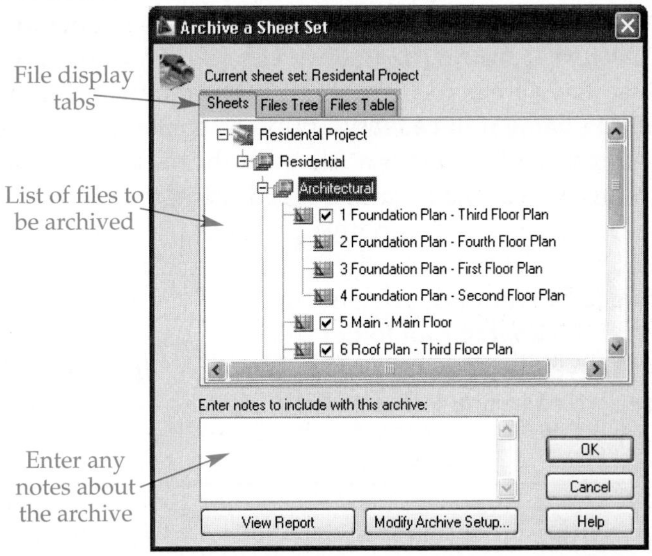

Figure 33-36.
Documents that relate to a project can be archived along with the AutoCAD files.

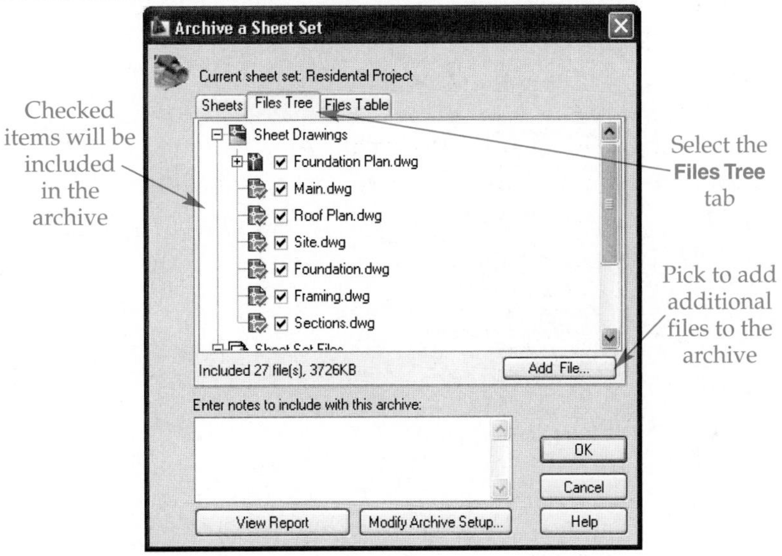

Checked items will be included in the archive

Select the **Files Tree** tab

Pick to add additional files to the archive

to Archive dialog box. Any type of file can be added to the archive—the archive is not limited to AutoCAD files. You can include them in the archive by typing them in the **Enter notes to include with this archive** text box. The **View Report** button lists all of the files included in the archive. To save this information to a text file, pick the **Save As...** button.

The location where the archive is saved, the type of archive that is created, and additional settings are specified in the **Modify Archive Setup** dialog box. See **Figure 33-37**. To open this dialog box, pick the **Modify Archive Setup...** button.

Use the **Archive package type** drop-down list to specify the archive format. Choose the **Folder (set of files)** option to copy all of the archived files into a single folder. Select the **Self-extracting executable (*.exe)** option to compress all of the files into a self-extracting *zip file*. Self-extracting zip files have an EXE extension. The files can be extracted later by double-clicking on the file. Choose the **Zip (*.zip)** option to compress all of the files into a normal zip file. A program that works with zip files must be used to extract the files.

Use the **File Format** drop-down list to select an earlier version of AutoCAD to convert the archived files to the selected version. The **Archive file folder** drop-down list defines where the archive is saved. Select a location from the list or pick the **Browse...** button to choose a different location.

The **Archive file name** drop-down list provides options for naming the archive. Choose the **Prompt for a filename** option to display the **Specify Zip File** dialog box so that you can specify a name for the archive package. Pick the **Overwrite if necessary** option automatically overwrite the file name if a file with the same name already exists. Select the **Increment file name if necessary** option to create a new file with an incremental number added to the file name if a file with the same name already exists. Multiple versions of the archive package can be saved using this option.

Additional settings for the archive package are specified in the **Archive Options** area. The first option determines how the folder structure is saved. If the **Use organized folder structure** radio button is selected, the archive file duplicates the folder structure for the files, and the **Source root folder** setting is used to determine the root folder for files that use relative paths, such as xrefs. To archive all of the files into one single folder, pick the **Place all files in one folder** radio button. Select the **Keep files and folders as is**

zip file: A file that contains one or more files that have been compressed using the Windows ZIP file format.

Figure 33-37.
The archive file settings are specified in the **Modify Archive Setup** dialog box.

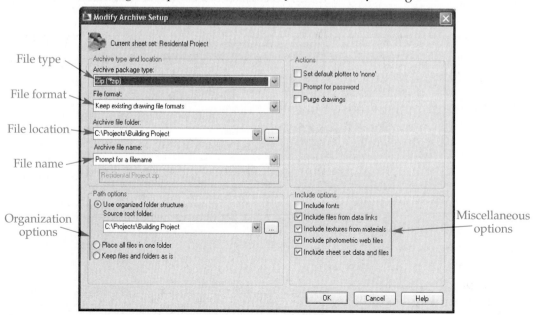

AutoCAD and Its Applications—Basics

radio button to use the same folder structure for all the files in the sheet set. Pick the **Include fonts** check box to include all fonts used in the drawings in the archive. The **Set default plotter to 'none'** check box disassociates the plotter name from the drawing files. This is useful if the files are sent to someone using a different plotter. Select the **Prompt for password** check box to set a password for the archive. The password is then needed to open the archive package. Pick the **Include sheet set data and files** check box to include the sheet set data file with the archive package.

> **NOTE**
>
> Right-click on a sheet set name and select the **eTransmit** option to display the **Create Transmittal** dialog box for use with the **eTransmit** feature. This option is very similar to the **Archive** option. It is used to package files and associated files for Internet exchange. The **Transmittal Setups** option displays the **Transmittal Setups** dialog box, which is used to configure **eTransmit** settings.

Chapter Test

Answer the following questions. Write your answers on a separate sheet of paper or complete the electronic chapter test on the Student CD.

1. What is a sheet set?
2. What does the term *sheet* refer to in relation to a sheet set and a drawing file?
3. What wizard is used to create a sheet set? What two types of ways can a new sheet set be created?
4. What file extension is applied to sheet sets?
5. What are subsets in relation to a sheet set?
6. What is the purpose of the **Create subsets based on folder structure** option in the **Import Options** dialog box?
7. Explain how to create a new subset in a sheet set and specify a template file and layout for creating new sheets in the subset.
8. List two ways to open a sheet from the **Sheet Set Manager.**
9. What is the purpose of the **Import Layouts as Sheets** dialog box?
10. How do you modify a sheet name or number?
11. Briefly explain how to publish a sheet set to a DWF file. How are the sheets organized in the resulting file?
12. How do you create a sheet selection set?
13. What are sheet views and how can they be referenced to each other within a sheet set?
14. What tab in the **Sheet Set Manager** is used to manage sheet views?
15. Briefly explain how to create a view category for a sheet set and associate callout blocks to the category.
16. Explain how to add a drawing file to a sheet set so that views in the drawing can be placed on a sheet.
17. What information is typically provided by the upper and lower values displayed in a callout block?
18. Explain why AutoCAD callout blocks and view labels are automatically updated when changes are made to the related sheet set.
19. Explain how to insert a callout block into a drawing.
20. Give three examples of fields that can be used in a sheet set.

21. What is the purpose of custom sheet set properties?
22. How do you add a custom property to a sheet set?
23. What is a sheet list table?
24. Explain how to add a column heading to a sheet list table.
25. How can a table be updated to reflect changes that are made in the **Sheet Set Manager**?
26. What happens to edits made manually to a sheet list table when the **Update Sheet List Table** tool is used?
27. What is the purpose of archiving a sheet set?
28. What is a zip file?
29. List the three packaging types available for archiving a sheet set.
30. How can you password-protect an archive?

Drawing Problems

Note: Some of the following problems refer to drawings created in previous chapters. If you have not yet created those drawings, you will need to do so before working these problems.

▼ Basic

1. Create a new sheet set using the **Create Sheet Set** wizard and an example sheet set. Use the Civil Imperial Sheet Set example sheet set. Name the new sheet set Civil Sheet Set. Finish creating the sheet set.

2. Create a new sheet set using the **Create Sheet Set** wizard and an example sheet set. Use the New Sheet Set example sheet set. Name the new sheet set My Sheet Set. Finish creating the sheet set.

▼ Intermediate

3. Create a new sheet set using the **Create Sheet Set** wizard and the **Existing drawings** option. Name the new sheet set Schematic Drawings. On the **Choose Layouts** page, pick the **Browse...** button and browse to the folder where the P29-8.dwg file from Chapter 29 is saved. Import all of the layouts from the file into the new sheet set. Continue creating the sheet set as follows:
   A. In the **Sheet Set Properties** dialog box, assign the layout named ISO A1 Layout from the Tutorial-mMfg.dwt template file in the AutoCAD 2009 Template folder as the sheet creation template.
   B. Open a new drawing file using the template of your choice and create a block for a view label. Save the drawing file and then assign the block to the sheet set using the **Label block for views** setting in the **Sheet Set Properties** dialog box.
   C. Create a new view category and name it Schematics.
   D. Open the 3 Wire Control layout, create a new view, and add it to the Schematics view category. Double-click on the new view name in the **Sheet Views** tab and insert the view label block you previously created. Renumber the view and save the drawing.
   E. Add a custom property to the sheet set named Checked by and set the **Owner** type to **Sheet**. Add another custom property named Client and set the **Owner** type to **Sheet Set**.

4. Create a new sheet set using the **Create Sheet Set** wizard and an example sheet set. Use the Architectural Imperial Sheet Set example sheet set. Name the new sheet set Floor Plan Drawings. Finish creating the sheet set. Under the Architectural subset, create a new sheet named Floor Plan. Number the sheet A1. In the **Model Views** tab, add a new location by browsing to the folder where the P19-16.dwg file from Chapter 19 is saved. Open the P19-16.dwg file and continue as follows:

   A. Create three model space views named Kitchen, Living Room, and Dining Room. Orient each display as needed to describe the area of the floor plan. Save and close the drawing.

   B. Open the A1-Floor Plan sheet. Create a new layer named Viewport and set it current.

   C. In the **Model Views** tab, expand the listing under the P19-16.dwg file. Right-click on each view name and select **Place on Sheet**. Insert each view into the layout. Delete the default view labels inserted with the views. Double-click inside each viewport and set the viewport scale as desired.

   D. In the **Sheet Views** tab, renumber the views. Insert a new view label block under each view.

   E. Save and close the drawing.

5. Open the Floor Plan Drawings sheet set created in Problem 33-4. Create an archive of the sheet set using the self-extracting zip executable (EXE) file format.

▼ Advanced

6. Use a word processor to write a report of approximately 250 words explaining the purpose of sheet sets. Cite at least three examples from actual industry applications of using sheet sets to help a set of drawings. Use at least two sketches to illustrate your report.

7. Plan a new shopping center for your area. Determine how many stores will be included. If possible, obtain a copy of a survey for vacant land in your area on which the shopping center could be built. Determine the components of a complete set of plans for the shopping center, including a site plan, floor plans, foundation plans, roof plans, elevations, and any needed sections. Establish the components for a new sheet set to organize the drawings and layouts.

8. Plan a new residence with approximately 3500–4000 square feet, four bedrooms, three baths, a den/office, kitchen, dining room, nook, family room, and three-car garage. Create a complete set of plans for the residence, including a site plan, floor plans, foundation plans, roof plans, elevations, and any needed sections. Prepare layouts for each drawing. Then create a new sheet set to organize the drawings and layouts. Archive the final sheet set.

joining, 339
joining other objects to, 412
making breaks in, 413–414
moving vertex, 415
opening and closing, 412
setting width, 406
straightening all segments, 418
straightening segments or arcs, 415
undoing previously drawn segments, 407
polyline arcs, 407–409
polyline vertex, 413
pop-up menus, 33
portrait paper orientation, 168
positional tolerance, 620
prefix, 496–497
preset views, 188
primary units, setting, 593
printers, 166
printing. *See* plotting
produced size, 607
projected tolerance zone, 617, 620, 622
projection plane, 231
PROJECTNAME system variable, 878
prompts
coordinate display, 86
dynamic input, 86–88
for numbers, 82
point entry methods, 83–85
previously picked points, 93
responding to, 81–94
using command line, 88–90
using direct distance entry, 91–92
properties, matching, 393
Properties palette, 388–393
annotation scales, 857–859
annotative text, 850
attributes, 826–827, 829
General category, 389–390
Geometry category, 390
layer property overrides, 810
linear parameters, 730, 732–733
making existing objects annotative, 847
overriding dimension style settings, 574
point parameters, 727–729
and **QuickCalc**, 465
rotation angle, 738
setting annotation scale, 849
Text category, 391–392
viewport and annotation scale, 853
visibility states, 746
PROPERTIES tool, 39–40

property filter, 157–158
Property Settings dialog box, 393–394
PSLTSCALE system variable, 805, 850
publishing, 911–912
Publish shortcut menu, 911–912
purge, 712–713
Purge dialog box, 712–713
PURGE tool, 712

Q

QDIM tool, 516–517, 572
QLEADER tool, 614, 618–620, 625
QNEW tool, 55
QSAVE tool, 56
QSELECT tool, 396–398
quadrant, 202
Quadrant object snap, 198, 202–203
quadratic curve, 417
Quick Access toolbar, 37
Quick Properties panel, 386–387
quick save, 56–58
Quick Select dialog box, 396–398
Quick View Drawings tool, 64–67, 768
Quick View Layouts tool, 766–768
QuickCalc, 458–466
additional options, 466
advanced calculations, 461
clearing input and history areas, 460
converting units, 462
entering expressions, 459–460
palette vs. window, 464
using drawing values, 464
using variables, 462–463
using with object properties, 465
using with tools, 464
QVDRAWING tool, 768
QVLAYOUT tool, 766–768

R

RAY tool, 230
rays, 228
modifying, 230
read-only drawings, 64
real block, 696
realtime panning, 180
realtime zooming, 178, 817
Recent Actions menu, 35–36
Recent Documents menu, 62–63

dex–Basics